Connecting with the Past

The D. C. Heath Document Sets for Western Civilization

to accompany

The Challenge of the West

Hunt • Martin • Rosenwein • Hsia • Smith

VOLUME I: TO 1787

D. C. Heath and Company
Lexington, Massachusetts   Toronto

Address editorial correspondence to:

D. C. Heath and Company
125 Spring Street
Lexington, MA 02173

Cover illustration: Cuneiform tablet, Ashur, recording sale of female slave named Kilanu. Lowie Museum of Anthropology, University of California, Berkeley.

Published simultaneously in Canada.

Printed in the United States of America.

International Standard Book Number: 0-669-39640-0

10 9 8 7 6 5 4 3 2 1

Preface

Connecting with the Past: The D. C. Heath Document Sets in Western Civilization represents an exciting new way of supplying instructors with the source material they need for teaching the survey course by taking full advantage of modern technology. We hope that you not only will be pleased with the result, but will begin a real partnership with us in developing this project in the years to come.

For generations, most teachers have agreed that an essential dimension of training students in history is to allow them to read and interpret the fundamental material with which every working historian must grapple—the documents. Recognizing this need, educational publishers have long made available edited collections of documents and documentary extracts. Many textbooks have featured "sidebar" source readings and, in recent years, many instructors have braved the difficulties of securing permissions and assembled their own sets of primary and secondary reading material—"self-publishing" through copy shops. *Connecting with the Past* not only draws on all these ways of placing documents into students' hands, but also combines elements of all of them to uniquely widen your options.

First, *Connecting with the Past* is a large, two-volume anthology that can stand on its own as a Western Civilization reader; its contents range from the earliest creation myths of the ancient Near East to the fall of Communism. The documents have been chosen not only to offer students a generous selection of readings from classic texts in the Western cultural, intellectual, and political tradition, but also to provide rich insights into the lives of ordinary men and women who lived through the times that the seminal thinkers and artists interpreted in their writings. Juxtaposing private experiences with the milestones of Western culture has been a primary organizing principle in assembling these readings.

Second, we have planned this version of *Connecting with the Past* to coordinate closely with

the structure of the Western Civilization textbook that D. C. Heath is publishing this year: *The Challenge of the West*, by Lynn Hunt and others. Every chapter of *Connecting with the Past* corresponds to one of the chapters in *The Challenge of the West*, so that students who are studying Western Civilization with the Hunt et al. textbook can easily find parallel, closely coordinated source readings in the equivalent chapter of *Connecting with the Past*. In this sense, *Connecting with the Past* can serve as a large *collection* of sidebars to *The Challenge of the West*, offering far more supplementary readings—and longer, more substantive ones—than ever could be accommodated within the textbook itself.

Minor exceptions to the chapter-by-chapter correlation with the Hunt et al. text do occur. For example, *The Challenge of the West* begins its treatment of the Enlightenment at the end of Chapter 18 and continues the discussion at the beginning of Chapter 19; *Connecting with the Past* concentrates its source materials on this topic in Chapter 19. And *Connecting with the Past*'s Chapter 29 corresponds to Chapters 29 and 30 of *The Challenge of the West*.

Third, *Connecting with the Past* is not, so to speak, a "finished product" that will stand unchanged until the next edition is published. Recent advances in custom publishing make it possible for D. C. Heath to offer instructors the opportunity to customize the anthology to suit their own courses. For details on how to customize *Connecting with the Past*, see the note that follows this preface. Feel free, as well, to discuss this matter with your D. C. Heath campus representative.

We look forward to working with you, and hope that you and your students enjoy *Connecting with the Past*.

James Miller, Ph.D.
Senior Editor, History
D. C. Heath and Company

Creating a Heath Custom Book Version of Connecting with the Past

You can easily create a *Heath Custom Book* version of *Connecting with the Past* by selecting portions of *Connecting with the Past* and adding your own original materials (such as course outlines), parts of other D. C. Heath ancillaries, and even selections from other sources. In this way you can provide your students with exactly those material you want them to have—no more, no less.

To learn how to do this, contact your D. C. Heath sales representative or call (800) 235–3565 and ask for a copy of our *D. C. Heath Custom Book Author's Guide.* Your custom books should be in your bookstore within six to eight weeks of our receiving your chosen materials.

Contents

CHAPTER 2
New Paths for Western Civilization, c. 1000–500 B.C.   24

CHAPTER 3

The Greek Golden Age, c. 500–403 B.C.   55

CHAPTER 5
The Rise and Fall of the Roman Republic, c. 800–44 B.C.   104

CHAPTER 6
The Roman Empire, 44 B.C.–A.D. 284   116

CHAPTER 7

The Fragmentation and Transformation of the Late Roman Empire, 284–568   161

CHAPTER 9
The Remaking of Three Societies, 756–1054   193

CHAPTER 10
Vitality and Reform, 1054–1144   210

CHAPTER 11
An Age of Confidence, 1144–1215   236

CHAPTER 12
The Quest for Order and Control, 1215–1320   259

CHAPTER 13
The Collapse of Medieval Order, 1320–1430   292

CHAPTER 14
Renaissance Europe, 1430–1493   321

CHAPTER 16
Religious Warfare and Crises of Authority, 1560–1640   399

CHAPTER 18
New Societies and the Early Enlightenment, 1690-1740   469

CHAPTER 19
The Promise of a New Order, 1740–1787   485

I

The First Civilizations in the West

DOCUMENT SET 1.1
Gods and the Creation

As far back in time and as dispersed in space as historians and anthropologists have discovered evidence of human intellectual efforts, they have found men and women brooding on the mysteries of life and death. By the time the first civilizations emerged, primitive speculation about pervasive spiritual forces had evolved into complicated theologies explaining how deities had created the world and ruled human destiny.

In Document A we can read how second-millennium Mesopotamian priests recorded their civilization's explanation for the creation of life by the high gods, whose identities had evolved from personified natural phenomena. Although the document comes down to us in a relatively late cuneiform, it is unlikely the substance of the myth had changed much since Sumerian times. Documents B and C are Egyptian hymns—respectively, the hymn to Aton and the king, and the hymn to the supreme god Amon-Re. The Aton hymn represents a short-lived revolution in ancient Egyptian religion carried out by the pharaoh Akhenaton (*1379–1362), who saw himself as the divine manifestation on earth of the supreme sun-god Aton, and as such the upholder of truth-justice (*maat*) and mediator between humanity and Aton. The hymn to Amon-Re was composed by priests of ancient Egypt's "mainstream" religious tradition, which both preceded and survived Akhenaton's attempted religious transformation. Document D, the Hebrew account of the Creation and the Book of Genesis, presented here in the King James English translation, dates from much later. Its various strands originated

between the tenth and the fifth centuries B.C., absorbing many Near Eastern religious ideas as well as the Hebrew oral tradition.

In reading these documents, remember first of all that they were set down in writing by religious authorities. How do they express the relationship between the creator-deity and humanity? Do you see any evidence of how those who wrote down these accounts incorporated—consciously or unconsciously—their own understanding of the world around them? What value do you see in these accounts as historical documents?

A. An Akkadian Creation Epic

Nothing there was but primordial Fresh-Water
  (Apsu), their begetter,
And Mother-Sea (Mummu-Tiamat), she who bore
  them all,
Their waters commingling as a single body;
No reed hut had been matted, no marsh land had
  appeared,
When no gods whatever had been brought into being,
Uncalled by name, their destinies undetermined—
Then it was that the gods were formed within
  them. . . .
Then struggled the Sea-Goddess (Tiamat) and the
  Sun-God (Marduk), wisest of gods.

"An Akkadian Creation Epic" from James B. Pritchard, *Ancient Near Eastern Texts Relating to the Old Testament*, 3/e, pp. 60–68, Copyright © 1969 by Princeton University Press. Reprinted by permission of Princeton University Press.

They strove in single combat, locked in battle. . . .
He released the arrow, it tore her belly,
It cut through her insides, splitting the heart.
Having thus subdued her, he extinguished her life.
He cast down her carcass to stand upon it. . . .
He split her like a shellfish into two parts:
Half of her he set up as the sky,
Pulled down the bar and posted guards.
He bade them to allow not her waters to escape.
He crossed the heavens and surveyed the regions. . . .
Opening his mouth, he addresses his father (Ea)
To impart the plan he had conceived in his heart:
"Blood I will mass and cause bones to be.
I will establish a savage, *man* shall be his name.
Truly, savage-man I will create.
He shall be charged with the service of the gods
That they might be at ease!"

B. A Hymn to Aton

Praise to thee! When thou risest in the horizon, O living Aton, Lord of eternity. Obeisance to thy rising in heaven, to illuminate every land, with thy beauty. Thy rays are upon thy beloved son. Thy hand has a myriad of jubilees for the King of Upper and Lower Egypt, Neferkheprure-Wanre, thy child who came forth from thy rays. Thou assignest to him thy lifetime and thy years. Thou hearest for him that which is in his heart. He is thy beloved, thou makest him like Aton. When thou risest, eternity is given him; when thou settest, thou givest him everlastingness. Thou begettest him in the morning like thine own forms; thou formest him as thy emanation, like Aton, ruler of truth, who came forth from eternity, son of Re, wearing his beauty, who offers to him the product of his rays; King of Upper and Lower Egypt, living in truth, Lord of the Two Lands, Neferkheprure-Wanre; the Great King's-Wife, Nefernefruaton-Nofretete; living forever and ever.

C. A Hymn to Amon-Re

Adoration of Amon-Re, the Bull Residing in Heliopolis, chief of all gods, the good god, the beloved, who gives life to all that is warm and to all good cattle.

Hail to thee, Amon-Re,
Lord of the Thrones of the Two Lands, Presiding over Karnak,
Bull of His Mother,[1] Presiding over His Fields!
Far-reaching of stride, presiding over Upper Egypt,
Lord of the Madjoi and ruler of Punt,[2]
Eldest of heaven, first-born of earth,
Lord of what is, enduring in all things, enduring in all things.
UNIQUE IN HIS NATURE LIKE THE *FLUID* of the gods,
The goodly bull of the Ennead, chief of all gods,
The Lord of truth and father of the gods.
Who made mankind and created the beasts,
Lord of what is, who created the fruit tree,
Made herbage, and gave life to cattle.
The goodly daemon whom Ptah made,
                    (ii)
The goodly beloved youth to whom the gods give praise,
Who made what is below and what is above,
Who illuminates the Two Lands
And crosses the heavens in peace:
The King of Upper and Lower Egypt: Re, the triumphant,[3]
Chief of the Two Lands,
Great of strength, Lord of reverence,
The chief one, who made the entire earth.
MORE DISTINGUISHED IN NATURE THAN any (other) god,
In whose beauty the gods rejoice,
To whom is given jubilation in the Per-wer,
Who is given ceremonial appearance in the Per-nezer.[4]
Whose fragrance the gods love, when he comes from Punt,
Rich in perfume, when he comes down (from) Madjoi,
The Beautiful of Face who comes (from) God's Land.[5]
The gods FAWN (at) his feet,
According as they recognize his majesty as their Lord,
The Lord of fear, great of dread,
Rich in might, terrible of appearances,
Flourishing in offerings and making provisions.

---

[1] As sun-god, Amon-Re recreated himself every day.
[2] Regions to the south and southeast of Egypt.
[3] Written as though Amon-Re were a former pharaoh.
[4] The *Per-wer*, "Great House," was the religious capital of Upper Egypt at el-Kab; the *Per-nezer* was the counterpart for Lower Egypt at Buto.
[5] "God's Land" was the east generally, the land of the rising sun. The countries south and east of Egypt were the incense-bearing lands.

Jubilation to thee who made the gods,
Raised the heavens and laid down the ground!

D. The Hebrew Account of the Creation

In the beginning God created the heaven and the earth. And the earth was without form, and void; and darkness was upon the face of the deep. And the Spirit of God moved upon the face of the waters. And God said, Let there be light: and there was light. And God saw the light, that it was good: and God divided the light from the darkness. And God called the light Day, and the darkness he called Night. And the evening and the morning were the first day.

And God said, Let there be a firmament in the midst of the waters, and let it divide the waters from the waters. And God made the firmament, and divided the waters which were under the firmament from the waters which were above the firmament: and it was so. And God called the firmament Heaven. And the evening and the morning were the second day.

And God said, Let the waters under the heaven be gathered together unto one place, and let the dry land appear: and it was so. And God called the dry land Earth; and the gathering together of the waters called he Seas: and God saw that it was good. And God said, Let the earth bring forth grass, the herb yielding seed, and the fruit tree yielding fruit after his kind, whose seed is in itself, upon the earth: and it was so. And the earth brought forth grass, and herb yielding seed after his kind, and the tree yielding fruit, whose seed was in itself, after his kind: and God saw that it was good. And the evening and the morning were the third day.

And God said, Let there be lights in the firmament of the heaven to divide the day from the night; and let them be for signs, and for seasons, and for days, and years: And let them be for lights in the firmament of the heaven to give light upon the earth: and it was so. And God made two great lights; the greater light to rule the day, and the lesser light to rule the night: he made the stars also. And God set them in the firmament of the heaven to give light upon the earth. And to rule over the day and over the night, and to divide the light from the darkness: and God saw that it was good. And the evening and the morning were the fourth day. And God said, Let the waters bring forth abundantly the moving creature that hath life, and fowl that may fly above the earth in the open firmament of heaven. And God created great whales, and every living creature that moveth, which the waters brought forth abundantly, after their kind, and every winged fowl after his kind: and God saw that it was good. And God blessed them, saying, Be fruitful, and multiply, and fill the waters in the seas, and let fowl multiply in the earth. And the evening and the morning were the fifth day.

And God said, Let the earth bring forth the living creature after his kind, cattle, and creeping thing, and beast of the earth after his kind: and it was so. And God made the beast of the earth after his kind, and cattle after their kind, and every thing that creepeth upon the earth after his kind: and God saw that it was good.

And God said, Let us make man in our image, after our likeness: and let them have dominion over the fish of the sea, and over the fowl of the air, and over the cattle, and over all the earth, and over every creeping thing that creepeth upon the earth. So God created man in his own image, in the image of God created he him; male and female created he them. And God blessed them, and God said unto them, Be fruitful, and multiply, and replenish the earth, and subdue it: and have dominion over the fish of the sea, and over the fowl of the air, and over every living thing that moveth upon the earth.

And God said, Behold, I have given you every herb bearing seed, which is upon the face of all the earth, and every tree, in the which is the fruit of a tree yielding seed; to you it shall be for meat. And to every beast of the earth, and to every fowl of the air, and to every thing that creepeth upon the earth, wherein there is life, I have given every green herb for meat: and it was so. And God saw every thing that he had made, and, behold, it was very good. And the evening and the morning were the sixth day.

Thus the heavens and the earth were finished, and all the host of them. And on the seventh day God ended his work which he had made; and he rested on the seventh day from all his work which he had made. And God blessed the seventh day, and sanctified it: because that in it he had rested from all his work which God created and made.

These are the generations of the heavens and of the earth when they were created, in the day that the Lord God made the earth and the heavens, And every plant of the field before it was in the earth, and every herb of the field before it grew: for the Lord God had not caused it to rain upon the earth, and there was not a man to till the ground. But there went up a mist from the earth, and watered the whole face of the ground. And the Lord God formed man of the dust of the ground, and breathed into his nostrils, the breath of life; and man became a living soul.

Document Set 1.1 References

A. An Akkadian Creation Epic
   E. A. Speiser and J. B. Pritchard, eds., *Ancient Near Eastern Texts: Relating to the Old Testment,* 3rd ed. (Princeton, N.J.: Princeton University Press, 1969), 60–68.
B. A Hymn to Aton
   James Breasted, *Ancient Records of Egypt* (Chicago: University of Chicago Press, 1906), 2:409–411.
C. A Hymn to Amon-Re
   Speiser and Pritchard, 365–367.
D. The Hebrew Account of the Creation
   Genesis 1:1–31; 2:1–7.

DOCUMENT SET 1.2
Gods and Humanity

These documents complement Set 1.1 by presenting early visions of the relationship between gods and the human race. The famous Egyptian Book of the Dead (an extract from which constitutes Document A) took shape in the Middle Kingdom, approximately 2100–1800 B.C., and advises a person facing postmortem judgment on how to account for his or her conduct in life. Part formulaic ritual and part ethical handbook, this is a key document explaining the ancient Egyptian understanding of life and death. Document B is an excerpt of the Mesopotamian epic poem Gilgamesh, which dates to somewhere between 2700 and 2500 B.C., although the extant version was copied on clay tablets about 650 B.C. The epic tells the tale of the King Gilgamesh's vain search for immortality. In the scene here, Gilgamesh learns from the guardian of the underworld, Utnapishtim, of the impassable gulf separating mortal humanity from the immortal gods. Equally tragic—and epic in its grandeur—is the story of the Fall of Man in Genesis, the passage that comes immediately after the Creation (Set 1.1).

Bear in mind that the Adam and Eve story, at least in the version we possess, is some 1,000 to 1,500 years more recent than Gilgamesh. You can contrast even more directly an ancient Mesopotamian myth and a later Hebrew version of the same story in Documents D and E; first the account of the Flood as it appears in Gilgamesh, and then the Hebrew account of Noah and the Flood from Genesis. Finally, Documents F and G contain two versions of the laws that the Hebrews' deity, Yahweh, revealed through Moses: the famous Ten Commandments (the fundamental rules of conduct in the Judeo-Christian tradition) and various other ordinances governing everyday transactions. Both extracts are given in the Book of Exodus, which recounts the Hebrews' deliverance from Egyptian bondage and their nomadic wandering in the desert under Moses's leadership, sometime during the thirteenth century B.C. (Exodus was assembled from various Hebrew traditions between the tenth and the fifth centuries B.C.)

What kind of societies do these documents reveal? What view of human destiny? How can documents such as these reveal significant information to historians, and what kinds of questions must scholars ask of these sources?

A. The Egyptian Book of the Dead Describes the Day of Reckoning

The Declaration of Innocence

To be said on reaching the Hall of the Two Truths so as to purge N of any sins committed and to see the face of every god:

Hail to you, great God, Lord of the Two Truths!
I have come to you, my Lord,
I was brought to see your beauty.
I know you, I know the names of the forty-two gods,
Who are with you in the Hall of the Two Truths,
Who live by warding off evildoers,
Who drink of their blood,
On that day of judging characters before Wennofer.
Lo, your name is "He-of-Two-Daughters,"
(And) "He-of-Maat's-Two-Eyes."
Lo, I come before you,
Bringing Maat to you,
Having repelled evil for you.

I have not done crimes against people,
I have not mistreated cattle,
I have not sinned in the Place of Truth.
I have not known what should not be known,
I have not done any harm.
I did not begin a day by exacting more than my due,
My name did not reach the bark of the mighty ruler.
I have not blasphemed a god,
I have not robbed the poor.
I have not done what the god abhors,
I have not maligned a servant to his master.
I have not caused pain,
I have not caused tears.
I have not killed,
I have not ordered to kill,
I have not made anyone suffer.
I have not damaged the offerings in the temples,
I have not depleted the loaves of the gods,
I have not stolen the cakes of the dead.
I have not copulated nor defiled myself.
I have not increased nor reduced the measure,
I have not diminished the arura.
I have not cheated in the fields.

Excerpt from "Book of the Dead" from *Ancient Egyptian Literature*, Vol. 1, by Miriam Litchheim, pp. 124–126. Copyright © 1973–1980 Regents of the University of California. Reprinted by permission of the University of California Press.

I have not added to the weight of the balance,
I have not falsified the plummet of the scales.
I have not taken milk from the mouth of children,
I have not deprived cattle of their pasture.
I have not snared birds in the reeds of the gods,
I have not caught fish in their ponds.
I have not held back water in its season,
I have not dammed a flowing stream,
I have not quenched a needed fire.
I have not neglected the days of meat offerings,
I have not detained cattle belonging to the god,
I have not stopped a god in his procession.
I am pure, I am pure, I am pure, I am pure!
I am pure as is pure that great heron in Hnes.
I am truly the nose of the Lord of Breath,
Who sustains all the people,
On the day of completing the Eye in On,
In the second month of winter, last day,
In the presence of the lord of this land.
I have seen the completion of the Eye in On!
No evil shall befall me in this land,
In this Hall of the Two Truths;
For I know the names of the gods in it,
The followers of the great God!

B. Gilgamesh Fails to Find Eternal Life

. . . So Utnapishtim looked at him and said, 'What is your name, you who come here wearing the skins of beasts, with your cheeks starved and your face drawn? Where are you hurrying to now? For what reason have you made this great journey, crossing the seas whose passage is difficult? Tell me the reason for your coming.'

He replied, 'Gilgamesh is my name. I am from Uruk, from the house of Anu.' Then Utnapishtim said to him, 'If you are Gilgamesh, why are your cheeks so starved and your face drawn? Why is despair in your heart and your face like the face of one who has made a long journey? Yes, why is your face burned with heat and cold; and why do you come here, wandering over the wilderness in search of the wind?

Gilgamesh said to him, 'Why should not my cheeks be starved and my face drawn? Despair is in my heart and my face is the face of one who has made a long journey. It was burned with heat and with cold. Why should I not wander over the pastures? My friend, my younger brother who seized and killed the Bull of Heaven and overthrew Humbaba in the cedar forest, my friend who was very dear to me and endured dangers beside me, Enkidu, my brother whom I loved, the end of mortality has overtaken him. I wept for him seven days and nights till the worm fastened on him. Because of my brother I am afraid of death; because of my brother I stray through the wilderness. His fate lies heavy upon me. How can I be silent, how can I rest? He is dust and I shall die also and be laid in the earth for ever.' Again Gilgamesh said, speaking to Utnapishtim, 'It is to see Utnapishtim whom we call the Faraway that I have come this journey. For this I have wandered over the world, I have crossed many difficult ranges, I have crossed the seas, I have wearied myself with travelling; my joints are aching, and I have lost acquaintance with sleep which is sweet. My clothes were worn out before I came to the house of Siduri. I have killed the bear and hyena, the lion and panther, the tiger, the stag and the ibex, all sorts of wild game and the small creatures of the pastures. I ate their flesh and I wore their skins; and that was how I came to the gate of the young woman, the maker of wine, who barred her gate of pitch and bitumen against me. But from her I had news of the journey; so then I came to Urshanabi the ferryman, and with him I crossed over the waters of death. Oh, father Utnapishtim, you who have entered the assembly of the gods, I wish to question you concerning the living and the dead, how shall I find the life for which I am searching?'

Utnapishtim said, 'There is no permanence. Do we build a house to stand for ever, do we seal a contract to hold for all time? Do brothers divide an inheritance to keep for ever, does the flood-time of rivers endure? It is only the nymph of the dragon-fly who sheds her larva and sees the sun in his glory. From the days of old there is no permanence. The sleeping and the dead, how alike they are, they are like a painted death. What is there between the master and the servant when both have fulfilled their doom? When the Anunnaki, the judges, come together, and Mammetun the mother of destinies, together they decree the fates of men. Life and death they allot but the day of death they do not disclose.'

C. The Fall of Man: Adam and Eve

And the Lord God planted a garden eastward in Eden; and there he put the man whom he had formed. And out of the ground made the Lord God to grow every tree that is pleasant to the sight, and good for food; the tree of life also in the midst of the garden, and the tree of knowledge of good and evil. . . . And the Lord God took the man, and put him into the garden of Eden to dress it and to keep it. And the Lord God commanded the man, saying, Of every tree of the garden thou mayest freely eat: But of the tree of the knowledge of good and evil, thou shalt not eat of it: for in the day that thou eatest thereof thou shalt surely die.

And the Lord God said, It is not good that the man should be alone; I will make him a help meet for him. And out of the ground the Lord God formed every beast of the field, and every fowl of the air; and brought them unto Adam to see what he would call them: and whatsoever Adam called every living creature, that was the name thereof. And Adam gave names to all cattle, and to the fowl of the air, and to every beast of the field; but for Adam there was not found a help meet for him. And the Lord God caused a deep sleep to fall upon Adam, and he slept; and he took one of his ribs, and closed up the flesh instead thereof. And the rib, which the Lord God had taken from man, made he a woman, and brought her unto the man. And Adam said, This is now bone of my bones, and flesh of my flesh: she shall be called Woman, because she was taken out of man. Therefore shall a man leave his father and his mother, and shall cleave unto his wife: and they shall be one flesh. And they were both naked, the man and his wife, and were not ashamed.

Now the serpent was more subtile than any beast of the field which the Lord God had made. And he said unto the woman, Yea, hath God said, Ye shall not eat of every tree of the garden? And the woman said unto the serpent, We may eat of the fruit of the trees of the garden: But of the fruit of the tree which is in the midst of the garden, God hath said, Ye shall not eat of it, neither shall ye touch it, lest ye die. And the serpent said unto the woman, Ye shall not surely die: For God doth know that in the day ye eat thereof, then your eyes shall be opened, and ye shall be as gods, knowing good and evil. And when the woman saw that the tree was good for food, and that it was pleasant to the eyes, and a tree to be desired to make one wise, she took of the fruit thereof, and did eat, and gave also unto her husband with her; and he did eat. And the eyes of them both were opened, and they knew that they were naked; and they sewed fig leaves together, and made, themselves aprons. And they heard the voice of the Lord God walking in the garden in the cool of the day: and Adam and his wife hid themselves from the presence of the Lord God amongst the trees of the garden. And the Lord God called unto Adam, and said unto him, Where art thou? And he said, I heard thy voice in the garden, and I was afraid, because I was naked; and I hid myself. And he said, Who told thee that thou wast naked? Hast thou eaten of the tree, whereof I com-

manded thee that thou shouldest not eat? And the man said, The woman whom thou gavest to be with me, she gave me of the tree, and I did eat. And the Lord God said unto the woman, What is this that thou hast done? And the woman said, The serpent beguiled me, and I did eat. And the Lord God said unto the serpent, Because thou hast done this, thou art cursed above all cattle, and above every beast of the field; upon thy belly shalt thou go, and dust shalt thou eat all the days of thy life: And I will put enmity between thee and the woman, and between thy seed and her seed; it shall bruise thy head, and thou shalt bruise his heel. Unto the woman he said, I will greatly multiply thy sorrow and thy conception; in sorrow thou shalt bring forth children; and thy desire shall be to thy husband, and he shall rule over thee. And unto Adam he said, Because thou hast hearkened unto the voice of thy wife, and hast eaten of the tree, of which I commanded thee, saying, Thou shalt not eat of it: cursed *is* the ground for thy sake; in sorrow shalt thou eat of it all the days of thy life; Thorns also and thistles shall it bring forth to thee; and thou shalt eat the herb of the field: In the sweat of thy face shalt thou eat bread, till thou return unto the ground; for out of it wast thou taken: for dust thou art, and unto dust shalt thou return. And Adam called his wife's name Eve; because she was the mother of all living. Unto Adam also and to his wife did the Lord God make coats of skins, and clothed them.

And the Lord God said, Behold, the man is become as one of us, to know good and evil: and now, lest he put forth his hand, and take also of the tree of life, and eat, and live for ever: Therefore the Lord God sent him forth from the garden of Eden, to till the ground from whence he was taken. So he drove out the man: and he placed at the east of the garden of Eden cherubim, and a flaming sword which turned every way, to keep the way of the tree of life.

D. The Babylonian Account of the Flood

'You know the city Shurrupak, it stands on the banks of Euphrates? That city grew old and the gods that were in it were old. There was Anu, Lord of the firmament, their father, and warrior Enlil their counsellor, Ninurta the helper, and Ennugi watcher over canals; and with them also was Ea. In those days the world teemed, the people multiplied, the world bellowed like a wild bull, and the great god was aroused by the clamour. Enlil heard the clamour and he said to the gods in council, "The uproar of mankind is intolerable and sleep is no longer possible by reason of the babel." So the gods agreed to exterminate mankind. Enlil did this, but Ea because of his oath warned me in a dream. He whispered their words to my house of reeds, "Reed-house, reed-house! Wall, O wall, hearken reed-house, wall reflect; O man of Shurrupak, son of Ubara-Tutu; tear down your house and build a boat, abandon possessions and look for life, despise worldly goods and save your soul alive. Tear down your house, I say, and build a boat. These are the measurements of the barque as you shall build her: let her beam equal her length, let her deck be roofed like the vault that covers the abyss; then take up into the boat the seed of all living creatures."

'When I had understood I said to my Lord, "Behold, what you have commanded I will honour and perform, but how shall I answer the people, the city, the elders?" Then Ea opened his mouth and said to me, his servant, "Tell them this: I have learnt that Enlil is wrathful against me, I dare no longer walk in his land nor live in his city; I will go down to the Gulf to dwell with Ea my Lord. But on you he will rain down abundance, rare fish and shy wild-fowl, a rich harvest-tide. In the evening the rider of the storm will bring you wheat in torrents."

'In the first light of dawn all my household gathered round me, the children brought pitch and the men whatever was necessary. On the fifth day I laid the keel and the ribs, then I made fast the planking. The ground-space was one acre, each side of the deck measured on hundred and twenty cubits, making a square. I built six decks below, seven in all, I divided them into nine sections with bulkheads between. I drove in wedges where needed, I saw to the punt-poles, and laid in supplies. The carriers brought oil in baskets, I poured pitch into the furnace and asphalt and oil; more oil was consumed in caulking, and more again the master of the boat took into his stores. I slaughtered bullocks for the people and every day I killed sheep. I gave the shipwrights wine to drink as though it were river water, raw wine and red wine and oil and white wine. There was feasting then as there is at the time of the New Year's festival; I myself anointed my head. On the seventh day the boat was complete.

'Then was the launching full of difficulty; there was shifting of ballast above and below till two thirds was submerged. I loaded into her all that I had of gold and of living things, my family, my kin, the beast of the field both wild and tame, and all the craftsmen. I sent them on board, for the time that Shamash had ordained was already fulfilled when he said, "In the evening, when the rider of the storm sends down the destroying rain, enter the boat and batten her down." The time was fulfilled, the evening came, the rider of the storm sent down the rain. I looked out at the weather and it was terrible, so I too boarded the boat and battened her down. All was now complete, the battening and the caulking; so I handed the tiller to Puzur-Amurri the steersman, with the navigation and the care of the whole boat.

'With the first light of dawn a black cloud came from the horizon; it thundered within where Adad, Lord of the storm was riding. In front over hill and plain Shullat and Hanish, heralds of the storm, led on. Then the gods of the abyss rose up; Nergal pulled out the dams of the nether waters, Ninurta the war-Lord threw down the dykes, and the seven judges of hell, the Annunaki, raised their torches, lighting the land with their livid flame. A stupor of despair went up to heaven when the god of the storm turned daylight to darkness, when he smashed the land like a cup. One whole day the tempest raged, gathering fury as it went, it poured over the people like the tide of battle; a man could not see his brother nor the people be seen from heaven. Even the gods were terrified at the flood, they fled to the highest heaven, the firmament of Anu; they crouched against the walls, cowering like curs. Then Ishtar the sweet-voiced Queen of Heaven cried out like a woman in travail: "Alas the days of old are turned to dust because I commanded evil; why did I command this evil in the council of all the gods? I commanded wars to destroy the people, but are they not my people, for I brought them forth? Now like the spawn of fish they float in the ocean." The great gods of heaven and of hell wept, they covered their mouths.

'For six days and six nights the winds blew, torrent and tempest and flood overwhelmed the world, tempest and flood raged together like warring hosts. When the seventh day dawned the storm from the south subsided, the sea grew calm, the flood was stilled; I looked at the face of the world and there was silence, all mankind was turned to clay. The surface of the sea stretched as flat as a roof-top; I opened a hatch and the light fell on my face. Then I bowed low, I sat down and I wept, the tears streamed down my face, for on every side was the waste of water. I looked for land in vain, but fourteen leagues distant there appeared a mountain, and there the boat grounded; on the mountain of Nisir the boat held fast, she held fast and did not bulge. One day she held, and a second day on the mountain of Nisir she held fast and did not budge. A third day, and a fourth day she held fast on the mountain and did not budge; a fifth day and a sixth day she held fast on the mountain. When the seventh day dawned I loosed a dove and let her go. She flew away, but finding no resting-place she returned. Then I loosed a swallow, and she flew away but finding no resting-place she returned. I loosed a raven, she saw that the waters had retreated, she ate, she flew around, she cawed, and she did not come back. Then I threw everything open to the four winds, I made a sacrifice and poured out a libation on the mountain top. Seven and again seven cauldrons I set up on their stands, I heaped up wood and cane and cedar and myrtle. When the gods smelled the sweet savour, they gathered like flies over the sacrifice. Then, at least, Ishtar also came, she lifted her necklace with the jewels of heaven that once Anu had made to please her. "O you gods here present, by the lapis lazuli round my neck I shall remember these days as I remember the jewels of my throat; these last days I shall not forget. Let all the gods gather round the sacrifice, except Enlil. He shall not approach this offering, for without reflection he brought the flood; he consigned my people to destruction."

'When Enlil had come, when he saw the boat, he was wrath and swelled with anger at the gods, the host of heaven, "Has any of these mortals escaped? Not one was to have survived the destruction." Then the god of the wells and canals Ninurta opened his mouth and said to the warrior Enlil, "Who is there of the gods that can devise without Ea? It is Ea alone who knows all things." Then Ea opened his mouth and spoke to warrior Enlil, "Wisest of gods, hero Enlil, how could you so senselessly bring down the flood?

> *Lay upon the sinner his sin,*
> *Lay upon the transgressor his transgression,*
> *Punish him a little when he breaks loose,*
> *Do not drive him too hard or he perishes;*
> *Would that a lion had ravaged mankind*
> *Rather than the flood,*
> *Would that a wolf had ravaged mankind*
> *Rather than the flood,*
> *Would that famine had wasted the world*
> *Rather than the flood,*
> *Would that pestilence had wasted mankind*
> *Rather than the flood.*

It was not I that revealed the secret of the gods; the wise man learned it in a dream. Now take your counsel what shall be done with him."

'Then Enlil went up into the boat, he took me by the hand and my wife and made us enter the boat and kneel down on either side, he standing between us. He touched our foreheads to bless us saying, "In time past Utnapishtim was a mortal man; henceforth he and his wife shall live in the distance at the mouth of the rivers." Thus it was that the gods took me and placed me here to live in the distance, at the mouth of the rivers.'

E. Biblical Account of the Flood

The earth also was corrupt before God; and the earth was filled with violence. And God looked upon the earth, and, behold, it was corrupt; for all flesh had corrupted his way upon the earth. And God said unto Noah, The end of all flesh is come before me; for the earth is filled with violence through them; and, behold, I will destroy them with the earth.

Make thee an ark of gopher wood; rooms shalt thou make in the ark, and shalt pitch it within and without with pitch. And this is the fashion which thou shalt make it of: . . . And, behold, I, even I, do bring a flood of waters upon the earth, to destroy all flesh, wherein is the breath of life, from under heaven; and every thing that is in the earth shall die. But with thee will I establish my covenant; and thou shalt come into the ark, thou, and thy sons, and thy wife, and thy sons' wives with thee. And of every living thing of all flesh, two of every sort shalt thou bring into the ark, to keep them alive with thee; they shall be male and female. Of fowls after their kind, and of cattle after their kind, of every creeping thing of the earth after his kind; two of every sort shall come unto thee, to keep them alive. And take thou unto thee of all food that is eaten, and thou shalt gather it to thee; and it shall be for food for thee, and for them. Thus did Noah; according to all that God commanded him, so did he.

And the Lord said unto Noah, Come thou and all thy house into the ark; for thee have I seen righteous before me in this generation. Of every clean beast thou shalt take in thee by sevens, the male and his female: and of beasts that are not clean by two, the male and his female. Of fowls also of the air by sevens, the male and the female; to keep seed alive upon the face of all the earth. For yet seven days, and I will cause it to rain upon the earth forty days and forty nights; and every living substance that I have made will I destroy from off the face of the earth. And Noah did according unto all that the Lord commanded him. And Noah was of six hundred years old when the flood of waters was upon the earth.

And Noah went in, and his sons, and his wife, and his sons' wives with him, into the ark, because of the waters of the flood. Of clean beasts, and of beasts that *are* not clean, and of fowls, and of every thing that creepeth upon the earth. There went in two and two unto Noah into the ark, the male and the female, as God, had commanded Noah. And it came to pass after seven days, that the waters of the flood were upon the earth.

In the six hundredth year of Noah's life, in the

second month, the seventeenth day of the month, the same day were all the fountains of the great deep broken up, and the windows of heaven were opened. And the rain was upon the earth forty days and forty nights. In the selfsame day entered Noah, and Shem, and Ham, and Japheth, the sons of Noah, and Noah's wife, and the three wives of his sons with them, unto the ark; They, and every beast after his kind, and all the cattle after their kind, and every creeping thing that creepeth upon the earth after his kind, and every fowl after his kind, every bird of every sort. And they went in unto Noah into the ark, two and two of all flesh, wherein is the breath of life. And they that went in, went in male and female of all flesh, as God had commanded him: and the Lord shut him in. And the flood was forty days upon the earth; and the waters increased, and bare up the ark, and it was lifted up above the earth. And the waters prevailed, and were increased greatly upon the earth; and the ark went upon the face of the waters. And the waters prevailed exceedingly upon the earth; and all the high hills, that were under the whole heaven, were covered. Fifteen cubits upward did the waters prevail; and the mountains were covered. And all flesh died that moved upon the earth, both of fowl, and of cattle, and of beast, and of every creeping thing that creepeth upon the earth, and every man: All in whose nostrils was the breath of life, of all that was in the dry land, died. And every living substance was destroyed which was upon the face of the ground, both man, and cattle, and the creeping things, and the fowl of the heaven; and they were destroyed from the earth: and Noah only remained alive, and they that were with him in the ark. And the waters prevailed upon the earth a hundred and fifty days.

And God remembered Noah, and every living thing, and all the cattle that was with him in the ark: and God made a wind to pass over the earth, and the waters assuaged. The fountains also of the deep and the windows of heaven were stopped, and the rain from heaven was restrained. And the waters returned from off the earth continually: and after the end of the hundred and fifty days the waters were abated. And the ark rested in the seventh month, on the seventeenth day of the month, upon the mountains of Ararat. . . .

And it came to pass at the end of forty days, that Noah opened the window of the ark which he had made: And he sent forth a raven, which went forth to and fro, until the waters were dried up from off the earth. Also he sent forth a dove from him, to see if the waters were abated from off the face of the ground. But the dove found no rest for the sole of her foot,

and she returned unto him into the ark; for the waters were on the face of the whole earth. . . .

And it came to pass in the six hundredth and first year, in the first month, the first day of the month, the waters were dried up from off the earth: and Noah removed the covering of the ark, and looked, and, behold, the face of the ground was dry. And in the second month, on the seven and twentieth day of the month, was the earth dried.

And God spake unto Noah, saying, Go forth of the ark, thou, and thy wife, and thy sons, and they sons' wives with thee. Bring forth with thee every living thing that is with thee, of all flesh, both of fowl, and of cattle, and of every creeping thing that creepeth upon the earth; that they may breed abundantly in the earth, and be fruitful, and multiply upon the earth. And Noah went forth, and his sons, and his wife, and his sons' wives with him: Every beast, every creeping thing, and every fowl, and whatsoever creepeth upon the earth, after their kinds, went forth out of the ark.

And Noah builded an altar unto the Lord; and took of every clean beast, and of every clean fowl, and offered burnt offerings on the altar. And the Lord smelled a sweet savor; and the Lord said in his heart, I will not again curse the ground any more for man's sake; for the imagination of man's heart is evil from his youth: neither will I again smite any more every thing living, as I have done. While the earth remaineth, seedtime and harvest, and cold and heat, and summer and winter, and day and night shall not cease.

And God blessed Noah and his sons, and said unto them, Be fruitful, and multiply, and replenish the earth.

F. Yahweh Prescribes the Ten Commandments

And it came to pass on the third day in the morning, that there were thunders and lightnings, and a thick cloud upon the mount, and the voice of the trumphet exceeding loud; so that all the people that was in the camp trembled. And Moses brought forth the people out of the camp to meet with God; and they stood at the nether part of the mount. And mount Sinai was altogether on a smoke, because the Lord descended upon it in fire: and the smoke thereof ascended as the smoke of a furnace, and the whole mount quaked greatly. And when the voice of the trumphet sounded long, and waxed louder and louder, Moses spake, and God answered him by a voice. And the Lord came down upon mount Sinai, on the top of the mount: and the Lord called Moses up to the top of the mount; and Moses went up. And the Lord said unto Moses, Go down, charge the people, lest they break through unto the Lord to gaze, and many of them perish. And let the priests also, which come near to the Lord, sanctify themselves, lest the Lord break forth upon them. And Moses said unto the Lord, The people cannot come up to mount Sinai: for thou chargedst us, saying, Set bounds about the mount, and sanctify it. And the Lord said unto him, Away, get thee down, and thou shalt come up, thou, and Aaron with thee: but let not the priests and the people break through to come up unto the Lord, lest he break forth upon them. So Moses, went down unto the people, and spake unto them.

And God spake all these words, saying, I am the Lord thy God, which have brought thee out of the land of Egypt, out of the house of bondage. Thou shalt have no other gods before me. Thou shalt not make unto thee any graven image, or any likeness of any thing that is in heaven above, or that is in the earth beneath, or that is in the water under the earth: Thou shalt not bow down thyself to them, nor serve them: for I the Lord thy God am a jealous God, visiting the iniquity of the fathers upon the children unto the third and fourth generation of them that hate me; And showing mercy unto thousands of them that love me, and keep my commandments. Thou shalt not take the name of the Lord thy God in vain: for the Lord will not hold him guiltless that taketh his name in vain. Remember the sabbath day, to keep it holy. Six days shalt thou labor, and do all thy work: But the seventh day is the sabbath of the Lord thy God: in it thou shalt not do any work, thou, nor thy son, nor thy daughter, thy manservant, nor thy maidservant, nor thy cattle, nor thy stranger that is within thy gates: For in six days the Lord made heaven and earth, the sea, and all that in them is, and rested the seventh day: wherefore the Lord blessed the sabbath day, and hallowed it.

Honor thy father and thy mother: that thy days may be long upon the land which the Lord thy God giveth thee. Thou shalt not kill. Thou shalt not commit adultery. Thou shalt not steal. Thou shalt not bear false witness against thy neighbor. Thou shalt not covet thy neighbor's house, thou shalt not covet thy neighbor's wife, nor his manservant, nor his maidservant, nor his ox, nor his ass, nor any thing that is thy neighbor's.

And all the people saw the thunderings and the lightnings, and the noise of the trumphet, and the mountain smoking: and when the people saw it, they removed, and stood afar off. And they said unto Moses, Speak thou with us, and we will hear: but let not God speak with us, lest we die. And Moses said unto the people, Fear not: for God is come to prove you, and that his fear may be before your faces, that ye sin not. And the people stood afar off, and Moses drew near unto the thick darkness where God was.

G. Yahweh's Laws for the Hebrews

If thou buy a Hebrew servant, six years he shall serve: and in the seventh he shall go out free for nothing. . . .

And if a man sell his daughter to be a maidservant, she shall not go out as the menservants do. . . .

And if a man smite his servant, or his maid, with a rod, and he die under his hand; he shall be surely punished. Not withstanding, if he continue a day or two, he shall not be punished: for he is his money. . . .

And if a man smite the eye of his servant, or the eye of his maid, that it perish; he shall let him go free for his eye's sake. And if he smite out his manservant's tooth, or his maidservant's tooth; he shall let him go free for his tooth's sake. . . .

Thou shalt neither vex a stranger, nor oppress him: for ye were strangers in the land of Egypt.

Ye shall not afflict any widow, or fatherless child. If thou afflict them in any wise, and they cry at all unto me, I will surely hear their cry; And my wrath shall wax hot, and I will kill you with the sword; and your wives shall be widows, and your children fatherless.

Document Set 1.2 References

A. The Egyptian Book of the Dead Describes the Day of Reckoning
   Miriam Lichtheim, trans. and ed., *Ancient Egyptian Literature* (Berkeley: University of California Press, 1973), 2:124–131.
B. Gilgamesh Fails to Find Eternal Life
   The Epic of Gilgamesh, trans. N. K. Sanders (Baltimore: Penguin, 1960), 105–107.
C. The Fall of Man: Adam and Eve
   Genesis 2:8–9, 15–25; 3:1–24.
D. The Babylonian Account of the Flood
   Epic of Gilgamesh, 108–113.
E. Biblical Account of the Flood
   Genesis 6:1–15, 17–22; 7:1–24; 8:1–4, 6–9, 13–22.
F. Yahweh Prescribes the Ten Commandments
   Exodus 19:16–25; 20:1–21.
G. Yahweh's Laws for the Hebrews
   Exodus 21:2, 7, 20–21, 26–27; 22:21–24.

DOCUMENT SET 1.3
Mesopotamian Kings and People

With this set we move to the purely human realm. Document A is another extract from Gilgamesh, in which the anonymous poet juxtaposes civilization and nature. Gilgamesh's friend Enkidu, representing humanity's pre-civilized condition, is seduced by an urban prostitute and rejected by his companions in the wild, and has to join Gilgamesh in a city over which the latter is king. It is remarkable to find so early in history the theme of the contrast of the freedom of nature with the confines of civilization. Note also how it is a woman (like the Hebrews' Eve) who seduces man out of his virtuous state of nature with an invitation to attain god-like wisdom.

Document B, dating from the middle of the third millennium B.C., gives another glimpse of the "early blessings" of civilization: incessant war, in this case waged between the Sumerian cities of Lagash and Umma. This theme continues in Document C, a clay tablet recording the rise and fall of the empire of Sargon of Akkad (*c. 2335–2280 B.C.)

The succeeding documents afford glimpses of early Mesopotamian society at work. In Document D, a Sumerian father exhorts his son to apply himself to the exacting task of becoming a scribe. Two excerpts from Hammurabi's Code (about 1800 B.C.) instruct tax collectors to deal justly with the people (Document E) and attempt to ensure that surgeons will perform only successful operations (Document F). Two Babylon contracts from the era of Hammurabi compose Document G.

Studying the documents in this set should give you an opportunity to assess the tensions and challenges of the earliest form of civilization to emerge in the Western world. Using these documents and *The Challenge of the West,* write a brief essay assessing the costs and benefits of Mesopotamia's breakthrough to civilization and urban society.

A. Civilization and Nature in the Gilgamesh Epic

The creeping creatures came, their heart delighting in water.
But as for him, Enkidu, born in the hills—
With the gazelles he feeds on grass,
With the wild beasts he drinks at the watering place,

With the creeping creatures his heart delights in water—
The woman beheld him, the savage-man,
The barbarous fellow from the depths of the steppe.

The woman freed her breasts, bared her bosom,
And he possessed her ripeness.

After he had had his fill of her charms,
He set his face toward his wild beasts.
On seeing him, Enkidu, the gazelles ran off,
The wild beasts of the steppe drew away from his body.
Startled was Enkidu, as his body became taut,
His knees were motionless—for his wild beasts had gone.
Enkidu had to slacken his pace—it was not as before;
But he now had wisdom, broader understanding.

The woman says to him, to Enkidu:
"You are wise, Enkidu, you are become like a god!
Why with the wild creatures do you roam over the steppe?
Come, let me lead you to ramparted Uruk,
To the holy temple, abode of Anu and Ishtar,
Where lives Gilgamesh, accomplished in strength,
And like a wild ox lords it over the folk."

B. War Ravages the Cities of Sumer

Enlil [leading deity of the Sumerian pantheon],[1] the king of all the lands, the father of all the gods, marked off the boundary for Ningirsu [the patron deity of Lagash], and Shara [the patron deity of Umma] by his steadfast word, (and) Mesilim, the king of Kish, measured it off in accordance with the word of Sataran, (and) erected a stele there. (But) Ush, the *ishakku* of Umma, violated (both) the decree (of the gods) and the word (given by man to man), ripped out its [the boundary's] stele, and entered the plain of Lagash.

(Then) did Ningirsu, Enlil's foremost warrior, do battle with (the men of) Umma in accordance with his [Enlil's] straightforward word; by the word of Enlil he hurled the great net upon them, and heaped up their skeleton (?) piles in the plain in their (various) places. (As a result) Eannatum, the *ishakku* of Lagash, the uncle of Entemena, the *ishakku* of Lagash, marked off the boundary with Enakalli, the *ishakku* of Umma; led out its [the boundary's] ditch from the Idnun [canal] to the Guedinna; inscribed (several) steles along that ditch; restored Mesilim's stele to its [former] place; (but) did not enter the plain of Umma, He (then) built there the Imdubba of

"Gilgamesh: Civilization and Nature," adapted from James B. Pritchard, *Ancient Near Eastern Texts Relating to the Old Testament,* 3/e, p. 75, Copyright © 1969 by Princeton University Press. Reprinted by permission of Princeton University Press.

[1]Brackets indicate explanatory insertions; parentheses supply missing words.

Ningirsu, the Namnunda-kigarra, (as well as) the shrine of Enlil, the shrine of Ninhursag [the Sumerian "mother" goddess], the shrine of Ningirsu, (and) the shrine of Utu (the sun-god).

(Moreover, following the boundary settlement) the Ummaites could eat the barley of (the goddess) Nanshe [another patron deity of Lagash] (and) the barley of Ningirsu to the amount of one *karu* (for each Ummaite, and only) for interest; (also) he (Eannatum) levied a tax on them, (and thus) brought in for himself (as revenue) 144,000 "large" *karu*.

Because this barley remained unpaid—(besides,) Ur-Lumma, the *ishakku* of Umma, deprived the boundary ditch of Ningirsu (and) the boundary ditch of Nanshe of water; ripped out its [the boundary ditch's] steles (and) put them to fire; destroyed the dedicated (?) shrines of the gods which had been built in the Namnunda-kigarra; obtained (the help of) the foreign lands; and (finally) crossed the boundary ditch of Ningirsu—Enannatum fought with him in the Gana-ugigga (where are) the fields and farms of Ningirsu, (and) Entemena, Enannatum's beloved son, defeated him. Ur-Lumma (then) fled, (while) he (Entemena) slew (the Ummaite forces) up into Umma (itself); (moreover) his (Ur-Lumma's) elite force (consisting of) 60 soldiers he wiped out (?) on the bank of the Lummagirnunta canal. (As for) its (Umma's fighting) men, he (Entemena) left their bodies in the plain (for the birds and beasts to devour) and (then) heaped up their skeleton (?) piles in five (separate) places.

At that time (however) Il, the temple-head of Zabalam, ravaged (?) (the land) from Girsu to Umma. It took to himself the *ishakku*-ship of Umma; deprived of water the boundary ditch of Ningirsu, the boundary ditch of Nanshe, the Imdubba of Ningirsu, that tract (of arable land) of the Girsu tracts which lies toward the Tigris, (and) the Namnunda-kigarra of Ninhursag; (and) paid (no more than) 3600 *karu* of the barley (due) Lagash. (And) when Entemena, the *ishakku* of Lagash, repeatedly sent (his) men to Il because of that (boundary) ditch, Il, the *ishakku* of Umma, the plunderer of fields and farms, the speaker of evil, said: "The boundary ditch of Ningirsu, (and) the boundary ditch of Nanshe are mine"; (indeed) he (even) said: "I shall exercise control from the Antasurra to the Dimgal-abzu temple." (However) Enlil and Ninhursag did not grant this to him.

Entemena, the *ishakku* of Lagash, whose name was pronounced by Ningirsu, made this (boundary) ditch from the Tigris to the Idnun in accordance with the straightforward word of Enlil, in accordance with the straightforward word of Ningirsu, (and) in accor-

dance with the straightforward word of Nanshe, (and) restored it for his beloved king Ningirsu and for his beloved queen Nanshe (after) he had constructed of bricks the foundation of the Namnunda-kigarra. May Shulutula, the (personal) god of Entemena, the *ishakku* of Lagash, whom Enlil gave the scepter, whom Enki (the Sumerian god of wisdom) gave wisdom, whom Nanshe fixed upon (in her) heart, the great *ishakku* of Ningirsu, the man who had received the words of the gods, step forward (in prayer) for the life of Entemena before Ningirsu and Nanshe unto distant days.

The Ummaite who (at any future time) will cross the boundary ditch of Ningirsu (and) the boundary ditch of Nanshe in order to take to himself fields and farms by force, whether he be (really) an Ummaite or a foreigner—may Enlil destroy him; may Ningirsu, after hurling his great net on him, bring down on him his lofty hand (and) his lofty foot; may the people of his city, having risen in rebellion, strike him down in the midst of his city.

c. The Rise of Sargon's Empire: An Akkadian Chronicle

Sargon, king of Agade, rose (to power) in the era of Ishtar and had neither rival nor opponent. He spread his terror-inspiring glamor over all the countries. He crossed the Sea in the East and he, himself, conquered the country of the West, in its full extent, in the 11th year (of his rule). He established there a central government [lit., he made its mouth be one]. He erected his stelae in the West. Their booty [i.e., the booty of the countries in the Eastern and Western Seas] he ferried over on rafts. He made his court officials live (around his residence, thus covering an area) of five double-miles, and held sway over the totality of the countries, without exception.

He marched against the country of Kazalla and turned Kazalla into ruin-hills and heaps (of rubble). He (even) destroyed (there every possible) perching place for a bird.

Afterwards, in his old age, all the countries revolted against him and they besieged him in Agade. (But) Sargon made an armed sortie and defeated them, knocked them over, and crushed their vast army.

Later on, Subartu rose with its multitudes, but it bowed to his military might. Sargon made sedentary this nomadic society. Their possessions he brought into Agade. He took away earth from the (foundation) pits of Babylon and he built upon it a(nother) Babylon beside the town of Agade. On account of the sacrilege he (thus) committed, the great lord

Marduk became enraged and destroyed his people by hunger. From the East to the West he alienated (them) from him and inflicted upon [him] (as punishment) that he could not rest (in his grave).

D. A Sumerian Father Demands That His Son Cease Carousing and Apply Himself to Learning the Scribe's Trade

"Where did you go?"

"I did not go anywhere."

"If you did not go anywhere, why do you idle about? Go to school, stand before your 'school-father,' recite your assignment, open your schoolbag, write your tablet, let your 'big brother' write your new tablet for you. After you have finished your assignment and reported to your monitor, come to me, and do not wander about in the street. Come now, do you know what I said?"

"I know, I'll tell it to you."

"Come, now, repeat it to me."

"I'll repeat it to you."

"Tell it to me.

"Come on, tell it to me."

"You told me to go to school, recite my assignment, open my schoolbag, write my tablet, while my 'big brother' is to write my new tablet. After finishing my assignment, I am to proceed to my work and to come to you after I have reported to my monitor. That's what you told me."

The father now continues with a long monologue:

"Come now, be a man. Don't stand about in the public square, or wander about the boulevard. When walking in the street, don't look all around. Be humble and show fear before your monitor. When you show terror, the monitor will like you."

. . . . *[About fifteen lines destroyed.]*

"You who wonder about in the public square, would you achieve success? Then seek out the first generations. Go to school, it will be of benefit to you. My son, seek out the first generations, inquire of them.

"Perverse one over whom I stand watch—I would not be a man did I not stand watch over my son—I spoke to my kin, compared its men, but found none like you among them.

"What I am about to relate to you turns the fool into a wise man, holds the snake as if by charms, and will not let you accept false phrases. Because my heart had been sated with weariness of you, I kept away from you and heeded not your fears and grumblings—no, I heeded not your fears and grumblings. Because of your clamorings, yes, because of your clamorings—I was angry with you—yes, I was angry with you. Because you do not look to your humanity, my heart was carried off as if by an evil wind. Your grumblings have put an end to me, you have brought me to the point of death.

"I, never in all my life did. I make you carry reeds to the canebrake. The reed rushes which the young and the little carry, you, never in your life did you carry them. I never said to you 'Follow my caravans.' I never sent you to work, to plow my field. I never sent you to work to dig up my field. I never sent you to work as a laborer. 'Go, work and support me,' I never in my life said to you.

"Others like you support their parents by working. If you spoke to your kin, and appreciated them, you would emulate them. They provide 10 gur [72 bushels] barley each—even the young ones provided their fathers with 10 gur each. They multiplied barley for their father, maintained him in barley, oil, and wool. But you, you're a man when it comes to perverseness, but compared to them you are not a man at all. You certainly don't labor like them—they are the sons of fathers who make their sons labor, but me—I didn't make you work like them.

"Perverse one with whom I am furious—who is the man who can really be furious with his son—I spoke to my kin and found something hitherto unnoticed. The words which I shall relate to you, fear them and be on your guard because of them. Your partner, your yokemate—you failed to appreciate him; why do you not emulate him? Your friend, your companion—you failed to appreciate him; why do you not emulate him? Emulate your older brother. Emulate your younger brother. Among all mankind's craftsmen who dwell in the land, as many as Enki (the god of arts and crafts) called by name (brought into existence), no work as difficult as the scribal art did he call by name. For if not for song (poetry)—like the banks of the sea, the banks of the distant canals, is the heart of song distant—you wouldn't be listening to my counsel, and I wouldn't be repeating to you the wisdom of my father. It is an accordance with the fate decreed by Enlil for man that a son follows the work of his father.

"I, night and day am I tortured because of you. Night and day you waste in pleasures. You have accumulated much wealth, have expanded far and wide, have become fat, big, broad, powerful, and puffed. But your kin waits expectantly for your misfortune, and will rejoice at it because you looked not to your humanity."

E. Hammurabi Instructs Tax Collectors to Deal Justly with People

To Sin-iddinam say, thus Hammurabi: Concerning the chief collector, Shêp-Sin, I wrote to thee, saying, "send him with one thousand eight hundred gur of sesame and nineteen minas of silver, due from him, as well as Sin-mushtal, the chief collector, with eighteen hundred gur of sesame and seven minas of silver, due from him, send them to Babylon, and send with them the market rate (?) . . ." But thou didst say that these chief collectors had said, "Just now is harvest-time, after harvest we will go." Thus they said, and thou didst tell me. Now the harvest is over. On receipt of this tablet, when I have sent to thee, send Shêp-Sin, the chief collector, with one thousand eight hundred gur of sesame and nineteen minas of silver, his due, and Sin-mushtal, the chief collector, with one thousand eight hundred gur of sesame and seven minas of silver, his due, to Babylon; and with them thy trustworthy guard, and with all their property let them come and appear before me. . . .

To Sin-iddinam say, thus saith Hammurabi: Lalu, the *kadurru*, hath informed me thus, saith he, "Ani-ellati, the governor *rabiânu*, has laid claim to [alienated] the field which I have held since . . . and [taken] the corn of the field." Thus he hath informed me. The tablet can be seen in the palace. Lalu holds two gan of land. Why has Ani-ellati, the governor, laid claim to Lalu's field? Inquire into the matter. If Ani-ellati has lent on mortgage to Lalu, the *kadurru*, grant him his debt and lay the blame on Ani-ellati, who lent on pledge.

F. Hammurabi's Code Lays Down the Law for Surgeons

215. If a physician performed a major operation on a freeman with a bronze lancet and has saved the freeman's life, or he opened up the eye-socket of a freeman with a bronze lancet and has saved the freeman's eye, he shall receive ten shekels[2] of silver.
216. If it was a commoner, he shall receive five shekels of silver.
217. If it was a freeman's slave, the owner of the slave shall give two shekels of silver to the physician.
218. If a physician performed a major operation on a freeman with a bronze lancet and has caused the freeman's death, or he opened up the eye-socket of a freeman and has destroyed the freeman's eye, they shall cut off his hand.

[2] A shekel is a measurement of weight (substantially less than an ounce), not a coin. A hired laborer earned about ten shekels in a year. The average price of a slave was about twenty shekels.

219. If a physician performed a major operation on a commoner's slave with a bronze lancet and has caused his death, he shall make good slave for slave.
220. If he opened up [the slave's] eye-socket with a bronze lancet and has destroyed his eye, he shall pay half his value in silver.

G. Business in the Age of Hammurabi: A Partnership and a Contract for Renting a Field

Erib-Sin and Nûr-Shamash entered into partnership and came into the temple of Shamash and made their plan. Silver, merchandise, man-servant, and maid-servant, abroad or at home, altogether they shared. Their purpose they realized. Money for money, man-servant and maid-servant, merchandise abroad or at home, from mouth to interest, brother with brother will not dispute. By Shamash and Malkat, by Marduk and Hammurabi, they swore. [Then follow seventeen witnesses. The document is not dated.]

. . . Amat-Shamash, a votary, rented out six oxen, among them two-cows; an irrigator, Amêl-Adadi; two tenders of an ox-watering machine, his nephews; three watering-machines for oxen; a female servant who tended the machines; half a gan of land for corn-growing; to Gimillu and Ilushu-banî. They shall make the yield of the field according to the average(?). They shall cause the corn to grow and measure it out to Amat-Shamash, daughter of Marduk-mushallim. In the time of harvest they shall measure out the corn to Amat-Shamash.

Document Set 1.3 References

A. Civilization and Nature in the Gilgamesh Epic
Adapted from E. A. Speiser and James B. Pritchard, eds., *Ancient Near Eastern Texts Relating to the Old Testament*, 3rd ed. with supplement (Princeton, N.J.: Princeton University Press, 1969), 75.
B. War Ravages the Cities of Sumer
Samuel Noah Kramer, *History Begins at Sumer* (Garden City, N.Y.: Doubleday, 1959), 41–43.
C. The Rise of Sargon's Empire: An Akkadian Chronicle
Speiser and Pritchard, 266.
D. A Sumerian Father Demands That His Son Cease Carousing and Apply Himself to Learning the Scribe's Trade
Kramer, 13–16.
E. Hammurabi Instructs Tax Collectors to Deal Justly with the People
Claude Herman Walter Johns, ed. and trans., *Babylonian and Assyrian Laws* (Edinburgh: T. & T. Clark, 1904), 325, 321.
F. Hammurabi's Code Lays Down the Law for Surgeons
Adapted from Speiser and Pritchard, 175.
G. Business in the Age of Hammurabi: A Partnership and a Contract for Renting a Field
Johns, 288–289, 196.

DOCUMENT SET 1.4
Egyptian Kings

One of the consistent themes of Egypt's immensely long history was the central role of the king in ensuring and keeping order in the valley of the Nile. When no strong central monarch reigned (as in the Old Kingdom's Ninth and Tenth dynasties, around 2100 B.C.), local rulers known as nomarchs tried to fill this kingly role, as we can see from the inscription of Nomarch Kheti II erected to proclaim his good intentions and generous deeds (Document A). The Nineteenth Dynasty king Harmhab (*1348–1320 B.C.) similarly announced his intention to do justice (Document B). Significantly this inscription comes from a period when traditional Egyptian values were being restored after Akhenaton's failed religious revolution. Finally, in Document C a royal official named Nu from the mid-second millennium B.C. wishes his moral qualities to be summed up as preparation for divine judgment after death.

It would be easy to dismiss these documents as hypocritical cant. Whether or not Nomarch Kheti, King Harmhab, and Nu actually behaved as decently as they claimed, the more interesting question is what values they saw fit to uphold. Moreover, these documents give a glimpse of the problems facing the Egyptian people. Write an essay outlining those values and social concerns as suggested by these documents.

A. The Old Kingdom Nomarch Kheti II Proclaims His Beneficent Intentions and Merciful Deeds

New Canal

I brought a gift for this city, in which there were no families of the Northland, nor people of Middle Egypt; making a monument in ———— I substituted a channel of ten cubits. I excavated for it upon the arable land. I equipped a gate for its ———— it in the ground of —— in one building, free from ——. I was liberal as to the monument —— —— ————. I sustained the life of the city, I made the —— with grain-food, to give water at midday, to —— —— ————. I supplied water in the highland district, I made a water-supply for this city of Middle Egypt in the mountain, which had not seen water. I secured the borders —— —— —— ——. I made the elevated land a swamp. I caused the water of the Nile to flood over the ancient landmarks, I made the arable land —— —— water. Every neighbor was supplied with water, and every citizen had Nile water to his heart's desire; I gave waters to his neighbors, and he was content with them.

Wealth and Generosity

I was rich in grain. When the land was in need, I maintained the city with kha and with heket. I allowed the citizen to carry away for himself grain; and his wife, the widow and her son. I remitted all imposts which I found counted by my fathers. I filled the pastures with cattle, every man had many colors; the cows brought forth twofold, the folds were full of calves. I was kind to the cow, when she said, "It is ——." I was one rich in bulls —— his ox; —— —— he lived well.

Kheti's Monuments

I was one rich in monuments of the temple, ———— who increased that which he found, who repeated offerings. I was a favorite, ————.

His Army

I was one strong with the bow, mighty with his sword, great in fear among his neighbors. I made a troop of soldiers ———— as commander of Middle Egypt.

His Fleet

I had goodly ships, —— —— —— —— a favorite of the king when he sailed up-river.

His Tomb

I was one vigilant in that which he said; with a determined heart on the evil day. I had a lofty tomb with a wide stair before the chamber.

Kheti's Childhood

I was a favorite of the king, a confidant of his princes, his exalted ones before Middle Egypt. He caused that I should rule as a child of a cubit (in height); he advanced my seat as a youth. He had me instructed in swimming along with the royal children. I was one correct of speech, free from opposition to his lord, who brought him up as a child. Siut was satisfied with my administration; Heracleopolis praised god for me. Middle Egypt and the Northland (Delta) said: "It is the instruction of a king."

B. A Middle Kingdom Egyptian Monarch Promises Justice

Introduction: The King's Zeal for the Relief of the People

His majesty took counsel with his heart how he might ————— expel evil and suppress lying. The plans of his majesty were an excellent refuge, repelling violence behind ————— and delivering the Egyptians from the oppressions which were among them. Behold, his majesty spent the whole time seeking the welfare of Egypt and searching out instances of oppression in the land. ————— came the scribe of his majesty. Then he seized palette and roll; he put it into writing according to all that his majesty, the king himself said. He spoke as follows: "My majesty commands ————— concerning all instances of oppression in the land.

Enactment Against Robbing the Poor of Dues for the Royal Breweries and Kitchens

If the poor man made for himself a craft with its sail, in order to be able to serve the Pharaoh, L. P. H., loading it with the dues for the breweries and kitchens of the Pharaoh, and he was robbed of the craft and the dues, the poor man stood reft of his goods and stripped of his many labors. This is wrong, and the Pharaoh will suppress it by his excellent measures. If there be a poor man who pays the dues of the breweries and kitchens of the Pharaoh, L. P. H., to the two deputies, and he be robbed of his goods and his craft, my majesty commands: that every officer who seizeth the dues and taketh the craft of any citizen of the army or of any person who is in the whole land, the law shall be executed against him, in that his nose shall be cut off, and he shall be sent to Tharu.

Against Robbing the Poor of Wood Due the Pharaoh

Furthermore, concerning the impost of wood, my majesty commands that if any officer find a poor man without a craft, then let him bring to him a craft for his impost from another, and let him send him to bring for him the wood; thus he shall serve the Pharaoh.

Against Exacting Dues from a Poor Man Thus Robbed

Furthermore, my majesty commands that if any poor man be oppressed by robbery, his cargo be emptied by theft of them, and the poor man stand reft of his goods, no further exactions for dues shall be made

from him when he has nothing. For it is not good, this report of very great injustice. My majesty commands that restitution be made to him; behold, ————————.

Against Robbing the Poor of Dues for the Harem or the Gods by the Soldiers

Furthermore, as for those who ————— and those who bring to the harem, likewise for the offerings of all gods, paying dues to the two deputies of the army and ————— my majesty commands that if any officer is guilty of extortions or thefts, the law shall be executed against him, in that his nose shall be cut off, and (he) shall be sent to Tharu likewise.

Against Unlawful Appropriation of Slave Service

When the officers of the Pharaoh's house of offerings have gone about tax-collecting in the towns, to take katha plant, they have seized the slaves of the people, and kept them at work for 6 days or 7 days, without one's being able to depart from them afar, so that it was an excessive detention indeed. It shall be done likewise against them. If there by any place where the stewards shall be tax-collecting, and any one shall hear, saying: "They are tax-collecting, to take katha-plant for themselves," and another shall come to report, saying: "My man slave (or) my female slave has been taken away and detained many days at work by the stewards;" it shall be done likewise against them.

Against Stealing of Hides by the Soldiers

The two divisions of troops which are in the field, one in the southern region, the other in the northern region, stole hides in the whole land, passing a year, without applying the brand of the royal house to cattle which were not due to them, thereby increasing their number, and stealing that which was stamped from them. They went out from house to house, beating and plundering without leaving a hide for the people —————. Then the officer of Pharaoh went about to each one, to collect the hides charged against him and came to the people demanding them, but the hides were not found with them (although) the amount charged against them could be established. They satisfied them, saying: "They have been stolen from us." A wretched case is this, therefore it shall be done likewise.

When the overseer of the cattle of Pharaoh, L. P. H., goes about to attend to the loan-herds in the whole land, and there be not brought to him the hides of the ———— which are on the lists, he shall not hold the people responsible for the hides if they have them not, but they shall be released by command of his majesty, according to his just purposes. As for any citizen of the army, (concerning) whom one shall hear, saying: "He goeth about stealing hides," beginning with this day, the law shall be executed against him, by beating him a hundred blows, opening five wounds, and taking from him by force the hides which he took.

Against Connivance of Dishonest Inspectors with Thievish Tax-Collectors, for a Share of the Booty

Now, as for this other instance of evil which the official staff were accustomed to commit, when they held inspection in the land, of that which happened against the law, the table-scribe of the queen and the table-scribe of the harem went about after the official staff, punishing them and investigating the affair —— —— of the one who sailed down- or up-river. One investigated it among the officials in the time of the King Menkheperre (Thutmose III). Now, when the one who sailed down- or up-river whom they took; and when the superior officials of the king, Menkheperre, went about after these officials each year, that they might make an expedition to the city, and that these superior officials might come to these officials, saying: "Give thou to us the consideration for the careless expedition;" then, behold, the Pharaoh, L. P. H., made the expedition at the feast of Opet each year without carelessness. One prepared the way before the Pharaoh and questioned the local magistrate, wherever he landed, concerning the corrupt official causing him to —— —— what he (the corrupt official) was like. As for the one who goes about again, afterward, to seek the consideration —— ——, then these officials shall go about with the expedition concerning the affairs of these poor people —————— ——————. My majesty commands to prevent that one shall do thus, beginning with this day —————— the landing; he is the one against whom one shall prosecute it.

Against Stealing Vegetables Under Pretense of Collecting Taxes

Likewise the collection of vegetables for the breweries and kitchens of the Pharaoh and ————— Extortion was practiced, and the officials plundered the poor, taking the best of their vegetables, saying: "They are for the impost of the Pharaoh." Thus they robbed the poor of their labors, so that a double impost was levied. Now, my majesty commands that as for any officials who come to collect vegetables for the impost of Pharaoh, L. P. H., in the arbors, and the —— houses of the estates of Pharaoh, L. P. H., and the —— of Pharaoh which contain vegetables, (concerning whom) one shall hear, saying: "They —— for

any —— of any citizen of the army, or any people, beginning with this day, the law shall be executed against them ——————— —— —— —— transgressing commands. . . .

Narratives of the King's Reforms, Containing also an Enactment Against Corrupt Judges

Appointment of Two Judges

I have improved this entire land —— —— —— I have sailed it, as far as south of the wall, I have given —————, I have learned its whole interior, I have traveled it entirely in its midst, I have searched in ————— and I have sought two officials perfect in speech, excellent in good qualities, knowing how to judge the innermost heart, hearing the words of the palace, the laws of the judgment-hall. I have appointed them to judge the Two Lands, to satisfy those who are in —————. I have given to each one his seat; I have set them in the two great cities of the South and the North; every land among them cometh to him without exception; I have put before them regulations in the daily register of the palace ————— —— —— I have directed them to the way of life, I lead them to the truth, I teach them, saying: "Do not associate with others of the people; do not receive the reward of another, not hearing —— —— —— ——. How, then, shall those like you judge others, while there is one among you committing a crime against justice.

Now, as to the obligation of silver and gold ————— —— —— my majesty remits it, in order that there be not collected an obligation of anything from the official staff of the South and North.

Punishment of Bribery

Now, as for any official or any priest (concerning whom) it shall be heard, saying: "He sits, to execute judgment among the official staff appointed for judgment, and he commits a crime against justice therein;" it shall be against him a capital crime. Behold, my majesty has done this, to improve the laws of Egypt, in order to cause that another should not be —— —— —————.

Appointment of Local Courts

Behold, my majesty appointed the official staff of the divine fathers, the prophets of the temples, the officials of the court of this land and the priests of the gods who comprise the official staff out of desire that they shall judge the citizens of every city. My majesty is legislating for Egypt, to prosper the life of its inhabitants; when he appeared upon the throne of Re.

Behold, the official staffs have been appointed in the whole land —— all —— to comprise the official staffs in the cities according to their rank.

The King's Audiences and Largesses

———————— They went around —— times a month, which he made for them like a feast; every man sat down at a portion of every good thing, of good bread, and meat of the storehouses, of royal provision ——————; their voices reached heaven, praising all benefits —— the heart of all the soldiers of the army. The king appeared to the people —— —— throwing (gifts) to them from the balcony while every man was called by his name by the king himself. They came forth from the presence rejoicing, laden with the provision of the royal house; yea, they took grain-heaps in the granary, every one of them bore barley and spelt, there was not found one who had nothing —————— their cities. If they did not complete the circuit therein within three days, —— —— their khetkhet-officers hastened after them to the place where they were immediately. They were found there ————.

C. An Egyptian Official Expresses His Ethical Concerns

"I have not done evil to mankind. I have not oppressed the members of my family, I have not produced evil in the place of right and truth. I have had no knowledge of worthless men. I have not wrought evil. I have not made to be the first consideration of each day that excessive labor should be performed for me. I have not brought forward my name for exaltation to honors. I have not ill-treated servants. I have not thought scorn of God. I have not defrauded the oppressed one of his property. I have not done that which is an abomination unto the gods. I have not caused harm to be done to the servant by his chief. I have not caused pain. I have made no one to weep. I have done no murder. I have not given the order for murder to be done for me. I have not inflicted pain upon mankind. I have not defrauded the temples of their offerings. I have not stolen the cakes of the gods. I have not committed fornication. . . . I have not turned back water at the time when it should flow. . . . I have not repulsed God in his manifestations. I am pure. I am pure. I am pure. . . . I have given bread to the hungry man, and water to the thirsty man, and clothes to the naked man, and a boat to the marooned sailor. I have made holy offerings to the gods, and funeral offerings to the dead."

Document Set 1.4 References

A. The Old Kingdom Nomarch Kheti II Proclaims His Beneficent Intentions and Merciful Deeds
   James Breasted, ed., *Ancient Records of Egypt* (Chicago: University of Chicago Press, 1906), 1:188–190.
B. A Middle Kingdom Egyptian Monarch Promises Justice
   Breasted, 3:111–119.
C. An Egyptian Official Expresses His Ethical Concerns
   Adapted from Epiphanius Wilson, ed., *Egyptian Literature* (London: The Colonial Press, 1901), 102–103.

DOCUMENT SET 1.5
Everyday Life in Egypt

These documents extend the themes explored in Set 1.4. Document A, the famous "Hymn to the Nile," gives an idea of how profoundly Egyptians felt themselves dependent on the life-giving floods that their great river brought them every year. Incidentally, it also reveals much about the conditions of everyday life. The hymns seem to date from about 1350 to 1100 B.C., but parts may be much older. With Document B we catch a glimpse of love and desire as felt by ancient Egyptians; the fact that this (and many other similar poems) amorously address a "sister" does not necessarily imply what we would today call an incestuous relationship; "sister" was apparently a term of endearment not to be taken literally. On the other hand, it is known that brother-sister marriages did occur not only among royalty but also among commoners. Document C, a text apparently intended as a model for copying by schoolboys aiming at a scribal career, extols the scribe's lucrative profession and gives a very dismal view of the lives endured by the rest of humanity.

Use these documents to analyze the concerns that ordinary Egyptians faced in their daily lives. You can extend your essay by also incorporating evidence from earlier sets.

A. The Hymn to the Nile

Worship of the Nile

Hail to thee, O Nile, that issues from the earth and comes to keep Egypt alive! Hidden in his form of appearance, a darkness by day, to whom minstrels have sung. He that waters the meadows which Re created, in order to keep every kid alive. He that makes to drink the desert and the place distant from water: that is his dew coming down (from) heaven. The beloved of Geb, the one who controls Nepri, and the one who makes the craftsmanship of Ptah to flourish.

The lord of fishes, he who makes the marsh-birds to go upstream. There are no birds which come down because of the hot winds. He who makes barley and brings emmer into being, that he may make the tem-

"Hymn to the Nile" from James B. Pritchard, *Ancient Near Eastern Texts Relating to the Old Testament,* 3/e, pp. 372–373, Copyright © 1969 by Princeton University Press. Reprinted by permission of Princeton University Press.

ples festive. If he is sluggish, (xii I) the nostrils are stopped up, and everybody is poor. If there be (thus) a cutting down in the food-offerings of the gods, then a million men perish among mortals, covetousness is practised, the entire land is in a fury, and great and small are on the execution-block. (But) people are different when he approaches. Khnum constructed him. When he rises, then the land is in jubilation, then every belly is in joy, every backbone takes on laughter, and every tooth is exposed.

The bringer of food, rich in provisions, creator of all good, lord of majesty, sweet of fragrance. What is in him is satisfaction. He who brings grass into being for the cattle and (thus) gives (5) sacrifice to every god, whether he be in the underworld, heaven, or earth, him who is under his authority. He who takes in possession the Two Lands, fills the magazines, makes the granaries wide, and gives things (to) the poor.

He who makes every beloved tree to grow, without lack of them. He who brings a ship into being by his strength, without hewing in stone. The enduring image with the White Crown. He cannot be seen; (he has) no taxes; he has no levies; no one can read of the mystery; no one knows the place where he is; he cannot be found by the power of writing. (He has) no shrines; he has no portion. He has no service of (his) desire. (But) generations of thy children jubilate for thee, and men give thee greeting as a king, stable of laws, coming forth (at) his season and filling Upper and Lower Egypt. (xiii I) (Whenever) water is drunk, every eye is in him, who gives an excess of his good.

He who was sorrowful is come forth gay. Every heart is gay, Sobek, the child of Neith, laughs, and the Ennead, in which thou art, is exalted. Vomiting forth and making the field to drink. Anointing the whole land. Making one man rich and slaying another, (but) there is no coming to trial with him, who makes satisfaction without being thwarted, for whom no boundaries are made.

A maker of light when issuing from darkness, a fat for his cattle. His limits are all that is created. There is no district which can live without him. Men are clothed (5) with flax from his meadows, for (he) made Hedj-hotep for his service. (He) made anointing with his unguents, being the associate of Ptah in his nature, bringing into being all service in him, all writings and divine words, his responsibility in Lower Egypt.

Entering into the underworld and coming forth above, loving to come forth as a mystery. If thou art (too) heavy (to rise), the people are few, and one begs for the water of the year. (Then) the rich man looks like him who is worried, and every man is seen (to be) carrying his weapons. This is no companion backing up a companion. There are no garments for clothing; there are no ornaments for the children of nobles. There is no listening at night, that one may answer with coolness. There is no anointing for anybody.

He who establishes truth in the heart of men, for it is said: "Deceit comes after poverty." If one compares thee with the great green sea, which does not (xiv I) control the Grain-God, whom all the gods praise, there are no birds coming down from his desert. His hand does not beat with gold, with making ingots of silver. No one can eat genuine lapis lazuli. (But) barley is foremost and lasting.

Men began to sing to thee with the harp, and men sing to thee with the hand. The generations of thy children jubilate for thee. Men equip messengers for thee, who come (back) bearing treasures (to) ornament this land. He who makes a ship to prosper before mankind; he who sustains hearts in pregnant women; he who loves a multitude of all (kinds of) his cattle.

When thou risest in the city of the ruler, then men are satisfied with the goodly produce of the meadows. (5) Oh for the little lotus-blossoms, everything that pours forth upon earth, all (kinds of) herbs in the hands of children! They have (even) forgotten how to eat. Good things are strewn about the houses. The land comes down frolicking.

When the Nile floods, offering is made to thee, oxen are sacrificed to thee, great oblations are made to thee, birds are fattened for thee, lions are hunted for thee in the desert, fire is provided for thee. And offering is made to every (other) god, as is done for the Nile, with prime incense, oxen, cattle, birds, and flame. The Nile has made his cavern in Thebes, and his name is no (longer) known in the underworld. Not a god will come forth in his form, if the plan is ignored.

O all men who uphold the Ennead, (10) fear ye the majesty which his son, the All-Lord, has made, (by) making verdant the two banks. So it is "Verdant art thou!" So it is "Verdant art thou!" So it is "O Nile, verdant art thou, who makest man and cattle to live!"

It has come to a good and successful end.

B. "The Love of My Sister Is on Yonder Side": An Egyptian Love Song

The love of my sister is on yonder side,
A stream lies between us,
And a crocodile waits in the shallows.
But when I go down into the water,
I wade the current,
My heart is great upon the stream,
And the waves are like land unto my feet.
It is the love of her that makes me steady,
For it makes a water-charm for me!
When I see my sister coming,
My heart dances,
And my arms open wide to embrace her, . . .
When the *mistress* comes to me.
THE END.

C. "Be a Scribe!" A School Text Contrasts Ordinary Peoples' Lives with That of the Scribe

1. Title

[Beginning of the instruction in letter-writing made by the royal scribe and chief overseer of the cattle of Amen-Re, King of Gods, Nebmare-nakht] for his apprentice, the scribe Wenemdiamun.

2. Praise of the Scribe's Profession

[The royal scribe] and chief overseer of the cattle of Amen-[Re, King of Gods, Nebmare-nakht speaks to the scribe Wenemdiamun]. [Apply yourself to this] noble profession. "Follower of Thoth" is the good name of him who exercises it. —————. He makes friends with those greater than he. Joyful ————. Write with your hand, read with your mouth. Act according to my words. —————, my heart is not disgusted. —————. ————— to my instructing you. You will find it useful. ————— [with bread and] beer. You will be advanced by your superiors. You will be sent on a mission —————. Love writing, shun dancing; then you become a worthy official. Do not long for the marsh ticket. Turn your back on throw stick and chase. By day write with your fingers; recite by night. Befriend the scroll, the palette. It pleases more than wine. Writing for him who knows

Excerpt from "Papyrus Lansing: A Schoolbook" from *Ancient Egyptian Literature*, Vol. 3, by Miriam Litchheim, pp. 168–172. Copyright © 1973–1980 Regents of the University of California. Reprinted by permission of the University of California Press.

it is better than all other professions. It pleases more than bread and beer, more than clothing and ointment. It is worth more than an inheritance in Egypt, than a tomb in the west.

3. Advice to the Unwilling Pupil

Young fellow, how conceited you are! You do not listen when I speak. Your heart is denser than a great obelisk, a hundred cubits high, ten cubits thick. When it is finished and ready for loading, many work gangs draw it. It hears the words of men; it is loaded on a barge. Departing from Yebu it is conveyed, until it comes to rest on its place in Thebes.

So also a cow is bought this year, and it plows the following year. It learns to listen to the herdsman; it only lacks words. Horses brought from the field, they forget their mothers. Yoked they go up and down on all his majesty's errands. They become like those that bore them, that stand in the stable. They do their utmost for fear of a beating.

But though I beat you with every kind of stick, you do not listen. If I knew another way of doing it, I would do it for you, that you might listen. You are a person fit for writing, though you have not yet known a woman. Your heart discerns, your fingers are skilled, your mouth is apt for reciting.

Writing is more enjoyable than enjoying a basket of *b3y* and beans; more enjoyable than a mother's giving birth, when her heart knows no distaste. She is constant in nursing her son; her breast is in his mouth every day. Happy is the heart (of) him who writes; he is young each day. . . .

5. All Occupations Are Bad Except That of the Scribe

See for yourself with your own eye. The occupations lie before you.

The washerman's day is going up, going down. All his limbs are weak, (from) whitening his neighbors' clothes every day, from washing their linen.

The maker of pots is smeared with soil, like one whose relations have died. His hands, his feet are full of clay; he is like one who lives in the bog.

The cobbler mingles with vats. His odor is penetrating. His hands are red with madder, like one who is smeared with blood. He looks behind him for the kite, like one whose flesh is exposed.

The watchman prepares garlands and polishes vase-stands. He spends a night of toil just as one on whom the sun shines.

The merchants travel downstream and upstream. They are as busy as can be, carrying goods from one town to another. They supply him who has wants. But the tax collectors carry off the gold, that most precious of metals.

The ships' crews from every house (of commerce), they receive their loads. They depart from Egypt for Syria, and each man's god is with him. (But) not one of them says: "We shall see Egypt again!"

The carpenter who is in the shipyard carries the timber and stacks it. If he gives today the output of yesterday, woe to his limbs! The shipwright stands behind him to tell him evil things.

His outworker who is in the fields, his is the toughest of all the jobs. He spends the day loaded with his tools, tied to his tool-box. When he returns home at night, he is loaded with the tool-box and the timbers, his drinking mug, and his whetstones.

The scribe, he alone, records the output of all of them. Take note of it!

6. The Misfortunes of the Peasant

Let me also expound to you the situation of the peasant, that other tough occupation. [Comes] the inundation and soaks him ———, he attends to his equipment. By day he cuts his farming tools; by night he twists rope. Even his midday hour he spends on farm labor. He equips himself to go to the field as if he were a warrior. The dried field lies before him; he goes out to get his team. When he has been after the herdsman for many days, he gets his team and comes back with it. He makes for it a place in the field. Comes dawn, he goes to make a start and does not find it in its place. He spends three days searching for it; he finds it in the bog. He finds no hides on them; the jackals have chewed them. He comes out, his garment in his hand, to beg for himself a team.

When he reaches his field he finds (it) [broken up]. He spends time cultivating, and the snake is after him. It finishes off the seed as it is cast to the ground. He does not see a green blade. He does three plowings with borrowed grain. His wife has gone down to the merchants and found nothing for [barter.] Now the scribe lands on the shore. He surveys the harvests. Attendants are behind him with staffs, Nubians with clubs. One says (to him): "Give grain." "There is none." He is beaten savagely. He is bound, thrown in the well, submerged head down. His wife is bound in his presence. His children are in fetters. His neighbors abandon them and flee. When it's over, there's no grain.

If you have any sense, be a scribe. If you have learned about the peasant, you will not be able to be one. Take note of it! . . .

8. The Scribe Does Not Suffer Like the Soldier

Furthermore. Look, I instruct you to make you sound; to make you hold the palette freely. To make you become one whom the king trusts; to make you gain entrance to treasury and granary. To make you receive the ship-load at the gate of the granary. To make you issue the offerings on feast days. You are dressed in fine clothes; you own horses. Your boat is on the river; you are supplied with attendants. You stride about inspecting. A mansion is built in your town. You have a powerful office, given you by the king. Male and female slaves are about you. Those who are in the fields grasp your hand, on plots that you have made. Look, I make you into a staff of life! Put the writings in your heart, and you will be protected from all kinds of toil. You will become a worthy official.

Do you not recall the (fate of) the unskilled man? His name is not known. He is ever burdened (like an ass carrying) in front of the scribe who knows what he is about.

Come, (let me tell) you the woes of the soldier, and how many are his superiors: the general, the troop-commander, the officer who leads, the standard-bearer, the lieutenant, the scribe, the commander of fifty, and the garrison-captain. They go in and out in the halls of the palace, saying: "Get laborers!" He is awakened at any hour. One is after him as (after) a donkey. He toils until the Aten sets in his darkness of night. He is hungry, his belly hurts; he is dead while yet alive. When he receives the grain-ration, having been released from duty, it is not good for grinding.

He is called up for Syria. He may not rest. There are no clothes, no sandals. The weapons of war are assembled at the fortress of Sile. His march is uphill through mountains. He drinks water every third day; it is smelly and tastes of salt. His body is ravaged by illness. The enemy comes, surrounds him with missiles, and life recedes from him. He is told: "Quick, forward, valiant soldier! Win for yourself a good name!" He does not know what he is about. His body is weak, his legs fail him. When victory is won, the captives are handed over to his majesty, to be taken to Egypt. The foreign woman faints on the march; she hangs herself (on) the soldier's neck. His knapsack drops, another grabs it while he is burdened with the woman. His wife and children are in their village; he dies and does not reach it. If he comes out alive, he is worn out from marching. Be he at large, be he detained, the soldier suffers. If he leaps and joins the deserters, all his people are imprisoned. He dies on the edge of the desert, and there is none to perpetuate his name. He suffers in death as in life. A big sack is brought for him; he does not know his resting place.

Be a scribe, and be spared from soldiering! You call and one says: "Here I am." You are safe from torments. Every man seeks to raise himself up. Take note of it!

Document Set 1.5 References

A. The Hymn to the Nile
   E. A. Speiser and J. B. Pritchard, eds., *Ancient Near Eastern Texts: Relating to the Old Testment,* 3rd ed. with supplement (Princeton, N.J.: Princeton University Press, 1969), 372–373.
B. "The Love of My Sister Is on Yonder Side": An Egyptian Love Song
   Speiser and Pritchard, 365–367.
C. "Be a Scribe!" A School Text Contrasts Ordinary Peoples' Lives with That of the Scribe
   Miriam Lichtheim, trans. and ed., *Ancient Egyptian Literature* (Berkeley: University of California Press), 3:168–172.

CHAPTER

2

New Paths for Western Civilization,
c. 1000–500 B.C.

DOCUMENT SET 2.1
Assyria and Neo-Babylon

The Assyrian empire arose after the ancient Near East's "time of troubles" at the beginning of the first millennium B.C., and it endured until the early sixth century B.C. It left its mark on Western civilization as a state founded on ruthlessly employed military power. Some sense of Assyrian ferocity can be garnered from Document A, a long inscription in which the ninth-century B.C. king Ashurnasirpal II boasts of his power and prowess. Inscriptions like this were meant to intimidate and so probably exaggerate a bit. Nor was Assyrian society occupied only with war, as the brief extracts from everyday contracts attest (Document B). How the busy commerce of the capital city Nineveh appeared to a rural Hebrew prophet may be gauged from Document C, an extract from the biblical Book of Nahum.

Predicting the future by carefully studying the position and movement of celestial bodies—what we now call astrology—was a highly developed pursuit in ancient Babylonia, and aside from whatever success the stargazers had in assuaging their customers' worries (Document D), their labors resulted in highly accurate observations and in some important mathematical advances.

A. A Year in the Reign of Assur-Nasir-Pal, a Busy Assyrian Conqueror

Year 4. A Third Campaign Against Zamua

In the eponymy of Limutti-adur, while I was staying in Nineveh, men brought me word that Ameka and Arashtua had withheld the tribute and forced labor due unto Assur, my lord. At the word of Assur, the great lord, my lord, and of Nergal, my leader, on the first day of the month of *Simânu* I ordered a call to arms for the third time against the land of Zamua. I did not wait for my chariots and hosts; I departed from the city of Kakzi, the Lower Zab I crossed. I entered the pass of Babite, I crossed the Radânu, drawing nearer every day to the foot of Mount Simaki. Cattle, sheep and wine, the tribute of the land of Dagara, I received. The ———— chariots and picked cavalry (men) I took with me, and all the night, until the dawn, I marched from (along?) the foot of the mountain of Simaki. I crossed the Turnat, and with all haste(?) to the city of Ammali, the stronghold of Arashtu, I drew near. With battle and assault I stormed the city, I took (it). 800 of their fighting men I struck down with the sword, with their corpses I filled the streets of their city, with their

Excerpt from "Annals of Assur-Nasir-Pal" from D. D. Luckenbill, ed., *Ancient Records of Assyria and Babylonia* Vol. 1, pp. 151–154. Copyright © 1926 University of Chicago Press. Reprinted by permission of the publisher.

blood I dyed their houses. Many men I captured alive with my hand, and I carried off great spoil from them; the city I destroyed, I devastated, I burned with fire.

The city of Hudun and twenty cities of its neighborhood I captured; I slew the inhabitants thereof, their spoil, their cattle, and their sheep I carried off; their cities I destroyed, I devastated, I burned with fire; their young men and their maidens I burned in the flames. The city of Kisirtu, their stronghold, ruled by (lit., of) Sabini, together with ten cities of its neighborhood, I captured, I slew their inhabitants, their spoil I carried away. The cities of the Bâreans, which were ruled by Kirtiara, and those of the men of Dûra and of Bunisa, as far as the pass of Hashmar, I destroyed, I devastated, I burned with fire, I turned them into mounds and ruins. I departed from the cities of Arashtua, I entered the pass between the steep mountains of Lâra and Bidirgi, which for the passage of chariots and hosts was not suited (lit., laid), to Zamri, the royal city of Ameka of the land of Zamua, I drew near.

Ameka became afraid before my mighty weapons and my fierce battle array, and occupied a steep mountain. The goods of his palace and his chariot I carried away; from the city of Zamri I departed. I crossed the Lallû and marched to Mount Etini, a difficult region, which was not suited (lit., laid) for the passage of chariots and armies, and unto which none among the kings, my fathers, had come nigh. The king, together with his armies, climbed up into Mount Etini. His goods and his possessions, many copper utensils, a copper wild-ox, vessels of copper, bowls of copper, cups of copper, the wealth of his palace, his heaped-up treasures, I carried out of the mountain, returned to my camp and spent the night. With the help of Assur and Shamash, the gods, my helpers, I departed from that camp, and I set out after him. I crossed the Edir River and in the midst of the mighty mountains of Sû and Elaniu I slew multitudes of them. His goods and his possessions, a copper wild-ox, vessels of copper, bowls of copper, dishes of copper; many copper utensils, tables which were overlaid with gold, their cattle and their flocks, their possessions, their heavy spoil, from the foot of Mount Elaniu I carried off. I took his horse from him. Ameka, to save his life, climbed up into Mount Sabua.

The cities of Zamru, Arasitku, Ammaru, Parsindu, Iritu, and Suritu, his strongholds, together with 150 cities which lay round about, I destroyed, I devastated, I burned with fire, into mounds and ruin heaps I turned them. While I was staying before the city of Parsindi, I placed in reserve the cavalry and pioneers (sappers). Fifty of Ameka's warriors I slew in the field, I cut off their heads and bound them to the tree trunks within his palace court. Twenty men I captured alive and I immured them in the wall of his palace. From the city of Zamri I took with me the cavalry and pioneers, and marched against the cities of Ata, of Arzizu, unto which none among the kings my fathers had come nigh. The cities of Arzizu and Arsindu, his strongholds, together with ten cities which lay round about on the steep mountain of Nispi, I captured. I slew the inhabitants thereof; the cities I destroyed, I devastated, I burned with fire, and returned to my camp.

At that time I received copper,—*tabbili* of copper, and rings(?) of copper, and many *shariâte* from the land of Sipirmena who(se inhabitants?) speak like women.

From the city of Zamri I departed and into the difficult mountain of Lâra, which was not suited for the passage of chariots and armies, with hatchets of iron I cut and with axes of bronze I hewed (a way), and I brought over the chariots and troops and came down to the city of Tukulti-Assur-asbat, which the men of the land of Lullu call Arakdi. All the kings of the land of Zamua were affrighted before the fury of my arms and the terror of my dominion, and embraced my feet. Tribute and tax,—silver, gold, lead, copper, vessels of copper, garments of brightly colored wool, horses, cattle, sheep, and wine I laid upon them (in greater measure) than before and used their forced laborers in the city of Calah. While I was staying in the land of Zamua, the men of the cities Huduni, Hartishi, Hubushkia and Gilzani were overwhelmed with the terrifying splendors of Assur, my lord, and they brought me tribute and tax,—silver, gold, horses, garments of brightly colored wool, cattle, flocks, and wine. The people, such as had fled from before my arms, climbed up into the mountains. I pursued them. Between the mountains of Aziru and Simaki they had settled themselves, and had made the city of Mesu their stronghold. Mount Aziru I destroyed, I devastated, and from the midst of Mount Simaki as far as the river Turnat I strewed their corpses. 500 of their warriors I slew and carried off their heavy spoil, the cities I burned with fire.

At that time, in the land of Zamua, the city of Atlila, which for the scepter of the king of Karduniash they had seized, had decayed and had become (lit., turned into) a mound and ruin heap. Assur-nâsir-pal restored it. I surrounded it with a wall, and I erected therein a palace for my royal dwelling, I adorned it and made it glorious and greater than it was before. Grain and straw from the whole land I heaped up within it, and I called its name Dûr-Assur.

B. Everyday Life in Assyria: A Labor Contract, a Loan Secured by Land and Slaves, and a Theft

Nâmir-nûrshu from Rutum, Rîsh-Shamash, son of Marduk-nâsir, for wages, for one year, has hired. His wages for one year, twenty-four *KA* of oil, he shall pay, and he shall clothe him. In Elul he shall enter, in Tirinu he shall leave. Two witnesses. Dated in the reign of Hammurabi.

Shamash-bâni-aplu, Latubashâni, Ukîn-abîa, Ahu . . . in all four workmen. Two talents of bronze, three homers one *SE* of cooked corn. On the tenth of the month they shall do the work. All the repairs and the beams they shall make fast. They shall fix the balks, and set up the roof. If the bricks are not sufficient . . . the month they do not give, they shall work and finish. Then follow seven witnesses. Dated on the sixth of some month, B.C. 734.

The lady Addati, the *šakintu*, lends two minas of silver, Carchemish standard, exact sum, to D, the deputy of the chief of the city. In lieu of the two minas of silver, a plot of twelve homers of land in the outskirts of Nineveh, Kurdi-Adadi, his wife and three sons, Kandilânu and his wife, in all seven people, and twelve homers of land, are pledged. On the day that one returns the money, the other shall release the land and people. Dated the first of Marchesvan, B.C. 694. Ten witnesses.

Amêl-Ninsah sues Garudu for the rent of a field. The debtor not paying was ejected. Apíl-Sin.

Shûmi-ersitim sues for right to a sheep and some corn, the *naptânu* of a god. Judges grant him half share. Hammurabi 9.

Judges summon Ibik-iltum before Elali-bânî to account for corn. He purges himself on oath. N. D.

Amat-Shamash claims to be the adopted daughter of Shamash-gâmil and his wife Ummi-Arahtum. Her witnesses proving unsatisfactory, her claim was disallowed on the oath of Ummi-Arahtum that they had never adopted her. Hammurabi (?).

Ilushu-abushu hired a pack-ass, *imer bilti*, of Ardi-Sin and Silli-Ishtar and lost it. The judges awarded them sixteen shekels of silver as compensation. Apil-Sin 5.

Babilîtum sued Erish-Saggil, Ubar-Nabium, and Markuk-nâsir for a share of her family possessions, *bît abiša*. The judges assigned her a share. Samsu-iluna 5.

Nidnusha and Shamash-abilu sue the daughter of Sin-eribam about property which she claimed to have inherited. They charge her with having forged the will of Amti-Shamash in her favor. The judges went to Gagim, where the property was, and examined witnesses who proved that Amti-Shamash had left the property to the daughter of Sin-eribam. The judges therefore confirmed her title. N. D.

Mâr-ersitim left a female slave Damiktum to Erib-Sin. His wife Mazabatum and his brother Ibni-Shamash dispute this legacy. The judges inspect a document by which Erib-Sin, on the suit of Mârersitim, had granted Damiktum to Mazabatum and Ibni-Shamash. The judges return Damiktum to Mazabatum. Hammurabi (?).

Thus: a scribe A prosecuted a farmer B for the theft of a bull. They came before Nabû-zêr-kênish-lîshir, the deputy *hazânu* of Nineveh. Restitution, bull for bull, was imposed on the defendant, who meantime was held for the fine. "On the day that he shall have made good the value of the bull he shall go free." Dated the 12th of Elul. Eponymy of Mushallim-Ashur. Twelve witnesses.

Again: A stole four slaves of B, who summoned him before the *sukallu*. The judge laid on him a fine to two hundred and ten minas of copper. B then deposited a pledge with A, either himself, or a slave, to perform work equivalent to the amount of the debt. If B, or any representative of his, pays the money, the pledge is void. "Whoever shall withdraw from this agreement, Ashur and Shamash shall be his judges, he shall pay ten minas of silver and ten minas of gold, he shall pay it in the treasury of Bêlit." Dated the 10th of Adar, b.c. 678. Eleven witnesses.

C. The Hebrew Prophet Nahum Denounces Nineveh for Its Whoredom and Commerce

Woe to the bloody city! it is all full of lies and robbery; the prey departeth not; The noise of a whip, and the noise of the rattling of the wheels, and of the prancing horses, and of the jumping chariots. The horseman lifeth up both the bright sword and the glittering spear: and there is a multitude of slain, and a great number of carcasses; and there is none end of their corpses; they stumble upon their corpses:

Because of the multitude of the whoredoms of the well-favored harlot, the mistress of witchcrafts, that selleth nations through her whoredoms, and families through her witchcrafts. Behold, I am against thee, saith the Lord of hosts; and I will discover thy skirts upon thy face, and I will show the nations thy nakedness, and the kingdoms thy shame. And I will cast abominable filth upon thee, and make thee vile, and will set thee as a gazingstock. And it shall come to pass, that all they that look upon thee shall flee from thee, and say, Nineveh is laid waste: who will bemoan her? whence shall I seek comforters for thee? . . .

Thou hast multiplied thy merchants above the stars of heaven: the cankerworm spoileth, and fleeth away. They crowned are as the locusts, and thy captains as the great grasshoppers, which camp in the hedges in the cold day, but when the sun ariseth they flee away, and their place is not known where they are. Thy shepherds slumber, O king of Assyria: thy nobles shall dwell in the dust: thy people is scattered upon the mountains, and no man gathereth them. There is no healing of thy bruise; thy would is grievous: all that hear the bruit of thee shall clap the hands over thee: for upon whom hath not thy wickedness passed continually?

D. Foreseeing the Future: A Babylonian Astrological Text

1. From this omen one learns the following: the city of the king and his men in the hand of the foe are; corpses [and famine]
2. . . . .on thy tablet the number (which) thou statest he shall state to thee and with. . . . . . .
3. A collection of 25 tablets of the signs of heaven and earth, according to their good presage and their bad [presage. . . . .]
4. The omens as many as in heaven are, and on earth are recorded. . . . . . .
5. This [is] the record. . . . .
6. Twelve months to each year, (6 × 60 =) 360 days, in order are recorded by the hand. . . . .
7. during the middle of the day a deficiency of the sight of the non-existent star. . . . . .
8. the appearance at the beginning of the year of the star Icu, the sight of the Moon and the Sun which in. . .
9. The rising and appearances of the Moon during the month one observes; . . . . . .

10. The balancing of the stars and the Moon one watches; and the opposition . . . . . .
11. of the year its months, of the months their days the announcement; and of peace the making. . . . . .
12. Then [follows] at the appearance of the Moon, during the day rain falls; all. . . . .
13. Next: during the middle of the day rain falls; all . . . .
14. for the {section/discernment} of the centre (of the heavens) and the observation of the divisions of the watches
15. and of the year [the rest is wanting]
16. The 12 months at the time of beginning [and] ending, according to the division of the day generally. . . . . .
17. The balancing of the stars and the Moon according to the tokens of beginning [and] ending.
18. The places of setting are announced; and the dark days.
Life [and] peace
19. during the year establish thou; and its continuance perfect. . . . .

Document Set 2.1 References

A. A Year in the Reign of Assur-Nasir-Pal, a Busy Assyrian Conqueror
D. D. Luckenbill, ed., *Ancient Records of Assyria and Babylonia* (Chicago: University of Chicago Press, 1926), 1:151–154.
B. Everyday Life in Assyria: A Labor Contract, a Loan Secured by Land and Slaves, and a Theft
Claude Herman Walter Johns, ed. and trans., *Babylonian and Assyrian Laws* (Edinburgh: T. & T. Clark, 1904), 273, 263, 107.
C. The Hebrew Prophet Nahum Denounces Nineveh for Its Whoredom and Commerce
Nahum 3:1–7, 16–19.
D. Foreseeing the Future: A Babylonian Astrological Text
A. H. Sayce, *Astronomy and Astrology of the Babylonians*, reprinted from the *Transactions of the Society of Biblical Archaeology*, vol. 3, part 1, 1874 (San Diego: Wizard's Bookshelf, 1981), 154–157.

DOCUMENT SET 2.2
Israel and Its Neighbors

Documents in previous sets have already acquainted you with the Hebrew accounts of the Creation and the Fall of Man (1.1, 1.2), with Yahweh's laws (1.2), and with the prophet Nahum's disapproving view of Nineveh (2.1). In this set we examine the Hebrew kingdoms of Israel and Judah.

Document A, from the First Book of Kings, gives a glimpse of the great King Solomon (mid-tenth century B.C.), under whom Israel briefly became a considerable power in the ancient Near East. What signs do you detect here of tension between Hebrew monotheism and Near Eastern religious traditions? In Document B, the prophet Ezekiel denounces the great Phoenician city-state of Tyre (in present-day Lebanon) for its commercial wealth. How the great Hebrew prophets responded to the disparities and abuses of wealth at home emerges clearly from Document C, the opening chapter of the Book of Isaiah. The prophet lived in the eighth century B.C., and this portion of the text reached its present version by the fifth century B.C. In Isaiah's searing vision, a demand for social justice flows directly into a call for spiritual renewal.

The final pair of documents (D and E) present a remarkable juxtaposition of Assyrian and Hebrew accounts—the latter from the Book of Isaiah—of the same event: the unsuccessful attempt of the Assyrian king Sennacherib (*704–681 B.C.) to take Jerusalem by seige. Comparing the two accounts (a most unusual opportunity in ancient history) is a fascinating exercise. Notice in particular Sennacherib's attempt to minimize his setback, which perhaps followed an outbreak of disease among his troops.

The northern Jewish kingdom of Israel had fallen to the Assyrians in the early seventh century B.C., and the southern kingdom (Judah, with Jerusalem its capital) was finally destroyed by the Neo-Babylonian king Nebuchadrezzar in 586 B.C. Most of the Hebrew population was deported to what is today Iraq. It was in this Babylon Exile that much of the Old Testament text was edited into the form that we now possess and that understanding of the Hebrews' God as the universal deity, controlling all human events and upholding justice for all Creation, came fully into focus. One product of the Exile was the Psalms, a collection of hymns in praise of God. Psalm 113 (Document F) encapsulates this powerful and moving vision.

A. King Solomon's Monarchy and His Accommodations with Alien Gods

And Solomon reigned over all kingdoms from the river unto the land of the Philistines, and unto the border of Egypt: they brought presents, and served, Solomon all the days of his life.

And Solomon's provision for one day was thirty measures of fine flour, and threesome measures of meal, Ten fat oxen, and twenty oxen out of the pastures, and a hundred sheep, besides harts, and roebucks, and fallow deer, and fatted fowl. For he had dominion over all the region on this side the river, from Tiphsah even to Azzah, over all the kings on this side the river: and he had peace on all sides round about him. And Judah and Israel dwelt safely, every man under his vine and under his fig tree, from Dan even to Beersheba, all the days of Solomon.

And Solomon had forty thousand stalls of horses for his chariots, and twelve thousand horsemen. And those officers provided victuals for king Solomon, and for all that came unto king Solomon's table, every man in his month: they lacked nothing. Barley also and straw for the horses and dromedaries brought they unto the place where the officers were, every man according to his charge.

And God gave Solomon wisdom and understanding exceeding much, and largeness of heart, even as the sand that is on the seashore. . . .

And it came to pass in the four hundred and eightieth year after the children of Israel were come out of the land of Egypt, in the fourth year of Solomon's reign over Israel, in the month Zif, which is the second month, that he began to build the house of the Lord. And the house which king Solomon built for the Lord, the length thereof was threescore cubits, and the breadth thereof twenty cubits, and the height thereof thirty cubits. And the porch before the temple of the house, twenty cubits was the length thereof, according to the breadth of the house; and ten cubits was the breadth thereof before the house. And for the house he made windows of narrow lights. . . .

But Solomon was building his own house thirteen years, and he finished all his house. . . .

Then he made a porch for the throne where he might judge, even the porch of judgment: and it was covered with cedar from one side of the floor to the other.

And his house where he dwelt had another court within the porch, which was of the like work. Solomon made also a house for Pharaoh's daughter, whom he had taken to wife, like unto this porch. All these were of costly stones, according to the measures of hewed stones, sawed with saws, within and without, even from the foundation unto the coping, and so on the outside toward the great court.

And the foundation was of costly stones, even great stones, stones of ten cubits, and stones of eight cubits.

And above were costly stones, after the measures of hewed stones, and cedars. And the great court round about was with three rows of hewed stones, and a row of cedar beams, both for the inner court of the house of the Lord, and for the porch of the house. . . .

And when the queen of Sheba heard of the fame of Solomon concerning the name of the Lord, she came to prove him with hard questions. And she came to Jerusalem with a very great train, with camels that bare spices, and very much gold, and precious stones: and when she was come to Solomon, she communed with him of all that was in her heart. And Solomon told her all her questions: there was not any thing hid from the king, which he told her not. And when the queen of Sheba had seen all Solomon's wisdom, and the house that he had built. And the meat of his table, and the sitting of his servants, and the attendance of his ministers, and their apparel, and his cupbearers, and his ascent by which he went up unto the house of the Lord; there was no more spirit in her. And she said to the king, It was a true report that I heard in mine own land of thy acts and of thy wisdom. . . .

Now the weight of gold that came to Solomon in one year was six hundred threescore and six talents of gold, Besides that he had of the merchant-men, and of the traffic of the spice merchants, and of all the kings of Arabia, and of the governors of the country.

And king Solomon made two hundred targets of beaten gold: six hundred shekels of gold went to one target. And he made three hundred shields of beaten gold; three pounds of gold went to one shield: and the king put them in the house of the forest of Lebanon.

Moreover, the king made a great throne of ivory, and overlaid it with the best gold. The throne had six steps, and the top of the throne was round behind: and there were stays on either side on the place of the seat, and two lions stood beside the stays. And twelve lions stood there on the one side and on the other upon the six steps: there was not the like made in any kingdom.

And all king Solomon's drinking vessels were of gold, and all the vessels of the house of the forest of Lebanon were of pure gold; none were of silver: it was nothing accounted of in the days of Solomon. . . .

But king Solomon loved many strange women, together with the daughter of Pharaoh, women of the Moabites, Ammonites, Edomites, Zidonians, and Hittites; Of the nations concerning which the Lord said unto the children of Israel, Ye shall not go in to them, neither shall they come in unto you: for surely they will turn away your heart after their gods: Solomon clave unto these in love. And he had seven hundred wives, princesses, and three hundred concubines: and his wives turned away his heart. For it came to pass, when Solomon was old, that his wives turned away his heart after other gods; and his heart was not perfect with the Lord his God, as was the heart of David his father. For Solomon went after Ashtoreth the goddess of the Zidonians, and after Milcom the abomination of the Ammonites. And Solomon did evil in the sight of the Lord, and went not fully after the Lord, as did David his father. Then did Solomon build a high place for Chemosh, the abomination of Moab, in the hill that is before Jerusalem, and for Molech, the abomination of the children of Ammon. And likewise did he for all his strange wives, which burnt incense and sacrificed unto their gods.

And the Lord was angry with Solomon, because his heart was turned from the Lord God of Israel, which had appeared unto him twice, And had commanded him concerning this thing, that he should not go after other gods: but he kept not that which the Lord commanded. Wherefore the Lord said unto Solomon, Forasmuch as this is done of thee, and thou hast not kept my covenant and my statutes, which I have commanded thee, I will surely rend the kingdom from thee, and will give it to thy servant. Notwithstanding, in thy days I will not do it for David thy father's sake: but I will rend it out of the hand of thy son.

B. The Prophet Ezekiel on Tyre

. . . O thou that art situate at the entry of the sea, which art a merchant of the people for many isles, Thus saith the Lord God; O Tyrus, thou hast said, I am of perfect beauty. Thy borders are in the midst of the seas, thy builders have perfected thy beauty. They have made all thy ship boards of fir trees of Senir: they have taken cedars from Lebanon to make masts for thee. Of the oaks of Bashan have they made thine oars; the company of the Ashurites have made thy benches of ivory, brought out of the isles of Chittim. Fine linen with broidered work from Egypt was that which thou spreadest forth to be thy sail; blue and purple from the isles of Elishah was that which covered thee. The inhabitants of Zidon and Arvad were thy mariners: thy wise men, O Tyrus, that were in thee, were thy pilots. The ancients of Gebal and the wise men thereof were in thee thy calkers: all the ships of the sea with their mariners were in thee to occupy thy merchandise. They of Persia and of Lud and of Phat were in thine army, thy men of war: they hanged the shield and helmet in thee; they set forth thy comeliness. The men of Arvad with thine army were upon thy walls round about, and the Gammadim were in thy towers: they hanged their shields upon thy walls round about; they have made thy beauty perfect. Tarshish was thy merchant by reason of the multitude of all kind of riches; with silver, iron, tin, and lead, they traded in thy fairs. Javan, Tubal, and Meshech, they were thy merchants: they traded the persons of men and vessels of brass in thy market. They of the house of Togarmah traded in thy fairs with horses and horsemen and mules. The men of Dedan were thy merchants; many isles were the merchandise of thine hand: they brought thee for a present, horns of ivory and ebony. Syria was thy merchant by reason of the multitude of the wares of thy making: they occupied in thy fairs with emeralds, purple, and broidered work, and fine linen, and coral, and agate. Judah, and the land of Israel, they were thy merchants: they traded in thy market wheat of Minnigh, and Pannag and honey, and oil, and balm. Damascus was thy merchant in the multitude of the wares of thy making for the multitude of all riches; in the wine of Helbon, and white wool. Dan also and Javan going to and fro occupied in thy fairs: bright iron, cassia and calamus, were in thy market. Dedan was thy merchant in precious clothes for chariots. Arabia, and all the princes of Kedar, they occupied with thee in lambs, and rams, and goats: in these were they thy merchants. The merchants of Sheba and Raamah, they were thy merchants: they occupied in thy fairs with chief of all spices, and with all precious stones, and gold. Haran, and Canneh, and Eden the merchants of Sheba, Asshur, and Chillmad, were thy merchants. These were thy merchants in all sorts of things, in blue clothes, and broidered work, and in chests of rich apparel, bound with cords, and made of cedar, among thy merchandise. The ships of Tarshish did sing of thee in thy market: and thou wast replenished, and made very glorious in the midst of the seas.

Thy rowers have brought thee into great waters: the east wind hath broken thee in the midst of the seas. Thy riches, and thy fairs, thy merchandise, thy mariners, and thy pilots, thy calkers, and the occupiers of thy merchandise, and all thy men of war, that are in thee, and in all thy company which in the midst of thee, shall fall into the midst of the seas in the day of thy ruin. The suburbs shall shake at the sound of the cry of thy pilots.

C. Prophesy and Social Protest: Isaiah

The vision of Isaiah the son of Amoz, which he saw concerning Judah and Jerusalem in the days of Uzziah, Jotham, Ahaz, and Hezekiah, kings of Judah. Hear, O heavens, and give ear, O earth: for the Lord hath spoken; I have nourished and brought up children, and they have rebelled against me. The ox knoweth his owner, and the ass his master's crib: but Israel doth not know, my people doth not consider. Ah sinful nation, a people laden with iniquity, a seed of evildoers, children that are corrupters: they have foresaken the Lord, they have provoked the Holy One of Israel unto anger, they are gone away backward.

Why should ye be stricken any more? ye will revolt more and more: the whole head is sick, and the whole heart faint. From the sole of the foot even unto the head there is no soundness in it; but wounds, and bruises, and putrifying sores: they have not been closed, neither bound up, neither mollified with ointment. Your country is desolate, your cities are burned with fire: your land, strangers devour it in your presence, and it is desolate, as overthrown by strangers. And the daughter of Zion is left as a cottage in a vineyard, as a lodge in a garden of cucumbers, as a besieged city. Except the Lord of hosts had left unto us a very small remnant, we should have been as Sodom, and we should have been like unto Gomorrah.

Hear the word of the Lord, ye rulers of Sodom; give ear unto the law of our God, ye people of Gomorrah. To what purpose is the multitude of your sacrifices unto me? saith the Lord: I am full of the burnt offerings of rams, and the fat of fed beasts; and I delight not in the blood of bullocks, or of lambs, or of he goats. When ye come to appear before me, who hath required this at your hand, to tread my courts? Bring no more vain oblations; incense is an abomination unto me; the new moons and sabbaths, the calling of assemblies, I cannot away with; it is iniquity, even the solemn meeting. Your new moons and your appointed feasts may soul hateth: they are a trouble unto me; I am weary to bear them. And when ye spread forth your hands, I will hide mine eyes from you; yea, when ye make many prayers, I will not hear: your hands are full of blood.

Wash ye, make you clean; put away the evil of your doings from before mine eyes; cease to do evil; Learn to do well; seek judgment, relieve the oppressed, judge the fatherless, plead for the widow. Come now, and let us reason together, saith the Lord; though your sins be as scarlet, they shall be as white as snow; though they be red like crimson, they shall be as wool. If ye be willing and obedient, ye shall eat the good of the land: But if ye refuse and rebel, ye shall be devoured with the sword: for the mouth of the Lord hath spoken it.

How is the faithful city become a harlot! it was full of judgment; righteousness lodged in it; but now murderers. Thy silver is become dross, thy wine mixed with water: They princes are rebellious, and companions of thieves: every one loveth gifts, and followeth after rewards: they judge not the fatherless, neither doth the cause of the widow come unto them. Therefore saith the Lord, the Lord of hosts, the Mighty One of Israel, Ah, I will ease me of mine adversaries, and avenge me of mine enemies.

And I will turn my hand upon thee, and purely purge away thy dross, and take away all thy tin: And I will restore thy judges as at the first, and thy counselors as at the beginning: afterward thou shalt be called, The city of righteousness, the faithful city. Zion shall be redeemed with judgment, and her converts with righteousness.

And the destruction of the transgressors and of the sinners shall be together, and they that forsake the Lord shall be consumed. For they shall be ashamed of the oaks which ye have desired, and ye shall be confounded for the gardens that ye have chosen. For ye shall be as an oak whose leaf fadeth, and as a garden that hath no water. And the strong shall be as tow, and the maker of it as a spark, and they shall both burn together, and none shall quench them.

D. Sennacherib Describes His Seige of Jerusalem

In my third campaign I marched against Hatti. Luli, king of Sidon, whom the terror-inspiring glamor of my lordship had overwhelmed, fled far overseas and perished. The awe-inspiring splendor of the "Weapon" of Ashur, my lord, overwhelmed his strong cities (such as) Great Sidon, Little Sidon, Bit-Zitti, Zaribtu, Mahalliba, Ushu (i.e. the mainland settlement of Tyre), Akzib (and) Akko, (all) his fortress cities, walled (and well) provided with feed and water for his garrisons, and they bowed in submission to my feet. I installed Ethbaal upon the throne to be their king and imposed upon him tribute (due) to me (as his) overlord (to be paid) annually without interruption.

As to all the kings of Amurru—Menahem from Samsimuruna, Tubalu from Sidon, Abdiliti from Arvad, Urumilki from Byblos, Mitinti from Ashdod, Buduili from Beth-Ammon, Kammusun-adbi from Moab (and) Aiarammu from Edom, they brought sumptuous gifts and—fourfold—their heavy *tâmartu*-presents to me and kissed my feet. Sidqia, however, king of Ashkelon, who did not bow to my yoke, I deported and sent to Assyria, his family-gods, himself, his wife, his children, his brothers, all the male descendants of his family. I set Sharruludari, son of Rukibtu, their former king, over the inhabitants of Ashkelon and imposed upon him the payment of tribute (and of) *katrû*-presents (due) to me (as) overlord—and he (now) pulls the straps (of my yoke)!

In the continuation of my campaign I besieged Beth-Dagon, Joppa, Banai-Barqa, Azuru, cities belonging to Sidqia who did not bow to my feet quickly (enough); I conquered (them) and carried their spoils away. The officials, the patricians and the (common) people of Ekron—who had thrown Padi, their king, into fetters (because he was) loyal to (his) solemn oath (sworn) by the god Ashur, and had handed him over to Hezekiah, the Jew (and) he (Hezekiah) held him in prison, unlawfully, as if he (Padi) be an enemy—had become afraid and had called (for help) upon the kings of Egypt (and) the bowmen, the chariot(-corps) and the cavalry of the king of Ethiopia, an army beyond counting—and they (actually) had come to their assistance. In the plain of Eltekeh, their battle lines were drawn up against me and they sharpened their weapons. Upon a trust (-inspiring) oracle (given) by Ashur, my lord, I fought with them and inflicted a defeat upon them. In the mêlée of the battle, I personally captured alive the Egyptian charioteers with the (ir) princes and (also) the charioteers of the king of Ethiopia. I besieged Eltekeh (and) Timnah, conquered (them) and carried their spoils away. I assaulted Ekron and

"Sennacherib's Account of How He Besieges Jerusalem" from James B. Pritchard, *Ancient Near Eastern Texts Relating to the Old Testament*, 3/e, pp. 287–288, Copyright © 1969 by Princeton University Press. Reprinted by permission of Princeton University Press.

killed the officials and patricians who had committed the crime and hung their bodies on poles surrounding the city. The (common) citizens who were guilty of minor crimes, I considered prisoners of war. The rest of them, those who were not accused of crimes and misbehavior, I released. I made Padi, their king, come from Jerusalem and set him as their lord on the throne, imposing upon him the tribute (due) to me (as) overlord.

As to Hezekiah, the Jew, he did not submit to my yoke, I laid siege to 46 of his strong cities, walled forts and to the countless small villages in their vicinity, and conquered (them) by means of well-stamped (earth-)ramps, and battering-rams brought (thus) near (to the walls) (combined with) the attack by foot soldiers, (using) mines, breeches as well as sapper work. I drove out (of them) 200,150 people, young and old, male and female, horses, mules, donkeys, camels, big and small cattle beyond counting, and considered (them) booty. Himself I made a prisoner in Jerusalem, his royal residence, like a bird in a cage. I surrounded him with earthwork in order to molest those who were leaving his city's gate. His towns which I had plundered, I took away from his country and gave them (over) to Mitinti, king of Ashdod, Padi, king of Ekron, and Sillibel, king of Gaza. Thus I reduced his country, but I still increased the tribute and the *katrû*-presents (due) to me (as his) overlord which I imposed (later) upon him beyond the former tribute, to be delivered annually. Hezekiah himself, whom the terror-inspiring splendor of my lordship had overwhelmed and whose irregular and elite troops which he had brought into Jerusalem, his royal residence, in order to strengthen (it), had deserted him, did send me, later, to Nineveh, my lordly city, together with 30 talents of gold, 800 talents of silver, precious stones, antimony, large cuts of red stone, couches (inlaid) with ivory, *nîmedu*-chairs (inlaid) with ivory, elephant-hides, ebony-wood, boxwood (and) all kinds of valuable treasures, his (own) daughters, concubines, male and female musicians. In order to deliver the tribute and to do obeisance as a slave he sent his (personal) messenger.

E. Isaiah Describes Sennacherib's Siege of Jerusalem

Now it came to pass in the fourteenth year of king Hezekiah, that Sennacherib king of Assyria came up against all the defensed cities of Judah, and took them. And the king of Assyria sent Rabshakeh from Lachish to Jerusalem unto king Hezekiah with a great army. And he stood by the conduit of the upper pool in the highway of the fuller's field. Then came forth unto him Eliakim, Hilkiah's son, which was over the house, and Shebna the scribe, and Joah, Asaph's son, the recorder.

And Rabshakeh said unto them, Say ye now to Hezekiah, Thus saith the great king, the king of Assyria, What confidence is this wherein thou trustest? I say, sayest thou, (but they are but vain words) I have counsel and strength for war: now on whom dost thou trust, that thou rebellest against me? Lo, thou trusted in the staff of this broken reed, on Egypt; whereon if a man lean, it will go into his hand, and pierce it: so is Pharaoh king of Egypt to all that trust in him. But if thou say to me, We trust in the Lord our God: is it not he, whose high places and whose altars Hezekiah hath taken away, and said to Judah and to Jerusalem, Ye shall worship before this altar? Now therefore give pledges, I pray thee, to my master the king of Assyria, and I will give thee two thousand horses, if thou be able on thy part to set riders upon them. How then wilt thou turn away the face of one captain of the least of my master's servants, and put thy trust on Egypt for chariots and for horsemen? And am I now come up without the Lord against this land to destroy it? the Lord said unto me, Go up against this land, and destroy it.

Then said Eliakim and Shebna and Joah unto Rabshakeh, Speak, I pray thee, unto they servants in the Syrian language; for we understand it: and speak not to us in the Jews' language, in the ears of the people that are on the wall.

But Rabshakeh said, Hath my master sent me to thy master and to thee to speak these words? hath he not sent me to the men that sit upon the wall, that they may eat their own dung, and drink their own piss with you? Then Rabshakeh stood, and cried with a loud voice in the Jews' language, and said, Hear ye the words of the great king, the king of Assyria. Thus saith the king, Let not Hezekiah deceive you; for he shall not be able to deliver you. Neither let Hezekiah make you trust in the Lord, saying, The Lord will surely deliver us: this city shall not be delivered into the hand of the king of Assyria. Hearken not to Hezekiah: for thus saith the king of Assyria, Make an agreement with me by a present, and come out to me: and eat ye every one of his vine, and every one of his fig tree, and drink ye every one the waters of his own cistern; Until I come and take you away to a land like your own land, a land of corn and wine, a land of bread and vineyards. Beware lest Hezekiah persuade you, saying, The Lord will deliver us. Hath any of the gods of the nations delivered his land out of the hand of the king of Assyria? Where are the gods of Hamath and Arphad? where are the gods of

Sepharvaim? and have they delivered Samaria out of my hand? Who are they among all the gods of these lands, that have delivered their land out of my hand, that the Lord should deliver Jerusalem out of my hand? But they held their peace, and answered him not a word: for the king's commandment was, saying, Answer him not.

Then came Eliakim, the son of Hilkiah, that was over the household, and Shebna the scribe, and Joah, the son of Asaph, the recorder, to Hezekiah with their clothes rent, and told him the words of Rabshakeh.

And it came to pass, when king Hezekiah heard it, that he rent his clothes, and covered himself with sackcloth, and went into the house of the Lord. And he sent Eliakim, who was over the household, and Shebna the scribe, and the elders of the priests, covered with sackcloth, unto Isaiah the prophet the son of Amoz. And they said unto him, Thus saith Hezekiah, This day is a day of trouble, and of rebuke, and of blasphemy: for the children are come to the birth, and there is not strength to bring forth. It may be the Lord thy God will hear the words of Rabshakeh, whom the king of Assyria his master hath sent to reproach the living God, and will reprove the words which the Lord thy God hath heard: wherefore lift up thy prayer for the remnant that is left. So the servants of king Hezekiah came to Isaiah.

And Isaiah said unto them, Thus shall ye say unto your master, Thus saith the Lord, Be not afraid of the words that thou hast heard, wherewith the servants of the king of Assyria have blasphemed me. Behold, I will send a blast upon him, and he shall hear a rumor, and return to his own land; and I will cause him to fall by the sword in his own land.

So Rabshakeh returned, and found the king of Assyria warring against Libnah: for he had heard that he was departed from Lachish. And he heard say concerning Tirhakah king of Ethiopia, He is come forth to make war with thee. And when he heard it, he sent messengers to Hezekiah saying, Thus shall ye speak to Hezekiah king of Judah, saying, Let not thy God, in whom thou trustest, deceive thee, saying, Jerusalem shall not be given into the hand of the king of Assyria. Behold, thou hast heard what the kings of Assyria have done to all lands by destroying them utterly; and shalt thou be delivered? Have the gods of the nations delivered them which my fathers have destroyed, as Gozan, and Haran, and Rezeph, and the children of Eden which were in Telassar? Where is the king of Hamath, and the king of Arphad, and the king of the city of Sepharvaim, Hena, and Ivah?

And Hezekiah received the letter from the hand of the messengers, and read it: and Hezekiah went up unto the house of the Lord, and spread it before the Lord. And Hezekiah prayed unto the Lord saying, O Lord of hosts, God of Israel, that dwellest between the cherubim thou art the God, even thou alone, of all the kingdoms of the earth: thou hast made heaven and earth. Incline thine ear, O Lord, and hear; open thine eyes, O Lord, and see: and hear all the words of Sennacherib, which hath sent to reproach the living God. Of a truth, Lord, the kings of Assyria have laid waste all the nations, and their countries, And have cast their gods into the fire: for they were no gods, but the work of men's hands, wood and stone: therefore they have destroyed them. Now therefore, O Lord our God, save us from his hand, that all the kingdoms of the earth may know that thou art the Lord, even thou only.

Then Isaiah the son of Amoz sent unto Hezekiah, saying, Thus saith the Lord God of Israel, Whereas thou hast prayed to me against Sennacherib king of Assyria: This is the word which the Lord hath spoken concerning him; The virgin, the daughter of Zion, hath despised thee, and laughed thee to scorn; the daughter of Jerusalem hath shaken her head at thee. Whom hast thou reproached and blasphemed? and against whom hast thou exalted thy voice, and lifted up thine eyes on high? even against the Holy One of Israel. By thy servants hast thou reproached the Lord, and hast said, By the multitude of my chariots am I come up to the height of the mountains, to the aides of Lebanon; and I will cut down the tall cedars thereof, and the choice fir trees thereof: and I will enter into the height of his border, and the forest of his Carmel. I have digged, and drunk water; and with the sole of my feet have I dried up all the rivers of the besieged places. Hast thou not heard long ago, how I have done it; and of ancient times, that I have formed it? now have I brought it to pass, that thou shouldest be to lay waste defensed cities into ruinous heaps. Therefore their inhabitants were of small power, they were dismayed and confounded: they were as the grass of the field, and as the green herb, as the grass on the housetops, and as corn blasted before it be grown up. But I know thy abode, and thy going out, and thy coming in, and thy rage against me. Because thy rage against me, and thy tumult, is come up into mine ears, therefore will I put my hook in thy nose, and my bridle in thy lips, and I will turn thee back by the way by which thou camest. And this shall be a sign unto thee, Ye shall eat this year such as groweth of itself; and the second year that which springeth of the same: and in the third year sow ye, and reap, and plant vineyards, and eat the fruit thereof. And the remnant that is escaped of the house of

Judah shall again take root downward, and bear fruit upward: For out of Jerusalem shall go forth a remnant, and they that escape out of mount Zion: the zeal of the Lord of hosts shall do this. Therefore thus saith the Lord concerning the king of Assyria, He shall not come into this city, nor shoot an arrow there, nor come before it with shields, nor cast a bank against it. By the way that he came, by the same shall be return, and shall not come into this city, saith the Lord. For I will defend this city to save it for mine own sake, and for my servant David's sake. Then the angel of the Lord went forth, and smote in the camp of the Assyrians a hundred and fourscore and five thousand: and when they arose early in the morning, behold, they were all dead corpses.

So Sennacherib king of Assyria departed, and went and returned, and dwelt at Nineveh. And it came to pass, as he was worshipping in the house of Nisroch his god, that Adrammelech and Sharezer his sons smote him with the sword; and they escaped into the land of Armenia: and Esarhaddon his son reigned in his stead.

F. The Hebrews Praise God as the Universal Deity

Psalm 113

Praise ye the Lord, Praise, O ye servants of the Lord, praise the name of the Lord. Blessed be the name of the Lord from this time forth and for evermore. From the rising of the sun unto the going down of the same the Lord's name is to be praised. The Lord is high above all nations, and his glory above the heavens. Who is like unto the Lord our God, who dwelleth on high, Who humbleth himself to behold the things that are in heaven, and in the earth! He raiseth up the poor out of the dust, and lifteth the needy out of the dunghill; That he may set him with princes, even with the princes of his people. He maketh the barren woman to keep house, and to be a joyful mother of children. Praise ye the Lord.

Document Set 2.2 References

A. King Solomon's Monarchy and His Accommodations with Alien Gods
I Kings 4:21–29; 6:1–4; 7:1, 7–12; 10:1–6, 14–21; 11:1–12.
B. The Prophet Ezekiel on Tyre
Ezekiel 27:3–28.
C. Prophesy and Social Protest: Isaiah
Isaiah 1:1–31.
D. Sennacherib Describes His Siege of Jerusalem
E. A. Speiser and James B. Pritchard, *Ancient Near Eastern Texts Relating to the New Testament,* 3rd ed. (Princeton, N.J.: Princeton University Press, 1969), 287–288.
E. Isaiah Describes Sennacherib's Siege of Jerusalem
Isaiah 36 and 37.
F. The Hebrews Praise God as the Universal Deity
Psalm 113.

DOCUMENT SET 2.3
Homeric Greece

The *Iliad* and the *Odyssey,* epics born in the oral tradition of Mycenaean and Dark Age Greece, were committed to writing sometime in the ninth or early eighth century B.C., authorship being attributed to Homer, a blind bard (singer of epic tales). Homer worked at the moment when a written culture was gradually arising alongside (and eventually replacing) the older oral culture in which laboriously memorized wisdom was passed down by word of mouth. The two Homeric epics became cultural norms on which later generations of Greek youths grew up. The heroic striving yet ultimate submission to the whims of the gods that the great figures of the Homeric epics display sums up their *arete,* or excellence—a central concept of the Greek mind. In Document A, from the Iliad, the Trojan hero Hector bids farewell to his family before he faces Achilles in a fight he is doomed to lose. In Document B, from the Odyssey, the hero Odysseus enters the palace of the ruler Alcinous after years of battling various supernatural hardships around the Mediterranean; in Document C, also from the Odyssey, we meet Alcinous's daughter Nausicaa, who boldly ministers to the exhausted Odysseus when he is washed up on her father's shore. Read all three documents for evidence of the arete that Homer considers appropriate for each of his characters to display. And, particularly in Document B, look also for evidence of how the males and females of the Greek upper class of Homer's time lived and demonstrated their authority.

A. The Hero Hector Bids Farewell to His Family

Then great Hector of the glancing helm answered her: "Surely I take thought for all these things, my wife; but I have very sore shame of the Trojans and Trojan dames with trailing robes, if like a coward I shrink away from battle. Moreover mine own soul forbiddeth me, seeing I have learned ever to be valiant and fight in the forefront of the Trojans, winning my father's great glory and mine own.

"Yea of a surety I know this in heart and soul; the day shall come for holy Ilios to be laid low and Priam and the folk of Priam of the good ashen spear. Yet doth the anguish of the Trojans hereafter not so much trouble me, neither Hekabe's own, neither King Priam's, neither my brethren's, the many and brave that shall fall in the dust before their foemen, as doth thy anguish in the day when some mailclad Achaian shall lead thee weeping and rob thee of the light of freedom. So shalt thou abide in Argos and play the loom at another woman's bidding, and bear water from fount Messeis or Hypereia, being grievously entreated, and sore constraint shall be laid upon thee. And then shall one say that beholdeth thee weep: 'This is the wife of Hector, that was foremost in battle of the horse-taming Trojans when men fought about Ilios.' Thus shall one say hereafter, and fresh grief shall be thine for lack of such an husband as thou hadst to ward off the day of thraldom. But me in death may the heaped-up earth be covering, ere I hear thy crying and thy carrying into captivity."

So spake glorious Hector, and stretched out his arm to his boy. But the child shrunk crying to the bosom of his fair-girdled nurse, dismayed at his dear father's aspect, and in dread at the bronze and horsehair crest that he beheld nodding fiercely from the helmet's top. Then his dear father laughed aloud, and his lady mother; forthwith glorious Hector took the helmet from his head, and laid it, all gleaming, upon the earth; then kissed he his dear son and dandled him in his arms, and spake in prayer to Zeus and all the gods: "O Zeus and all ye gods, vouchsafe ye that this my son may likewise prove even as I, preëminent amid the Trojans, and as valiant in might, and be a great king of Ilios. Then may men say of him, 'Far greater is he than his father,' as he returneth home from battle; and may he bring with him bloodstained spoils from the foeman that he has slain, and may his mother's heart be glad."

So spake he, and laid his son in his dear wife's arms; and she took him to her fragrant bosom, smiling tearfully. And her husband had pity to see her, and caressed her with his hand, and spake and called upon her name: "Dear one, I pray thee be not of oversorrowful heart; no man against my fate shall hurl me to Hades; only destiny, I ween, no man hath escaped, be he coward or be he valiant, when once he hath been born. But go thou to thine house and see to mine own tasks, the loom and distaff, and bid thy handmaidens ply their work; but for war shall men provide, and I in chief of all men that dwell in Ilios."

So spake glorious Hector, and took up his horsehair crested helmet; and his dear wife departed to her home, oft looking back, and letting fall big tears.

B. Odysseus at the Palace of Alcinous

So saying, flashing-eyed Athene departed over the unresting sea, and left lovely Scheria. She came to Marathon and broad-wayed Athens, and entered the well-built house of Erectheus; but Odysseus went to the glorious palace of Alcinous. There he stood, and his heart pondered much before he reached the threshold of bronze; for there was a gleam as of sun or moon over the high-roofed house of great-hearted Alcinous. Of bronze were the walls that stretched this way and that from the threshold to the innermost chamber, and around was a cornice of cyanus. Golden were the doors that shut in the well-built house, and doorposts of silver were set in a threshold of bronze. Of silver was the lintel above, and of gold the handle. On either side of the door there stood gold and silver dogs, which Hephaestus had fashioned with cunning skill to guard the palace of great-hearted Alcinous; immortal were they and ageless all their days. Within, seats were fixed along the wall on either hand, from the threshold to the innermost chamber, and on them were thrown robes of soft fabric, cunningly woven, the handiwork of women. On these the leaders of the Phaeacians were wont to sit drinking and eating, for they had unfailing store. And golden youths stood on well-built pedestals, holding lighted torches in their hands to give light by night to the banqueters in the hall. And fifty slave-women he had in the house, of whom some grind the yellow grain on the millstone, and others weave webs, or, as they sit, twirl the yarn, like unto the leaves of a tall poplar tree: and from the closely-woven linen the soft olive oil drips down. For as the Phaeacian men are skilled above all others in speeding a swift ship upon the sea, so are the women cunning workers at the loom, for Athene has given to them above all others skill in fair handiwork, and an understanding heart. But without the courtyard, hard by the door, is a great orchard of four acres, and a hedge runs about it on either side. Therein grow trees, tall and luxuriant, pears and pomegranates and apple-trees with their bright fruit, and sweet figs, and luxuriant olives. Of these the fruit perishes not nor fails in winter or in summer, but lasts throughout the year; and ever does the west wind, as it blows, quicken to life some fruits, and ripen others; pear upon pear waxes ripe, apple upon apple, cluster upon cluster, and fig upon fig. There, too, is his fruitful vineyard planted, one part of which, a warm spot on level ground, is being dried in the sun, while other grapes men are gathering, and others, too, they are treading; but in front are unripe grapes that are shedding the blossom, and others that are turning purple. There again, by the last row of the vines, grow trim garden beds of every sort, blooming the year through, and therein are two springs, one of which sends its water throughout all the garden, while the other, over against it, flows beneath the threshold of the court toward the high house; from this the townsfolk drew their water. Such were the glorious gifts of the gods in the palace of Alcinous.

C. The Excellence of Nausicaa

. . . [T]he goodly Odysseus came forth from beneath the bushes, and with his stout hand he broke from the thick wood a leafy branch, that he might hold it about him and hide therewith his nakedness. Forth he came like a mountain-nurtured lion trusting in his might, who goes forth, beaten with rain and wind, but his two eyes are ablaze: into the midst of the kine he goes, or of the sheep, or on the track of the wild deer, and his belly bids him go even into the close-built fold, to make an attack upon the flocks. Even so Odysseus was about to enter the company of the fair-tressed maidens, naked though he was, for need had come upon him. But terrible did he seem to them, all befouled with brine, and they shrank in fear, one here, one there, along the jutting sand-spits. Alone the daughter of Alcinous kept her place, for in her heart Athene put courage, and took fear from her limbs. She fled not, but stood and faced him; and Odysseus pondered whether he should clasp the knees of the fair-faced maid, and make his prayer, or whether, standing apart as he was, he should beseech her with gentle words, in hope that she might show him the city and give him raiment. And, as he pondered, it seemed to him better to stand apart and beseech her with gentle words, lest the maiden's heart should be wroth with him if he clasped her knees; so straight-way he spoke a gentle word and crafty:

"I beseech thee, O queen,—a goddess art thou, or art thou mortal? If thou art a goddess, one of those who hold broad heaven, to Artemis, the daughter of great Zeus, do I liken thee most nearly in comeliness and in stature and in form. But if thou art one of mortals who dwell upon the earth, thrice-blessed then are they father and thy honoured mother, and thrice-blessed thy brethren. Full well, I ween, are their hearts ever warmed with joy because of thee, as they see thee entering the dance, a plant so fair. But he again is blessed in heart above all others, who shall prevail with his gifts of wooing and lead thee to his home. For never yet have mine eyes looked upon a mortal such as thou, whether man or woman; amazement holds me as I look on thee. Or a truth in Delos once I saw such a thing, a young shoot of a palm springing up beside the altar of Apollo—for thither, too, I went, and much people followed with me, on that journey on which evil woes were to be my portion;—even so, when I saw that, I marvelled long at heart, for never yet did such a tree spring up from the earth. And in like manner, lady, do I marvel at thee, and am amazed, and fear greatly to touch thy knees; but sore grief has come upon me. Yesterday, on the twentieth day, I escaped from the wine-dark sea, but ever until then the wave and the swift winds bore me from the island of Ogygia; and now fate has cast me ashore here, that here too, haply, I may suffer some ill. For not yet, methinks, will by troubles cease, but the gods ere that will bring many to pass. Nay, O queen, have pity; for it is to thee first that I am come after many grievous toils, and of the others who possess this city and land I know not one. Shew me the city, and give me some rag to throw about me, if thou hadst any wrapping for the clothes when thou camest hither. And for thyself, may the gods grant thee all that thy heart desires; a husband and a home may they grant thee, and oneness of heart—a goodly gift. For nothing is greater or better than this, when man and wife dwell in a home in one accord, a great grief to their foes and a joy to their friends; but they know it best themselves."

Then white-armed Nausicaa answered him; "Stranger, since thou seemest to be neither an evil man nor a witless, and it is Zeus himself, the Olympian, that gives happy fortune to men, both to the good and the evil, to each man as he will; so to thee, I ween, he has given this lot, and thou must in any case endure it. But now, since thou hast come to our city and land, thou shalt not lack clothing or aught else of those things which befit a sore-tried suppliant when he cometh in the way. The city will I shew thee, and will tell thee the name of the people. The Phaeacians possess this city and land, and I am the daughter of great-hearted Alcinous, upon whom depend the might and power of the Phaeacians."

She spoke, and called to her fair-tressed hand-maids: "Stand, my maidens. Whither do ye flee at the sight of a man? Ye do not think, surely, that he is an enemy? That mortal man lives not, or exists nor shall ever be born who shall come to the land of the Phaeacians as a foeman, for we are very dear to the immortals. Far off we dwell in the surging sea, the furthermost of men, and no other mortals have dealings with us. Nay, this is some hapless wanderer that has come hither. Him must we now tend; for from Zeus are all strangers and beggars; and a gift, though small, is welcome. Come, then, my maidens, give to the stranger food and drink, and bathe him in the river in a spot where there is shelter from the wind."

So she spoke, and they halted and called to each other. Then they set Odysseus in a sheltered place, as Nausicaa, the daughter of great-hearted Alcinous, bade, and beside him they put a cloak and a tunic for raiment, and gave him soft olive oil in the flask of gold, and bade him bathe in the streams of the river. Then among the maidens spoke goodly Odysseus: "Maidens, stand yonder apart, that by myself I may wash the brine from my shoulders, and anoint myself with olive oil; for of a truth it is long since oil came near my skin. But in your presence will I not bathe, for I am ashamed to make me naked in the midst of fair-tressed maidens.". . .

Document Set 2.3 References

A. The Hero Hector Bids Farewell to His Family
   Homer, *The Illiad*, bk. 21, in Fred Morrow Fling, ed., *A Source Book of Greek History* (Boston: D. C. Heath and Company, 1907), 6–7.
B. Odysseus at the Palace of Alcinous
   Homer, *The Odyssey*, trans. A. T. Murray (Cambridge: Mass.: Harvard University Press, Loeb Classical Library, 1919), 8:78–132.
C. The Excellence of Nausicaa
   Homer, *The Odyssey*, 6:125–220.

The documents in this set serve as milestones in the evolution of Greek society from the Dark Age to the early period of the *polis,* or city-state. Hesiod (fl. c. 800 B.C.) speaks for the Greek peasants on the eve of the breakthrough to the polis: his lengthy poem *Works and Days* (excerpted as Document A) is a jumble of speculations on human destiny, complaints about abuses inflicted by powerful men upon debtors, gloomy ruminations about women, comments about how to farm and how to trade (is it significant that the subject of commerce suddenly comes up?), and homely advice for minimizing the aches and pains of life. Hesiod's vision of humanity's degeneration from a legendary Age of Gold to his own "miserable Age of Iron" became for the Greeks a classic assessment of the human condition, which should be compared to the Hebrew story of the Fall of Man. The notion that history is the process of human decline from a vanished Golden Age will have enormous staying power in the Western tradition.

With Document B we are in the age of the polis. About 630 B.C. the city of There on Crete sent out a colony of its citizens to settle what became Cyrene in present-day Libya; in the fourth century the people of Cyrene set up this inscription to reaffirm their ties to their mother city at the same time attesting to the internal tensions in There that had necessitated colonization. In Document C we encounter another seminal Greek institution—the Olympic Games. There are no contemporary descriptions of the early games, but the account given here—an extract from a guidebook to Greece compiled in the second century A.D. by Pausanias—recalls some memorable moments from Olympiads of the distant past.

Study these documents and list the evidence they reveal of the Greeks' ideals and grievances in the Archaic Period, and signs of changes that were occurring. Feel free to draw upon *The Challenges of the West* for background and historical context.

A. Hesiod Recounts the Degeneration of the Human Race

. . . First of all the deathless gods who dwell on Olympus made a golden race of mortal men who lived in the time of Cronos when he was reigning in heaven. And they lived like gods without sorrow of heart, remote and free from toil and grief: miserable age rested not on them; but with legs and arms never failing they made merry with feasting beyond the reach of all evils. When they died, it was as though they were overcome with sleep, and they had all good things; for the fruitful earth unforced bare them fruit abundantly and without stint. They dwelt in ease and peace upon their lands with many good things, rich in flocks and loved by the blessed gods.

But after the earth had covered this generation—they are called pure spirits dwelling on the earth, and are kindly, delivering from harm, and guardians of mortal men; for they roam everywhere over the earth, clothed in mist and keep watch on judgements and cruel deeds, givers of wealth; for this royal right also they received;—then they who dwell on Olympus made a second generation which was of silver and less noble by far. It was like the golden race neither in body nor in spirit. A child was brought up at his good mother's side an hundred years, an utter simpleton, playing childishly in his own home. But when they were full grown and were come to the full measure of their prime, they lived only a little time and that in sorrow because of their foolishness, for they could not keep from sinning and from wronging one another, nor would they serve the immortals, nor sacrifice on the holy altars of the blessed ones as it is right for men to do wherever they dwell. Then Zeus the son of Cronos was angry and put them away, because they would not give honour to the blessed gods who live on Olympus.

But when earth had covered this generation also—they are called blessed spirits of the underworld by men, and, though they are of second order, yet honour attends them also—Zeus the Father made a third generation of mortal men, a brazen race, sprung from ash-trees; and it was in no way equal to the silver age, but was terrible and strong. They loved the lamentable works of Ares and deeds of violence; they ate no bread, but were hard of heart like adament, fearful men. Great was their strength and unconquerable the arms which grew from their shoulders on their strong limbs. Their armour was of bronze, and their houses of bronze, and of bronze were their implements: there was no black iron. These were destroyed by their own hands and passed to the dank house of chill Hades, and left no name: terrible though they were, black Death seized them, and they left the bright light of the sun.

But when earth had covered this generation also, Zeus the son of Cronos made yet another, the fourth, upon the fruitful earth, which was nobler and more righteous, a god-like race of hero-men who are called demi-gods, the race before our own, throughout the boundless earth. Grim war and dread battle destroyed a part of them, some in the land of Cadmus at seven-gated Thebe when they fought for the flocks of Oedipus, and some, when it had brought them in ships over the great sea gulf to Troy for rich-haired Helen's sake: there death's end enshrouded a part of them. But to the others father Zeus the son of Cronos gave a living and an abode apart from men, and made them dwell at the ends of earth. And they live untouched by sorrow in the islands of the blessed along the shore of deep swirling Ocean, happy heroes for whom the grain-giving earth bears honey-sweet fruit flourishing thrice a year, far from the deathless gods, and Cronos rules over them; for the father of men and gods released him from his bonds. And these last equally have honour and glory.

And again far-seeing Zeus made yet another generation, the fifth, of men who are upon the bounteous earth.

Thereafter, would that I were not among the men of the fifth generation, but either had died before or been born afterwards. For now truly is a race of iron, and men never rest from labour and sorrow by day, and from perishing by night; and the gods shall lay sore trouble upon them. But, notwithstanding, even these shall have some good mingled with their evils. And Zeus will destroy this race of mortal men also when they come to have grey hair on the temples at their birth. The father will not agree with his children, nor the children with their father, nor guest with his host, nor comrade with comrade; nor will brother be dear to brother as aforetime. Men will dishonour their parents as they grow quickly old, and will carp at them, chiding them with bitter words, hard-hearted they, not knowing the fear of the gods. They will not repay their aged parents the cost of their nurture, for might shall be their right: and one man will sack another's city. There will be no favour for the man who keeps his oath or for the just or for the good; but rather men will praise the evil-doer and his violent dealing. Strength will be right and reverence will cease to be; and the wicked will hurt the worthy man, speaking false words against him, and will swear an oath upon them. Envy, foul-mouthed, delighting in evil, with scowling face, will go along with wretched men one and all. And then Aidôs and Nemesis, with their sweet forms wrapped in white robes, will go from the wide-pathed earth and forsake mankind to join the company of the deathless gods: and bitter sorrows will be left for mortal men, and there will be no help against evil. . . .

You princes, mark well this punishment you also;

for the deathless gods are near among men and mark all those who oppress their fellows with crooked judgements, and reck not the anger of the gods. For upon the bounteous earth Zeus has thrice ten thousand spirits, watchers of mortal men, and these keep watch on judgements and deeds of wrong as they roam, clothed in mist, all over the earth. And there is virgin Justice, the daughter of Zeus, who is honoured and reverenced among the gods who dwell on Olympus, and whenever anyone hurts her with lying slander, she sits beside her father, Zeus the son of Cronos, and tells him of men's wicked heart, until the people pay for the mad folly of their princes who, evilly minded, pervert judgement and give sentence crookedly. Keep watch against this, you princes, and make straight your judgements, you who devour bribes; put crooked judgements altogether from your thoughts.

He does mischief to himself who does mischief to another, and evil planned harms the plotter most.

The eye of Zeus, seeing all and understanding all, beholds these things too, of so he will, and fails not to mark what sort of justice is this that the city keeps within it. Now, therefore, may neither I myself be righteous among men, nor my son—for then it is a bad thing to be righteous—if indeed the unrighteous shall have the greater right. But I think that all-wise Zeus will not yet bring that to pass. . . .

Mark, when you hear the voice of the crane who cries year by year from the clouds above, for she gives the signal for ploughing and shows the season of rainy winter; but she vexes the heart of the man who has no oxen. Then is the time to feed up your horned oxen in the byre; for it is easy to say: "Give me a yoke of oxen and a waggon," and it is easy to refuse: "I have work for my oxen." The man who is rich in fancy thinks his waggon as good as built already—the fool! he does not know that there are a hundred timbers to a waggon. Take care to lay these up beforehand at home.

So soon as the time for ploughing is proclaimed to men, then make haste, you and your slaves alike, in wet and in dry, to plough in the season for ploughing, and bestir yourself early in the morning so that your fields may be full. Plough in the spring; but fallow broken up in the summer will not belie your hopes. Sow fallow land when the soil is still getting light: fallow land is a defender from harm and a soother of children. . . .

But if desire for uncomfortable sea-faring seize you; when the Pleiades plunge into the misty sea to escape Orion's rude strength, then truly gales of all kinds rage. Then keep ships no longer on the sparkling sea, but bethink you to till the land as I bid you. Haul up your ship upon the land and pack it closely with stones all round to keep off the power of the winds which blow damply, and draw out the bilge-plug so that the rain of heaven may not rot it. Put away all the tackle and fittings in your house, and stow the wings of the sea-going ship neatly, and hang up the well-shaped rudder over the smoke. You yourself wait until the season for sailing is come, and then haul your swift ship down to the sea and stow a convenient cargo in it, so that you may bring home profit, even as your father and mine, foolish Perses, used to sail on shipboard because he lacked sufficient livelihood. And one day he came to this very place crossing over a great stretch of sea; he left Aeolian Cyme and fled, not from riches and substance, but from wretched poverty which Zeus lays upon men, and he settled near Helicon in a miserable hamlet, Ascra, which is bad in winter, sultry in summer, and good at no time.

But you, Perses, remember all works in their season but sailing especially. Admire a small ship, but put your freight in a large one; for the greater the lading, the greater will be your piled gain, if only the winds will keep back their harmful gales.

If ever you turn your misguided heart to trading and wish to escape from debt and joyless hunger, I will show you the measures of the loud-roaring sea, though I have no skill in sea-faring nor in ships; for never yet have I sailed by ship over the wide sea, but only to Euboea from Aulis where the Achaeans once stayed through much storm when they had gathered a great host from divine Hellas for Troy, the land of fair women. Then I crossed over to Chalcis, to the games of wise Amphidamas where the sons of the great-hearted hero proclaimed and appointed prizes. And there I boast that I gained the victory with a song and carried off an handled tripod which I dedicated to the Muses of Helicon, in the place where they first set me in the way of clear song. Such is all my experience of many-pegged ships; nevertheless I will tell you the will of Zeus who holds the aegis; for the Muses have taught me to sing in marvellous song. . . .

B. A Greek City Dispatches a Colony

Since Apollo of Delphi spontaneously told Battus and the Therans to settle Cyrene, the Therans decided to send Battus to North Africa as leader and king and for the Therans to sail as his companions. They are to sail on equal and fair terms according to their household and one adult son [from each family] is to be conscripted, [and those who are to be chosen are to be those who are the adults, and of the other Therans only those who are free are to sail.] And if the colonists establish the settlement, men who sail later to North Africa shall share in citizenship and magistracies and shall be given portions from the land which has no owner. But if they do not establish the settlement and the Therans are unable to give it assistance and the colonists are oppressed by hardship for five years, they shall depart without fear from the land to Thera, to their own property, and they shall be citizens. And if any man is unwilling to leave when the *polis* sends him, he shall be subject to the death penalty and his property shall be confiscated. Any man who harbors or hides him, whether he is a father helping his son, or a brother his brother, is to suffer the same penalty as the man who is unwilling to sail. A sworn agreement was made on these conditions by those who stayed and those who sailed to found the colony, and they invoked curses against those who break it or fail to keep it, whether they were those who settled in North Africa or those who remained behind.

C. Pausanias Recalls Early Olympic Champions

From the time the Olympian games were revived continuously, prizes were first instituted for running, and Corœbus of Elis was the victor. His statue is at Olympia and his grave is on the borders of Elis. And in the 14th Olympiad afterwards the double course was introduced, when Hypenus, a native of Pisa, won the wild olive crown, and Acanthus the second. And in the 18th Olympiad they remembered the pentathlon and the wrestling. . . . And in the 23rd Olympiad they ordained prizes for boxing. . . . And in the 25th Olympiad they had a race of full-grown horses. . . . And in the 8th Olympiad late they introduced the pancratium and the riding race. The horse of Crannonian Crauxidas got in first, and the competitors for the pancratium were beaten by the Syracusan Lygdamus, who has his sepulchre at the stone quarries of Syracuse. And I don't know whether Lygdamus was really as big as the Theban Hercules, but that is the tradition at Syracuse. And the contest of the boys was not a revival of ancient usage, but the people of Elis instituted it because the idea pleased them. So prizes were instituted for running and wrestling among boys in the 307th Olympiad. . . . And in the 41st Olympiad afterwards they invited boxing boys. . . . And the race in heavy armor was tried in the 65th Olympiad as an exercise for war, I think; and of those who ran with their shields Damaretus of Heræum was the victor. . . .

The order of the games in our day is to sacrifice victims to the god and then to contend in the pentathlon and horse-race, according to the programme established in the 77th Olympiad, for before this horses and men contended on the same day. And at that period the pancrataists did not appear till night, for they could not compete sooner, so much time being taken up by the horse-races and pentathlon. . . . But in the 25th Olympiad afterwards nine general umpires were appointed, three for the horses, three to watch the pentathlon, and three to preside over the remaining games. And in the 2d Olympiad after this a tenth umpire was appointed. And in the 103d Olympiad, as the people of Elis had twelve tribes, a general umpire was appointed by each.

He won they say the horse-race at Olympia, when Hercules the Theban established the Olympian games. Why a crown of wild olive was given to the victor at Olympia I have shown in my account of Elis, and why of laurel at Delphi I shall show hereafter. And at the Isthmian games pine, at the Nemean games parsley, were wont to be the prize, as we know from the cases of Palæmon and Archemorus. But most games have a crown of palm as the prize, and everywhere the palm is put into the right hand of the victor.

Document Set 2.4 References

A. Hesiod Recounts the Degeneration of the Human Race
Hesiod, *Works and Days,* trans. H. G. Evans-White (Cambridge, Mass.: Harvard University Press, Loeb Classical Library, 1914), 109–199, 249–275, 448–465, 618–663.
B. A Greek City Dispatches a Colony
M. Crawford and D. Whitehead, *Archaic and Classical Greece* (Cambridge: Cambridge University Press, 1983), no. 16.
C. Pausanias Recalls Early Olympic Champions
Pausanius, 1:316, 318, in Fred Morrow Fling, ed. *A Source Book of Greek History* (Boston: D. C. Heath and Company, 1907), 47–48.

DOCUMENT SET 2.5
Sparta

The severe discipline by which the city-state of Sparta preserved its unique institutions and dominated the Peloponnese facinated the ancient Greeks, even if they were also repelled by the harshness of Spartan life. Essentially this was a society that chose to maintain its domination in the face of overwhelming odds by imposing fanatical austerities on its own citizenry, exercising a pitiless despotism over its subject population, and shunning outside influence. In the aftermath of the Peloponnesian War (431–404 B.C.) the disillusioned Athenian aristocrat Xenophon conceived (like many other Greek conservatives) a profound admiration for the Spartan way of life, which he described in the extract forming Document A. In Document B we go back several hundred years earlier, to the period when the austere Spartan way of life was beginning to take shape; Sparta at this time was still able to produce the great poet Tyrtaeus (fl. ca. 650 B.C.), whose powerful verse celebrated the ethos by which the Spartan citizen-soldier lived and died.

But not all Greeks admired Sparta. The philosopher Aristotle (384–322 B.C.), in his *Politics*, condemned Sparta for an unexpected reason—that it gave too much freedom to women!

The documents in this set should enable you to write a brief essay exploring Spartan values and explaining why they could appear attractive to non-Spartans. *The Challenge of the West* gives you additional background to consider.

A. Xenophon Describes the Upbringing of Spartan Boys and Girls

. . . Take for example—and it is well to begin at the beginning—the whole topic of the birth and rearing of children. Throughout the rest of the world the young girl, who will one day become a mother (and I speak of those who may be held to be well brought up), is nurtured on the plainest food attainable, with the scantiest addition of meat or other condiments; whilst as to wine they train them either to total abstinence or to take it highly diluted with water. And in imitation, as it were, of the handicraft type, since the majority of artificers are sedentary, we, the rest of the Hellenes, are content that our girls should sit quietly and work wools. That is all we demand of them. But how are we to expect that women nurtured in this fashion should produce a splendid offspring?

Lycurgus[1] pursued a different path. Clothes were things, he held, the furnishing of which might well enough be left to female slaves. And believing that the highest function of a free woman was the bearing of children, in the first place he insisted on the training of the body as incumbent no less on the female than the male; and in pursuit of the same idea instituted rival contests in running and tests of strength for women as for men. His belief was that where both parents were strong their progeny would be found to be more vigorous. . . .

So opposed to those of the rest of the world are the principles which Lycurgus devised in reference to the birth of children. Whether they enabled him to provide Sparta with a race of men superior to all in size and strength any one who desires may examine.

After this exposition of the customs in connection with the birth of children, I wish now to explain the systems of education in fashion there and elsewhere. Throughout the rest of Hellas the custom on the part of those who claim to educate their sons in the best way is as follows. As soon as the children are of an age to understand what is said to them they are immediately placed under the charge of Paidagogoi (boy-escorts), who are also attendants, and sent off to the school of some teacher to be taught "letters," "music," and the concerns of the palæstra. Besides this they are given shoes to wear which tend to make their feet tender, and their bodies are made soft by various changes of clothing. As for food, the only measure recognized is that which is fixed by appetite.

But when we turn to Lycurgus, instead of leaving it to each member of the state privately to appoint a slave to be his son's escort, he set over the young Spartans a public guardian, the paidonómos or "manager of boys" to give him his proper title, with complete authority over them. This guardian was selected from those who fill the highest magistracies. He had authority to hold musters of the boys, and as their overseer, in case of any misbehavior, to chastise severely. The legislator further provided him with a body of youths in the prime of young manhood and bearing whips, to inflict punishment when necessary, with this happy result that in Sparta reverence and obedience ever go hand in hand, nor is there lack of either.

1 The legendary law-giver who, Greeks believed, had created Sparta's institutions.

Instead of softening their feet with shoes, his rule was to make them hardy through going barefoot. This habit, if practised, would, as he believed, enable them to go up steep ascents more easily and to go down descending slopes with less danger. In fact, with his feet so trained the young Spartan would leap and jump high and run faster unshod than another shod in the ordinary way.

Instead of pampering them with a variety of clothes, his rule was to habituate them to a single garment the whole year through, thinking that so they would be better prepared to withstand the variations of heat and cold.

Again, as regards food, according to his regulation the Eirên, or head of the flock, must see that his messmates gathered to the club meal, with such moderate food as to avoid that heaviness which is engendered by repletion, and yet not to remain altogether unacquainted with inadequate sustenance. His belief was that by such training they would be better able when it proved necessary to undergo hardships without food. They would be all the fitter, if the word of command were given, to remain on the stretch for a long time without extra dieting. The craving for a finer dish would be less, the readiness to take any victual set before them greater, and, in general, the régime would be found more healthy. Under it he thought the lads would increase in stature and shape into finer men, since, as he maintained, a dietary which gave suppleness to the limbs must be more conducive to both ends than one which added thickness to the bodily parts by feeding.

On the other hand, in order to guard against a too great pinch of starvation, though he did not actually allow the boys to help themselves without trouble to what they needed more, he did give them permission to steal this thing or that in the effort to alleviate their hunger. It was not of course from any real difficulty how else to supply them with nutriment that he left it to them to provide themselves by this crafty method. Nor can I conceive that any one will so misinterpret the custom. Clearly its explanation lies in the fact that he who would live the life of a robber must forego sleep by night, and in the daytime he must enjoy shifts and lie in ambuscade; he must prepare and make ready his scouts, and so forth, if he is to succeed in capturing the quarry.

It is obvious, I say, that the whole of this education tended, and was intended, to make the boys craftier and more inventive in getting supplies, whilst at the same time it cultivated their warlike instincts. An objector may retort: "But if he thought it so fine a feat to steal, why did he inflict many blows on the unfortunate who was caught?" My answer is: for the self-same reason which induces people, in other matters which are taught, to punish the mal-performance of a service. So they, the Lacedæmonians, visit penalties on the boy who is caught thieving as being but poor thieves. So to steal as many cheeses as possible off the shrine of Orthia was a feat to be encouraged; but, at the same moment, others were enjoined to scourge the thief, which would point a moral not obscurely, that by pain endured for a brief season a man may earn the joyous reward of lasting glory. Herein, too, it is plainly shown that where speed is requisite the sluggard will win for himself much trouble and scant good.

Furthermore, and in order that the boys should not want a ruler, even in case the overseer himself about absent, he gave to any citizen who chanced to be present authority to lay upon them injunctions for their good, and to chastise them if they failed in anything. By so doing he brought it about that boys of Sparta were more respectful. Indeed there is nothing which, whether as boys or men, they respect more highly than the ruler. Lastly, and with the same intention, that the boys must never be bereft of a ruler, even if by chance there were no grown man present, he laid down the rule that in such a case the most seasoned of the Leaders or Prefects was to become ruler for the nonce, each of his own division. The conclusion is that under no circumstances whatever are the boys of Sparta destitute of one to rule them. . . .

Coming to the critical period at which a boy ceases to be a boy and becomes a youth, we find that it is just then that the rest of the world proceed to emancipate their children from the boy-escorts and from the teachers, and without substituting any further ruler, are content to launch them into absolute independence.

Here, again, Lycurgus took an entirely opposite view of the matter. This, if observation might be trusted, was the season when the greatest conceit is developed in them, and insolence most luxuriates, when, too, the strongest desires for pleasures arise. At this point he imposed very many hardships upon them and devised the largest occupation. By a crowning enactment, which said that he who shrank from the duties imposed on him would forfeit henceforth all claim to the glorious honors of the state, he caused, not only the public authorities, but those personally interested in each of them to take serious pains so that no single individual of them should by an act of craven cowardice find himself dishonored within the body politic.

Furthermore, in his desire firmly to implant in their youthful souls a root of modesty he imposed upon these bigger boys a special rule. In the very streets they were to keep their two hands within the folds of the cloak; they were to walk in silence and without turning their heads to gaze, now here, now there, but rather to keep their eyes fixed upon the ground before them. There also it has become manifest that, even in the matter of self-control, the males are stronger than the nature of females. At any rate, you might sooner expect a stone image to utter a sound than one of those Spartan youths; to divert the eyes of some bronze statue were less difficult. As to quiet bearing, no bride ever stepped in bridal bower with more natural modesty. Note them when they have reached the public table. The plainest answer to the question asked,—that is all you need expect to hear from their lips.

But if he was thus careful in the education of the stripling, the Spartan lawgiver showed a still greater anxiety in dealing with those who had reached the prime of opening manhood; considering their immense importance to the city in the scale of good, if only they proved themselves the men they should be. He had only to look around to see that wherever the spirit of emulation was most deeply seated, there, too, their choruses and gymnastic contests would present alike the highest charm to eye and ear. On the same principle he persuaded himself that he needed only to match is youthful warriors in the rivalry of excellence, and with like result. They also, in their degree, might be expected to attain to the fullest measure of manly virtue.

What method he adopted to engage these combatants I will now explain. Their ephors select three men out of the whole body of the citizens in the prime of life. These three are named hippagretæ, or masters of the horse. Each selects one hundred others, being bound to explain for what reason he prefers some and rejects others. The result is that those who fail to obtain the distinction are now at open war, not only with those who rejected them, but with those who were chosen in their stead; and they keep ever a jealous eye on one another to detect some slip of conduct contrary to the high code of honor there held customary. Thus is set on foot that strife, in truest sense acceptable to heaven, and for the purposes of state most politic. It is a strife in which not only is the pattern of a brave man's conduct fully set forth, but where each of them separately train themselves for the highest efficiency, and if there be any need, they will individually come to the aid of the commonwealth with all their strength.

Necessity, moreover, is laid upon them to study a good habit of the body, coming as they do to blows with their fists on account of their feud wherever

they meet. Albeit any one present has a right to separate the combatants, and, if obedience is not shown to the peacemaker, the manager of boys hales the delinquent before the ephors, and the ephors inflict heavy damages, since they will have it plainly understood that rage must never override obedience to law.

With regard to those who have already passed the vigor of early manhood, and on whom the highest magistracies henceforth devolve, there is a like contrast. In Hellas generally we find that at this age the need of further attention to physical strength is removed, although the imposition of military service continues. But Lycurgus made it customary for men of that age to regard hunting as the highest honor suited to their time of life; albeit not to the exclusion of any public duty. His aim was that they might be equally able to undergo the fatigues of campaigning with those in the prime of early manhood. . . .

B. Tyrtaeus Sings of the Spartan Citizen-Warrior's Steadfastness

A

I would not say anything for a man nor
    take account of him
for any speed of his feet or wrestling
    skill he might have,
not if he had the size of a Cyclops and
    strength to go with it,
not if he could outrun Bóreas, the
    North Wind of Thrace,
not if he were more handsome and
    gracefully formed than Tithónos,
or had more riches than Midas had, or
    Kinyras too,
not if he were more of a king than
    Tantalid Pelops,
or had the power of speech and
    persuasion Adrastos had,
not if he had all splendors except for a
    fighting spirit.

B

For no man ever proves himself a good
    man in war unless he can endure to
    face the blood and the slaughter,
go close against the enemy and fight
    with his hands.
Here is courage, mankind's finest
    possession, here is
the noblest prize that a young man
    can endeavor to win,

and it is a good thing his city and all the
people share with him
when a man plants his feet and stands
in the foremost spears
relentlessly, all thought of foul flight
completely forgotten,
and has well trained his heart to be
steadfast and to endure,

C

and with words encourages the man who
is stationed beside him.
Here is a man who proves himself to
be valiant in war.
With a sudden rush he turns to flight
the rugged battalions
of the enemy, and sustains the beating
waves of assault.
And he who so falls among the
champions and loses his sweet life,
so blessing with honor his city, his father, and all his people,
with wounds in his chest, where the spear
that he was facing has transfixed
that massive guard of his shield, and
gone through his breastplate as well,
why, such a man is lamented alike by the
young and the elders,
and all his city goes into mourning and
grieves for his loss.
His tomb is pointed out with pride, and so
are his children,
and his children's children, and afterward all the race that is his.
His shining glory is never forgotten, his
name is remembered,

D

and he becomes an immortal, though he
lies under the ground,
when one who was a brave man has been
killed by the furious War God
standing his ground and fighting hard for
his children and land.
But if he escapes the doom of death, the
destroyer of bodies,
and wins his battle, and bright renown
for the work of his spear,
all men give place to him alike, the youth
and the elders,
and much joy comes his way before he
goes down to the dead.

Aging he has reputation among his citizens. No one tries to interfere with his
honors or all he deserves;
all men withdraw before his presence, and
yield their seats to him.
and youth, and the men of his age, and
even those older than he.
Thus a man should endeavor to reach this
high place of courage
with all his heart, and, so trying, never
be backward in war.

c. Aristotle Deplores the Freedom of Spartan Women

The licence of the Lacedaemonian [Spartan] women defeats the intention of the Spartan constitution, and is adverse to the good order of the state. For a husband and a wife, being each a part of every family, the state may be considered as about equally divided into men and women; and, therefore, in those states in which the condition of the woman is bad, half the city may be regarded as having no laws. And this is what has actually happened at Sparta; the legislator wanted to make the whole state hardy and temperate, and he has carried out his intention in the case of the men, but he has neglected the women, who live in every sort of intemperance and luxury. The consequence is that in such a state wealth is too highly valued, especially if the citizens fall under the dominion of their wives, after the manner of all warlike races, except the Celts and a few others who openly approve of male loves. The old mythologer would seem to have been right in uniting Ares and Aphrodite, for all warlike races are prone to the love either of men or of women. This was exemplified among the Spartans in the days of their greatness; many things were managed by their women. But what difference does it make whether women rule, or the rulers are ruled by women? The result is the same. Even in regard to courage, which is of no use in daily life, and is needed only in war, the influence of the Lacedaemonian women has been most mischievous. . . . This licence of the Lacedaemonian women existed from the earliest times, and was only what might be expected. For, during the wars of the Lacedaemonians, first against the Argives, and afterwards against the Arcadians and Messenians, the men were long away from home, and, on the return of peace, they gave themselves into the legislator's hand, already prepared by the discipline of a soldier's life (in which there are many elements of virtue), to receive his enactments. But, when

Lycurgus, as tradition says, wanted to bring the women under his laws, they resisted, and he gave up the attempt. They, and not he, are to blame for what then happened, and this defect in the constitution is clearly to be attributed to them. We are not, however, considering what is or is not to be excused, but what is right or wrong, and the disorder of the women, as I have already said, not only of itself gives an air of indecorum to the state, but tends in a measure to foster avarice. . . .

Document Set 2.5 References

A. Xenophon Describes the Upbringing of Spartan Boys and Girls
   Xenophon, *Constitution of the Lacedaemonians,* trans., E. G. Sihler in G. W. Botsford and E. G. Sihler, eds., *Hellenic Civilization* (New York: Columbia University Press, 1915), 131–136.
B. Tyrtaeus Sings of the Spartan Citizen-Warrior's Steadfastness
   Richmond Lattimore, trans., *Greek Lyrics* (Chicago: University of Chicago Press, 1955), 14–15.
C. Aristotle Deplores the Freedom of Spartan Women
   Aristotle, *Politics,* trans. Benjamin Jowett in Mary R. Lefkowitz and Maureen B. Fant, eds., *Women's Life in Greece and Rome,* 2d ed. (Baltimore: Johns Hopkins University Press, 1982), 64–65.

DOCUMENT SET 2.6
Early Athens

The polis of Athens was ideally suited by its geographical location and silver mines to develop a money economy and a far-flung commercial network, which inevitably spawned social and political tension. Document A records the severe laws imposed by the early Athenian legislator Draco about 620 B.C. meant to bring order to a tense, unruly society. Document B is one of the poems composed by another earlier Athenian lawgiver, Solon (c. 630–c. 580 B.C.), justifying measures he took to reestablish social justice. Use these documents to extract whatever evidence you can find that details the sources and manifestations of tension in the early Athenian polis.

A. Draco Prescribes the Law on Homicide

. . . First Table. And if anyone shall kill another without premeditation, [he shall be exiled.] The kings shall administer justice on a charge of murder or [if anyone charges another with contriving it (?)] and the *ephetae* shall decide. If there is a father or a brother or sons, all shall forgive, or else the opposition of one shall prevail; [if there are no] such persons, the relatives as far as the degree of first cousin [may forgive, if all of them] are willing, after swearing the oath. If there is not any one of these persons and the homicide was involuntary and the fifty-one ephetae decide that it was involuntary, the slayer shall be admitted (to the country) by ten members of the phratry, if they are willing. These persons shall be chosen by the fifty-one from those of noble birth. This ordinance shall be applicable also to those who have committed homicide previously. The warning to the slayer shall be given, in the market-place, by the relatives nearer than the degree of first cousin, but first cousins and sons of first cousins and sons-in-law and fathers-in-law and members of the phratry shall aid in the prosecution.

(Then follow several lines which cannot be restored.)

If anyone shall kill the murderer or cause him to be slain while he is keeping away from the market-place on the frontier, from (public) games, and from amphictyonic sanctuaries, such a person shall be subject to the same penalties as one who has killed an Athenian, and the decision shall rest with the ephetæ. It shall be allowable to kill or arrest murderers in our own country, but not to mistreat them or to take a ransom, under penalty of paying double the amount of the damage. *(The next line is lost.)*

If anyone shall kill another in self-defence . . . if the homicide is involuntary, the kings shall try the case on a charge of murder, and the ephetæ shall decide. [One who has killed a slave shall be subject to trial for murder in the same way as one who has killed] a free man. If anyone in his own defence shall kill on the spot one who is forcibly and unlawfully plundering, the homicide shall not be punished. *(The remaining ten lines cannot be restored.)*

B. Solon Defends His Reforms

My purpose was to bring my scattered people back together. Where did I fall short of my design? I call to witness at the judgment seat of time one who is noblest, mother of Olympian divinities, and greatest of them all, Black Earth. I took away the mortgage stones stuck in her breast, and she, who went a slave before, in now set free. Into this sacred land, our Athens, I brought back a throng of those who had been sold, some by due law, though others wrongly; some by hardship pressed to escape the debts they owed; and some of these no longer spoke Attic, since they had drifted wide around the world, while those in the country had the shame of slavery upon them, and they served their masters' moods in fear. These I set free; and I did this by strength of hand, welding right law with violence to a single whole. So have I done, and carried through all that I pledged. I have made laws, for the good man and the bad alike, and shaped a rule to suit each case, and set it down. Had someone else not like myself taken the reins, some ill-advised or greedy person, he would not have held the people in. Had I agreed to do what pleased their adversaries at that time, or what they themselves planned to do against their enemies, our city would have been widowed of her men. Therefore, I put myself on guard at every side, and turned among them like a wolf inside a pack of dogs.

Document Set 2.6 References

A. Draco Prescribes the Law on Homicide
    Athenian inscriptions, in G. W. Botsford and E. G. Sihler, eds., *Hellenic Civilization* (New York: Columbia University Press, 1915), 289–291.
B. Solon Defends His Reforms
    Richmond Lattimore, trans., *Greek Lyrics,* 2d ed. (Chicago: University of Chicago Press, 1960), 22.

DOCUMENT SET 2.7
Gods, the Creation, and the Beginning of Philosophy

With the documents of this set we move from the Homeric world of gods casually meting out life and death to their favorite human beings to the beginning of Greek philosophy and science. Document A, from the *Iliad,* shows Zeus pulling all the cosmic strings that determine the fate of mortal heroes. Document B, from another poem attributed to Hesiod, *Theogony,* provides archaic Greek counterpart to the creation myths already encountered in the ancient Near East. (Cronos, the last creature mentioned by Hesiod, later begot Olympian gods who eventually overthrew him.) With Document C we have traversed some two hundred of years since Hesiod's time to the great lyric poet Sappho of Lesbos (c. 610–c. 580 B.C.); her hymn to the goddess of love, Aphrodite, reveals a far more accessible divinity.

Document D and the short selections grouped together as Document E are among the oldest known true philosophical writings. In Document D, the Ionic poet Xenophon of Colophon (c. 580–480 B.C.) characteristically expresses some of the novel ideas about the gods that occurred to him and other thinkers of his time, rejecting the apparent moral failings of the gods of Homer and Hesiod. The extracts in Document E are in some cases virtually all we know of the earliest Greek philosophers—Thales, Anaximander, Heraclitus, and Democritus—who speculated about the nature of the ultimate substance or idea that lies behind the transitory flux of everyday phenomena. In the case of Thales and Anaximander, the passages quoted here come from accounts of their ideas as reported much later by Aristotle; and Democritus's ideas similarly are reported by the later philosopher Diogenes Laertius.

As a first step in analyzing these documents, try to establish how Homer and Hesiod view the gods and their doings. Then using both the intenal evidence of the documents and insights that you glean from reading *The Challenge of the West,* try to appreciate how vast a change in human understanding of the gods had occurred by the time of Sappho and Xenophon. Finally, study the philosophical fragments to extract a basic understanding of how the early Greek philosophers tried to apply reason to make sense of the world as observed by the cosmos? How do they differ? What place do they leave for the gods?

A. Homer's Zeus Ponders How to Favor Achilles

. . . Now all other gods and chariot-driving men slept all night long, only Zeus was not holden of sweet sleep; rather was he pondering in his mind how he should do honor to Achilles and destroy many beside the Achaians' ships.

And this design seemed to his mind the best, to wit, to send a baneful dream upon Agamemnon, son of Atreus. So he spake and uttered to him winged words: "Come now, thou baneful Dream, go to the Achaians' fleet ships, enter into the hut of Agamemnon, son of Atreus, and tell him every word plainly as I charge thee. Bid him call to arms the flowing-haired Achaians with all speed, for that now he may take the wide-wayed city of the Trojans." . . .

And they did sacrifice each man to one of the everlasting gods, praying for escape from death and the tumult of battle. But Agamemnon, king of men, slew a fat bull of five years to most mighty Kronion, and called the elders, the princes of the Achaian host. . . . Then stood they around the bull and took the barley meal, and Agamemnon made his prayer in their midst and said: "Zeus most glorious, most great god of the storm cloud, that dwellest in the heavens, vouchsafe that the sun set not upon us, nor the darkness come near until I have laid low upon the earth Priam's palace smirched with smoke and burnt the doorways thereof with consuming fire, and rent on Hector's breast his doublet, cleft with the blade; and about him may full many of his comrades, prone in the dust, bit the earth." . . .

B. Hesiod's Creation Myth

First verily was created Chaos, and then broad-bosomed Earth, the habitation unshaken forever of all the deathless gods who keep the top of snowy Olympus, and misty Tartarus within the wide-wayed Earth, and Love (Eros) which is the fairest among the deathless gods; which looseth the limbs and overcometh within the breasts of all gods and all men their mind and counsel wise.

From Chaos sprang Erebus and black Night; and from Night in turn sprang Bright Sky (Ether) and Day, whom Night conceived and bare after loving union with Erebus. Earth first bare the starry Heaven, of equal stature to herself, that he might cover her utterly about, to the end that there might be for the blessed gods a habitation steadfast forever; and she bare the lofty Hills, the pleasant haunts of the goddess Nymphs who dwell among the gladed Hills. Also she bare the unharvested deep with raging flood, even the Sea (Pontus), without the sweet rites of love. And then in the couch of Heaven (Ouranos) she bare the deep-eddying Oceanus, and Cœus and Crius, and Hyperion and Iapetus and Theia and Rhea and Themis and Mnemosyne and Thebe of the golden crown and lovely Tethys. After these was born her youngest son, even Cronos of crooked counsels, of all her children most terrible, and he hated his lusty sire.

C. Sappho's Hymn to Aphrodite

Aphrodite on your intricate throne, immortal, daughter of Zeus, weaver of plots, I beg you, do not tame me with pain or my heart with anguish

but come here, as once before when I asked you, you heard my words from afar and listened, and left your father's golden house and came

you yoked your chariot, and lovely swift sparrows brought you, fast whirling over the dark earth from heaven through the midst of the bright air

and soon they arrived. And you, o blessed goddess, smiled with your immortal face and asked what was wrong with me, and why did I call now,

and what did I most want in my maddened heart to have for myself. 'Who now am I to persuade to your love, who, Sappho, has done you wrong? For if she flees, soon she'll pursue you, and if she won't take gifts, soon she'll give them, and if she won't love, soon she will love you, even if she doesn't want to.'

Come to me now again, release me from my cruel anxiety, accomplish all that my heart wants accomplished. You yourself join my battle.

D. Xenophanes of Colophon Thinks New Thoughts About the Gods

There is one god, greatest among gods and men, similar to mortals neither in shape nor in thought . . . But mortals think that the gods are born, and have clothes and speech and shape like their own . . .

But if cows and horses or lions had hands
or could draw with their hands and make the things
  humans can make,
then horses would draw the forms of gods like
  horses,
cows like cows, an they would make their bodies
similar in shape to those which each had themselves.

E. Pre-Socratic Philosophers: Fragments from Thales, Anaximander, Heraclitus, and Democritus

Thales

Some say that the earth rests on water. We have ascertained that the oldest statement of this character is the one accredited to Thales the Milesian, to the effect that it rests on water, floating like a piece of wood or something else of that sort. [Aristotle]

And Thales, according to what is related of him, seems to have regarded the soul as something endowed with the power of motion, if indeed he said that the loadstone has a soul because it moves iron. [Aristotle]

Anaximander

The beginning of that which is, is the boundless but whence that which is arises, thither must it return again of necessity; for the things give satisfaction and reparation to one another for their injustice, as is appointed according to the ordering of time.

For some who hold that the real, the underlying substance, is a unity, either one of the three [elements] or something else that is denser than fire and more rarefied than air, teach that other things are generated by condensation and rarefaction. . . . And others believe that existing opposites are separated from the unity, as Anaximander says. . . . [Aristotle]

There is no beginning of the infinite, for in that case it would have an end. But it is without beginning and indestructible, as being a sort of first principle; for it is necessary that whatever comes into existence should have an end, and there is a conclusion of all destruction. Wherefore as we say, there is no first principle of this [i.e., the infinite], but it itself seems to be the first principle of all other things and to surround all and to direct all, as they say who think that there are no other causes besides the infinite (such as mind, or friendship), but that it itself is divine; for it is immortal and indestructible, as Anaximander and most of the physicists say. [Aristotle]

Heraclitus

. . . Hear first the four roots of all things: bright Zeus, life-giving Hera (air), and Aidoneus (earth), and Nestis who moistens the springs of men with her tears. . . .

And a second thing I will tell thee: There is no origination of anything that is mortal, nor yet any end in baneful death; but only mixture and separation of what is mixed, but men call this "origination." . . .

But when light is mingled with air in human form, or in form like the race of wild beasts or of plants or of birds, then men say that these things have come into being; and when they are separated, they call them evil fate; this is the established practice, and I myself also call it so in accordance with the custom. . . .

Fools! for they have no far-reaching studious thoughts who think that what was not before comes into being or that anything dies and perishes utterly. . . .

For from what does not exist at all it is impossible that anything come into being, and it is neither possible nor perceivable that being should perish completely; for things will always stand wherever one in each case shall put them. . . .

Twofold is the truth I shall speak; for at one time there grew to be one alone out of many, and at another time, however, it separated so that there were many out of the one. Twofold is the coming into being, twofold the passing away, of perishable things; for the latter (*i.e.* passing away) the combining of all things both begets and destroys, and the former (*i.e.* coming into being), which was nurtured again out of parts that were being separated, is itself scattered. . . .

And these (elements) never cease changing place continually, now being all united by Love into one, now each borne apart by the hatred engendered of Strife, until they are brought together in the unity of the all, and become subject to it. Thus inasmuch as one has been wont to arise out of many and again with the separation of the one the many arise, so things are continually coming into being and there is no fixed age for them; and farther inasmuch as they (the elements) never cease changing place continually, so they always exist within an immovable circle. . . .

But come, hear my words, for truly learning causes the mind to grow. For as I said before in declaring the ends of my words: Twofold is the truth I shall speak; for at one time there grew to be the one alone out of many, and at another time it separated

so that there were many out of the one; fire and water and earth and boundless height of air, and baneful Strife apart from these, balancing each of them, and Love among them, their equal in length and breadth. Upon her do thou gaze with thy mind, nor yet sit dazed in thine eyes; for she is wont to be implanted in men's members, and through her they have thoughts of love and accomplish deeds of union, and call her by the names of Delight, and Aphrodite; no mortal man has discerned her with them (the elements) as she moves on her way. But do thou listen to the undeceiving course of my words. . . .

For these (elements) are equal, all of them, and of like ancient race; and one holds one office, another another, and each has his own nature. . . . For nothing is added to them, nor yet does anything pass away from them; for if they were continually perishing they would no longer exist. . . . Neither is any part of this all empty, nor over full. For how should anything cause this all to increase, and whence should it come? And whither should they (the elements) perish, since no place is empty of them? And in their turn they prevail as the cycle comes round, and they disappear before each other, and they increase each in its allotted turn. But these (elements) are the same; and penetrating through each other they become one thing in one place and another in another, while ever they remain alike (*i.e.*, the same). . . .

For they two (Love and Strife) were before and shall be, nor yet, I think, will there ever be an unutterably long time without them both. . . .

But come, gaze on the things that bear farther witness to my former words, if in what was said before there be anything defective in form. Behold the sun, warm and bright on all sides, and whatever is immortal and is bathed in its bright ray, and behold the rain-cloud, dark and cold on all sides; from the earth there proceed the foundations of things and solid bodies. In Strife all things are, endured with form and separate from each other, but they come together in Love and are desired by each other. For from these (elements) come all things that are or have been or shall be; from these there grew up trees and men and women, wild beasts and birds and water-nourished fishes, and the very gods, long-lived, highest in honour. . . .

But when mighty Strife was nurtured in its members and leaped up to honour at the completion of the time, which has been driven on by them both in turn under a mighty oath. . . .

And if your faith be at all lacking in regard to these (elements), how from water and earth and air and sun (fire) when they are mixed, arose such colours and forms of mortals things, as many as now have arisen under the uniting power of Aphrodite. . . .

Hair and leaves and thick feathers of birds are the same thing in origin, and reptiles' scales, too, on strong limbs. . . .

This is indeed remarkable in the mass of human members; at one time all the limbs which form the body, uniting into one by Love, grow vigorously in the prime of life; but yet at another time, separated by evil Strife, they wander each in different directions along the breakers of the sea of life. Just so it is with plants and with fishes dwelling in watery halls, and beasts whose lair is in the mountains, and birds borne on wings. . . .

Democritus

The first principles of the universe are atoms and empty space; everything else is merely thought to exist. The worlds are unlimited; they come into being and perish. Nothing can come into being from that which is not nor pass away into that which is not. Further, the atoms are unlimited in size and number, and they are borne along in the whole universe in a vortex, and thereby generate all composite things—fire, water, air, earth; for even these are conglomerations of given atoms. And it is because of their solidity that these atoms are impassive and unalterable. The sun and the moon have been composed of such smooth and spherical masses, i.e. atoms, and so also the soul, which is identical with reason. We see by virtue of the impact of images upon our eyes.

All things happen by virtue of necessity, the vortex being the cause of the creation of all things, and this he calls necessity. The end of action is tranquillity, which is not identical with pleasure, as some by a false interpretation have understood, but a state in which the soul continues calm and strong, undisturbed by any fear of superstition or any other emotion. This he calls well-being and many other names; the qualities of things exist merely by convention; in nature there is nothing but atoms and void space. These, then, are his opinions. [Diogenes Laertius]

Document Set 2.7 References

A. Homer's Zeus Ponders How to Favor Achilles
Homer, *Iliad,* bk. 1, in Fred Morrow Fling, ed., *A Source Book of Greek History* (Boston: D. C. Heath and Company, 1907), 20–21.
B. Hesiod's Creation Myth
Hesiod, *Theogony,* 116–138, in G. W. Botsford and E. G. Sihler, eds., *Hellenic Civilization* (New York: Columbia University Press, 1915), 109–110.
C. Sappho's Hymn to Aphrodite
Sappho, "To Aphrodite," in Mary R. Lekowitz and Maureen B. Fant, eds., *Women's Life in Greece and Rome,* 2d ed. (Baltimore: Johns Hopkins University Press, 1982), 4.
D. Xenophanes of Colophon Thinks New Thoughts About the Gods
Xenophanes of Colophon, from Clement, *Miscellanies* V: xiv, 109:1–3; translation slightly adapted from Jonathan Barnes, *Early Greek Philosophy,* (Harmondworth, England: Penguin, 1987), 95.
E. Pre-Socratic Philosophers: Fragments from Thales, Anaximander, Heraclitus, and Democritus
T. V. Smith, *From Thales to Plato* (Chicago: University of Chicago Press, 1934), 6–7, 28–31, 45.

DOCUMENT SET 2.8
Women and Men, Love and Death

The last set in this chapter tries to bring the Greek people of the Archaic Period alive through vividly contrasting poetry. Most of the lyric poets represented here were aristocrats and (perhaps including Sappho) polis citizens. Some of their works were meant to be sung or chanted in a public recitation accompanied by a lyre. Semonides (Document A), a native of Samos, flourished about 660 B.C. and founded a colony on the small Aegean island of Amargos. Does his bitter-sounding sarire reflect resentment at women becoming more assertive? And what do you make of the final "type" of woman, of whom he approves? Sappho became famous all over the sixth-century Greek world for her lyrics celebrating female love and transient beauty—a secluded world that men seldom glimpsed. Her lyrics commonly addressed young women whom she encountered as an educator. Little is known about her life except that she had a daughter and was forced into exile by the tyrant who ruled her city, perhaps because she or her family had been involved in opposition activity; the position of women in her society may have differed considerably from that of other Greek communities. Mimnermus of Colophon (fl. c. 630 B.C., Document D) was an Ionian about whom very little is known save the beautiful, wistful elegies he composed on the theme of life's fleeting joys. Theognis (Document E), an aristocrat and outspoken enemy of democracy from Megara, near Athens, flourished in the sixth and early fifth centuries. Many of his verses address his young male lover, Kurnos, and display a full range of thoughts, from advice on how a true aristocrat should bear a misfortune to bitter reproaches to his lover for abandoning him; these selections represent only a small portion of his known output. Finally, Document F offers a poem (translated here in prose) of Archilochus of Paros (c. 680–640 B.C.), a swaggering mercenary and wandering adventurer. The little seduction he describes here seems a characteristic event in a turbulent life graced with a talent for vivid expression.

This poetry flourished in between the age of Homeric epic and the subsequent "classical" era of great drama and philosophy. Combining your reading of this poetry with what you have learned from *The Challenge of the West*'s account of archaic Greece, try to summarize the values and emotions that gave rise to such brief, intense verse.

A. Simonides Offers a Bitter View of Women

Not even if in angry fit he'd break her teeth with a
   stone
Nor even if to gentle speech resorteth he
Nor either if 'mid guest-friends she should chance to
   sit,
But firmly does she hold her ineffectual scream.

Another the Olympians shaped of earth
And then bestowed on man—half-witted she
Nor evil nor the good such woman knows;
Of works she only knows how to eat;
Not even when God an evil tempest makes,
Though shivering will she draw her chair closer to the
   fire. . . .

Another from the ashen-colored and much beaten
   ass,
Which whether by constraint or by the urging call
Is satisfied to do all her toilsom task,
With full complacence: meanwhile she munches in a
   corner
All night, all day, she eateth by the hearth. . . .

Another one a dainty steed with flowing mane
   produced,
Who turns aside from servile work and toil.
A gristmill she'd not touch nor sieve
Would lift, nor dirt throw from the house,
Nor sit by the fire, keeping from me soot:
It is by sheer constraint she wins her husband's
   friendship.
On every day she washes off each spot
Twice, sometimes thrice; with ointments fragrant is:
And always wears her manelike tresses combed
Deep; with blossoms shades she them.
A comely thing to see is such a wife
For others, but to him who weds her proves an ill,
Unless he be a prince or sceptered sovereign,
Who with such things his fancy doth adorn. . . .

The other from the bee; fortunate he who gets her:
For she alone to censure furnishes no occasion,
But by her life doth bloom and doth increase;
Dear to her loving spouse she groweth old.
Often hath she given birth to children fair and famed.
Distinguished is she among the women all—

A grace divine doth play about her form.
Nor does she pleasure take to sit among the women,
Where they do hold converse of scandals bold.
Such are the wives which Zeus doth grant to men
A boon of grace, the best there are, the wisest of the
    sex.

For Zeus did make this greatest evil,
The woman; for even if they seem to furnish
    usefulness,
To him who weds them most they prove a bane.
For never he with cheerful spirit passes through a day
Complete, who with a woman is. . . .
And when the husband most does seem to please his
    mood
At home abiding, be it fate divine or kindliness of
    man,
She finds some word of censure, helms herself to
    fight.
For where a woman is, not even into the home
With willing mind (the husband) would receive a
    stranger
Who arrives. . . .

B. Sappho Longs for an Absent Lover

Equal to the gods does he appear,
that man who sits close to you,
hears the sound of your sweet voice,
—intently near—

and your delightful laughter. That sight,
I swear, sets my heartbeat pounding;
the slightest glance at you puts my
speech to flight!

My tongue unhinges, a delicate
flame slips racing beneath my skin,
I see nothing, am blinded, my ears
ring, pulsate,

a cold sweat commands me, dread
grasps at my heart. More pallid
than grass, I appear to myself
nearly dead.

C. Sappho Meditates on Death

Yea, thou shalt die,
And lie
    Dumb in the silent tomb;

Nor of thy name
Shall there be any fame
    In ages yet to be or years to come:
For of the flowering Rose,
Which on Pieria blows,
    Thou hast no share:
But in sad Hades' house,
Unknown, inglorious.
    'Mid the dim shades that wander there
Shalt thou flit forth and haunt the filmy air.

D. Mimnermus Contemplates the Transient Joys of Love

What living is there and what charm without gold
    Aphrodite?
I would be dead, when no more these things were my
    concern. . . .
If youth's blossoms may be plucked
For men and for women; but when there comes on
Lamentable age, which renders ugly even the comely
    man,
Ever his mind is ground by evil cares about,
Nor does he rejoice in gazing at beams of the sun,
But he is hateful to boys, unhonored by women,
So grievous has God rendered old age.

Our growth is like the leaves in the season of much-
    blossoming
Spring; when swiftly they do increase in the beams of
    the sun,
Like unto these, for a mere ell of time youth's
    blossoms
Do we enjoy, from gods knowing nor evil
Nor good. The murky Fates stand by our side,
This one holding goal of troublesome old age,
And the other, of death; slender the measure of the
Harvest of youth; as far as the sun sheds his light on
    the earth.
But when this consummation of bloom has passed,
Straightway to die is better than living;
For many evils ensue in the spirit; one time one's
    house
Is ruined, lamentable are the works of poverty;
Another again lacks children, yearning chiefly for
    whom
He passes under the earth to Hades' realm;
Another has a disease that consumes his spirit, nor is
    there
Any of men to whom Zeus gives not evils abundant.

E. Theognis Shows How an Aristocrat Bears Misfortune

I give you wings. You'll soon be lifted up
Across the land, across the boundless crests
Of ocean; where men dine and pass the cup,
You'll light there, on the lips of all the guests,
Where lithe, appealing lads will praise you, swelling
Their song to match the piper's sweet, shrill tone.
At length, my boy, you'll enter Hades' dwelling,
That black hole where departed spirits moan,
But even then your glory will not cease,
Your well-loved name will stay alive, unworn;
You'll skim across the mainland, over Greece,
Over the islands and the sea, not borne
By horses, Kurnos; you'll be whirled along
By violet-crowned maids, the Muses; yours
Will be each practised singer's finest song,
As long as light exists and earth endures.
I give you this, for what? To be reviled—
To be betrayed and lied to, like a child. . . .

Don't be too grieved in bad times, nor too glad
In good; a gentleman bears everything.

F. An Old Story: Seduction and Birth Control in Archaic Greece

"But if you are in hurry and desire drives you on, there is in our house a girl who is eager . . . young and delicate. I think she has a perfect figure. You . . . her."

So she spoke, and I answered: "Daughter of Amphimedo (she was a good woman, though now she lies beneath the broad earth), there are many other pleasures for young men besides the Sacred Act. One of those will do. The rest you and I will discuss at leisure when . . . I'll follow your orders: beneath the lintel and below the gate—don't begrudge me, dear; I'll put ashore at your garden's grass. But realise this: another man can have Neobule. Alas, she's overripe; her girlhood's flower has fallen, and the charm she had before; [she can't get] enough—a mad-woman who shows no measure . . . she can go to hell . . . If I had such a wife I'd give my neighbors pleasure. I much prefer you. You aren't faithless or two-faced; she's more bitter and takes on too many. I'm afraid that in my haste I'd hurry to produce blind and premature offspring, like a bitch."

Those were my words. I took the girl and laid her down among the flowers. I covered her with my soft cloak and held my arm around her neck. She stopped trembling like a fawn; I touched her breasts gently with my hand; she revealed her new young skin. I touched her fair body everywhere and sent my white force aside, touching her blonde hair.

Document Set 2.8 References

A. Simonides Offers a Bitter View of Women
Trans. E. G. Sihler, in G. W. Botsford and E. G. Sihler, eds., *Hellenic Civilization* (New York: Columbia University Press, 1915), 188–191.
B. Sappho Longs for an Absent Lover
Sappho no. 31 (*Greek Lyrics,* vol. 1, Loeb Classical Library) in Jeffrey M. Duban, trans., *Ancient and Modern Images of Sappho* (Lanham, Md.: University Press of America, 1983), 51.
C. Sappho Meditates on Death
Trans. J. A. Symonds, in Botsford and Sihler, 196.
D. Mimnermus Contemplates the Transient Joys of Love
Trans. E. G. Sihler in Botsford and Sihler, 191.
E. Theognis Shows How an Aristocrat Bears Misfortune
Theognis, *Elegies,* lines 237–254, 658–659, in Dorothea Wender, trans. and ed., *Hesiod and Theognis* (Baltimore: Penguin, 1973), 105–109.
F. An Old Story: Seduction and Birth Control in Archaic Greece
Paros, recorded by Archilochus, in Mary R. Lefkowitz and Maureen B. Fant, eds., *Women's Life in Greece and Rome,* 2d ed. (Baltimore: Johns Hopkins University Press, 1982), 178.

The Greek Golden Age,
c. 500–403 B.C.

DOCUMENT SET 3.1
The Values of the Polis

As *The Challenge of the West* emphasizes, the city-state, or polis, became the central focus of ancient Greek life—the only setting, indeed, where Greeks thought that one could live a just and civilized life. The documents in this set provide varying insights into how Greeks of the classical era viewed the polis, focusing mainly on the best-known and largest city-state, Athens.

Document A presents an extract from *The Eumenides* by the great tragedian Aeschylus (c. 525–c. 456 B.C.). *The Eumenides* is the last of the three dramas of the Oresteia trilogy, which explores the consequences of Agamemnon's murder by his wife Clytemnestra, the vengeance that their son Orestes took on Clytemnestra, and finally the expiation of Orestes' guilt. In this climactic scene Athena (the goddess of wisdom) appears before the Athenians who are judging Orestes; she casts the deciding vote in his favor. Read this scene with an eye to Athenian attitudes towards women and Aeschylus's praise of the Athenian polis as the ultimate seat of justice.

The Athenian historian Thucydides, who died sometime after 426 B.C., constructed his *Peloponnesian War* as a kind of extended dramatic tragedy, recounting the arrogant pride (*hubris*) with which Athens came to dominate its empire, and as a consequence suffered a devastating defeat. Early in his history, Thucydides presents the Athenian leader Pericles delivering the funeral oration that appears as Document B (this, like all speeches in the work, was written by Thucydides, who assures us that he has

preserved the essence of the speakers' words). Read the funeral oration as an expression of the values that classical-age Athenians believed were embodied in their polis.

Documents C and D, drawn from classical literature, broaden our inquiry to encompass the purpose of civilized life itself. Document C is a fragment from the Theban poet Pindar (c. 520–c. 438 B.C.) that somberly meditates on death as it comes even to the virtuous citizen; contrast this with Document D, an extract from *Antigone* (translated here in prose rather than in verse) by another great Athenian tragedian, Sophocles (c. 496–c. 406 B.C.), extolling human potential within the context of polis life.

With Document E we return to Thucydides, reading the historian's account of the horrendous plague that struck Athens not long after Pericles delivered his funeral oration. (Pericles was one of the plague's victims.) Consider here the ways in which a disaster could shake the solidarity of even the strongest polis. (We shall encounter another such plague, the Black Death of fourteenth-century Europe, in Chapter 13.)

Document F comes from after the Peloponnesian War; it is an extract from the *Politics* of the philosopher Aristotle, a foreigner who for much of his career taught at Athens. Although the polis was by Aristotle's time declining (see *The Challenge of the West,* Chapter 4), Aristotle still upheld it as the key to living "the good life." In this passage he provides the classical explanation of the processes by which states decay—an analysis that Europeans would admire and repeat down to the eighteenth century. Read this extract carefully to ascertain Aristotle's attitude toward democracy.

The final document (Document G) gives a glimpse of the Athenian state in practice; it is an inscription recording a law, enacted shortly before the Peloponnesian War, providing for the repayment by the polis of a loan it had contracted from funds controlled by the temples on the Acropolis. Piety, in other words, begot contributions to the temples, from which the state could borrow at interest, but the loans had to be repaid out of taxes and the tribute rendered to Athens by its allies.

Use these documents, supplementing the account given in *The Challenge of the West,* to write an essay on the classical polis in theory and practice.

A. Aeschylus Vindicates Athenian Justice

Athena. Now judges, as your judgment is, I charge you,
  So vote the doom. Words we have had enough.
Chorus. Our quiver's emptied. We await the doom.
Athena. How should the sentence fall to keep me free
  Of your displeasure?
Chorus. What we said we said.
  Even as your heart informs you, nothing fearing,
  So judges justly vote, the oath revering.
Athena. Now, hear my ordinance, Athenians! Ye,
  In this first strife of blood, umpires elect,
  While age on age shall roll, the sons of Aegeus
  This Council shall revere. Here, on this hill,
  The embattled Amazons pitched their tents of yore,
  What time with Theseus striving, they their tents
  Against these high-towered infant walls uptowered.
  To Mars they sacrificed, and, to this day,
  This Mars' Hill speaks their story. Here, Athenians,
  Shall reverence of the gods, and holy fear,
  That shrinks from wrong, both night and day possess,
  A place apart, so long as fickle change
  Your ancient laws disturbs not; but, if this
  Pure fount with muddy streams ye trouble, ye
  Shall draw the draught in vain. From anarchy
  And slavish masterdom alike my ordinance
  Preserve my people! Cast not from your walls
  All high authority; for where no fear
  Awful remains, what mortal will be just?
  This holy reverence use, and ye possess
  A bulwark, and a safeguard of the land,
  Such as no race of mortals vaunteth, fa:
  In Borean Scythia, or the land of Pelops.
  This council I appoint intact to stand
  From gain, a venerated conclave, quick
  In pointed indignation, when all sleep
  A sleepless watch. These words of warning hear,

My citizens for ever. Now ye judges
  Rise, take your pebbles, and by vote decide,
  The sacred oath revering. I have spoken.

The AEROPAGITES *advance; and, as each puts his pebble into the urn, the* CHORUS *and* APOLLO *alternately address them as follows:*

Chorus. I warn ye well: the sisterhood beware,
  Whose wrath hangs heavier than the land may bear.
Apollo. I warn ye well: Jove is my father; fear
  To turn to nought the words of me, his seer.
Chorus. If thou dost plead, where thou hast no vocation,
  For blood, will men respect thy divination?
Apollo. Must then my father share thy condemnation,
  When first he heard Ixion's supplication?
Chorus. Thou say'st. But I, if justice be denied me,
  Will sorely smite the land that so defied me.
Apollo. Among the gods the elder, and the younger,
  Thou hast no favour; I shall prove the stronger.
Chorus. Such were thy deeds in Pheres' house, deceiving
  The Fates, and mortal men from death reprieving.
Apollo. Was it a crime to help a host? to lend
  A friendly hand to raise a sinking friend?
Chorus. Thou the primeval Power didst undermine,
  Mocking the hoary goddesses with wine.
Apollo. Soon, very soon, when I the cause shall gain,
  Thou'lt spit thy venom on the ground in vain.
Chorus. Thou being young, dost jeer my ancient years
  With youthful insolence; till the doom appears,
  I'll patient wait; my hot-spurred wrath I'll stay,
  And even-poised betwixt two tempers sway.
Athena. My part remains; and I this crowning pebble
  Drop to Orestes; for I never knew
  The mother's womb that bore me. I give honor,
  Save in my virgin nature, to the male
  In all things; all my father lives in me.
  Not blameless be the wife, who dared to slay
  Her husband, lord and ruler of her home.
  My voice is for Orestes; though the votes
  Fall equal from the urn, my voice shall save him.
  Now shake the urn, to whom this duty falls,
  And tell the votes.
Orest. O Phœbus, how shall end
  This doubtful issue?
Chorus. O dark Night, my mother,
  Behold these things!
Orest. One moment blinds me quite,
  Or to a blaze of glory opes my eyes.
Chorus. We sink to shame, or to more honor rise.
Apollo. Judges, count well the pebbles as they fall,
  And with just jealousy divide them. One
  Being falsely counted works no simple harm.
  One little pebble saves a mighty house.
Athena. Hear now the doom. This man from blood is free.

The votes are equal; he escapes by me.
Orest. O Pallas, Saviour of my father's house,
  Restorer of the exile's hope, Athena,
  I praise thee! Now belike some Greek will say,
  The Argive man revisiteth the homes
  And fortunes of his father, by the aid
  Of Pallas, Loxias, and Jove the Saviour
  All-perfecting, who pled the father's cause,
  Fronting the wrathful Furies of the mother!
  I now depart: and to this land I leave,
  And to this people, through all future time,
  An oath behind me, that no lord of Argos
  Shall ever brandish the well-pointed spear
  Against this friendly land. When, from the tomb,
  I shall perceive who disregards this oath
  Of my sons' sons, I will perplex that man
  With sore perplexities inextricable;
  Ways of despair, and evil-birded paths
  Shall be his portion, cursing his own choice.
  But if my vows be duly kept, with those
  That in the closely-banded league shall aid
  Athena's city, I am present ever.
  Then fare thee well, thou and thy people! Never
  May foe escape thy grasp! When thou dost struggle,
  Safety and victory attend thy spear!

                    [Exit.

B. Pericles Praises Athens's War Dead and the Cause for Which They Fell

Most of my predecessors in this place have commended him who made this speech part of the law, telling us that it is well that it should be delivered at the burial of those who fall in battle. For myself, I should have thought that the worth which had displayed itself in deeds, would be sufficiently rewarded by honours also shown by deeds; such as you now see in this funeral prepared at the people's cost. And I could have wished that the reputations of many brave men were not to be imperilled in the mouth of a single individual, to stand or fall according as he spoke well or ill. For it is hard to speak properly upon a subject where it is even difficult to convince your hearers that you are speaking the truth. . . .

Our constitution does not copy the laws of neighbouring states; we are rather a pattern to others than imitators ourselves. Its administration favours the many instead of the few; this is why it is called a democracy. If we look to the laws, they afford equal justice to all in their private differences; if to social standing, advancement in public life falls to reputation for capacity, class considerations not being allowed to interfere with merit; nor again does poverty bar the way, if a man is able to serve the state, he is not hindered by the obscurity of his condition. The freedom which we enjoy in our government extends also to our ordinary life. There, far from exercising a jealous surveillance over each other, we do not feel called upon to be angry with our neighbor for doing what he likes, or even to indulge in those injurious looks which cannot fail to be offensive, although they inflict no positive penalty. But all this ease in our private relations does not make us lawless as citizens. Against this fear is our chief safeguard, teaching us to obey the magistrates and the laws, particularly such as regard the protection of the injured, whether they are actually on the statute book, or belong to that code which, although unwritten, yet cannot be broken without acknowledged disgrace.

Further, we provide plenty of means for the mind to refresh itself from business. We celebrate games and sacrifices all the year round, and the elegance of our private establishments forms a daily source of pleasure and helps to banish the spleen; while the magnitude of our city draws the produce of the world into our harbour, so that to the Athenian the fruits of other countries are as familiar a luxury as those of his own.

If we turn to our military policy, there also we differ from our antagonists. We throw open our city to the world, and never by alien acts exclude foreigners from any opportunity of learning or observing, although the eyes of an enemy may occasionally profit by our liberality; trusting less in system and policy than to the native spirit of our citizens; while in education, where our rivals from their very cradles by a painful discipline seek after manliness, at Athens we live exactly as we please, and yet are just as ready to encounter every legitimate danger. In proof of this it may be noticed that the Lacedaemonians [Spartans] do not invade our country alone, but bring with them all their confederates; while we Athenians advance unsupported into the territory of a neighbour, and fighting upon a foreign soil usually vanquish with ease men who are defending their homes. Our united force was never yet encountered by any enemy, because we have at once to attend to our marine and to despatch our citizens by land upon a hundred different services; so that, wherever they engage with some such fraction of our strength, a success against a detachment is magnified into a victory over the nation, and a defeat into a reverse suffered at the hands of our entire people. And yet if with habits not of labour but of ease, and courage not of art but of nature, we are still willing to encounter danger, we have the double advantage of escaping the experience of hardships in anticipation and of facing them in the hour of need as fearlessly as those who are never free from them. . . .

In short, I say that as a city we are the school of Hellas [Greece] while I doubt if the world can produce a man, who where he has only himself to depend upon, is equal to so many emergencies, and graced by so happy a versatility as the Athenian. And that this is no mere boast thrown out for the occasion, but plain matter of fact, the power of the state acquired by these habits proves. For Athens alone of her contemporaries is found when tested to be greater than her reputation, and alone gives no occasion to her assailants to blush at the antagonist by whom they have been worsted, or to her subjects to question her title by merit to rule. . . .

Turning to the sons or brothers of the dead, I see an arduous struggle before you. When a man is gone, all are wont to praise him, and should your merit be ever so transcendent, you will still find it difficult not merely to overtake, but even to approach their renown. The living have envy to contend with, while those who are no longer in our path are honoured with a goodwill into which rivalry does not enter. On the other hand, if I must say anything on the subject of female excellence to those of you who will now be in widowhood, it will be all comprised in this brief exhortation. Great will be your glory in not falling short of your natural character; and greatest will be hers who is least talked of among the men whether for good or for bad.

My task is now finished. I have performed it to the best of my ability, and in words, at least, the requirements of the law are now satisfied. If deeds be in question, those who are here interred have received part of their honours already, and for the rest, their children will be brought up till manhood at the public expense: the state thus offers a valuable prize, as the garland of victory in this race of valour, for the reward both of those who have fallen and their survivors. And where the rewards for merit are greatest, there are found the best citizens.

And now that you have brought to a close your lamentations for your relatives, you may depart.

C. Pindar Broods on Life and Death

For all creatures the body goes the way of Death in
  his strength,
but there is still left a living image of the life. This
  alone
comes from the gods. It sleeps in the action of the
  limbs, but as we sleep in dream after dream
it shows the judgment between pleasures and
  hardships advancing upon us.

D. Sophocles Ponders Human Potential

Wonders are many, and none is more wonderful than man; the power that crosses the white sea, driven by the stormy southwind, making a path under surges that threaten to engulf him; and Earth, the eldest of the gods, the immortal, the unwearied, doth he wear, turning the soil with the offspring of horses, as the ploughs go to and fro from year to year.

And the light-hearted race of birds, and the tribes of savage beasts, and the sea-brood of the deep, he snares in the meshes of his woven toils, he leads captive, man excellent in wit. And he masters by his arts the beast whose lair is in the wilds, who roams the hills; he tames the horse of shaggy mane, he puts the yoke upon its neck, he tames the tireless mountain bull.

And speech and swift-winged thought and all the moods that mould a state, hath he taught himself; and how to flee the arrows of the frost, when 'tis hard lodging under the clear sky, and the arrows of the rushing rain; yea, he hath resource for all; without resource he meets nothing that must come; only against Death shall he call for aid in vain; but from baffling maladies he hath devised escapes.

Cunning beyond fancy's dream is the fertile skill which brings him now to evil, now to good. When he honors the laws of the land, and that justice which he hath sworn by the gods to uphold, proudly stands his city; no city hath he who for his rashness dwells with sin. Never may he share my hearth, never think my thoughts, who doth these things!

E. Thucydides Analyzes How the Plague Shook the Athenian Polis to Its Foundations

As soon as summer returned, the Peloponnesian army, comprising as before two-thirds of the force of each confederate state, under the command of the Lacedemonian king Archidamus, the son of Zeuxidamus, invaded Attica, where they established themselves and ravaged the country. They had not been there many days when the plague broke out at Athens for the first time. A similar disorder is said to have previously smitten many places, particularly Lemnos, but there is no record of such a pestilence occurring elsewhere, or of so great a destruction of human life. For a while physicians, in ignorance of the nature of the disease, sought to apply remedies; but it was in vain, and they themselves were among the first victims, because they oftenest came into contact with it. No human art was of any avail, and as to supplications in temples, inquiries of oracles, and the like, they were utterly useless, and at last men were overpowered by the calamity and gave them all up.

The disease is said to have begun south of Egypt in Ethiopia; thence it descended into Egypt and Libya, and after spreading over the greater part of the Persian empire, suddenly fell upon Athens. It first attacked the inhabitants of the Piræus, and it was supposed that the Peloponnesians had poisoned the cisterns, no conduits having as yet been made there. It afterwards reached the upper city, and then the mortality became far greater. As to its probable origin or the causes which might or could have produced such a disturbance of nature, every man, whether a physician or not, will give his own opinion. But I shall describe its actual course, and the symptoms by which any one who knows them beforehand may recognize the disorder should it ever reappear. For I was myself attacked, and witnessed the sufferings of others.

The season was admitted to have been remarkably free from ordinary sickness; and if anybody was already ill of any other disease, it was absorbed in this. Many who were in perfect health, all in a moment, and without any apparent reason, were seized with violent heats in the head and with redness and inflammation of the eyes. Internally the throat and the tongue were quickly suffused with blood, and the breath became unnatural and fetid. There followed sneezing and hoarseness; in a short time the disorder, accompanied by a violent cough, reached the chest; then fastening lower down, it would move the stomach and bring on all the vomits of bile to which physicians have ever given names; and they were very distressing. An ineffectual retching producing violent convulsions attacked most of the suffers; some as soon as the previous symptoms had abated, others not until long afterwards. The body externally was not so very hot to the touch, nor yet pale; it was of a livid color inclining to red, and breaking out in pustules and ulcers. But the internal fever was intense; the sufferers could not bear to have on them even the finest linen garment; they insisted on being naked, and there was nothing which they longed for more eagerly than to throw themselves into cold water. And many of these who had no one to look after them actually plunged into the cisterns, for they were tormented by unceasing thirst, which was not in the least assuaged whether they drank little or much. They could not sleep; a restlessness which was intolerable never left them. While the disease was at its height the body, instead of wasting away, held out amid these sufferings in a marvellous manner, and either they died on the seventh or ninth day, not of weakness, for their strength was not exhausted, but of internal fever, which was the end of most; . . .

The general character of the malady no words can describe, and the fury with which it fastened upon each sufferer was too much for human nature to endure. There was one circumstance in particular which distinguished it from ordinary diseases. The birds and animals which feed on human flesh, although so many bodies were lying unburied, either never came near them, or died if they touched them. This was proved by a remarkable disappearance of the birds of prey, which were not to be seen either about the bodies or anywhere else; while in the case of the dogs the result was even more obvious, because they live with man.

Such was the general nature of the disease: I omit many strange peculiarities which characterized individual cases. None of the ordinary sicknesses attacked any one while it lasted, or, if they did, they ended in the plague. Some of the sufferers died from want of care, others equally who were receiving the greatest attention. No single remedy could be deemed a specific; for that which did good to one did harm to another. No constitution was of itself strong enough to resist or weak enough to escape the attacks; the disease carried off all alike and defied every mode of treatment. Most appalling was the despondency which seized upon any one who felt himself sickening; for he instantly abandoned his mind to despair, and, instead of holding out, absolutely threw away his chance of life. Appalling, too, was the rapidity with which men caught the infection; dying like sheep if they attended on one another; and this was the principal cause of mortality. When they were afraid to visit one another, the sufferers died in their solitude, so that many houses were empty because there had been no one left to take care of the sick; or if they ventured they perished, especially those who aspired to heroism. For they went to see their friends without thought of themselves and were ashamed to leave them, at a time when the very relations of the dying were at last growing weary and ceased even to make lamentations, overwhelmed by the vastness of the calamity. But whatever instances there may have been of such devotion, more often the sick and the dying were tended by the pitying care of those who had recovered, because they knew the course of the disease and were themselves free from apprehension. For no one was ever attacked a second time, or not with a fatal result. All men congratulated them, and they themselves, in the excess of their joy at the moment, had an innocent fancy that they could not die of any other sickness.

The crowding of the people out of country into the city aggravated the misery; and the newly arrived suffered most. For, having no houses of their own, but inhabiting in the height of summer stifling huts, the mortality among them was dreadful, and they perished in wild disorder. The dead lay as they died, one upon another, while others hardly alive wallowed in the streets and crawled about every fountain craving for water. The temples in which they lodged were full of the corpses of those who died in them; for the violence of the calamity was such that men, not knowing where to turn, grew reckless of all law, human and divine. The customs which had hitherto been observed at funerals were universally violated, and they buried their dead each one as best he could. Many, having no proper appliances, because the deaths in their household had been so numerous already, lost all shame in the burial of the dead. When one man had raised a funeral pile, others would come, and throwing on their dead first, set fire to it; or when some other corpse was already burning, before they could be stopped, would throw their own dead upon it and depart.

There were other and worse forms of lawlessness which the plague introduced at Athens. Men, who had hitherto concealed what they took pleasure in, now grew bolder. For, seeing the sudden change,—how the rich died in a moment, and those who had nothing immediately inherited their property,—they reflected that life and riches were alike transitory, and they resolved to enjoy themselves while they could, and to think only of pleasure. Who would be willing to sacrifice himself to the law of honor when he knew not whether he would ever live to be held in honor? The pleasure of the moment and any sort of thing which conduced to it took the place both of honor and of expediency. No fear of Gods or law of man deterred a criminal. Those who saw all perishing alike, thought that the worship or neglect of the gods made no difference. For offences against human law no punishment was to be feared; no one would live long enough to be called to account. Already a far heavier sentence had been passed and was hanging over a man's head; before that fell, why should he not take a little pleasure?

Such was the grievous calamity which now afflicted the Athenians; within the walls their people were dying, and without, their country was being ravaged. . . .

F. Aristotle Describes the Three Good and Three Bad Kinds of State

Having established these particulars, we come to consider next the different number of governments which there are, and what they are; and first, what are their excellencies: for when we have determined this, their defects will be evident enough.

It is evident that every form of government or administration, for the words are of the same import, must contain a supreme power over the whole state, and this supreme power must necessarily be in the hands of one person, or a few, or many; and when either of these apply their power for the common good, such states are well governed; but when the interest of the one, the few, or the many who enjoy this power is alone consulted, then ill; for you must either affirm that those who make up the community are not citizens, or else let these share in the advantages of government. We usually call a state which is governed by one person for the common good, a kingdom; one that is governed by more than one, but by a few only, an aristocracy; either because the government is in the hands of the most worthy citizens, or because it is the best form for the city and its inhabitants. When the citizens at large govern for the public good, it is called a state; which is also a common name for all other governments, and these distinctions are consonant to reason; for it will not be difficult to find one person, or a very few, of very distinguished abilities, but almost impossible to meet with the majority of a people eminent for every virtue; but if there is one common to a whole nation it is valour; for this is created and supported by numbers: for which reason in such a state the profession of arms will always have the greatest share in the government.

Now the corruptions attending each of these governments are these; a kingdom may degenerate into a tyranny, an aristocracy into an oligarchy, and a state into a democracy. Now a tyranny is a monarchy where the good of one man only is the object of government, an oligarchy considers only the rich, and a democracy only the poor; but neither of them have a common good in view. . . .

It may also be a doubt where the supreme power ought to be lodged. Shall it be with the majority, or the wealthy, with a number of proper persons, or one better than the rest, or with a tyrant? But whichever of these we prefer some difficulty will arise. For what? shall the poor have it because they are the majority? they may then divide among themselves what belongs to the rich: nor is this unjust; because truly it has been so judged by the supreme power. But what avails it to point out what is the height of injustice if this is not? Again, if the many seize into their own hands everything which belongs to the few, it is evident that the city will be at an end. But virtue will never destroy what is virtuous; nor can what is right be the ruin of the state: therefore such a law can never be right, nor can the acts of a tyrant ever be wrong, for of necessity they must all be just; for he, from his unlimited power, compels every one to obey his command, as the multitude oppress the rich. Is it right then that the rich, the few, should have the supreme power? and what if they be guilty of the same rapine and plunder the possessions of the majority, that will be as right as the other: but that all things of this sort are wrong and unjust is evident. Well then, these of the better sort shall have it: but must not then all the other citizens live unhonoured, without sharing the offices of the city; for the offices of a city are its honours, and if one set of men are always in power, it is evident that the rest must be without honour. Well then, let it be with one person of all others the fittest for it: but by this means the power will be still more contracted, and a greater number than before continue unhonoured. But some one may say, that it is wrong to let man have the supreme power and not the law, as his soul is subject to so many passions. But if this law appoints an aristocracy, or a democracy, how will it help us in our present doubts? for those things will happen which we have already mentioned.

G. Turning Piety to Practical Effect: The Athenian Polis Borrows from the Temple Funds

Be it resolved by the Boulê and the Demus: That the moneys owed shall be repaid to the gods, since there have been brought up into the Acropolis for Athena the three thousand talents in our own coin, as had been voted. The repayment shall be made from the moneys which have been voted for repaying the gods; namely, the sums now in the hands of the Hellenic Treasurers, the remainder that belongs to these funds, and the proceeds of the tithe, when it shall have been farmed out. The thirty accountants now in office shall audit with exactness the sums due to the gods, and the boulê shall have full power to convoke the accountants. The prytaneis, together with the (whole) boulê, shall repay the moneys and shall cancel (the indebtedness) upon making payment, searching for the tablets and the account books and whatever other records there may be. The priests, the commissioners of sacrifices, and any other person who has knowledge, shall be obliged to produce the records. Treasurers of these funds shall be taken by lot at the same time as the other magistrates and upon the same terms as the Treasurers of the Sacred Funds of Athena. They shall deposit the funds of the gods, so far as is possible and allowable, in the Opisthodomos on the Acropolis, and they shall join with the Treasurers of Athena in opening and closing and sealing the doors of the Opisthodomos. The funds (received) from the present treasurers and the superintendents and the commissioners of sacrifices in the temples, who have the management at present, shall be counted and weighed out in the presence of the boulê on the Acropolis by the Treasurers to be appointed, and these officers shall receive the funds from the persons now in office and shall record them all on a single stele, both the amounts belonging to each of the gods respectively and the sum total, the silver and the gold separately. And in future the Treasurers for the time being shall make record upon a stele and shall account to the auditors for the funds at hand and for those accruing to the gods, and for whatever is expended during the year. They shall submit to examination,—and shall render their account from Panathenæa to Panathenæa, like the Treasurers of Athena. The Treasurers shall place on the Acropolis the stelæ on which they record the sacred funds. When the moneys shall have been repaid to the gods, the surplus shall be used for the dockyard and the fortifications.

Document Set 3.1 References

A. Aeschylus Vindicates Athenian Justice
Aeschylus, *Eumenides* (from final scene), trans. John Stuart Blackie (New York: E. P. Dutton, 1906), 162–165.
B. Pericles Praises Athens's War Dead and the Cause for Which They Fell
Thucydides, *Peloponnesian War,* bk. 2, in G. W. Botsford and E. G. Sihler, eds., *Hellenic Civilization* (New York: Columbia University Press, 1915), 239–246.
C. Pindar Broods on Life and Death
Pindar, no. 13, in Richmond Lattimore, *Greek Lyrics,* 2d ed. (Chicago: University of Chicago Press, 1960), 62.
D. Sophocles Ponders Human Potential
Sophocles, *Antigone,* in Botsford and Sihler, 328.
E. Thucydides Analyzes How the Plague Shook the Athenian Polis to Its Foundations
Thucydides, *Peloponnesian War* 2:48–54 in Fred Morrow Fling, ed., *A Source Book of Greek History* (Boston: D. C. Heath, 1907), 186–190.
F. Aristotle Describes the Three Good and Three Bad Kinds of State
Aristotle, *Politics* 3:7, 10, trans. J. E. C. Welldon (London: Macmillan, 1883), 78–79, 84.
G. Turning Piety to Practical Effect: The Athenian Polis Borrows from the Temple Funds
P. J. Rhodes, ed., *The Greek City-States: A Source Book* (Norman: University of Oklahoma Press, 1986), 133.

DOCUMENT SET 3.2
Greeks and Persians

The Greeks' war with the Persians has always stood out in the history of Western civilization as one of those climactic episodes when western freedom confronted eastern despotism. That was certainly how the Greeks themselves saw the issue; we do not have the Persian side. But these documents can help us evaluate the struggle.

Document A is a Persian inscription in which Xerxes (*485–465 B.C.) proclaims his own greatness and the justice of his rule as sanctioned by the supreme Zoroastrian god Ahuramazda. In Document B the Greek historian Herodotus (c. 485–c. 425 B.C.), whose *Persian Wars* is our main narrative source for the conflict, attempts to explain the "barbarian" Persians' religion to Greek readers. Xerxes' famous crossing of the Hellespont in 480 B.C. is narrated by Herodotus in Document C. How the Persians' invasion was regarded by those Greek cities that chose to resist may be gauged by Document D, recording a temple inscription at Corinth in which that city's women beseeched Aphrodite to inspire their men with courage. The women's act of going into the temple rather than praying outside it took extraordinary bravery; normally deities like Aphrodite expected more deference from their worshipers.

Document E, however, records the Persians' characteristic policy of tolerating the religious cults of peoples they dominated; here the Persian emperor Darius about 500 B.C. instructs an official charged with enforcing Persian rule over the Greek poleis of Ionia in western Asia Minor.

Using these documents and consulting *The Challenge of the West,* write as balanced an account as you can of the fundamental issues at the heart of the Greco-Persian confrontation. Be sure to consider what you have learned from Set 3.1 about the values of the polis.

A. Xerxes Lauds His Own Greatness, and God's

Ahuramazda is the great god who gave (us) this earth, who gave (us) that sky, who gave (us) mankind, who gave to his worshipers prosperity, who made Xerxes,

the king, (rule) the multitudes (as) only king, give alone orders to the other (kings). . . .

I am Xerxes, the great king, the . . . king of kings, the king of (all) countries (which speak) all kinds of languages, the king of this (entire) big and far(-reaching) earth,—the son of king Darius, the Achaemenian, a Persian, son of a Persian, an Aryan (*ar-ri-i*) of Aryan descent. . . .

Thus speaks king Xerxes: These are the countries—in addition to Persia—over which I am king under the "shadow" of Ahuramazda, over which I hold sway, which are bringing their tribute to me— whatever is commanded them by me, that they do and they abide by my law(s)—: Media, Elam, Arachosia, . . . Armenia, Drangiana, Parthia, (H)aria, Bactria, Sogdia, Chorasmia, Babylonia, Assyria, Sattagydia, Sardis, Egypt, the Ionians who live on the salty sea and (those) who live beyond . . . the salty sea, Maka, Arabia, Gandara, India, Cappadocia, Da'an, the Amyrgian Cimmerians. . . , the Cimmerians (wearing) pointed caps, the Skudra, the Akupish, Libya, Banneshu (Carians) (and) Kush.

Thus speaks king Xerxes: After I became king, there were (some) among these countries (names of . which) are written above, which revolted (but) I crushed (lit.: killed) these countries, after Ahuramazda had given me his support, under the "shadow" of Ahuramazda, and I put them (again) into their (former political) status. Furthermore, there were among these countries (some) which performed (religious) service (lit.: festival) to the "Evil (God)s," (but) under the "shadow" of Ahuramazda I destroyed (lit.: eradicated) these temples of the "Evil (God)s" and proclaimed (as follows): "You must not perform (religious) service to the 'Evil (God)s' (any more)!" Wherever formerly (religious) service was performed to the "Evil (God)s," I, myself, performed a (religious) service to Ahuramazda and the *arta* (cosmic order) reverently. Furthermore, there were other things which were done in a bad way, and these (too) I made in the correct way.

All these things which I did, I performed under the "shadow" of Ahuramazda and Ahuramazda gave me his support until I had accomplished everything.

Whosoever you are, in future (days) who thinks (as follows): "May I be prosperous in this life and blessed after my death!"—do live according to this law which Ahuramazda has promulgated: "Perform (religious) service (only) for Ahuramazda and the *arta* (cosmic order) reverently." A man who lives according to this law which Ahuramazda has promulgated, and (who) performs (religious) service (only) to Ahuramazda and the *arta* (cosmic order) reverently, will be prosperous while he is alive and—(when) dead—he will become blessed.

Thus speaks king Xerxes: May Ahuramazda protect me, my family and these countries from all evil. This I do ask of Ahuramazda and this Ahuramazda may grant me!

B. Herodotus Explains Persian Religion

These are the customs, so far as I know, which the Persians practise: Images and temples and altars they do not account it lawful to erect, nay they even charge with folly those who do these things; and this, as it seems to me, because they do not account the gods to be in the likeness of men, as do the Hellenes. But it is their wont to perform sacrifices to Zeus: and they sacrifice to the sun and the moon and the earth, to fire and to water and to the winds: these are the only gods to whom they have sacrificed ever from the first; but they have learnt also to sacrifice to Aphrodite Urania, having learnt it both from the Assyrians and the Arabians; and the Assyrians call Aphrodite Mylitta, the Arabians Alitta, and the Persians Mitra.

Now this is the manner of sacrifice for the gods aforesaid which is established among the Persians: They make no altars neither do they kindle fire; and when they mean to sacrifice they use no libation nor music of the pipe nor chaplets nor meal for sprinkling; but when a man wishes to sacrifice to any one of the gods, he leads the animal for sacrifice to an unpolluted place and calls upon the god, having his tiara wreathed round generally with a branch of myrtle. For himself alone separately the man who sacrifices may not request good things in his prayer, but he prays that it may be well with all the Persians and with the king; for he himself also is included of course in the whole body of Persians. And when he has cut up the victim into pieces and boiled the flesh, he spreads a layer of the freshest grass and especially clover, upon which he places forthwith all the pieces of flesh; and when he has placed them in order, a magian man stands by them and chants over them a theogony (for of this nature they say that their incantation is), seeing that without a magian it is not lawful for them to make sacrifices. Then after waiting a short time the sacrificer carries away the flesh and uses it for whatever purpose he pleases.

C. Xerxes Crosses the Hellespont

. . . In the mean while those who were appointed had joined the Hellespont from Asia to Europe. There is in the Chersonese on the Hellespont, between the city of Sestos and Madytus, a craggy shore extending into the sea, directly opposite Abydos: there, not long after these events, under Xanthippus, son of Ariphron, a general of the Athenians, having taken Artayctes, a Persian, governor of Sestos, they impaled him alive against a plank; for he, having brought women into the temple of Protesilaus at Elæus, committed atrocious crimes.

To this shore, then, beginning at Abydos, they, on whom this task was imposed, constructed bridges, the Phœnicians one with white flax, and the Egyptians the other with papyrus. The distance from Abydos to the opposite shore is seven stades. When the strait was thus united, a violent storm arising, broke in pieces and scattered the whole work. When Xerxes heard of this, being exceeding indignant, he commanded that the Hellespont should be stricken with three hundred lashes with a scourge, and that a pair of fetters should be let down into the sea. I have moreover heard that with them he likewise sent branding instruments to brand the Hellespont. He certainly charged those who flogged the waters to utter these barbarous and impious words: "Thou bitter water! thy master inflicts this punishment upon thee, because thou hast injured him, although thou hadst not suffered any harm from him. And king Xerxes will cross over thee, whether thou wilt or not; it is with justice that no man sacrifices to thee, because thou art both a deceitful and briny river!" He accordingly commanded them to chastise the sea in this manner, and to cut off the heads of those who had to superintend the joining of the Hellespont.

They on whom this thankless office was imposed, carried it into execution; and other engineers constructed bridges; and they constructed them in the following manner. They connected together penteconters and triremes, under that towards the Black Sea, three hundred and sixty; and under the other, three hundred and fourteen, obliquely in respect of the Pontus, but in the direction of the current in respect of the Hellespont, that it might keep up the tension of the cables. Having connected them together, they let down very long anchors, some on the one bridge towards the Pontus, on account of the winds that blew from it within; others on the other bridge towards the west and the Aegean, on account of the south and south-east winds. They left an opening as a passage through between the penteconters, and that in three places, that any one who wished might be able to sail into the Pontus in light vessels, and from the Pontus outwards. Having done this, they stretched the cables from the shore, twisting them with wooden capstans, not as before using the two kinds separately, but assigning to each two of white flax and four of papyrus. The thickness and quality was the same, but those of flax were stronger in proportion, every cubit weighing a full talent. When the passage was bridged over, having sawn up trunks of trees, and having made them equal to the width of the bridge, they laid them regularly upon the extended cables; and having laid them in regular order, they then fastened them together. And having done this, they put brush-wood on the top; and having laid the brush-wood in regular order they put earth over the whole; and having pressed down the earth, they drew a fence on each side, that the beasts of burden and horses might not be frightened by looking down upon the sea. . . .

D. The Women of Corinth Beseech the Gods as the Persians Approach

Theopompus says that the women of Corinth prayed to Aphrodite to inspire their husbands with the love of fighting the Persians for the sake of Greece. (In order to do this,) they entered the temple of Aphrodite, which they say was founded by Medea at the command of Hera. The verses inscribed exist even now, positioned on the left as one enters the temple: "On behalf of the Greeks and their own citizen-warriors these women stood in prayer to Lady Kypris (i.e., Aphrodite under one of her several titles). For shining Aphrodite did not wish to give over to the bow-carrying Persians the acropolis of the Greeks."

E. The Persians Tolerate Greek Religion

The king of kings, Darius, the son of Hystaspes, to his slave Gadatas says thus:—I learn that thou dost not obey my commands in all respects. In that thou cultivatest my land by transplanting the fruits (of the country) beyond the Euphrates to the lower parts of Asia, I commend thy purpose, and by reason of this there shall be laid up for thee great favor in the king's house. But, in that thou settest at naught my policy towards the gods, I will give thee, if thou dost not change, a proof of my wronged feelings; for thou didst exact a payment from the sacred gardeners of Apollo and didst command them to dig unhallowed ground, not knowing the mind of my forefathers towards the god, who hath told the Persians the whole truth. . . .

Document Set 3.2 References

A. Xerxes Lauds His Own Greatness, and God's
E. A. Speiser and J. B. Pritchard, eds., *Ancient Near Eastern Texts Relating to the Old Testament,* 3rd ed. (Princeton, N.J.: Princeton University Press, 1969), 316–317.
B. Herodotus Explains Persian Religion
Herodotus, *Histories* 1:131, in Fred Morrow Fling, ed., *A Source Book of Greek History* (Boston: D. C. Heath, 1907), 98–99.
C. Xerxes Crosses the Hellespont
Herodotus, *Histories* 7:33–35, trans. Henry Cary (London: Routledge, 1891), 348–349.
D. The Women of Corinth Beseech the Gods as the Persians Approach
Scholion to Pindar, *Olympian Ode* 13:22–23b, in Charles Fornara, ed., *Translated Documents of Greece and Rome,* vol. 1: *Archaic Times to the End of the Peloponnesian War,* 2d ed. (Cambridge: Cambridge University Press, 1983), no. 53.
E. The Persians Tolerate Greek Religion
G. W. Botsford and E. G. Sihler, eds., *Hellenic Civilization* (New York: Columbia University Press, 1915), 162.

DOCUMENT SET 3.3
The Sophists and Socrates

Cultural sophistication and the diversifying effects of commercial and demographic growth produced a vibrant, contentious society in fifth-century Athens. A demand for training in the arts of quick reasoning and eloquent, persuasive speech were direct consequences of the emergence of a bustling, litigating community. The teachers who stepped forward to teach these arts were called sophists.

Protagoras (c. 485–c. 410 B.C.) was a prominent sophist. He taught that a well-trained orator ought to be prepared to argue either side of a case, presumably so that (like a lawyer today) he can serve any client who needs his services. Because Protagoras also insisted that human beings needed to develop a sense of justice in order to survive, he was probably not a cynical advocate of using glib words to undermine social stability. But that was the way his teachings were presented for a wider audience—as in Document A, an extract from an anonymous handbook of the late fifth century called *Double Arguments,* showing how common sense could be stood on its head.

Although he was also a sophist in the sense that he taught reasoning, Socrates (c. 470–399 B.C.) accepted no fees, insisted that he knew nothing save how to ask penetrating questions, and stood forth as the great opponent of "sophistic" logic-twisting. The admiring reminiscences of one of his pupils, Xenophon (431–c. 350 B.C.), an extract of which constitutes Document B, gives a vivid though perhaps idealized portrait of Socrates. In Documents C and D, Socrates speaks for himself. Document C is an extract from the *Apology,* an account by Socrates' most famous disciple, Plato (c. 438–348), describing the old philosopher's self-defense before a jury of his fellow Athenians who had put him on trial for "corrupting" the city's youth—questioning traditional ideas, in other words. In Document D from the *Symposium* (a dialogue set at an all-male drinking party), Socrates tells how he learned the meaning of love from a temple priestess, Diotema. Finally, in Document E we have a glimpse of how conservative Athenians (like the aristocratic comic dramatist Aristophanes, c. 450–c. 388 B.C.) thought about Socrates. Here, in an extract from Aristophanes's *The Clouds,* Socrates is ridiculed as a wafty spinner of fantasies.

Studying these documents, look for evidence of why the sophists and Socrates could so thoroughly alarm their traditionalist contemporaries.

A. Protagoras Inspires Arguments on Both Sides of a Case

Double arguments concerning the good and the bad are put forward in Greece by those who philosophize. Some say that the good is one thing and the bad another, but others say that they are the same, and that a thing might be good for some persons but bad for others, or at one time good and at another time bad for the same person. I myself agree with those who hold the latter opinion, which I shall examine using as an example human life and its concern for food, drink, and sexual pleasures: these things are bad for a man if he is sick but good if he is healthy and needs them. And, further, overindulgence in these things is bad for the overindulger but good for those who make a profit by selling these things. And again, sickness is bad for the sick but good for the doctors. And death is bad for those who die but good for the undertakers and makers of grave monuments. . . . Shipwrecks are bad for the shipowners but good for the shipbuilders. When tools are blunted and worn away it is bad for others but good for the blacksmith. And if a pot gets smashed, this is bad for everyone else but good for the potter. When shoes wear out and fall apart it is bad for others but good for the shoemaker. . . . In the *stadion* race for runners, victory is good for the winner but bad for the losers.

B. Xenophon Recalls Socrates' Manner of Teaching

. . . He was constantly in public, for he went in the morning to the places for walking and the gymnasia; at the time when the market was full he was to be seen there; and the rest of the day he was where he was likely to meet the greatest number of people; he was generally engaged in discourse, and all who pleased were at liberty to hear him; yet no one ever either saw Socrates doing, or heard him saying, anything impious or profane; for he did not dispute about the nature of things as most other philosophers disputed, speculating how that which is called by sophists *the world* was produced, and by what necessary laws everything in the heavens is effected, but endeavored to show that those who chose such subjects of contemplation were foolish; and he used in the first place to inquire of them whether they thought that they already knew sufficient of human affairs, and therefore proceeded to such subjects of meditation, or whether, when they neglected human affairs entirely, and speculated on celestial matters, they thought that they were doing what became them. . . .

C. Socrates on Relieving the Fear of Death

Let us consider in another way also how there is good reason to hope that death is a good thing. For being dead is one of two things: either it is virtually nothingness, so that the dead person has no consciousness of anything, or it is, as people say, a change and migration of the soul from this to another place. And if it is unconsciousness, like a sleep in which the sleeping person does not even dream, death would be a wonderful gain. For I think if anyone were to pick out that night in which he slept a dreamless sleep and, comparing it with the other days and nights of his life, were to say, after due consideration, how many days and nights in his life had passed more pleasantly than that night—I believe that not only any private individual, but even the Great King of Persia himself would find that they were few in comparison with the other days and nights. If this, then, is the nature of death, I count it a gain: for then all time will seem to be no longer than one night. On the other hand, if death is, as it were, a move from here to some other place, and if what we are told is true, that all the dead are there, what greater blessing could there be. . . ? For if a man when he reaches the other world, after leaving behind these who claim to be judges, shall find there those who are truly judges, who are said to sit in judgment there . . . and were said to be just men in their lives, would the move be undesirable? Or, again, what would any of you give to meet with Orpheus and Musaeus and Hesiod and Homer? I am willing to die many times over, if these things are true. . . .

D. Diotima Teaches Socrates About Love

And now, taking my leave of you, I will rehearse a tale of love which I heard from Diotima of Mantineia, a woman wise in this and in many other kinds of knowledge, who in the days of old, when the Athenians offered sacrifice before the coming of the plague, delayed the disease ten years. She was my instructress in the art of love. . . . First I said to her . . . that Love was a mighty god, and likewise fair; and she proved to me as I proved to him that, by my own showing, Love was neither fair nor good. 'What do you mean, Diotima,' I said, 'is love then evil and foul?' 'Hush,' she cried; 'must that be foul which is not fair?' . . . 'Well,' I said, 'Love is surely admitted by all to be a great god.' 'By those who know or by those who do not know?' 'By all.' 'And how, Socrates,' she said with a smile, 'can Love be acknowledged to be a great god by those who say that he is not a god at all?' 'And who are they?' I said, 'You and I are two of them,' she replied. 'How can that be?' I said. 'It is quite intelligible,' she replied; 'for you yourself would acknowledge that the gods are happy and fair—of course you would—would you dare to say that any god was not?' 'Certainly not,' I replied. 'And you mean by the happy, those who are the possessors of things good or fair?' 'Yes.' And you admitted that Love, because he was in want, desires those good and fair things of which he is in want?' 'Yes, I did.' 'But how can he be a god who has no portion in what is either good or fair?' 'Impossible.' 'Then you see that you also deny the divinity of Love.'

'What then is Love?' I asked; 'Is he mortal?' 'No.' 'What then?' 'As in the former instance, he is neither mortal nor immortal, but in a mean between the two.' 'What is he, Diotima?' 'He is a great spirit, and like all spirits he is intermediate between the divine and the mortal.' 'And what,' I said, 'is his power?' 'He interprets,' she replied, 'between gods and men, conveying and taking across to the gods the prayers and sacrifices of men, and to men the commands and replies of the gods; he is the mediator who spans the chasm which divides them, and therefore in him all is bound together, and through him the arts of the prophet and the priest, their sacrifices and mysteries and charms, and all prophecy and incantation, find their way. For God mingles not with man; but through Love all the intercourse and converse of god with man, whether awake or asleep, is carried on. The wisdom which understands this is spiritual; all other wisdom, such as that of arts and handicrafts, is mean and vulgar. Now these spirits or intermediate powers are many and diverse, and one of them is Love.' . . .

I said: 'O thou stranger woman, thou sayest well; but, assuming Love to be such as you say, what is the use of him to men?' 'That, Socrates,' she replied, 'I will attempt to unfold: of his nature and birth I have already spoken; and you acknowledge that love is of the beautiful. But some one will say: Of the beautiful in what, Socrates and Diotima?—or rather let me put the question more clearly, and ask: When a man loves the beautiful, what does he desire?' I answered her 'That the beautiful may be his.' 'Still,' she said, 'the answer suggests a further question: What is given by the possession of beauty?' 'To what you have asked,'

I replied, 'I have no answer ready.' 'Then,' she said, 'let me put the word "good" in the place of the beautiful, and repeat the question once more: If he who loves loves the good, what is it then that he loves?' 'The possession of the good,' I said, 'And what does he gain who possesses the good?' 'Happiness,' I replied; 'there is less difficulty in answering that question.' 'Yes,' she said, 'the happy are made happy by the acquisition of good things. Nor is there any need to ask why a man desires happiness; the answer is already final.' 'You are right,' I said. 'And is this wish and this desire common to all? and do all men always desire their own good, or only some men?—what say you?' 'All men,' I replied; 'the desire is common to all.' 'Why, then,' she rejoined, 'are not all men, Socrates, said to love, but only some of them? whereas you say that all men are always loving the same things.' 'I myself wonder,' I said, 'why this is.' 'There is nothing to wonder at,' she replied; 'the reason is that one part of love is separated off and receives the name of the whole, but the other parts have other names.' 'Give an illustration,' I said. She answered me as follows: 'There is poetry, which, as you know, is complex and manifold. All creation or passage of non-being into being is poetry or making, and the processes of all art are creative; and the masters of arts are all poets or makers.' 'Very true.' 'Still,' she said, 'you know that they are not called poets, but have other names; only that portion of the art which is separated off from the rest, and is concerned with music and metre, is termed poetry, and they who possess poetry in this sense of the word are called poets.' 'Very true,' I said. 'And the same holds of love. For you may say generally that all desire of good and happiness is only the great and subtle power of love; but they who are drawn towards him by any other path, whether the path of money-making or gymnastics or philosophy, are not called lovers—the name of the whole is appropriated to those whose affection takes one form only—they alone are said to love, or to be lovers.' 'I dare say,' I replied, 'that you are right.' 'Yes,' she added, 'and you hear people say that lovers are seeking for their other half; but I say that they are seeking neither for the half of themselves, nor for the whole, unless the half or the whole be also a good. And they will cut off their own hands and feet and cast them away, if they are evil; for they love not what is their own, unless perchance there be some one who calls what belongs to him the good, and what belongs to another the evil. For there is nothing which men love but the good. Is there anything?' 'Certainly, I should say, that there is nothing.' 'Then,' she said, 'the simple truth is, that men love the good.' 'Yes,' I said. 'To which must be added that they love the possession of the good?' 'Yes, that must be added.' 'And not only the possession, but the everlasting possession of the good?' 'That must be added too.' 'Then love,' she said, 'may be described generally as the love of the everlasting possession of the good?' 'That is most true.'

E. Aristophanes Irreverently Spoofs Socrates

Strepsiades: Then, woe to you! And who is this man suspended up in a basket?
Disciple: 'Tis *he himself.*
Strepsiades: Who himself?
Disciple: Socrates.
Strepsiades: Socrates! Oh! I pray you, call him right loudly for me.
Disciple: Call him yourself; I have no time to waste.
Strepsiades: Socrates! my little Socrates!
Socrates: Mortal, what do you want with me?
Strepsiades: First, what are you doing up there? Tell me, I beseech you.
Socrates: I traverse the air and contemplate the sun.
Strepsiades: Thus 'tis not on the solid ground, but from the height of this basket, that you slight the gods, if indeed. . .
Socrates: I have to suspend my brain and mingle the subtle essence of my mind with this air, which is of the like nature, in order to clearly penetrate the things of heaven. I should have discovered nothing, had I remained on the ground to consider from below the things that are above; for the earth by its force attracts the sap of the mind to itself. 'Tis just the same with the water-cress.
Strepsiades: What? Does the mind attract the sap of the water-cress? Ah! my dear little Socrates, come down to me! I have come to ask you for lessons.
Socrates: And for what lessons? . . .
Socrates: Do you really wish to know the truth of celestial matters?
Strepsiades: Why, truly, if 'tis possible.
Socrates: . . . and to converse with the clouds, who are our genii?
Strepsiades: Without a doubt.
Socrates: Then be seated on this sacred couch.
Strepsiades: I am seated.
Socrates: Now take this chaplet.
Strepsiades: Why a chaplet? Alas! Socrates, would you sacrifice me, like Athamas?
Socrates: No, these are the rites of initiation.
Strepsiades: And what is it I am to gain?
Socrates: You will become a thorough rattle-pate, a hardened old stager, the fine flour of the talkers. . . . But come, keep quiet.

Strepsiades: By Zeus! You lie not! Soon I shall be nothing but wheat-flour, if you powder me in this fashion.

Socrates: Silence, old man, give heed to the prayers.... Oh! most mighty king, the boundless air, that keepest the earth suspended in space, thou bright Aether and ye venerable goddesses, the Clouds, who carry in your loins the thunder and the lightning, arise, ye sovereign powers and manifest yourselves in the celestial spheres to the eyes of the sage.

Strepsiades: Not yet! Wait a bit, till I fold my mantle double, so as not to get wet. And to think that I did not even bring my travelling cap! What a misfortune!

Socrates: Come, oh! Clouds, whom I adore, come and show yourselves to this man, whether you be resting on the sacred summits of Olympus, crowned with hoar-frost, or tarrying in the gardens of Ocean, your father, forming sacred choruses with the Nymphs; whether you be gathering the waves of the Nile in golden vases or dwelling in the Mæotic marsh or on the snowy rocks of Mimas, hearken to my prayer and accept my offering. May these sacrifices be pleasing to you.

Chorus: Eternal Clouds, let us appear, let us arise from the roaring depth of Ocean, our father; let us fly towards the lofty mountains, spread our damp wings over their forest-laden summits, whence we will dominate the distant valleys, the harvest fed by the sacred earth, the murmur of the divine streams and the resounding waves of the sea, which the unweary-ing orb lights up with its glittering beams. But let us shake off the rainy fogs, which hide our immortal beauty and sweep the earth from afar with our gaze.

Socrates: Oh, venerated goddesses, yes, you are answering my call! (*To Strepsiades.*) Did you hear their voices mingling with the awful growling of the thunder?

Strepsiades: Oh! adorable Clouds, I revere you and I too am going to let off *my* thunder, so greatly has your own affrighted me. Faith! whether permitted or not, I must, I must crap!

Socrates: No scoffing; do not copy those accursed comic poets. Come, silence! a numerous host of goddesses approaches with songs. . . .

Document Set 3.3 References

A. Protagoras Inspires Arguments on Both Sides of a Case
   Dissoi Logoi, 1.1–6, in Rosamund Kent Sprague, ed., *The Older Sophists* (Columbia: University of South Carolina Press, 1972), 279–280.
B. Xenophon Recalls Socrates' Manner of Teaching
   Xenophon, *Memorabilia,* in Fred Morrow Fling, ed., *A Source Book of Greek History* (Boston: D. C. Heath, 1907), 241.
C. Socrates on Relieving the Fear of Death
   Plato, *Apology* 40c–41a, trans. H. N. Fowler, Loeb Classical Library (Cambridge, Mass.: Harvard University Press, 1977).
D. Diotima Teaches Socrates About Love
   Plato, *Symposium,* trans. Benjamin Jowett (Oxford: Clarendon Press, 1892), 327–328, 329–330.
E. Aristophanes Irreverently Spoofs Socrates
   Aristophanes, *The Clouds,* in *Eleven Comedies,* trans. anon. (New York: Liveright, 1943), 310–314.

DOCUMENT SET 3.4
Women and Slaves

Document A, taken from a speech written by the orator Lysias (c. 450–380 B.C.), himself a good example of the cosmopolitan sophist, records the arguments presented to an Athenian jury by a man accused of having killed his wife's lover, one Eratosthenes. We do not know the trial's outcome. Read the argument, however, for the details it presents on Athenian domestic life, as well as for the insights it affords into ordinary Greek men's notions of honor and husbandly prerogatives.

Document B by contrast suggests how radically different were the ideas of Plato (and, perhaps, of Socrates). Here, in *The Republic,* Plato puts into Socrates' mouth a plan for the total overhaul of all society, including making women eligible to join the ranks of elite philosopher-kings, or guardians. What do you think of Plato's reasoning?

Aristotle, Plato's pupil, rejected the ideal state of *The Republic* as fantastic; his more conservative (and socially acceptable) ideas of how women should be governed appear in Document C, an extract from his *Politics.*

Using *The Challenge of the West* as a resource, evaluate the documents in this set as sources of reliable information about gender relations in classical Athens.

A. An Athenian Husband Testifies How He Killed His Wife's Lover

Members of the jury: when I decided to marry and had brought a wife home, at first my attitude towards her was this: I did not wish to annoy her, but neither was she to have too much of her own way. I watched her as well as I could, and kept an eye on her as was proper. But later, after my child had been born, I came to trust her, and I handed all my possessions over to her, believing that this was the greatest possible proof of affection.

Well, members of the jury, in the beginning she was the best of women. She was a clever housewife, economical and exact in her management of everything. But then, my mother died; and her death has proved to be the source of all my troubles, because it was when my wife went to the funeral that this man

Eratosthenes saw her; and as time went on, he was able to seduce her. . . .

Now first of all, gentlemen, I must explain that I have a small house which is divided into two—the men's quarters and the women's—each having the same space, the women upstairs and the men downstairs.

After the birth of my child, his mother nursed him; but I did not want her to run the risk of going downstairs every time she had to give him a bath, so I myself took over the upper storey, and let the women have the ground floor. And so it came about that by this time it was quite customary for my wife often to go downstairs and sleep with the child, so that she could give him the breast and stop him from crying.

This went on for a long while, and I had not the slightest suspicion. . . .

Time passed, gentlemen. One day, when I had come home unexpectedly from the country, after dinner, the child began crying and complaining. Actually it was the maid who was pinching him on purpose to make him behave so because—as I found out later—this man was in the house.

Well, I told my wife to go and feed the child, to stop his crying. But at first she refused, pretending that she was glad to see me back after my long absence. At last I began to get annoyed, and I insisted on her going.

'Oh, yes!' she said. 'To leave *you* alone with the maid up here! You mauled her about before, when you were drunk!'

I laughed. She got up, went out, closed the door—pretending that it was a joke—and locked it. As for me, I thought no harm of all this, and I had not the slightest suspicion. I went to sleep, glad to do so after my journey from the country.

Towards morning, she returned and unlocked the door.

I asked her why the doors had been creaking during the night. She explained that the lamp beside the baby had gone out, and that she had then gone to get a light from the neighbours.

I said no more. I thought it really was so. But it did seem to me, members of the jury, that she had done up her face with cosmetics, in spite of the fact that her brother had died only a month before. Still, even so, I said nothing about it. I just went off, without a word. . . . [Eratosthenes' former mistress sends word to the husband of what is going on.] At once I

Excerpt from "An Athenian Husband's Defense" from Lefkowitz and Fant, eds., *Women's Life in Greece and Rome: A Sourcebook in Translation,* Johns Hopkins University Press, 1982, pp. 41–47. Reprinted by permission of the publisher.

was overwhelmed. Everything rushed into my mind, and I was filled with suspicion. I reflected how I had been locked into the bedroom. I remembered how on that night the middle and outer doors had creaked, a thing that had never happened before; and how I had had the idea that my wife's face was rouged. All these things rushed into my mind, and I was filled with suspicion.

I went back home, and told the servant to come with me to market. I took her instead to the house of one of my friends; and there I informed her that I had discovered all that was going on in my house.

'As for you,' I said, 'two courses are open to you: either to be flogged and sent to the tread-mill, and never be released from a life of utter misery; or to confess the whole truth and suffer no punishment, but win pardon from me for your wrongdoing. Tell me no lies. Speak the whole truth.'

At first, she tried denial, and told me that I could do as I pleased—she knew nothing. But when I named Eratosthenes to her face, and said that he was the man who had been visiting my wife, she was dumbfounded, thinking that I had found out everything exactly. And then at last, falling at my feet and exacting a promise from me that no harm should be done to her, she denounced the villain. . . . [The husband demands that his wife break off with Eratosthenes and hush up the affair. But Eratosthenes sneaks into the house a few nights later. Suspecting what is afoot, the husband goes out to round up some of his friends. They return.]

We forced the bedroom door. The first of us to enter saw him still lying beside my wife. Those who followed saw him standing naked on the bed.

I knocked him down, members of the jury, with one blow. I then twisted his hands behind his back and tied them. And then I asked him why he was committing this crime against me, of breaking into my house.

He answered that he admitted his guilt; but he begged and besought me not to kill him—to accept a money-payment instead.

But I replied: 'It is not I who shall be killing you, but the law of the state, which you, in transgressing, have valued less highly than your own pleasure. You have preferred to commit this great crime against my wife and my children, rather than to obey the law and be of decent behaviour.'

Thus, members of the jury, this man met the fate which the laws prescribe for wrongdoers of his kind. . . .

To the Clerk of the Court: Read the law.

The Law of Solon is read, that an adulterer may be put to death by the man who catches him.

He made no denial, members of the jury. He admitted his guilt, and begged and implored that he should not be put to death, offering to pay compensation. But I would not accept his estimate. I preferred to accord a higher authority to the law of the state, and I took that satisfaction which you, because you thought it the most just, have decreed for those who commit such offences. Witnesses to the preceding, kindly step up.

The witnesses come to the front of the court, and the Clerk reads their depositions. . . .

You hear, members of the jury, how it is expressly decreed by the Court of the Areopagus itself, which both traditionally and in your own day has been granted the right to try cases of murder, that no person shall be found guilty of murder who catches an adulterer with his wife and inflicts this punishment. The lawgiver was so strongly convinced of the justice of these provisions in the case of married women, that he applied them also to concubines, who are of less importance. Yet obviously, if he had known of any greater punishment than this for cases where married women are concerned, he would have provided it. . . .

You have heard the witnesses, members of the jury. Now consider the case further in your own minds, inquiring whether there had ever existed between Eratosthenes and myself any other enmity but this. You will find none. He never brought any malicious charge against me, nor tried to secure my banishment, nor prosecuted me in any private suit. Neither had he knowledge of any crime of which I feared the revelation, so that I desired to kill him; nor by carrying out this act did I hope to gain money. So far from ever having had any dispute with him, or drunken brawl, or any other quarrel, I had never even set eyes on the man before that night. What possible object could I have had, therefore, in running so great a risk, except that I had suffered the greatest of all injuries at his hands? . . .

It is my belief, members of the jury, that this punishment was inflicted not in my own interests, but in those of the whole community. Such villains, seeing the rewards which await their crimes, will be less ready to commit offences against others if they see that you too hold the same opinion of them. Otherwise it would be far better to wipe out the existing laws and make different ones, which will penalise those who keep guard over their own wives, and grant full immunity to those who criminally pursue them. This would be a far more just procedure than to set a trap for citizens by means of the laws, which urge the man who catches an adulterer to do with him whatever he will, and yet allow the injured party to undergo a trial far more perilous than that which faces the lawbreaker who seduces other men's wives. Of this, I am an example—I, who now stand in danger of losing life, property, everything, because I have obeyed the laws of the state.

B. Plato Argues for Female Equality in His Ideal State

Next, we shall ask our opponent how, in reference to any of the pursuits or arts of civic life, the nature of a woman differs from that of a man?

That will be quite fair.

And perhaps he, like yourself, will reply that to give a sufficient answer on the instant is not easy; but after a little reflection there is no difficulty.

Yes, perhaps.

Suppose then that we invite him to accompany us in the argument, and then we may hope to show him that there is nothing peculiar in the constitution of women which would affect them in the administration of the State.

By all means....

And can you mention any pursuit of mankind in which in which the male sex has not all these gifts and qualities in a higher degree than the female? Need I waste time in speaking of the art of weaving, and the management of pancakes and preserves, in which womankind does really appear to be great, and in which for her to be beaten by a man is of all things the most absurd?

You are quite right, he replied, in maintaining the general inferiority of the female sex: although many women are in many things superior to many men, yet on the whole what you say is true.

And if so, my friend, I said, there is no special faculty of administration in a state which a woman has because she is a woman, or which a man has by virtue of his sex, but the gifts of nature are alike diffused in both; all the pursuits of men are the pursuits of women also, but in all of them a woman is inferior to a man.

Very true.

Then are we to impose all our enactments on men and none of them on women?

That will never do.

One woman has a gift of healing, another not; one is a musician, and another has no music in her nature?

Very true.

And one woman has a turn for gymnastic and military exercises, and another is unwarlike and hates gymnastics?

Certainly.

And one woman is a philosopher, and another is an enemy of philosophy; one has spirit, and another is without spirit?

That is also true.

Then one woman will have the temper of a guardian, and another not. Was not the selection of the male guardians determined by differences of this sort?

Yes.

Men and women alike possess the qualities which make a guardian; they differ only in their comparative strength or weakness.

Obviously.

And those women who have such qualities are to be selected as the companions and colleagues of men who have similar qualities and whom they resemble in capacity and in character?

Very true.

And ought not the same natures to have the same pursuits?

They ought.

Then, as we were saying before, there is nothing unnatural in assigning music and gymnastic to the wives of the guardians—to that point we come round again.

Certainly not....

Well, and may we not further say that our guardians are the best of our citizens?

By far the best.

And will not their wives be the best women?

Yes, by far the best.

And can there be anything better for the interests of the State than that the men and women of a State should be as good as possible?

There can be nothing better.

And this is what the arts of music and gymnastic, when present in such manner as we have described, will accomplish?

Certainly.

Then we have made an enactment not only possible but in the highest degree beneficial to the State?

True.

Then let the wives of our guardians strip, for their virtue will be their robe, and let them share in the toils of war and the defence of their country; only in the distribution of labours the lighter are to be assigned to the women, who are the weaker natures, but in other respects their duties are to be the same. And as for the man who laughs at naked women exercising their bodies from the best of motives, in his laughter he is plucking

'A fruit of unripe wisdom,'

and he himself is ignorant of what he is laughing at, or what he is about;—for that is, and ever will be, the best of sayings, *That the useful is the noble and the hurtful is the base.*

C. Aristotle on the Governance and *Arete* of Women, Children, and Slaves

It was laid down, then, that there are three parts of domestic government; one, that of the master, of which we have already treated; another of the father, and a third that of the husband.

Now the government of the wife and children, should both be that of free persons, but not the same; for the wife should be treated as the member of a state, but the children should be under kingly rule; for the male is by nature made to rule over the female, except when something happens contrary to the usual course of nature; as the elder and full-grown is superior to the younger and imperfect. . . .

It is evident then that, in the due government of a family, greater attention should be paid to its several members than to the mere gaining of inanimate things; and to the virtues of the former rather than of the latter, (and this we term wealth;) and greater regard to those of freemen than of slaves. But here some one may question whether there is any other virtue in a slave than his mechanical services, and of higher estimation than these, as temperance, fortitude, justice, and other such like habits, or whether slaves possess none beyond mere bodily qualities. Each side of the question has its difficulties; for if they possess these virtues, wherein will they differ from freemen? and since they are men, and partakers of reason, it is absurd to say that they do not. Nay, nearly the same inquiry may be made concerning a woman, and a child, whether these also have their proper virtues, whether a woman ought to be temperate, brave, and just, and whether a child can be unbridled and temperate or not; and indeed this inquiry ought to be made in general, whether the virtues of those who by nature either govern or are governed, are the same, or different. For if it is necessary that both of them should partake of noble character, why is it necessary that the one should always govern, the other always be governed? Surely this difference cannot be merely one of degree; for to govern, and to be governed, are things different in species, but *more* or *less* are not. And yet it is strange that the one party ought to have them, and the other not; for if he who is to govern shall not be temperate and just, how can he govern well? or if he is to be governed, how can he be governed well? for he who is intemperate and a coward, will never do what he ought. It is evident, then, that both parties ought to

partake of virtue, but that there must be some difference of virtue between them, as there is between those who by nature command and those who by nature obey. This is suggested by the soul; for in this there is implanted by nature one part that rules and one that obeys; and the virtues of these we say are different, as are those of a rational and an irrational being. It is plain then that the same principle may be extended to the case of the others, so that there is by nature a variety of things which govern and are governed. Now a freeman governs his slave in one manner, the male governs the female in another, and in another manner the father governs his child; and all these have the different parts of the soul within them, but in a different manner. Thus a slave can have no deliberative faculty, a woman but a weak one, a child an imperfect one. Thus also must it necessarily be with respect to moral virtues; it must be supposed that all must possess them, though not in the same manner, but as is best suited to the several ends of each. Hence, by the way, he who is to govern ought to be perfect in moral virtue,—(for his business is entirely that of a master artificer, and reason is the master artificer;)—while others want only that portion of it which may be sufficient for their station: and hence it is evident, that although moral virtue is common to all those of whom we have spoken, yet the temperance of a man and of a woman are not the same, nor their courage, nor their justice, as Socrates thought; for the courage of the man consists in commanding, the woman's in obedience. And the same is true in all other particulars, and this will be evident to those who will examine the matter in detail; for those who use general terms deceive themselves, when they say that virtue consists in a good disposition of mind, or in doing what is right, or something of this sort. They do much better who enumerate the different virtues as Georgias did, than those who thus define them, and hence we ought to think of all persons, as the poet [Sophocles] says of a woman,

"Silence is woman's ornament,"

but it is not the ornament of man.

Document Set 3.4 References

A. An Athenian Husband Testifies How He Killed His Wife's Lover
   Mary R. Lefkowitz and Maureen B. Fant, eds., *Women's Life in Greece and Rome* (Baltimore: Johns Hopkins University Press, 1982), 41–47.
B. Plato Argues for Female Equality in His Ideal State
   Plato, *Republic* 5, trans. Benajmin Jowett, *Dialogues of Plato* (Oxford, Clarendon Press, 1892), 147–150.
C. Aristotle on the Governance and *Arete* of Women, Children, and Slaves
   Aristotle, *Politics* 12, trans. J. E. C. Welldon (London: Macmillan, 1883), 28–31.

Democratic fifth-century Athens was indisputably an aggressive, imperialistic power, feared and hated by other poleis. Admirable as may be Athenian democracy from our contemporary perspective, the Athenians' willingness to trample the liberties of fellow Greeks seems unsettling. Evaluate and try to explain this using the documents of this set (and other sets in this chapter). Do you find the Athenian conjuncture of democracy and imperialism ironic, paradoxical, even hypocritical? Why, or why not?

Document A is an inscription recording requirements for the payment of tribute by "allies," set up between 448 and 425 B.C. Document B contains the regulations that Athens imposed on the little polis of Chalcis after its rebellion had been put down in 446 B.C. What do you make of the procedural rights that Athens still allowed to the defeated Chalcidians? Far more brutal was the fate dealt by the Athenians to the polis of Melos in 418, which merely tried to maintain neutrality during the Peloponnesian War. This extract (Document C) is one of the most memorable passages from Thucydides' *Peloponnesian War.* Is it reasonable to ask how a democratic state could treat another community in such a way?

A. Athens Prescribes Regulations for Its Allies to Pay Tribute

Gods. Resolved by the Boule and the People. The Boule, the governors in the cities and the episkopoi shall see to it that the tribute payments be collected each year and be brought to Athens. Identification seals shall be made for the cities, so that it will be impossible that fraud be committed by those bringing the tribute payments. And after the city has inscribed in an account book whatever tribute payment it is sending, and has set its seal to it, let it be sent off to Athens. Let those bringing it give up the account book in the Boule, to be read at the same time as they are paying in the tribute money. And let the Prytaneis, after the Dionysia, summon an Assembly for the Hellenotamiai to make known to the Athenians which of the cities paid the tribute money in full and which fell short; these separately, as many. Let the Athenians select men, four in number, and send them to the cities to give a receipt for the tribute payment made and to demand what was not remitted two of them to sail to the cities of the islands and of Ionia on a swift trireme, the other two to sail to those of the Hellespont and of Thrace. The Prytaneis shall

bring up this matter in the Boule and in the Assembly at once after the Dionysia, and they shall consider it without interruption until a decision has been taken. And if any Athenian or ally is guilty of wrongdoing in respect to the tribute which it is required for those carrying it (the culprit) may be indicted before the Prytaneis by anyone who wishes, Athenian or ally. The Prytaneis shall bring before the Boule whatever indictment may have been drawn up, or they shall be called to account for bribery and (be liable to a fine of) drachmas each. As to the man charged by the Boule, sentence on him shall not be in its hands, but he shall be brought before the law court immediately. If and when he shall be found guilty, judgment shall be passed by the Prytaneis as to what seems proper for him as a punishment or as a fine. And as to the bringing of the cow or the panoply, if anyone commits a wrong, a similar indictment shall lie against him and the penalty shall be the same. The Hellenotamiai, after registering it on a notice board whitened over, shall publish both the assessment of the tribute and write down. [Approximately ten lines lost] Boule entering office. All those who have brought (payment) to Athens and who on the notice board are listed as owing publish to the People. If any of the cities raises any dispute about the tribute payment, claiming to have paid it the government (?) of the city the cities and not be permitted let the liability be the accuser's. The indictment shall be lodged with the Polemarch in the month of Gamelion. If anyone disputes prosecutions, the Boule, having considered. Let the Eisagogeis bring into court those whose tribute to the Athenians is owing, in the order of the list of denunciations of the current year's tribute and of the previous year's the Boule, framing a preliminary decree, shall refer is concerned at the next day's meeting of the election to transact [*The rest of the line is lost*].

B. The Athenians Punish a Rebellious Ally

The oath shall be taken as follows by the Athenian Council and all the jurors: 'I shall not deport Chalcidians from Chalcis or devastate the city or deprive any individual of his rights or punish him with exile or imprison him or kill him or take property from anyone unheard in trial without (the concurrence of) the People [i.e., the assembly] of the Athenians. I shall not have a vote taken, without summons to attend trial, against either the government or any private individual whatever. When an embassy has arrived, I shall introduce it to the Council and People within ten days when I am in charge of the procedure, to the best of my power. This I shall guarantee the Chalcidians if they obey the People of the Athenians.'

The Chalcidians shall take the following oath: 'I shall not rebel against the People of the Athenians either by artifice or by device of any kind either by word or by deed. Nor shall I follow anyone in rebellion and if anyone does rebel, I shall denounce him to the Athenians. I shall pay the dues to the Athenians which I persuade them [to assess], and as an ally I shall be the best and truest possible. And I shall assist the People of the Athenians and defend them if anyone does injury to the People of the Athenians, and I shall obey the People of the Athenians.'

C. Melos Meets Its Doom

. . . The Athenians also made an expedition against the isle of Melos with thirty ships of their own, six Chian, and two Lesbian vessels, sixteen hundred heavy infantry, three hundred archers, and twenty mounted archers from Athens, and about fifteen hundred heavy infantry from the allies and the islanders. The Melians are a colony of Lacedaemon [Sparta] that would not submit to the Athenians like the other islanders, and at first remained neutral and took no part in the struggle, but afterwards upon the Athenians using violence and plundering their territory, assumed an attitude of open hostility. Cleomedes, son of Lycomedes, and Tisias, son of Tisimachus, the generals, encamping in their territory with the above armament, before doing any harm to their land, sent envoys to negotiate. These the Melians did not bring before the people, but bade them state the object of their mission to the magistrates and the few; upon which the Athenian envoys spoke as follows: . . .

Athenians. For ourselves, we shall not trouble you with specious pretences—either of how we have a right to our empire because we overthrew the Mede, or are now attacking you because of wrong that you have done us—and make a long speech which would not be believed; and in return we hope that you, instead of thinking to influence us by saying that you did not join the Lacedaemonians, although their colonists, or that you have done us no wrong, will aim at what is feasible, holding in view the real sentiments of us both; since you know as well as we do that right, as the world goes, is only in question between equals in power, while the strong do what they can and the weak suffer what they must.

Melians. As we think, at any rate, it is expedient—we speak as we are obliged, since you enjoin us to let right alone and talk only of interest—that you should not destroy what is our common protection, the privilege of being allowed in danger to invoke what is fair and right, and even to profit by arguments not strictly valid if they can be got to pass current. And you are as much interested in this as any, as your fall would be a signal for the heaviest vengeance and an example for the world to meditate upon.

Athenians. The end of our empire, if end it should, does not frighten us: a rival empire like Lacedaemon, even if Lacedaemon was our real antagonist, is not so terrible to the vanquished as subjects who by themselves attack and overpower their rulers. This, however, is a risk that we are content to take. We will now proceed to show you that we are come here in the interest of our empire, and that we shall say what we are now going to say, for the preservation of your country; as we would fain exercise that empire over you without trouble, and see you preserved for the good of us both.

Melians. And how, pray, could it turn out as good for us to serve as for you to rule?

Athenians. Because you would have the advantage of submitting before suffering the worst, and we should gain by not destroying you.

Melians. So that you would not consent to our being neutral, friends instead of enemies, but allies of neither side.

Athenians. No; for your hostility cannot so much hurt us as your friendship will be an argument to our subjects of our weakness, and your enmity of our power.

Melians. Is that your subjects' idea of equity, to put those who have nothing to do with you in the same category with peoples that are most of them your own colonists, and some conquered rebels?

Athenians. As far as right goes they think one has as much of it as the other, and that if any maintain their independence it is because they are strong, and that if we do not molest them it is because we are afraid; so that besides extending our empire we should gain in security by your subjection; the fact that you are islanders and weaker than others rendering it all the more important that you should not succeed in baffling the masters of the sea.

[The debate continues. The Melians point out that Athens cannot afford to make every neutral an enemy, and trust that the gods will protect them. Eventually the Athenian envoys brusquely demand that the Melians stop talking and submit honorably:]

You will not think it dishonourable to submit to the greatest city in Hellas, when it makes you the moderate offer of becoming its tributary ally; without ceasing to enjoy the country that belongs to you; nor when you have the choice given you between war and security, will you be so blinded as to choose the worse. And it is certain that those who do not yield to their equals, who keep terms with their superiors, and are moderate towards their inferiors, on the whole succeed best. Think over the matter, therefore, after our withdrawal, and reflect once and again that it is for your country that you are consulting, that you have not more than one, and that upon this one deliberation depends its prosperity or ruin.

The Athenians now withdrew from the conference; and the Melians, left to themselves, came to a decision corresponding with what they had maintained in the discussion, and answered: 'Our resolution, Athenians, is the same as it was at first. We will not in a moment deprive of freedom a city that has been inhabited these seven hundred years; but we put our trust in the fortune by which the gods have preserved it until now, and in the help of men, that is, of the Lacedaemonians; and so we will try and save ourselves. Meanwhile we invite you to allow us to be friends to you and foes to neither party, and to retire from our country after making such a treaty as shall seem fit to us both.

Such was the answer of the Melians. The Athenians now departing from the conference said: 'Well, you alone, as it seems to us, judging from these resolutions, regard what is future as more certain than what is before your eyes, and what is out of sight, in your eagerness, as already coming to pass; and as you have staked most on, and trusted most in, the Lacedaemonians, your fortune, and your hopes, so will you be most completely deceived.

The Athenian envoys now returned to the army; and the Melians showing no signs of yielding, the generals at once betook themselves to hostilities, and drew a line of circumvallation round the Melians, dividing the work among the different states. Subsequently the Athenians returned with most of their army, leaving behind them a certain number of their own citizens and of the allies to keep guard by land and sea. The force thus left stayed on and besieged the place. . . .

[For a while Athens had to fight on other fronts while also besieging Melos.]

Summer was now over. The next winter the Lacedaemonians intended to invade the Argive territory, but arriving at the frontier found the sacrifices for crossing unfavourable, and went back again. This intention of theirs gave the Argives suspicions of certain of their fellow citizens, some of whom they arrested; others, however, escaped them. About the same time the Melians again took another part of the Athenian lines which were but feebly garrisoned. Reinforcements afterwards arriving from Athens in consequence, under the command of Philocrates, son of Demeas, the siege was now pressed vigorously; and some treachery taking place inside, the Melians surrendered at discretion to the Athenians, who put to death all the grown men whom they took, and sold the women and children for slaves, and subsequently sent out five hundred colonists and inhabited the place themselves.

Document Set 3.5 References

A. Athens Prescribes Regulations for Its Allies to Pay Tribute
Charles Fornara, ed., *Translated Documents of Greece and Rome*, vol. 1: *Archaic Times to the End of the Peloponnesian War*, 2d ed. (Cambridge: Cambridge University Press, 1983), 104.
B. The Athenians Punish a Rebellious Ally
Fornara, 104–105.
C. Melos Meets Its Doom
Thucydides, *Peloponnesian War* 5:17, trans. Richard Crawley (New York, E.P Dutton), 303–306.

4

Remaking the Mediterranean World, 403–30 B.C.

DOCUMENT SET 4.1
Plato and Aristotle

This document set in some respects continues the issues raised in Set 3.3. In Document A, for example, Plato in Book X of *The Republic* has Socrates insist that justice and virtue offer the only proper foundation for a well-ordered society. This is the central point of Plato's teaching, as perhaps it also was of Socrates'. In Document B, taken from *The Politics,* Aristotle offers a rather similar definition of the good life, although his means for achieving it are a good deal less drastic. To what extent do these two thinkers, on the evidence presented here, fit into larger patterns of Greek society, politics, and culture?

A. Plato Insists That Only Justice and Virtue Can Give a Satisfying Human Existence

There is a thing which you call good and another which you call evil?

Yes, he replied.

Would you agree with me in thinking that the corrupting and destroying element is the evil, and the saving and improving element the good?

Yes.

And you admit that everything has a good and also an evil; as ophthalmia is the evil of the eyes and disease of the whole body; as mildew is of corn, and rot of timber, or rust of copper and iron: in everything, or in almost everything, there is an inherent evil and disease?

Yes, he said.

And anything which is infected by any of these evils is made evil, and at last wholly dissolves and dies?

True.

The vice and evil which is inherent in each is the destruction of each; and if this does not destroy them there is nothing else that will; for good certainly will not destroy them, nor again, that which is neither good nor evil.

Certainly not.

If, then, we find any nature which having this inherent corruption cannot be dissolved or destroyed, we may be certain that of such a nature there is no destruction?

That may be assumed.

Well, I said, and is there no evil which corrupts the soul?

Yes, he said, there are all the evils which we were just now passing in review: unrighteousness, intemperance, cowardice, ignorance.

But does any of these dissolve or destroy her?— and here do not let us fall into the error of supposing that the unjust and foolish man, when he is detected, perishes through his own injustice, which is an evil of the soul. Take the analogy of the body: The evil of the body is a disease which wastes and reduces and annihilates the body; and all the things of which we were just now speaking come to annihilation through their own corruption attaching to them and inhering in them and so destroying them. Is not this true?

Yes.

Consider the soul in like manner. Does the injustice or other evil which exists in the soul waste and consume her? do they by attaching to the soul and inhering in her at last bring her to death, and so separate her from the body?

Certainly not.

And yet, I said, it is unreasonable to suppose that anything can perish from without through affection of external evil which could not be destroyed from within by a corruption of its own?

It is, he replied.

Consider, I said, Glaucon, that even the badness of food, whether staleness, decomposition, or any other bad quality, when confined to the actual food, is not supposed to destroy the body; although, if the badness of food communicates corruption to the body, then we should say that the body has been destroyed by a corruption of itself, which is disease, brought on by this; but that the body, being one thing, can be destroyed by the badness of food, which is another, and which does not engender any natural infection—this we shall absolutely deny?

Very true.

And, on the same principle, unless some bodily evil can produce an evil of the soul, we must not suppose that the soul, which is one thing, can be dissolved by any merely external evil which belongs to another?

Yes, he said, there is reason in that.

Either, then, let us refute this conclusion, or, while it remains unrefuted, let us never say that fever, or any other disease, or the knife put to the throat, or even the cutting up of the whole body into the minutest pieces, can destroy the soul, until she herself is proved to become more unholy or unrighteous in consequence of these things being done to the body; but that the soul, or anything else if not destroyed by an internal evil, can be destroyed by an external one, is not to be affirmed by any man. . . .

But the soul which cannot be destroyed by an evil, whether inherent or external, must exist for ever, and if existing for ever, must be immortal?

Certainly.

That is the conclusion, I said; and, if a true conclusion, then the souls must always be the same, for if none be destroyed they will not diminish in number. Neither will they increase, for the increase of the immortal natures must come from something mortal, and all things would thus end in immortality.

Very true.

But this we cannot believe—reason will not allow us—any more than we can believe the soul, in her truest nature, to be full of variety and difference and dissimilarity.

What do you mean? he said.

The soul, I said, being, as is now proven, immortal, must be the fairest of compositions and cannot be compounded of many elements?

Certainly not.

B. Aristotle Sums Up the Good Life in a Well-Ordered Polis

. . . Since our proposed object is to inquire what government is best, namely, that by which a state may be best administered, and that state would seem best administered where the people are the happiest, it is evident that the nature of happiness is a thing which ought not to escape us. Now, we have already said in our treatise on Ethics, (if there be any use in what we there said,) that happiness consists in the energy and perfect practice of virtue, and this not relatively, but simply. I mean by relatively, what is necessary in some certain circumstances; by simply, what is good in itself. Of the first sort are just punishments and restraints in a just cause; for they arise from virtue, and are necessary, and on that account are virtuous; (though it is more desirable, that neither any state or any individual should stand in need of such things:) but those actions which are directed to procure either honours or wealth are simply best. For the one are eligible as tending to remove an evil: these actions, on the contrary, are the foundation and means of producing relative good. A worthy man indeed will bear poverty, disease, and other unfortunate accidents, with a noble mind, but happiness consists in the contrary to these. Now we have already determined in our treatise on Ethics, that he is a man of worth who considers what is good because it is virtuous, as what is simply good: it is evident, therefore, that the using these things in such a manner must be worthy and simply good. This has led some persons to conclude that the cause of happiness was external goods; which would be as if any one should attribute to the lyre itself a brilliant and noble performance, and not to the art itself. It necessarily follows from what has been said, that some things should be ready at hand and others procured by the legislator: for which reason, we earnestly wish that the constitution of the state may have those things which are under the dominion of fortune—(for over some things we admit her to be supreme);—but for a state to be worthy and great is not the work of fortune only, but of knowledge and deliberate choice as well. But for a state to be worthy, it is necessary that those citizens who are in the administration should be worthy also: but in our city every citizen has a share in the state. And so we must consider how a man may become worthy. For if the whole body could become worthy, and not some individuals only, it would be more desirable; for then it would follow, that what might be done by one, might be done by all. Men are worthy and good in three ways; and these are, by nature, by custom, by reason. In the first place, each one ought to be born a man, and not any other animal; that is to say, he ought to be of a particular disposition both in body and soul. But as to some things, it avails not to be born with them, for custom makes great alterations: for there are some things in nature capable of alteration either way, and which are fixed by custom, either for the better or the worse. Now, other animals live chiefly a life of mere nature, and in very few things according to custom; but man lives according to reason also, with which he alone is endowed; wherefore he ought to make all these accord with each other: for if they are persuaded that it is best to follow some other way, men oftentimes act contrary to nature and custom. . . .

Document Set 4.1 References

A. Plato Insists That Only Justice and Virtue Can Give a Satisfying Human Existence
Plato, *Republic,* trans. Benjamin Jowett, *Dialogues of Plato* (Oxford: Clarendon Press, 1892), 3:324–328.

B. Aristotle Sums Up the Good Life in a Well-Ordered Polis
Aristotle, *Politics* 7:3, 13, trans. J. E. C. Welldon (London: Macmillan, 1883), 256–259.

DOCUMENT SET 4.2
Hellenistic Thinkers

As Chapter 4 of *The Challenge of the West* explains, the Hellenistic Age was a period of extensive cultural interaction throughout the ancient Mediterranean and Persian worlds, combined with a restless quest for personal security in a competitive world. Hellenistic intellectual life, with its prominent philosophical-religious schools promising the road to security, must be assessed in its larger social and cultural context. Similarly, Hellenistic science was primarily abstract and theoretical, although capable of considerable ingenuity.

Document A is a surviving fragment of the teachings of Zeno of Citium (342–270 B.C.), the founder of the Stoic school. Probably born in Phoenicia, he settled in Athens and taught that although virtue is absolutely good, the material world can be only relatively good; hence the virtuous sage can rise above it. Notice his insistence on the universality of natural law.

Document B shows the sophistication of Hellenistic science at Alexandria in Egypt. Here the mathematician Eratosthenes (276–194 B.C.) computes the circumference of the globe with an accuracy surpassed only in the nineteenth century. Another seemingly prophetic Hellenistic scientist was the Alexandrian astronomer Aristarchus of Samos (fl. 280–264 B.C.), who—like Copernicus almost 1,800 years later—challenged "common-sense" perceptions by insisting that the earth revolves around the sun. A report of his unorthodox idea (by the famous engineer Archimedes), which appears as Document C, also suggests why Aristarchus's hypothesis was rejected by his contemporaries. Why should it be that Aristarchus's idea seemed to frighten other Greeks, and hence was allowed to drop into obscurity?

With Document D we return to the world of the Hellenistic philosophers, summing up the "principal doctrines" of Epicurus (341–270 B.C.). An enormously successful and influential teacher at Athens, Epicurus devised a philosophy whose principal aim was the securing of pleasure and the avoidance of pain and fear; study the summary of his teachings to see how he suggested that his followers attain these seemingly hedonistic goals (were they so in practice?). Document E is a fragment from the first-century A.D. Hellenistic philosopher Epictetus that conveys well the Stoic ideal of enduring and transcending suffering, armed with the inner fortitude of one's faith in justice and virtue.

All the philosophers, scholars, scientists, and speculators of the Hellenistic world whose works have survived were male. That women could under certain circumstances also follow an intellectual bent and hold their own in a discussion of the fashionable ideas of the era is apparent from Document F, an extract from the ancient biographer Diogenes Laertius's *Lives and Opinions of Eminent Philosophers*. The woman he describes, Hipparchia, was the sister of a philosopher of the austere Cynic school.

A. Zeno Preaches on Universal Truth and Justice: A Stoic Fragment

The element of all the things which exist is Fire, and the origins of this Fire are Stuff and God. Both of these are bodily substances: God the active substance, and Stuff the passive substance. At certain destined periods of time the whole universe is turned to fire; then again it is once more constituted an ordered manifold world. But the primal fire subsists in it like a kind of seminal fluid, containing in itself the formulas and causes of all the things which have been and are and shall be; the concatenation and sequence of these things is Destiny or Understanding or Truth, an inevitable and ineluctable Law of things. Thus the whole universe is governed excellently well, like a city-state in which Law reigns supreme.

B. Eratosthenes Computes the Earth's Circumference

Under the same meridian, he [Eratosthenes] says, lie Syene and Alexandria. Since then the greatest (lines) in the universe are the meridians, the spherical lines lying under them on the earth must necessarily be the greatest. Consequently whatever extent the theory (of Eratosthenes) will demonstrate for the spherical line running through Syene and Alexandria, so extensive also will be the greatest spherical line of the earth. He then says: And it is so, that Syene lies under the summer solstice. Whenever therefore the sun, having passed into Cancer and, effecting the summer solstice, is precisely at the zenith point of the sky, the gnomon of the sundial necessarily becomes shadowless, in accordance with the exact perpendicular of the sun standing overhead; and it is reasonable that this should happen to the extent of three hundred stadia in diameter. At Alexandria at the same hour the gnomons of the sun-dials cast a shadow, since this city lies more to the north than Syene. Inasmuch as these cities lie under the same meridian and the greatest spherical line, if we draw the arc from the apex of the shadow of the sun-dial to the base itself of the sun-dial which is in Alexandria, this arc will prove a segment of the greatest spherical line in the concave sun-dial, since the concave surface of the sun-dial lies under the largest spherical line. If consequently we were to conceive straight lines extended through the earth from each of the sun-dials, they will meet at the centre of the earth. Since then the sun-dial at Syene lies perpendicularly under the sun, if we conceive in addition a straight line drawn from the sun to the apex of the style of the sun-dial, then the line drawn from the sun to the centre of the earth will prove *one* straight line. If then we conceive another straight line from the apex of the shadow of the gnomon drawn up to the sun from the concave dial in Alexandria, this one and the aforesaid straight line will prove to be parallel, passing from different parts of the sun to different parts of the earth. Into these (lines), which are parallel, the line drawn from the centre of the earth to the dial at Alexandria falls as a straight line, so as to render the alternate angles equal. Of these (angles) the one is at the centre of the earth through the meeting of the straight lines which were drawn from the apex of its shadow. The other angle results through the meeting of (the lines drawn) from the apex of the dial at Alexandria and the line drawn upward from the apex of its shadow to the sun through the contact with it. Upon this is constructed the circular line which has been circumscribed from the apex of the shadow of the gnomon to its base; and upon that at the centre of the earth the (line) which passes from Syene to Alexandria. Similar then are the arcs to each other, namely, those based on equal angles. The relation therefore which the line in the concave has to its own circle is the same as the relation of the line drawn from Syene to Alexandria. The line in the concave is to be 1/50 of its own circle; therefore necessarily also the distance from Syene to Alexandria must be 1/50 of the largest circle of earth; and this is (a distance) of 5,000 stadia. The whole circle therefore amounts to 250,000 stadia.

Such is the computation of Eratosthenes.

C. Aristarchus Proposes a Heliocentric Theory of the Cosmos

The term world, as it is defined by most astronomers, is here designed to signify a sphere of the heavens, whose center coincides with the center of the earth, and whose semi-diameter is the distance from the center of the earth to the center of the sun. This definition of the term world, as given in the writings of other astronomers, Aristarchus of Samos refutes, and has given it a far more extensive signification; for according to his hypothesis, neither the fixed stars nor the sun are subject to any motion; but the earth annually revolves round the sun in the circumference of a circle, in the centre of which the sun remains fixed. The sphere of the fixed stars, too, whose center he supposes to coincide with the sun's, is of such immense magnitude that the circle, in whose periphery the earth is supposed to revolve round the sun, bears no greater proportion to the distance of the fixed stars than the center of a sphere does to its superficies.

D. Epicurus: A Summary of His "Principal Doctrines"

1. The blessed and immortal nature knows no trouble itself nor causes trouble to any other, so that it is never constrained by anger or favour. For all such things exist only in the weak.
2. Death is nothing to us: for that which is dissolved is without sensation; and that which lacks sensation is nothing to us. . . .
4. Pain does not last continuously in the flesh, but the acutest pain is there for a very short time, and even that which just exceeds the pleasure in the flesh does not continue for many days at once. But chronic illnesses permit a predominance of pleasure over pain in the flesh.
5. It is not possible to live pleasantly without living prudently and honourably and justly, nor again to live a life or prudence, honour, and justice without living pleasantly. And the man who does not possess the pleasant life, is not living prudently and honourably and justly, and the man who does not possess the virtuous life, cannot possibly live pleasantly. . . .
7. Some men wished to become famous and conspicuous, thinking that they would thus win for themselves safety from other men. Wherefore if the life of such men is safe, they have obtained the good which nature craves; but if it is not safe, they do not possess that for which they strove at first by the instinct of nature.
8. No pleasure is a bad thing in itself: but the means which produce some pleasures bring with them disturbances many times greater than the pleasures. . . .
10. If the things that produce the pleasures of profligates could dispel the fears of the mind about the phenomena of the sky and death and its pains, and

also teach the limits of desires and of pains, we should never have cause to blame them: for they would be filling themselves full with pleasures from every source and never have pain of body or mind, which is the evil of life. . . .

12.   A man cannot dispel his fear about the most important matters if he does not know what is the nature of the universe but suspects the truth of some mythical story. So that without natural science it is not possible to attain our pleasures unalloyed. . . .

15.   The wealth demanded by nature is both limited and easily procured; that demanded by idle imaginings stretches on to infinity. . . .

17.   The just man is most free from trouble, the unjust most full of trouble. . . .

21.   He who has learned the limits of life knows that that which removes the pain due to want and makes the whole of life complete is easy to obtain; so that there is no need of actions which involve competition. . . .

27.   Of all the things which wisdom acquires to produce the blessedness of the complete life, far the greatest is the possession of friendship. . . .

31.   The justice which arises from nature is a pledge of mutual advantage to restrain men from harming one another and save them from being harmed. . . .

33.   Justice never is anything in itself, but in the dealings of men with one another in any place whatever and at any time it is a kind of compact not to harm or be harmed. . . .

E. Epictetus Points the Way to the Good Life

When you are going in to any great personage, remember that another also from above sees what is going on, and that you ought to please him above all others. He then who sees from above asks you: In the schools what used you to say about exile, and bonds, and death, and disgrace? I used to say that they are things indifferent (neither good nor bad). What then do you say of them now? Are they changed at all? No. Are you changed then? No. Tell me then what things are indifferent? The things which are independent of the will. Tell me, also, what follows from this. The things which are independent of the will are nothing to me. Tell me also about the Good; what did you hold it to be? A will such as we ought to have and also a right use of things about us. And our aim, what is it? To follow thee. Do you say this now also? I say the same now also.

Then go in to the great personage boldly and

remember these things; and you will see what a youth is who has studied these things when he is among men who have not studied them. . . .

If the things are true which are said by the philosophers about the kinship between God and man, what else remains for men to do than what Socrates did? Never say, in reply to the question, To what country do you belong? that you are an Athenian, or a Corinthian, but that you are a citizen of the world. . . . He who has observed with intelligence the administration of the world, and has learned that the greatest and the supreme and the most comprehensive community is that which is composed of men and God, . . . why should not such a man call himself a citizen of the world, why not a son of God, and why should he be afraid of anything which happens among men? Is kinship with the emperor or with any other of the powerful in Rome sufficient to enable us to live in safety, and above contempt and without any fear at all? But to have God for your maker, and father, and guardian, shall not this release us from our sorrows and fears?

F. An Intellectual Woman

Hipparchia, the sister of Metrocles, was charmed along with others by the doctrines of this school. She and Metrocles were natives of Maroneia. She fell in love with the doctrines and the manners of Crates, and could not be diverted from her regard for him either by the wealth or the high birth or the personal beauty of any of her suitors; but Crates was everything to her. She threatened her parents to make away with herself, if she were not given in marriage to him. When entreated by her parents to dissuade her from this resolution, Crates did all he could; and at last, as he could not persuade her, he arose and placing all his furniture before her, he said: "This is the bridegroom whom you are choosing, and this is the whole of his property. Consider these facts; for it will not be possible for you to become his partner, if you do not apply yourself to the same studies and conform to the same habits as he does." The girl chose him; and assuming the same dress as he wore, went with him as her husband, and appeared with him in public everywhere, and went to all entertainments in his company.

Once when she went to sup at the house of Lysimachus, she attacked Theodorus, who was surnamed the Atheist. To him she proposed the following sophism: "What Theodorus could not be called wrong for doing, that same thing Hipparchia could not be called wrong for doing. But Theodorus does no wrong when he beats himself; therefore

Hipparchia does no wrong when she beats Theodorus." He made no reply to what she said, but only pulled her gown. Hipparchia was neither offended nor ashamed, as many a woman would have been; but when he said to her:—

> Who is the woman who has left the shuttle
> So near the warp? [Euripides]

She replied: "I, Theodorus, am the person; but do I seem to you to have come to a wrong decision, if I devote that time to philosophy which otherwise I should have spent at the loom?" These and many other sayings are reported of this female philosopher.

Document Set 4.2 References

A. Zeno Preaches on Universal Truth and Justice: A Stoic Fragment
   C. K. Barrett, ed., *The New Testament Background* (London: S. P. C. K., 1956), 62.
B. Eratosthenes Computes the Earth's Circumference
   Cleomedes, *Concerning the Circular Motion of the Heavenly Bodies,* in G. W. Botsford and E. G. Sihler, eds., *Hellenic Civilization* (New York: Columbia University Press, 1915), 636–637.
C. Aristarchus Proposes a Heliocentric Theory of the Cosmos
   Botsford and Sihler, 640.
D. Epicurus: A Summary of His "Principal Doctrines"
   Whitney H. Oates, ed., *The Stoic and Epicurean Philosophers* (New York: Modern Library, 1940), 35–39.
E. Epictetus Points the Way to the Good Life
   James Harvey Robinson, ed., *Readings in European History* (Boston: Ginn, 1904), 1:15–17.
F. An Intellectual Woman
   Botsford and Sihler, 665.

DOCUMENT SET 4.3
Greek Cities After the Peloponnesian War

Democracy did not disappear from the Greek city-states of the Hellenistic world—it remained important in Athens, for example, well into the Roman era—but this was not an age propitious to popular rule. Indeed, the most characteristic form of government was absolute, often bureaucratic, monarchy, which owed much to the traditions of ancient kingship in Egypt, Persia, and Mesopotamia.

Document A, another extract from Aristotle's *Politics,* attests to the declining prestige of democracy by the fourth century B.C.; compare Aristotle's attitude with Pericles' *Funeral Oration* (Set 3.1, Document B). Notice one of Aristotle's criticisms of democratic city-states—that they incite class hatred or redistribute income from rich to poor—and compare this to Document B, an extract from the geographer Strabo's description of the oligarchic commercial city of Rhodes. Why do you suppose that an oligarchy would continue to maintain something of a welfare state? What it meant to be on the dole in fourth-century Athens can be learned from Document C, another of Lysias's speeches, this time purporting to be an impoverished cripple's claim for receiving his tiny daily allotment.

In Document D we have the complaint of a rich Athenian (once again Lysias supplies the words) about the heavy burden he bears in the form of liturgies—forced expenditures for the public good imposed by the polis. Document E presents still another extract from Lysias: this time a speech pleading for the regulation of Athens's grain trade by the polis in order to bypass the supposedly excessive speculative profits earned by the *metics* (resident aliens) who normally dealt in this commodity.

After reading these documents, write a brief analysis of social welfare policy in the late classical polis.

A. Aristotle Deplores Democracies' Tendency to Court the Poor, Spend on Social Welfare, and Threaten the Rich

It is also the business of the legislator, and all those who would establish a government of this sort, not to make it too great a work or too perfect, but to aim only at rendering it stable. For, let a state be constituted ever so badly, there is no difficulty in its con-

tinuing for two or three days: they should therefore endeavour to procure its safety by all those ways which we have described in assigning the causes of the preservation and destruction of governments; avoiding what is hurtful, and framing such laws, both written and unwritten, as shall contain those things which chiefly tend to the preservation of the state; and they should not suppose that any thing is useful either for a democratic or an oligarchic form of government, which contributes to make it more purely so, but what will contribute to its duration. But our demagogues at present, to flatter the people, occasion frequent confiscations in the courts. For which reason those who have the welfare of the state really at heart should act on the opposite side, and enact a law to prevent forfeitures from being divided amongst the people or paid into the treasury, but to have them set apart for sacred uses. For those who are of a bad disposition would not then be the less cautious, as their punishment would be the same; and the community would not be so ready to condemn those on whom they sit in judgment, when they are about to get nothing by it. They should also take care that the causes which are brought before the public should be as few as possible, and punish with the utmost severity those who bring an action against any one without cause; for it is not the commons, but the nobles, whom they are wont to prosecute. But in all things the citizens of the same state ought to be affectionate to each other, or at the least not to treat those who have the chief power in it as their enemies. Now, as the democracies which have been lately established are very numerous, and it is difficult to get the common people to attend the public assemblies unless they are paid for it, this is against the interest of the nobles, when there is not a sufficient public revenue. For the deficiencies must be necessarily made up by taxes, confiscations, and fines imposed by corrupt courts of justice: things which have already destroyed many democracies. Whenever, then, the revenues of the state are small, there should be but few public assemblies; and the courts of justice should have extensive jurisdiction, but continue sitting a few days only; for by this means the rich will not fear the expense, although they receive nothing for their attendance, though the poor do; and judgment also will be given much better; for the rich will not choose to be long absent from their own affairs, but will willingly be so for a short time. And, when there are sufficient revenues, a different conduct ought to be pursued from what the demagogues at present follow; for now they divide the surplus of the public money amongst the poor; these receive it, and again want the same supply; while the giving such help to the poor is like pouring water into a sieve. But the true patriot in a democracy ought to take care that the majority are not too poor, for this is the cause of rapacity in that government. He should endeavour, therefore, that they may enjoy a lasting plenty; and as this also is advantageous to the rich, what can be saved out of the public money should be put by, and then divided at once among the poor, if possible, in such a quantity as may enable every one of them to purchase a little field; or, if that cannot be done, at least to give each of them enough to procure the implements of trade and husbandry; and if there is not enough for all to receive so much at once, then to divide it according to tribes, or any other allotment. In the mean time, let the rich pay them for the necessary attendance, and cease from lavishing them on useless shows. And something like this was the manner in which they manage at Carthage, and so preserve the affections of the people; for, by continually sending some of their community into colonies, they procure plenty. It is also worthy of a sensible and generous nobility, to divide the poor amongst them, and to induce them to work by supplying them with what is necessary; or to imitate the conduct of the people at Tarentum: for by permitting the poor to partake in common of every thing which is needful for them, they gain the affections of the commonality. They have also two different ways of electing their magistrates; for some are chosen by vote, others by lot; by the last, that the people at large may have some share in the administration; by the former, that the state may be well governed. It is also possible to accomplish the same thing, if of the same magistrates some are chosen by vote, and others by lot. And thus much for the manner in which democracies ought to be established.

B. The Oligarchy at Rhodes Provides for the Poor

Although their form of government is not democratic, the Rhodians are attentive to the welfare of the people, and exert themselves to support the masses of the poor. The people receive allowances of grain and the rich support the needy in accordance with an ancient usage. The state has public offices, whose object is to procure and distribute provisions, that the poor may obtain subsistence, and the city may not suffer for want of persons to serve her especially in manning her fleets.

C. On the Dole: An Athenian Welfare-Seeker Answers His Critics

My father left me nothing, and I ceased to support my mother only three years ago when she died, and my children are not yet old enough to support me. I have a trade which brings me scant returns, which I now carry on with great difficulty, and am unable to find any one to take it off my hands. I have no income besides this (allowance), and if you take it from me, I shall run the risk of falling into the direst straits. . . . It would be unreasonable, Council, if when my misfortune was single I should receive this dole but should be deprived of it when old age and diseases and their attendant evils have been added to my lot. . . .

(My adversary) asserts that I am insolent and violent and possessed of an excessively unbridled temper, as though he could only speak the truth if he used terrible words, and could not do so if he used only mild words and abstained from exaggeration. But I fancy, Council, that you know well how to distinguish between men whose part it is to be insolent and men to whom such a thing is unbecoming. It is not reasonable that the poor and the desperately needy should be insolent; that rather falls to the lot of those who possess far more than a competence; nor the disabled in body but those rather who trust to their physical strength; nor those who have far advanced in age, but the young and the possessors of youthful dispositions. For the wealthy with their money purchase exemption from the danger of punishment, whereas the poor are forced to sobriety by their present need. . . .

Do not because of this man (my accuser) deprive me of the only part or lot in my country that fortune has granted me. . . . For since, Council, the deity (Daimon) has debarred us from the highest offices, the state has voted us this money, considering that the chances of good and ill are common to all. How then should I not be the most wretched of all men, if through my misfortune I should be deprived of the noblest and greatest things, and then through my accuser should lose what the state has bestowed in its forethought for men who are situated as I am?

D. A Rich Athenian Pays His Liturgies

I was appointed choregos for tragedies and spent thirty minas; two months later, at the Thargelia, I was victorious with a men's chorus at a cost of two thousand drachmae. In the archonship of Glaucippus [410–409] I spent eight hundred drachmae on pyrrhic dancers at the Great Panathenaea; in the same archonship I was victorious with a men's chorus at the Dionysia, and my expenditure including the dedication of the tripod was five thousand drachmae. In the archonship of Diocles [409–408] I spent three hundred drachmae on a cyclic chorus at the Lesser Panathenaea. In the meantime I was trierarch for seven years, and spent six talents. . . . Of all these sums which I have listed, if I had been prepared to perform liturgies simply according to what is written in the law, I should not have spent a quarter.

E. Lysias Pleads for State Regulation of the Grain Trade

. . . First, stand up and tell me, are you a metic? "Yes." And are you a metic with the expectation of obeying the laws of the commonwealth, or of doing what you like? "Of obeying." Do you deserve anything else but death, if you have done anything contrary to the laws—any act on which the death-penalty is set? "I do not." Answer me then, whether you admit having bought up more grain than fifty phormi, which the law allows? "I bought it up under orders of the officials."

If then he demonstrates, gentlemen of the jury, that a statute exists, which orders the grain dealers to buy up the grain in case the officials order them to do so, acquit him; but it not, it is just that you should find him guilty. For we presented to you the statute which prohibits anyone in the commonwealth from buying up more grain than fifty phormi.

This charge then, gentlemen of the jury, ought to be sufficient, since this man admits that he bought it up, but the law appears as prohibiting that, and you have sworn to give your verdict according to the laws. It is necessary, however, to speak more at length about them. When these men shifted the blame upon the grain inspectors, we called upon the latter and interrogated them. Two of them said they knew nothing of the matter, but Anytus explained that last winter when grain was high, and when these men bid up the price against one another, and fought among themselves, he had advised them to cease wrangling, thinking it advantageous to you who bought from them, that they should make their purchases at as fair a figure as possible: for it was necessary for them to sell at a rise of no more than one obol. . . .

It seems outrageous to me, if whenever a tax is to be paid, of which all are bound to have knowledge, they are unwilling but allege poverty as a pretext, yet in a matter in which death is set as a penalty and it is profitable for them to escape notice, they say they committed these illegal acts from devotion to you. Still you all know that it behooves these men least of all to make such statements. For their advantage is the opposite to that of others: their gains are largest when upon the arrival of some bad news they sell their grain to the community at a high figure. So gladly therefore do they see your troubles that some of them they ascertain earlier than others, and some they invent themselves, either that the ships in the Black Sea have perished, or while sailing out were captured by the Lacedæmonians, or that the harbors are closed, or that the truce is about to be cancelled. . . .

Remember, gentlemen of the jury, that you have condemned to death many men already who were subject to this charge and furnished witnesses, deeming more reliable the statements of the accusers. Why would it not be strange, if while sitting in judgment on the same misdemeanors you are eager to impose penalty on those who make denial? In fact, gentlemen of the jury, I think it is clear to all that the contests about such things happen to be of the widest concern in common to every one in the community, so that they are going to discover what opinion you entertain about them, thinking, if you condemn them to death, the others will be more seemly; but if you let them go scotfree, you will have voted them ample immunity to do what they like.

But it is necessary, gentlemen of the jury, to chastise them not only for the sake of the past, but also as an example for the future; for as things now are, they will be hardly endurable. And consider that in consequence of this vocation very many already have stood trial for their life; and so great are the emoluments which they derive from it that they prefer to risk their life every day rather than cease to draw from you unjust profits. And indeed not even if they entreat you and supplicate, would you justly pity them, but much rather the citizens who perished on account of their wickedness, and the importers against whom they made a combination. The importers you will gratify and cheer, if you impose a penalty on the dealers. Otherwise what opinion do you think they will have, when they learn that you acquitted the retailers who admitted plotting against the skippers?

I do not know what I should say further; for concerning other evildoers one must learn from the prosecutors at the time of trial, but the wickedness of these men you all know. If then you shall condemn them, you will act justly and you will buy grain cheaper; otherwise, dearer.

Document Set 4.3 References

A. Aristotle Deplores Democracies' Tendency to Court the Poor, Spend on Social Welfare, and Threaten the Rich
  Aristotle, *Politics* 6:5, trans. J. E. C. Welldon (London: Macmillan, 1883), 221–224.

B. The Oligarchy at Rhodes Provides for the Poor
  G. W. Botsford and E. G. Sihler, eds., *Hellenic Civilization* (New York: Columbia University Press, 1915), 686.

C. On the Dole: An Athenian Welfare-Seeker Answers His Critics
  Botsford and Sihler, 424–425.

D. A Rich Athenian Pays His Liturgies
  P. J. Rhodes, ed., *The Greek City-States: A Source Book* (Norman: University of Oklahoma Press, 1986), 134.

E. Lysias Pleads for State Regulation of the Grain Trade
  Botsford and Sihler, 426–430.

Philip and Alexander

The documents of this set all offer perspectives on the meteoric rise of the empire of Philip of Macedonia (*359–336 B.C.) and his world-conquering son Alexander (*336–323 B.C.)

In Document A, the Athenian orator Isocrates (436–338 B.C.) appeals to Philip to unify the Greeks and attack Persia. Did such a policy necessarily compromise the autonomy of the polis, to which Isocrates also claimed to be devoted?

Alexander could be by turns brutal, extravagant, and lenient; compare the policies he followed and the assessments of his personality in Documents B–E. The two contemporary writers quoted here (Ephippus of Olynthus, in C, and Diodorus of Sicily, in E), were both strongly biased against Alexander. Make use of *The Challenge of the West*'s account of Alexander's career in considering your own verdict on this extraordinary man.

A. Isocrates Proposes That Philip Become the Leader of the Greeks

For these reasons I think that it is to your interest, when everyone else is so cowardly minded, to put yourself at the head of the expedition against the King. And while it is the duty of the others, who are descendants of Heracles, and are united by polity and laws, to love *that* state in which they happen to dwell, it behoves you, as one who has been released from individual obligations, to look upon the whole of Hellas as your fatherland, in the same manner as the father of your race, and to be ready to face danger on its behalf as readily as on behalf of those who are your especial care.

Perhaps some of those who are fit to do nothing else may venture to blame me, because I have chosen to exhort you to undertake the campaign against the barbarians and the care of all the Hellenes, and have passed over my own city. Now, if I were undertaking to address myself on these points to others rather than to my own native city, which has thrice freed Hellas, twice from the barbarians, and once from the rule of Lacedæmon, I would allow that I was wrong; but, as it is, it will be seen that I have exhorted Athens before all other cities, with the greatest earnestness of which I was capable, to undertake the task, but, when

I perceived that she thought less of what I said than of those who rave upon the platform, I left her alone, but, notwithstanding, did not abandon my efforts. Wherefore all might fitly praise me because, as far as the powers I possess permitted me, I have persistently waged war against the barbarians, accused those who did not hold the same opinion as myself, and endeavoured to induce those, whom I hope will be best able to do so, to render some service to the Hellenes, and to deprive the barbarians of their present prosperity. For this reason I now address my words to you, well aware that many will be jealous of them when uttered by me, but that all will rejoice alike at the same undertakings when accomplished by you. For, although no one has taken part in what I have proposed, everyone will think that he is entitled to a share in the advantages that will result from it.

B. Alexander Warns the Conquered People of Chios

From Alexander to the demus of the Chians. The exiles from Chios are to return, all of them, and the form of government of Chios is to be a democracy. Law-givers are to be chosen who shall write the laws and set them in order in such a way that nothing in them shall oppose the democracy or the return of the exiles. When arranged or written the laws are to be referred to Alexander.

The Chians are to furnish twenty triremes, with a full complement for them, and these are to sail so long as the rest of the naval force of the Hellenes shall sail with us.

Of those who betrayed the city to the barbarians, as many as may already have escaped, are to be exiled from all the cities which have shared in the peace, and they are to be considered as outlaws according to the decree of the Hellenes. As many as may be captured, are to be brought before the Council of the Hellenes for judgment.

If any difficulty arises between the restored exiles and those in the city, they are to receive judgment in this matter in our presence. Until the Chians shall be reconciled, a garrison is to be stationed among them from Alexander, the king, as many as may be necessary. And the Chians shall support this garrison.

C. Ephippus of Olynthus's Unflattering Recollections of Alexander

Concerning the luxury of Alexander the Great, Ephippus of Olynthus, in his treatise *On the Burial of Alexander and Hephaestion,* relates that he had in his park a golden throne and couches with silver feet, on which he used to sit while transacting business with his companions. Nicobule says, moreover, that while he was at supper all the dancers and athletes sought to amuse the king. At his very last banquet, Alexander, remembering an episode in the *Andromeda* of Euripides, recited it in a declamatory manner, and then drank a cup of unmixed wine with great zest, and compelled all the rest to do the same. Ephippus tells us, too, that Alexander used to wear at his entertainments even the sacred vestments. Sometimes he would put on the purple robe, cloven sandals, and horns of Ammon, as if he had been the god. Sometimes he would imitate Artemis, whose dress he often wore while driving in his chariot; at the same time he had on a Persian robe, which displayed above his shoulders the bow and javelin of the goddess. At times also he would appear in the guise of Hermes; at other times, and in fact nearly every day, he would wear a purple cloak, a chiton shot with white, and a cap with a royal diadem attached. When too he was in private with his friends he wore the sandals of Hermes, with the petasus on his head and the caduceus in hand. Often however he wore a lion's skin and carried a club like Heracles. . . .

Alexander used also to have the floor sprinkled with exquisite perfumes and with fragrant wine; and myrrh and other kinds of incense were burned before him, while all the bystanders kept silence or spoke words only of good omen because of fear. For he was an extremely violent man with no regard for human life, and gave the impression of a man of choleric temperament. . . .

D. Alexander Rules in Egypt by Proxy

When Cleomenes of Alexandria was satrap of Egypt and a great famine raged in other countries, but only a moderate one in Egypt, Cleomenes put a stop to the export of grain. The nomarchs asserted that they were unable to pay the tribute because they could not export the grain. Cleomenes therefore gave them the right to export, but placed a high price upon the grain, so that he received a high revenue, although little grain was exported, and put an end to the excuses of the nomarchs.

When Cleomenes was travelling by boat through the nome in which the crocodile is a god, one of his slaves was seized by a crocodile. Summoning the priests he stated that a wrong had been done him and that he wished to punish the crocodiles. So he gave orders to hunt them. In order that their god might not be subjected to insult the priests brought together all the money that they could collect and gave it to him, and so put an end to the affair.

When King Alexander bade Cleomenes build a city near Pharos and locate there the market which had formerly been at the Canopic mouth of the Nile, Cleomenes sailed down the river to Canopus and went to the priests and the wealthy citizens and said that he had come there in order to settle them elsewhere. The priests and inhabitants of Canopus brought money and gave it to him in order to induce him to leave the market in their district. He took the money and sailed away. Later, when he was quite ready to begin the building, he sailed down again and demanded an immense sum from them, saying that it was a great advantage to him to have the market at the other place rather than at Canopus. When they said that they could not possibly pay the money, he took them away as colonists.

When grain was selling in the country at ten drachmas he summoned those engaged in the grain business and asked them at what price they were willing to sell to him. they responded that they would sell it at a lower price than that at which they sold to the retailers. He ordered them to deliver it to him at the same price at which they sold to the others. He then fixed the price of grain at thirty-two drachmas and disposed of it at that price.

He called the priests to him and said that the expenditure upon the temples throughout the country was very great, and that the number of temples and priests must therefore be decreased. The priests individually and in common gave him the sacred treasures, thinking that Cleomenes was in truth about to decrease the number and each one wishing that his own temple should be left and he himself remain its priest.

E. Alexander Dies, Leaving His Empire "To the Strongest"

Just when it seemed that he was at the peak of his power and good fortune, Fate cut off the time allowed him by nature to remain alive. Straightway heaven also began to foretell his death, and many strange portents and signs occurred. . . . [Details follow.]

He recalled the prediction of the Chaldaeans and was angry with the philosophers who had persuaded him to enter Babylon. He was impressed anew with the skill of the Chaldaeans and their insight, and generally railed at those who used specious reasoning to argue away the power of Fate.

A little while later heaven sent him a second portent about his kingship. He had conceived the desire to see the great swamp of Babylonia and set sail with his friends in a number of skiffs. For some days his boat became separated from the others and he was lost and alone, fearing that he might never get out alive. As his craft was proceeding through a narrow channel where the reeds grew thickly and overhung the water, his diadem was caught and lifted from his head by one of them and then dropped into the swamp. One of the oarsmen swam after it and, wishing to return it safely, placed it on his head and so swam back to the boat. After three days and nights of wandering, Alexander found his way to safety just as he had again put on his diadem when this seemed beyond hope. Again he turned to the soothsayers for the meaning of all this.

They bade him sacrifice to the gods on a grand scale and with all speed, but he was then called away by Medius, the Thessalian, one of his Friends, to take part in a comus. There he drank much unmixed wine in commemoration of the death of Heracles, and finally, filling a huge beaker, downed it at a gulp. Instantly he shrieked aloud as if smitten by a violent blow and was conducted by his Friends, who led him by the hand back to his apartments. His chamberlains put him to bed and attended him closely, but the pain increased and the physicians were summoned. No one was able to do anything helpful and Alexander continued in great discomfort and acute suffering. When he, at length, despaired of life, he took off his ring and handed it to Perdiccas. His Friends asked: "To whom do you leave the kingdom?" and he replied: "To the strongest." He added, and these were his last words, that all of his leading Friends would stage a vast contest in honour of his funeral. This was how he died after a reign of twelve years and seven months. He accomplished greater deeds than any, not only of the kings who had lived before him but also of those who were to come later down to our time.

Document Set 4.4 References

A. Isocrates Proposes That Philip Become the Leader of the Greeks
Isocrates, *Philippus* 5:127–131, in G. W. Botsford and E. G. Sihler, eds., *Hellenic Civilization* (New York: Columbia University Press, 1915), 407–420.
B. Alexander Warns the Conquered People of Chios
Botsford and Sihler, 568–569.
C. Ephippus of Olynthus's Unflattering Recollections of Alexander
Botsford and Sihler, 682–683.
D. Alexander Rules in Egypt by Proxy
Botsford and Sihler, 584–585.
E. Alexander Dies, Leaving His Empire "To the Strongest"
Diodorus of Sicily, *Bibliotheca Historica* 17:115.5–117.5, trans. C. H. Oldfather, Loeb Classical Library (Cambridge, Mass.: Harvard University Press, 1963).

DOCUMENT SET 4.5
Hellenistic Kings

We have already seen (Set 4.4, Document D) how Alexander administered his conquered kingdom of Egypt as an absentee monarch. The documents in Set 4.5 focus on the mechanism of rule in the Hellenistic monarchies.

In Ptolemaic Egypt, the arable land was divided into great estates (called land gifts) parceled out to royal favorites, who sublet the estates but left ultimate jurisdiction over the peasants to the state. Document A shows a peasant appealing (nominally to the king but in fact to the local state official, the *strategus*) against another peasant. Document B conveys the rather hyperbolic praise of Ptolemy V (*205–280 B.C.) proclaimed by priests of the traditional Egyptian religion. How much of the ancient Egyptian tradition do you perceive in this document? How much evidence of the royal land monopoly and extensive bureaucracy of the Ptolemaic kings do you detect? (This is the document, incidentally, that is engraved on the famous Rosetta Stone; by comparing the Greek and Egyptian texts, Jean Champollion [1790–1831] first deciphered ancient Egyptian).

Documents C and D both refer to the Seleucid king Antiochus Soter ("the Savior," *280–260 B.C.): the first advertising his glory and the second being a perhaps more realistic Babylonian account of his reign. Compare the two documents, and set them in the broader context of Hellenistic society that you are evolving through your study.

A. A Farmer in Ptolemaic Egypt Petitions the King for Justice

To King Ptolemy, greeting, from Idomeneus, one of the cultivators upon the Land Gift of Chrysermus, from the village Camenoë. I am being wronged by Petobastis, son of Taos, and Horus, son of Keleësis, belonging to the same village. For I lease from the Gift of Chrysermus 2 arouræ and sowed my plot in vetches. But the aforesaid Petobastis and Horus flooded my seed so that my vetch crop was spoiled and I cannot furnish the payments resting upon the plot. I beg of you, therefore, O King, if it seem good to you, to order Diophanes the strategus to write to Hephaetion the epistates to send Petobastis and Horus, who did the flooding, to Crocodilopolis, so that I may accuse them in the court of Diophanes, and, if I prove that they have flooded my seed, compel them to take over my seed land and pay the rental,

and give to me in place of what they have flooded an equal share of the land which they cultivate. In that case by having recourse to you, O King, I shall be able to pay my rentals to Chrysermus and shall have met with kindness from you.

I wish you good fortune.

To Hephaestion. Above all try to reconcile them. If not, send them to us upon the 10th of Choiax that the case may be decided before the proper tribunal.

B. Egyptian Priests Honor Ptolemy V: The Rosetta Stone Text

In the reign of the young one, who has received royalty from his father, the lord of crowns, whose glory is great, who established Egypt and is pious towards the gods, the conqueror of his enemies, who restored the life of men, the lord of the Thirty-Year festivals, like Hephaestus (i.e. Ptah) the Great, a king like the Sun (= Rā), the great king of the upper and lower regions, son of the Father-Loving Gods, approved by Hephaestus, to whom the Sun granted victory, the living image of Zeus, (= Amun) son of the Sun, Ptolemy the everliving, beloved of Ptah, . . . the chief priests, the prophets, those who enter the holy of holies for the robing of the gods . . . declared: since King Ptolemy the everliving, beloved of Ptah, God Manifest and Beneficent, born of King Ptolemy and Queen Arsinoe, Father-Loving Gods, has conferred many benefits on the temples and those who dwell in them and on all the subjects in his kingdom, being a god born of a god and goddess—just as Horus son of Isis and Osiris, who avenged his father Osiris—and being benevolently disposed towards the gods, has dedicated to the temples revenues in money and corn, and has sustained many expenses to bring Egypt to a state of prosperity and to establish the temples, and has given away freely from his own means, and of the revenues and dues he receives from Egypt some he has completely remitted and others he has reduced, so that the people and all others might enjoy prosperity during his reign, and he has remitted the debts to the crown which were owed by the people in Egypt and those in the rest of his kingdom, which were considerable, and he has freed those who were in the prisons and who were under accusation for a long time from the charges against them; and he has ordered that the revenues of the temples and the grants which are made to them annually in corn and money, and also the proper quota (*apomoira*) which is assigned to the gods from vineyards and gardens and the other possessions of the gods, should remain as they were in his father's time; and with regard to the priests he has ordered that they should pay no more as their fee for consecration than they were required to pay under his father and up to the first year (sc. of Ptolemy V's reign); and he has released the members of the priestly class from the annual obligation to sail down the river (i.e. the Nile) to Alexandria; and he has ordered that men shall no longer be pressganged for the navy, and has remitted two-thirds of the tax on byssus cloth paid by the temples to the royal treasury, and has restored to order whatever things were neglected in former times, taking care that the customary celebrations should be offered to the gods as is fitting; and he has also dispensed justice to everybody, just like Hermes (i.e. Thoth) the Great and Great; and he has ordered further that those soldiers who come back, and the others who were rebellious during the period of disturbances, should return and keep possession of their own property; and he had made sure that the cavalry and infantry forces and ships should be sent out against those attacking Egypt by sea and by land, and has sustained great expenses in money and corn so that the temples and all the people in the land might be in safety; and having gone to Lycopolis in the Busirite nome, which had been occupied and fortified for a siege with an abundant stock of weapons and other supplies—for the disaffection was now of long standing among the impious men who had gathered there and who had done much harm to the temples and the inhabitants of Egypt—and having encamped against it he surrounded it with mounds and trenches and massive fortifications; and when the Nile rose to a great height in the 8th year (198–197) and was about to flood the plains as usual, he held it in check by damming in many places the mouths of the canals, for which he spent no small sum of money, and having stationed cavalry and infantry to guard them, in a short while he took the city by storm and destroyed all the impious men in it, just as Hermes (= Thoth) and Horus, the son of Isis and Osiris, subdued formerly those who had rebelled in the same places. When he came to Memphis to avenge his father and his own royalty, he punished in a fitting way all the leaders of those who rebelled in his father's time, who had [disturbed] the country and done harm to the temples, at the time when he came there for the performance of the appropriate ceremonies for his reception of royalty; and he has remitted the debts of the temples to the royal treasury up to the 8th year (198–197), which was no small amount of corn and

money, [and] similarly the dues on the byssus cloth which had not been delivered to the royal treasury and of those delivered (he has remitted) the cost of checking them, up to the same period; and he has freed the temples from the (tax of one) artaba for each arura of sacred land, and also the (tax of one) jar of wine for each arura of vineyards; and he has bestowed many gifts on Apis and Mnevis and the other sacred animals in Egypt, much more than the kings before him, showing consideration for what belonged [to] them in every respect, and for their burials he gave what was needed lavishly and splendidly, and what was paid to their special shrines, with sacrifices and religious assemblies and the other [customary observances], and he has maintained the privileges of the temples and of Egypt in accordance with the laws, and has adorned the temple of Apis with lavish work, spending on it no small sum of gold [and silver] and precious stones, and he has founded temples and shrines and altars, and has restored those in need of repair, in the spirit of a beneficent god in matters relating [to] religion; and having discovered what temples were held in the highest honour, he has restored them during his own reign, as is fitting; in return for these things the gods have granted him health, victory, power and [all] other blessings, and his royalty shall remain with him and his children for all time. . . .

C. Antiochus Soter, a Seleucid King, 280–260 B.C., Extols His Own Virtues

I am Antiochus the great king, the legitimate king, the king of the world, king of Babylon, king of all countries, the caretaker of the temples Esagila and Ezida, the first(-born) son of king Seleucus, the Macedonian king of Babylon.

When I conceived the idea of (re)constructing Esagila and Ezida, I formed with my august hands (when I was still) in the country Hatti the (first) brick for Esagila and Ezida with the finest oil and brought (it with me) for the laying of the foundation of Esagila and Ezida. And in the month of Addaru, the 20th day, the 43rd year (of the Seleucid era), I did lay the foundation of Ezida, the (only) true temple of Nebo which is in Borsippa.

O Nebo, lofty son, (most) wise among the gods, splendid (and) worthy of all praise, first-born son of Marduk, child of Arua, the queen who fashioned all creation, do look friendly (upon me) and may—upon your lofty command which is never revoked—the overthrow of the country of my enemy, the fulfillment of (all) my wishes against my foes, constant predominance, a kingdom (ruled) in justice (to all), an orderly government, years of happiness, enough progeny (lit.: to be sated with progeny) be your permanent gift to the (joint) kingship of Antiochus and his son, king Seleucus!

When you, prince Nebo, born in Esagila, firstborn of Marduk, child of Arua the queen, enter—under jubilant rejoicings—Ezida, the (only) true temple, the temple (befitting) your position as Anu (i.e. highermost of the gods), the seat which gladdens your heart, may—upon your trustworthy command which cannot be made void—my days (on earth) be long, my years many, my throne firm, my rule lasting, under your lofty scepter which determines the borderline between the heaven and the nether world. May (only words of) favor be on your sacred lips with regard to me, and may I personally conquer (all) the countries from sunrise to sunset, gather their tribute and bring it (home) for the perfection of Esagila and Ezida.

O Nebo, foremost son, when you enter Ezida, the (only) true temple, may there be on your lips (words of) favor for Antiochus, the king of all countries, for Seleucus, the king, his son (and) for Stratonike, his consort, the queen!

D. A Somber Babylonian Account of Two Years in the Reign of Antiochus Soter, 276–274 B.C.

... In that year [276/5 B.C.] the king (Antiochus I) left his court, his wife and the crown prince in Sapardu to keep a strong guard. He went to the province Ebirnari [Syria] and marched against the Egyptian army which was camped in Ebirnari. The Egyptian army fled before him. In Adar [a month] on the 24th the governor of Akkad despatched a great quantity of silver, cloth stuffs, furniture and gear from Babylon and Seleucia, the royal city, and 20 elephants which the governor of Bactria had sent to the king, to Ebirnari to the king. . . . In that month the general assembled the royal army which was in Akkad from its head to its . . . , and in Nisan marched to Ebirnari

to assist the king. In that year they paid current prices in Babylon and the cities in copper coins of Greece. In that year there was much scabies in the country. In the 37th year (= 275/4), Antiochus (I) and Seleucus. In the month of Adar on the 9th the governor of Akkad and the town magistrates of the king who went to Sapardu in the 36th year (= 276/5) to the king returned to Seleucia, the royal city on the Tigris. They wrote (?) their rescripts to the Babylonians. In Teshri on the 12th they brought the Babylonians out to Seleucia. In that month the governor of Akkad acquired the seed-land, which they gave in the 32nd year (= 280/79) according to the king's wish for the food supply of the inhabitants of Babylon. Borsippa and Kuthah, and the oxen, sheep and everything whatever which in the towns and cities according to the king's wish unto the Babylonians they gave, for the king's household. In that year a quantity of bricks for rebuilding Esagila were made above and below Babylon . . . with sun-dried brick in . . . There was a famine in Akkad. The people hired their children for silver. The people died of hunger. In that year there was much scabies in the country. They paid current prices in Babylon and the cities in copper coins of Greece. In the 38th year (= 274/3), reigns of Antiochus (I) and Seleucus . . . Observation of the firmament (?) from Teshri of the 38th year to the end of Adar of the 38th year, in the reign of Antiochus and Seleucus. [. . .]

Document Set 4.5 References

A. A Farmer in Ptolemaic Egypt Petitions the King for Justice
G. W. Botsford and E. G. Sihler, eds., *Hellenic Civilization* (New York: Columbia University Press, 1915), 594.
B. Egyptian Priests Honor Ptolemy V: The Rosetta Stone Text
M. M. Austin, ed., *The Hellenistic World from Alexander to the Roman Conquest: A Selection of Ancient Sources in Translation* (Cambridge: Cambridge University Press, 1981), 374–376.
C. Antiochus Soter, a Seleucid King, 280–260 B.C., Extols His Own Virtues
E. A. Speiser and J. B. Pritchard, ed., *Ancient Near Eastern Texts Relating to the New Testament*, 3rd ed. (Princeton, N.J.: Princeton University Press, 1969), 317.
D. A Somber Babylonian Account of Two Years in the Reign of Antiochus Soter, 276–274 B.C.
Austin, 240–241.

A Cosmopolitan World

These documents are meant to shed some light on cultural and demographic diffusion in the Hellenistic world. Document A, from a "letter" of the Greek writer Alciphron (fl. 180 B.C.) supposedly conveys the thoughts of ordinary people; in this piece he imagines the thoughts of a peasant resolved to flee the land and try his luck as a trader. It also offers thoughts on the subject that Hellenistic Greeks and Romans worried about endlessly—the rule of chance over human affairs. Why this preoccupation? In Document B, we read of the introduction of the Egyptian-derived cult of the god Serapis into a Greek community about 200 B.C. Serapis was regarded by his many Greek-speaking devotees as a benevolent savior-god; what was the attraction of such a cult to Hellenistic Greeks? And what was the significance of a religion of Egyptian origin gaining an important following among Hellenistic Greeks?

Document C reveals another side of cultural diffusion: the strong sense of ethnic hierarchy in a "cosmopolitan" society such as Ptolemaic Egypt; in this document a well-to-do Egyptian woman was evidently not cowed by a threat by a Greek named Apollodorus and appealed to the authorities. (As with Set 4.5, Document A, it is doubtful whether Ptolemy spent his time reading such appeals; most likely matters were handled locally by his officials.)

Considering all these documents, as well as information furnished by your textbook, what conclusions can you draw about the "cosmopolitanism" of the Hellenistic Age?

A. A Greek Peasant Gives Up on Farming and Turns to Commerce

As the earth repays me nothing equivalent to my toils, I have resolved to devote myself to the sea and the waves. Life and death are the common lot of us all, and there is no possibility of escape, even if a man should lock himself up in a little room and stay there. The day of fate is not idle, and we cannot escape payment when it is due. Life therefore does not hang upon such circumstances but is determined by Chance. Some on land have proved short-lived whereas upon the sea others have lived to a good old age. Knowing full well that this is true, I am going on a voyage, and shall keep company with the winds and the waves. It is better to return from Bosporos and Propontis with new-earned wealth than to stay in the border fields of Attica and complain of hunger and thirst.

B. The Cult of Serapis Is Introduced at Delos

Apollonius the priest had (this text) inscribed in accordance with an injunction from the god. For Apollonius, my grandfather, who was an Egyptian from the priestly class came from Egypt with his god, and continued to celebrate the cult in accordance with ancestral tradition; he lived, it is thought, to the age of 97. My father Demetrius succeeded him and worshipped the gods in the same way; because of his piety he was honoured by the god with a bronze statue which is dedicated in the temple of the god. He lived 61 years. When I inherited the sacred objects and devoted myself carefully to his cult, the god told me in my sleep that a Serapeum of his own must be dedicated to him and that he must not be as before in a rented building; he said he would find a spot himself where he should be set and that he would point it out. And that is what happened. Now this spot was full of dirt and was advertised for sale on a little notice (displayed) in the passage to the agora. As the god wanted this the purchase was completed and the sanctuary was rapidly built in six months. And when some men joined against us and the god, and introduced a public suit against the sanctuary and me involving a penalty or a fine, the god promised to me in my sleep that we would be victorious. Now that the trial is completed and we have won a victory worthy of the god, we praise the gods and repay them adequate thanks.

C. Ethnic Hierarchy Takes Shape in Ptolemaic Egypt

"To King Ptolemy greetings from Tetosiris. I have a lawsuit pending . . . against Apollodorus over a house . . . Needing witnesses for the trial, I obtained from the clerk of the court a letter instructing the police chief, Herakleodorus, to take sworn depositions from the witnesses I would bring to him. Apollodorus, bringing a gang [?] with him, burst in and terrorized all my witnesses, saying he would beat them and me within an inch of our lives and drive us out of the village. He even abused [a Greek, whose name is incompletely preserved], a land holder who was going to testify for me, and he said he would beat him up too, for which reason he did not testify for me. As the others who were going to testify for me are Egyptians, they were intimidated and ran away and did not testify. I therefore ask and beg you, O king, not to allow justice to be delayed thereby . . . but to instruct Diophanes, the regional administrator, to write to Herakleodorus to send up to Diophanes those who, as I will inform him, built this house— hod carriers, carpenters, masons [?]—so that he may take their sworn depositions . . . when that has been done I, O king, fleeing for refuge with you, the common benefactor of all, will experience your benevolence. Farewell."

Document Set 4.6 References

A. A Greek Peasant Gives Up on Farming and Turns to Commerce
   G. W. Botsford and E. G. Sihler, eds., *Hellenic Civilization* (New York: Columbia University Press, 1915), 522.
B. The Cult of Serapis Is Introduced at Delos
   M. M. Austin, ed., *The Hellenistic World from Alexander to the Roman Conquest: A Selection of Ancient Sources in Translation* (Cambridge: Cambridge University Press, 1981), 226–227.
C. Ethnic Hierarchy Takes Shape in Ptolemaic Egypt
   Ptolemaic papyrus, c. 221 B.C., adapted from Naphtali Lewis, *Greeks in Ptolemaic Egypt* (Oxford: Clarendon Press, 1986), 60–61.

DOCUMENT SET 4.7
Hellenistic People

These documents continue some of the concerns of the materials in Set 4.6 while at the same time shedding light on everyday Hellenistic life.

Document A—another of Alciphron's letters, which convey what a man of letters thought an ordinary person would think—ruminates on the well-established practice at lending money at interest. How credible is this source? Document B is also a literary source, an extract from an oration by the Athenian Aeschines (386–314 B.C.) scornfully recounting the downward lurch of a man who has squandered his generous inheritance. What does it tell you about Hellenistic life?

The next pair of selections—collectively, Document C—consists first of a will executed about 148 B.C. by Dryton, a Greek settled in Ptolemaic Egypt, and second of a court case arising out of a dispute among Dryton's surviving daughters. Wills and litigation are a prime source to historians in reconstructing everyday life, but they are exceedingly rare in ancient history. Use this pairing of documents to disentangle what you can of Dryton's family and property.

The last pair of documents (D and E) illustrate slavery in Ptolemaic Egypt. (Like Document C, these rare items were written on papyrus that managed to survive thanks to a dry climate.) The sources in Document D are manumission documents, issued after the slave in question had amassed enough capital as a trader or artisan to buy freedom. In Document E, a slave has undertaken to "emancipate" himself by running away.

A. A Contract Specifying Interest

Agelarchides to Pytholaus:

The usurers in the city, kind friend, are a great nuisance. I do not know what was the matter with me when I ought to have gone to you or some other of my country neighbors, at the time I was in need of money for purchasing a farm at Colonus. On that occasion a man of the city went with me to the house of Byrtius to introduce me to him. There I found an old man looking wrinkled and with brows contracted, holding in his hand an antique paper, rotted by time and half-eaten by moths and bugs. Forthwith he spoke to me in brusquest fashion, as though he considered talking a loss of time. But when my voucher said I wanted money, he asked how many talents. Then when I expressed surprise at his mention of so

large a sum, he forthwith spat, and showed ill temper. Nevertheless he gave the money, demanded a note, required a heavy interest on the principal, and placed a mortgage on my house. A great nuisance indeed are these men who reckon with pebbles and crooked fingers. Never, ye spirits who watch over the farmers, never may it again be my lot to behold a wolf or a usurer!

B. An Athenian Spendthrift

When this (property) [which had come to his use through his connections with a certain Hegesander] too had disappeared and had been squandered in gambling and gluttony . . . and his abominable and wicked nature always maintained the same appetites, and in an excess of incontinence imposed command upon command and dissipated wealth in his daily life, then he turned to consuming his paternal estate. Thus not only did he eat it up, but if one may use the expression, he even drank it up. Not for a proper price did he alienate his several possessions, nor did he wait for the opportunity of gain or advantage, but he used to sell for whatever price a thing would bring, so strenuously did he pursue his pleasures. His father had left him an estate from which another man might even have discharged the expensive and gratuitous public functions (liturgies), but he could not even maintain it for his own advantage. He had a house behind the Acropolis, another in the outlying district, in the deme Sphettus; in the deme Alopecê another place, and in addition slaves who were skilled in the shoemaker's trade, nine or ten of them, each of whom brought this man an income of two obols a day, and the foreman of the shop three obols; also a woman slave who understood how to weave the fibre of Amorgos, and a man slave who was a broiderer. There were some, too, who owed him money, and besides he possessed personal property. . . . The house in town he sold to Nausicrates the comic poet, and afterward Cleænetus the trainer of choruses bought it of Nausicrates for twenty minas. The estate in the country was sold to Mnesitheus of the deme Myrrhinus. It was a large farm, but fearfully run to weeds under the management of the accused. As to the farm at Alopecê, which is eleven or twelve stadia distant from the walls (of Athens), when his mother entreated and begged him, as I learn, to let it alone and not sell it, but if nothing else, to leave it for her to be buried in,—for all that, even from this place he did not abstain, but his farm too he sold, for 2000 drachmas. Furthermore of the woman slaves and the domestic slaves he left not one, but has sold everything.

C. An Alexandrian Will Gives Rise to Litigation

. . . Being in good health and of sound mind, Dryton, son of Pamphilus, Cretan, ranking as a Successor and Hipparch in the Troops of the Reserve.

So long as health remains to me I am to remain in control of my property; but in case of death, I hereby leave and bequeath the real estate and furniture and herds belonging to me and whatsoever else I may possess, as follows:

My war-horse and all my arms to Esthladas, the son born to me and Sarapias, daughter of Esthladas, son of Theon, citizeness, with whom I lived as my wife, in accordance with the laws and a will (deposited) at the record office in Diospolis Parva before Dionysius the agoranomus in the sixth year in the time of Philometor. This will makes the rest clear and has established . . . (?) And of the four household slaves Esthladas is to have the two whose names are Myrsine and . . . The remaining two female slaves, whose names are Irene and Ampelion, are to go to Apollonia and her four sisters, making five in all; likewise, the vineyard belonging to me in the (district of ?) Pathyris, and the well of burnt brick and the other appurtenances, and the wagon with the cow, . . . one dove-cote and a second one unfinished, a yard, next to which on the south are waste fields of the beforementioned Esthladas, on the north a vaulted chamber of Apollonia the Younger, on the east a waste place belonging to Petrasis (?) . . . son of Esthladas, on the west a waste field of Esthladas up to the open doorway upon the west (?). The house to the west and bowls . . . and waste field up to the dove-cote stretching away below the doorway of Esthladas and to the left of the vaulted chamber, I give to Apollonia and Aristo and Aphrodisia and Nicarion and Apollonia the younger, making five daughters born to me and Apollonia, also called Semmonthis, with whom I lived as legal wife. Let them share equally in the two female slaves and the cow and the houses, according as I have made the division. Let Esthladas have the waste field already given him, facing his doorway from east to west, four strips extending to the place of the earthern pot. Of the remaining buildings and empty lots in Diospolis Magna in the Ammonium and among the potter's shops let Esthladas have one

half, and Apollonia and her sisters one half, and all my other belongings, contracts for loans in money or wheat, and furniture, let them share by halves. Let Esthladas and Apollonia with her sisters pay the expenditures for building the aforementioned dovecote, until it be completed. And to Apollonia also called Semmonthis, my wife, let them pay for four years, if she remains at home and without reproach, for the support of herself and the second and third daughters, 2 1/2 artabæ of wheat, 1/12 artaba of croton, and 200 copper drachmæ each month. And let them give the same amounts out of the common stock to the two youngest daughters for eleven years. And to Tachratis let them give out of the common stock 12 talents in copper as her dowry. Whatsoever additional income Semmonthis appears to have made while living with Dryton, of this she is to have absolute possession, and any one who starts acting against her regarding this income . . . (will suffer such and such a penalty).

To Phommoutis, the King's Cousin and Epistrategus and Strategus of the Thebaid.

From Apollonia also called Senmouthis, and Aphrodisia also called Tachratis, both daughters of Dryton dwelling in Pathyris. To us and to our sisters, Aristo also called Senmonthis, and Nicarion also called Thermouthis, and Apollonia the younger also called Senpelais, belongs a half share of our father's estates of which there are four in the Peri-Theban nome and the Pathyrite nome, likewise the household slaves. Included in these estates, in Cochlax on the Arabian side (eastern bank of the Nile) of the beforementioned Pathyrite nome, is a half share of a vineyard amounting to 2 1/2 arouræ, or as much more as it may be, and the orchard to the east of this, and wells and buildings and . . . and barren land and other land without the . . . , and their appurtenances, all of which our father owned while he lived, and we, his relics, own since his death. . . . Ariston, son of Athenodotus, living in Diospolis Magna has forcibly taken possession of the beforementioned vineyard and its appurtenances in the period when communication ceased (between the two banks of the Nile) and unjustly maintains possession of the half share belonging to us and has planted a certain part in vines, knowing that we are women and that we dwell in another place and cannot easily take action against the possession above stated. Therefore we deem it right to appeal to you, if it seems best, to examine him, and if the matter be as we declare it, to compel him to leave the half share of the vineyard which clearly belongs to us and the vines planted upon it and the places belonging with it, and to pay back the produce which he has taken away from them, and in return for his violent behavior to arrest him as a rogue that we may receive satisfaction. Farewell.

D. Manumissions of Slaves: Conditional and Unconditional

(a) Unconditional manumission

In the archonship of Tharres, in the month of Panagyrius, as reckoned by the people of Amphissa, and in the archonship of Damostratus at Delphi, in the month of Poitropius (144 B.C.), Telon and Cleto, with the approval of their son Straton, sold to Pythian Apollo a male slave whose name is Sosus, of Cappadocian origin, for the price of 3 minas of silver. Accordingly Sosus entrusted the sale to the god, on condition of his being free and not to be claimed as a slave by anyone for all time. Guarantor in accordance with the law and the contract; Philoxenus son of Dorotheus of Amphissa. The previous sale of Sosus to Apollo which took place in the archonship of Thrasycles at Delphi, and the provisions of the sale, namely that Sosus should remain with Telon and Cleto for as long as they live, shall be null and void. Witnesses: the priests of Apollo, Praxias and Andronicus, and the archon Pyrrhias son of Archelaus, and the Amphissians Charixenus son of Ecephylus, Polycritus, Aristodamus son of Callicles, Euthydamus son of Polycritus, Dorotheus son of Timesius, Demetrius son of Monimus. The contract is kept by the priest Praxias and Andronicus, and the Amphissians Polycritus and [Charixenus] son of Ecephylus.

(b) Conditional manumission

When Panaetolus and Phytaeus were generals of the Aetolians, in the month of Homoloius, and in the archonship of Xeneas at Delphi and the month Bysius (167 B.C.), Critodamus son of Damocles, of Physce, sold to Pythian Apollo a male slave whose name is Maiphatas, of Galatian origin, and a female (slave) whose name is Ammia, of Illyrian origin, for the price of seven minas of silver. Maiphatas and Ammia shall remain with Critodamus for as long as Critodamus lives, doing for Critodamus what they are told to; if they do not remain and do what they are told to, the sale shall be null and void. When Critodamus dies, Maiphatas and Ammia shall be free and the sale shall remain with the god on condition that they are free and not to be claimed as slaves by anyone for their whole life, doing whatever they wish and going wherever they wish. Guarantors in accor-

dance with the law and the contract: Philon son of Aristeas, Astoxenus son of Dionysius. Witnesses: the priests Amyntas and Tarantinus; private citizens: Dexicrates, Sotimus, Callimachus, Euangelus, . . . chaeus, of Delphi, Lyciscus and Menedamus, of Physce.

E. An Owner Seeks Runaway Slaves in Alexandria

. . . A slave of Aristogenes son of Chrysippus, of Alabanda, ambassador, has escaped in Alexandria, by name Hermon also called Nilus, by birth a Syrian from Bambyce, about 18 years old, of medium stature, beardless, with good legs, a dimple on the chin, a mole by the left side of the nose, a scar above the left corner of the mouth, tattooed on the right wrist with two barbaric letters. He has taken with him 3 octadrachms of coined gold, 10 pearls, an iron ring on which an oil-flask and strigils are represented, and is wearing a cloak and a loincloth. Whoever brings back this slave shall receive 3 talents of copper; if he points him out in a temple, 2 talents; if in the house of a substantial and actionable man, 5 talents. Whoever wishes to give information shall do so to the agents of the strategus.

There is also another who has escaped with him, Bion, a slave of Callicrates, one of the chief stewards at court, short of stature, broad at the shoulders, stout-legged, bright-eyed, who has gone off with an outer garment and a slave's wrap and a woman's dress (?) worth 6 talents 5000 drachmae of copper. . . .

Whoever brings back this slave shall receive the same rewards as for the above-mentioned. Information about this one also is to be given to the agents of the strategus.

Document Set 4.7 References

A. A Contract Specifying Interest
   G. W. Botsford and E. G. Sihler, eds., *Hellenic Civilization* (New York: Columbia University Press, 1915), 521–522.
B. An Athenian Spendthrift
   Botsford and Sihler, 508–509.
C. An Alexandrian Will Gives Rise to Litigation
   Botsford and Sihler, 603–606.
D. Manumissions of Slaves: Conditional and Unconditional
   M. M. Austin, ed., *The Hellenistic World from Alexander to the Roman Conquest: A Selection of Ancient Sources in Translation* (Cambridge: Cambridge University Press, 1981), 221–222.
E. An Owner Seeks Runaway Slaves in Alexandria
   A. S. Hunt and C. C. Edgar, trans., *Selected Papyri*, Loeb Classical Library (Cambridge, Mass.: Harvard University Press, 1934), 2:135, 139.

DOCUMENT SET 4.8
Men, Women, and Children

These documents should enable you to draw some conclusions about Hellenistic attitudes towards women and children. Document A is a satirical verse describing the artifices used by urban streetwalkers to lure customers.

No one knows whether the author of Document B was male or female, but it certainly represents the viewpoint of the Pythagorean religious and philosophical movement. Pythagoras was a sixth-century thinker possibly influenced by such Indian ideas as cycles of existence, reincarnation, and numerical symbolism. He made important discoveries in mathematics and taught a way of life based on strict purity and observing mystical numerical ratios. (None of his writings survive.) His movement, which endured for centuries, admitted both men and women. Document B's stress on moderation and the avoidance of luxury fits Pythagorean tenets; but the concerns it expresses for rearing a child in a manner worthy of a "free person" are characteristically Greek. What resonances do you find for this concern in some other materials you have read from ancient Greek? Ask the same questions of Document C, a second-century B.C. inscription from the Ionian city of Teos, and also consider the rich man who provided the endowment for the school. What did he expect to gain?

The next three documents all illustrate various aspects of family relationships. Document D is a marriage contract from first-century B.C. Alexandria; read it for insights into the conditions under which prosperous urban Hellenistic Greeks entered into marriage. Document E is a strikingly revealing letter from an Alexandrian husband to his wife (who may or may not have been his sister; the word was often but not always used as a mere term of endearment) instructing her as to the fate of their unborn child. Document F shows a father in a completely different—and to him no doubt humiliating—position of dependence upon his grown daughter and her husband. (Though formally directed to the king this petition would actually have been read by local officials.) In closing, consider Document G, an inscription memorializing a presumably unmarried woman who died young; it should be set against the other evidence you have seen, in this set and elsewhere, of women's relatively low esteem in this society.

A. Streetwalkers Entice Customers

For first of all, to earn themselves great gain,
And better to plunder all the neighboring men,
They use a lot of adventitious aids—
They plot to take in every one. And when
By subtle artifice they've made some money,
They enlist fresh girls and add recruits, who ne'er
Have tried the trade, unto their cunning troop,
And drill them so that they are very soon
Different in manners and in look and semblance
From all they were before. Suppose one's short,
They put cork soles within the heels of her shoes;
If any one's too tall, she wears a slipper
Of thinnest substance, and with head depressed
Between her shoulders, walks the public streets,
And so takes off from her superfluous height.
If any one's too lean about the flank,
They hoop her with a bustle, so that all
Who see her marvel at her fair proportions.
Has any one too prominent a stomach,
They crown it with false bosom, such as perchance
At times you may in comic actors see;
And what is still too prominent, they force
Back, ramming it as if with scaffolding.
Has any one red brows, those they smear
With soot. Has any one a dark complexion,
White lead will that correct. This girl's too fair,
They rub her well with rich vermillion.
Is she a splendid figure, then her charms
Are shown in unclad beauty to the purchaser.
Has she good teeth, then she is forced to laugh,
That all the bystanders may see her mouth,
How beautiful it is; and if she be
But ill inclined to laugh, then she is kept
Close within doors whole days, and all the things
Which cooks keep by them when they sell goats' heads,
Such as a stick of myrrh, she's forced to keep
Between her lips, till they have learned the shape
Of the required smile. And by such arts
They make their charms and persons up for market.

B. Neopythagorean Experts Advise on the Care of Infants

Since you have become a mother . . . , I want to give you the following advice. Choose someone for a wet nurse who is suitable and well-groomed, modest, not prone to sleep or drunkenness. Such a nurse would make the best judgments as to how to rear children in a manner worthy of a free person . . . For . . . the first and foremost part of one's entire life depends upon the nurse's knowledge of good nursing so that she does the right things at the right time. She should [nurse] not according to whim, but with some forethought; in this way she will guide the infant toward good health . . . If possible, she should be a Greek woman rather than a foreigner.

It is best if the infant is pleasantly filled with milk and thus falls asleep. Such a feeding is a sweet relaxation for newborns and best for their digestion. If you give any other sort of food, it must be of the simplest sort. In general, you should refrain from using the strong force of wine, or only occasionally put in a small amount (together with milk) in mixing the afternoon meal. . . . In all of these matters [pertaining to bathing and clothing the infant], nature yearns for what is fitting, not what is expensive.

C. The Hellenistic City of Teos Founds a School

So that all the free children might be educated just as Polythrus son of Onesimos in his foresight promised to the people, wishing to establish a most fair memorial of his own love of glory, he made a gift for this purpose of 34,000 drachmas . . . Three school teachers are to be appointed, who will teach the boys and the girls. The person appointed to the uppermost class shall receive an annual salary of 600 drachmas; to the next class, 550 drachmas; and to the youngest class, 500 drachmas. Two physical trainers are also to be appointed, at 500 drachmas a year. A lute player . . . is also to be appointed, at 700 drachmas a year. He shall teach music and playing the lute . . . to the children whom it is fitting to select for the higher class and those who are a year younger than they, and he shall teach music to the adolescent boys. The superintendent of children shall decide about the ages of these children . . . The superintendent of children and the leader of the gymnasium shall also hire a drillmaster [at 300 drachmas a year] and a teacher of archery and javelin throwing [at 250 drachmas a year], subject to ratification by the people; they shall teach the adolescent boys and the children who have been registered to learn music . . . The superintendent of children and the leader of the gymnasium shall see to it that the children and the adolescent boys practice their studies carefully, as each of them is instructed to do according to the laws.

D. An Alexandrian Marriage Contract

Year 22, Mecheir 11 [92 B.C.]. Philiscus son of Apollonius, Persian of the Epigone acknowledges to Apollonia also called Kellauthis, daughter of Heraclides, Persian, having with her as guardian her brother Apollonius, that he has received from her in copper money 2 talents 4000 drachmae, the dowry for herself, Apollonia, agreed upon with him.

Apollonia shall live with Philiscus, obeying him as a wife should her husband, owning their property in common with him. All necessaries and clothing and whatever else is proper for a wedded wife Philiscus shall supply to Apollonia, whether he is at home or abroad, in proportion to their means. It shall not be lawful for Philiscus to bring in another wife besides Apollonia, nor to keep a concubine or boy, nor to have children by another woman while Apollonia lives, nor to inhabit another house over which Apollonia is not mistress, nor to eject or insult or ill-treat her, nor to alienate any of their property to the detriment of Apollonia. If he is proved to be doing any of these things or fails to supply her with necessaries or clothing or other things as stated, Philiscus shall forthwith forfeit to Apollonia the dowry of 2 talents 4000 drachmae of copper. In like manner it shall not be lawful for Apollonia to spend the night or day away from the house of Philiscus without Philiscus's consent or to consort with another man or to dishonour the common home or to cause Philiscus to be shamed by any act that brings shame upon a husband. If Apollonia chooses of her own will to separate from Philiscus, Philiscus shall repay her the bare dowry within ten days from the date of the demand. If he does not repay as stated, he shall forthwith forfeit to her one and a half-times the amount of the dowry which he has received. . . . [A list of witnesses, all described as Macedonians, follows.] . . . Keeper of the contract: Dionysius. . . .

Selection D: Reprinted by permission of the publishers and the Loeb Classical Library from A. S. Hunt and C. C. Edgar, eds., pp. 5, 7, 9, Cambridge, Mass.: Harvard University Press, 1932, 1934.

E. An Alexandrian Husband Instructs His Pregnant Sister(?)/Wife on How to Deal with Her Baby

Hilarion to his sister Alis very many greetings, like-wise to my lady Berous and Apollonarion. Know that we are still in Alexandria. Do not be anxious; if they really go home, I will remain in Alexandria. I beg and entreat you, take care of the little one, and as soon as we receive our pay I will send it up to you. If by chance you bear a child, if it is a boy, let it be, if it is a girl, cast it out. You have said to Aphrodisias "Do not forget me." How can I forget you? I beg you then not to be anxious. The 29th year of Caesar, Pauni 23 [1 B.C.] (Addressed) Deliver to Alis from Hilarion.

F. A Father Complains of Not Being Supported by His Adult Daughter

To King Ptolemy greeting from Ctesicles. I am being wronged by Dionysius and my daughter Nice. For though I had nurtured her, being my own daughter, and educated her and brought her up to womanhood, when I was stricken with bodily infirmity and my eyesight enfeebled she would not furnish me with any of the necessaries of life. And when I wished to obtain justice from her in Alexandria, she begged my pardon and in year 18 she gave me in the temple of Arsinoe Actia a written oath by the king that she would pay me twenty drachmae every month by means of her own bodily labour; if she failed to do so or transgressed any of the terms of her bond, she was to forfeit to me 500 drachmae on pain of incurring the consequences of the oath. Now, however, corrupted by Dionysius, who is a comedian, she is not keeping any of her engagements to me, in contempt of my old age and my present infirmity. I beg you therefore, O king, not to suffer me to be wronged by my daughter and Dionysius the comedian who has corrupted her, but to order Diophanes the strategus to summon them and hear our case; and if my words are true, let Diophanes deal with her corrupter as seems good to him and compel my daughter Nice to yield me my rights. . . . For by this means I shall no longer be wronged, but having sought your protection, O king, I shall obtain justice. . . .

G. A Tribute to an Accomplished Woman

This stone marks a woman of accomplishment and beauty. Who she is the Muses' inscriptions reveal: Menophila. Why she is honoured is shown by a carved lily and an alpha, a book and a basket, and with these a wreath. The book shows that you were wise, the wreath that you wore on your head shows that you were a leader; the letter alpha that you were an only child; the basket is a sign of your orderly excellence; the flower shows the prime of your life, which Fate stole away. May the dust lie light on you in death. Alas; your parents are childless; to them you have left tears.

Document Set 4.8 References

A. Streetwalkers Entice Customers
   M. M. Austin, ed., *The Hellenistic World from Alexander to the Roman Conquest: A Selection of Ancient Sources in Translation* (Cambridge: Cambridge University Press, 1981), 662–663.
B. Neopythagorean Experts Advise on the Care of Infants
   J. M. Snyder, *The Woman and the Lyre* (Carbondale: Southern Illinois University Press, 1989), 111–112.
C. The Hellenistic City of Teos Founds a School
   Austin, 599–601.
D. An Alexandrian Marriage Contract
   A. S. Hunt and C. C. Edgar, trans., *Selected Papyri*, Loeb Classical Library (Cambridge, Mass.: Harvard University Press, 1934), 5, 7, 9.
E. An Alexandrian Husband Instructs His Pregnant Sister(?)/Wife on How to Deal with Her Baby
   Hunt and Edgar, 1:295.
F. A Father Complains of Not Being Supported by His Adult Daughter
   Hunt and Edgar, 2:268.
G. A Tribute to an Accomplished Woman
   Mary R. Lefkowitz and Maureen B. Fant, eds., *Women's Life in Greece and Rome* (Baltimore: Johns Hopkins University Press, 1982), 24–25.

DOCUMENT SET 4.9
Greeks and Jews

As *The Challenge of the West* explains, it was the fate of the second-century B.C. Jews of Palestine to be subject to Hellenization by the Seleucid king Antiochus IV (*175–164 B.C.). His erection of a Greek temple in Jerusalem outraged Jewish religious feelings, culminating in the successful Maccabean revolt.

The Book of Daniel (Document A), though it purports to deal with a prophet of the era of the Babylonian captivity, actually dates (at least in the final form) from the era of Antiochus IV. It attests to the growing apocalyptic mentality in Judaism—the expectation that God would send an avenging Messiah to vindicate the chosen people and destroy the heathen. Such faith was destined to play an enormous role in Christianity. In what ways can you interpret Daniel's vision as a commentary on gentile rule over the Jews?

The revolt itself is narrated in Document B, an extract of the Book of Maccabees. On the other hand, a very different kind of relationship between a Hellenistic king and his Jewish subjects is shown in Document C, an account of how Ptolomy II (*285–236 B.C.) sponsored the translation of the Hebrew scriptures into Greek, followed by the same king's acknowledgment of the wealth of this important Jewish community in Hellenistic Egypt.

A. The Prophet Daniel Beholds the Beast with Four Heads and Seven Horns

In the first year of Belshazzar king of Babylon, Daniel had a dream and visions of his head upon his bed: then he wrote the dream, and told the sum of the matters. Daniel spake and said, I saw in my vision by night, and, behold, the four winds of the heaven strove upon the great sea. And four great beasts came up from the sea, diverse one from another. The first was like a lion, and had eagle's wings: I beheld till the wings thereof were plucked, and it was lifted up from the earth, and made stand upon the feet as a man, and a man's heart was given to it. And behold another beast, a second, like to a bear, and it raised up itself on one side, and it had three ribs in the mouth of it between the teeth of it: and they said thus unto it, Arise, devour much flesh. After this I beheld, and lo another, like a leopard, which had upon the back of it four wings of a fowl; the beast had also four heads; and dominion was given to it. After this I saw in the night visions, and behold a fourth beast, dreadful and terrible, and strong exceedingly; and it had great iron teeth: it devoured and brake in pieces, and stamped the residue with the feet of it: and it was diverse from all the beasts that were before it; and it had ten horns. I considered the horns, and, behold, there came up among them another little horn, before whom there were three of the first horns plucked up by the roots: and, behold, in this horn were eyes like the eyes of man, and a mouth speaking great things.

I beheld till the thrones were cast down, and the Ancient of days did sit, whose garment was white as snow, and the hair of his head like the pure wool: his throne was like the fiery flame, and his wheels as burning fire. A fiery stream issued and came forth from before him: thousand thousands ministered unto him, and ten thousand times ten thousand stood before him: the judgment was set, and the books were opened. I beheld then, because of the voice of the great words which the horn spake: I beheld even till the beast was slain, and his body destroyed, and given to the burning flame. As concerning the rest of the beasts, they had their dominion taken away: yet their lives were prolonged for a season and time. I saw in the night visions, and, behold, one like the Son of man came with the clouds of heaven, and came to the Ancient of days, and they brought him near before him. And there was given him dominion, and glory, and a kingdom, that all people, nations, and languages, should serve him: his dominion is an everlasting dominion, which shall not pass away, and his kingdom that which shall not be destroyed.

I Daniel was grieved in my spirit in the midst of my body, and the visions of my head troubled me. I came near unto one of them that stood by, and asked him the truth of all this. So he told me, and made me know the interpretation of the things. These great beasts, which are four, are four kings, which shall arise out of the earth. But the saints of the Most High shall take the kingdom, and possess the kingdom for ever, even for ever and ever. Then I would know the truth of the fourth beast, which was diverse from all the others, exceeding dreadful, whose teeth were of iron, and his nails of brass; which devoured, brake in pieces, and stamped the residue with his feet; And of the ten horns that were in his head, and of the other which came up, and before whom three fell; even of that horn that had eyes, and a mouth that spake very great things, whose look was more stout than his fellows. I beheld, and the same horn made war with the saints, and prevailed against them; Until the Ancient of days came, and judgment was given to the saints of the Most High; and the time came that the saints possessed the kingdom. Thus he said, The fourth beast shall be the fourth kingdom upon earth, which shall be diverse from all kingdoms, and shall devour the whole earth, and shall tread it down, and break it in pieces. And the ten horns out of this kingdom are ten kings that shall arise: and another shall rise after them; and he shall be diverse from the first, and he shall subdue three kings. And he shall speak great words against the Most High, and shall wear out the saints of the Most High, and think to change times and laws: and they shall be given into his hand until a time and times and the dividing of time. But the judgment shall sit, and they shall take away his dominion, to consume and to destroy it unto the end. And the kingdom and dominion, and the greatness of the kingdom under the whole heaven, shall be given to the people of the saints of the Most High, whose kingdom is an everlasting kingdom, and all dominions shall serve and obey him. Hitherto is the end of the matter. As for me Daniel, my cogitations much troubled me, and my countenance changed in me: but I kept the matter in my heart.

B. Antiochus IV Persecutes the Jews

From them came forth a sinful shoot, Antiochus Epiphanes, son of King Antiochus (III), who after being a hostage in Rome became king in year 137 of the kingdom of the Greeks. In those days there came forth from Israel a lawless generation who persuaded many others by saying, 'Come, let us make a treaty with the peoples around us, since many evils have fallen upon us from the time we separated from them.' This proposal seemed good in their eyes, and some of the people eagerly went to the king, who granted them permission to practise the customs of the heathen. And they built a gymnasium in Jerusalem in accordance with the customs of the nations. They became uncircumcised, gave up the holy covenant to join the yoke of the gentiles, and sold themselves to cause evil. And when Antiochus felt his kingdom was firmly established, he decided to become ruler of the land of Egypt so as to reign over both kingdoms. He invaded Egypt with a massive army of chariots and elephants and a large fleet. He waged war on Ptolemy king of Egypt, and Ptolemy turned away before him and fled, and many men were wounded and fled. They seized the

Egyptian strongholds and captured the spoils of the land of Egypt. After defeating Egypt Antiochus returned in the year 143 (= 169); he marched against Israel and entered Jerusalem with a massive army. In his arrogance he penetrated the sanctuary, and seized the golden altar and the lamp for the light with all its fittings, and the table for the offering of the loaves, the libation vases, the cups, the golden censers, the veil, the crowns, the golden ornaments on the facade of the Temple which he stripped off completely. He seized the silver and gold and the precious vessels and took away the hidden treasures he found. He went away to his country taking everything, shedding much blood and uttering words of extreme arrogance. [. . .]

The king then issued a proclamation to the whole of his kingdom that they should all form one people and that they should each give up their own customs. All the nations acquiesced in the royal edict. Many Israelites accepted his worship and sacrificed to idols and profaned the Sabbath. The king also sent letters by messenger to Jerusalem and the cities of Juda that they should follow customs alien to their land, banish holocausts, sacrifices and libations from the sanctuary and profane the sabbaths and festivals, defile the sanctuary and the holy men, build altars and sacred enclosures and idol's temples, sacrifice pigs and unclean animals, leave their sons uncircumcised, defile themselves with every king of impurity and abomination, so as to forget the Law and change all their ordinances. Anyone who did not conform to the king's edict would be punished with death. In accordance with all these instructions he sent letters to the whole of his kingdom; he set up inspectors over the whole people and ordered the cities of Juda to sacrifice in each and every city. Many of the people joined with them, whoever abandoned the Law, and they caused great evil in the land, and drove Israel into all its secret hiding places. On the 15th day of Chislev in the year 145 (= December 167), he (sc. Antiochus) built the 'abomination of desolation' on the altar, and in the cities of Juda around they built altars, and offered incense at the doors of houses and in the streets. Any books of the Law that were found were torn up and burnt.

C. The Ptolemies Deal with the Egyptian Jews

When Demetrius of Phalerum was placed in charge of the king's Library he was provided with large sums of money to collect, if possible, all the books in the world. He purchased some and transcribed others, and brought to completion the king's design as far as he was able. When he was asked in my presence, 'How many thousands of books are there?' he replied, 'Over 200,000, Sire, and I shall endeavour in a short while to bring up the number to 500,000 with the remainder. I have been told that the laws of the Jews deserve to be transcribed and included in your Library.' 'What then prevents you from doing this,' the king said, 'everything you need is at your disposal.' Demetrius replied, 'A translation is needed; in their country the Jews use their own script, just as the Egyptians use their arrangements of letters, and they also have their own language. They are believed to use Syrian [Aramaic], but this is not so, and their dialect is different.' When the king learnt of these details he said a letter would be sent to the High Priest of the Jews to bring the above-mentioned design to completion.[. . .]

King Ptolemy to Eleazar the High-Priest, greetings and good health. Since it happens that many Jews have been settled in our country, some of whom were transplanted from Jerusalem by the Persians during their period of rule, and others came as captives to Egypt in our father's train—of those he enrolled many in the army at high rates of pay, and similarly when he judged their leading men to be reliable he founded fortresses which he gave them, in order to keep the Egyptian people in fear; and since we have taken over the kingdom, we deal with all men in a very humane way, but particularly so with your own countrymen–we have given their freedom to over 100,000 prisoners of war paying their owners the proper value in money and putting right any harm done through the impulses of the crowd. It was our intention to perform a pious deed and to dedicate a thank-offering to the greatest god, who has kept our kingdom in peace and in the greatest renown throughout the whole inhabited world. We have enrolled in the army those in the prime of age, and those capable of being in our service and who are deserving of trust at the court we have appointed to official positions. Now as we wish to show favour to them, to all the Jews in the inhabited world and to those of future generations, we have decided to have your Law translated from the Hebrew language you use into Greek, so that they too may be available in our Library together with the other royal books. It would therefore be a good action on your part and one worthy of our zeal if you selected elders of distinguished life, experienced in the Law and capable of translating, six from each tribe, so that agreement may be reached among the majority, since the enquiry concerns a matter of great importance. We believe that the completion of this task will bring us great fame. Concerning this matter we have sent Andreas, one of the *archisomatophylakes,* and Aristeas, men we hold in esteem, to discuss the question with you, and to bring dedications to the Temple and 100 talents of silver for sacrifices and other expenses. You would do us a favour and do a friendly act if you wrote to us about anything you desire, and your wishes shall be fulfilled as quickly as possible. Farewell.

Document Set 4.9 References

A. The Prophet Daniel Beholds the Beast with Four Heads and Seven Horns
   Daniel 7.
B. Antiochus IV Persecutes the Jews
   Josephus, *Jewish Antiquities* 12:138–153, in M. M. Austin, ed., *The Hellenistic World from Alexander to the Roman Conquest: A Selection of Ancient Sources in Translation* (Cambridge: Cambridge University Press, 1981), 278–279.
C. The Ptolemies Deal with the Egyptian Jews
   Letter of Aristeus to Philocrates, in Austin, 440–442.

CHAPTER

5

The Rise and Fall of the Roman Republic, c. 800–44 B.C.

DOCUMENT SET 5.1
Foundations of Roman Society

Apart from increasingly important and rich archaeological finds, the most sources for early Roman history are the legends and written laws. Document A is the traditional story of the rape of the Roman matron Lucretia, as narrated by the historian Livy (59 B.C.–A.D. 17). Basically uncritical of his sources, Livy retold his old stories primarily to illustrate the themes that his history emphasized: the sturdy virtue of the ancient republicans that he admired. By idealizing early Rome in beautiful Latin prose, Livy gave to the Western world a republican myth that for two millennia repeatedly exerted a powerful influence. As you read Livy's version of the Lucretia story look for elements of the republican myth, as well as for the Roman ideal of womanly virtue.

Document B contains a group of laws from early Rome (including the famous fundamental Laws of the Twelve Tables) focusing specifically on the position of women. Contrast these severe legal restrictions with Livy's idealized portrait of Lucretia. Contrast, again, the phrase for a deceased wife in the inscription quoted in Document C, which appears on a tombstone beneath a sculptured depiction of a man and woman holding hands. The virtues that the husband praises were those considered appropriate for a Roman woman. Moreover, these particular inscriptions provide a rare glimpse into the lives of a first-century B.C. ex-slave woman. (Most likely the former slaves mentioned here were Greeks who managed to buy their freedom out of their earnings.)

Document D presents a no doubt idealized portrait of one of the classic Old Romans, Cato the Elder

(234–149 B.C.), as drawn by the Greek biographer Plutarch (A.D. 46–120). Plutarch's primary purpose was to hold up character traits for emulation, but his short biographies can be valuable (if used critically) as sources of information about Greek and Roman statesman. Read this extract from Plutarch's life of Cato the Elder for its insight into the conservation Roman values as upheld by a man known to have been a relentless critic of "contamination" of Rome by Greek cultural influences.

A. The Rape of Lucretia Has Unexpected Consequences

. . . A few days after, Sextus Tarquinius, without the knowledge of Collatinus, went to Collatia, with only a single attendant: he was kindly received by the family, who suspected not his design, and, after supper, conducted to the chamber where guests were lodged. Then, burning with desire, as soon as he thought that every thing was safe, and the family all at rest, he came with his sword drawn to Lucretia, where she lay asleep, and, holding her down, with his left hand pressed on her breast, said, "Lucretia, be silent: I am Sextus Tarquinius; my sword is in my hand, if you utter a word, you die."

Terrified at being thus disturbed from sleep, she saw no assistance near, and immediate death threatening her. Tarquinius then acknowledged his passion, entreated, mixed threats with entreaties, and used every argument likely to have effect on a woman's mind: but finding her inflexible, and not to be moved, even by the fear of death, he added to that fear, the dread of dishonour, telling her that, after killing her he would murder a slave, and lay him naked by her side, that she might be said to have been slain in base adultery. The shocking apprehension, conveyed by this menace, overpowering her resolution in defending her chastity, his lust became victorious; and Tarquinius departed, applauding himself for this triumph over a lady's honour.

But Lucretia plunged by such a disaster into the deepest distress, despatched a messenger to Rome to her father, with orders to proceed to Ardea to her husband, and to desire them to come to her, each with one faithful friend; to tell them, that there was a necessity for their doing so, and speedily, for that a dreadful affair had happened. Spurius Lucretius came with Publius Valerius, the son of Volesus; Collatinus with Lucius Junius Brutus, in company with whom he chanced to be returning to Rome, when he was met by his wife's messenger.

They found Lucretia sitting in her chamber, melancholy and dejected: on the arrival of her friends, she burst into tears, and on her husband's asking, "Is all well?" "Far from it," said she, "for how can it be well with a woman who has lost her chastity? Collatinus, the impression of another man is in your bed; yet my person only has been violated, my mind is guiltless as my death will testify. But give me your right hands, and pledge your honour that the adulterer shall not escape unpunished. He is Sextus Tarquinius, who, under the appearance of a guest, disguising an enemy, obtained here last night, by armed violence, a triumph deadly to me, and to himself also, if ye be men."

They all pledged their honour, one after another, and endeavoured to comfort her distracted mind, acquitting her of blame, as under the compulsion of force, and charging it on the violent perpetrator of the crime, told her, that "the mind alone was capable of sinning, not the body, and that where there was no such intention, there could be no guilt."

"Is it your concern," said she, "to consider what is due to him; as to me, though I acquit myself of the guilt, I cannot dispense with the penalty, nor shall any woman ever plead the example of Lucretia, for surviving her chastity." Thus saying, she plunged into her heart a knife which she had concealed under her garment, and falling forward on the wound, dropped lifeless. The husband and father shrieked aloud.

But Brutus, while they were overpowered by grief, drawing the knife, from the wound of Lucretia, and holding it out, reeking with blood, before him, said, "By this blood, most chaste until injured by royal insolence, swear, and call you, O ye gods, to witness, that I will prosecute to destruction, by sword, fire, and every forcible means in my power, both Lucius Tarquinius the proud, and his impious wife, together with their entire race, and never will suffer one of them, nor any other person whatsoever, to be king in Rome." He then delivered the knife to Collatinus, afterwards to Lucretius, and Valerius, who were filled with amazement, as at a prodigy, and at a loss to account for this unusual elevation of sentiment in the mind of Brutus.

However, they took the oath as directed, and converting their grief into rage, followed Brutus, who put himself at their head, and called on them to proceed instantly to abolish kingly power.

They brought out the body of Lucretia from the house, conveyed it to the forum, and assembled the people, who came together quickly, in astonishment, as may be supposed at a deed so atrocious and unheard of. Every one exclaimed with vehemence against the villany and violence of the prince: they were deeply affected by the grief of her father, and also by the discourse of Brutus, who rebuked their tears and ineffectual complaints, and advised them, as became men, as became Romans, to take up arms against those who had dared to treat them as enemies. The most spirited among the youth offered themselves with their arms, and the rest followed their example. On which, leaving half their number at the gates to defend Collatia, and fixing guards to prevent any intelligence of the commotion being carried to the princes, the rest, with Brutus at their head, marched to Rome.

When they arrived there, the sight of such an armed multitude spread terror and confusion wherever they came: but, in a little time, when people observed the principal men of the state marching at their head, they concluded, that whatever the matter was, there must be good reason for it. Nor did the heinousness of the affair raise less violent emotions in the minds of the people at Rome, than it had at Collatia: so that, from all parts of the city, they hurried into the forum; where, as soon as the party arrived, a crier summoned the people to attend the tribune of the celeres, which office happened at that time to be held by Brutus.

He there made a speech, no way consonant to that low degree of sensibility and capacity, which until that day, he had counterfeited; recounting the violence and lust of Sextus Tarquinius, the shocking violation of Lucretia's chastity, and her lamentable death; the misfortune of Tricipitinus, in being left childless, who must feel the cause of his daughter' death as a greater injury and cruelty, than her death itself: to these representations he added the pride of the king himself, the miseries and toils of the commons, buried under ground to cleanse sinks and sewers, saying, that "that citizens of Rome, the conquerors of all the neighbouring nations, were, from warriors, reduced to labourers and stone cutters;" mentioned the barbarous murder of king Servius Tullius, his abominable daughter driving in her carriage over the body of her father, and invoked the gods to avenge the cause of parents.

By descanting on these and other, I suppose, more forcible topics, which the heinousness or present injuries suggested at the time, but which it is difficult for writers to repeat, he inflamed the rage of the multitude to such a degree, that they were easily persuaded to deprive the king of his government, and to pass an order for the banishment of Lucius Tarquinius, his wife, and children. Brutus himself, having collected and armed such of the young men as voluntarily gave in their names, set out for the camp at Ardea, in order to excite the troops there to take part against the king. The command in the city he left to Lucretius, who had some time before been appointed by the king to the office of prefect of the city. During this tumult Tullia fled from her house; both men and women, wherever she passed, imprecating curses on her head, and invoking the furies, the avengers of parents. . . .

B. Early Roman Laws Regulate the Family and Women

11. If a daughter-in-law strikes her father-in-law she shall be dedicated as a sacrifice to his ancestral deities.

Laws attributed to Numa Pompilius; traditional dates, 716–673 B.C.

9. On the vestal virgins he conferred high honours, among which was the right of making a will while their fathers lived and of doing all other juristic acts without a guardian.
12. A royal law forbids the burial of a pregnant woman before the child is extracted from the womb. Whoever violates this law is deemed to have destroyed the child's expectancy of life along with the mother.
13. A concubine shall not touch the Altar of Juno. If she touches it she shall sacrifice, with her hair unbound, a ewe lamb to Juno.

The Twelve Tables. Rome; traditional dates, 450 B.C.

Table IV. Paternal power

1. A notably deformed child shall be killed immediately.
3. To repudiate his wife her husband shall order her . . . to have her own property for herself, shall take the keys, shall expel her.
4. A child born within ten months of the father's death shall enter into the inheritance . . .

Table V. Inheritance and guardianship

1. . . . Women, even though they are of full age, because of their levity of mind shall be under guardianship . . . except vestal virgins, who . . . shall be free from guardianship.
2. The conveyable possessions of a woman who is under guardianship of male agnates shall not be acquired by prescriptive right unless they are transferred by the woman herself with the authorisation of her guardian . . .
4. If anyone who has no direct heir dies intestate the nearest male agnate shall have the estate.

C. A Bereaved Husband Lauds a Beloved Wife

The inscription on the left reads:

Lucius Aurelius Hermia, freeman of Lucius, a butcher from the Viminal Hill

My wife, who died before me, chaste in body, my one and only, a loving woman who possessed my heart, she lived as a faithful wife to a faithful husband with affection equal to my own, since she never let avarice keep her from her duty.

The inscription on the right reads:

Aurelia Philmatio, free woman of Lucius

When I was alive I was called Aurelia Philmatio. I was chaste and modest; I did not know the crowd. I was faithful to my husband. He whom, alas, I have lost was my fellow-freedman and was truly more than a father to me. When I was seven years old, he took me to his bosom; now, at forty, I am possessed by violent death. He, though my diligent performance of duty, flourished at all times . . . (The rest of the inscription has not survived.)

D. Plutarch Describes Cato's Views on the Goals of Education

He was also a good father, an excellent husband to his wife, and an extraordinary economist[1]; and as he did not manage his affairs of this kind carelessly, and as things of little moment, I think I ought to record a little further whatever was commendable in him in these points. He married a wife more noble than rich; being of opinion that the rich and the high-born are equally haughty and proud; but that those of noble blood would be more ashamed of base things, and consequently more obedient to their husbands in all that was fit and right. A man who beat his wife or child laid violent hands, he said, on what was most sacred; and a good husband he reckoned worthy of more praise than a great senator; and he admired the ancient Socrates for nothing so much as for having lived a temperate and contented life with a wife who was a scold, and children who were half-witted.

As soon as he had a son born, though he had never such urgent business upon his hands, unless it were some public matter, he would be by when his wife washed it and dressed it in its swaddling clothes. For she herself suckled it, nay, she often too gave her breast to her servant's children, to produce, by suckling the same milk, a kind of natural love in them to her son. When he began to come to years of discretion, Cato himself would teach him to read, although he had a servant, a very good grammarian, called Chilo, who taught many others; but he thought not fit, as he himself said, to have his son reprimanded by a slave, or pulled, it may be, by the ears when found tardy in his lesson: nor would he have him owe to a servant the obligation of so great a thing as his learning; he himself, therefore (as we were saying), taught him his grammar, law, and his gymnastic exercises. Nor did he only show him, too, how to throw a dart, to fight in armour, and to ride, but to box also and to endure both heat and cold, and to swim over the most rapid and rough rivers. He says, likewise, that he wrote histories, in large characters, with his own hand, that so his son, without stirring out of the house, might learn to know about his countrymen and forefathers; nor did he less abstain from speaking anything obscene before his son, than if it had been in the presence of the sacred virgins, called vestals. Nor would he ever go into the bath with him; which seems indeed to have been the common custom of the Romans. Sons-in-law used to avoid bathing with fathers-in-law, disliking to see one another naked; but having, in time, learned of the Greeks to strip before men, they have since taught the Greeks to do it even with the women themselves.

Thus, like an excellent work, Cato formed and fashioned his son to virtue; nor had he any occasion to find fault with his readiness and docility; but as he proved to be of too weak a constitution for hardships, he did not insist on requiring of him any very austere way of living. However, though delicate in health, he proved a stout man in the field, and behaved himself valiantly when Paulus Æmilius fought against Perseus; where when his sword was struck from him by a blow, or rather slipped out of his hand by reason of its moistness, he so keenly resented it, that he turned to some of his friends about him, and taking them along with him again fell upon the enemy; and having by a long fight and much force cleared the place, at length found it among great heaps of arms, and the dead bodies of friends as well as enemies piled one upon another. Upon which Paulus, his general, much commended the youth; and there is a letter of Cato's to his son, which highly praised his honourable eagerness for the recovery of his sword. Afterwards he married Tertia, Æmilius Paulus's daughter, and sister to Scipio; nor was he admitted into this family less for his own worth than his father's. So that Cato's care in his son's education came to a very fitting result.

Document Set 5.1 References

A. The Rape of Lucretia Has Unexpected Consequences
Livy, *History* 1:58–59, trans. George Baker (Philadelphia: T. Wardle, 1840).
B. Early Roman Laws Regulate the Family and Women
Mary R. Lefkowitz and Maureen B. Fant, eds., *Women's Life in Greece and Rome* (Baltimore: Johns Hopkins University Press, 1982), 173–174.
C. A Bereaved Husband Lauds a Beloved Wife
Lefkowitz and Fant, 134–135.
D. Plutarch Describes Cato's Views on the Goals of Education
Plutarch, *Lives,* "Cato the Elder," trans. John Dryden, rev. Arthur Hugh Clough (New York: Modern Library, n.d.), 425–427.

[1] household manager

DOCUMENT SET 5.2
The Roman State and Army

The Greek Polybius (205–c. 123 B.C.) originally came to Rome as a political hostage but became a close friend of the Roman general Scipio Aemilianus, who helped him collect sources for the massive history whose writing occupied most of Polybius's life. His purpose was to show how and why the civilized world of his day was falling under Roman rule, and his famous analysis of the Republic's constitution (Document A) contains the heart of his explanation for Rome's success.

The extract from Livy in Document B conveys well the panic felt by the Roman Senate when in 186 B.C. it learned of the popularity of secret Greek cults in honor of the god Dionysius (whom the Romans called Bacchus). Clearly Livy also believed such cults to be a threat to Roman ways. Read this document with the question in mind of why the Senate should fear rites that appealed primarily to slaves, women, and lower-class free citizens. Keep this document in mind, too, when in Chapter 6 you study the Roman reaction to early Christianity. Document C is an extract from Flavius Vegetius Renatus's *Epitome of the Military Art*—dating from the fourth century A.D., but thoroughly based on (lost) earlier sources and so can be rather safely regarded as a valid description of republican-era Roman military life. It gives a good idea of the rigorous training to which all citizen-soldiers were subjected. Document D, another extract from Polybius describing the duties of the centurions in maintaining discipline, reinforces this impression. Desertion or cowardly conduct was punishable at least by life-long disgrace and often by death.

How Roman toughness came out in political life is exemplified by Document E, another extract from Plutarch's biography telling the well-known story of how Cato the Elder repeatedly called for Carthage's total destruction—a deed that would in fact be carried out at the end of the Third Punic War, which Cato helped incite. Using these documents, as well as what you have learned from studying *The Challenge of the West,* write a brief analysis of the values that Romans considered important to maintaining their republic.

A. The Secret of Political Stability: Polybius Praises the Balanced Roman Constitution

As for the Roman constitution, it had three elements, each of them possessing sovereign powers: and their respective share of power in the whole state had been regulated with such a scrupulous regard to equality and equilibrium, that no one could say for certain, not even a native, whether the constitution as a whole were an aristocracy or democracy or despotism. And no wonder: for if we confine our observation to the power of the Consuls we should be inclined to regard it as despotic; if on that of the Senate, as aristocratic; an if finally one looks at the power possessed by the people it would seem a clear case of a democracy.

B. The Senate Responds to an Influx of "Uncontrolled Foreign Cults" in the Second Century B.C.

This pestilential evil spread to Rome like a contagious disease. At first the size of the city, with room and tolerance for such evils, concealed it, but information at length reached the consul Postumius. . . . He laid the matter before the Senate . . . The senators were seized by a panic of fear, both for the public safety, lest these secret conspiracies and nocturnal gatherings contain some hidden harm or danger, and for themselves individually, lest some relatives be involved in this vice. They decreed a vote of thanks to the consul for having investigated the matter so diligently and without creating any public disturbance. Then they commissioned the consuls to conduct a special inquiry . . . and to offer rewards to induce other informers to come forward. The priests of these rites, whether men or women, were to be sought out not only in Rome, but in every place . . . Edicts were to be published in the city of Rome and throughout Italy, ordering that none who had been initiated into the Bacchic rites should be minded to gather or come together for the celebration of these rites, or to perform any such ritual; and, above all, an inquiry was to be conducted regarding those persons who had gathered together or conspired to promote debauchery or crime.

A copy has survived of the report that the consuls wrote to record the Senate's edict.

"Let no one be minded to perform ceremonies in secret; nor let anyone be minded to perform ceremonies, whether in public or private or outside the city, without approaching the urban praetor and obtaining his authorization with the approval of the Senate. . . . Let no one be minded to hold services in a group larger than five men and women together, and let not more than two men and three women be minded to attend, except on authorization of the urban praetor and the Senate as recorded above."

C. Flavius Vegetius Describes Basic Training in the Roman Army

The Recruits Must Be Taught the Military Step, Run, and Jump

In the first order of practice the recruits must be taught the military step. For nothing is more important both on the march and in the battle line than that all the soldiers observe the order of advancing. This is not able to be done unless by constant practice they learn to walk swiftly and in step. For a divided and unorganized army has always sustained most severe danger from the enemy. By using the military step, therefore, twenty thousand paces ought to be completed within five hours, at least, while on campaigns. However, by the full step, which is faster, twenty-four thousand paces ought to be covered in the same number of hours. Whenever you increase this, then the soldier is running, and the exact distance covered is not able to be defined. But the recruits also ought to become accustomed to running, so that they might attack the enemy with greater force, and in order that they might occupy the better places quickly when the opportunity presents, itself; or that they might get possession of a place before the enemy who is trying to do the same; in order that they might carry out scouting activities quickly and return more quickly; and that they might overtake those fleeing more easily. The recruits must be trained for jumping also, by which ditches are crossed or any high obstacle is overcome, so that whenever they come upon difficulties of this sort, they might be able to overcome them without effort. Furthermore, in the battle itself and in a skirmish with spears the soldier approaching with a leap and a jump dazzles the eyes and deters the mind of the adversary, and thus without doubt he prepares himself for defense and resistance before the enemy even strikes a blow. Sallust recalls that Gnaeus Pompeius the Great in his training, "completed with the agile in jumping, with the speedy in running, and with the strong in carrying." For otherwise he would have been no equal for Sertorius except that he had prepared both himself and his soldiers for battle by frequent training.

D. Polybius Analyzes Roman Military Discipline

The Romans wish the centurions to be not so much venturesome daredevils as natural leaders of a steady and sedate spirit, not so much men who will initiate attacks and open the battle as men who will hold their ground when worsted and hard pressed and be ready to die at their posts . . . The troops [whom centurions command] often face certain death, refusing to leave their ranks even when vastly outnumbered, owing to dread of the punishment they would meet with [if they did]. And, again, men who have lost a shield or sword or any of their other arms in battle unexpectedly throw themselves into the midst of the enemy, hoping either to recover the lost object or to escape by death inevitable disgrace and the insults of their relatives. Even those [delinquent in their duty] who manage to escape [after a court martial] are not saved thereby: impossible! For they are not allowed to return to their homes, and none of his relatives would dare to receive such a man in his house. So that those who have once fallen into this misfortune are utterly ruined.

E. Cato Urges the Destruction of Carthage

Some will have the overthrow of Carthage to have been one of his last acts of state; when, indeed, Scipio the younger did by his valour give it the last blow, but the war, chiefly by the counsel and advice of Cato, was undertaken on the following occasion. Cato was sent to the Carthaginians and Masinissa, King of Numidia, who were at war with one another, to know the cause of their difference. He, it seems, had been a friend of the Romans from the beginning; and they, to, since they were conquered by Scipio, were of the Roman confederacy, having been shorn of their power by loss of territory and a heavy tax. Finding Carthage, not (as the Romans thought) low and in an ill condition, but well manned, full of riches and all sorts of arms and ammunition, and perceiving the Carthaginians carry it high, he conceived that it was not a time for the Romans to adjust affairs between them and Masinissa; but rather that they themselves would fall into danger, unless they should find means to check this rapid new growth of Rome's ancient irreconcilable enemy. Therefore, returning quickly to Rome, he acquainted the Senate that the former defeats and blows given to the Carthaginians had not so much diminished their strength, as it had abated their imprudence and folly; that they were not become weaker, but more experienced in war, and did only skirmish with the Numidians to exercise themselves the better to cope with the Romans: that the peace and league they had made was but a kind of suspension of war which awaited a fairer opportunity to break out again.

Moreover, they say that, shaking his gown, he took occasion to let drop some African figs before the Senate. And on their admiring the size and beauty of them, he presently added, that the place that bore them was but three days' sail from Rome. Nay, he never after this gave his opinion, but at the end he would be sure to come out with this sentence, "Also, CARTHAGE OUGHT UTTERLY TO BE DESTROYED." But Publius Scipio Nasica would always declare his opinion to the contrary, in these words, "It seems requisite to me that Carthage should still stand." For seeing his countrymen to be grown wanton and insolent, and the people made, by their prosperity, obstinate and disobedient to the Senate, and drawing the whole city, whither they would, after them, he would have had the fear of Carthage to serve as a bit to hold the contumacy of the multitude; and he looked upon the

Carthaginians as too weak to overcome the Romans, and too great to be despised by them. On the other side, it seemed a perilous thing to Cato that a city which had been always great, and was now grown sober and wise, by reason of its former calamities, should still lie, as it were in wait for the follies and dangerous excesses of the over-powerful Roman people; so that he thought it the wisest course to have all outward dangers removed, when they had so many inward ones among themselves.

Thus Cato, they say, stirred up the third and last war against the Carthaginians: but no sooner was the said war begun, than he died. . . .

Document Set 5.2 References

A. The Secret of Political Stability: Polybius Praises the Balanced Roman Constitution
   Polybius, *Histories,* 6:11, trans. Evelyn S. Schuckburgh (Bloomington: Indiana University Press, 1962), 1:468–469).
B. The Senate Responds to an Influx of "Uncontrolled Foreign Cults" in the Second Century B.C.
   Naphtali Lewis and Meyer Reinhold, eds., *Roman Civilization: Selected Readings* (New York: Columbia University Press, 1951), 1:470, 472–473.
C. Flavius Vegetius Describes Basic Training in the Roman Army
   Flavius Vegetius, *Epiitoma rei militaris,* trans. and ed. Leo F. Stelten (New York: Peter Lang, 1990), 23–25.
D. Polybius Analyzes Roman Military Discipline
   Lewis and Reinhold, 1:435, 437.
E. Cato Urges the Destruction of Carthage
   Plutarch, *Lives,* "Cato the Elder," trans. John Dryden, rev. Arthur Hugh Clough (New York: Modern Library, n.d.), 430–431.

DOCUMENT SET 5.3
The Social and Civil Struggle

The Roman revolution was a century-long crisis set in motion by the Gracchus brothers' attempt to halt the declining economic status of lower-class citizen-farmers and culminating in the civil wars that followed the assassination of Julius Caesar in 44 B.C. Throughout the struggle, the Roman political elite desperately sought wealth, intrigued and maneuvered for power, and frequently fought one another.

The historian Sallust (86–34 B.C.), himself an adherent of Caesar and not above corruption and extortion, in his *Catiline War* paints a devastating portrait of the adventurer Catilina (108–62 B.C.), who tried to incite a revolt at Rome. Sallust's account is valuable for its description of the desperadoes to whom Catilina appealed—notice the presence of a talented and daring woman among them—and for its analysis of Catilina's character. Do you find it credible that such personalities could be stirred to action under revolutionary conditions?

Julius Caesar (100–44 B.C.) speaks for himself in Document B. In an extract from his "Commentaries on the Civil War," Caesar recalls the arguments he used to urge his troops to fight his enemy, Pompey. What does this extract tell you about the motivations of the men (leaders and followers alike) who waged Rome's civil wars? Plutarch reflects upon Caesar's aim to become king in Document C. Because of the Romans' deep abhorrence of kingship (not even the most despotic of emperors in the centuries that followed dared to revive the title), it may be that Caesar's royal ambition was more a figment of his enemies' rhetoric than an actual fact. Nonetheless, Caesar plainly aimed at ending the Civil War by creating a one-man dictatorship; and it was for this offense against Rome's republican tradition that in 44 B.C. he was assassinated, in a conspiracy that Marcus Brutus joined. Analyze the convoluted motives that Plutarch ascribes to the various actors described here. (You may notice how closely Plutarch's account was followed by Shakespeare in his tragedy *Julius Caesar*.)

The final selection, Document D, comes from an oration that Cicero (106–44 B.C.) delivered shortly after Caesar's assassination, before the political consequences of that event were becoming clear. Cicero had involuntarily retired from politics when Caesar was killed and at first tried to stay neutral; his first speech on returning (which appears here) was equivocal. Soon, however, he opposed Antony openly and tried to work for the restoration of his beloved Republic, for which offense he was executed on the orders of the Second Triumvirate. In Document D, note Cicero's fears about the forces that Caesar's assassination may have unleashed.

Using these document and referring to *The Challenge of the West,* write a brief essay on the forces propelling participants in Rome's civil wars.

A. Sallust Condemns Catilina and His Disreputable Crew

Lucius Catilina, scion of a noble family, had great vigour both of mind and of body, but an evil and depraved nature. From youth up he revelled in civil wars, murder, pillage, and political dissension, and amid these he spent his early manhood. His body could endure hunger, cold and want of sleep to an incredible degree; his mind was reckless, cunning, treacherous, capable of any form of pretence or concealment. Covetous of others' possessions, he was prodigal of his own; he was violent in his passions. He possessed a certain amount of eloquence, but little discretion. His disordered mind ever craved the monstrous, incredible, gigantic.

After the domination of Lucius Sulla the man had been seized with a mighty desire of getting control of the government, recking little by what manner he should achieve it, provided he made himself supreme. His haughty spirit was goaded more and more every day by poverty and a sense of guilt, both of which he had augmented by the practices of which I have already spoken. He was spurred on, also, by the corruption of the public morals, which were being ruined by two great evils of an opposite character, extravagance and avarice. . . . [There follows a long digression on how Rome's ancient republican virtues had become corrupted by wealth and personal ambition.]

In a city so great and so corrupt Catiline found it a very easy matter to surround himself, as by a bodyguard, with troops of criminals and reprobates of every kind. For whatever wanton, glutton, or gamester had wasted his patrimony in play, feasting, or debauchery; anyone who had contracted an immense debt that he might buy immunity from disgrace or crime; all, furthermore, from every side who had been convicted of murder or sacrilege, or feared prosecution for their crimes; those, too, whom hand and tongue supported by perjury or the blood of their fellow citizens; finally, all who were hounded by disgrace, poverty, or an evil conscience—all these were nearest and dearest to Catiline. And if any guiltless man did chance to become his friend, daily intercourse and the allurements of vice soon made him as bad or almost as bad as the rest. But most of all Catiline sought the intimacy of the young; their minds, still pliable as they were and easily moulded, were without difficulty ensnared by his wiles. For carefully noting the passion which burned in each, according to his time of life, he found harlots for some or bought dogs and horses for others; in fine, he spared neither expense nor his own decency, provided he could make them submissive and loyal to himself. I am aware that some have believed that the young men who frequented Catiline's house set but little store by their chastity; but that report became current rather for other reasons than because anyone had evidence of its truth. . . .

To the young men whom he had ensnared, as I have described, he taught many forms of wickedness. From their number he supplied false witnesses and forgers; he bade them make light of honour, fortune, and dangers; then, when he had sapped their good repute and modesty, he called for still greater crimes. If there was no immediate motive for wrong doing, he nevertheless waylaid and murdered innocent as well as guilty, indeed, he preferred to be needlessly vicious and cruel rather than to allow their hands and spirits to grow weak through lack of practice.

Relying upon such friends and accomplices as these, Catiline formed the plan of overthrowing the government, both because his own debt was enormous in all parts of the world and because the greater number of Sulla's veterans, who had squandered their property and now thought with longing of their former pillage and victories, were eager for civil war. There was no army in Italy; Gnaeus Pompeius was waging war in distant parts of the world; Catiline himself had high hopes as a candidate for the consulship; the senate was anything but alert; all was peaceful and quiet; this was his golden opportunity. . . .

Accordingly, when the elections had been held Marcus Tullius and Gaius Antonius were proclaimed consuls, and this at first filled the conspirators and consternation. And yet Catiline's frenzy did not abate. On the contrary, he increased his activity every day, made collections of arms at strategic points in Italy, and borrowed money on his own credit or that of his friends, sending it to Faesulae to a certain Manlius, who afterwards was the first to take the field. At that time Catiline is said to have gained the support of many men of all conditions and even of some women; the latter at first had met their enor-

mous expenses by prostitution, but later, when their time of life had set a limit to their traffic but not to their extravagance, had contracted a huge debt. Through their help Catiline believed that he could tempt the city slaves to his side and set fire to Rome; and then either attach the women's husbands to his cause or make away with them.

XXV. Now among these women was Sempronia, who had often committed many crimes of masculine daring. In birth and beauty, in her husband also and children, she was abundantly favoured by fortune; well read in the literature of Greece and Rome, able to play the lyre and dance more skilfully than an honest woman need, and having many other accomplishments which minister to voluptuousness. But there was nothing which she held so cheap as modesty and chastity; you could not easily say whether she was less sparing of her money or her honour; her desires were so ardent that she sought men more often than she was sought by them. Even before the time of the conspiracy she had often broken her word, repudiated her debts, been privy to murder; poverty and extravagance combined had driven her headlong. Nevertheless, she was a woman of no mean endowments; she could write verses, bandy jests, and use language which was modest, or tender, or wanton; in fine, she possessed a high degree of wit and of charm. . . .

B. Caesar Rallies His Troops to Fight Pompey

When this was known Caesar addresses his troops. He relates all the wrongs that his enemies had ever done him, and complains that Pompeius had been led astray and corrupted by them through jealousy and a desire to detract from his credit, though he had himself always supported and aided his honour and dignity. He complains that a new precedent had been introduced into the state whereby the right of tribunicial intervention, which in earlier years had been restored by arms, was now being branded with ignominy and crushed by arms. Sulla, he said, though stripping the tribunicial power of everything, had nevertheless left its right of intervention free, while Pompeius, who had the credit of having restored the privileges that were lost, had taken away even those that they had before. There had been no instance of the decree that the magistrates should take measures to prevent the state from suffering harm (the declaration and decision of the senate by which the Roman people are called to arms) except in the case of pernicious laws, tribunicial violence, a popular secession, or the seizure of temples and elevated positions: and he explains that these precedents of a former age had been expiated by the downfall of Saturninus and of the Gracchi. No event of this kind had occurred at the time in question or had even been thought of. He exhorts them to defend from his enemies the reputation and dignity of the commander under whose guidance they have administered the state with unfailing good fortune for nine years, fought many successful battles, and pacified the whole of Gaul and Germany. Thereupon the men of the Thirteenth Legion, which was present (he had called this out at the beginning of the disorder; the rest had not yet come together), exclaim that they are ready to repel the wrongs of their commander and of the tribunes.

c. Plutarch Recounts Caesar's Overweening Ambition

But that which brought upon him the most apparent and mortal hatred was his desire of being king; which gave the common people the first occasion to quarrel with him, and proved the most specious pretence to those who had been his secret enemies all along. Those who would have procured him that title gave it out that it was foretold in the Sibyls' books[1] that the Romans should conquer the Parthians when they fought against them under the conduct of a king, but not before. And one day, as Caesar was coming down from Alba to Rome, some were so bold as to salute him by the name of king; but he, finding the people disrelish it, seemed to resent it himself, and said his name was Caesar, not king. Upon this there was a general silence, and he passed on looking not very well pleased or contented. Another time, when the senate had conferred on him some extravagant honours, he chanced to receive the message as he was sitting on the rostra, where, though the consuls and prætors themselves waited on him, attended by the whole body of the senate, he did not rise, but behaved himself to them as if they had been private men, and told them his honours wanted rather to be retrenched then increased. This treatment offended not only the senate, but the commonalty too, as if they thought the affront upon the senate equally reflected upon the whole republic; so that all who could decently leave him went off, looking much discomposed. Caesar, perceiving the false step he had made, immediately retired home; and laying his throat bare, told his friends that he was ready to offer this to any one

would give the stroke. But afterwards he made the malady from which he suffered [epilepsy] the excuse for his sitting, saying that those who are attacked by it lose their presence of mind if they talk much standing; that they presently grow giddy, fall into convulsions, and quite lose their reason. But this was not the reality, for he would willingly have stood up to the senate, had not Cornelius Balbus, one of his friends, or rather flatterers, hindered him. "Will you not remember," said he, "you are Cæsar, and claim the honour which is due to your merit?"

He gave a fresh occasion of resentment by his affront to the tribunes. The Lupercalia were then celebrated, a feast at the first institution belonging, as some writers say, to the shepherds, and having some connection with the Arcadian Lycae. Many young noblemen and magistrates run up and down the city with their upper garments off, striking all they meet with thongs of hide, by way of sport; and many women, even of the highest rank, place themselves in the way, and hold out their hands to the lash, as boys in a school do to the master, out of a belief that it procures an easy labour to those who are with child, and makes those conceive who are barren. Caesar, dressed in a triumphal robe, seated himself in a golden chair at the rostra to view this ceremony. Antony, as consul, was one of those who ran this course, and when he came into the forum, and the people made way for him, he went up and reached to Caesar a diadem wreathed with laurel. Upon this there was a shout, but only a slight one, made by the few who were planted there for that purpose; but when Caesar refused it, there was universal applause. Upon the second offer, very few, and upon the second refusal, all again applauded. Caesar finding it would not take, rose up, and ordered the crown to be carried into the capitol. Caesar's statues were afterwards found with royal diadems on their heads. Flavius and Marullus, two tribunes of the people, went presently and pulled them off, and having apprehended those who first saluted Caesar asking committed them to prison. The people followed them with acclamations, and called them by the name of Brutus, because Brutus was the first who ended the succession of kings,[2] and transferred the power which before was lodged in one man into the hands of the senate and people. Caesar so far resented this, that he displaced Marullus and Flavius; and in urging his charges against them, at the same time ridiculed the people, by himself giving the men more than once the names of Bruti and Cumæi.

This made the multitude turn their thoughts to

---

[1] prophetic writings, widely read in ancient Rome

[2] a reference to Marcus Brutus's ancestor, see Set 5.1, Document A

Marcus Brutus, who, by his father's side, was thought to be descended from that first Brutus, and by his mother's side from the Servilii, another noble family, being besides nephew and son-in-law to Cato. But the honours and favours he had received from Cæsar took off the edge from the desires he might himself have felt for overthrowing the new monarchy. For he had not only been pardoned himself after Pompey's defeat at Pharsalia, and had procured the same grace for many of his friends, but was one in whom Cæsar had a particular confidence. He had at that time the most honourable prætorship for the year, and was named for the consulship four years after, being preferred before Cassius, his competitor. Upon the question as to the choice, Cæsar, it is related, said that Cassius had the fairer pretensions, but that he could not pass by Brutus. Nor would he afterwards listen to some who spoke against Brutus, when the conspiracy against him was already afoot, but laying his hand on his body, said to the informers, "Brutus will wait for this skin of mine," intimating that he was worthy to bear rule on account of his virtue, but would not be base and ungrateful to gain it. Those who desired a change, and looked on him as the only, or at least the most proper, person to effect it, did not venture to speak with him; but in the night-time laid papers about his chair of state, where he used to sit and determine causes, with such sentences in them as, "You are asleep, Brutus," "You are no longer Brutus." Cassius, when he perceived his ambition a little raised upon this, was more instant than before to work him yet further, having himself a private grudge against Cæsar for some reasons that we have mentioned in the Life of Brutus. Nor was Cæsar without suspicions of him, and said once to his friends, "What do you think Cassius is aiming at? I don't like him, he looks so pale." And when it was told him that Antony and Dolabella were in a plot against him, he said he did not fear such fat, luxurious men, but rather the pale, lean fellows, meaning Cassius and Brutus.

D. Cicero Cautiously Defends Caesar's Assassination

. . . The speech Marcus Antonius made that day was a noble one; his good will too was conspicuous; in a word, it was through him and his sons that peace was established with our most illustrious citizens.

And with these beginnings the sequel agreed. To the deliberations he held at his house on public affairs he invited the chief men of the State; to this our body he made the most favourable reports; nothing then but what was known to all men was being found in Caius Caesar's note-books; with the greatest decision he replied to the questions put to him. Were any exiles recalled? One, he said; beyond the one, nobody. Were any exemptions from taxation given? None, he replied. He even wished us to assent to the motion of Servius Sulpicius, a man of great distinction, that from the Ides of March no notice of any decree or grant of Caesar's should be posted. Much, and that excellent, I pass over, for there is one particular act of Marcus Antonius which I must mention at once. The dictatorship, which had already usurped the might of regal authority, he abolished utterly out of the State; about that we did not even debate. He brought in draft the decree he wished passed, and when this was read we followed his recommendation with the greatest enthusiasm, and passed him a vote of thanks in the most complimentary terms.

It seemed almost as if light had been shed upon us, now there had been removed, not merely despotism—that we had endured—but also the dread of despotism; and a great assurance had been given by him to the State of his wish that it should be free, in that he had utterly abolished the title of dictator—an office often established by law—on account of men's recollection of the perpetual dictatorship. A few days after, the Senate was relieved from the peril of proscription; the fugitive slave who had usurped the name of Marius was executed. And all these things were done jointly with his colleague; other things afterwards were Dolabella's own acts,[3] yet I believe that, had not Dolabella's colleague been absent, they would have been the joint acts of the two. For when an illimitable evil was creeping into the State, and spreading day by day more widely, and when the same men were building an altar in the Forum who had carried out that burial that was no burial, and when daily more and more scoundrels, together with slaves like themselves, were threatening the dwellings and temples of the city, so signal was the punishment Dolabella inflicted not only on audacious and rascally slaves, but also on debauched and wicked freemen, and so prompt was his upsetting of that accursed column, that it seems to me marvellous how greatly the time that followed differed from that one day.

For look you: on the Kalends of June, on which they had summoned us to sit, all was changed: nothing was done through the Senate, much—and that important—was done through the people, and in the absence of the people and against its will. The consuls elect said they dared not come into the Senate; the lib-

---

[3] Dolabella was a member of the Senate.

erators of their country were exiles from the city from whose neck they had struck off the yoke of slavery, while none the less the consuls themselves, both in public meetings and in common talk, were passing eulogies upon them. Those that claimed the name of veterans, for whom this our body had been most carefully solicitous, were being incited, not to preserve what they already possessed, but to hope for new plunder. As I preferred to hear of these things rather than to see them, and held an honorary commission as legate, I departed with the intention of being at home on the Kalends of January, which seemed the first likely date for a meeting of the Senate.

Document Set 5.3 References

A. Sallust Condemns Catilina and His Disputable Crew
Sallust, *Catiline War*, trans. C. Wolfe, Loeb Classical Library (London: Heinemann, 1921), 9–11, 17–25, 27–29, 43–45.

B. Caesar Rallies His Troops to Fight Pompey
Julius Caesar, *Commentaries on the Civil War*, 1:17, trans. A. G. Peskett, Loeb Classical Library (London: Heinemann, 1914).

C. Plutarch Recounts Caesar's Overweening Ambition
Plutarch, *Lives*, "Cato the Elder," trans. John Dryden, rev. Arthur Hugh Clough (New York: Modern Library, n.d.), 888–890.

D. Cicero Cautiously Defends Caesar's Assassination
Cicero, Philippius, trans. Walter A. C. Ker, Loeb Classical Library (Cambridge, Mass.: Harvard University Press, 1926), 21–25.

CHAPTER

6

The Roman Empire,
44 B.C.—A.D. 284

DOCUMENT SET 6.1
The Principate

The documents in this set offer sources for understanding the Principate, the regime established by Augustus at the conclusion of the civil wars and the foundation for the imperial system. Bear in mind that although the Republic was now dead, Augustus was careful to mask its demise—and his own status as virtually a crowned head—with the fiction that revered old institutions were being but slightly adapted.

Examine Document A as a sample of Augustus's image building. This document is an extract from a long inscription that Augustus erected in Asia Minor to glorify his accomplishments and justify his reign. (Similar inscriptions probably appeared throughout the Roman world.) What evidence does this document reveal about the conditions of life as Rome emerged from decades of turmoil into the stability that Augustus promised? How useful to modern historians do you think such a document is? Document B is another inscription, this one raised by Emperor Vespasian (*A.D. 70–79) celebrating his patronage in the Spanish city of Sabora. How does this document supplement what you have learned from Document A?

In Document C you can read part of the assessment of Augustus's reign by a Roman historian who lived a century later, Suetonius (A.D. 75–160). Not an uncritical admirer of Augustus, Suetonius was realistic about the need for a conservative regime that would reinstate traditional Roman values. Compare Suetonius's account with Augustus's own in Document A, and notice too the stress that Suetonius

lays on Augustus's sponsorship of public works and entertainments.

Document D is an extract from another great Roman historian, Tacitus (A.D. 55–120). Here, at the opening of his *Histories,* Tacitus gives a general overview of the disasters unleashed upon the death of the tyrannical Emperor Nero in A.D. 68. What does this document reveal about the values of a conservative Roman aristocrat like Tacitus?

Document E comes from a later date. The Roman legal scholar Ulpian (A.D. 170–223), born in what is today Lebanon, wrote nearly 280 books explaining Roman laws and its relevance to contemporary issues. He lived through the tumultuous, despotic reign of the early third-century tyrant Caracalla, and he was murdered by the Praetorian Guard for advocating reforms contrary to their interests. Here he characteristically pleads for fairness as the basis of the law.

Using *The Challenge of the West* as a guide, extract from these documents an analysis of the theory and practice of government in the first two centuries of the Roman Empire.

A. Augustus Proclaims His Restoration of Good Government

Below is a copy of the deeds of the divine Augustus, by which he subjected the whole world to the dominion of the Roman people, and of the amounts which he expended upon the commonwealth and the Roman people, as engraved upon two brazen columns which are set up at Rome.

In my twentieth year, acting upon my own judgment and at my own expense, I raised an army by means of which I restored to liberty the commonwealth which had been oppressed by the tyranny of a faction. On account of this the senate by laudatory decrees admitted me to its order, in the consulship of Gaius Pansa and Aulus Hirtius, and at the same time gave me consular rank in the expression of opinion, and gave me the *imperium*. It also voted that I as propraetor, together with the consuls, should see to it that the commonwealth suffered no harm.

Those who killed my father I drove into exile by lawful judgments, avenging their crime, and afterwards, when they waged war against the commonwealth, I twice defeated them in battle.

I undertook civil and foreign wars by land and sea throughout the whole world, and as victor I showed mercy to all surviving citizens. Foreign peoples, who could be pardoned with safety, I preferred to preserve rather than to destroy. About five hundred thousand Roman citizens took the military oath of allegiance to me. Of these I have settled in colonies or sent back to their *municipia*, upon the expiration of their terms of service, somewhat over three hundred thousand, and to all these I have given lands purchased by me, or money for farms, out of my own means.

The dictatorship which was offered to me by the people and the senate, both when I was absent and when I was present, in the consulship of Marcus Marcellus and Lucius Arruntius, I did not accept. At a time of the greatest dearth of grain I did not refuse the charge of the food supply, which I so administered that in a few days, at my own expense, I freed the whole people from the anxiety and danger in which they then were. The annual and perpetual consulship offered to me at that time I did not accept. . . .

. . . In my sixth consulship, with Marcus Agrippa as colleague, I made a census of the people. I performed the lustration [a census] after forty-one years. In this lustration the number of Roman citizens was four million and sixty-three thousand. . . . By new legislation I have restored many customs of our ancestors which had now begun to fall into disuse, and I have myself also committed to posterity many examples worthy of imitation. . . .

Close to the temples of Honor and Virtue, near the Capena gate, the senate consecrated in honor of my return an altar to Fortune the Restorer, and upon this altar it ordered that the *pontifices* [priests] and the Vestal virgins should offer sacrifice yearly on the anniversary of the day on which I returned into the city from Syria, in the consulship of Quintus Lucretius and Marcus Vinucius, and it called the day the Augustalia, from our cognomen. . .

To each man of the Roman *plebs* I paid three hundred sesterces in accordance with the last will of my father; and in my own name, when consul for the fifth time, I gave four hundred sesterces from the spoils of the wars; again, moreover, in my tenth consulship I gave from my own estate four hundred sesterces to each man by way of *congiarium;* and in my eleventh consulship I twelve times made distributions of food, buying grain at my own expense; and in the twelfth year of my tribunitial power I three times gave four hundred sesterces to each man. These my donation have never been made to less than two hundred and fifty thousand men. In my twelfth consulship and the eighteenth year of my tribunitial power I gave to three hundred and twenty thousand of the city *plebs* sixty *denarii* apiece. In the colonies of my soldiers, when consul for the fifth time, I gave to each man a thousand sesterces from the spoils; about a hundred and twenty thousand men in the colonies received that triumphal donation. When consul for the thirteenth time I gave sixty *denarii* to the *plebs* who were at that time receiving public grain; these men were a little more than two hundred thousand in number.

For the lands which in my fourth consulship, and afterwards in the consulship of Marcus Crassus and Cnæus Lentulus, the augur, I assigned to soldiers, I paid money to the *municipia*. . . . Of all those who have established colonies of soldiers in Italy or in the provinces I am the first and only one within the memory of my age, to do this. . . .

Four times I have aided the public treasury from my own means, to such extent that I have furnished to those in charge of the treasury one hundred and fifty million sesterces. And in the consulship of Marcus Lepidus and Lucius Arruntius I paid onto the military treasury which was established by my advice that from it gratuities might be given to soldiers who have served a term of twenty or more years, one hundred and seventy million sesterces from my own estate.

Beginning with that year in which Cnæus and Publius Lentulus were consuls, when the imposts failed, I furnished aid sometimes to a hundred thousand men, and sometimes to more, by supplying grain or money for the tribute from my own land and property. . . .

[There follows a list of temples Augustus established in Rome and Palestine.]

The Capitol and the Pompeian theatre have been restored by me at enormous expense for each work, without any inscription of my name. Aqueducts which were crumbling in many places by reason of age I have restored, and I have doubled the water which bears the name Marcian by turning a new spring into its course. The Forum Julium and the basilica which was between the temple of Castor and the temple of Saturn, works begun and almost completed by my father, I have finished; and when that same basilica was consumed by fire, I began its reconstruction on an enlarged site, inscribing it with the names of my sons; and if I do not live to complete it, I have given orders that it be completed by my heirs. In accordance with a decree of the senate, while consul for the sixth time, I have restored eighty-two temples of the gods, passing over none which was at that time in need of repair. In my seventh consulship I constructed the Flaminian way from the city to Ariminum, and all the bridges except the Mulvian and Minucian. . . .

[Augustus mentions other temples and other public works that he has restored, built, or endowed.]

Three times in my own name, and five times in that of my sons or grandsons, I have given gladiatorial exhibitions; in these exhibitions about ten thousand men have fought. Twice in my own name, and three times in that of my grandson, I have offered the people the spectacle of athletes gathered from all quarters. I have celebrated games four times in my own name, and twenty-three times in the turns of other magistrates. In behalf of the college of quindecemvirs, I, as master of the college, with my colleague Agrippa, celebrated the Secular Games in the consulship of Gaius Furnius and Gaius Silanus. When consul for the thirteenth time, I first celebrated the Martial games, which since that time the consuls have given in successive years. Twenty-six times in my own name, or in that of my sons and grandsons, I have given hunts of African wild beasts in the circus, the forum, the amphitheatres, and about thirty-five hundred beasts have been killed.

I gave the people the spectacle of a naval battle beyond the Tiber, where now in the grove of the Cæsars. For this purpose an excavation was made eighteen hundred feet long and twelve hundred wide. In this contest thirty beaked ships, triremes or biremes, were engaged, besides more of smaller size. About three thousand men fought in these vessels in addition to the rowers. . . .

I have freed the sea from pirates. In that war with the slaves I delivered to their masters for punishment about thirty thousand slaves who had fled from their masters and taken up arms against the state. The whole of Italy voluntarily took the oath of allegiance to me, and demanded me as leader in that war in which I conquered at Actium. The provinces of Gaul, Spain, Africa, Sicily and Sardinia swore the same allegiance to me. There were more than seven hundred senators who at that time fought under my standards, and among these, up to the day on which these words are written, eighty-three have either before or since been made consuls, and about one hundred and seventy have been made priests.

I have extended the boundaries of all the provinces of the Roman people which were bordered by nations not yet subjected to our sway. I have reduced to a state of peace the Gallic and Spanish provinces, and Germany, the lands enclosed by the ocean from Gades to the mouth of the Elbe. The Alps from the region nearest the Adriatic as far as the Tuscan Sea I have brought into a state of peace, without waging an unjust war upon any people. My fleet has navigated the ocean from the mouth of the Rhine as far as the boundaries of the Cimbri, where before that time no Roman had ever penetrated by land or sea; and the Cimbri and Charydes and Semnones and other German peoples of that section, by means of legates, sought my friendship and that of the Roman people. By my command and under my auspices two armies at almost the same time have been led into Ethiopia and into Arabia, which is called "the Happy," and very many of the enemy of both peoples have fallen in battle, and many towns have been captured. Into Ethiopia the advance was as far as Nabata, which is next to Meroe. In Arabia the army penetrated as far as the confines of the Sabaei, to the town Mariba.

I have added Egypt to the empire of the Roman people. Of greater Armenia, when its king Artaxes was killed I could have made a province, but I preferred, after the example of our fathers, to deliver that kingdom to Tigranes, the son of king Artavasdes, and grandson of king Tigranes; and this I did through Tiberius Nero, who was then my son-in-law. And afterwards, when the same people became turbulent and rebellious, they were subdued by Gaius, my son, and I gave the sovereignty over them to king Ariobarzanes, the son of Artabazes, king of the Medes, and after his death to his son Artavasdes. When he was killed I sent into that kingdom Tigranes, who was sprung from the royal house of the Armenians. I recovered all the provinces across the Adriatic Sea, which extend toward the east, and

Cyrenaica, at that time for the most part in the possession of kings, together with Sicily and Sardinia, which had been engaged in a servile war.

I have established colonies of soldiers in Africa, Sicily, Macedonia, the two Spains, Achaia, Asia, Syria, Gallia Narbonensis and Pisidia. Italy also has twenty-eight colonies established under my auspices, which within my lifetime have become very famous and populous.

I have recovered from Spain and Gaul, and from the Dalmatians, after conquering the enemy, many military standards which had been lost by other leaders. I have compelled the Parthians to give up to me the spoils and standards of three Roman armies, and as suppliants to seek the friendship of the Roman people. Those standards, moreover, I have deposited in the sanctuary which is in the temple of Mars the Avenger.

The Pannonian peoples, whom before I became *princeps,* no army of the Roman people had ever attacked, were defeated by Tiberius Nero, at that time my son-in-law and legate; and I brought them under subjection to the empire of the Roman people, and extended the boundaries of Illyricum to the bank of the river Danube. When an army of the Dacians crossed this river, it was defeated and destroyed, and afterwards my army, led across the Danube, compelled the Dacian people to submit to the sway of the Roman people. . . .

[There follows a list of kings and other potentates who have "betaken themselves as suppliants" to Augustus.] . . . Since I have been *princeps* very many other races have made proof of the good faith of the Roman people, who never before had had any interchange of embassies and friendship with the Roman people.

In my sixth and seventh consulships, when I had put an end to the civil wars, after having obtained complete control of affairs by universal consent, I transferred the commonwealth from my own dominion to the authority of the senate and Roman people. In return for this favor on my part I received by decree of the senate the title Augustus, the door-posts of my house were publicly decked with laurels, a civic crown was fixed above my door, and in the Julian Curia was placed a golden shield, which, by its inscription, bore witness that it was given to me by the senate and Roman people on account of my valor, clemency, justice and piety. After that time I excelled all others in dignity, but of power I held no more than those also held who were my colleagues in any magistracy.

While I was consul for the thirteenth time the senate and the equestrian order and the entire Roman people gave me the title of father of the fatherland, and decreed that it should be inscribed upon the vestibule of my house and in the Curia, and in the Augustan Forum beneath the quadriga which had been, by decree of the senate, set up in my honor. When I wrote these words I was in my seventy-sixth year. . . .

[A supplementary inscription follows, listing other temples that Augustus built or restored.]

B. Revenue Sharing: Provincial Cities Receive Imperial Aid for Public Works

The Emperor Caesar Vespasian Augustus, *pontifex maximus,* holding the tribunician power for the ninth year, acclaimed *imperator* eighteen times, eight times consul, father of his country, sends greetings to the *quattuorviri* and decurions [local officials] of Sabora. Since you inform me that you are impoverished and beset by many difficulties, I permit you to build the town under my name in the plain, as you wish. The revenues which you say you were granted by the deified Augustus I reaffirm; if you desire to add any new ones, you must apply to the proconsul therefor, since I can make no decision if there is no appeal. I received your decree on July 25 and dismissed your envoys on the 29th of the same. Farewell.

The duovirs, Gaius Cornelius Severus and Marcus Septimius Severus, had this inscribed on bronze at public expense.

C. Suetonius Assesses Augustus's Reign

He was for ten years a member of the triumvirate for restoring the State to order, and though he opposed his colleagues for some time and tried to prevent a proscription, yet when it was begun, he carried it through with greater severity than either of them. . . .

While he was triumvir, Augustus incurred general detestation by many of his acts. For example, when he was addressing the soldiers and a throng of civilians had been admitted to the assembly, noticing that Pinarius, a Roman knight, was taking notes, he ordered that he be stabbed on the spot, thinking him an eaves-dropper and a spy. . . .

Selection B: Excerpt from "Imperial Intervention" from *Roman Civilization,* Vol. 2 by N. Lewis and M. Reinhold. Copyright © 1990 by Columbia University Press, excerpts from pp. 341–342. Reprinted with permission of the publisher.

He twice thought of restoring the republic; first immediately after the overthrow of Antony, remembering that his rival had often made the charge that it was his fault that it was not restored; and again in the weariness of a lingering illness, when he went so far as to summon the magistrates and the senate to his house, and submit an account of the general condition of the empire. Reflecting, however, that as he himself would not be free from danger if he should retire, so too it would be hazardous to trust the State to the control of the populace, he continued to keep it in his hands; and it is not easy to say whether his intentions or their results were the better. . . .

Since the city was not adorned as the dignity of the empire demanded, and was exposed to flood and fire, he so beautified it that he could justly boast that he had found it built of brick and left it in marble. He made it safe too for the future, so far as human foresight could provide for this.

He built many public works, in particular the following: his forum with the temple of Mars the Avenger, the temple of Apollo on the Palatine, and the fane of Jupiter the Thunderer on the Capitol. . . .

He divided the area of the city into regions and wards, arranging that the former should be under the charge of magistrates selected each year by lot, and the latter under "masters" elected by the inhabitants of the respective neighbourhoods. To guard against fires he devised a system of stations of night watchmen, and to control the floods, he widened and cleared out the channel of the Tiber, which had for some time been filled with rubbish and narrowed by jutting buildings. . . .

He restored sacred edifices which had gone to ruin through lapse of time or had been destroyed by fire, and adorned both these and the other temples with most lavish gifts. . . .

After he finally had assumed the office of pontifex maximus, . . . he collected whatever prophetic writings of Greek or Latin origin were in circulation anonymously or under the names of authors of little repute, and burned more than two thousand of them, . . . Inasmuch, as the calendar, which had been set in order by the Deified Julius, had later been confused and disordered through negligence, he restored it to its former system; and in making this arrangement he called the month Sextilis by his own surname, rather than his birth-month September. . . . He increased the number and importance of the priests, and also their allowances and privileges, in particular those of the Vestal virgins. . . .

Next to the immortal Gods he honoured the memory of the leaders who had raised the estate of the Roman people from obscurity to greatness.

Accordingly he restored the works of such men with their original inscriptions, and in the two colonnades of his forum dedicated statues of all of them in triumphal garb. . . .

Many pernicious practices militating against public security had survived as a result of the lawless habits of the civil wars, or had even arisen in time of peace. Gangs of footpads openly went about with swords by their sides, ostensibly to protect themselves, and travellers in the country, freemen and slaves alike, were seized and kept in confinement in the workhouses of the land owners; numerous leagues, too, were formed for the commission of crimes of every kind, assuming the title of some new guild. Therefore to put a stop to brigandage, he stationed guards of soldiers wherever it seemed advisable, inspected the workhouses, and disbanded all guilds, except such as were of long standing and formed for legitimate purposes. He burned the records of old debts to the treasury, which were by far the most frequent source of blackmail. . . . To prevent any action for damages or on a disputed claim from falling through or being put off, he added to the term of the courts thirty more days, which had before been taken up with honorary games. . . .

He himself administered justice regularly and sometimes up to nightfall, having a litter placed upon the tribunal, if he was indisposed, or even lying down at home. In his administration of justice he was both highly conscientious and very lenient; for to save a man clearly guilty of parricide from being sewn up in the sack, a punishment which was inflicted only on those who pleaded guilty, he is said to have put the question to him in this form: "You surely did not kill your father, did you?" . . .

He revised existing laws and enacted some new ones, for example, on extravagance, on adultery and chastity, on bribery, and on the encouragement of marriage among the various classes of citizens. Having made somewhat more stringent changes in the last of these than in the others, he was unable to carry it out because of an open revolt against its provisions, until he had abolished or mitigated a part of the penalties, besides increasing the rewards and allowing a three years' exemption from the obligation to marry after the death of a husband or wife. . . . And on finding that the spirit of the law was being evaded by betrothal with immature girls and by frequent changes of wives, he shortened the duration of betrothals and set a limit on divorce.

Since the number of the senators was swelled by a low-born and ill-assorted rabble, . . . he restored it to its former limits and distinction by two enrolments. . . . On questions of special importance he called upon the senators to give their opinions, not according to the order established by precedent, but just as he fancied, to induce each man to keep his mind on the alert, as if he were to initiate action rather than give assent to others. . . .

To enable more men to take part in the administration of the State, he devised new offices: the charge of public buildings, of the roads, of the aqueducts, of the channel of the Tiber, of the distribution of grain to the people, as well as the prefecture of the city, a board of three for choosing senators, and another for reviewing the companies of the knights whenever it should be necessary. He appointed censors, an office which had long been discontinued. . . .

He was not less generous in honouring martial prowess, for he had regular triumphs voted to above thirty generals, and the triumphal regalia to somewhat more than that number. . . .

He reviewed the companies of knights at frequent intervals, reviving the custom of the procession after long disuse. But he would not allow an accuser to force anyone to dismount as he rode by, as was often done in the past; and he permitted those who were conspicuous because of old age or any bodily infirmity to send on their horses in the review, and come on foot to answer to their names whenever they were summoned. . . .

Having obtained ten assistants from the senate, he compelled each knight to render an account of his life, punishing some of those whose conduct was scandalous and degrading others; but the greater part he reprimanded with varying degrees of severity. The mildest form of reprimand was to hand them a pair of tablets publicly, which they were to read in silence on the spot. He censured some because they had borrowed money at low interest and invested it at a higher rate. . . .

He revised the lists of the people street by street, and to prevent the commons from being called away from their occupations too often because of the distributions of grain, he determined to give out tickets for four months' supply three times a year; . . .

Considering it also of great importance to keep the people pure and unsullied by any taint of foreign or servile blood, he was most chary of conferring Roman citizenship and set a limit to manumission. . . .

He desired also to revive the ancient fashion of dress, and once when he saw in an assembly a throng of men in dark cloaks, he cried out indignantly, "Behold them, Romans, lords of the world, the nation clad in the toga," and he directed the aediles [local police] never again to allow anyone to appear in the Forum or its neighbourhood except in the toga and without a cloak.

He often showed generosity to all classes when occasion offered. For example, by bringing the royal treasures to Rome in his Alexandrian triumph he made ready money so abundant, that the rate of interest fell, and the value of real estate rose greatly; and after that, whenever there was an excess of funds from the property of those who had been condemned, he loaned it without interest for fixed periods to any who could give security for double the amount. He increased the property qualification for senators, requiring one million two hundred thousand sesterces, instead of eight hundred thousand, and making up the amount for those who did not possess it. He often gave largess to the people, but usually of different sums. . . . In times of scarcity too he often distributed grain to each man at a very low figure, sometimes for nothing, and he doubled the money tickets.

But to show that he was a prince who desired the public welfare rather than popularity, when the people complained of the scarcity and high price of wine, he sharply rebuked them . . . Once indeed in a time of great scarcity when it was difficult to find a remedy, he expelled from the city the slaves that were for sale, as well as the schools of gladiators, all foreigners with the exception of physicians and teachers, and a part of the household slaves; and when grain at last became more plentiful, he writes: "I was strongly inclined to do away forever with distributions of grain, because through dependence on them agriculture was neglected; but I did not carry out my purpose, feeling sure that they would one day be renewed through desire for popular favour." But from that time on he regulated the practice with no less regard for the interests of the farmers and grain-dealers than for those of the populace.

He surpassed all his predecessors in the frequency, variety, and magnificence of his public shows. He says that he gave games four times in his own name and twenty-three times for other magistrates, who were either away from Rome or lacked means. He gave them sometimes in all the wards and on many stages with actors in all languages, and combats of gladiators not only in the Forum or the amphitheatre, but in the Circus and in the Saepta; sometimes however, he gave nothing except a fight with wild beasts. . . . Besides he gave frequent performances of the game of Troy by older and younger boys, thinking it a time-honoured and worthy custom for the flower of the nobility to become known in this way. . . .

He sometimes employed even Roman knights in scenic and gladiatorial performances, but only before it was forbidden by decree of the senate. After that he exhibited no one of respectable parentage. . . . He did however on the day of one of the shows make a display of the first Parthian hostages that had ever been sent to Rome, by leading them through the middle of the arena and placing them in the second row above his own seat. Furthermore, if anything rare and worth seeing was ever brought to the city, it was his habit to make a special exhibit of it in any convenient place on days when no shows were appointed. For example a rhinoceros in the Saepta, a tiger on the stage and a snake of fifty cubits in the Comitium.

D. Tacitus Describes the Turmoil Following Nero's Downfall

I enter upon a time rich in catastrophes, full of fierce battles and civic strife, a time when even peace had horrors of its own; a time during which four Emperors perished by the sword; in which there were three Civil Wars, several foreign wars, and some that partook of both characters; a time of good fortune in the East, and of disaster in the West: a time when Illyricum was in revolt, Gaul wavering in her allegiance, Britain subdued and forthwith abandoned; when the Sarmatian and Suebish nations were in arms against us; when the Dacians gained glory alike from defeats inflicted and sustained, and when even Parthia was nearly moved to arms by a vain pretender to the name of Nero. Italy was smitten by calamities unknown before, or recurring after many generations, which swallowed up or overwhelmed cities in the fairest regions of Campania. Rome was devastated by fires which destroyed her most ancient Temples; the Capitol itself was burnt down by the hands of citizens. I shall have to tell of holy rites profaned, of adulteries in high places, of seas crowded with exiles, of islands stained with blood, and of horrors in the city greater still, where high birth, wealth, the acceptance of office, or the refusal of it, were accounted crimes, and where virtue proved the surest road to death.

Nor were the rewards of accusers less hateful than their villainies: some gained Consulships and Priesthoods as their spoils, some Procuratorships, others influence of a more secret kind, overturning everything, carrying all before them, by the forces of hate and terror. Slaves were bribed to betray their masters, clients their patrons; those who had no enemies were ruined by their friends.

And yet the age was not so barren of all virtue as not to exhibit some noble examples. Mothers followed their sons, wives their husbands, into exile; some kinsmen showed courage, some sons-in-law were faithful; there were slaves who held out staunchly even against torture, and illustrious men who bore their doom with fortitude; there were death-scenes as noble as those celebrated by antiquity.

And in addition to these manifold disasters in human affairs, there were prodigies in earth and sky; there were warnings from lightning, there were presages for the future, some of good, some of evil, some obscure, some not to be misunderstood: for never did the people of Rome endure calamities more grievous, never witness more convincing proof that the Gods care much for our chastisement, for our happiness not at all. . . .

The death of Nero was at first welcomed with transports of delight. But it gave rise to many reflections, not only in the city—in the minds of the Fathers, the people, and the Urban troops—but also among the Legions and their Generals; for now the secret of the Empire had been divulged, that Emperors could be made elsewhere than at Rome.

The Fathers were well pleased, making at once full use of their freedom as towards a new and absent Prince; hardly less was the satisfaction of the leading Knights. Hope ran high among the sounder part of the populace—those who were attached to great houses, or were the clients and freedmen of condemned or banished patrons; while the degraded rabble which haunts the theatres and the circus, the lowest class of slaves, as well as those persons of squandered fortunes who had been shamefully maintained by Nero, observed an attitude of sullen and greedy expectancy.

E. Ulpian Extols the Law

The term law [ius, to quote the Latin of Ulpian] derives its name from justice [justitia]. Law is the art of the good and the fair . . . We cherish justice and profess the knowledge of the good and the fair, separating the fair from the unfair, judging between the permitted and the forbidden, wanting to make people good, not only by the fear of penalties, but also by the incentives of rewards . . . The subject of law has two categories, public and private. Public law concerns the constitution of the Roman state; private law looks to the interest of individuals . . . Public law is concerned with sacred rites, with priests, with public officials. Private law is derived from the rules of natural law, the law of nations, and civil law. Natural law is what all animals have been taught by nature; this law is not confined to the human race, but is common to all animals which are produced on land or sea, and to the birds as well. From it comes the union of male and female, which we call marriage, and the procreation and rearing of children . . . Acquaintance with this law affects animals in general, even wild beasts. The law of nations is that which the various peoples of humanity observe.

Document Set 6.1 References

A. Augustus Proclaims His Restoration of Good Government
Translations and Reprints from the Original Sources of European History, vol. 5 (Philadelphia: University of Pennsylvania Press, 1898).

B. Revenue Sharing: Provincial Cities Receive Imperial Aid for Public Works
Naphtali Lewis and Meyer Reinhold, eds., *Roman Civilization: Selected Readings* (New York: Columbia University Press, 1951), 341–342.

C. Suetonius Assesses Augustus's Reign
Suetonius *Lives of the Caesars*, 2:27–35, 37–43, trans. J. C. Rolfe, Loeb Classical Library (London: Heinemann, 1920).

D. Tacitus Describes the Turmoil Following Nero's Downfall
Tacitus, *Histories*, 1:1–15, trans. George Gilbert Ramsey (London: J. Murray, 1915).

E. Ulpian Extols the Law
Lewis and Reinhold, 2:543.

DOCUMENT SET 6.2
Forgotten Values and Virtuous Barbarians

Lamenting the passing of the good old virtuous days seems to have been an almost universal theme of Roman writers—at least in those writings that have survived. This set offers a variety of examples. Document A is a prose translation from one of the odes of Horace (65 B.C.–8 B.C.): these poems date from the reign of Augustus and characteristically deplore the decline of olden values.

In Document B we return to the writings of Tacitus. Having lived some years in Roman-occupied Germany, Tacitus wrote his *Germania* not only to inform his fellow citizens about the northern "barbarians" but also to scold Romans for having degenerated from the ancient values that German tribesman still upheld. Tacitus's *Agricola* (Document C) has a somewhat similar purpose: he tries to shame his Roman contemporaries by holding up for admiration his own father-in-law, Agricola, the conqueror of Britain. Although the book is of questionable value as a biography, do you suppose that it might have other value as a source for historians?

In Document D we remain on Rome's northern frontier, looking over the shoulder of Rome's philosopher-emperor Marcus Aurelius (*A.D. 161–181), who spent much of his reign fighting off barbarian tribes. His *Meditations,* from which this extract is taken, express a Stoic's resignation in the face of life's tribulations: if ever there was a Roman ruler who truly embodied the ancient virtues, it was Marcus Aurelius.

A. Horace Laments the Decline of Roman Family Values

Thy fathers' sins, O Roman, thou, though guiltless, shalt expiate, till thou dost restore the crumbling temples and shrines of the gods and their statues soiled with grimy smoke. 'Tis by holding thyself the servant of the gods that thou dost rule; with them all things begin; to them ascribe the outcome! Outraged, they have visited unnumbered woes on sorrowing Hesperia. Already twice Monaeses and the band of Pacorus have crushed our ill-starred onslaughts, and now beam with joy to have added spoil from us to their paltry necklaces. Beset with civil strife, the City has narrowly escaped destruction at the hands of Dacian and of Aethiop, the one sore dreaded for his fleet, the other better with the flying arrow. Teeming with sin, our times have sullied first the marriage-bed, our offspring, and our homes; sprung from this source, disaster's stream has overflowed the folk and fatherland. The maiden early takes delight in learning Grecian dances, and trains herself in coquetry e'en now, and plans unholy amours, with passion unrestrained. Soon midst her husband's revels she seeks younger paramours, nor stops to choose on whom she swiftly shall bestow illicit joys when lights are banished; but openly, when bidden, and not without her husband's knowledge, she rises, be it some peddler summons her, or the captain of some Spanish ship, lavish purchaser of shame.

Not such the sires of whom were sprung the youth that dyed the sea with Punic blood, and struck down Pyrrhus and great Antiochus and Hannibal, the dire; but a manly brood of peasant soldiers, taught to turn the clods with Sabine hoe, and at a strict mother's bidding to bring cut firewood, when the sun shifted the shadows of the mountain sides and lifted the yoke from weary steers, bringing the welcome time of rest with his departing car.

What do the ravages of time not injure! Our parents' age, worse than our grandsires', has brought forth us less worthy and destined soon to yield an offspring still more wicked.

B. Noble Savages: Tacitus Encounters the Germans

In general the country, though varying here and there to appearance, is covered over with wild forests or filthy swamps, being more humid on the side of Gaul but bleaker toward Noricum and Pannonia.[1] It is suitable enough for grain but does not permit the cultivation of fruit trees; and though rich in flocks and herds these are for the most part small, the cattle not even possessing their natural beauty nor spreading horns. The people take pride in possessing a large number of animals, these being their sole and most cherished wealth. Whether it was in mercy or wrath that the gods denied them silver and gold, I know not. . . .

They choose their kings on account of their ancestry, their generals for their valor. The kings do not have free and unlimited power and the generals lead by example rather than command, winning great admiration if they are energetic and fight in plain

[1] that is, toward what is today Austria, Hungary, and Croatia

sight in front of the line. But no one is allowed to put a culprit to death or to imprison him, or even to beat him with stripes except the priests, and then not by way of a punishment or at the command of the general but as though ordered by the god who they believe aids them in their fighting. Certain figures and images taken from their sacred groves they carry into battle, but their greatest incitement to courage is that a division of horse or foot is not made up by chance or by accidental association but is formed of families and clans; and their dear ones are close at hand so that the wailings of the women and the crying of the children can be heard during the battle. These are for each warrior the most sacred witnesses of his bravery, these his dearest applauders. They carry their wounds to their mothers and their wives, nor do the latter fear to count their number and examine them while they bring them food and urge them to deeds of valor.

It is related how on certain occasions their forces already turned to flight and retreating have been rallied by the women who implored them by their prayers and bared their breasts to their weapons, signifying thus the captivity close awaiting them, which is feared far more intensely on account of their women than for themselves; to such an extent indeed that those states are more firmly bound in treaty among whose hostages maidens of noble family are also required. Further, they believe that the sex has a certain sanctity and prophetic gift, and they neither despise their counsels nor disregard their answers. . . .

Concerning minor matters the chiefs deliberate, but in important affairs all the people are consulted, although the subjects referred to the common people for judgment are discussed beforehand by the chiefs. Unless some sudden and unexpected event calls them together they assemble on fixed days either at the new moon or the full moon, for they think these the most auspicious times to begin their undertakings. They do not reckon time by the number of days, as we do, but by the number of nights. So run their appointments, their contracts; the night introduces the day, so to speak. A disadvantage arises from their regard for liberty in that they do not come together at once as if commanded to attend, but two or three days are wasted by their delay in assembling. When the crowd is sufficient they take their places fully armed. Silence is proclaimed by the priests, who have on these occasions the right to keep order. Then the king or a chief addresses them, each being heard according to his age, noble blood, reputation in warfare and eloquence, though more because he has the power to persuade than the right to command. If an opinion is displeasing they reject if by shouting; if

they agree to it they clash with their spears. The most complimentary form of assent is that which is expressed by means of their weapons.

It is also allowable in the assembly to bring up accusations, and to prosecute capital offenses. Penalties are distinguished according to crime. Traitors and deserters are hung to trees. Weaklings and cowards and those guilty of infamous crimes are cast into the mire of swamps. . . .

They undertake no business whatever either of a public or a private character save they be armed. But it is not customary for any one to assume arms until the tribe has recognized his competence to use them. Then in a full assembly some one of the chiefs or the father or relatives of the youth invest him with the shield and spear. This is the sign that the lad has reached the age of manhood; this is his first honor. . . .

In the intervals of peace they spend little time in hunting but much in idleness, given over to sleep and eating; all the bravest and most warlike doing nothing, while the hearth and home and the care of the fields is given over to the women, the old men and the various infirm members of the family. . . .

It is well known that none of the German tribes live in cities, nor even permit their dwellings to be closely joined to each other. They live separated and in various places, as a spring or a meadow or a grove strikes their fancy. They lay out their villages not as with us in connected or closely-joined houses, but each one surrounds his dwelling with an open space, either as a protection against conflagration or because of their ignorance of the art of building. They do not even make use of rough stones or tiles. They use for all purposes undressed timber, giving no beauty or comfort. Some parts they plaster carefully with earth of such purity and brilliancy as to form a substitute for painting and designs in color. They are accustomed also to dig out subterranean caves which they cover over with great heaps of manure as a refuge against the cold and a place for storing grain, for retreats of this sort render the extreme cold of their winters bearable and, whenever an enemy has come upon them, though he lays waste the open country he is either ignorant of what is hidden underground or else it escapes him for the very reason that is has to be searched for.

Generally their only clothing is a cloak fastened with a clasp, or if they haven't that, with a thorn; this being their only garment, they pass whole days about the hearth or near a fire. The richest of them are distinguished by wearing a tunic . . . There are those, also, who wear the skins of wild beasts, those nearest the Roman border in a careless manner, but those further back more elegantly, as those do who have no better clothing obtained by commerce. They select certain animals, and stripping off their hides sew on them patches of spotted skins taken from those strange beasts that the distant ocean and the unknown sea bring forth. The women wear the same sort of dress as the men except that they wrap themselves in linen garments which they adorn with purple stripes and do not lengthen out the upper part of the tunic into sleeves, but leave the arms bare the whole length. The upper part of their breasts is also exposed. However, their marriage code is strict, and in no other part of their manners are they to be praised more than in this. For almost alone among barbarian peoples they are content with one wife each, expecting those few who because of their high position rather than out of lust enter into more than one marriage engagement.

The wife does not bring a dowry to the husband, but the husband to the wife. . . .

Thus they live in well-protected virtue, uncorrupted by the allurements of shows or the enticement of banquets. Men and women alike know not the secrecy of correspondence. Though the race is so numerous, adultery is very rare, its punishment being immediate and inflicted by the injured husband. He cuts off the woman's hair in the presence of her kinsfolk, drives her naked from his house and flogs her through the whole village. Indeed, the loss of chastity meets with no indulgence. . . . To limit the number of children or to put any of the later children to death is considered a crime, and with them good customs are of more avail than good laws elsewhere.

In every household the children grow up naked and unkempt into that lusty frame and those sturdy limbs that we admire. Each mother nurses he own children; they are not handed over to servants and paid nurses. The lord and the slave are in no way to be distinguished by the delicacy of their bringing up. They live among the same flocks, they lie on the same ground, until age separates them and valor distinguishes the free born. The young men marry late and their vigor is thereby unimpaired. Nor is the marriage of girls hastened. They have the same youthful vigor, the same stature as the young men. Thus well-matched and strong when they marry, the children reproduce the robustness of their parents. . . .

A German is required to adopt not only the feuds of his father or of a relative, but also their friendships, though the enmities are not irreconcilable. For even homicide is expiated by the payment of a certain number of cattle, and the whole family accept the satisfaction, a useful practice as regards the state because feuds are more dangerous where there is no strong legal control.

No other race indulges more freely in entertainments and hospitality. It is considered a crime to turn any mortal man away from one's door. . . .

As soon as they awake from sleep, which they prolong till late in the day, they bathe, usually in warm water as their winter lasts a great part of the year. After the bath they take food, each sitting in a separate seat and having a table to himself. Then they proceed to their business or not less often to feasts, fully armed. It is no disgrace to spend the whole day and night in drinking . . .

To trade with capital and to let it out at interest is unknown, and so it is ignorance rather than legal prohibition that protects them. Land is held by the villages as communities according to the number of the cultivators, and is then divided among the freemen according to their rank. The extent of their territories renders this partition easy. They cultivate fresh fields every year and there is still land to spare. They do not plant orchards nor lay off meadow-lands nor irrigate gardens so as to require of the soil more than it would naturally being forth of its own richness and extent. Grain is the only tribute exacted from their land, whence they do not divide the year into as many seasons as we do. The terms winter, spring and summer have a meaning with them, but the name and blessings of autumn are unknown.

There is no pomp in the celebration of their funerals. The only custom they observe is that the bodies of illustrious men should be burned with certain kinds of wood. . . .

c. The Upright Imperial Governor: Tacitus Describes His Father-In-Law Agricola

. . . Agricola was aware of the temper of the provincials, and took to heart the lesson which the experience of others suggested, that little was accomplished by force if injustice followed. He decided therefore to eliminate the causes of war. He began with himself and his own people: he put in order his own house, a task not less difficult for most governors than the government of a province. He transacted no public business through freedmen or slaves: he admitted no officer or private to his staff from personal likings, or private recommendation, or entreaty: he gave his confidence only to the best. He made it his business to know everything; if not, always, to follow up his knowledge: he turned an indulgent ear to small offences, yet was strict to offences that were serious: he was satisfied generally with penitence instead of punishment: to all offices and positions he preferred to advance the men not likely to offend rather than to condemn them after offences.

Demands for grain and tribute he made less burdensome by equalising the burdens: he abolished all the profit-making dodges which we re more intolerable than the tribute itself. As a matter of fact, the natives used to be compelled to go through the farce of dancing attendance at locked granaries, buying grain to be returned, and so redeeming their obligations at a price: side-roads or distant districts were named in the governor's proclamations, so that the tribes with winter quarters close at hand delivered at a distance and across country, and ultimately a task easy for everyone became a means of profit to a few. . . .

In order that a population scattered and uncivilised, and proportionately ready for war, might be habituated by comfort to peace and quiet, he would exhort individuals, assist communities, to erect temples, market-places, houses: he praised the energetic, rebuked the indolent, and the rivalry for his compliments took the place of coercion. Moreover he began to train the sons of the chieftains in a liberal education, and to give a preference to the native talents of the Briton as against the trained abilities of the Gaul. As a result, the nation which used to reject the Latin language began aspire to rhetoric: further, the wearing of our dress became a distinction, and the toga came into fashion, and little by little the Britons went astray into alluring vices: to the promenade, the bath, the well-appointed dinner table. The simple natives gave the name of "culture" to this factor of their slavery.

D. Marcus Aurelius Does His Duty

Begin the morning by saying to thyself, I shall meet with the busybody, the ungrateful, arrogant, deceitful, envious, unsocial. These are so by reason of their ignorance of what is good and evil. But I who have seen the nature of the good, that it is beautiful, and of the bad, that it is ugly, and the nature of him who does wrong, that he is akin to me, not only of the same blood and origin, but that he participates in the same intelligence and the same portion of the divinity, I can neither be injured by any of those I meet, for no one can fix on me what is ugly, nor can I be angry with my kinsman, nor hate him. For we are made for coöperation, like feet, like hands, like eyelids, like the rows of the upper and lower teeth. To act against one another then is contrary to nature; and it is acting against one another to be vexed and to turn away. . . .

If thou workest at that which is before thee, following right reason seriously, vigorously, calmly, without allowing anything else to distract thee, but keeping thy divine part pure, as if thou shouldest be bound to give it back immediately; if thou holdest to this, expecting nothing, fearing nothing, but satisfied with thy present activity according to nature, and with heroic truth in every word and sound which thou utterest, thou wilt live happy. And there is no man who is able to prevent this.

Document Set 6.2 References

A. Horace Laments the Decline of Roman Family Values
   Horace, *Odes and Epodes,* 3:6, trans. C. E. Bennett, Loeb Classical Library (Cambridge, Mass: Harvard University Press, 1968).
B. Noble Savages: Tacitus Encounters the Germans
   Tacitus, *Germania,* in *Translation and Reprints from the Original Sources of European History* (Philadelphia: University of Pennsylvania Press, 1898), vol. 6/2, 5–14.
C. The Upright Imperial Governor: Tacitus Describes His Father-In-Law Agricola
   Tacitus, *Agricola,* 19–21, trans. Maurice Hutton, Loeb Classical Library (London: Heinemann, 1914).
D. Marcus Aurelius Does His Duty
   Marcus Aurelius, *Meditations,* in James Harvey Robinson, ed., *Readings in European History* (Boston: Ginn, 1904), 1:17.

DOCUMENT SET 6.3
Rich and Poor

Satire is one of our best literary sources for coming face-to-face with the realities of everyday Roman life. Yet it must be read with care, for satirists almost invariably exaggerate for literary or didactic effect. We also possess a few revealing scraps of evidence in which ordinary Romans speak directly to posterity. Evaluate the sources in this set with these qualifications in mind.

Document A—a letter to a friend by the Roman philosopher and author Seneca (4 B.C.–A.D. 65)—gives a lively picture of the range of activities available at baths, which were extremely popular in the cities of the Roman Empire. On this occasion, Seneca had to endure a great deal of noise because he had rented an apartment over a public bath during a stay at a resort in southern Italy. Document B comes from another fashionable resort—Pompeii, which was destroyed by the eruption of Mt. Vesuvius in A.D. 79. Archaeologists excavating the ruins have found many graffiti on Pompeii's walls: everything from plugs for local political candidates to prostitutes' offers complete with their rates.

Another perspective on urban life comes from the Athenian sophist Philostratus (A.D. 170–245) who wrote an idealized biography of a famous Pythagorean sage of the first century A.D. This passage from the "Life of Apollonius of Tyana" (Document C) describes a bread riot—the threat of which hung constantly over Roman cities—in Asia Minor.

One way in which wealthy citizens were expected to keep order in Roman cities was through philanthropy. Document D is an inscription recording the good works that the Roman writer Pliny the Younger (A.D. 62–114) provided for his home town of Como in northern Italy. In Document E, Pliny comments on another (to us rather ironic) dimension of philanthropy: the wealthy patron's obligation to provide his less-fortunate fellow citizens with such gaudy spectacles as gladiatorial and wild-animal fights. Document F is another inscription honoring a successful Roman equestrian (a rich man of non-senatorial descent) providing posterity with a sketch of the "career-path" that such a man might hope for and the rewards he could expect.

Satire returns in Document G, a brief extract from the racy story "Trimalchio's Dinner Party," by the first-century Roman writer Petronius, who perhaps was the same Petronius who helped arrange Nero's licen-

tious merry-making. Trimalchio is a fantastically rich old businessman who made his fortune disreputably and enjoys it extravagantly: perhaps with some exaggeration, this is how wealthy playboys actually lived.

Contrast the selections in this set with those of Set 6.2, and draw your own conclusions.

A. Seneca Comments on a Scene at a Roman Bath

I live over a bath. Imagine the variety of voices, enough noise to make you sick. When the stronger fellows are working out with heavy weights, when they are working hard or pretending to work hard, I hear their grunts; and whenever they exhale, I hear their hissing and panting. Or when some lazy type is getting a cheap rubdown, I hear the slap of the hand pounding his shoulders . . . If a serious ballplayer comes along and starts keeping score out loud, that's the end for me . . . And there's the guy who always likes to hear his own voice when washing, or those people who jump into the swimming pool with a tremendous splash . . . The hair plucker keeps up a constant chatter to attract customers, except when he is plucking armpits and making his customer scream instead of screaming himself. It would be disgusting to list all the cries from the sausage seller, and the fellow hawking cakes, and all the food vendors yelling out what they have to sell, each with own special intonation.

B. Voices of the People: Graffiti from the Walls of Pompeii

The fruit dealers together with Helvius Vestalis unanimously urge the election of Marcus Holconius Priscus as duovir with judicial power.

I ask you to elect Gaius Julius Polybius aedile. He gets good bread.

The muleteers urge the election of Gaius Julius Polybius as duovir.

"Local Election Graffiti" from *Roman Civilization*, Vol. 2 by N. Lewis and M. Reinhold. Copyright © 1990 by Columbia University Press, excerpts from pp. 326–327, 338–339, 353–354, 359–360. Reprinted with permission of the publisher.

The worshippers of Isis unanimously urge the election of Gnaeus Helvius Sabinus as aedile.

Proculus, make Sabinus aedile and he will do as much for you.

His neighbors urge you to elect Lucius Statius Receptus duovir with judicial power; he is worthy. Aemilius Celer, a neighbor, wrote this. May you take sick if you maliciously erase this!

Satia and Petronia support and ask you to elect Marcus Casellius and Lucius Albucius aediles. May we always have such citizens in our colony!

I ask you to elect Epidius Sabinus duovir with judicial power. He is worthy, a defender of the colony, and in the opinion of the respected judge Suedius Clemens and by agreement of the council, because of his services and uprightness, worthy of the municipality. Elect him! . . .

I ask you to elect Marcus Cerrinius Vatia the aedileship. All the late drinkers support him. Florus and Fructus wrote this.

The petty thieves support Vatia for the aedileship.

I ask you to elect Aulus Vettius Firmus aedile. He is worthy of the municipality. I ask you to elect him, ballplayers. Elect him!

I wonder, O, wall, that you have not fallen in ruins from supporting the stupidities of so many scribblers.

Twenty pairs of gladiators of Decimus Lucretius Satrius Valens, lifetime *flamen* of Nero son of Caesar Augustus, and ten pairs of gladiators of Decimus Lucretius Valens, his son, will fight at Pompeii on April 8, 9, 10, 11, 12. There will be a full card of wild beast combats, and awnings [for the spectators]. Aemilius Celer [painted this sign], all alone in the moonlight.

Market days: Saturday in Pompeii, Sunday in Nuceria, Monday in Atella, Tuesday in Nola, Wednesday in Cumae, Thursday in Puteoli, Friday in Rome.

6th: cheese 1, bread 8, oil 3, wine 3
7th: bread 8, oil 5, onions 5, bowl 1, bread for the slave[?] 2, wine 2
8th: bread 8, bread for the slave[?] 4, grits 3

9th: wine for the winner 1 *denarius*, bread 8, wine 2, cheese 2
10th: . . . 1 *denarius*, bread 2, for women 8, wheat 1 *denarius*, cucumber 1, dates 1, incense 1, cheese 2, sausage 1, soft cheese 4, oil 7

Pleasure says: "You can get a drink here for an *as* [a small coin], a better drink for two, Falernian for four.

A copper pot is missing from this shop. 65 sesterces reward if anybody brings it back, 20 sesterces if he reveals the thief so we can get our property back.

The weaver Successus loves the inkeeper's slave girl, Iris by name. She doesn't care for him, but he begs her to take pity on him. Written by his rival. So long.
[Answer by the rival:] Just because you're bursting with envy, don't pick on a handsomer man, a lady-killer and a gallant.
[Answer by the first writer:] There's nothing more to say or write. You love Iris, who doesn't care for you.

Take your lewd looks and flirting eyes off another man's wife, and show some decency on your face!

Anybody in love, come here. I want to break Venus' ribs with a club and cripple the goddess' loins. If she can pierce my tender breast, why can't I break her head with a club?

I write at Love's dictation and Cupid's instruction;
But damn it! I don't want to be a god without you.

[A prostitute's sign:] I am yours for 2 *asses* cash.

C. A Bread Riot Erupts

When he came to Aspendus in Pamphylia . . . he found nothing but vetch on sale in the market, and the citizens were feeding upon this and on anything else they could get; for the rich men had locked up all the grain and were holding it for export from the country. Consequently an excited crowd of all ages had set upon the chief magistrate and was lighting a fire to burn him alive even though he was clinging to the statues of the emperor, which were at that time more dreaded and a more inviolable sanctuary than that of Zeus in Olympia. . . . Apollonius turned to the bystanders and beckoned to them that they must listen; and they not only held their tongues from wonderment at him, but they placed their fire on the altars that were there. The chief magistrate then plucked up courage and said, "So-and-so and So-and-so," naming several, "are to blame for the famine which has arisen, for they have taken away the grain and are keeping it in different parts of the country." A hue and cry thereupon arose among the Aspendians to make for these men's estates, but Apollonius shook his head to tell them not to do that but rather to summon those who were to blame and obtain the grain from them with their consent. And when they arrived, he very nearly broke out in speech against them, so affected was he by the tears of the crowd— for the children and women had all flocked together, and the old men were groaning as if they were on the point of dying of hunger. However, he respected his vow of silence and wrote his indictment on a writing board, and handed it to the chief magistrate to read aloud; and his indictment ran as follows: "Apollonius to the grain dealers of Aspendus. The earth is the mother of us all, for she is just; but you, because you are unjust, have made her the mother of yourselves alone, and if you do not stop I will not permit you to remain upon her." They were so terrified by these words that they filled the market place with grain, and the city revived.

D. Pliny Proclaims His Philanthrophy: An Inscription

Gaius Plinius Caecilius Secundus son of Lucius, of the Oufentine tribe; consul; augur; legate with rank of praetor in the province of Pontus and Bithynia sent to that province with consular power in accordance with a decree of the senate by the Emperor Caesar Nerva TRAJAN Augustus Germanicus Dacicus, father of his country; commissioner of the bed and banks of the Tiber and of the sewers of the city; prefect of the treasury of Saturn; prefect of the soldiers' bonus fund; praetor; tribune of the plebs; quaestor of the emperor; member of the board of six of the Roman *equites*; military tribune of Legion III Gallica; member of the board of fifteen for judging lawsuits. He left . . . sesterces in his will for the construction of baths, with an additional 300,000[plus?] sesterces for decoration, and in addition to that 200,000 sesterces for upkeep; and for the support of his freedmen, a hundred persons, he likewise bequeathed to the municipality 1,866,666 sesterces, the income from which desired to have applied there-

after to an annual banquet for the public. In his lifetime he also gave 500,000 sesterces for the support of the boys and girls of the lower class, and also a library and 100,000 sesterces for the upkeep of the library.

E. Trajan Commends a Friend for Putting on a Gladiatorial Show

Gaius Plinius to his dear Maximus, greeting.

You were right to promise a combat of gladiators to our good friends the people of Verona, by whom you have so long been loved, admired, and honored. It was from there, too, that you took your wife most dear and lovely, to whose memory some public monument or show was due, preferably this exhibition, which is especially appropriate for commemorating the dead. Besides, you were so unanimously pressed to do so, that to refuse would have seemed not constancy but obstinacy. It was a distinguished gesture, too, that you were so ready, so generous in providing them; for these, too, are the marks of a noble spirit. I am sorry the many African panthers you had purchased did not arrive in time; but even though they were delayed by bad weather and failed to appear, it was nevertheless understood, as you deserved, that it was not your fault that you did not exhibit them. Farewell.

F. An Inscription Honors a Second-Century Equestrian

To Titus Flavius Germanus son of Titus; superintendent of the most fortunate second German triumph of the Emperor Caesar Lucius Aurelius Commodus Augustus; honored by the same with the most illustrious priesthood of minor pontiff; procurator of the five-percent tax on inheritances; procurator of the imperial estate bureau; procurator of the Great Games; procurator of the Morning Games; procurator of the districts of the city with the added charge of paving streets in two parts of the city; procurator of the five-percent tax on inheritances for Umbria, Etruria, Picenum, and the district of Campania; procurator for child assistance in Lucania, Bruttium, Calabria, and Apulia; commissioner of public works and religious edifices in good repair; aedile; *duovir;* flamen of the deified Augustus; *duovir quinquennalis;* patron of the colony. Cerdo, his freedman, [dedicated this to him], patron incomparable, together with his sons, Flavius Maximinus, Germanus, and Rufinus, honored with equestrian rank.

G. A Vulgar Display: Trimalchio's Dinner

"Don't you know whose house you're going to visit to-day? Trimalchio's. He's stinking with money. Why, the man's got a clock in his dining room with a live trumpeter attachment, uniform and all, as part of the works, so he can discover at any second how fast life's dripping."

We jettisoned all our troubles, put on our clothes as dandyishly as we could, and [went] to the Baths. . . . [There they first encounter the rich, eccentric, and vulgar Trimalchio.]

In a proper state of amaze by now, we took our places and followed, and by Agamemnon's side reached the doorway of [Trimalchio's] house. There on one of the pillars was a notice announcing:

ANY SLAVE GOING OUT OF DOORS WITHOUT LEAVE OF ABSENCE WILL GET 100 LASHES.

Right in the entrance lounged a porter in a green uniform with a cherry coloured belt, shelling peas into a basin of silver. Above the door swung a golden cage, and in it a speckled magpie which chattered a welcome at us.

While I was gaping at all these things my knees almost gave way under me as though tapped from behind by terror. On the left, close by the porter's lodge, was a monstrous dog chained up . . . in paint on the wall, with BEWARE THE DOG printed in capital letters over it. My companions, needless to say, didn't let me off their derision, but I pulled myself together and went on inspecting the rest of the frescoes. One depicted a Slave market, price tickets and everything complete; another Trimalchio himself with a mop of hair on his head and Mercury's wand in his hand, being ushered into Rome by Minerva; the next related how he had learned bookkeeping and been installed as bailiff. To the series the conscientious artist had appended an elaborate verbal analysis. Towards the end of the gallery Mercury was shown elevating Trimalchio by the leverage of a hand under the chin into an imposing judgment seat, about which hovered the Goddess Fortune with her Horn that bubbles out eternal plenty, and the Trio of Fates spinning with thread of gold. I saw also in this hall a flock of runners being put through their paces by a trainer; and in one corner a great cupboard arrangement where in a miniature shrine were silver images of the House gods and a marble Venus statue and a gold casket of no puny size in which, I was told, was preserved the first Snippets of the Beard of Trimalchio.

We had extracted all the humour we could from these items of interest and were about to step into the room, when a slave, placed there for this particular office, bawled out, "Right foot first, please." We stood in a tremble of indecision, afraid that one of us would lift the wrong foot and transgress the ordinance. And when we all at last gingerly moved out right feet forward as if we were being drilled, a slave, stript for the whip, grovelled before us, begging us to intercede for him. Only a little fault, that was all, he said, that had ruined him. The steward had had his clothes stolen at the Baths, and they were not worth more than a shilling or two. So we withdrew our right feet, and put in a word for him to the steward who was counting out gold in the hall. Let him off the flogging, we asked.

With majestic deliberateness the steward raised his head to look at us. "It's not that the clothes are gone," he said, "I don't mind that. It's the negligence of the shiftless trash. It was my dinner suit he let go, and I value it—a birthday gift from a client, you know, a hanger on of mine—genuine Tyrian it was, and not been sent to the laundry more than once. Well, what does it matter? Sirs, the man is yours. I give him to you."

The patronizing air of magnanimity with which he conferred this benefit left us speechless. We drifted back to the dining room, and there came upon the very slave we had rescued. He surprised us with a fluster of grateful kisses and exclamation. "You'll soon find," he said, "who it was you were so good to. The master's private wine is the waiter's present."

At last we lay down in our places. Water cooled with snow was sluiced over our hands by Alexandrian slave boys, while others applied themselves to our feet, trimming the toe nails with the ease of accomplished artistry. But even this difficult pedicure did not obsess their minds; as they worked they sang. I wondered if the whole household were choristers also, and out of curiosity asked for a drink. A boy at once burst into song in a piercing treble and brought it to me. Indeed, any request you made was carried out to the same melodious setting. It was much more like being among a ballet of warbling vaudevillists than at dinner in a reputable person's place.

However, in they brought a relish, a very appetizing dish too. By now Trimalchio was the sole absentee. Following the newest fashion, the first seat was kept for his special occupance. Among the dinner plate stood a small wrought ass of Corinthian bronze, panniered with olives—the black one side, the white the other. Over the ass were fixed two salvers, around the edges of which were engraved Trimalchio's name and the weight of the silver. And there were two contraptions of iron soldered on, formed like bridges, which offered dormice sauced with poppy seeds and honey. Sausage steamed on a silver gridiron, underneath which lay black Damascus plums and pomegranate seeds from Carthage.

We were eating away when Trimalchio in person was borne aloft into the room, welcomed with a noise of music and tucked into a lot of dainty little cushions. Taken off their guard, some laughed. The globe of his shaven poll was balanced loosely on the scarlet mass of his cloak, his neck was hidden in shawls, and he had dressed up in a linen robe with a broad stripe and a fringe of tassels dingle dangling. A gilt ring bulged from his left little finger, but on the last joint of the finger next to it he wore a smaller ring which I thought at first flash to be solid gold, but which was really spangled with star tips of steel. To make it quite clear that he owned more jewellery still, his right arm was bared and clasped with a circlet of gold and an ivory bangle jointed with a glitter of gold metal.

First of all he picked his teeth thoroughly with a silver tooth pick. Then he spoke:

"My dear friends, had I consulted my own inclinations I would not have come so early to dinner, but as I feared my absence might cast a blight over the party, I put my personal wishes aside and came along. Still, I don't expect you'll object to me finishing my game."

Behind him entered a slave with an inlaid board of terebinth and a set of crystal men; and I noted in chief one typical lavish detail. He had substituted gold and silver money for the black and white counters. While he was still swearing away heatedly to himself and we were finishing off the relishes, a tray with a basket on it was fetched in. Inside the basket reposed a hen carved in wood and her wings cuddled round her as though she were on the cluck of dropping an egg.

Straightaway two slaves came up, and amid the squawks of the protesting orchestra began to feel through the straw and pick out pea hens' eggs, which they handed round among the company. Trimalchio looked up over his game at this by play.

"My friends," he said, "I gave orders for that hen to sit on a clutch of pea hens' eggs. I assure you I'm half of a mind that she's gone and all but hatched them. The best thing to do is to break the shells bravely and see if your stomachs can stand what you find."

We took up our spoons (incidentally a clear half-pound each) and struck the eggs—only to discover that they were imitations kneaded from a rich paste. For myself, I almost threw my egg away, for it seemed to have a chick's foetus in it. But I heard a guest, who knew the house's routine of surprises, saying, "There's sure to be something pretty good in here." And so I continued peeling the layers until I came across a tiny but fleshy fig pecker buried in the midst of a well peppered yoke.

Here Trimalchio concluded his game, called for everything he had missed, and announced loudly that there was a second cup of mead ready for anyone with an empty glass. Then, abruptly, at a signalling bang from the band, the choric waiters bustled all the course away. But in the scramble a side dish happened to be bumped to the ground, and a slave lifted it up. Trimalchio perceived the action and commanded that the boy's ears be tweaked and the dish dropped back. A groom came in with a broom and swept up the silver dish as well as the scraps of food spilled from it.

Next two long haired Ethiopians appeared with small skins similar to those employed for strewing sand down the arena, and drenched our hands with wine. No one was offered anything like vulgar water. We commended the rare refinement of our host's taste.

"Fair play's a jewel," he replied. "So think Mars and I. And that's why each of you had a table to himself. It's less stuffy if the slaves can get about without sweating against each other."

Glass wine bottles, elaborately sealed with gypsum, came in at the tail of this discourse. There was a label about their necks:

FALERNIAN CONSUL OPIMIUS 100 YEARS OLD

As we perused these inscriptions Trimalchio slapped his hands together and ejaculated, "Alas, seeing is believing, wine outspans us poor mannikins. So gargle it down. Wine is Life, it is. And this is guaranteed Opimian I'm giving you. I didn't produce anything so good yesterday though the people I had here were much better class than any of you."

Document Set 6.3 References

A. Seneca Comments on a Scene at a Roman Bath
   Naphtali Lewis and Meyer Reinhold, eds., *Roman Civilization: Selected Readings* (New York: Columbia University Press, 1951), 2:228.

B. Voices of the People: Graffiti from the Walls of Pompeii
   Lewis and Reinhold, 2:326–327, 359–360.

C. A Bread Riot Erupts
   Philostratus, *Life of Apollinius of Tyana*, 1:15, in Lewis and Reinhold, 2:338–339.

D. Pliny Proclaims His Philanthropy: An Inscription
   Lewis and Reinhold, 2:35–354.

E. Trajan Commends a Friend for Putting on a Gladiatorial Show
   Pliny, *Letters*, 6:34, in Lewis and Reinhold, 2:349.

F. An Inscription Honors a Second-Century Equestrian
   Lewis and Reinhold, 2:128.

G. A Vulgar Display: Trimalchio's Dinner
   Pertronius, *Trimalchio's Dinner Party*, trans. Jack Lindsay (New York: Rarity Press, 1932), 16–21.

DOCUMENT SET 6.4
Labor—Free and Slave

The Petronius extract in Set 6.3 gives one glimpse of first-century Roman slavery in action. The documents in this set deal directly with both free and slave labor.

Document A is a contract (preserved on a wax tablet) obligating a free man to labor in the gold mines of Dacia, today Romania, and gives some idea of the working conditions. Incidentally, though the contract describes the worker as illiterate, he was able to sign his name at the end. Document B also concerns free labor: it is an apprenticeship agreement from Roman Egypt, preserved on papyrus.

In Document C the first-century B.C. Roman writer Columella, author of a long treatise on agricultural technique and estate administration, advises his upper-class readers on how best to manage their mixed labor force of slaves and free tenants.

Document D records a slave sale in Roman Egypt, documented on a papyrus preserved by the dry climate there. In Document E (also a papyrus from Roman Egypt) we can see the conditions under which a slave was emancipated.

Most Romans—including, apparently, the Christian apostle Paul—accepted slavery as a fact of life. One who did not was the philosopher Seneca, an extract from whose "Moral Epistles" appears as Document F.

Drawing on these documents and *The Challenge of the West,* write a brief assessment of slavery in the early Roman empire.

A. A Labor Contract from Asia Minor, A.D. 164

In the consulship of Macrinus and Celsus, May 20, [A.D. 164]. I, Flavius Secundinus, at the request of Memmius son of Asclepius (because he declared that he was illiterate) have here recorded the fact that he declared that he had let, and he did in fact let, his labor in the gold mine to Aurelius Adjutor from this day to November 13 next for seventy *denarii* and board. He shall be entitled to receive his wages in installments. He shall be required to render healthy and vigorous labor to the above-mentioned employer. If he wants to quit or stop working against the employer's wishes, he shall have to pay five sesterces

for each day, deducted from his total wages. If a flood hinders operations, he shall be required to prorate accordingly. If the employer delays payment of the wages when the time is up, he shall be subject to the same penalty after three days of grace.

B. An Apprenticeship Contract from Egypt, A.D. 66

Tryphon son of Dionysius son of Tryphon and of Thamounis daughter of Onnophris, and Ptolemaeus son of Pausirion son of Ptolemaeus and of Ophelous daughter of Theon, weaver, both being inhabitants of Oxyrhynchus, mutually acknowledge that Tryphon has apprenticed to Ptolemaeus his son Thoonis, whose mother is Saraeus daughter of Apion, and who is not yet of age, for a period of one year from the present day, to serve and to follow all the instructions given to him by Ptolemaeus in the art of weaving as far as he himself knows it, the boy to be fed and clothed for the whole period by his father Tryphon, who will also be responsible for all the taxes on him, on the condition that Ptolemaeus will pay to him monthly an account of food 5 drachmae and at the close of the whole period on account of clothing 12 drachmae, nor shall Tryphon have the right to remove the boy from Ptolemaeus until the completion of the period, and for whatever days therein the boy play truant, he shall send him to work for the like number at the end of it or else forfeit one drachma of silver for each day, and for removing him within the period he shall pay a penalty of 100 drachmae and the like sum to the Treasury. If Ptolemaeus fails to instruct the boy fully, he shall be liable to the same penalties. This contract of apprenticeship is valid. The 13th year of Nero Claudius Caesar Augustus Germanicus Imperator, the 21st of the month Sebastus. (Signed) I, Ptolemaeus son of Pausirion son of Ptolemaeus and of Ophelous daughter of Theon, will do everything in the one year. I, Zoilus son of Horus son of Zoilus and of Dieus daughter of Sokeus have written for him, as he is illiterate. The 13th year of Nero Claudius Caesar Augustus Germanicus Imperator, Sebastus 21 [A.D. 66].

C. Columella Advises Estate Owners How to Treat Their Free and Servile Laborers

After all these arrangements [for buildings, tools, etc.] have been acquired or contrived, especial care is demanded of the master not only in other matters, but most of all in the matter of the persons in his service; and these are either tenant-farmers or slaves, whether unfettered or in chains. He should be civil in dealing with his tenants, should show himself affable, and should be more exacting in the matter of work than of payments, as this gives less offence yet is, generally speaking, more profitable. . . .

The next point is with regard to slaves—over what duty it is proper to place each and to what sort to tasks to assign them. So my advice at the start is not to appoint an overseer from that sort of slaves who are physically attractive, and certainly not from that class which has busied itself with the voluptuous occupations of the city. . . .

But be the overseer what he may, he should be given a woman companion to keep him within bounds and yet in certain matters to be a help to him; and this same overseer should be warned not to become intimate with a member of the household, and much less with an outsider, yet at times he may consider it fitting, as a mark of distinction, to invite to his table on a holiday one whom he has found to be constantly busy and vigorous in the performance of his tasks. He shall offer no sacrifice except by direction of the master. Soothsayers and witches, two sets of people who incite ignorant minds through false superstition to spending and then to shameful practices, he must not admit to the place. He must have no acquaintance with the city or with the weekly market, except to make purchases and sales in connection with his duties. . . .

In the case of the other slaves, the following are, in general, the precepts to be observed, and I do not regret having held to them myself: to talk rather familiarly with the country slaves, provided only that they have not conducted themselves unbecomingly, more frequently than I would with the town slaves; and when I perceived that their unending toil was lightened by such friendliness on the part of the master, I would even jest with them at times and allow them also to jest more freely. Nowadays I make it a practice to call them into consultation on any new work, as if they were more experienced, and to discover by this means what sort of ability is possessed by each of them and how intelligent he is. Furthermore, I observe that they are more willing to set about a piece of work on which they think that their opinions have been asked and their advice followed.

D. A Slave Is Sold, Egypt, A.D. 129

The 13th year of the Emperor Caesar Trajanus Hadrianus Augustus [A.D. 129]. Pauni 29, at Oxyrhynchus in . . . Agathodaemon also called Dionysius son of Dionysius son of Dionysius, his mother being Hermione, of Oxyrhynchus, acknowledges to Gaius Julius Germanus son of Gaius Julius Domitianus, in the street, that he hereby confirms the autograph contract which the acknowledging party Agathodaemon also called Dionysius made with Julius Germanus on Tubi 25 of the current 13th year for the sale of a female slave called Dioscorous, aged about 25 years, without distinguishing marks, who became his property by purchase and formerly belonged to Heraclides also called Theon son of Machon, of the Sosicosmian tribe and the Althaean deme, which slave Julius Germanus did then take over from him just as she was, not repudiable except for epilepsy or seizure by a claimant, for the price of 1200 drachmae of silver, which Agathodaemon also called Dionysius then received from Julius Germanus in full on the making of the autograph contract, out of which price Julius Germanus paid the tax on the sale of the said slave Dioscorous on Phamenoth 3 of the said year according to the receipt issued to him; and it is incumbent on Agathodaemon also called Dionysius to guarantee the sale of the said slave Dioscorous in every respect, as the autograph contract states. If the contract should happen to be lost or destroyed in some other way, Julius Germanus shall not require . . .

E. A Slave Is Emancipated, First Century A.D.

Achilleus, aged about 20 years, of medium height, with fair complexion, long face, and a scar in the middle of his forehead, and Carapas, aged about . . . years, of medium height, with fair complexion, long face, and a scar on his left . . ., both sons of . . . son of

Reprinted by permission of the publishers and the Loeb Classical Library from *Columella I,* trans. by Harrison Boyd Ash, pp. 79, 82–93, Cambridge, Mass.: Harvard University Press, 1941.

Selection D: Reprinted by permission of the publishers and the Loeb Classical Library from A. S. Hunt and C. C. Edgar, eds., Vol. I, pp. 97, 99, 35, 37, Cambridge, Mass.: Harvard University Press, 1934.

Ammonius, their mother being Sarapous daughter of
. . ., all of Oxyrhynchus, have set free under sanction
of Zeus, Earth, and Sun, by deed drawn up in the
street, the third part which they jointly own of the
female slave who has already been freed as regards the
other two thirds, namely Apollonous, aged about 26
years, of medium height, with fair complexion, long
face, and a scar on the right foot; and whereas she has
already been freed to the extent of two thirds for . . .
talents, the sum payable in respect of the third part
now being freed consists of a fee of . . . drachmae 4
obols of coined silver and of the ransom paid to
Achilleus and Sarapas by Heraclas son of Tryphon
son of . . ., his mother being Taonnophris daughter of
Panesies, of the said city, aged about 31 years, of
medium height, with fair complexion, long face, and
a scar above the right knee, namely 200 drachmae of
Imperial silver coin and . . . talents 1000 drachmae of
copper; and it shall not be lawful for Achilleus or
anyone else on his behalf to demand the aforesaid
ransom from Apollonous or her assigns or to . . .
Certifier of the manumission: . . . son of . . . son of
Peteesis, his mother being . . ., of the said city, aged
about 40 years, of medium height, with fair complexion, long face, and a scar on the . . . shin, in the street
as said.

F. Seneca Condemns the Abuses of Slavery

The master eats more than he can hold, and with
monstrous greed loads his belly until it is stretched
and at length ceases to do the work of a belly; so that
he is at greater pains to discharge all the food than he
was to stuff it down. All this time the poor slaves may
not move their lips, even to speak. The slightest murmur is repressed by the rod; even a chance sound,—a
cough, a sneeze, or a hiccup,—is visited with the lash.
There is a grievous penalty for the slightest breach of
silence. All night long they must stand about, hungry
and dumb.

The result of it all is that these slaves, who may
not talk in their master's presence, talk about their
master. But the slaves of former days, who were permitted to converse not only in their master's presence, but actually with him, whose mouths were not
stitched up tight, were ready to bare their necks for
their master, to bring upon their own heads any danger that threatened him; they spoke at the feast, but
kept silence during torture. Finally, the saying, in
allusion to this same high-handed treatment, becomes
current: "As many enemies as you have slaves." They
are not enemies when we acquire them; we make
them enemies. . . .

Kindly remember that he whom you call your
slave sprang from the same stock, is smiled upon by
the same skies, and on equal terms with yourself
breathes, lives, and dies. It is just as possible for you
to see in him a free-born man as for him to see in you
a slave. As a result of the massacres in Marius's day,
many a man of distinguished birth, who was taking
the first steps toward senatorial rank by service in the
army, was humbled by fortune, one becoming a shepherd, another a caretaker of a country cottage.
Despise, then, if you dare, those to whose estate you
may at any time descend, even when you are despis-
ing them.

I do not wish to involve myself in too large a
question, and to discuss the treatment of slaves,
towards whom we Romans are excessively haughty,
cruel, and insulting. But this is the kernel of my
advice: Treat your inferiors as you would be treated
by your betters. And as often as you reflect how
much power you have over a slave, remember that
your master has just as much power over you. "But I
have no master," you say. You are still young; perhaps
you will have one. Do you not know at what age
Hecuba entered captivity, or Croesus, or the mother
of Darius, of Plato, or Diogenes?

Associate with your slave on kindly, even on
affable, terms; let him talk with you, plan with you,
live with you. I know that at this point all the exquis-
ites will cry out against me in a body; they will say:
"There is nothing more debasing, more disgraceful,
than this." But these are the very persons whom I
sometimes surprise kissing the hands of other men's
slaves. Do you not see even this,—how our ancestors,
removed from masters everything invidious, and
from slaves everything insulting? They called the
master "father of the household," and the slaves
"members of the household," a custom which still
holds in the mime. They established a holiday on
which masters and slaves should eat together,—not as
the only day for this custom, but as obligatory on
that day in any case. They allowed the slaves to attain
honours in the household and to pronounce judgment; they held that a household was a miniature
commonwealth.

"Do you mean to say," comes the retort, "that I
must seat all my slaves at my own table?" No, not
any more than that you should invite all free men to
it. You are mistaken if you think that I would bar
from my table certain slaves whose duties are more
humble, as, for example, yonder muleteer or yonder
herdsman; I propose to value them according to their
character, and not according to their duties. . . .

"He is a slave." His soul, however, may be that of
a freeman. "He is a slave." But shall that stand in his

way? Show me a man who is not a slave; one is a slave to lust, another to greed, another to ambition, and all men are slaves to fear. I will name you an ex-consul who is slave to an old hag, a millionaire who is slave to a serving-maid; I will show you youths of the noblest birth in serfdom to pantomine players! No servitude is more disgraceful than that which is self-imposed.

Document Set 6.4 References

A. A Labor Contract from Asia Minor, A.D. 164
  Naphtali Lewis and Meyer Reinhold, eds., *Roman Civilization: Selected Readings* (New York: Columbia University Press, 1951), 2:194–195.

B. An Apprenticeship Contract from Egypt, A.D. 66
  A. S. Hunt and C. C. Edgar, trans., *Selected Papyri,* Loeb Classical Library (Cambridge, Mass.: Harvard University Press, 1934), 2:268.

C. Columella Advises Owners How to Treat Their Free and Servile Laborers
  Columella, *On Agriculture,* 1:7–8, trans. Harrison Boyd Ash, Loeb Classical Library (Cambridge, Mass.: Harvard University Press, 1941).

D. A Slave Is Sold, Egypt, A.D. 129
  Hunt and Edgar, 1:32.

E. A Slave Is Emancipated, First Century A.D.
  Hunt and Edgar, 1:12.

F. Seneca Condemns the Abuses of Slavery
  Seneca, *Moral Epistles,* 47, trans. Richard M. Gummere, Loeb Classical Library (Cambridge, Mass.: Harvard University Press, 1917).

DOCUMENT SET 6.5
Men and Women

Under the Empire, the ideal of womanly deportment continued to be the virtuous maidens and matrons of the early Republic; naturally, then, the fact that rich women increasingly managed to enjoy themselves in less than virtuous ways provoked angry comment from (male) moralists like the Stoic satirist Juvenal (55–c. 140). Document A is a small extract of his long denunciation of the "emancipated" upper-class Roman woman of his day.

Midwifery and wet nursing were two female professions whose services most well-off Romans found it necessary to employ. The skill involved in midwifery, and its attendant dignity, is conveyed in Document B, an extract from the Roman physician Soranus's *Gynecology,* from the second century A.D. It suggests the opposite extreme from the kind of emancipated woman at whom Juvenal directed his darts. That women had an independent place in the work world is also attested by Document C, a contract from Roman Egypt.

Using these documents, as well as other resources (such as Set 5.1) and information gleaned from *The Challenge of the West,* write a brief essay on the situation of Roman women under the Empire.

A. Juvenal Deplores the Emancipated Roman Woman

Money, the nurse of debauchery, was the first that introduced foreign manners, and enervating riches sapped the sinews of the age with foul luxury. For what cares Venus in her cups? All difference of head or tail is alike to her who at very midnight devours huge oysters, when unguents mixed with neat Falernian foam, when she drains the conch, when from her dizziness the roof seems to reel, and the table to rise up with the lights doubled in number. . . .

And yet that woman is more offensive still, who, as soon as she has taken her place at table, praises Virgil, and excuses the suicide of Dido: matches and compares poets together: in one scale weighs Maro in the balance, and Homer in the other. The grammarians yield; rhetoricians are confuted; the whole company is silenced; neither lawyer nor crier can put in a word, nor even another woman. Such a torrent of words pours forth, you would say so many basins or bells were all being struck at once. Henceforth let no one trouble trumpets or brazen vessels; she will be able singly to relieve the moon when suffering an eclipse. The philosopher sets a limit even to those things which are good in themselves. For she that desires to appear too learned and eloquent, ought to wear a tunic reaching only to the middle of the leg, to sacrifice a pig to Sylvanus, and bathe for a quadrans. Let not the matron that shares your marriage-bed possess a set style of eloquence, or hurl in well-rounded sentence the enthymeme curtailed of its premiss; nor be acquainted with all histories. But let there be some things in books which she does not understand. I hate her who is forever poring over and studying Palæmon's treatise; who never violates the rules and principles of grammar; and skilled in antiquarian lore, quotes verses I never knew; and corrects the phrases of her friend as old-fashioned, which men would never heed. A husband should have the privilege of committing a solecism.

There is nothing a woman will not allow herself, nothing she holds disgraceful, when she has encircled her neck with emeralds, and inserted earrings of great size in her ears, stretched with their weight. Nothing is more unbearable than a rich woman!

Meanwhile her face, shocking to look at, or ridiculous from the large poultice, is all swollen; or is redolent of rich Poppæan unguents, with which the lips of her wretched husband are glued up. She will present herself to her adulterer with skin washed clean. When does she choose to appear beautiful at home? It is for the adulterers her perfumes are prepared. It is for these she purchases all that the slender Indians send us. At length she uncases her face and removes the first layer. She begins to be herself again; and bathes in that milk, for which she carries in her train she-asses, even if sent an exile to Hyperborean climes. But that which is overlaid and fomented with so many and oft-changed cosmetics, and receives poultices of boiled and damp flour, shall we call it a face, or a sore?

It is worth while to find out exactly what their occupations and pursuits are through the livelong day. If her husband has gone to sleep with his back toward her, the housekeeper is half killed—the tire-women are stripped to be whipped—the Liburnian slave is accused of having come behind his time, and is forced to pay the penalty of another's sleep; one has rods broken about him, another bleeds from the whips, a third from the cowhide. Some women pay a regular salary to their torturers. While he lashes she is employed in enameling her face. She listens to her friend's chat, or examines the broad gold of an embroidered robe. Still he lashes. She pores over the items in her long diary. Still he lashes. Until at length, when the torturers are exhausted, "Begone!" she thunders out in awful voice, the inquisition being now complete.

The government of her house is no more merciful than the court of a Sicilian tyrant. For if she has made an assignation, and is anxious to be dressed out more becomingly than usual, and is in a hurry, and has been some time already waited for in the gardens, or rather near the chapels of the Isiac procuress; poor Psecas arranges her hair, herself with disheveled locks and naked shoulders and naked breasts.

B. A Midwife Learns Her Profession

A suitable person . . . must be literate in order to be able to comprehend the art through theory too: she must have her wits about her so that she may easily follow what is said and what is happening: she must have a good memory to retain the imparted instructions (for knowledge arises from memory of what has been grasped). She must love work in order to persevere through all vicissitudes (for a woman who wishes to acquire such vast knowledge needs manly patience). She must be respectable since people will have to trust their household and the secrets of their lives to her and because to women of bad character the semblance of medical instruction is a cover for evil scheming. She must not be handicapped as regards her senses since there are things which she must see, answers which she must hear when questioning, and objects which she must grasp by her sense of touch. She needs sound limbs so as not to be handicapped in the performances of her work and she must be robust, for she takes a double task upon herself during the hardship of her professional visits. Long and slim fingers and short nails are necessary to touch a deep lying inflammation without causing too much pain. This skill, however, can also be acquired through zealous endeavour and practice in her work . . .

We call a person the best midwife if she is trained in all branches of therapy (for some cases must be treated by diet, others by surgery, while still others must be cured by drugs); if she is moreover able to prescribe hygienic regulations for her patients, to observe the general and the individual features of the case, and from this to find out what is expedient, not from the causes or from the repeated observations of what usually occurs or something of the kind. Now

to go into detail: she will not change her methods when the symptoms change, but will give her advice in accordance with the course of the disease: she will be unperturbed, unafraid in danger, able to state clearly the reasons for her measures, she will bring reassurance to her patients, and be sympathetic. And it is not absolutely essential for her to have borne children, as some people contend, in order that she may sympathise with the mother, because of her experience with pain; for [to have sympathy] is not more characteristic of a person who has given birth to a child. She must be robust on account of her duties but not necessarily young as some people maintain, for sometimes young persons are weak whereas on the contrary older persons may be robust. She will be well disciplined and always sober, since it is uncertain when she may be summoned to those in danger. She will have a quiet disposition, for she will have to share many secrets of life. She must not be greedy for money, lest she give an abortive wickedly for payment; she will be free from superstition so as not to overlook salutary measures on account of a dream or omen or some customary rite or vulgar superstition. She must also keep her hands soft, abstaining from such wool-working as may make them hard, and she must acquire softness by means of ointments if it is not present naturally. Such persons will be the best midwives.

C. A Woman Contracts to Work in an Oil-Press Enterprise, Egypt, A.D. 99

Phaophi 18 [A.D. 99]. . . . Thenetkouis daughter of Heron, olive-carrier, Persian, aged about 26 years, with a scar on the right shin, having with her as guardian her kinsman Leontas son of Hippalus, aged about 54 years, with a scar on the right side of the forehead, acknowledges to Lucius Bellenus Gemellus, discharged legionary, with a scar on the left wrist, that she has received from him directly by hand from his house 16 drachmae of silver as irrepudiable earnest-money. Thenetkouis thereby bound to carry at the olive-press belonging to Lucius Bellenus Gemellus at Euhemeria from whatever day he orders her the olive crop included in the current third, year, doing all that is required of a carrier until the completion of the entire oil-manufacture, and receiving from Lucius Bellenus her daily wage at the same rate as the similar carriers in the village; and Lucius shall deduct the 16 drachmae of silver by instalments from the wages to be paid. If Thenetkouis does not act in accordance with the conditions above written, she shall pay back to Lucius double, the earnest-money, Lucius Bellenus having the right of execution upon the acknowledging party and upon all her property as if by legal decision. Signatory on behalf of Thenetkouis: Leontas the aforesaid. (Subscribed) I, Thenetkouis daughter of Heron, Persian, leaving with me as guardian my kinsman Leontas son of Hippalus, acknowledge that I have received from Lucius the 16 drachmae of silver forming the earnest-money, and I will carry at the olive-press from whatever day you order me, receiving from you, Lucius, my wages at the same rate as similar carriers, and I will do everything as stated above. I, Leontas, have written for Thenetkouis also, as she is illiterate.

Document Set 6.5 References

A. Juvenal Deplores the Emancipated Roman Women
   Juvenal, *Satires,* 6, trans. Lewis Evans (New York: Harper, 1861).
B. A Midwife Learns Her Profession
   Mary R. Lefkowitz and Maureen B. Fant, eds., *Women's Life in Greece and Rome* (Baltimore: Johns Hopkins University Press, 1982), 162–163.
C. A Woman Contracts to Work in an Oil-Press Enterprise, Egypt, A.D. 99
   A. S. Hunt and C. C. Edgar, trans., *Selected Papyri,* Loeb Classical Library (Cambridge, Mass.: Harvard University Press, 1934), 1:17.

DOCUMENT SET 6.6
Learning and Religion

Compared to classical Greece or medieval Europe, imperial Rome was not one of the great cradles of Western philosophy. Yet the philosophical schools we encountered in the Hellenistic era left a deep imprint on Roman culture. Extracts you have read in earlier sets from Epictetus (Set 4.2, Document E), Marcus Aurelius (Set 6.2, Document D), and Seneca (Set 6.4, Document F) attest to this influence.

Seneca's Stoic faith in divine providence and universal law is well expressed in Document A, an extract from his book *On Benefits.* Marcus Aurelius's ruminations on the same theme in his *Meditations,* written in Greek (Document B), convey as well a sense of the human being's small place in the cosmic scheme of things.

The foremost scientist of the Roman era who attempted to explain the cosmos mathematically was the Alexandrian astronomer and geographer Ptolemy (90–168), who pulled together and corrected the work of his Babylonian and Greek predecessors. His cosmology essentially reflected a common-sense view of the universe—does not the sun encircle the earth every day?—which at the same time fit in well with the view of Plato and Aristotle that the heavens were the seat of all perfection and the earth the abode of corruption and decay toward which all material things sink. Document C, an extract from Ptolemy's astronomical work known by its medieval Arabic translation, *The Almagest,* expounds his cosmic vision.

The final three documents in this set pertain to "pagan" religion. Document D is a prayer from the Mithraic faith, a formidable competitor to Christianity in that it offered believers hope for regeneration through belief in a savior and envisioned the deity as essentially a monotheistic, transcendent being. Like Christianity, Mithraism was imported in the Roman world (in this case from Persia); unlike Christianity, it was quite compatible with Rome's official imperial cult. The prayer quoted reveals the same hope of spiritual rebirth that Christianity kindled. Document E comes from a literary work, *The Golden Ass,* by Apuleius, a second-century Roman writer who traveled widely and was initiated into many salvation cults; here he describes the initiation rite of Isis, an extremely popular faith of Egyptian origin. Finally, Document F is an inscription from a town in Asia Minor paying tribute to the virtues of a pagan priestess.

Using these documents as well as other relevant materials in this chapter, discuss pagan religion and non-Christian philosophy in the early Roman Empire.

A. Seneca Expounds the Universal Goodness and Bounty of the Stoics' God

Doth not God bestow all benefits upon us? From whence then hast thou all those things whereof thou are possessed? which thou givest? which thou deniest? which thou keepest? which thou takest unjustly? From whence come the infiniteness of things that delight the eye, affect the ear, and please the understanding? . . . From when have we so many trees, bearing sundry sorts of savory fruit, so many wholesome herbs, for the maintenance of our health, such variety of meats, strong for all seasons through the whole year, so that an idle sluggard may pick up without effort sufficient sustenance upon the earth to feed and nourish him? . . .

If a man should give thee money, and fill thy coffer (for that seemeth a great thing in thy sight) thou wouldst term it a benefit. And thinkest thou it no favor, that God hath hidden so many metals in the earth, spread so many rivers on the sands, which floating, discover ingots of massy gold, silver, brass, and iron, which he hath hidden everywhere; that he hath given thee means and knowledge to find it out, by setting marks of his covert riches on the upper face of the earth? If a man should give thee a house enriched with marble pillars, if the cover thereof were resplendent, and painted with gold and goodly colors, thou wouldst highly esteem this present of his: God hath builded thee a great palace, without any danger or fear of falling down, wherein thou seest not little pieces, smaller than the chisel itself wherewith they were carved, but entire huge masses or precious stone, all fastened and fashioned after divers manners, the least piece whereof maketh thee wonder at the beauty of the same: the roof whereof shineth after one sort by day and after another by night: and wilt thou then deny that thou hast received any benefit at all? . . .

It is Nature, saith one, that communicateth and giveth me all these things. But understandest thou not that in speaking after this manner, thou only changest the name of God? For what else is Nature but God, a divine being and reason, which by his searching assistance resideth in the world, and all the parts thereof? . . .

To bestow a favor in hope to receive another, is a contemptible and base usury. How badly soever thy former favors have fallen out, yet persevere thou in bestowing others. They are best hoarded in the hands of the ungrateful, whom either shame, or occasion, or imitation, may at length fashion to be grateful. Persevere continually, and cease not to be bountiful: accomplish that good work which thou hast begun, and perform the duty of a good man. Relieve this man with thy goods, another with thy credit; that man by thy favor, this with thy good counsels and wholesome precepts.

B. Ptolemy Explains Why the Earth Must Be Stationary

That the Earth Performs No Progressive Motion

In the same way it will be proved by what precedes that the earth cannot make a contrary motion to the aforementioned lateral sides, or ever be displaced at all from its position in the center [of the universe] . . . The earth occupies the central position in the cosmos, and all heavy objects move toward if. . . . If it had any one movement in common with the other heavy bodies, it would outstrip them all in its descent because its size is so much bigger. It would leave living creatures behind, and partly dense bodies floating on the air. For its part, it would swiftly drop out of the heavens, altogether. . . .

For let us grant them what is unnatural: the lightest and least dense bodies [the stars] do not move at all . . . while the densest and heaviest bodies execute their own swift and uniform motion. . . . The geokineticist [those who suppose that the earth moves] would then admit that of all the motions in the earthly region the swiftest is the rotation of the earth. In a short time it performs so vast a rotation. As a result, everything not attached to it would appear to be always moving in the direction opposite the earth's. Not a cloud nor any other thing flying or thrown upward would ever be floating eastward. For the earth would always outstrip them all as it overtook them in its eastward motion. Consequently all other bodies would seem to be traveling westward as they were left behind.

On the other hand, the geokineticists might say that the air is carried around with the earth in the same direction and at the same speed. Nevertheless, whatever bodies are caught up in the air would always be seen falling behind the speed of both the earth and the air. Or if these bodies were carried around as though united with the air, they would no longer be seen either moving ahead or falling behind. On the contrary, they would always maintain the same position. Neither in the things flying or thrown would there be any dislodgment or displacement. [Yet] we do see all these things happening with such clarity that no part at all of their slowness or swiftness is attributable to the earth's failure to stand still.

C. Marcus Aurelius Meditates on God's Ways

Full of Providence are the works of the Gods, nor are Fortune's works independent of Nature or of the woven texture and interlacement of all that is under the control of Providence. Thence are all things derived; but Necessity too plays its part and the Welfare of the whole Universe of which thou art a portion. But good for every part of Nature is that which the Nature of the Whole brings about, and which goes to preserve it. Now it is the changes not only of the elements but of the things compounded of them that preserve the Universe. Let these reflections suffice thee, if thou hold them as principles. But away with thy thirst for books, that thou mayest die not murmuring but with a good grace, truly and from thy heart grateful to the Gods.

Call to mind how long thou deferrest these things, and how many times thou hast received from the Gods grace of the appointed day and thou usest it not. Yet now, if never before, shouldest thou realize of what Universe thou art a part, and as an emanation from what Controller of that Universe thou dost subsist; and that a limit has been set to thy time, which if thou use not to let daylight into thy soul, it well be gone—and thou!—and never again shall the chance be thine.

Every hour make up thy mind sturdily as a Roman and a man to do what thou hast in hand with scrupulous and unaffected dignity and love of thy kind and independence and justice; and to give thyself rest from all other impressions. And thou wilt give thyself this, if thou dost execute every act of thy life as though it were thy last, divesting thyself of all aimlessness and all passionate antipathy to the convictions of reason, and all hypocrisy and self-love and dissatisfaction with thy allotted share. Thou seest how few are the things, by mastering which a man may lead a life of tranquillity and godlikeness; for the Gods also will ask no more from him who keeps these precepts. . . .

This must always be borne in mind, what is the

Nature of the whole Universe, and what mine, and how this stands in relation to that, being too what sort of a part of what sort of a whole; and that no one can prevent thee from doing and saying always what is in keeping with the Nature of which thou are a part. . . .

Let thine every deed and word and thought be those of a man who can depart from life this moment. But to go away from among men, if there are Gods, is nothing dreadful; for they would not involve thee in evil. But if indeed there are no Gods, or if they do not concern themselves with the affairs of men, what boots it for me to live in a Universe empty of Gods or empty of Providence? Nay, but there *are* Gods, and they *do* concern themselves with human things; and they have put it wholly in man's power not to fall into evils that are truly such. And had there been any evil in what lies beyond, for this too would they have made provision, that it should be in every man's power not to fall into it. But how can that make a man's life worse which does not make the man worse? Yet the Nature of the Whole could not have been guilty of an oversight from ignorance or, while cognizant of these things, through lack of power to guard against or amend them; nor could it have gone so far amiss either from inability or unskilfulness, as to allow good and evil to fall without any discrimination alike upon the evil and the good. Still it is a fact that death and life, honour and dishonour, pain and pleasure, riches and penury, do among men one and all betide the Good and the Evil alike, being in themselves neither honourable nor shameful. Consequently they are neither good nor evil.

D. Born Again: A Mithraic Prayer

"First origin of my origin, first beginning of my beginning, spirit of spirit, firstfruit of the spirit within me, fire which art god-given to my mixing, the mixing of the mixings within me, firstfruit of the fire within me, water of water, firstfruit of the water within me, earthy substance, firstfruit of the earthy substance within me, whole body of me, A, son of my mother B, framed by the honourable arm and incorruptible right had in a world unilluminated yet bright, with no living soul, yet with a living soul: if it seem good to you to give me, held as I am by my underlying nature, to immortal bitch, in order that, after the present need which presses sore upon me, I may behold by deathless spirit the deathless Beginning, by deathless water, by solid earth and air, that I may be born anew by Thought, that I may be initiated and that the sacred spirit may breathe in me,

that I may marvel at the holy fire, that I may behold the terrible great deep of the Day-spring, that the life-giving and surrounding Aether may hear me; for-to-day I am to gaze with deathless eyes, I who was born mortal from a mortal womb, but transformed by might power and an incorruptible right hand. . . .

. . . But you shall see how the gods gaze upon you, and influence you. Lay at once your right [fore] finger upon your mouth and say, "Silence! Silence! Silence!" (a symbol of the living, incorruptible god). "Guard me, Silence!" Then whistle long, then sneeze, and say . . . and then you will see the gods looking graciously upon you, and no longer influencing you but going upon their own course of business. . . .

"O Lord, hail, great in power, king great in sovereignty, greatest of gods, Helios, Lord of heaven and earth, god of gods, mighty is thy breath, mighty is thy power. Lord, if it please thee, announce me to the greatest god, who hath begotten and made thee; for I am a man, A, the son of my mother B, born of the mortal womb of B and of lifegiving seed, and this day by thee who hast been regenerated, who out of so many thousands have been brought into immortality in this hour by the counsel of god, who is good beyond measure—a man who wills and prays to worship thee according to his human power." When you have said this, he will come into the vault of heaven and you will see him walking as on a road.

. . . Gaze on the god, groan long, and greet him thus: "O Lord, hail, ruler of water, hail, founder of earth, hail, sovereign of spirit. Lord, having been born again I depart; increasing and having been increased I die; born of a life-giving birth I am set free for death and go on my way, as thou didst ordain, as thou didst enact and didst make the mystery."

E. A Vision of the Goddess Isis

Behold me, Lucius; moved by thy prayers, I appear to thee; I, who am Nature, the parent of all things, the mistress of all the elements, the primordial offspring of time, the supreme among Divinities, the queen of departed spirits, the first of the celestials, and the uniform manifestation of the Gods and Goddesses; who govern by my nod the luminous heights of heaven, the salubrious breezes of the ocean, and the anguished silent realms of the shades below: whose one sole divinity the whole orb of the earth venerates under a manifold form, with different rites, and under a variety of appellations. Hence the Phrygians, that primæval, race, call me Pessinuntica, the Mother of the Gods; the Aborigines of Attica, Cecropian Minerva; the Cyprians, in their sea-girt isle, Paphian

Venus; the arrow-bearing Cretans, Diana Dictynna; the three-tongued Sicilians, Stygian Proserpine; and the Eleusinians, the ancient Goddess Ceres. Some call me Juno, others Bellona, others Hecate, and others Rhamnusia. But those who are illumined by the earliest rays of that divinity, the Sun, when he rises, the Æthiopians, the Arii, and the Egyptians, so skilled in ancient learning, worshipping me with ceremonies quite appropriate, call me by my true name, Queen Isis. Behold then, commiserating your calamities, I am come to thy assistance; favouring and propitious I am come. Away, then, with tears; leave your lamentations; cast off all sorrow. Soon, through my providence, shall the day of deliverance shine upon you. Listen, therefore, attentively to these my instructions.

Eternal religion has consecrated to me the day which will be born from this night; to-morrow my priests offer to me the first fruits of the opened navigation, and dedicate to me a new ship, for that the wintry tempests are now appeased, and the stormy waves of the ocean lulled, and the sea itself has become navigable. That sacred ceremonial you must await, with a mind neither full of anxiety, nor intent upon subjects that are profane. For the priest, at my command, will carry in the procession a crown of roses, attached to the sistrum in his right hand. Without delay, then, pushing the crowd aside, join my procession, and put your trust in my gracious disposition; then, having approached close, as though to kiss the hand of the priest, gently pluck the roses, and at once divest yourself of the hid of that abominable beast, which I have long looked upon with detestation.

"Nor hold in dread anything pertaining to my concerns as difficult. For even at this very same instant of time in which I appear to you here present, I am giving orders also to my priest how to bring about the things that are to take place hereafter. By my command, the dense crowds of people shall give way before you. Neither, amid the joyous rites and festive scenes, will any one view with abhorrence the unsightliness of the figure which you bear, or malignantly accuse you, by putting a sinister interpretation on the sudden change of your form. Only remember, and always keep it fast in the very depths of your heart, that the remaining period of your life must be dedicated to me, even the moment of your latest breath. Nor is it unjust that you should devote your whole life to that goddess, by whose assistance you will have been restored to human form. But under my protection you will live happy, you will live glorious: and when, having passed through the allotted period of your life, you shall descend to the realms beneath, there, also in the subterranean hemisphere,

you, dwelling in the Elysian fields, shall frequently adore me whom you now behold, thus propitious to you, and shall there see me shining amidst the darkness of Acheron, and reigning in the Stygian realms. And further, if you shall be found to deserve the protection of my divinity by sedulous obedience, religious devotion, and inviolable chastity, you shall be sensible that it is possible for me, and me alone, to extend your life beyond the limits that have been appointed to it by our destiny."

F. A City Pays Tribute to Its Virtuous Priestess, Second Century A.D.

The council and the people and the senate honour with first-rank honours Tata, daughter of Diodorus son of Diodorus son of Leon, reverend priestess of Hera for life, mother of the city, who became and remained the wife of Attalus son of Pytheas the *stephanephorus,* herself a member of an illustrious family of the first rank, who, as priestess of the imperial cult a second time, twice supplied oil for athletes in hand-bottles, filled most lavishly from basins for the better part of the night as well [as in the day], who became a *stephanephorus,* offered sacrifices throughout the year for the health of the imperial family, who held banquets for the people many times with couches provided for the public, who herself, for dances and plays, imported the foremost performers in Asia and displayed them in her native city (and the neighbouring cities could also come to the display of the performance), a woman who spared no expense, who loved honour, glorious in virtue and chastity.

Document Set 6.6 References

A. Seneca Expounds the Universal Goodness and Bounty of the Stoics' God
Seneca, on *Benefits,* in James Harvey Robinson, ed., *Readings in European History* (Boston: Ginn, 1904), 1:17.
B. Ptolemy Explains Why the Earth Must Be Stationary
Edward Rosen, ed., *Copernicus and the Scientific Revolution* (Malabar, Florida: Krieger, 1984), 139–140.
C. Marcus Aurelius Meditates on God's Ways
Marcus Aurelius, *Meditations,* 2:3–5, 9, 11, trans. C. R. Haines, Loeb Classical Library (London: Heinemann, 1916).
D. Born Again: A Mithraic Prayer
C. K. Barrett, *The New Testament Background* (London: S. P. C. K., 1956), 103–104.
E. A Vision of the Goddess Isis
Apuleis, *The Golden Ass,* 11, trans. William Addington (London: 1853), 226–227.
F. A City Pays Tribute to Its Virtuous Priestess, Second Century A.D.
Mary R. Lefkowitz and Maureen B. Fant, eds., *Women's Life in Greece and Rome* (Balitmore: Johns Hopkins University Press, 1982), 260.

DOCUMENT SET 6.7
Judaism in the Early Empire

Probably the most important written sources of knowledge about Jews in the first century A.D. are the Dead Sea Scrolls and the writings of Flavius Josephus (37–?100 A.D.), a Jew who witnessed the great Jewish Revolt of 67–70 A.D. Josephus, a Pharisee and son of a priest, initially supported the insurrection, but when he realized its hopelessness he accommodated himself with the Romans. Nevertheless, his books on the revolt and on Jewish history attempted to present his people favorably to a basically anti-Jewish Greco-Roman public. In Document A, taken from *The Jewish War,* he describes the three leading Jewish sects of the day—the Pharisees, Sadducees, and Essenes (each of which embraced only a small part of the Jewish population).

In Document B we read an extract from the Dead Sea Scrolls, a large body of parchments first discovered in a desert cave in Palestine in 1947 and still being pieced together and deciphered. The scrolls emanated from a quasi-monastic Essene community that had established itself in the desert to prepare for the coming of the Messiah. The Essenes believed that they could hasten Israel's deliverance by the strictest possible observance of the Jewish law and by maintaining rigid discipline within their ranks; the extract from their Manual of Discipline conveys the spirit of their movement.

In Document C we return to Josephus's *Jewish War,* in which he narrates one of the most dramatic and affecting incidents of the uprising: the fall of the last Jewish outpost at Masada. The document testifies to the intense faith and desperation of the Zealots, as the Jewish guerrillas were called.

A. Josephus Describes Essenes, Pharissees, and Saducees

Among the Jews there are three schools of thought, whose adherents are called Pharisees, Sadducees, and Essenes respectively. The Essenes profess a severer discipline: they are Jews by birth and are peculiarly attached to each other. They eschew pleasure-seeking

"Josephus on the Essenes" from *Jewish War,* translated by G. A. Williamson, revised by E. Mary Smallwood (Penguin Classics 1959, Second revised edition, 1981) copyright © G. A. Williamson, 1959, 1969 revisions copyright © E. M. Smallwood, 1981. Reprinted by permission of Penguin Books, Ltd.

as a vice and regard temperance and mastery of the passions as virtue. Scorning wedlock, they select other men's children while still pliable and teachable, and fashion them after their own pattern—not that they wish to do away with marriage as a means of continuing the race, but they are afraid of the promiscuity of women and convinced that none of the sex remains faithful to one man. Contemptuous of wealth, they are communists to perfection, and none of them will be found to be better off than the rest: their rule is that novices admitted to the sect must surrender their property to the order, so that among them all neither humiliating poverty nor excessive wealth is ever seen, but each man's possessions go into the pool and as with brothers their entire property belongs to them all. . . .

In general they take no action without orders from the supervisors, but two things are left entirely to them - personal aid, and charity; they may of their own accord help any deserving person in need or supply the penniless with food. But gifts to their own kinsfolk require official sanction. Showing indignation only when justified, they keep their tempers under control; they champion good faith and serve the cause of peace. Every word they speak is more binding than an oath; swearing they reject as something worse than perjury, for they say a man is already condemned if he cannot be believed without God being named. They are wonderfully devoted to the work of ancient writers, choosing mostly books that can help soul and body; from them in their anxiety to cure disease they learn all about medicinal roots and the properties of stones. . . .

It is indeed their unshakable conviction that bodies are corruptible and the material composing them impermanent, whereas souls remain immortal for ever. Coming forth from the most rarefied ether they are trapped in the prison-house of the body as if drawn down by one of nature's spells; but once freed from the bonds of the flesh, as if released after years of slavery, they rejoice and soar aloft. Teaching the same doctrines as the sons of Greece, they declare that for the good souls there waits a home beyond the ocean, a place troubled by neither rain nor snow nor heat, but refreshed by the zephyr that blows ever gentle from the ocean. Bad souls they consign to a darksome, stormy abyss, full of punishments that know no end. I think the Greeks had the same notion when they assigned to their brave men, whom they call heroes or demigods, the Islands of the Blest, and to the souls of the wicked the place of the impious in Hades, where according to their stories certain people undergo punishment—Sisyphus and Tantalus, Ixion and Tityus, and the like. They tell these tales firstly because they believe souls to be immortal, and secondly in the hope of encouraging virtue and discouraging vice, since the good become better in their lifetime through the hope of a reward after death, and the propensities of the bad are restrained by the fear that, even if they are not caught in this life, after their dissolution they will undergo eternal punishment. This then is the religious teaching of the Essenes about the soul, providing an inescapable inducement to those who have once tasted their wisdom.

Some of them claim to foretell the future, after a lifelong study of sacred literature, purifications of different kinds, and the aphorisms of prophets; rarely if ever do their predictions prove wrong.

There is a second order of Essenes, which agrees with the other in its way of life, customs, and rules, and differs only in its views on marriage. They think that the biggest thing in life—the continuance of the race—if forfeited by men who do not marry, and further, if everyone followed their example mankind would rapidly disappear. However, they put their brides on probation for three years, and do not marry them till the regularity of their periods proves them capable of child-bearing. When conception has taken place intercourse ceases—proof that the object of the marriage was not pleasure but the begetting of children. When women bathe they wear a dress just as the men wear a loincloth. Such are the customs of the order. . .

Of the two schools named first, the Pharisees are held to be the most authoritative exponents of the Law and count as the leading sect. They ascribe everything to Fate or to God: the decision whether or not to do right rests mainly with men, but in every action Fate takes some part. Every soul is incorruptible, but only the souls of good men pass into other bodies, the souls of bad men being subjected to eternal punishment. The Sadducees, the second order, deny Fate altogether and hold that God is incapable of either committing sin or seeing it; they say that men are free to choose between good and evil, and each individual must decide which he will follow. The permanence of the soul, punishments in Hades, and rewards they deny utterly. Again, Pharisees are friendly to one another and seek to promote concord with the general public, but Sadducees, even towards each other, show a more disagreeable spirit, and in their relations with men like themselves they are as harsh as they might be to foreigners.

B. A Dead Sea Scroll: The Essenes' Standard of Righteousness

Anyone who refuses to enter the (ideal) society of God and persists in walking in the stubbornness of his heart shall not be admitted to this community of God's truth. For inasmuch as his soul has revolted at the discipline entailed in a knowledge of God's righteous judgments, he has shown no real strength in amending his way of life, and therefore cannot be reckoned with the upright. The mental, physical and material resources of such a man are not to be introduced into the stock of the community, for such a man 'plows in the slime of wickedness' and 'there are stains on his repentance'. He is not honest in resolving the stubbornness of his heart. On paths of light he sees but darkness. Such a man cannot be reckoned as among those essentially blameless. He cannot be cleared by mere ceremonies of atonement, nor cleansed by any waters of ablution, nor sanctioned by immersion in lakes or rivers, nor purified by any bath. Unclean, unclean he remains so long as he rejects the government of God and refuses the discipline of communion with Him. For it is only through the spiritual apprehension of God's truth that man's ways can be properly directed. Only thus can all his iniquities be shriven so that he can gaze upon the true light of life. Only through the holy spirit can he achieve union with God's truth and be purged of all his iniquities. Only by a spirit of uprightness and humility can his sin be atoned. Only by the submission of his soul to all the ordinances of God can his flesh be made clean. Only thus can it really be sprinkled with waters of ablution. Only thus can it really be sanctified by waters of purification. And only thus can he really direct his steps to walk blamelessly through all the vicissitudes of his destiny in all the ways of God in the manner which He has commanded, without turning either to the right or to the left and without overstepping any of God's words. Then indeed will he be acceptable before God like an atonement-offering which meets with His pleasure, and then indeed will he be admitted to the covenant of the community for ever.

C. The Jewish Guerillas' Last Stand: Josephus Narrates the Fall of Masada

[The guerrilla leader Eleazar speaks:]
My loyal followers, long age we resolved to serve nei-

Excerpt from "Cleaning-Up Operations" from *Jewish War*, pp. 385–386, 390–391, translated by G. A. Williamson, revised by E. Mary Smallwood (Penguin Classics 1959, Second revised edition, 1981) copyright © G. A. Williamson, 1959, 1969. Reprinted by permission of Penguin Books Ltd.

ther the Romans nor anyone else but only God, who alone is the true and righteous Lord of men: now the time has come that bids us prove our determination by our deeds. At such a time we must not disgrace ourselves: hitherto we have never submitted to slavery, even when it brought no danger with it: we must not choose slavery now, and with it penalties that will mean the end of everything if we fall alive into the hands of the Romans. For we were the first of all to revolt, and shall be the last to break off the struggle. And I think it is God who has given us this privilege, that we can die nobly and as free men, unlike others who were unexpectedly defeated. In our case it is evident that daybreak will end our resistance, but we are free to choose an honourable death with our loved ones. This our enemies cannot prevent, however earnestly they may pray to take us alive; nor can we defeat them in battle.

From the very first, when we were bent on claiming our freedom but suffered such constant misery at each other's hands and worse at the enemy's, we ought perhaps to have read the mind of God and realized that His once beloved Jewish race had been sentenced to extinction. For if He had remained gracious or only slightly indignant with us, He would not have shut His eyes to the destruction of so many thousands or allowed His most holy City to be burnt to the ground by our enemies. We hoped, or so it would seem, that of all the Jewish race we alone would come through safe, still in possession of our freedom, as if we had committed no sin against God and taken part in no crime—we who had taught the others! Now see how He shows the folly of our hopes, plunging us into miseries more terrible than any we had dreamt of. Not even the impregnability of our fortress has sufficed to save us, but though we have food in abundance, ample supplies of arms, and more than enough of every other requisite, God Himself without a doubt has taken away all hope of survival. The fire that was being carried into the enemy lines did not turn back of its own accord towards the wall we had built: these things are God's vengeance for the many wrongs that in our madness we dared to do to our own countrymen.

For those wrongs let us pay the penalty not to our bitterest enemies, the Romans, but to God—by our own hands. It will be easier to bear. Let our wives die unabused, our children without knowledge of slavery: after that, let us do each other an ungrudging kindness, preserving our freedom as a glorious winding-sheet. But first let our possessions and the whole fortress go up in flames: it will be a bitter blow to the Romans, that I know, to find our persons beyond their reach and nothing left for them to loot. One

thing only let us spare our store of food: it will bear witness when we are dead to the fact that we perished, not through want but because, as we resolved at the beginning, we chose death rather than slavery. . . .

[Apparently, Josephus continues, not all the defenders were yet ready to follow Eleazar into mass suicide, so he had to resort to even more powerful oratory. Then, in a tremendous rush of emotion, the defenders realized that they had no other option.]

. . . As if possessed they rushed off, everyone anxious to be quicker than the next man, and regarding it as proof positive of manliness and wisdom not be found among the last: so irresistible a desire had seized them to slaughter their wives, their little ones, and themselves. It might have been thought that as they approached their task their determination would have weakened; but they clung resolutely to the purpose they had formed while listening to the appeal, and while they all retained feelings of personal affection, reason, which had urged what was best for their dear ones, won the day. For at the very moment when with streaming eyes they embraced and caressed their wives, and taking their children in their arms pressed upon them the last, lingering kisses, hands other than their own seemed to assist them and they carried out their purpose, the thought of the agonies they would suffer at the hands of the enemy consoling them for the necessity of killing them. In the end not a man failed to carry out his terrible resolve, but one and all disposed of their entire families, victims of cruel necessity who with their own hands murdered their wives and children and felt it to be the lightest of evils! . . .

[All the men thereupon drew lots, every tenth one slitting the throats of the other nine, until all had perished next to the bodies of their wives and children. Only two women and five children who had hidden lived to relate what had happened. In all, 960 men, women, and children died.]

. . . Expecting further resistance, the Romans armed themselves at dawn and with gangways bridge the gap between platform and ramparts, then made their assault. Seeing no enemy, but dreadful solitude on every side, fire within, and silence, they were at a loss to guess what had happened. At last, as if giving the signal for a volley, they shouted, in the hope that some of those inside would show themselves. The noise came to the ears of the women, who emerged from the conduits and gave the Romans a detailed account of what had happened, the second of them providing a lucid report of Eleazar's speech and the action that had followed. They found it difficult to believe her and were sceptical of such astounding resolution; but they attempted to extinguish the blaze and quickly cut a way through to the inside of the palace. When they came upon the rows of dead bodies, they did not exult over them as enemies but admired the nobility of their resolve, and the way in which so many had shown in carrying out without a tremor an utter contempt of death.

Document Set 6.7 References

A. Josephus Describes Essenes, Pharissees, and Saducees
Josephus, *The Jewish War,* trans. G. A. Williamson (Harmondsworth: Penguin, 1959), 125–130.

B. A Dead Sea Scroll: The Essenes' Standard of Righteousness
T. H. Gaster, ed., *The Dead Sea Scrolls in English Translation,* rev. ed. (Garden City, N.Y.: Anchor Books, 1964), 49–50.

C. The Jewish Guerrillas' Last Stand: Josephus Narrates the Fall of Masada
Josephus, 385–386, 390–392.

DOCUMENT SET 6.8
Earliest Christianity

The sources for earliest Christianity are extraordinarily hard to interpret. For one thing, the Gospels—accounts of the life of Jesus Christ—are not biographies in the modern sense but interpretations of his teachings, reflecting the different traditions of early Christian groups. Moreover, the Gospels were written at least one generation after his death, and perhaps even more. Scholars believe that there were several early Christian groups, some of which adhered closely to Jewish practices while others—notably the communities established in the Greek-speaking world by the Apostle Paul—abandoned most of the Jewish ceremonial traditions in an effort to accommodate converts of gentile origin. Probably only after the Roman destruction of Jerusalem in A.D. 70 did Paul's groups predominate. Nevertheless, almost everything that can be said about the history of early Christianity is subject to great controversy.

Document A presents what many scholars believe to be the teaching of Jesus of Nazareth, if not his actual words, as they were remembered sometime after the middle of the first century. This is the Sermon on the Mount taken from the Gospel of St. Matthew, probably written down by followers of Paul. Jesus' message here seems to be directed to his fellow Jews ("Ye are the salt of the earth"), not to the gentile world at large.

Contemporary materials from non-Christian sources that shed light on the beginnings of Christianity are exceedingly rare. One of the principal exceptions to this is Josephus's writings. In the *Jewish War* he describes the Roman governor (procurator) of Judaea, Pontius Pilate, under whose authority Jesus was crucified. The first passage in Document B is of unquestioned authenticity, but the passage set in italics in highly controversial. It is not found in the Greek text but comes from a manuscript written in medieval Slavic, which may in turn have been translated from the (now lost) ancient Hebrew or Aramaic version of Josephus's book. Do a little detective work on the passage and see whether you think it sounds authentic. Could it be a later Christian forgery? Does it support Christian interpretations of Jesus' life and crucifixion? Or does it suggest a genuinely different perspective? Whatever your answer, realize that some qualified scholars will agree with you, and others will disagree.

Document C may be the oldest extant authentic Christian text: The Epistle (Letter) of the Apostle Paul to the small Christian community of Thessalonika in northern Greece, about A.D. 50—some twenty years after Jesus' crucifixion. The entire short epistle (I Thessalonians) gives a vivid picture of the concerns of this small Christian group and of the kind of faith of Jesus as redeemer that Paul was striving to stimulate.

Document D dates from the mid-second century A.D. Its author, Justin Martyr (c. 100–165), was a sophisticated man, well trained in Stoic and Platonic philosophy. He converted to Christianity as an adult; eventually, as his name indicates, he was put to death. His *Apology,* of which this is an extract, defends Christianity against critics who spread rumors of the obscene secret purposes of Christian gatherings. Here Justin describes how Christians actually conducted themselves at worship and what they believed.

The last two documents of this set refer to the Christian heresy (as it was defined by the victorious side) of Gnosticism. Here the foremost early Christian opponent of the Gnostics, Irenaeus (c. 130–200), condemns the teachings of Marcion of Pontus. In Document F, another extract from the same work (*Against Heretics*), Irenaeus describes the doings of another Gnostic preacher, Marcus. Allowing for the fact that this is contentious writing, what can you learn about the Gnostics and why "orthodox" Christianity opposed them?

Piece together from these documents and from *The Challenge of the West* an essay revealing your understanding of early Christianity. It will enrich your account if you also draw on the document sets about Roman paganism and the mystery religions.

A. Jesus of Nazareth Admonishes His Fellow Jews: Sermon on the Mount

Blessed are the poor in spirit: for theirs is the kingdom of heaven. Blessed are they that mourn: for they shall be comforted. Blessed are the meek: for they shall inherit the earth. Blessed are they which do hunger and thirst after righteousness: for they shall be filled. Blessed are the merciful: for they shall obtain mercy. Blessed are the pure in heart: for they shall see God. Blessed are the peacemakers: for they shall be called the children of God. Blessed are they which are persecuted for righteousness' sake: for theirs is the kingdom of heaven. Blessed are ye, when men shall revile you, and persecute you, and shall say all manner of evil against you falsely, for my sake. Rejoice, and be exceeding glad: for great is your reward in heaven: for so persecuted they the prophets which were before you.

Ye are the salt of the earth: but if the salt have lost his savor, wherewith shall it be salted? it is thenceforth good for nothing, but to be cast out, and to be trodden under foot of men. Ye are the light of the world. A city that is set on a hill cannot be hid. Neither do men light a candle, and put it under a bushel, but on a candlestick; and it giveth light unto all that are in the house. Let your light so shine before men, that they may see your good works, and glorify your Father which is in heaven.

Think not that I am come to destroy the law, or the prophets: I am not come to destroy, but to fulfil. For verily I say unto you, Till heaven and earth pass, one jot or one tittle shall in no wise pass from the law, till all be fulfilled. Whosoever therefore shall break one of these least commandments, and shall teach men so, he shall be called the least in the kingdom of heaven: but whosoever shall do and teach them, the same shall be called great in the kingdom of heaven. For I say unto you, That except your righteousness shall exceed the righteousness of the scribes and Pharisees, ye shall in no case enter into the kingdom of heaven.

Ye have heard that it was said by them of old time, Thou shalt not kill; and whosoever shall kill shall be in danger of the judgment: But I say unto you, That whosoever is angry with his brother without a cause shall be in danger of the judgment: and whosoever shall say to his brother, Raca, shall be in danger of the council: but whosoever shall say, Thou fool, shall be in danger of hell fire. Therefore if thou bring thy gift to the altar, and there rememberest that thy brother hath aught against thee; Leave there thy gift before the altar, and go thy way; first be reconciled to thy brother, and then come and offer thy gift. Agree with thine adversary quickly, while thou art in the way with him; lest at any time the adversary deliver thee to the judge, and the judge deliver thee to the officer, and thou be cast into prison. Verily I say unto thee, Thou shalt by no means come out thence, till thou hast paid the uttermost farthing.

Ye have heard that it was said by them of old time, Thou shalt not commit adultery: But I say unto you, That whosoever looketh on a woman to lust after her hath committed adultery with her already in his heart. And if thy right eye offend thee, pluck it out, and cast it from thee: for it is profitable for thee that one of thy members should perish, and not that thy whole body should be cast into hell. And if thy right hand offend thee, cut it off, and cast it from thee: for it is profitable for thee that one of thy members should perish, and not that thy whole body should be cast into hell. It hath been said, Whosoever shall put away his wife, let him give her a writing of divorcement: But I say unto you, That whosoever shall put away his wife, saving for the cause of fornication, causeth her to commit adultery: and whosoever shall marry her that is divorced committeth adultery.

Again, ye have heard that it hath been said by them of old time, Thou shalt not forswear thyself, but shalt perform unto the Lord thine oaths: But I say unto you, Swear not at all; neither by heaven; for it is God's throne: Nor by the earth; for it is his footstool: neither by Jerusalem; for it is the city of the great King. Neither shalt thou swear by thy head, because thou canst not make one hair white or black. But let your communication be, Yea, yea; Nay, nay: for whatsoever is more than these cometh of evil.

Ye have heard that it hath been said, An eye for an eye, and a tooth for a tooth: But I say unto you, That ye resist not evil: but whosoever shall smite thee on thy right cheek, turn to him the other also. And if any man will sue thee at the law, and take away thy coat, let him have thy cloak also. And whosoever shall compel thee to go a mile, go with him twain. Give to him that asketh thee, and from him that would borrow of thee turn not thou away.

Ye have heard that it hath been said, Thou shalt love thy neighbor, and hate thine enemy. But I say unto you, Love your enemies, bless them that curse you, do good to them that hate you, and pray for them which despitefully use you, and persecute you; That ye may be the children of your Father which is in heaven: for he maketh his sun to rise on the evil and on the good, and sendeth rain on the just and on the unjust. For if ye love them which love you, what reward have ye? do not even the publicans the same? And if ye salute your brethren only, what do ye more than others? do not even the publicans so? Be ye therefore perfect, even as your Father which is in heaven is perfect.

B. Josephus Describes Pilate, Including a Controversial Passage on the Crucifixion of Jesus

As procurator of Judaea Tiberius sent Pilate, who during the night, secretly and under cover, conveyed

Excerpt from "Antipas and the Two Agrippas" from *Jewish War*, pp. 130–131, 398–399, translated by G. A. Williamson, revised by E. Mary Smallwood (Penguin Classics 1959, Second revised edition, 1981) copyright © G. A. Williamson, 1959, 1969 revisions copyright © E. M. Smallwood, 1981. Reprinted by permission of Penguin Books Ltd.

to Jerusalem the images of Caesar known as *signa*. When day dawned this caused great excitement among the Jews; for those who were near were amazed at the sight, which meant that their laws had been trampled on—they do not permit any graven image to be set up in the City—and the angry City mob were joined by a huge influx of people from the country. They rushed off to Pilate in Caesarea, and begged him to remove the *signa* from Jerusalem and to respect their ancient customs. When Pilate refused, they fell prone all round his house and remained motionless for five days and nights.

The next day Pilate took his seat on the tribunal in the Great Stadium and summoned the mob on the pretext that he was ready to give them an answer. Instead he gave a pre-arranged signal to the soldiers to surround the Jews in full armour, and the troops formed a ring three deep. The Jews were dumbfounded at the unexpected sight, but Pilate, declaring that he would cut them to pieces unless they accepted the images of Caesar, nodded to the soldiers to bare their swords. At this the Jews as though by agreement fell to the ground in a body and bent their necks, shouting that they were ready to be killed rather than transgress the Law. Amazed at the intensity of their religious fervour, Pilate ordered the *signa* to be removed from Jerusalem forthwith.

It was at the time that a man appeared—if 'man' is the right word—who had all the attributes of a man but seemed to be something greater. His actions, certainly, were superhuman, for he worked such wonderful and amazing miracles that I for one cannot regard him as a man; yet in view of his likeness to ourselves I cannot regard him as an angel either. Everything that some hidden power enabled him to do he did by an authoritative word. Some people said that their first Lawgiver had risen from the dead and had effected many marvellous cures; other thought he was a messenger from heaven. However, in many ways he broke the Law—for instance, he did not observe the Sabbath in the traditional manner. At the same time his conduct was above reproach. He did not need to use his hands: a word sufficed to fulfill his every purpose.

Many of the common people flocked after him and followed his teaching. There was a wave of excited expectation that he would enable the Jewish tribes to throw off the Roman yoke. As a rule he was to be found opposite the City on the Mount of Olives, where also he healed the sick. He gathered round him 150 assistants and masses of followers. When they saw his ability to do whatever he wished by a word, they told him that they wanted him to enter the City, destroy the Roman troops, and make himself king; but he took no notice.

When the suggestion came to the ear of the Jewish authorities, they met under the chairmanship of the high priest and exclaimed: 'We are utterly incapable of resisting the Romans; but as the blow is about to fall we'd better go and tell Pilate what we've heard, and steer clear of trouble, in case he gets to know from someone else and confiscates our property, puts us to death, and turns our children adrift.' So they went and told Pilate, who sent troops and butchered many of the common people. He then had the Miracle-worker brought before him, held an inquiry, and expressed the opinion that he was a benefactor, not a criminal or agitator or a would-be king. Then he let him go, as he had cured Pilate's wife when she was at the point of death.

Returning to his usual haunts he resumed his normal work. When the crowds grew bigger than ever, he earned by his actions an incomparable reputation. The exponents of the Law were mad with jealousy, and gave Pilate 30 talents to have him executed. Accepting the bribe, he gave them permission to carry out their wishes themselves. So they seized him and crucified him in defiance of all Jewish tradition.

C. The First Authentic Christian Text: Paul Instructs the Thessalonians

Furthermore then we beseech you, brethren, and exhort you by the Lord Jesus, that as ye have received of us how ye ought to walk and to please God, so ye would abound more and more. For ye know what commandments we gave you by the Lord Jesus. For this is the will of God, even your sanctification, that ye should abstain from fornication: The every one of you should know how to possess his vessel in sanctification and honor; Not in the lust of concupiscence, even as the Gentiles, which know not God: That no man go beyond and defraud his brother in any matter: because that the Lord is the avenger of all such, as we also have forewarned you and testified. For God's hath not called us unto uncleanness, but unto holiness. . . . But I would not have you to be ignorant, brethren, concerning them which are asleep, that ye sorrow not, even as others which have no hope. For if we believe that Jesus died and rose again, even so them also which sleep in Jesus will God bring with him. For this we say unto you by the word of the Lord, that we which are alive and remain unto the coming of the Lord shall not prevent them which are asleep. For the Lord himself shall descend from heaven with a shout, with the voice of the archangel, and with the trump of God: and the dead in Christ shall rise first: Then we which are alive and remain shall be caught up together with them in the clouds, to meet the Lord in the air: and so shall we ever be with the Lord. Wherefore comfort one another with these words.

D. Justin Martyr Describes Early Christian Worship

All who are convinced and believe that what is taught and said by us is true, and promise that they are able to live accordingly, are taught to pray and with fasting to ask forgiveness of God for their former sins; and we pray and fast with them. Then they are brought by us to where there is water, and they are reborn in the same manner as we ourselves were reborn. For in the name of God, the Father and Lord of the universe, and of our Savior Jesus Christ, and of the Holy Ghost, they then are washed in the water. . . .

After thus washing the one who has been convinced and has given his assent, we conduct him to the place where those who are called the brethren are assembled, to offer earnest prayers in common for ourselves, for him who has been enlightened, and for all others everywhere, so that we, now that we have learned the truth, may by our works also be deemed worthy of being found to be good practitioners and keepers of the commandments, and thus be saved with eternal salvation. When we end our prayers we greet each other with a kiss. Then bread and a chalice of wine mixed with water are brought to the one who presides over the brethren; and he takes it, and offers up praise and glory to the Father of the universe, through the name of the Son and the Holy Ghost; and he gives thanks at length for our being deemed worthy of these things by Him. When he has finished the prayers and thanksgiving, all the people present express their assent, saying "Amen.". . . And when he who presides has celebrated the eucharist [thanksgiving], and all the people have expressed their assent, those called among us deacons allow each one of those present to partake of the bread and wine and water for which thanks have been given, and they bring it also to those not present. And this food is called among us the eucharist. . . .

And on the day called Sunday there is a gathering in one place of all who dwell in the cities or in the country places, and the memoirs of the Apostles or the writings of the prophets are read as long as time

"Justin Martyr on Early Christian Worship" from *Roman Civilization*, Vol. 2 by N. Lewis and M. Reinhold. Copyright © 1990 by Columbia University Press, excerpts from pp. 589–590. Reprinted with permission of the publisher.

allows. Then when the reader his finished, he who presides gives oral admonition and exhortation to imitate these excellent examples. Then we all rise together, and offer prayers; and, as stated before, when we have ended our praying, bread and wine and water are brought. And he who presides similarly offers up prayers and thanksgiving, as far as lies in his power, and the people express their approval by saying "Amen." And each receives a share and partakes of the food for which thanks have been given, and through the deacons some is sent to those not present. The prosperous, if they so desire, each contribute what they wish, according to their own judgment, and the collection is entrusted to the one who presides. And he assists orphans and widows, and those who are in need because of illness or any other reason, and those who are in prison, and strangers sojourning with us; in short, all those in need are his care.

E. The Gnostic Teachings of Marcion of Pontus

Marcion of Pontus . . . advanced the most daring blasphemy against Him who is proclaimed as God by the law and the prophets, declaring Him to be the author of evils, to take delight in war, to be infirm of purpose, and even to be contrary to Himself. But Jesus being derived from that father who is above the God that made the world, and coming in Judaea in the times of Pontius Pilate the governor, who was the procurator of Tiberius Caesar, was manifested in the form of a man to those who were in Judaea, abolishing the prophets and the law, and all the works of that God who made the world, whom also he calls Cosmocrator. Besides this, he mutilates the Gospel which is according to Luke, removing all that is written respecting the generation of the Lord, and setting aside a great deal of the teaching of the Lord, in which the Lord is recorded as most clearly confessing that the Maker of this universe is His Father. He likewise persuaded his disciples that he himself was more worthy of credit than are those apostles who have handed down the Gospel to us, furnishing them not with the Gospel, but merely a fragment of it. In like manner, too, he dismembered the Epistles of Paul, removing all that is said by the apostle respecting that God who made the world, to the effect that He is the Father of our Lord Jesus Christ, and also those passages from the prophetical writings which the apostle quotes, in order to teach us that they announced beforehand the coming of the Lord.

Salvation will be the attainment only of those

souls which had learned his doctrine; while the body, as having been taken from the earth, is incapable of sharing in salvation. In addition to his blasphemy against God Himself, he advanced this also, truly speaking as with the mouth of the devil, and saying all things in direct opposition to the truth,—that Cain, and those like him, and the Sodomites, and the Egyptians, and others like them, and, in fine, all the nations who walked in all sorts of abomination, were saved by the Lord, on His descending into Hades, and on their running unto Him, and that they welcomed Him into their kingdom. But the serpent which was in Marcion declared that Abel, and Enoch, and Noah, and those other righteous men who sprang from the patriarch Abraham, with all the prophets, and those who were pleasing to God, did not partake in salvation. For since these men, he says, knew that their God was constantly tempting them, so now they suspected that He was tempting them, and did not run to Jesus, or believe His announcement: and for this reason he declared that their souls remained in Hades.

F. A Gnostic Guru Works His Wiles on Women

There is another among these heretics, Marcus by name, who boasts himself as having improved upon his master. He is a perfect adept in magical impostures, and by this means drawing away a great number of men, and not a few women, he has induced them to join themselves to him, as to one who is possessed of the greatest knowledge and perfection, and who has received the highest power from the invisible and ineffable regions above. Thus it appears as if he really were the precursor of Antichrist. For, joining the buffooneries of Anaxilaus to the craftiness of the *magi*, as they are called, he is regarded by his senseless and cracked-brain followers as working miracles by these means.

Pretending to consecrate cups mixed with wine, and protracting to great length the word of invocation, he contrives to give them a purple and reddish colour, so that Charis who is one of those that are superior to all things, should be thought to drop her own blood into that cup through means of his invocation, and that thus those who are present should be led to rejoice to taste of that cup, in order that, by so doing, the Charis, who is set forth by this magician, may also flow into them. Again, handing mixed cups to the women, he bids them consecrate these in his presence. When this has been done, he himself produces another cup of much larger size than that which the deluded woman has consecrated, and pouring from the smaller one consecrated by the woman into that which has been brought forward by himself, he at the same time pronounces these words: "May that Charis who is before all things, and who transcends all knowledge and speech, fill thine inner man, and multiply in thee her own knowledge, by sowing the grain of mustard seed in thee as in good soil." Repeating certain other like words, and thus goading on the wretched woman [to madness], he then appears a worker of wonders when the large cup is seen to have been filled out of the small one, so as even to overflow by what has been obtained from it. By accomplishing several other similar things, he has completely deceived many, and drawn them away after him.

It appears probable enough that his man possesses a demon as his familiar spirit, by means of whom he seems able to prophesy, and also enables as many as he counts worthy to be partakers of his Charis themselves to prophesy. He devotes himself especially to women, and those such as are well-bred, and elegantly attired, and of great wealth, whom he frequently seeks to draw after him, by addressing them in such seductive words as these: "I am eager to make thee a partaker of my Charis, since the Father of all doth continually behold thy angel before His face. Now the place of thy angel is among us: it behoves us to become one. Receive first from me and by me [the gift of] Charis. Adorn thyself as a bride who is expecting her bridegroom, that thou mayest be what I am, and I what thou art. Establish the germ of light in thy nuptial chamber. Receive from me a spouse, and become receptive of him, while thou art received by him. Behold Charis has descended upon thee; open thy mouth and prophesy." On the woman replying, "I have never at any time prophesied, nor do I know how to prophesy;" then engaging, for the second time, in certain invocations, so as to astound his deluded victim, he says to her, "Open thy mouth, speak whatsoever occurs to thee, and thou shalt prophesy." She then, vainly puffed up and elated by these words, and greatly excited in soul by the expectation that it is herself who is to prophesy, her heart beating violently [from emotion], reaches the requisite pitch of audacity, and idly as well as impudently utters some nonsense as it happens to occur to her, such as might be expected from one heated by an empty spirit. (Referring to this, one superior to me has observed, that the soul is both audacious and impudent when heated with empty air.) Henceforth she reckons herself a prophetess, and expresses her thanks to Marcus for having imparted to her of his own Charis. She then makes the effort to reward him, not only by the gift of her possessions (in which way he has collected a very large fortune), but also by yielding up to him her person, desiring in every way to be united to him, that she may become altogether one with him.

Document Set 6.8 References

A. Jesus of Nazareth Admonishes His Fellow Jews: The Sermon on the Mount
Matthew 5.

B. Josephus Describes Pilate, Including a Controversial Passage on the Crucifixion of Jesus
Josephus, *The Jewish War,* trans. G. A. Williamson (Harmondsworth, England: Penguin, 1959), 130–131, 398–399.

C. The First Authentic Christian Text: Paul Instructs the Thessalonians
I Thessalonians 4, 1–7, 13–18.

D. Justin Martyr Describes Early Christian Worship
Naphtali Lewis and Meyer Reinhold, eds., *Roman Civilization: Selected Readings* (New York: Columbia University Press, 1951), 2:589–590.

E. The Gnostic Teachings of Marcion of Pontus
Tertullian, *Against Marcion,* 1:27, in Alexander Roberts and James Donaldson, eds., *The Ante-Nicene Fathers,* Edinburgh Edition (reprinted Grand Rapids, Mich.: Wm. B. Eerdmans, 1978–1979), vol. 3

F. A Gnostic Guru Works His Wiles on Women
Irenaeus, *Against Heretics,* 1:13, in *Ante-Nicene Fathers,* vol. 1, (reprinted Grand Rapids, Mich.: Wm. B. Eerdmans Publishing Co., 1978–1979).

The Persecution of Christianity

The earliest large-scale persecution of Christianity by the Roman authorities occurred about A.D. 64 under Emperor Nero, who blamed this unpopular and obscure sect for setting the great fire that had recently devastated Rome. The conservative moralist Tacitus had little regard for the Christians or Jews, but he also condemned Nero for his sadistic cruelty. His account, an extract from his *Annals*, appears as Document A.

How the first-century Christians reacted to repeated waves of persecution may be gauged from the apocalyptic New Testament book of Revelation (Document B). It is in the tradition of the Jewish Book of Daniel (Set 4.9 Document A). Who wrote it and to what Christian group he belonged is much debated.

Even the relatively clement and reflective Emperor Trajan and his friend Pliny the Younger regarded Christianity as subversive of public order, as can be seen in Document C, dating from about 112 B.C. (So too did Marcus Aurelius, also a brutal persecutor of the Christians in 177.) In Document D, a second-century martyr, St. Perpetua, speaks for herself in an account taken down shortly before her execution.

After reading these source materials and also considering other sets in Chapters 5 and 6, you should be able to analyze why the Roman authorities repeatedly singled out Christianity for ferocious persecution, as well as how the fledgling Christian groups managed to withstand these efforts to extirpate them. In what ways did Christianity challenge fundamental Roman values—as well as the authority of the Roman state as symbolized by the imperial cult, to which all subjects were expected to offer sacrifice as testimony of their loyalty?

A. Tacitus Describes Nero's Persecution of Christians

. . . Those, who were called Christians by the mob and hated for their moral-enormities, were substituted in his place as culprits by Nero and afflicted with the most exquisite punishments. Christ, from whom the name was given, was put to death during the reign of Tiberius, by the procurator Pontius Pilate. Although checked for the time, this pernicious superstition broke out again not only in Judea, where the evil originated, but throughout the City, in which the atrocities and shame from all parts of the world cen-

ter and flourish. Therefore those who confessed were first seized, then on their information a great multitude were convicted, not so much of the crime of incendiarism, as of hatred of the human race. The victims who perished also suffered insults, for some were covered with the skins of wild beasts and torn to pieces by dogs, while others were fixed to crosses and burnt to light the night when daylight had failed. Nero had offered his gardens for the spectacle and was giving a circus show, mingling with the people in the dress of a driver, or speeding about in a chariot. Although they were criminals who deserved the most severe punishment, yet a feeling of pity arose since they were put to death not for the public good but to satisfy the rage of an individual.

B. Christian Apocalypse: The Book of Revelation

And I saw when the Lamb opened one of the seals, and I heard, as it were the noise of thunder, one of the four beasts saying, Come and see. And I saw, and behold a white horse: and he that sat on him had a bow; and a crown was given unto him: and he went forth conquering, and to conquer. And when he had opened the second seal, I heard the second beast say, Come and see. And there went out another horse that was red: and power was given to him that sat thereon to take peace from the earth, and that they should kill one another: and there was given unto him a great sword. And when he had opened the third seal, I heard the third beast say, Come and see. And I beheld, and lo a black horse; and he that sat on him has a pair of balances in his hand. And I heard a voice in the midst of the four beasts say, A measure of wheat for a penny, and three measures of barley for a penny; and see thou hurt not the oil and the wine. And when he had opened the fourth seal, I heard the voice of the fourth beast say, Come and see. And I looked, and behold a pale horse: and his name that sat on him was Death, and Hell followed with him. And power was given unto them over the fourth part of the earth, to kill with sword, and with hunger, and with death, and with the beasts of the earth. And when he had opened the fifth seal, I saw under the altar the souls of them that were slain for the word of God, and for the testimony which they held: And they cried with a loud voice, saying, How long, O Lord, holy and true, dost thou not judge and avenge our blood on them that dwell on the earth? And white robes were given unto every one of them; and it was said unto them, that they should rest yet for a little season, until their fellow servants also and their brethren, that should be killed as they were, should be fulfilled. And I beheld when he had opened the sixth seal, and, lo, there was a great earthquake; and the sun became black as sackcloth of hair, and the moon became as blood; And the stars of heaven fell unto the earth, even as a fig tree casteth her untimely figs, when she is shaken of a mighty wind. And the heaven departed as a scroll when it is rolled together; and every mountain and island were moved out of their places. And the kings of the earth, and the great men, and the rich men, and the chief captains, and the mighty men, and every bondman, and every free man, hid themselves in the dens and in the rocks of the mountains; And said to the mountains and rocks, Fall on us, and hide us from the face of him that sitteth on the throne, and from the wrath of the Lamb: For the great day of his wrath is come; and who shall be able to stand?

c. Trajan and Pliny Discuss How to Handle Accusations Against Suspected Christians

It is my custom, my lord, to refer to you all things concerning which I am in doubt. For who can better guide my indecision or enlighten my ignorance?

I have never taken part in the trials of Christians: hence I do not know for what crime or to what extent it is customary to punish or investigate. I have been in no little doubt as to whether any discrimination is made for age, or whether the treatment of the weakest does not differ from that of the stronger; whether pardon is granted in case of repentance, or whether he who has ever been a Christian gains nothing by having ceased to be one; whether the name itself without the proof of crimes, or the crimes, inseparably connected with the name, are punished. Meanwhile I have followed this procedure in the case of those who have been brought before me as Christians. I asked them whether they were Christians a second and a third time and with threats of punishment, I questioned those who confessed, I ordered those who were obstinate to be executed. For I did not doubt that, whatever it was that they confessed, their stubbornness and inflexible obstinacy ought certainly to be punished. There were others of similar madness, who because they were Roman citizens, I have noted for sending to the City. Soon, the crime spreading, as is usual when attention is called to

it, more cases arose. An anonymous accusation, containing many names, was presented. Those who denied that they were or had been Christians, ought, I thought, to be dismissed since they repeated after me a prayer to the gods and made supplication with incense and wine to your image, which I had ordered to be brought for the purpose together with the statues of the gods, and since besides they cursed Christ, not one of which things they say, those who are really Christians can be compelled to do. Others, accused by the informer, said that they were Christians and afterwards denied it; in fact, they had been but had ceased to be, some many years ago, some even twenty years before. All both worshipped your image and the statues of the gods, and cursed Christ. They continued to maintain that this was the amount of their fault or error that, on a fixed day, they were accustomed to come together before daylight and to sing by turns a hymn to Christ as a god, and that they bound themselves by oath, not for some crime but that they would not commit robbery, theft, or adultery, that they would not betray a trust or deny a deposit when called upon. After this it was their custom to disperse and to come together again to partake of food, of an ordinary and harmless kind, however; even this they ceased to do after the publication of my edict in which according to your command I had forbidden associations. Hence I believed it the more necessary to examine two female slaves, who were called deaconesses, in order to find out what was true, and to do it by torture. I found nothing but a vicious, extravagant superstition. Consequently I postponed the examination and make haste to consult you. For it seemed to me that the subject would justify consultation, especially on account of the number of those in peril. For many of all ages, of every rank, and even of both sexes are and will be called into danger. The infection of this superstition has not only spread to the cities but even to the villages and country districts. It seems possible to stay it and bring about a reform. It is plain enough that the temples, which had been almost deserted, have begun to be frequented again, that the sacred rites, which had been neglected for a long time, have begun to be restored, and that fodder for victims, for which till now there was scarcely a purchaser, is sold. From which one may readily judge what a number of men can be reclaimed if repentance is permitted.

Trajan's Reply

You have followed the correct procedure, my Secundus, in conducting the cases of those who were accused before you as Christians for no general rule can be laid down as a set form. They ought not to be sought out; if they are brought before you and convicted they ought to be punished; provided that he who denies that he is a Christian, and proves this by making supplication to our gods, however much he may have been under suspicion in the past, shall secure pardon on repentance. In the case of no crime should attention be paid to anonymous charges, for they afford a bad precedent and are not worthy of our age.

D. St. Perpetua Describes Her Impending Martyrdom

The young catechumens, Revocatus and his fellow-servant Felicitas, Saturninus and Secundulus, were apprehended. And among them also was Vivia Perpetua, respectably born, liberally educated, a married matron, having a father and mother and two brothers, one of whom, like herself, was a catechumen, and a son an infant at the breast. She herself was about twenty-two years of age. From this point onward she shall herself narrate the whole course of her martyrdom, as she left it described by her own hand and with her own mind.

"While," says she, "we were still with the persecutors, and my father, for the sake of his affection for me, was persisting in seeking to turn me away, and to cast me down from the faith,—'Father,' said I, 'do you see, let us say, this vessel lying here to be a little pitcher, or something else?' And he said, 'I see it to be so.' And I replied to him, 'Can it be called by any other name than what it is?' And he said, 'No,' 'Neither can I call myself anything else than what I am, a Christian.' Then my father, provoked at this saying, threw himself upon me, as if he would tear my eyes out. But he only distressed me, and went away overcome by the devil's arguments. Then, in a few days after I had been without my father, I gave thanks to the Lord; and his absence became a source of consolation to me. In that same interval of a few days we were baptized, and to me the Spirit prescribed that in the water *of baptism* nothing else was to be sought for than bodily endurance. After a few days we are taken into the dungeon, and I was very much afraid, because I had never felt such darkness. O terrible day! O the fierce heat of the shock of the soldiery, because of the crowds! I was very unusually distressed by my anxiety for my infant. There were present there Tertius and Pomponius, the blessed deacons who ministered to us, and had arranged by means of a gratuity that we might be refreshed by being sent out for a few hours into a pleasanter part of the prison. Then going out of the dungeon, all

attended to their own wants. I suckled my child, which was now enfeebled with hunger. In my anxiety for it, I addressed my mother and comforted my brother, and commended to their care my son. I was languishing because I had seen them languishing on my account. Such solicitude I suffered for many days, and I obtained leave for my infant to remain in the dungeon with me; and forthwith I grew strong and was relieved from distress and anxiety about my infant; and the dungeon became to me as it were a palace, so that I preferred being there to being elsewhere. . . . [Perpetua: brother vainly tries to persuade her to renounce Christianity.]

"After a few days there prevailed a report that we should be heard. And then my father came to me from the city, worn out with anxiety. He came up to me, that he might cast me down, saying, 'Have pity my daughter, on my grey hairs. Have pity on your father, if I am worthy to be called a father by you. If with these hands I have brought you up to this flower of your age, if I have preferred you to all your brothers, do not deliver me up to the scorn of men. Have regard to your brothers, have regard to your mother and your aunt, have regard to your son, who will not be able to live after you. Lay aside your courage, and do not bring us all to destruction; for none of us will speak in freedom if you should suffer anything.' These things said my father in his affection, kissing my hands, and throwing himself at my feet; and with tears he called me not Daughter, but Lady. And I grieved over the grey hairs of my father, that he alone of all my family would not rejoice over my passion. And I comforted him, saying, 'On that scaffold whatever God wills shall happen. For know that we are not placed in our own power, but in that of God.' And he departed from me in sorrow.

"Another day, while we were at dinner, we were suddenly taken away to be heard, and we arrived at the town-hall. At once the rumour spread through the neighbourhood of the public place, and an immense number of people were gathered together. We mount the platform. The rest were interrogated, and confessed. Then they came to me, and my father immediately appeared with my boy, and withdrew me from the step, and said in a supplicating tone, 'Have pity on your babe.' And Hilarianus the procurator, who had just received the power of life and death in the place of the proconsul Minucius Timinianus, who was deceased, said, 'Spare the grey hairs of your father, spare the infancy of your boy, offer sacrifice for the well-being of the emperors.' And I replied, 'I will not do so.' Hilarianus said, 'Are you a Christian?' And I replied, 'I am a Christian.' And as my father stood there to cast me down *from the faith,* he was ordered by Hilarianus to be thrown down, and was beaten with rods. And my father's misfortune grieved me as if I myself had been beaten, I so grieved for his wretched old age. The procurator then delivers judgment on all of us, and condemns us to the wild beasts, and we went down cheerfully to the dungeon. Then, because my child had been used to receive suck from me, and to stay with me in the prison, I send Pomponius the deacon to my father to ask for the infant, but my father would not give it him. And even as God willed it, the child no long desired the breast, nor did my breast cause me uneasiness, lest I should be tormented by care of my babe and by the pain of my breasts at once. . . . [After several other appeals from her father, and after experiencing several visions to encourage her resistance, she dies in the arena with the other condemned Christians.]

Document Set 6.9 References

A. Tacitus Describes Nero's Persecution of Christians
   Tacitus, *Annals,* 15:44, in *Translation and Reprints from the Original Sources of European History* (Philadelphia: University of Pennsylvania Press, 1898), 4/1:4.
B. Christian Apocalypse: The Book of Revelation
   Revelation 6.
C. Trajan and Pliny Discuss How to Handle Accusations Against Suspected Christians
   Pliny the Younger, *Letters,* 10.96, 97, in *Translations and Reprints,* 4/1:8–10.
D. St. Perpetua Describes Her Impending Martyrdom
   Alexander Roberts and James Donaldson, eds., *The Ante-Nicene Fathers,* Edinburgh Edition (reprinted Grand Rapids, Mich.: Wm. B. Eerdmans, 1978–1979), 3:699–701.

DOCUMENT SET 6.10
The Imperial Crisis Begins

The events that gradually overwhelmed the Roman Empire in the third century A.D. are illustrated by the documents in this set bearing on political, economic, and social turmoil. An early sign of the coming trouble was the sad story of General Pertinax, who was acclaimed emperor by this troops after the murder of Marcus Aurelius's wastrel son Commodus in 193. Pertinax was assassinated within three months by the Praetorian Guard. The story is narrated in Document A, an ancient summary ("epitome") of a lost book of the Roman history by Dio Cassius. (The Greens referred to here were a faction of fans in the Roman coliseum.) Pertinax's inability to put Rome's domestic house in order foreshadowed much that went wrong over the succeeding century. Some of these problems are illustrated by the next group of documents. Document B, from an Egyptian papyrus, attests to one of the Empire's most intractable problems, the flight of tax-paying peasants from the countryside into the cities, where they often found themselves unemployable; this document is a directive from Emperor Caracalla to his officials in Egypt. Document C gives further evidence of the breakdown of law and order in the provinces, in this case Thrace, in modern northern Greece and Bulgaria. Losses of revenue, occasioned by such disorders, in turn worsened the problem of currency debasement, as illustrated by Document D, another Roman-Egyptian papyrus. And Document E offers insights into local officials' vain efforts to stem the problems they faced.

Considering these sources and the synthesis offered by *The Challenge of the West,* write an essay on the third-century crisis of the Roman Empire.

A. The Swift Rise and Swifter Fall of Emperor Pertinax, 192

While Pertinax was still in Britain, after that great revolt which he quelled, and was being accounted worthy of praise on all sides, a horse named Pertinax won a race at Rome. It belonged to the Greens and was favoured by Commodus. So, when its partisans raised a great shout, crying, "It is Pertinax!" the others, their opponents, in disgust at Commodus, likewise prayed,—with reference to the man rather than to the horse,—"Would that it were so!" Later, when this same horse had left the race-track because of age and was in the country, it was sent for by Commodus, who brought it into the Circus after gilding its hoofs and adorning its back with a gilded skin. And the people, suddenly seeing it, cried out again: "It is Pertinax!" This very expression was doubtless an omen in itself, occurring, as it did, at the last horse-race that year; and immediately afterward the throne passed to Pertinax. Similar views were expressed also concerning the incident of the club; for Commodus when about to contend on the final day had given it to Pertinax.

It was in this manner that Pertinax came into power. And he obtained all the customary titles pertaining to the office, and also a new one to indicate his wish to be democratic; for he was styled Chief of the Senate in accordance with the ancient practice. He at once reduced to order everything that had previously been irregular and confused; for he showed not only humaneness and integrity in the imperial administration, but also the most economical management and the most careful consideration for the public welfare. . . .

At this time, then, there was such a dearth of funds in the imperial treasury that only a million sesterces could be found. Pertinax therefore raised money as best he could from the statues, the arms, the horses, the furniture, and the favourites of Commodus, and gave to the Pretorians all that he had promised and to the populace a hundred denarii per man. . . .

Since now, neither the soldiers were allowed to plunder any longer nor the imperial freedmen to indulge in lewdness, they both hated him bitterly. The freedmen, for their part, attempted no revolt, being unarmed; but the Pretorian troops and Laetus formed a plot against him. [The soldiers break into his palace and threaten him with death.] . . .

Hoping to overawe them by his appearance and to win them over by his words, he went to meet the approaching band, which was already inside the palace; for no one of their fellow soldiers had barred the way, and the porters and other freedmen, so far from making any door fast, had actually opened absolutely all the entrances. The soldiers on seeing him were at first abashed, all save one, and kept their eyes on the ground, and they thrust their swords back into their scabbards; but that one man leaped forward, exclaiming, "The soldiers have sent you this sword," and forthwith fell upon him and wounded him. Then his comrades no longer held back, but struck down their emperor together with Eclectus.

The latter alone had not deserted him, but defended him as best he could, even wounding several of his assailants; hence I, who felt that even before that he had shown himself an excellent man, now thoroughly admired him. The soldiers cut off the head of Pertinax and fastened it on a spear, glorying in the deed. Thus did Pertinax, who undertook to restore everything in a moment, come to his end. He failed to comprehend, though a man of wide practical experience, that one cannot with safety reform everything at once, and that the restoration of a state, in particular, requires both time and wisdom. He had lived sixty-seven years, lacking four months and three days, and had reigned eighty-seven days.

B. Flight from the Land, Egypt, 215

All Egyptians in Alexandria, especially countryfolk, who have fled other parts and can easily be detected, are by all manner of means to be expelled, with the exception, however, of pig-dealers and river boatmen and the men who bring down reeds for heating the baths. But expel all the others, as by the numbers of their kind and their uselessness they are disturbing the city. I am informed that at the festival of Sarapis and on certain other festal days Egyptians are accustomed to bring down bulls and other animals for sacrifice, or even on other days; they are not to be prohibited for this. The persons who ought to be prohibited are those who flee from their own districts to escape rustic toil, not those, however, who congregate here with the object of viewing the glorious city of Alexandria or come down for the sake of enjoying a more civilized life or for incidental business.

A further extract: For genuine Egyptians can easily be recognized among the linen-weavers by their speech, which proves them to have assumed the appearance and dress of another class; moreover in their mode of life their far from civilized manners reveal them to be Egyptian countryfolk.

C. Law and Order Collapse in Thrace, 238

To the Emperor Caesar Marcus Antonius Gordian Pius Felix Augustus, petition from the villagers of Scaptopara and Gresa[?]. During the most fortunate and eternal time of your reign you have often stated in rescripts that the villages should be inhabited and improved instead of having the inhabitants driven from their homes. Such a policy is conducive to the security of your subjects and the advantage of your most sacred treasury. Wherefore we too convey a just

supplication to your divinity, praying that you may graciously grant our petition to this effect.

We dwell in and are property owners in the afore-mentioned village, which is exposed to wanton damage because it possesses the advantage of hot springs and is situated between two of the army camps which are in your Thrace. And in the past, as long as the inhabitants remained undisturbed and unharmed, they paid their tribute and other levies unexceptionably. But when certain parties began at times to proceed to insolence and employ violence, then indeed the village began to decline. A famous festival is celebrated two miles from our village, and those who visit there for fifteen days for the festival do not remain at the site of the festival but leave it and descend upon our village, forcing us to provide them with hospitality and furnish many other things for their entertainment without payment. In addition to these, soldiers too, when sent elsewhere, leave their proper routes and come to us, and likewise compel us to provide them with hospitality and supplies and pay us no money. And the governors of the province and even your procurators for the most part visit here for the benefit of the waters. We are continually entertaining the authorities, as we needs must; but, unable to bear the burden of the others, we appealed repeatedly to the governors of Thrace, who in accordance with the divine ordinances gave orders that we be left undisturbed. For we pointed out that we could no longer abide it, but actually had a mind to abandon even our ancestral hearths on account of the violence of those who descend upon us—and in truth we have declined from many home owners to a very few.

For some time the edicts of the governors prevailed, and no one disturbed us with a demand either for hospitality or for provision of supplies; but as time went on, the whole throng who are contemptuous of our defenselessness again dared to foist themselves upon us. Since, therefore, we can no longer endure the oppression, and since in truth we, too, like the rest, are in danger of having to abandon the abode of our forefathers, on this account we beg you, O invincible Augustus, that by your sacred rescript you give orders that everyone proceed by his proper route, and that they not leave the other villages to come to us and force us to furnish them with supplies free of charge, or even to provide hospitality to those to whom we are not obliged to—for the governors have more than once issued orders that hospitality is not to be provided for any but those sent by the governors and procurators on government service. And if we are oppressed, we will flee from our homes, and the treasury will be involved in very great loss. But pitied through your divine foresight, we will remain in our places of origin and be able to provide the sacred tribute and the other taxes. And this will come out about for us in the most fortunate times of your reign, if you give orders for your divine letter to be inscribed on a stele and set up in public, so that we shall be able, if we obtain this, to acknowledge our thanks to your fortune. . . .

D. Fiscal Crisis, 260: Egyptian Bankers Are Forced to Accept Debased Roman Coins

From Aurelius Ptolemaeus also called Nemesianus, strategus of the Oxyrhynchite nome. Since the officials have assembled and accused the bankers of the banks of exchange of having closed these through their unwillingness to accept the divine coin of the Emperors, it has become necessary that an injunction should be issued to all the owners of the banks to open these and to accept and change all coin except what is clearly spurious and counterfeit, and not to them only, but to all who engage in business transactions of any kind whatever, understanding that if they disobey this injunction they will experience the penalties which in former years his highness the praefect ordained for their case. Signed by me. The 1st year, Hathur 28 [A.D. 260].

E. An Attempt to Stem Disorders in Egypt, 278

Aurelius Harpoeration, strategus of the Oxyrhynchite nome, to the *decemprimi* of the nome greeting. A copy of the circular letter addressed to us, the strategi and *decemprimi* of the Heptanomia and the Arsinoite nome, by his excellency the dioecetes, Ulpius Aurelius, concerning the consolidation of the dykes and the cleansing of the canals is sent to you, dear friends, in order that you may know and follow his instructions. Whoever of you first receives this order should transmit it to the others. I pray for your health, dear friends. The 3rd year of our lord Marcus Aurelius Probus Augustus, Pharmouthi[.].

Ulpius Aurelius to the strategi and *decemprimi* of the Heptanomia and the Arsinoite nome greeting.

The season for the consolidation of the dykes and the cleansing of the canals having arrived, I thought it necessary to instruct you by this letter that all the cultivators and . . . ought now to carry out these operations and all zeal on the . . . belonging to them, with a view both to the public good and to their own private advantage. For I am persuaded that everyone is aware of the benefit resulting from these works. Therefore let it be the care of you, the strategi and *decemprimi*, both to urge all to take in hand this most necessary labour and to see that the overseers usually elected for the purpose are chosen from magistrates or even private individuals, their task being to compel everyone to perform his proper work in person, according to the rule given in the constitution of the appointment, without enmity or favour, so that the dykes are brought up to the prescribed height and breadth and the breaches filled in, to enable them to withstand the flood of the most sacred Nile auspiciously approaching, and that, the canals are cleansed to the depth of the so-called standards and the usual width, in order that they may easily absorb the coming influx of water for the irrigation of the fields, this being a matter of public utility, and that in no case is money exacted from any person instead of work. If anyone dares to attempt such a thing or disregards these orders, let him know that by impairing measures designed for the welfare of the whole of Egypt he will put to stake not only his property but his very life.

Document Set 6.10 References

A. The Swift Rise and Swifter Fall of Emperor Pertinax, 192
Dio Cassius, *Roman History,* epitome of bk 74, trans. Earnest Cary, Loeb Classical Library, vol. 9 (Cambridge, Mass.: Harvard University Press, 1977).
B. Flight from the Land of Egypt, 215
A. S. Hunt and C. C. Edgar, trans., *Selected Papyri,* Loeb Classical Library (Cambridge, Mass.: Harvard University Press, 1934), 2:215.
C. Law and Order Collapse in Thrace, 238
Naphtali Lewis and Meyer Reinhold, eds., *Roman Civilization: Selected Readings* (New York: Columbia University Press, 1951), 2:439–440.
D. Fiscal Crisis, 260: Egyptian Bankers Are Forced to Accept Debased Roman Coins
Hunt and Edgar, 2:230.
E. An Attempt to Stem Disorders in Egypt, 278
Hunt and Edgar, 2:225.

7

The Fragmentation and Transformation of the Late Roman Empire, 284–568

DOCUMENT SET 7.1
The Empire in Crisis

This set in many respects represents a continuation of the questions framed by Document Set 6.10. Document A is an Egyptian papyrus recording a list of apparently typical questions submitted by anxious supplicants to an oracle's temple about A.D. 300; it gives an idea of problems on the minds of ordinary people. While in itself unremarkable, this source should be remembered when reading the other documents of this set, such as Document B (still another Egyptian papyrus). What does it reveal about the cause and consequences of peasant flight? Document C—an extract from Diocletian's decree establishing rigid price controls—shows the authorities' desperate attempt to regain economic stability, and it also reveals what they thought to be the causes of the Empire's economic woes. What do you think of their explanation and proposed cure? Although it comes more than a generation later, Document D shows the kind of pressure local officials used in trying to enforce price controls such as this. In Document E, the authorities in Roman Egypt attempt to compel prosperous citizens to meet their public responsibilities as "curiales," which formerly they had performed more or less voluntarily.

By the fifth century, "barbarians" like the Germanic Goths and Vandals as well as the steppe-raider Scythians began to seem a less fearful alternative to the decaying Roman government, at least according to the two witnesses in Documents F and G—respectively, the Christian poet Salvian (about 440) and the imperial diplomat Priscus (about 448). Use these documents to help assess the crisis of

public order in the Roman world in the era of Diocletian and Constantine, as well as its long-term consequences.

A. Anxieties: Questions Put to an Egyptian Oracle, 300

72, shall I receive the allowance? 73, shall I remain where I am going? 74, am I to be sold? 75, am I to obtain benefit from my friend? 76, has it been granted me to make a contract with another person? 77, am I to be reconciled(?) with my offspring(?)? 78, am I to get furlough? 79, shall I get the money? 80, is he who left home alive? 81, am I to profit by the transaction? 82, is my property to be put up to auction? 83, shall I find a means of selling? 84, am I able to carry off what I have in mind? 85, am I to become a beggar(?)? 86, shall I be a fugitive? 87, shall I be an ambassador(?)? 88, am I to become a senator? 89, is my flight to be stopped? 90, am I to be divorced from my wife? 91, have I been poisoned? 92, am I to get my own?

B. A Deserted Egyptian Village, 332

To his eminence Flavius Hyginus, praefect of Egypt, from the community of the village of Theadel-

Reprinted by permission of the publishers and the Loeb Classical Library from A. S. Hunt and C. C. Edgar, eds., Vol. I, pp. 437, 439, Cambridge, Mass.: Harvard University Press, 1934.

Reprinted by permission of the publishers and the Loeb Classical Library from A. S. Hunt and C. C. Edgar, eds., Vol. I, pp. 301–303, Cambridge, Mass.: Harvard University Press, 1934.

phia. . . . We the aforesaid, our lord praefect, are a group of three persons in the village who pay taxes on behalf of all the village for five hundred arurae which are not even being ploughed up and for a roll of twenty-five individuals including the employees of the Treasury, so that from this state of things our village is reduced to great straits. Setting out in search of our fellow-villagers in the Oxyrhynchite nome we discovered at the farmstead of Eulogius son of Nidas, of the hamlet of Serenus, five nominated (?) men, Dionysius, Hor, Ammon, Soucheidas, Apol, and Sabbaeus, with their families; and their landlord Eulogius, together with Arion, a vine-dresser, and Scrapion, a cultivator, did not allow us even to approach the door of the farmstead, repulsing us with violence. We also found three migrants in the Cynopolite nome, Gerontius, Pathas, and Heron, holding between them a hundred arurae and more of Crown land. Therefore we, humble and solitary men, beseech your excellency to give orders to the superintendent of public security to deliver up to us our fellow-villagers with their families, in order that we may be enabled by this measure of relief to remain in our village and may for ever feel grateful to your illustrious fortune. Farewell. (Signed) We, the Aurelii Sakaon and Heron and Kanaoug, have presented this petition. I, Aurelius Maximus, wrote for them, as they are illiterate.

C. The Imperial Authorities Try to Impose Price Controls

The Emperor Caesar . . . Augustus, [and others] . . .

. . . We have decided that maximum prices of articles for sale must be established. We have not set down fixed prices, for we do not deem it just to do this, since many provinces occasionally enjoy the good fortune of welcome low prices and the privilege, as it were, of prosperity. Thus, when the pressure of high prices appears anywhere—may the gods avert such a calamity!—avarice . . . will be checked by the limits fixed in our statute and by the restraining curbs of the law.

It is our pleasure, therefore, that the prices listed in the subjoined schedule be held in observance in the whole of our Empire. And every person shall take note that the liberty to exceed them at will has been ended, but that the blessing of low prices has in no way been impaired in those places where supplies actually abound. . . .

Anyone who resists the measures of this statute shall be subject to a capital penalty for daring to do so. And let no one consider the statute harsh, since

there is at hand a ready protection from danger in the observance of moderation. . . . We therefore exhort the loyalty of all, so that a regulation instituted for the public good may be observed with willing obedience and due scruple, especially as it is seen that by a statute of this kind provision has been made, not for single municipalities and peoples and provinces but for the whole world. . . .

The prices for the sale of individual items which no one may exceed are listed below.

I.					
Wheat	1 army *modius*		100	*denarii*
Barley	1	”	”	60	”
Rye	1	”	”	60	”
Millet, ground	1	”	”	100	”
Millet, whole	1	”	”	50	”
Panic grass	1	”	”	50	”
Spelt, hulled	1	”	”	100	”
. . . .					
Beans, crushed	1	”	”	100	”
Beans, not ground	1	”	”	60	”
Lentils	1	”	”	100	”
Pulse	1	”	”	80	”
Peas, split	1	”	”	100	”
Peas, not split	1	”	”	60	”
. . . .					
Rice, cleaned	1 army *modius*		200	”
Barley grits, cleaned	1 *modius*		100	”
Spelt grits, cleaned	1 *modius*		200	”
Sesame	1 army *modius*		200	”
. . . .					

II. Likewise, for wines:				
Picene	1 Italian *sextarius*		30	”
Tiburtine	1	”	”	30	”
Sabine	1	”	”	30	”
. . . .					
Falernian	1	”	”	30	”
Likewise, aged wine, first quality	1	”	”	24	”
Aged wine, second quality	1	”	”	16	”
Ordinary	1	”	”	8	”
Beer, Gallic or Pannonian	1	”	”	4	”
Beer, Egyptian	1	”	”	2	”
. . . .					

III. Likewise, for oil:				
From unripe olives	1	”	”	40	”
Second quality	1	”	”	24	”
. . . .					
Salt	1 army *modius*		100	”

Spiced salt	1 Italian *sextarius*			8	”
Honey, best quality	1 ”	”		40	”
Honey, second quality	1 ”	”		24	”

. . . .

IV. Likewise, for meat:

Pork	1 Italian pound			12	”
Beef	1 ”	”		8	”

. . . .

Leg of pork, Menapic or Cerritane, best	1 ”	”		20	”

. . . .

Pork mince-meat	1 ounce			2	”
Beef mince-meat	1 Italian pound			10	”
Pheasant, fattened				250	”
Pheasant, wild				125	”

. . . .

D. Egyptian Brewers Swear That They Are Observing Controlled Prices, 338

To Flavius Eusebius, logistes of the Oxyrhynchite nome, from the guild of beer-sellers of Oxyrhynchus through us, Aurelius Salaminus son of Apollo and Aurelius Eulogius son of Gela[. . . .]. We declare that by our own estimate the price of the commodities which we handle is as given below for the present month, and we swear the divine oath that our statement is correct. The price is: for 1 artaba of barley 13 talents 500 denarii. In the consulship of Flavius Ursus and Flavius Polemius the most illustrious, Hathur 30 [A.D. 338]. We, Aurelius Salaminus and Aurelius Eulogius, make the foregoing declaration. Written by me, Theon, as they are illiterate.

E. Compulsory Public Service, Third-Century Egypt

We present and report at our own risk the persons mentioned below, being well-to-do and suitable, for the performance of the services of the year. They are as follows. For Cynopolis: for the cleaning of canals Gikon son of Diodorus, aged about 46 years, having property worth 600 drachmae; for the guarding of crops the persons previously nominated to superintend flooding, watering, sowing, and all other public works, Patron, without patronymic, his mother being Protous, aged about 30, having property worth 1000

drachmae, Aphrodas son of Nepheros, aged about 45, having house-sites worth 1000 drachmae; and for the guarding of threshing-floors Hekusis son of Sanpas, aged about 25, having property worth 600 drachmae, Latron son of Anoubas, having similarly 600 drachmae; and for taking care that the government wheat when delivered is pure and unadulterated Anoubas son of Nepheros, aged about 40, having house-sites worth 600 drachmae, Petenouphis son of Maximus, having similarly 600 drachmae; and for taking charge of the public granaries and sealing (receipts?) along with the sitologi Petenouphis son of Sarapion, age about 35, having property worth 1000 drachmae; Heron son of Heron, aged about 35, having similarly 1000 drachmae; and for the guard of the strategus Horion son of Arius, aged about 25, having similarly 600 drachmae. Similarly for the village of Lysimachis: for the throwing up of dykes Ischyras son of Pakemis surnamed Ages, having house-sites worth 600 drachmae; for the cleaning of canals Stotoetis son of Sokmenis; and for the guarding of crops the persons previously nominated to superintend flooding, watering, sowing, and all other public works, Herieus son of Zoilus, Hermes son of Apunchis; and for the guarding of threshing-floors Polion son of Ptolemaeus, Euporion son of Dioscorus; and for taking care that the government wheat when delivered is pure and unadulterated . . .

F. Salvian Compares Roman and Barbarian Rule in Gaul

In what respects can our customs be preferred to those of the Goths and Vandals, or even compared with them? And first, to speak of affection and mutual charity (which, our Lord teaches, is the chief virtue, saying, "By this shall all men know that ye are my disciples, if ye have love one to another"), almost all barbarians, at least those who are of one race and kin, love each other, while the Romans persecute each other. For what citizen does not envy his fellow-citizen? What citizen shows to his neighbor full charity?

[The Romans oppress each other with exactions] nay, not each other: it would be quite tolerable, if each suffered what he inflicted. It is worse than that; for the many are oppressed by the few, who regard public exactions as their own peculiar right, who carry on private traffic under the guise of collecting the taxes. And this is done not only by nobles, but by men of lowest rank; not by judges only, but by judges' subordinates. For where is the city—even the town or village—which has not as many tyrants as it has curials? . . . What place is there, therefore, as I have said, where the substance of widows and orphans, nay even of the saints, is not devoured by the chief citizens? . . . None but the great is secure from the devastations of these plundering brigands, except those who are themselves robbers.

[Nay, the state has fallen upon such evil days that a man cannot be safe unless he is wicked] Even those in a position to protest against the iniquity which they see about them dare not speak lest they make matters worse than before. So the poor are despoiled, the widows sigh, the orphans are oppressed, until many of them, born of families not obscure, and liberally educated, flee to our enemies that they may no longer suffer the oppression of public persecution. They doubtless seek Roman humanity among the barbarians, because they cannot bear barbarian inhumanity among the Romans. And although they differ from the people to whom they flee in manner and in language; although they are unlike as regards the fetid odor of the barbarians' bodies and garments, yet they would rather endure a foreign civilization among the barbarians than cruel injustice among the Romans.

So they migrate to the Goths, or to the Bagaudes, or to some other tribe of the barbarians who are ruling everywhere, and do not regret their exile. For they would rather live *free* under an appearance of slavery than live as captives under an appearance of liberty. The name of Roman citizen, once so highly esteemed and so dearly bought, is now a thing that men repudiate and flee from. . . .

It is urged that if we Romans are wicked and corrupt, that the barbarians commit the same sins, and are not so miserable as we. There is, however, this difference, that if the barbarians commit the same crimes as we, yet we sin more grievously. . . . All the barbarians, as we have already said, are pagans or heretics. The Saxon race is cruel, the Franks are faithless, the Gepidae are inhuman, the Huns are unchaste,—in short, there is vice in the life of all the barbarian peoples. But are their offenses as serious as ours? Is the unchastity of the Hun so criminal as ours? Is the faithlessness of the Frank so blameworthy as ours? Is the intemperance of the Alemanni so base as the intemperance of the Christians? Does the greed of the Alani so merit condemnation as the greed of the Christians? If the Hun or the Gepid cheat, what is there to wonder at, since he does not know that cheating is a crime? If a Frank perjures himself, does he do anything strange, he who regards perjury as a way of speaking, not as a crime?

G. Priscus Meets a Greek Who Prefers the Scythians to Civilization

A man whom, from his Scythian dress, I took for a barbarian, came up and addressed me in Greek, with the word "Hail!" I was surprised at a Scythian speaking Greek. For the subjects of the Huns, swept together from various lands, speak, beside their own barbarous tongue, either Hunnic or Gothic, or—as many as have commercial dealings with the western Romans—Latin; but none of them speak Greek readily, except captives from the Thracian or Illyrian seacoast; and these last are easily known to any stranger by their torn garments and the squalor of their head, as men who have met with a reverse. This man, on the contrary, resembled a well-to-do Scythian, being well dressed, and having his hair cut in a circle after Scythian fashion.

Having returned his salutation, I asked him who he was and whence he had come into a foreign land and adopted Scythian life. When he asked me why I wanted to know, I told him that his Hellenic speech had prompted my curiosity. Then he smiled and said that he was born a Greek and had gone as a merchant to Viminacium, on the Danube, where he had stayed a long time, and married a very rich wife. But the city fell a prey to the barbarians, and he was stripped of his prosperity, and on account of his riches was allotted to Onegesius [a Hunnish leader] in the division of the spoil, as it was the custom among the Scythians for the chiefs to reserve for themselves the rich prisoners. Having fought bravely against the Romans and the Acatiri, he had paid the spoils he won to his master, and so obtained freedom. He then married a barbarian wife and had children, and had the privilege of partaking at the table of Onegesius.

He considered his new life among the Scythians better than his old life among the Romans, and the reasons he urged were as follows: "After war the Scythians live at leisure, enjoying what they have got, and not at all, or very little, disturbed. The Romans, on the other hand, are in the first place very liable to be killed, if there are any hostilities, since they have to rest their hopes of protection on others, and are not allowed, by their tyrants, to use arms. And those who do use them are injured by the cowardice of their generals, who cannot properly conduct war.

"But the condition of Roman subjects in time of peace is far more grievous than the evils of war, for the exaction of the taxes is very severe, and unprincipled men inflict injuries on others because the laws are practically not valid against all classes. A transgressor who belongs to the wealthy classes is not punished for his injustice, while a poor man, who does not understand business, undergoes the legal penalty,—that is, if he does not depart this life before the trial, so long is the course of lawsuits protracted, and so much money is expended on them. The climax of misery is to have to pay in order to obtain justice. For no one will give a hearing to the injured man except he pay a sum of money to the judge and the judge's clerks."

In reply to this attack on the empire, I asked him to be good enough to listen with patience to the other side of the question. "The creators of the Roman Republic," I said, "who were wise and good men, in order to prevent things from being done at haphazard, made one class of men guardians of the laws, and appointed another class to the profession of arms, who were to have no other object than to be always ready for battle, and to go forth to war without dread, as though to their ordinary exercise, having by practice exhausted all their fear beforehand. Others again were assigned to attend to the cultivation of the ground, to support themselves and those who fight in their defense by contributing the military corn supply. . . . To those who protect the interests of the litigants a sum of money is paid by the latter, just as a payment is made by the farmers to the soldiers. Is it not fair to support him who assists and requite him for his kindness? . . .

"Those who spend money on a suit and lose it in the end cannot fairly put it down to anything but the injustice of their case. And as to the long time spent on lawsuits, that is due to anxiety for justice, that judges may not fail in passing accurate judgments by having to give sentence offhand; it is better that they should reflect, and conclude the case more tardily, than that by judging in a hurry they should both injure man and transgress against the Deity, the institutor of justice. . . .

"The Romans treat their slaves better than the king of the Scythians treats his subjects. They deal with them as fathers or teachers, admonishing them to abstain from evil and follow the lines of conduct which they have esteemed honorable; they reprove them for their errors like their own children. They are not allowed, like the Scythians, to inflict death on their slaves. They have numerous ways of conferring freedom; they can manumit not only during life, but also by their wills, and the testamentary wishes of a Roman in regard to his property are law."

My interlocutor shed tears, and confessed that the laws and constitution of the Romans were fair, but deplored that the officials, not possessing the spirit of former generations, were ruining the state.

Document Set 7.1 References

A. Anxieties: Questions Put to an Egyptian Oracle, 300
A. S. Hunt and C. C. Edgar, trans., *Selected Papyri*, Loeb Classical Library (Cambridge, Mass.: Harvard University Press, 1934), 1:195.
B. A Deserted Egyptian Village, 332
Hunt and Edgar, 2:295.
C. The Imperial Authorities Try to Impose Price Controls Diocletian's Edict on Maximum Prices, in Naphtali Lewis and Meyer Reinhold, eds., *Roman Civilization: Selected Readings* (New York: Columbia University Press, 1951), 2:454–466.
D. Egyptian Brewers Swear That They Are Observing Controlled Prices, 338
Hunt and Edgar, 2:332.
E. Compulsory Public Service, Third-Century Egypt
Hunt and Edgar, 2:343.
F. Salvian Compares Roman and Barbarian Rule in Gaul
James Harvey Robinson, ed., *Readings in European History* (Boston: Ginn, 1904), 1:28–30.
G. Priscus Meets a Greek Who Prefers the Scythians to Civilization
Robinson, 1:30–33. (Boston: Ginn, 1904) Vol. I.

The Beginning of the East Roman Empire

The documents of this set provide insights into the kind of urban society that the founders of the Eastern Roman Empire faced in the fourth through the sixth centuries. Document A describes the long-standing problem of political violence in Constantinople, institutionalized (as it were) in the rival factions of racing fans known as the Blues and Greens. (Compare Set 6.10, Document A, for similar factions at Rome.) This extract comes from a history by Procopius (499–565), an official highly honored by Justinian but who also wrote a "secret history" graphically detailing the moral corruption that he alleged to be rampant at the court of Justinian and Theodora. After reading Procopius's account, consider Justinian's promise to rule justly (Document B)—what was likely to be the fate of peasants pouring into Constantinople, and how could the authorities keep them in line?

Some insights into how the East Roman state tried to deal with the problems of family breakdown should emerge from Documents C and D. One gives a "micro" view of the problem, as an injured wife in Egypt petitions for redress against her husband; the other is an extract from Justinian's abridged law code (Codex), which summarized, interpreted, and in some cases reformed ancient Roman law. How Justinian regarded law in general is apparent in Document E, from the preface to the enormous "Corpus of Civil Law."

A. Politicized Fans: Procopius Describes Constantinople's Blues and Greens

. . . In every city the population has been divided for a long time past into the Blue and the Green factions; but within comparatively recent times it has come about that, for the sake of these names and the seats which the rival factions occupy in watching the games, they spend their money and abandon their bodies to the most cruel tortures, and even do not think it unworthy to die a most shameful death. And they fight against their opponents knowing not for what end they imperil themselves, but knowing well that, even if they overcome their enemy in the fight, the conclusion of the matter for them will be to be carried off straightway to the prison, and finally, after suffering extreme torture, to be destroyed. So there grows up in them against their fellow men a hostility which has no cause, and at no time does it cease or disappear, for it gives place neither to the ties of marriage nor of relationship nor of friendship, and the case is the same even though those who differ with respect to these colours be brothers or any other kin. They care neither for things divine nor human in comparison with conquering in these struggles; and it matters not whether a sacrilege is committed by anyone at all against God, or whether the laws and the constitution are violated by friend or by foe; nay even when they are perhaps ill supplied with the necessities of life, and when their fatherland is in the most pressing need and suffering unjustly, they pay no heed if only it is likely to go well with their "faction"; for so they name the bands of partisans. And even women join with them in this unholy strife, and they not only follow the men, but even resist them if opportunity offers, although they neither go to the public exhibitions at all, nor are they impelled by any other cause; so that I, for my part, am unable to call this anything except a disease of the soul. This, then, is pretty well how matters stand among the people of each and every city.

B. Justinian Announces His Intention of Dealing Philanthropically and Justly With Subjects Fleeing the Countryside to Constantinople

With the aid of God, we continually possess complete foresight so that the object which has been given to us for our philanthropy [i.e., the people] is preserved unharmed. Then, so as to take care of the people, we have established laws of complete justice, and that which little by little declines we strive to repair. Especially do we design administrative acts which correct the lesser evils of the ones who commit offenses. Therefore we have established praetors of the people in this great city—a most useful provision for all types of matters—provisions approved by all the inhabitants of this our imperial city. As a result of this practice, we have thought to regulate something else which requires attention and to establish justice by law and authority.

We have found that little by little the provinces are becoming denuded of their inhabitants, and this great city of ours becomes disturbed by a great multitude of all kinds of people, especially those from the rural areas, who have left their own towns and their agricultural pursuits in order to take refuge here.

C. Justinian Codifies Roman Laws on Women and the Family

The *lex Julia* declares that wives have no right to bring criminal accusations for adultery against their husbands, even though they may desire to complain of the violation of the marriage vow, for while the law grants this privilege to men it does not concede it to women . . .

The *lex Julia* relating to chastity forbids the two parties guilty of adultery, that is to say, the man and the woman, to be prosecuted at the same time, and in the same case, but they can both be prosecuted in succession . . .

No one doubts that a husband cannot accuse his wife of adultery if he continues to retain her in marriage . . . Under the new law, however, he can do so, and if the accusation is proved to be true, he can then repudiate her, and he should file a written accusation against her. If, however, the husband should not be able to establish the accusation of adultery which he brought, he will be liable to the same punishment which his wife would have undergone if the accusation had been proved . . .

You can resume marital relations with your wife without fear of being liable to the penalty prescribed by the *lex Julia* for the suppression of adultery, as you did nothing more than file the written accusation, for the reason that you assert that you afterwards ascertained that you were impelled by groundless indignation to accuse her; for he alone will be liable to the penalty specifically mentioned by the law who is aware that his wife has been publicly convicted of adultery, or that she is an adulteress, as he cannot simulate ignorance of the fact, and retain her as his wife . . .

There is no doubt that he who has two wives at once is branded with infamy, for, in a case of this kind, not the operation of the law by which our citizens are forbidden to contract more than one marriage at a time, but the intention, should be considered; and therefore he who pretended to be unmarried, but had another wife in the province, and asked you to marry him, can lawfully be accused of the crime of fornication, for which you are not liable, for the reason that you thought that you were his wife. You can obtain from the governor of the province the return of all your property of which you deplore the loss on account of the fraudulent marriage, and which should be restored to you without delay. But how can you recover what he promised to give you as his betrothed? . . .

The laws punish the detestable wickedness of women who prostitute their chastity to the lusts of others, but do not hold those liable who are compelled to commit fornication through force, and against their will. And, moreover, it has very properly been decided that their reputations are not lost, and that their marriage with others should not be prohibited on this account . . .

If a woman whom you have carnally known indiscriminately sold herself for money, and prostituted herself everywhere as a harlot, you did not commit the crime of adultery with her . . .

Slaves cannot accuse their wives of adultery for violation of conjugal faith.

If you should be accused of adultery by her with whom you have lived in violation of law, you can defend yourself by an innumerable number of expedients.

D. A Wife Petitions Against an Abusive Husband, Egypt, 458

To Flavius Valerius the most learned *defensor* of the city of Oxyrhynchus from Aurelia Sophia daughter of Anouthius, of the said city. My husband having been cast out by his own father and charged by him with debts amounting to fourteen solidi, these I was able to honour by selling the articles of my dowry and the nuptial gift, and toiling together with him my husband I was able also to procure for ourselves a home; but he, failing to preserve a kindly attitude towards me, seeks on every occasion to cast me out, though no fault can be found against me. For this reason I humbly beseech your erudition to command that he be brought before you and compelled to restore both the gift and the dowry, and I beg you to give me an order concerning the marriage, most learned lord *defensor*. (Signed) I, Aurelia, Sophia, have presented this petition. (Dated) In the consulship of our master Flavius Leon, eternal Augustus, for the 1st time, Mesore 10.

E. Justinian Describes the Sources of Law

Natural Law is that which nature has taught to all animals, for this law is not peculiar to the human race, but applies to all creatures which originate in the air, on the earth, and in the sea. Hence arises the union of the male and the female which we designate marriage; and hence are derived the procreation and the education of children: for we see that other animals act as though endowed with knowledge of this law.

The Civil Law and the Law of Nations are divided as follows. All peoples that are governed by laws and customs make use of the law which is partly peculiar to themselves and partly pertaining to all men; for what each people has established for itself is peculiar to that State, and is styled the Civil Law, being, as it were, the special law of that individual commonwealth. But the law which natural reason has established among all mankind and which is equally observed among all peoples, is called the Law of Nations, as being that which all nations make use of . . .

Our Law, which We make use of is either written or unwritten, just as among the Greeks written and unwritten laws exist . . .

Whatever is approved by the sovereign has also the force of law . . . Some [of the Emperor's decisions] are personal and are not considered as precedents, because the sovereign does not wish them to be such; for any favor he grants on account of merit, or where he inflicts punishment upon anyone or affords him

unusual assistance, this affects only the individual concerned. . . .

Document Set 7.2 References

A. Politicized Fans: Procopius Describes Constantinople's Blues and Greens
Procopius, *History of the Persian Wars,* 14, trans. H. B. Dewing, Loeb Classical Library (London: Heinemann, 1914).

B. Justinian Announces His Intention of Dealing Justly and Philanthropically With Subjects Fleeing the Countryside to Constantinople
Deno John Geanokoplos, ed., *Byzantium: Church, Society, and Civilization Seen Through Contemporary Eyes* (Chicago: University of Chicago Press, 1984), 257.

C. Justinian Codifies Roman Laws on Women and the Family
Mary R. Lefkowitz and Maureen B. Fant, eds., *Women's Life in Greece and Rome* (Balitmore: Johns Hopkins University Press, 1982), 182–184.

D. A Wife Petitions Against an Abusive Husband, Egypt, 458
A. S. Hunt and C. C. Edgar, trans., *Selected Papyri,* Loeb Classical Library (Cambridge, Mass.: Harvard University Press, 1934), 2:297.

E. Justinian Describes the Sources of Law
Justinian, *Institutes,* trans. J. B. Moyle, in *The Middle Ages,* vol. 1 of *The Sources of Medieval History,* ed. Brian Tierney (New York: Alfred A. Knopf, 1973), 52–53.

DOCUMENT SET 7.3
Christianity Becomes the State Religion

This set should be considered essentially a continuation of the two preceding sets: it shows how the founders of the East Roman Empire tried to use religious uniformity as an instrument in reversing the imperial crisis.

In Document A, the last of the great pagan emperors, Diocletian (*284–305, d. 313), attempts to stamp out the by now flourishing—though still minority—religion of Christianity, replacing it with an invigorated imperial cult. This account, it should be noted, was written a generation later by the Christian historian Eusebius, and it should be evaluated for possible bias.

Document B reverses Diocletian's persecutions: it is the Edict of Milan (313), which accorded official tolerance to Christianity. Toleration was, however, a pragmatic tactic and did not imply a modern acceptance of pluralism. What deeper motives does the document reveal?

Why did Constantine turn to the Christian God and set the Roman Empire—and the Western world—on the course to Christianity? Historians still debate his motives, relying heavily on sources such as Eusebius's "Life of Constantine," an extract from which appears as Document C. Bear in mind that Eusebius was a fervent Christian and that this account was written well after the events it describes. Allowing for this bias, what does Eusebius reveal about Constantine's conversion?

Uniformity of belief and worship, however, scarcely ever ceased to be the objective of imperial policy. Once Christianity became Rome's quasi-official religion, the complicated question arose of what kind of standards to apply to those who had lapsed in their Christian faith under Diocletian's persecutions. Those known as the Novatians wanted to exclude such backsliders, but would this be a suitable stance for an official church to take? Document D shows how the Council of Nicaea (324), held under Constantine's leadership and with his active participation, answered this question, thereby helping set the precedent for many centuries of enforced uniformity in Christianity. By the late fourth century, the Christian church had grown powerful enough within Roman society to permit one of the great Christian leaders, Bishop Ambrose of Milan, to bring the emperor Theodosius to heel with the threat of excommunication (Document E). And in 392 the same Theodosius formally outlawed pagan sacrifice, thus completing the elevation of Christianity to Rome's

state religion (Document F). In what respect can this be said to completely reverse the terms of public worship that in previous centuries had underlain the persecution of Christianity by the Roman state?

An extract from one of the great documents in the history of Christianity, the monumental *City of God,* written by St. Augustine (354–430), constitutes Document G. In it Augustine tries to persuade the remaining non-Christian Roman upper class that the tribulations the empire was suffering resulted not from the old gods' vengeance on the city for abandoning them but rather were God's retribution for earlier Roman "devil worship"; he tried to show how all that had been admired in the old Roman philosophy found its logical culmination in Christianity. The broader thesis of *The City of God* was that the Christian's "true" city, or ultimate allegiance, was not of this world.

Given such an attitude toward the visible world, what was to be the proper function of secular authority? Documents H and I reveal two Christian answers: Emperor Justinian's forthright insistence on imperial headship over the church, and the assertion by Pope Gelasius I of the superiority of spiritual authority over secular power.

Considering the readings in this set and in set 7.2 as a group and drawing upon *The Challenge of the West,* write an essay on how the rulers of the Roman Empire sought to surmount the third-century crisis by shoring up imperial power and co-opting Christianity as a new foundation of public authority—and how Christianity was in turn reshaped.

A. Diocletian Outlaws Christianity

This was the nineteenth year of the reign of Diocletian, in Dystrus (which the Romans call March), when the feast of the Saviour's passion was near at hand, and royal edicts were published everywhere, commanding that the churches should be razed to the ground, the Scriptures destroyed by fire, those who held positions of honor degraded, and the household servants, if they persisted in the Christian profession, be deprived of their liberty.

And such was the first decree against us. But issuing other decrees not long after, the emperor commanded that all the rulers of the churches in every place should be first put in prison and afterwards compelled by every device to offer sacrifice. . . .

Then as the first decrees were followed by others commanding that those in prison should be set free, if they would offer sacrifice, but that those who refused should be tormented with countless tortures, who could again at that time count the multitude of martyrs throughout each province, and especially throughout Africa and among the race of the Moors, in Thebais and throughout Egypt, from which having already gone into other cities and provinces, they became illustrious in their martyrdoms!

B. The Edict of Milan Promises Toleration for All Religions

When I, Constantine Augustus, as well as I, Licinius Augustus, had fortunately met near Mediolanum (Milan), and were considering everything that pertained to the public welfare and security, we thought that among other things which we saw would be for the good of many, that those regulations pertaining to the reverence of the Divinity ought certainly to be made first, so that we might grant to the Christians and to all others full authority to observe that religion which each preferred; whence any Divinity whatsoever in the seat of the heavens may be propitious and kindly disposed to us, and all who are placed under our rule. And thus by this wholesome counsel and most upright provision, we thought to arrange that no one whatever should be denied the opportunity to give his heart to the observance of the Christian religion or of that religion which he should think best for himself, so that the supreme Deity, to whose worship we freely yield our hearts, may show in all things his usual favor and benevolence. Therefore, your Worship should know that it has pleased us to remove all conditions whatsoever, which were in the rescripts formerly given to you officially, concerning the Christians, and now any one of these who wishes to observe the Christian religion may do so freely and openly, without any disturbance or molestation. . . . When you see that this has been granted to them by us, your Worship will know that we have also conceded to other religions the right of open and free observance of their worship for the sake of the peace of our times, that each one may have the free opportunity to worship as he pleases; this regulation is made that we may not seem to detract aught from any dignity or any religion. . . .

C. Eusebius Narrates the Conversion of Constantine

Being convinced, however, that he needed some more powerful aid than his military forces could afford him, on account of the wicked and magical enchantments which were so diligently practiced by the tyrant, he sought Divine assistance, deeming the possession of arms and a numerous soldiery of secondary importance, but believing the co-operating power of Deity invincible and not to be shaken. He considered, therefore, on what God he might rely for protection and assistance. While engaged in this enquiry, the thought occurred to him, that, of the many emperors who had preceded him, those who had rested their hopes in a multitude of gods, and served them with sacrifices and offerings, had in the first place been deceived by flattering predictions, and oracles which promised them all prosperity, and at last had met with an unhappy end, while not one of their gods had stood by to warn them of the impending wrath of heaven; while one alone who had pursued an entirely opposite course, who had condemned their error, and honored the one Supreme God during his whole life, had found him to be the Saviour and Protector of his empire, and the Giver of every good thing. Reflecting on this, and well weighing the fact that they who had trusted in many gods had also fallen by manifold forms of death, without leaving behind them either family or offspring, stock, name, or memorial among men: while the God of his father had given to him, on the other hand, manifestations of his power and very many tokens: and considering farther that those who had already taken arms against the tyrant, and had marched to the battle-field under the protection of a multitude of gods, had met with a dishonorable end (for one of them had shamefully retreated from the contest without a blow, and the other, being slain in the midst of his own troops, became, as it were, the mere sport of death); reviewing, I say, all these considerations, he judged it to be folly indeed to join in the idle worship of those who were no gods, and, after such convincing evidence, to err from the truth; and therefore felt it incumbent on him to honor his father's God alone.

Accordingly he called on him with earnest prayer and supplications that he would reveal to him who he was, and stretch forth his right hand to help him in his present difficulties. And while he was thus praying with fervent entreaty, a most marvelous sign appeared to him from heaven, the account of which it might have been hard to believe had it been related by any other person. But since the victorious emperor himself long afterwards declared it to the writer of this history, when he was honored with his acquaintance and society, and confirmed his statement by an oath, who could hesitate to accredit the relation, especially since the testimony of after-time has established its truth? He said that about noon, when the day was already beginning to decline, he saw with his own eyes the trophy of a cross of light in the heavens, above the sun, and bearing the inscription, CONQUER BY THIS. At this sight he himself was struck with amazement, and his whole army also, which followed him on this expedition, and witnessed the miracle.

D. The Council of Nicea Condemns a Christian Heresy

With respect to those who at one time style themselves "the Pure" [i.e. Novatians], but afterward seek admission to the catholic and apostolic church, the holy and great Synod has seen fit to decree that they may remain in the clerical office, provided that they receive imposition of hands. But, first of all, they must make confession in writing that they will agree to the decrees of the catholic and apostolic church, and follow them: that is, by having fellowship with those who have married a second time, and also with those who have lapsed in persecution, if the church has appointed for such a season of penance and a definite time when they can return to fellowship. They will thus give evidence that they will follow all the decrees of the catholic church. Wherever, then, either in villages or cities, those who have received ordination shall be found to be entirely confined to their sect, the men thus found in the clerical office shall retain the same status as before. But if certain [Novatian] clerics seek admission to the catholic church when it already has a bishop or presbyter of its own appointment, it is plain that the bishop of the church shall retain the dignity of "bishop," while he who is styled "bishop" by the so-called "Pure," shall have the rank of presbyter: this, at least, unless the bishop be pleased to grant him a share in the honorary title of "bishop;" if he is not so minded, he should certainly find a place for him as rural bishop or presbyter, that he may seem to retain fully his clerical status. This provision, then, is made to prevent the anomaly of two ruling bishops in one city.

E. St. Ambrose Threatens Emperor Theodosius with Excommunication

I have written these things, indeed, not to confound you, but that the example of these kings might induce you to put away this sin from your kingdom, which

you will accomplish by humiliating your soul to God. You are a man and temptation has come to you; confess it. Sin is not put away except by tears and penitence. Neither an angel can do it nor an archangel; the Lord himself, who alone can say, "I am with you," does not forgive us if we have sinned except we be penitent.

I persuade, I beg, I exhort, I admonish; because it is a grief to me that you who were an example of unusual piety, who were the very personification of clemency, who would not allow guilty individuals to be brought into danger, that you do not grieve at the death of so many innocent persons. Although you have fought battles most successfully, although in other things also you are worthy of praise, yet the crown of all your work was always piety. This the devil envied you, since it was your ever present possession. Conquer him while as yet you have wherewith you may conquer. Do not add another sin to your sin, that you may practice what it has injured many to practice.

I, indeed, though in all other things a debtor to your kindness which I can never be ungrateful for, which kindness surpassed that of many emperors and was equalled by the kindness of one only, I, I say, have no cause for a charge of contumacy against you, but I have a cause for fear; I dare not offer the sacrifice if you will to be present. Is that which is not allowed after shedding the blood of one innocent person to be allowed after shedding the blood of many? I do not think so.

F. Theodosius Outlaws Pagan Sacrifice, 392

No person at all, of any class or order whatsoever of men or of dignitaries . . . shall sacrifice an innocent victim to senseless images in any place at all or in any city. . . . But if any man should dare to immolate a victim for purpose of sacrifice, or to consult the quivering entrails, according to the example of a person guilty of high treason, he shall be reported by an accusation which is permitted to all persons, and he shall receive the appropriate sentence, even though he has inquired nothing contrary to, or with reference to, the welfare of the emperors.

G. Augustine Exhorts Romans to Abandon Demon-Inspired Paganism and Embrace Christianity

Cicero, a weighty man, and a philosopher in his way, when about to be made edile, wished the citizens to understand that, among the other duties of his magistracy, he must propitiate Flora by the celebration of games. And these games are reckoned devout in proportion to their lewdness. In another place, and when he was now consul, and the state in great peril, he says that games had been celebrated for ten days together, and that nothing had been omitted which could pacify the gods: as if it had not been more satisfactory to irritate the gods by temperance, than to pacify them by debauchery; and to provoke their hate by honest living, than soothe it by such unseemly grossness. . . .

They, then, are but abandoned and ungrateful wretches, in deep and fast bondage to that malign spirit, who complain and murmur that men are rescued by the name of Christ from the hellish thraldom of these unclean spirits, and from a participation in their punishment, and are brought out of the night of pestilential ungodliness into the light of most healthful piety. Only such men could murmur that the masses flock to the churches and their chaste acts of worship, where a seemly separation of the sexes is observed; where they learn how they may so spend this earthly life, as to merit a blessed eternity hereafter; where Holy Scripture and instruction in righteousness are proclaimed from a raised platform in presence of all, that both they who do the word may hear to their salvation, and they who do it not may hear to judgment. And though some enter who scoff at such precepts, all their petulance is either quenched by a sudden change, or is restrained through fear or shame. For no filthy and wicked action is there set forth to be gazed at or to be imitated; but either the precepts of the true God are recommended, His miracles narrated, His gifts praised, or His benefits implored.

This, rather, is the religion worthy of your desires, O admirable Roman race,—the progeny of your Scævolas and Scipios, of Regulus, and of Fabricius. This rather covet, this distinguish from that foul vanity and crafty malice of the devils. If there is in your nature any eminent virtue, only by true piety is it purged and perfected, while by impiety it is wrecked and punished. Choose now what you will pursue, that your praise may be not in yourself, but in the true God, in whom is no error. For of popular glory you have had your share; but by the secret providence of God, the true religion was not offered to your choice. Awake, it is now day; as you have already awaked in the persons of some in whose perfect virtue and sufferings for the true faith we glory: for they, contending on all sides with hostile powers, and conquering them all by bravely dying, have purchased for us this country of ours with their blood; to which country we invite you, and exhort you to add yourselves to the number of the citizens of this city, which also has a sanctuary of its own in the true remission of sins. Do not listen to those degenerate sons of thine who slander Christ and Christians, and impute to them these disastrous times, though they desire times in which they may enjoy rather impunity for their wickedness than a peaceful life. Such has never been Rome's ambition even in regard to her earthly country. Lay hold now on the celestial country, which is easily won, and in which you will reign truly and for ever. For there shalt thou find no vestal fire, no Capitoline stone, but the one true God.

> "No date, no goal will here ordain:
> But grant an endless, boundless reign."

No longer, then, follow after false and deceitful gods; abjure them rather, and despise them, bursting forth into true liberty. Gods they are not, but malignant spirits, to whom your eternal happiness will be a sore punishment.

H. Justinian Defines Imperial Authority Over the Church

The greatest blessings of mankind are the gifts of God which have been granted us by the mercy on high: the priesthood and the imperial authority. The priesthood ministers to things divine; the imperial authority is set over, and shows diligence in, things human; but both proceed from one and the same source, and both adorn the life of man. Nothing, therefore, will be a greater matter of concern to the emperor than the dignity and honor of the clergy; the more as they offer prayers to God without ceasing on his behalf. For if the priesthood be in all respects without blame, and full of faith before God, and if the imperial authority rightly and duly adorn the commonwealth committed to its charge, there will ensue a happy concord which will bring forth all good things for mankind. We therefore have the greatest concern for true doctrines of the Godhead and the dignity and honor of the clergy; and we believe that if they maintain that dignity and honor we shall gain thereby the greatest of gifts, holding fast what we already have and laying hold of what is yet to come. "All things," it is said, "are done well and truly if they start from a beginning that is worthy and pleasing in the sight of God." We believe that this will come to pass if observance be paid to the holy rules which have been handed down by the Apostles—those righteous guardians and ministers of the Word of God, who are ever to be praised and adored—and have since been preserved and interpreted by the holy Fathers.

I. Pope Gelasius I Claims Superiority for the Spiritual Authority

. . . There are two powers, august Emperor, by which this world is chiefly ruled, namely, the sacred authority of the priests and the royal power. Of these, that of the priests is the more weighty, since they have to render an account for even the kings of men in the divine judgment. You are also aware, dear son, that while you are permitted honorably to rule over human kind, yet in things divine you bow your head humbly before the leaders of the clergy and await from their hands the means of your salvation. In the reception and proper disposition of the heavenly mysteries you recognize that you should be subordinate rather than superior to the religious order, and that in these matters you depend on their judgment rather than wish to force them to follow your will.

If the ministers of religion, recognizing the supremacy granted you from heaven in matters affecting the public order, obey your laws, lest otherwise they might obstruct the course of secular affairs by irrelevant considerations, with what readiness should you not yield them obedience to whom is assigned the dispensing of the sacred mysteries of religion. Accordingly, just as there is no slight danger in the case of the priests if they refrain from speaking when the service of the divinity requires, so there is no little risk for those who disdain—which God forbid—when they should obey. And if it is fitting that

the hearts of the faithful should submit to all priests in general who properly administer divine affairs, how much the more is obedience due to the bishop of that see which the Most High ordained to be above all others, and which is consequently dutifully honored by the devotion of the whole Church.

Document Set 7.3 References

A. Diocletian Outlaws Christianity
Translations and Reprints from the Original Sources of European History (Philadelphia: University of Pennsylvania Press, 1898), 4/1:26–28.
B. The Edict of Milan Promises Toleration for All Religions
Translations and Reprints, 4/1:29.
C. Eusebius Narrates the Conversion of Constantine
Eusebius, *Life of Constantine,* in E. C. Richardson, ed., *Library of Nicene and Post-Nicene Fathers,* 2d ser. (New York, 1890), 1:489–491.
D. The Council of Nicea Condemns a Christian Heresy
Translations and Reprints, 4/1:6–7.
E. St. Ambrose Threatens Emperor Theodosius with Excommunication
Translations and Reprints, 4/1:23–24.
F. Theodosius Outlaws Pagan Sacrifice, 392
Deno John Geanokoplos, ed., *Byzantium: Church, Society, and Civilization Seen Through Contemporary Eyes* (Chicago: University of Chicago Press, 1984), 130.
G. Augustine Exhorts Romans to Abandon Demon-Inspired Paganism and Embrace Christianity
Augustine, *City of God,* 27–29, in Richardson, 1st ser., 3:41–43.
H. Justinian Defines Imperial Authority Over the Church
Corpus Iuris Civilis, novella 6, in Geanokoplos, 130.
I. Pope Gelasius I Claims Superiority for the Spiritual Authority
James Harvey Robinson, ed., *Readings in European History* (Boston: Ginn, 1904), 1:72.

DOCUMENT SET 7.4
The Quest for Religious Certainty

Religion permeated every aspect of life in the late Roman Empire, and quasi-religious practices propitiating sacred—and warding off evil—cosmic forces that lurked everywhere were central to almost everyone's well being. A non-Christian example of this quest appears as Document A, an Egyptian papyrus of the fourth century invoking Sarapis and other pagan divinities.

Document B is an extract from St. Augustine's autobiography, *The Confessions,* a masterpiece of psychological insight that also breathes the spiritual obsessions of the fourth century. Here Augustine recalls his search for truth as a young man, when he followed the Persian-influenced Manichean faith with its insistence on the duality of Creation, divided between a sanctified spiritual cosmos and a corrupt, devilish material world.

Document C attests to Christians' attempts to heighten their spiritual self-assurance through intense asceticism. Once the threat of martyrdom no longer hung over believers and the state itself had become Christian, psychological pressures mounted on devout Christians to flee the secular world and seek the solitude of the desert to mediate and fend off temptation. Women as well as men were drawn to such a life, as can be seen from "Desert Mother" Syncletica's biblical learning (the mark of a dedicated Christian since the second century). But such individual piety was not the only ascetic life the Christians embraced; indeed because it was individualistic and essentially anarchistic, it was not viewed as wholly desirable by the early church. The Rule of St. Benedict, of which Document D is a brief extract, was formulated about 515 by the western hermit St. Benedict of Nursia (c. 480–c. 547). His rules for the organized, disciplined monastic communities, which the emerging papacy encouraged, proved to be normative for Latin Christendom.

A. The Secrets of Divination: A Fourth-Century Formula

[To be wrought by the help] of a boy, with a lamp, a bowl, and a stand. I invoke thee, O Zeus, Helius, Mithra, Sarapis, unconquerable, possessor of honey, Melicertes, father of honey, abraalbabachambechi, baibeizoth, ebaibeboth, . . . [etc.], the great, great Sarapis; samasphreth, odargazas, . . . [etc.], appear and give heed to him who has manifested before fire and snow, bainphoooch, for thou art he who didst manifest light and snow, terrible-eyed-thundering-and-lightning-swift-footed one, pintouche, etomthoout, opsianaeak, arourongoa, paphtha, enosade, iae, iaoai, aoiao, oeu. . . .

The dismissal: Depart, lord, to thine own world, and to thine own thrones, to thine own orbits, and guard me and this boy unhurt, in the name of the most high god Samasphreth. Perform [this divination] when the moon is in a firm sign of the zodiac in conjunction with beneficent stars, or when she is in favorable limits, not when she is at the full, for thus it is better, and thus is the divination performed in orderly fashion. But in other versions it has been recorded that it should be performed when the moon is full.

B. Augustine Recalls His Youthful Search for Truth

Those impostors, then, whom they designate Mathematicians, I consulted without hesitation, because they used no sacrifices, and invoked the aid of no spirit for their divinations, which art Christian and true piety fitly rejects and condemns. For good it is to confess unto Thee, and to say, "Be merciful unto me, heal my soul, for I have sinned against Thee;" and not to abuse Thy goodness for a license to sin, but to remember the words of the Lord, "Behold, thou art made whole; sin no more, lest a worse thing come unto thee." All of which salutary advice they endeavour to destroy when they say, "The cause of thy sin is inevitably determined in heaven;" and, "This did Venus, or Saturn, or Mars;" in order that man, forsooth, flesh and blood, and proud corruption, may be blameless, while the Creator and Ordainer of heaven and stars is to bear the blame. And who is this but Thee, our God, the sweetness and well-spring of righteousness, who renderest "to every man according to his deeds," and despisest not "a broken and a contrite heart!"

There was in those days a wise man, very skilful in medicine, and much renowned therein, who had with his own proconsular hand put the Agonistic garland upon my distempered head, not, though, as a physician; for this disease Thou alone healest, who resistest the proud, and givest grace to the humble. But didst Thou fail me even by that old man, or forbear from healing my soul? For when I had become more familiar with him, and hung assiduously and fixedly on his conversation (for though couched in simple language, it was replete with vivacity, life, and earnestness), when he had perceived from my discourse that I was given to books of the horoscope-casters, he, in a kind and fatherly manner, advised me to throw them away, and not vainly bestow the care and labour necessary for useful things upon these vanities; saying that he himself in his earlier years had studied that art with a view to gaining his living by following it as a profession, and that, as he had understood Hippocrates, he would soon have understood this, and yet he had given it up, and followed medicine, for no other reason than that he discovered it to be utterly false, and he, being a man of character, would not gain his living by beguiling people. "But thou," saith he, "who hast rhetoric to support thyself by, so that thou followest this of free will, not of necessity—all the more, then, oughtest thou to give me credit herein, who laboured to attain it so perfectly, as I wished to gain my living by it alone." When I asked him to account for so many true things being foretold by it, he answered me (as he could) "that the force of chance, diffused throughout the whole order of nature, brought this about. For if when a man by accident opens the leaves of some poet, who sang and intended something far different, a verse oftentimes fell out wondrously apposite to the present business, it were not to be wondered at," he continued, "if out of the soul of man, by some higher instinct, not knowing what goes on within itself, an answer should be given by chance, not art, which should coincide with the business and actions of the questioner."

And thus truly, either by or through him, Thou didst look after me. And Thou didst delineate in my memory what I might afterwards search out for myself. But at that time neither he, nor my most dear Nebridius, a youth most good and most circumspect, who scoffed at that whole stock of divination, could persuade me to forsake it, the authority of the authors influencing me still more; and as yet I had lighted upon no certain proof—such as I sought—whereby it might without doubt appear that what had been truly foretold by those consulted was by accident or chance, not by the art of the star-gazers.

C. A "Desert Mother" Praises Christian Asceticism

Mother Syncletica said, "In the beginning there are a great many battles and a good deal of suffering for those who are advancing towards God and, afterwards, ineffable joy. It is like those who wish to light a fire; at first they are choked by the smoke and cry, and by this means obtain what they seek (as it is said: 'Our God is a consuming fire' [*Heb.* 12.24]): so we also must kindle the divine fire in ourselves through tears and hard work."

She also said, "Just as the most bitter medicine drives out poisonous creatures, so prayer joined to fasting drives evil thoughts away."

She also said, "Do not let yourself be seduced by the delights of the riches of the world, as though they contain something useful on account of vain pleasure. Worldly people esteem the culinary art, but you, through fasting and thanks to cheap food, go beyond their abundance of food. It is written: 'He who is sated loathes honey.' [*Prov.* 27.7] Do not fill yourself with bread and you will not desire wine."

Blessed Syncletica was asked if poverty was a perfect good. She said, "For those who are capable of it, it is a perfect good. Those who can sustain it receive suffering in the body but rest in the soul, for just as one washes coarse clothes by trampling them underfoot and turning them about in all directions, even so the strong soul becomes much more stable thanks to voluntary poverty."

D. "Work and Pray": The Rule of St. Benedict ~ 515

Concerning the daily manual labour. Idleness is the enemy of the soul. And therefore, at fixed times, the brothers ought to be occupied in manual labour; and again, at fixed times, in sacred reading. Therefore we believe that, according to this disposition, both seasons ought to be arranged; so that, from Easter until the Calends of October, going out early, from the first until the fourth hour they shall do what labour may be necessary. Moreover, from the fourth hour until about the sixth, they shall be free for reading. After the meal of the sixth hour, moreover, rising from table, they shall rest in their beds with all silence; or, perchance, he that wishes to read may so read to himself that he do not disturb another. And the nona (the second meal) shall be gone through with more moderately about the middle of the eighth hour; and again they shall work at what is to be done until Vespers. But, if the exigency or poverty of the place demands that they be occupied by themselves in picking fruits, they shall not be dismayed: for then they are truly monks if they live by the labours of their hands; as did also our fathers and the apostles. Let all things be done with moderation, however, on account of the faint-hearted. . . . [There follows a slightly different schedule for the winter months from October to Easter.] But in the days of Lent, from dawn until the third full hour, they shall be free for their readings; and, until the tenth full hour, they shall do the labour that is enjoined on them. In which days of Lent they shall all receive separate books from the library; which they shall read entirely through in order. These books are to be given out on the first day of Lent. Above all there shall certainly be appointed one or two elders, who shall go round the monastery at the hours in which the brothers are engaged in reading, and see to it that no troublesome brother chance to be found who is open to idleness and trifling, and is not intent on his reading; being not only of no use to himself, but also stirring up others. If such a one—may it not happen—be found, he shall be admonished once and a second time. If he do not amend, he shall be subject under the Rule to such punishment that the others may have fear. . . . On feeble or delicate brothers such a labour or art is to be imposed, that they shall neither be idle, nor shall they be so oppressed by the violence of labour as to be driven to take flight. Their weakness is to be taken into consideration by the abbot. *(responsibility)*

Document Set 7.4 References

A. The Secrets of Divination: A Fourth-Century Formula
Naphtali Lewis and Meyer Reinhold, eds., *Roman Civilization: Selected Readings* (New York: Columbia University Press, 1951), 2:569.
B. Augustine Recalls His Youthful Search for Truth
Augustine, *Confessions*, 4:3.4–3.6, in E. C. Richardson, ed., *Library of Nicene and Post-Nicene Fathers*, 1st ser., vol. 3 (Buffalo, 1896).
C. A "Desert Mother" Praises Christian Asceticism
Ross E. Kraemer, *Maenads, Martyrs, Matrons, Monastics: A Sourcebook on Women's Religions in the Greco-Roman World* (Philadelphia: Fortress Press, 1988), 118.
D. "Work and Pray": The Rule of St. Benedict
E. F. Henderson, ed., *Select Historical Documents of the Middle Ages* (London: G. Bell, 1892), 597–598.

8

The Heirs of the Roman Empire, 568–756

DOCUMENT SET 8.1
The Byzantine Church and Piety

Byzantine piety ran very deep, matching and counter-balancing the worldly sophistication of Byzantine economic and political life and the complexities of Constantinople's social structure. Document A is a sixth-century description of the crowning glory of Byzantine architecture, the great church of St. Sophia, erected by Justinian to the glory of God and of his earthly representative, the Roman emperor. Philanthropy, or service to one's fellow man, part of the traditional ethos of the polis and the Roman city (see Set 4.3, Document D; Set 6.3, Document D; and Set 7.1, Document E), took on a strongly religious character in the Byzantine world, though it continued to lend vital support to imperial social policy as well. In Document B a notable sixth-century saint, John the Almsgiver, is lauded for his good works among the urban poor. Document C, one of the most famous and powerful Byzantine hymns, also dates from the sixth century. Its quasi-hypnotic effect, when chanted, is best appreciated against the background of a mental image of St. Sophia.

A. The Glories of St. Sophia

Above all rises into the immeasurable air the great helmet [of the dome], which, bending over, like the radiant heavens, embraces the church. And at the highest part, at the crown, was depicted the cross, the protector of the city. And wondrous it is to see how the dome gradually rises, wide below, and growing less as it reaches higher. It does not however spring upwards to a sharp point, but is like the firmament which rests on air, though the dome is fixed on the strong backs of the arches. . . . Everywhere the walls glitter with wondrous designs, the stone for which came from the quarries of seagirt Proconnesus. The marbles are cut and joined like painted patterns, and in stones formed into squares or eight-sided figures the veins meet to form devices; and the stones show also the forms of living creatures. . . .

A thousand others [lamps] within the temple show their gleaming light, hanging aloft by chains of many windings. Some are placed in the aisles, others in the centre or to east and west, or on the crowning walls, shedding the brightness of flame. Thus the night seems to flout the light of day, and be itself as rosy as the dawn. . . .

Thus through the spaces of the great church come rays of light, expelling clouds of care, and filling the mind with joy. The sacred light cheers all: even the sailor guiding his bark on the waves, leaving behind him the unfriendly billows of the raging Pontus, and winding a sinuous course amidst creeks and rocks, with heart fearful at the dangers of his nightly wanderings—perchance he has left the Aegean and guides his ship against adverse currents in the Hellespont, awaiting with taut forestay the onslaught of a storm from Africa—does not guide his laden vessel by the light of Cynosure, or the circling Bear, but by the divine light of the church itself. Yet not only does it guide the merchant at night, like the rays from the Pharos on the coast of Africa, but it also shows the way to the living God.

B. Byzantine Philanthropy: John the Almsgiver

Another good habit this Saint also adopted, namely sleeping on the cheapest of beds and using only very poor coverings in his own cell. One of the city's landowners once went into the Patriarch's room and saw that he was only covered with a torn and worn quilt, so he sent him a quilt costing 36 nomismata and besought him earnestly to cover himself with that in memory he said, of the giver.

John took and used it for one night because of the giver's insistence, but throughout the night he kept saying to himself (for so his chamber-attendant related), "Who shall say that humble John"—for he ever called himself that—"was lying under a coverlet costing 36 nomismata whilst Christ's brethren are pinched with cold? How many are there at this minute grinding their teeth because of the cold? and how many have only a rough blanket half below and half above them so that they cannot stretch out their legs but lie shivering, rolled up like a ball of thread? How many are sleeping on the mountain without food or light, suffering twofold pangs from cold and hunger? How many would like to be filled with the outer leaves of the vegetables which are thrown away from my kitchen? Verily, if you live like that and pass your life in such ease, do not expect to enjoy the good things prepared for us on high; but you will certainly be told as was that other rich man: Thou in thy life-time receivedst thy good things, but the poor evil things; and now they are comforted, but thou art in anguish. Blessed be God! You shall not cover humble John a second night. For it is right and acceptable to God that 144 of your brothers and masters should be covered rather than you, one miserable creature." For four rough blankets could be bought for one nomisma. Early on the following morning, therefore, he sent it to be sold, but the man who had given it saw it and bought it for 36 nomismata and again brought it to the Patriarch. But when he saw it put up for sale again the next day he bought it once more and carried it to the Patriarch and implored him to use it. When he had done this for the third time the Saint said to him jokingly, "Let us see whether you or I will give up first!" For the man was exceedingly well-to-do, and the Saint took pleasure in getting money out of him, and he used to say that if with the object of giving to the poor anybody were able, without ill-will, to strip the rich right down to their shirts, he would not do wrong more especially if they were heartless skinflints. For thereby he gets a twofold profit, firstly he saves their souls, and secondly he himself will gain no small reward therefrom. And to confirm this saying he would adduce as trustworthy evidence the tale about St. Epiphanius and John the Patriarch of Jerusalem—to with that the former would skilfully steal away the Patriarch John's silver and give it to the poor.

C. Byzantine Devotion: The Akathistos Hymn

To thee, protectress, leader of my army, victory.
I, thy city, from danger freed
   this song of thanks
inscribe to thee,
   mother of God.
Since thou hast an unconquerable power,
free me from all danger,
that I may sing to thee:
Hail mother undefiled.

A prince of angels
was sent from heaven
to greet the Mother of God,
and upon his unbodied word,
seeing thee, O Lord,
   take body,
he stood in ecstasy and
cried to thee this greeting:

Hail by whom gladness will be enkindled;
hail by whom the curse
   will be quenched.
Hail righting
   of the fallen Adam;
hail ransom
   of Eve's tears.
Hail height unscaled
   by human reasonings;
hail depth inscrutable
   even to angel's eyes.
Hail for thou art
   the king's seat;
hail for thou bearest him,
   who beareth all.
Hail thou star
   that makest the sun to shine;
hail thou womb
   of God's incarnation.
Hail thou by whom
   all creation is renewed;
hail thou through whom
   the Creator became a babe.
Hail mother undefiled.

The blessed virgin,
seeing herself chaste,
said unto Gabriel resolutely:
"The contradiction in thy assertion
seems very hard
  to my soul.
Thou foretellest me a childbirth
by seedless conception, and criest:
  Alleluia!"

The virgin, yearning to know,
the unknowable knowledge,
exclaimed to the servant:
"From my maiden womb
how may a child be born?
  Tell me."
to her he answered
timorously, crying out:

Hail! initiated
  into the unspeakable counsel;
hail! faith
  in what has to remain secret.
Hail! of Christ's wonders
  the beginning;
hail! of all tenets about him
  the summary.
Hail! heavenly ladder
  by which God came down;
hail! bridge that carries
  the earth-born into heaven.

Hail! marvel much spoken of
  by the angels;
hail! wounding most lamentable
  for the demons.
Hail! who mysteriously
  gavest birth to the light
hail! who the manner
  to none hast taught.
Hail, who outsoarest
  the learning of the wise;
hail! who enlightenest
  the mind of the faithful.
Hail! mother undefiled.

The power from on high
overshadowed then
unto conception the undefiled maid,
and converted her fruitless womb
into a meadow sweet
  to all men,
who sought to reap
salvation by singing thus:
  Alleluia!

Document Set 8.1 References

A. The Glories of St. Sophia
  Deno John Geanokoplos, ed., *Byzantium: Church, Society,
  and Civilization Seen Through Contemporary Eyes* (Chicago:
  University of Chicago Press, 1984), 197.
B. Byzantine Philanthropy: John the Almsgiver
  Geanokoplos, 312.
C. Byzantine Devotion: The Akathistos Hymn
  Geanakoplos, 193–195.

The worldly sophistication of the Byzantine state, and some of the practical problems that it faced with the relentless "barbarian" Slavic incursions across its Balkan frontier, are illustrated by the documents of this set.

Document A was written by the tenth-century Emperor Constantine VII Porphyrogenitus. Although some elements of his account are mythic rather than factual, he accurately emphasized the great ethnic mix prevailing in the Balkans and the clan-based organization of Slavic society. Document B also comes from a work by a Byzantine emperor, Maurice (*582–602), who advises how the state should buy off as well as militarily confront the Balkan tribesmen. In Document C an advisor to several emperors, Theophylact Simocattes (610–641), suggests the respect with which Byzantine statesmen regarded training in the lessons of history and the heritage of ancient Greek culture.

After reading these extracts from those who sat on or near the throne, it may come as a bit of a surprise to read Document D, in which a sausage maker in Byzantine-ruled Egypt promises to remain faithful to his craft. In what ways would this humble man's fate interest the rulers in far-away Constantinople?

Considering together the documents of Sets 8.1 and 8.2, write a brief essay explaining how Byzantium may be regarded as an heir of Greco-Roman antiquity.

A. Constantine Porphyrogenitus Describes Ethnic Transformations in the Seventh-Century Balkans

[And the Avars] thereafter made themselves masters of all the country of Dalmatia and settled down in it. Only the townships on the coast held out against them, and continued to be in the hands of the Romans, because they obtained their livelihood from the sea. The Avars, then seeing this land to be most fair, settled down in it. But the Croats at this time were dwelling beyond Bavaria, where the Belocroats [White Croats] are now. From them split off a family of five brothers, Kloukas and Lobelos and Kosentzis and Mouchlo and Chrobatos, and two sisters, Touga and Bouga, who came with their folk to Dalmatia and found the Avars in possession of that land. After they had fought one another for some years, the Croats prevailed and killed some of the Avars and the remainder they compelled to be subject to them.

B. Emperor Maurice Advises How to Deal with the Balkan Barbarians

The yellow-haired nations are rash and dauntless in battle when it is a question of liberty. Being daring and reckless, they look disdainfully on even a short retreat as a sign of cowardice, and they calmly despise death, fighting violent hand-to-hand combat either on horse or on foot. When they are in a tight situation during a cavalry battle, they will dismount and arrange themselves in a single mass on foot; even if they are few, they do not decline battle against a greater number of cavalry. They are armed with shields and pikes and with broad swords which are carried on their shoulders. They take pleasure in infantry battles and in making raiding incursions. In these battles they arrange themselves—whether on foot or on horseback—into no formal divisions or order, neither into *moiras* or *mere* [smaller units in the Byzantine army], but only according to tribal affiliation, with bonds of kinship and friendship among their fellow soldiers. (For this reason in times of crisis, when [close] friends or relatives have been left behind [i.e., dead], they often plunge into the battle in order to avenge them.) In battle they make the face [front] of their battle formations equal and densely packed; their attacks, whether on horseback or on foot, are vehement and uncontrollable, as they alone of all peoples shun every form of timidity. Since they are disobedient to their officers and without [a sense of] responsibility, since they lack cunning, [concern for] safety, and any conception of their own best interest, they despise ordered tactics [i.e., discipline], especially when fighting on horseback.

They are easily corrupted by bribes, since they are lovers of gain. Ill-fate and [military] reverses trouble them grievously. For while they are of brave and bold spirit, their bodies are well taken care of, and soft and unable to bear hardship easily. Heat, cold, rain, a lack of provisions and especially wine—the excesses of war—bother them. In time of cavalry combat, bad terrain and forests are unfavorable to their fighting. But they calmly endure ambushes against the flanks or rear of their formation, and they do not even bother with guards and other security. Their ranks are broken easily through the tactics of feigned withdrawal and sudden counterattacks. Nocturnal raids by archers are also often effective against them, causing them to flee in disorder. Therefore, in battle one must, above all, not advance against them in clear formation, especially in the opening stage, but rather lie in wait in good order and utilize especially stealth and cunning, protracting and length of battle and not drawing up [our troops] opposite them in a disadvantageous manner, so that through lack of provisions or the extremities of heat or cold, their bravery and passion may be diminished.

Such conditions occur best when the [Byzantine] army is encamped in a fortified place or in rugged terrain, so that the enemy spears cannot be utilized easily against the defenders' position. If an opportunity arises, however, for formal battle array, the troops should be drawn up as we have elucidated in our [previous] discussion of battle formations.

C. Theophylact Simocattes Insists That a Ruler Must Be Trained in History and the Use of Reason

Man is adorned not only by the endowments of nature but also by the fruits of his own efforts. For reason, which he possesses, is an admirable and divine trait by which he renders to God his adoration and homage. Through reason he enters into knowledge of himself and does not remain ignorant of the ordering of his creation. Accordingly, through reason men come together with each other and, turning away from external considerations, they direct their thoughts toward the mystery of their own nature.

Reason has given many good things to men and is an excellent helpmate of nature. The things which nature has withheld from man, reason provides in the most effective manner, embellishing those things which are seen, adding spice to those that are tasted, roughening or softening things to the touch, composing poetry and music for the ear, soothing the soul by lessening discord, and bringing sounds into concord. Is not reason also the most persuasive master of the crafts?—reason which has made a well-woven tunic from wool, which from wood has constructed carts for farmers, oars for sailors, and small wicker shields for soldiers as protection against the dangers of the battlefield.

Most important of all, reason provides the hearer with that pleasure which reflects the greatest amount of experience, the study of history, which is the instructor of the spirit. Nothing can be more seductive than history for the minds of those who desire to learn. It is sufficient to cite an example from Homer to demonstrate this: Soon after he had been thrown on the beach by violent waves of the sea, the son of Laertes, Odysseus, almost naked and with his body emaciated from the mishap of the shipwreck, was graciously received at the court of Alcinous. There he was clothed in a bright robe and given a place at the table of the king. Although only just arrived, he was granted permission to speak and an opportunity to relate his adventures. His recital pleased the Phocaeans so much that the banquet seemed to have changed into a theater. Indeed, they lent him an attention altogether remarkable, nor did they feel during his long narration any tedium, although he described the many misfortunes he had suffered. For listening brings an overwhelming desire [to hear more] and thus easily accepts a strange tale.

It is for this reason that in learning the poets are considered most estimable, for they realize that the spirits of men are fond of stories, always yearning to acquire knowledge and thirsty for strange narrations. Thus the poets create myths for men and clothe their phrases with adornments, fleshing out the fables with method, and embellishing their nonsense with meter as if with enchanted spells. This artifice has succeeded so well that poets are considered to be theologians, intimately associated with the gods. It is believed that through the poets' mouths the gods reveal their own personal affairs and also whether a felicitous or a calamitous event will happen to men in their lifetime.

This being so, one may term history the common teacher of all men: it shows which course to follow and which to avoid as profitless. The most competent generals are those who have been instructed by history, for history reveals how to draw up troops and by what means to outmaneuver the enemy through ambush. History renders these generals more prudent because they know about the misfortunes of others, and it directs them through observation of the mistakes of others. Similarly, it has shown that men become happier through good conduct, pushing men to higher peaks of virtue through gradual advances. For the old man history is his support and staff, while for the young, it is the fairest and wisest instructor, applying [the fruit of] great experience to new situations and thus anticipating somewhat the lessons of time. I now dedicate my own zeal and efforts to history, although I know that I am undertaking a greater task than I am able to fulfill effectively, since I lack elegance of expression, profundity of thought, purity of syntax, and skill in composition. If any parts of my work should prove pleasing in any way, let this be ascribed rather to the result of chance than to my own skill.

D. A Continuing Social and Economic Crisis: An Egyptian Sausage Maker Promises Not to Abandon His Trade and His Customers, 566

In the 1st year of the reign of our most godlike master Flavius Justinus the eternal Augustus and Imperator, the 25th year after the consulship of the most honourable Flavius Basilius, Phamenoth 21, . . . To the administration of the market through you, Philemon, chief assistant at Antinoe, from Flavius Sarapammon also called Colluthus, of Antinoe. I acknowledge voluntarily and of my own accord that I accept at your hands the charge of and responsibility for Aurelius . . ., sausage-maker, of Antinoe, engaging that he shall remain here in Antinoe pursuing his trade of sausage-making without fault, and shall devote himself to it from the holy Easter day of the present 14th indiction to the time of taking over in the (D.V.) 15th indiction, and shall in no circumstances leave his work. If he should leave his work, and I shall fail to bring him when he is wanted and deliver him to you in a public place, debarred from the protection of sacred precincts and sacred images and Sundays and holidays, I as his surety will pay you for his evasion 1 gold solidus. This deed of surety is valid and guaranteed, and in answer to the formal question I have given my assent on every point. (Signed) I, Flavius Sarapammon also called Colluthus, accept the charge and I agree to everything as aforesaid. I, Aurelius Stephanus son of Horus . . ., of Antinoe, wrote for him by request, as he is illiterate. (Subscribed) Executed by me, Cosmas, private notary.

Document Set 8.2 References

A. Constantine Porphyrogenitus Describes Ethnic Transformations in the Seventh-Century Balkans
John V. A. Fine, Jr., *The Early Medieval Balkans* (Ann Arbor: University of Michigan Press, 1983), 50.

B. Emperor Maurice Advises How to Deal with the Balkan Barbarians
Deno John Geanokoplos, ed., *Byzantium: Church, Society, and Civilization Seen Through Contemporary Eyes* (Chicago: University of Chicago Press, 1984), 103–104.

C. Theophylact Simocattes Insists That a Ruler Must Be Trained in History and the Use of Reason
Geanakoplos, 396–397.

D. A Continuing Social and Economic Crisis: An Egyptian Sausage Maker Promises Not to Abandon His Trade and His Customers, 566
A. S. Hunt and C. C. Edgar, trans., *Selected Papyri*, Loeb Classical Library (Cambridge, Mass.: Harvard University Press, 1934), 455, 457.

DOCUMENT SET 8.3
Early Islam

The Holy Qur'an is one of the world's great spiritual treasures, a powerful testimony to the religious inspiration that enabled the Prophet Mohammed to rally the feuding clans and trading communities of seventh-century Arabia into a fighting force that conquered most of the East Roman Empire and all of Persia within a generation. The central message of the Qur'an is an apocalyptic vision of God's wrath towards the wicked and of his merciful willingness to redeem those who accept the saving word of his Prophet: themes summarized by the extracts in Document A.

Document B hints at another reason for Islam's lightning spread through Arabia: the way in which the new community of believers transcended blood relationships to forge new unities of compassion and faith. How could this serve to protect and empower the individual? Notice too the relatively favorable position promised the Jews, evidently an important element in the population of Medina in Mohammad's time. It was the successful creation of an Islamic community at Medina that first signaled the Prophet's success in establishing his message.

Jihad—the obligation laid individually on every Muslim and collectively on the whole Islamic community to wage a holy struggle on behalf of the faith—is described in Document C, another extract from the Qur'an. Beyond the obvious confidence that such a teaching put into the hearts of men fighting for their cause, what other elements of strength would jihad lend to the Islamic community? In answering this question, consider also Documents D and E—respectively, the terms granted to Jerusalem when in 636 a Muslim army conquered that hitherto-Byzantine city, and a document from A.D. 710 in which the Muslim governor of Egypt calls on the people of a certain village to pay their overdue taxes. What elements of continuity and change do you detect in these documents?

A. The Holy Qur'an Proclaims God's Majesty and Justice

In the Name of God, the Compassionate, the Merciful

Praise be to God, the Lord of the Worlds!
The Compassionate, the Merciful!

King of the day of judgment!
Thee we worship, and Thee we ask for help.
Guide us in the straight way,
The way of those to whom Thou art gracious;
Not of those upon whom is Thy wrath, nor of the erring.

In the name of the merciful and compassionate God. That is the book! there is no doubt therein; a guide to the pious, who believe in the unseen, and are steadfast in prayer, and of what we have given them expend in alms; who believe in what is revealed to thee, and what was revealed before thee, and of the hereafter they are sure. These are in guidance from their Lord, and these are the prosperous.

Verily, those who misbelieve, it is the same to them if ye warn them or if ye warn them not, they will not believe. God has set a seal upon their hearts and on their hearing; and on their eyes is dimness, and for them is grievous woe. There are, indeed, those among men who say, "We believe in God and in the last day"; but they do not believe. They would deceive God and those who do believe; but they deceive only themselves and they do not perceive. In their hearts is a sickness, and God has made them still more sick, and for them is grievous woe because they lied. . . .

And if ye are in doubt of what we have revealed unto our servant, then bring a chapter like it, and call your witnesses other than God if ye tell truth. But if ye do it not, and ye shall surely do it not, then fear the fire, whose fuel is men and stones, prepared for misbelievers. But bear the glad tidings to those who believe and work righteousness, that for them are gardens beneath which rivers flow. Whenever they are provided with fruit therefrom they say, "This is what we were provided with before, and they shall be provided with the like; and there are pure wives for them therein, and they shall dwell therein for aye.". . .

In the Name of God, the Compassionate, the Merciful

Have we not made the earth as a bed? And the mountains as tent-pegs? and created you in pairs, and made you sleep for rest, and made the night for a mantle, and made the day for bread-winning, and built above you seven firmaments, and put therein a burning lamp, and sent down water pouring from the squeezed clouds to bring forth grain and herb withal, and gardens thick with trees?

Lo! the Day of Decision is appointed—the day when there shall be a blowing of the trumpet, and ye shall come in troops, and the heavens shall be opened, and be full of gates, and the mountains shall be removed, and turn into midst. Verily hell lieth in wait, the goal for rebels, to abide therein for ages; they shall not taste therein coolness nor drink, save scalding water and running sores,—a meet reward! Verily they did not expect the reckoning, and they denied our signs with lies; but everything have we recorded in a book:—

Then the people of the right hand—what people of good omen! And the people of the left hand—what people of ill omen! And the outstrippers, still outstripping:—these are the nearest [to God], in gardens of delight; a crowd of the men of yore, and a few of the latter days; upon inwrought couches, reclining thereon face to face. Youths ever young shall go unto them round about with goblets and ewers and a cup of flowing wine,—their heads shall not ache with it, neither shall they be confused; and fruits of their choice, and flesh of birds of their desire; and damsels with bright eyes like hidden pearls,—a reward for what they have wrought. They shall hear no folly therein, nor any sin, but only the greeting, "Peace! peace!"

And the people of the right hand—what people of good omen! Amid thornless lote-trees, and bananas laden with fruit, and shade outspread, and water flowing, and fruit abundant, never failing, nor forbidden, . . . But the people of the left hand—what people of ill omen!—amid burning wind and scalding water, and a shade of black smoke, not cool or grateful! Verily before that they were prosperous; but they persisted in the most grievous sin, and used to say, "When we have died, and become dust and bones, shall we indeed be raised again, and our fathers, the men of yore." Say: Verily those of yore and of the latter days shall surely be gathered to the trysting-place of a day which is known. Then ye, O ye who err and call it a lie, shall surely eat of the tree of Zakkum, and fill your bellies with it, and drink upon it scalding water,—drink like the thirsty camel:—this shall be their entertainment on the Day of Judgment!

B. The Constitution of Medina Reveals the Position of Jews in Earliest Islamic Society

The Messenger of God wrote a document, concerning the emigrants from Mecca and the helpers of Medina, in which he reconciled the Jews and convenanted with them, letting them act freely in the religion and possessions which they had, and stated reciprocal obligations.

In the name of God, the Merciful, the Compassionate!

This document is from Muhammad the Prophet, governing relations among the Believers and the Muslims of Quraysh and Yathrib (Medina) and those who followed them and joined with them and struggled with them.

1. They are one Community (umma) to the exclusion of all other men. . . .

11. The Believers shall not desert any poor person among them, but shall pay his redemption or blood-money, as is proper.

12. No Believer shall seek to turn the auxiliary of another Believer against him.

13. God-fearing Believers will be against whoever among them is rebellious or whoever seeks to sow injustice or sin or enmity among the Believers; every man's hand shall be against him, though he were the son of one of them.

14. No Believer shall kill a Believer for the sake of an unbeliever, or aid an unbeliever against a Believer.

15. The protection of God is one: even the least of them may extend it to a stranger. The Believers are friends to each other, to the exclusion of all other men.

16. The Jews who follow us shall have aid and equality, except those who do wrong or aid the enemies of the Muslims.

17. The peace of the Believers is one: no Believer shall make peace separately where there is fighting for God's sake. Conditions (of peace) must be just and equitable to all.

18. In every raid, the riders shall ride close together.

19. And the Believers shall avenge one another's blood, if shed for God's sake, for the God-fearing have the best and strongest guidance.

20. No idolator (of Medina) shall take Qurayshī property or persons under his protection, nor shall he turn anyone against a Believer.

21. Whoever kills a Believer shall also be killed, unless the next of kin of the slain man is otherwise satisfied, and the Believers shall be against him altogether; no one is permitted to act otherwise.

22. No Believer who accepts this document and

Excerpt from The Constitution of Medina from *Themes of Islamic Civilization* by John A. Williams, pp. 12–15, University of California Press, 1971. Reprinted by permission of the author.

believes in God and Judgment is permitted to aid a criminal or give him shelter. The curse of God and His wrath on the Day of Judgment shall fall upon whoever aids or shelters him, and no repentance or compensation shall be accepted from him if he does.

23. Whenever you differ about a case, it shall be referred to God and to Muhammad.

24. The Jews shall bear expenses with the Muslims as long as they fight along with them.

25. The Jews of the Banu 'Awf are one community with the Believers; the Jews have their religion and the Muslims have theirs. This is so for them and their clients, except for one who does wrong or treachery; he hurts only himself and his family. . . .

46. Everyone shall have his portion from the side to which he belongs; the Jews of al—Aws, their clients and themselves, are in the same position as the people of this document. Honorable dealing is without treachery.

47. Whoever acquires any (guilt) does not acquire it for any but himself. God is the most just and loyal fulfiller of what is in this document. This writing will not protect a wrongdoer or a traitor. Whoever goes out is safe, and he who stays at home is safe in the town, unless he has done wrong or treachery. God is the protecting neighbour (*jā r*) of whoever does good and fears Him, and Muhammad is the Messenger of God. Verily God is wrathful when His covenant is broken. Peace be upon you.

C. Jihad: The Qur'an Commands the Faithful to Wage Holy War

Fight in the path of God against those who fight you, but do not transgress, for God does not love transgressors.

Kill them wherever you encounter them, and expel them from whence they have expelled you, for dissension [*fitna*] is worse than killing. But do not fight them by the Sacred Mosque unless they fight you first, and if they do fight you, then kill them. Such is the recompense of the unbelievers.

But if they desist, then God is forgiving and merciful.

Fight them until there is no more dissension, and religion is God's. If they desist, there is no enmity, save against the unjust.

When you meet those who are infidels, strike their necks until you have overwhelmed them, tighten their bonds, and then release them, either freely or for ransom, when war lays down its burdens. Thus it is, and if God wished, He would crush them Himself, but He tests you against one another. Those who are killed in the path of God, He does not let their good deeds go for nothing.

D. The Arab Conqueror Grants Terms to Jerusalem, 636

In the name of God the Merciful and the Compassionate.

This is the safe-conduct accorded by the servant of God 'Umar, the Commander of the Faithful, to the people of Aelia [Jerusalem].

He accords them safe-conduct for their persons, their property, their churches, their crosses, their sound and their sick, and the rest of their worship.

Their churches shall neither be used as dwellings nor destroyed. They shall not suffer any impairment, nor shall their dependencies, their crosses, nor any of their property.

No constraint shall be exercised against them in religion nor shall any harm be done to any among them.

No Jew shall live with them in Aelia.

The people of Aelia must pay the *jizya* in the same way as the people of other cities.

They must expel the Romans and the brigands [?] from the city. Those who leave shall have safe-conduct for their persons and property until they reach safety. Those who stay shall have safe-conduct and must pay the *jizya* like the people of Aelia.

Those of the people of Aelia who wish to remove their persons and effects and depart with the Romans and abandon their churches and their crosses shall have safe-conduct for their persons, their churches, and their crosses, until they reach safety.

The country people who were already in the city before the killing of so-and-so may, as they wish, remain and pay the *jizya* the same way as the people of Aelia or leave with the Romans or return to their families. Nothing shall be taken from them until they have gathered their harvest.

This document is placed under the surety of God and the protection [*dhimma*] of the Prophet, the Caliphs and the believers, on condition that the inhabitants of Aelia pay the *jizya* that is due from them.

Witnessed by Khālid ibn al-Walīd, 'Amr ibn al-'Ā s, Abd al-Rahmān ibn 'Awf, Mu'āwiya ibn Abī Sufyān, the last of whom wrote this document in the year 15 [A.D. 636].

E. The Arab Governor of Egypt Demands Payment of Taxes

In the name of God, Kurrah ibn Sharik, governor, to Basilius, administrator of the village of Aphrodito. We give thanks to God, and to proceed, we have manifestly written to you many times about the two-thirds part of the gold taxes in your district, and we supposed that you had already paid this. Now when we ordered the secretaries to look into the books of the treasury to learn what you had paid into it, we found that your performance is inadequate and of no account and that in this matter you are behaving badly. For we did not send you to pass your time in gormandizing, but we sent you rather to fear God and keep faith and fulfil the claims of the Amir al Muminin. And neither you nor those in your district have an excuse of any kind. For the produce of the fields has been abundant, and God has blessed it and increased it twofold more than it was before, and the wheat has fetched a good price and it has been sold by the inhabitants. Now, as has been said, you have no excuse of any kind. Look therefore to the arrears of the two-thirds part of the gold taxes in your district and complete them with all expedition, not omitting a single farthing. For God knows that the way you have acted in the matter of these same taxes did not please us; indeed we had a mind to repay you for this.

If therefore there is any good in you, complete with all haste, as we have said, your district's arrears of this same two-thirds part of the gold taxes and dispatch them. For it is to the interest of the inhabitants to deliver their dues promptly and not to be left in peace until they are saddled with an accumulation of claims and are hard put to it to pay. We know that the official whose conduct is inadequate and unprofitable seeks excuses for the shortcomings of his work. Do not therefore act in that way and give us cause to threaten your life. Behold, we solemnly warn you. Written on Pauni 7 of the 9th indiction. [A.D. 710]

Document Set 8.3 References

A. The Holy Qur'an Proclaims God's Majesty and Justice
   James Harvey Robinson, ed., *Readings in European History* (Boston: Ginn, 1904), 1:116–120.
B. The Constitution of Medina Reveals the Position of Jews in Earliest Islamic Society
   J. A. Williams, *Themes in Islamic Civilization* (Berkeley and Los Angeles: University of California Press, 1971), 11–15.
C. Jihad: The Qur'an Commands the Faithful to Wage Holy War
   Bernard Lewis, ed., *Islam: From the Prophet Muhammed to the Capture of Constantinople* (New York: Walker, 1987), 1:209–210.
D. The Arab Conqueror Grants Terms to Jerusalem, 636
   Lewis, 2:225–230.
E. The Arab Governor of Egypt Demands Payment of Taxes
   A. S. Hunt and C. C. Edgar, trans., *Selected Papyri*, Loeb Classical Library (Cambridge, Mass.: Harvard University Press, 1934), 2:434.

Reprinted by permission of the publishers and the Loeb Classical Library from A. S. Hunt and C. C. Edgar, eds., Vol. 2, pp. 597, 599, 601, Cambridge, Mass.: Harvard University Press, 1934.

DOCUMENT SET 8.4
The Conversion of the Barbarian West and the Early Papacy

The strengths and limitations of the papacy in further-ing the reconstruction of society in the "barbarian" West is nowhere better illustrated than in the volumi-nous writings of Pope Gregory the Great (B.C. 540 *590–604). Son of a noble Roman family, he was as well educated as any westerner of his time and had spent some time as a monk and would-be missionary before being acclaimed pope. As pontiff, he applied his formidable organizational talents to giving the western church a new sense of mission. As Document A reveals, he was deeply pessimistic about the future of the world (had you lived in his day would you have agreed or disagreed?). But his instructions to the missionaries he dispatched to con-vert heathen Britain to Christianity (Document B) also reveal an abundance of practical sense and certainly had enduring results.

The Ecclesiastical History of the English People, by the learned Anglo-Saxon monk known as the Venerable Bede (c. 673–735), is the chief written source for the earliest history of Christian Britain. The events described in Document C, dating from A.D. 642, concern the doings of a converted king in the northern English territory of Northumbria, where Bede himself lived in a monastery. Besides recording a mix-ture of legends, miracles, and verifiable events, Bede's work strikingly conveys the mentality of the age, including its mystical faith in the saving power of saints' relics. How pagan north Europeans were con-verted by missionaries dispatched from Rome is sug-gested by Documents D and E, both dealing with St. Boniface (c. 680–754), the English-born "Apostle of Germany," who was eventually martyred.

A. Gregory the Great Expects the Imminent End of the World

Gregory to Leander, bishop of Seville:
With all my heart I have wished to answer you better, but the burden of my pastoral calls so overpowers me that I would rather weep than speak,—as your rever-ence undoubtedly gathers from the very character of my correspondence when I am remiss in addressing one whom I warmly love. In fact, so beaten about am I by the billows in this corner of the world, that I can in no wise bring to harbor the ancient, rolling ship at whose helm I stand through God's mysterious dispensation.

Now the waves break over us from the front, now at the side the foaming mountains of the sea swell high, now in the rear the tempest pursues us. Beset by all these perils, I am forced first to steer directly in the face of the storm, again to swerve the vessel and to receive obliquely the onset of the waters. I groan, because I know that if I am negligent the bilge water of vice is deepening, and that if the storm assails us furiously at that instant the decaying planks forebode shipwreck. Fearful, I remember that I have lost my quiet shore of peace, and sighing I gaze toward the land which, while the wind of circum-stances blows contrarily, I cannot gain. So, dearest brother, if you love me, stretch forth the hand of prayer to me amid these floods, and, as you aid me in my troubles, thus as a reward shall you come forth more valiantly from yours. . . .

. . . Some [portents of the end of the world] we see already accomplished; the others we dread as close upon us. For we now see that nation rises against nation, and that they press and weigh upon the land in our own times as never before in the annals of the past. Earthquakes overwhelm countless cities, as we often hear from other parts of the world. Pestilence we endure without interruption. It is true that as yet we do not behold signs in the sun and moon and stars; but that these are not far off we may infer from the changes in the atmosphere. Before Italy was given over to be desolated by the sword of a heathen foe, we beheld fiery ranks in heaven, and even the streaming blood of the human race as it was afterwards split.

B. Gregory the Great Instructs the Missionaries to England

When Almighty God shall bring you to the most rev-erend Bishop Augustine, our brother, tell him what I have, after mature deliberation on the affairs of the English, determined upon, namely, that the temples of the idols in that nation ought not to be destroyed, but let the idols that are in them be destroyed; let holy water be made and sprinkled in the said temples; let altars be erected, and relics placed. For if those temples are well built, it is requisite that they be con-verted from the worship of devils to the service of the true God; that the nation, seeing that their temples are not destroyed, may remove error from their hearts and, knowing and adoring the true God, may the more familiarly resort to the places to which they have been accustomed.

And because they have been used to slaughter many oxen in the sacrifices to devils, some solemnity must be substituted for them on this account, as, for instance, that on the day of the dedication, or of the nativities of the holy martyrs whose relics are there deposited, they may build themselves huts of the boughs of trees about those churches which have been turned to that use from temples, and celebrate the solemnity with religious feasting, no more offering beasts to the devil, but killing cattle to the praise of God in their eating, and returning thanks to the Giver of all things for their sustenance; to the end that, whilst some outward gratifications are permitted them, they may the more easily consent to the inward consolations of the grace of God.

For there is no doubt that it is impossible to efface everything at once from their obdurate minds, because he who endeavors to ascend to the highest place rises by degrees or steps and not by leaps. Thus the Lord made himself known to the people of Israel in Egypt; and yet he allowed them to use the sacrifices which they were wont to offer to the devil in his own worship, commanding them in his sacrifice to kill beasts to the end that, changing their hearts, they might lay aside one part of the sacrifice, whilst they retained another; that whilst they offered the same beasts which they were wont to offer, they should offer them to God, and not to idols, and thus they would no longer be the same sacrifices.

C. Bede Describes the Power of Saints

Oswald, the most Christian king of the Northumbrians, reigned nine years, including that year which is to be held accursed for the brutal impiety of the king of the Britons, and the apostasy of the English kings; for, as was said above, it is agreed by the unanimous consent of all, that the names of the apostates should be erased from the catalogue of the Christian kings, and no date ascribed to their reign. After which period, Oswald was killed in a great battle, by the same pagan nation and pagan king of the Mercians, who had slain his predecessor Edwin, at a place called in the English tongue Maserfield, in the thirty-eighth year of his age, on the fifth day of the month of August.

How great his faith was towards God, and how remarkable his devotion, has been made evident by miracles since his death; for, in the place where he was killed by the pagans, fighting for his country, infirm men and cattle are healed to this day. Whereupon many took up the very dust of the place where his body fell, and putting it into water, did much good with it to their friends who were sick. This custom came so much into use, that the earth being carried away by degrees, there remained a hole as deep as the height of a man. Nor is it to be wondered that the sick should be healed in the place where he died; for, whilst he lived, he never ceased to provide for the poor and infirm, and to bestow alms on them, and assist them. Many miracles are said to have been wrought in that place, or with the earth carried from thence; but we have thought it sufficient to mention two, which we heard from our ancestors.

It happened, not long after his death, that a man was travelling near that place, when his horse on a sudden began to tire, to stand stock still, hang down his head, and foam at the mouth, and, at length, as his pain increased, he fell to the ground; the rider dismounted, and throwing some straw under him, waited to see whether the beast would recover or die. At length, after much rolling about in extreme anguish, the horse happened to come to the very place where the aforesaid king died. Immediately the pain ceased, the beast gave over his struggles, and, as is usual with tired cattle, turned gently from side to side, and then starting up, perfectly recovered, began to graze on the green herbage; which the man observing, being an ingenious person, he concluded there must be some wonderful sanctity in the place where the horse had been healed, and left a mark there, that he might know the spot again. After which he again mounted his horse, and repaired to the inn where he intended to stop. On his arrival he found a girl, niece to the landlord, who had long languished under the palsy; and when the friends of the family, in his presence, lamented the girl's calamity, he gave them an account of the place where his horse had been cured. In short, she was put into a cart and carried and laid down at the place. At first she slept awhile, and when she awaked found herself healed of her infirmity. Upon which she called for water, washed her face, put up her hair, and dressed her head, and returned home on foot, in good health, with those who had brought her.

D. St. Boniface Destroys the Oak of Thor

Many of the people of Hesse were converted [by Boniface] to the Catholic faith and confirmed by the grace of the spirit: and they received the laying on of hands. But some there were, not yet strong of soul, who refused to accept wholly the teachings of the true faith. Some men sacrificed secretly, some even openly, to trees and springs. Some secretly practiced divining, soothsaying, and incantations, and some openly. But others, who were of sounder mind, cast aside all heathen profanation and did none of these things; and it was with the advice and consent of these men that Boniface sought to fell a certain tree of great size, at Geismar, and called, in the ancient speech of the region, the oak of Jove [i.e. Thor].

The man of God was surrounded by the servants of God. When he would cut down the tree, behold a great throng of pagans who were there cursed him bitterly among themselves because he was the enemy of their gods. And when he had cut into the trunk a little way, a breeze sent by God stirred overhead, and suddenly the branching top of the tree was broken off, and the oak in all its huge bulk fell to the ground. And it was broken into four parts, as if by the divine will, so that the trunk was divided into four huge sections without any effort of the brethren who stood by. When the pagans who had cursed did see this, they left off cursing and, believing, blessed God. Then the most holy priest took counsel with the brethren: and he built from the wood of the tree an oratory, and dedicated it to the holy apostle Peter.

E. St. Boniface Swears Allegiance to the Papacy

I, Boniface, bishop by the grace of God, promise to you, the blessed Peter, chief of the apostles, and to thy vicar, the blessed Pope Gregory, and to his successors, by the Father and the Son and the Holy Ghost, the indivisible Trinity, and by this thy most holy body, that, God helping me, I will maintain all the belief and the purity of the holy Catholic faith, and I will remain steadfast in the unity of this faith in which the whole salvation of Christians lies, as is established without doubt.

I will in no wise oppose the unity of the one universal Church, no matter who may seek to persuade me. But as I have said, I will maintain my faith and purity and union with thee and the benefits of thy Church, to whom God has given the power to loose and to bind, and with thy vicar and his successors, in all things. And if it comes to my knowledge that priests have turned from the ancient practices of the holy fathers, I will have no intercourse nor connection with them; but rather, if I can restrain them, I will. If I cannot, I will at once faithfully make known the whole matter to my apostolic lord.

Document Set 8.4 References

A. Gregory the Great Expects the Imminent End of the World
   James Harvey Robinson, ed., *Readings in European History* (Boston: Ginn, 1904), 1:75–76.
B. Gregory the Great Instructs the Missionaries to England
   Robinson, 1:100–101.
C. Bede Describes the Power of Saints
   Bede, *A History of the English Church and People,* trans. Leo Sherley-Price (Baltimore: Penguin, 1965), 155–157.
D. St. Boniface Destroys the Oak of Thor
   Robinson, 1:106–107.
E. St. Boniface Swears Allegiance to the Papacy
   O. J. Thatcher and E. H. McNeal, eds., *A Source Book for Medieval History* (New York: Scribner, 1905), 94–95.

DOCUMENT SET 8.5
Barbarian Kings and Their People

The documents of this set are meant to convey a sense of the texture of life in the "barbarian" western kingdoms. Gregory of Tours (c. 538–594), a Roman nobleman, wrote *The History of the Franks,* largely on the basis of his first-hand experiences at the court of the new Frankish kings in his native Gaul; the extract in Document A suggests something of the position of women at the early Merovingian royal court, as well as its moral tone.

The beginnings of feudalism can be traced to the Germanic kingdoms that arose on the wreckage of Roman imperial authority. Document B is a formula of commendation—that is, a declaration of personal subjugation to a more powerful protector—by which the seventh-century Franks tried to create enforceable bonds of interdependence. What does the fact that this document contains a formula rather than the actual testimony of a certain individual's dependency tell you about its reliability as a historical document?

Document C reveals evidence of another persistent problem in the Dark Ages—that of maintaining law and order through reliable procedures of meting out justice to offenders. This extract, from Gregory of Tours's *History,* describes a rough-and-ready way used by the Franks (as well as other Germanic peoples) to ensure that justice was being done. (How literally would you take this story?) It also reveals the persistence of Arianism in Northern Europe: the belief (to which the ancient Goths had been converted) that Jesus Christ was metaphysically inferior to God the Father. Arianism had long been condemned as a heresy by the church.

How the power of the Merovingian line of Frankish kings came to an end in the eighth-century is narrated in Document D by Einhard (c. 770–845), Charlemagne's biographer. What does this document reveal about the symbolism and the substance of royal authority in sixth- to eighth-century western Europe?

A. Gregory of Tours Comments on Merovingian Women

King Lothar had seven sons by his various wives. By Ingund he had Gunthar, Childeric, Charibert, Guntram, Sigibert and a daughter called Chlothsind; by Aregund, who was the sister of Ingund, he had Chilperic; and by Chunsina he had Chramn. I had better tell you how he came to marry the sister of his own wife. When he had already married Ingund and loved her with all his heart, she made the following suggestion to him: "My lord, you have already done what you wished with me, your handmaiden, and you have taken me to bed with you. To complete my happiness, listen now to what I have to say. I ask you to choose for my sister, who is also a member of your household, a competent and wealthy husband, so that I need not be ashamed of her, but rather that she may be a source of pride to me, so that I may serve you even more faithfully." Lothar was too much given to woman-chasing to be able to resist this. When he heard what Ingund had to say, he was filled with desire for Aregund. He went off to the villa where she lived and married her. When he had slept with her, he came back to Ingund. "I have done my best to reward you for the sweet request which you put to me," he said. "I have looked everywhere for a wealthy and wise husband whom I could marry to your sister, but I could find no one more eligible than myself. You must know, then, that I myself have married her. I am sure that this will not displease you." "You must do as you wish," answered Ingund. "All I ask is that I may retain your good favour."

B. Personal Dependence Spreads: A Seventh-Century Frankish Formula of Commendation

To that magnificent Lord — , I , —. Since it is known familiarly to all how little I have whence to feed and clothe myself, I have therefore petitioned your Piety, and your good will has permitted me to hand myself over or commend myself to your guardianship, which I have thereupon done; that is to say, in this way, that you should aid and succor me as well with food as with clothing, according as I shall be able to serve you and deserve it.

And so long as I shall live I ought to provide service and honor to you, suitably to my free condition; and I shall not during my lifetime have the ability to withdraw from your power or guardianship, but must remain during the days of my life under your power or defense. Wherefore it is proper that if either of us shall wish to withdraw himself from these agreements, he shall pay—shillings to his companion, and this agreement shall remain unbroken.

Wherefore it is fitting that they should make or confirm between themselves two letters drawn up in the same form on this matter; which they have thus done.

It is right that those who offer to us unbroken fidelity should be protected by our aid. And since —, a faithful one of ours, by the favor of God, coming here in our palace with his arms, has seen fit to swear trust and fidelity to us in our hand, therefore we herewith decree and command that for the future — —, above mentioned, be reckoned among the number of the antrustions [i.e. followers]. And if any one perchance should presume to kill him, let him know that he will be judged guilty of his weregild of six hundred shillings.

C. A Quest for Certainty: Germanic Judicial Ordeals

An Arian presbyter disputing with a deacon of our religion made venemous assertions against the Son of God and the Holy Ghost, as is the habit of that sect. But when the deacon had discoursed a long time concerning the reasonableness of our faith and the heretic, blinded by the fog of unbelief continued to reject the truth, according as it is written, "Wisdom shall not enter the mind of the wicked," the former said: "Why weary ourselves with long discussions? Let acts approve the truth; let a kettle be heated over the fire and someone's ring be thrown into the boiling water. Let him who shall take it from the heated liquid be approved as a follower of the truth, and afterwards let the other party be converted to the knowledge of this truth. And do thou also understand, O heretic, that this our party will fulfil the conditions with the aid of the Holy Ghost; thou shalt confess that there is no discordance, no dissimilarity in the Holy Trinity." The heretic consented to the proposition and they separated after appointing the next morning for the trial. But the fervor of faith in which the deacon had first made this suggestion began to cool through the instigation of the enemy. Rising with the dawn he bathed his arm in oil and smeared it with ointment. But nevertheless he made the round of the sacred places and called in prayer on the Lord. What more shall I say? About the third hour they met in the market place. The people came together to see the show. A fire was lighted, the kettle was placed upon it, and when it grew very hot the ring was thrown into the boiling water. The deacon invited the heretic to take it out of the water first. But he promptly refused, saying, "Thou who didst propose this trial art the one to take it out." The deacon all of a tremble bared his arm. And when the heretic presbyter saw it besmeared with ointment he cried out: "With magic arts thou hast thought to protect

thyself, that thou hast made use of these salves, but what thou hast done will not avail." While they were thus quarreling there came up a deacon from Ravenna named Iacinthus and inquired what the trouble was about. When he learned the truth he drew his arm out from under his robe at once and plunged his right hand into the kettle. Now the ring that had been thrown in was a little thing and very light so that it was thrown about by the water as chaff would be blown about by the wind; and searching for it a long time he found it after about an hour. Meanwhile the flame beneath the kettle blazed up mightily so that the greater heat might make it difficult for the ring to be followed by the hand; but the deacon extracted it at length and suffered no harm, protesting rather that at the bottom the kettle was cold while at the top it was just pleasantly warm. When the heretic beheld this he was greatly confused and audaciously thrust his hand into the kettle saying, "My faith will aid me." As soon as his hand had been thrust in all the flesh was boiled off the bones clear up to the elbow. And so the dispute ended.

D. Einhard Recalls the Weakness of the Merovingian Kings

The Franks in olden times were wont to choose their kings from the family of the Merovingians. This royal line is considered to have come to an end in the person of Childeric III, who was deposed from the throne by command of Stephen, the Roman pontiff; his long hair was cut off and he was thrust into a monastery.

Although the line of the Merovingians actually ended with Childeric, it had nevertheless for some time previously been so utterly wanting in power that it had displayed no mark of royalty except the empty kingly title.

All the resources and power of the kingdom had passed into the control of the prefects of the palace, who were called the "mayors of the palace," and who employed the supreme authority. Nothing was left to the king. He had to content himself with his royal title, his flowing locks, and long beard. Seated in a chair of state, he was wont to display an appearance of power by receiving foreign ambassadors on their arrival, and, on their departure, giving them, as if on his own authority, those answers which he had been taught or commanded to give.

Thus, except for his empty title, and an uncertain allowance for his subsistence, which the prefect of the palace used to furnish at his pleasure, there was nothing that the king could call his own, unless it were the income from a single farm, and that a very small one, where he made his home, and where such servants as were needful to wait on him constituted his scanty household. When he went anywhere he traveled in a wagon drawn by a yoke of oxen, with a rustic oxherd for charioteer. In this manner he proceeded to the palace, and to the public assemblies of the people held every year for the dispatch of the business of the kingdom, and he returned home again in the same sort of state. The administration of the kingdom, and every matter which had to be undertaken and carried through, both at home and abroad, was managed by the mayor of the palace.

Document Set 8.5 References

A. Gregory of Tours Comments on Merovingian Women
   Gregory of Tours, *History of the Franks,* trans. L. Thorpe (Baltimore: Penguin, 1974), 197–198.
B. Personal Dependence Spreads: A Seventh-Century Frankish Formula of Commendation
   James Harvey Robinson, ed., *Readings in European History* (Boston: Ginn, 1904), 1:175–176.
C. A Quest for Certainty: Germanic Judicial Ordeals
   Translations and Reprints from the Original Sources of European History (Philadelphia: University of Pennsylvania Press, 1898), 1/4:10, 17.
D. Einhard Recalls the Weakness of the Merovingian Kings
   Robinson, 1:120.

9

The Remaking of Three Societies, 756–1054

DOCUMENT SET 9.1
Byzantium and Russia

As *The Challenge of the West* explains, the greatest internal crisis that the Byzantine Empire faced in the eighth century revolved around the issue of whether icons—holy pictures of God, Christ, and the saints—should be venerated as miraculous or destroyed as idolatrous. Documents A and B will help you sort out the issues of this question, which shook Byzantium to its core. Why should such a controversy have mattered?

The worldly side of Byzantine life is the subject of Documents C to E. The awesome splendor of the Byzantine court was calculated to have just the effect on barbarian emissaries that in 949 the western ambassador Luitprand of Cremona describes. Byantine's material wealth and commercial interests are suggested by Document D, an early eighth-century set of regulations for silk merchants. What does this document also tell you about the conditions of economic production in imperial Constantinople? In Document E, the masterful tenth-century Emperor Basil II (known as the Bulgar Slayer for his devastating campaigns against Byzantium's northern neighbor) directs his attention to the empire's peasant population. Before 1050, Byzantine emperors were strong enough to slow—but not to stop—the subjugation of the peasantry by a powerful aristocracy. Here, Basil guarantees peasants' right to sue these *dynastoi* (powerful men) no matter how long ago the land had been taken. Why, however, should the Byzantine emperor have been so solicitous of his peasant subjects?

Byzantine influence in Russia is apparent in Document F, a selection from the *Russian Primary Chronicle,* compiled by monks. Here the pagan prince Vladimir in 987 tries to decide which of the neighboring religions he should adopt—Islam from the Turkic Bulgars of the Volga valley (not to be confused with the Bulgarians of the Balkans); Judaism from another Turkic tribe of the steppes, the Khazars; Latin Christianity from the Germans; or Byzantine Christianity. How would you evaluate his choice?

Byzantine influence is, however, very distant in the final selection of this set, an extract from the Russian epic *The Lay of Igor's Host,* a nearly contemporary account of the endemic warfare that tenth- and eleventh-century Kievan princes waged with steppe invaders. Document G does, however, suggest other influences on early Russia. How do you account for it?

Using these sources as well as *The Challenge of the West,* write a brief analysis of Byzantium as a center of civilization and state power in the ninth and tenth centuries.

A. John of Damascus Defends the Veneration of Icons *Focus*

For the invisible things of God since the creation of the world are made visible through images. We see images in creation which remind us faintly of God, as *not real* when, for instance, we speak of the holy and adorable

Trinity, imaged by the sun, or light, or burning rays, or by a running fountain, or a full river, or by the mind, speech, or the spirit within us, or by a rose tree, or a sprouting flower, or a sweet fragrance.

Again, an image is expressive of something in the future, mystically shadowing forth what is to happen. For instance, the ark represents the image of Our Lady, Mother of God; so does the staff and the earthen jar. The serpent brings before us Him who vanquished on the cross the bite of the original serpent; the sea, water, and the cloud the grace of baptism.

Again, things which have taken place are expressed by images for the remembrance either of a wonder, or an honour, or dishonour, or good or evil, to help those who look upon it in after times that we may avoid evils and imitate goodness. If is of two kings, the written image in books, as when God had the law inscribed on tablets, and when He enjoined that the lives of holy men should be recorded and sensible memorials be preserved in remembrance; as, for instance, the earthen jar and the staff in the ark. So now we preserve in writing the images and the good deeds of the past. Either, therefore, take away images altogether and be out of harmony and God who made these regulations, or receive them with the language and in the manner which befits them. In speaking of the manner let us go into the question of worship.

Worship is the symbol of veneration and of honour. Let us understand that there are different degrees of worship. First of all the worship . . . which we show to God, who alone by nature is worthy of worship. Then, for the sake of God who is worshipped by nature, we honour His saints and servants, as Joshua and Daniel worshipped an angel, and David His holy places, when he says, "Let us go the place where His feet have stood." Again, in His tabernacles, as when all the people of Israel adored in the tent, and standing round the temple in Jerusalem, fixing their gaze upon it from all sides, and worshiping from that day to this, or in the rulers established by Him, as Jacob rendered homage to Esau, his elder brother, and to Pharoah, the divinely established ruler. Joseph was worshipped by his brothers. I am aware that worship was based on honour, as in the case of Abraham and the sons of Emmor. Either, then, do away with worship, or receive it altogether according to its proper measure. . . .

Of old, God the incorporeal and uncircumscribed was never depicted. Now, however, when God is seen clothed in flesh, and conversing with men, I make an image of the God whom I see. I do not worship matter, I worship the God of matter, who became matter for my sake, and designed to inhabit matter, who worked out my salvation through matter. I will not cease from honouring that matter which works my salvation. I venerate it, though not as God. How could God be born out of lifeless things? And if God's body is God by union, it is immutable. The nature of God remains the same as before, the flesh created in time is quickened by a logical and reasoning soul. I honour all matter besides, and venerate it. Through it, filled, as it were, with a divine power and grace, my salvation has come to me. Was not the thrice happy and thrice blessed wood of the Cross matter? Was not the sacred the holy mountain of Calvary matter? What of the life-giving rock, the Holy Sepulchre, the source of our resurrection: was it not matter? Is not the most holy book of the Gospels matter? Is not the blessed table matter which gives us the Break of Life? Are not the gold and silver matter out of which crosses and altar-plate and chalices are made? And before all these things, is not the body and blood of our Lord matter? Either do away with the veneration and worship due to all these things, or submit to the tradition of the Church in the worship of images, honouring God and His friends, and following in this the grace of the Holy Spirit.

B. Emperor Leo V Demands the Destruction of Icons

Why are the Christians suffering defeat at the hands of the pagans? It seems to me it is because the icons are worshipped and nothing else. And (for this reason) I intend to destroy them. For you see that those emperors who accepted and worshipped them [the icons] died either as a result of exile or in battle. But those alone who have not worshiped them died each one in his own bed and after death were buried with honor in the imperial tombs at the Church of the Holy Apostles. Thus I too wish to imitate these latter emperors and destroy the icons in order that I and my son may live for a long time, and that our line may reign until the fourth and fifth generation.

C. Luitprand of Cremona Is Awestruck by the Byzantine Court

Adjoining the imperial palace in Constantinople there is a hall of extraordinary size and beauty. . . . The emperor Consantine [VII] had this hall arranged in the following manner for the reception of the recently arrived Spanish ambassador, as well as of Liutfrid [ambassador of Otto I] and myself. In front of the emperor's throne stood a tree of gilded iron, whose branches were filled with birds of various kinds, made of iron and gilded, which gave forth the different sorts of birds' notes. The throne itself was so cunningly constructed that at one instant it looked low, the next, higher, and a moment later had risen to a great elevation. It was guarded on either side by huge lions, I know not whether of metal or wood, but covered with gold, which lashed their tails on the floor and, with open mouth and moving. tongue, roared aloud.

In this hall, and accompanied by two eunuchs, I was brought before the emperor. At my entrance the lions roared and the birds sang, each after his kind; but I was neither frightened nor even astonished, since I had taken pains to learn beforehand about these things from those who knew about them. When I raised my head, after prostrating myself before the emperor for the third time, I beheld him, whom before I had seen seated at a moderate height above me, elevated almost to the roof of the hall and clad in different garments. How this was managed I do not know, unless by means of something like the screw of a press. All this time the emperor spoke no word; indeed, even had he wished to do so, it would have been undignified from so great a height. He inquired, however, through his chamberlain, after Berengar's health and pursuits. After I had replied in a fitting manner I retired, at a sign from the interpreter, and was conducted to the inn where quarters had been assigned me.

D. The Guild of Silk Merchants at Constantinople Is Regulated, c. 911

1. The raw-silk dealers are not to exercise another craft [in addition to their own], but they are to practice their own publicly in the place established for them. And whoever does not do so is to be beaten, shaved, and banished.

2. A raw-silk dealer who engages a journeyman is not to make a contract for a duration longer than one month, nor is he to pay salary in advance for longer than thirty working days, but [he is to pay] only for what the journeyman can accomplish by working the whole month. Whoever pays a salary for more than the appointed period is to lose this [extra amount].

3. A raw-silk dealer is not to engage the journeyman of another before the journeyman has accomplished the work he undertook for his [previous] salary. Whoever does otherwise is to be fined the amount of the [unearned] salary.

4. [The raw-silk dealers] are to pay only one *keration* in each hundred-weights to the exarchs [of the gild]. Whoever possesses scales or weights[?] not marked with the seal of the Prefect is to be beaten and shaved.

5. Those who come to the *mitata* from outside with raw silk are not to pay duties except for rent and lodgings. Likewise, those who buy [from them] are not to be asked to pay duties.

6. Whoever is going to be admitted to [the gild of] the raw-silk dealers must obtain the testimony of honorable and reliable men in regard to his good reputation. Then, upon giving two nomismata to the gild, he is to be enrolled.

7. If a raw-silk dealer wants to put his slave in his place in his business, he is to be jointly [liable] with him, assuming the risk if [the slave] should do something wrong.

8. The entire community of the gild at the time of the market is to make a deposit, each member according to his means. And the apportionment is to be effected according to the deposit of each member.

9. If a rich [raw-silk dealer] who has bought from outsider must sell [silk] to others who are poorer, he is to take a profit of only one ounce per nomisma.

10. If a raw-silk dealer deals in silk under his own name for a powerful or rich man or even a cloth maker, and does so for a salary, he is to be beaten and shaved and expelled from the gild.

11. Whoever embezzles the earnest given him for the purchase of silk and raises its price is to be fined the amount of that earnest.

12. If a raw-silk dealer is caught traveling to buy silk, he is to be expelled from the gild.

13. The raw-silk dealers must not sell unworked silk in their homes but in the market, so that the silk may not be forwarded secretly to those who are forbidden to buy it. Whoever does so is to pay 15 nomismata to the gild.

14. The raw-silk dealers are not to have a license to spin silk, but only to buy and to sell it. Whoever is caught [transgressing this provision] is to be punished by the penalty of being flogged and shaved.

15. The so-called *melathrarioi* are not to buy pure silk either secretly or openly. Whoever does so is to be subject to the aforesaid penalty.

16. The raw-silk dealers are not to sell silk to Jews or to [other] merchants for resale outside the city. Whoever does so is to be beaten and shaved.

E. Basil II Attempts to Protect Byzantine Peasants from Over-Powerful Lords

We have been very disturbed on behalf of the poor, and we have observed with our own eyes (when we traverse the themes of our empire and set out on campaigns) the avarice the injustices every day perpetrated against the poor . . .

For when one who happens to be powerful acquires property in communities of peasant villages or enlarges his property with more land, and when his successors take over his authority as well as his wealth and provide no opportunity for the poor man to take legal action against them for the things they have evilly expropriated and taken from him, it is clear that whatever amount of time may elapse in these matters, the poor man ought in no case to be prevented from seeking and gaining the return of his own property.

F. Vladimir Accepts Byzantine Christianity in Russia

[A.D.] 987 (6495) Vladimir summoned together his vassals and the city elders, and said to them: "Behold, the Bulgarians came before me urging me to accept their religion. Then came the Germans and praised their own faith; and after them came the Jews. Finally the Greeks appeared, criticizing all other faiths but commending their own, and they spoke at length, telling the history of the whole world from its beginning. Their words were artful, and it was wondrous to listen and pleasant to hear them. They preach the existence of another world. 'Whoever adopts our religion and then dies shall arise and live forever. But whosoever embraces another faith, shall be consumed with fire in the next world.' What is your opinion on this subject, and what do you answer?" The vassals and the elders replied: "You know, O Prince, that no man condemns his own possessions, but praises them instead. If you desire to make certain, you have servants at your disposal. Send them to inquire about the ritual of each and how he worships God."

Their counsel pleased the prince and all the people, so that they chose good and wise men to the number of ten, and directed them to go first among the Bulgarians [i.e., the Turkic Volga Bulgars] and inspect their faith. The emissaries went their way, and

Excerpt from Chapter 9 of *Medieval Russia's Epics, Chronicles, and Tales*, Serge A. Zenovsky, ed., E. P. Dutton, 1963, pp. 66–68, 69, 146. Reprinted by permission.

when they arrived at their destination they beheld the disgraceful actions of the Bulgarians and their worship in the mosque; then they returned to their own country. Vladimir then instructed them to go likewise among the Germans, and examine their faith, and finally to visit the Greeks. They thus went into Germany, and after viewing the German ceremonial, they proceeded to Constantinople where they appeared before the emperor. He inquired on what mission they had come, and they reported to him all that had occurred. When the emperor heard their words, he rejoiced, and did them great honor on that very day.

On the morrow, the emperor sent a message to the patriarch to inform him that a Russian delegation had arrived to examine the Greek faith, and directed him to prepare the church and the clergy, and to array himself in his sacerdotal robes, so that the Russians might behold the glory of the God of the Greeks. When the patriarch received these commands, he bade the clergy assemble, and they performed the customary rites. They burned incense, and the choirs sang hymns. The emperor accompanied the Russians to the church, and placed them in a wide space, calling their attention to the beauty of the edifice, the chanting, and the offices of the archpriest and the ministry of the deacons, while he explained to them the worship of his God. The Russians were astonished, and in their wonder praised the Greek ceremonial. Then the Emperors Basil and Constantine invited the envoys to their presence, and said, "Go hence to your native country," and thus dismissed them with valuable presents and great honor.

Thus they returned to their own country, and the prince called together his vassals and the elders. Vladimir then announced the return of the envoys who had been sent out, and suggested that their report be heard. He thus commanded them to speak out before his vassals. The envoys reported: "When we journeyed among the Bulgarians, we beheld how they worship in their temple, called a mosque, while they stand ungirt. The Bulgarian bows, sits down, looks hither and thither like one possessed, and there is no happiness among them, but instead only sorrow and a dreadful stench. Their religion is not good. Then we went among the Germans, and saw them performing many ceremonies in their temples; but we beheld no glory there. Then we went on to Greece, and the Greeks led us to the edifices where they worship their God, and we knew not whether we were in heaven or on earth. For on earth there is no such splendor or such beauty, and we are at a loss how to describe it. We know only that God dwells there among men, and their service is fairer than the cere-

physical splendor.

monies of other nations. For we cannot forget that beauty. Every man, after tasting something sweet, is afterward unwilling to accept that which is bitter, and therefore we cannot dwell longer here." Then the vassals spoke and said, "If the Greek faith were evil, it would not have been adopted by your grandmother Olga, who was wiser than all other men." Vladimir then inquired where they should all accept baptism, and they replied that the decision rested with him. [However, Vladimir was not yet ready for baptism. He captured the Greek city of Kherson in the Crimea and demanded that the Byzantine emperor give him his daughter in marriage. The emperor refused unless Vladimir became a Christian. He gave his promise and the princess was dispatched to Russia, but still he refused to go through with the ceremony.]

By divine agency, Vladimir was suffering at that moment from a disease of the eyes, and could see nothing, being in great distress. The princess declared to him that if he desired to be relieved of this disease, he should be baptized with all speed, otherwise it could not be cured. When Vladimir heard her message, he said, "If this proves true, then of a surety is the God of the Christians great," and gave order that he should be baptized. The Bishop of Kherson, together with the princess's priests, after announcing the tidings, baptized Vladimir, and as the bishop laid his hand upon him, he straightway received his sight. Upon experiencing this miraculous cure, Vladimir glorified God, saying, "I have now perceived the one true God." When his followers beheld this miracle, many of them were also baptized.

G. Warfare on the Russian Steppes: The Igor Tale

And so it used to be.
There were battles and campaigns,
but there had never been such battle as this.
From early morning to night,
from evening to dawn
there flew tempered arrows,
swords rained down upon helmets,
Frankish lances resound,
and all this in the unknown prairie,
in the human land.

The black earth under the hooves
was strewn with bones,
was covered with blood.
Grief overwhelmed the Russian land.

What noise do I hear?
What clinking comes to my ears
so early in the morning, before the dawn?
It is Prince Igor who has led away his troops.
He is saddened by the fate of his brother, Vsevolod.
They fought for one day.
They fought for another day.
At noon on the third day Igor's banners fell.
Here, on the shores of the swift river Kaiala,
the brothers parted.
The wine of this bloody banquet was drunk to the
    last drop.
The Russians gave their guests to drink from the same
    cup.
They died for the Russian land.
    The grass withered from sorrow,
    and the saddened trees drooped earthward.

Document Set 9.1 References

A. John of Damascus Defends the Veneration of Icons
   Allies, M. H. trans., *St. John of Damascene on Holy Images* (London: Burns and Oates Ltd., 1898), 10–17.
B. Emperor Leo V Demands the Destruction of Icons
   Deno John Geanokoplos, ed., *Byzantium: Church, Society, and Civilization Seen Through Contemporary Eyes* (Chicago: University of Chicago Press, 1984), 157.
C. Luitprand of Cremona Is Awestruck by the Byzantine Court
   James Harvey Robinson, ed., *Readings in European History* (Boston: Ginn, 1904), 1:340.
D. The Guild of Silk Merchants at Constantinople Is Regulated, c. 911
   Robert S. Lopez and Irving W. Raymond, *Medieval Trade in the Mediterranean World* (New York: Columbia University Press, 1930s), 20–22.
E. Basil II Attempts to Protect Byzantine Peasants from Over-Powerful Lords
   Geanokoplos, 246.
F. Vladimir Accepts Byzantine Christianity in Russia
   Serge A. Zenkovsky, ed., *Medieval Russia's Epics, Chronicles and Tales* (New York: 1963), 66–72.
G. Warfare on the Russian Steppes: The Igor Tale
   Zenkovsky, 142–146.

DOCUMENT SET 9.2
Islam

Having overrun the ancient Near East and established the Caliphate at Damascus, the first Muslim dynasty, the Umayyads (661–750) faced the problem of governing long-civilized lands and of adapting to the needs of a relatively advanced empire of the Islamic faith that had unified the Bedouins and townspeople of Arabia. How Muslims grappled with this transition is suggested by Document A, which purports to record how the early Islamic conqueror Umar (d. 644) governed the faithful justly. Umar lives on in Muslim memory as the "perfect caliph."

The Abbasid dynasty (750–c. 1100), which supplanted the Umayyads, was still more worldly and sophisticated. Under the great caliph Harun al-Rashid (786–809), the Abbasids consolidated their grip on the Near East despite several Byzantine attempts at a comeback. An episode from this conflict is narrated from the Muslim perspective in Document B. The Byzantine empress Irene (*797–802), the first woman to rule the empire in her own right, preferred buying off the Arabs rather than fighting them; the secretary who overthrew her became Emperor Nicephorus (*802–811), a soldier and administrator as capable as Harun al-Rashid. Document B also attests to the continuing importance of traditional Arabian poetry at the caliph's court. Document C, an extract from the ninth-century political leader and poet Ibrahim ibn al-Mahdi, not only continues Document B's testimony to the high cultural tone of the Abbasid court but also illustrates both the possibilities and the limits of women's power at Baghdad. The scene opens with several of Harun's wives sitting together on a large Armenian carpet. Suddenly Murayyah, the widow of a Umayyad caliph, enters to complain that she has fallen on hard times.

A. The "Perfect Caliph" Described: Umar, c. A.D. 720

When 'Umar was dying, he left this advice: "I advise my successor to fear God, and to respect the rights and the merits of the first emigrants to Medina; and as to the Ansār, who lived in Medina, and in the Faith, to accept their good deeds and to be indulgent to the bad among them. As to the people of the garrison towns, (*amsār*), they are the help of Islam, the fury of the enemy, and the bringers of wealth, so he should take only their superfluity, and by their agreement. I advise him as to the beduins that they are the source

of the Arabs, and the raw stuff of Islam, and he should take only a little of their possessions, to return to the poorest among them. As to the protected peoples, let him fulfill his agreement with them and fight their enemies and not burden them beyond their endurance."

And 'Umar wrote to Abū Mūsā al-Ash'arī (whom he had made governor of Basra). "The happiest shepherd with God will be the one whose flock was happy. Take care not to stray, or your subordinates will stray too, and in God's eyes you will be like a brute, who looks only at the green stuff of the earth, grazing upon it to fatten itself, and dying with its fat."

Ismā'īl al-Bajalī told me from 'Abd al-Mālik ibn 'Umayr that a man of the Thaqīf tribe said, "(the caliph) 'Ali made me tax-collector for 'Ukbarā', and said to me while the people of that place were with me listening, 'See that you take what they owe in taxes; beware of lessening it for them in any way, and beware of showing any weakness.' Then he sent for me that noon, and I went to him and he said, 'I only advised you thus before the people because they are a deceitful lot. But see when you are over them that you do not sell (to raise tax money) a single garment of theirs, summer or winter, or the provisions they eat, or a work animal, and that you do not strike anyone even a blow, for tax money, or hang him up by one leg to extort money, or sell any of their land to raise taxes, for we have only been ordered to take the abundance. If you act contrary to my orders, it is God who will punish you in my stead, and if I hear that you do, I shall remove you.' I told him, 'Then I shall leave here as I came.' He said, 'And what if you do?" Then he went, and I did as he ordered, yet the tax collection did not suffer in any respect."

B. An Islamic Historian Describes the War Between Harun al-Rashid and Byzantium

A woman came to rule over the Romans because at the time she was the only one of their royal house who remained. She wrote to the Caliphs al-Mahdī

"The Abbasids" from *Islam: From the Prophet Muhammad to the Capture of Constantinople*, Volume II by Bernard Lewis, pp. 27–30. Copyright © 1974 by Bernard Lewis. Reprinted by permission of HarperCollins Publishers, Inc.

and al-Hādī and to al-Rashīd at the beginning of his Caliphate with respect and deference and showered him with gifts. When her son [Constantine VI] grew up and came to the throne in her place, he brought trouble and disorder and provoked al-Rashīd. The empress, who knew al-Rashīd and feared his power, was afraid lest the kingdom of the Romans pass away and their country be ruined. She therefore overcame her son by cunning and put out his eyes so that the kingdom was taken from him and returned to her. But the people of their kingdom disapproved of this and hated her for it. Therefore Nikephoros, who was her secretary, rose against her, and they helped and supported him so that he seized power and became the ruler of the Romans.

When he was in full control of his kingdom, he wrote to al-Rashīd, "From Nikephoros, the king of Romans, to al-Rashīd, the king of the Arabs, as follows: That woman put you and your father and your brother in the place of kings and put herself in the place of a commoner. I put you in a different place and am preparing to invade your lands and attack your cities, unless you repay me what that woman paid you. Farewell!"

When his letter reached al-Rashīd, he replied, "In the name of God, the Merciful and the Compassionate, from the servant of God, Hārūn, Commander of the Faithful, to Nikephoros, the dog of the Romans, as follows: I have understood your letter, and I have your answer. You will see it with your own eye, not hear it." Then he at once sent an army against the land of the Romans of a size the like of which was never heard before and with commanders unrivaled in courage and skill. When news of this reached Nikephoros, the earth became narrow before him and he took counsel. Al-Rashid advanced relentlessly into the land of the Romans, killing, plundering, taking captives, destroying castles, and obliterating traces, until they came to the narrow roads before Constantinople, and when they reached there, they found that Nikephoros had already had trees cut down, thrown across these roads, and set on fire. The first who put on the garments of the naphtha-throwers was Muhammad ibn Yazīd ibn Mazyad. He plunged boldly through, and then the others followed him.

Nikephoros sent gifts to al-Rashīd and submitted to him very humbly and paid him the poll tax for himself as well as for his companions.

On this Abu'l-'Atāhiya said:

*O Imam of God's guidance, you have become the
    guardian of religion, quenching the thirst of all who
    pray for rain.*
You have two names drawn from righteousness [rashād]

*and guidance [hudā], for you are the one called
    Rashīd and Mahdī,*
*Whatever displeases you becomes loathsome; if
    anything pleases you, the people are well pleased
    with it.*
*You have stretched out the hand of nobility to us,
    east and west, and bestowed bounty on both
    easterner and westerner.*
*You have adorned the face of the earth with gen-
    erosity and munificence, and the face of the
    earth is adorned with generosity.*
*O, Commander of the Faithful, brave and pious,
    you have opened that part of benevolence which
    was closed!*
*God has destined that the kingdom should remain
    to Hārūn, and God's destiny is binding on
    mankind.*
*The world submits to Hārūn, the favored of God,
    and Nikephoros has become the* dhimmi *of
    Hārūn.*

Then al-Rashīd went back, because of what Nikephoros had given him, and got as far as Raqqa. When the snow fell and Nikephoros felt safe from attack, he took advantage of the respite and broke the agreement between himself and al-Rashīd and returned to his previous posture. Yahyā ibn Khālid [the vizier], let alone any other, did not dare to inform al-Rashīd of the treachery of Nikephoros. Instead, he and his sons offered money to the poets to recite poetry and thereby inform al-Rashīd of this. But they all held back and refrained, except for one poet from Jedda, called Abū Muhammad, who was very proficient, strong of heart and strong of poetry, distinguished in the days of al-Ma'mūn and of very high standing. He accepted the sum of 100,000 dirhams from Yahyā and his sons and then went before al-Rashīd and recited the following verses:

*Nikephoros has broken the promise he gave you,
    and now death hovers above him.*
*I bring good tidings to the Commander of the
    Faithful, for Almighty God is bringing you a
    great victory.*
*Your subjects hail the messenger who brings the
    good news of his treachery*
*Your right hand craves to hasten to that battle
    which will assuage our souls and bring a memo-
    rable punishment.*
*He paid you his poll tax and bent his cheek in fear
    of sharp swords and in dread of destruction.*
*You protected him from the blow of swords which
    we brandished like blazing torches.*

You brought all your armies back from him and he to
whom you gave your protection was secure and
happy.

Nikephoros! If you played false because the Imam
was far from you, how ignorant and deluded you
were!
Did you think you could play false and escape? May
your mother mourn you! What you thought is
delusion.
Your destiny will throw you into its brimming depths;
seas will envelop you from the Imam.
The Imam has power to overwhelm you, whether
your dwelling be near or far away.
Though we may be neglectful the Imam does not
neglect that which he rules and governs with his
strong will.
A king who goes in person to the holy war! His enemy
is always conquered by him.
O you who seek God's approval by your striving,
nothing in your inmost heart is hidden from God.
No counsel can avail him who deceives his Imam, but
counsel from loyal counsellers deserves thanks.
Warning the Imam is a religious duty, an expiation
and a cleansing for those who do it.

When he recited this, al-Rashīd asked, "Has he done that?" and he learned that the viziers had used this device to inform him of it. He then made war against Nikephoros while the snow still remained and conquered Heraclea at that time.

C. Tale of al-Mahdi Regarding Women at the Court of Harun al-Rashid

Now Zainab saw that Khaizuran's eyes were filling with tears. So she cut short Murayyah's speech and said, "Oh mother of the Commander of the Faithful, beware lest any compassion for this accursed woman penetrate your heart. She turned to Murayyah and said, "May you instead remain in your present condition. You seem to forget the time I visited you [when your husband was Caliph]. You were seated on this very rug. I stood then on the spot where you now stand. You looked at me with a scowl on your face and said, 'What have women to do with the affairs of men?' Then you rudely ordered my dismissal."

Murayyah said, "What she has related about me is true. It is that behaviour which has placed me in this position. Fortunate is he who learns from the experience of others." So saying she left.

Khaizuran, after the departure of Zainab, sent for Murayyah. She treated her kindly and was so generous to her that she was better off than in the time of the Umayyads.

Document Set 9.2 References

A. The "Perfect Caliph" Described: Umar, c. A.D. 720
J. A. Williams, *Themes of Islamic Civilization* (Berkeley: University of California Press, 1971), 69–73.
B. An Islamic Historian Describes the War Between Huran al-Rashid and Byzantium
Lewis, *Islam: From the Prophet Muhammed to the Capture of Constantinople* (New York: Walker, 1987), 1:27–30.
C. Tale of al-Mahdi Regarding Women at the Court of Harun al-Rashid
Charis Waddy, *Women in Muslim History* (London: Longman, 1980), 39.

DOCUMENT SET 9.3
From Charlemagne to the Vikings

A contemporary of Harun al-Rashid, Irene, and Nicephorus, Charlemagne (*768–814) struggled mightily to restore political stability and cultural life in the West. The documents of this set help place his achievements and limitations in perspective and also afford the basis of comparison with the Byzantine and Arab worlds of his day.

Document A is an extract from the biography of Charlemagne by Einhardt (c. 770–840), a scholar and official at his court. Document B, a capitulary, or imperial decree, reveals the great emperor in his role of conqueror and forcible Christianizer of the pagans Saxons in what today is eastern Germany. Charlemagne in general tried to impose rational standards other than drastic ordeals for his law courts in meeting out justice, but in Document C he shows what courts could do in especially intractable cases. (The ordeal of the cross was a relatively tame procedure, requiring the opponents to stand with their arms stretched out; the first to drop his arms lost the case. Compare the ordeal described by Gregory of Tours in Set 8.5, Document C.)

The kind of resources Charlemagne could command, the indeed the level of economic development of the ninth-century West, stand out vividly in Document D: an extract from Charlemagne's capitulary *De villis* and the inventory of an imperial estate. Remember that estates such as these were built to maintain the emperor and his entourage as they made their rounds. To what extent does the actual inventory meet the standards specified in the capitulary?

The revival of learning that Charlemagne stimulated by gathering scholars from the monasteries of the British Isles, Gaul, and Germany is exemplified in Document E. The commentaries, biographies, letters, and other works of these scholars—including Paschasius Radbertus (c. 865), represented here—demonstrated great familiarity with the Christian and pagan classics. Here in his biography of a cousin of Charlemagne, Paschasius uses a dialogue form modeled on Plato and Gregory the Great.

The Carolingian world all but collapsed in the century after Charlemagne's death, falling victim to raids by Vikings, Magyars, and Arabs that the successor kingdoms to Charles's empire could not fend off. There are two extracts in Document F: the first describes a Viking raid on Nantes in 843, from the chronicle *Annals of St. Bertin*; the second narrates a similar attack the next year in northern Germany, from the *Annals of Xanten*.

Use these documents in conjunction with your study of *The Challenge of the West* to weigh the strengths and weaknesses of the Carolingian-era revival of the West. You might want to broaden your inquiry by introducing, as a comparative dimension, the contemporary worlds of Byzantium and Islam (Sets 9.1 and 9.2).

A. Einhard Describes Charlemagne

Charles was large and robust, of commanding stature and excellent proportions, for it appears that he measured in height seven times the length of his own foot. The top of his head was round, his eyes large and animated, his nose somewhat long. He had a fine head of gray hair, and his face was bright and pleasant; so that, whether standing or sitting, he showed great presence and dignity. Although his neck was thick and rather short, and his belly too prominent, still the good proportions of his limbs concealed these defects. His walk was firm, and the whole carriage of his body was manly. His voice was clear, but not so strong as his frame would have led one to expect. . . .

He took constant exercise in riding and hunting, which was natural for a Frank, since scarcely any nation can be found to equal them in these pursuits. . . .

He wore the dress of his native country, that is, the Frankish; [and] he thoroughly disliked the dress of foreigners, however fine; and he never put it on except at Rome. . . .

In his eating and drinking he was temperate; more particularly so in his drinking, for he had the greatest abhorrence of drunkenness in anybody, but more especially in himself and his companions. He was unable to abstain from food for any length of time, and often complained that fasting was injurious to him. On the other hand, he very rarely feasted, only on great festive occasions, when there were very large gatherings. The daily service of his table consisted of only four dishes in addition to the roast meat, which the hunters used to bring in on spits, and of which he partook more freely than of any other food.

While he was dining he listened to music or reading. History and the deeds of men of old were most often read. He derived much pleasure from the works of St. Augustine, especially from his book called *The City of God*. . . .

While he was dressing and binding on his sandals, he would receive his friends; and also, if the count of the palace announced that there was any case which could only be settled by his decision, the suitors were immediately ordered into his presence, and he heard the case and gave judgment as if sitting in court. And this was not the only business that he used to arrange at that time, for he also gave orders for whatever had to be done on that day by any officer or servant.

He was ready and fluent in speaking, and able to express himself with great clearness. He did not confine himself to his native tongue, but took pains to learn foreign languages, acquiring such knowledge of Latin that he could make an address in that language as well as in his own. Greek he could better understand than speak. Indeed, he was so polished in speech that he might have passed for a learned man.

He was an ardent admirer of the liberal arts, and greatly revered their professors, whom he promoted to high honors. In order to learn grammar, he attended the lectures of the aged Peter of Pisa, a deacon; and for other branches he chose as his preceptor Albinus, otherwise called Alcuin, also a deacon,—a Saxon by race, from Britain, the most learned man of the day, with whom the king spent much time in leaving rhetoric and logic, and more especially astronomy. He learned the art of determining the dates upon which the movable festivals of the Church fall, and with deep thought and skill most carefully calculated the courses of the planets.

Charles also tried to learn to write, and used to keep his tablets and writing book under the pillow of his couch, that when he had leisure he might practice his hand in forming letters; but he made little progress in this task, too long deferred and begun too late in life.

B. Charlemagne Forcibly Christianizes the Saxons

First, concerning the greater chapters it has been enacted.

It was pleasing to all that the churches of Christ, which are now being built in Saxony and consecrated to God, should not have less, but greater and more illustrious honor, than the fanes of the idols had had.

2. If any one shall have fled to a church for refuge, let no one presume to expel him from the church by violence, but he shall be left in peace until he shall be brought to the judicial assemblage; and on account of the honor due to God and the saints, and the reverence due to the church itself, let his life and all his members be granted to him. Moreover, let him plead has cause as best he can and he shall be judged; and so let him be led to the presence of the lord king, and the latter shall send him where it shall have seemed fitting to his clemency.

3. If any one shall have entered a church by violence and shall have carried off anything in it by force or theft, or shall have burned the church itself, let him be punished by death.

4. If any one, out of contempt for Christianity, shall have despised the holy Lenten fast and shall have eaten flesh, let him be punished by death. But, nevertheless, let it be taken into consideration by a priest, lest perchance any one from necessity has been led to eat flesh.

5. If any one shall have killed a bishop or priest or deacon, let him likewise be punished capitally.

6. If any one deceived by the devil shall have believed, after the manner of the pagans, that any man or woman is a witch and eats men, and on this account shall have burned the person, or shall have given the person's flesh to others to eat, or shall have eaten it himself, let him be punished by a capital sentence.

7. If any one, in accordance with pagan rites, shall have caused the body of a dead man to be burned and shall have reduced his bones to ashes, let him be punished capitally.

8. If any one of the race of the Saxons hereafter concealed among them shall have wished to hide himself unbaptized, and shall have scorned to come to baptism and shall have wished to remain a pagan, let him be punished by death.

9. If any one shall have sacrificed a man to the devil, and after the manner of the pagans shall have presented him as a victim to the demons, let him be punished by death.

10. If any one shall have formed a conspiracy with the pagans against the Christians, or shall have wished to join with them in opposition to the Christians, let him be punished by death; and whosoever shall have consented to this same fraudulently against the king and the Christian people, let him be punished by death.

11. If any one shall have shown himself unfaithful to the lord king, let him be punished with a capital sentence.

12. If any one shall have ravished the daughter of his lord, let him be punished by death.

13. If any one shall have killed his lord or lady, let him be punished in a like manner.

14. If, indeed, for these mortal crimes secretly committed any one shall have fled of his own accord to a priest, and after confession shall have wished to

do penance, let him be freed by the testimony of the priest from death.

15. Concerning the lesser chapters all have consented. To each church let the parishioners present a house and two *mansi* of land, and for each one hundred and twenty men, noble and free, and likewise *liti*, let them give to the same church a man-servant and a maid-servant. . . .

17. Likewise, in accordance with the mandate of God, we command that all shall give a tithe of their property and labor to the churches and priests; let the nobles as well as the freemen, and likewise the *liti*, according to that which God shall have given to each Christian, return a part to God. . . .

19. Likewise, it has been pleasing to insert in these decrees that all infants shall be baptized within a year; and we have decreed this, that if any one shall have despised to bring his infant to baptism within the course of a year, without the advice or permission of the priest, if he is a noble he shall pay 120 *solidi* to the treasury, if a freeman 60, if a *litus* 30.

20. If any one shall have made a prohibited or illegal marriage, if a noble 60 *solidi,* if a freeman 30, if a *litus* 15.

21. If any one shall have made a vow at springs or trees or groves, or shall have made any offering after the manner of the heathen and shall have partaken of a repast in honor of the demons, if he shall be a noble 60 *solidi,* if a freeman 30, if a *litus* 15. If, indeed, they have not the means of paying at once, they shall be given into the service of the church until the *solidi* are paid.

22. We command that the bodies of Saxon Christians shall be carried to the church cemeteries and not to the mounds of the pagans.

23. We have ordered that diviners and soothsayers shall be given to the churches and priests. . . .

29. Let all the counts strive to preserve peace and unity with one another; and if perchance any discord or disturbance shall have arisen between them, they shall not on this account neglect either our aid or profit.

30. If any one shall have killed or shall have aided in the murder of a count, his property shall go to the king, and he shall become the serf of the latter. . . .

34. We have forbidden that all the Saxons shall hold public assemblies in general, unless perchance our *missus* shall have caused them to come together in accordance with our command; but each count shall hold judicial assemblies and administer justice in his jurisdiction. And this shall be cared for by the priests, lest it be done otherwise.

C. Charlemagne Permits the "Ordeal of the Cross" in Insoluble Judicial Cases

If a dispute, contention, or controversy shall arise between the parties regarding the boundaries or limits of their kingdoms of such a nature that it cannot be settled or terminated by human evidence, then we desire that for the decision of the matter the will of God and the truth of the dispute may be sought by means of the judgment of the cross, nor shall any sort of battle or duel ever be adjudged for the decision of any such question.

D. Inspecting the Imperial Domains: The Capitulary "De Villis" and an Estate Inventory

62. That each steward shall make an annual statement of all our income: an account of our lands cultivated by the oxen which our plowmen drive and of our lands which the tenants of farms ought to plow . . .

22. In each of our estates our stewards are to have as many cowhouses, piggeries, sheep-folds, stables for goats, as possible, and they ought never to be without these. And let them have in addition cows furnished by our serfs for performing their service, so that the cow-houses and plows shall be in no way weakened by the service on our demense. And when they have to provide meat, let them have steers lame, but healthy, and cows and horses which are not mangy, or other beasts which are not diseased and, as we have said, our cow-houses and plows are not to be weakened for this.

34. They must provide with the greatest care, that whatever is prepared or made with the hands, that is, lard, smoked meat, salt meat, partially salted meat, wine vinegar, mulberry wine, cooked wine, *garns,* mustard, cheese, butter, malt, beer, mead, honey, wax, flour, all should be prepared and made with the greatest cleanliness.

40. That each steward on each of our domains shall always have, for the sake of ornament, swans, peacocks, pheasants, ducks, pigeons, partridges, turtle-doves.

42. That in each of our estates, the chambers shall be provided with counterpanes, cushions, pillows, bed-clothes, coverings for the tables and benches; vessels of brass, lead, iron and wood; andirons, chains, pot-hooks, adzes, axes, augers, cutlasses and all other kinds of tools, so that it shall never be necessary to go elsewhere for them, or to borrow them.

And the weapons, which are carried against the enemy, shall be well cared for, so as to keep them in good condition; and when they are brought back they shall be placed in the chamber.

gender separation in labor

43. For our women's work they are to give at the proper time, as has been ordered, the materials, that is the linen, wool, woad, vermillion, madder, wool-combs, teasels, soap, grease, vessels and the other objects which are necessary.

44. Of the food-products other than meat, two-thirds shall be sent each year for our own use, that is of the vegetables, fish, cheese, butter, honey, mustard vinegar, millet, panic, dried and green herbs, radishes, and in addition of the wax, soap and other small products; and they tell us how much is left by a statement, as we have said above; and they shall not neglect this as in the past; because from those two-thirds, we wish to know how much remains.

45. That each steward shall have in his district good workmen, namely, blacksmiths, gold-smith, sil-ver-smith, shoe-makers, turners, carpenters, sword-makers, fishermen, foilers, soap-makers, men who know how to make beer, cider, berry, and all the other kinds of beverages, bakers to make pastry for our table, net-makers who know how to make nets for hunting, fishing and fowling, and the other who are too numerous to be designated.

functional not fancy

We found in the domain estate of Asnapium a royal house built of stone in the best manner, 3 rooms; the whole house surrounded with balconies, with 11 apartments for women; beneath 1 cellar; 2 porticoes; 17 other houses built of wood within the court-yard with as many rooms and other appurte-nances, well built; 1 stable, 1 kitchen, 1 mill, 1 gra-nary, 8 barns.

The yard surrounded carefully with a hedge and stone gateway and above a balcony from which to make distributions. An inner yard, likewise enclosed within a hedge, arranged in a suitable manner planted with various kinds of trees.

Vestments: coverings for 1 bed, 1 table cloth, 1 towel.

Utensils: 2 brass kettles, 2 drinking cups, 2 brass cauldrons, 1 iron one, 1 frying-pay, 1 gramalmin, 1 pair of andirons, 1 lamp, 2 hatchets, 1 chisel, 2 augers, 1 axe, 1 knife, 1 large plane, 1 plane, 2 scythes, 2 sick-les, 2 spades tipped with iron. Enough wooden uten-sils for use.

Farm produce: [an inventory follows, listing bas-kets of grain, honey, butter, cheese, etc.]

Of cattle; . . . [an inventory follows, enumerating 51 head of "larger cattle," horses, lambs, chickens, and 22 peacocks.]

In another villa. We found domain buildings and a yard surrounded by a hedge and within 3 barns, 1 arpent of vines, 1 garden with trees, 15 geese, 20 chickens.

In a third villa, domain buildings. It has 2 barns, 1 granary, 1 garden, 1 yard well enclosed by a hedge.

We found all the dry and liquid measures just as in the palace. We did not find any goldsmiths, silver-smiths, blacksmiths, huntsmen or persons engaged in other services.

The garden herbs which we found were . . . [list follows]

E. Paschasius Radbertus Praises Carolingian Scholarship

Paschasius: The truth is that from boyhood Prior Arsenius extended his fame by soldiery and high office. He was a first cousin of the greatest of the august ones [Charlemagne] and dearer to him than all others. He was "in speech truthful" (as is said of one whose ashes recently brought among us have glis-tened with many miracles), upright in judgment, far-sighted in counsel, and most faithful in trust." In meetings of the senate he was by his talent more capa-ble than all the others. If he were questioned about any kind of transaction, he replied immediately what-ever could be said or devised, and his words flowed as if from a fountain of wisdom. Already his virtue was the loftiest, his authority vastly extended, both rec-ommended by goodness and nobility of character and nation. . . .

Adeodatus: If he was that kind of man, why did he so often lament that he was begotten as "a man of strife and discord," although you say that he was beloved by everyone?

F. The Viking Onslaught: Chronicle Extracts

Lothaire and Louis dwelt each in the confines of his own kingdom and kept the peace. Charles was marching about Aquitaine. . . . In the terrible and increasing calamities of the time and the general dev-astation, many men in various parts of Gaul were forced to eat a kind of bread made of earth and a lit-tle flour. It was an abominable crime that men should be reduced to eat earth, when the horses of those who were devastating the land were plentifully supplied with fodder.

Pirates of the Northmen's race came to the city of Nantes. They killed the bishop of many of the clergy and laity, both men and women, and plundered the city. Then they marched away to lay waste the land of lower Aquitaine. Finally they reached a certain island [Rhé, near Rochelle], and took thither from the mainland materials to build them houses; and they settled there for the winter as if it were a fixed habitation.

Charles betook himself to a rendezvous with his brothers, and joined them at Verdun; and there they divided the land among them. Louis had as his portion everything beyond the Rhine, and on this side of the Rhine the cities and districts of Speyer, Worms, and Mayence. Lothaire received the territory between the Rhine and the Scheldt to their emptying into the sea, besides Cambria, Hennegau, Lomatschgau, and the provinces on the left bank of the Maas, and further on to the place where the Saône joins the Rhone, and the counties along the Rhone on both banks to the sea. The other lands to the confines of Spain they ceded to Charles. When each had given his oath to the others they parted.

Twice in the canton of Worms there was an earthquake; the first in the night following Palm Sunday, the second in the holy night of Christ's Resurrection. In the same year the heathen broke in upon the Christians at many points, but more than twelve thousand of them were killed by the Frisians. Another party of invaders devastated Gaul; of these more than six hundred men perished. Yet owing to his indolence Charles agreed to give them many thousand pounds of gold and silver if they would leave Gaul, and this they did. Nevertheless the cloisters of most of the saints were destroyed and many of the Christians were led away captive.

After this had taken place King Louis once more led a force against the Wends. When the heathen had learned this they sent ambassadors, as well as gifts and hostages, to Saxony, and asked for peace. Louis then granted peace and returned home from Saxony. Thereafter the robbers were afflicted by a terrible pestilence, during which the chief sinner among them, by the name of Reginheri, who had plundered the Christians and the holy places, was struck down by the hand of God. They then took counsel and threw lots to determine from which of their gods they should seek safety; but the lots did not fall out happily, and on the advice of one of their Christian prisoners that they should cast their lot before the God of the Christians, they did so, and the lot fell happily. Then their king, by the name of Rorik, together with all the heathen people, refrained from meat and drink for fourteen days, when the plague ceased, and they sent back all their Christian prisoners to their country.

Document Set 9.3 References

A. Einhard Describes Charlemagne
   Einhard, *Life of Charlemagne*, in James Harvey Robinson, ed., *Readings in European History* (Boston: Ginn, 1904), 1:126–128.
B. Charlemagne Forcibly Christianizes the Saxons
   From Capitulary "De Partibus Saxoniae," in *Translations and Reprints from the Original Sources of European History* (Philadelphia: University of Pennsylvania Press, 1898), 4/2:2–5.
C. Charlemagne Permits the "Ordeal of the Cross" in Insoluble Judicial Cases
   Translations and Reprints, 4/4:16.
D. Inspecting the Imperial Domains: The Capitulary "De Villis" and an Estate Inventory
   Translations and Reprints, 3/2:2–5.
E. Paschasius Radbertus Praises Carolingian Scholarship
   Allen Cabaniss, trans., *Charlemagne's Cousins: Contemporary Lives of Adalard and Wala* (Syracuse: Syracuse University Press, 1967), 88–89.
F. The Viking Onslaught: Chronicle Extracts
   Robinson, 1:157–159.

[handwritten margin note: To obtain labor — land grants (commendation)]

DOCUMENT SET 9.4
Monasteries, Lords, and Kings: The Origins of Feudalism

With the Carolingian collapse, Western Europeans desperately sought other foundations on which to erect a viable social and political order. Although the seductive imperial ideal was pursued by German kings after the mid-tenth century, it was feudalism that provided the from-the-ground-up basics for establishing a semblance of order. The roots of feudalism run at least as far back as the seventh-century Frankish practice of commendation (see Set 8.5, Document B), and with the West inundated by alien marauders and local desperadoes, pressures were intense for communities and monasteries to establish strongly reciprocal ties with whoever might plausibly offer protection. The documents of this set illustrate the process; read them with a view to writing a brief analysis of the origins of feudalism.

Document A is a model document for granting a *vill* (an estate with its attached peasants) to a man able to defend it and binding the grantee to render obedience or aid to the monastery or territorial lord who bestows the grant. What significance do you attach to the fact that this is a fill-in-the-blanks form?

An early and well-documented case study in a chartered medieval institution is afforded by the monastery of Cluny, founded in 910 by a Burgundian lord (Document B); notice the eloquent threats of divine vengeance on any who may violate its terms. Document C shows how Cluny grew with subsequent donations by other lords.

Law enforcement remained highly tenuous. Raoul Glabar, a chronicler active around the year 1000, relates how King Robert of France tried in vain to keep his feudal subordinates in line (Document D); and in Document E, an extract from a German chronicle for the year 1033 describes what happened when recourse was had in the "judicial duel," in which God was expected to reveal which party was in the right. About 1020 the bishop of Chartres, Fulbert, wrote to the Duke of Aquitaine describing how feudal relations ought to be observed (Document F). And the coronation oath sworn in 978 by the Anglo-Saxon King Ethelred II (Document G) succinctly promises to maintain peace and contractual obligations in his realm. Both were theoretical expressions of how the emerging feudal society ought to operate. Using the documents in this set and what you have learned in studying *The Challenge of the West,* write a brief essay on how feudalism came into being.

A. Granting a Vill to a Layman: A Feudal Formula

[handwritten note: Generic]

Therefore, may your Greatness . . . know that we have seen fit to concede by our ready will to — —, an illustrious man, the vill named —, situated in the district of —, completely, with its whole proper boundary, as it has been possessed by — —, or by our treasury, or is possessed at this present time. Wherefore, by this our present command, we have decreed forever that the person aforesaid should have the abovementioned vill, in its entirety, with the lands, houses, buildings, villeins, slaves, vineyards, woods, field, meadows, pastures, waters or watercourses, gristmills, additions, appurtenances, including any class of men who are subjected to our treasury who dwell there; in entire immunity, and without the entrance of any one of the judges for the purpose of exacting fines for any kind of case. He shall have, hold, and possess it in proprietary right and without expecting the entrance of any of our judges; and may with our good will leave it to his posterity, by the aid of God, or to whom he will; by our permission he shall hereafter be free to do with it what he will. And in order that this concession may be observed the more strictly, we have determined that it should be corroborated below with our own hand.

B. Count William Charters the Monastery of Cluny

[handwritten note: 910]

To all right thinkers it is clear that the providence of God has so provided for certain rich men that, by means of their transitory possessions, if they use them well, they may be able to merit everlasting rewards. As to which . . . I, William, count and duke by the grace of God, diligently pondering this, and desiring to provide for my own safety while I am still able, have considered it advisable—nay, most necessary, that from the temporal goods which have been conferred upon me I should give some little portion for the gain of my soul. I do this, indeed, in order that I who have thus increased in wealth, may not, perchance, at the last be accused of having spent all in caring for my body, but rather may rejoice, when fate at last shall snatch all things away, in having reserved something for myself. Which end, indeed, seems attainable by no more suitable means than that . . . I should support at my own expense a congregation of monks. And this is my trust, this my hope, indeed, that although I myself am unable to despise all things, nevertheless, by receiving despisers of the world, whom I believe to be righteous, I may receive the reward of the righteous. Therefore be it known to all . . . that, for the love of God and of our Saviour Jesus Christ, I hand over from my own rule to the holy apostles, Peter, namely, and Paul, the possessions over which I hold sway, the town of Cluny, namely, with the court and demesne manor, and the church in honour of St. Mary the mother of God and of St. Peter the prince of the apostles, together with all the things pertaining to it, the vills, indeed, the chapels, the serfs of both sexes, the vines, the fields, the meadows, the woods, the waters and their outlets, the mills, the incomes and revenues, what is cultivated and what is not, all in their entirety. Which things are situated in or about the country of Macon, each one surrounded by its own bounds. I give, moreover, all these things to the aforesaid apostles—I, William, and my wife Ingelberga—first for the love of God; then for soul of my lord king Odo, of my father and my mother; for myself and my wife—for the salvation, namely, of our souls and bodies;—and not least for that of Ava who left me these things in her will; for the souls also of our brothers and sisters and nephews, and of all our relatives of both sexes; for our faithful ones who adhere to our service; for the advancement, also, and integrity of the catholic religion. Finally, since all of us Christians are held together by one bond of love and faith, let this donation be for all,—for the ortho-dox, namely, of past, present or future times. I give these things, moreover, with this understanding, that in Cluny a regular monastery shall be constructed in honour of the holy apostles Peter and Paul, and that there the monks shall congregate and live according to the rule of St. Benedict, and that they shall possess, hold, have and order these same things unto all time. . . . [The monks are to be under the protection of the pope, and no one—not even the pope—is to dare to violate Cluny's rights.] ← removed from normal church hierarchy.

If any one—which Heaven forbid, and which, through the mercy of God and the protection of the apostles I do not think will happen,—whether he be a neighbour or a stranger, no matter what his condition or power, should, through any kind of wile, attempt to do any act of violence contrary to his deed of gift which we have ordered to be drawn up for love of almighty God and for reverence of the chief apostles Peter and Paul: first, indeed, let him incur the wrath of almighty God, and let God remove him from the land of the living and wipe out his name from the book of life, and let his portion be with those who said to the Lord God: Depart from us; and, with Dathan and Abiron whom the earth, opening its jaws, swallowed up, and hell absorbed while still alive, let him incur everlasting damnation. And being made a companion of Judas let him be kept thrust down there with eternal tortures, and, lest it seem to human eyes that he pass through the present world with impunity, let him experience in his own body, indeed, the torments of future damnation, sharing the double disaster with Heliodorus and Antiochus, of whom one being coerced with sharp blows scarcely escaped alive; and the other struck down by the divine will, his members putrefying and swarming with vermin, perished most miserably. . . .

I, William, commanded this act to be made and drawn up, and confirmed it with my own hand.

(Signed by Ingelberga and a number of bishops and nobles.)

C. A Donation to Cluny, 910

To the holy place, accessible to our prayers [et cetera]. I, Rotrudis, and [my husband] Josseran, and my sons, all of us give to God and his holy Apostles, Peter and Paul, [the saints to whom Cluny was dedicated] and at the place Cluny, half of a church that is located in the Mâconnais [the region in which Cluny was located], named in honor of St. Peter, along with everything that belongs to it, wholly and completely. And we give [property in] the *villa* that is called Curtil-sous-Buffières. There [we give] a field and a meadow that go together and have the name *ad Salas*. This land borders at the east on a road and a man-made wall; at the south on a meadow; at the west on a road, and similarly at the north. [I make this gift] for the salvation of the soul of my husband Josseran, and [for the soul of my son] Bernard. Done at Cluny. Witnesses: Rotrudis, Josseran, Bernard, Israel, Erleus, Hugo, Odo, Raimbert, Umbert. Ingelbald wrote this in the 28th year of the reign of King Lothar [i.e. in 981–982].

D. King Robert of France Struggles with His Unruly Vassals

King Robert, to whom the kingdom of the Franks then fell, was frequently subjected to the outrages of certain of his insolent subjects, especially of those whom Hugh, his father, and Hugh, his grandfather, or he himself, had, in spite of their base origin, raised from a humble condition to the highest dignities. At their head stood Eudes, the son of Thibaut of Chartres, known as the Trickster, who, with a great number of other less dangerous lords, seemed to revolt with the more pride the more clear their duty was to show themselves humble and submissive. Among these was Eudes II [count of Blois and of Chartres], son of the Eudes just mentioned, who outdid all others in power and perfidy. Now the count of Troyes and of Meaux, son of Heribert, and the king's cousin, having left no children, Eudes took possession, in spite of the king's opposition, of these vast domains, which ought in justice to have become part of the patrimony of King Robert. This same Eudes became involved in long contests and foreign wars with Foulques of Anjou. Both of them were puffed up with pride, and consequently were rarely in a pacific frame of mind.

E. The Embarrassing Outcome of a Judicial Ordeal by Combat in Eastern Germany

The emperor having levied a force in Saxony marched upon the Luitzes, a people who were formerly half Christians but who have wickedly apostatized and are now become thorough pagans. In their district he put an end to an implacable strife in a wonderful manner. Between the Saxons and the pagans at that time fighting and raids were being carried on incessantly, and when the emperor came he began to inquire which side had first broken the peace that had long been observed inviolate between them. The pagans said that the peace had been disturbed first by the Saxons, and they would prove this by the duel if the emperor would so direct. On the other side the Saxons pledged themselves to refute the pagans in like manner by single combat, though as a matter of fact their contention was untrue. The emperor after consulting his princes permitted the matter to be settled between them by a duel, though this was not a very wise act. Two champions, each selected by his own side, immediately engaged. The Christian, trusting in his faith alone, though faith without the works of justice if dead, began the attack fiercely without diligently considering that God who is the Truth, who maketh His sun to shine upon the evil and the good, and the rain to fall upon the just and the unjust, decides all things by a true judgment. The pagan on the other hand resisted stoutly, having before his eyes only the consciousness of the truth for which he was fighting. Finally the Christian fell wounded by the pagan. Thereupon his party were seized with such

elation and presumption that, had the emperor not been present, they would forthwith have rushed upon the Christians; but the emperor constructed the fortress Werben in which he place a garrison of soldiers to check their incursions and bound the Saxon princes by an oath and by the imperial commands to a unanimous resistance against the pagans. Then he returned to Franconia.

F. Fulbert of Chartres Explains the Mutual Duties of Vassals and Lords, 1020

Asked to write something concerning the form of fealty, I have noted briefly for you, on the authority of the books, the things which follow. He who swears fealty to his lord ought always to have these six things in memory: what is harmless, safe, honorable, useful, easy, practicable. *Harmless,* that is to say, that he should not injure his lord in his body; *safe,* that he should not injure him by betraying his secrets or the defenses upon which he relies for safety; *honorable,* that he should not injure him in his justice or in other matters that pertain to his honor; *useful,* that he should not injure him in his possessions; *easy* and *practicable,* that that good which his lord is able to do easily he make not difficult, nor that which is practicable he make not impossible to him.

That the faithful vassal should avoid these injuries is certainly proper, but not for this alone does he deserve his holding; for it is not sufficient to abstain from evil, unless what is good is done also. It remains, therefore, that in the same six things mentioned above he should faithfully counsel and aid his lord, if he wishes to be looked upon as worthy of his benefice and to be safe concerning the fealty which he has sworn.

The lord also ought to act toward his faithful vassal reciprocally in all these things. And if he does not do this, he will be justly considered guilty of bad faith, just as the former, if he should be detected in avoiding or consenting to the avoidance of his duties, would be perfidious and perjured.

I would have written to you at greater length, if I had not been occupied with many other things, including the rebuilding of our city and church, which was lately entirely consumed in a terrible fire; from which loss, though we could not for a while be diverted, yet by the hope of God's comfort and of yours we breathe again.

compare to 8.5.B + 9.4 A

reciprocity: mutual relationship

G. The Coronation Oath of Ethelred II, 978

In the name of the Holy Trinity, three things do I promise to this Christian people, my subjects; first, that I will hold God's church and all the Christian people of my realm in true peace; second, that I will forbid all rapine and injustice to men of all conditions; third, that I promise and enjoin justice and mercy in all judgments, in order that a just and merciful God may give us all His eternal favor, who liveth and reigneth.

Document Set 9.4 References

A. Granting a Vill to a Layman: A Feudal Formula
James Harvey Robinson, ed., *Readings in European History* (Boston: Ginn, 1904), 1:172–173.
B. Count William Charters the Monastery of Cluny
E. F. Henderson, *Select Historical Documents of the Middle Ages* (London: 1892), 329–333.
C. A Donation to Cluny, 910
Trans. Barbara H. Rosenwein, 1993, n.p.
D. King Robert of France Struggles with His Unruly Vassals
Robinson, 196–197.
E. The Embarrassing Outcome of a Judicial Ordeal by Combat in Eastern Germany
Translations and Reprints from the Original Sources of European History (Philadelphia: University of Pennsylvania Press, 1898), 4/4:19–20.
F. Fulbert of Chartres Explains the Mutual Duties of Vassals and Lords, 1020
Translations and Reprints, 4/3:184–185.
G. The Coronation Oath of Ethelred II, 978
Translations and Reprints, 4/6:2.

CHAPTER
10

Vitality and Reform, 1054–1144

Papal Reform

The papacy reached its nadir in the tenth century, when it was controlled by the chief potentate of the Roman region, an unscrupulous and powerful Germanic prince named Alberic, who put his own son Octavian on the throne as Pope John XII in 955. The chronicle excerpted as Document A describes this pope's behavior and the circumstances under which Otto the Great, the Saxon king of Germany, intervened to put a more seemly but utterly dependent pope on the throne.

Consider this background when reading the documents that follow, all of which relate to the eleventh-century church reform movement headed by Pope Gregory VII. Document B records the condemnation of simony and clerical marriage by a synod (church council) under Gregory's leadership in 1074; why did these offenses become the focal point of reform efforts? In Documents C and D, Gregory sets forth his exalted conception of papal authority; again, how do such sweeping claims fit with the evident need to rout out corruption from the church? (Document D dates from 1081 and is addressed to a German bishop, justifying the papal excommunication and deposition of Emperor Henry IV.)

Document E deals with another clash between the papacy and its opponents: the mutual excommunications of the pope and the Orthodox patriarch in 1054. How do they fit into the pattern of papal-led reform?

A. Chronicles Reveal the Sorry State of the Tenth-Century Papacy

Octavian was elected to the holy see and was called John XII. He led a life so licentious and so openly wicked that he might have been a heathen. He hunted constantly, not as a pope but like a wild man. He was given over to vain desires and surrounded himself with a crowd of evil women. So great was his iniquity that it cannot be told.

Now there were in the city of Rome a deacon of the holy Roman church named John, and Azzo, a papal scribe, who hated the pontiff. Because his life was so evil, we consulted how we might call the Saxon kings into Italy to possess the Roman power. John and Azzo were sturdy men, and they were of one heart and one mind,—that it were better to do the pontiff to death than to let him live, and that the Roman power should be bestowed upon the Saxon king, to the end that he might rule justly as the protector of holy Church. They sent legates to Otto, the first Saxon king, asking him to come and possess Italy and the Roman power.

The pope heard of this plot. He seized John the deacon and Azzo the scribe. He ordered the hand to be cut off with which Azzo had written the letter to Otto, and had John the deacon's nose cut off. . . .

Otto the king came into Italy [961] with a great multitude of people that well-nigh filled the face of the earth like locusts. He had with him many nations whose tongues the people did not know. The Roman people met him, together with the pontiff, and

Connection to crusades?

47
63

received him honorably. Masses were celebrated in the church of the chief of the apostles. Otto was extolled with high praises, and was called "August." In this wise was the Italian kingdom, or the Roman power, made subject to the Saxon king.

The king and the queen, whose name was Adelaide, were crowned in the church of the chief of the apostles; and they gave many gifts throughout the holy Roman church. Then much trouble came upon the Italian kingdom, for it was devastated by pestilence, famine, fire, and sword. The cattle perished, the land became a wilderness, and the famine ever increased.

A great conflict arose between the emperor and the pope,—how, we do not say. John withdrew into Campania, leaving the apostolic see for fear of the emperor. The Romans were in great confusion, and they begged the emperor that he would elect a certain Leo pope. This seemed good to the emperor, and Leo was elected and enthroned in the most holy see. . . .

The Romans, as was their ancient habit, were divided among themselves; and John the pope was recalled from Campania, and entered Rome with a strong army. Leo took flight and withdrew to a distance. They say he went across the Alps. Not long afterward the emperor returned with the pope and a great army into Italy. John the pope heard of the king's furious onslaughts: he left Rome and fled to Campania. [Soon after, he died.] The Romans elected Benedict, the subdeacon, pope, a prudent man well versed in grammar.

The emperor heard of this schism and grew very angry. How swore by his royal power that he would besiege the city of Rome on all sides unless Benedict would give way to the rightful pope [Leo]. Rome was surrounded by the people of the Lombards, the Saxons, and the Gauls, in a great circle, so that none dared to go beyond the walls. Fire and sword caused great famine in Rome, and the hearts of the people quailed within them because their strength was brought to naught. There was but one voice among them from the least to the greatest. Forced by dire need, they took Benedict the pope and gave him into the hands of the emperor, and said to one another: "It is better for one alone to die for all, that we may save all other lives from destruction by hunger." The emperor sent the pontiff into exile in Saxony, and Leo returned to the most sacred seat, amid the praises of the Roman people. . . .

Woe unto thee, Rome, oppressed and trodden under foot by so many nations! Thou art taken captive by the Saxon king, thy people are put to the sword, thy strength is brought to naught. Thy gold and thy silver are carried away in their purses. The mother thou wast—a daughter thou hast become. What thou hadst, thou hast lost. Thou art despoiled of thy former strength. . . .

Formerly, glorying in thy power, thou hast triumphed over nations, hast cast the world into the dust, hast strangled the kings of the earth. Thou hast grasped the scepter and wielded great power. Now art thou plundered and utterly despoiled by the Saxon king. As some wise men say, and as it will be found written in thy histories, thou didst once fight with foreign nations and conquer them from north to south. Now the people of Gaul have encamped in the midst of thee. Thou wast too beautiful.

B. The Roman Council of 1074 Condemns Simony and Clerical Marriage

buying or selling of church offices.

Pope Gregory [VII] held a synod in which he anathematized all who were guilty of simony. He also forbade all clergy who were married to say mass, and all laymen were forbidden to be present when such a married priest should officiate. In this he seemed to many to act contrary to the decisions of the holy fathers who have declared that the sacraments of the church are neither made more effective by the good qualities, nor less effective by the sins, of the officiating priest, because it is the Holy Spirit who makes them effective.

stability
God over man

create stability ← Established authority over other rulers.

C. Gregory VII's *Dictatus Papae* Outlines the Papal Reform Program

Clarification -

1074
↑
after Great Schism

The Roman church was founded by God alone.

The Roman bishop alone is properly called universal.

before secular rulers.

He alone may depose bishops and reinstate them.

His legate, though of inferior grade, takes precedence, in a council, of all bishops and may render a decision of deposition against them.

He alone may use the insignia of empire.

The pope is the only person whose feet are kissed by all princes.

His title is unique in the world.

He may depose emperors.

No council may be regarded as a general one without his consent.

No book or chapter may be regarded as canonical without his authority.

A decree of his may be annulled by no one; he alone may annul the decrees of all.

He may be judged by no one.

No one shall dare to condemn one who appeals to the papal see.

infallability

The Roman church has never erred, nor ever, by the witness of Scripture, shall err to all eternity.

He may not be considered Catholic who does not agree with the Roman church.

The pope may absolve the subjects of the unjust from their allegiance.

1081

D. Gregory VII Justifies Reform to Bishop Hermann of Metz

Who does not remember the words of our Lord and Savior Jesus Christ: "Thou are Peter and on this rock I will build my Church, and the gates of hell shall not prevail against it. And I will give thee the keys of the kingdom of heaven and whatsoever thou shalt bind on earth shall be bound in heaven and whatsoever thou shalt loose on earth shall be loosed in heaven."

religious over secular

Are kings excepted here? Or are they not of the sheep which the Son of God committed to St. Peter? . . .

Who does not know that kings and princes derive their origin from men ignorant of God who raised themselves above their fellows by pride, plunder, treachery, murder—in short by every kind of crime—at the instigation of the Devil, the prince of this world, men blind with greed and intolerable in their audacity? If, then, they strive to bend the priests of God to their will, to whom may they more properly be compared than to him who is chief over all the sons of pride? . . .

Every Christian king when he approaches his end asks the aid of a priest as a miserable supplicant that he may escape the prison of hell, may pass from darkness into light and may appear at the judgment seat of God freed from the bonds of sin. But who, layman or priest, in his last moments has ever asked the help of any earthly king for the safety of his soul? And what king or emperor has power through his office to snatch any Christian from the might of the Devil by the sacred rite of baptism, to confirm him among the sons of God and to fortify him by the holy chrism? Or—and this is the greatest thing in the Christian religion—who among them is able by his own word to create the body and blood of the Lord? or to whom among them is given the power to bind and loose in Heaven and upon earth? From this it is apparent how greatly superior in power is the priestly dignity.

E. The Papacy Looks Eastward: The Mutual Excommunications of 1054

A. Humbert's Anathema of Cerularius

Humbert, by the grace of God cardinal-bishop of the Holy Roman Church . . .:

. . . We have perceived a very great evil because of which we are extremely saddened. . . . Although admonished by our Lord Pope Leo regarding these errors . . ., Michael [Cerularius] himself has with contempt disregarded these warnings. . . . Indeed, . . . he cursed the Apostolic See, in opposition to which he signed himself "ecumenical patriarch." Wherefore, not putting up with this unheard-of slander and insult to the first, holy Apostolic See, and seeing the Catholic faith assaulted in many ways, we, . . . whatever our most reverend lord the pope has denounced in Michael and his followers, unless they repent, we declare to be anathematized:

"May Michael, false neophyte patriarch, . . . and . . . Leo the archdeacon . . ., and all their followers in the aforesaid errors and presumptions, be anathematized. . . .

B. Michael Cerularius and the Standing Synod Anathema of the Papal Legation

Decree in response to the bull of excommunication cast before the holy altar by the legates of Rome against the most Holy Patriarch Michael . . .:

When Michael, our most holy despot and ecumenical patriarch was presiding [over the Orthodox church] certain impious and disrespectful men . . . coming out of the darkness (they were begotten of the West)—came to this pious and God-protected city [Constantinople] from which the springs of orthodoxy flow. . . . To this city they came like a thunderbolt, or an earthquake, or a hailstorm, or . . . like wild wolves trying to defile the Orthodox belief. . . . Setting aside the Scriptures, they deposited [an excommunication] on the holy altar. . . .

. . . Moreover, they do not wish to comprehend and insist that the Holy Spirit proceeds not only from the Father but also from the Son, . . . [a] blasphemy against the holy doctrine.

In accordance with the foresight of our most pious emperor, that impious document [Humbert's Anathema] and those who deposited it or gave an opinion on its composition were placed under anathema. . . ."

Cluny

Bishop- no legitimate children
→ lands return to original owner

Document Set 10.1 References

A. Chronicles Reveal the Sorry State of the Tenth-Century
   Papacy
   James Harvey Robinson, ed., *Readings in European History*
   (Boston: Ginn, 1904), 1:253–255.
B. The Roman Council of 1074 Condemns Simony and Clerical
   Marriage
   O. J. Thatcher and E. H. McNeal, *A Source Book of Medieval
   History* (New York: Scribners, 1905), 134.
C. Gregory VII's *Dictatus Papae* Outlines the Papal Reform
   Program
   Robinson, 1:274–275.
D. Gregory VII Justifies Reform to Bishop Hermann of Metz
   Ephraim Emerton, ed. and trans., *The Correspondence of Pope
   Gregory VII* (New York: W. W. Norton, 1960), 167–171.
E. The Papacy Looks Eastward: The Mutual Excommunications
   of 1054
   Deno John Geanokoplos, ed., *Byzantium: Church, Society,
   and Civilization Seen Through Contemporary Eyes* (Chicago:
   University of Chicago Press, 1984), 208–212.

This page is blank because permission was denied to use a particular document. It will be corrected in a subsequent printing.

DOCUMENT SET 10.2
The Investiture Conflict

Document A, taken from the chronicle of Ekkehard of Aurach, provides a vivid and generally reliable account of the state of affairs in the Germany of Emperor Henry IV. In Document B, Gregory VII in 1076 takes on Henry over his refusal to accept the papacy's reform decrees; Henry gives Gregory an appropriately hostile response. What claims to authority does each put forward?

Document C, dating from 1078, is a crucial Roman decree forbidding lay investiture. It is directed primarily against the authority of Henry IV to control the church in areas under his rule. And Document D spells out the terms of the final compromise—the Concordant of Worms, between Pope Calixtus II and Emperor Henry V in 1122.

The Investiture Conflict was once viewed by historians as primarily a church-state affair. Using the documents in this set (and also those in Set 10.1), assess the extent to which "church" and "state" are adequate terms with which to define the contending sides.

A. Ekkehard of Aurach Chronicles the Early Years of Henry IV's Reign

In the year of our Lord 1064, Siegfried, bishop of Mayence, Gunther of Babenberg, and William of Utrecht, along with many other bishops and noblemen, set forth with a great following on a pilgrimage to Jerusalem. Here they suffered much from the attacks of the barbarians, but finally, having happily reached their goal they returned, greatly reduced in numbers and strength. . . .

In the year of our Lord 1066, a comet glowed long over the whole earth[1]. In the same year England was terribly desolated by the Norman William and finally subjugated, and he had himself made king. He then drove almost all the bishops of the said kingdom into banishment and had the nobles killed. The commons he gave over in bondage to his knights, and he compelled the wives of the natives to marry the invaders.

In the year of our Lord 1067, King Henry took to wife Bertha, daughter of a certain Otto, an Italian, and of Adelheid; and he celebrated the wedding at Tribur. Conrad, councilor of the church of Cologne,

[1] Haley's comet.

whom King Henry had designated as bishop of Treves, was taken prisoner by Theodoric, count of that city, and was carried into the forest by his followers and thrown down three times from the top of a mountain, but since he still remained unhurt, they dispatched him with a sword.

In the year of our Lord 1068, King Henry, with youthful recklessness, began to reside in Saxony alone of all the Roman Empire, to despise the princes, oppress the nobles, exalt the lowborn, and to devote himself (as was said) to the chase, to gaming and other occupations of this kind, more than to the administration of justice. He married the daughters of the nobles to his favorites of low origin, and, full of distrust against the powerful of the empire, he began to build certain castles. By thus recklessly sowing the seeds of discord it fell out that the number of those who proposed to deprive the king not only of his kingdom but even of his life grew rapidly. However, as he had not yet fully reached the years of maturity, many judged that the responsibility did not fall so much upon him as upon Archbishop Adelbert of Bremen, since everything was done on his advice.

In the year of our Lord 1069, the Empress Agnes, mother of King Henry, through vexation, or better, through divine inspiration, surrendered the duchy of Bavaria, and, discarding the reins of government in her devotion to Christ, betook herself to Rome, where, with marvelous humility, she brought forth the fruits of repentance and after a few years closed this earthly life in the Lord.

B. Henry IV and Gregory VII Trade Curses, 1076

Bishop Gregory, servant of the servants of God, to King Henry, greeting and apostolic benediction: —that is, if he be obedient to the apostolic chair as beseems a Christian king:

For we cannot but hesitate to send thee our benediction when we seriously consider the strictness of the Judge to whom we shall have to render account for the ministry intrusted to us by St. Peter, chief of the apostles. For thou art said knowingly to associate with men excommunicated by a judgment of the apostolic chair and by sentence of a synod. If this be true, thou thyself dost know that thou mayest not receive the favor of the divine, nor of the apostolic benediction, unless those who have been excommunicated be separated from thee and compelled to do penance, and thou, with condign repentance and satisfaction, obtain absolution and pardon for thy misdeeds. Therefore we counsel thy Highness that, if thou dost feel thyself guilty in this matter, thou shouldst seek the advice of some devout bishop, with prompt confession. He, with our permission, enjoining on thee a proper penance for this fault, shall absolve thee, and shall take care to inform us by letter, with thy consent, of the exact measure of thy penance.

In the next place, it seems strange to us that although thou dost so often send us such devoted letters; and although thy Highness dost show such humility in the messages of thy legates,—calling thyself the son of holy mother Church and of ourselves, subject in the faith, foremost in love and devotion;—although, in short, thou dost commend thyself with all the sweetness of devotion and reverence, yet in conduct and action thou dost show thyself most stubborn, and in opposition to the canonical and apostolic decrees in those matters which the religion of the Church deems of chief importance. . . . And now, indeed, inflicting wound upon wound, thou hast, contrary to the rules of the apostolic chair, given the churches of Fermo and Spoleto—if indeed a church can be given or granted by a mere man—to certain persons not even known to us, on whom, unless they are previously well known and proven, it is not lawful regularly to perform the laying on of hands.

It would have beseemed thy royal dignity, since thou dost confess thyself a son of the Church, to have treated more respectfully the master of the Church,—that is, St. Peter, the chief of the apostles. For to him, if thou art of the Lord's sheep, thou wast given over by the Lord's voice and authority to be fed; Christ himself saying, "Peter, feed my sheep." And again: "To thee are given over the keys of the kingdom of heaven; and whatsoever thou shalt bind on earth shall be bound in heaven; and whatsoever thou shalt loose on earth shall be loosed in heaven."

Inasmuch as in his seat and apostolic ministration we, however sinful and unworthy, do, by the providence of God, act as the representative of his power, surely he himself is receiving whatever, in writing or by word of mouth, thou hast sent to us. And at the very time when we are either perusing thy letters or listening to the voices of those who speak for thee, he himself is observing, with discerning eye, in what spirit the instructions were issued. Wherefore thy Highness should have seen to it that no lack of good will should appear toward the apostolic chair in they words and messages. . . .

In this year a synod was assembled about the apostolic chair, over which the heavenly dispensation willed that we should preside, and at which some of thy faithful subjects were present. Seeing that the good order of the Christian religion has now for some time been disturbed, and that the chief and proper methods of winning souls have, at the instigation of the devil, long been neglected and suppressed, we, struck by the danger and impending ruin of the Lord's flock, reverted tome decrees and teachings of the holy fathers,—decreeing nothing new, nothing of our own invention. . . .

Lest these things should seem unduly burdensome or unjust to thee, we did admonish thee, through thy faithful servants, that the changing of an evil custom should not alarm thee; that thou shouldst send to us wise and religious men from thy land, to demonstrate or prove, if they could, by any reasoning, in what respects, saving the honor of the Eternal King and without danger to our soul, we might moderate the decree as passed by the holy fathers, and we would yield to their counsels. Even without our friendly admonitions it would have been but right that, before thou didst violate apostolic decrees, thou shouldst reasonably have appealed to us in cases where we oppressed thee or infringed thy prerogatives. But how little thou didst esteem our commands or the dictates of justice is shown by those things which thou afterwards didst.

But since the long-suffering patience of God still invites thee to amend thy ways, we have hopes that thy understanding may be awakened, and thy heart and mind be bent to obey the mandates of God: we exhort thee with paternal love to recognize the dominion of Christ over thee and to reflect how dangerous it is to prefer thine own honor to his.

Henry, King not by usurpation but by holy ordination of God, to Hildebrand, now no Pope but false monk:

Such greeting as this hast thou merited through thy disturbances, for there is no rank in the Church but thou hast brought upon it, not honor but disgrace, not a blessing but a curse. To mention a few notable cases out of the many, thou hast not only dared to assail the rulers of the holy Church, the anointed of the Lord,—archbishops, bishops, and priests,—but thou hast trodden them under foot like slaves ignorant of what their master is doing. By so crushing them thou hast won the favor of the common herd; thou hast regarded them all as knowing nothing,—thyself alone as knowing all things. Yet this knowledge thou hast exerted, not for their advantage but for their destruction; so that with reason we believe St. Gregory, whose name thou hast usurped, prophesied of thee when he said, "The pride of the magistrate commonly waxes great if the number of those subject to him be great, and he thinks that he can do more than they all."

We, forsooth, have endured all this in our anxiety to save the honor of the apostolic see, but thou hast mistaken our humility for fear, and hast, accordingly, ventured to attack the royal power conferred upon us by God, and threatened to divest us of it. As if we had received our kingdom from thee! As if the kingdom and the empire were in thy hands, not in God's! For our Lord Jesus Christ did call us to the kingdom, although he has not called thee to the priesthood: that thou hast attained by the following steps.

By craft abhorrent to the profession of monk, thou hast acquired wealth; by wealth, influence; by influence, arms; by arms, a throne of peace. And from the throne of peace thou hast destroyed peace; thou hast turned subjects against their governors, for thou, who wert not called of God, hast taught that our bishops, truly so called, should be despised. Thou hast put laymen above their priests, allowing them to depose or condemn those whom they themselves had received as teachers from the hand of God through the laying on of bishops' hands.

Thou hast further assailed me also, who, although unworthy of anointing, have nevertheless been anointed to the kingdom, and who, according to the traditions of the holy fathers, am subject to the judgment of God alone, to be deposed upon no charge save that of deviation from the faith,—which God avert! For the holy fathers by their wisdom committed the judgment and deposition of even Julian the Apostate not to themselves but to God alone. Likewise the true pope, Peter, himself exclaims: "Fear God. Honor the king." But thou, who dost not fear God, art dishonoring me, his appointed one. Wherefore, St. Paul, since he spared not an angel of heaven if he should preach other than the gospel, has not excepted thee, who dost teach other doctrine upon earth. For he says, "If any one, whether I, or an angel from heaven, shall preach the gospel other than that which has been preached to you, he shall be damned."

Thou, therefore, damned by this curse and by the judgment of all our bishops and ourselves, come down and relinquish the apostolic chair which thou hast usurped. Let another assume the seat of St. Peter, who will not practice violence under the cloak of religion, but will teach St. Peter's wholesome doctrine. I, Henry, king by the grace of God, together with all our bishops, say unto thee: "Come down, come down, to be damned throughout all eternity!"

biblical references

C. Gregory VII Condemns Lay Investiture, 1078

Inasmuch as we have learned that, contrary to the ordinances of the holy fathers, the investiture with churches is, in many places, performed by lay persons, and that from this cause many disturbances arise in the Church by which the Christian religion is degraded, we decree that no one of the clergy shall receive the investiture with a bishopric, or abbey, or church, from the hand of an emperor, or king, or of any lay person, male or female. If he shall presume to do so, let him know that such investiture is void by apostolic authority, and that he himself shall lie under excommunication until fitting satisfaction shall have been made.

D. A Compromise Settles the Investiture Conflict, 1122

I, Bishop Calixtus, servant of the servants of God, do grant to thee, beloved son Henry, by the grace of God emperor august of the Romans, permission to hold the elections of the bishops and abbots of the German realm who belong to the kingdom, in thy presence, without simony or show of violence; with the understanding that, should any discord arise among those concerned, thou, by the counsel and judgment of the metropolitan and the suffragan bishops, shalt give support and aid to the party which appears to have the better case. Moreover the one elected may receive the regalia from thee through the scepter, subject to no exactions; and he shall perform his lawful duties to thee for them.

He who is consecrated in other parts of the empire [i.e. in Burgundy or Italy] shall, within six months and subject to no exactions, receive the regalia from thee through the scepter, and shall perform his lawful duties for them, saving all rights which are known to pertain to the Roman Church. In whatever cases thou shalt make complaint to me and ask my help, I, as my office requires, will furnish thee aid. I grant, moreover, to thee, and to all those who are or have been of thy party during this conflict, a true peace.

In the name of the holy and indivisible Trinity, I, Henry, by the grace of God emperor august of the Romans, for the love of God and of the holy Roman Church and of our lord, Pope Calixtus, and for the cleansing of my soul, do surrender to God and to the holy apostles of God, Peter and Paul, and to the holy Catholic Church, all investiture through the ring and the staff; and do agree that in all churches throughout my kingdom and empire there shall be canonical elections and free consecration.

All the property and regalia of St. Peter which have been seized upon from the beginning of this conflict until this day and which I now hold I restore to that same holy Roman Church; and will faithfully aid in the restoration of that which is not in my own hands. The goods also of all other churches and princes and of every one, whether lay or ecclesiastical, which have been lost in the struggle, I will restore, as far as I hold them, according to the counsel of the princes and the behests of justice. I will also faithfully promote the restoration of that which I do not hold.

And I grant a true peace to our master, Pope Calixtus, and to the holy Roman Church, and to all those who are or have been on its side. In matters where the holy Roman Church shall seek assistance, I will faithfully render it, and whensoever it shall appeal to me I will see that justice is done.

All this has been done by the consent and counsel of the princes, whose names are here added. . . .

Document Set 10.2 References

A. Ekkehard of Aurach Chronicles the Early Years of Henry IV's Reign
   James Harvey Robinson, ed., *Readings in European History* (Boston: Ginn, 1904), 1:267–268.
B. Henry IV and Gregory VII Trade Curses, 1076
   Robinson, 1:267–268.
C. Gregory VII Condemns Lay Investiture, 1078
   Robinson, 1:275.
D. A Compromise Settles the Investiture Conflict, 1122
   Concordat or Worms, in Robinson, 1:292–293.

DOCUMENT SET 10.3
Lay Piety and Rebelliousness

The documents in this set demonstrate some discussions of the reforming Western church's relationship with lay society in the eleventh and twelfth centuries.

Document A is a "truce of God," one of many such agreements sponsored by the church, in this case injured by the Synod of Clermont in 1095—the same gathering at which Pope Urban II launched the First Crusade (see Set 10.4).

One of the most far-reaching activities of bishops at this time was the chartering of urban institutions in their cathedral towns. Document B shows the Bishop of Speyer (a German town on the Rhine River) bestowing on Jews the right to settle in that town. What benefit did the bishop derive from this arrangement, and how does it appear that the townspeople felt about it?

In 1074, the town of Cologne, also on the Rhine, was ruled by an archbishop whose interests and prerogatives often clashed with those of the townspeople. Document C shows the merchants leading an uprising against the archbishop. Though it was not successful, another uprising in 1106 drove the archbishop out of the city and established a measure of urban self-government.

The last two documents reveal the growing piety of Western lay people. Christina of Markyate (c. 1096–c. 1155) came from a well-to-do English family. She fled from a marriage to which she had been forced and lived first as a recluse, then as a nun. Here, in about 1122, her unknown biographer describes one of her many visions. Notice the significance of the Virgin Mary and of the symbolism of light, both characteristic of spiritual writings of the age. Document E describes the parallel experience of the Englishman St. Godric of Finchdale (c. 1065–1170), who began life as a peddler and possibly a pirate and ended it as a hermit. What does St. Godric's short biography tell you about his age and the kind of religious experience that a successful man of the world could undergo? Notice the references to St. Godric's pilgrimages. How do the documents of this set fit in with the overall pattern of church-led reforms with which earlier sets in this chapter have dealt?

A. An Attempt to Control Disorder: A Truce of God

Be it enacted, that monks, clergymen, women, and those who may be with them, shall remain in peace every day; farther, on three days, viz., the second, third and fourth days of the week, an injury done to any one shall not be considered an infraction of the Peace; but on the remaining four days, if any one injures another, he shall be considered a violator of the Sacred Peace, and shall be punished in the manner decreed.

B. The Bishop of Speyer Issues a Charter to the Jews of Speyer, 1084

1. In the name of the holy and undivided Trinity. I, Rudeger, by cognomen Huozman, humble bishop of Speyer, when I wished to make a city of my village of Speyer, thought that it would greatly add to its honor if I should establish some Jews in it. I have therefore collected some Jews and located them in a place apart from the dwellings and association of the other inhabitants of the city; and that they may be protected from the attacks and violence of the mob, I have surrounded their quarter with a wall. The land for their dwellings I had acquired in a legal way; for the hill [on which they are to live] I secured partly by purchase and partly by trade, and the valley [which I have given them] I received as a gift from the heirs who possessed it. I have given them this hill and valley on condition that they pay every year three and one-half pounds of money coined in the mint of Speyer, for the use of the brothers [monks of some monastery which is not named here].

2. I have given them the free right of changing gold and silver coins and of buying and selling everything they wish within their own walls and outside the gate clear up to the beat landing [on the Rhine] and also on the wharf itself. And they have the same right throughout the whole city.

3. Besides, I have given them a piece of the land of the church as a burial-ground. This land they shall hold forever.

4. I have also granted that, if a Jew comes to them from some other place and is their guest for a time, he shall pay no tolls [to the city].

5. The chief priest of their synagogue shall have the same position and authority among them as the

mayor of the city has among the citizens. He shall judge all the cases which arise among them or against them. If he is not able to decide any case it shall be taken before the bishop or his chamberlain.

6. They are bound to watch, guard, and defend only their own walls, in which work their servants may assist them.

7. They may hire Christian nurses and Christian servants.

8. The meats which their law forbids them to eat they may sell to Christians, and the Christians may buy them.

9. To add to my kindness to them I grant them the most favorable laws and conditions that the Jews have in any city of the German kingdom. . . .

C. Cologne Revolts Against Its Archbishop

The archbishop spent Easter in Cologne with his friend, the bishop of Munster, whom he had invited to celebrate this festival with him. When the bishop was ready to go home, the archbishop ordered his servants to get a suitable boat ready for him. They looked all about, and finally found a good boat which belonged to a rich merchant of the city, and demanded it for the archbishop's use. They ordered it to be got ready at once and threw out all the merchandise with which it was loaded. The merchant's servants, who had charge of the boat, resisted, but the archbishop's men threatened them with violence unless they immediately obeyed. The merchant's servants hastily ran to their lord and told him what had happened to the boat, and asked him what they should do. The merchant had a son who was both bold and strong. He was related to the great families of the city, and, because of his character, very poplar. He hastily collected his servants and as many of the young men of the city as he could, rushed to the boat, ordered the servants of the archbishop to get out of it, and violently ejected them from it. . . . The riot in the city was finally quieted a little, but the young man, who was very angry as well as elated over his first success, kept on making all the disturbance he could. He went about the city making speeches to the people about the harsh government of the archbishop, and accused him of laying unjust burdens on the people, [and] of depriving innocent persons of their property.

D. Christina of Markyate, a Twelfth-Century English Nun, Beholds the Virgin

A wonderful thing, more wonderful than any wonder, happened. For once when [Christina] was at prayer and was shedding tears through her longing for heaven, she was suddenly snatched above the clouds up to heaven, where she saw the queen of heaven sitting on a throne and angels in brightness seated about her. Their brightness exceeded that of the sun by as much as the radiance of the sun exceeds that of the stars. Yet the light of the angels could not be compared to the light which surrounded her who was the mother of the Most High. How great, then, do you think was the brightness of her countenance which outshone all the rest? Yet as [Christina] gazed first at the angels and then at the mistress of the angels, by some marvellous power she was better able to see through the splendor that surrounded the mistress than through that which shone about the angels, even though the weakness of human sight finds brighter things harder to bear. She saw [Mary's] countenance, therefore, more clearly than those of the angels. And while [Christina] gazed upon [Mary's] beauty more avidly and was filled with delight, the Queen turned to one of the angels standing by and said: "Ask Christina what she wants, because I will give her whatever she asks."

E. From Merchant to Monk: The Career of St. Godric of Finchdale

When the boy had passed his childless years quietly at home, then, as he began to grow to manhood, he began to follow more prudent ways of life, and to learn carefully and persistently the teachings of worldly forethought. Wherefore he chose not to follow the life of a husbandman [farmer] but rather to study, learn, and exercise the rudiments of more subtle conceptions. For this reason, aspiring to the merchant's trade, he began to follow the chapman's [peddler] way of life, first learning how to gain in small bargains and things of insignificant price; and thence, while yet a youth, his mind advanced little by little to buy and sell and gain from things of greater expense. For, in his beginnings, he was wont to wander with small wares around the villages and farmsteads of his own neighbourhood; but, in process of time, he gradually associated himself by compact with city merchants. Hence, within a brief space of time, the youth who had trudged for many weary hours from village to village, from farm to farm, did so profit by his increase of age and wisdom as to travel with associates of his own age through towns and boroughs, fortresses and cities, to fairs and to all the various booths of the market-place, in pursuit of his public chaffer [bargaining]. He went along the highway, neither puffed up by the good testimony of his conscience nor downcast in the nobler part of his soul by the reproach of poverty. . . .

Yet in all things he walked with simplicity; and, in so far as he yet knew how, it was ever his pleasure to follow in the footsteps of the truth. For, having learned the Lord's Prayer and the Creed from his very cradle, he oftentimes turned them over in his mind, even as he went alone on his longer journeys; and, in so far as the truth was revealed to his mind, he clung thereunto most devoutly in all his thoughts concerning God. At first, he lived as a chapman [peddler] for four years in Lincolnshire, going on foot and carrying the smallest wares; then he travelled abroad, first to St. Andrews in Scotland and then for the first time to Rome. On his return, having formed a familiar friendship with certain other young men who were eager for merchandise, he began to launch upon bolder courses and to coast frequently by sea to the foreign lands that lay around him. Thus, sailing often to and fro between Scotland and Britain, he traded in many divers wares and, amid these occupations, learned much worldly wisdom. . . .

Then he purchased the half of a merchant-ship with certain of his partners in the trade; and again by his prudence he bought the fourth part of another ship. At length, by his skill in navigation, wherein he excelled all his fellows, he earned promotion to the post of steersman. . . .

For he was vigorous and strenuous in mind, whole of limb and strong in body. He was of middle stature, broad-shouldered and deep-chested, with a long face, grey eyes most clear and piercing, bushy brows, a broad forehead, long and open nostrils, a nose of comely curve, and a pointed chin. His beard was thick, and longer than the ordinary, his mouth well-shaped, with lips of moderate thickness; in youth his hair was black, in age as white as snow; his neck was short and thick, knotted with veins and sinews; his legs were somewhat slender, his instep high, his knees hardened and horny with frequent kneeling; his whole skin rough beyond the ordinary, until all this roughness was softened by old age. . . .

And now he had lived sixteen years as a merchant, and began to think of spending on charity, to God's honour and service, the goods which he had so laboriously acquired. He therefore took the cross as a

pilgrim to Jerusalem, and, having visited the Holy Sepulchre, came back to England by way of St. James [of Compostella]. Not long afterwards he became steward to a certain rich man of his own country, with the care of his whole house and household. But certain of the younger household were men of iniquity, who stole their neighbours' cattle and thus held luxurious feasts, whereas Godric, in his ignorance, was sometimes present. Afterwards, discovering the truth, he rebuked and admonished them to cease; but they made no account of his warnings; wherefore he concealed not their iniquity, but disclosed it to the lord of the household, who, however, slighted his advice. Wherefore he begged to be dismissed and went on a pilgrimage, first to St. Gilles and thence to Rome the abode of the Apostles, that thus he might knowingly pay the penalty for those misdeeds wherein he had ignorantly partaken. I have often seen him, even in his old age, weeping for this unknowing transgression. . . .

Godric, when he had restored his mother safe to his father's arms, abode but a brief while at home; for he was now already firmly purposed to give himself entirely to God's service. Wherefore, that he might follow Christ the more freely, he sold all his possessions and distributed them among the poor. Then, telling his parents of this purpose and receiving their blessing, he went forth to no certain abode, but whithersoever the Lord should deign to lead him; for above all things he coveted the life of a hermit.

Document Set 10.3 References

A. An Attempt to Control Disorder: A Truce of God
William of Malmesbury, *The First Canon of the Council of Clermont*, in *Translations and Reprints from the Original Sources of European History* (Philadelphia: University of Pennsylvania Press, 1898), 1/2:8.
B. The Bishop of Speyer Issues a Charter to the Jews of Speyer, 1084
O. J. Thatcher and E. H. McNeal, *A Source Book of Mediaeval History* (New York: Scribners, 1905), 577–578.
C. Cologne Revolts Against Its Archbishop
Adapted from Thatcher and McNeal, 585–586.
D. Christina of Markyate, a Twelfth-Century English Nun, Beholds the Virgin
Adapted from C. H. Talbot, *The Life of Christina of Markyate, a Twelfth-Century Recluse* (Oxford: Clarendon Press, 1959), 109–110.
E. From Merchant to Monk: The Career of St. Godric of Finchdale
Reginald of Durham, "Life of St. Godric of Finchdale," in G. G. Coulton, *Social Life in Britain from the Conquest to the Reformation* (Cambridge: Cambridge University Press, 1918), 415–420.

1071 — Islam gains Asia Minor.

DOCUMENT SET 10.4
The First Crusade

Fall of Jerusalem. ~635   *Pilgrimages*   *Permission Byzantium relics*

One of the objectives of this set is to look for evidence of the connection between Western church reform and the First Crusade. Another is to understand the crusade as a manifestation of the restless, aggressive enterprise of Western lay people.

Document A is one of several known versions of the speech Pope Urban II delivered at the Synod of Clermont in south-central France in 1095, at which the First Crusade began. (It is interesting to compare Urban's call for holy war with the Qu'ran's injunction to *Jihad*; see Set 8.4, Document D.) Though Urban's appeal was to the Franks, ardor for crusading quickly spread to Germany. Document B contains an extract from the Chronicle of Ekkehard of Aurach (compare Set 10.2, Document A), who after going on pilgrimage to Jerusalem in 1101 added to his history a retrospective account of the First Crusade. Notice his mention of "impudent critics" of the crusade—what do you make of their attitude? What does his account add to your understanding?

Document C gives a completely different perspective—that of Anna Comnena, the shrewd and well-educated daughter of Byzantine Emperor Alexius I, who wrote a full-scale history of his reign, from which this extract is taken.

Use these documents and *The Challenge of the West* to place the First Crusade in its political, social, and cultural context.

A. Robert the Monk Reports Urban II's Speech Launching the First Crusade

"Oh, race of Franks, race from across the mountains, race beloved and chosen by God,—as is clear from many of your works,—set apart from all other nations by the situation of your country as well as by your Catholic faith and the honor which you render to the holy Church: to you our discourse is addressed, and for you our exhortations are intended. We wish you to know what a grievous cause has led us to your country, for it is the imminent peril threatening you and all the faithful which has brought us hither.

From the confines of Jerusalem and from the city of Constantinople a grievous report has gone forth and has repeatedly been brought to our ears; namely, that a race from the kingdom of the Persians, an accursed race, a race wholly alienated from God, 'a generation that set not their heart aright, and whose spirit was not steadfast with God,' has violently invaded the lands of those Christians and has depopulated them by pillage and fire. They have led away a part of the captives into their own country, and a part they have killed by cruel tortures. They have either destroyed the churches of God or appropriated them for the rites of their own religion. They destroy the altars, after having defiled them with their uncleanness. . . . The kingdom of the Greeks is now dismembered by them and has been deprived of territory so vast in extent that it could not be traversed in two months' time.

On whom, therefore, is the labor of avenging these wrongs and of recovering this territory incumbent, if not upon you,—you, upon whom, above all other nations, God has conferred remarkable glory in arms, great courage, bodily activity, and strength to humble the heads of those who resist you? Let the deeds of your ancestors encourage you and incite your minds to manly achievements:—the glory and greatness of King Charlemagne, and of his son Louis, and of your other monarchs, who have destroyed the kingdoms of the Turks and have extended the sway of the holy Church over lands previously pagan. Let the holy sepulcher of our Lord and Saviour, which is possessed by the unclean nations, especially arouse you, and the holy places which are now treated with ignominy and irreverently polluted with the filth of the unclean. Oh, most valiant soldiers and descendants of invincible ancestors, do not degenerate, but recall the valor of your progenitors.

But if you are hindered by love of children, parents, or wife, remember what the Lord says in the Gospel, 'He that loveth father or mother more than me is not worthy of me.' 'Every one that hath forsaken houses, or brethren, or sisters, or father, or mother, or wife, or children, or lands, for my name's sake, shall receive an hundredfold, and shall inherit everlasting life.' Let none of your possessions retain you, nor solicitude for your family affairs. For this land which you inhabit, shut in on all sides by the seas and surrounded by the mountain peaks, is too narrow for your large population; nor does it abound in wealth; and it furnishes scarcely food enough for its cultivators. Hence it is that you murder and devour one another, that you wage war, and that very many among you perish in intestine strife.

Let hatred therefore depart from among you, let your quarrels end, let wars cease, and let all dissen-

sing

s

alty

sions and controversies slumber. Enter upon the road to the Holy Sepulcher; wrest that land from the wicked race, and subject it to yourselves. That land which, as the Scripture says, 'floweth with milk and honey' was given by God into the power of the children of Israel. Jerusalem is the center of the earth; the land is fruitful above all others, like another paradise of delights. This spot the Redeemer of mankind has made illustrious by his advent, has beautified by his sojourn, has consecrated by his passion, has redeemed by his death, has glorified by his burial.

This royal city, however, situated at the center of the earth, is now held captive by the enemies of Christ and is subjected, by those who do not know God, to the worship of the heathen. She seeks, therefore, and desires to be liberated and ceases not to implore you to come to her aid. From you especially she asks succor, because, as we have already said, God has conferred upon you above all other nations great glory in arms. Accordingly, undertake this journey eagerly for the remission of your sins, with the assurance of the reward of imperishable glory in the kingdom of heaven."

When Pope Urban had urbanely said these and very many similar things, he so centered in one purpose the desires of all who were present that all cried out, "It is the will of God! It is the will of God!" When the venerable Roman pontiff heard that, with eyes uplifted to heaven, he gave thanks to God and, commanding silence with his hand, said:

"Most beloved brethren, to-day is manifest in you what the Lord says in the Gospel, 'Where two or three are gathered together in my name, there am I in the midst of them'; for unless God had been present in your spirits, all of you would not have uttered the same cry; since, although the cry issued from numerous mouths, yet the origin of the cry was one. Therefore I say to you that God, who implanted this in your breasts, has drawn it forth from you. Let that then be your war cry in combats, because it is given to you by God. When an armed attack is made upon the enemy, let this one cry be raised by all the soldiers of God: 'It is the will of God! It is the will of God!' [*Deus vult! Deus vult!*]

B. Ekkehard of Aurach Describes Spreading Enthusiasm for the First Crusade in Germany

Here I am very anxious to add certain details concerning these military undertakings, which are due to divine rather than human inspiration. This I do for the especial purpose of refuting those imprudent—or,

better, impudent—critics, who, bound by prejudice, take it upon themselves with insolent lips to blame this novel enterprise, so necessary to a world that is growing old and nearing its end. They, like the Epicureans, prefer the broad way of pleasure to the narrow way of God's service. To them love of the world is wisdom and those who despise it are fools. . . . I, however, since I trust in the Lord and strive not for present but for future things, would, although only as an idle spectator yet a kindly well-wisher, exalt the glorious men of our time who have overcome the kingdoms of this world and who, for the sake of the blessed Shepherd who sought the hundredth sheep that was lost, have left wife and child, principalities and riches, and have taken their lives in their hands. . . .

[After Urban had aroused the spirits of all by the promise of forgiveness to those who undertook the expedition with single-hearted devotion,] toward one hundred thousand men were appointed to the immediate service of God from Aquitaine and Normandy, England, Scotland, Ireland, Brittany, Galicia, Gascony, France, Flanders, Lorraine, and from other Christian peoples, whose names I no longer retain. It was truly an army of "crusaders," for they bore the sign of the cross on their garments as a reminder that they should mortify the flesh, and in the hope that they would in this way triumph over the enemies of the cross of Christ, as it had once come to pass in the case of the great Constantine. Thus, through the marvelous and unexampled working of divine dispensation, all these members of Christ, so different in speech, origin, and nationality, were suddenly brought together as one body through their love of Christ.

While they were all under one king, Christ, the several peoples nevertheless were led by their several leaders, namely Godfrey of Lorraine and . . . [various other nobles named here]. Over all of these the above-mentioned pope placed Bishop Hademar, a man of venerable holiness and wisdom. To him the pope granted the right to exercise in his stead the power transmitted by St. Peter to the Roman see of binding and loosing. . . .

The West Franks were easily induced to leave their fields, since France had, during several years, been terribly visited now by civil war, now by famine, and again by sickness. . . . Among the other nations, the common people, as well as those of higher rank, related that, aside from the apostolic summons, they had in some instances been called to the land of promise by certain prophets who had appeared among them, or through heavenly signs and revelations. Others confessed that they had been induced to pledge themselves by some misfortune. A great part of them started forth with wife and child and laden with their entire household equipment.

The summons, however, failed altogether to reach the East Franks, Saxons, Thuringians, Bavarians, and Alemannians. This was due especially to the division between the civil government and the priesthood, which from the time of Pope Alexander [II] to the present day has, alas, made us as hated and offensive to the Romans as the Romans are to us. So it came about that almost the whole German people were, at the beginning of the expedition, quite unacquainted with the reasons for it. Consequently the many legions of horsemen who passed through their land, the hosts of people on foot, the crowds of country people, women and children, were viewed by them with contempt as persons who had altogether lost their wits.

Those bound for the Holy Land seemed to them to be leaving the land of their birth and sacrificing what they already had for a vain hope. The promised land offered no certainty but danger, yet they deserted their own possessions in a greedy struggle for those of others. Nevertheless, although our people are far more arrogant than others, the fury of the Teutons finally gave way in view of the divine mercy, and after they had thoroughly discussed the matter with the multitude of pilgrims, they too inclined their hearts.

Moreover the signs in the sun and the wonders which appeared, both in the air and on the earth, aroused many who had previously been indifferent. It seems to us useful to interweave an account of a few of these signs, although it would carry us too far to enumerate them all. For example, we beheld a comet on the 7th of October to the south, and its brilliancy slanting down seemed like a sword. . . . [Various other celestial visions also appeared.]

Many, moreover, displayed, either on their clothing, or upon their forehead, or elsewhere on their body, the sign of the cross, which had been divinely imprinted, and they believed themselves on this account to have been destined to the service of God. Others likewise were induced, through some sudden change of spirit or some nocturnal vision, to sell all their property and possessions and to sew the sign of mortification on their mantles. Among all these people who pressed into the churches in incredible numbers, swords were distributed with the priestly benediction, according to the new usage, along with the pilgrim's staff and wallet.

I may also report that at this time a woman after two years gestation finally gave birth to a boy who was able to talk; and that a child with a double set of limbs, another with two heads, and some lambs with two heads were also born; and that colts came into the world with great teeth, which we ordinarily call horses' teeth and which nature only grants to three-year old horses.

While through these and similar signs the whole creation seemed to offer its services to the Creator, the watchful enemy, who takes occasion when others sleep to sow his tares amongst the good seed, raised up also false prophets and mixed false brethren and degraded women among the Lord's host under the appearance of religion. In this way the armies of Christ were defiled not only through hypocrisy and lies but through shameless uncleanness, so that the prophecy of the Good Shepherd might be fulfilled, that even the elect may be led astray.

c. Anna Comnena Sniffs at the Crusaders

When the Franks had all come together and had taken an oath to the emperor, there was one count who had the boldness to sit down upon the throne. The emperor, well knowing the pride of the Latins, kept silent, but Baldwin approached the Frankish count and taking him by the hand said, "You ought not to sit there; that is an honor which the emperor permits to no one. Now that you are in this country, why do you not observe its customs?" The insolent count made no reply to Baldwin, but said in his barbarous language, as if talking to himself, "This must be a rude fellow who would alone remain seated when so many brave warriors are standing up." Alexis noted the movement of the man's lips and called an interpreter in order to learn what he had said; but when the interpreter had told him he did not complain to the Franks, although he did not forget the matter.

When the counts came to take leave of the emperor he retained this haughty knight and asked him who he was. "I am a Frank," he replied, "of the most high and ancient nobility. I know but one thing, an that is that there is in my country a church built at the crossroads where all those betake themselves who hope to show their valor in single combat, and there make their prayer to God while they await an enemy; I remained there a long time without anybody daring to measure swords with me."

Alexis was on his guard against accepting this challenge. "If you then waited without being able to show your bravery," he said to him, "you now have a chance to fight; and if I may give you a word of advice, it will be not to put yourself either at the head nor rear of the army but in the middle. The experience which I have had of the way in which the Turks make war has convinced me that that is the best place."

Document Set 10.4 References

A. Robert the Monk Reports Urban II's Speech Launching the First Crusade
   James Harvey Robinson, ed., *Readings in European History* (Boston: Ginn, 1904), 1:312–315.
B. Ekkehard of Aurach Describes Spreading Enthusiasm for the First Crusade in Germany
   Robinson, 1:320.
C. Anna Comnena Sniffs at the Crusaders
   Robinson, 1:320–321.

DOCUMENT SET 10.5
Two Feudal Monarchs: Louis the Fat and William the Conqueror

In Set 9.4 we encountered manifestations of the origin of feudalism; the documents here pertain to the more mature feudal institutions and customs that had taken shape by the late eleventh and twelfth centuries. Document A describes how Count Charles of Flanders (in present-day Belgium) received the homage of his vassals in 1127. In Document B, Abbot Suger, one of the most notable statesmen and historians of his day, recounts how his friend Louis VI the Fat, king of France (*1108–1137), as a younger and presumably more physically fit man brought under tighter control some of the more unruly vassals of the French crown. (When these events took place, Louis was still the crown prince.) Notice also Suger's account of how Louis cooperated with the church in trying to bring order to the land.

The most formidable feudal monarchy was that created in England by William the Conqueror (*1066–1087), who had the advantage of being able to name a great number of new, loyal vassals. William's brief coronation oath (Document C) hints at the new king's relative freedom of action. Document D, taken from the *Anglo-Saxon Chronicle,* describes how William and his *witan* (royal council) gathered an unprecedented amount of information about the resources available to him as sovereign lord through the compilation of the famous Domesday Book in 1806 (an excerpt of which appears as Document E). Document D also gives an interesting sketch of the Conqueror's character and policy in imposing his will. Keep in mind that the chronicle was compiled by Anglo-Saxon monks who had been on the losing side.

An even more striking illustration of what it meant to have been defeated by William the Conqueror can be seen in Document F, an extract from the Chronicle of Abbington Abbey. Dating from the early thirteenth century, it records the monks' unavailing efforts to regain lands that William had confiscated.

As a commentary on feudal values as perceived in the early twelfth century, see Document G, a brief extract from the French epic *The Song of Roland*, which tells us a greatly idealized story of how lords Roland and Oliver, and Bishop Turpin, were faithful unto death to their lord, Charlemagne, who had charged them with holding a pass against the Moors in Spain.

Use these documents and *The Challenge of the West* to analyze feudal monarchy.

A. A Twelfth-Century Ceremony of Homage and Fealty

Through the whole remaining part of the day those who had been previously enfeoffed by the most pious Count Charles did homage to the [new] count, taking up now again their fiefs and offices and whatever they had before rightfully and legitimately obtained. On Thursday, the seventh of April, homages were again made to the count, begin completed in the following order of faith and security.

First they did their homage thus. The count asked the vassal if he were willing to become completely his man, and the other replied, "I am willing": and with hands clasped, placed between the hands of the count, they were bound together by a kiss. Secondly, he who had done homage gave his fealty to the representative of the count in these words, "I promise on my faith that I will in future be faithful to Count William, and will observe my homage to him completely against all persons, in good faith and without deceit." And, thirdly, he took his oath to this upon the relics of the saints. Afterward the count, with a little rod which he held in his hand, gave investitures to all who by this agreement had given their security and accompanying oath.

B. Suger Describes Louis VI's Efforts to Strengthen Royal Authority in France

The young hero, Prince Louis, gay, gracious, and so friendly to all that he passed with some for a person of no force, had hardly come to man's estate when he proved himself an illustrious and courageous defender of his father's realm. He provided for the needs of the Church, and strove to secure peace for those who pray, for those who work, and for the poor. And no one had done this for a long time.

Now it came to pass at this time that certain disputes arose between Adam, the venerable abbot of St. Denis, and a nobleman, Burchard, lord of Montmorency [his vassal], concerning certain customs. The controversy waxed so hot and reached such extremes of irritation that all ties of homage were broken between vassal and lord, and the two disputants betook themselves to arms, war, and fire.

When the affair came to the ears of Lord Louis he

was sorely vexed. He delayed not, but ordered the aforesaid Burchard, duly summoned, to appear before his father in the castle of Poissy for judgment. Burchard lost his cause, but refused to submit to the judgment. He was not taken prisoner, for that is not the custom of the French, but having withdrawn to his estates, he straightway learned what manner of injury and calamity the king's majesty can inflict on his disobedient subjects. For this famous youth [Prince Louis] carried arms thither against him and his criminal allies, Matthew, count of Beaumont, and Dreux of Mouchy-le-châtel, vigorous and warlike men. He laid waste the land of Burchard with fire, famine, and the sword; and overthrew all the defenses and buildings, except the castle itself, and razed them to the ground. When his enemies undertook to defend themselves in the castle he besieged them with the French and the Flemish troops of his uncle Robert, as well as with his own. By these and other means he brought the humiliated Burchard to repentance, bent him to his will and pleasure, and satisfactorily adjusted the dispute which had given rise to the trouble. . . .

A king, when he takes the royal power, vows to put down with his strong right arm insolent tyrants whensoever he sees them vex the state with endless wars, rejoice in rapine, oppress the poor, destroy the churches, give themselves over to lawlessness which, and it be not checked, would flame out into ever greater madness; for the evil spirits who instigate them are wont cruelly to strike down those whom they fear to lose, but give free rein to those whom they hope to hold, while they add fuel to the flames which are to devour their victims to all eternity. . . .

It is known that kings have long arms; and to show that the king's strength was not confined within the narrow boundaries of certain places, a man, Alard de Guillebaut by name, a clever man, with an oily tongue, came from the frontiers of Berri to the king. He laid the grievance of his stepson before his lord the king, and entreated him right humbly, that he would summon by his royal authority a certain noble baron, Aymon by name, surnamed Vais-Vache, lord of Bourbon, who refused to do him justice. Moreover he asked that the king should restrain Aymon from despoiling, with presumptuous audacity, his nephew, the son of his older brother, Archambaut, and to fix according to French custom what portion of goods each of them ought to have.

Now the king loved justice and had compassion on the churches and the poor. And he feared lest these wars should make wickedness flourish, and lest the poor might be vexed and bear the punishment for the pride of others. So, after vainly summoning Aymon,

who would not trust himself to trial and refused to obey the summons, Louis gave way neither to pleasure nor to sloth, but marched with a great army toward the territory of Bourges. There he directed his forces against Aymon's castle of Germigni, which was well fortified, and strove to reduce it by a vigorous assault.

Then did Aymon see that he could not hold out, and he gave over hoping to save himself or his castle. He saw only this one way to safety—that he should throw himself at the king's feet. There he prostrated himself again and again, while all the crowd marveled, and prayed the king to have compassion upon him. He gave up his castle, and, humble now as he had once been proud, submitted himself utterly to the king's justice. The king kept the castle and took Aymon into France to be judged there; and right justly and piously, by the decision and arbitration of the French, did he settle the dispute which had arisen between the uncle and nephew.

King Louis spent freely both of money and the sweat of his brow to relieve the sufferings and oppressions of many. He was used to make many such expeditions throughout the country for the relief of churches and of the poor, but we must pass over these, as it would but weary the reader to narrate them. . . .

C. William the Conqueror's Coronation Oath and Guarantees to London, 1066

Church over State

Having first, as the archbishop required, sworn before the altar of St. Peter the Apostle, in the presence of the clergy and people, to defend the holy churches of God and their governors, and also to rule over the whole people subject to him justly and with royal providence; to enact and to preserve right law, and straitly to forbid violence and unjust judgments.

D. William the Conqueror and the Domesday Book: A Contemporary Description

At Midwinter the king was at Gloucester with his "witan," and there held his court five days; and afterwards the archbishop and clergy had a synod three days. There was Maurice chosen bishop of London, and William, of Norfolk, and Robert, of Cheshire. They were all the king's clerks. After this the king had a great council, and very deep speech with his "witan" about this land, how it was peopled, or by what men; then he sent his men over all England, into every shire, and caused to be ascertained how many hundred hides were in the shire, or what land the king himself had, and cattle within the land, or what dues he ought to have, in twelve months, from the shire. Also he caused to be written how much land his archbishops had, and his suffragan bishops, and his abbots, and his earls: and—though I may narrate somewhat prolixly—what or how much each man had who was a landholder in England, in land, or in cattle, and how much money it might be worth. So very narrowly he caused it to be traced out, that there was not one single hide, nor one yard of land, nor even—it is shame to tell, though it seemed to him no shame to do—an ox, nor a cow, nor a swine, left that was not set down in his writ.

King William, about whom we speak, was a very wise man, and very powerful, more dignified and strong than any of his predecessors were. He was mild to the good men who loved God, and beyond all measure severe to the men who gainsaid his will. . . . He was also very dignified; thrice every year he wore his crown, as oft as he was in England. At Easter he wore it in Winchester; at Pentecost, in Westminster; at Midwinter, in Gloucester. And then were with him all the great men over all England, archbishops and suffragan bishops, abbots and earls, thanes and knights.

So also was he a very rigid and cruel man, so that no one durst do anything against his will. He had earls in bonds who had acted against his will; bishops he cast from their bishoprics, and abbots from their abbacies, and thanes into prison; and at last he spared not his own brother, named Odo: he was a very rich bishop in Normandy; at Bayeux was his episcopal see; and he was the foremost man besides the king; and he had an earldom in England, and when the king was in Normandy, then was he the most powerful in this land: and him the king put in prison.

Among other good things is not to be forgotten the good peace that he made in this land; so that a man who had any confidence in himself might go over his realm, with his bosom full of gold, unhurt. Nor durst any man slay another man had he done ever so great evil to the other. He reigned over England, and by his sagacity so thoroughly surveyed it that there was not a hide of land within England that he knew not who had it, or what it was worth, and afterwards set it in his writ.

Brytland (Wales) was in his power, and therein he built castles, and completely ruled over that race of men. In like manner he also subjected Scotland to him by his great strength. The land of Normandy was naturally his, and over the country which is called Le

Maine he reigned; and if he might yet have lived two years he would, by his valor, have won Ireland, and without any weapons.

Certainly in his time men had great hardship and very many injuries. Castles he caused to be made, and poor men to be greatly oppressed. The king was very rigid, and took from his subjects many a mark of gold, and more hundred pounds of silver, all which he took, by right and with great unright, from his people, for little need. He had fallen into covetousness, and altogether loved greediness.

He planted a great preserve for deer, and he laid down laws therewith, that whosoever should slay hart or hind should be blinded. He forbade the harts and also the boars to be killed. As greatly did he love the tall deer as if he were their father. He also ordained concerning the hares that they should go free. His great men bewailed it, and the poor men murmured thereat; but he was so obdurate that he recked not of the hatred of them all; but they must wholly follow the king's will if they would live, or have land, or property, or even his peace. Alas that any man should be so proud, so raise himself up, and account himself above all men! May the Almighty God show mercy to his soul, and grant him forgiveness of his sins!

E. The Domesday Book Inventories a Manor, 1086

Peter de Valence holds in domain Hecham, which Haldane a freeman held in the time of King Edward, as a manor, and as 5 hides. There have always been 2 ploughs in the demesne, 4 ploughs of the men. At that time there were 8 villeins, now 10; then there were 2 bordars, now 3; at both times 4 *servi*, woods for 300 swine, 18 acres of meadow. Then there were 2 fish ponds and a half, now there are none. At that time there was 1 ox, now there are 15 cattle and 1 small horse and 18 swine and 2 hives of bees. At that time it was worth 69s., now 4£ 10s. When he received this manor he found only 1 ox, and 1 acre planted. Of those 5 hides spoken of above, one was held in the time of King Edward by 2 freemen, and was added to this manor in the time of King William. It was worth in the time of King Edward 10s., now 22s., and William holds this from Peter de Valence.

F. The Abington Chronicle Reveals the Consequences of Being on the Losing Side of the Conquest

William obtained the crown of England. Some submitted to him and swore fealty, but not a few departed into exile, hoping that they might find for themselves homes in other lands. Abbot Ealdred at first joined the former of these parties and swore fealty to the king. But when many, including the mother of the slain king, changed over and joined the latter party, the abbot also left England taking with him among others a priest named Blacheman. This priest, as has earlier been mentioned in connection with Abbot Ordric, was a man of the church of Abingdon and held from the monastery Sandford and Chilton and Leverton. When he left England, everything which he possessed was taken into the hands of the king since he was held to be a renegade, and it was with the greatest difficulty that the abbot secured the restoration of his lands to the church.

As the abbot was successful in this instance, so also in other cases where lands had been alienated from the church he might perhaps have vindicated his right if he had not to his own loss and to the loss of the church incurred the enmity of the king. Of this we shall learn more later. A certain rich man, Turchill by name, with the witness and consent of Earl Harold, had performed homage to the church and to Abbot Ordric for his land which was called Kingston. For then a freeman was allowed so to act that the lordship of the aforesaid village might ever after pertain to the church. When this man fell in the famous battle [of Hastings] Henry of Ferrières seized his land for himself despite the protests of the abbot, and despite the fact that the lordship of this land had been vested in the church a long time before this battle. A similar usurpation took place at Fyfield. There, a certain Godric, who was sheriff, had held from the church on a lease for three lives, on the understanding that whatever mischance might befall the tenants, the church should suffer no loss therefrom. But when Godric likewise was killed in the same battle, Henry of Ferrières added this village also to his possessions.

In these days not only was the abbey thus robbed of its estates, but the ornaments of the sanctuary itself were stolen. An order came that the most precious of these should be sent to the queen. The abbot and the monks took counsel what should be done in this matter, and planned to send to the queen certain ornaments. But she declined those which were offered and demanded more precious treasures. Wherefore the abbot and monks, oppressed by fear of their new rulers from overseas, decided that their orders must in some measure be obeyed. To meet the wishes of the queen they therefore made a compromise, and sent a chasuble wonderfully embroidered throughout with gold and the best ceremonial cope, and an alb with a stole, and a gospel book decorated with gold and precious gems.

Meanwhile many plots were hatched in the kingdom of England by those who resented the unaccustomed yoke of a foreign rule. Some of them hid in woods and islands, living like outlaws and plundering and attacking those who came their way. Others besought the Danes to come to England. And when the Danes came in answer to this call, they in their turn plundered the land and laid it waste by fire, and took away many into captivity. But they were not strong enough to wage a pitched battle or to subdue the kingdom, and so with their task unaccomplished they returned to their own land.

Men of all ranks and classes took part in these attempts. Aethelwine, bishop of Durham, for instance, was found amongst those who were taken prisoner, and having been brought to Abingdon he ended his days there in captivity. The men of the abbey of Abingdon, although they ought to have sustained the cause of King William, listened to the opposite advice and went armed to join a gathering of the enemies of the king. Being intercepted on their journey, they were captured and imprisoned and grievously punished. For this reason the king was incensed against their lord, that is to say, Abbot Ealdred, also named Brichwin, who was therefore thrown into prison immediately in Wallingford Castle. After being kept for some time in that place, he was at length taken thence and given into the charge of Walkelin, bishop of Winchester, with whom he remained for the rest of his life.

At this time, owing to the changed state of the kingdom, many treasures were deposited in the monastery of Abingdon in the hope that, being protected by the custody of the abbey, they might escape plunder. But when the officers of the court obtained knowledge of this through informers, everything that had been secretly sent, and everything that was found so stored, was taken away. Besides this, whatever was found in the treasure chests of the monks was removed. Thus much of what had been contributed for the honour and use of the church was removed, gold and silver, vestments, books and vessels. No respect was paid to the threshold of the holy places, and no pity was shown to the afflicted monks. Outside, with a similar lack of respect, the villages were widely devastated. How much of the property of the abbey was lost at this time it would be hard to reckon. . . .

G. The Song of Roland Exalts Feudal Faithfulness

LXXXVII

Heroic Roland and wise Oliver,
Each a great vassal of prodigious courage.
Since they have mounted horses, taken arms,
Neither will shun the battle, fleeing death;
The counts are noble, lofty are their words.
In zealous wrath the wicked pagans ride,
Says Oliver, 'See in what strength they come!
They're close to us but Charles is far away.
You did not deign to sound the olifant;
Were the king here, our loss were not so great.
But glance up there towards the pass to Spain
And you will see the rearguard's melancholy;
Who fights this day will never fight another.'
Roland replies, 'Speak no outrage to honour!
Woe to the heart turned coward in the breast!
We'll stand in our positions on this spot,
And we shall strike the blows and wield the swords.'

LXXXVIII

When Roland sees the battle near at hand,
His courage swells, more fierce than lion or leopard.
He calls the French and shouts to Oliver,
'My lord companion, friend, hold back such words!
The emperor who left these French with us
—His own selection of some twenty thousand—
Was well assured no coward was among them.
A man should suffer greatly for his lord,
Endure both biting cold and sweltering heat
And sacrifice for him both flesh and blood.
Strike with your lance as I with Durendal,
My own good sword, a present from the king.
If I die here, whoever has it next
May say it was a noble vassal's sword.'

LXXXIX

Archbishop Turpin, far across the field,
Spurs on his horse and gallops up a hill.
He calls the French and speaks these words to them:
'Barons, my lords, King Charles has left us here.
We should die well and nobly for our king.
Offer your help to succour Christendom!
You will have battle; be quite sure of that;
With your own eyes you saw the Saracens.
Confess your sins and ask the grace of God.
I shall absolve you to protect your souls.
If you die here, you will be holy martyrs.
You will have seats in highest paradise.'
The French dismount and kneel upon the ground;
In God's name the archbishop blesses them
And for their penance orders them to fight.

Document Set 10.5 References

A. A Twelfth-Century Ceremony of Homage and Fealty
James Harvey Robinson, ed., *Readings in European History* (Boston: Ginn, 1904), 1:179–180.

B. Suger Describes Louis VI's Efforts to Strengthen Royal Authority in France
Robinson, 1:199–205.

C. William the Conqueror's Coronation Oath and Guarantees to London, 1066
Translations and Reprints from the Original Sources of European History (Philadelphia: University of Pennsylvania Press, 1897), 1/6:2.

D. William the Conqueror and the Domesday Book: A Contemporary Description
Robinson, 1:229–231.

E. The Domesday Book Inventories a Manor, 1086
Translations and Reprints, 3/5:3–4.

F. The Abington Chronicle Reveals the Consequences of Being on the Losing Side of the Conquest
David C. Douglas and George W. Greenaway, ed., *English Historical Documents* (London: Methuen, 1953), vol. 2, doc. 223, 899–303.

G. The Song of Roland Exalts Feudal Faithfulness
Howard S. Roberts, trans., *The Song of Roland* (London: Dent, 1972), §§88–90, 33–34.

Excerpt from *The Song of Roland,* trans. by Howard S. Robertson, J. M. Dent, Everyman's Library, 1972, pp. 33–34. Reprinted by permission of David Campbell Publishers Ltd.

DOCUMENT SET 10.6
The Intellectual Revival

What would become the Western intellectual revival of the High Middle Ages, with its veneration for Aristotle's logic, actually began in the Islamic world. Document A presents an extract from the autobiography of Ibn Sina (known to the West as Avicenna, 980–1037), born near Bokhara in what is today Uzbekistan. Evidently he was first stimulated intellectually by debates at home over Shi'ite and Sunni Muslim doctrine. Notice how this early experience kindled his eagerness to explore the richness of Greek philosophy and his eventual progression to Aristotelian logic. Avicenna exerted a powerful influence throughout the Islamic world, including Muslim Spain, from which a few Western scholars began transplanting word of Aristotle's philosophy to the Latin world.

Neoplatonism, as filtered through the writings of St. Augustine, continued however to be the foundation of philosophical inquiry in eleventh-century Christian Europe. One of the most influential thinkers at that time was St. Anselm, the Italian-born archbishop of Canterbury (1033–1109). Claiming that "I believe in order to understand," Anselm, like other scholars of his time, sought to explain and deepen his faith through logic, as exempliefied through his proof of God's existence (Document B).

Fascination with logic as a method for clarifying vexed problems of faith surged to the fore with Peter Abelard (1079–1142). Son of a Breton noble, Abelard in effect substituted intellectual dueling for literal swordsmanship as a means of making his way in the world. Document C, taken from his *Autobiography*, suggests something of his contentious, ambitious personality; Document D, an extract from his *Sic et Non* (Yes or No), is a compilation of 158 theological and philosophical questions on which the authorities he cited contradicted each other. Because he insisted on human reason's capacity to resolve these disturbing issues, Abelard shocked many of his contemporaries. An example of the hostility he aroused can be seen in Document E, an extract of Otto Freising's important contemporary history. Otto alludes to one of Abelard's most formidable critics, St. Bernard of Clairvaux.

At 38, Abelard fell in love with one of his pupils, Heloise, the niece of a cathedral canon, and he secretly married her. As a result, he was castrated on orders from her uncle. Thereafter Heloise became a nun and Abelard took up monastic life without, however, being any less a focus of intellectual controversy. The two maintained a correspondence; an extract from the first letter to him from Heloise constitutes Document F. In addition to revealing a human dimension all too rare in sources from this period, the Heloise-Abelard correspondence also speaks eloquently of the spiritual concerns of the era and of the situation in which an intelligent, educated woman with "normal" human desires found herself.

A. The Arab Philosopher Ibn Sina (Avicenna) Describes His Exhilarating Discovery of Ancient Greek Learning

My father was one of those who had responded to propaganda for the Egyptians and was counted among the Ismā'īlīs. He had accepted their teachings on the soul and the mind, as had my brother. They often discussed it with one another. I listened to them and understood what they said, and they tried to win me over to this doctrine. Sometimes they also used to discuss philosophy, geometry, and Indian arithmetic, and my father decided to send me to a certain grocer who knew Indian arithmetic so that I could learn it from him.

Then Abū 'Abdallāh al-Nātilī, who claimed to be a philosopher, came to Bukhārā. My father lodged him in our house in the hope that I would learn something from him. Before he came, I was studying jurisprudence under Ismā'īl al-Zāhid [the Hermit], and I was one of his best pupils. I became proficient in the different methods of questioning and of objection to the respondent, in accordance with the customary procedures. Then, under the guidance of al-Nātilī, I began to read the *Isagoge* [of Aristotle]. When he told me the definition of *genus*, that is, that which is said of a number of things which differ in species in answer to the question "What is it?" I began to give greater precision to this definition in a way the like of which he had never heard before. He was full of admiration for me and persuaded my

[marginal annotation: education as commodity]

"Poets, Scholars, and Physicians" from *Islam: From the Prophet Muhammad to the Capture of Constantinople*, Volume II by Bernard Lewis, pp. 177–181. Copyright © 1974 by Bernard Lewis. Reprinted by permission of HarperCollins Publishers, Inc.

father to let me devote myself entirely to learning. Whatever problem he put to me, I resolved better than he could himself. Thus I learned from him the broad principles of logic. but he knew nothing of the subtleties. Then I began to read books and study commentaries on my own until I mastered logic. I also read the geometry of Euclid. . . . Then I took up medicine and began to read books written on this subject. Medicine is not one of the difficult sciences, and in a very short time I undoubtedly excelled in it, so that physicians of merit studied under me. I also attended the sick, and the doors of medical treatments based on experience opened before me to an extent that cannot be described. At the same time I carried on debates and controversies in jurisprudence. At this point I was sixteen years old. . . .

Then I returned to the study of the divine science. I read the book called *Metaphysics,* but could not understand it, the aim of its author remaining obscure for me. I read the book forty times, until I knew it by heart, but I still could not understand its meaning or its purpose. I despaired of understanding it on my own and said to myself, "There is no way to understand this book." Then one afternoon I happened to be in the market of the booksellers, and a crier was holding a volume in his hand and shouting the price. He offered it to me, and I rejected it impatiently, believing that there was no profit in this science. He persisted and said, "Buy this book from me, it is cheap. I will sell it to you for three dirhams because its owner needs the money." I bought it and found that it was Abu'l-Nasr al-Fārābī's book, explaining the meaning of the *Metaphysics.* I returned to my house and made haste to read it. Immediately the purposes of this book became clear to me because I already knew it by heart. I was very happy at this, and the next day I gave much alms to the poor in thanksgiving to Almighty God. . . .

B. St. Anselm Proves God's Existence

I began to ask myself whether there might be found a single argument which would require no other for its proof than itself alone; and alone would suffice to demonstrate that God truly exists, and that there is a supreme good requiring nothing else, which all other things require for their existence and well-being, and whatever [else] we believe regarding the divine Being. . . . One day . . . the proof of which I had despaired offered itself . . . [namely:] It is possible to conceive of a being which cannot be conceived not to exist; and this is greater than one which can be conceived not to exist. Hence, if that, than which nothing

greater can be conceived, can be conceived not to exist, it is not that, than which nothing greater can be conceived. But this is an irreconcilable contradiction. There is, then, so truly a being than which nothing greater can be conceived to exist, that it cannot even be conceived not to exist; and this being thou art, O Lord, our God.

C. Abelard Describes His Quest for Knowledge

. . . I traversed the various provinces, engaging in disputation and visiting all those places where I heard that the art of logic flourished. I came finally to Paris, where this art was wont to be most cultivated, to William of Champeaux, my preceptor, who at that time was quite justly famous in his profession. I remained with him for a time and was at first favorably received; later he came to dislike me heartily, when I attempted to oppose certain of his opinions. I began frequently to argue against him, and sometimes appeared to get the better of him in debate. Moreover those among my fellow-students who stood highest were especially indignant with me, since I was reckoned of slight consequence owing to my youth and the brief period I had been studying. Here my calamities had their beginning and they still continue. . . .

At my first lecture few were present, since it seemed absurd to them all that I, hitherto almost wholly inexperienced in the Scriptures, should undertake the task so suddenly. However, all who came were so pleased that, one and all, they praised my words and urged me to proceed with my comments according to my interpretation. As the affair became known, those who had not been present at the first lecture began to come in great numbers to the second and third. All were, moreover, eager to make notes from the very beginning, upon the explanation which I had given the first day.

D. "Yes and No": Abelard Asks Some Hard Questions

Should human faith be based upon reason, or no?
Is God one, or no?
Is God a substance, or no?
Does the first Psalm refer to Christ, or no?
Is sin pleasing to God, or no?
Is God the author of evil, or no?
Is God all-powerful, or no?
Can God be resisted, or no?

Has God free will, or no?

Was the first man persuaded to sin by the devil, or no?

Was Adam saved, or no?

Did all the apostles have wives except John, or no?

Are the flesh and blood of Christ in very truth and essence present in the sacrament of the altar, or no?

Do we sometimes sin unwillingly, or no?

Does God punish the same sin both here and in the future, or no?

Is it worse to sin openly than secretly, or no?

E. Abelard's Brash Rationalism Leaves Conservatives Aghast

This Peter was a native of that province of France which is now called by its inhabitants Brittany. This region is productive of clerics endowed with keen intellects, well adapted to the arts but almost witless for other matters, such as the two brothers Bernard and Thierry, very learned men. This Peter, I say, had from an early age been devoted to literary studies and other trifles, but was so conceited and had such confidence in his own intellectual power that he would scarcely so demean himself as to descend from the heights of his own mind to listen to his teachers. However, he first had a teacher named Roscellinus who was the first in our times to teach in logic the nominalistic doctrine. Afterward he betook himself to those very distinguished men, Anselm of Laon and William of Champeaux, bishop of Châlons-sur-Marne, but did not long endure the weight of their words, judging them to be devoid of cleverness and subtlety. Then he became a teacher and went to Paris, showing great capacity by his originality in discovering matters not only of importance for philosophy but also conducive to social amusements and pastimes. On a certain sufficiently well-known occasion he was very roughly dealt with, and became a monk in the monastery of St. Denis. There devoting himself day and night to reading and meditation, from being a keen thinker he became keener, from being a learned man he became more learned, to such a degree that after some time he was released from obedience to his abbot, came forth in public, and again assumed the office of teacher. Accordingly, holding to the doctrine of nominalism in natural philosophy, he rashly carried it over into theology. Therefore, in teaching and in writing of the Holy Trinity he minimized too much the three persons which Holy Church has up to the present time piously believed

and faithfully taught to be not merely empty names but distinct entities and differentiated by their properties. The analogies he used were not good, for he said among other things: "Just as the same utterance is the major premise, the minor premise, and the conclusion, so the same being is Father, Son, and Holy Spirit." On this account a provincial synod was assembled against him at Soissons in the presence of a legate of the Roman see [1121]. He was adjudged a Sabellian heretic by those excellent men and acknowledged masters, Alberic of Rheims and Letald of Novara, and was forced by the bishops to cast into the fire with his own hand the books that he had published. No opportunity of making a reply was granted him because his skill in disputation was mistrusted by all. These things were done under Louis the Elder, king of France.

(xlviii). Then, after he had lectured again for a long time and had attracted a very great throng of pupils to him, while Innocent was pope at Rome, and in France Louis, the son of the former Louis, was king, he was again summoned by the bishops and by Abbot Bernard to a hearing at Sens, in the presence of King Louis and Thibaud, the count palatine, and other nobles and countless numbers of the people [1140]. While his faith was being discussed there, fearing an uprising of the people, he asked that he might appear before the Roman see. But the bishops and the abbot sent a deputation to the Roman Church along with the articles because of which he was assailed and demanded a sentence of condemnation, in a letter of which this is a copy:

"... Peter Abelard strives to make vain the merit of the Christian faith, since he believes he can comprehend by human reason all that is God: he mounts up to the heaven, he goes down again to the depths; there is nothing that is hid from him, whether in the depth of hell or in the height above. The man is great in his own eyes, disputing concerning the faith against the faith, exercising himself in great matters and in things too high for him, a searcher of his own glory, a contriver of heresies. In the past he composed a book about the Holy Trinity, but by the authority of a legate of the Roman Church it was tried by fire because iniquity was found in it.

"Cursed be he who rebuilds the ruins of Jericho. That book of his has risen from the dead, and with it the heresies of many that were asleep have risen and have appeared to many. Finally now she sends out her boughs unto the sea and her shoots unto Rome. This is the man's boast, that his book hath where to lay its head in the Roman court; by this is his error strengthened and confirmed. Hence he preaches with confidence everywhere the word of iniquity.

"Therefore, when the abbot of Clairvaux, armed with zeal for justice and for the faith, accused him of these matters in the presence of the bishops, he neither confessed nor made denial, but that he might prolong his iniquity, he appealed, without suffering any hurt or oppression, from the time, the place, and the judge that he had himself selected for himself, to the apostolic see.

F. Heloise Writes to Abelard of Their Past Love and Present Miseries

To her master, nay father, to her husband, nay brother; his handmaid, nay daughter, his spouse, nay sister: to ABELARD, HELOISE. . . .

Thou hast written to thy friend the comfort of a long letter, considering his difficulties, no doubt, but treating of thine own. Which diligently recording, whereas thou didst intend them for his comfort, thou hast added greatly to our desolation, and while thou wert anxious to heal his wounds hast inflicted fresh wounds of grief on us and made our former wounds to ache again. Heal, I beseech thee, the wounds that thou thyself hast given, who art so busily engaged in healing the wounds given by others. Thou hast indeed humoured thy friend and comrade, and paid the debt as well of friendship as of comradeship; but by a greater debt thou hast bound thyself to us, whom if behoves thee to call not friends but dearest friends, not comrades but daughters, or by a sweeter and a holier name, if any can be conceived. . . .

How many grave treatises in the teaching, or in the exhortation, or for the comfort of holy women the holy Fathers composed, and with what diligence they composed them, thine excellence knows better than our humility. Wherefore to no little amazement thine oblivion moves the tender beginnings of our conversion, that neither by reverence for God, nor by love of us, nor by the examples of the holy Fathers hast thou been admonished to attempt to comfort me, as I waver and am already crushed by prolonged grief, either by speech in thy presence or by a letter in thine absence. And yet thou knowest thyself to be bound to me by a debt so much greater in that thou art tied to me more closely by the pact of the nuptial sacrament; and that thou art the more beholden to me in that I ever, as is known to all, embraced thee with an unbounded love. Thou knowest, dearest, all men

know what I have lost in thee, and in how wretched a case that supreme and notorious betrayal took me myself also from me with thee, and that my grief is immeasurably greater from the manner in which I lost thee than from the loss of thee. . . .

And if the name of wife appears more sacred and more valid, sweeter to me is ever the word friend, or, if thou be not ashamed, concubine or whore. To wit that the more I humbled myself before thee the fuller grace I might obtain from thee, and so also damage less the fame of thine excellence. And thou thyself wert not wholly unmindful of that kindness in the letter of which I have spoken, written to thy friend for his comfort. Wherein thou hast not disdained to set forth sundry reasons by which I tried to dissuade thee from our marriage, from an ill-starred bed; but wert silent as to many, in which I preferred love to wedlock, freedom to a bond. I call God to witness, if *Augustus*, ruling over the whole world, were to deem me worthy of the honour of marriage, and to confirm the whole world to me, to be ruled by me for ever, dearer to me and of greater dignity would it seem to be called thy strumpet than his empress.

For who among kings or philosophers could equal thee in fame? What kingdom or city or village did not burn to see thee? Who, I ask, did not hasten to gaze upon thee when thou appearedst in public, nor on the departure with straining neck and fixed eye follow thee? What wife, what maiden did not yearn for thee in thine absence, nor burn in thy presence? What queen or powerful lady did not envy me my joys and my bed? There were two things, I confess, in thee especially, wherewith thou couldst at once captivate the heart of any woman; namely the arts of making songs and of singing them. Which we know that other philosophers have seldom followed. Wherewith as with a game, refreshing the labour of philosophic exercise, thou hast left many songs composed in amatory measure or rhythm, which for the suavity both of words and of tune being oft repeated, have kept thy name without ceasing on the lips of all; since even illiterates the sweetness of thy melodies did not allow to forget thee. It was on this account chiefly that women sighed for love of thee. And as the greater part of thy songs descanted of our love, they spread my fame in a short time through many lands, and inflamed the jealousy of many women against me. For what excellence of mind or body did not adorn thy youth? What woman who envied me then does not my calamity now compel to pity one deprived of such delights? What man or women, albeit an enemy at first, is not now softened by the compassion due to me?

. . . While with thee I enjoyed carnal pleasures, many were uncertain whether I did so from love or from desire. But now the end shews in what spirit I began. I have forbidden myself all pleasures that I might obey thy will. I have reserved nothing for myself, save this, to be now entirely thine. Consider therefore how great is thine injustice, if to me who deserve more thou payest less, nay nothing at all, especially when it is a small thing that is demanded of thee, and right easy for thee to perform.

And so in His Name to whom thou hast offered thyself, before God I beseech thee that in whatsoever way thou canst thou restore to me thy presence, to wit by writing me some word of comfort. To this end alone that, thus refreshed, I may give myself with more alacrity to the service of God. When in time past thou soughtest me out for temporal pleasures, thou visitedst me with endless letters, and by frequent songs didst set thy *Heloise* on the lips of all men. With me every public place, each house resounded. How more rightly shouldst thou excite me now towards God, whom thou excitedst then to desire. Consider, I beseech thee, what thou owest me,

pay heed to what I demand; and my long letter with a brief ending I conclude. Farewell, my all.

Document Set 10.6 References

A. The Arab Philosopher Ibn Sina (Avicenna) Describes His Exhilarating Discovery of Ancient Greek Learning
Lewis, *Islam: From the Prophet Muhammed to the Capture of Constantinople* (New York: Walker, 1987), 2:177–180.

B. St. Anselm Proves God's Existence
Adapted from *St. Anselm: Basic Writings*, trans. S. N. Deane (Lasalle, Ill: Open Court, 1966), 1–2, 8–9.

C. Abelard Describes His Quest for Knowledge
Abelard, *Autobiography*, in James Havey Robinson, ed., *Readings in European History* (Boston: Ginn, 1904), 1:447–449.

D. "Yes and No": Abelard Asks Some Hard Questions
Abelard *Yea and Nay*, in Robinson, 1:451–452.

E. Abelard's Brash Rationalism Leaves Conservatives Aghast
Otto of Freising, in C. C. Mierow, ed., *The Deeds of Frederick Barbarossa* (New York: Columbia University Press, 1935), 83–85.

F. Heloise Writes to Abelard of Their Past Love and Present Miseries
The Letters of Abelard and Heloise, trans. C. F. Scott Montcrieff (New York: Knopf, 1942), 53–61.

11

An Age of Confidence,
1144–1215

early corporations

DOCUMENT SET 11.1
Universities and Gothic Architecture

In Set 10.6 we examined sources from the beginnings of the revival of Western learning; this set continues the theme. Document A, a brief extract from the voluminous writings of the Spanish Muslim scholar Ibn Roushd (Averroes), attests to his near-fanatical veneration for Aristotle. Averroes interpreted the entire Qu'ran to accord with Aristotelian philosophy (much to the distress of conservative Muslims), and he went considerably further than most Christian thinkers were willing to go in accepting many Aristotelian propositions that were difficult or impossible to reconcile with Judeo-Christian and Muslim teachings.

The granting of corporate privileges to teachers and students—the normal way of incorporating an interest-group into medieval society—began in the twelfth century. In Document B, dated 1158, Emperor Frederick I Barbarossa grants such recognition to the wandering scholars of the Holy Roman Empire, at the same time attesting to the hardships and value of their work.

Opposition to the "new learning" never let up. Bishop Stephen of Tournai addressed to the pope an outraged letter in Document C sometime between 1192 and 1203, protesting with picturesque invectives against the ambitions of intellectuals such as those assembling at Paris to subject Christianity to logical scrutiny. What do you make of Bishop Stephen's blast against "adolescents with long hair" and "beardless youths" displacing senior masters? Document D, an official document (as opposed to

Bishop Stephen's blowing off of steam), contains specific denunciations of allegedly heretical doctrines; but exactly what the teachings were, and how close they may have come to definitely non-Christian ideas of Aristotle, is unknown.

The University of Paris received its statute in 1215 (Document E). What evidence do you see here of attempts by the authorities to control intellectual inquiry?

The last two documents attest to the powerful outburst of artistic creativity that paralleled the intellectual revival, manifesting itself in the building of cathedrals and the composition of religious poetry. In Document F, the Archbishop of Rouen writes to his colleague, the Bishop of Amiens, in 1145 to describe the spirit with which a splendid new cathedral was arising in Chartres—acknowledged today as one of the great masterworks of Gothic architecture. Document G is part of the cycle of songs (*symphonia*) written over many decades by German Abbess Hildegard of Bingen (1098–1179). Living an intensely personal and creative religious life, in her poetry (written for liturgical use) she captured the music she heard in visionary concerts of "the voice of a multitude singing in harmony, in praise of the celestial hierarchy."

Do you see any common threads linking medieval intellectuals, cathedral builders, and hymn writers?

A. The Muslim Philosopher Ibn Roushd (Averroes) Lauds Aristotle as Almost Divine

Aristotle was the wisest of the Greeks and constituted and completed logic, physics, and metaphysics. I say that he constituted these sciences, because all the works on these subjects previous to him do not deserve to be mentioned and were completely eclipsed by his writings. I say that he put the finishing touches on these sciences, because none of those who have succeeded him up to our time, to wit, during nearly fifteen hundred years, have been able to add anything to his writings or find in them any error of any importance. Now that all this should be found in one man is a strange and miraculous thing, and this privileged being deserves to be called divine rather than human.

B. Emperor Frederick Barbarossa Promises Protection to Students and Scholars, 1158

After a careful consideration of this subject by the bishops, abbots, dukes, counts, judges, and other nobles of our sacred palace, we, out of our piety, have granted this privilege to all scholars who travel for the sake of study, and especially to the professors of divine and sacred laws, namely: that they may go in safety to the places in which the studies are carried on, both they themselves and their messengers, and may dwell there in security. For we think it fitting that, so long as they conduct themselves with propriety, those should enjoy our approval and protection who, by their learning, enlighten the world and mold the life of our subjects to obey God and us, his minister. By reason of our special regard we desire to defend them from all injuries.

For who does not pity those who exile themselves through love for learning, who wear themselves out in poverty in place of riches, who expose their lives to all perils and often suffer bodily injury from the vilest men,—yet all these vexatious things must be endured by the scholar. Therefore, we declare, by this general and ever-to-be-valid law, that in the future no one shall be so rash as to venture to inflict any injury on scholars, or to occasion any loss to them on account of a debt owed by an inhabitant of their province,—a thing which we have learned is sometimes done, by an evil custom. And let it be known to the violators of this decree, and also to those who shall at the time be the rulers of the places where the offense is committed, that a fourfold restitution of property shall be exacted from all those who are guilty and that, the mark of infamy being affixed to them by the law itself, they shall lose their office forever.

Moreover, if any one shall presume to bring a suit against them on account of any business, the choice in this matter shall be given to the scholars, who may summon the accusers to appear before their professors, or before the bishop of the city, to whom we have given jurisdiction in this matter. But if, in sooth, the accuser shall attempt to drag the scholar before another judge, even though his cause is a very just one, he shall lose his suit for such an attempt.

C. Stephen of Tournai Denounces the "New Learning," End of the Twelfth Century

Having obtained indulgence, let us speak to our lord, whose gentleness emboldens us, whose prudence sustains our inexperience, whose patience promises impunity. To this the authority of our ancestors compels us and a disease gradually insinuating whose ills, if not met at the start, will be incurable in the end. Nor do we say this, father, as if we wished to be censors of morals, or judges of doctors, or debaters of doctrines. This load requires stouter shoulders, and this battle awaits the robust frames of spiritual athletes. We merely wish to indicate the sore spot to your holy paternity, to whom God has given both the power to uproot errors and the knowledge to correct them.

The studies of sacred letters among us are fallen into the worship of confusion, while both disciples applaud novelties alone and masters watch out for glory rather than learning. They everywhere compose new and recent *summulae* and commentaries, by which they attract, detain, and deceive their hearers, as if the works of the holy fathers were not still sufficient, who, we read, expounded holy scripture in the same spirit in which we believe the apostles and prophets composed it. They prepare strange and exotic courses for their banquet, when at the nuptials of the son of the king of Taurus his own flesh and blood are killed and all prepared, and the wedding guests have only to take and eat what is set before them. Contrary to the sacred canons there is public

From *University Records and Life in the Middle Ages,* edited by Lynn Thorndike, pp. 23–24, 26–27. Copyright © 1944 by Columbia University Press. Reprinted with permission of the publisher.

disputation as to the incomprehensible deity; concerning the incarnation of the Word, verbose flesh and blood irreverently litigates. The indivisible Trinity is cut up and wrangled over in the trivia [introductory courses], so that now there are as many errors as doctors, as many scandals as classrooms, as many blasphemies as squares. Again, if a case comes up which should be settled by canon law either under your jurisdiction or within that of the ordinary judges, there is produced from the vendors an inextricable forest of decretals presumably under the name of pope Alexander of sacred memory, and older canons are cast aside, rejected, expunged. When this plunder has been unrolled before us, those things which were wholesomely instituted in councils of holy fathers neither impose form on councils nor an end to cases, since letters prevail which perchance advocates for hire invented and forged in their shops or cubicles under the name of Roman pontiffs. A new volume composed of these is solemnly read in the schools and offered for sale in the forum to the applause of a horde of notaries, who rejoice that in copying suspect opuscula [small books] both their labor is lessened and their pay increased. Two woes are the aforesaid, and lo, a third remains: faculties called liberal having lost their pristine liberty are sunk in such servitude that adolescents with long hair impudently usurp their professorships, and beardless youths sit in the seat of their seniors, and those who don't yet know how to be disciples strive to be named masters. And they write their *summulae* moistened with drool and dribble but unseasoned with the salt of philosophers. Omitting the rules of the arts and discarding the authentic books of the artificers, they seize the flies of empty words in their sophisms like the claws of spiders. Philosophy cries that her garments are torn and disordered and, modestly concealing her nudity for a few specific tatters, neither is consulted nor consoles as of old. All these things, father, call for the hand of apostolic correction, that the disorder in teaching, learning and disputing may be reduced to due form by your authority, that the divine word be not cheapened by vulgar handling, that it be not said on the street corners, "Lo Christ is here or lo He is there," lest what is holy be given to dogs and pearls be trodden under foot by swine.

D. The Bishop of Paris Condemns Heretical Ideas Circulating at the University, 1210

Let the body of master Amaury be removed from the cemetery and cast into unconsecrated ground, and the same be excommunicated by all the churches of the entire province. Bernard, William of Arria the goldsmith, Stephen priest of Old Corbeil, Stephen priest of Cella, John priest of Occines, master William of Poitiers, Dudo the priest, Dominicus de Triangulo, Odo and Elinans clerks of St. Cloud—these are to be degraded and left to the secular arm. Urricus priest of Lauriac and Peter of St. Cloud, now a monk of St. Denis, Guarinus priest of Corbeil, and Stephen the clerk are to be degraded and imprisoned for life. The writings of David of Dinant are to be brought to the bishop of Paris before the Nativity and burned.

Neither the books of Aristotle on natural philosophy nor their commentaries are to be read at Paris in public or secret, and this we forbid under penalty of excommunication. He in whose possession the writings of David of Dinant are found after the Nativity shall be considered a heretic.

As for the theological books written in French we order that they be handed over to the diocesan bishops, both *Credo in deum* and *Pater noster* in French except the lives of the saints, and this before the Purification, because [then] he who shall be found with them shall be held a heretic.

E. The Church Authorities Lay Down New Regulations for the University of Paris, 1215

R., servant of the cross of Christ, by the divine mercy cardinal priest with the title of St. Stephen in Monte Celio and legate of the apostolic seat, to all the masters and scholars at Paris—eternal safety in the Lord.

Let all know, that having been especially commanded by the lord pope to devote our energy effectively to the betterment of the condition of the students at Paris, and wishing by the advice of good men to provide for the tranquility of the students in the future, we have ordered and prescribed the following rules:

No one is to lecture at Paris in arts before he is twenty years old. He is to listen in arts at least six years, before he begins to lecture. He is to promise that he will lecture for at least two years, unless he is prevented by some good reason, which he ought to prove either in public or before the examiners. He must not be smirched by any infamy. When he is ready to lecture, each one is to be examined according to the form contained in the letter of lord P. bishop of Paris (in which is contained the peace established between the chancellor and the students by the judges appointed by the lord pope, approved and confirmed namely by the bishop and deacon of Troyes and by P. the bishop, and J. the chancellor of Paris).

The treatises of Aristotle on logic, both the old and the new, are to be read in the schools in the regular and not in the extraordinary courses. The two Priscians, or at least the second, are also to be read in the schools in the regular courses. On the feast-days nothing is to be read except philosophy, rhetoric, *quadrivialia,* the Barbarisms, the Ethics, if one so chooses, and the fourth book of the Topics. The books of Aristotle on Metaphysics or Natural Philosophy, or the abridgements of these works, are not to be read, nor "the doctrine" of master David de Dinant, of the heretic Almaric, or of Maurice of Spain.

In the inceptions and meetings of the masters and in the confutations or arguments of the boys or youths there are to be no festivities. But they may call in some friends or associates, but only a few. We also advise that donations of garments and other things be made, as is customary or even to a greater extent, and especially to the poor. No master lecturing in arts is to wear anything except a cope, round and black and reaching to the heels—at least, when it is new. But he may well wear a pallium. He is not to wear under the round cope embroidered shoes and never any with long bands.

If any one of the students in arts or theology dies, half of the masters of arts are to go the funeral, and the other half to the next funeral. They are not to withdraw until the burial is completed, unless they have some good reason. If any master of arts or theology dies, all the masters are to be present at the vigils, each one is to read the psalter or have it read. Each one is to remain in the church, where the vigils are celebrated, until midnight or later, unless prevented by some good reason. On the day when the master is buried, no one is to lecture or dispute.

We fully confirm to them the meadow of St. Germain in the condition in which it was adjudged to them.

Each master is to have jurisdiction over his scholars. No one is to receive either schools or a house without the consent of the occupant, if he is able to obtain it. No one is to receive a license from the chancellor or any one else through a gift of money, or furnishing a pledge or making an agreement. Also, the masters and students can make among themselves or with others agreements and regulations, confirmed by a pledge, penalty or oath, about the following matters: namely, if a student is killed, mutilated or receives some outrageous injury and if justice is not done; for taxing the rent of *Hospitia;* concerning the

dress, burial, lectures and disputations; in such a manner, however, that the university is not scattered nor destroyed on this account.

We decide concerning the theologians, that no one shall lecture at Paris before he is thirty-five years old, and not unless he has studied at least eight years, and has heard the books faithfully and in the schools. He is to listen in theology for five years, before he reads his own lectures in public. No one of them is to lecture before the third hour on the days when the masters lecture. No one is to be received at Paris for the important lectures or sermons unless he is of approved character and learning. There is to be no student at Paris who does not have a regular master.

In order moreover that these may be inviolably observed, all who presume contumaciously to violate these our statutes, unless they take care, within fifteen days from the date of the transgression, to correct their presumption in the presence of the university of masters and scholars, or in the presence of some appointed by the university, by the authority of the legation with which we are entrusted, we bind with the bond of excommunication.

Done in the year of grace 1215, in the month of August.

F. The Building of Chartres Cathedral

Hugo, priest of Rouen, to the Reverend Father Thierry, Bishop of Amiens, may he prosper always in Christ. Great is the work of the Lord, excellent in all of His will. The inhabitants of Chartres have combined to aid in the construction of their church by transporting the material; our Lord has rewarded their humble zeal by miracles which have roused the Normans to imitate the piety of their neighbors. People of our land, therefore, having received blessing from us, set out continuously for that place and fulfill their vows. Since then, the faithful of our diocese and of other neighboring regions have formed associations for the same object; they admit no one into their company unless he has been to confession, has renounced enmities and revenges, and has reconciled himself with his enemies. That done, they elect a chief, under whose direction they conduct their waggons in silence and with humility, and present their oblations not without discipline and tears. These three things which we set forth, confession with penitence, concord in place of all malevolence, and humility with obedience—we require from those who are about to come to us; if they defer to these three, we receive them piously, absolve and bless them. While thus instructed they travel on their way, and whenever they bring their sick with them great miracles are very frequently wrought in our church, and they lead away as well those who came with them as invalids. And we allow our own people to go outside our regions, but we prohibit them from entering among the excommunicated or the interdicted. Given in this year of the Incarnate Word, 1145. Farewell.

G. Hildegard of Bingen's Liturgical Verses

Antiphon for the Virgin

Banished Eve and Adam blushing
    watched as their children fell,
        helplessly rushing
            toward hell.
            Mary!
        you plead for all:
    lift up your voice and carry
our souls above on the wings of your call.

Antiphon for Divine Love

Charity rising
from the vast abyss
past the stars above
abounds in all worlds,
unbounded love,
and with spousal kiss
disarms the sky—king.

Document Set 11.1 References

A. The Muslim Philosopher Ibn Roushd (Averroes) Lauds Aristotle as Almost Divine
James Harvey Robinson, ed., *Readings in European History* (Boston: Ginn, 1904), 1:456.

B. Emperor Frederick Barbarossa Promises Protection to Students and Scholars, 1158
Robinson, 1:452

C. Stephen of Tournai Denounces the "New Learning," End of the Twelfth Century
Lynn Thorndike, ed., *University Records and Life in the Middle Ages* (New York: Columbia University Press, 1944), 23–24.

D. The Bishop of Paris Condemns Heretical Ideas Circulating at the University, 1210
Thorndike, 26–27.

E. The Church Authorities Lay Down New Regulations for the University of Paris, 1215
Translations and Reprints from the Original Sources of European History (Philadelphia: University of Pennsylvania Press, 1898), 2/3:12–15.

F. The Building of Chartres Cathedral
Hugo of Rouen, letter, in Elizabeth G. Holt, *Documentary History of Art* (Princeton: Princeton University Press, 1981), 1:51.

G. Hildegard of Bingen's Liturgical Verses
Quoted in Barbara Newman, *Saint Hildegard of Bingen. Symphonia* (Ithica, NY: Cornell University Press, 1988), 7–8, 119, 141.

DOCUMENT SET 11.2
Courtly Love

The source readings in this set should be read not for their intellectual sophistication but for fun, for they were intended to be works of entertainment and instruction in the art of love. Try, however, to ferret out evidence of how male-female relations were viewed by the upper-class audiences for which these works were created, and ascertain to what extent the literature of courtly love may have had a prescriptive purpose.

Document A is a nineteenth-century English rendering of a song by the Provençal troubadour Bernard de Ventadorn. Document B is an extract from the lengthy romance *Lancelot* by Chrétien de Troyes. In Document C, a twelfth-century writer known as Andreas Capellanus (Andrew the Chaplain) sets down in quasi-logical form a set of propositions for the proper pursuit of the beloved in the spirit of courtly love.

A. Agonies of Love as Endured by the Troubadour Bernart de Ventadorn

Whene'er the lark's glad wings I see
    Beat sunward 'gainst the radiant sky
Till, lost in joy so sweet and free,
    She drops, forgetful how to fly,—
        Ah, when I view such happiness
           My bosom feels so deep an ache,
        Meseems for pain and sore distress
           My longing heart will straightway break.

Alas, I thought I held the key
    To love! How ignorant am I!
For her that ne'er will pity me
    I am not able to defy;
        My loving heart, my faithfulness,
           Myself, my world, she deigns to take,
        Then leaves me bare and comfortless
           To longing thoughts that ever wake.

B. Sir Lancelot Seeks His True Love

When they had risen from the table, the damsel said to the knight: "Sire, if you do not object, go outside and amuse yourself; but, if you please, do not stay after you think I must be in bed. Feel no concern or embarrassment; for then you may come to me at once, if you will keep the promise you have made." And he replies: "I will keep my word, and will return when I think the time has come." Then he went out, and stayed in the courtyard until he thought it was time to return and keep the promise he had made.

Going back into the hall, he sees nothing of her who would be his mistress; for she was not there. Not finding or seeing her, he said: "Wherever she may be, I shall look for her until I find her." He makes no delay in his search, begin bound by the promise he had made her.

Entering one of the rooms, he hears a damsel cry aloud, and it was the very one with whom he was about to lie. At the same time, he sees the door of another room standing open, and stepping toward it, he sees right before his eyes a knight who had thrown her down, and was holding her naked and prostrate upon the bed. She, thinking that he had come of course to help her, cried aloud: "Help, help, thou knight, who art my guest. If thou dost not take this man away from me, I shall find no one to do so; if thou dost not succour me speedily, he will wrong me before thy eyes. Thou art the one to lie with me, in accordance with thy promise; and shall this man by force accomplish his wish before thy eyes? Gentle knight, exert thyself, and make haste to bear me aid."

He sees that the other man held the damsel brutally uncovered to the waist, and he is ashamed and angered to see him assault her so; yet it is not jealousy he feels, nor will he be made a cuckold by him. At the door there stood as guards two knights completely armed and with swords drawn. Behind them there stood four men-at-arms, each armed with an axe—the sort with which you could split a cow down the back as easily as a root of juniper or broom. The knight hesitated at the door, and thought: "God, what can I do? I am engaged in no less an affair than the quest of Queen Guinevere. I ought not to have the heart of a hare, when for her sake I have engaged in such a quest. If cowardice puts its heart in me, and if I follow its dictates, I shall never attain what I seek. I am disgraced, if I stand here; indeed, I am ashamed even to have thought of holding back. My heart is very sad and oppressed: now I am so ashamed and distressed that I would gladly die for having hesitated here so long. I say it not in pride: but may God have mercy on me if I do not prefer to die honourably rather than live a life of shame! If my path were unobstructed, and if these men gave me leave to pass through without restraint, what honour would I gain? Truly, in that case the greatest coward alive would pass through; and all the while I hear this poor creature calling for help constantly, and reminding me of my promise, and reproaching me with bitter taunts."

Then he steps to the door, thrusting in his head and shoulders; glancing up, he sees two swords descending. He draws back, and the knights could not check their strokes: they had wielded them with such force that the swords struck the floor, and both were broken in pieces. When he sees that the swords are broken, he pays less attention to the axes, fearing and dreading them much less. Rushing in among them, he strikes first one guard in the side and then another. The two who are nearest him he jostles and thrusts aside, throwing them both down flat; the third missing his stroke at him, but the fourth, who attacked him, strikes him so that he cuts his mantle and shirt, and slices the white flesh on his shoulder so that the blood trickles down from the wound. But he, without delay, and without complaining of his wound, presses on more rapidly, until he strikes between the temples him who was assaulting his hostess. Before he departs, he will try to keep his pledge to her. He makes him stand up reluctantly. Meanwhile, he who has missed striking him comes at him as fast as he can, and, raising his arm again, expects to split his head to the teeth with the axe. But the other, alert to defend himself, thrusts the knight toward him in such a way that he receives the axe just where the shoulder joins the neck, so that they are cleaved apart. Then the knight seizes the axe, wresting it quickly from him who holds it; then he lets go the knight whom he still held, and looks to his own defence; for the knights from the door, and the three men with axes are all attacking him fiercely. So he leaped quickly between the bed and the wall, and called to them: "Come on now, all of you. If there were thirty-seven of you, you would have all the fight you wish, with me so favourably placed; I shall never be overcome by you." And the damsel watching him, exclaimed: "By my eyes, you need have no thought of that henceforth where I am." Then at once she dismisses the knights and the men-at-arms, who retire from there at once, without delay or objection. And the damsel continues: "Sire you have well defended me against the men of my household. Come now, and I'll lead you on." Hand in hand they enter the hall, but he was not at all pleased, and would have willingly dispensed with her.

In the midst of the hall a bed had been set up, the sheets of which were by no means soiled, but were white and wide and well spread out. The bed was not of shredded straw or of coarse spreads. But a covering of two silk cloths had been laid upon the couch. The damsel lay down first, but without removing her chemise. He had great trouble in removing his hose and in untying the knots. He sweated with the trouble of it all; yet, in the midst of all the trouble, his promise impels and drives him on. Is this then an actual force? Yes, virtually so; for he feels that he is in duty bound to take his place by the damsel's side. It is his promise that urges him and dictates his act. So he lies down at once, but like her, he does not remove his shirt. He takes good care not to touch her; and when he is in bed, he turns away from her as far as possible, and speaks not a word to her, like a monk to whom speech is forbidden. Not once does he look at her, nor show her any courtesy. Why not? Because his heart does not go out to her. She was certainly very fair and winsome, but not every one is pleased and touched by what is fair and winsome. The knight has only one heart, and this one is really no longer his, but has been entrusted to some one else, so that he cannot bestow it elsewhere.

Love, which holds all hearts beneath its sway, requires it to be lodged in a single place. All hearts? No, only those which it esteems. And he whom love deigns to control ought to prize himself the more. Love prized his heart so highly that it constrained it in a special manner, and made him so proud of this distinction that I am not inclined to find fault with him, if he lets alone what love forbids, and remains fixed where it desires.

The maiden clearly sees and knows that he dislikes her company and would gladly dispense with it, and that, having no desire to win her love, he would not attempt to woo her. So she said: "My lord, if you will not feel hurt, I will leave and return to bed in my own room, and you will be more comfortable. I do not believe that you are pleased with my company and society. Do not esteem me less if I tell you what I think. Now take your rest all night, for you have so well kept your promise that I have no right to make further request of you. So I commend you to God, and shall go away."

Thereupon she arises: the knight does not object, but rather gladly lets her go, like one who is the devoted lover of some one else; the damsel clearly perceived this, and went to her room, where she undressed completely and retired, saying to herself: "Of all the knights I have ever known, I never knew a single knight whom I would value the third part of an angevin in comparison with this one. As I understand the case, he has on hand a more perilous and grave affair than any ever undertaken by a knight;

and may God grant that he succeed in it." Then she fell asleep, and remained in bed until the next day's dawn appeared.

c. Andreas Capellanus Codifies the Rules of Courtly Love

I. Marriage is no real excuse for not loving.

II. He who is not jealous cannot love.

III. No one can be bound by a double love.

IV. It is well known that love is always increasing or decreasing.

V. That which a lover takes against the will of his beloved has no relish.

VI. Boys do not love until they arrive at the age of maturity.

VII. When one lover dies, a widowhood of two years is required of the survivor.

VIII. No one should be deprived of love without the very best of reasons.

IX. No one can love unless he is impelled by the persuasion of love.

X. Love is always a stranger in the home of avarice.

XI. It is not proper to love any woman whom one would be ashamed to seek to marry.

XII. A true lover does not desire to embrace in love anyone except his beloved.

XIII. When made public love rarely endures.

XIV. The easy attainment of love makes it of little value; difficulty of attainment makes it prized.

XV. Every lover regularly turns pale in the presence of his beloved.

XVI. When a lover suddenly catches sight of his beloved his heart palpitates.

XVII. A new love puts to flight an old one.

XVIII. Good character alone makes any man worthy of love.

XIX. If love diminishes, it quickly fails and rarely revives.

XX. A man in love is always apprehensive.

XXI. Real jealousy always increases the feeling of love.

XXII. Jealousy, and therefore love, are increased when one suspects his beloved.

XXIII. He whom the thought of love vexes eats and sleeps very little.

XXIV. Every act of a lover ends in the thought of his beloved.

XXV. A true lover considers nothing good except what he thinks will please his beloved.

XXVI. Love can deny nothing to love.

XXVII. A lover can never have enough of the solaces of his beloved.

XXVIII. A slight presumption causes a lover to suspect his beloved.

XXIX. A man who is vexed by too much passion usually does not love.

XXX. A true lover is constantly and without intermission possessed by the thought of his beloved.

XXXI. Nothing forbids one woman being loved by two men or one man by two women.

Document Set 11.2 References

A. Agonies of Love as Endured by the Troubadour Bernart de Ventadorn
   James Harvey Robinson, ed., *Readings in European History* (Boston: Ginn, 1904), 1:437.
B. Sir Lancelot Seeks His True Love
   Chrétian de Troyes, *Arthurian Romances,* trans. W. W. Comfort (Everyman's Library, 1914), 283–286.
C. Andreas Capellanus Codifies the Rules of Courtly Love
   Andreas Capellanus, *Art of Courtly Love,* trans. J. J. Perry (New York: Columbia University Press, 1941).

DOCUMENT SET 11.3
Feudalism and Monarchy: England and France

The documents in this set continue Set 10.5's inquiry into feudal monarchy. Document A is (apart from Domesday Book) one of the oldest English estate inventories. It gives a representative example of the kind of property and peasants (villeins) at the disposal of a feudal lord, in this case Peterborough Abbey. Document B is a brief extract from another kind of feudal-era register, a *coutumier,* or listing of "customary" dues owed to the local lord—here the Duke of Normandy—by his vassals. "Aids" are obligations that the vassal owed, theoretically on pain of losing his holding. Such feudal obligations as the requirement that a vassal obtain his lord's permission before marrying could be seriously enforced: see Document C, an extract from a chronicle from what is today Belgium, dated 1151.

Documents D and E show how two feudal rulers made themselves effective monarchs. In Document D a contemporary biographer describes (not correctly in all details but overall accurately enough) how kings of France like Philip Augustus (*1180–1223) were steadily building up the royal domain. How did claims of feudal rights figure in this process? Document E is an extract from the Assize of Clarendon (1166), an assembly at which England's Henry II (*1154–1189) laid down—"with the assent of the archbishops, bishops, abbots, earls, and barons of all England"—basic procedures for the maintenance of justice by English courts. Notice the provision made for twelve-man juries to investigate alleged crimes and render verdicts, and also the role of sheriffs, the appointed royal representatives in each shire. Notice too the final provision, directed against heretics, the first such legislation in England.

How Henry II's law courts functioned is suggested by Document F, a selection of "pleas of the crown" dating from 1201–1214. Ordeals, it is apparent, were still resorted to, though they would be forbidden after 1219.

Using these source materials and *The Challenge of the West,* write a brief essay analyzing how the French and English monarchies worked in practice in approximately the years 1050–1215.

A. An English Manor, c. 1125

In Werminton are 7 hides at the taxation of the king. And of this land 20 full villeins and 29 half-villeins hold 34 virgates and a half; and for these the full villeins work 3 days a week through the year; and the half tenants as much as corresponds to their tenancies. And all these men have 16 plows, and they plow 68 acres and a half, and besides this they do 3 boon-works with their plows, and they ought to bring from the woods 34 wagon loads of wood. And all these men pay 4£. 11s.4d. And to the love feast of St. Peter 10 rams and 400 loaves and 40 platters and 34 hens and 260 eggs. And there are 8 socmen who have 6 plows. In the demesne of the court are 4 plows of 32 oxen, and 9 cows and 5 calves, and 1 riding horse and 129 sheep and 61 swine and 1 draught-horse and 1 colt. And there is 1 mill with 1 virgate of land and 6 acres which pays 60s. and 500 eels. And Ascelin the clerk holds the church, with 2 virgates of land, from the altar of St. Peter of Borough. Robert, son of Richard, has 2 virgates and a half. In this vill 100 sheep can be placed.

B. The "Three Customary Aids" in Twelfth-Century Normandy

Next it is proper to see the chief aids of Normandy, which are called chief because they should be paid to the chief lords.

In Normandy there are three chief aids. One is to make the oldest son of his lord a knight; the second, to marry his oldest daughter; the third to ransom the body of his lord from prison when he is taken in the Duke's war.

C. A Vassal Tries to Marry Without His Lord's Consent, 1151

Then the young man Aegidius, son of Gerard Maufilatre married a wife, Bertha by name, half-sister of Count Baldwin of Hainault and took her without his assent. The count, extremely angry at this, immediately took up arms against him at the beginning of the month of October. Thus from the time in which he had married her till Whitsunday, with or without consent, he kept her closely by force and arms at his house. But Aegidius having been attacked by a severe fever, which troubled him sharply every day, compelled by the counsel of his friends, who had helped him honorably in all things in his war, dismissed and openly abjured her; and peace was thus restored with the count, and the land was peaceful which had been long troubled by wars.

D. Philip Augustus Extends the Royal Domain of France, 1184

In the year of our Lord's Incarnation 1184, the fifth year of Philip Augustus' reign and the twentieth of his age, a dispute arose, as is not uncommon in times of change, between Philip, most Christian king of the French, and Philip, count of Flanders, about a certain district commonly called Vermandois.

The king claimed that all Vermandois, with its castles, villages, and vills, belonged by right of inheritance and succession to the kings of the French; and he offered to prove it all by the testimony of clergy and laity,—archbishops, bishops, counts, viscounts, and other nobles.

The count of Flanders replied that he had held the land in question during the lifetime of the most Christian king Louis, of blessed memory, and had possessed it in peace, without any dispute, during many years, and was firmly resolved never to give it up so long as he lived. For the count believed that, since the king was but a lad, he could easily divert his mind from this project by promises and flattering words. Besides, it is said that many nobles were ready to support him; but, as the proverb says, "They are sons of the winds, they weave cobwebs."

At length Philip Augustus followed the advice of the princes and barons and called together all the nobles of his lands in the beautiful castle of Karnopalis, commonly called Compiègne. He took counsel with them, and collected a very large army at the city which is called Amiens.

When the count of Flanders heard of the king's coming his heart rejoiced. He collected an army to oppose Philip, directed his forces against his lord, the king, and swore by the strength of his arm that he could defend himself against all men. Thus in the fifth year of his reign and the twentieth of his age the king entered into that land with his army, which covered the face of the earth like locusts. When the count of Flanders saw the king's army, that it was very great and strong, his spirit was troubled, and the hearts of his people became as water, so that they sought safety in flight. Then the count took counsel with his own, and sent messengers to call to his presence Theobald, count of Blois, chief of the king's knights and seneschal of France, and William, archbishop of Rheims—both uncles of the king, to whom the direction of affairs had been intrusted at this time because they were faithful to the king.

The count of Flanders used them as intermediaries and through them addressed the king in this wise: "Let thine anger toward us cease, Lord. Come to us in peaceful guise, and use our service as shall be pleasing in thy sight. The land which thou desirest, my lord king, Vermandois, with all the castles and vills belonging to it, I will restore to thee, my lord king, in its entirety, freely, and without delay. But if it shall please your royal majesty, I beg that the castle of St. Quentin and the castle of Péronne may be granted to me as a kingly gift to be held so long as I live. After my death they shall, without controversy, devolve upon thee or thy successors, the kings of the French."

When Philip, most Christian king of the French, had heard this message, he called together all the archbishops, bishops, abbots, counts, viscounts, and all the barons who had come with one accord to subdue the insolence of the count of Flanders and to humble his pride. He took counsel with them, and they answered as with one voice that this which the count of Flanders proposed to the king should be done. When this decision had been reached, the count of Flanders was introduced, and before all the nobles and the throng gathered there, he restored to Philip, the lawful king, the land he had so long wrongfully held; and then and there, after he had restored the land before them all, he put the king in possession of it.

Further, he promised the king upon his oath to make good, without delay, and according to the king's will, all the losses he had inflicted upon Baldwin, count of Hainault, and other friends of the king. And thus was peace restored between the king the count as by a miracle, for it was concluded without shedding human blood. And when all the people heard of these things they were filled with great joy, and praised and blessed God who saves those who put their hope in him.

E. Henry II Prescribes Law and Order in England: The Assizes of Clarendon, 1166

1. In the first place, the aforesaid King Henry, with the consent of all his barons, for the preservation of the peace and the keeping of justice, has enacted that inquiry should be made through the several counties and through the several hundreds, by twelve of the most legal men of the hundred and by four of the most legal men of each manor, upon their oath that they will tell the truth, whether there is in their hundred or in their manor, any man who has been accused or publicly suspected of himself being a robber, or murderer, or thief, or of being a receiver of robbers, or murderers, or thieves, since the lord king has been king. And let the justices make this inquiry before themselves, and the sheriffs before themselves.

2. And let anyone who has been found by the oath of the aforesaid, to have been accused or publicly suspected of having been a robber, or murderer, or thief, or a receiver of them, since the lord king has been king, be arrested and go to the ordeal of water and let him swear that he has not been a robber, or murderer, or thief, or receiver of them since the lord king has been king, to the value of five shillings, so far as he knows. . . .

4. And when a robber, or murderer, or thief, or receiver of them shall have been seized through the above-mentioned oath, if the justices are not to come very soon into that county where they have been arrested, let the sheriffs send word to the nearest justice by some intelligent man that they have arrested such men, and the justices will send back word to the sheriffs where they wish that these should be brought before them; and the sheriffs shall bring them before the justices; and along with these they shall bring from the hundred and the manor where they have been arrested, two legal men to carry the record of the county and of the hundred as to why they were seized, and there before the justice let them make their law. . . .

7. And in the several counties where there are no jails, let such be made in a borough or in some castle of the king, from the money of the king and from his forest, if one shall be near, or from some other neighboring forest, on the view of the servants of the king; in order that in them the sheriffs may be able to detain those who have been seized by the officials who are accustomed to do this or by their servants. . . .

10. And in cities and boroughs, let no one have men or receive them in his house or in his land or his soc, whom he does not take in hand that he will produce before the justice if they shall be required, or else let them be under a frankpledge.

11. And let there be none in a city or borough or in a castle or without, or even in the honor of Wallingford, who shall forbid the sheriffs to enter into his land or his jurisdiction to arrest those who have been charged or publicly suspected of being robbers or murderers or thieves or receivers of them, or outlaws, or persons charged concerning the forest; but he requires that they should aid them to capture these.

12. And if any one is captured who has in his possession the fruits of robbery or theft, if he is of bad reputation and has an evil testimony from the public, and has not a warrant, let him not have law. And if he shall not have been accused on account of the possession which he has, let him go to the water. . . .

15. And the lord king forbids any vagabond, that is a wandering or an unknown man, to be sheltered anywhere except in a borough, and even there he shall be sheltered only one night, unless he shall be sick there, or his horse, so that he is able to show an evident excuse.

16. And if he shall have been there more than one night, let him be arrested and held until his lord shall come to give securities for him, or until he himself shall have secured pledges; and let him likewise be arrested who has sheltered him. . . .

20. The lord king moreover prohibits monks and canons and all religious houses from receiving any one of the lesser people as a monk or canon or brother, until it is known of what reputation he is, unless he shall be sick unto death.

21. The lord king moreover forbids any one in all England to receive in his land or his jurisdiction or in a house under him any one of the sect of those renegades who have been excommunicated and branded at Oxford. And if anyone shall have received them, he will be at the mercy of the lord king, and the house in which they have been shall be carried outside the village and burned. And each sheriff will take this oath that he will hold this, and will make all his servants swear this, and the stewards of the barons, and all knights and free tenants of the countries. . . .

F. Criminal Cases Tried Before the English Royal Courts, 1201–1214

Denise, who was wife of Anthony, summons Nicholas Kam for the death of Anthony, her husband, as having wickedly killed her husband; and this she offers to prove against him under award of the court. And Nicholas denies it all. It is adjudged that Denise has no right of summons, because she does not claim in her accusation that she saw it. The jurors being asked say that they suspect him of it, and the whole county likewise suspects him. Let Nicholas purge himself by water, according to the assize. He has found sureties.

Hugh of Ruperes summons John of Ashby because he in the king's peace and wickedly came into his meadows and pastured his cattle on them, and this he offers, etc. And John comes and denies it all. And since it has been testified by the sheriff and by the guardians of the pleas of the crown, that he had previously summoned John for the pasturing of his meadows and for the beating of his men, and now is not willing to pursue his accusation concerning the men, but only concerning the meadows, and moreover an accusation of the pasturing of meadows does not pertain to the king's crown, it is judged that the accusation is of no effect, and therefore let Hugh be in mercy and John be declared quit. Hugh is in custody because he cannot find securities.

Hereward, the son of William, accuses Walter, the son of Hugh, of assaulting him, in the king's peace, and wounding him in the arm with a certain iron fork, and giving him another wound on the head; and this he offers to prove on his body, as the court shall approve. And Walter denies it all, on his body. And it is testified by the coroners and by the whole county that the same Hereward showed his wounds at the proper time, and has made sufficient suit. And it is therefore adjudged that a battle should be made. The securities of Walter are Peter of Gosberton church and Richard, the son of Hereward; the securities of Hereward are William, his father, and the Prior of Pinchbeck. Let them come armed, a fortnight from St. Swithin's day, at Leicester.

Lambert, the miller, complains that Clarice, wife of Lawrence, the son of Walter, sold him beer by a false gallon, and produces testimony which report that they were present when she thus sold by that gallon, that is to say, three gallons for a penny. Clarice comes and denies that she sold by a false gallon, or that she sold by that gallon which he said was hers as being a whole gallon, but as being a half-gallon. Let her defend herself with twelve hands on the coming of the justices. She has given securities. Security for her law, William, son of Ascelin; securities of Lambert to prosecute, William Sanguinel, Richard, son of Geoffrey, Dennis, son of Lambert, and Walter the miller.

A certain Lemis is suspected by the jurors of being present when Reinild of Hemchurch was slain, and of having given aid and consent to her death. And she denies it. Therefore let her purge herself by the ordeal of iron; but as she is ill, let it be postponed until she recovers.

Walter Trenchebof was asserted to have handed to Inger of Faldingthrope the knife with which he killed Guy Foliot, and is suspected of it. Let him purge himself by water that he did not consent to it. He has failed and is hanged.

Simon, the son of Robert, who was captured in company with thieves and was held in prison because he was under age must likewise purge himself by water. He has purged himself and abjured the realm.

Document Set 11.3 References

A. An English Manor, c. 1125
   Translations and Reprints from the Original Sources of European History (Philadelphia: University of Pennsylvania Press, 1902), 3/5:4.
B. The "Three Customary Aids" in Twelfth-Century Normandy
   Translations and Reprints (1898), 4/3:28.
C. A Vassal Tries to Marry Without His Lord's Consent, 1151
   Robinson, 25.
D. Philip Augustus Extends the Royal Domain of France, 1184
   From Rigord, *Life of Philip Augustus,* in James Harvey Robinson, ed., *Readings in European History* (Boston: Ginn, 1904), 5:207–209.
E. Henry II Prescribes Law and Order in England: The Assizes of Clarendon, 1166
   Translations and Reprints, 1/6:22–26.
F. Criminal Cases Tried Before the English Royal Courts, 1201–1214
   Translations and Reprints, (1897), 30–31.

DOCUMENT SET 11.4
Feudalism, Imperialism, and the Commune: Frederick Barbarossa Confronts the Italians

Both documents in this set come from Bishop Otto of Freising's *Deeds of Frederick I*, a study of Barbarossa's early years written by his uncle—a man of considerable learning and acute judgment, if not lacking in bias. In Document A, Barbarossa and emissaries of the city of Rome debate whether Rome's ancient republican traditions still have validity in the face of the Holy Roman Emperor's assertion of imperial authority. (This incident is related at the beginning of Chapter 11 of *The Challenge of the West*.) Document B narrates how Barbarossa, temporarily triumphant over the north Italian communes, attempted to impose a centralized system of justice and carried out a review of existing legal rights.

How does Barbarossa's view of royal authority compare with what you have studied of feudal monarchy in Sets 10.5 and 11.4?

A. The Roman Commune and Barbarossa Debate the Restoration of Rome's Ancient Republic

"We the ambassadors of the City—no insignificant part of the City—O Excellent King, have been sent to Your Excellency by the senate and people of Rome. Hear with calm mind and gracious ears. . . .

Now you know that the city of Rome, by the wisdom of the senatorial dignity and the valor of the equestrian order, sending out her boughs from sea to sea, has not only extended her empire to the ends of the earth but has even added to her world the islands that lie beyond the world, and planted there the shoots of her dominion. The boisterous waves of the seas could not protect those, nor could the rugged and inaccessible crags of the Alps defend these: indomitable Roman valor has subdued all. But, for our sins, since our princes dwelt at a great distance from us, that noble token of our antiquity—I refer to the senate—was given over to neglect by the slothful carelessness of certain men. As wisdom slumbered, strength too was of necessity diminished. I have

arisen to reinstate the holy senate of the holy City and the equestrian order, to enhance your glory and that of the divine republic, that by the decree of the one and the arms of the other its ancient splendor may return to the Roman empire and to your person. Should this not please Your Nobility? Will not so notable a deed and one so in keeping with your authority be judged even worthy of reward? Hear then, O Prince, with patience and with clemency a few matters that have to do with your justice and with mine! About yours, however, before I speak of mine. For 'the beginning is from Jove.' You were a stranger. I made you a citizen. You were a newcomer from the regions beyond the Alps. I have established you as prince. What was rightfully mine I gave to you. You ought therefore first afford security for the maintenance of my good customs and ancient laws, strengthened for me by the emperors your predecessors, that they may not be violated by the fury of barbarians. To my officials, who must acclaim you on the Capitol, you should give as much as five thousand pounds as expense money. You should avert harm from the republic even to the extent of the shedding of your blood, and safeguard all this by privileges, and establish it by the interposition of an oath with your own hand."

Hereupon the king, inflamed with righteous anger by the tenor of a speech, as insolent as it was unusual, interrupted the flow of words of those ambassadors concerning the jurisdiction of their republic and of the empire, as they were about to spin out their oration in the Italian fashion by lengthy and circuitous periods. Preserving his royal dignity with modest bearing and charm of expression he replied without preparation but not unprepared.

"We have heard much heretofore concerning the wisdom and the valor of the Romans, yet more concerning their wisdom. Wherefore we cannot wonder enough at finding your words insipid with swollen pride rather than seasoned with the salt of wisdom. You set forth the ancient renown of your city. You extol to the very stars the ancient status of your sacred republic. Granted, granted! To use the words of your own writer, 'There was, *there was once* virtue in this republic.' 'Once,' I say. And O that we might truthfully and freely say 'now'! Your Rome—nay, ours also—has experienced the vicissitudes of time. She could not be the only one to escape a fate ordained by the Author of all things for all that dwell beneath the orb of the moon. What shall I say? It is clear how first the strength of your nobility was transferred from this city of ours to the royal city of the East, and how for the course of many years the thirsty Greekling sucked the breasts of your delight. Then came the Frank, truly noble, in deed as in name, and forcibly possessed himself of whatever freedom was still left to you. Do you wish to know the ancient glory of your Rome? The worth of the sensatorial dignity? The impregnable disposition of the camp? The virtue and the discipline of the equestrian order, its unmarred and unconquerable boldness when advancing to a conflict? Behold our state. All these things are to be found with us. All these have descended to us, together with the empire. Not in utter nakedness did the empire come to us. It came clad in its virtue. It brought its adornments with it. With us are your consuls. With us is your senate. With us is your soldiery. These very leaders of the Franks must rule you by their counsel, these very knights of the Franks must avert harm from you with the sword. You boastfully declare that by you I have been summoned, that by you I have been made first a citizen and then the prince, that from you I have received what was yours. How lacking in reason, how void of truth this novel utterance is, may be left to your own judgment and to the decision of men of wisdom! . . .

B. Barbarossa Imposes Imperial Overlordship and Local Feudal Authority in Italy

During the following days the emperor was occupied from morning until evening, in full and solemn court, dispensing judgments and justice. He listened attentively to complaints and appeals of rich and poor alike. He had four judges, . . . eloquent and pious men, most learned in the law, doctors of law in the city of Bologna and teachers of many students. With these and other jurists present from various cities, he heard, deliberated, and decided matters. Remarking the great number of those who carried crosses—for this is the custom of the Italians, that those who have grievances carry a cross in their hands—he felt sorry for them and said that he marveled at the wisdom of the Latins, who gloried much in their knowledge of law, yet were so often found to be its transgressors. How niggardly they were of justice was clearly apparent from the number of those who were hungering and thirsting for righteousness. Therefore, by divine inspiration, he appointed particular judges for

each diocese, not, however, from its own city, but either from the court or from another city. He did so for this reason: he feared that if a citizen were appointed to judge his own fellow citizens, he might readily be diverted from the truth by favor or hatred. And so it came about that of this great number of plaintiffs, there was scarcely any who did not rejoice at having secured either a complete victory in his suit, or his rights, or a satisfactory agreement with his adversary.

Then the emperor spoke earnestly about the justice of the realm and the regalia which, for a long time past, had been lost to the empire, either by reason of the impudence of usurpers or through royal neglect. As they could find no defense whereby to excuse themselves, both the bishops and the secular leaders and cities with one voice and one accord restored the regalia into the hand of the emperor. The people of Milan were the first of those who resigned them. Upon being asked what this right included, they assigned to him dukedoms, marches, counties, consulates, mints, market tolls (*thelonea*), forage tax (*fodrum*), wagon tolls (*vectigalia*), gate tolls (*portus*), transit tolls (*pedatica*), mills, fisheries, bridges, all the use of accruing from running water, and the payment of an annual tax, not only on the land, but also on their own persons.

When all these had been assigned to the imperial treasury, the prince displayed such generosity toward the former holders that whoever had documentary proof that he possessed any of these things by royal grant, he should even now, by imperial grant and in the name of the empire, hold the same in perpetuity. However, from those who had appropriated regalia unjustifiably, by sheer presumption, there accrued to the public revenues annually thirty thousand talents, more or less.

Furthermore, this also was adjudicated to him by all and recognized as his right: that he should himself select, with the consent of the people, the podestas, consuls, and all other magistrates, who (being both loyal and wise) would know how to maintain both the emperor's honor and due justice for the citizens and their native state.

Moreover, that all these agreements might be accepted and observed in good faith and without deceit, all the states bound themselves under oath and furnished hostages at the emperor's pleasure. Next, a common peace was sworn, that city would not war on city, nor man on man, save at the emperor's command.

Finally, with reference to feudal law, because it had not yet been satisfactorily expressed in writing among the Latins and almost all had converted the justice of the fiefs into injustice, he promulgated laws the provisions of which we have set down in the present chronicle:

[These provisions sought to ensure that all feudal relationships of lord and vassal would be strictly enforced. Among his other conditions, the emperor also tried to prevent Italian towns from forming communes and other associations:]

"We also absolutely forbid that there be associations and any sworn brotherhoods, in and outside the cities, even on the ground of blood relationship, whether between city and city, person and person, or a city and a person, and we abolish those formed in the past, individual members of the sworn brotherhoods to be assessed a fine of one pound of gold. . . .

Document Set 11.4 References

A. The Roman Commune and Barbarossa Debate the Restoration of Rome's Ancient Republic
C. C. Mierow, ed., *The Deeds of Frederick Barbarossa* (New York: Columbia University Press, 1935), 145–147.
B. Barbarossa Imposes Imperial Overlordship and Local Feudal Authority in Italy
Mierow, 237–239, 242.

DOCUMENT SET 11.5
The Later Crusades

Like the First Crusade (Set 10.4), the Second Crusade was stimulated by the papacy through the agency of such preachers as St. Bernard of Clairvaux (Document A). The crusade failed, owing to the rivalry of the two leading crusaders, the king of France and the Holy Roman Emperor. Bernard of Clairvaux seems to have gone out of his way to try to keep the crusaders' attention focused on the Muslims in the Holy Land rather than on the Jews in western Europe; how do you explain this?

The Fourth Crusade of 1204 was, as you have learned from *The Challenge of the West,* a scandalous atrocity in which the Venetians maneuvered the none-too-reluctant Western crusaders into attacking Constantinople. Document B provides two contrasting extracts, from Western and Byzantine chronicles, describing the sack of Constantinople.

Crusades were waged not only in the Near East but also against the Muslims of Spain (the *Reconquista*) and non-Christian Slavic and Baltic peoples of northeastern Europe. Document C, taken from *The Chronicle of the Slavs* by the twelfth-century German writer Helmhold, describes how German settlers poured into the region east of the Elbe River, in present-day eastern Germany, after the land had been forcibly wrested from its pagan Slavic native population. Notice the presence here of "Hollanders" skilled in reclaiming swampy land for cultivation. This influx of German settlers across the Elbe marked the beginning of what Germans call the *Drang nach Osten,* the "push to the east," that was to continue in a variety of ways (sometimes peaceful, sometimes not) until the calamitous Nazi quest for "living space" in eastern Europe in World War II. In Document D, Muslim traveler Ibn Jubayr of Valencia comments (c. 1217) on the conditions of Muslims living under Christian rule in the Crusader States and Sicily. Document E provides a vivid thirteenth-century Muslim report on the barbarous-seeming people of "Frank-land," whence the crusaders came repeatedly to harry Islam. Judging by the knowledge you have gained in your study of medieval history, how do you respond to this Muslim assessment?

A. Bernard of Clairvaux Preaches the Second Crusade

Behold, brethren, now is the accepted time, now is the day of salvation. The earth also is moved and has trembled, because the God of heaven has begun to destroy the land which is his. . . . And now, for our sins, the enemies of the Cross have raised blaspheming heads, ravaging with the edge of the sword the land of promise. . . . Alas! they rage against the very shrine of the Christian faith with blasphemous mouths, and would enter and trample down the very couch on which, for us, our Life lay down to sleep in death.

What are you going to do then, O brave men? What are you doing, O servants of the Cross? Will you give what is holy to the dogs, and cast your pearls before swine? How many sinners there, confessing their sins and tears, have obtained pardon, after the defilement of the heathen had been purged by the swords of your fathers! . . .

What are we then to think, brethren? Is the Lord's arm shortened so that it cannot save, because he calls his weak creatures to guard and restore his heritage? Can he not send more than twelve legions of angels, or merely speak the word, and the land shall be set free? It is altogether in his power to effect what he wishes; but I tell you, the Lord, your God, is trying you. He looks upon the sons of men to see if there be any to understand, and seek, and bewail his error. For the Lord hath pity upon his people, and provides a sure remedy for those that are afflicted. . . .

But now, O brave knight, now, O warlike hero, here is a battle you may fight without danger, where it is glory to conquer and gain to die. If you are a prudent merchant, if you are a desirer of this world, behold I show you some great bargains; see that you lost them not. Take the sign of the cross, and you shall gain pardon for every sin that you confess with a contrite heart. The material itself, being bought, is worth little; but if it be placed on a devout shoulder, it is, without doubt, worth no less than the kingdom of God. Therefore they have done well who have already taken the heavenly sign: well and wisely also will the rest do, if they hasten to lay upon their shoulders, like the first, the sign of salvation.

Besides, brethren, I warn you, and not only I, but God's apostle, "Believe not every spirit." We have heard and rejoice that the zeal of God abounds in you, but it behooves no mind to be wanting in wisdom. The Jews must not be persecuted, slaughtered, nor even driven out. Inquire of the pages of Holy Writ. I know what is written in the Psalms as prophecy about the Jews. "God hath commanded me," says the Church, 'Slay them not, lest my people forget.' "

They are living signs to us, representing the Lord's passion. For this reason they are dispersed into all regions, that now they may pay the just penalty of so great a crime, and that they may be witnesses of our redemption. Wherefore the Church, speaking in the same Psalm, says, "Scatter them by thy power; and bring them down, O Lord, our shield." So has it been. They have been dispersed, cast down. They undergo a hard captivity under Christian princes. Yet they shall be converted at even-time, and remembrance of them shall be made in due season. Finally, when the multitude of the Gentiles shall have entered in, then "all Israel shall be saved," saith the apostle. Meanwhile he who dies remains in death.

I do not enlarge on the lamentable fact that where there are no Jews there Christian men *judaize* even worse than they in extorting usury,—if, indeed, we may call them Christians and not rather baptized Jews. Moreover, if the Jews be utterly trampled down, how shall the promised salvation or conversion profit them in the end? . . .

B. A Latin Leader and a Greek Bishop Comment on the Sack on Constantinople, 1204

From Geoffrey of Villehardouin's chronicle

The booty gained was so great that none could tell you the end of it: gold and silver, and vessels and precious stones, and samite and cloth of silk, and robes vair and grey, and ermine, and every choicest thing found upon the earth . . . That which was brought to the churches was collected together and divided, in equal parts, between the Franks and the Venetians . . . After the division had been made [the Crusaders] paid out of their share fifty thousand marks of silver to the Venetians, and then divided at least one hundred thousand marks among themselves.

From Nicholas Mesarites

And so the streets, squares, houses of two and three stories, sacred places, nunneries, houses for nuns and monks, sacred churches, even the Great Church of God and the imperial palace, were filled with men of the enemy, all of them maddened by war and murderous in spirit, all clad in armor, and bearing spears, swords and lances, archers and horsemen boasting terribly, barking like Cerberus and exhaling like

Charon, as they sacked the sacred places and trampled on the divine things [and] ran riot over the holy vessels . . . Moreover, they tore children from their mothers and mothers from their children, and they defiled the virgins in the holy chapels, fearing neither God's anger nor man's vengeance.

C. German Settlers Colonize Lands Conquered from Pagan Slavs

At that time Albert, the margrave whose by-name is the Bear, held eastern Slavia. By the favor of God he also prospered splendidly in the portion of his lot; for he brought under his sway all the country of the Brizani, the Stoderani, and the many tribes dwelling along the Havel and the Elbe, and he curbed the rebellious ones among them. In the end, as the Slavs gradually decreased in number, he sent to Utrecht and to places lying on the Rhine, to those, moreover, who live by the ocean and suffer the violence of the sea—to wit, Hollanders, Zeelanders, Flemings—and he brought large numbers of them and had them live in the strongholds and villages of the Slavs. The bishopric of Brandenburg, and likewise that of Havelberg, was greatly strengthened by the coming of the foreigners, because the churches multiplied and the income from the tithes grew enormously. At the same time foreigners from Holland also began to settle on the southern bank of the Elbe; the Hollanders received all the swamp and open country, the land which is called Balsamerlande and Marscinerlande, together with very many cities and villages from the city of Salzwedel clear to the Bohemian woodland. These lands, indeed, the Saxons are said to have occupied of old—namely in the time of the Ottos—as can be seen from the ancient levees which had been constructed in the lowlands of the Balsami along the banks of the Elbe. But afterwards, when the Slavs got the upper hand, the Saxons were killed and the land has been held by the Slavs down to our own times. Now, however, because God gave plentiful aid and victory to our duke and to the other princes, the Slavs have been everywhere crushed and driven out. A people strong and without number have come from the bounds of the ocean, and taken possession of the territories of the Slavs. They have built cities and churches and have grown in riches beyond all estimation.

D. An Islamic Traveler Bemoans the Fate of Muslims Under Christian Rule, 1217

We moved from Tibnin (in Syria)—may God destroy it—through continuous farms and ordered settlements whose inhabitants were all Muslims, living comfortably with the Franks. God protect us from such temptation. They surrender half their crops to the Franks at harvest time, and pay as well a poll-tax of one dinār and five *qirāt* for each person. Other than that, they are not interfered with, save for a light tax on the fruits of trees. Their houses and all their effects are left to their full possession. All the coastal cities occupied by the Franks are managed in this fashion, their rural districts, the villages and farms, belonging to the Muslims. But their hearts have been seduced, for they observe how unlike them in ease and comfort are their brethren in the Muslim regions under their (Muslim) governors. This is one of the misfortunes afflicting the Muslims. The Muslim community bewails the injustice of a landlord of its own faith, and applauds the conduct of its opponent and enemy and is accustomed to justice from him. He who laments this state must turn to God.

During our stay in Tyre, we rested in one of the Mosques that remained in Muslim hands. One of the Muslim elders of Tyre told us that it had been wrested from them in the year 518 (June 27, 1124). They thereupon decided to abandon the town, and to make good their escape. So it happened, and they dispersed among the Muslim lands. But there were some whose love of native land impelled them to return and, under the conditions of a safeguard which was written for them, to live amongst the infidels. "God is the master of His affair" (12:21). Glorious is God, and great is His power. His will overcomes all impediments.

There can be no excuse in the eyes of God for a Muslim to stay in any infidel country, save when passing through it, while the way lies clear in Muslim lands. They will face pains and terrors such as the abasement and destitution of the capitation (tax) and more especially, amongst the base and lower orders, the hearing of what will distress the heart in the reviling of him (Muhammad) whose memory God has sanctified, and whose rank He has exalted; there is also the absence of cleanliness, the mixing with the pigs, and all the other prohibited matters too numerous to be related or enumerated. Beware, beware of entering their lands. May God Most High grant His beneficent indulgence for this sin into which our feet have slipped (of setting foot there), but His forgiveness in not given save after accepting our penitence. Glory be unto God, the Master. There is no Lord but He.

The (Muslim) people of the island of Sicily suffer, amongst other tribulations, one that is very sore. Should a man show anger to his son or wife, or a woman to her daughter, the one who is the object of displeasure may perversely throw himself into a church, and there be baptised and turn Christian. Then there will be for the father no way of approaching his son, or the mother her daughter. Conceive now the state of one so afflicted in his family, or even in his son. The dread of their falling to this temptation would alone shorten his life. The Muslims of Sicily therefore are most watchful. The most clear-sighted of them fear that it shall chance to them all as it did in earlier times to the Muslim inhabitants of Crete. There a Christian despotism so long visited them with one (painful) circumstance after another that they were all constrained to turn Christian, only those escaping whom God decreed. But the word of chastisement shall fall upon these infidels. God's will shall prevail: there is indeed no God but He. . . .

We came upon another striking example of their state, such as breaks the spirit in pity and melts the heart in compassion. One of the notables of this town of Trapani sent his son to one of our pilgrim companions, desiring of him that he would accept of him his daughter, a young virgin who was nearing the age of puberty. Should he be pleased with her, he could marry her; if not, he could marry her to any one of his countrymen who liked her. She would go with them, content to leave her father and her brothers, desiring only to escape from the temptation (of apostasy), and to live in the lands of the Muslims. The man sought after, in order to win a heavenly reward, accepted the offer, and we helped him to seize an opportunity which would lead him to the felicities both of this world and the next.

We ourselves were filled with wonder at a situation which would lead a man to give up so readily a trust tied to his heart, and to surrender her to one strange to her, to bear in patience the want of her, and to suffer longings for her and loneliness without her. We were likewise amazed at the girl—may God protect her—and at her willingness to leave her kin for her love of Islam.

E. "Frank-land": A Thirteenth-Century Islamic View

Frank-land, a mighty land and a broad kingdom in the realms of the Christians. Its cold is very great, and its air is thick because of the extreme cold. It is full of good things and fruits and crops, rich in rivers, plentiful of produce, possessing tillage and cattle, trees and honey. There is a wide variety of game there and also silver mines. They forge very sharp swords there, and the swords of Frank-land are keener than the swords of India.

Its people are Christians, and they have a king possessing courage, great numbers, and power to rule. He has two or three cities on the shore of the sea on this side, in the midst of the lands of Islam, and he protects them from his side. Whenever the Muslims send forces to them to capture them, he sends forces from his side to defend them. His soldiers are of mighty courage and in the hour of combat do not even think of flight, rather preferring death. But you shall see none more filthy than they. They are a people of perfidy and mean character. They do not cleanse or bathe themselves more than once or twice a year, and then in cold water, and they do not wash their garments from the time they put them on until they fall to pieces. They shave their beards, and after shaving they sprout only a revolting stubble. One of them was asked as to the shaving of the beard, and he said, "Hair is a superfluity. You remove it from your private parts, so why should we leave it on our faces?"

Document Set 11.5 References

A. Bernard of Clairvaux Preaches the Second Crusade
James Harvey Robinson, ed., *Readings in European History* (Boston: Ginn, 1904), 1:330–333.

B. A Latin Leader and a Greek Bishop Comment on the Sack on Constantinople, 1204
Deno John Geanokoplos, ed., *Byzantium: Church, Society, and Civilization Seen Through Contemporary Eyes* (Chicago: University of Chicago Press, 1984), 368–369.

C. German Settlers Colonize Lands Conquered from Pagan Slavs
Helmhoid, *Christianizing of the Slavs,* trans. Francis Joseph Tschan (New York: Columbia University Press, 1935), 235–236.

D. An Islamic Traveler Bemoans the Fate of Muslims Under Christian Rule, 1217
J. A. Williams, *Themes of Islamic Civilization* (Berkeley: University of California Press, 1971), 45–46.

E. "Frank-land": A Thirteenth-Century Islamic View
Al-Qazwini, *Athar al-bilad,* in Lewis, *Islam: From the Prophet Muhammed to the Capture of Constantinople* (New York: Walker, 1987), 2:123.

DOCUMENT SET 11.6
Twelfth-Century Townspeople

The documents in this set offer perspectives on the place of towns and urban populations in four very different European societies during the twelfth and early thirteenth centuries.

Document A is from Russia. It is an extract from the Novgorod Chronicle, dated 1156, describing how that proud city, which called itself Lord Novgorod the Great, asserted its authority to name its own "posadnik," or chief administrative official, rather than submit to any territorial prince. The city also successfully named its own bishop. How did these actions compare with Western towns' defense of their interests, such as efforts by Cologne (Set 10.3, Document 4) or Liège in present-day Belgium (Document B, below)?

West European townspeople almost invariably bitterly hated the Jews they found in their midst, seeing in them not only despised religious outcasts, but also bitter economic rivals. Usually the Jews were settled in towns under charters granted by the territorial rulers (see Set 10.3, Document B), who saw a material advantage in keeping "their" Jews prosperous taxpayers. Occasionally, however, a ruler desperate for quick wealth would agree to expel Jews from his jurisdiction, taking a generous helping of the Jews' forfeited property. Such an expulsion, on a national scale, occurred in late twelfth-century France on orders from Philip Augustus (Document C). What does this document reveal about the Jews' situation in France prior to their expulsion, and about the king's reasons for taking the step?

The greatest commercial city in all of Europe remained Constantinople. Document D is an extract from a late twelfth-century description of it by a Jewish traveler from Muslim Spain. Is it likely that Jews or other outsiders to the European "mainstream" would suffer harassment here?

A. "Lord Novgorod the Great" Defends Its Autonomy, 1156–1157

The Novgorodians expelled Sudila, the *posadnik* of the city, and he died five days later. And they gave the position of *posadnik* to Yakun Miroslavovich. In the same spring, on April 29th, Archbishop Nifont passed away. Before he died he went to Kiev to oppose the metropolitan bishop, but many people say that he went to Constantinople after having plundered the Cathedral (St. Sophia in Kiev). They say many things about him, but it is their sin for doing so.

We should remember that he was the one who embellished the Cathedral (St. Sophia of Novgorod), who decorated the porches, who made the icon case, and who adorned the church on the outside. He also built the Church of the Holy Savior in Pskov and the Church of St. Clement in Ladoga. I believe that God, because of our sins, did not desire that we should have his grave for our consolation and so he sent him to Kiev, where he died. And he was buried in the Crypt Monastery.

In the same year the whole populace of the city gathered and decided to elect as bishop a holy man, Arkady, who was chosen by God. And all the people went to the Monastery of the Holy Mother of God and took him, Prince Mstislav, the entire clergy of the Cathedral of St. Sophia, and all the priests, abbots, and monks of the city and brought them to the court of St. Sophia. And they entrusted the bishopric to Arkady until the Metropolitan of Russia should arrive and consecrate him. And in the same year the merchants from over the seas erected the Church of Good Friday on the market square.

1157 (6665) There was malice among the people, and they rose against Prince Mstislav Yurievich and began to drive him from Novgorod, but the merchants took up arms for him. And brother quarreled with brother. The bride over the river Volkhov was seized. Guards took their stand on either side of the town gates, and it nearly came to the shedding of blood between them. And then Sviatoslav Rostislavich and David Rostislavich arrived. That very night Mstislav fled from Novgorod. And in three days Rostislav himself arrived. And the brothers came together, and no harm came of it.

In the spring Prince George died at Kiev, and the people of Kiev set Iziaslav Davidovich on the throne. In the same year Andrew, Abbot of the Church of the Holy Mother of God, died. And Alexis was appointed in his place. And in the fall the weather was fearsome with thunder and lightning, and on November 7th, at five in the night, there was hail of the size of apples.

B. Liège Resists Its Archbishop, 1203

In this year [1203] the burghers of Huy rose against their bishop [of Liège] on account of a certain due which he had claimed in an unjust manner. They took possession of the apparatus for carrying on a siege, which was coming by ship from Namur. The vessel they dragged overland to the market place; they barricaded the entrance and exit to the burg. But soon they repented and all betook themselves to Liege, where they rendered satisfaction barefooted to the bishop in the presence of the clergy and people.

A bitter feud broke out between Duke Henry of Louvain and Count Louis of Los over a certain due paid by the town of St. Trond. This town belonged to the bishop of Metz; he had taken it from the count of Los and given it to the duke. But the people of St. Trond rose in opposition and would not yield to the duke. Now Count Louis of Los proceeded to grant all his towns, namely, Montenaken, Brusthem, Hallut, and all the land he controlled, to [the church of] St. Lambert. He offered all these at the altar of the church as a legal gift before clergy and people, and in the presence of the bishop, Duke Henry of Ardennerland and Count Henry of Moha. He then received the lands again from the hand of the bishop as a fief. The bishop took possession on St. John's day of the aforementioned towns and the lands.

As the harvest approached the duke [of Louvain] summoned his forces and proposed to lay siege to the town of St. Trond. He set up his tent in the village of Landen and remained a week there, destroyed the crops in the region in a manner hard to believe, and assembled a great number of soldiers. The count of Los, however, went to the bishop, whose man he had lately become, and asked his help. He also got together from his own lands and elsewhere heavy reenforcements. The bishop ordered his dependents— knights, burghers, and those of his household—to defend him, and ordered the count to be at a village called Waremme on a certain day. They all came together accordingly and took their station in the said village. There they awaited the outcome, hoping rather for war than peace. In the meantime negotiations were carried on for a week at a place between Montenaken and Landen, but in spite of the intervention of the clergy, who tried to bring about an adjustment, no peaceful settlement could be reached. At last the count of Namur intervened and effected an armistice, which the others had been unable to arrange.

[During the succeeding years there was no end of disorder, due mainly to feudal complications. Finally, in 1212,] on the 1st of May the burghers of Liege sallied forth to fight Duke Henry of Brabant. But the next day they returned in disorder and fright. The third day the town was invested and immediately taken and pillaged. On the fourth and fifth days the enemy robbed the people of all their gold, silver, and everything in the way of valuables; women and girls

were carried off to the enemy's camp and many burghers taken prisoners. On the sixth day the burghers who were left concluded a peace, but a miserable one; on the seventh day the army withdrew from Liege; on the eighth it laid siege to Musal, but did not take the town. Waleffe, on the contrary, was turned over deserted to the duke. A week after Ascension day the army of the duke returned home. The count of Namur demanded some security that the duke would keep the peace, for he feared the duke's power. The bishop kept in hiding with a few followers.

C. Philip Augustus Expels the Jews from France, 1182

[Philip Augustus had often heard] that the Jews who dwelt in Paris were wont every year on Easter day, or during the sacred week of our Lord's Passion, to go down secretly into underground vaults and kill a Christian as a sort of sacrifice in contempt of the Christian religion. For a long time they had persisted in this wickedness, inspired by the devil, and in Philip's father's time many of them had been seized and burned with fire. St. Richard, whose body rests in the church of the Holy Innocents-in-the-Fields in Paris, was thus put to death and crucified by the Jews, and through martyrdom went in blessedness to God. Wherefore many miracles have been wrought by the hand of God through the prayers and intercessions of St. Richard, to the glory of God, as we have heard.

And because the most Christian King Philip inquired diligently, and came to know full well these and many other iniquities of the Jews in his forefathers' days, therefore he burned with zeal, and in the same year in which he was invested at Rheims with the holy governance of the kingdom of the French, upon a Sabbath, the first of March, by his command, the Jews throughout all France were seized in their synagogues and then bespoiled of their gold and silver and garments, as the Jews themselves had spoiled the Egyptians at their exodus from Egypt. This was a harbinger of their expulsion, which by God's will soon followed. . . .

At this time a great multitude of Jews had been dwelling in France for a long time past, for they had flocked thither from divers parts of the world, because peace abode among the French, and liberality; for the Jews had heard how the kings of the French were prompt to act against their enemies, and were very merciful toward their subjects. And therefore their elders and men wise in the Law of Moses, who were called by the Jews *didascali*, made resolve to come to Paris.

When they had made a long sojourn there, they grew so rich that they claimed as their own almost half of the whole city, and had Christians in their houses as menservants and maidservants, who were open backsliders from the faith of Jesus Christ, and *judaized* with the Jews. And this was contrary to the decree of God and the law of the Church. And whereas the Lord has said by the mouth of Moses in Deuteronomy (xxiii. 19, 20), "Thou shalt not lend upon usury to thy brother," but "to a stranger," the Jews in their wickedness understood by "stranger" every Christian, and they took from the Christians their money at usury. And so heavily burdened in this wise were citizens and soldiers and peasants in the suburbs, and in the various towns and villages, that many of them were constrained to part with their possessions. Others were bound under oath in houses of the Jews in Paris, held as if captives in prison.

The most Christian King Philip heard of these things, and compassion was stirred within him. He took counsel with a certain hermit, Bernard by name, a holy and religious man, who at that time dwelt in the forest of Vincennes, and asked him what he should do. By his advice the king released all Christians of his kingdom from their debts to the Jews, and kept a fifth part of the whole amount for himself.

Finally came the culmination of their wickedness. Certain ecclesiastical vessels consecrated to God—the chalices and crosses of gold and silver bearing the image of our Lord Jesus Christ crucified—had been pledged to the Jews by way of security when the need of the churches was pressing. These they used so vilely, in their impiety and scorn of the Christian religion, that from the cups in which the body and blood of our Lord Jesus Christ was consecrated they gave their children cakes soaked in wine. . . .

In the year of our Lord's Incarnation 1182, in the month of April, which is called by the Jews Nisan, an edict went forth from the most serene king, Philip Augustus, that all the Jews of his kingdom should be prepared to go forth by the coming feast of St. John the Baptist. And then the king gave them leave to sell each his movable goods before the time fixed, that is, the feast of St. John the Baptist. But their real estate, that is, houses, fields, vineyards, barns, winepresses, and such like, he reserved for himself and his successors, the kings of the French.

When the faithless Jews heard this edict some of them were born again of water and the Holy Spirit and converted to the Lord, remaining steadfast in the faith of our Lord Jesus Christ. To them the king, out of regard for the Christian religion, restored all their possessions in their entirety, and gave them perpetual liberty.

Others were blinded by their ancient error and persisted in their perfidy; and they sought to win with gifts and golden promises the great of the land,—counts, barons, archbishops, bishops,—that through their influence and advice, and through the promise of infinite wealth, they might turn the king's mind from his firm intention. But the merciful and compassionate God, who does not forsake those who put their hope in him and who doth humble those who glory in their strength, . . . so fortified the illustrious king that he could not be moved by prayers nor promises of temporal things. . . .

The infidel Jews, perceiving that the great of the land, through whom they had been accustomed easily to bend the king's predecessors to their will, had suffered repulse, and astonished and stupefied by the strength of mind of Philip the king and his constancy in the Lord, exclaimed, "Scema Israhel!" and prepared to sell all their household goods. The time was now at hand when the king had ordered them to leave France altogether, and it could not be in any way prolonged. Then did the Jews sell all their movable possessions in great haste, while their landed property reverted to the crown. Thus the Jews, having sold their goods and taken the price for the expenses of their journey, departed with their wives and children and all their households in the aforesaid year of the Lord 1182.

D. Constantinople Attracts the World's Merchants

All kinds of merchants come [to Constantinople] from Babylon and Shin'ar, from Persia and Medea, from all the kingdoms of Egypt, from the land of Canaan, from the kingdom of Russia, from Hungary, from the land of the Petchenegs, from Khazaria, from Lombardy and from Spain. It is a tumultuous city; men come to trade there from all countries by land and by sea. There is none like it in all the world except for Baghdad, the great city which is Ishmael's. . . . Constantinople has countless buildings. Year by year tribute is brought to it from all the land of Greece, whereby castles are filled with garments of silk, purple and gold. Such buildings, such riches can be seen nowhere else in Greece. They say that the city's daily income, what with the rent from shops and markets and what with the customs levied on merchants coming by sea and by land, reaches twenty thousand gold pieces.

Document Set 11.6 References

A. "Lord Novgorod the Great" Defends Its Autonomy,
1156–1157
Serge A. Zenkovsky, ed., *Medieval Russia's Epics, Chronicles and Tales* (New York: Dutton, 1963), 163–164.

B. Liège Resists Its Archbishop, 1203
Reiner, *Annals of St. James in Liège,* in James Harvey Robinson, ed., *Readings in European History* (Boston: Ginn, 1904), 1:300–301.

C. Philip Augustus Expels the Jews from France, 1182
Rigord, *Life of Philip Augustus,* in James Harvey Robinson, ed., *Readings in European History* (Boston: Ginn, 1904), 1:426–428.

D. Constantinople Attracts the World's Merchants
Deno John Geanokoplos, ed., *Byzantium: Church, Society, and Civilization Seen Through Contemporary Eyes* (Chicago: University of Chicago Press, 1984), 278.

The Quest for Order and Control, 1215–1320

DOCUMENT SET 12.1
The New Piety

Whether it manifested itself as orthodoxy or heresy, Christian religious devotion deepened markedly among ordinary lay people in the twelfth and thirteenth centuries. However varied the causes, written and visual sources from this period bespeak powerful religious feelings and a vividness of imagery.

One of the most striking signs of the new piety was the Franciscan movement. St. Francis of Assisi (c. 1181–1226), the pleasure-loving son of a wealthy urban merchant, experienced a radical conversion in 1206 and quickly gained an enthusiastic band of followers for what became a new religious order emphasizing utter poverty and service to the poor and the outcast. Francis kept his movement within the bounds of orthodoxy, though after his death the Franciscans split into orthodox and heretical branches (the former gradually abandoning the rigors of strict poverty, and the latter adhering more faithfully to their founder's ideals). Francis's own account of the mission to which he felt himself divinely called is excerpted in Document A, dictated shortly before his death. A number of great Roman Catholic hymns still used in the liturgy are of thirteenth-century Franciscan origin. One is Thomas of Celano's *Dies Irae* (Day of Wrath), the central text of the traditional Catholic Requiem Mass. Numerous translations have been attempted of this terse and terrifyingly vivid Latin text, describing the resurrected soul's experience at the Day of Judgment: the one appearing here as Document B dates from the nineteenth century.

The improbable event recounted in Document C comes from a collection of anecdotes used for popular preaching by the Dominican Stephen of Bourbon (d. 1261).

Using *The Challenge of the West* as a reference and incorporating these sources, write a brief analysis of the heightening of religious feeling in this era. Consider such factors as the development of an urban society and the appearance of new preaching orders (Franciscans and Dominicans).

A. St. Francis Implores the Franciscans to Remain Faithful to His Ideals

When the Lord gave me the care of some brothers, no one showed me what I ought to do, but the Most High himself revealed to me that I ought to live according to the model of the holy gospel. I caused a short and simple formula to be written, and the lord pope confirmed it for me.

Those who presented themselves to follow this kind of life distributed all they might have to the poor. They contented themselves with one tunic, patched within and without, with the cord and breeches, and we desired to have nothing more. The clerics said the office like other clerics, and the laymen repeated the paternoster[the Lord's Prayer].

We loved to live in poor and abandoned churches, and we were ignorant, and were submissive to all. I worked with my hands and would still do so, and I firmly desire also that all the other brothers work, for this makes for goodness. Let those who know no trade learn one, but not for the purpose of receiving the price of their toil, but for their good example and to flee idleness. And when we are not given the price of our work, let us resort to the table of the Lord, begging our bread from door to door. The Lord revealed to me the salutation which we ought to give: "God give you peace!"

Let the brothers take great care not to accept churches, habitations, or any buildings erected for them, except as all is in accordance with the holy poverty which we have vowed in the Rule; and let them not live in them except as strangers and pilgrims. I absolutely interdict all the brothers, in whatsoever place they may be found, from asking any bull from the court of Rome, whether directly or indirectly, in the interest of church or convent, or under pretext of preaching, nor even for the protection of their bodies. If they are not received anywhere, let them go of themselves elsewhere, thus doing penance with the benediction of God.

I firmly desire to obey the minister general of this brotherhood, and the guardian whom he may please to give me. I desire to put myself entirely into his hands, to go nowhere and do nothing against his will, for he is my lord. Though I be simple and ill, I would, however, have always a clerk who will perform the office, as it is said in the Rule. Let all the other brothers also be careful to obey their guardians and to do the office according to the Rule.

If it come to pass that there are any who do not the office according to the Rule, and who desire to make any other change, or if they are not Catholics, let all the brothers, wherever they may be, be bound by obedience to present them to the nearest custodian. Let the custodians be bound by obedience to keep such a one well guarded, like a man who is in bonds, day and night, so that he may not escape from their hands until they personally place him in the minister's hands. And let the minister be bound by obedience to send him, by brothers who will guard him as a prisoner day and night, until they shall have placed him in the hands of the lord bishop of Ostia, who is the lord protector, and the corrector of all the brotherhood.

And let the brothers not say, "This is a new Rule"; for this is only a reminder, a warning, an exhortation; it is my last will and testament, that I, little Brother Francis, make for you, my blessed brothers, in order that we may observe in a more Catholic way the Rule which we promised the Lord to keep. Let the ministers general, all the other ministers, and the custodians be held by obedience to add nothing to and take nothing away from these words. Let them always keep this writing near them beside the Rule; and in all the assemblies which shall be held, when the Rule is read, let these words be read also.

I interdict absolutely by obedience all the brothers, clerics and laymen, to introduce comments in the Rule, or in this will, under pretext of explaining it. But since the Lord has given me to speak and to write the Rule and these words in a clear and simple manner, so do you understand them in the same way without commentary, and put them in practice until the end.

And whoever shall have observed these things, may he be crowned in heaven with the blessings of the heavenly Father, and on earth with those of his well-beloved Son and of the Holy Spirit, the Consoler, with the assistance of all the heavenly virtues and all the saints.

And I, little Brother Francis, your servitor, confirm to you, so far as I am able, this most holy benediction. Amen.

B. A Vision of the Last Judgment: The *Dies Irae*

Day of wrath, that day of burning,
Seer and Sibyl speak concerning,
All the world to ashes turning.

Oh, what fear shall it engender,
When the Judge shall come in splendor,
Strict to mark and just to render!

Trumpet, scattering sounds of wonder,
Rending sepulchres asunder,
Shall resistless summons thunder.

All aghast then Death shall shiver,
And great Nature's frame shall quiver,
When the graves their dead deliver.

Volume, from which nothing's blotted,
Evil done nor evil plotted,
Shall be brought and dooms allotted.

When shall sit the Judge unerring,
He'll unfold all here occurring,
Vengeance then no more deferring.

What shall I say, that time pending?
Ask what advocate's befriending,
When the just man needs defending?

Dreadful King, all power possessing,
Saving freely those confessing,
Save thou me, O Fount of Blessing!

Think, O Jesus, for what reason
Thou didst bear earth's spite and treason,
Nor me lose in that dread season!

Seeking me Thy worn feet hasted,
On the cross Thy soul death tasted:
Let such travail not be wasted!

Righteous Judge of retribution!
Make me gift of absolution
Ere that day of execution!

Culprit-like, I plead, heart-broken,
On my cheek shame's crimson token:
Let the pardoning word be spoken!

Thou, who Mary gav'st remission,
Heard'st the dying Thief's petition,
Cheer'st with hope my lost condition.

Though my prayers be void of merit,
What is needful, Thou confer it,
Lest I endless fire inherit!

Be there, Lord, my place decided
With Thy sheep, from goats divided,
Kindly to Thy right hand guided!

When th' accursed away are driven,
To eternal burnings given,
Call me with the blessed to heaven!

I beseech Thee, prostrate lying,
Heart as ashes, contrite, sighing,
Care for me when I am dying!

Day of tears and late repentance,
Man shall rise to hear his sentence:
Him, the child of guilt and error,
Spare, Lord, in that hour of terror!

C. The Bees and the Eucharist: A Thirteenth-Century Popular Tale

I have heard that a certain rustic, wishing to become wealthy and having many hives of bees, asked certain evil men how he could get rich and increase the number of his bees. He was told by some one that if he retained the sacred host on Easter and placed it in some one of his hives, he would entice away all of his neighbor's bees, which, leaving their own hives, would come to the place where the body of our Lord was and there would make honey. So he did this.

Then all the bees came to the hive where the body of Christ was, and just as if they felt sorrow for the irreverence done to it, by their labor they began to construct a little church and to erect foundations, and bases, and columns, and an altar; then with the greatest reverence they placed the body of our Lord upon the altar. And within their little beehive they formed the little church with wonderful and most beautiful workmanship. The bees of the vicinity, leaving their hives, came to that one; and over that work they sang in their own manner certain wonderful melodies like hymns.

The rustic, hearing this, marveled. But waiting until the fitting time for collecting the honey, he found nothing in his hives. Finding himself impoverished through the means by which he had expected to be enriched, he went to the hive where he had placed the host, and where he saw the bees had come together. But when he approached, just as if they wished to vindicate the insult to our Saviour, the bees rushed upon the rustic and stung him so severely that he escaped with difficulty and in great agony. Going to the priest, he related all that he had done, and what the bees had done.

The priest, by the advice of the bishop, collected his parishioners and made a procession to that place. Then the bees, leaving the hive, rose in the air, making sweet melody. Raising the hive, they found inside the noble structure of that little church and the body of our Lord placed upon the altar. Then, returning thanks, they bore to their own church that little church of the bees, constructed with such skill and elegance, and placed it on the altar.

By this deed those who do not reverence, but offer insult instead, to the sacred body of Christ, or the sacred place where it is, ought to be put to great confusion.

Document Set 12.1 References
A. St. Francis Implores the Franciscans to Remain Faithful to His Ideals
  James Harvey Robinson, ed., *Readings in European History* (Boston: Ginn, 1904), 1:393–395.
B. A Vision of the Last Judgment: The *Dies Irae*
  Pages 5–8.
C. The Bees and the Eucharist: A Thirteenth-Century Popular Tale
  Stephen of Bourbon, in James Harvey Robinson, ed., *Readings in European History* (Boston: Ginn, 1904), 1:355–356.

As pointed out in the introduction to Set 12.1, the line between orthodox religious fervor and heresy was none too clear. Tightening up its own organization and doctrines meant that the Catholic church thereby defined heresy all the more rigidly.

The great theologian St. Thomas Aquinas not only gave sharp definition to many Catholic teachings but also argued uncompromisingly for harsh treatment for those convicted of heresy (Document A). As everywhere in his formal writings, Aquinas begins by citing the opposing viewpoint, then points out the contradictions, and finally as in the section quoted here, gives his own finding.

The most important institution that the church used to rout out heresy was the Inquisition, in which Aquinas's fellow Dominicans took an especially active role. In Document B a Dominican inquisitor of the early fourteenth century, Bernard of Gui, gives a relentlessly hostile picture of the Albigensians whom he was persecuting in the south of France. Bernard characterizes them as "Manicheans," that is, proponents of the dualist idea that the material world is evil and only the invisible world of the spirit was created by God. Notwithstanding Bernard's evident bias, look for evidence that he provides of the heretics' critique of Catholic institutions and practices.

Document C offers a rare glimpse into the world of the ordinary people who found themselves the objects of both heretical and orthodox exhortations. A little before 1320, a young woman named Grazida Lizier was accused of Albigensianism and called to testify before inquisitors. Not educated, rich, or worldly (she had spent her entire life in a small village in the Pyrenees in southern France), she nevertheless reveals in her testimony a lively mind and sense of individuality. Her words demonstrate that a period of apparent conformity teemed with diverse ideas, few of which have been recorded. What do you make of her understanding of the questions at issue in the conflict between heresy and orthodoxy?

State authority almost invariably came down heavyhandedly on the side of religious orthodoxy. Document E, dating from 1228, shows Louis IX of France—St. Louis—unequivocally backing the suppression of heresy. Consider the Albigensian Crusade of 1208 (*The Challenge of the West* provides details), which brought southern France under much tighter royal control; does this alone explain why the secular authorities so consistently backed religious orthodoxy?

Document E provides another dimension of the church's drive toward religious conformity. On this occasion—as on several others—the handful of Christian scholars who had learned Hebrew became convinced that the Talmud contained blasphemous or heretical ideas dangerous to Christianity and thus demanded its destruction. This incident occurred in St. Louis's reign, and one of the instigators was a Catalan Dominican learned in both Jewish and Muslim lore.

A. St. Thomas Aquinas Answers the Question, "Should Heretics Be Tolerated?"

I reply that heretics must be considered from two points of view, namely, as regards the heretic himself, and secondly, as regards the church. As for the heretics themselves, there is their sin for which they deserve not only to be separated from the Church by excommunication, but to be sent out of the world by death. It is, indeed, a much more serious offence to corrupt the faith, upon which depends the life of the soul, than to falsify coin, by means of which the temporal life is sustained. Hence, if counterfeiters and other malefactors are justly hurried to death by secular rulers, much the more may those who are convicted of heresy not only be excommunicated but justly put to a speedy death. But on the side of the Church, there is mercy looking for the conversion of the erring. She does not therefore condemn immediately, but only after a first and second admonition, as the Apostle teaches. Should the heretic still prove stubborn, the Church, no longer hoping for his conversion, shall provide for the safety of others by separating him from herself by a sentence of excommunication. She further relinquishes him to the secular judgment to be put out of the world by death. Jerome also says (on the passage in Galatians v.—"*a little leaven;*"), and it is stated in 24. qu. 3, cap. 16, "*Foul flesh must be cut away, and mangy sheep must be kept from the fold lest the whole house be burned, the whole mass corrupted, the whole body be destroyed. Arius was but a spark in Alexandria, but since this spark was not promptly quenched, the whole world has been devastated by the flames.*"

B. The Inquisitor Bernard of Gui Describes the Albigensians' Heresies

It would take too long to describe in detail the manner in which these same Manichæan heretics preach and teach their followers, but it must be briefly considered here.

In the first place, they usually say of themselves that they are good Christians, who do not swear, or lie, or speak evil of others; that they do not kill any man or animal, nor anything having the breath of life, and that they hold the faith of the Lord Jesus Christ and his gospel as Christ and his apostles taught. They assert that they occupy the place of the apostles, and that, on account of the above-mentioned things, they of the Roman Church, namely the prelates, clerks, and monks, and especially the inquisitors of heresy, persecute them and call them heretics, although they are good men and good Christians, and that they are persecuted just as Christ and his apostles were by the Pharisees.

Moreover they talk to the laity of the evil lives of the clerks and prelates of the Roman Church, pointing out and setting forth their pride, cupidity, avarice, and uncleanness of life, and such other evils as they know. They invoke, with their own interpretation and according to their abilities, the authority of the Gospels and the Epistles against the condition of the prelates, churchmen, and monks, whom they call Pharisees and false prophets, who say, but do not.

Then they attack and vituperate, in turn, all the sacraments of the Church, especially the sacrament of the eucharist, saying that it cannot contain the body of Christ, for had this been as great as the largest mountain Christians would have entirely consumed it before this. They assert that the host comes from straw, that it passes through the tails of horses, to wit, when the flour is cleaned by a sieve (of horse hair); that, moreover, it passes through the body and comes to a vile end, which, they say, could not happen if God were in it.

Of baptism, they assert that water is material and corruptible, and is therefore the creation of the evil power and cannot sanctify the soul, but that the churchmen sell this water out of avarice, just as they sell earth for the burial of the dead, and oil to the sick when they anoint them, and as they sell the confession of sins as made to the priests.

Hence they claim that confession made to the priests of the Roman Church is useless, and that, since the priests may be sinners, they cannot loose nor bind, and, being unclean themselves, cannot make others clean. They assert, moreover, that the cross of Christ should not be adored or venerated, because, as they urge, no one would venerate or adore the gallows upon which a father, relative, or friend had been hung. They urge, further, that they who adore the cross ought, for similar reasons, to worship all thorns and lances, because as Christ's body was on the cross during the passion, so was the crown of thorns on his head and the soldier's lance in his side. They proclaim many other scandalous things in regard to the sacraments.

Moreover they read from the Gospels and the Epistles in the vulgar tongue, applying and expounding them in their favor and against the condition of the Roman Church in a manner which it would take too long to describe in detail; but all that relates to this subject may be read more fully in the books they have written and infected, and may be learned from the confessions of such of their followers as have been converted.

C. Testimony of an Albigensian Woman Before the Inquisition

Seven years ago, or thereabouts, in summer, Pierre Clergue [a priest] came to my mother's house—she was out reaping—and incited me to let him make love with me. I consented; I was still a virgin then, fourteen years old I think, or perhaps fifteen. He took me in the barn where the straw is kept, but not at all violently. Afterwards he made love with me often, till the next January, and this always in my mother's house. She knew, and tolerated it. It was mostly in the daytime.

Then in January he gave me in marriage to Pierre Lizier, my late husband. And after that he still often lay with me, in the four years my husband was alive: my husband knew about it, and did not put up resistance . . .

At the time we made love together, both before I was married and after, as our love-making in all that time gave joy to us both, I did not think I sinned, nor does it seem so to me now. But now there'd be no joy in it for me—so, if I were to make love with him now, I believe it would be a sin . . .

I don't know, but I've heard it said that there is a paradise, and I believe it; I've also heard there is a hell, but that I don't believe, though I won't urge it is untrue . . . I've often heard that we shall rise again—after death—I don't believe that, though I don't discredit it.

D. St. Louis Proclaims an Edict Against the Albigensians

Moreover, since the keys of the church are often despised in that country [Languedoc], we command that excommunicated persons shall be avoided according to the canonical provisions, and that if any one shall contumaciously remain in a state of excommunication for a year, he shall be forced by material means to return to the unity of the Church, in order that those who are not induced to leave their evil way by the law of God, may be brought back by temporal penalties. We therefore order that our bailiffs shall, after one year, seize all the property, both real and personal, of all such excommunicated persons. And on no account shall such property be in any way returned to such persons, until they have been absolved and have rendered satisfaction to the church, and then only by our special order.

E. Pope Innocent IV Condemns the Talmud, 1244

Innocent, bishop, servant of the servants of God, to his cherished son Louis, illustrious king of France, greeting and apostolic benediction. The impious perfidy of the Jews—from whose hearts because of the enormity of their crimes our Redeemer did not lift the veil but still permits them to remain, as is fitting, in the blindness which is characteristic of Israel—not regarding the fact that Christian piety receives them only out of pity and patiently endures dwelling together with them, commits those enormities which stupefy hearers and horrify narrators. For these ingrates to the Lord Jesus Christ, who patiently awaits their conversion out of the richness of His long-suffering, showing no shame for their fault nor respecting the honor of the Christian faith, and omitting or scorning the Mosaic law and the prophets, follow certain traditions of their seniors concerning which the Lord rebukes them in the Gospel, saying: Why do you transgress the mandate of God and irritate Him by your traditions, teaching human doctrines and mandates?

Upon this sort of traditions, which in Hebrew are called the *Talmud*—and there is a great book among them exceeding the text of the Bible in length, in which are manifest blasphemies against God and

Christ and the blessed Virgin, intricate fables, erroneous abuses, and unheard-of stupidities—they nourish and teach their sons and render them utterly alien from the doctrine of the law and the prophets, fearing lest, if they knew the truth, which is in the law and the prophets, and which testifies openly that the only begotten son of God will come in the flesh, they would be converted to the faith and humbly return to their Redeemer. And not content with these things, they make Christian women nurses of their sons in contumely of the Christian faith, with whom they commit many shameful things. On which account the faithful should be afraid lest they incur divine wrath while they unworthily allow them to perpetrate acts which bring confusion upon our faith.

And although our cherished son, the chancellor of Paris, and the doctors teaching at Paris in holy writ, by the mandate of pope Gregory, our predecessor of happy memory, after reading and examining the said abusive book and certain others with all their glosses, publicly burned them in the presence of clergy and people to the confusion of the perfidy of the Jews, as we have seen stated in their letters, to whom you as catholic king and most Christian prince rendered suitable aid and favor in this, for which we commend your royal excellency with praises in the Lord and pursue with acts of grace: because nevertheless the profane abuse of the Jews themselves has not yet quieted nor has persecution yet given them understanding, we earnestly ask, admonish, and beseech your highness in the Lord Jesus Christ that against detestable and enormous excesses of this sort committed in contumely of the Creator and in injury to the Christian name, as you piously began, you laudably continue to proceed with due severity. And that you order both the aforesaid abusive books condemned by the same doctors and generally all the books with their glosses which were examined and condemned by them to be burned by fire wherever they can be found throughout your entire kingdom, strictly forbidding that Jews henceforth have Christian nurses or servants, that the sons of a free woman may not serve the sons of a handmaid, but as servants condemned by the Lord, whose death they wickedly plotted, they at least outwardly recognize themselves as servants of those whom the death of Christ made free and themselves slaves. So we may commend the zeal of your sincerity in the Lord with due praises. Given at the Lateran, May 9, in the first year of our pontificate.

Document Set 12.2 References

A. St. Thomas Aquinas Answers the Question, "Should Heretics Be Tolerated?"
St. Thomas Aquinas, in *Translations and Reprints from the Original Sources of European History* (Philadelphia: University of Pennsylvania Press, 1898), 3/6:18–19.

B. The Inquisitor Bernard of Gui Describes the Albigensians' Heresies
Bernard of Gui, *Inquisitor's Guide,* in James Harvey Robinson, ed., *Readings in European History* (Boston: Ginn, 1904), 1:381–383.

C. Testimony of an Albigensian Woman Before the Inquisition
Peter Dronke, *Women Writers of the Middle Ages* (Cambridge: Cambridge University Press, 1984), 204–205.

D. St. Louis Proclaims an Edict Against the Albigensians
Translations and Reprints from the Original Sources of European History (Philadelphia: University of Pennsylvania Press, 1898), 3/6:15.

E. Pope Innocent IV Condemns the Talmud, 1244
Lynn Thorndike, ed., *University Records and Life in the Middle Ages* (New York: Columbia University Press, 1944), 49–50.

DOCUMENT SET 12.3
The Institutional Church at Its Apogee

As we have seen, in its zeal to define heresy the Latin church of the High Middle Ages was systematically strengthening its claims to extraordinary powers. Aquinas was in the forefront of this effort: what are the implications of his opinion in the matter of the priest's role in consecrating the Eucharist (Document A)? Against the background of such claims, however, read Document B, an extract from the Record of Inspection of Parishes in the diocese that the bishop of Rouen carried out from 1248 to 1269. What pattern of clerical behavior emerges? And what significance do you attach to the fact that such inspections were carried out at all?

Document C illustrates the enormous sweep of papal claims over secular rulers by the beginning of the thirteenth century. Admittedly, King John of England, who was the recipient of this missive from Pope Innocent III, was one of the weakest and most vulnerable of medieval English rulers. He was simultaneously under attack by both bishops and barons for infringing on English liberties (see Set 12.4, Documents A and B). Even more far-reaching was Boniface VIII's papal bull *Unam Sanctam* (1302), which asserted spiritual and temporal lordship over the entire earth. Boniface, a less shrewd politician than Innocent III, made the fatal mistake of launching his attack against the ruthless and masterful French king Philip IV (*1285–1314). But despite Boniface's personal downfall, papal power to intervene in secular affairs remained formidable, as the successful imposition of an interdict against Venice in 1309 shows (Document E). In reading this account (which describes the effects of the interdict), ask yourself what value the papacy's control of a purely religious sanction carried as a political weapon.

The poet Dante Alighieri (1265–1321) was a notable opponent of papal claims of lordship over the secular authorities which Dante saw as equally divinely sanctioned. Dante's veneration of Aquinas's theology (Set 12.7, Document D) did not prevent him from consigning Boniface VIII and other recent popes to a most picturesque damnation in the first part of his Divine Comedy, *Hell* (Document F). The punishment he describes here torments the simoniacs, church men who bought and sold church offices. Nor were the Byzantines impressed by papal powers: see the brief extract in Document G.

Drawing on *The Challenge of the West* for background and context, use the documents of Sets 12.1 through 12.3 to analyze the Western church's consolidation of authority in the thirteenth and early fourteenth centuries, the factors facilitating this consolidation, and the opposition it aroused.

A. St. Thomas Aquinas Defines the Priest's Sacred Office

The dispensing of Christ's body belongs to the priest for three reasons. First, because, as was said above, he consecrates as in the person of Christ. But as Christ consecrated His body at the supper, so also He gave it to others to be partaken of by them. Accordingly, as the consecration of Christ's body belongs to the priest, so likewise does the dispensing belong to him. Secondly, because the priest is the appointed intermediary between God and the people; hence as it belongs to him to offer the people's gifts to God, so it belongs to him to deliver consecrated gifts to the people. Thirdly, because out of reverence towards this sacrament, nothing touches it, but what is consecrated; hence the corporal and the chalice are consecrated, and likewise the priest's hands, for touching this sacrament. Hence it is not lawful for anyone else to touch it except from necessity, for instance, if it were to fall upon the ground, or else in some other case of urgency.

B. Church Inspectors Uncover Reality Among the Norman Clergy

On the fourteenth day before the Kalends of April [1248] we visited the chapter of Rouen. We found that they talked in the choir, in violation of their rule. Clerks wandered about the church and chatted with women while the service was going on. They did not observe the rule in regard to entering the choir, and chanted the psalms too fast without making the pauses. . . . In short, they failed to observe many other of the rules, and their temporalities were badly managed.

As for the canons themselves, we found that Master Michael of Berciac was accused of incontinence, likewise Lord Benedict. Likewise Master William of Salmonville of incontinence, theft, and homicide. Likewise Master John of St. Laud of incontinence. Likewise Master Alain of frequenting taverns, drunkenness, and gaming. Likewise Peter of Auleige of carrying on business.

On the *nones* of May [1256] we visited the chapter of St. Firmat. There are fifteen secular canons and a prior there; six canons in residence. Firmin, the vicar of the prior, farms the prebends of the said canons. Morell, the choir clerk, is a rough fellow (*percussor*). Regnaud of Stampis is accused of incontinence, and has a boy with him whom he supports. Bartholomew, the vicar of the cantor, sometimes gets drunk and then does not get up to matins. Roger, one of the canons, occasionally frequents taverns. John, the vicar of the dean, is a tipsy fellow. We accordingly admonished Bartholomew, the cantor's vicar, for his drinking, and likewise John, the dean's vicar, and Roger, the canon, for going to the tavern, and Regnaud of Stampis for his licentiousness, and bade the said Bartholomew, John, Roger, and Regnaud to avoid these offenses. Likewise we ordered that Morell, the choir clerk, who was given to striking and evil speaking, should be corrected as he deserved, and also Firmin, the vicar, for farming the prebends, else we should come down upon them with a heavy hand.

On the Kalends of May [1258] we visited the nunnery of St. Savior. There were sixty-three nuns. They did not have books enough: we ordered that these should be procured. The rule of silence was not properly observed: we commanded that it should be. We admonished them to go to confession every month. We enjoined that they should not keep dogs, birds, or squirrels, and should send away those that they had. Each nun has a chest of her own. We ordered the abbess to see what these contained, and that she should have them opened, and that the iron fastenings should be removed. When they receive new gowns they do not return the old ones. We ordered that no nun should dare to give away her old gown without the permission of the abbess.

C. Innocent III Forces King John to Acknowledge Papal Lordship Over England, 1214

Innocent, bishop, servant of the servants of God, to his well-beloved son in Christ, John illustrious king of the English, and to his legitimate free-born heirs for ever.

The King of kings and Lord of lords, Jesus Christ, a priest for ever after the order of Melchisedech, has so established in the Church His kingdom and His priesthood that the one is a kingdom of priests and the other a royal priesthood, as is testified by Moses in the Law and by Peter in his Epistle; and over all He has set one whom He has appointed as His Vicar on earth [the Pope], so that, as

every knee is bowed to Jesus, of things in heaven, and things in earth, and things under the earth, so all men should obey His Vicar and strive that there may be one fold and one shepherd. All secular kings for the sake of God so venerate this Vicar, that unless they seek to serve him devotedly they doubt if they are reigning properly. To this, dearly beloved son, you have paid wise attention; and by the merciful inspiration of Him in whose hand are the hearts of kings which He turns whithersoever He wills, you have decided to submit in a temporal sense yourself and your kingdom to him to whom you knew them to be spiritually subject, so that kingdom and priesthood, like body and soul, for the great good and profit of each, might be united in the single person of Christ's Vicar. He has deigned to work this wonder, who being alpha and omega has caused the end to fulfill the beginning and the beginning to anticipate the end, so that those provinces which from of old have had the Holy Roman Church as their proper teacher in spiritual matters should now in temporal things also have her as their peculiar sovereign. You, whom God has chosen as suitable minister to effect this, by a devout and spontaneous act of will and on the general advice of your barons have offered and yielded, in the form of an annual payment of a thousand marks, yourself and your kingdoms of England and Ireland, with all their rights and appurtenances, to God and to SS Peter and Paul His apostles and to the Holy Roman Church and to us and our successors, to be our right and our property.

D. Boniface VIII Asserts Papal Domination Over the Whole Earth, 1302

That there is one holy Catholic and apostolic Church we are impelled by our faith to believe and to hold—this we do firmly believe and openly confess—and outside of this there is neither salvation nor remission of sins, as the bridegroom proclaims in Canticles, "My dove, my undefiled is but one; she is the only one of her mother, she is the choice one of her that bare her." The Church represents one mystic body, and of this body Christ is the head; of Christ, indeed, God is the head. In it is one Lord, and one faith, and one baptism. In the time of the flood there was one ark of Noah, prefiguring the one Church, finished in one cubit, having one Noah as steersman and commander. Outside of this all things upon the face of the earth were, as we read, destroyed. This Church we venerate and this alone. . . . It is that seamless coat of the Lord, which was not rent but fell by lot.

Therefore, in this one and only Church there is one body and one head,—not two heads as if it were a monster,—namely, Christ and Christ's vicar, Peter and Peter's successor; for the Lord said to Peter himself, "Feed my sheep." "*My* sheep," he said, using a general term and not designating these or those sheep, so that we must believe that all the sheep were committed to him. If, then, the Greeks, or others, shall say that they were not intrusted to Peter and his successors, they must perforce admit that they are not of Christ's sheep, as the Lord says in John, "there is one fold, and one shepherd."

In this Church and in its power are two swords, to wit, a spiritual and a temporal, and this we are taught by the words of the Gospel; for when the apostles said, "Behold, here are two swords" (in the Church, namely, since the apostles were speaking), the Lord did not reply that it was too many, but enough. And surely he who claims that the temporal sword is not in the power of Peter has but ill understood the word of our Lord when he said, "Put up again thy sword into his place." Both the spiritual and the material swords, therefore, are in the power of the Church, the latter indeed to be used for the Church, the former by the Church, the one by the priest, the other by the hand of kings and soldiers, but by the will and sufferance of the priest.

It is fitting, moreover, that one sword should be under the other, and the temporal authority subject to the spiritual power. For when the apostle said, "there is no power but of God: the powers that be are ordained of God," they would not be ordained unless one sword were under the other, and one, as inferior, was brought back by the other to the highest place. For, according to St. Dionysius, the law of divinity is to lead the lowest through the intermediate to the highest. Therefore, according to the law of the universe, things are not reduced to order directly and upon the same footing, but the lowest through the intermediate, and the inferior through the superior. It behooves us, therefore, the more freely to confess that the spiritual power excels in dignity and nobility any form whatsoever of earthly power, as spiritual interests exceed the temporal in importance. All this we see fairly from the giving of tithes, from the benediction and sanctification, from the recognition of this power and the control of these same things.

Hence, the truth bearing witness, it is for the spiritual power to establish the earthly power and judge it, if it be not good. Thus, in the case of the Church and the power of the Church, the prophecy

of Jeremiah is fulfilled: "See, I have this day set thee over the nations and over the kingdoms," etc. Therefore, if the earthly power shall err, it shall be judged by the spiritual power; if the lesser spiritual power err, it shall be judged by the higher. But if the supreme power err, it can be judged by God alone and not by man, the apostles bearing witness, saying, The spiritual man judges all things, but he himself is judged by no one. Hence this power, although given to man and exercised by man, is not human, but rather a divine power, given by the divine lips to Peter, and founded on a rock for him and his successors in him (Christ) whom he confessed, the Lord saying to Peter himself, "Whatsoever thou shalt bind," etc.

Whoever, therefore, shall resist this power, ordained by God, resists the ordination of God, unless there should be two beginnings [i.e. principles], as the Manichæan imagines. But this we judge to be false and heretical, since, by the testimony of Moses, not in the *beginnings* but in the *beginning*, God created the heaven and the earth. We, moreover, proclaim, declare, and pronounce that it is altogether necessary to salvation for every human being to be subject to the Roman pontiff.

E. Venice Incurs a Papal Interdict, 1309

And since a just quarrel had arisen because of such great sin on the part of the doge of Venice and the Venetian senate he smote them with the anathema, especially mentioning by name Giovanni Soranzo who had wrested the domain of Ferrara away from the church, and Vitali Michieli who was ruling Ferrara in the name of the republic, and ordered them to restore the rule of the Roman church. He deprived all the Venetian territory of the use of the sacraments and of the rights of trade; he branded the magistrates with infamy and pronounced them deprived of the benefits and privileges of the law; and ordered ecclesiastics to leave the Venetian domains except such as were needed to baptize infants and to receive the confessions of the dying. Finally, if they persisted in their present course beyond the time fixed for submission, be pronounced the doge deprived of his authority and all the property of the Venetians confiscated, and declared that the kings of Europe would be summoned to direct their arms against them until they should restore Ferrara to the church.

F. Dante Predicts Boniface VIII's Damnation

I saw the gulley, both its banks and ground,
  Thickset with holes, all of the selfsame size,
  Pierced through the livid stone; and each was round,

Seeming nor more nor less wide to mine eyes
  Than those in my own beautiful St John,
  Made for the priests to stand in, to baptize; . . .

From each hole's mouth stuck out a sinner's feet
  And legs up to the calf; but all the main
  Part of the body was hid within the pit.

The soles of them were all on fire, whence pain
  Made their joints quiver and thrash with such
    strong throes,
  They'd have snapped withies and hempen ropes in
    twain.

And as on oily matter the flame flows
  On the outer surface only, in lambent flashes,
  So did it here, flickering from heels to toes. . . .

"Oh thou, whoever thou art, unhappy shade,
  Heels over head thus planted like a stake,
  Speak if thou canst." This opening I essayed

And stood there like the friar who leans to take
  Confession from the treacherous murderer
  Quick-buried, who calls him back for respite's sake.

He cried aloud: "Already standing there?
  Art standing there already, Boniface?
  Why then, the writ has lied by many a year.

What! so soon sated with the gilded brass
  That nerved thee to betray and then to rape
  The Fairest among Women that ever was?"

Then I became like those who stand agape,
  Hearing remarks which seem to make no sense,
  Blank of retort for what seems jeer and jape.

But Virgil now broke in: "Tell him at once:
  'I am not who thou think'st, I am not he' ";
  So I made answer in obedience.

G. The Byzantines Reject the Latin Church, 1274

Instead of a conflict of words, instead of refutative proof, instead of arguments drawn from the Scriptures, what we envoys constantly hear [from the Byzantine people] is, *"Frangos kathestekas"* (["By accepting union with Rome] You have become a Frank . . ."). Should we who are pro-unionists, simply because we favor union with Rome, be subjected to being called supporters of a foreign nation and not Byzantine patriots?

Document Set 12.3 References

A. St. Thomas Aquinas Defines the Priest's Sacred Office
   St. Thomas Aquinas, *Summa Theologica*, pt. 3, q. 82, art. 3., trans. Fathers of the English Dominican Province (London, 1912).
B. Church Inspectors Uncover Reality Among the Norman Clergy
   Eudes Rigaud, in James Harvey Robinson, ed., *Readings in European History* (Boston: Ginn, 1904), 1:378–379.
C. Innocent III Forces King John to Acknowledge Papal Lordship Over England, 1214
   Innocent III, letter to King John, April 1214, in Lacey Baldwin Smith and Jean Reeder Smith, eds., *The Past Speaks, Sources and Problems in English History*, 2d ed. (Lexington, Mass.: D. C. Heath, 1993), 2:84–85.
D. Boniface VIII Asserts Papal Domination Over the Whole Earth, 1302
   Boniface VIII, *Unam Sanctam*, in James Harvey Robinson, ed., *Readings in European History* (Boston: Ginn, 1904), 1:346–348.
E. Venice Incurs a Papal Interdict, 1309
   Baronius, *Annales*, in *Translations and Reprints from the Original Sources of European History* (Philadelphia: University of Pennsylvania Press, 1898), 4/4:30–31.
F. Dante Predicts Boniface VIII's Damnation
   Dante, *Hell*, canto 19, trans. D. Sayers (Penquin, 1949), 188–191.
G. The Byzantines Reject the Latin Church, 1274
   Metochites, in Deno John Geanokoplos, ed., *Byzantium: Church, Society, and Civilization Seen Through Contemporary Eyes* (Chicago: University of Chicago Press, 1984), 219.

DOCUMENT SET 12.4
The Limits of Monarchical Power

The documents of this set parallel those of the previous set in that they illustrate the limits of power encountered by thirteenth-century monarchs. King John of England's confrontation with his barons and his concession of the Magna Carta in 1215 (Documents A and B) is a dramatic story of tremendous significance for the long-term history of the English-speaking peoples. Based on your reading of Roger Wendover's *Chronicle* (Document A), assess the motives that the English nobility expressed in forcing the king to terms. Remember throughout that the rights assured by Magna Carta applied only to freemen, not to villeins (serfs). A king who managed his public relations much better than King John—and who had a relatively extensive domain from which he could "live of his own" rather than merely squeeze revenue from his subjects—was Louis IX of France (*1226–1270). Louis also took seriously his responsibility to govern justly. In 1254, returning from a crusade, he began a series of reforms that included a thoroughgoing reconstruction of the administration of Paris. Document C, from Joinville's *Life of St. Louis,* shows how the interests of good government and fiscal well-being went hand in hand. Document D, an extract from the legal reforms that Louis promulgated, also illustrates how the king responded to his nobles' constant preoccupation with obtaining justice.

Documents E through G deal with the colorful and always-controversial "wonder of the world," Emperor Frederick II (*1211–1250). He was determined to make Italy his power base; in Naples and Sicily, where he inherited Byzantine and Arab institutions, he was able to overpower opposition. Frederick then conceded extensive liberties to the German bishops and princes in return for their fiscal and military support for his successful efforts to ensure absolute bureaucratic rule in southern Italy (Document E). The reforms he promulgated in Sicily were not merely despotic but also contained a strong dose of rationalism (Document F)—a trait that, in sometimes bizarre ways, he also manifested in his private life, here commented on by a contemporary observer (Document G).

The turmoil that engulfed Germany after Frederick's death in 1250, when his son Conrad IV weakly held the imperial crown, is reflected in the mutual-defense pact that four north German towns made among themselves in 1253 (Document H). It was in such regional compacts that the famous Hanseatic League of northern towns later emerged.

To keep in perspective the vicissitudes of Western monarchies in the thirteenth century, it is useful to recall the fate of the Russian lands at the same time. A massive, irresistible invasion by the Mongols in 1240 devastated all the Russian lands (as well as Hungary and Poland), and for more than 200 years thereafter Russia would be subjugated beneath what has become known as the "Mongol Yoke." Document I, extracted from an anonymous lament composed in the late thirteenth century, gives some sense of the situation.

With the final document in this set, we return to England. Document J is one of Edward I's (*1272–1307) summons of shire and town representatives to Parliament in 1295. Edward's reign was marked by frequent consultations with representatives of his subjects in order to enact legislation and raise revenue; in 1295 the king convoked what has become known as the "Model Parliament," representing the propertied classes as well as the great lords of the land, according to the famous formula, "what concerns all should be approved by all."

Considering all the issues raised by your reading of the sources in this set, in what ways can you see the creation of representative institutions as a means of strengthening state authority?

A. The Barons of England Force King John to Grant Magna Carta, 1215

In the year of our Lord 1215, which was the seventeenth year of the reign of King John, he held his court at Winchester at Christmas for one day, after which he hurried to London, and took up his abode at the New Temple; and at that place the above-mentioned nobles came to him in gay military array, and demanded the confirmation of the liberties and laws of King Edward [the Confessor], with such other liberties granted to them and to the kingdom and church of England as were contained in the charter and the above-mentioned laws of Henry the First. They also asserted that at the time of his absolution at Winchester he had promised to restore those laws and ancient liberties, and was bound by his own oath to observe them. The king, hearing the bold tone of the barons in making this demand, much feared an attack from them, as he saw that they were prepared for battle; he however made answer that their demands were a matter of importance and difficulty, and he therefore asked a truce till the end of Easter, that he might, after due deliberation, be able to satisfy them as well as the dignity of his crown. . . .

In Easter week of this same year the above-mentioned nobles assembled at Stamford with horses and arms, since they had now induced almost all the nobility of the whole kingdom to join them and constituted a very large army. There were computed to be two thousand knights, besides horse soldiers, attendants, and foot soldiers, who were variously equipped. . . . All of these were united by oath, and were supported by the concurrence of Stephen, archbishop of Canterbury, who was at their head. The king at this time was awaiting the arrival of his nobles at Oxford.

On the Monday next after the octaves of Easter the said barons assembled in the town of Brackley; and when the king learned of them, he sent the archbishop of Canterbury and William Marshall, earl of Pembroke, with some other prudent men, to them, to inquire what the laws and liberties were which they demanded. The barons then delivered to the messengers a paper, containing in great measure the laws and ancient customs of the kingdom, and declared that unless the king immediately granted them and confirmed them under his own seal they would, by taking possession of his fortresses, force him to give them sufficient satisfaction as to their before-named demands.

The archbishop with his fellow-messengers then carried the paper to the king and read to him all the heads of the paper, one by one. The king, when he heard the purport of these heads, derisively said, with the greatest indignation, "Why, amongst all these unjust demands, did not the barons ask for my kingdom also? Their demands are vain and visionary, and are unsupported by any plea of reason whatever." And at length he angrily declared, with an oath, that he would never grant them such liberties as would render him their slave. . . .

King John, when he saw that he was deserted by almost all, so that out of his regal superabundance of followers he scarcely retained seven knights, was much alarmed lest the barons should attack his castles and reduce them without difficulty, as they would find no obstacle to their so doing. So he deceitfully pretended to make peace for a time with the aforesaid barons, and sent William Marshall, earl of Pembroke, with other trustworthy messengers, to them, and told them that, for the sake of peace and for the exaltation and honor of the kingdom, he would willingly grant them the laws and liberties they required; he also sent word to the barons by these same messengers, to

appoint a fitting day and place to meet and carry all these matters into effect.

The king's messengers then came in all haste to London, and without deceit did report to the barons all that had been deceitfully imposed on them; they, in their great joy, appointed the 15th of June for the king to meet them at a field lying between Staines and Windsor. Accordingly, at the time and place pre-agreed upon, the king and nobles came to the appointed conference, and when each party had stationed themselves apart from the other, they began a long discussion about terms of peace and the aforesaid liberties. . . . At length, after various points on both sides had been discussed, King John, seeing that he was inferior in strength to the barons, without raising any difficulty, granted the underwritten laws and liberties and confirmed them by his charter as follows:

B. Magna Carta Defines Free-Born English Subjects' Liberties

John, by the grace of God, king of England, lord of Ireland, duke of Normandy and Aquitaine, and count of Anjou, to the archbishops, bishops, abbots, earls, barons . . . and faithful subjects, greeting . . .

We have . . . granted to all free men of our kingdom, for ourselves and our heirs, for ever, all the liberties written below, to be had and held by them and their heirs of us and our heirs . . .

No widow shall be forced to marry so long as she wishes to live without a husband, provided that she gives security not to marry without our consent if she holds [a fief] of us, or without the consent of her lord of whom she holds, if she holds of another.

No scutage [payment in lieu of performing military service] or aid shall be imposed in our kingdom unless by common counsel of our kingdom, except for ransoming our person, for making our eldest son a knight, and for once marrying our eldest daughter; and for these only a reasonable aid shall be levied . . .

Neither we nor our bailiffs will take, for castles or other works of ours, timber which is not ours, except with the agreement of him whose timber it is.

We will not hold for more than a year and a day the lands of those convicted of felony, and then the lands shall be handed over to the lords of the fiefs.

No free man shall be arrested or imprisoned or disseised [dispossessed] or outlawed or exiled or in any way victimized, neither will we attack him or send anyone to attack him, except by the lawful judgment of his peers or by the law of the land.

To no one will we sell, to no one will we refuse or delay right or justice.

We will not make justices, constables, sheriffs or bailiffs save of such as know the law of the kingdom and mean to observe it well.

C. St. Louis Reforms the Goverment of Paris

At that time the provostship of Paris used to be sold to the citizens of Paris or to any persons; those who bought it shielded their children and nephews in their misdeeds . . . In addition there were so many criminals and thieves in Paris and elsewhere that the whole country was full of them. The King, who always laboured for the protection of the poor, knew the truth. He refused accordingly to have the provostship of Paris sold, and gave a generous salary to those who should hold it in future. He stamped out all the evil customs by which the people could be oppressed, and everywhere throughout the Kingdom he had enquiries made to find a man who would deal out fair and firm justice, sparing the rich no more than the poor.

Stephen Boileau, then, was brought to his notice; and he maintained and upheld the provostship so effectively that there was no malefactor or thief or murderer who dared to remain in Paris who was not forthwith hanged or exterminated. Neither kinship, nor birth, nor gold, nor silver could save him. The state of the King's realm began to improve, and people came to it for the good justice to be obtained. Population and prosperity so increased that the revenue from sales of land, death duties, commerce and other sources was double what the King received before.

D. Royal Justice in St. Louis's France

If a baron is summoned to the court of the king for any question of an inheritance and shall say, "I am not willing to be judged in this matter except by my peers," then at least three others ought to be summoned, and the king's justice shall try the suit along with these and any other nobles.

E. Frederick II Concedes Freedom to the German Princes, 1231

In the name of the holy and undivided Trinity. Frederick II, by divine mercy emperor of the Romans, Augustus, king of Jerusalem, king of Sicily. . . .

1. No new castles or cities shall be erected by us or by anyone else to the prejudice of the princes.

2. New markets shall not be allowed to interfere with the interests of former ones.

3. No one shall be compelled to attend any market against his will. . . .

5. We will not exercise jurisdiction within the ban-mile of our cities.

6. Each prince shall possess and exercise in peace according to the customs of the land the liberties, jurisdiction, and authority over counties and hundreds which are in his own possession or are held as fiefs from him. . . .

12. The serfs of princes, nobles, ministerials, and churches shall not be admitted to our cities.

13. Lands and fiefs of princes, nobles, ministerials, and churches, which have been seized by our cities, shall be restored and shall never again be taken.

14. The right of the princes to furnish safe-conduct within the lands which they hold as fiefs from us shall not be infringed by us or by anyone else.

15. Inhabitants of our cities shall not be compelled by our judges to restore any possessions which they may have received from others before they moved there.

16. Notorious, condemned, and proscribed persons shall not be admitted to our cities; if they have been, they shall be driven out.

17. We will never cause any money to be coined in the land of any of the princes which shall be injurious to his coinage.

18. The jurisdiction of our cities shall not extend beyond their boundaries, unless we possess special jurisdiction in the region.

19. In our cities the plaintiff shall bring suit in the court of the accused.

20. Lands or property which are held as fiefs shall not be pawned without the consent of the lord from whom they are held.

21. No one shall be compelled to aid in the fortifying of cities unless he is legally bound to render that service.

22. Inhabitants of our cities who hold lands outside shall pay to their lords or advocates the regular dues and services, and they shall not be burdened with unjust exactions.

23. If serfs, freemen subject to advocates, or vassals of any lord, shall dwell within any of our cities, they shall not be prevented by our officials from going to their lords.

F. Frederick II Abolishes Judicial Ordeals

The laws which are called by certain ingenuous persons *paribiles,* which neither regard nature nor give heed to the truth, We, who investigate the true science of laws and reject their errors, abolish from our tribunals; forbidding by the edict published under sanction of our name all the judges of our kingdom ever to impose on any of our faithful subjects these *paribiles* laws, which ought rather to be called laws that conceal the truth; but let them be content with ordinary proofs such as are prescribed in the ancient laws and in our constitutions. Indeed, we consider that they deserve ridicule rather than instruction who have so little understanding as to believe that the natural heat of red-hot iron grows mild, nay, (what is more foolish) even turns to coldness without the working of an adequate cause; or who assert that on account of a troubled conscience alone a criminal does not sink into the cold water, when rather it is the holding in of sufficient air that does not allow of his being submerged.

G. Salimbine Records Frederick II's Bizarre Rationalism

Of faith in God he had none; he was crafty, wily, avaricious, lustful, malicious, wrathful; and yet a gallant man at times, when he would show his kindness or courtesy; full of solace, jocund, delightful, fertile in devices. He knew to read, write, and sing, and to make songs and music. He was a comely man, and well-formed, but of middle stature. I have seen him, and once I loved him, for on my behalf he wrote to Bro. Elias, Minister-General of the Friars Minor, to send me back to my father. Moreover, he knew to speak with many and varied tongues, and, to be brief, if he had been rightly Catholic, and had loved God and His Church, he would have had few emperors his equals in the world. . . .

When he saw the Holy Land, (which God had so oft-times commended as a land flowing with milk and honey and most excellent above all lands,) it pleased him not, and he said that if the God of the Jews had seen *his* lands of Terra di Lavoro, Calabria, Sicily, and Apulia, then He would not so have commended the land which He promised to the Jews. . . .

He enclosed a living man in a cask that he might die there, wishing thereby to show that the soul perished utterly, as if he might say the word of Isaiah "Let us eat and drink, for to-morrow we die." For he was an Epicurean; wherefore, partly of himself and partly through his wise men, he sought out all that he could find in Holy Scripture which might make for the proof that there was no other life after death, as for instance "Thou shalt destroy them, and not build them up and again Their sepulchres shall be their houses for ever."

H. Four German Towns Ally to Cope with Rampant Disorders, 1253

In the name of the holy and indivisible Trinity, Amen. The magistrates, consuls, and the whole community of burghers and citizens in Münster, Dortmund, Soest, and Lippstadt, to all who may read this document, greeting:

We hereby make known to all men, now and in the future, that because of the manifold dangers to which we are constantly exposed, of capture, robbery, and many other injuries, we have, by common counsel and consent, decided to unite in a perpetual confederation under the following terms, and we have mutually given and received word and oath:

First, that if any man shall take captive one of our citizens or seize his goods without just cause, we will altogether deny to him opportunity to trade in all our cities aforesaid. And if the castellan of any lord shall be the author of an injury that has been done, the afore-mentioned privileges shall be altogether withheld from the lord of that castellan, and from all his soldiers and servants, and all others dwelling with him in his castle. . . .

If any robber has taken goods from one of our citizens . . . and the injured man shall go to any one of our [federated] cities seeking counsel and aid, in order that justice may be done upon the malefactor, the citizens of that city shall act as they would be obliged to act if executing justice for a similar crime committed against one of their own fellow-citizens.

And if any of our burgesses shall chance to go to any of our cities and fear to go forth because of peril to life and property, the burgesses of that city shall conduct him to a place whence his fellow-citizens can receive him in safety.

If a knight shall be denounced to us on reasonable grounds as a violator of faith and honor, we will denounce him in all our cities, and will by mutual consent withhold from him all privileges in our cities until he shall pay the whole debt for which he broke his word.

If any one of us shall buy goods taken from any of our confederates by theft or robbery, . . . he shall not offer the goods at retail anywhere and shall be held guilty with the thief and robber.

I. A Lament on Russia's Conquest by the Mongols

O Russian land, brightest of the bright,
most beautifully adorned,
thou art marvelous to us, with thy many beauties.
Marvelous are thy numerous lakes,
thy rivers and venerated springs,
steep mountains, high hills,
oak forests, beautiful fields,
many beasts and countless birds,
great cities, wonderful villages, and monastery
   gardens,
honorable boyars and countless lords,
Christian churches and stern princes.
Thou, Russian land, art rich in wealth
and the Orthodox Christian faith.
Thou spreadest from Hungary to Poland
   and Bohemia,
from Bohemia to the land of the Yatvags,
from the land of the Yatvags to the Lithuanians
   and Germans,
from the land of the Germans to Karelia,
from Karelia to Ustiug
where live the pagan Toymians,
and beyond the breathing sea,
and from the sea to the Bulgars,
from the Bulgars to the Burtasians,
from the Burtasians to the Cheremiss, and
from the Cheremiss to the Mordvians.
All these vast areas and the people that live on them
were subjugated by God to the Christian people (of
   Russia)
and to Great Prince Vsevolod
and to his father, Yury, Prince of Kiev,
and to his grandfather, Vladimir Monomakh,
with whose name the Kumans frightened
   their children in their cradles,
and in whose reign the Lithuanians
did not dare show themselves from their swamps,
and in whose reign the Hungarians fortified
the stone walls of their cities with their iron gates
so that great Vladimir might not pass through.
And at that time the Germans did rejoice
in being so far (from the Russians) beyond the sea.
And the Burtasians, Cheremiss, Votiaks, and
   Mordvians
worked hard to pay tribute to Vladimir the Great.
And even the Emperor of Byzantium, Manuel,
fearing lest Vladimir the Great take Constantinople,
was sending rich presents to him.

And so it used to be.
But now a great misfortune has befallen the Russian
   land, . . .

J. Edward I Summons Representatives of the Shires and Towns to England's Model Parliament, 1295

The king to the sheriff of Northamptonshire. Since we intend to have a consultation and meeting with the earls, barons and other principal men of our kingdom with regard to providing remedies against the dangers which are in these days threatening the same kingdom; and on that account have commanded them to be with us on the Lord's day next after the feast of St. Martin in the approaching winter, at Westminster, to consider, ordain, and do as may be necessary for the avoidance of these dangers; we strictly require you to cause two knights from the aforesaid county, two citizens from each city in the same county, and two burgesses from each borough, of those who are especially discreet and capable of laboring, to be elected without delay, and to cause them to come to us at the aforesaid time and place.

Moreover, the said knights are to have full and sufficient power for themselves and for the community of the aforesaid county, and the said citizens and burgesses for themselves and the communities of the aforesaid cities and boroughs separately, then and there for doing what shall then be ordained according to the common counsel in the premises; so that the aforesaid business shall not remain unfinished in any way for defect of this power. And you shall have there the names of the knights, citizens and burgesses and this writ.

Witness the king at Canterbury on the third day of October.

Document Set 12.4 References

A. The Barons of England Force King John to Grant Magna
   Carta, 1215
   Roger Wendover, *Chronicle*, in James Harvey Robinson, ed.,
   Readings in European History (Boston: Ginn, 1904), 231–233.
B. Magna Carta Defines Free-Born English Subjects' Liberties
   David C. Douglas, ed., *English Historical Documents*, vol. 3,
   ed. Harry Rothwell (London: Eyre and Spottiswoode, 1975),
   316–321.
C. St. Louis Reforms the Goverment of Paris
   Jean de Joinville, *The Character of St. Louis* (Coronado Press,
   1968), 43–44.
D. Royal Justice in St. Louis's France
   Viollet, *Lives*, in *Translations and Reprints from the Original
   Sources of European History* (Philadelphia: University of
   Pennsylvania Press, 1898), 33.
E. Frederick II Concedes Freedom to the German Princes, 1231
   O. J. Thatcher and E. H. McNeal, *A Source Book of
   Mediaeval History* (New York: Scribners, 1905), 238–240.
F. Frederick II Abolishes Judicial Ordeals
   Translations and Reprints, 4/4:18.

G. Salimbine Records Frederick II's Bizarre Rationalism
   G. C. Coulton, *St. Francis to Dante* (London: 1906), 242–243.
H. Four German Towns Ally to Cope with Rampant Disorders, 1253
   James Harvey Robinson, ed., *Readings in European History* (Boston: Ginn, 1904), 1:413.

I. A Lament on Russia's Conquest by the Mongols
    Orison on the Downfall of Russia, in Serge A. Zenkovsky, ed., *Medieval Russia's Epics, Chronicles and Tales* (New York: 1963), 173–174.
J. Edward I Summons Representatives of the Shires and Towns to England's Model Parliament, 1295
    Translations and Reprints, 1/6:5.

DOCUMENT SET 12.5
The Thirteenth-Century English Manor

As we have seen, the liberties conceded by King John in the Magna Carta were intended only for his free subjects; the documents of this set demonstrate what it meant to be a serf in medieval England.

Document A is an extract from the inventory of a manor of Edward I's day, Alwalton, belonging to the monastery of Peterborough. Document B, from almost the same time, shows the Abbot of Peterborough manumitting (freeing) a serf, or *villein,* almost certainly in return for a cash payment; what conditions and constraints are still imposed upon the freed man? How would you compare his situation with that of the villeins and cotters at Alwalton?

Document C presents a variety of cases heard in a lord's manorial court in 1246–1249, all involving serfs accused of offenses or accusing each other of violation of rights. Notice in particular the enforcement of marriage rules; why should the lord have interested himself in such a matter?

Documents D and E give a glimpse of how the lord of the manor lived and tried to extract a profit from his or her position. How comfortable do you suppose life was for the lord of a manor such as Document D describes?

Using these documents, write a brief summary of the lives of a lord, his serfs, and his free tenants.

A. An English Manor Is Inventoried, 1279

The abbot of Peterborough holds the manor of Alwalton and vill from the lord king directly; which manor and vill with its appurtenances the lord Edward, formerly king of England gave to the said abbot and convent of that place in free, pure, and perpetual alms. And the court of the said manor with its garden contains one half an acre. And to the whole of the said vill of Alwalton belong 5 hides and a half and 1 virgate of land and a half; of which each hide contains 5 virgates of land and each virgate contains 25 acres. Of these hides the said abbot has in demesne 1 hide and a half of land and half a virgate, which contain as above. Likewise he has there 8 acres of meadow. Also he has there separable pasture which contains 1 acre. Likewise he has there 3 water mills. Likewise he has there a common fish pond with a fish-weir on the bank of the Nene, which begins at Wildlake and extends to the mill of Newton and contains in length 2 leagues. Likewise he has there a ferry with a boat.

Free Tenants. Thomas le Boteler holds a messuage with a court yard which contains 1 rood, and 3 acres of land, by charter, paying thence yearly to the said abbot 14s.

Likewise the rector of the church of Alwalton holds 1 virgate of land with its appurtenances, with which the said church was anciently endowed. Likewise the said rector has a holding the tenant of which holds 1 rood of ground by paying to the said rector yearly 1d.

And the abbot of Peterborough is patron of the church.

Villeins. Hugh Miller holds 1 virgate of land in villenage paying thence to the said abbot 3s. 1d. Likewise the same Hugh works through the whole year except 1 week at Christmas, 1 week at Easter, and 1 at Whitsuntide, that is in each week 3 days, each day with 1 man, and in autumn each day with 2 men, performing the same works at the will of the said abbot as in plowing and other work. Likewise he gives 1 bushel of wheat for benseed and 18 sheaves of oats for foddercorn. Likewise he gives 3 hens and 1 cock yearly and 8 eggs at Easter. Likewise he does carrying to Peterborough and to Jakele and no where else, at the will of the said abbot. Likewise if he sells a brood mare in his court yard for 10s. or more, he shall give to the said abbot 4d., and if for less he shall give nothing to the aforesaid. He gives also merchet and heriot, and is tallaged at the feast of St. Michael, at the will of the said abbot. There are also there 17 other villeins, . . . each of whom holds 1 virgate of land in villenage, paying and doing in all things, each for himself, to the said abbot yearly just as the said Hugh Miller. There are also 5 other villeins, . . . each of whom holds half a virgate of land by paying and doing in all things half of the whole service which Hugh Miller pays and does.

Cotters. Henry, son of the miller, holds a cottage with a croft which contains 1 rood, paying thence yearly to the said abbot 2s. Likewise he works for 3 days in carrying hay and in other works at the will of the said abbot, each day with 1 man and in autumn 1 day in cutting grain with 1 man.

Likewise . . . [thirty-three other cotters, all named, who have either a full or a half-rood croft and who provide similar monetary and labor payments. A number of these cotters are widows.]

Likewise each of the said cottagers, except the widows, gives yearly after Christmas a penny which is called head-penny.

B. An English Villein Becomes a Free Man, 1278

To all the faithful of Christ to whom the present writing shall come, Richard by the divine permission abbot of Peterborough and the convent of the same place, eternal greeting in the Lord. Let all know that we have manumitted and liberated from all yoke of servitude William, the son of Richard of Wythington whom previously we have held as our born bondman, with his whole progeny and all his chattels, so that neither we nor our successors shall be able to require or exact any right or claim in the said William, his progeny, or his chattels. But the same William with his whole progeny and all his chattels will remain free and quit and without disturbance, exaction, or any claim on the part of us or our successors by reason of any servitude, forever. We will moreover and concede that he and his heirs shall hold the messuages, land, rents and meadows in Wythington which his ancestors held from us and our predecessors, by giving and performing the fine which is called merchet for giving his daughter in marriage and tallage from year to year according to our will—that he shall have and hold these for the future from us and our successors freely, quietly, peacefully, and hereditarily, by paying thence to us and our successors yearly 40s. sterling, at the four terms of the year, namely; at St. John the Baptist's day, 10s., at Michaelmas, 10s., at Christmas, 10s., and at Easter, 10s., for all service, exaction, custom, and secular demand; saving to us nevertheless attendance at our court of Castre every three weeks, wardship and relief, and outside service of our lord the king, when they shall happen. And if it shall happen that the said William or his heirs shall die at any time without an heir, the said messuage, land, rents, and meadows with their appurtenances shall return fully and completely to us and our successors. Nor will it be allowed to the said William or his heirs the said messuage, land, rents, meadows, or any part of them to give, sell, alienate, mortgage, or in any way encumber by which the said messuage, land, rents, and meadows should not return to us and our successors in the form declared above. But if this should occur later their deed shall be declared null and what is thus alienated shall come to us and our successors. In testimony of which duplicate seals are appended to this writing, formed as a chirograph, for the sake of greater security. These being witnesses, etc. Given at Borough, for the love of lord Robert of good memory, once abbot, our predecessor and maternal uncle of the said William, and at the instance of the good man brother Hugh of Mutton, relative of the said abbot Robert; A. D. 1278, on the eve of Pentecost.

C. Manorial Court Records Reveal Everyday Experiences, 1246–1249

John Sperling complains that Richard of Newmere on the Sunday next before St. Bartholomew's day last past with his cattle, horses, and pigs wrongfully destroyed the corn of his [John's] land to his damage to the extent of one thrave of wheat, and to his dishonour to the extent of two shillings; and of this he produces suit. And Richard comes and defends all of it. Therefore let him go to the law six handed. His pledges, Simon Combe and Hugh Frith.

Hugh Free in mercy for his beast caught in the lord's garden. Pledges, Walter Hill and William Slipper. Fine 6d.

[The] twelve jurors say that Hugh Cross has right in the bank and hedge about which there was a dispute between him and William White. Therefore let him hold in peace and let William be distrained for his many trespasses. (Afterwards he made fine for 12d.)

Roger Pleader is at his law against Nicholas Croke [to prove] that neither he [Roger] nor his killed [Nicholas's] peacock. Pledges, Ringer and Jordan. Afterwards he made his law and therefore is quit.

From the whole township of Little Ogbourne, except seven, for not coming to wash the lord's sheep, 6s, 8d.

Gilbert Richard's son gives 5s. for licence to marry a wife. Pledge, Seaman. Term [for payment,] the Purification.

William Jordan in mercy for bad ploughing on the lord's land. Pledge, Arthur. Fine, 6d.

The parson of the Church is in mercy for his cow caught in the lord's meadow. Pledges, Thomas Ymer and William Coke.

From Martin Shepherd 6d. for the wound that he gave Pekin.

Ragenhilda of Bec gives 2s. for having married without licence. Pledge, William of Primer.

Walter Hull gives 13s. 4d. for licence to dwell on the land of the Prior of Harmondsworth so long as he shall live and as a condition finds pledges, to wit, William Slipper, John Bisuthe, Gilbert Bisuthe, Hugh

Tree, William Johnson, John Hulle, who undertake that the said Walter shall do to the lord all the services and customs which he would do if he dwelt on the lord's land, and that his heriot shall be secured to the lord in case he dies there [i.e. at Harmondsworth].

The Court presented that William Noah's son is the born bondman of the lord and a fugitive and dwells at Dodford. Therefore he must be sought. They say also that William Askil, John Parsons and Godfrey Green have furtively carried off four geese from the vill of Horepoll.

It was presented that Robert Carter's son by night invaded the house of Peter Burgess and in felony threw stones at his door so that the said Peter raised the hue. Therefore let the said Robert be committed to prison. Afterwards he made fine with 2s.

All the ploughmen of Great Ogbourne are convicted by the oath of twelve men . . . because by reason of their default [the land] of the lord was ill-ploughed whereby the lord is damaged to the amount of 9s. . . . And Walter Reaper is in mercy for concealing [i.e. not giving information as to] the said bad ploughing. Afterwards he made fine with the lord with 1 mark.

D. How the Lord Lived: An English Manor House, c. 1256

He received also a sufficient and handsome hall well ceiled with oak. On the western side is a worthy bed, on the ground a stone chimney, a wardrobe, and a certain other small chamber; at the eastern end is a pantry and a buttery. Between the hall and the chapel is a side room. There is a decent chapel covered with tiles, a portable altar, and a small cross. In the hall are four tables on trestles. There are likewise a good kitchen well covered with tiles, with a furnace and ovens, one large, the other small, for cakes, two tables, and alongside the kitchen a small house for baking. Also a new granary covered with oak shingles, and a building in which the dairy is contained, though it is divided. Likewise a chamber suited for clergymen and a necessary chamber. Also a henhouse. These are within the inner gate.

Likewise outside of that gate are an old house for the servants, a good stable, long and divided, and to the east of the principal building, beyond the smaller stable, a solar for the use of the servants. Also a building in which is contained a bed; also two barns, one for wheat and one for oats. These buildings are enclosed with a moat, a wall, and a hedge. Also beyond the middle gate is a good barn, and a stable for cows and another for oxen, these old and ruinous. Also beyond the outer gate is a pigsty.

E. Walter of Henley Advises "How a Lord or Lady Can . . . Live Yearly of Their Own," c. 1240

The fourth rule teaches how a lord or lady can further examine into their estate, that is to say, how he or she can live yearly of their own

In two ways by calculation can you inquire your estate. First this, command strictly that in each place at the leading of your corn there be thrown in a measure at the entrance to the grange the eighth sheaf of each kind of corn, and let it be threshed and measured by itself. And by calculating from that measure you can calculate all the rest in the grange. And in doing this I advise you to send to the best manors of your lands those of your household in whom you place most confidence to be present in August at the leading in of the corn, and to guard it as is aforesaid. And if this does not please you, do it in this way. Command your seneschal that every year at Michaelmas he cause all the stacks of each kind of corn, within the grange and without, to be valued by prudent, faithful, and capable men, how many quarters there may be, and then how many quarters will be taken for seed and servants on the land, and then of the whole amount, and of what remains over and above the land and the servants, set the sum in writing, and according to that assign the expenses of your household in bread and ale. Also see how many quarters of corn you will spend in a week in dispensable bread, how much in alms. That is if you spend two quarters a day, that is fourteen quarters a week, that is seven hundred and fourteen quarters a year. And if to increase your alms you spend two quarters and a half every day, that is seventeen quarters and a half in the week, and in the year eight hundred and fifty three quarters and a half. And when you have subtracted this sum from the sum total of your corn, then you can subtract the sum for ale, according as weekly custom has been for the brewing in your household. And take care of the sum which will remain from sale. And with the money from your corn, and from your rents, and from the issues of pleas in your courts, and from your stock, arrange the expenses of your kitchen and your wines and your wardrobe and the wages of servants, and subtract your stock. But on all manors take care of your corn, that it be not sold out of season nor without need; that is, if your rents and other returns will suffice for the expenses of your chamber and wines and kitchen, leave your store of corn whole until you have the advantage of the corn of another year, not more, or at the least, of half [a year].

Document Set 12.5 References

A. An English Manor Is Inventoried, 1279
   Rotuli Hundredorum, in *Translations and Reprints from the Original Sources of European History* (Philadelphia: University of Pennsylvania Press, 1902), 3/5:4–7.
B. An English Villein Becomes a Free Man, 1278
   Dugdale, *Monasticon,* in *Translations and Reprints,* 3/5:31–32.
C. Manorial Court Records Reveal Everyday Experiences, 1246–1249
   G. G. Coulton, *Social Life in Britain from the Conquest to the Reformation* (London: 1918), 306–308.
D. How the Lord Lived: An English Manor House, c. 1256
   James Harvey Robinson, ed., *Readings in European History* (Boston: Ginn, 1904), 1:404–405.
E. Walter of Henley Advises "How a Lord or Lady Can . . . Live Yearly of Their Own," c. 1240
   Walter of Henley, in H. E. S. Fisher and A. R. J. Jurica, eds., *Documents in English Economic History* (London: G. Bell, 1977), 1:402–403.

DOCUMENT SET 12.6
Medieval Students

This set is devoted to university students and student life in the thirteenth century. Read these documents with an eye to the consolidation of the church and the sharpening definition of heresy (Sets 12.1 and 12.2), two trends that exerted considerable influence on medieval academia. Consider also your own situation as a student; in what ways have students' lives changed over the intervening centuries, and do you still recognize any continuing concerns?

Document A is a set of extracts from student letters home or—in two cases—of parental admonitions to a son away at school. Document B is an extract of the life of Richard of Chichester, later sainted, a student of impeccable devotion to his studies (how many were like him?). In Document C, Jacques de Vitry, a thirteenth-century French preacher, shakes his finger at the misconduct of students flocking to Paris. Document D concerns a perennial issue, the price and reliability of textbooks. (Before the age of printing, which began in the late fifteenth century, did students have textbooks as we now know them? What does Document D suggest?) Document E describes the kind of student merrymaking that the university authorities tried to suppress; and Document F—in a nineteenth-century translation of the *Gaudeamus igitur,* a student song beloved in Germany down to our own time—hints at what students thought of such rules.

On the basis of these documents, as well as those in Set 11.1, prepare a brief paper on what it meant to be a medieval student.

A. Students Write Home

Safe Arrival

After my departure from your gracious presence the circumstances of my journey continued to improve until by divine assistance I arrived safely in the city of Brünn [Moravia], where I have had the good fortune to obtain lodgings with a certain citizen who has two boys in school and provides me with food and clothing in sufficient amount. I have also found here an upright and worthy master, of distinguished reputation and varied attainments, who imparts instruction faithfully; all my fellow pupils, too, are modest, courteous, and of good character, cherishing no hatred but giving mutual assistance in the acquirement of knowledge and in honour preferring one another.

Hard at Work

To their very dear and respected parents M. Martre, knight, and M. his wife, M. and S. their sons send greetings and filial obedience. This is to inform you that, by divine mercy, we are living in good health in the city of Orleans and are devoting ourselves wholly to study, mindful of the words of Cato, "To know anything is praiseworthy," etc. We occupy a good and comely dwelling, next door but one to the schools and market-place, so that we can go to school every day without wetting our feet. We have also good companions in the house with us, well advanced in their studies and of excellent habits—an advantage which we well appreciate, for as the Psalmist says, "With an upright man thou wilt show thyself upright," etc. (Psalms, xviii. 25). Wherefore lest production cease from lack of material, we beg your paternity to send us by the bearer, B., money for buying parchment, ink, a desk, and the other things which we need in sufficient amount that we may suffer no want on your account (God forbid!) but finish our studies and return home with honour. The bearer will also take charge of the shoes and stockings which you have to send us, and any news as well.

Send Money

B. to his venerable master A., greeting. This is to inform you that I am studying at Oxford with the greatest diligence, but the mater of money stands greatly in the way of my promotion, as it is now two months since I spent the last of what you sent me. The city is expensive and makes many demands; I have to rent lodgings, buy necessaries, and provide for many other things which I cannot now specify. Wherefore I respectfully beg your paternity that by the promptings of divine pity you may assist me, so that I may be able to complete what I have well begun. For you must know that without Ceres [bread] and Bacchus [wine] Apollo [the god of Wisdom] grows cold.

In Debt

Well-beloved father, I have not a penny, nor can I get any save through you, for all things at the University are so dear: nor can I study in my Code or my Digest [law books], for they are all tattered. Moreover, I owe ten crowns in dues to the Provost, and can find no man to lend them to me; I send you word of greetings and of money.

The Student hath need of many things if he will profit here; his father and his kin must needs supply him freely, that he be not compelled to pawn his books, but have ready money in his purse, with gowns and furs and decent clothing, or he will be damned for a beggar; wherefore, that men may not take me for a beast, I send you word of greetings and of money.

Wines are dear, and hostels, and other good things; I owe in every street, and am hard bested to free myself from such snares. Dear father, deign to help me! I fear to be excommunicated; already have I been cited, and there is not even a dry bone in my larder. If I find not the money before this feast of Easter, the church door will be shut in my face: wherefore grant my supplication, for I send you word of greetings and of money.

Report Card

I have learned—not from your master, although he ought not to hide such things from me, but from a certain trustworthy source—that you do not study in your room or act in the schools as a good student should, but play and wander about, disobedient to your master and indulging in sport and in certain other dishonorable practices which I do not now care to explain by letter.

Party Time

To his son G. residing at Orleans P. of Besançon sends greeting with paternal zeal. It is written, 'He also that is slothful in his work is brother to him that is a great waster.' I have recently discovered that you live dissolutely and slothfully, preferring license to restraint and play to work and strumming a guitar while the others are at their studies, whence it happens that you have read but one volume of law while your more industrious companions have read several. Wherefore I have decided to exhort you herewith to repent utterly of your dissolute and careless ways, that you may no longer be called a waster and that your shame may be turned to good repute.

Graduation

Sing unto the Lord a new song, praise him with stringed instruments and organs, rejoice upon the high-sounding cymbals, for your son has held a glorious disputation [in Bologna], which was attended by a great number of teachers and scholars. He answered all questions without a mistake, and no one could get the better of him or prevail against his arguments. Moreover he celebrated a famous banquet, at which both rich and poor were honoured as never before, and he has duly begun to give lectures which are already so popular that others' classrooms are deserted and his own are filled.

B. St. Richard of Chichester, a Good Student

Richard therefore hastily left both [his father's] lands and the lady, and all his friends, and betook himself to the University of Oxford and then to that of Paris, where he learned logic. Such was his love of learning, that he cared little or nothing for food or raiment. For, as he was wont to relate, he and two companions who lodged in the same chamber had only their tunics, and one gown between them, and each of them a miserable pallet. When one, therefore, went out with the gown to hear a lecture, the others sat in their room, and so they went forth alternately; and bread with a little wine and pottage sufficed for their food. For their poverty never suffered them to eat flesh or fish, save on the Sunday or on some solemn holy day or in presence of companions or friends; yet he hath oftentimes told me how, in all his days, he had never after led so pleasant and delectable a life.

C. Jacques de Vitry Finds Most Students Unworthy, c. 1240

Almost all the students at Paris, foreigners and natives, did absolutely nothing except learn or hear something new. Some studied merely to acquire knowledge, which is curiosity; others to acquire fame, which is vanity; still others for the sake of gain, which is cupidity and the vice of simony. Very few studied for their own edification or that of others. They wrangled and disputed not merely about the various factions and subjects of discussions; but the differences between the countries also caused dissensions, hatreds and virulent animosities among them, and they impudently uttered all kinds of affronts and insults against one another.

They affirmed that the English were drunkards and had tails; that the sons of France were proud, effeminate and carefully adorned like women. They said that the Germans were furious and obscene at their feasts; the Normans, vain and boastful; the Poitevins, traitors and always adventurers. The Burgundians they considered vulgar and stupid. The Bretons were reported to be fickle and changeable and were often reproached for the death of Arthur. The Lombards were called avaricious, wicked and cowardly; the Romans, seditious, turbulent and slanderous; the Sicilians, tyrannical, brigands and ravishers; the Flemings, fickle, prodigal, gluttonous, yielding as butter, and slothful. After such insults as these in words they often came to blows.

D. The University of Paris Cracks Down on the Bookstores, 1270

The university of masters and students at Paris as a perpetual reminder. Since that field is known to bring forth rich fruit, for which the care of the farmer *colonus* provides painstakingly in all respects, lest we, laboring in the field of the Lord to bring forth fruit a hundredfold in virtues and science, the Lord disposing, should be molested or impeded, especially by those who by a bad custom hang about the university of Paris for the sake of gain, which they make in mercenary works and assistance, we ordain by decree and decree by ordinance that the stationers who vulgarly are called booksellers (*librarii*), shall each year or every second year or whenever they shall be required by the university, give personal oath that, in receiving books to sell, storing, showing, and selling the same and in their other functions in connection with the university, they will conduct themselves faithfully and legitimately.

Also, since some of the aforesaid booksellers, given to insatiable cupidity, are in a way ungrateful and burdensome to the university itself, when they put obstacles in the way of procuring books whose use is essential to the students and by buying too cheaply and selling too dearly and thinking up other frauds make the same books too costly, although as those who hold an office of trust they ought to act openly and in good faith in this matter, which they would better observe if they would not simultaneously act as buyer and seller, we have decreed that the same booksellers swear, as has been stated above, that within a month from the day on which they receive books to sell they will neither make nor pretend any contract concerning those books to keep them for themselves, nor will they suppress or conceal them in order later to buy or retain them, but in good faith, immediately they have received the books or other things, they will offer them for sale at an opportune place and time. And if they shall be asked by the sellers, they shall estimate and state in good faith at how much they really believe the books offered for sale can be sold at a just and legitimate price, and they shall also put the price of the book and the name of the seller somewhere on the book so that it can be

seen by one looking at it. They shall also swear that, when they sell the books, they will not assign or transfer them entirely to the purchasers nor receive the price for them until they have communicated to the seller or his representative what price he is going to receive, and that concerning the price offered for the book they will tell the pure and simple truth without fraud and deceit, nor otherwise in any way shall they attempt anything about their office by cupidity or fraud, whence any detriment could come to the university or the students.

Also, while the laborer is worthy of his hire, which too he licitly seeks by civil law (*Proxenetica*), since nevertheless the standard which should be maintained in such matters is frequently exceeded by the booksellers, we have decreed that the stationers swear that they will not demand for books sold beyond four pence in the pound and a smaller quantity *pro rata* as their commission, and these they shall demand not from the seller but the purchaser.

Also, since many damages come from corrupt and faulty exemplars, we have decreed that the said booksellers swear that they will apply care and pains with all diligence and toil to have true and correct exemplars, and that for exemplars they shall not demand from anyone anything beyond the just and moderate rent or gain or beyond that which shall have been assessed by the university or its deputies.

Also, we have decreed that, if perchance the said booksellers shall be unwilling to swear to the aforesaid or any of the aforesaid, or after having sworn shall have committed fraud in connection with them, or shall not have diligently observed them all and each, not only shall they be utterly ousted from the grace and favor of the university but also henceforth they shall not have the liberty of exercising the office which they exercised before on behalf of the university. So that no master or scholar shall presume to have any business or contract whatever with the said booksellers, after it has been established that the said booksellers have committed a violation of the aforesaid rules or any one of them. But if any master or scholar shall presume to contravene this, he shall be deprived of the society of the masters and scholars until he shall have been reinstated by the university itself. Acted on after deliberation and decreed are these in the general congregation at Paris in the convent of the Friars Preachers and sealed with the seal of the university on December 8, 1275 A.D.

From *University Records and Life in the Middle Ages,* edited by Lynn Thorndike, pp. 101–102. Copyright © 1944 by Columbia University Press. Reprinted with permission of the publisher.

E. King's College, Cambridge, Forbids Students to Cavort in the Streets, c. 1250

It is decreed and ordained that no feast of any nation be henceforth celebrated in any church solemnly and with the accustomed assembly of Masters and Scholars or other acquaintance (except so far as any man desireth to celebrate devoutly the feast of some saint of his own diocese in the church of his own parish, but without inviting the Masters or Scholars or any other of his acquaintance from another parish, even as none such are invited on the feasts of St. Catherine, St. Nicholas, and so forth). We command also the observance of this [following] decree, with the authority of the Chancellor, under pain of the greater excommunication: that no [master or scholar] dance with masks, or with any noise whatsoever, in the churches or the streets, nor go about garlanded or crowned with a crown woven of leaves or the like, under pain of excommunication which we hereby pronounce, and of long imprisonment.

F. Students Raise Their Voices in "Gaudeamus Igitur"

Let us live then and be glad
    While young life's before us!
        After youthful pastime had,
        After old age hard and sad,
    Earth will slumber o'er us.

Where are they who in this world,
    Ere we kept, were keeping?
        Go ye to the gods above;
        Go to hell; inquire thereof:
    They are not; they're sleeping.

Brief is life, and brevity
    Briefly shall be ended:
        Death comes like a whirlwind strong,
        Bears us with his blast along;
    None shall be defended.

Live this university,
    Men that learning nourish;
        Live each member of the same,
        Long live all that bear its name;
    Let them ever flourish!

Live the commonwealth also,
    And the men that guide it!
        Live our town in strength and health,
        Founders, patrons, by whose wealth
    We are here provided!

Live all girls! A health to you,
    Melting maids and beauteous!
        Live the wives and women too,
        Gentle, loving, tender, true,
    Good, industrious, duteous!

Perish cares that pule and pine!
    Perish envious blamers!
        Die the Devil, thine and mine!
        Die the starch-necked Philistine!
    Scoffers and defamers!

Document Set 12.6 References

A. Students Write Home
   Charles Homer Haskins, *Studies in Medieval Culture* (Oxford: Oxford University Press, 1929; revised ed. Ithaca, N.Y.: Cornell University Press, 1957), 10, 15–18, 28.
B. St. Richard of Chichester, a Good Student
   John Capgrave, *Acta Sanctorum Bolland,* in G. G. Coulton, *Social Life in Britain from the Conquest to the Reformation* (London: 1918), 61.
C. Jacques de Vitry Finds Most Students Unworthy, c. 1240
   Jacques de Vitry, *The History of the West,* in James Harvey Robinson, ed., *Readings in European History* (Boston: Ginn, 1904), 1:454–455.
D. The University of Paris Cracks Down on the Bookstores, 1270
   Lynn Thorndike, ed., *University Records and Life in the Middle Ages* (New York: Columbia University Press, 1944), 100–102.
E. King's College, Cambridge, Forbids Students to Cavort in the Streets, c. 1250
   Anstey, *Munimenta Academica,* in G. G. Coulton, *Social Life in Britain from the Conquest to the Reformation* (London: 1918), 67–68.
F. Students Raise Their Voices in "Gaudeamus Igitur"
   J. A. Symonds, trans., *Wine, Women, and Song: Medieval Latin Student Songs* (1884), 165–167.

DOCUMENT SET 12.7
Scholasticism

Metaphysics, the study of philosophical questions beyond the scope of what can tangibly be apprehended by the senses, was the stuff of medieval philosophy. These documents come for the "Golden Age" of high medieval philosophy, and they illustrate some of the concerns with which the great minds of the age wrestled and some of the constraints they encountered.

Moses Maimonides (1135–1204), the great medieval Jewish Aristotelian thinker, was born in Islamic Spain and eventually settled at Cairo. In his famous *Guide for the Perplexed* (Document A), he provided a moving essay on the difficulties of unraveling the subtle metaphysical questions with which the great scholastic philosophers contended. Moreover, philosophers in the Christian West had to reckon with the constraints that the church authorities placed on their inquiry (Document B). Among these condemned propositions were ideas of Eastern Orthodox, Arian, and Manichean origin, and also ideas derived from ancient Greek thought. Document C is an extract from St. Thomas Aquinas's *Summa Theologica,* intended to illustrate scholastic method. It represents the first article, or problem for study, from Aquinas's analysis of the perpetually intractable problem of free will: are human beings responsible for their actions as freely chosen, or have they been "programmed" (as we would say today) to act in such a way? Notice how Aquinas first marshals citations from the Bible and Aristotle ("The Philosopher") denying freedom of the will; then he presents his own response ("I answer that . . .") and proceeds to counterattack the opening statements. This method (repeated throughout the entire *Summa*) reflected disputations within the university. Do you find it a convincing argument? Dante certainly did, in describing his mystical meeting with Aquinas in heaven in (*Divine Comedy, Paradise,* Canto XIII). This passage (Document D) shows how Dante's poetry interweaves scholastic philosophy and mystical ecstasy. Dante's heaven, incidentally, is taken directly from Aristotle's description of the universe: a series of crystalline spheres within spheres, on each of which one of the planets circles.

A. The Jewish Philosopher Moses Maimonides Warns Beginners to Be Wary of Metaphysics

There are five reasons why instruction should not begin with Metaphysics, but should at first be restricted to pointing out what is fitted for notice and what may be made manifest to the multitude.

First Reason.—The subject itself is difficult, subtle and profound. . . . Instruction should not begin with abstruse and difficult subjects. . . . He who can swim may bring up pearls from the depth of the sea, he who is unable to swim will be drowned, therefore only such persons as have had proper instruction should expose themselves to the risk.

Second Reason.—The intelligence of man is at first insufficient; for he is not endowed with perfection at the beginning, but at first possesses perfection only *in potentiâ*, not in fact. . . . There are many things which obstruct the path to perfection, and which keep man away from it. Where can he find sufficient preparation and leisure to learn all that is necessary in order to develop that perfection which he has *in potentiâ*?

Third Reason.—The preparatory studies are of long duration, and man, in his natural desire to reach the goal, finds them frequently too wearisome, and does not wish to be troubled by them. Be convinced that, if man were able to reach the end without preparatory studies, such studies would not be preparatory but tiresome and utterly superfluous. Suppose you awaken any person, even the most simple, as if from sleep, and you say to him, Do you not desire to know what the heavens are, what is their number and their form; what beings are contained in them; what the angels are; how the creation of the whole world took place; what is its purpose, and what is the relation of its various parts to each other; what is the nature of the soul; how it enters the body; whether it has an independent existence, and if so, how it can exist independently of the body; by what means and to what purpose, and similar problems. He would undoubtedly say "Yes," and show a natural desire for the true knowledge of these things; but he will wish to satisfy that desire and to attain to that knowledge by listening to a few words from you. Ask him to interrupt his usual pursuits for a week, till he learn all this, he would not do it, and would be satisfied and contented with imaginary and misleading notions; he would refuse to believe that there is anything which requires preparatory studies and persevering research.

There is still another urgent reason why the preliminary disciplines should be studied and understood. During the study many doubts present themselves, and the difficulties, or the objections raised against certain assertions, are soon understood, just as the demolition of a building is easier than its erection; while, on the other hand, it is impossible to prove an assertion, or to remove any doubts, without having recourse to several propositions taken from these preliminary studies. He who approaches metaphysical problems without proper preparation is like a person who journeys towards a certain place, and on the road falls into a deep pit, out of which he cannot rise, and he must perish there; if he had not gone forth, but had remained at home, it would have been better for him. . . .

The majority of scholars, that is to say, the most famous in science, are afflicted with this failing, viz., that of hurrying at once to the final results, and of speaking about them, without treating of the preliminary disciplines. Led by folly or ambition to disregard those preparatory studies, for the attainment of which they are either incapable or too idle, some scholars endeavour to prove that these are injurious or superfluous. On reflection the truth will become obvious.

The Fourth Reason is taken from the physical constitution of man. It has been proved that moral conduct is a preparation for intellectual progress, and that only a man whose character is pure, calm and steadfast, can attain to intellectual perfection; that is, acquire correct conceptions. Many men are naturally so constituted that all perfection is impossible. . . .

Fifth Reason.—Man is disturbed in his intellectual occupation by the necessity of looking after the material wants of the body, especially if the necessity of providing for wife and children be superadded; much more so if he seeks superfluities in addition to his ordinary wants, for by custom and bad habits these become a powerful motive. Even the perfect man to whom we have referred, if too busy with these necessary things, much more so if busy with unnecessary things, and filled with a great desire for them— must weaken or altogether lose his desire for study, to which he will apply himself with interruption, lassitude, and want of attention. He will not attain to that for which he is fitted by his abilities, or he will acquire imperfect knowledge, a confused mass of true and false ideas. For these reasons it was proper that the study of Metaphysics should have been exclusively cultivated by privileged persons, and not entrusted to the common people. It is not for the beginner, and he should abstain from it, as the little child has to abstain from taking solid food and from carrying heavy weights.

B. The University of Paris Condemns Twelve Errors, 1241

These are the articles rejected as contrary to true theology and condemned by Odo, the chancellor of Paris, and the masters ruling in theology at Paris, in the year of our Lord 1240, on the second Sunday after the octaves of Christmas.

The first [error] is, that the Divine essence in itself will not be seen by any man or angel.

We condemn this error, and by the authority of William, the bishop, we excommunicate those who assert and defend it. Moreover, we firmly believe and assert that God in His essence or substance will be seen by the angels and all saints, and is seen by glorified spirits.

The second, that although the Divine essence is one in Father, Son and Holy Ghost, nevertheless that as far as regards form it is one in Father and Son, but not one in these with the Holy Ghost, and yet this form is the same as the Divine essence.

We condemn this error, for we firmly believe that the essence or substance is one in the Father and Son and Holy Ghost, and the essence is the same in regard to form.

The third, that the Holy Ghost, as it is a bond of affection or love, does not proceed from the Son, but only from the Father.

We condemn this error, for we firmly believe that as it is a bond of affection or love, it proceeds from both.

The fourth, that glorified spirits are not in the empyreal heaven with the angels, nor will the glorified bodies be there, but in the aqueous or crystalline heaven, which is above the firmament; which they also presume to think concerning the blessed Virgin.

We condemn this error, for we firmly believe that angels and sanctified souls and corporeal bodies will occupy the same corporeal place, namely, the empyreal heaven.

The fifth, that the bad angel was bad from his very creation, and never was anything but bad.

We condemn this error, for we firmly believe that he was created good, and afterward through sinning he became bad.

The sixth, that an angel can at the same moment be in different places and can be omnipresent if he chooses.

We condemn this error, for we firmly believe that an angel is in one definite place; so that, if he is here, he is not elsewhere at the same moment; for it is impossible that he should be omnipresent, for this is peculiar to God alone.

The seventh, that many truths, which are not God, have existed eternally.

We condemn this error, for we firmly believe that one truth alone, which is God, has existed eternally.

The eighth, that the beginning, the present time, the creation and the passion may not have been created.

We condemn this error, for we firmly believe that each is both created and creature.

The ninth, that he who has greater talents, will of necessity have greater grace and glory.

We condemn this error, for we firmly believe that God will give grace and glory to each one according to what he has decided and fore-ordained.

The tenth, that the bad angel never had ground whereon he was able to stand, nor even Adam in his state of innocence.

We condemn this error, for we firmly believe that each one had ground whereon he was able to stand, but not anything by which he was able to profit.

C. Scholastic Method: St. Thomas Aquinas Asserts the Freedom of the Will

We proceed thus to the First Article:—Objection 1. It would seem that man has not free will. For whoever has free will does what he wills. But man does not what he wills; for it is written (Rom. vii. 19): *For the good which I will I do not, but the evil which I will not, that I do.* Therefore man has not free will.

Obj. 2. Further, whoever has free will has in his power to will or not to will, to do or not to do. But this is not in man's power: for it is written (Rom. ix. 16): *It is not of him that willeth*—namely, to will— *nor of him that runneth*—namely, to run. Therefore man has not free will.

Obj. 3. Further, what is *free is cause of itself,* as the Philosopher [Aristotle] says (*Metaph.* i. 2). Therefore what is moved by another is not free. But God moves the will, for it is written (Prov. xxi. 1): *The heart of the king is in the hand of the Lord; whithersoever He will He shall turn it;* and (Phil. ii. 13): *It is God Who worketh in you both to will and to accomplish.* Therefore man has not free will.

Obj. 4. Further, whoever has free will is master of his own actions. But man is not master of his own actions: for it is written (Jer. x. 23): *The way of a man*

is not his: neither is it in a man to walk. Therefore man has not free will.

Obj. 5. Further, the Philosopher says (Ethic. iii. 5): *According as each one is, such does the end seem to him.* But it is not in our power to be of one quality or another; for this comes to us from nature. Therefore it is natural to us to follow some particular end, and therefore we are not free in so doing.

On the contrary, It is written (Ecclus. xv. 14): *God made man from the beginning, and left him in the hand of his own counsel; and the gloss adds: That is of his free will.*

I answer that, Man has free will: otherwise counsels, exhortations, commands, prohibitions, rewards and punishments would be in vain. In order to make this evident, we must observe that some things act without judgment; as a stone moves downwards; and in like manner all things which lack knowledge. And some act from judgment, but not a free judgment; as brute animals. For the sheep, seeing the wolf, judges it a thing to be shunned, from a natural and not a free judgment, because it judges, not from reason, but from natural instinct. And the same thing is to be said of any judgment of brute animals. But man acts from judgment, because by his apprehensive power he judges that something should be avoided or sought. But because this judgment, in the case of some particular act, is not from a natural instinct, but from some act of comparison in the reason, therefore he acts from free judgment and retains the power of being inclined to various things. For reason in contingent matters may follow opposite courses, as we see in dialectic syllogisms and rhetorical arguments. Now particular operations are contingent, and therefore in such matters the judgment of reason may follow opposite courses, and is not determinate to one. And forasmuch as man is rational is it necessary that man have a free will.

Reply Obj. 1. As we have said above (Q. 81, A. 3, *ad* 2), the sensitive appetite, though it obeys the reason, yet in a given case can resist by desiring what the reason forbids. This is therefore the good which man does not when he wishes—namely, *not to desire against reason,* as Augustine says (*ibid.*).

Reply Obj. 2. Those words of the Apostle [St. Paul] are not to be taken as though man does not wish or does not run of his free will, but because the free will is not sufficient thereto unless it be moved and helped by God.

Reply Obj. 3. Free will is the cause of its own movement, because by his free will man moves himself to act. But it does not of necessity belong to liberty that what is free should be the first cause of itself, as neither for one thing to be cause of another need it be the first cause. God, therefore, is the first cause, Who moves causes both natural and voluntary. And just as by moving natural causes He does not prevent their acts being natural, so by moving voluntary causes He does not deprive their actions of being voluntary: but rather is He the cause of this very thing in them; for He operates in each thing according to its own nature.

Reply Obj. 4. Man's way is said *not to be his* in the execution of his choice, wherein he may be impeded, whether he will or not. The choice itself, however, is in us, but presupposes the help of God.

Reply Obj. 5. Quality in man is of two kinds: natural and adventitious. Now the natural quality may be in the intellectual part, or in the body and its powers. From the very fact, therefore, that man is such by virtue of a natural quality which is in the intellectual part, he naturally desires his last end, which is happiness. Which desire, indeed, is a natural desire, and is not subject to free will, as is clear from what we have said above (Q. 82, AA. 1, 2). But on the part of the body and its powers man may be such by virtue of a natural quality, inasmuch as he is of such a temperament or disposition due to any impression whatever produced by corporeal causes, which cannot affect the intellectual part, since it is not the act of a corporeal organ. And such as a man is by virtue of a corporeal quality, such also does his end seem to him, because from such a disposition a man is inclined to choose or reject something. But these inclinations are subject to the judgment of reason, which the lower appetite obeys, as we have said (Q. 81, A. 3). Wherefore this is in no way prejudicial to free will.

The adventitious qualities are habits and passions, by virtue of which a man is inclined to one thing rather than to another. And yet even these inclinations are subject to the judgment of reason. Such qualities, too, are subject to reason, as it is in our power either to acquire them, whether by causing them or disposing ourselves to them, or to reject them. And so there is nothing in this that is repugnant to free will.

D. Dante Meets St. Thomas Aquinas in Heaven

If you would understand what I now write
    of what I saw next in that Heaven, imagine
    (and hold the image rock-fast in your sight)
the fifteen brightest stars the heavens wear
    in their living crown, stars of so clear a ray
    it pierces even the mist-thickened air . . .
[Thomas said]: Now open your eyes to what I shall say here
    and see your thought and my words form one truth,
    like the center and circumference of a sphere.
All things that die and all that cannot die
    are the reflected splendor of the Form
    our Father's love brings forth beyond the sky.
For the Living Light that streams forth from the Source
    in such a way that it is never parted
    from Him, nor from the Love whose mystic force
joins them in Trinity, lets its grace ray down,
    as if reflected, through nine subsistant natures
    [the angels who guard the spheres]
    that sempiternally remain as one.

Document Set 12.7 References

A. The Jewish Philosopher Moses Maimonides Warns Beginners to Be Wary of Metaphysics
Moses Maimonides, *Guide for the Perplexed,* trans. M. Friedlander (London: 1910), 44–49.
B. The University of Paris Condemns Twelve Errors, 1241
Translations and Reprints from the Original Sources of European History (Philadelphia: University of Pennsylvania Press, 1898), 2/3:17–19.
C. Scholastic Method: St. Thomas Aquinas Asserts the Freedom of the Will
St. Thomas Aquinas, *Summa Theologica,* pt. 1, q. 83, art. 1, trans. Fathers of the English Dominican Province (London, 1912).
D. Dante Meets St. Thomas Aquinas in Heaven
Dante, *Paradise,* canto 13, trans. John Ciardi (Mentor, 1970), 150–152.

DOCUMENT SET 12.8
Trade, Usury, and Morality

The medieval mind saw economic questions overwhelmingly from the standpoint of morality and ethics: there was a just price at which goods ought to be sold, and to insist on more was to cheat and sin. Notice the reasoning that St. Thomas brings to bear in making this argument in Document A. Usury—the lending of money at interest—was morally wrong; not only had it been forbidden by the Old Testament (notice the qualification in Deuteronomy) and the Qur'an (Document B), but it also violated common sense and Greek philosophy to suppose that a debt could increase over time. Christians did negotiate with Jews to borrow funds at up to specified rates of interest (Document C), and Christian merchants frequently borrowed and lent at interest, both openly (Document D) and through a variety of clever legal dodges. Creditors risked having a usurious debt annulled, however, as well as feeling remorse over committing a sin (Document E). The Catalan merchant who lay dying at Constantinople in 1281 (Document F) obviously felt the need for much soul-searching before he died, considering the sins he may have committed in a life of commerce. But no documentary evidence suggests that anyone considered the slave trade (Document G) morally questionable.

Using these documents as well as *The Challenge of the West*, write a brief essay on the causes and consequences of medieval people's efforts to run their economic life from an ethical viewpoint.

A. St. Thomas Aquinas on the Just Price

It is altogether sinful to have recourse to deceit in order to sell a thing for more than its just price, because this is to deceive one's neighbor so as to injure him. Hence Tully says (*De Offic.* iii. 15): *Contracts should be entirely free from double-dealing: the seller must not impose upon the bidder, nor the buyer upon one that bids against him.*

But, apart from fraud, we may speak of buying and selling in two ways. First, as considered in themselves, and from this point of view, buying and selling seem to be established for the common advantage of both parties, one of whom requires that which belongs to the other, and vice versa, as the Philosopher states (*Polit.* i. 3). Now whatever is established for the common advantage, should not be more of a burden to one party than to another, and consequently all contracts between them should observe equality of thing and thing. Again, the quality of a thing that comes into human use is measured by the price given for it, for which purpose money was invented, as stated in *Ethic.* v. 5. Therefore if either the price exceed the quantity of the thing's worth, or, conversely, the thing exceed the price, there is no longer the equality of justice: and consequently, to sell a thing for more than its worth, or to buy it for less than its worth, is in itself unjust and unlawful.

Secondly we may speak of buying and selling, considered as accidentally tending to the advantage of one party, and to the disadvantage of the other: for instance, when a man has great need of a certain thing, while another man will suffer if he be without it. In such a case the just price will depend not only on the thing sold, but on the loss which the sale brings on the seller. And thus it will be lawful to sell a thing for more than it is worth in itself, though the price paid be not more than it is worth to the owner. Yet if the one man derive a great advantage by becoming possessed of the other man's property, and the seller be not at a loss through being without that thing, the latter ought not to raise the price, because the advantage accruing to the buyer, is not due to the seller, but to a circumstance affecting the buyer. Now no man should sell what is not his, though he may charge for the loss he suffers.

On the other hand if a man find that he derives great advantage from something he has bought, he may, of his own accord, pay the seller something over and above: and this pertains to his honesty.

B. Deuteronomy and the Qur'an Condemn Usury

Deuteronomy:

Thou shalt not lend upon usury to thy brother; usury of money, usury of victuals, usury of any thing that is lent upon usury. Unto a stranger thou mayest lend upon usury; but unto thy brother thou shalt not lend upon usury: that the Lord thy God may bless thee in all that thou settest thine hand to in the land whither thou goest to possess it.

The Qur'an

Those who feed on usury will not rise again [on the Day of Judgment], but will be as those whom the Devil has overthrown by his touch. This is because they claim that trade and usury are the same. But God has permitted trade and forbidden usury. He to whom there comes an admonition from his Lord, and who desists, may keep his past gains, and his case is with God, but those who revert will be dwellers in hellfire for evermore.

C. Jewish Merchants Contract to Settle in Siena and Lend at Interest, 1309

Mosè [son] of Diodato, Salomone [son] of Ser Manuele, and Rosso Levi, Jews residing in the city of Siena, to the men of great nobility and wisdom, their lordships . . . the Twelve Defenders of the Commune of San Gimignano: Greetings and increase of desired happiness!

In regard to taking up residence in your territory and in regard to the pacts and negotiations undertaken between us and you, just as we had suggested to you, we made it our concern to answer you briefly by the present letter that it is our intention as best we can to please you and every individual person in everything, but that we suggest as a pact that we should be allowed to receive six deniers per pound as interest and no more from anyone; for you know well that on a small amount it would not be convenient to receive less than six deniers [per pound]. In regard to large sums everyone could make a pact with us, and it is our intention to receive [interest] up to the said amount in accordance with the pact. And [we request] that all the articles, pacts, and conditions included in our petition be accepted by you in their entirety. And if it be your pleasure to have the aforesaid carried out, be pleased to give orders in regard to the aforesaid to the Syndic of your Commune, and let the Syndic himself come to us with a legal mandate, and on our side we shall have everything carried out in the name of God. And we transmit to you that petition enclosed in the present letter, and the petition itself is of the same tenor as the other petition consigned to you at another time, although at that time we were divided among ourselves because we were not yet in mutual agreement, but at present we are unanimous in the aforesaid.

D. A Genoese Contract of 1161 Openly Mentions Usury

[Genoa,] July 16, 1161

Witnesses: Oberto de Insula, Ansaldo Cintraco, Gozzo and Oberto de Chiberra, Atto Scuvalo. I, Embrone, have taken in loan (*mutuum*) from you, Salvo of Piacenza, £ 100 Genoese, for which I shall pay you or your messenger, personally or by my messenger, £ 120 within one year; but if I wish to pay you the aforesaid £ 100 and accrued interest before the next feast of the Purification, you must accept them and for that purpose have your messenger in Genoa. If I do not so observe [these conditions], I promise you, making the stipulation, the penalty of the double. And on account of this I place in your power all my goods as security, so that if I do not so observe [these conditions], you may then enter [into possession] of whatever of my goods you want in consideration of the capital and the penalty, and you may have estimates made for yourself of an equivalent amount, and this estimated [amount] you may possess by title of sale and you may do with it whatever you please—this, indeed, without decree of the consuls and without objection on my part or of anyone [acting] in my behalf, by your authority alone. I also swear to pay, personally or by my messenger, to you or your messenger, that debt as written above, and [I swear] not on any account to do anything to prevent its being paid except by just impediment or by your permission or by that of your accredited agent—if by impediment, up to its removal, if by permission, up to the expiration of the granted delay or delays. [And I promise] not to deduct anything [from the debt], and I shall not claim release from its payment on account of the emperor or of [any] discord which may exist between our city and yours, or of [interference from] any person. And for so long a time from then as you leave that money with me, I shall protect it in your behalf against all men and I shall pay you whenever you ask.

I, Simone d'Oria, constitute myself as the proper and principal debtor to you, the said creditor, in regard to this debt, so that unless this is so [observed] I shall then pay within eight days the penalty of the double, etc.—waiving [the exception] under the law according to which the first debtor is sued before the second.

Done in the chapter house, July 16, 1161, eighth indiction.

E. A Demand for the Restitution of Usury, 1220

Ugolino and Arduino, brothers, [sons] of the late Ildebrandino, feeling weighed down by usuries which Genovese, [recently] deceased, had extracted from them, therefore appealed to the Supreme Pontiff, [asking] that Filippo, priest [and] rector of the Church of S. Pietro Somaldi, must not bury him before they are satisfied in regard to the usuries which they had asked him to return. This was done in Lucca, in the court of S. Pietro Somaldi, in the portico, in the presence of Gaiascone, [son] of the late Orlando Guasone, and of Guido, [son] of the late Orlandino. 1220, the third [day] before the Ides of March.

[I], Benedetto, judge and notary of the lord emperor, took part in this entire [transaction], and I wrote this as a record.

F. A Catalan Merchant at Constantinople Lists His Assets and Liabilities, and Makes Provision for His Soul

Pera [Constantinople], July 17, 1281

I, Nicolau de Palacio, Catalan, being sick of body and of sound mind, fearing the judgment of God if I die intestate, in contemplation of my last will make the following disposition of my person and goods: First, if I am to die, I elect that my body be buried at the Church of Saint Mary in Constantinople, and to this church I bequeath for my burial and for my funeral rites, for [the salvation of] my soul, 10 assayed gold hyperpers. Also, I bequeath for my soul to the *bailo* of Venice 1 hyperper; also, I bequeath for my soul to the hospital of Pera 2 assayed gold hyperpers; also, I bequeath for my soul to the hospital of the [Knights of] Jerusalem in Acre 5 assayed gold hyperpers; also, I bequeath for the souls of those from whom I believe I have taken [interest] unjustly 20 hyperpers, to be distributed by my executors (*fideicommissarii*); also, I bequeath for my soul all my personal clothing to be distributed by my executors. And I also bequeath to Irene, my woman and the one who is serving me during my present illness, for my soul, 5 assayed gold hyperpers, one old cover, two sheets, one interwoven blanket, and the other utensils and furniture of my house which are not put down in writing below. I also declare that I am to recover from the persons mentioned below the sums of money written below under the pledges written below. First,

from Bernardo Trincia, Pisan, 10 hyperpers, in regard to which I affirm that there is a [notarial] instrument; also, from Pere Goxabis, Spaniard, 9 hyperpers; also, from Ximen, Spaniard, 1 hyperper; also, from Guido of Bologna, my partner and godfather, 60 hyperpers which he had in *accomendacio* from me and of which I affirm that there is a public instrument; also from a certain woman of Pera, under pledge of two scarlet mantles which I have, 10 gold hyperpers; also from Domingo, Spaniard, under pledge of one cape and one sword, 6 hyperpers and 12 keratia; also, from a certain Valeros Megadoukas, under pledge of one tunic of half. . . . I cannot remember the name, under pledge of one tunic with lace . . . also, from a certain Spaniard, whose name I do not know, under pledge of one [piece of] green cloth . . . to give 4 hyperpers and 3 1/2 keratia . . . [and so on, naming a number of other men.] Also, I declare that I have as my own the goods written below: First, one carpet. . . . Also, I will that Bernardo da Ponte, furrier, Bernat of Montpellier, and Lord Martí be the distributors of the said legacies and goods of mine and my executors in regard to my aforesaid goods. . . . My other remaining goods which I have in these regions of Constantinople and the Black Sea, and which may remain after my aforesaid legacies, I bequeath for my soul to my son Joan, son of Maria, if he is alive. And if he is not alive, I will that the said Maria, his mother, shall have from my aforesaid goods 10 assayed gold hyperpers and no more, and I will that my remaining goods, which I have in these parts and the Black Sea, shall be given and distributed for my soul by my said executors wherever it shall seem best to them that they be distributed. This is my last will. . . .

G. Slave Trading, 1248

Genoa, May 11, 1248

I, Giunta, son of the late Bonaccorso of Florence, sell, give, and deliver to you, Raimondo Barbiere, a certain white slave of mine, called Maimona, formerly from Malta, for the price of £ 5 s.10 Genoese, which I acknowledge that I have received for her from you. . . . And I call myself fully paid and quit from you, waiving the exception that the money has not been counted and received. I acknowledge that I have given you power and physical domination [over the slave], promising you that I shall not interfere nor take away the aforesaid slave in any way, but rather I shall protect [her] for you and keep her out [of the power] of any person [under penalty] of £ 20 Genoese which I promise you, making the stipulation, the promise remaining as settled. And I pledge for that. Waiving the privilege of [selecting] the tribunal. And I, said Maimona, acknowledge that I am a slave, and I wish to be delivered and sold to you, Raimondo. And I acknowledge that I am more than ten [years old]. Witnesses called: Oberto de Cerredo, notary, and Antonio of Piacenza, notary. Done in Genoa behind the Church of Saint Laurent, 1248, fifth indiction, on May 11, before terce.

Document Set 12.8 References

A. St. Thomas Aquinas on the Just Price
   Summa Theologica, pt. 2, q. 77, art. 1., trans. Fathers of the English Dominican Province (London, 1912).
B. Deuteronomy and the Qur'an Condemn Usury
   Deuteronomy 23:19–20; excerpt from the *Qur'an* in Lewis, *Islam: From the Prophet Muhammed to the Capture of Constantinople* (New York: Walker, 1987), 124.
C. Jewish Merchants Contract to Settle in Siena and Lend at Interest, 1309
   Lopez and Raymond, 105.
D. A Genoese Contract of 1161 Openly Mentions Usury
   Lopez and Raymond, 116.
E. A Demand for the Restitution of Usury, 1220
   Lopez and Raymond, 159.
F. A Catalan Merchant at Constantinople Lists His Assets and Liabilities, and Makes Provision for His Soul
   Lopez and Raymond, 106–107.
G. Slave Trading, 1248
   Robert S. Lopez and Irving W. Raymond, *Medieval Trade in the Mediterranean World* (New York: Columbia University Press), 158–159.

13

The Collapse of Medieval Order, 1320–1430

DOCUMENT SET 13.1
The Black Death and Social Control

Documents A and B trace the social disintegration caused by the Black Death and the flagellant movement. Although it dates from a generation before the Black Death, a chronicle entry for the year 1310 (Document A) shows how frightening an outbreak of flagellantism could be to late medieval people; study this passage to understand the fear and hopes involved. Boccaccio's famous account of the plague in the *Decameron* rivals Thucydides' description of a similar disaster in fourth-century B.C. Athens (Set 3.1, Document E). Read Boccaccio's document for an understanding of both the epidemic itself and its social consequences.

The last three documents in this set address the issue of maintaining late medieval social control. In 1245, shortly before the Black Death struck, the London Guild of Spurriers (spur-makers) tightened regulations for bidding, excessive competition, and the taking of shortcuts in producing wares. Why? How would such behavior be regulated today? In Document D, the Statute of Laborers (1351), the English government responds to staggering population losses; read this document for an understanding of how drastically the plague altered social and economic relationships and how those in authority tried to maintain old hierarchies. Document E, from the Florentine archives, does not deal with the plague; still, how does this attempt to regulate townspeople's dress speak to the issue of social control?

A. Flagellants Come to Florence, 1310

In the said year [1310] a great marvel made its appearance. It began in Piedmont, advanced through Lombardy and the Genoese littoral, and spread thence to Tuscany and almost covered all Italy. Many people of the commoner sort, men and women and children without number, left their occupations and their cares behind them and, with the cross to point the way, went from place to place beating their bodies and crying *misericordia* ["God have mercy"] and turning people to penance by persuading them to make peace with one another. The Florentines and the inhabitants of a few other cities refused to let them enter their territory and drove them away saying that they were an augury of evil to the land.

B. Giovanni Boccaccio Describes the Black Death

"Dear ladies . . . here we tarry, as if, I think, for no other purpose than to bear witness to the number of the corpses that are brought here for internment. . . . And if we quit the church, we see dead or sick folk carried about, or we see those, who for their crimes were of late condemned to exile . . . but who, now . . . well knowing that their magistrates are a prey to death or disease, have returned, and traverse the city in packs, making it hideous with their riotous antics; or else we see the refuse of the people, fostered on our blood, becchini, as they call themselves, who for our torment go prancing about . . . making mock of our miseries in scurrilous songs. . . . Or go we home, what see we there? . . . where once were servants in plenty, I find none left but my maid, and shudder with terror, and feel the very hairs of my head to stand on end; and turn or tarry where I may, I encounter the ghosts of the departed. . . . None . . . having means and place of retirement as we have, stays here . . . or if any such there be, they are of those . . . who make no distinction between things honorable and their opposites, so they but answer the cravings of appetite, and, alone or in company, do daily and nightly what things soever give promise of most gratification. Nor are these secular persons alone, but such as live recluse in monasteries break their rule, and give themselves up to carnal pleasures, persuading themselves that they are permissible to them, and only forbidden to others, and, thereby thinking to escape, are become unchaste and dissolute.

c. Social Control Before the Black Death: English Guild Regulations, 1345

Be it remembered, that on Tuesday, the morrow of [the feast of] St. Peter's bonds, in the nineteenth year of the reign of King Edward III, the articles underwritten were read before John Hammond, mayor, Roger de Depham, recorder, and the other aldermen; and seeing that the same were deemed befitting, they were accepted and enrolled in these words.

In the first place, that no one of the trade of spurriers shall work longer than from the beginning of the day until curfew rings out at the church of St. Sepulcher, without Newgate; by reason that no man can work so neatly by night as by day. And many persons of the said trade, who compass how to practice deception in their work, desire to work by night rather than by day; and then they introduce false iron, and iron that has been cracked, for tin, and also they put gilt on false copper, and cracked.

And further, many of the said trade are wandering about all day, without working as all at their trade; and then, when they have become drunk and frantic, they take to their work, to the annoyance of the sick, and all their neighborhood as well, by reason of the broils that arise between them and the strange folk who are dwelling among them. And then they blow up their fires so vigorously, that their forges begin all at once to blaze, to the great peril of themselves and of all the neighborhood around. And then, too, all the neighbors are much in dread of the sparks, which so vigorously issue forth in all directions from the mouths of the chimneys in their forges.

By reason thereof it seems unto them that working by night should be put an end to, in order to avoid such false work and such perils; and therefore the mayor and the aldermen do will, by the assent of the good folk of the said trade and for the common profit, that from henceforth such time for working, and such false work made in the trade, shall be forbidden. And if any person shall be found in the said trade to do the contrary hereof, let him be amerced, the first time in forty pence, one half to go to the use of the Chamber of the Guildhall of London, and the other half to the use of the said trade; the second time, in half a mark; and the third time, in ten shillings, to the use of the same Chamber and trade; and the fourth time, let him forswear the trade forever.

Also, that no one of the said trade shall hang his spurs out on Sundays, or on any other days that are double feasts; but only a sign indicating his business; and such spurs as they shall so sell, they are to show and sell within their shops, without exposing them without or opening the doors or windows of their shops, on the pain aforesaid.

Also, that no one of the said trade shall keep a house or shop to carry on his business, unless he is free of the city; and that no one shall cause to be sold, or exposed for sale, any manner of old spurs for new ones, or shall garnish them or change them for new ones.

Also, that no one of the said trade shall take an apprentice for a less term than seven years, and such apprentice shall be enrolled according to the usages of the said city.

Also, that if any one of the said trade, who is not a freeman, shall take an apprentice for a term of years, he shall be amerced as aforesaid.

Also, that no one of the said trade shall receive the apprentice, serving man, or journeyman of another in the same trade, during the term agreed upon between his master and him, on the pain aforesaid.

Also, that no alien of another country, or foreigner of this country, shall follow or use the said trade, unless he is enfranchised before the mayor, aldermen, and chamberlain; and that, by witness and surety of the good folk of the said trade, who will go surety for him, as to his loyalty and his good behavior.

D. Social Control After the Black Death: The English Ordinance Concerning Laborers, 1351

The king to the sheriff of Kent, greeting. Because a great part of the people, and especially of workmen and servants, have lately died in the pestilence, many seeing the necessities of masters and great scarcity of servants, will not serve unless they may receive excessive wages, and others preferring to beg in idleness rather than by labor to get their living; we, considering the grievous incommodities which of the lack especially of ploughmen and such laborers may hereafter come, have upon deliberation and treaty with the prelates and the nobles and learned men assisting us, with their unanimous counsel ordained:

That every man and woman of our realm of England, of what condition he be, free or bond, able in body, and within the age of sixty years, not living in merchandize, nor exercising any craft, nor having of his own whereof he may live, nor land of his own about whose tillage he may occupy himself, and not serving any other; if he be required to serve in suitable service, his estate considered, he shall be bound to serve him which shall so require him; and take only the wages, livery, meed, or salary which were accustomed to be given in the places where he oweth to serve, the twentieth year of our reign of England, or five or six other common years next before. Provided always, that the lords be preferred before others in their bondmen or their land tenants, so in their service to be retained; so that, nevertheless, the said lords shall retain no more than be necessary for them. And if any such man or woman being so required to serve will not do the same, and that be proved by two true men before the sheriff, bailiff, lord, or constable of the town where the same shall happen to be done, he shall immediately be taken by them or any of them, and committed to the next gaol, there to remain under strait keeping, till he find surety to serve in the form aforesaid.

If any reaper, mower, other workman or servant, of what estate or condition he be, retained in any man's service, do depart from the said service without reasonable cause or license, before the term agreed, he shall have pain of imprisonment; and no one, under the same penalty, shall presume to receive or retain such a one in his service.

No one, moreover, shall pay or promise to pay to any one more wages, liveries, meed, or salary than was accustomed, as is before said; nor shall any one in any other manner demand or receive them, upon pain of doubling of that which shall have been so paid, promised, required or received, to him who thereof shall feel himself aggrieved; and if none such will sue, then the same shall be applied to any of the people that will sue; and such suit shall be in the court of the lord of the place where such case shall happen.

And if lords of towns or manors presume in any point to come against this present ordinance, either by them or by their servants, then suit shall be made against them in the form aforesaid, in the counties, wapentakes, and trithings, or such other courts of ours, for the penalty of treble that so paid or promised by them or their servants. And if any before this present ordinance hath covenanted with any so to serve for more wages, he shall not be bound, by reason of the said covenant, to pay more than at another time was wont to be paid to such a person; nor, under the same penalty, shall presume. to pay more.

Item. Saddlers, skinners, white tawyers, cordwainers, tailors, smiths, carpenters, masons, tilers, shipwrights, carters, and all other artificers and workmen, shall not take for their labor and workmanship above the same that was wont to be paid to such persons the said twentieth year, and other common years next preceding, as before is said, in the place where they shall happen to work; and if any man take more he shall be committed to the next gaol, in manner as before is said.

Item. That butchers, fishmongers, hostelers, brewers, bakers, poulterers, and all other sellers of all manner of victuals, shall be bound to sell the same victuals for a reasonable price, having respect to the price that such victuals be sold at in the places adjoining, so that the same sellers have moderate gains, and not excessive, reasonably to be required according to the distance of the place from which the said victuals be carried; and if any sell such victuals in any other manner, and thereof be convicted, in the manner and form aforesaid, he shall pay the double of the same that he so received to the party injured, or in default of him, to any other that will sue in this behalf. And the mayors and bailiffs of cities, boroughs, merchant towns, and others, and of the ports and maritime places, shall have power to inquire of all and singular, which shall in any thing offend against this, and to levy the said penalty to the use of them at whose suit such offenders shall be convicted. And in case the same mayors and bailiffs be negligent in doing execution of the premises, and thereof be convicted before our justices, by us to be assigned, then the same mayors and bailiffs shall be compelled by the same justices to pay the treble of the thing so sold to the party injured, or in default of him, to any other that will sue; and nevertheless they shall be grievously punished on our part.

And because many strong beggars, as long as they may live by begging, do refuse to labor, giving themselves to idleness and vice, and sometimes to theft and other abominations; none upon the said pain of imprisonment, shall, under the color of pity or alms, give anything to such, who are able to labor, or presume to favor them in their idleness, so that thereby they may be compelled to labor for their necessary living.

E. Florence Imposes Sumptuary Legislation, 1378

It is well known to all that the worthy men, Benozzo di Francesco di Andrea . . . [and fifteen others] . . . have been selected to discover ways and means by which money will accrue to the Commune. . . . Considering the Commune's need for revenue to pay current expenses . . . they have enacted . . . the following:

First, all women and girls, whether married or not, whether betrothed or not, of whatever age, rank, and condition . . . who wear—or who wear in future—any gold, silver, pearls, precious stones, bells, ribbons of gold or silver, or cloth of silk brocade on their bodies or heads . . . for the ornamentation of their bodies . . . will be required to pay each year . . . the sum of 50 florins . . . to the treasurer of the gabelle on contracts. . . . [The exceptions to this prohibition are] that every married woman may wear on her hand or hands as many as two rings. . . . And every married woman or girl who is betrothed may wear . . . a silver belt which does not exceed fourteen ounces in weight. . . .

So that the gabelle is not defrauded, and so that citizens—on account of clothing already made—are not forced to bear new expenditures, [the officials] have decreed that all dresses, gowns, coats, capes, and other items of clothing belonging to any women or girls above the age of ten years, which were made up to the present day and which are decorated in whatever manner, may be worn for ten years in the future without the payment of any *gabelle*. . . .

Document Set 13.1 References

A. Flagellants Come to Florence, 1310
   Giovanni Villani, *Chronicle,* in Kenneth R. Bartlett, ed., *The Civilization of the Italian Renaissance: A Sourcebook* (Lexington, Mass.: D. C. Heath, 1992), 40.
B. Giovanni Boccaccio Describes the Black Death
   Giovanni Boccaccio, *The Decameron,* ed. Edward Hutton (London, 1955), 1:13–14.
C. Social Control Before the Black Death: English Guild Regulations, 1345
   Articles of the Spurriers of London, in James Harvey Robinson, ed., *Readings in European History* (Boston: Ginn, 1904), 1:409–411.
D. Social Control After the Black Death: The English Ordinance Concerning Laborers, 1351
   Translations and Reprints from the Original Sources of European History (Philadelphia: University of Pennsylvania Press, 1898), 2/5:3–5.
E. Florence Imposes Sumptuary Legislation, 1378
   Gene Brucker, *The Society of Renaissance Florence* (New York: Harper & Row, 1971), 46–47.

Rome – "upon this rock"
Jesus to Peter

1046 – 3 popes
1080s – 2 popes

bad politics: fights over papal states
–pope stays in Avignon for safety
–Papal bureaucracy (1° office building)

Destruction of Papal Unity → shocked Europe
connected to Black D

DOCUMENT SET 13.2
Who Shall Rule the Church? The Great Schism

The crisis of the papacy tore at the heart of late medieval Western society. It was scandalous that the popes left Rome for Avignon and there built a bureaucracy that seemed much more interested in raising money and pursuing secular political goals than in guiding Christians safely to salvation. Things grew even worse after 1378, when two and then even three rival popes roared maledictions at each other and at their enemies' adherents.

Lay people at many levels tried to respond to this dangerous situation. One of the most important medieval political philosophers, Marsilius of Padua (1270–1336?), wrote *Defender of Peace* to argue the case of having the civil authority (here represented by the would-be Holy Roman Emperor, Louis of Bavaria) impose order on the church and bring peace to Christendom (Document A). What potential for the expansion of the secular state do you detect in his proposal—which the papacy furiously condemned in 1327 (Document B)?

In the East, meanwhile, the Byzantine Empire found itself increasingly beleaguered by encircling Ottoman Turkish forces. Although reunion with the Latin West appeared one possible way of getting aid, a Byzantine ambassador to the pope in 1339 insisted (Document C) that such a reunion could come only on the Eastern church's terms. What does this say for the papacy's claim to lead all Christendom?

Document D comes from the era of the Great Schism, when after 1378 Latin Christendom found itself divided between rival popes. An Avignon cleric called Nicholas Clamanges cited a long list of complaints against a worldly church establishment that, he charged, had lost sight of its real mission. But consider also how the church authorities might have handled the flood of business pouring into Avignon *without* becoming bureaucratic and materialistic.

The University of Paris took the lead in calling for a church council to settle the schism and put Christendom aright. Its 1393 plan appears in Document E. And when in 1415 such a council finally convened at Constance (Document F), the balance of power in the Church had apparently shifted against the papal monarchy. (How do you suppose Marsilius of Padua would have responded?) But such a shift did not become permanent. The early fifteenth-century councils like those at Constance and Basel (1431–1449) failed to head off arrangements between the papacy and the kings of western Europe.

Branding as heretical appeals to "future councils," *"weak fai*...* popes like Pius II (*1458–1464) were able to kill off the conciliar movement, which by then had lost its prestige (Document G).

Drawing upon these documents and your reading of *The Challenge of the West*, prepare an analysis of the rise and fall of conciliarism. Why did it fail?

A. Marsilius of Padua Calls for Popular Sovereignty in Church and State, 1327

Only peace can furnish the necessary conditions for progress, for peace is the mother of all the higher arts. The evils of discord and strife have nearly all been described by Aristotle; but one great and important cause of trouble naturally escaped him,—a potent, hidden influence which interferes with the welfare not only of the empire but of all the governments of Europe. . . .

The power of making the laws should belong to the whole body of citizens, for there is no lawgiver among men superior to the people themselves. The argument that there are an infinite number of fools in the world may be met by pointing out that "foolish" is a relative term, and that the people know their own needs best and will not legislate against their own interests. Any particular class of people is, however, likely to be self-seeking, as is shown by the decrees of the popes and the clergy, where the self-interest of the lawmaker is only too apparent.

The actual administration must, nevertheless, be in the hands of a single person or group of persons. Perhaps a king is the best head for the state, but the monarch should be elected and not hold his office hereditarily, and should be deposed if he exceed his powers. . . .

The bishops of Rome have extended their jurisdiction not only over the clergy but, since the Donation of Constantine, over secular rulers as well. This is illustrated by the acts of the popes of the time (including the famous bull *Unam Sanctam*) and of the existing bishop of Rome, John XXII, who claims, both in Italy and Germany, to have supreme jurisdiction over the emperor and over the lesser princes and communities, even in purely temporal and feudal matters.

In its original meaning the "church" meant all

believers in Christ,—all those for whom he shed his blood. "Churchmen" then include all the faithful, whether they be priests or not. The assumed supremacy of the bishop of Rome is without foundation. Even if Peter was ever in Rome,—which is doubtful,—there is no reason to suppose that he handed down any exceptional power to the succeeding bishops.

B. Pope John XXII Condemns Marsilius's Heresy, 1327

(1) When Christ ordered the coin which was taken from the fish's mouth to be paid to the tax collector, he paid tribute to Caesar; and he did this not out of condescension or kindness, but because he had to pay it. From this it is clear that all temporal powers and possessions of the church are subject to the emperor, and he may take them as his own.

(2) That St. Peter had no more authority than the other apostles, and was not the head over the other apostles; and that Christ left behind no head of the church, and did not appoint anyone as his vicar.

(3) That the emperor has the right to make and depose popes and to punish them.

(4) That all priests, whether pope or archbishop or simple priest, are, in accordance with the appointment of Christ, of equal authority and jurisdiction.

(6) That the whole church together can not punish any man with coactive punishment, without the permission of the emperor.

The above articles are contrary to the holy scriptures and hostile to the catholic faith and we declare them to be heretical and erroneous, and the aforesaid Marsilius and John [of Jandun] to be open and notorious heretics, or rather heresiarchs.

C. The Byzantines Insist That Only an Ecumenical Council Can Restore Christian Unity, 1339

The emperor does not dare to manifest publicly that he desires union with you. If he did declare this, a great number of princes and men of the people, in the fear that he would renew the experience of Michael Palaeologus would seek an occasion to put him to death. . . . You have two means peacefully to realize the union. You can either convince the scholars, who in their turn will convince the people, or persuade both people and learned men at the same time. To convince the learned men is easy, since both they and you seek only the truth. But when the scholars return

home they will be able to do absolutely nothing with the people. Some men will arise who, either from jealousy or from vainglory, and perhaps believing they act rightly, will teach all exactly the opposite of what you will have defined. They will say to the Greeks, "Do not let yourselves be seduced by these men who have sold themselves for gold and are swelled up with pride; let them say what they wish, do not change anything of your faith." And they will listen to them. . . .

To persuade therefore both the people and the learned men together there is only one way: a general council to be held in the East. For the Greeks admit that all that has been determined in a general council conforms to the faith. You will object, saying that already at Lyons a council to treat of union was held. But no one of the Greeks will accept that the Council of Lyons was ecumenical unless another council declares it so. The Greeks present at Lyons had been delegated neither by the four patriarchs who govern the Eastern church nor by the people, but by the emperor alone, who, without seeking to gain their consent, wanted to achieve union by force. Therefore send legates to the four patriarchs; under their presidency a general council will be held which will make union. And all of us who will have been present at this council will say to the people, "Here is what the Holy General Council has decreed. It is your duty to observe its decisions." And all will submit.

D. The Downfall of the Church: An Avignon Clergyman Exposes Avarice and Corruption

After the great increase of worldly goods, the virtues of our ancestors being quite neglected, boundless avarice and blind ambition invaded the hearts of the churchmen. As a result they were carried away by the glory of their position and the extent of their power, and soon gave way to the degrading effects of luxury. Three most exacting and troublesome masters had now to be satisfied. *Luxury* demands sundry gratifications,—wine, sleep, banquets, music, debasing sports, courtesans, and the like. *Display* requires fine houses, castles, towers, palaces, rich and varied furniture, expensive clothes, horses, servants, and the pomp of luxury. Lastly is *Avarice*, which carefully brings together vast treasures to supply the demands of the above-mentioned vices or, if these are otherwise provided for, to gratify the eye by the vain contemplation of the coins themselves.

So insatiable are these lords, and so imperious are their demands, that the Golden Age of Saturn, which we hear of in stories, should it now return, would hardly suffice to meet the requirements. Since it is impossible, however rich the bishop and ample his revenue, to satisfy these rapacious harpies with that alone, he must cast about for other sources of income.

For carrying on these exactions and gathering the gains into the camera, or Charybdis, as we may better call it, the popes appoint their *collectors* in every province,—those, namely, whom they know to be most skillful in extracting money, owing to peculiar energy, diligence, or harshness of temper, those, in short, who will neither spare nor except but would squeeze gold from a stone. To these the popes grant, moreover, the power of anathematizing any one, even prelates, and of expelling from the communion of the faithful every one who does not, within a fixed period, satisfy their demands for money. What ills these collectors have caused, and the extent to which poor churches and people have been oppressed, are questions best omitted, as we could never hope to do the matter justice. From this source come the laments of the unhappy ministers of the Church, which reach our ears, as they faint under the insupportable yoke,—yea, perish of hunger. Hence come suspensions from divine service, interdicts from entering a church, and anathemas, a thousandfold intensified in severity.

Such things were resorted to in the rarest instances by the fathers [i.e., by the early church], and then only for the most horrible of crimes; for by these penalties a man is separated from the companionship of the faithful and turned over to Satan. But nowadays these inflictions are so fallen in esteem that they are used for the lightest offense, often for no offense at all, so that they no longer bring terror but are objects of contempt.

To the same cause is to be ascribed the ruin of numerous churches and monasteries and the leveling to the ground, in so many places, of sacred edifices, while the money which was formerly used for their restoration is exhausted in paying these taxes. But it even happens, as some well know, that holy relics in not a few churches—crosses, chalices, feretories, and other precious articles—go to make up this tribute.

Who does not know how many abbots and other prelates, when they come to die, are, if they prove obnoxious to the papal camera on account of their poverty, refused a dignified funeral, and even denied burial, except perchance in some field or garden, or other profane spot, where they are secretly disposed of. Priests, as we all can see, are forced, by reason of their scanty means of support, to desert their parishes and their benefices and, in their hunger, seek bread where they may, performing profane services for lay-

men. Some rich and hitherto prosperous churches have, indeed, been able to support this burden, but all are now exhausted and can no longer bear to be cheated of their revenue.

E. The University of Paris Tries to Settle the Great Schism, 1393

The first way. Now the first way to end the schism is that both parties should entirely renounce and resign all rights which they may have or claim to have to the papal office. . . .

The second way. But if both cling tenaciously to their rights and refuse to resign, as they have done up to now, we would propose the way of arbitration. That is, that they should together choose worthy and suitable men, or permit such to be chosen in a regular and canonical way, and these shall have the full power and authority to discuss the case and decide it, and if necessary and expedient, and approved by those who according to the canon law have the authority [that is, the cardinals], they may also have the right to proceed to the election of a pope.

The third way. If the rival popes, after being urged in a brotherly and friendly manner, will not accept either of the above ways, there is a third way which we propose as an excellent remedy for this sacrilegious schism. We mean that the matter shall be left to a general council. This general council might be composed, according to canon law, only of prelates, or, since many of them are very illiterate, and many of them are bitter partisans of one or the other pope, there might be joined with the prelates an equal number of masters and doctors of theology and law from the faculties of approved universities. Or if this does not seem sufficient to anyone, there might be added besides one or more representatives from cathedral chapters and the chief monastic orders, in order that all decisions might be rendered only after most careful examination and mature deliberation.

F. The Council of Constance Imposes Reform, 1415–1417

This holy synod of Constance, constituting a general council for the extirpation of the present schism and the union and reformation of the Church of God in head and members, legitimately assembled in the Holy Ghost, to the praise of omnipotent God, in order that it may the more easily, safely, effectively, and freely bring about the union and reformation of the Church of God, hereby determines, decrees, ordains, and declares what follows:

New pope appointed.

Church lost credibility

It first declares that this same council, legitimately assembled in the Holy Ghost, forming a general council and representing the Catholic Church militant, has its power immediately from Christ, and every one, whatever his position or rank, even if it be the papal dignity itself, is bound to obey it in all those things which pertain to the faith, to the healing of the schism, and to the general reformation of the Church of God in head and members.

It further declares that any one, whatever his position, station, or rank, even if it be the papal, who shall contumaciously refuse to obey the mandates, decrees, ordinances, or instructions which have been, or shall be, issued by this holy council, or by any other general council legitimately summoned, which concern, or in any way relate to, the above-mentioned objects, shall, unless he repudiate his conduct, be subjected to condign penance and be suitably punished, having recourse, if necessary, to the resources of the law. . . .

A frequent celebration of general councils is an especial means for cultivating the field of the Lord and effecting the destruction of briers, thorns, and thistles, to wit, heresies, errors, and schism, and of bringing forth a most abundant harvest. The neglect to summon these fosters and develops all these evils, as may be plainly seen from a recollection of the past and a consideration of existing conditions. Therefore, by a perpetual edict, we sanction, decree, establish, and ordain that general councils shall be celebrated in the following manner, so that the next one shall follow the close of this present council at the end of five years. The second shall follow the close of that, at the end of seven years, and councils shall thereafter be celebrated every ten years in such places as the pope shall be required to designate and assign, with the consent and approbation of the council, one month before the close of the council in question, or which, in his absence, the council itself shall designate. Thus, with a certain continuity, a council will always be either in session, or be expected at the expiration of a definite time.

This term may, however, be shortened on account of emergencies, by the supreme pontiff, with the counsel of his brethren, the cardinals of the holy Roman Church, but it may not be hereafter lengthened. The place, moreover, designated for the future council may not be altered without evident necessity. If, however, some complication shall arise, in view of which such a change shall seem necessary, as, for example, a state of siege, a war, a pest, or other obstacles, it shall be permissible for the supreme pontiff, with the consent and subscription of his said brethren, or two thirds of them, to select another appropriate place near the first, which must be within the same country, unless such obstacles, or similar ones, shall exist throughout the whole nation. In that case, the council may be summoned to some appropriate neighboring place, within the bounds of another nation. To this the prelates, and others, who are wont to be summoned to a council, must betake themselves as if that place had been designated from the first. Such change of place, or shortening of the period, the supreme pontiff is required legitimately and solemnly to publish and announce one year before the expiration of the term fixed, that the said persons may be able to come together, for the celebration of the council, within the term specified. . . . [1417]

The holy council of Constance decrees and ordains that the supreme pontiff who shall next, by the grace of God, assume office, shall, in conjunction with this holy council, or with the deputies of the several "nations," reform the Church, before the council dissolves, in head and members, as well as the Roman curia, in accordance with justice and the proper organization of the Church, in all the respects enumerated below, and which are submitted by the "nations" as requiring reform:

The number, character, and nationality of the lords cardinals.

The reservations [of benefices] made by the apostolic see.

The annates, both the *servitia communia* and the *servitia minuta.*

The collation to benefices and expectative favors.

What cases are to be brought before the Roman curia and what not.

Appeals to the Roman curia.

The functions of the [papal] chancery and penitentiary.

Exemptions and incorporations made during the schism.

Benefices *in commendam.*

Confirmation of elections.

Income during vacancies.

The non-alienation of the possessions of the Roman church or other churches.

For what reasons and in what manner a pope shall be corrected or deposed.

The extirpation of heresy.

Dispensations.

The means of support of pope and cardinals.

Indulgences.

Tenths.

When the above-mentioned deputies shall have been appointed by the "nations," it shall be free to the others, with the permission of the pope, to return home. [1417]

G. Papal Monarchy Triumphant: Pope Pius II Forbids Appeals to Future Church Councils, 1459

The execrable and hitherto unknown abuse has grown up in our day, that certain persons, imbued with the spirit of rebellion, and not from a desire to secure a better judgment, but to escape the punishment of some offence which they have committed, presume to appeal from the pope to a future council, in spite of the fact that the pope is the vicar of Jesus Christ and to him, in the person of St. Peter, the following was said: "Feed my sheep" [John 21:16] and "Whatsoever thou shalt bind on earth shall be bound in heaven" [Matt. 16:18]. Wishing therefore to expel this pestiferous poison from the church of Christ and to care for the salvation of the flock entrusted to us, and to remove every cause of offence from the fold of our Saviour, with the advice and consent of our brothers, the cardinals of the holy Roman church, and of all the prelates, and of those who have been trained in the canon and civil law, who are at our court, and with our own sure knowledge, we condemn all such appeals and prohibit them as erroneous and detestable.

Document Set 13.2 References

A. Marsilius of Padua Calls for Popular Sovereignty in Church and State, 1327
   Marsilius of Padua, *Defender of Peace*, in James Harvey Robinson, ed., *Readings in European History* (Boston: Ginn, 1904), 1:491–492.
B. Pope John XXII Condemns Marsilius's Heresy, 1327
   O. J. Thatcher and E. H. McNeal, *A Source Book of Mediaeval History* (New York: Scribners, 1905), 324.
C. The Byzantines Insist That Only an Ecumenical Council Can Restore Christian Unity, 1339
   Barlaam's address to the Pope, in Deno John Geanokoplos, ed., *Byzantium: Church, Society, and Civilization Seen Through Contemporary Eyes* (Chicago: University of Chicago Press, 1984), 220–221.
D. The Downfall of the Church: An Avignon Clergyman Exposes Avarice and Corruption
   Nicholas Clamanges, *The Downfall of the Church,* in Robinson, 1:508–510.
E. The University of Paris Tries to Settle the Great Schism, 1393
   Thatcher and McNeal, 326–327.
F. The Council of Constance Imposes Reform, 1415–1417
   Council of Constance, in Robinson, 1:511–514.
G. Papal Monarchy Triumphant: Pope Pius II Forbids Appeals to Future Church Councils, 1459
   Pius II, "Execrabilis," in Thatcher and McNeal, 332.

DOCUMENT SET 13.3
Spiritual Tensions

Battles over who should rule the church had no effect on popular piety. How deeply felt were the efforts of ordinary Christians to expiate their sins and placate divine wrath may be judged from the documents of this set.

William Langland (c. 1332–c. 1400), an English cleric in minor orders who shared the life of the London poor, composed the long allegorical poem *Piers Plowman* (in Document A translated into modern English prose), which criticized the clergy and spoke for the anxieties of ordinary people. Forming religious confraternities was one way that lay people could "pool" their devotions and increase their sense of security; one such organization from Norwich, England, is described in Document B.

Although most Christians managed to stay within prescribed bounds of belief and practice, heretical groups also thrived. In Italy most Franciscan friars made their compromises with "the world," but a minority, called *Fraticelli* ("little brothers"), continued to preach stringent asceticism and total poverty, and they were condemned as heretical. Document C shows how Florence in 1389 punished one of the Fraticelli. One of the traps that could lead one into heresy, indeed, was the belief that sacraments (like penance and communion) performed by sinful priests had no validity. This view, which if accepted would have undermined the whole institutional church (for who was to judge what priests were guilty?), was roundly condemned by churchmen like the author of a 1444 tract (Document D) against the heretical Waldensian movement.

To help to pull together this material and understand late medieval religious anxieties, consider also Document E, one of the sonnets of the great, restless Italian poet Petrarch (1304–1374). The poem describes the decision of Petrarch's brother to enter the especially strict Carthusian Order after his lady-love's death in 1343. No one in late-medieval Europe could ever forget the prospect of sudden death and judgment for one's sins; use the documents of this set and *The Challenge of the West* to evoke this melancholy foreboding and to analyze the means by which lay Christians sought to deal with it.

A. Piers Plowman Prefers Individual Piety to Reliance on the Church

And all this maketh me think upon my dream. And how the priest found no pardon like Do-well and thought that Do-well surpassed indulgences, saying mass two or three years for departed souls, and bishops' letters; and how Do-well shall be worthier received at the day of doom, and shall surpass all the pardons of St. Peter's church.

Now the pope hath power to grant people the power to pass into heaven without any penance. This is our belief, as learned men teach us. ("Whatsoever you shall bind on earth, it shall be bound in heaven," etc.) And so I truly believe (Lord forbid otherwise!) that pardon and penance and prayers indeed cause souls to be saved which have sinned deadly seven times. But to trust these three-year masses methinketh truly is not so safe for the soul, certes, as is Do-well.

Therefore, I counsel you, ye men who are rich on this earth and have three-year masses in trust of your treasure, be ye never the bolder to break the ten commandments; and especially, ye masters, mayors, judges, who are held for wise men and have the wealth of this world and can purchase pardon and the pope's bulls. At the dreadful doom when the dead shall rise and all come before Christ to render account,—how thou didst lead thy life here and didst keep his laws, and how thou didst do day by day, the doom will declare. And bagful of pardons there, or provincial letters,—or though ye be found in the fraternity of all the four monastic orders, and have doublefold indulgences,—except Do-well help you, I set your letters and pardons at the worth of a pea shell!

B. A Religious Confraternity in England Organizes Communal Devotion, 1389

In the first place with one assent it is ordained that all the brethren and sisters of this gild shall come together to the parish church of St. Simon and St. Jude, in Norwich, on the day of St. Katharine, to go in the procession with their candle, which is borne before them, and to hear the mass of St. Katharine in the aforesaid church; and at that mass every brother and sister shall offer a half-penny.

And also it is ordained that what brother or sister shall be absent at the procession aforesaid, or at mass, or at offering, he shall pay to the chattels of the gild two pounds of wax, but they may be excused reasonably.

And also it is ordained, that where a brother or a sister is dead, and every brother and sister shall come to *dirige*[1] and to mass; and at the mass, each shall offer a half-penny, and give a half-penny to alms; and for a mass to be sung for the soul of the dead, a penny. And at the *dirige*, every brother and sister that is lettered shall say, for the soul of the dead, *placebo* and *dirige*, in the place where they shall come together; and every brother and sister that is not lettered shall say for the soul of the dead, twenty times, the *Paternoster*, with *ave Maria*; and from the chattels of the gild shall there be two candles of wax, of sixteen pounds weight, about the body of the dead.

And also it is ordained, that if any brother or sister die out of the city of Norwich, within eight miles, six of the brethren that have the chattels of the gild in keeping, shall go to that brother or sister that is dead; and if it be lawful, they shall carry it to Norwich, or else it be buried there; and if the body be buried out of Norwich, all the brethren and sisters shall be warned to come to the foresaid church of St. Simon and St. Jude, and there shall be done for the soul of the dead all service, light and offering as if the body were there present. And what brother or sister be absent at *placebo* and *dirige*, or at mass, he shall pay two pounds of wax to the chattels of the gild, unless he be reasonably excused. And nevertheless he shall do for the dead as it is said before. . . .

And also it is ordained that if any brother or sister fall into poverty, through adventure of the world, his estate shall be helped by every brother and sister of the gild, with a farthing in the week.

And also it is ordained by common assent that if there be any discord between brothers and sisters, that discord shall be first showed to other brothers and sisters of the gild, and by them shall accord be made, if it may be skillfully. And if they cannot be so brought to accord, it shall be lawful to them to go to the common law, without any maintenance. And whoso does against this ordinance, he shall pay two pounds of wax to the light.

Also it is ordained, by common assent, that if any brother of this gild be chosen into office and refuse it, he shall pay two pounds of wax to the light of St. Katharine.

Also it is ordained, by common assent, that the brethren and sisters of this gild, in the worship of St. Katharine, shall have a livery of hoods in suit, and eat together in their gild day, at their common cost; and whoso fails, he shall pay two pounds of wax to the light.

Also it is ordained, by common assent, that no brother or sister shall be received into this gild but by the alderman and twelve brethren of the gild. . . .

C. One of the Florentine *Fraticelli* Is Burned at the Stake, 1389

This is the condemnation of Giovanni, called Fra Michele di Berti of Calci, in the territory of Pisa, a man of low condition, evil conversation, life, and reputation, and a heretic against the Catholic faith, against whom we have proceeded by means of inquisition. . . . It has come to our attention that this Giovanni . . . with the spirit and intent of being a heretic, had relations with the Fraticelli, called the Little Brothers of Poverty, heretics and schismatics and denounced by the Holy Roman Church, and that he joined that depraved sect in a place called the grotto of the *Dieci Yoffensi*, in which place they congregated and stayed. . . .

Now everything which I here describe, I who write both saw or heard. Fra Michele, having come into the courtyard, waited attentively to hear the condemnation. And the vicar [general of the bishop] spoke: "The bishop and the Inquisitor have sent me here to tell you that if you wish to return to the Holy Church and renounce your errors, then do so, in order that the people may see that the church is merciful." And Fra Michele replied, "I believe in the poor crucified Christ, and I believe that Christ, showing the way to perfection, possessed nothing. . . ." Having read his confession, the judge turned his back upon Fra Michele . . . and the guards seized him and with great force pushed him outside of the gate of the judge's palace. He remained there alone, surrounded by scoundrels, appearing in truth as one of the martyrs. And there was such a great crowd that one could scarcely see. And the throng increased in size, shouting: "You don't want to die!" And Fra Michele replied, "I will die for Christ." And the crowd answered: "Oh! You aren't dying for Christ! You don't believe in God!" And Fra Michele replied: "I believe in God, in the Virgin Mary, and in the Holy Church!" And someone said to him, "You wretch! The devil is pushing you from behind!" . . .

. . . And at the Mercato Nuovo, the shouts grew louder: "Repent, repent!" And he replied, "Repent of your sins; repent of your usury and your false mer-

[1] Various prayers in the Latin liturgy are named in this document.

chandising. . . ." And at the Piazza del Grano, there were many women in the windows of the houses who cried to him: "Repent, repent!" And he replied, "Repent of your sins, your usury, your gambling, your fornication. . . ." When he arrived at S. Croce, near the gate of the friars, the image of St. Francis was shown to him and he raised his eyes to heaven and said, "St. Francis, my father, pray to Christ for me. . . ."

And when he arrived at the gate near the place of execution, one of the faithful began to cry, "Remain firm, martyr of Christ, for soon you will receive the crown. . . ." And arriving at the place of execution, there was a great turmoil and the crowd urged him to repent and save himself and he refused. . . . And the guards pushed the crowd back and formed a circle of horsemen around the pyre so that no one could enter. I myself did not enter but climbed upon the river bank to see, but I was unable to hear. . . . And he was bound to the stake . . . and the crowd begged him to recant, except one of the faithful, who comforted him. . . . And they set fire to the wood . . . and Fra Michele began to recite the Te Deum. . . . And when he had said, "In your hands, O Lord, I commend my spirit," the fire burned the cords which bound him and he fell dead . . . to the earth.

And many of the onlookers said, "He seems to be a saint." Even his enemies whispered it . . . and then they slowly began to return to their homes. They talked about Michele and the majority said that he was wrong and that no one should speak such evil of the priests. And some said, "He is a martyr," and others said, "He is a saint," and still others denied it. And there was a greater tumult and disturbance in Florence than there had ever been. . . .

D. Are Sacraments Performed by an Unworthy Priest Valid?

Since the sin of adultery does not take from a king the royal dignity, if otherwise he is a good prince who righteously executes justice in the earth, so neither can it take the sacerdotal dignity from the priest, if otherwise he performs the sacraments rightly and preaches the word of God. Who doubts that a licentious king is more noble than a chaste knight, although not more holy? . . . No one can doubt that Nathaniel was more holy than Judas Iscariot; nevertheless Judas was more noble on account of the apostleship of the Lord, to which Judas and not Nathaniel was called.

But thou, heretic, wilt say: "Christ said to his disciples, 'Receive ye the Holy Ghost. Whosoever sins ye remit, they are remitted unto them'; therefore the priest who does not receive the Holy Ghost because he is wicked cannot absolve." Even if a wicked priest has neither charity nor the Holy Ghost as a private man, nevertheless his priesthood is worthy as far as the efficacy of the sacraments goes, though he himself may be unworthy of the priesthood. . . .

For example, a red rose is equally red in the hands of an emperor or of a dirty old woman; likewise a carbuncle in the hand of a king or of a peasant; and my servant cleans the stable just as well with a rusty iron hoe as with a golden one adorned with gems. No one doubts that in the time of Elijah there were many swans in the world, but the Lord did not feed the prophet by swans, but by a black crow. It might have been pleasanter for him to have had a swan, but he was just as well fed by a crow. And though it may be pleasanter to drink nectar from a golden goblet than from an earthen vessel, the draught intoxicates just the same, wherever it comes from.

E. Petrarch Broods on Love and Death

Thy lady fair, whom thou didst love so well,
Hath from amongst us suddenly withdrawn,
And unto heav'n—that dare I hope—is gone;
Such pleasantness and softness round her fell.
'Tis therefore time, that in thy keeping dwell
Thy heart's two keys, which living she did own;
Thou shouldst pursue her, by straight path, anon,
And from thee all the weight of earth dispel.
Thou art from thy chief hinderance now freed,
And may'st whate'er remains lay down with ease,
And like unloaded pilgrims, may'st emerge.
Thou see'st now well, how every creature flees
Always to death, and how the soul hath need
To step, with lightness, to that perilous verge.

Document Set 13.3 References

A. Piers Plowman Prefers Individual Piety to Reliance on the Church
James Harvey Robinson, ed., *Readings in European History* (Boston: Ginn, 1904), 1:477.
B. A Religious Confraternity in England Organizes Communal Devotion, 1389
Translations and Reprints from the Original Sources of European History (Philadelphia: University of Pennsylvania Press, 1902), 34–35.
C. One of the Florentine *Fraticelli* Is Burned at the Stake, 1389
Alessandro D'Ancona in Gene Brucker, ed., *The Society of Renaissance Florence* (New York: Harper & Row, 1971), 253–257.
D. Are Sacraments Performed by an Unworthy Priest Valid?
Pilichdorfer, *Against the Wilderness*, in Robinson, 1:383–384.
E. Petrarch Broods on Love and Death
Petrarch, Sonnet 70, trans. C. B. Cayley.

DOCUMENT SET 13.4
Wycliffe, Hus, and Their Followers

This set continues to deal with lay concerns for religious safeguards as expressed in Set 13.3, but with a focus on how John Wycliffe in England and Jan Hus in Bohemia took stands that the church declared heretical.

Both Wycliffe (c. 1329–1384) and Hus (c. 1369–1415) were priests and university teachers who became deeply aware of abuses in the church through their sympathetic contacts with ordinary people. The ideas of Wycliffe, a generation older than Hus, probably became known to the latter through direct contacts between the universities of Oxford and Prague and also through the presence in Prague of Englishmen associated with the English-born queen of Bohemia. Wycliffe survived because the church, divided by schism, could not prevail on the English authorities (among whom he had many sympathizers) to hand him over. Hus was martyred by the Council of Constance, which although it had deposed popes, was not about to tolerate "Wycliffite" attacks on central church dogmas like transubstantiation (the doctrine that the priest transforms the communion bread and wine into the actual body and blood of Christ).

The central message of Wycliffe's and Hus's teaching was that the clergy could not mediate between the individual Christian and God. Document A is a brief extract from Wycliffe's voluminous writings on this theme, translated into modern English; in Document B, Hus writes from his prison cell in Constance to justify his position and protest against the council's attempt to silence him. In Document C the consequences of Hus's revolt become apparent: the Czech people rose in arms to resist their king, Sigismund, who had betrayed Hus and now was attempting to enforce the council's decrees on religious conformity. In this document a member of the Prague City Council, a moderate Hussite, describes how radical Hussites founded a community they called Tabor. His account combines sympathy for the persecuted with a rejection of the social and religious radicalism of the sectarians, who fervently believed they were ushering in the reign of God's righteousness on earth.

A. John Wycliffe Attacks the Clergy for Withholding the Gospel from the People

We should put on the armor of Christ, for the antichrist has turned these clergy to covetousness and worldly love, and has so blinded the people and decried the law of Christ that his servants be thick [many], and few be on Christ's side. And always they despise that men should know Christ's life, for by his life and his teaching should help arise on his side, and priests should be ashamed of their lives, and especially these high priests, for they reverse Christ both in word and deed.

And therefore the great Bishop of England, as men say, is ill-pleased that God's law be written in English for laymen; and he pursues a priest for writing to men this English, and summons him and persecutes him, so that he is hard pressed to cry out. And thus he pursues another priest by the help of Pharisees, for he preached Christ's gospel freely without distortions.

B. Jan Hus, on the Eve of His Execution, Writes "to the Entire Christian World," 1415

I, Master John Hus, in hope a servant of Jesus Christ, heartily desiring that Christ's faithful after my decease should have no occasion to be offended on account of my death by judging me as if I were an obstinate heretic; and taking Christ Jesus as witness, for Whose law I desire to die, write this as a memorial to the friends of truth.

First, that in the very many private hearings and later in the public hearings of the Council I protested my willingness to submit to instruction and direction, revocation and punishment, were I taught that anything I had written, taught, or said in reply was contrary to the truth. And fifty doctors, delegates of the Council, as they said, often rebuked by me even in the public hearing of the Council because of their false abstracting of the articles, were not willing to give me any private instruction; yea, they were not willing even to confer with me, saying: "You must stand by the decision of the Council." As for the Council, when I adduced in the public hearing Christ's Scripture or [the opinion] of the holy doctors, they either mocked me or said that I understood it wrongly, while the doctors said that I adduced it inappropriately. Also a certain cardinal, the highest in the Council and delegated by the Council, taking out a paper, said at a public hearing: "Look, a certain master of sacred theology presented me this argument: answer it!" It was an argument about the common essence which I had conceded to exist in divine things. Afterward, when he floundered, although he is reputed to be a most eminent doctor of theology, I spoke to him about the common created essence which is the first created being and is communicated to every individual creature. From this he wished to prove the remanence of the material bread. But being obviously reduced to the utmost lack of knowledge of the argument, he became silent.

Immediately thereafter an English doctor began to argue, but he similarly floundered, and another English doctor, who at a private hearing said to me that Wyclif had wished to destroy all knowledge and that in every one of his books and his treatises of logic he had committed errors; he, rising, began to argue about the multiplication of the body of Christ in the host. Failing in the argument, when they told him to keep still, he said: "Look! he [Hus] astutely deceives the Council! Beware, lest the Council be deceived as it was deceived by Berengar!"[1] When he became silent, someone began to argue noisily about the common created essence; but he was shouted down by the crowd. I, however, standing up, asked to be accorded a hearing, saying to him: "Argue boldly; I shall gladly answer you." But he likewise gave up and ill-temperedly added: "It is a heresy!"

What clamor then, what mocking, jeering, and reviling arose against me in that assembly is known to lords Wenceslas of Dubá and John of Chlum and his notary Peter, the most steadfast knights and lovers of God's truth. Hence even I, being often overwhelmed by such clamor, spoke these words: "I had supposed that in this Council would be greater reverence, piety, and discipline." Then they all listened because the king ordered silence. The cardinal presiding over the Council said: "You spoke more humbly in the castle!" I said: "Because then nobody shouted at me; while now all are shouting against me." And he added: "Look! the Council requests whether you are willing to submit to instruction." I said: "Most gladly am I willing, in accordance with my declaration." And he said: "Yea, this constitutes your instruction,

that the doctors declare the articles drawn from your books to be erroneous. You must revoke them and abjure those which were deposed against you by the witnesses." The king then said: "They will be shortly written for you, and you will reply." And the cardinal said: "This will be done at the next hearing." And immediately the Council rose up. God knows what great temptings I suffered afterward!

C. Lawrence of Brezová Describes the Founding of Tabor

In these times therefore the faithful Czechs, both clergy and laity, who favored communion in both kinds and devotedly promoted it, and who grieved at the unjust death of Master John Hus . . . suffered very great difficulties, tribulations, anguish, and torment throughout the Kingdom of Bohemia, at the hands of the enemies and blasphemers of the Truth. . . . For these enemies of the Truth hunted down priests and laymen who ardently supported the chalice in various parts of the realm and brought them to the men of Kutná Hora,[2] to whom they sold some for money. The Kutná Horans—Germans and cruel persecutors and enemies of the Czech—afflicted them with various blasphemies and diverse punishments, and inhumanly threw them—some alive, some first decapitated—into deep mine shafts, especially into the mine shaft near the church of St. Martin near the Kourim gate, which shaft the Kutná Horans called "Tabor." . . . In a short time more than 1,600 utraquists [those who took communion in both kinds] were killed . . . the executioners often being exhausted by the fatigue of slaughter. . . .

During this time certain Taborite priests were preaching to the people a new coming of Christ, in which all evil men and enemies of the Truth would perish and be exterminated, while the good would be preserved in five cities. . . . They urged that all those desiring to be saved from the wrath of Almighty God, which in their view was about to be visited on the whole globe, should leave their cities, castles, villages, and towns, as Lot left Sodom, and should go to the five cities of refuge. . . . And many simple folk . . . sold their property, taking even a low price, and flocked to these priests from various parts of the Kingdom of Bohemia and . . . Moravia, with their wives and children, and they threw their money at the feet of the priests.

---

[1] A French theologian (c. 999–1088) whose views denying transubstantiation were condemned by the church in the eleventh century.

[2] A rich mining town near Prague, inhabited by a mixed Czech-German population

Document Set 13.4 References

A. John Wycliffe Attacks the Clergy for Withholding the Gospel from the People
   John Wycliffe, adapted from James Harvey Robinson, ed., *Readings in European History* (Boston: Ginn, 1904), 1:497–498.

B. Jan Hus, on the Eve of His Execution, Writes "to the Entire Christian World," 1415
   M. Spinka, *John Hus and the Council of Constance* (New York: 1965), 293–294.

C. Lawrence of Brezová Describes the Founding of Tabor
   Lawrence of Brezová in Howard Kaminsky, *A History of the Hussite Revolution* (Berkeley: University of California Press, 1967), 310–312.

DOCUMENT SET 13.5
Domination

The three documents of this set reflect upper-class views of the social hierarchy in late medieval society. Read them to extract the values they express.

Document A is an extract from the prologue to *The Canterbury Tales* of Geoffrey Chaucer, which introduces the characters who will subsequently tell their stories as they journey on a pilgrimage to the great shrine at Canterbury. Chaucer's Prologue sets before us the complete social hierarchy, and it should be read in its entirety, if possible. Read Document B—an extract from Christine de Pizan's (1364–c. 1430) *The Book of the City of Ladies*—for her views on how a "wise princess" should keep the women in her charge under control. Christine was an accomplished woman of her day, a professional writer patronized by the queen of France, and she understood well the secluded world of court women whose chain-of-command paralleled that of men of comparable rank. Finally consider the tournament, staged in 1390 during the Hundred Years' War, as described in the *Chronicles* of Sir John Froissart (1333?–1400). Such entertainments brought together men and women of the court and the town to enjoy a display of knightly prowess.

A. Geoffrey Chaucer Idealizes "a Truly Perfect, Gentle Knight"

A knight there was, and he a worthy man,
Who, from the moment that he first began
To ride about the world, loved chivalry,
Truth, honour, freedom and all courtesy.
Full worthy was he in his liege-lord's war,
And therein had he ridden (none more far)
As well in Christendom as heathenesse,
And honoured everywhere for worthiness.
  At Alexandria, he, when it was won;
Full oft the table's roster he'd begun
Above all nations' knights in Prussia.
In Latvia raided he, and Russia,
No christened man so oft of his degree.
In far Granada at the siege was he
Of Algeciras,[1] and in Belmarie.
At Ayas was he and at Satalye
When they were won; and on the Middle Sea
At many a noble meeting chanced to be.

1 Various campaigns against the Muslims in Southern Spain and North Africa are named here.

Of mortal battles he had fought fifteen,
And he'd fought for our faith at Tramissene
Three times in lists, and each time slain his foe.
This self-same worthy knight had been also
At one time with the lord of Palatye
Against another heathen in Turkey:
And always won he sovereign fame for prize.
Though so illustrious, he was very wise
And bore himself as meekly as a maid.
He never yet had any vileness said,
In all his life, to whatsoever wight.
He was a truly perfect, gentle knight.
But now, to tell you all of his array,
His steeds were good, but yet he was not gay.
Of simple fustian wore he a jupon
Sadly discoloured by his habergeon;
For he had lately come from his voyage
And now was going on this pilgrimage.

B. Christine de Pizan Advises "How the Wise Princess Will Keep the Women of Her Court in Good Order"

17. The sixth teaching: how the wise princess will keep the women of her court in good order.

Just as the good shepherd takes care that his lambs are maintained in health, and if any of them becomes mangy, separates it from the flock for fear that it may infect the others, so the princess will take upon herself the responsibility for the care of her women servants and companions, who she will ensure are all good and chaste, for she will not want to have any other sort of person around her. Since it is the established custom that knights and squires and all men (especially certain men) who associate with women have a habit of pleading for love tokens from them and trying to seduce them, the wise princess will so enforce her regulations that there will be no visitor to her court so foolhardy as to dare to whisper privately with any of her women or give the appearance of seduction. If he does it or if he is noticed giving any sign of it, immediately she should take such an attitude towards him that he will not dare to importune them any more. The lady who is chaste will want all her women to be so too, on pain of being banished from her company.

She will want them to amuse themselves with decent games, such that men cannot mock, as they do the games of some women, though at the time the men laugh and join in. The women should restrain themselves with seemly conduct among knights and squires and all men. They should speak demurely and sweetly and, whether in dances or other amusements, divert and enjoy themselves decorously and without wantonness. They must not be frolicsome, forward, or boisterous in speech, expression, bearing or laughter. They must not go about with their heads raised like wild deer. This kind of behaviour would be very unseemly and greatly derisory in a woman of the court, in whom there should be more modesty, good manners and courteous behaviour than in any others, for where there is most honour there ought to be the most perfect manners and behaviour. Women of the court in any country would be deceiving themselves very much if they imagined that it was more appropriate for them to be frolicsome and saucy than for other women. For this reason we hope that in time to come our doctrine in this book may be carried into many kingdoms, so that it may be valuable in all places where there might be any shortcoming.

We say generally to all women of all countries that it is the duty of every lady and maiden of the court, whether she be young or old, to be more prudent, more decorous, and better schooled in all things than other women. The ladies of the court ought to be models of all good things and all honour to other women, and if they do otherwise they will do no honour to their mistress nor to themselves. In addition, so that everything may be consistent in modesty, the wise princess will wish that the clothing and the ornaments of her women, though they be appropriately beautiful and rich, be of a modest fashion, well fitting and seemly, neat and properly cared for. There should be no deviation from this modesty nor any immodesty in the matter of plunging necklines or other excesses.

In all things the wise princess will keep her women in order just as the good and prudent abbess does her convent, so that bad reports about it may not circulate in the town, in distant regions or anywhere else. This princess will be so feared and respected because of the wise management that she will be seen to practise that no man or woman will be so foolhardy as to disobey her commands in any respect or to question her will, for there is no doubt that a lady is more feared and respected and held in greater reverence when she is seen to be wise and chaste and of firm behaviour. But there is nothing wrong or inconsistent in her being kind and gentle, for the mere look of the wise lady and her subdued reception is enough of a sign to correct those men and women who err and to inspire them with fear.

C. Sir John Froissart Describes the Pageantry of a Joust, 1390

The King of England and his three uncles had received the fullest information of the splendid feasts and entertainments made for Queen Isabella's public entry into Paris; and in imitation of it, they ordered grand tournaments and feasts to be holden in the city of London, where sixty knights should be accompanied by sixty noble ladies richly ornamented and dressed. The sixty knights were to tilt for two days; that is to say, on the Sunday after Michaelmas day, and the Monday following, in the year of grace 1390. They were to set out at two o'clock in the afternoon from the Tower of London with their ladies, and parade through the streets, down Cheapside, to a large square called Smithfield. There they were to wait on the Sunday the arrival of any foreign knights who might be desirous of tilting; and this feast of the Sunday was called the challengers'.

The same ceremonies were to take place on the Monday, and the sixty knights to be prepared for tilting courteously, with blunted lances, against all comers. The prize for the best knight of the opponents was a rich crown of gold, that for the tenants of the lists a very rich golden clasp. They were to be given to the most gallant tilter, according to the judgment of the ladies who should be present with the Queen of England, and the great barons, as spectators. On Tuesday the tournaments were to be continued by squires against others of the same rank who wished to oppose them. The prize for the opponents was a courser saddled and bridled, and for the tenants of the lists a falcon. Accordingly when Sunday came, about three o'clock, there paraded from the Tower of London, which is situated in the square of St. Catherine, on the banks of the Thames, sixty barbed coursers ornamented for the tournament, and on each was mounted a squire of honour. . . .

Document Set 13.5 References

A. Geoffrey Chaucer Idealizes "a Truly Perfect, Gentle Knight" Geoffrey Chaucer, *Canterbury Tales,* trans., J. U. Nicolson (Garden City, N.Y.: Garden City Publishing Co., 1934), 2–3.
B. Christine de Pizan Advises "How the Wise Princess Will Keep the Women of Her Court in Good Order" Christine de Pizan, *The Book of the City of Ladies,* in Sarah Lawson, trans., *Treasuries of the City of Ladies* (Penguin, 1985), 74–76.
C. Sir John Froissart Describes the Pageantry of a Joust, 1390 John Froissart, *The Chronicles of England, France and Spain* (London: Dutton, 1906), 481.

DOCUMENT SET 13.6
Violence and Revolt

The inverse of displays of upper-class authority, examined in Set 13.5, was the frequent eruption of lower-class violence. The fourteenth and early fifteenth centuries were an age of brutal conflict both between rival monarchies and within them. Document A describes an insurrection in the Byzantine city of Thessalonika (in present-day northern Greece) in 1346. How do you account for the religious coloration evidenced in this account of the rioters' behavior?

Froissart's account of a tournament (Set 13.5, Document C) presents one side of the Hundred Years' War; Documents B and C of this set show another aspect. How do you account for the brutality of the sack of Limoges, a French town, as Froissart describes it (Document B), or for the speculations in ransomed prisoners (Document C)? Draw upon *The Challenge of the West* in answering such questions. The English Peasant Rebellion of 1381 climaxed a long period of rural oppression—serfdom itself, compounded by taxation and the lords' desperate attempts to maintain their accustomed dominance in the face of a severe labor shortage after the Black Death. The law "against the excess of the villeins [serfs]" enacted in 1377 (Document D) shows how Parliament tried to control this explosive situation, and the short extract from the peasants' embattled leader, John Ball, evokes the rebels' elemental demand for justice and order.

A. An Urban Insurrection: The Zealot Revolt in Thessalonika, 1345

In Thessalonika, since the *protostrator*, as we said, was doubtful over which emperor to associate himself with and openly pondered the matter, something even more reprehensible occurred—he tolerated the so-called Zealots, who chose to fight on behalf of the Palaeologan emperor against the Emperor Cantacuzene and who were gradually increasing in numbers. He did this on the one hand lest he should seem openly favorable to the side of Emperor Cantacuzene. For his wife and daughter, who were in Byzantium, . . . caused him great indecision, lest on account of him they be subjected to many misfortunes. This also made him indifferent [toward the Zealots], the fact that not only the garrison of Thessalonika, which was not small, but also the powerful members of the citizenry had chosen the side of the Emperor Cantacuzene (citizens whom he believed confidently would, whenever they might wish, suppress the Zealots).

And then, when the Zealots, on account of his [the *protostrator's*] neglect, became somewhat greater in number, and when they incited the people [*demos*] against the rich [*dynatoi*], and when the *protostrator* was recognized as doing the bidding of the Emperor Cantacuzene, the Zealots attacked in a mob and drove out from the city about a thousand people. A small crowd formed as a result of the skirmishing, in which a few even of the household of the *protostrator* were wounded, and they also captured some of the rich [*dynatoi*] who were unable to escape along with the others at the time of the first attack. After the Zealots had taken possession of the city, they rushed to the houses of the fugitives and razed them and seized their goods and did other things, things that men would do who were driven by poverty and urged on to reckless violence on account of the immense wealth [of the rich]. They came to such a point of murder and audacity that some dared even the most terrible things. Seizing the cross from the holy sanctuary, they used it as a banner and said they were fighting under it (although they were actually led by the enemy of the cross). And if someone was involved in legal dispute with another, he, seizing the cross, displayed it alongside his opponent's house as if the cross itself had given a signal. And at once, it was [deemed] necessary to raze the house to its foundation, since the people [*demos*] were driven by irrational force and hope of profit.

For two or three days Thessalonika was devoured as if by enemy soldiers, and nothing was done there which was not customary for captured cities. The victors, at night and during the day, roved around in groups, expressed themselves with cries and shouting, and plundered and carried away the property of the vanquished. The victims, lamenting, hid in intolerable places, accepting the situation as inescapable, [fearing] lest suddenly they might be killed. Since the revolt would cease when corrupt citizens were lacking, the Zealots, who from the poorest and most ignoble status had suddenly become rich and arrogant, seized everything for themselves, and either drew the middle class toward them or forced them (reluctantly) to accept them. Or the Zealots condemned wisdom and reasonableness as being "Cantacuzenism." In Thessalonika, then, such things were happening.

B. Sir John Froissart Describes the Sack of Limoges, 1370

[Having mined the town walls,] the miners set fire into their mine, and so the next morning, as the prince had ordained, there fell down a great piece of the wall and filled the moats, whereof the Englishmen were glad and were ready armed in the field to enter the town. the foot-men might well enter at their ease, and so they did, and ran to the gate and beat down the fortifying and barriers, for there was no defense against them: it was done so suddenly that they of the town were not aware thereof.

Then the prince, the duke of Lancaster, the earl of Cambridge, the earl of Pembroke, Sir Guichard d'Angle, and all the others, with their companies, entered into the city, and all other foot-men ready apparelled to do evil, and to pill and rob the city, and to slay men, women, and children; for so it was commanded them to do. It was a great pity to see the men, women, and children that kneeled down on their knees before the prince for mercy. But he was so inflamed with ire that he took no heed of them, so that none was heard, but all put to death as they were met withal, and such as were nothing culpable.

There was no pity taken of the poor people who wrought never no manner of treason, yet they bought it dearer than the great personages, such as had done the evil and trespass. There was not so hard a heart within the city of Limoges and if he had any remembrance of God, but that wept piteously for the great mischief that they saw before their eyen, for more than three thousand men, women, and children were slain that day. God have mercy on their souls, for I trow they were martyrs.

And thus entering into the city, a certain company of Englishmen entered into the bishop's palace, and there they found the bishop; and so they brought him to the prince's presence, who beheld him right fiercely and felly, and the best word that he could have of him was how he would have his head stricken off, and so he was had out of his sight. . . .

Thus the city of Limoges was pilled, robbed, and clean brent and brought to destruction.

C. War for Profit: An English Knight Speculates in Ransomed French Prisoners, 1376

A.D. 1376. To all persons who these letters shall see or hear, William de Beauchaumpe, greeting. Whereas Messire Thomas de Feltone is bound unto me, and obligated, in 4000 silver marks, by reason of the purchase of Messire Berard de la Bret, my prisoner, I do will and grant that the said Messire Thomas, his heirs, and his executors, shall be acquitted and discharged by these present letters; and that I myself, my heirs, and my executors, be ousted for ever hereby from all manner of action by reason of the said statute, or by reason of the purchase of the said Messire Berard, my prisoner.

D. King Richard II and John Ball: Two Views of the English Peasant Revolt, 1381

King Richard II:

At the grievous complaint of the lords and commons of the realm, as well men of holy church as other, made in this Parliament, of that in many lordships and parts of the realm of England, the villains and land tenants in villainage, who owe services and customs to their said lords, have now late withdrawn and do daily withdraw their services and customs due to their said lords; by comfort and procurement of other their counsellors, maintainers and abettors in the country, which have taken hire and profit of the said villains and land tenants by color of certain exemplifications made out of the book of Domesday of the manors and towns where they have been dwelling, and by virtue of the same exemplifications and their evil interpretations of the same, they affirm them to be quit and utterly discharged of all manner of serfdom, due as well of their body as of their said tenures, and will not suffer any distress or other justice to be made upon them; but do menace the servants of their lords of life and member, and, which is more, gather themselves together in great routs, and agree by such confederacy, that every one shall aid other to resist their lords with strong hand; and much other harm they do in sundry ways, to the great damage of their said lords and evil example to others to begin such riots; so that if due remedy be not the rather provided upon the same rebels, greater mischief, which God prohibit, may thereofspring through the realm. It is ordained and established that the lords which feel themselves grieved, shall have special commission under the great seal to the justices of the peace, or to other sufficient persons, to inquire of all such rebels, and of their offences, and their counsellors, procurers, maintainers and abettors, and to imprison all those that shall be thereof indicted before them, as well for the time past as for the time to come, without delivering them out of prison by mainprise, bail or otherwise, without assent of their lords, till they be attainted or acquitted thereof; and that the same justices have power to hear and determine as well at the king's suit as at the suit of the party.

And as to the said exemplifications, made and purchased as afore is said, which were caused to come in the Parliament, it is declared in the said Parliament that the same may not nor ought to avail, or hold place to the said villains or land tenants, as to the franchise of their bodies; nor to change the condition of their tenure and customs of old time due; nor to do prejudice to the said lords, to have their services and customs as they were wont of old time; and it is ordained that upon this declaration the said lords shall have letters patent under the great seal, as many and such as they shall need, if they the same require.

John Ball:

John Schep, som tyme Seynt Marie prest of York, and now of Colchester, greteth welle Johan Nameles,[1] and Johan the Mullere, and Johan Cartere, and biddeth hem that thei ware of gyle in borugh [i.e., who had entered the town by guile], and stondeth togiddir in Goddis name, and biddeth Peres Ploughman go to his werke, and chastise welle Hobbe the robber, and taketh with you Johan Trewman, and alle his felaws, and no mo, and loke scharpe you to on heved, and no mo.

Johan the Muller hath ygrownde [grown] smal, smal, smal;

The Kyngis sone of hevene [i.e., Jesus] shalle pay for alle.

Be ware or ye be wo.

Knoweth your frende fro youre foo,

Haveth ynowe [enough], and seythe "Hoo;"

And do welle and bettre, and fleth synne,

And seketh pees [peace], and holde therynne [there in].

And so biddeth Johan Trewman and alle his felawes.

Document Set 13.6 References

A. An Urban Insurrection: The Zealot Revolt in Thessalonika, 1345
   John Cantacuzene, *Historia,* in Deno John Geanokoplos, ed., *Byzantium: Church, Society, and Civilization Seen Through Contemporary Eyes* (Chicago: University of Chicago Press, 1984), 271–272.
B. Sir John Froissart Describes the Sack of Limoges, 1370
   John Froissart, *The Chronicles of England, France and Spain,* in James Harvey Robinson, ed., *Readings in European History* (Boston: Ginn, 1904), 1:472–473.
C. War for Profit: An English Knight Speculates in Ransomed French Prisoners, 1376
   H. T. Riley, *Memorials of London* (1868), 392.
D. King Richard II and John Ball: Two Views of the English Peasant Revolt, 1381
   Translations and Reprints from the Original Sources of European History (Philadelphia: University of Pennsylvania Press, 1898), 2/5:17–19.

[1] Johan [John] Nameles[s] and other names given here are allegorical names standing for members of various groups.

DOCUMENT SET 13.7
Fears of the Occult

It was not enough for late-medieval society to fear religious anxiety, status insecurity, sudden death, war, and lower-class violence; the occult world of black magic, alchemy, and witchcraft also fed the lurking sense of unease. In Document A, the University of Paris's Faculty of Theology paused amid its other labors in 1398 to crack down on the black arts it had learned were being practiced in its own citadel of learning. The Florentine authorities regarded with equal horror an alchemist who in 1402 defrauded some gullible citizens (Document B) and a woman who in 1427 used witchcraft to keep her lovers (Document C).

Perhaps the most celebrated accusation of witchcraft in these years was that lodged against Joan of Arc by her English and Burgundian captors, who burned her at the stake in 1431. Did they genuinely feel that her charismatic career resulted from a diabolical pact? Did they mean simply to discredit the nineteen-year-old "Maid"? Testifying to her inquisitors, Joan insisted on her divine inspiration, and two contemporaries testified to her bravery and her religious calling. Using *The Challenge of the West,* write a brief essay that puts her case into the perspective of fifteenth-century hopes, fears, and aspirations.

A. The University of Paris Condemns Magic, 1398

Considering the feat or principal operation and its makeup in itself and all its accompanying circumstances, namely, the great circle conscribed with divers unknown names and marked with various characters, the little wooden wheel raised on four wooden feet and a stake in the midst of the same great circle and the bottle placed upon the said wheel, above which bottle on a little paper scroll were written certain names, whose meaning is unknown to us, forsooth Garsepin, Oroth, Carmesine, Visoc, with the sign of the cross and certain characters interposed between the said names, and also thrones, earthen pots, a fire kindled, suffumigations, lights, swords and many other characters and figures and divers names and unknown words and also the naming or writing of four kings on four small paper wheels, for-

From *University Records and Life in the Middle Ages,* by Lynn Thorndike, pp. 260–266. Copyright © 1944 by Columbia University Press. Reprinted with permission of the publisher.

sooth, king Galtinus of the north, king Baltinus of the east, king Saltinus of the south, king Ultinus of the west, with certain characters written in red interposed between the names of the said kings; considering also the time and the suspect place and the behavior of those who were present at the said work and participated in it and the things they did after oaths had been taken by them many times as to making a legal division of the treasures to be found, also repeated after the declaration of the said work by the principal actor of that artifice, as appears from their confessions, from which it is learned that in a certain room in which were the said instruments, superstitious in themselves, with lights lit and suffumigations about the bottle and circles, in which were the said inscriptions and said characters, the said coworkers, stripped to the waist in their smallclothes, holding swords by their hilts each one before a throne, sometimes fixing the points in the earth and sometimes circling about with the said swords near the thrones and circles and bottle, raising the points of the swords to the sky, and sometimes placing their hands together with the hand of the protagonist over the bottle, which he called holy and in which, as they said, should come the spirit who would reveal and make known hidden treasures; in view of all the aforesaid and their accompaniments our deliberate conclusion is as follows, that not only those who use such figments and sorceries to find hidden treasure or learn and know things secret and occult, but also all professed Christians in possession of reason who voluntarily operate and employ such things in such manner are to be held superstitious in the Christian religion, are to be deemed idolaters, are to be deemed invokers of demons and strongly suspect in the faith.

To all devotees of the orthodox faith the chancellor of Paris and the faculty of theology in the dear university of Paris, our mother, with full honor of divine worship, to have hope in the Lord and not look upon vanities and false insanities. From olden darkness a foul flood of errors newly emerging has warned us to recall, that often catholic truth which escapes others is quite clear to those studious in sacred writ, since certainly every art has this property of being clear to those trained in it, so that thence comes that maxim, "Believe the man who is skilled in his art. . . .

Moreover, the first article is that by magic arts and sorceries and nefarious invocations to seek the intimacy and friendship and aid of demons is not idolatry. An error.

Second article, that to give or offer or promise to demons such-and-such a thing in order that they may fulfill a man's desire, or in their honor to kiss or carry something, is not idolatry. Error.

Third article, that to enter on a pact with demons, tacit or express, is not idolatry or a species of idolatry and apostasy. Error. . . .

Twenty-first article, that images of copper or lead or gold or white or red wax or other material baptized, exorcized and consecrated, or rather execrated, according to the said arts and on certain days, have marvelous virtues which are recited in the books of such arts. An error in faith, in natural philosophy, and in true astrology.

Twenty-second article, that to use such and believe in them is not idolatry and infidelity. An error.

Twenty-third article, that some demons are good, some benign, some omniscient, some neither saved nor damned. An error. . . .

Twenty-sixth article, that the intelligence which moves the heaven influences the rational soul just as the body of the heaven influences the human body. An error.

Twenty-seventh article, that our intellectual cogitations and inner volitions are caused immediately by the sky, and that by a magic tradition such can be known, and that thereby it is licit to pass certain judgment as to them. An error.

Twenty-eighth article, that by certain magic arts we can reach the vision of the divine essence or of the holy spirits. An error. . . .

B. An Alchemist Defrauds Some Florentines, 1402

. . . We condemn . . . Master Antonio di Luca of Messina in Sicily, a perpetrator of fraud and a man of evil condition. . . . He attempted to defraud the following men: Michele di Messer Vanni Castellani, Otto di Messer Mainardo Cavalcanti, Messer Tommaso of Città di Castello and Ser Francesco of Gubbio. . . . He had a conversation with Michele and Otto . . . and another with Messer Tommaso and Ser Francesco, saying to them: "If you wish, and if you furnish me the means, I will perform . . . an act of alchemy for you, in the following manner. I will transform and reduce copper from its color into a very white color [i.e., like silver]. . . . But to do this, I must have some gold, and the more the better, and we will place it on the fire and liquify it and then reduce

it to powder. With this powder, we will be able to transform the copper from its original color and state to a white substance."

Having no doubts about these words of Master Antonio but rather accepting them credulously, Tommaso, Michelino, Otto, and Ser Francesco . . . brought the abovementioned sums of money and hastily prepared the pots in the following manner. Michelino and Otto . . . brought 1,000 gold florins in an earthern cooking pot, with the intention of placing that pot on the fire to liquify these coins in a kiln which had been built by Master Antonio in his house. . . . When Michelino and Otto brought this pot holding the money to the kiln, Master Antonio instructed them to place the copper in certain receptacles so that they might be placed in the oven. Then, Master Antonio secretly took the pot containing the money and replaced it with another pot, similar in size and appearance. . . . Into that pot Master Antonio placed the following ingredients: sublimate silver, cinnabar, saltpeter, sulphur, and many other things, which he placed . . . upon the fire in the oven. But the pot containing the money he secretly took away . . . and hid it in an underground room of the house. . . .

Item, Tommaso and Ser Francesco brought a pot containing 400 florins to Master Antonio for the purpose of liquifying and pulverizing them . . . in an earthern oven. . . . And on a certain day . . . Master Antonio went to Tommaso's house, pretending to inspect the project and to see how it was progressing. . . . He secretly took the pot and hid it in the sleeves of his jacket, and replaced it in the oven with another pot in which he had put silver, saltpeter, sublimate silver, sulphur, cinnabar, and many other ingredients. . . .

Then, Master Antonio . . . had a conversation with Pierotto and Corsino . . . and said to them: "If you wish, and if you give me the means, I will make you an indigo dye so strong that it can be used a hundred times [for dyeing cloth] and it will be worth 60 florins or more. If we begin [this project], I want to make a large quantity. And so that you don't think that I will trick you, I will invest 200 florins of my own money, and you will invest 1,000 florins. And each of us will share the profit and loss according to his investment. It is necessary to place these florins in a pot on the fire to liquify them. . . . Then we shall mix this molten metal with other ingredients necessary to make the indigo dye." Pierotto and Corsino . . . told Master Antoni that they were willing if he would invest 200 florins. . . . So Master Antonio took some of the money which he had stolen and counted out 200 florins and gave it to Pierotto and Corsino. [Antonio was captured and imprisoned by the captain of the *popolo*.] To avoid paying the penalty for his crimes, he took his belt . . . and made a noose and placed it around his neck. Then he suspended himself from the iron bars of a prison window, and had he not been rescued by a prison guardian, we would have died. [Antonio was condemned to be burned at the stake; the sentence was executed.]

C. Florence Condemns a Witch, 1427

. . . We condemn . . . Giovanna called Caterina, daughter of Francesco called El Toso, a resident of the parish of S. Ambrogio of Florence . . . who is a magician, witch, and sorceress, and a practitioner of the black arts. . . . It happened that Giovanni Ceresani of the parish of S. Jacopo tra le Fosse was passing by her door and stared at her fixedly. She thought that she would draw the chaste spirit of Giovanni to her for carnal purposes by means of the black arts. . . . She went to the shop of Monna Gilia, the druggist, and purchased from her a small amount of lead . . . and then she took a bowl and placed the lead in it and put it on the fire so that the lead would melt. With this melted lead she made a small chain and spoke certain words which have significance for this magical and diabolical art (and which, lest the people learn about them, shall not be recorded). . . . All this which was done and spoken against Giovanni's safety by Giovanna was so powerful that his chaste spirit was deflected to lust after her, so that willynilly he went several times to her house and there he fulfilled her perfidious desire. . . .

In the time when Giovanna was menstruating, she took a little of her menses, that quantity which is required by the diabolical ceremonies, and placed it in a small beaker . . . and then poured it into another flask filled with wine . . . and gave it to Giovanni to drink. And on account of this and other things described above, Giovanni no longer has time for his affairs as he did in the past, and he has left his home and his wife and son . . . and does only what pleases Giovanna. . . .

Several years ago, Giovanna was the concubine of Niccolò di Ser Casciotto of the parish of S. Giorgio, and she had three children by him. Having a great affection for Niccolò, who was then in Hungary, she wanted him to return to her in Florence. . . . So she planned a diabolical experiment by invoking a demon, to the detriment of Niccolò's health. . . . She went to someone who shall not be identified . . . and asked him to go to another diabolical woman, a sorceress (whose name shall not be publicized, for the public good), and asked her to make for Giovanna a wax image in the form of a woman, and also some pins and other items required by this diabolical experiment. . . . Giovanna took that image and placed it in a chest in her house. When, a few days later, she had to leave that house and move to another, she left the image in the chest. Later it was discovered by the residents of the house, who burned it. . . .

She collected nine beans, a piece of cloth, some charcoal, several olive leaves which had been blessed and which stood before the image of the Virgin Mary, a coin with a cross, and a grain of salt. With these in her hand she genuflected . . . [before the image] and recited three times the Pater Noster and the Ave Maria, spurning the divine prayers composed for the worship of God and his mother the Virgin Mary. Having done this, she placed these items on a piece of linen cloth and slept over them for three nights. And afterwards, she took them in her hand and thrice repeated the Pater Noster and the Ave Maria. . . . And thus Giovanna knew that her future husband would not love her. And so it happened, for after the celebration and the consummation of the marriage, her husband Giovanni stayed with her for a few days, and then left her and has not yet returned. [Giovanna confessed to these crimes and was beheaded.]

D. Joan of Arc Faces Her Inquisitors, 1431

Joan [to her inquisitors]: When I was thirteen years old, I had a voice from God to help me govern my conduct. And the first time I was very fearful. And came this voice, about the hour of noon, in the summer-time, in my father's garden. . . . I heard the voice on the right-hand side . . . and rarely do I hear it without a brightness. . . . It has taught me to conduct myself well, to go habitually to church. . . . The voice told me that I should raise the siege laid to the city of Orleans . . . and me, I answered it that I was a poor girl who knew not how to ride nor lead in war.

Jean Pasquerel [priest, Joan's confessor]: "On the morrow, Saturday, I rose early and celebrated mass. And Joan went out against the fortress of the bridge where was the Englishman Classidas. And the assault lasted there from morning until sunset. In this assault . . . Joan . . . was struck by an arrow above the breast, and when she felt herself wounded she was afraid and wept. . . . And some soldiers, seeing her so wounded, wanted to apply a charm to her wound, but she would not have it, saying: "I would rather die than do a thing which I know to be a sin or against the will of God." . . . But if to her could be applied a remedy without sin, she was very willing to be cured. And they put on to her wound olive oil and lard. And after that had been applied, Joan made her confession to me, weeping and lamenting."

Count Dunois: "The assault lasted from the morning until eight . . . so that there was hardly hope of victory that day. So that I was going to break off and . . . withdraw. . . . Then the Maid came to me and required me to wait yet a while. She . . . mounted her horse and retired alone into a vineyard. . . . And in this vineyard she remained at prayer. . . . Then she came back . . . at once seized her standard in hand and placed herself on the parapet of the trench, and the moment she was there the English trembled and were terrified. The king's soldiers regained courage and began to go up, charging against the boulevard without meeting the least resistance."

Jean Pasquerel: "Joan returned to the charge, crying and saying: 'Classidas, Classidas, yield thee, yield thee to the King of Heaven; thou hast called me 'whore'; I take great pity on thy soul and thy people's! Then Classidas, armed from head to foot, fell into the river of Loire and was drowned. And Joan, moved by pity, began to weep much for the soul of Classidas and the others who were drowned in great numbers." . . .

Document Set 13.7 References

A. The University of Paris Condemns Magic, 1398
Eduard Winkelmann, in Lynn Thorndike, ed., *University Records and Life in the Middle Ages* (New York: Columbia University Press, 1944), 261–266.
B. An Alchemist Defrauds Some Florentines, 1402
Gene Brucker, ed., *The Society of Renaissance Florence* (New York: Harper & Row, 1971), 157–159.
C. Florence Condemns a Witch, 1427
Brucker, 270–273.
D. Joan of Arc Faces Her Inquisitors, 1431
Régine Pernoud, *Joan of Arc, By Herself and Her Witnesses* (New York: 1966), 30, 90–92.

DOCUMENT SET 13.8
Florence on the Eve of the Renaissance

Florence, where early humanism first became a coherent cultural movement towards the end of the fourteenth and the beginning of the fifteenth centuries, was one of the largest and richest cities in Europe. Some sense of the great city's resources on the eve of the Black Death emerges from Document A, the *Florentine Chronicle* of Giovanni Villani (who died in the Black Death along with perhaps a third of the population). Notice in particular the continuing presence of old aristocrats (magnates and knights), whose violent tendencies the commune kept in check, and the curious imbalance in the number of male and female babies baptized; how do you account for this? Above all, consider Villani's statistical precision and the wealth he describes; do you see any connection between mind-set and enterprise here?

Petrarch, a transitional figure between medieval piety and modern individualism (compare Set 13.3, Document G), was obsessed with his reputation. His "Letter to Posterity" (Document B) reflects some of the ambiguities of his character. He also felt acutely that he lived in a degenerate age—an attitude that made him a leader in the budding campaign to revive ancient standards of Latin eloquence, which we now call humanism.

Humanism was definitely an elite phenomenon, and to understand the Florentine elite we must keep in mind the turbulent, mercilessly exploited lower class, the *Ciompi*, or day laborers in the wool industry. Their uprising in 1378 was barely contained by the savage efforts of the combined forces of the city's upper and artisan classes; in Document C, the Ciompi explain their cause.

A climactic event in the emergence of Florence's characteristic brand of humanism was the city's lonely struggle against the despotic Milanese Galeazzo Visconti, who until 1402 seemed likely to bring most of northern and central Italy under his sway. His unexpected defeat—described in Document D by the Florentine humanist Coluccio Salutati and his associates to exalt Roman republicanism as the fitting ideal for Florence, breaking the long-medieval tradition of venerating Julius Caesar and imperial Rome.

The creation of appropriate works of public art was always a matter of concern for the Florentine commune and the elite who dominated it, as the 1424 letter (Document E) from the man of letters Leonardo Bruni attests. The occasion was the commissioning of a second set of bronze doors for the Florentine Baptistery, part of the city's cathedral. An enthusiastic humanist who in 1427–1444 served as the Florentine chancellor, Bruni wished to guide the artisan who would execute the work, and he had in mind more than a mere copy of traditional medieval iconography. The sculptor Lorenzo Ghiberti (c. 1378–1455), whose first set of doors had already been triumphantly completed, responded with one of the great masterpieces of early Florentine Renaissance art, the "Gates of Paradise." In what ways do you see Bruni articulating specifically humanist values?

A. Giovanni Villani Recounts "the Greatness and State and Magnificence of the Commune of Florence," c. 1338

Since we have spoken about the income and expenditure of the Commune of Florence in this period, I think it is fitting to mention this and other great features of our city, so that our descendants in days to come may be aware of any rise, stability, and decline in condition and power that our city may undergo, and also so that, through the wise and able citizens who at the time shall be in charge of its government, [our descendants] may endeavor to advance it in condition and power, seeing our record and example in this chronicle. We find after careful investigation that in this period there were in Florence about 25,000 men from the ages of fifteen to seventy fit to bear arms, all citizens. And among them were 1,500 noble and powerful citizens who as magnates gave security to the Commune. There were in Florence also some seventy-five full-dress knights. To be sure, we find that before the second popular government now in power was formed there were more than 250 knights; but from the time that the people began to rule, the magnates no longer had the status and authority enjoyed earlier, and hence few persons were knighted. From the amount of bread constantly needed for the city, it was estimated that in Florence there were some 90,000 mouths divided among men, women,

From *Medieval Trade in the Mediterranean World* by Lopez and Raymond, pp. 71–74. Copyright © 1955 by Columbia University Press. Reprinted with permission of the publisher.

and children, as can readily be grasped [from what we shall say] later; and it was reckoned that in the city there were always about 1,500 foreigners, transients, and soldiers, not including in the total the citizens who were clerics and cloistered monks and nuns, of whom we shall speak later. It was reckoned that in this period there were some 80,000 men in the territory and district of Florence. From the rector who baptized the infants—since he deposited a black bean for every male baptized in San Giovanni and a white bean for every female in order to ascertain their number—we find that at this period there were from 5,500 to 6,000 baptisms every year, the males usually outnumbering the females by 300 to 500. We find that the boys and girls learning to read [numbered] from 8,000 to 10,000, the children learning the abacus and algorism from 1,000 to 1,200, and those learning grammar and logic in four large schools from 550 to 600. . . .

The workshops of the *Arte della Lana* [the cloth guild] were 200 or more, and they made from 70,000 to 80,000 pieces of cloth, which were worth more than 1,200,000 gold florins. And a good third [of this sum] remained in the land as [the reward] of labor, without counting the profit of the entrepreneurs. And more than 30,000 persons lived by it. [To be sure,] we find that some thirty years earlier there were 300 workshops or thereabouts, and they made more than 100,000 pieces of cloth yearly; but these cloths were coarser and one half less valuable, because at that time English wool was not imported and they did not know, as they did later, how to work it.

The *fondachi* [warehouses] of the *Arte di Calimala,* dealing in French and Transalpine cloth, were some twenty, and they imported yearly more than 10,000 pieces of cloth, worth 300,000 gold florins. And all these were sold in Florence, without counting those which were reexported from Florence.

The banks of money-changers were about eighty. The gold coins which were struck amounted to some 350,000 gold florins and at times 400,000 [yearly]. And as for deniers of four petty each, about 20,000 pounds of them were struck yearly. . . .

Merchants and mercers were a large number; the shops of shoemakers, slipper makers, and wooden-shoe makers were so numerous they could not be counted. . . .

[Florence] within the walls was well built, with many beautiful houses, and at that period people kept building with improved techniques to obtain comfort and richness by importing designs of every kind of improvement. [They built] parish churches and churches of friars of every order, and splendid monasteries. And besides this, there was no citizen, whether commoner or magnate, who had not built or was not building in the country a large and rich estate with a very costly mansion and with fine buildings, much better than those in the city—and in this they all were committing sin, and they were called crazy on account of their wild expenses. And yet, this was such a wonderful sight that when foreigners, not accustomed to [cities like] Florence, came from abroad, they usually believed that all of the costly buildings and beautiful palaces which surrounded the city for three miles were part of the city in the manner of Rome—not to mention the costly palaces with towers, courts, and walled gardens farther distant, which would have been called castles in any other country. To sum up, it was estimated that within a six-mile radius around the city there were more than twice as many rich and noble mansions as in Florence.

B. Petrarch Writes to Posterity

Greeting.—It is possible that some word of me may have come to you, though even this is doubtful, since an insignificant and obscure name will scarcely penetrate far in either time or space. If, however, you should have heard of me, you may desire to know what manner of man I was, or what was the outcome of my labors, especially those of which some description or, at any rate, the bare titles may have reached you.

To begin with myself, then: the utterances of men concerning me will differ widely, since in passing judgment almost every one is influenced not so much by truth as by preference, and good and evil report alike know no bounds. I was, in truth, a poor mortal like yourself, neither very exalted in my origin, nor, on the other hand, of the most humble birth, but belonging, as Augustus Caesar says of himself, to an ancient family. As to my disposition, I was not naturally perverse or wanting in modesty, however the contagion of evil associations may have corrupted me.

My youth was gone before I realized it; I was carried away by the strength of manhood; but a riper age brought me to my senses and taught me by experience the truth I had long before read in books, that youth and pleasure are vanity,—nay, that the Author of all ages and times permits us miserable mortals, puffed up with emptiness, thus to wander about, until finally, coming to a tardy consciousness of our sins, we shall learn to know ourselves.

In my prime I was blessed with a quick and active body, although not exceptionally strong; and while I do not lay claim to remarkable personal beauty, I was comely enough in my best days. I was possessed of a clear complexion, between light and dark, lively eyes, and for long years a keen vision, which however deserted me, contrary to my hopes, after I reached my sixtieth birthday, and forced me, to my great annoyance, to resort to glasses. Although I had previously enjoyed perfect health, old age brought with it the usual array of discomforts.

My parents were honorable folk, Florentine in their origin, of medium fortune, or, I may as well admit it, in a condition verging upon poverty. They had been expelled from their native city, and consequently I was born in exile, at Arezzo, in the year 1304 of this latter age, which begins with Christ's birth, July the 20th, on a Monday, at dawn.... In my familiar associations with kings and princes, and in my friendship with noble personages, my good fortune has been such as to excite envy. But it is the cruel fate of those who are growing old that they can commonly only weep for friends who have passed away. The greatest kings of this age have loved and courted me. They may know why; I certainly do not. With some of them I was on such terms that they seemed in a certain sense my guests rather than I theirs; their lofty position in no way embarrassing me, but, on the contrary, bringing with it many advantages. I fled, however, from many of those to whom I was greatly attached; and such was my innate longing for liberty, that I studiously avoided those whose very name seemed incompatible with the freedom that I loved.

I possessed a well-balanced rather than a keen intellect,—one prone to all kinds of good and wholesome study, but especially inclined to moral philosophy and the art of poetry. The latter, indeed, I neglected as time went on, and took delight in sacred literature. Finding in that a hidden sweetness which I had once esteemed but lightly, I came to regard the works of the poets as only amenities.

Among the many subjects which interested me, I dwelt especially upon antiquity, for our own age has always repelled me, so that, had it not been for the love of those dear to me, I should have preferred to have been born in any other period than our own. In order to forget my own time, I have constantly striven to place myself in spirit in other ages, and consequently I delighted in history. The conflicting statements troubled me, but when in doubt I accepted what appeared most probable, or yielded to the authority of the writer.

C. The Ciompi Demand Their Place in the Commune, 1378

[July 21, 1378] When the *popolo* [ordinary working people] and the guildsmen had seized the palace [of the podestà, or chief magistrate], they sent a message to the Signoria [Florentine government] . . . that they wished to make certain demands by means of petitions, which were just and reasonable. . . . They said that, for the peace and repose of the city, they wanted certain things which they had decided among themselves . . . and they begged the priors to have them read, and then to deliberate on them, and to present them to their colleges. . . .

The first chapter [of the petition] stated that the Lana [cloth-merchants'] guild would no longer have a [police] official of the guild. Another was that the combers, carders, trimmers, washers, and other cloth workers would have their own [guild] consuls, and would no longer be subject to the Lana guild. Another chapter [stated that] the Commune's funded debt would no longer pay interest, but the capital would be restored [to the shareholders] within twelve years. . . . Another chapter was that all outlaws and those who had been condemned by the Commune . . . except rebels and traitors would be pardoned. Moreover, all penalties involving a loss of a limb would be cancelled, and those who were condemned would pay a money fine. . . . Furthermore, for two years none of the poor people could be prosecuted for debts of 50 florins or less. For a period of six months, no forced loans were to be levied. . . . And within that six months' period, a schedule for levying direct taxes [*estimo*] was to be compiled. . . .

The *popolo* entered the palace and [the podestà] departed, without any harm being done to him. They ascended the bell tower and placed there the emblem of the blacksmiths' guild, that is, the tongs. Then the banners of the other guilds, both great and small, were unfurled from the windows of the [palace of] the podestà, and also the standard of justice, but there was no flag of the Lana guild. Those inside the palace threw out and burned . . . every document which they found. And they remained there, all that day and night, in honor of God. Both rich and poor were there, each one to protect the standard of his guild.

The next morning the *popolo* brought the standard of justice from the palace and they marched, all armed, to the Piazza della Signoria, shouting: "Long live the *popolo minuto!*" [lit., "little people"] . . . Then they began to cry "that the Signoria should leave, and if they didn't wish to depart, they would be taken to their homes." Into the piazza came a certain Michele di Lando, a wool-comber, who was the son of Monna

Simona, who sold provisions to the prisoners in the Stinche . . . and he was seized and the standard of justice placed in his hands. . . . Then the *popolo* ordered the priors to abandon the palace. It was well furnished with supplies necessary [for defense] but they were frightened men and they left [the palace], which was the best course. Then the *popolo* entered, taking with them the standard of justice . . . and they entered all the rooms and they found many ropes which [the authorities] had bought to hang the poor people. . . . Several young men climbed the bell tower and rang the bells to signal the victory which they had won in seizing the palace, in God's honor. Then they decided to do everything necessary to fortify themselves and to liberate the *popolo minuto*. Then they acclaimed the wool-comber, Michele di Lando, as *signore* [lord] and standard-bearer of justice, and he was *signore* for two days. . . . Then [the *popolo*] decided to call other priors who would be good comrades and who would fill up the office of those priors who had been expelled. And so by acclamation, they named eight priors and the Twelve and the [Sixteen] standard-bearers. . . .

When they wished to convene a council, these priors called together the colleges and the consuls of the guilds. . . . This council enacted a decree that everyone who had been proscribed as a Ghibelline since 1357 was to be restored to Guelf status. . . . And this was done to give a part to more people, and so that each would be content, and each would have a share of the offices, and so that all of the citizens would be united. Thus poor men would have their due, for they have always borne the expenses [of government], and only the rich have profited.

. . . And they deliberated to expand the lower guilds, and where there had been fourteen, there would now be seventeen, and thus they would be stronger, and this was done. The first new guild comprised those who worked in the woolen industry: factors, brokers in wool and in thread, workers who were employed in the dye shops and the stretching sheds, menders, sorters, shearers, beaters, combers, and weavers. These were all banded together, some nine thousand men. . . . The second new guild was made up of dyers, washers, carders, and makers of combs. . . . In the third guild were menders, trimmers, stretchers, washers, shirtmakers, tailors, stockingmakers, and makers of flags. . . . So all together, the lower guilds increased by some thirteen thousand men.

The lord priors and the colleges decided to burn the old Communal scrutiny lists, and this was done. Then a new scrutiny was held. The Offices were divided as follows: the [seven] greater guilds had

three priors; the fourteen [lower] guilds had another three, and the three new guilds had three priors. And so a new scrutiny was completed, which satisfied many who had never before had any share of the offices, and had always borne the expenses.

D. Coluccio Salutati Narrates Florence's Defense of Republican Liberty Against the Milanese Despotism, 1402

The following year, which was 1402, great battles were fought around Bologna. Even before the emperor's complete withdrawal, Galeazzo, elated by the way things were going for him, sent part of his forces into Bolognese territory, to overthrow if possible the new lord of that city. The arrival of these forces immediately put the city in great peril, for there were enough powerful exiles to make the castles and towns of the area rise up, and the citizens inside the city were not all happy about the government of the lord of Bologna either. The Florentines responded to the danger by sending the captain Bernardone with a large number of troops. They added more troops in time, as they learned of reinforcements sent to the enemy. Large forces were sent to the aid of Bologna by the lord of Padua and other allies, and the lord of Padua sent two of his sons along. All the forces of the Florentine people and of their allies, and all the forces of the enemy, were finally gathered around Bologna. Both sides made encampments around the city. . . .

Bologna after the return of the exiles received a civil government. A formal republic and formal liberty were restored. This indeed was what Galeazzo had promised the exiles. The pleasure only lasted two or three days, however. Then certain persons sent by the duke with a military force ran through the city shouting the name of Galeazzo, usurped the authority of the city's officials, and proclaimed the entire lordship of Milan. The people and the exiles were disappointed, but they had to bend their necks to the yoke of servitude.

When the Florentines heard that the army had been defeated and . . . that Bologna too had fallen, they were even more terrified, expecting the enemy from hour to hour. Without the general and the army, they seemed to despair completely. Had the enemy approached promptly to follow up his victory, the city could not have withstood him. The enemy, however, whether because of weariness or internal discord, let the time for action pass in useless settling down. . . .

. . .The enemy seemed to want to make peace after taking Bologna, and sent representatives to Venice to propose rather reasonable conditions. The Florentines suspected deception and fraud, and finally decided to agree to the peace and to the Venetian alliance at the same time, thinking that if the peace began at the same time as the alliance, the peace would be more durable and the conditions demanded by the Venetians less important. They instructed their representatives to sign, with the addition of a few corrections, peace with the enemy and an alliance with Venice.

While the city was just doing this, word came through that Galeazzo was dead. The death was first announced by Paolo Guinisi, lord of Lucca, but it was not considered a certainty. Later it was repeated as a certainty, but a deep secret. At once letters were sent to the representatives in Venice not to agree to the peace nor to the alliance. The Venetians learned of the duke's death only from the Florentine embassy, having heard nothing before. There had been signs, however, such as some forces sent towards Tuscany through Piacenza and Lunigiana being suddenly recalled. The leaders of the army, who were still before Bologna, had received orders not to move from the spot. It now proved that Galeazzo had become ill soon after Bologna was taken. He had died somewhat later of the same illness, at the Milanese castle of Marignano. These facts had been kept secret at first. Eventually they had to be made public, and there was a magnificent funeral. It also came out that Galeazzo, while he lay ill, had passionately desired peace with Florence. Hence the attempt to send a mission to Venice and to make a new peace. He realized that his sons were still young and were being left in the midst of great danger. So he was in a hurry to make peace before he would leave the world. This would have been accomplished, too, if he had lived just a little longer. His sudden death brought such a reversal of things that those who before had hardly any hope left for their own safety were now filled with high confidence, while those who had just considered themselves victorious lost all hope of being able to resist.

E. Leonardo Bruni Describes the Making of Ghiberti's Baptistery Doors, 1424

I consider that the twenty stories, which you have decided are to be chosen from the Old Testament, should have two qualities principally, being both resplendent and significant. By 'resplendent' I mean that they should delight the eye with the variety of their design; by 'significant' that they should be important enough to rest in the memory. With these two presuppositions in my mind, I have chosen according to my judgement twenty stories, which I am sending to you noted down on paper. It will be necessary for whoever does them to be well instructed about each story, so that he can render well both the persons and the actions which occur in it, and that he has a lightness of touch so that he can adorn them well. In addition to the twenty stories, I have made a note of eight prophets, as you see on the paper. Now I do not doubt that this work, as I have planned it, will succeed excellently. But I would very much like to be with whoever has the job of designing it, to make sure that he takes into account the whole significance of each story. I recommend myself to you.

Your Leonardo of Arezzo

Document Set 13.8 References

A. Giovanni Villani Recounts "the Greatness and State and Magnificence of the Commune of Florence," c. 1338
Giovanni Villani, *Chronicle,* in Robert S. Lopez and Irving W. Raymond, *Medieval Trade in the Mediterranean World* (New York: Columbia University Press, 1930s), 71–74.

B. Petrarch Writes to Posterity
Petrarch, *Letter to Posterity*, in James Harvey Robinson, ed., *Readings in European History* (Boston: Ginn, 1904), 1:524–526.

C. The Ciompi Demand Their Place in the Commune, 1378
Gene Brucker, ed., *The Society of Renaissance Florence* (New York: Harper & Row, 1971), 236–239.

D. Coluccio Salutati Narrates Florence's Defense of Republican Liberty Against the Milanese Despotism, 1402
Coluccio Salutati, *History of Florence,* in Kenneth R. Bartlett, ed., *The Civilization of the Italian Renaissance: A Sourcebook* (Lexington, Mass.: D. C. Heath, 1992), 99–102.

E. Leonardo Bruni Describes the Making of Ghiberti's Baptistery Doors, 1424
Leonardo Bruni to Niccolò da Uzzano in D. S. Chambers, *Patrons and Artists in the Italian Renaissance* (Columbia, S.C.: University of South Carolina Press, 1971), 48.

14

Renaissance Europe,
1430–1493

DOCUMENT SET 14.1
Humanism

The Italian word *umanista* (humanist) was originally medieval student slang for a teacher of elementary subjects such as grammar and rhetoric, which a university student took before studying technical subjects like logic, law, and theology. In the fourteenth and fifteenth centuries, however, the prestige of the lowly humanities courses rose. As *The Challenge of the West* explains (Chapters 14 and 15), an educated, prosperous middle class was emerging, interested in classical literature and history. Moreover, governments increasingly felt it necessary to employ high officials who could speak and write elegant Latin.

The six documents in this set chart the humanities' rising prestige. In Document A, the fifteenth-century Florentine bookseller Vespasiano da Bisticci—who wrote short biographies of many of his eminent customers—sketches the character of the prominent humanist Nicolò Nicoli (d. 1437), whose inherited wealth let him live for the life of a collector and patron. Document B is an extract from an educational treatise by one of Renaissance Italy's great pedagogues, Battista Guarino (1370?–1460), who ran a boarding school for the sons of prominent families. Education in the humanities—which prepared one for a public career and enhanced family prestige—was overwhelmingly a male pursuit. Yet a few young women (often educators' daughters) also managed to get such training. One was Laura Cereta (d. 1499), whose outspoken *Defense of the Liberal Instruction of Women* (Document C) protests against male humanists' typical scorn for women's intellectual capacity.

Document D, Giovanni Pico della Mirandola's (1463–1494) famous *Oration on the Dignity of Man,* on the other hand, should be read as a vindication of the potential for human self improvement. A minor Italian princeling, Pico spent his entire short life feverishly pursuing wisdom, not only through well-known classical literature and philosophy but also through esoteric ancient magical lore and the mystical Hebrew *cabala.* He wrote his *Oration* to open a public debate on his ideas, but the pope condemned some of these ideas as heretical, and Pico died as a more orthodox Christian.

The final two documents throw additional light on fifteenth-century humanism. Document E records the determination of the city fathers of Ferrara to improve the teaching of grammar in that Italian city's schools. In Document F, the German scholar Conrad Celtes (1459–1508), who made a considerable stir by traveling from one German university to another propagating Italian-style humanism, receives a stinging rebuke from the undergraduates⁻ of the University of Ingolstadt in Bavaria.

Using these documents and also drawing upon *The Challenge of the West,* you should be able to write a brief essay on the program of Italian Humanism. What did the Humanists claim as the value of their type of education? How does it differ from what you have learned about medieval education? How would you evaluate humanist education from your late twentieth-century perspective?

A. Nicolò Nicoli Collects the Classics

Nicolò may justly be called the father and the benefactor of all students of letters, for he gave them protection and encouragement to work, and pointed out to them the rewards which would follow. If he knew of any Greek or Latin book which was not in Florence he spared neither trouble nor cost until he should procure it; indeed, there are numberless Latin books which the city possesses through his care. He gained such high reputation amongst men of letters that Messer Leonardo sent him his *Life of Cicero* and pronounced him to be the censor [i.e., foremost critic] of the Latin tongue.

He was a man of upright life who favored virtue and censured vice. He collected a fine library, not regarding the cost, and was always searching for rare books. He bought all these with the wealth which his father had left, putting aside only what was necessary for his maintenance. He sold several of his farms and spent the proceeds on his library. He was a devoted Christian, who specially favored monks and friars, and was the foe of evildoers. He held his books rather for the use of others than of himself, and all lettered students of Greek or Latin would come to him to borrow books, which he would always lend.... If he heard of students going to Greece or to France or elsewhere he would give them the names of books which they lacked in Florence, and procure for them the help of Cosimo de' Medici who would do anything for him. When it happened that he could only get the copy of a book he would copy it himself, either in current or shaped characters, all in the finest script, as may be seen in San Marco, where there are many books from his hand in one lettering or the other. He procured at his own expense the works of Tertullian and other [ancient] writers which were not in Italy. He also found an imperfect copy of Ammianus Marcellinus and wrote it out with his own hand. The *De Oratore* and the *Brutus* [by Cicero] were sent to Nicolò from Lombardy, having been brought by the envoys of Duke Filippo when they went to ask for peace in the time of Pope Martin. The book was found in a chest in a very old church; this chest had not been opened for a long time, and they found the book, a very ancient example, while searching for evidence concerning certain ancient rights. *De Oratore* was found broken up, and it is through the care of Nicolò that we find it perfect today. He also rediscovered many sacred works and several of Tully's [Cicero's] orations.

Through Nicolò Florence acquired many fine works of sculpture, of which he had great knowledge as well as of painting. A complete copy of Pliny did not exist in Florence, but when Nicolò heard that there was one in Lübeck, in Germany, he secured it by Cosimo's aid, and thus Pliny came to Florence. All the young men he knew in Florence used to come to him for instruction in letters, and he cared for the needs of all those who wanted books or teachers. He did not seek any office in Florence [although] he was made an official in the University; many times he was selected for some governorship, but he refused them all, saying that they were food for the vultures, and he would let these feed on them. He called vultures those who went into the alehouses and devoured the poor....

B. Battista Guarino Outlines a Course of Liberal Studies

... From the first, stress must be laid upon distinct and sustained enunciation, both in speaking and in reading. But at the same time utterance must be perfectly natural; if affected or exaggerated the effect is unpleasing. The foundation of education must be laid in Grammar. Unless this be thoroughly learnt subsequent progress is uncertain—a house built upon treacherous ground. Hence let the knowledge of nouns and verbs be secured early, as the starting point for the rest. The master will employ the devices of repetition, examination, and the correction of erroneous inflexions purposely introduced....

I have said that ability to write Latin verse is one of the essential marks of an educated person. I wish now to indicate a second, which is of at least equal importance, namely, familiarity with the language and literature of Greece. The time has come when we must speak with no uncertain voice upon this vital requirement of scholarship. I am well aware that those who are ignorant of the Greek tongue decry its necessity, for reasons which are sufficiently evident. But I can allow no doubt to remain as to my own conviction that without a knowledge of Greek Latin scholarship itself is, in any real sense, impossible....

Our scholar should make his first acquaintance with the Poets through Homer, the sovereign master of them all. For from Homer our own poets, notably Vergil, drew their inspiration; and in reading the *Iliad* or the *Odyssey* no small part of our pleasure is derived from the constant parallels we meet with. Indeed in them we see as in a mirror the form and manner of the *Aeneid* figured roughly before us, the incidents, not less than the simile or epithet which describe them, are, one might say, all there. In the same way, in his minor works Vergil has borrowed from Theocritus or Hesiod. After Homer has been attempted the way lies open to the other Heroic poets and to the Dramatists.

In reading of this wider range a large increase of vocabulary is gained, and in this the memory will be greatly assisted by the practice of making notes, which should be methodically arranged afterwards. . . .

But whilst a beginning is being thus made with Greek, continued progress must at the same time be secured in Latin. For instance the broader rules of grammar which sufficed in the earlier stages must give place to a more complete study of structure, such as we find in Priscian, and irregularities or exceptions, hitherto ignored, must be duly noted. At the same time the *Epistles* of Cicero will be taken in hand for purposes of declamation. Committed to memory they serve as one of the finest possible aids to purity, directness, and facility of style, and supply admirable matter in no less admirable form for adaptation to our own uses. Yet I would not be understood to claim the *Letters* of Cicero as alone offering a sufficient training in style. For distinction of style is the fruit of a far wider field of study. To quote Horace once more:

> *Of writing well, be sure, the secret lies*
> *In wisdom: therefore study to be wise.*

But we are now passing from the first, or elementary, to the second, or more advanced, stage of grammar which I called "Historice," which is concerned with the study of continuous prose authors, more particularly the Historians. Here we begin with a short but comprehensive view of general history, which will include that of the Roman people, by such writers as Justin or Valerius Maximus. The latter author is also valuable as affording actual illustrations of virtuous precepts couched in attractive style. The scholar will now devote his attention to the Historians in regular order. By their aid he will learn to understand the manners, laws and institutions of different types of nation, and will examine the varying fortunes of individuals and states, the sources of their success and failure, their strength and their weakness. Not only is such Knowledge of interest in daily intercourse but it is of practical value in the ordering of affairs.

Side by side with the study of history a careful reading of the poets will be taken in hand. The true significance of poetic fiction will now be appreciated. . . .

The course of study which I have thus far sketched out will prove an admirable preparation for that further branch of scholarship which constitutes Rhetoric, including the thorough examination of the great monuments of eloquence, and skill in the oratorial art itself. The first work to claim our attention in this subject is the *Rhetoric* of Cicero, in which we find all the points of Oratory concisely but comprehensively set forth. The other rhetorical writings of Cicero will follow, and the principles therein laid down must be examined in the light of his own speeches. Indeed the student of eloquence must have his Cicero constantly in his hand; the simplicity, the lofty moral standard, the practical temper of his writings render them a peculiarly noble training for a public speaker. Nor should the admirable Quintilian be neglected in this same connection.

It will be desirable also to include the elements of Logic in our course of studies, and with that the *Ethics* of Aristotle, and the Dialogues of Plato; for these are necessary aids to the proper understanding of Cicero.

C. Laura Cereta Defends the Liberal Education of Women

My ears are wearied by your carping. You brashly and publicly not merely wonder but indeed lament that I am said to possess as fine a mind as nature ever bestowed upon the most learned man. You seem to think that so learned a woman has scarcely before been seen in the world. You are wrong on both counts, Sempronius, and have clearly strayed from the path of truth and disseminate falsehood. I agree that you should be grieved; indeed, you should be ashamed, for you have ceased to be a living man, but have become an animated stone; having rejected the studies which make men wise, you rot in torpid leisure. Not nature but your own soul has betrayed you, deserting virtue for the easy path of sin.

You pretend to admire me as a female prodigy, but there lurks sugared deceit in your adulation. You wait perpetually in ambush to entrap my lovely sex, and overcome by your hatred seek to trample me underfoot and dash me to the earth. It is a crafty ploy, but only a low and vulgar mind would think to halt Medusa with honey. You would better have crept up on a mole than on a wolf. For a mole with its dark vision can see nothing around it, while a wolf's eyes glow in the dark. For the wise person sees by [force of] mind, and anticipating what lies ahead, proceeds by the light of reason. For by foreknowledge the thinker scatters with knowing feet the evils which litter her path.

I would have been silent, believe me, if that savage old enmity of yours had attacked me alone. For the light of Phoebus cannot be befouled even in the mud. But I cannot tolerate your having attacked my entire sex. For this reason my thirsty soul seeks revenge, my sleeping pen is aroused to literary struggle, raging anger stirs mental passions long chained by silence. With just cause I am moved to demonstrate how great a reputation for learning and virtue women have won by their inborn excellence, manifested in every age as knowledge, the [purveyor] of honor. Certain, indeed, and legitimate is our possession of this inheritance, come to us from a long eternity of ages past....

D. Pico della Mirandola Exalts Human Dignity

... At last it seems to me I have come to understand why man is the most fortunate of creatures and consequently worthy of all admiration and what precisely is that rank which is his lot in the universal chain of Being—a rank to be envied not only by brutes but even by the stars and by minds beyond this world. It is a matter past faith and a wondrous one. Why should it not be? For it is on this very account that man is rightly called and judged a great miracle and a wonderful creature indeed....

O supreme generosity of God the Father, O highest and most marvelous felicity of man! To him it is granted to have whatever he chooses, to be whatever he wills. Beasts as soon as they are born (so says Lucilius) bring with them from their mother's womb all they will ever possess. Spiritual beings, either from the beginning or soon thereafter, become what they are to be for ever and ever. On man when he came into life the Father conferred the seeds of all kinds and the germs of every way of life. Whatever seeds each man cultivates will grow to maturity and bear in him their own fruit. If they be vegetative, he will be like a plant. If sensitive, he will become brutish. If rational, he will grow into a heavenly being. If intellectual, he will be an angel and the son of God. And if, happy in the lot of no created thing, he withdraws into the center of his own unity, his spirit, made one with God, in the solitary darkness of God, who is set above all things, shall surpass them all. Who would not admire this our chameleon? Or who could more greatly admire aught else whatever? It is man who Asclepius of Athens, arguing from his mutability of character and from his self-transforming nature, on just grounds says was symbolized by Proteus in the mysteries. Hence those metamorphoses renowned among the Hebrews and the Pythagoreans....

E. Ferrara Condemns Ignorant School Teachers

There exists at this time in this city a seminary of evil learning and ignorance. Our citizens desire to instruct their sons and their adolescents in good letters, and they are sunk in I know not what pit from which they can never extricate themselves. That is, certain barbarous teachers—who, far from knowing, never even saw, any good literature—have invaded our city, opened schools, and professed grammar. Citizens ignorant of these men's ignorance entrust their sons to them to be educated. They want them to learn and to graduate learned, but they learn those things which later they must unlearn. Lest this calamity and pest progress further, they decree that no one take scholars to train, nor hold a school, unless first he shall have demonstrated that he is acquainted with good literature or has been approved by the board of the Twelve Wise as suited to open a school. If anyone shall dare to do different, let him be ejected from the city as a pestiferous beast.

F. His Students Denounce the German Humanist Conrad Celtes as a Windbag

By your long and incessant scoldings, with which you frequently consume half the hour, you force us to make some reply in the name of truth. You accuse us of madness and charge that we are stupid barbarians, and you call wild beasts those whose fees support you.... This we might have borne with better grace, but for the fact that you yourself abound in the faults of which you accuse us. For what of the fact that, while you carp about us, you yourself are so torpid from dissipation that in private conversation your drowsy head droops to your elbow like a figure eight. You touch on many points in questions, but you speak neither plain argument nor cultured speech nor elegant Latin expositions; nor do you observe true coherence and order of speaking. Yet you have at hand the motto, "He teaches clearly who understands clearly." Either you lack understanding—a shameful thing in a doctor—or you think us unworthy of your learning, which is incredible. For you certainly experience daily studious auditors, sometimes learned men, calculated to adorn you with great praise. Or you dislike the labor of lecturing, as we clearly comprehend, understand and see. In this one point you both derogate from your own reputation and seem to us all deficient. But now we have clearly expressed ourselves on that point. Wherefore, if you are ready and willing to vindicate the name and dignity of a preceptor and doctor, to fulfill your professional duties, we will be more attentive. If first, as befits you, you clear yourself of the fault you impute to us, you will make us more diligent by your diligence, which has now long been lacking, if you can conquer and overcome your dislike of study and tardiness in work. If you do less, we shall have to take more stringent measures.

Document Set 14.1 References

A. Nicolò Nicoli Collects the Classics
Vespasiano, *Lives,* in Kenneth R. Bartlett, ed., *The Civilization of the Italian Renaissance: A Sourcebook* (Lexington, Mass.: D. C . Heath, 1992), 89–90.

B. Battista Guarino Outlines a Course of Liberal Studies
Battista Guarino, "On the Means of Teaching and Learning," in Bartlett, 283–288.

C. Laura Cereta Defends the Liberal Education of Women
Laura Cereta, "In Defense of the Liberal Instruction of Women," in M. L. King and Albert Rabil, Jr., eds., *Selected Works By and About the Woman Humanists of Quattrocento Italy* (Binghamton, N.Y.: Medieval and Renaissance Texts and Studies, 1983), 81–84.

D. Pico della Mirandola Exalts Human Dignity
Pico della Mirandola, "Oration on the Dignity of Man," in Bartlett, 130–133.

E. Ferrara Condemns Ignorant School Teachers
Borsetti, *History of the Ferrara Schools,* in Lynn Thorndike, ed., *University Records and Life in the Middle Ages* (New York: Columbia University Press, 1944), 337.

F. His Students Denounce the German Humanist Conrad Celtes as a Windbag
Thorndike, 366.

DOCUMENT SET 14.2
The Quattrocento Artist

Artist-patron relationships are of great importance in cultural history, tracing not only changes in taste but also attesting to the degree of control that patrons exercised over artists. The documents in this set testify to the varying conditions under which fifteenth-century artists worked. In Document A, for example, Duke Philip the Good of Burgundy offers with some deference his patronage to the famous Netherlands master Jan van Eyck (d. 1441). The extracts from Document B bespeak a far greater degree of patronly control over a commissioned work of art, in this case an altarpiece being executed at Avignon in the south of France. Document C, an order issued by Duke Galeazzo Maria Sforza of Milan in 1463, suggests something of that potentate's method of dealing with subordinates.

The last three documents all concern famous Italian Renaissance painters. Document D speaks much for the touchy relationship between the painter Andrea Mantegna (1431?–1506) and Duke Federico I of Mantua (who in this 1480 letter addresses the Duchess of Milan). In Document E, the neo-Platonist Florentine philosopher Marsilio Ficino writes to his patron, Lorenzo the Magnificent, describing an elaborate allegorical painting similar to Sandro Botticelli's masterpiece *La Primavera* (Spring), which was executed for the Medicis in 1477–1478. (Scholars debate whether Botticelli painted it under Ficino's direction.) Document F dates from 1550: it comes from Giorgio Vasari's collection of biographies of Renaissance painters and describes how in 1495–1497 Leonardo da Vinci painted his fresco *The Last Supper* in Milan.

Taken together, these documents offer insights into the artist's transition from relatively humble medieval artisan to "inspired genius." They will be particularly rewarding if you write a brief essay analyzing this transition, not only through the documents of this set but also through Sets 14.1, 14.4, and 14.5.

A. The Duke of Burgundy Extends His Patronage to Jan van Eyck

Jan van Eyck, former painter and equerry of the late Lord John, Duke of Bavaria, was known for his ability and craftsmanship by my said lord [Philip the Good] who had heard thereof from several of his people and which he knew to be true, being acquainted personally with the said Jan van Eyck. Confident of his loyalty and probity, my lord has retained said Jan as his painter and equerry, with the customary honors, prerogatives, franchises, liberties, rights, profits and usual emoluments pertaining to this position. And to the end that he shall be held to work for him in painting whenever it pleases him, my lord has ordered him to have and to take on his general receipt from Flanders, the sum of 100 parisis in Flemish money in two settlements yearly, half at Christmas and the other half at Saint John's, of which he wishes the first payment to be at Christmas 1425 and the other at Saint John's, and so from year to year and payment to payment, as long as it shall please him. Ordering to the masters of his household and his other officers that all his present honors, rights, prerogatives, profits and emoluments above mentioned they shall make and allow the said Jan to enjoy peaceably without prevention or disturbance; in addition ordering to his said receiver general of Flanders, present and future, that he shall pay, give and deliver every year the said sum of 100 Parisian pounds per year on the above declared terms to the said Jan, his painter and equerry, so all that is said on these matters may appear more plainly in the letters patent of my beforementioned lord, given in his city of Bruges, the 19th day of May in the year 1425. By virtue of that attestation is briefly given here to make payment for the term of Christmas 1425, and that which will follow to make a payment of 50 pounds on his quittance.

For the terms of St. John and Christmas 1426 together is made payment of 100 pounds on his quittance.

B. An Avignon Priest Contracts to Have an Altarpiece Painted, 1453

On the 25th day of April [1453], Master Enguerrand Quarton, of the diocese of Laon, painter, resident in Avignon, made a contract and agreement with the said Dominus Jean de Montagnac—both contracting parties being present—for painting an altarpiece according to the manner, form, and prescription contained and set forth article by article on a sheet of paper, which they passed over to me, written in French, whose tenor follows and is such:

Here follows the list of items of the altarpiece that Messer Jean de Montagnac has commissioned from Master Enguerrand, painter, to be placed in the church of the Carthusians, Villeneuve-les-Avignon, on the altar of the Holy City.

First: There should be the form of Paradise, and

in that Paradise should be the Holy Trinity, and there should not be any difference between the Father and the Son; and the Holy Ghost in the form of a dove; and Our Lady in front as it will seem best to Master Enguerrand; the Holy Trinity will place the crown on the head of Our Lady.

Item: The vestments should be very rich; those of Our Lady should be white-figured damask according to the judgement of said Master Enguerrand; and surrounding the Holy Trinity should be cherubim and seraphim. . . .

Item: On the left side will be Hell, and between Purgatory and Hell will be a mountain, and from the part of Purgatory below the mountain will be an angel comforting the souls of Purgatory; and from the part of Hell will be a very disfigured devil turning his back to the angel and throwing certain souls into Hell, given him by other devils.

Item: In Purgatory and Hell will be all the estates according to the judgement of said Master Enguerrand.

Item: Said altarpiece shall be made in fine oil colors and the blue should be fine blue of Acre, except that which will be put on the frame, that should be fine German blue, and the gold that will be used on the frame as well as around the altarpiece should be fine gold and burnished.

Item: Said Master Enguerrand will show all his knowledge and skill in the Holy Trinity and in the Blessed Virgin Mary, and will be governed by his conscience. . . .

A promise was given, I declare, by the same Master Enguerrand to execute these things faithfully and according to the foregoing description, from the next [feast of] St. Michael, for the next one continuous year, for the price of one hundred and twenty florins, each at the value of XXIII *sous* of the currency at Avignon. . . .

C. Galeazzo Maria Sforza Orders His Painter About

To Vincenzo of Brescia, painter

We want you when you receive these letters to come to us here, and bring with you the picture you received from Papi, our chamberlain as your model for a portrait of Our Lady. Come whether or not your own work is finished, because we want to employ you in other matters. Come at once with the said picture.

Milan, 3 March 1463

D. The Gonzagas Find Mantegna a Temperamental Artist

Most illustrious Excellency, I have received the portrait painting that Your Excellency sent me and have done my utmost to make Mantegna make a small reproduction in elegant form. He says this would almost be the work of a miniature-painter, and because he is not accustomed to painting small figures he would much rather do a Madonna, or something the length of a *braccia* [an arm] or a *braccia* and a half, if it were pleasing to Your Most illustrious Highness. My Lady, if I might know what Your Ladyship wants me to do, I shall endeavour to satisfy your wish, but usually these painters have a touch of the fantastic and it is advisable to take what they offer one; but if Your Ladyship is not served as quickly as you wished, I beseech you to excuse me; in your good grace etc.

E. The Philosopher Marsilio Ficino Suggests the Theme for Botticelli's *Primavera*

My immense love for you, excellent Lorenzo [patron of Botticelli], has long prompted me to make you an immense present. For anyone who contemplates the heavens, nothing he sets eyes upon seems immense but the heavens themselves. If, therefore, I make you a present of the heavens themselves what would be its price? But I would rather not talk of the price; for Love, born from the Graces, gives and accepts everything without payment; nor indeed can anything under heaven fairly balance against heaven itself.

The astrologers have it that the happiest man is he for whom Fate has so disposed the heavenly signs that Luna is not contrary in aspect to Mars and Saturn, that furthermore she is in a favourable aspect to Sol and Jupiter, Mercury and Venus. And just as the astrologers call happy the man for whom Fate has thus arranged the heavenly bodies, so the theologians deem him happy who has disposed his own self in a similar way. You may well wonder whether this is not asking too much—it certainly is much, but nevertheless, my gifted Lorenzo, go forward to the task with good cheer, for he who made you is greater than the heavens, and you too will be greater than the heavens as soon as you resolve to face them. We must not look for these matters outside ourselves, for all the heavens are within us and the fiery vigour in us testifies to our heavenly origin.

First Luna—what else can she signify in us but that continuous motion of the soul and of the body? Mars stands for speed, Saturn for tardiness, Sol for God, Jupiter for the Law, Mercury for Reason, and Venus for Humanity.

Onward, then, great-minded youth, gird yourself, and, together with me, dispose your own heavens. Your Luna—the continuous motion of your soul and body—should avoid the excessive speed of Mars and the tardiness of Saturn, that is, it should leave everything to the right and opportune moment, and should not hasten unduly, nor tarry too long. Furthermore, this Luna within you should continuously behold the Sun, that is God himself, from whom she ever receives the life-giving rays, for you must honour him above all things to whom you are beholden, and make yourself worthy of the honour. Your Luna should also behold Jupiter, the laws human and divine, which should never be transgressed—for a deviation of the laws by which all things are governed is tantamount to perdition. She should also direct her gaze on Mercury, that is on good counsel, reason and knowledge, for nothing should be said or done for which no plausible reason can be adduced. A man not versed in science and letters is considered blind and deaf. Finally she should fix her eyes on Venus herself, that is to say on Humanity. This serves us as an exhortation and a reminder that we cannot possess anything great on this earth without possessing the men themselves from whose favour all earthly things spring. Men, however, cannot be caught by any other bait but that of Humanity. Be careful, therefore, not to despise it, thinking perhaps that *humanitas* is of earthly origin.

For Humanity herself is a nymph of excellent comeliness, born of heaven and more than others beloved by God all highest. Her soul and mind are Love and Charity, her eyes Dignity and Magnanimity, the hands Liberality and Magnificence, the feet Comeliness and Modesty. The whole, then, is Temperance and Honesty, Charm and Splendour. Oh, what exquisite beauty! How beautiful to behold! My dear Lorenzo, a nymph of such nobility has been given wholly into your hands. If you were to unite with her in wedlock and claim her as yours she would make all your years sweet.

In fine, then, to speak briefly, if you thus dispose the heavenly signs and your gifts in this way, you will escape all the threats of fortune, and, under divine favour, will live happy and free from cares.

F. Leonardo da Vinci Paints *The Last Supper*

Leonard also executed in Milan, for the Dominicans of Santa Maria delle Grazie, a marvellous and beautiful painting of the Last Supper. Having depicted the heads of the apostles full of splendor and majesty, he deliberately left the head of Christ unfinished, convinced he would fail to give it the divine spirituality it demands. . . . It is said that the prior used to keep pressing Leonardo, in the most importunate way, to hurry up and finish the work, because he was puzzled by Leonardo's habit of sometimes spending half a day at a time contemplating what he had done so far; if the prior had had his way, Leonardo would have toiled like one of the laborers hoeing in the garden and never put his brush down for a moment. Not satisfied with this, the prior then complained to the duke [Ludovico Sforza], making such a fuss that the duke was constrained to send for Leonardo. . . . Leonardo, knowing he was dealing with a prince of acute and discerning intelligence, was willing (as he never had been with the prior) to explain his mind at length. . . . He explained that men of genius sometimes accomplish most when they work the least. . . . Leonardo then said that he still had two heads to paint: the head of Christ was one, and for this he was unwilling to look for any human model. . . . Then, he said, he had yet to do the head of Judas, and this troubled him since he did not think he could imagine the features that would form the countenance of a man who, despite all the blessings he had been given, could so cruelly steel his will to betray his own master and the creator of the world. However, added Leonardo, he would try to find a model for Judas, and if he did not succeed in doing so, why then he was not without the head of that tactless and importunate prior. The duke roared with laughter at this and said that Leonardo had every reason in the world for saying so.

Document Set 14.2 References

A. The Duke of Burgundy Extends His Patronage to Jan van Eyck
   Elizabeth G. Holt, *A Documentary History of Art* (New York: Doubleday, 1957), 1:303–304.

B. An Avignon Priest Contracts to Have an Altarpiece Painted, 1453
   Holt, 298, 301–302.

C. Galeazzo Maria Sforza Orders His Painter About
   D. S. Chambers, *Patrons and Artists in the Italian Renaissance* (Columbia, S. C.: University of South Carolina Press, 1971), 154.

D. The Gonzagas Find Mantegna a Temperamental Artist
   Federico I. Gonzaga, in Chambers, 120.

E. The Philosopher Marsilio Ficino Suggests the Theme for Botticelli's *Primavera*
   Marsilio Ficino, in Chambers, 98–99.

F. Leonardo da Vinci Paints *The Last Supper*
   Giorgio Vasari, *Artists of the Renaissance: A Selection from "Lives of the Artists,"* trans. George Bull (New York: Penguin, 1978), 187–188.

Family Life

All the documents in this set come from Florence, where the evolution of family life can be studied using an unusually rich collection of documents and literary works. Document A consists of extracts from letters from the widow Alessandra Strozzi to her son Filippo in 1464–1465; they reveal Alessandra (assuming the role normally taken by the family patriarch) negotiating a suitable match for her son—a process in which the bride had no say at all. They illustrate the extreme seriousness with which upper-class families took the business of continuing their lineage. Document B is taken from the diary kept by the head of the Panzone family. Noting his wife's death with genuine emotion, Luca di Matteo da Panzone incidentally reveals clues about family relationships and the public-private dichotomy of Florentine life. Document C, an extract from a similar record book kept by Bernardo Machiavelli (1475), tells part of the story of what happened when the servant girl in a respectable family became pregnant. Many details of Bernard's account have been omitted for reasons of space, including the outcome: fearing a public scandal, the Machiavelli family came up with a small dowry to marry Nencia off in her hometown, unusually lenient treatment. What happened when another young woman of modest circumstances committed a sexual transgression can be seen in Document D, an official court record. Keep in mind these records of private life when reading Document E, in which the humanist Francesco Barbaro comments on conjugal love, in a literary work that puts forward some ideas a bit in advance of their time.

A. Marriage Negotiations in the Strozzi Family

[April 20, 1464] . . . Concerning the matter of a wife [for Filippo], it appears to me that if Francesco di Messer Guglielmino Tanagli wishes to give his daughter, that it would be a fine marriage. . . . Now I will speak with Marco [Parenti, Alessandra's son-in-law], to see if there are other prospects that would be better. . . . Francesco Tanagli has a good reputation, and he has held office, not the highest, but still he has been in office. You may ask: "Why should he give her to someone in exile?" There are three reasons. First, there aren't many young men of good family who have both virtue and property. Secondly, she has only a small dowry, 1,000 florins, which is the dowry of an artisan. . . . Third, I believe that he will give her away, because he has a large family and he will need help to settle them. . . .

[August 17, 1465] . . . Sunday morning I went to the first mass at S. Reparata . . . to see the Adimari girl, who customarily goes to that mass, and I found the Tanagli girl there. Not knowing who she was, I stood beside her. . . . She is very attractive, well proportioned, as large or larger than Caterina [Alessandra's daughter]. . . . She has a long face, and her features are not very delicate, but they aren't like a peasant's. From her demeanor, she does not appear to me to be indolent. . . . I walked behind her as we left the church, and thus I realized that she was one of the Tanagli. . . .

[September 13, 1465] . . . Marco came to me and said that he had met with Francesco Tanagli, who had spoken very coldly, so that I understand that he had changed his mind. . . . I believe that this is the result of the long delay in our replying to him, both yours and Marco's. Now that this delay has angered him, and he has at hand some prospect that is more attractive. . . . I am very annoyed by this business. . . .

[Filippo Strozzi eventually married Fiametta di Donato Adimari, in 1466]

B. Luca di Matteo da Panzone Records His Wife's Death, 1447

November 5, 1445. I record that my wife Lucrezia, from whom I have eleven children alive today, died this day, Friday evening, two and one-half hours after sunset. This has caused me as much grief as though I were dying, for we have lived together for twenty years, one month, and eleven days. I pray to God most fervently that He pardon her. She died in labor; the child was apparently stillborn. But since the child was said to be breathing, it was baptized and named Giovanni. We buried it in the church of S. Simone.

We dressed my daughter Gostanza and Monna Caterina, the wife of Filippo di Ghezzi, with fourteen yards of cloth for a cloak, and a pair of veils and handkerchiefs. On Saturday morning at 11 o'clock, we held a vigil in our house with priests and friars. We buried her that day in S. Croce, in the vault of Messer Luca [Luca's grandfather] next to the fount of holy water. On the 8th, we had a mass said for her soul in S. Croce, with candles and as much pomp as possible. A large number of friends and relatives attended.

The loss of this woman was a grievous blow; she was mourned by the entire populace of Florence. She was a good woman, sweet-tempered and well-mannered, and was loved by everyone who knew her. I believe that her soul has gone to sit at the feet of God's servants. For she bore her final sufferings with patience and humility. She lay ill for two weeks after the child was born. May God with His great mercy make a place for her with angels.

On May 16, 1446, I, Luca da Panzano, ordered thirty masses of St. Gregory to be said, one each morning on consecutive days, for the salvation of my wife Lucrezia's soul. I commissioned my confessor, Fra Altaviano del Mangano, a friar of S. Croce in Florence [to say these masses]. Today I gave him two wax candles weighing a pound each to keep lighted during these masses. And for his services, I gave Fra Altaviano approximately one-half yard of Alexandria velvet.

C. The Machiavellis' Servant Girl Nencia Gets Pregnant, 1475

My wife told me that from certain signs which she had observed, our servant girl Lorenza, also called Nencia di Lazerino, had missed her period and that she appeared to be pregnant.... I told her to confront the girl alone and to use threats and persuasions to find out the truth from her. I had to go away, and upon my return in the evening, she told me that she had the girl alone in a room and that, after cajoling and threatening her, she had learned that the girl was pregnant by Niccolò di Alessandro Machiavelli. When asked how this had happened, she said that after we had returned from the country last year, on November 8, she had often gone at night through the window over the roof, and then through the little window next to the kitchen hearth to Niccolò's house to stay with him....

The truth was that he, Niccolò, had never had anything to do with her. Francesco had done this, and his only fault had been his failure to tell me.

In reply, I complained bitterly of his [Niccolò's] injury to me, which would have been grave in any event, but which was even worse, since he was my neighbor ... and a close blood relation. [I said] that I had never done anything similar to him or his father, and that I did not understand how he could have held me in such low esteem. For both here [in Florence] and at the villa, he was often in my company and had never said anything to me so that I might prevent my house from becoming a bordello. He should also consider the nature of this affair, for this girl was not

a slut but came from a good but impoverished family of Pistoia, and her father and brothers were men of some worth. I did not want the girl in my house any longer, and I had no choice but to inform Giovanni Nelli, who had given her to me, or to arrange for her father and mother to come for her. Niccolò replied that he was aware that he had injured me, but that it was Francesco who had harmed the girl, and that his error had been in not telling me....

D. Monna Francesca Commits Infanticide, 1404

... We [the magistrates] condemn ... Monna Francesca, the daughter of Cristofano Ciuti of Villa Caso, the wife of Cecco Arrighi of Ponte Boccio.... During the months of April, May, and June of the past year, Francesca lived at Montemurlo ... on a farm belonging to Buonaccorso Strozzi. There she had conversations with a certain Jacopo of Romagna, Buonaccorso's servant, who told her that he wanted to take her for his wife. So Francesca, persuaded by his words and his arguments, allowed herself to become intimate with him on several occasions ... so that she became pregnant by Jacopo....

Then Francesca, knowing herself to be pregnant ... promised to marry ... Cecco Arrighi of Ponte Boccio ... in the month of October.... Cecco did not realize that Francesca was pregnant by Jacopo ... although she had been questioned by Cecco and his brothers about her swollen stomach....

In the month of March of the present year, Francesca ... gave birth to a healthy male child.... But inspired by an evil spirit and so that no one would know that she had given birth to that child, she threw him in the river ... and as a result this son and creature of God was drowned.

[Francesca confessed. She was led through the streets of Pistoia on a donkey, with the corpse of her child tied to her neck, and was then burned to death.]

E. Francesco Barbaro Commends Conjugal Love

Now we shall speak of conjugal love, whose great power and high dignity almost always created—as we know from many great thinkers—a pattern of perfect friendship. I must omit a great many topics so that I may speak primarily about what is to be observed most. I should like a wife to love her husband with such great delight, faithfulness, and affection that he can desire nothing more in diligence, love, and goodwill. Let her be so close to him that nothing seems good or pleasant to her without her husband. Indeed, I think that true love will be of the greatest help in this matter. In all matters there is no better, no shorter path than being exactly what we seem to be. . . .

In the first place, let wives strive so that their husbands will clearly perceive that they are pensive or joyful according to the differing states of their husbands' fortunes. Surely congratulations are proper in times of good fortune, just as consolations are appropriate in times of adversity. Let them openly discuss whatever is bothering them, provided it is worthy of prudent people, and let them feign nothing, dissemble nothing, and conceal nothing. Very often sorrow and trouble of mind are relieved by means of discussion and counsel that ought to be carried out in a friendly fashion with the husband. If a husband shares all the pressures of her anxieties, he will lighten them by participating in them and make their burden lighter, but if her troubles are very great or deeply rooted, they will be relieved as long as she is able to sigh in the embrace of her husband. I would like wives to live with their husbands in such a way that they can always be in agreement, and if this can be done, then, as Pythagoras defines friendship, the two are united in one. Now that this could be accomplished more easily, the people of Crete, who have for several centuries now lived under our dominion, used to permit their daughters to marry only those men with whom as virgins they had expressed mutual signs of love. The Cretans believe that those men would be more

beloved by their wives if they were loved by them even before marriage. They recall that nature has so arranged and usage proven that all actions require time with few exceptions. It certainly happens that we may touch something hot and we are not immediately burned, or sometimes wood that is thrown into a fire does not always burst into flame right away. Hence, they think it is necessary for the girl to choose a husband suited to her own personality, just as one does in forming a friendship. The Cretans believe that a couple cannot properly know each other or fall passionately in love immediately. Whether the custom is a good one, I leave it to everyone to decide, but I cannot deny that it is well suited to the joy and constancy of love. . . .

Document Set 14.3 References

A. Marriage Negotiations in the Strozzi Family
Gene Brucker, ed., *The Society of Renaissance Florence* (New York: 1971), 37–40.

B. Luca di Matteo da Panzone Records His Wife's Death, 1447
Panzone, *Diary,* in Brucker, 44–45.

C. The Machiavellis' Servant Girl Nencia Gets Pregnant, 1475
Bernardo Machiavelli, *Libro di Ricordi,* in Brucker, 218–220.

D. Monna Francesca Commits Infanticide, 1404
Brucker, 156–157.

E. Francesco Barbaro Commends Conjugal Love
Francesco Barbaro, in Kenneth R. Bartlett, ed., *The Civilization of the Italian Renaissance: A Sourcebook* (Lexington, Mass.: D. C. Heath, 1992), 144–145.

DOCUMENT SET 14.4
Wealth

Urban Italy probably boasted the greatest concentration of wealth in fifteenth-century Europe; the documents in this set comment on that prosperity. Document A juxtaposes the assets and debts reported by a rich merchant against those of a humble worker in Florence in 1427—data compiled in connection with *Catasto* calculations of residents' wealth. Although not everyone filled out these precursors of an IRS form with scrupulous honesty, *Catasto* documents demonstrate typical disparities in economic standing. In Document B a rich patrician of the Ruccellai family reveals his thoughts on making, keeping, and wisely spending money; while reading this document, keep in mind what you have learned already about Florentines' ideas of family prestige.

Documents C and D come from Naples and Milan and attest to the diligence with which fifteenth-century merchants kept track of transactions. Double-entry bookkeeping was developed in Renaissance Italy; Document D gives a good example.

Studying these documents and reading Chapter 14 of *The Challenge of the West* should help you write a brief report on how wealth was gained and spent in Renaissance Italy.

A. A Rich Man and a Wool Carder Report Their Assets and Liabilities in the Florentine *Catasto*, 1427

The Declaration of Conte di Giovanni Compagni

[Figures are in florins, soldi, denari.]

Assets of Conte di Giovanni Compagni. . .

A house with furnishings which I inhabit, located in the parish of S. Trinita on the street of the Lungarno

> [not taxable]   0

A house in the parish of S. Trinita on the street of the Lungarno . . . which is rented to Niccolò and Tommaso Soderini for 24 florins per year, [capitalized] at 7 percent   342-17-2

A house on the Lungarno in that parish . . . rented to Giovanni di Simone Vespucci for 24 florins per year, [capitalized] at 7 percent   342-17-2

A house located in that street . . . rented to Michele di Piero Dini for 12 florins per year. . . .   171-8-9

Two shops . . . with courtyards and basements for

selling wine, located in the parish of S. Agostino in the Via de' Terni . . . rented to Daddo di Zanobi, wineseller, for 20 florins per year. . . .   285-14-6

One-half of two-thirds of some shops in the palace of the Aretti of Pisa. . . . My share [of the rent] is 28 florins per year, more or less. . . .   400-0-0

A farm in the parish of S. Maria a Quarto . . . 238-11-6

A farm in the parish of S. Giorgio in the *contado* of Prato, with laborer's cottage, including several plots of vineyard and pieces of woodland adjacent to the farm. . . . Bartolomeo di Filippo cultivates this farm; he has borrowed 38 1/2 florins [from me] and he keeps a pair of oxen at his risk. . . . [The farm is valued at]   353-15-2

A small farm in the Valdimarina in the parish of S. Margherita a Torre with a villa and a laborer's cottage and olive trees and woods [valued at]139-13-0

A piece of woodland [valued at]   35-14-0

He [Conte] has invested in a shop of the Lana [woolen cloth manufacturers] guild in the company of Michele di Benedetto di Ser Michele, the sum of   2000-0-0

In another account with Michele in that shop, he is to receive   911-0-0

And in another account, he is to receive   66-0-0

Money which is owed to him by:

Francesco and Niccolò Tornabuoni	1130-0-0
Bartolomeo Peruzzi and company	335-5-0
Lorenzo di Messer Palla Strozzi and company	465-0-0
Michele Dini	75-0-0
Lorenzo di Messer Palla [Strozzi] and company	500-0-0
Michele di Benedetto di Ser Michele	325-0-0
Giovanni and Rinaldo Peruzzi and company	17-2-0

[Compagni estimated his holdings in *Monte* shares (communal bonds) and accrued interest at   4390-3-0

He also estimated that he would collect only 500 florins of some 1,079 florins owed to him by delinquent debtors.]   500-0-0

Obligations

Money owed to:

Creditors of Gino	39-0-0
Giovanni and Rinaldo di Rinieri Peruzzi	33-0-0

Lorenzo di Messer Palla [Strozzi] and company	118-18-6
Lorenzo di Messer Palla and company	45-11-0
Baldo, my servant	12-0-0
Marco di Bernardo and company, druggists	15-0-0
Monna Guida of the Mugello, my servant	10-0-0
[other obligations]	128-11-6

Personal exemptions:

Conte, aged 61	200-0-0
Monna Nanna, his wife	200-0-0
Ilarione, his son, aged 15	200-0-0
Giovanni, his son, aged 11	200-0-0
[Total estimated value of Conte's taxable assets]	13,039-6-3
[Total debts and exemptions]	1,202-1-0
[Net assets subject to taxation]	11,837-5-3 . . .

The Declaration of Biagio di Niccolò, Wool Carder

He owns one-third of a house in the parish of _____; his father bought it for 30 florins. . . . He lives in it.   0

One-half of a cottage located in the Via delle Romite. He receives 3 1/4 florins of rent annually   46-0-0

Next to the cottage is a small piece of garden . . .   0-8-8

Obligations

He owes Braccio di Giovanni, cloth manufacturer   20-0-0

Personal exemptions:

Biagio di Niccolò	200-0-0
Monna Fiora, his wife	200-0-0
Gemma, his daughter, aged 9	200-0-0
Chola, his daughter, aged 5	200-0-0
He pays rent on the two-thirds of his house which he does not own . . .	14-5-0
[Biagio's taxable assets]	65-18-8
[His obligations and exemptions]	834-5-10

B. A Rich Florentine Comments on Getting and Keeping Wealth, c. 1460

Now I shall discuss the best way to invest money: whether it should be all in cash, or all in real estate and communal bonds, or some in one and some in the other. Now it is true that money is very difficult to conserve and to handle; it is very susceptible to the whims of fortune, and few know how to manage it.

But whoever possesses a lot of money and knows how to manage it is, as they say, the master of the business community because he is the nerve center of all of the trades and commercial activities. For in every moment of adverse fortune, in times of exile and those disasters which occur in the world, those with money will suffer less than those who are well provided with real estate. . . . I would not wish to deny, however, that real estate is more secure and more durable [than money], although occasionally it has been damaged and even destroyed by war, by enemies with fire and sword. Real estate holdings are particularly useful for minors and for others who have no experience in banking. . . . There is nothing easier to lose, nothing more difficult to conserve, more dangerous to invest, or more troublesome to keep, than money. . . . The prudent family head will consider all of his property, and will guard against having it all in one place or in one chest. If war or other disaster occur here, you might still be secure there; and if you are damaged there, then you may save yourself here. . . .

Let me warn you again that in our city of Florence, wealth is conserved only with the greatest difficulty. This is due to the frequent and almost continual wars of the Commune, which have required the expenditure of great sums, and the Commune's imposition of many taxes and forced loans. I have found no better remedy for defending myself than to take care not to gain enemies, for a single enemy will harm you more than four friends will help. I have always remained on good terms with my relatives and neighbors and the other residents of the district, so that whenever the taxes have been assessed, they have befriended me and taken pity on me. In this business, good friends and relatives are very useful. . . . So guard against making enemies or involving yourself in quarrels or disputes. And if someone with gall and arrogance tries to quarrel with you, you should treat him with courtesy and patience. . . .

With respect to good, honest, and virtuous friends, I again counsel you to serve them and be liberal with them. Lend to them, give to them, trust them. . . . And while being liberal and generous to friends, one should occasionally do the same to strangers, so that one will gain a reputation for not being miserly, and also will acquire new friends.

I have told you, my sons, how I have treated good friends, and also how I have treated the swindlers and beggars who daily petition me. Now I must tell you how to respond when, as happens every day, your close relatives make demands on you. It seems to me that one is obligated to help them, not so much with money, as with blood and sweat and whatever one can, even to sacrificing one's life for the honor of the family. One must know how to spend money and to acquire possessions. He who spends only in eating and dressing, or who does not know how to disburse money for the benefit and honor of his family, is certainly not wise. But in these matters, one must use good judgment, because it makes no sense to destroy one's own fortune in order to save that of a relative. . . .

Of necessity, the rich man must be generous, for generosity is the most noble virtue that he can possess, and to exercise it requires wisdom and moderation. Whoever wishes to be regarded as liberal must spend and give away his wealth, for which trait the rich are much liked. . . . But who gives beyond his means soon dissipates his fortune. But if you wish to acquire a reputation for liberality, consider well your resources, the times, the expenses which you must bear, and the qualities of men. According to your means, give to men who are in need and who are worthy. And whoever does otherwise goes beyond the rule of liberality, and does not acquire praise thereby. Whatever you give to the unworthy is lost, and whoever disburses his wealth beyond measure soon experiences poverty.

c. "On Commerce and the Perfect Merchant": A Neopolitan Businessman's Advice

The pen is an instrument so noble and excellent that it is absolutely necessary not only to merchants but also in any art, whether liberal, mercantile, or mechanical. And when you see a merchant to whom the pen is a burden or who is inept with the pen, you may say that he is not a merchant. And [a good merchant] not only must be skilled in writing but also must keep his records (*scritture*) methodically. And with these records we plan to deal in the present chapter. For no merchant ought to transact his business by heart, unless he were like King Cyrus, who could call by name every person in his entire army, which was innumerable. And in the same way Lucius Scipio, the Roman, and Cynea, the legate of Pyrrhus, the day after entering Rome, greeted every member of the senate by his name. But since this is not possible for everyone, we shall turn to the practice of [keeping] records. These not only preserve and keep in the memory [all] transactions, but they also are a means to avoid many litigations, quarrels, and scandals. And they also cause literate men to live thousands upon thousands of years. . . .

Mercantile records are the means to remember all that a man does, and from whom he must have, and to whom he must give, and the costs of wares, and the profits, and the losses, and every other transaction on which the merchant is at all dependent. And it should be noted that knowing how to keep good and orderly records teaches one how to draw contracts, how to do business, and how to obtain a profit. And undoubtedly a merchant must not rely upon memory, for such reliance has caused many persons to err. Of this speaks Averroes, the commentator. When he wished to chide Avicenna, who was relying upon his own intelligence, he said: "Two things cause men to err in natural matters, reliance upon [one's own] intelligence, and ignorance of logic."

Therefore the merchant ought to keep three books, that is, the ledger (*quaderno*), the journal (*giornale*), and the memorandum (*memoriale*). And the ledger ought to have its alphabetical [index] through which one may quickly find any account written in the said ledger. And it ought to be marked *A*; and on its first sheet [the merchant] ought to invoke the name of God and [to state] what it deals with and of how many sheets it consists. And he also will mark by the said [letter] *A* his journal, alphabetical [index], and memorandum.

In the journal you shall reconstruct methodically all [your] capital, item by item, and you shall carry it forward in the ledger. Then you shall be able, as you please, to begin your management with that capital and to do business with it. And when you have finished writing the said ledger, you shall settle all accounts opened in it, extract from them all balances (*resti*) to the debit or likewise to the credit, [and carry forward the balances] in the last sheet after the last account. Then, when you carry them forward in a new ledger, give every balance its separate account. And you shall mark that ledger by [the letter] *B*, also marking by the same [letter] the new journal, alphabetical [index], and memorandum [corresponding] to it. Always continue like that successively from one book to another, up to the last syllable of the alphabet, always invoking in the first sheet of a ledger the name of God, etc., as above.

In the memorandum you ought to note every evening or morning before you leave your home everything you have traded and transacted on that day because of your commerce or of [any] other necessary and incidental [expense]—such as sales, purchases, payments, receipts, remittances, orders of payment (*assegnamenti*), exchanges, expenses, promises, and any other business—before any account originates from it in the journal. For many things happen while [business] is transacted without making accounts in the journal.

And you should further note that you ought to keep always with you a small notebook (*libriccino piccolo delle ricordanze*) in which you shall note day by day and hour by hour even the minute [detail] of your transactions, so that later you may at your best convenience create accounts in the memorandum book or the journal. And always exert yourself to carry the accounts, or part of them, forward from the said memorandum into the journal the same day or the following one; then carry them forward in the ledger daily.

And at the end of every year you shall check the ledger against the accounts in the journal, making the trial balance (*bilancione*) of them, and carrying forward all profits or losses (*avanzi overo disavanzi*) in your capital account.

Further, you ought to keep two more books, one to copy the statements (*conti*) which are sent out, the other to copy the letters you sent, [including] even those of the smallest importance.

Also you must keep your writing desk in order, and note on all letters you receive where they come from, and of what year, and of what day according as you have received them daily. And then every month you shall make bundles of those letters, and you shall put away each bundle into the drawer of the proper class in your writing desk, together with all other records—such as contracts, instruments, chirographs, [bills of] exchange, statements, policies, etc.—keeping them there as true merchants are wont to do.

And for the sake of brevity let it be enough to have said this about the method [of keeping] books and records; for if I wanted to tell everything here in detail I would be too long-winded—and it is almost impossible to explain it, since one can hardly learn it from a book without oral instruction. And therefore I warn and encourage any merchant to take pleasure in knowing how to keep his books well and methodically. And whoever does not know [how to do this], let him get instruction, or else let him keep an adequate and expert young bookkeeper (*quaderniero*). Otherwise your commerce will be chaos, a confusion of Babel—of which you must beware if you cherish your honor and your substance.

D. Double-Entry Bookkeeping from Naples

1396

Alberico of Meda, maker of spurs, must give—Credited to the account of Marco Serrainerio on folio 6 on March 6—[for money] which he [Marco] paid to him
£ 9 s.– d.–

Item—[credited] to said Marco on folio 6 on March 11—[for money] deposited for Filippo, his [Alberico's] brother, in [the bank of] Paolino of Osnago
£ 15 s.– d.–

Item—[credited] to Giovanni of Dugnano, on folio 8 on March 24—[for money] which he [Giovannino] ordered to be given him [Alberico or Filippo?] in [the bank of] Andrea Monte
£ 18 s.– d.–

Item—[credited] to Marco Serrrainerio, on folio 6 on May 13—[for money] deposited in [the bank of] Mano, [son] of Ser Jacopo
£ 15 s.– d.–

Item—paid in his behalf on the aforesaid day to Pietrino Bazuella—posted in the cash account on folio 23   £ 10 s.– d.–

Item—for the [balance] posted to the credit account of the joint profit [of the partnership] on folio 20 on January 3, 1397
£ 4s.–8 d.–

1396

He [Alberico] must have—Debited to the account of Merceries on folio 15 on February 24—for 6 dozen fine jeweled spurs, at £ 4 s.10 imperial per dozen, amounting to
£ 27 s.– d.–

Item, posted as above, for 6 dozen small fine jeweled spurs, at s.54 per dozen   £ 16 s.4 d.–

Item, posted as above, for 6 dozen Cordovan spurs, at s.48 per dozen, amounting to £ 14 s.8 d.–

Item, posted as above, for 4 dozen spurs with a prick, at s.26 per dozen, amounting to £ 5 s.4 d.–

Item, posted as above, for 4 dozen quality spurs with thick arms, at s.23 per dozen   £ 4. s.12 d.–

Item, posted as above, for 4 dozen spurs of medium quality, at s.20 per dozen   £ 4 s.– d.–
Total £ 71s.8

Document Set 14.4 References

A. A Rich Man and a Wool Carder Report Their Assets and
  Liabilities in the Florentine *Catasto,* 1427
  Gene Brucker, ed., *The Society of Renaissance Florence* (New
  York: Harper & Row, 1971), 6–8, 13.
B. A Rich Florentine Comments on Getting and Keeping
  Wealth, c. 1460
  Giovanni Rucellai, in Brucker, 24–27.
C. "On Commerce and the Perfect Merchant": A Neapolitan
  Businessman's Advice
  Benedetto Cotrugli, in Robert S. Lopez and Irving W.
  Raymond, *Medieval Trade in the Mediterranean World* (New
  York: Columbia University Press, 1930s), 375–377.
D. Double-Entry Bookkeeping from Naples
  Lopez and Raymond, 372–373.

Faith in the supernatural infused every aspect of fifteenth-century life. However worldly minded an individual may have appeared, thoughts about how such behavior might affect one's standing with God almost invariably arose. The documents in this set focus directly on three dimensions of religious experience. In Document A, Thomas à Kempis conveys a sense of the individual piety permeating the *Devoto Moderna,* the lay (opposed to monastic) movement that spread widely across northern Europe. Document B testifies to a very different kind of piety: that of Florentine intellectuals who tried to reconcile newly rediscovered Platonic philosophy with their Christian beliefs. The author of this commentary, Marsilio Ficino, was a kind of "philosopher in residence" to the Medici family; you have already encountered him in Document Set 14.2. You should also refer back to Document Set 3.3 for Plato's account of the conversation about love between Socrates and Diotima, upon which Ficino comments.

Document C is taken from the *Commentaries* of Pope Pius II, a set of memoirs completed in 1462. Pius here describes his vigorous reaction to a French challenge to papal authority in 1438—following which he enjoys a delightful summer vacation.

All three documents reveal challenges to the medieval church and to traditional church-centered devotion that were building up during the fifteenth century. Identify and explain as many of these challenges as you can.

A. Thomas à Kempis Expresses the Piety of the Devotio Moderna

Evil ought not be done for anything in the world, nor for the love of any human being; but yet for the benefit of one that is in need, a good work is sometimes freely to be left undone, or rather to be changed for what is better.

For by this means a good work is not lost, but changed into a better.

Without charity, the outward work provideth nothing; but whatever is done out of charity, be it ever so little and contemptible, it is all made fruitful, inasmuch as God regardeth more out of how much love a man doth a work, than how much he doth.

2. He doth much who loveth much.

He doth much who doth well what he hath to do.

He doth well, who regardeth rather the common good than his own will.

Oftentimes that seemeth to be charity which is rather carnality; for natural inclination, self-will, hope of reward, study of our own interests, will seldom be absent.

3. He that hath true and perfect charity, seeketh himself in nothing, but only desireth God to be glorified in all things.

And he envieth no man, for he loveth no joy for himself alone.

Neither doth he desire to rejoice in himself, but wisheth to find his blessedness above all good things in God.

He attributeth nothing of good to any man, but referreth it all to God, from whom, as from their fountain, all things proceed, and in whom, as in their end, all the Saints repose in fruition.

Oh, if one had but a spark of real charity, truly would he feel that all earthly things are full of vanity!

B. Marsilio Ficino Attempts to Fuse Platonism and Christianity

". . . The beauty of any individual man, O Socrates, you will scorn if you compare it to that abstract concept of yours. You possess that concept not so much thanks to bodies as to your own soul. Therefore love that concept which your soul has created, and the soul itself, its creator, rather than that external beauty, which is defective and scattered.

"But what is it that I urge you to love in the soul? The beauty of the soul. The beauty of bodies is a light; the beauty of the soul is also a light. The light of the soul is truth, which is the only thing which your friend Plato seems to ask of God in his prayers:

Grant to me, O God, he says, *that my soul may become beautiful, and that those things which pertain to the body may not impair the beauty of the soul, and that I may think only the wise man rich.*

In this prayer Plato says that the beauty of the soul consists in truth and wisdom, and that it is given to men by God. Truth, which is given to us by God single and uniform, through its various effects acquires the names of various virtues. Insofar as it deals with divine things, it is called Wisdom (which Plato asked of God above all else); insofar as it deals with natural things, it is called Knowledge; with human things, Prudence. Insofar as it makes men equal, it is called Justice; insofar as it makes them invincible, Courage; and tranquil, Temperance. . . .

But we, my distinguished friends, shall love God not only without moderation, as Diotima is imagined as commanding, but God alone. For the Angelic Mind is to God as the vision of our eyes is to the sun. The eye desires not only light above all else, but light alone. If we do love bodies, souls, or angels, we shall not really be loving these things, but God in them. In loving bodies we shall really be loving the shadow of God; in souls, the likeness of God; in angels, the image of God. Thus in this life we shall love God in all things so that in the next we may love all things in God. For living in this way we shall proceed to the point where we shall see both God and all things in God, and love both Him, and all things which are in Him. And anyone who surrenders himself to God with love in this life will recover himself in God in the next life. Such a man will certainly return to his own Idea, the Idea by which he was created. There any defect in him will be corrected again; he will be united with his Idea forever. For the true man and the Idea of a man are the same. For this reason as long as we are in this life, separated from God, none of us is a true man, for we are separated from our own Idea or Form. To it, divine love and piety will lead us. Even though we may be dismembered and mutilated here, then, joined by love to our own Idea, we shall become whole men, so that we shall seem to have first worshipped God in things, in order later to worship things in God, and to worship things in God for this reason, in order to recover ourselves in Him above all, and in loving God we shall seem to have loved ourselves.

C. Pius II Tries to Restore Papal Power, Then Goes on Vacation, 1462

It was the sixteenth year of Charles's reign and the 1438th of the Incarnation of our Lord, when the prelates of France on July 7 presented the completed volume of the Pragmatic Sanction to this same Charles for his approval. Charles, apparently forgetting the divine grace which he had experienced through the Maid as well as the many benefits heaped upon him by the Apostolic See in sending the Cardinal of Santa Croce to reconcile the Burgundians with him, approved these impious and unjust enactments and commanded that they should be observed throughout his dominions on pain of most severe punishment.

This decree of the King together with the constitutions of the prelates received the name of the Pragmatic Sanction. The numerous envoys sent to France by the Apostolic See during the lives of Eugenius. Nicholas, and Calixtus to obtain its annulment accomplished nothing. It was twenty-four years before it was completely wiped out under Pius II.[1] As a result of this law the prelates of France, who thought they were going to be free, were reduced to the most abject servitude and became practically slaves of the laity. They were forced to give evidence in the French parliament in individual cases; to confer benefices at the pleasure of the king or other princes and powerful nobles; to advance to the priesthood minors, ignoramuses, monsters, and libertines; to remit the punishment of those they had condemned for misdeeds and to absolve the excommunicated without their making atonement. No independent right of censure was left them. Anyone who brought to France an apostolic letter opposing the Pragmatic Sanction was condemned to death. Cases concerning bishops, metropolitan churches, marriages, and heresy were investigated in parliament and the insolence of the laity ran riot in France, to such an extent that the most holy Body of Christ, when, as often happened, it was being carried in procession to be worshipped by the people or taken as viaticum for the sick, was ordered to halt by the supreme authority of the king. Bishops and other prelates and priests deserving of respect were haled off to public prisons: estates of the Church and all property of the clergy were confiscated on flimsy pretexts of the decision of a secular judge and given over to the laity. Thus many acts of folly were brought about by the Pragmatic Sanction and either enforced or permitted by an ungrateful king.

Meantime, when the summer was over, Pius, who had been invited by Giovanni, Cardinal of San Sisto, to visit the monastery of Subiaco over which he presided, set out with four cardinals on a trip for pleasure and refreshment. They crossed the Aniene at Tivoli, followed along its left bank, and spent the first night at Vicovaro, which some think means Varro's town and some Varus's. It lies on a high cliff and is triangular in shape. Two sides are protected by precipitous rocks divided on one side by a never-failing stream and on the other jutting out into the current of the Aniene. The third side is defended by a lofty tower, a strongly fortified citadel, and an artificial moat. It still retains traces of its early splendor. A good part of the wall constructed of huge blocks of

---

[1] Pius refers to himself throughout in the third person.

stone such as we see in ancient works is still standing, lying about are numerous columns and broken statues that yet give evidence of the talent of their sculptors. Francesco Orsini, when prefect of the city, began a noble chapel of gleaming white marble and adorned it with fine statues and flowers, works of art by no means despicable for our times. Death prevented his completing his work and his successors, who are contesting their inheritance by force of arms, have not yet put the finishing touches to it.

Pius granted the town indulgence that the chapel might be completed. He lodged in a house overlooking the Aniene which commanded a most delightful view, as did also the mountain on the other side of the river which was covered with forests still green and leafy. The land down by the river was either meadows or vineyards; the hills were clothed halfway up with vines and the rest of the way with acorn-bearing oaks.

From here they went to San Clemente some two miles distant. The people worship there with the greatest reverence and the monks are celebrated for their sanctity. The ground where the monastery stands is level but behind it the cliffs above the Aniene fall to such a depth that the eye can hardly see the water at their base. The Pope entered the chapel and prayed. Then after blessing the monks he continued his journey, . . .

Document Set 14.5 References

A. Thomas à Kempis Expresses the Piety of the Devotio Moderna
   Thomas à Kempis, *The Imitation of Christ*, ch. 15.
B. Marsilio Ficino Attempts to Fuse Platonism and Christianity
   Marsilo Ficino, in Kenneth R. Bartlett, ed., *The Civilization of the Italian Renaissance: A Sourcebook* (Lexington, Mass.: D. C. Heath, 1992), 122–125.
C. Pius II Tries to Restore Papal Power, Then Goes on Vacation, 1462
   Memoirs of a Renaissance Pope: Commentaries of Pius II: An Abridgement, trans. Florence A. Gragg, ed. Leona C. Gabel (New York: Capricorn, 1962), 210–212.

DOCUMENT SET 14.6
The State as a Work of Art

The nineteenth-century Swiss historian Jacob Burckhardt, who originated the idea of the Renaissance, used the expression "the state as a work of art" to refer to a key feature of Renaissance politics. As Chapter 14 of *The Challenge of the West* explains, this expression refers to the essentially contrived character of Renaissance state-building, which often involved imposing new forms of rule or nurturing new loyalties. The three documents of this set all speak to Renaissance state-building.

Document A is an ambassador's dispatch to the princely government of Milan (itself a newly created state) describing the Duke of Burgundy's use of the elaborate ritual of his Order of the Golden Fleece to win the loyalty of his nobles. The dispatch (partly written in cipher, indicated here in italics) also testifies to the new institutions and practices of diplomacy, a fifteenth-century Italian innovation. Document B records the sort of civic ritual that the Florentine Republic used to reinforce loyalty to the state. In Document C, Lorenzo the Magnificent, the head of the Medicis at the end of the fifteenth century and a prince in all but name, recalls the cost to his family of staging the lavish displays necessary to demonstrate its power and generosity—and finds it all worthwhile. (Detailed investigation of the Medici family's banking enterprises shows that overspending and neglect of business interests in favor of politics were already undermining the Medici fortune even as Lorenzo was making himself the virtual ruler of Florence.)

After examining these documents, consider afresh what Burckhardt meant by calling the Renaissance state an essentially "artistic creation." Consider also the evidence that you encountered in Sets 14.1 through 14.4.

A. The Duke of Burgundy Presides Over the Order of the Golden Fleece, 1461

For the rest, the ceremonies of the Golden Fleece have been celebrated. In these the Duke of Burgundy exemplified three themes: worship, lofty solemnity, ritual. Worship: the Duke remained most devoutly on his knees throughout the divine service, which lasted until two o'clock in the afternoon, constantly contemplating the arms and insignia of King Alfonso, [of Aragon, died 1458] which he had before his eyes as a mirror of the human condition. Lofty solemnity: in

that he has such revered princes who acknowledge him their Duke, Father, Lord, although he honors them in sharing the bond of brotherhood. Ritual: in the cult, divine and human, of the Highest.

The ordering of the celebration was as follows. In the stalls of the choir sat at the head and on the right the lord Duke, and along both sides of the choir were ranged the insignia, names, and titles of all the princes, barons, and knights of the Order. All wore the vestments of the Golden Fleece, scarlet hoods and scarlet mantels that reached to the feet and were fringed with gold, and had about their necks the collar of the Golden Fleece. In the stalls of those absent sat their proxies; in the stalls of the deceased were hung black cloths displaying their insignia, names, and titles. I was given the first place on the left side, beneath the head of the barons on that side. At the offertory, *Golden Fleece,* chief of the Duke's heralds, ceremoniously called the roll of the Order by name and title, except that there was announced the suspension of the Duke of Alençon on account of his being a prisoner, until his case, if indeed there was a case, is considered by the Order. Subsequently *Orléans'* name was called, *as Duke of Orléans and Count of Blois, but he was not given the accustomed title of Duke of Milan, at which point the Duke of Burgundy gave me a significant glance.*

The church, which is very large, was splendidly hung with arras depicting with magnificent artistry the Apocalypse. The choir was similarly embellished, with hangings of cloth of gold depicting various stories from the Old and New Testament. The altar, as a thing divine, was adorned with religious objects: namely, first a very large cross containing a piece of the True Cross; then eighteen images, of gold not silver, of the length of an arm; and in the middle the holy Fleur-de-Lys, more than an arm's length tall and almost as wide, which contained holy relics and was crusted with jewels, precious both in their quantity and quality. Of singers, heralds, and such appurtenances, there was an infinite number, all superbly contributing to the ceremonies.

The banquet hall, which is of the size of that of the most illustrious lady, the Duchess, but with a higher ceiling, was completely hung with tapestries of cloth of gold, as above, marvellous works depicting the whole story of how the golden fleece was sent down from heaven to Gideon as a sign that he was to undertake the salvation of the people of Israel. Behind the dais where sat the princes were silken hangings and other adornments of gold. Opposite was a display of plate, very rich and all of vessels of gold and silver gilt, four unicorn horns arranged in order of size like organ pipes, and many vessels of crystal and of other precious stones. This plate remained untouched that day because so much of it does the Duke have that there was plenty of additional plate for the dinner service.

At the banquet the Duke sat at the middle of the board with the others ranged on either side in accordance with their seniority in the Order. On the extreme right was my lord [Charles] of Charolais; at the other end [Antoine], the Bastard of Burgundy, both sons of the Duke. Each of the princes of the Golden Fleece had his own service, and the banquet consisted of fifty courses, each served by fifty servitors and the courses borne through the hall in a grand procession of trumpeters and other musicians, with the other nobles then being served. These ceremonies were held on May 2.

The number of the princes of the Order is established by the constitution at thirty-one. There are two main bases of the Order: a vow to defend Holy Church, and a vow to maintain all honor, morality, and good custom without stain, these vows being part of the articles of the Order, of which articles I hope to be able to obtain a copy because I think they are worthy and useful. Stemming from these vows is the requirement *that all members of the Order be in league, confraternity, and identity of wills with each other. The Duke of Burgundy finds this brotherhood of great value to him because he has their aid and counsel.*

To supply the places of the deceased members, six of them, many secret councils were held, as is customary, and according to what they themselves have told me, I believe that at present they will elect five *new members, unless they change their minds. I believe that, in honor of the late King of Aragon, they will not fill his place until they elect another King, and I think they are reserving the place for King Ferrante, if matters permit. This is my judgment of the situation.*

Considering then the nature of this Order of the Golden Fleece and the honor and prestige that it confers, I confess to have within me a strong desire for Count Galeazzo to be elected to it. Nonetheless since I do not know how Your Excellency feels about the matter and since I also do not know whether, in this procedure, indication of a desire to be elected does a service or disservice, I have contented myself with offering a certain indication, or rather a very small one. However, what I have been able to do, acting with discretion, I have done, such as calling upon these princes in order to speak with them about Your

Excellency and to describe your manners and modes of government, your justice, liberality, the grace and authority that all universally find in you, and similar things, and to explain how in these customs, with great and marvelous loftiness of spirit and intelligence, has been reared, and made knight, Count Galeazzo.

I believe that by these means I aroused the right feeling among these princes, and if the obstacle of the Duke of Orléans did not stand in the way, which I do not like to believe, I am not without some thought that they may have elected Count Galeazzo, although neither I nor others know for certain because it is a custom of the Order never to announce the names of outsiders who are chosen until they consent to become members, and this is for the honor of the Order. This is my view of the matter, reserving always the judgment of Your Excellency. Would that thus it was, because it would seem to me that in this honorable way, and without incurring the dislike of any lord in the world, you would acquire a league with the Duke of Burgundy and with the other lords of the Order without expense etc., which league could some time come in very handy, however things turn out. I can well assure Your Excellency that you have a greater reputation in these parts than—speaking always with permission—has had any other who has been Duke of Milan. Should Count Galeazzo be elected, the news will be brought to Your Excellency by a worthy emissary, to whom, if Your Excellency agrees, it will be well to pay high honors, etc. However, I offer no assurance about all this, for I would not want to send Your Excellency unbaked dough [i.e. opinion masquerading as fact]. *However, as I say, I have some hopes about the matter, and therefore I would strongly suggest that Count Galeazzo become acquainted, through letters and a little something more, with the son of the Duke of Burgundy.* I humbly recommend myself to Your Excellency. Given as above.

B. Florentines Celebrate a Communal Ritual

When springtime comes and the whole world rejoices, every Florentine begins to think about organizing a magnificent celebration on the feast day of St. John the Baptist [June 24]. . . . For two months in advance, everyone is planning marriage feasts or other celebrations in honor of the day. There are preparations for the horse races, the costumes of the retinues, the flags and the trumpets; there are the pennants and the wax candles and other things which the subject territories offer to the Commune. Messengers are sent to obtain provisions for the banquets, and horses come from everywhere to run in the races. The whole city is engaged in preparing for the feast, and the spirits of the young people and the women [are animated] by these preparations. . . . Everyone is filled with gaiety; there are dances and concerts and songfests and tournaments and other joyous activities. Up to the eve of the holiday, no one thinks about anything else.

Early on the morning of the day before the holiday, each guild has a display outside of its shops of its fine wares, its ornaments and jewels. There are cloths of gold and silk sufficient to adorn ten kingdoms. . . . Then at the third hour, there is a solemn procession of clerics, priests, monks, and friars, and there are so many [religious] orders, and so many relics of saints, that the procession seems endless. [It is a manifestation] of great devotion, on account of the marvelous richness of the adornments . . . and clothing of gold and silk with embroidered figures. There are many confraternities of men who assemble at the place where their meetings are held, dressed as angels, and with musical instruments of every kind and marvelous singing. They stage the most beautiful representations of the saints, and of those relics in whose honor they perform. They leave from S. Maria del Fiore [the cathedral] and march through the city and then return.

Then, after midday, when the heat has abated before sunset, all of the citizens assemble under [the banner of] their district, of which there are sixteen. Each goes in the procession in turn, the first, then the second, and so on with one district following the other, and in each group the citizens march two by two, with the oldest and most distinguished at the head, and proceeding down to the young men in rich garments. They march to the church of St. John [the Bapistery] to offer, one by one, a wax candle weighing one pound. . . . The walls along the streets through which they pass are all decorated, and there are . . . benches on which are seated young ladies and girls dressed in silk and adorned with jewels, pearls, and precious stones. This procession continues until sunset, and after each citizen has made his offering, he returns home with his wife to prepare for the next morning.

Whoever goes to the Piazza della Signoria on the morning of St. John's Day witnesses a magnificent, marvelous, and triumphant sight, which the mind can scarcely grasp. Around the great piazza are a hundred towers which appear to be made of gold. Some were brought on carts and others by porters. . . . [These towers] are made of wood, paper, and wax [and dec-

orated] with gold, colored paints, and with figures. . . . Next to the rostrum of the palace [of the Signoria] are standards . . . which belong to the most important towns which are subject to the Commune: Pisa, Arezzo, Pistoia, Volterra, Cortona, Lucignano. . . .

First to present their offering, in the morning, are the captains of the Parte Guelfa, together with all of the knights, lords, ambassadors, and foreign knights. They are accompanied by a large number of the most honorable citizens, and before them, riding on a charger covered with a cloth . . . is one of their pages carrying a banner with the insignia of the Parte Guelfa. Then there follow the abovementioned standards, each one carried by men on horseback . . . and they all go to make their offerings at the Baptistery. And these standards are given as tribute by the districts which have been acquired by the Commune of Florence. . . . The wax candles, which have the appearance of golden towers, are the tribute of the regions which in most ancient times were subject to the Florentines. In order of dignity, they are brought, one by one, to be offered to St. John, and on the following day, they are hung inside the church and there they remain for the entire year until the next feast day. . . . Then come . . . an infinite number of large wax candles, some weighing 100 pounds and others 50, some more and some less . . . carried by the residents of the villages [in the *contado*] which offer them. . . .

Then the lord priors and their colleges come to make their offerings, accompanied by their rectors, that is, the podestà, the captain [of the *popolo*], and the executor. . . . And after the lord [priors] come those who are participating in the horse race, and they are followed by the Flemings and the residents of Brabant who are weavers of woolen cloth in Florence. Then there are offerings by twelve prisoners who, as an act of mercy, have been released from prison . . . in honor of St. John, and these are poor people. . . . After all of these offerings have been made, men and women return home to dine. . . . [There follows a description of the horse race which takes place in the afternoon.]

C. Lorenzo de' Medici Totals up the Medicis' Spending on Public Display

To do as others had done, I held a joust in the Piazza S. Croce at great expense and with great pomp. I find we spent about 10,000 ducats. . . . Piero, our father, departed this life on July 2 . . . having been much tormented with gout. He would not make a will, but we drew up an inventory and found we possessed 237,988 scudi [a coin worth approximately a florin]. . . .

I find that from 1434 till now we have spent large sums of money, as appear in a small quarto notebook of the said year to the end of 1471. Incredible are the sums written down. They amount to 663,755 florins for alms, buildings, and taxes, let alone other expenses. But I do not regret this, for though many would consider it better to have a part of that sum in their purse, I consider that it gave great honor to our State, and I think the money was well expended, and am well pleased.

Document Set 14.6 References

A. The Duke of Burgundy Presides Over the Order of the Golden Fleece, 1461
Paul M. Kendall and Vincent Ilardi, eds., *Dispatches with Related Documents of the Milanese Ambassadors to France and Burgundy, 1450–1483* (Athens, Ohio: Ohio University Press, 1971), 2:346–354.
B. Florentines Celebrate a Communal Ritual
Gregorio Dati, in Gene Brucker, ed., *The Society of Renaissance Florence* (New York: Harper & Row, 1971), 75–78.
C. Lorenzo de' Medici Totals up the Medicis' Spending on Public Display
Lorenzo de' Medici, in J. Ross, *Lives of the Early Medicis* (Boston: 1911), 134–135.

DOCUMENT SET 14.7
The End of the Byzantine Empire

The year 1453 is an epochal date in European history, marking the end of Christian Constantinople, which for a thousand years had stood as the capital of the eastern empire. Henceforth the city would be known as Istanbul, and its population would be islamicized.

Document A suggests one reason for this outcome: the Byzantine people's refusal to subject themselves to papal religious leadership in order to win Western support against the Turks. (How much aid the West would likely have sent even if the Byzantines had submitted to Rome is something that you should think about as you read *The Challenge of the West*.) The Turkish conquest of Constantinople is described—and the contrasting Muslim and Christian emotions evoked—in Documents B and C. Drawing upon these selections and the account in Chapter 14, write a brief account of the fall of Constantinople from the viewpoints of all three heirs of the ancient world: Orthodox Eastern Christianity, Latin Western Christianity, and Islam.

A. The Byzantines Reject the Council of Florence, 1439

At this time the schismatic party went to the Monastery of the Pantocrator, to the cell of Gennadios, the former George Scholarios, and asked him "What are we to do?" He was in seclusion in his cell, and taking a piece of paper he expressed his thoughts and counsel in writing. His words were: "Wretched Romans, how you have gone astray! You have rejected the hope of God and trusted in the strength of the Franks; you have lost your piety along with your city which is about to be destroyed. Lord have mercy on me. I testify before you that I am innocent of such transgression. Know, wretched citizens, what you are doing. Along with your impending captivity, you have forsaken the faith handed down from your fathers [*patroparadoton*] and assented to impiety. Woe unto you, when you are judged!" This and many other things he had written, he placed on the door of his cell; he secluded himself inside and what he wrote was read.

Then all the nuns, who believed themselves to be pure and dedicated servants of God in Orthodoxy, in accordance with their own sentiment and that of their teacher Gennadios, cried out the anathema, and along with them the abbots and confessors and the remaining priests and laymen. They condemned the doctrinal definition of the council [of Florence] and all those who had acquiesced to it, all those who were now acquiescing, and all who would do so in the future. The common and low-born people, leaving the courtyard of the monastery, entered into the taverns and, holding bottles of unwatered wine in their hands, anathematized the unionists and drank to the intercession of the icon of the Mother of God [the *Hodegetria*]. And they beseeched her to guard and aid the city now against Mehmed, as she had formerly done against Chosroës, Kaghan, and the Arabs. "We need neither the aid of the Latins nor Union. Keep the worship of the azymites far from us."

B. The Turks Exalt in the Fall of Constantinople

The fighting went on, day and night, for fifty days. On the fifty-first day the Sultan ordered free plunder. They attacked. On the fifty-first day, a Tuesday, the citadel was captured. There was good booty and plunder. Gold and silver and jewels and fine stuffs were brought and stacked in the camp market. They began to sell them. They made the people of the city slaves and killed their Emperor, and the gāzīs [soldiers] embraced their pretty girls. . . .

This victory was achieved by Sultan Mehmed Khan in the year 857 of the Hijira [1453].

C. The Byzantines Lament the Fall of Constantinople

And the entire City [its inhabitants and wealth] was to be seen in the tents of the [Turkish] camp, the city deserted, lying lifeless, naked, soundless, without either form or beauty. O City, City, head of all cities! O City, City, center of the four corners of the world! O City, City, pride of the Romans, civilizer of the barbarians! O City, second paradise planted toward the west, possessing all kinds of vegetation, laden with spiritual fruits! Where is your beauty, O paradise, where the beneficent strength of the charms of your spirit, soul, and body? Where are the bodies of the Apostles of my Lord, which were implanted long ago in the always-green paradise, having in their midst the purple cloak, the lance, the sponge, the reed, which, when we kissed them, made us believe that we were seeing him who was raised on the Cross? Where are the relics of the saints, those of the martyrs? Where the remains of Constantine the Great and the other emperors? Roads, courtyards, crossroads, fields, and vineyard enclosures, all teem with the relics of saints, with the bodies of nobles, of the chaste, and of male and female ascetics. Oh what a loss! "The dead bodies of thy servants, O Lord, have they given to be meat unto the fowls of the heaven, the flesh of thy saints unto the beasts of the earth round about New Sion and there was none to bury them [Psalm 78:2–3]."

O temple [Hagia Sophia]! O earthly heaven! O heavenly altar! O sacred and divine places! O magnificence of the churches! O holy books and words of God! O ancient and modern laws! O tablets inscribed by the finger of God! O Scriptures spoken by his mouth! O divine discourses of angels who bore flesh! O doctrines of men filled with the Holy Spirit! O

teachings of semi-divine heroes! O commonwealth! O citizens! O army, formerly beyond number, now removed from sight like a ship sunk into the sea! O houses and palaces of every type! O sacred walls! Today I invoke you all, and as if incarnate beings I mourn with you, having Jeremiah as [choral] leader of this lamentable tragedy!

Document Set 14.7 References

A. The Byzantines Reject the Council of Florence, 1439
Ducas, *Historia Turcobyzantia, 1341–1462*, in Deno John Geanokoplos, ed., *Byzantium: Church, Society, and Civilization Seen Through Contemporary Eyes* (Chicago: University of Chicago Press, 1984), 225.

B. The Turks Exult in the Fall of Constantinople
Naphtali Lewis, *Islam: From the Prophet Muhammed to the Capture of Constantinople* (New York: Walker, 1987), 145–146.

C. The Byzantines Lament the Fall of Constantinople
Ducas, in Geanokoplos, 389.

DOCUMENT SET 14.8
Life in the Fifteenth-Century North

The documents in this chapter's final set can only hint at many important aspects of life north of the Alps. One way to read these six documents is to look for features that both recall late medieval life and point toward coming changes.

Document A is an account from the 1430s of the devastation that France suffered during the Hundred Years' War, a horrible experience that left the monarchy determined to consolidate its resources and overcome provincial disunity. Document B speaks to peacetime concerns in the ordinance of the Tailors' Guild in the English city of Exeter. It contrasts with much less settled conditions in Document C, which describes rural troubles that began when a Warwickshire gentleman, Henry Smith, converted common village lands to his private use in 1493, dispossessing the peasants. In Document D we return to France, where the "Spider King" Louis XI (1423–1483) is described in the memoirs of the observant French statesman Philippe de Commynes. Anything but a glamorous monarch, Louis ruthlessly gathered under tight central control the lands nominally subject to the French crown.

Document E originated in Germany but would exert a baleful influence throughout early modern Europe: an extract from the *Malleus Maleficarum* ("The Hammer of Witches") published with papal encouragement in 1486 by two Dominican friars, cataloging the alleged practices of witches and giving directions for their detection. (Notice how this document assumes that the accused is likely to be a woman.) Publication of the *Malleus Maleficarum* marked the onset of an obsessive, officially organized campaign against witchcraft that would convulse the West for 200 years. Equally disturbing (although it dates from the early sixteenth century), Document F, also from Germany, illustrates all too well the rampant antisemitism sweeping through that country's cities in the fifteenth century.

Using these documents in conjunction with your textbook, sketch out some elements of the popular "mentality" (a favorite historian's word) of north Europeans in this century marked by a waning of medieval culture and the first stirrings of the early modern era. Focus particularly on Europeans' anxieties—the changes and tensions in the air that convinced people that times were "out of joint" and evil forces were running rampant. Consider as well the evidence that you have extracted from Chapter 14's earlier sets. You will then have a good sense of European life on the eve of the Reformation.

A. France Emerges from the Hundred Years' War

. . . In his time, owing to the long wars which had raged within and without, the lethargy and cowardliness of the officers and commanders who were under him, the destruction of all military discipline and order, the rapacity of the troopers, and the general dissolution into which all things had fallen, such destruction had been wrought that from the river Loire to the Seine—even to the Somme,—the farmers were dead or had fled, and almost all the fields had for many years lain without cultivation or any one to cultivate them. A few districts might indeed be excepted, where if any agriculture remained, it was because they were far from cities, towns, or castles, and in consequence the constant excursions of the despoilers could not be extended to them. Lower Normandy, embracing the bishoprics of Bayeux and Coutances, which were under English rule, were far from the headquarters of the enemy, nor could they be easily reached by the depredators. They therefore remained somewhat better off in the matter of population and cultivators, but nevertheless were often afflicted by the greatest misfortunes, as will appear later.

We have ourselves beheld the vast regions of Champagne, Brie, Chartres, Perche, Beauvais, . . . Amiens, Abbeville, Soissons, Laon, and beyond toward Hainault, well-nigh deserted, untilled, without husbandmen, grown up to weeds and briers. In many places where fruit trees could flourish these had grown up into dense forests. The vestiges of such ruin, unless the divine clemency shall aid mere human endeavor, will, it is to be feared, last for long years to come.

If any kind of cultivation was still carried on in the regions enumerated, it could only be done close to cities, towns, or castles, no farther away than the watch could be seen, stationed on a high lookout, whence he could observe the robbers as they approached. He would then give the alarm by means of a bell, or a hunter's horn, to those in the fields or vineyard, so that they could betake themselves to a place of safety. This happened so frequently in many places that so soon as the oxen and plow animals were loosed, having heard the signal of the watch, they would, taught by long experience, rush to a place of safety in a state of terror. Even the pigs and sheep did the same.

B. The Tailors of Exeter Regulate Their Lives, 1466

To the worship of God and of our Lady Saint Mary, and of St. John the Baptist, and of all Saints; These be the ordinances made and established of the fraternity of the craft of tailors, of the city of Exeter, by assent and consent of the fraternity of the craft aforesaid gathered there together, for evermore to endure.

First, it is ordained, by virtue of the charter granted by our sovereign lord King Edward the Fourth, in the sixth year of his reign, that the master of the aforesaid craft for the time being, every Thursday shall be at the common hall, or else a deputy for him upon pain of two pounds of wax. And every warden that is absent without reasonable cause shall pay a pound of wax to the use and profit of the aforesaid fraternity; and that the aforesaid master and wardens be there every Thursday at nine of the clock, there to obtain and rule what may be for the welfare of the fraternity and craft aforesaid, and none to act without the other.

Also, it is ordained by the master and wardens and the common council aforesaid that every person who is privileged with the craft aforesaid who is of the value of £20 of goods and above, shall be of the masters' fellowship and clothing. And every person that is of the fellowship and the aforesaid craft shall pay, every year, for his feast, at Midsummer, 12d., and his offering; and for his clothing as it comes to, within a month from Midsummer day, upon pain of being put out of the aforesaid fraternity and craft for evermore. And every person that is so admitted shall pay a spoon of silver, weighing an ounce, and its fashioning.

Also, it is ordained that every out-brother, that is not privileged of the aforesaid fraternity and gild, shall pay every year 6d. at Midsummer. And if he refuse to pay this within a month from Midsummer, he is to be dismissed from the aforesaid fraternity and gild for evermore.

Also, it is ordained that all the fellowship of the bachelors shall hold their feast on St. John's day, in harvest. And every person that is a shop-holder of the aforesaid fellowship and craft shall pay to the aforesaid feast 8d. and his offering. And every servant that receiveth wages shall pay 6d. to the aforesaid feast. And every out-brother that is of the aforesaid fellow-

ship shall pay, every year, 4d. And if any of the fellowship and craft aforesaid, refuse to pay this, then their names shall be certified to the master and wardens, that they may do correction therein, as belongeth to them to do, according to charter granted by the sovereign lord, the King Edward the Fourth, the sixth year of his reign, by assent and consent of the mayor, the bailiffs, and commons of the city of Exeter, for ever to endure.

Also, it is ordained by the aforesaid master and wardens and fellowship of the fraternity and craft aforesaid that every servant that is of the aforesaid craft that taketh wages to the value of 20s. and above shall pay 20d. to be a free sewer, to the use and profit of the aforesaid fraternity; that no man of the aforesaid craft set any new sewer to work above the space of fifteen days without bringing him before the master and wardens there to pay his 20d. to be made a free sewer, or else to find a surety.

Also it is ordained by the master and wardens aforesaid that if any person of the aforesaid craft who is bound to pay any debt over to the aforesaid master and wardens, breaks his day by the space of half a year, he shall forfeit his whole bond. Provided, always, that if any person or persons aforesaid have fallen into poverty, and will testify so by his oath, he shall be discharged of his bond and debt and shall have sustenance by the foresaid craft as may be thought, by their discretion, convenient and reasonable.

Also, it is ordained by the foresaid master and wardens that if any brother of the aforesaid fraternity and craft despise another, calling him knave, or whoreson, or stupid, or any other misname, he shall pay at the first fault, 12d.; at the second fault, 20d.; and at the third fault, to be put out of the fraternity and craft for evermore.

Also, it is ordained by the foresaid master and wardens and the whole fellowship, that if any brother of the aforesaid craft take any clothing of any lord, knight or gentlemen, outside of the city without leave of the master and wardens, at the first fault, 40s., and at the second fault to be put out of the fraternity and craft for evermore.

Also, it is ordained by the foresaid master and wardens that there shall be four quarter-days that every brother of this craft shall assemble at our common-hall. And every shop-holder shall spend 2d. for a breakfast, or send his money by a deputy. And at that the oath and the ordinances and constitutions shall be read. The first day shall be the next Thursday after Twelfth day, and the second day shall be the second Thursday after Easter, and the third day shall be the second Thursday after the feast of St. John the

Baptist, and the fourth day shall be the next Thursday after St. Michael's day. And at every of these foresaid days, after dinner there shall come all free sewers and take the remains of the meat and drink that the aforesaid master and shopholders leave; and each of them shall spend 1d. to the welfare of the aforesaid fraternity and gild.

Also, it is ordained by the master and wardens that at every coste of ale that is given into the aforesaid fraternity and gild, every shopholder shall spend thereto 1d., aud every free sewer one farthing, and he that cometh not shall send his money by the beadle, upon pain of one pound of wax.

Also, it is ordained by the master and wardens and all the whole craft, that from henceforth no man of the said craft shall hold more than three servants and one apprentice at the most, without license of the master and wardens for the time being, upon pain of 40s. and he that pleadeth for him that doth against this ordinance shall forfeit 20s.

Also, it is ordained by the master and wardens and all the whole craft, that every person of the said craft that taketh an apprentice shall bring him before the master and wardens, there to have his indenture enrolled, the master to pay 12d. for his enrollment. This is to be done within a twelvemonth and a day or else he is to lose his freedom of the craft for evermore.

Also, it is ordained by the master and wardens and the craft aforesaid that every apprentice of the said craft that is enrolled and truly serveth his covenant shall pay a silver spoon weighing an ounce and its fashioning, and shall give a breakfast to the foresaid master and wardens before the day that he is able to be made freeman of the city aforesaid; and if he pay not a spoon worth 4s., then 4s. in money for the same.

Also, it is ordained by the master and wardens and the whole fellowship that every person that shall be made free of the craft by redemption shall pay 20s. to his fine without any pardon; and when he is enabled, shall give a breakfast to the master and wardens, before he is admitted free man of the city. And every person so enabled from henceforth shall have, the first year, but one servant, the second year, two, the third, three, and an apprentice if he be able. And he that doeth against this ordinance shall forfeit, at the first fault, 20s. at the second offense, 40s., at the third offense, he shall be put out of the fraternity and craft for evermore.

C. Enclosures Disrupt Late Fifteenth-Century England

And the aforesaid jurors say that Henry Smith was recently seised in his demesne as of fee of 12 mes-

suages and 4 cottages, 640 acres of arable land to the annual value of 55*l* with appurtenances in Stretton super Street in the aforesaid county, and with each of the aforesaid messuages 40 acres of arable land, suitable for and ordinarily in cultivation, were accustomed to be let, farmed and occupied from time immemorial. Thus was the same Henry Smith seised on the 6th. December 9 Henry VII. He enclosed the messuages, cottages and lands with ditches and banks and he wilfully caused the same messuages and cottages to be demolished and laid waste and he converted them from the use of cultivation and arable husbandry into pasture for brute animals. Thus he holds them to this day, on account of which 12 ploughs that were employed in the cultivation of those lands are withdrawn and 80 persons, who similarly were occupied in the same cultivation, and who dwelled in the said messuages and cottages, were compelled to depart tearfully against their will. Since then they have remained idle and thus they lead a miserable existence, and indeed they die wretched. What is more to be lamented is [that] the church of Stretton on that occasion fell into ruin and decay, so that the Christian congregation, which used to gather there to hear the divine offices, is no longer held there and the worship of God is almost at an end. In the church animals are sheltered from the storms of the air and brute animals feed among the tombs of Christian bodies in the churchyard. In all things the church and burial-place are profaned to the evil example of others inclined to act in such a manner.

D. Louis XI of France Hunts and Schemes

Small hopes and comfort ought poor and inferior people to have in this world, considering what so great a king suffered and underwent, and how he was at last forced to leave all, and could not, with all his care and diligence, protract his life one single hour. I knew him, and was entertained in his service in the flower of his age and at the height of his prosperity, yet I never saw him free from labor and care.

Of all diversions he loved hunting and hawking in their seasons, but his chief delight was in dogs. . . . In hunting, his eagerness and pain were equal to his pleasure, for his chase was the stag, which he always ran down. He rose very early in the morning, rode sometimes a great distance, and would not leave his sport, let the weather be never so bad. And when he came home at night he was often very weary and generally in a violent passion with some of his courtiers or huntsmen; for hunting is a sport not always to be managed according to the master's direction; yet, in the opinion of most people, he understood it as well as any prince of his time. He was continually at these sports, lodging in the country villages to which his recreations led him, till he was interrupted by business; for during the most part of the summer there was constantly war between him and Charles, duke of Burgundy, while in the winter they made truces. . . .

When his body was at rest his mind was at work, for he had affairs in several places at once, and would concern himself as much in those of his neighbors as in his own, putting officers of his own over all the great families, and endeavoring to divide their authority as much as possible. When he was at war he labored for a peace or a truce, and when he had obtained it he was impatient for war again. He troubled himself with many trifles in his government which he had better have let alone; but it was his temper, and he could not help it. Besides, he had a prodigious memory, and he forgot nothing, but knew everybody, as well in other countries as in his own. . . .

I am of opinion that if all the days of his life were computed in which his joys and pleasures outweighed his pain and trouble, they would be found so few, that there would be twenty mournful ones to one pleasant. He lived about sixty-one years, yet he always fancied he should never outlive sixty, giving this for a reason, that for a long time no king of France had lived beyond that age. . . .

E. The *Malleus Maleficarum* Tells How to Torture a Suspected Witch

The method of beginning an examination by torture is as follows: First, the jailers prepare the implements of torture, then they strip the prisoner (if it be a woman, she has already been stripped by other women, upright and of good report). This stripping is lest some means of witchcraft may have been sewed into the clothing—such as often, taught by the Devil, they prepare from the bodies of unbaptized infants, [murdered] that they may forfeit salvation. And when the implements of torture have been prepared, the judge, both in person and through other good men zealous in the faith, tries to persuade the prisoner to confess the truth freely; but, if he will not confess, he bids attendants make the prisoner fast to the strappado or some other implement of torture. The attendants obey forthwith, yet with feigned agitation. Then, at the prayer of some of those present, the prisoner is loosed again and is taken aside and once more

persuaded to confess, being led to believe that he will in that case not be put to death.

Here it may be asked whether the judge, in the case of a prisoner much defamed, convicted both by witnesses and by proofs, nothing being lacking but his own confession, can properly lead him to hope that his life will be spared—when, even if he confess his crime, he will be punished with death.

It must be answered that opinions vary. Some hold that even a witch of very ill repute, against whom the evidence justifies violent suspicion, and who, as a ringleader of the witches, is accounted very dangerous, may be assured her life, and condemned instead to perpetual imprisonment on bread and water, in case she will give sure and convincing testimony against other witches; yet this penalty of perpetual imprisonment must not be announced to her, but only that her life will be spared, and that she will be punished in some other fashion, perhaps by exile. And doubtless such notorious witches, especially those who prepare witch-potions or who by magical methods cure those bewitched, would be peculiarly suited to be thus preserved, in order to aid the bewitched or to accuse other witches, were it not that their accusations cannot be trusted, since the Devil is a liar, unless confirmed by proofs and witnesses.

Others hold, as to this point, that for a time the promise made to the witch sentenced to imprisonment is to be kept, but that after a time she should be burned.

A third view is, that the judge may safely promise witches to spare their lives, if only he will later excuse himself from pronouncing the sentence and will let another do this in his place. . . .

But if, neither by threats nor by promises such as these, the witch can be induced to speak the truth, then the jailers must carry out the sentence, and torture the prisoner according to the accepted methods, with more or less of severity as the delinquent's crime may demand. And, while he is being tortured, he must be questioned on the articles of accusation, and this frequently and persistently, beginning with the lighter charges—for he will more readily confess the lighter than the heavier. And, while this is being done, the notary must write down everything in his record of the trial—how the prisoner is tortured, on what points he is questioned, and how he answers.

And note that, if he confesses under the torture, he must afterward be conducted to another place, that he may confirm it and certify that it was not due alone to the force of the torture.

But, if the prisoner will not confess the truth satisfactorily, other sorts of tortures must be placed before him, with the statement that, unless he will confess the truth, he must endure these also. But, if not even thus he can be brought into terror and to the truth, then the next day or the next but one is to be set for a *continuation* of the tortures—not a *repetition,* for they must not be repeated unless new evidences be produced.

The judge must then address to the prisoners the following sentence: We, the judge, etc., do assign to you, —, such and such a day for the continuation of the tortures, that from your own mouth the truth may be heard, and that the whole may be recorded by the notary.

And during the interval, before the day assigned, the judge, in person or through approved men, must in the manner above described try to persuade the prisoner to confess, promising her (if there is aught to be gained by this promise) that her life shall be spared.

The judge shall see to it, moreover, that throughout this interval guards are constantly with the prisoner, so that she may not be left alone; because she will be visited by the Devil and tempted into suicide.

F. "How the Jews Were Driven from Regensburg"

Among the Christians were a few
Felt pity for the wretched Jew;
These loved not God and felt no urge
To venerate the Holy Church.
But other men were free of blame;
Among them Thomas Fuchs I name . . .

By murder and usury, the Jews
Had done our city grave abuse.
Stirred by laments from young and old,
By pleas from all the land, I'm told,
The council acted. Otherwise,
Had council members shut their eyes
And left the Jews in impunity
They would have wrecked our community.
May our brave councillors be blessed
For having rid us of this pest.
God's purpose was behind their action,
For our Lord feels satisfaction
Whenever Jews are driven from
A famous city in Christendom.
God heeds the cries of honest folk

Excerpt from "How the Jews Were Driven from Regensberg" from Gerald Strauss, *Manifestations of Discontent in Germany on the Eve of the Reformation,* pp. 124–129. Reprinted by permission of Indiana University Press.

Oppressed beneath the Jewish yoke.
No craftsmen's income is too small
For Jews to demand it all.
He needs a suit, a pair of shoes?

Off he goes trudging to the Jews;
There he finds pewter, silver plate,
Velvet and linen stuffs, brocade,
The things that he himself not owns
Jews hold as pledges for their loans,
Or buy from highwayman and thief
To make their pile from Christian grief.
Stolen or found, cheap stuff or rare,
Look at the Jew's; you'll find it there.
He's got the cash to lend on it,
No questions asked, depend on it.
A piece worth fifty gulden when
Bought new, the Jew gets it for ten,
Holds on to it two weeks or three,
Then claims it as his property,
Converts his house into a store
With pants and coats stuffed roof to floor;
A cobbler can't sell a pair of shoes,
Townfolk buy only from the Jews.

But these misdeeds, though they are cursed
By all the world, are not their worst.
A graver crime and fouler deed
Lies on this Godforsaken breed.
Obstinate, blind, faithless toward
Their patient, kind, forgiving Lord,
They've always sinned, never repent,
As we learn from the Old Testament.
The five books of Moses, the Book of Kings
Show how the Jew to his habits clings;
They prove it to satiety:
Jews are a race without piety.
We're told by wise old Jeremiah
That they killed their prophets with sword and fire.
David, among their kings the first,
They sent to hell despised and cursed.
Moses, a demigod to Jews,
They covered with hatred and abuse.
No wonder, given such behavior,
They crucified God's son, our savior.
They're in the dark, can't see the clearing,
They'll never give their prophets hearing,
Must live forever in God's ban;
Who gives them aid is no Christian man.

Jewish malignity was foretold
by the prophet Isaiah in days of old;
And if further evidence you desire,
Ask Doctor Balthasar Hubmair

To tell you why it is that we
Treat the Jews with such hostility.
He'll waste no time convincing you
(By quoting God's own Gospel, too)
That there's no punishment too painful
For a tribe so openly disdainful
Not only of Christ, their adversary,
But of his mother, the Virgin Mary.
For a Christian there's no sin so great
As to merit a Jew's love, not his hate.
Unceasingly the Jewish swine
Scheme how to violate, malign,
Dishonor the pure Virgin Maid,
Our Christian solace, hope, and aid,
Whose son died on the cross that we
Might live in bliss eternally.
No city therefore can fare well
Until it's sent its Jews to hell.

Now listen and pay careful heed
To a horrendous, bestial deed
Of Christian blood shed without pity
By murderous Jews in our city.
It happened in Emperor Frederick's reign;
Six children they killed with dreadful pain.
Into a dungeon then they threw them
To hide the bodies, bleeding and gruesome.
But soon their crime was indicated,
All of the Jews incarcerated,
And the burghers resolved, for the Virgin's sake,
To burn the damned Jews at the stake.
But—though to tell it is a disgrace—
The Jews found help in an exalted place.
Our council spent what money it could
To keep the Jews from winning their suit,
But with the emperor to defend
Their case, the Jews won in the end.
This caused complaints and lamentations;
Citizens sent deputations
To ask why Jewish dogs who spilled
Pure Christian blood should not be killed.
As for the Jews, they caught the drift
Of things, made many a handsome gift
Where money counts; their silver and gold
Regained for them their old foothold.
The burghers would have burned the Jews,
But the emperor saw fit to refuse.
The might and glory of his crown
Served to keep Jews in our town.
Our councillors resented this intervention,
Which frustrated their good intention
Of just revenge on the blaspheming Jew
For the innocent children whom they slew.

The gold sent abroad also caused them grief;
It could have been used for poor relief.
Three years they wasted in vain appeal,
But the emperor adhered to his deal.
Nothing the councilors could say
Would change his mind; the Jews must stay.

For forty years we pressed our case
Against the murderous Jewish race.
Of money paid out, the total score
Was a hundred and thirty-five thousand gulden or
    more;
The city registers record it.
Our citizens could scarcely afford it,
While the Jews, who had much more to spend,
Bribed the emperor's courtiers to pretend
To Maximilian, double-tongued,
That the Jews of Regensburg had been wronged.
Money makes lies like truth appear,
And the facts were kept from the emperor's ear.
Thus matters stood, justice defied,
Until the day Maximilian died,
And God eliminated a few
Of our Jew-loving burghers, too,
Which left the Jews without a friend
Their horrid actions to defend.
That's all I'll say about them here,
Their stubborn blindness cost them dear.
We're free at last of their oppressions;
May God forgive them their transgressions.

Document Set 14.8 References

A. France Emerges from the Hundred Years' War
   French account, in James Harvey Robinson, ed., *Readings in European History* (Boston: Ginn, 1904), 1:474–475.
B. The Tailors of Exeter Regulate Their Lives, 1466
   Ordinances of the Gild of the Tailors, in *Smith's English Gilds* (Early English Text Society, 1870), 312–316.
C. Enclosures Disrupt Late Fifteenth-Century England
   Government report, in H. E. S. Fisher and A. R. J. Jurica, eds., *Documents in English Economic History* (London: G. Bell, 1977), 1:117.
D. Louis XI of France Hunts and Schemes
   Commynes, *Memoirs*, in James Harvey Robinson, ed., *Readings in European History* (Boston: Ginn, 1904), 1:481–483.
E. The *Malleus Maleficarum* Tells How to Torture a Suspected Witch
   Translations and Reprints from the Original Sources of European History (Philadelphia: University of Pennsylvania Press, 1898), 3/2:11–13.
F. "How the Jews Were Driven from Regensburg"
   Anonymous verse, in Gerald Strauss, *Manifestations of Discontent in Germany on the Eve of the Reformation* (Bloomington: University of Indiana Press, 1971), 124–129.

15

The Struggle for Faith and Power, 1494–1560

DOCUMENT SET 15.1
Wider Horizons in the Old World: The Portuguese Explore Africa and the East

Seeking to outflank middlemen and trade for gold at the source, fifteenth-century Portuguese adventurers explored farther and farther south along the coast of West Africa as they simultaneously learned the vital skill of tacking back north against winds and currents. As early as the mid-fifteenth century, they began establishing trading posts in West Africa. Document A, by a Venetian who sailed with the Portuguese as far as present-day Mauretania, describes how the Europeans were also discovering a lucrative trade in African slaves. This is one of the earliest sources documenting the European-African encounter and the Atlantic slave trade; read it for evidence of the attitudes on both sides.

Document B was written three-quarters of a century later. The Portuguese had by then rounded the Cape, reached India, and blazed a commercial route to Canton (Guangchou) in southern China. It is instructive reading for the mind-sets that it reveals.

A. The Portuguese Encounter Africans and the Slave Trade, 1455–1456

You should also know that behind this Cauo Bianco on the land, is a place called Hoden,[1] which is about

[1] Wadan, an important desert market about 350 miles east of Arguim. Later, in 1487, when the Portuguese were endeavouring to penetrate the interior they attempted to establish a trading factory at Wadan which acted as a feeder to Arguim, tapping the northbound caravan traffic and diverting some of it to the west coast.

six days inland by camel. This place is not walled, but is frequented by Arabs, and is a market where the caravans arrive from Tanbutu [Timbuktu], and from other places in the land of the Blacks, on their way to our nearer Barbary. The food of the peoples of this place is dates, and barley, of which there is sufficient, for they grow in some of these places, but not abundantly. They drink the milk of camels and other animals, for they have no wine. They also have cows and goats, but not many, for the land is dry. Their oxen and cows, compared with ours, are small.

They are Muhammadans, and very hostile to Christians. They never remain settled, but are always wandering over these deserts. These are the men who go to the land of the Blacks, and also to our nearer Barbary. They are very numerous, and have many camels on which they carry brass and silver from Barbary and other things to Tanbuto and to the land of the Blacks. Thence they carry away gold and pepper, which they bring hither. They are brown complexioned, and wear white cloaks edged with a red stripe: their women also dress thus, without shifts. On their heads the men wear turbans in the Moorish fashion, and they always go barefooted. In these sandy districts there are many lions, leopards, and ostriches, the eggs of which I have often eaten and found good.

You should know that the said Lord Infante of Portugal [the crown prince, Henry the Navigator] has leased this island of Argin to Christians [for ten years], so that no one can enter the bay to trade with the Arabs save those who hold the license. These have dwellings on the island and factories where they buy and sell with the said Arabs who come to the coast to trade for merchandise of various kinds, such as woollen cloths, cotton, silver, and "alchezeli," that is, cloaks, carpets, and similar articles and above all, corn, for they are always short of food. They give in exchange slaves whom the Arabs bring from the land of the Blacks, and gold *tiber*. The Lord Infante therefore caused a castle to be built on the island to protect this trade for ever. For this reason, Portuguese caravels are coming and going all the year to this island.

These Arabs also have many Berber horses, which they trade, and take to the Land of the Blacks, exchanging them with the rulers for slaves. Ten or fifteen slaves are given for one of these horses, according to their quality. The Arabs likewise take articles of Moorish silk, made in Granata and in Tunis of Barbary, silver, and other goods, obtaining in exchange any number of these slaves, and some gold. These slaves are brought to the market and town of Hoden; there they are divided: some go to the mountains of Barcha, and thence to Sicily, [others to the said town of Tunis and to all the coasts of Barbary], and others again are taken to this place, Argin, and sold to the Portuguese leaseholders. As a result every year the Portuguese carry away from Argin a thousand slaves. Note that before this traffic was organized, the Portuguese caravels, sometimes four, sometimes more, were wont to come armed to the Golfo d'Argin, and descending on the land by night, would assail the fisher villages, and so ravage the land. Thus they took of these Arabs both men and women, and carried them to Portugal for sale: behaving in a like manner along all the rest of the coast, which stretches from Cauo Bianco to the Rio di Senega and even beyond. . . .

B. Portuguese Emissaries Reach China, 1517

God grant that these Chinese may be fools enough to lose the country; because up to the present they have had no dominion, but little by little they have gone on taking the land from their neighbours; and for this reason the kingdom is great, because the Chinese are full of much cowardice, and hence they come to be presumptuous, arrogant, cruel; and because up to the present, being a cowardly people, they have managed without arms and without any practice of war, and have always gone on getting the land from their neighbors, and not by force but by stratagems and deceptions; and they imagine that no one can do them harm. They call every foreigner a savage; and their country they call the kingdom of God. Whoever shall come now, let it be a captain with a fleet of ten or fifteen sail. The first thing will be to destroy the fleet if they should have one, which I believe they have not; let it be by fire and blood and cruel fear for this day, without sparing the life of a single person, every junk being burnt, and no one being taken prisoner, in order not to waste the provisions, because at all times a hundred Chinese will be found for one Portuguese. And this done, Nanto must be cleared, and at once they will have a fortress and provisions if they wish, because it will at once be in their power; and then with the whole fleet attack Aynācha, which lies at the bar of Tācoam, as I have already said above having a good port. Here the ships, which cannot enter the river, will be anchored, and whatever craft they may have will be burnt; and after it has been taken if it seem good the town can be burnt, in order to terrify the Chinese. . . .

Document Set 15.1 References

A. The Portuguese Encounter Africans and the Slave Trade, 1455–1456
Alvise da Ca' da Mosto, "Description of Capo Bianco and the Islands Nearest to It," in J. H. Parry, *European Reconnaissance: Selected Documents* (New York: Walker, 1968), 59–61.
B. Portuguese Emissaries Reach China, 1517
Letters from Canton, trans. and ed. D. Ferguson, *The Indian Antiquary* 31 (Jan. 1902): 10–30, in Perry, *European Reconnaissance*, 140.

DOCUMENT SET 15.2
New Worlds: America

Except for Brazil, the lands of the Western Hemisphere fell to explorers sent out by the Spanish rather than by the Portuguese crown. Document A, describing one of the earliest European contacts with Native Americans, is dated November 8, 1492. It is an extract from Christopher Columbus's log, entered one month after his first landfall in the Bahamas. Here he meets the native population of Cuba. In what ways does Columbus suggest what was to be the Indians' subsequent fate, and why?

By 1518, Spain had already done so thorough a job of carving out colonies in the Caribbean that Castilian adventurers like Hernando Cortés were itching to seek new lands to conquer. Mexico, which Cortés and his small band of soldiers attacked, was a sophisticated civilization and a highly organized state. Cortés's letters to Charles V reported the progress of his conquest, reflecting both admiration for the grandeur of Aztec urban civilization and disgust at the human sacrifices and cannibalism with which the Aztecs coerced their subjects. Evaluate his letters describing Tenochtitlán (today Mexico City) as a valuable source of early ethnography and a justification for imperialism.

The conduct of the new Spanish lords of the Caribbean was harshly criticized by Dominican friars like Fray Anton Montesino. Document C is taken from the famous account of another Dominican, Bartolomé de las Casas (1474–1566), who had first come to Hispaniola as a layman to join in its exploitation but was converted to becoming the Indians' defender by witnessing horrors such as Montesino here describes. Evaluate the source of the Dominicans' concerns and what they proposed to do to halt the atrocities.

Document D is an extract from a mid-sixteenth-century Venetian ambassador's report. The gold and silver pouring into Spain from the Americas astonished everyone, but its chief economic impact was to touch off sustained inflation throughout Europe as the Spanish monarchy turned its gold into money with which to settle the enormous debts that its wars and diplomacy incurred. Read this document for signs of the ambassador's understanding of what was occurring.

A. Christopher Columbus Reaches Land, 1492

It appears to me that it would be well to take some of these people . . . to the Sovereigns, in order that they might learn our language and we might learn what there is in this country. Upon return they may speak the language of the Christians and take our customs and Faith to their people. I see and know that these people have no religion whatever, nor are they idolaters, but rather, they are very meek and know no evil. They do not kill or capture others and are without weapons. They are so timid that a hundred of them flee from one of us. . . . They are very trusting; they believe that there is a God in Heaven, and they firmly believe that we come from Heaven. . . . Therefore, Your Highnesses must resolve to make them Christians. I believe that if this effort commences, in a short time a multitude of peoples will be converted to our Holy Faith, and Spain will acquire great domains and riches and all of their villages. Beyond doubt there is a very great amount of gold in this country. . . .

B. Hernando Cortez Approaches Tenochtitlán, 1521

This great city of Tenochtitlán is built on the salt lake. . . . It has four approaches by means of artificial causeways. . . . The city is as large as Seville or Cordoba. Its streets . . . are very broad and straight, some of these, and all the others, are one half land, and the other half water on which they go about in canoes. . . . There are bridges, very large, strong, and well constructed, so that, over many, ten horsemen can ride abreast. . . . The city has many squares where markets are held. . . . There is one square, twice as large as that of Salamanca, all surrounded by arcades, where there are daily more than sixty thousand souls, buying and selling . . . in the service and manners of its people, their fashion of living was almost the same as in Spain, with just as much harmony and order; and considering that these people were barbarous, so cut off from the knowledge of God and other civilized peoples, it is admirable to see to what they attained in every respect. [Second letter]

It happened . . . that a Spaniard saw an Indian . . . eating a piece of flesh taken from the body of an Indian who had been killed. . . . I had the culprit burned, explaining that the cause was his having killed that Indian and eaten him which was prohibited by Your Majesty, and by me in Your Royal name. I further made the chief understand that all the people . . . must abstain from this custom. . . . I came . . . to protect their lives as well as their property, and to teach them that they were to adore but one God . . . that they must turn from their idols, and the rites they had practised until then, for these were lies and deceptions which the devil . . . had invented. . . . I, likewise, had come to teach them that Your Majesty, by the will of Divine Providence, rules the universe, and that they also must submit themselves to the imperial yoke, and do all that we who are Your Majesty's ministers here might order them. . . . [Fifth letter]

C. Antón Montesino Preaches in Hispaniola

The Dominican friars had already pondered on the sad life and harsh captivity suffered by the natives on the island and had noticed the Spanish lack of concern for their fate except as a business loss which brought about no softening of their oppression. There were two kinds of Spaniards, one very cruel and pitiless, whose goal was to squeeze the last drop of Indian blood in order to get rich, and one less cruel, who must have felt sorry for the Indians; but in each case they placed their own interests above the health and salvation of those poor people. Of all those who used Indians, I knew only one man, Pedro de Rentería—of whom there will be much to say later, if God so wills—who was pious toward them. The friars, then, weighed these matters as well as the innocence, the inestimable patience and the gentleness of Indians, and deliberated on the following points among themselves. Weren't these people human beings? Wasn't justice and charity owed them? Had they no right to their own territory, their own kingdoms? Have they offended us? Aren't we under obligation to preach to them the Christian religion and work diligently toward their conversion? How is it that in fifteen or sixteen years their number has so decreased, since they tell us how crowded it was when they first came here? . . .

The most scholarly among them [the Dominicans] composed the first sermon on the subject by order of their superior, fray Pedro de Córdoba, and they all signed it to show that it represented common sentiment and not that of the preacher alone. They gave it to their most important preacher, Fray Antón Montesino, who was the second of three preachers the Order had sent here. Fray Antón Montesino's talent lay in a certain sternness when reproaching faults and a certain way of reading sermons both choleric and efficient, which was thought to reap great results. So then, as a very animated speaker, they gave him that first sermon on such a new theme; the novelty consisting in saying that killing a man is more serious than killing a beetle. They set aside the fourth week of Advent for the sermon, since the Gospel according to St. John that week is "The Pharisees asked St. John the Baptist who he was and he said: *Ego vox clamantis in deserto.*" ["I am a voice crying in the wilderness."] The whole city of Santo Domingo was to be there, including the admiral Diego Columbus, and all the jurists and royal officials, who had been notified each and every one individually to come and hear a sermon of great importance. They accepted readily, some out of respect for the virtue of the friars; others, out of curiosity to hear what was to be said that concerned them so much, though had they known, they would have refused to come and would have censured the sermon as well.

At the appointed time fray Antón Montesino went to the pulpit and announced the theme of the sermon: *Ego vox clamantis in deserto.* After the introductory words on Advent, he compared the sterility of the desert to the conscience of the Spaniards who lived on Hispaniola in a state of blindness, a danger of damnation, sunk deep in the waters of insensitivity and drowning without being aware of it. Then he said: "I have come here in order to declare it unto you, I the voice of Christ in the desert of this island. Open your hearts and your senses, all of you, for this voice will speak new things harshly, and will be frightening." For a good while the voice spoke in such punitive terms that the congregation trembled as if facing Judgment Day. "This voice," he continued, "says that you are living in deadly sin for the atrocities you tyrannically impose on these innocent people. Tell me, what right have you to enslave them? What authority did you use to make war against them who lived at peace on their territories, killing them cruelly with methods never before heard of? How can you oppress them and not care to feed or cure them, and work them to death to satisfy your greed? And why don't you look after their spiritual health, so that they should come to know God, that they should be baptized, and that they should hear Mass and keep the holy days? Aren't they human beings? Have they no rational soul? Aren't you obligated to love them as you love yourselves? Don't you understand? How can you live in such a lethargical dream? You may rest assured that you are in no better state of salvation than the Moors [Muslims of Spain] or the Turks who reject the Christian Faith." The voice had astounded them all; some reacted as if they had lost their senses, some were petrified and others showed signs of repentance, but no one was really convinced. After his sermon, he descended from the pulpit holding his head straight, as if unafraid—he wasn't the kind of man to show fear—for much was at stake in displeasing the audience by speaking what had to be said, and he went on to his thin cabbage soup and the straw house of his Order accompanied by a friend. . . .

[Although the settlers request that the Domini-cans apologize, Frey Montesino preaches again.]

To return to the subject: they left the church in a state of rage and again salted their meal that day with bitterness. Not bothering with the friars, since conversation with them had proved useless, they decided to tell the King [Ferdinand] on the first occasion that the Dominicans had scandalized the world by spreading a new doctrine that condemned them all to Hell because they used Indians in the mines, a doctrine that went against the orders of His Highness and aimed at nothing else but to deprive him of both power and a source of income. The King required an interview with the Castilian provincial of the Order—the friars of Hispaniola had not yet been granted a charter—and complained to him about his choice of friars, who had done him a great disservice by preaching against the state and causing disturbances all over the world. The King ordered him to correct this by threatening to take action. You see how easy it is to deceive a King, how ruinous to a kingdom it is to heed misinformation, and how oppression thrives where truth is not allowed a voice.

D. A Venetian Ambassador Reports on Spain's Apparent Wealth from the Gold of the Indies, 1559

From New Spain are obtained gold and silver, cochineal (little insects like flies), from which crimson dye is made, leather, cotton, sugar and other things; but from Peru nothing is obtained except minerals. The fifth part of all that is produced goes to the king, but since the gold and silver is brought to Spain and he has a tenth part of that which goes to the mint and is refined and coined, he eventually gets one-fourth of the whole sum, which fourth does not exceed in all four or five hundred thousand ducats, although it is reckoned not alone at millions, but at millions of pounds. Nor is it likely that it will long remain at this figure, because great quantities of gold and silver are no longer found upon the surface of the earth, as they have been in past years; and to penetrate into the bowels of the earth requires greater effort, skill and outlay, and the Spaniards are not willing to do the work themselves, and the natives cannot be forced to do so, because the Emperor has freed them from all obligation of service as soon as they accept the Christian religion. Wherefore it is necessary to acquire negro slaves, who are brought from the coasts of Africa, both within and without the Straits, and these are selling dearer every day, because on account of their natural lack of strength and the change of climate, added to the lack of discretion upon the part of their masters in making them work too hard and giving them too little to eat, they fall sick and the greater part of them die.

Document Set 15.2 References

A. Christopher Columbus Reaches Land, 1492
   The Log of Christopher Columbus, trans. Robert H. Fuson (Camden, Maine: International Marine, 1987), 106–107.
B. Hernando Cortez Approaches Tenochtitlán, 1521
   Letters of Cortes, trans. Francis A. MacNutt (New York: 1908), 1:256–257, 2:244.
C. Anton Montesino Preaches in Hispaniola
   B. de Las Casas, *History of the Indies,* trans. and ed. Andrée Collard (New York: Harper & Row, 1971), 181–187.
D. A Venetian Ambassador Reports on Spain's Apparent Wealth from the Gold of the Indies, 1559
   Michele Soriano, *Relazione di Spagna,* in *Translations and Reprints from the Original Sources of European History* (Philadelphia: University of Pennsylvania Press, 1898), 3/3:5–6.

DOCUMENT SET 15.3
New Worlds: The Cosmos

America, Africa, and the East were not the only "New Worlds" that Europeans encountered at the beginning of the sixteenth century. New vistas also opened as a handful of Western thinkers began to contemplate the universe anew. In his secret notebooks, the great artist and thinker Leonardo da Vinci (1452–1519) entered, at some unknown date, the cryptic speculations about the sun that form Document A. Exactly where Leonardo may have gotten his ideas (if they were not wholly original with him) is unclear, but it should be remembered that Leonardo was not formally trained in philosophy or science and hence was free, indeed scornful, of traditional learning based on ancient authority.

Nicholas Copernicus (1473–1543) differed from Leonardo in having received a thorough technical education in mathematics and astronomy, but he resembled the Italian artist in his wish to keep his speculations secret until they could be properly understood by the competent few. At some point in the early sixteenth century (experts differ as to the date), he set down his revolutionary thoughts about the cosmos in an unpublished manuscript known as the *Commentariolus* ("little commentary"), excerpted here as Document B. Copernicus proceeded to spend the rest of his life working out the mathematics to support his new hypothesis, while also carrying out the duties of a cathedral canon and administrator in a remote corner of what used to be called East Prussia. Notice Copernicus's reasoning in the *Commentariolus* and his profound awareness of the precedents of ancient Greek thought; all his life he thought himself merely the *corrector*, not the supplanter of Ptolemy. Copernicus was reluctant to publish his masterwork *On the Revolutions of the Heavenly Bodies,* in which he demonstrated his theories mathematically—probably he feared ridicule, and certainly he knew that only an expert could understand what he had to say. In 1542 a German scholar finally persuaded him to publish, and when the first copy came off the press in 1543, the author lay on his deathbed. The editor (Andreas Osiander) wrote a preface (Document C) that completely distorted what Copernicus meant the book to assert. The ways in which conventionally educated Europeans reacted to news that an obscure Polish astronomer had questioned the physical reality of Ptolemy's and Aristotle's universe may be gauged from Martin Luther's off-the-cuff remarks (Document D).

A. Leonardo da Vinci Speculates on the Cosmos

Demonstration that the Earth is a Star
In your discourse you must prove that the earth is a star much like the moon, and the glory of our universe; and then you must treat of the size of various stars according to the authors.

The sun does not move.

The sun has substance, shape, motion, radiance, heat, and generative power: and these qualities all emanate from it without its diminution.

The sun has never seen any shadow.

Praise of the Sun
If you look at the stars without their rays (as may be done by looking at them through a small hole made with the extreme point of a fine needle and placed so as almost to touch the eye), you will see these stars to be so minute that it would seem as though nothing could be smaller; it is in fact the great distance which is the reason of their diminution, for many of them are very many times larger than the star which is the earth with the water. Think, then, what this star of ours would seem like at so great a distance, and then consider how many stars might be set in longitude and latitude between these stars which are scattered throughout this dark expanse. I can never do other than blame many of those ancients who said that the sun was no larger than it appears; among these being Epicurus; and I believe that he reasoned thus from the effects of a light placed in our atmosphere equidistant from the centre; whoever sees it never sees it diminished in size at any distance. . . .

But I wish I had words to serve me to blame those who would fain extol the worship of men above that of the sun; for in the whole universe I do not see a body of greater magnitude and power than this, and its light illumines all the celestial bodies which are distributed throughout the universe. All vital force descends from it since the heat that is in living creatures comes from the soul (vital spark); and there is no other heat nor light in the universe. . . . And certainly those who have chosen to worship men as gods such as Jove, Saturn, Mars, and the like have made a very great error, seeing that even if a man were as large as our earth he would seem like one of the least of the stars which appears but a speck in the universe; and seeing also that men are mortal and subject to decay and corruption in their tombs.

The Spera and Marullo and many others praise the sun.

B. Nicholas Copernicus Explains His First Heliocentric Hypothesis, 1520s

Our ancestors assumed, I observe, a large number of celestial spheres for this reason especially, to explain the apparent motion of the planets by the principle of regularity. For they thought it altogether absurd that a heavenly body, which is a perfect sphere, should not always move uniformly. They saw that by connecting and combining regular motions in various ways they could make any body appear to move to any position.

Callippus and Eudoxus, who endeavored to solve the problem by the use of concentric spheres, were unable to account for all the planetary movements; they had to explain not merely the apparent revolutions of the planets but also the fact that these bodies appear to us sometimes to mount higher in the heavens, sometimes to descend; and this fact is incompatible with the principle of concentricity. Therefore it seemed better to employ eccentrics and epicycles, a system which most scholars finally accepted.

Yet the planetary theories of Ptolemy and most other astronomers, although consistent with the numerical data, seemed likewise to present no small difficulty. For these theories were not adequate unless certain equants were also conceived; it then appeared that a planet moved with uniform velocity neither on its deferent nor about the center of its epicycle. Hence a system of this sort seemed neither sufficiently absolute nor sufficiently pleasing to the mind.

Having become aware of these defects, I often considered whether there could perhaps be found a more reasonable arrangement of circles, from which every apparent inequality would be derived and in which everything would move uniformly about its proper center, as the rule of absolute motion requires. After I had addressed myself to this very difficult and almost insoluble problem, the suggestion at length came to me how it could be solved with fewer and much simpler constructions than were formerly used, if some assumptions (which are called axioms) were granted me. They follow in this order.

Assumptions

1. There is no one center of all the celestial circles or spheres.

2. The center of the earth is not the center of the universe, but only of gravity and of the lunar sphere.

3. All the spheres revolve about the sun as their mid-point, and therefore the sun is the center of the universe.

4. The ratio of the earth's distance from the sun to the height of the firmament is so much smaller than the ratio of the earth's radius to its distance from the sun that the distance from the earth to the sun is imperceptible in comparison with the height of the firmament.

5. Whatever motion appears in the firmament arises not from any motion of the firmament, but from the earth's motion. The earth together with its circumjacent elements performs a complete rotation on its fixed poles in a daily motion, while the firmament and highest heaven abide unchanged.

6. What appear to us as motions of the sun arise not from its motion but from the motion of the earth and our sphere, with which we revolve about the sun like any other planet. The earth has, then, more than one motion.

7. The apparent retrograde and direct motion of the planets arises not from their motion but from the earth's. The motion of the earth alone, therefore, suffices to explain so many apparent inequalities in the heavens.

Having set forth these assumptions, I shall endeavor briefly to show how uniformity of the motions can be saved in a systematic way. However, I have thought it well, for the sake of brevity, to omit from this sketch mathematical demonstrations, reserving these for my larger work. But in the explanation of the circles I shall set down here the lengths of the radii; and from these the reader who is not unacquainted with mathematics will readily perceive how closely this arrangement of circles agrees with the numerical data and observations.

Accordingly, let no one suppose that I have gratuitously asserted, with the Pythagoreans, the motion of the earth; strong proof will be found in my exposition of the circles. For the principal arguments by which the natural philosophers attempt to establish the immobility of the earth rest for the most part on the appearances; it is particularly such arguments that collapse here, since I treat the earth's immobility as due to an appearance.

C. Copernicus's Editor Distorts *De Revolutionibus*, 1543

To the Reader Concerning the Hypotheses of This Work:

There have already been widespread reports about the novel hypotheses of this work, which declares that the earth moves whereas the sun is at rest in the center of the universe. Hence certain scholars, I have no doubt, are deeply offended and believe that the liberal arts, which were established long ago on a sound basis, should not be thrown into confusion. But if these men are willing to examine the matter closely, they will find that the author of this work has done nothing blameworthy. For it is the duty of an astronomer to compose the history of the celestial motions through careful and expert study. Then he must conceive and devise the causes of these motions or hypotheses about them. Since he cannot in any way attain to the true causes, he will adopt whatever suppositions enable the motions to be computed correctly from the principles of geometry for the future as well as the past. The present author has performed both these duties excellently. For these hypotheses need not be true nor even probable. On the contrary, if they provide a calculus consistent with the observations, that alone is enough. Perhaps there is someone who is so ignorant of geometry and optics that he regards the epicycle of Venus as probable, or thinks that it is the reason why Venus sometimes precedes and sometimes follows the sun by forty degrees and even more. Is there anyone who is not aware that from this assumption it necessarily follows that the diameter of the planet at perigee should appear more than four times, and the body of the planet more than sixteen times, as great as at apogee? Yet this variation is refuted by the experience of every age. In this science there are some other no less important absurdities, which need not be set forth at the moment. For this art, it is quite clear, is completely and absolutely ignorant of the causes of the apparent nonuniform motions. And if any causes are devised by the imagination, as indeed very many are, they are not put forward to convince anyone that they are true, but merely to provide a reliable basis for computation. However, since different hypotheses are sometimes offered for one and the same motion (for example, eccentricity and an epicycle for the sun's motion), the astronomer will take as his first choice that hypothesis which is the easiest to grasp. The philosopher will perhaps rather seek the semblance of the truth. But neither of them will understand or state anything certain, unless it has been divinely revealed to him.

Therefore alongside the ancient hypotheses, which are no more probable, let us permit these new hypotheses also to become known, especially since they are admirable as well as simple and bring with them a huge treasure of very skillful observations. So far as hypotheses are concerned, let no one expect anything certain from astronomy, which cannot furnish it, lest he accept as the truth ideas conceived for another purpose, and depart from this study a greater fool than when he entered it. Farewell.

D. Martin Luther Hears About Copernicus

There was mention of a certain new astrologer who wanted to prove that the earth moves and not the sky, the sun, and the moon. This would be as if somebody were riding on a cart or in a ship and imagined that he was standing still while the earth and the trees were moving. [Luther remarked,] "So it goes now. Whoever wants to be clever must agree with nothing that others esteem. He must do something of his own. This is what that fellow does who wishes to turn the whole of astronomy upside down. Even in these things that are thrown into disorder I believe the Holy Scriptures, for Joshua commanded the sun to stand still and not the earth."

Document Set 15.3 References

A. Leonardo da Vinci Speculates on the Cosmos
  Selections from the Notebooks of Leonardo da Vinci, ed. Irma A. Richter (Oxford, England: Oxford University Press, 1977), 54–55.
B. Nicholas Copernicus Explains His First Heliocentric Hypothesis, 1520s
  Copernicus, "The Commentariolus," in Edward Rosen, *Three Copernican Treatises,* 3d. ed. (New York: Octagon, 1971), 57–59.
C. Copernicus's Editor Distorts *De Revolutionibus,* 1543
  Osiander, "Address to the Reader," Preface to Copernicus's *De Revolutionibus,* in Edward Rosen, ed., *Copernicus and the Scientific Revolution* (Melbourne, Fla.: Krieger, 1984), 195–196.
D. Martin Luther Hears About Copernicus
  Luther, *Table Talk,* in Rosen, *Copernicus and the Scientific Revolution,* 182–183.

DOCUMENT SET 15.4
The Dream of Renovation: Savonarola and the Christian Humanists

Girolamo Savonarola (1452–1498) was no humanist but a passionately committed Dominican moralist and preacher who in the 1490s exerted a magnetic spell over Florence, including many of its intellectuals and artists. A critic of the Medici regime, Savonarola was thrust into power by the French invasion of 1494, which he interpreted as God's judgment on a wicked society. His vision of Florence transformed into a just, godly community (Document A) bears strong resemblance to the kind of purified regime many Christian reformers would later try to impose on sixteenth-century cities. Was it a practical program?

The prince of humanists on the eve of the reformation was the Dutchman Desiderius Erasmus (1466–1536). Traveling to Italy in 1506, Erasmus saw for himself the corruption and pomp of the papacy and the devastation of the wars brought on in part by papal politics. The wonderfully wicked scene in Document B comes from a short Latin dialogue that Erasmus published anonymously in 1517. *Julius Excluded* enjoyed a huge success, much to the church's anger. What do you see in it that prefigures the critique reformers like Luther would soon launch against the Catholic church? Erasmus's greatest work of satire, *The Praise of Folly* (1509), like all great comedy, not only ridicules but also brings home enduring truths of human character. What elements of mockery and idealism do you see in the extract that forms Document C?

An equally devastating satire was published in 1515 by the German humanist Ulrich von Hutten, the *Letters of Obscure Men.* Occasioned by clerical attacks on a humanist who had tried to study the Hebrew scriptures and the mystical cabala, Hutten's *Letters* were written in the crabbed Latin style of old-fashioned scholastics and were intended to mock all conservative resistance to the new learning—and, incidentally, also the externals of traditional piety.

A. Savonarola Proposes to Make Florence Perfect

Every Florentine citizen who wants to be a good member of his city and to help her, as everyone should wish to do, must first of all believe that this council and this civil government were ordained by God. This is true, indeed, not only because all good government comes from God, but also and especially because of the providential care which God has recently manifested in preserving the city. No one who has lived here for the past three years and is not blind and devoid of judgment would deny that, but for the hand of God, this government would never have been created against so much and such powerful opposition, nor would it have maintained itself to this day among so many traitors and so few friends. God, however, demands of us that we ourselves use the intellect and the free will he has given us. He has made all that pertains to government imperfect at first, so that with his help we can improve it. This government is still imperfect and has many flaws. We have hardly more than the foundation. Every citizen, therefore, should strive to perfect it. It can be made perfect only if all or at least the majority are blessed with the following four virtues.

First, fear of God. . . . ①

Second, love of the common good. When they hold offices and other dignities, the citizens must put ② aside all private interests and all the special needs of their relatives and friends. They must think solely of the common good. . . .

Third, love of one another. The citizens must ③ drop feuds and forget all past offenses. Hatred, bad feelings, and envy blind the eye of the intellect and do not let it see the truth. Sitting in councils and in public offices, anyone who is not well purged in this regard will make many mistakes. . . .

Fourth, justice. Justice purges the city of bad ④ men, or makes them live in fear. The good and just endure in high authority because they are gladly elected to office by those who love justice. They are enlightened by God in legislation and in guiding the city to a happy state. Justice will make the city fill up with goodness because it always rewards goodness; and the good men, wanting to live where there is justice, will congregate there in great numbers. God, for justice also, will increase the city's empire, as he did that of the Romans. Because the Romans exercised strict and severe justice, He gave them imperial power over the whole world. He wanted justice to make his peoples righteous.

The Florentine citizens, if they deliberate and use rational judgment, will see that they require no other government than the one we have described. If they have faith, moreover, that it was given to them by God, and exercise the four virtues we have named, their government will doubtless be soon perfected. . . .

[handwritten note: Julius Exclusus]

B. Erasmus Shuts Pope Julius II Out of Heaven

[In this opening scene, Pope Julius finds heaven's gate locked and St. Peter, the gatekeeper, less than friendly.]

[handwritten note: arrogance.]

Julius: How about opening the door, you, right away! If you wanted to do your job right you would have come to meet me—with the whole parade of angels, in fact.

Peter: Pretty bossy, all right. But first, you tell me who you are. . . .

Julius: Cut out the foolishness, if you have any sense. For your information, I am the famous Julius the Ligurian, and I trust you recognize the letters P.M., unless you have forgotton the alphabet altogether.

Peter: I take it they stand for Pestilential Maximum . . .

Julius: Oh, come on—they stand for Pontifex Maximus, the supreme Pontiff. . . . Why don't you cut out the nonsense and open the door, unless you would rather have it battered down? In a word—do you see what a retinue I have?

Peter: To be sure, I see thoroughly hardened brigands. But in case you don't know it, these doors you must storm with other weapons.

Julius: Enough talk, I say! Unless you obey right away, I shall hurl—even against you—the thunderbolt of excommunication, with which I once terrified the mightiest of kings, or for that matter whole kingdoms. You see the Bull already prepared for this purpose?

Peter: What damned thunderbolt, what thunder, what Bulls, what bombast are you talking to me about, pray? We never heard anything of those matters from Christ.

C. Erasmus Mocks the Externals of Piety

To this same class of fools belong those who beguile themselves with the silly but pleasing notion that if they look upon a picture or image of St. Christopher,—that huge Polyphemus,—they will not die that day; or that he who salutes an image of St. Barbara with the proper form of address will come back from battle safe; or that one who approaches St. Erasmus on certain days with wax candles and prayers will soon be rich. They have found a new Hercules in St. George,—a sort of second Hippolytus. They seem to adore even his horse, which is scrupulously decked out with gorgeous trappings, and additional offerings are constantly being made in the hope of gaining new favors. His bronze helmet one would think half divine, the way people swear by it.

And what shall I say of those who comfortably delude themselves with imaginary pardons for their sins, and who measure the time in purgatory with an hourglass into years, months, days, and hours, with all the precision of a mathematical table? There are plenty, too, who, relying upon certain magical little certificates and prayers,—which some pious impostor devised either in fun or for the benefit of his pocket,—believe that they may procure riches, honor, future happiness, health, perpetual prosperity, long life, a lusty old age,—nay, in the end, a seat at the right hand of Christ in heaven; but as for this last, it matters not how long it be deferred: they will content themselves with the joys of heaven only when they must finally surrender the pleasures of this world, to which they lovingly cling. *[handwritten note in margin: like indulgences?]*

The trader, the soldier, and the judge think that they can clean up the Augean stable of a lifetime, once for all, by sacrificing a single coin from their ill-gotten gains. They flatter themselves that all sorts of perjury, debauchery, drunkenness, quarrels, bloodshed, imposture, perfidy, and treason can be compounded for by contract and so adjusted that, having paid off their arrears, they can begin a new score.

How foolish, or rather how happy, are those who promise themselves more than supernal happiness if they repeat the verses of the seven holy psalms! Those magical lines are supposed to have been taught to St. Bernard by a demon, who seems to have been a wag; but he was not very clever, and, poor fellow, was frustrated in his attempt to deceive the saint. These silly things which even I, Folly, am almost ashamed of, are approved not only by the common herd but even by the teachers of religion.

How foolish, too, for religious bodies each to give preference to its particular guardian saint! Nay, each saint has his particular office allotted to him, and is addressed each in his special way: this one is called upon to alleviate toothache; that, to aid in childbirth; others, to restore a stolen article, bring rescue to the shipwrecked, or protect cattle,—and so on with the rest, who are much too numerous to mention. A few indeed among the saints are good in more than one emergency, especially the Holy Virgin, to whom the common man now attributes almost more than to her Son. *[handwritten note in margin: Cult of Virgin]*

And for what, after all, do men petition the saints except for foolish things? Look at the votive offerings which cover the walls of certain churches and with which you see even the ceiling filled; do you find any one who expresses his gratitude that he has escaped

Folly or because he has become a whit wiser? One perhaps was saved from drowning, another recovered when he had been run through by his enemy; another, while his fellows were fighting, ran away with expedition and success; another, on the point of being hanged, escaped, through the aid of some saintly friend of thieves, and lived to relieve a few more of those whom he believed to be overburdened with their wealth. . . .

These various forms of foolishness so pervade the whole life of Christians that even the priests themselves find no objection to admitting, not to say fostering, them, since they do not fail to perceive how many tidy little sums accrue to them from such sources. But what if some odious philosopher should chime in and say, as is quite true: "You will not die badly if you live well. You are redeeming your sins when you add to the sum that you contribute a hearty detestation of evil doers: then you may spare yourself tears, vigils, invocations, fasts, and all that kind of life. You may rely upon any saint to aid you when once you begin to imitate his life."

As for the theologians, perhaps the less said the better on this gloomy and dangerous theme, since they are a style of man who show themselves exceeding supercilious and irritable unless they can heap up six hundred conclusions about you and force you to recant; and if you refuse, they promptly brand you as a heretic,—for it is their custom to terrify by their thunderings those whom they dislike. It must be confessed that no other group of fools are so reluctant to acknowledge Folly's benefits toward them, although I have many titles to their gratitude, for I make them so in love with themselves that they seem to be happily exalted to the third heaven, whence they look down with something like pity upon all other mortals, wandering about on the earth like mere cattle. . . .

D. Ulrich von Hutten Pokes Fun at the "Obscure Men" Who Block Reform

Henricus Schaffsmulius to Master Ortuin Gratius, many salutations:

When I first went to the Curia you told me that I should write to you frequently and address any theological questions to you, for you wished to answer them more satisfactorily than could those about the papal court at Rome. I, therefore, wish now to ask your opinion in the case of one who should on Friday, which is the sixth day, or upon any other fast day, eat an egg in which there is a chick. For we were recently dining at an inn in the Campo Fiore, and were eating eggs. And I, opening my egg, discovered that there was a chick within; but upon showing it to my companion, he urged me to swallow it straightway before the host caught sight of it, for otherwise I should have to pay a Carolinus or a Julius for a fowl, since it is the custom here to pay for everything the host places on the table, because they will take nothing back. Now if he saw that there was a chick in the egg he would say, "You must pay me for a fowl,"—for he would charge for a little one just as much as he would for a big one.

And I immediately swallowed the egg and the chick at the same time, and afterwards it occurred to me that it was Friday, and I said to my companion, "You have caused me to commit a mortal sin in eating meat on Friday."

But he said that is was not a mortal sin, nor even a venial sin, since a chick may not be considered other than an egg until it is born. And he remarked that it is just the same in the case of cheese in which there are worms, and of the worms in cherries, and in peas, and young beans; but they are eaten on the sixth day, and even on the vigils of the apostles. But inn proprietors are such rascals that they sometimes say that these are meat in order to gain thereby.

Then I went out and thought about it, and, by Heaven, Master Ortuin, I am much disturbed, and I do not know what I ought to do about it. It is true that I might take counsel with a member of the papal court, but I know that they have bad consciences. As for myself, it seems to me that chicks in the egg are meat, because the matter is already formed and shaped into the members and body of an animal, and it has animal life. It is otherwise in the case of worms in cheese and in other comestibles, for worms are accounted to be fish, as I have heard from a physician, who is also a very able scientist.

I beseech of you earnestly to reply to my question. For if you hold that it is a mortal sin, then I wish to seek absolution before I go to Germany; for you probably know that our lord, Jacob Hochstraten, borrowed a thousand florins from the bank, and I believe he would want to make something out of the case; and may the devil take that John Reuchlin and those other poets and men of law, who are trying to fight the Church of God—that is to say, the theologians, who are the real backbone of the Church, as Christ said, "Thou art Peter, and upon this rock will I build my church."

May the Lord God preserve you. Farewell.
Written in the city of Rome.

Document Set 15.4 References

A. Savonarola Proposes to Make Florence Perfect
Savanarola, in "Draft Constitution for Florence," in R. Watkins, ed., *Humanism and Liberty* (Columbia, S.C.: University of South Carolina Press, 1978), 253–260.

B. Erasmus Shuts Pope Julius II Out of Heaven
Desiderius Erasmus, *The Julius Exclusus of Erasmus,* trans. Paul Pascal (Bloomington, Ind.: University of Indiana Press, 1968), 45–49.

C. Erasmus Mocks the Externals of Piety
Erasmus, *The Praise of Folly,* in James Harvey Robinson, ed., *Readings in European History* (Boston: Ginn, 1904), 2:41–43.

D. Ulrich von Hutten Pokes Fun at the "Obscure Men" Who Block Reform
Ulrich Von Hutten, "Letters of Obscure Men." in Robinson 2:47–49.

DOCUMENT SET 15.5
Luther

The origins of Luther's mission as a reformer lie not in humanist "new learning" or in the moralists' attack on abuses, but in Luther's own solitary struggle with his conscience. Confronting his apparent inability to feel that his conduct would satisfy God and atone for the sinfulness that he could never expunge from his innermost character, Luther came to interpret St. Paul's Epistle to the Romans to mean that God would "justify" (redeem) those who had faith in divine mercy, without regard for the merit of their own feeble efforts. Read Documents A (from Paul's Epistle) and B (Luther's own recollections much later in life) in the light of this struggle. His new understanding in many ways recalled St. Augustine's solution a thousand years earlier and very likely the Apostle Paul's original spiritual battle between Jesus' teachings and Jewish law. Only after having arrived at this decision was Luther impelled to become a public critic of the abuses of indulgence-selling, which can be followed in Documents C and D. In Document C the newly elected Archbishop of Mainz gives instructions for an indulgence-selling campaign designed to strengthen his financial position (not the safeguards that the actual sellers apparently disregarded); in Document D, Luther posts his Ninety-five Theses, which you should read with an eye to how Luther is already attacking the foundations of papal power.

Document E is an excerpt from Luther's pamphlet *The Freedom of a Christian,* composed and published in 1520. Unlike Latin treatises for the intellectual elite, this pamphlet was published in German and reached a broad public through the printing press. It popularized Luther's idea of justification by faith. How can it be said to undermine the entire structure of Catholicism: clergy, sacraments, rules, and good works?

In recent years scholars have debated the extent to which Luther's reformation "succeeded." Prime evidence in this controversy is the surviving sermon and "visitation" material. (The latter are records of parish inspections and examinations of individuals, which were carried out by higher church officials.) What signs do these sources reveal to you of changes in behavior among ordinary Christians "reformed" by Protestantism? Document F summarizes one of Luther's own sermons to his congregation; Document G comes from a visitation report in north-central Germany, 1594. Judging from this evidence, how would you assess the practical outcome of the Lutheran Reformation?

A. St. Paul Writes to the Christians at Rome on Justification by Faith

Now we know that what things soever the law saith, it saith to them who are under the law: that every mouth may be stopped, and all the world may become guilty before God. Therefore by the deeds of the law there shall no flesh be justified in his sight: for by the law is the knowledge of sin.

But now the righteousness of God without the law is manifested, being witnessed by the law and the prophets; even the righteousness of God which is by faith in Jesus Christ unto all and upon all them that believe: for there is no difference: for all have sinned, and come short of the glory of God; being justified freely by his grace through the redemption that is in Christ Jesus: whom God hath set forth to be a propitiation through faith in his blood, to declare his righteousness for the remission of sins that are past, through the forbearance of God; to declare, I say, at this time his righteousness: that he might be just, and the justifier of him which believeth in Jesus.

Where is boasting then? It is excluded. By what law? Of works? Nay: but by the law of faith. Therefore we conclude that a man is justified by faith without the deeds of the law.

B. Luther Discovers the True Meaning of Paul's *Epistle to the Romans*

I greatly longed to understand Paul's Epistle to the Romans and nothing stood in the way but that one expression, "the justice of God," because I took it to mean that justice whereby God is just and deals justly in punishing the unjust. My situation was that, although an impeccable monk, I stood before God as a sinner troubled in conscience, and I had no confidence that my merit would assuage him. Therefore I did not love a just and angry God, but rather hated and murmured against him. Yet I clung to the dear Paul and had a great yearning to know what he meant.

Night and day I pondered until I saw the connection between the justice of God and the statement that "the just shall live by his faith." Then I grasped that the justice of God is that righteousness by which through grace and sheer mercy God justifies us through faith. Thereupon I felt myself to be reborn and to have gone through open doors into paradise. The whole of Scripture took on a new meaning, and whereas before the "justice of God" had filled me with hate, now it became to me inexpressibly sweet in greater love. This passage of Paul became to me a gate to heaven. . . .

If you have a true faith that Christ is your Saviour, then at once you have a gracious God, for faith leads you in and opens up God's heart and will, that you should see pure grace and overflowing love. This it is to behold God in faith that you should look upon his fatherly, friendly heart, in which there is no anger nor ungraciousness. He who sees God as angry does not see him rightly but looks only on a curtain, as if a dark cloud had been drawn across his face.

C. Archbishop Albert of Mainz Gives His Instructions for Indulgence-Selling, 1517

Here follow the four principal graces and privileges, which are granted by the apostolic bull, of which each may be obtained without the other. In the matter of these four privileges preachers shall take pains to commend each to believers with the greatest care, and, in-so-far as in their power lies, to explain the same.

The first grace is the complete remission of all sins; and nothing greater than this can be named, since man who lives in sin and forfeits the favor of God, obtains complete remission by these means and once more enjoys God's favor: moreover, through this remission of sins the punishment which one is obliged to undergo in Purgatory on account of the affront to the divine Majesty, is all remitted, and the pains of Purgatory completely blotted out. And although nothing is precious enough to be given in exchange for such a grace,—since it is the free gift of God and a grace beyond price,—yet in order that Christian believers may be the more easily induced to procure the same, we establish the following rules, to wit:

In the first place every one who is contrite in heart, and has made oral confession, or at all events has the intention of confessing at a suitable time, shall visit at least the seven churches indicated for this purpose, that is to say, those in which the papal arms are displayed, and in each church shall say devoutly five Paternosters and five Ave Marias in honor of the five wounds of our Lord Jesus Christ, whereby our salvation is won, or one *Miserere* [the prayer beginning "Lord have mercy"], which Psalm is particularly well adapted for obtaining forgiveness of sins. . . .

Respecting, now, the contribution to the chest, for the building of the said church of the chief of the apostles, the penitentiaries and confessors, after they have explained to those making confession the full remission and privileges, shall ask of them, for how much money or other temporal goods they would conscientiously go without the said most complete remission and privileges; and this shall be done in order that hereafter they may be brought the more easily to contribute. And because the conditions and occupations of men are so manifold and diverse that we cannot consider them individually, and impose specific rates accordingly, we have therefore concluded that the rates should be determined according to the recognized classes of persons.

Kings and Queens and their offspring, archbishops and bishops, and other great rulers as well, provided they seek the places where the cross is raised, or otherwise present themselves, shall pay at least five and twenty Rhenish guilders in gold. Abbots and the great prelates of Cathedral churches, counts, barons, and others of the higher nobility, together with their consorts, shall pay for each letter of indulgence ten such guilders. Other lesser prelates and nobles, as also the rectors of celebrated places, and all others, who, either from permanent incomes or merchandise, or otherwise, enjoy a total yearly revenue of five hundred gold guilders, shall pay six such guilders. Other citizens and tradespeople and artisans, who have individual incomes and families of their own, shall pay one such guilder; others of less means only a half. And where it is impossible to adhere rigidly to the schedule above indicated, then we declare that the said kings, bishops, dukes, abbots, prelates, counts, barons, members of the higher nobility and rectors, together with all others above mentioned, shall place or caused to be placed in the chest a sum in accordance with the dictates of sound reason, proportionate to their magnificence or generosity, after they have listened to the advice and council of the sub-commissioners and penitentiaries and of their confessors, in order that they may fully obtain the grace and privileges. All other persons are confided to the discretion of the confessors and penitentiaries, who should have ever in view the advancement of this building, and should urge their penitents to a freer contribution, but should let no one go away without some portion of grace, because the happiness of Christian believers is here concerned not less than the interests of the building. And those that have no money, they shall supply their contribution with prayer and fasting; for the Kingdom of Heaven should be open to the poor not less than to the rich.

And although a married woman may not dispose

of the husband's goods against his will, yet she shall be able to contribute in this instance against the will of her husband of her dowry or of her own private property, which has come to her in a regular manner. Where she has no such possessions, or is prevented by her husband, she shall then supply such contribution with prayer; and the same we wish to have understood concerning sons who still remain under parental control. . . .

The second signal grace is a confessional letter containing the most extraordinarily comforting and hitherto unheard of privileges, and which also retains its virtue even after our bull expires at the end of eight years, since the bull says: "they shall be participators now and for ever." The meaning of the same preachers and confessors shall explain and bring unto all possible prominence; for there will be granted in the confessional letter, to those who buy: first, the power to choose a qualified confessor, even a monk from the mendicant orders, who shall absolve them first and foremost, with the consent of the persons involved, from all censures by whomsoever imposed; in the second place, from each and every crime, even the greatest, and as well from those reserved to the apostolic see, once in a lifetime and in the hour of death; third, in those cases which are not reserved, as often as necessary; fourth, the chosen confessor may grant him complete forgiveness of all sins once in life, and at the hour of death, as often as it may seem at hand, although death ensue not; and, fifth, transform all kinds of vows, excepting alone those solemnly taken, into other works of piety (as when one has vowed to perform the journey to the Holy Land, or to visit the holy Apostles at Rome, to make a pilgrimage to St. James at Compostella, to become a monk, or to take a vow of chastity); sixth, the confessor may administer to him the sacrament of the alter at all seasons, except on Easter day, and in the hour of death. . . .

The third most important grace is the participation in all the possessions of the church universal, which consists herein, that contributors toward the said building, together with their deceased relations, who have departed this world in a state of grace, shall from now and for eternity, be partakers in all petitions, intercessions, alms, fastings, prayers, in each and every pilgrimage, even those to the Holy Land; furthermore, in the stations at Rome, in the masses canonical hours, flagellations, and all other spiritual goods which have been brought forth or which shall be brought forth by the universal, most holy church militant or by any of its members. Believers will become participants in all these things who purchase confessional letters. Preachers and confessors must insist with great perseverance upon these advantages,

and persuade believers that they should not neglect to acquire these along with their confessional letter.

We also declare that in order to acquire these two most important graces, it is not necessary to make confession, or to visit the churches and altars, but merely to purchase the confessional letter. . . .

The fourth distinctive grace is for those souls which are in purgatory, and is the complete remission of all sins, which remission the pope brings to pass through his intercession to the advantage of said souls, in this wise; that the same contribution shall be placed in the chest by a living person as one would make for himself. It is our wish, however, that our subcommissioners should modify the regulations regarding contributions of this kind which are given for the dead, and that they should use their judgment in all other cases, where in their opinion modifications are desirable. It is furthermore not necessary that the persons who place their contributions in the chest for the dead should be contrite in heart and have orally confessed, since this grace is based simply on the state of grace in which the dead departed, and on the contribution of the living, as is evident from the text of the bull. Moreover, preachers shall exert themselves to give this grace the widest publicity, since through the same, help will surely come to departed souls, and the construction of the Church of St. Peter will be abundantly promoted at the same time. . . .

D. Luther Posts His Ninety-five Theses, 1517

1. Our Lord and Master Jesus Christ in saying "Repent ye" (*poenitentiam agite*) etc., intended that the whole life of believers should be penitence (*poenitentia*).

2. This word cannot be understood as sacramental penance (*poenitentia*), that is, of the confession and satisfaction which are performed under the ministry of priests.

3. It does not, however, refer solely to inward penitence (*poenitentia*); nay such inward penitence is naught, unless it outwardly produces various mortifications of the flesh.

4. The penalty (*poena*) thus continues as long as the hatred of self (that is, true inward penitence); namely, till our entrance into the kingdom of heaven.

5. The Pope has neither the will nor the power to remit any penalties except those which he has imposed by his own authority, or by that of the canons.

6. The Pope has no power to remit any guilt, except by declaring and warranting it to have been remitted by God; or at most by remitting cases reserved for himself; in which cases, if his power were despised, guilt would certainly remain.

7. Certainly God remits no man's guilt without at the same time subjecting him, humbled in all things, to the authority of his representative the priest.

8. The penitential canons are imposed only on the living, and no burden ought to be imposed on the dying, according to them.

9. Hence, the Holy Spirit acting in the Pope does well for us in that, in his decrees, he always makes exception of the article of death and of necessity.

10. Those priests act unlearnedly and wrongly who, in the case of the dying, reserve the canonical penances for purgatory. . . .

20. Therefore the Pope, when he speaks of the plenary remission of all penalties, does not mean really of all, but only of those imposed by himself.

21. Thus those preachers of indulgences are in error who say that by the indulgences of the Pope a man is freed and saved from all punishment.

22. For in fact he remits to souls in purgatory no penalty which they would have had to pay in this life according to the canons.

23. If any entire remission of all penalties can be granted to any one it is certain that it is granted to none but the most perfect, that is to very few.

24. Hence, the greater part of the people must needs be deceived by this indiscriminate and high-sounding promise of release from penalties. . . .

26. The Pope acts most rightly in granting remission to souls not by the power of the keys (which is of no avail in this case) but by the way of intercession.

27. They preach man who say that the soul flies out of Purgatory as soon as the money thrown into the chest rattles.[1]

28. It is certain that, when the money rattles in the chest, avarice and gain may be increased, but the effect of the intercession of the Church depends on the will of God alone.

29. Who knows whether all the souls in purgatory desire to be redeemed from it—witness the story told of Saints Severinus and Paschal?

30. No man is sure of the reality of his own contrition, much less of the attainment of plenary remission.

31. Rare as is a true penitent, so rare is one who truly buys indulgences—that is to say, most rare.

32. Those who believe that, through letters of pardon, they are made sure of their own salvation will be eternally damned along with their teachers.

33. We must especially beware of those who say that these pardons from the Pope are that inestimable gift of God by which man is reconciled to God.

34. For the grace conveyed by these pardons has respect only to the penalties of sacramental satisfaction, which are of human appointment.

35. They preach no Christian doctrine who teach that contrition is not necessary for those who buy souls [out of purgatory] or buy confessional licenses.

36. Every Christian who feels true compunction has of right plenary remission of punishment and guilt even without letters of pardon.

37. Every true Christian, whether living or dead, has a share in all the benefits of Christ and of the Church, given him by God, even without letters of pardon.

38. The remission, however, imparted by the Pope is by no means to be despised, since it is, as I have said, a declaration of the divine remission.

39. It is a most difficult thing, even for the most learned theologians, to exalt at the same time in the eyes of the people the ample effect of pardons and the necessity of true contrition.

40. True contrition seeks and loves punishment; while the ampleness of pardons relaxes it, and causes men to hate it, or at least gives occasion for them to do so.

41. Apostolic pardons ought to be proclaimed with caution, lest the people should falsely suppose that they are placed before other good works of charity.

42. Christians should be taught that it is not the wish of the Pope that the buying of pardons should be in any way compared to works of mercy.

43. Christians should be taught that he who gives to a poor man, or lends to a needy man, does better than if he bought pardons.

44. Because by works of charity, charity increases, and the man becomes better; while by means of pardons, he does not become better, but only freer from punishment.

45. Christians should be taught that he who sees any one in need, and, passing him by, gives money for pardons, is not purchasing for himself the indulgences of the Pope but the anger of God.

46. Christians should be taught that, unless they have superfluous wealth, they are bound to keep what is necessary for the use of their own households, and by no means to lavish it on pardons.

47. Christians should be taught that while they are free to buy pardons they are not commanded to do so.

---

[1] This was the claim being made by the indulgence seller Tetzel in Luther's Saxony.

48. Christians should be taught that the Pope, in granting pardons, has both more need and more desire that devout prayer should be made for him than that money should be readily paid.

49. Christians should be taught that the Pope's pardons are useful if they do not put their trust in them, but most hurtful if through them they lose the fear of God.

50. Christians should be taught that, if the Pope were acquainted with the exactions of the Preachers of pardons, he would prefer that the Basilica of St. Peter should be burnt to ashes rather than that it should be built up with the skin, flesh, and bones of his sheep.

51. Christians should be taught that as it would be the duty so it would be the wish of the Pope even to sell, if necessary, the Basilica of St. Peter, and to give of his own money to very many of those from whom the preachers of pardons extract money.

52. Vain is the hope of salvation through letters of pardon, even if a commissary—nay, the Pope himself—were to pledge his own soul for them.

53. They were enemies of Christ and of the Pope who, in order that pardons may be preached, condemn the word of God to utter silence in other churches.

54. Wrong is done to the Word of God when, in the same sermon, an equal or longer time is spent on pardons than on it.

55. The mind of the Pope necessarily is that, if pardons, which are a very small matter, are celebrated with single bells, single processions, and single ceremonies, the Gospel, which is a very great matter, should be preached with a hundred bells, a hundred processions, and a hundred ceremonies.

56. The treasures of the Church, whence the Pope grants indulgences, are neither sufficiently named nor known among the people of Christ.

57. It is clear that they are at least not temporal treasures, for these are not so readily lavished, but only accumulated, by many of the preachers.

58. Nor are they the merits of Christ and of the saints, for these, independently of the Pope, are always working grace to the inner man, and the cross, death, and hell to the outer man. . . .

67. Those indulgences, which the preachers loudly proclaim to be the greatest graces, are seen to be truly such as regards the promotion of gain.

68. Yet they are in reality most insignificant when compared to the grace of God and the piety of the cross. . . .

75. To think that the Papal pardons have such power that they could absolve a man even if—by an impossibility—he had violated the Mother of God, is madness.

76. We affirm on the contrary that Papal pardons cannot take away even the least of venial sins, as regards its guilt.

77. The saying that, even if St. Peter were now Pope, he could grant no greater graces, is blasphemy against St. Peter and the Pope.

78. We affirm on the contrary that both he and any other Pope has greater graces to grant, namely, the Gospel, powers, gifts of healing, etc. (1 Cor. xii.)

79. To say that the cross set up among the insignia of the Papal arms is of equal power with the cross of Christ, is blasphemy.

80. Those bishops, priests and theologians who allow such discourses to have currency among the people will have to render an account.

81. This license in the preaching of pardons makes it no easy thing, even for learned men, to protect the reverence due to the Pope against the calumnies, or, at all events, the keen questionings of the laity.

82. As for instance: Why does not the Pope empty purgatory for the sake of most holy charity and of the supreme necessity of souls—this being the most just of all reasons—if he redeems an infinite number of souls for the sake of that most fatal thing, money, to be spent on building a basilica—this being a very slight reason?

83. Again; why do funeral masses and anniversary masses for the deceased continue, and why does not the Pope return, or permit the withdrawal of, the funds bequeathed for this purpose, since it is a wrong to pray for those who are already redeemed?

84. Again; what is this new kindness of God and the Pope, in that, for money's sake, they permit an impious man and an enemy of God to redeem a pious soul which loves God, and yet do not redeem that same pious and beloved soul out of free charity on account of its own need?

85. Again; why is it that the penitential canons, long since abrogated and dead in themselves, in very fact and not only by usage, are yet still redeemed with money, through the granting of indulgences, as if they were full of life?

86. Again; why does not the Pope, whose riches are at this day more ample than those of the wealthiest of the wealthy, build the single Basilica of St. Peter with his own money rather than with that of poor believers?

87. Again; what does the Pope remit or impart to those who through perfect contrition have a right to plenary remission and participation?

88. Again; what greater good could the Church receive than if the Pope, instead of once, as he does now, were to bestow these remissions and participations a hundred times a day on any one of the faithful?

89. Since it is the salvation of souls, rather than money, that the Pope seeks by his pardons, why does he suspend the letters and pardons granted long ago, since they are equally efficacious? . . .

91. If all these pardons were preached according to the spirit and mind of the Pope, all these questions would be resolved with ease; nay, would not exist. . . .

E. Luther Explains the True Freedom of a Christian, 1520

One thing, and only one thing, is necessary for Christian life, righteousness, and freedom. That one thing is the most holy Word of God, the gospel of Christ . . . it is easy to see from what source faith derives such great power and why a good work or all good works together cannot equal it. No good work can rely upon the Word of God or live in the soul, for faith alone and the Word of God rule in the soul. Just as the heated iron glows like fire because of the union of fire with it, so the Word imparts its qualities to the soul. It is clear, then, that a Christian has all that he needs in faith and needs no works to justify him; and if he has no need of works, he has no need of the law; and if he has no need of the law, surely he is free from the law. . . . This is that Christian liberty, our faith, which does not induce us to live in idleness or wickedness but makes the law and works unnecessary for any man's righteousness and salvation.

F. Luther Preaches to His Congregation, 1528

The sermon on the 8th of November, 1528, was on the lord who forgave his servant: This lord, said Luther, is a type of the Kingdom of God. The servant was not forgiven because he had forgiven his fellow servant. On the contrary he received forgiveness before he had done anything whatever about his fellow servant. From this we see that there are two kinds of forgiveness. The first is that which we receive from God; the second is that which we exercise by bearing no ill will to any upon earth. But we must not overlook the two administrations, the civil and the spiritual, because the prince cannot and should not forgive. He has a different administration than Christ,

who rules over crushed and broken hearts. The Kaiser rules over scoundrels who do not recognize their sins and mock and carry their heads high. That is why the emperor carries a sword, a sign of blood and not of peace. But Christ's kingdom is for the troubled conscience. He says, "I do not ask of you a penny, only this, that you do the same for your neighbor." And the lord in the parable does not tell the servant to found a monastery, but simply that he should have mercy on his fellow servants.

But now what shall I say to you Wittenbergers? It would be better that I preach to you the *Sachsenspiegel* [the imperial law], because you want to be Christians while still practicing usury, robbing and stealing. How do people who are so sunk in sins expect to receive forgiveness? The sword of the emperor really applies here, but my sermon is for crushed hearts who feel their sins and have no peace. Enough for this gospel.

I understand that this is the week for the church collection, and many of you do not want to give a thing. You ungrateful people should be ashamed of yourselves. You Wittenbergers have been relieved of schools and hospitals, which have been taken over by the common chest, and now you want to know why you are asked to give four pennies. They are for the ministers, schoolteachers, and sacristans. The first labor for your salvation, preach to you the precious treasure of the gospel, administer the sacraments, and visit you at great personal risk in the plague. The second train children to be good magistrates, judges, and ministers. The third care for the poor. So far the common chest has cared for these, and now that you are asked to give four miserable pennies you are up in arms. What does this mean if not that you do not want the gospel preached, the children taught, and the poor helped? I am not saying this for myself. I receive nothing from you. I am the prince's beggar. But I am sorry I ever freed you from the tyrants and the papists. You ungrateful beasts, you are not worthy of the treasure of the gospel. If you don't improve, I will stop preaching rather than cast pearls before swine.

And now another point: couples to be blessed by the curate before a wedding should come early. There are stated hours: in summer, mornings at eight and afternoons at three; in winter, mornings at nine and afternoons at two. If you come later, I will bless you myself, and you won't thank me for it. And the invited guests should prepare themselves in good time for the wedding and let not Miss Goose wait for Mrs. Duck.

G. Lutheran Church Officials Inspect a Parish, 1594

First, gruesome cursing and blaspheming, as for instance "by God," "by God's Holy Cross," "by God's Passion, -death, -flesh, -blood, -heart, -hand," etc., "A Thousand Sacraments," "by the Baptism," "element," "star," "thunder and hail," "earth." Also dreadful swearing by various fears, epidemics, and injuries. These oaths are very common among young and old, women as well as men. People cannot carry on a friendly chat, or even address their children, without the use of these words. And none of them considers it a sin to swear.

Everyone is lax about going to church, both young and old. Many have not been seen by their pastor in a year or more. . . . Those who come to service are usually drunk. As soon as they sit down they lean their heads on their arms and sleep through the whole sermon, except that sometimes they fall off the benches, making a great clatter, or women drop their babies on the floor. . . . At times the wailing of babies is so loud that the preacher cannot make himself heard in the church.

The moment the sermon ends, everyone runs out. No one stays for the hymn, prayer, and blessing. They behave as if they were at a dance, not a divine service. . . . On Sunday afternoons, hardly ten or fifteen of 150 householders come to catechism practice, nor do they oblige their children and servants to attend. Instead they loaf at home, or sit about gossiping. . . . In many places catechism preaching on holiday afternoons has had to be abandoned for lack of auditors.

Document Set 15.5 References

A. St. Paul Writes to the Christians at Rome on Justification by Faith
Romans 3:19–28.
B. Luther Discovers the True Meaning of Paul's *Epistle to the Romans*
Martin Luther, in Roland H. Bainton, *Here I Stand* (Nashville, Tenn.: Abington Press, 1950; Mentor Books edition), 49–50.
C. Archbishop Albert of Mainz Gives His Instructions for Indulgence-Selling, 1517
Gerdes, *Introductio in Historian Evangelii Seculo,* in *Translations and Reprints from the Original Sources of European History* (Philadelphia: University of Pennsylvania Press, 1898), 2/6:4–9.
D. Luther Posts His Ninety-five Theses, 1517
Martin Luther, "Ninety-five Theses," in *Translations and Reprints,* 2/6:12–18.
E. Luther Explains the True Freedom of a Christian, 1520
Martin Luther, *The Freedom of a Christian,* in *Luther's Works,* American Edition (Philadelphia: 1957), 31:345, 349–350.
F. Luther Preaches to His Congregation, 1528
Martin Luther, Sermon of November 8, 1528, in 274–275.
G. Lutheran Church Officials Inspect a Parish, 1594
Report of Visitation in Nassau-Wiesbaden, in Gerald Strauss, *Luther's House of Learning* (Baltimore: Johns Hopkins University Press, 1978), 283–284.

Reformation not particularly successful (not practiced devoutly)

strict austere

DOCUMENT SET 15.6
The Reformation of the Common Man: The Peasants' War and the Anabaptists

One reason that historians often cite for the declining acceptability of Luther's message among ordinary people (Section 15.5, Documents F and G) is the crisis of the 1520s, during which many unlettered German men and women did in fact try to implement their understanding of the Gospel. Read Document A, an extract from the Twelve Articles that formed the basis of villagers' demand in the Peasants' War of 1525, looking for both the grievances and the peasants' idea of justice; compare Document B, in which the Zurich town council debates tithing with the aggrieved local peasantry.

Documents C to F all come from the Peasants' War. Read them to answer such questions as why did the fighting spread so far and so fast in the spring of 1525? Who were the peasants' leaders and what (if any) organizations did they possess? What roles did Thomas Müntzer and Martin Luther play?

Document G comes from the same south German town of Rothenburg that two years earlier had experienced the full brunt of the Peasants' War. Did this trauma have something to do with the ferocity with which the town executed the gentle pacifist Michael Sattler for preaching Anabaptist ideas? In what ways were these ideas judged subversive by the authorities?

The final document of the set (H) dates from after the Anabaptist debacle at Münster; Obbe Philips, a Dutch Anabaptist, found himself forced by circumstance to conclude that *all* Anabaptist idealism—whether pacifist or violent—was somehow fatally flawed. Why, on the basis of the evidence you have read, did he reach that conclusion?

After studying the documents in this set, write a brief essay assessing the peasants' insurgence and the Anabaptists as represenatives of ordinary Germans in the Reformation Era.

A. The German Peasants Plead for Justice: The Twelve Articles

Peace to the Christian Reader and the Grace of God through Christ.

There are many evil writings put forth of late which take occasion, on account of the assembling of the peasants, to cast scorn upon the Gospel, saying: Is this the fruit of the new teaching, that no one should obey but all should everywhere rise in revolt, and rush together to reform, or perhaps destroy entirely, the authorities, both ecclesiastical and lay? The articles below shall answer these godless and criminal fault-finders, and serve in the first place to remove the reproach from the word of God and, in the second place, to give a Christian excuse for the disobedience or even the revolt of the entire Peasantry. In the first place the Gospel is not the cause of revolt and disorder, since it is the message of Christ, the promised Messiah, the Word of Life, teaching only love, peace, patience and concord. Thus, all who believe in Christ should learn to be loving, peaceful, long-suffering and harmonious. This is the foundation of all the articles of the peasants (as will be seen) who accept the gospel and live according to it. How then can the evil reports declare the Gospel to be a cause of revolt and disobedience? That the authors of the evil reports and the enemies of the Gospel oppose themselves to these demands is due not to the Gospel but to the Devil, the worst enemy of the Gospel, who causes this opposition by raising doubts in the minds of his followers; and thus the word of God, which teaches love, peace and concord, is overcome. In the second place, it is clear that the peasants demand that this Gospel be taught them as a guide in life, and they ought not to be called disobedient or disorderly. Whether God grant the peasants (earnestly wishing to live according to his word) their requests or no, who shall find fault with the will of the Most High? Who shall meddle in his judgments or oppose his majesty? Did he not hear the children of Israel when they called upon him and save them out of the hands of Pharaoh? Can he not save his own to-day? Yea, he will save them and that speedily. Therefore, Christian reader, read the following articles with care and then judge. Here follow the articles:

The First Article.—First, it is our humble petition and desire, as also our will and resolution, that in the future we should have power and authority so that each community should choose and appoint a pastor, and that we should have the right to depose him should he conduct himself improperly. The pastor thus chosen should teach us the Gospel pure and simple, without any addition, doctrine or ordinance of man. . . .

The Second Article.—According as the just tithe is established by the Old Testament and fulfilled in the New, we are ready and willing to pay the fair tithe of grain. The word of God plainly provides that in giving according to right to God and distributing to his people the services of a pastor are required. We will that for the future our church provost, whomsoever the community may appoint, shall gather and receive this tithe. From this he shall give to the pastor, elected by the whole community, a decent and sufficient maintenance for him and his (*im und den seynen*), as shall seem right to the whole community [*or,* with the knowledge of the community]. What remains over shall be given to the poor of the place, as the circumstances and the general opinion demand. Should anything farther remain, let it be kept, lest anyone should have to leave the country from poverty. Provision should also be made from this surplus to avoid laying any land tax on the poor. . . .

The Third Article.—It has been the custom hitherto for men to hold us as their own property, which is pitable enough, considering that Christ has delivered and redeemed us all, without exception, by the shedding of his precious blood, the lowly as well as the great. Accordingly, it is consistent with Scripture that we should be free and wish to be so. Not that we would wish to be absolutely free and under no authority. God does not teach us that we should lead a disorderly life in the lusts of the flesh, but that we should love the Lord our God and our neighbor. We would gladly observe all this as God has commanded us in the celebration of the communion. He has not commanded us not to obey the authorities, but rather that we should be humble, not only towards those in authority, but towards everyone. We are thus ready to yield obedience according to God's law to our elected and regular authorities in all proper things becoming to a Christian. We, therefore, take it for granted that you will release us from serfdom, as true Christians, unless it should be shown us from the Gospel that we are serfs.

The Fourth Article.—In the fourth place it has been the custom heretofore, that no poor man should be allowed to touch venison or wild fowl, or fish in flowing water, which seems to us quite unseemly and unbrotherly, as well as selfish and not agreeable to the word of God. In some places the authorities preserve the game to our great annoyance and loss, recklessly permitting the unreasoning animals to destroy to no purpose our crops, which God suffers to grow for the use of man, and yet we must remain quiet. This is neither godly nor neighborly. For when God created man he gave him dominion over all the animals, over the birds of the air and over the fish in the water. Accordingly it is our desire if a man holds possession of waters that he should prove from satisfactory doc-

uments that his right has been unwittingly acquired by purchase. . . .

The Fifth Article.—In the fifth place we are aggrieved in the matter of wood-cutting, for the noble folk have appropriated all the woods to themselves alone. If a poor man requires wood he must pay double for it, [*or perhaps,* two pieces of money]. . . .

The Sixth Article.—Our sixth complaint is in regard to the excessive services demanded of us, which are increased from day to day. We ask that this matter be properly looked into so that we shall not continue to be oppressed in this way, and that some gracious consideration be given us, since our forefathers were required only to serve according to the word of God.

The Seventh Article.—Seventh, we will not hereafter allow ourselves to be farther oppressed by our lords, but will let them demand only what is just and proper according to the word of the agreement between the lord and the peasant. The lord should no longer try to force more services or other dues from the peasant without payment, but permit the peasant to enjoy his holding in peace and quiet. The peasant should, however, help the lord when it is necessary, and at proper times, when it will not be disadvantageous to the peasant, and for a suitable payment.

The Eighth Article.—In the eighth place, we are greatly burdened by holdings which cannot support the rent exacted from them. The peasants suffer loss in this way and are ruined; and we ask that the lords may appoint persons of honor to inspect these holdings, and fix a rent in accordance with justice, so that the peasant shall not work for nothing, since the laborer is worthy of his hire.

The Ninth Article.—In the ninth place, we are burdened with a great evil in the constant making of new laws. We are not judged according to the offence, but sometimes with great ill will, and sometimes much too leniently. In our opinion we should be judged according to the old written law, so that the case shall be decided according to its merits, and not with partiality.

The Tenth Article.—In the tenth place, we are aggrieved by the appropriation by individuals of meadows and fields which at one time belonged to a community. . . .

The Eleventh Article.—In the eleventh place we will entirely abolish the due called *Todfall* [a payment owed upon a peasant's death by his heirs], and will no longer endure it, nor allow widows and orphans to be thus shamefully robbed against God's will, and in violation of justice and right, as has been done in many places, and by those who should shield and protect them. . . .

Conclusion.—In the twelfth place it is our conclusion and final resolution, that if any one or more of the articles here set forth should not be in agreement with the word of God, as we think they are, such article we will willingly recede from, when it is proved really to be against the word of God by a clear explanation of the Scripture. . . . For this we shall pray God, since he can grant this, and he alone. The peace of Christ abide with us all.

B. The Zurich City Council and Local Peasants Debate the Justice of Tithes, 1525

The peasants would not be peaceful and held a commune at Kloten and at Gossau, and would gladly have freed themselves from the tithe. But the lords of Zürich ordered that the tithe should be paid as before [issuing a mandate to that effect of 7 June 1525] . . . Such a mandate was unwelcome to the self-seeking crowd and many wanted to blame the preachers. They had taught that a Christian was free, etc. [arguing that] "the tithe in the New Testament is not divine law, etc." However, each Christian was to give what he was obliged to pay, and what had grown up of old . . . There was a public discussion about this dispute on the tithe, and an assembly of all the priests of the town and countryside of Zürich was held. The countryfolk also sent representatives to this meeting, intending that the peasants would be freed from the tithe, or, at the very least, the small tithe. But the lords of Zürich would not allow this, and after discussion issued an explanatory mandate . . . as follows:

Mandate of July 1, 1525: it has come to the notice of our lords, the Mayor, Council, and Great Council, that there is some misunderstanding among you about the tithe. Some think that when the seven crops—that is, corn, rye, oats, barley, wheat, wine, and hay (where this is customarily tithed)—have been paid, the small tithe and others are remitted. Our lords reply that all communes have received recent instructions (and since their reply to the communes is quite clear there can be no misunderstanding). Before the very eyes of our lords and of the priests of town and countryside, [the communes] dropped the articles they had written down, (for all the communes agreed to uphold the Word of God and clearly said that the disturbance about the tithe had arisen from the divisive preaching of the priests), and requested our lords . . . to deliberate whether the articles had any foundation and to remit those without foundation in the Word of God. Our lords therefore told the envoys that they should return home, and that they would deliberate on the articles as soon as business allowed . . . and, with the advice of master Ulrich Zwingli and other learned and knowledgeable men, they would weigh the matter thoroughly and see what they could redress according to the Word of God. Nonetheless, one should pay the tithe and rents due to various ecclesiastical and secular persons, according to the content of the last mandate issued on this matter.

Whereupon one person was deputed from each guild to sit in judgment on the peasant articles and to consider thoroughly what could be conceded. After lengthy discussion, the mandate was confirmed, that all rents and tithes should be paid as was obligatory by custom, even the small tithe except that wherever two crops were grown annually in a field, [for example,] the aftermath of hay, or turnips after hemp, or millet after winter barley, etc., only the first crop would be tithed and the second would be free, such as the second crop of hay, turnips, etc.

[The Zürich town council, however, first issued a mandate on the peasant articles and the tithe on 14 August 1525.]. . . We do not doubt that you have all been informed that some disagreement and dispute have arisen over the tithe, because of the conflicting sermons of our preachers, and misunderstanding on the part of some of our surrounding subjects (in our view out of self-interest). For this reason, some areas, namely, those from the county of Kyburg, the territory of Eglisau, of Grüningen, Greifensee, Andelfingen, Bülach, Neuamt, and Rümlang, appeared before us in the person of their envoys, together with their pastors and preachers, to discuss and negotiate extensively and in detail over the tithe. Finally, the envoys of the communes were told that such disturbance arose in their midst only on account of their priests and their conflicting preaching and that they had been instructed and taught by them. Therewith the matter was referred to us [the council] for a decision according to the Word of God, and to remit those articles which were not grounded in it.

Since we heard, saw, and felt that there were some who, out of self-seeking, persisted in their disobedience, from which great disadvantage might ensue for us and all of you in the eyes of God, our fellow confederates and other neighbors on our borders who receive tithes in our territories, so we nominated certain councillors and biblical scholars to read through and search the holy Scripture with especial diligence and industry. And we can find in no part of the divine Word, either according to God or the law, that anyone is obliged to give the tithe or to supply it, or [obliged] to renounce it. Thus, it is unfitting for us or any judge to refuse any holders, ecclesiastical or lay their tithes where they have been rendered and received in peaceful possession for many hundreds of years according to praiseworthy ancient tradition and good credentials, and thus to take or remove their property from them. But for many reasons which are godly, Christian, and founded in Scripture, we have decided, adjudged, and affirmed what we wish to be observed this year and each year henceforth:

1. All those who have holdings in our territories . . . whether they be residents or not, shall be bound and obliged to give the great tithe, not only on the seven crops . . . but also on all other items on which each commune or parish has been accustomed to pay the great tithe, wherever and to whom, secular and lay, it was previously given, without alteration or diminution.

2. On the small tithe, since it is unbecoming for us to wrest any possessions, inheritances, or estates from the hands of either natives or foreigners within our territories, we further declare that each parish and commune should deliver and pay the small tithe, together with whatever belonged to it of old, they have habitually rendered, this year and every year henceforth, without dimunition or alteration, but with this concession, that whenever anyone sows a field once during the year, a tithe should be given from it, but any further sowings during the year shall be free. Whoever transgresses the above provisions and is arraigned shall be punished with temporal penalties over and above what he may expect from God, so that he will chose to obey us as his sovereign authority, according to divine Scripture.

3. Nonetheless we will see to it with the help of Almighty God that the ecclesiastical tithes remaining in our lands which we administer shall be restored to a proper use according to the content of the divine Word, i.e. that pastors will be afforded a suitable competency, and that the remainder will be deployed in good time according to the will of God.

4. We are also willing to help to negotiate genuinely over the small tithe, so that where there is anyone, either native or foreigner, who has purchased a small tithe on a deed of redemption, then the parishes or communes may redeem it. But where there is neither a letter of purchase nor a sealed attestation, and the possession is only vested in peaceful ownership and praiseworthy tradition without a deed of redemption, we will apply ourselves amicable and do the best we can, so that the parishes and communes may achieve a reasonable redemption . . .

The peasants were not at all content with this explanation or in agreement with it. They had promised [earlier] . . . that they would commit their lives and goods for the Word of God, [believing that] their evangelical freedom would bring them some advantage. Many took the tithe into their own barns and were later punished for it. They laid all the blame for this on the preachers, since some of them were said to have proclaimed that the tithe was not demanded in the New Testament. Yet since they were ancient traditions, usages, and customs bequeathed to us, no Christian should refuse to pay them, but give the cloak as well as the coat. But this proposal vexed the peasants, who withdrew in great hatred of the preachers, where previously they would have given their right arm for the Gospel.

C. The Peasants' War Engulfs Rothenburg, 1525

Through the preachers here in Rothenburg,—namely, Caspar Cristian, a priest, and Brother Melchior, who married the blind monk's sister and held the wedding in Schwarzman's house,—also especially through the efforts of Hans Rotfuchs, the blind monk himself, and another fellow who gave himself out for a peasant, and through certain citizens here in Rothenburg who adhere to the heresy of Luther and Carlstadt,[1] it has come about that bad, false teaching has greatly got the upper hand, owing also to the dissimulation and concessions of some of the town authorities. Dr. Andreas Carlstadt has appeared in person, preached here, and asked to be received as a burgher.

On March 21, a Tuesday, thirty or forty peasants got together in a mob in Rothenburg, bought a kettledrum, and marched about the town, a part going to Pretheim and a part toward Orenbach. They got together again on Thursday and on Friday, as many as four hundred.

The working classes in the town now begin to revolt. They cease to obey the authorities and form a committee of thirty-six to manage affairs. Cunz Eberhardt and George Bermeter are meanwhile dispatched to learn what the peasants are doing; but the peasants will give no reply, for they say that they have not all got together yet. A letter is received from Margrave Casimir [of Brandenburg]. This is read to the community. He offers to aid the town authorities and if necessary come in person to reëstablish peace and harmony. The community and their committee of thirty-six treat this scornfully and do not accept the offer.

[1] Carlstadt was another preacher of reforms, originally an ally of Luther but later an opponent.

March 24. This evening between five and six o'clock some one knocked off the head of Christ's image on a crucifix and struck off the arms.

March 25. The town councils are in great danger and anxiety, for they are oppressed by the community and its committee of thirty-six.

March 27. The councilors are forced to pledge their obedience to the community, for they are taken out one by one, guarded by members of the committee of thirty-six. Each thought he was going to be killed, but after taking the pledge he was secretly sent home without his companions' knowledge.

March 26. Chrischainz, the baker, knocked the missal out of the priest's hand in the chapel of our Lady and drove away the priest from mass. To-day the peasants let themselves be seen in the field outside the Galgenthor.

The following Monday, while the priest was performing service in the parish church and chanting "Adjuva nos, deus salutaris noster" [Save us, Lord our salvation!], Ernfried Kumpf addressed him rudely, saying that if he wished to save himself he would better leave the altar. Kumpf then knocked the missal on to the floor and drove the scholars out of the choir.

On Tuesday eight hundred peasants came together. Those who would not join them willingly they forced to do so or took their property, as happened to a peasant at Wettring.

On Friday the peasants all gathered, as many as two thousand strong, and camped near Neusitz. Lorenz Knobloch went out to them, and they promised to make him a captain. The same day some of the peasants were sent into the town to give a report of their demands and plans. Meanwhile representatives of the emperor and of the Swabian League arrive with a hope of making peace, but they ride away without accomplishing anything, as did those from Nuremberg.

On this same day all the artisans were to lay all their complaints and demands before a committee. The taxes, wages, and methods of weighing were discussed. The peasants encamped near Santhof. Friday, April 7, Kueplein, during the sermon, threw the lighted oil lamps about the church. Some of the peasants came into Rothenburg and the neighboring towns, everywhere plundering cupboards and cellars.

On Good Friday all services were suspended in the churches of Rothenburg, for there was neither chanting nor preaching except that Dr. John Teuschel preached against emperor, kings, princes, and lords, ecclesiastical and lay, with foul abuse and slander, on the ground that they were hindering God's word.

On Saturday the blind monk, Hans Rotfuchs, spoke contemptuously of the holy sacrament, calling it idolatry and heresy.

On Holy Easter there was neither singing nor preaching. . . .

April 18. The reforms of the committee are proclaimed. The younger priests may, and should, marry, and may enjoy their benefices for three years. The old priests shall have theirs for life. There is a struggle between Kueplein and his followers, on the one hand, who want to destroy a picture of the Virgin, and the pious old Christians, on the other, who wish to protect it. Some knives are drawn.

April 19. The peasants take three casks of wine from the priest at Scheckenpach and drink it up.

April 20. The women here in Rothenburg take eleven measures of grain from the house of Conrad Volemar. George Bermeter [one of the revolutionists] is chosen burgomaster.

On the same day, Thursday after Easter, the women run up and down Hafengasse with forks and sticks, declaring that they will plunder all the priests' houses, but are prevented.

Friday. All priests are forced to become citizens, otherwise they would have lost all their goods. They are to take their share of guard duty and work on the fortifications.

On Wednesday (April 26) Lorenz Knobloch was hewn to pieces by the peasants at Ostheim, and then they pelted one another with the fragments. They said he was a traitor and that he wanted to mislead them. Divine retribution! He had said he would not die until he had killed three priests, but, thank God, not one fell into his hands.

April 30. The monastery of Anhausen was plundered and burned in the night, also that near Dinkelsbühl. The peasants also attacked the monastery of Schwarzach, and the castle of Reichelsberg was burned.

May 6. Early in the morning the great bell rang three times, summoning the people to hear a message from Margrave Casimir, brought by three noblemen, and inviting all to take refuge in Rothenburg under his protection. The greater part refused, and some were noted by the margrave's representative, and afterward lost their heads.

Monday. The peasants approach Neuhaus, and next day plunder and burn.

In Rothenburg the citizens are summoned to decide whether, like the neighboring towns of Heilbronn, Dinkelsbühl, and Wimfen, they will aid the peasants. The majority decide to send them guns and pikes, powder and lead.

May 12. The clergy forced to take arms like the rest. All monks are compelled to lay aside their cowls and the nuns their veils.

May 15. The bell summoned the community. In spite of the protests of the old Christians, they are forced to obey the majority, and Rothenburg that day fell away from the empire and joined the peasants. In the meantime a gallows was erected in the market place as a warning, according to their ideas of brotherhood. Supplies were sent to the camp.

May 15. The peasants attack the castle of Würzburg and scale the walls, but are all killed. The peasants attempt to get possession of Rothenburg by conspiracy, but are ejected without bloodshed.

May 21. Certain Hohenlohe peasants burn their lord's castle.

On the next Monday Margrave Casimir proceeds with his forces to subdue and punish the peasants. Hans Krelein the older, priest at Wernitz, was beheaded, with four peasants, at Leutershausen. Seven have their fingers cut off. Likewise at Neuenstat eighteen burghers and peasants are beheaded. At Kitzingen fifty-eight have their eyes put out and are forbidden to enter the town again.

On Friday before Whitsuntide the forces of the Swabian League slay four thousand peasants at Königshofen.

On Monday after Whitsunday eight thousand peasants are slaughtered by the troops of the League near Büttart and Sulzdorf. In all these battles the League lost not over one hundred and fifty men.

On June 6 messengers are sent from Rothenburg to Casimir to ask for pardon. Next day others are sent to the League, but they are told that they must surrender unconditionally.

On Thursday following, after the League had retaken the town of Würzburg, they beheaded sixty-two.

After the League had attacked Bamberg they beheaded twenty-one.

On Friday after Corpus Christi, mass was once more chanted in Rothenburg, as formerly.

June 17. Vespers, complines, and matins are once more sung.

On June 23 Dr. John Teuschel and the blind monk Hans are taken and shut up, but several others, including Dr. Andreas Carlstadt, who had done most to stir up trouble, secretly escape.

On the eve of Peter and Paul's day Margrave Casimir rides into Rothenburg with four hundred horsemen, a thousand footmen, and two hundred wagons full of arms and equipments.

Next day four hundred foot soldiers belonging to the margrave and the League divide into two parts. One went to the village of Orenbach, which they plundered, and burned the church to the ground. The

other went to Pretheim, a fine village. This they plundered, killing a number of people, including the innkeeper, behind a table. They burned the village, including the church, and carried off six hundred head of cattle and thirty carts full of plunder.

June 30. The citizens of Rothenburg are summoned to the market place by a herald and surrounded by pikemen. They are accused of deserting the empire and joining the peasants, and are threatened with the vengeance they deserve.

The names of a number of citizens are read off, and they are beheaded on the spot. Their bodies are left on the market place all day. Some got away through the ring of soldiers: Lorenz Diem, the sexton, Joseph Schad, a tanner, Fritz Dalck, a butcher, and others, but were nevertheless executed.

July 1. Fifteen more are beheaded in the market place, including the blind monk. All the bodies are left on the market place all day, then buried. All of these died without confession or the last sacrament, and did not even ask for it.

D. A Peasant Band Pressures a Reluctant Community, 1525

Dear brothers in Christ, our friendly greetings. You have probably heard that our assembly has met at Rappertsweiler on the hill and that we have entered a Christian undertaking. . . . We have heard that some in Hofsteig speak ill of our Christian undertaking, which displeases and disturbs us, and we once again hope that you, the magistrate and entire community, will do as many other Christian people have done and support and not oppose us, and will confirm this in writing. If that does not happen, we must suppose that what has been reported to us is true, and that we will neither tolerate nor endure. Therefore, dear brothers and neighbors, think it over carefully and aid us in our Christian enterprise, and we will commit our lives, honor, and goods to you as Christian brothers. You should do the same for us. Dated in haste at Tettnang on the Tuesday after Invocavit, anno 25.

E. Thomas Müntzer Exhorts His Parishioners, 1525

May the pure fear of God be with you, dear brothers. How long are you going to slumber, how long are you going to resist God's will . . . ? If you are unwilling to suffer for the sake of God, then you will have to be martyrs for the devil. . . . The whole of

Germany, France, Italy is awake; the master wants to set the game in motion, the evildoers are for it. At Fulda four abbeys were laid waste during Easter week, the peasants in the Klettgau and the Hegau in the Black Forest have risen, three thousand strong. . . .

Even if there are only three of you whose trust in God is imperturbable and who seek his name and honor alone, you need have no fear of a hundred thousand. So go to it, go to it, go to it! The time has come, the evildoers are running like scared dogs! . . . Pay no attention to the cries of the godless . . . they will whimper and wheedle like children. Show no pity, as God has commanded in the words of Moses, Deuteronomy 7:[1–5] . . . Alert the villages and towns and especially the mineworkers and other good fellows who will be of use. We cannot slumber any longer.

. . . The time has come. Let Balthasar and Barthel Krump, Valentin and Bischof lead the dance! Let this letter go out to the miners . . .

Go to it, go to it, while the fire is hot. Hammer away ding-dong on the anvils of Nimrod [i.e. the princes and lords], cast down their tower to the ground! As long as they live it is impossible for you to rid yourselves of the fear of men . . . Go to it, go to it, while it is day. God goes before you; follow, follow . . .

This is what God says, "You should have no fear. You should not shrink from this great host; it is not your fight, but the Lord's." . . .

Mühlhausen, in the year 1525.

Thomas Müntzer, a servant of God against the godless.

F. Luther Rages "Against the Murdering and Robbing Bands of Peasants"

In my preceding pamphlet [on the "Twelve Articles"] I had no occasion to condemn the peasants, because they promised to yield to law and better instruction, as Christ also demands (Matt. vii. 1). But before I can turn around, they go out and appeal to force, in spite of their promises, and rob and pillage and act like mad dogs. From this it is quite apparent what they had in their false minds, and that what they put forth under the name of the gospel in the "Twelve Articles" was all vain pretense. In short, they practice mere devil's work, and it is the arch-devil himself who reigns at Mühlhausen,[1] indulging in nothing but rob-

[1] Thomas Münzer

bery, murder, and bloodshed; as Christ says of the devil in John viii. 44, "he was a murderer from the beginning." Since, therefore, those peasants and miserable wretches allow themselves to be led astray and act differently from what they declared, I likewise must write differently concerning them; and first bring their sins before their eyes, as God commands (Isa. lviii. 1; Ezek. ii. 7), whether perchance some of them may come to their senses; and, further, I would instruct those in authority how to conduct themselves in this matter.

With threefold horrible sins against God and men have these peasants loaded themselves, for which they have deserved a manifold death of body and soul.

First, they have sworn to their true and gracious rulers to be submissive and obedient, in accord with God's command. . . . But since they have deliberately and sacrilegiously abandoned their obedience, and in addition have dared to oppose their lords, they have thereby forfeited body and soul, as perfidious, perjured, lying, disobedient wretches and scoundrels are wont to do. . . .

Second, they cause uproar and sacrilegiously rob and pillage monasteries and castles that do not belong to them, for which, like public highwaymen and murderers, they deserve the twofold death of body and soul. It is right and lawful to slay at the first opportunity a rebellious person, who is known as such, for he is already under God's and the emperor's ban. Every man is at once judge and executioner of a public rebel; just as, when a fire starts, he who can extinguish it first is the best fellow. Rebellion is not simply vile murder, but is like a great fire that kindles and devastates a country; it fills the land with murder and bloodshed, makes widows and orphans, and destroys everything, like the greatest calamity. Therefore, whosoever can, should smite, strangle, and stab, secretly or publicly, and should remember that there is nothing more poisonous, pernicious, and devilish than a rebellious man. Just as one must slay a mad dog, so, if you do not fight the rebels, they will fight you, and the whole country with you.

Third, they cloak their frightful and revolting sins with the gospel, call themselves Christian brethren, swear allegiance, and compel people to join them in such abominations. Thereby they become the greatest blasphemers and violators of God's holy name, and serve and honor the devil under the semblance of the gospel, so that they have ten times deserved death of body and soul, for never have I heard of uglier sins. And I believe also that the devil foresees the judgment day, that he undertakes such an unheard-of measure; as if he said, "It is the last and therefore it shall be the worst; I'll stir up the dregs and knock the very bottom out." May the Lord restrain him! Lo, how mighty a prince is the devil, how he holds the world in his hands and can put it to confusion: who else could so soon capture so many thousands of peasants, lead them astray, blind and deceive them, stir them to revolt, and make them the willing executioners of his malice. . . .

And should the peasants prevail (which God forbid!),—for all things are possible to God, and we know not but that he is preparing for the judgment day, which cannot be far distant, and may purpose to destroy, by means of the devil, all order and authority and throw the world into wild chaos,—yet surely they who are found, sword in hand, shall perish in the wreck with clear consciences, leaving to the devil the kingdom of this world and receiving instead the eternal kingdom. For we are come upon such strange times that a prince may more easily win heaven by the shedding of blood than others by prayers.

G. Rothenburg Condemns the Anabaptist Michael Sattler, 1527

"In regard to the articles relating to me and my brethren and sisters, hear this brief answer:

"First, that we have acted contrary to the imperial mandate, we do not admit. For the same says that the Lutheran doctrine and delusion is not to be adhered to, but only the gospel and the Word of God. This we have kept. For I am not aware that we have acted contrary to the gospel and the Word of God. I appeal to the words of Christ.

"Secondly, that the real body of Christ the Lord is not present in the sacrament, we admit. For the Scripture says: Christ ascended into heaven and sitteth on the right hand of his Heavenly Father, whence he shall come to judge the quick and the dead, from which it follows that, if he is in heaven and not in the bread, he may not be eaten bodily.

"Thirdly, as to baptism we say infant baptism is of no avail to salvation. For it is written [Rom. 1:17] that we live by faith alone. Again [Mark 16:16]: He that believeth and is baptized shall be saved. Peter says the same [I, ch. 3:21]: Which doth also now save you in baptism (which is signified by that [Ark of Noah]), not the putting away of the filth of the flesh but rather the convenant of a good conscience with God by the resurrection of Jesus Christ. . . .

[He goes on to deny having insulted the Blessed Virgin.]

"Sixthly, we hold that we are not to swear before the authorities, for the Lord says [Matt. 5:34]: Swear not, but let your communication be, Yea, yea; nay, nay.

"Seventhly, when God called me to testify of his Word and I had read Paul and also considered the unchristian and perilous state in which I was, beholding the pomp, pride, usury, and great whoredom of the monks and priests, I went and took unto me a wife, according to the command of God; for Paul well prophesies concerning this to Timothy [I, ch. 4:3]: In the latter time it shall come to pass that men shall forbid to marry and command to abstain from meats which God hath created to be received with thanksgiving.

"Eighthly, if the Turks should come, we ought not to resist them. For it is written [Matt. 5:21]: Thou shalt not kill. We must not defend ourselves against the Turks and others of our persecutors, but are to beseech God with earnest prayer to repel and resist them. . . .

"In conclusion, ministers of God, I admonish you to consider the end for which God has appointed you, to punish the evil and to defend and protect the pious. Whereas, then, we have not acted contrary to God and the gospel, you will find that neither I nor my brethren and sisters have offended in word or deed against any authority. Therefore, ministers of God, if you have neither heard nor read the Word of God, send for the most learned men and for the sacred books of the Bible in whatsoever language they may be and let them confer with us in the Word of God. If they prove to us with the Holy Scriptures that we err and are in the wrong, we will gladly desist and recant and also willingly suffer the sentence and punishment for that of which we have been accused; but if no error is proven to us, I hope to God that you will be converted and receive instruction."

Upon this speech the judges laughed and put their heads together, and the town clerk of Ensisheim said: "Yes, you infamous, desperate rascal of a monk, should we dispute with you? The hangman will dispute with you, I assure you!"

Michael said: "God's will be done."

The town clerk said: "It were well if you had never been born."

Michael replied: "God knows what is good."

The town clerk: "You archheretic, you have seduced pious people. If they would only now forsake their error and commit themselves to grace!"

Michael: "Grace is with God alone."

One of the prisoners also said: "We must not depart from the truth."

The town clerk: "Yes, you desperate villain, you archheretic, I say, if there were no hangman here, I would hang you myself and be doing God a good service thereby."

Michael: "God will judge aright."

[While the judges were deliberating, Sattler was mocked and insulted by the soldiers guarding him.]

The judges having returned to the room, the sentence was read. It was as follows: . . . [J]udgment is passed that Michael Sattler shall be delivered to the executioner, who shall lead him to the place of execution and cut out his tongue, then forge him fast to a wagon and thereon with red-hot tongs twice tear pieces from his body; and after he has been brought outside the gate, he shall be plied five times more in the same manner. . . .

After this had been done in the manner prescribed, he was burned to ashes as a heretic. His fellow brethren were executed with the sword, and the sisters drowned. His wife, also after being subjected to many entreaties, admonitions, and threats, under which she remained steadfast, was drowned a few days afterward. Done the 21st day of May, A.D. 1527.

H. The Anabaptist Obbe Philips Sorrowfully Recants

Just as John Matthijs was truly Enoch with the true commission and apostolic office, so he also came to his end and received his reward according to his works. Melchior died in prison and did not come out again as the prophets and prophetesses had predicted, and all his intentions with all his following toppled to the ground and came to nothing more. John Matthijs, as an apostle and Enoch, was beaten before the gates of Münster in a skirmish or hostile encounter, for he daily strode there in his armor and with his musket like a wild man out of his senses. He was so fierce and bloodthirsty that he brought various people to their deaths; yea, and he was so violent that even his enemies for their part were terrified of him, and when finally in a tumult they became too powerful for him, they were so incensed that they did not just kill him like other people but hacked and chopped him into little pieces, so that his brethren had to carry him in a basket when the tumult was over. Yet some of the brethren insisted that, following the prophecy of Enoch and Elijah, he would be resurrected on the fourth day and before all people he would rise up to heaven or be carried away by a cloud. So blind with such frightful blindness were some of them smitten. . . .

O how many times were some of us so distressed to death that the heart in our bodies turned cold, and we did not know where to turn, nor what best to do; the whole world pursued us to death with fire, water, sword, and bloody tyranny for our belief. The prophecies deceived us on all sides and the letter of the Scriptures took us prisoner. . . .

. . . I shall be silent about all the false commissions, prophecies, visions, dreams, revelations, and unspeakable spiritual pride which immediately from the first hour stole in among the brethren. For those baptized one day cried on the morrow about all the godless, that they must be rooted out. And actually, as soon as anyone was baptized, he was at once a pious Christian and slandered all people and admitted no one on earth to be good but himself and his fellow brethren. Was that not a great and terrible pride? And who can express the great wrangling and dissension among the congregations, of debating and arguing about the Tabernacle of Moses, the cloven claw, about the commission, the armor of David, about the thousand-year Kingdom of Christ on earth, about the incarnation, baptism, belief, Supper, the promised David, second marriage, free will, predestination, the conscious sin unto death. And all this occurred with ban, condemnations, blasphemy, slander, the blackening of reputation, backbiting, judging, and adjudication, [the labeling of others] as heretical, godless, papistical, Lutheran, Zwinglian. And this the brethren did among each other, the one as much as the other, the one this and the other that. . . .

Document Set 15.6 References

A. The German Peasants Plead for Justice: The Twelve Articles
Translations and Reprints from the Original Sources of European History (Philadelphia: University of Pennsylvania Press, 1898), 2/6:25–30.

B. The Zurich City Council and Local Peasants Debate the Justice of Tithes, 1525
Johannes Stumpf, *Reformation Chronicle*, in Tom Scott and Bob Scribner, eds., *The German Peasants' War* (Atlantic Highlands, N.J.: Humanities Press International, 1991), 111–113.

C. The Peasants' War Engulfs Rothenburg, 1525
Michael Eisenhart, in James Harvey Robinson, ed., *Readings in European History* (Boston: Ginn, 1904), 2:106.

D. A Peasant Band Pressures a Reluctant Community, 1525
Captain and Councillors in Tettnang, in Scott and Scribner, 135.

E. Thomas Müntzer Exhorts His Parishioners, 1525
Müntzer, open letter, in Scott and Scribner, 238.

F. Luther Rages "Against the Murdering and Robbing Bands of Peasants"
Martin Luther, in Robinson, 2:106–108.

G. Rothenburg Condemns the Anabaptist Michael Sattler, 1527
Martyrs' Mirror, excerpted in Library of Christian Classics, vol. 25: *Spiritual and Anabaptist Writers*, ed. G. H. Williams (Philadelphia: Westminster Press, n.d.), 138–144.

H. The Anabaptist Obbe Philips Sorrowfully Recants
"Obbe Philips: A Confession," trans. C. T. Lievstro, Library of Christian Classics, 25:221–225.

DOCUMENT SET 15.7
Calvin and the Radicals

In many respects John Calvin (1509–1564) was the heir of the Christian humanist reformers; indeed, he began his career as a humanist, editing Seneca. In his *Institutes of the Christian Religion* (first published in 1536 and revised and expanded several times during his lifetime), Calvin emphatically rejected the charge of "innovator," raised by his Catholic opponents to discredit him (Document A). In the case of Document B, an extract from the *Institutes* in which Calvin spells out his doctrine of predestination, the reformer would likewise have indignantly rejected the label "innovator." Judging from this evidence, why was it so important for sixteenth-century reformers of all camps to insist that they were not innovators but, rather, their opponents were?

Documents C to E all refer to the rigorous regime over which Calvin presided at Geneva. Assess its aims and methods in indoctrinating and coercing (where necessary) the people of Geneva. Would you have liked to live there? Consider your answer both from a twentieth-century perspective and from that of the sixteenth century. In what ways does this regime show Calvin to be an heir of humanism—and, perhaps, of Savonarola (see Set 15.4, Document A)?

Both in Geneva and in east-central Europe the Calvinist movement bore the brunt of defending theological orthodoxy against a growing array of radical critics who attacked such ideas as the Trinity (that is, the teaching that Christianity's One God consisted of three equal manifestations, Father, Son, and Holy Spirit). The Spanish physician Miguel Servetus (1511–1553) was one of the principal preachers of the antitrinitarian position (that God, the Father, is the sole God and that Jesus, the Son, was a man mystically raised to something approaching divinity). Servetus's arguments were difficult to refute without simply reverting to the decrees of ancient church bodies like the fourth-century Council of Nicaea (see Chapter 7). Document F details the charges that the Genevan authorities made against him when Servetus was discovered in that city. Calvin approved the death sentence but tried in vain to have it carried out in a less horrifying manner than burning at the stake, which was Servetus's eventual fate. Document G suggests how readily Servetus's ideas, as well as other radical and Anabaptist teachings, spread in the late sixteenth century in Poland-Lithuania, where central authority was generally too weak (and usually disinclined) to persecute. The Polish-Lithuanian com-

monwealth, indeed, became a kind of test case for the variety of ways in which complex Christian teachings were understood by unsophisticated lay people (such as were the local gentry, who decided what faith would be preached in their local parish church). The author of this document, Andrzej Lubieniecki, was a nobleman who belonged to a sect that eventually coalesced in a communistic community at the little town of Raków, Poland. What, in your opinion, were the sources of these radical ideas, and how do they relate to the impulses set in motion by Servetus?

A. Calvin Rejects the Charge of "Innovation," 1536

[Our detractors call our teaching] new, and lately forged they cavil that it is doubtful and uncertain; they demand by what miracle it is confirmed; they ask whether it be meet that it should prevail against the consent of so many holy fathers and the most ancient customs; they press upon us to confess it to be schismatical, which moveth war against the Church, or that the true Church hath lain dead through the many ages in which no such thing hath been heard of. Last of all, they say that they need no arguments, for (say they) it may be judged by its fruits of what sort it is, which, namely, hath bred so big a heap of sects, so many turmoils of sedition, so great licentiousness of vices. Truly, full easy it is for them to triumph over a forsaken cause among the credulous and ignorant multitude, but if we might also have our turn to speak, verily this sharp haste would soon be cooled wherewith they do, licentiously and with full mouth, foam against us.

First, whereas they call it new, they do great wrong to God, whose holy word deserves not to be accused of newness. To them indeed I nothing doubt that it is new, to whom Christ is new, and his gospel is new. But they that know the preaching of Paul to be old, and that Jesus Christ died for our sins and rose again for our justification, shall find nothing new among us. Secondly, that it hath long lain hidden, unknown, and buried,—that is the fault of the ungodliness of men. Sith it is by the bountifulness of God restored to us, it ought at least, by right of full restitution, to receive the title of anciety.

They may mock at the uncertainty of our teachings, but if they were driven to steal their own doctrine with their own blood and with the loss of their lives, men might see how much they set by it. Far other is our faith, which dreadeth neither the terrors of death nor yet the very judgment seat of God. . . .

As for the dilemma into which they would drive us, to compel us to confess that either the Church hath lain dead a certain time, or that we have controversy against the real Church: truly the Church of Christ hath lived and shall live so long as Christ shall reign at the right hand of the father. . . . But they err not a little from the truth when they acknowledge no church but that which they see with the present eye, and when they affirm that the form of the Church is always to be seen; for they set the true form of the Church in the see of Rome and in the order of their prelates. We, on the contrary side, affirm both that the Church may consist of no visible form, and that the form itself is not contained in that outward splendor which they foolishly admire, but hath a far other indication, namely, the pure teaching of the word of God and the right ministration of the sacraments. . . .

Thus, O King, is the venomous injustice of slanders so largely spread abroad that you should not too easily believe their reports. . . . Your mind, though it be now turned away and estranged from us, yea, even inflamed against us, yet we trust that we shall be able to recover the favor thereof. But if the whisperings of the malicious do so possess your ears that there is no place for accused men to speak for themselves; and if those outrageous furies do still, with your winking at them, exercise cruelty, with prisoning, tormenting, mutilating, and burning,—then shall we indeed, as sheep appointed to the slaughter, be brought to all extremities, yet so that in our patience we shall possess our soul and wait for the strong hand of the Lord, which shall without doubt be present in time and stretch forth itself armed, both to deliver the poor out of affliction and to take vengeance on the despisers which now triumph with so great assuredness.

The Lord, the King of kings, establish your throne with righteousness and your seat with equity, most noble King.

At Basel, the tenth day before the Kalends of September.

B. Calvin Explains Predestination

Therefore we say that the Scripture shows that God, by His eternal and immutable counsel once for all determined both those whom He desired one day to admit to salvation and those whom He would give back to destruction. We affirm that this counsel as to the elect is founded upon His gratuitous mercy, with-out any respect to human merit; but to those whom He had handed over to damnation, by His just and blameless though incomprehensible judgment, the way of life is closed.

In the case of the elect we regard calling as an evidence of election, and justification another token of its manifestation, until they arrive in glory, where its fulness shall be found. Just as God seals His elect by calling and justification, so by shutting out the rejected ones either from the knowledge of His name or the sanctification of His spirit He makes known to them the judgment that awaits them.

C. Calvin Plans the Regeneration of Geneva, 1537

Our Lord established excommunication as a means of correction and discipline, by which those who led a disordered life unworthy of a Christian, and who despised to mend their ways and return to the strait way after they had been admonished, should be expelled from the body of the church and cut off as rotten members until they come to themselves and acknowledge their fault. . . . We have an example given by St. Paul (1 Tim. i and 1 Cor. v), in a solemn warning that we should not keep company with one who is called a Christian but who is, none the less, a fornicator, covetous, an idolater, a railer, a drunkard, or an extortioner. So if there be in us any fear of God, this ordinance should be enforced in our Church.

To accomplish this we have determined to petition you [i.e. the town council] to establish and choose, according to your good pleasure, certain persons [namely, the elders] of upright life and good repute among all the faithful, likewise constant and not easy to corrupt, who shall be assigned and distributed in all parts of the town and have an eye on the life and conduct of every individual. If one of these see any obvious vice which is to be reprehended, he shall bring this to the attention of some one of the ministers, who shall admonish whoever it may be who is at fault and exhort him in a brotherly way to correct his ways. If it is apparent that such remonstrances do no good, he shall be warned that his obstinacy will be reported to the church. Then if he repents, there is in that alone excellent fruit of this form of discipline. If he will not listen to warnings, it shall be time for the minister, being informed by those who have the matter in charge, to declare publicly to the congregation the efforts which have been made to bring the sinner to amend, and how all has been in vain.

Should it appear that he proposes to persevere in

his hardness of heart, it shall be time to excommunicate him; that is to say, that the offender shall be regarded as cast out from the companionship of Christians and left in the power of the devil for his temporal confusion, until he shall give good proofs of penitence and amendment. In sign of his casting out he shall be excluded from the communion, and the faithful shall be forbidden to hold familiar converse with him. Nevertheless he shall not omit to attend the sermons in order to receive instruction, so that it may be seen whether it shall please the Lord to turn his heart to the right way.

The offenses to be corrected in this manner are those named by St. Paul above, and others like them. When others than the said deputies—for example, neighbors or relatives—shall first have knowledge of such offenses, they may make the necessary remonstrances themselves. If they accomplish nothing, then they shall notify the deputies to do their duty.

This then is the manner in which it would seem expedient to us to introduce excommunication into our Church and maintain it in its full force; for beyond this form of correction the Church does not go. But should there be insolent persons, abandoned to all perversity, who only laugh when they are excommunicated and do not mind living and dying in that condition of rejection, it shall be your affair to determine whether you should long suffer such contempt and mocking of God to pass unpunished. . . .

If those who agree with us in faith should be punished by excommunication for their offenses, how much more should the Church refuse to tolerate those who oppose us in religion? The remedy that we have thought of is to petition you to require all the inhabitants of your city to make a confession and give an account of their faith, so that you may know who agree with the gospel and who, on the contrary, would prefer the kingdom of the pope to the kingdom of Jesus Christ.

D. Genevan Children Learn Calvinist Doctrine

Concerning the Lord's Supper.

The minister. Have we in the supper simply a signification of the things above mentioned, or are they given to us in reality?

The child. Since Jesus Christ is truth itself there can be no doubt that the promises he has made regarding the supper are accomplished, and that what is figured there is verified there also. Wherefore according as he promises and represents I have no doubt that he makes us partakers of his own substance, in order that he may unite us with him in one life.

The minister. But how may this be, when the body of Jesus Christ is in heaven, and we are on this earthly pilgrimage?

The child. It comes about through the incomprehensible power of his spirit, which may indeed unite things widely separated in space.

The minister. You do not understand then that the body is enclosed in the bread, or the blood in the cup?

The child. No. On the contrary, in order that the reality of the sacrament be achieved our hearts must be raised to heaven, where Jesus Christ dwells in the glory of the Father, whence we await him for our redemption; and we are not to seek him in these corruptible elements.

The minister. You understand then that there are two things in this sacrament: the natural bread and wine, which we see with the eye, touch with the hand and perceive with the taste; and Jesus Christ, through whom our souls are inwardly nourished?

The child. I do. In such a way moreover that we have there the very witness and so say a pledge of the resurrection of our bodies; since they are made partakers in the symbol of life.

E. Geneva Suppresses Catholic Piety, 1546

[August 31, 1546]. The sister of Sr. Curtet, Lucresse, to whom remonstrances have been made on account of her going with certain monies to have masses said at Nessy by the monks of St. Claire. Questioned whether she has no scruples as to what she says. Replied that her father and mother have brought her up to obey a different law from the one now in force here: however she does not despise the present law. Asked as to when was the festival of St. Felix, she replied that it was yesterday. Asked if she had not fasted, she replied that she fasted when it pleased her. Asked if she did not desire to pray to a single God; said that she did. Asked if she did not pray to St. Felix; said that she prayed to St. Felix and other saints who interceded for her. She is very obstinate. Decision that she be sent to some minister of her choice every sermon day and that the Lord's supper be withheld from her. *Calvin present.*

F. Calvin's Secretary Presses the Orthodox Case Against the Antitrinitarian Michael Servetus

Nicholas de la Fontaine asserts that he has instituted proceedings against Michael Servetus, and on this account he has allowed himself to be held prisoner in criminal process.

1. In the first place that about twenty-four years ago the defendant commenced to annoy the churches of Germany with his errors and heresies, and was condemned and took to flight in order to escape the punishment prepared for him.

2. *Item,* that on or about this time he printed a wretched book, which has infected many people.

3. *Item,* that since that time he has not ceased by all means in his power to scatter his poison, as much by his construction of biblical text, as by certain annotations which he has made upon Ptolemy.

4. *Item,* that since that time he has printed in secrecy another book containing endless blasphemies.

5. *Item,* that while detained in prison in the city of Vienne [in France], when he saw that they were willing to pardon him on condition of his recanting, he found means to escape from prison.

Said Nicholas demands that said Servetus be examined upon all these points.

And since he is able to evade the question by pretending that his blasphemies and heresies are nought else than good doctrine, said Nicholas proposes certain articles upon which he demands said heretic be examined.

6. To wit, whether he has not written and falsely taught and published that to believe that in a single essence of God there are three distinct persons, the Father, the Son, and the Holy Ghost, is to create four phantoms, which cannot and ought not to be imagined.

7. *Item,* that to put such distinction into the essence of God is to cause God to be divided into three parts, and that this is a threeheaded devil, like to Cerberus, whom the ancient poets have called the dog of hell, a monster, and things equally injurious. . . .

9. *Item,* whether he does not say that our Lord Jesus Christ is not the Son of God, except in so much as he was conceived of the Holy Ghost in the womb of the virgin Mary.

10. *Item,* that those who believe Jesus Christ to have been the word of God the Father, engendered through all eternity, have a scheme of redemption which is fanciful and of the nature of sorcery.

11. *Item,* that Jesus Christ is God, insomuch as God has caused him to be such. . . .

27. *Item,* that the soul of man is mortal, and that the only thing which is immortal is an elementary breath, which is the substance that Jesus Christ now possesses in heaven and which is also the elementary and divine and incorruptible substance of the Holy Ghost. . . .

32. *Item,* that the baptism of little children is an invention of the Devil, an infernal falsehood tending to the destruction of all Christianity. . . .

37. *Item,* that in the person of M. Calvin, minister of the word of God in the Church of Geneva, he has defamed with printed book the doctrine which he preached, uttering all the injurious and blasphemous things which it is possible to invent. . . .

G. Radical Sects Proliferate in Poland-Lithuania

. . . Within a period so short [1562–1572], and in a corner of the world so small as this our land, we saw a mass of various worships the like of which could have been seen but in heathen times: Roman Catholics, Greeks or Armenians, Jewish, Tartar, Karaimian.

There were many tritheists who, rejecting the word Holy Trinity, worshipped three divine beings: God the Father, God the Son, and the Holy Ghost. Such were the Wilno group, the Lithuania and Podlasie groups, and others [in Lithuania].

There were ditheists, who did not recognize the Holy Ghost as a person and claimed the Son and Father were one in essence, out of the Father. Others said that the Son had been born of the Holy Ghost centuries back, and thought him a minor being.

And those were most markedly split in two.

For there were those who baptized infants, and whose leaders were . . . [several named]; and of them, there is no trace. And second were those who did not baptize infants, and whose leaders were . . . [several named], they too are gone or have been dispersed among other denominations.

Then there were those in the Kujawia [in Poland] who held that Jesus had been with the Father for ages; they baptized adults, differed from the ones above in the instruction of exculpation, and followed a rigorous discipline among themselves; their leaders were then . . . [several named].

Besides them were the Dutch Neo-baptists who had come to settle in [West] Prussia, whose ideas they shared and tried to inculcate in the group; they did not fare well either.

There were those who introduced and propagated Moravian communism[1] and concepts, whom the Moravians themselves were helping to bring in; but they accomplished little, and are not heard of any more.

There were also those who spoke of the Scripture as a dead letter and a daub of printer's ink and, wishing to imitate Schwenkfeld[2], held that dreams, visions, and ideas were the things most necessary in religious practice and for salvation; and to them, sins not contravening civil law did not preclude attendance in churches, temples, and synagogues—as offenses committed in body did not matter if spirits were pure.

There were those who condemned all officiating at any religious service, claiming that nobody was fit to officiate or instruct unless he had had a divine revelation and had either witnessed miracles or performed them. Such were . . . [names listed]; and they too were wiped out by the Lord Jesus.

There were also those who were loutish themselves, walked, lay, and labored in uncouth manner—claiming their ways to be favored by God; and, preening themselves because of them, thought other people undeserving of eternal life. They too are gone and are not seen any more.

There were those who incited godly and honest men to relinquish their offices, put away their arms, refuse litigation regardless of the wrong sustained, and who forbade the repeating of an oath. Many decent men left their offices and sold their estates or scattered their possessions.

But also there were some whose transgression was the worst—and whom Satan strew most thickly throughout Lithuania, White Russia [Belarus], Podlasie, Wolynia [northern Ukraine], and the Ukraine—for they did not believe in Jesus Christ. Some mingled together the Old Testament and the Gospel; others placed the Old Testament above the Gospel and introduced Judaism. And of those, some had taken to celebrate the Sabbath, or did not eat dishes not eaten by Jews. But they too were routed by Jesus Christ through his servants, and moreover wiped out so completely that none remained in our lands.

But God's will was done in the last days of [King Sigismund] Augustus' reign [1569–1572], sapping the strength of all the sects or else destroying them. For when people got weary of controversies and quarrels, of the public bickering going on in the Diets and in the synods held nearly every year, there were men who came out to say they had sickened of all worldly affairs and wished to go away some place in a band so as to live together, practice their religion, and await death in peace. At that time, Mr. Sienieński [a Polish nobleman] founded [the town of] Raków, to which flocked people of the same faith—noblemen, burghers, ministers, and countless others, foreigners and scholars. There was no peace, day or night, for three years (1569–1572), for the various debates went on without respite, until, finally, a fair number were converted through the arguments propounded, while the remainder, unconvinced, went on their way and later perished. The ones who stayed on in Raków were those known as Christians; they continued to live together in peace, having elaborated their doctrine and humbled their hearts, or—as they called it—yielded them to the Lord Jesus. Among them were scores of ministers later assigned to different places: ten were brought by Mr. Kiszka to his Podlasie estates in Lithuania, the Wojewoda Sieniawski took some to Ruthenia [the western Ukraine], Prince Zbaraski had others go to Wolynia, and various noblemen also distributed them throughout their estates.

Document Set 15.7 References

A. Calvin Rejects the Charge of "Innovation," 1536
John Calvin, letter to Francis I, in James Harvey Robinson, ed., *Readings in European History* (Boston: Ginn, 1904), 2:124–126.
B. Calvin Explains Predestination
John Calvin, *Institutes of the Christian Religion,* in *Translations and Reprints from the Original Sources of European History* (Philadelphia: University of Pennsylvania Press, 1898), 3/2:7–8.
C. Calvin Plans the Regeneration of Geneva, 1537
John Calvin's Proposal to Geneva Town Council, in Robinson, 2:130–132.
D. Genevan Children Learn Calvinist Doctrine
John Calvin, *The Genevan Catechism,* in *Translations and Reprints,* 3/2:8–9.
E. Geneva Suppresses Catholic Piety, 1546
Geneva Consistory on Heresy Case, in *Translations and Reprints,* 3/2:9.
F. Calvin's Secretary Presses the Orthodox Case Against the Antitrinitarian Michael Servetus
Nicholas de la Fontaine, in *Translations and Reprints,* 3/2:12–15.
G. Radical Sects Proliferate in Poland-Lithuania
Andrew Lubieniecki, *Polonoeutychia,* in Stanislaw Kot, *Socinianism in Poland,* trans. E. M. Wilbur (Boston: Starr King, 1957), xv–xvii.

[1] A reference to religious and social radicals who established a Hussite- and Anabaptist-influenced community in Moravia (modern Czech Republic) that practiced communism.
[2] Casper Schwenkfeld (1489–1561) was a nobleman who founded a spiritualist movement in Germany that dissented equally from the Lutherans and the Zwinglians; his followers formed small, secret brotherhoods.

DOCUMENT SET 15.8
The Catholic Reformers

This document set, as well as the whole tradition of Erasmian reform (Set 15.4), shows that critics within the Catholic church were conscious of abuses well before Luther appeared. The author of the excerpt in Document A, Gasparo Contarini (1483–1542), a clergyman from a noble Venetian family, remained within the Catholic church and eventually became cardinal. He advocated making concessions that would induce at least the moderate Protestant reformers to return, but his viewpoint did not prevail. Document A, taken from his book *On the Office of Bishops* (1516), appealed to the clergy to root out superstition and encourage "true piety." The Spaniard St. Ignatius de Loyola (1491–1556), the founder of the Jesuit Order, demanded of his followers unswerving obedience to the pope and—as Document B shows—intense devotion, though not asceticism to the point of damaging health. What stand does Loyola take on the great doctrinal issues of the day? The Jesuits were later to become famous for their insistence that individuals could exercise free will to choose repentance and good works, and thus merit salvation; what evidence do you see for this in Loyola's rules?

Document C is an extract from the Council of Trent's final decrees. The Council condemned heresy in terms calculated to draw the sharpest possible line between Catholicism and Protestant "heresy." What evidence for this do you see in Document C? Compare the Council of Trent's approach to thirteenth-century efforts to tighten up church discipline (Set 12.2). Do you see any common threads, and if so, what are they?

A. Gasparo Contarini Attacks Superstition and Impiety, 1516

The other sin . . . is superstition which is what I might call an exaggeration [*excessus*] of religion. . . . Therefore let all superstition be diligently destroyed, so that when the saints dwelling in heaven are invoked or their relics are venerated or likenesses of the Lord, the Most Blessed Virgin, and other saints are depicted in the churches everything be done with the greatest propriety and in good order. Such practices ought to lead the people to the worship of the one God as if they were leading them step by step by hand, so to speak. But if any abuse in these matters does creep in, it will be well for the prudent Bishop and ecclesiastic to do away with it gradually, lest, if we are carried along hastily or without consideration, we destroy the very worship of God, faith in the sacraments, and also the hierarchical order of the Church as heretics have done. Consequently, let the people often be taught that in all things God must be loved and worshipped; also, that all exists because of God without whom nothing has been made; and that the saints themselves are nothing. Thus, let every action and thought proceed from Him and to Him finally return, as the Alpha and Omega. If men have recourse to the saints, let them know why they are doing it and in addition what has been most wisely decreed and explained by the Councils. But if anyone, either because of avarice or for some other reason, should make wrong use of relics or sacred images, let such plagues at once be kept far from the Church of God and let a heavy penalty be imposed, lest Christian purity be corrupted by these perversions.

When the error of superstition and the sin of impiety have been avoided, the people can be easily kept in the right religious path. Nevertheless, let the Bishop take care that everyone frequent the sacraments of Penance and the Eucharist at least at the proper times, and let him inquire about this of the priests in charge of the districts of the city and the villages. If anyone fails in this obligation, let the Bishop first endeavor, having summoned the offender before him, to call him back to his duty and the right path of piety by persuasion and gentle rebuking. But if he observes that anyone obstinately persists in his wrongdoing and refuses to be corrected, then let him judge him guilty before others and subject to the ecclesiastical fines and censures, lest others also be infected by contact with the evil of that man.

Further, let the Bishop attend to the education of the young people, and let him not allow, as far as he is able, the souls of boys from their youth to be corrupted by the licentiousness of poets and other authors of this kind. If the young drink in such wantonness in their childhood years, it will be almost impossible to summon them again at a maturer age to greater virtue. . . .

B. St. Ignatius Loyola Codifies the Rules for Thinking with the Catholic Church

In order to think truly, as we ought, in the church militant, the following rules are to be observed.

Laying aside all private judgment, we ought to keep our minds prepared and ready to obey in all things the true Spouse of Christ our Lord, which is our Holy Mother, the Hierarchical Church.

The second is to praise confession made to a priest, and the reception of the Most Holy Sacrament, once a year, and what is much better once a month, and much better still every eight days, always with the requisite and due dispositions.

The third is to praise the frequent hearing of Mass, also hymns, psalms, and long prayers, both in and out of the church, and likewise the hours ordained at fixed times for all the Divine Office, for prayers of any kind, and all the canonical hours.

The fourth, to praise greatly religious orders, and a life of virginity and continency, and not to praise the married state as much as any of these.

The fifth is to praise the vows of religion, of Obedience, Poverty, and Chastity, and vows to perform other works of perfection and supererogation; and it is to be noticed that as a vow is made in matters more nearly approaching evangelical perfection, so in matters which depart from it a vow ought not to be made, *e.g.*, to become a merchant or to enter the marriage state. &c.

The sixth is to praise the relics of saints, showing veneration to the relics, and praying to the saints, and to praise likewise the Stations, pilgrimages, indulgences, jubilees, Bulls of the *Cruciata* [crusade], and candles lighted in churches.

The seventh is to praise the precepts with regard to fasts and abstinences, as those of Lent, Ember days, Vigils, Fridays, and Saturdays; likewise not only interior but also exterior penances.

To praise the building and the ornaments of churches; and also images, and to venerate them according to what they represent.

Finally, to praise all the precepts of the Church, keeping our minds ready to seek reasons to defend, never to impugn them. . . .

To attain the truth in all things, we ought always to hold that we believe what seems to us white to be black, if the Hierarchical Church so defines it; believing that between Christ our Lord the Bridegroom and the Church His Bride there is one and the same Spirit, which governs and directs us to the salvation of our souls; for our Holy Mother the Church is guided and ruled by the same Spirit and Lord that gave the Ten Commandments.

Although it is very true that no one can be saved without being predestined, and without having faith and grace, we must be very careful in our manner of speaking and treating of all this subject.

We ought not habitually to speak of much of Predestination; but if sometimes mention be made of it in any way, we must so speak that the common people may not fall into error, as happens sometimes when they say: "It is already fixed whether I am to be saved or damned, and there cannot be any other result whether I do good or ill"; and, becoming slothful in consequence, they neglect works conducive to their salvation, and to the spiritual profit of their souls.

In the same way it is to be noticed that we must take heed lest by speaking much with great earnestness on Faith, without any distinction or explanation, occasion be given to the people to become slothful and sluggish in good works, whether it be before or after that faith is formed in charity.

In like manner we ought not to speak or to insist on the doctrine of Grace so strongly, as to give rise to that poisonous teaching that takes away free-will. Therefore, we may treat of Faith and Grace, as far as we may with the help of God, for the greater praise of His Divine Majesty; but not in such a way, especially in these dangerous times of ours, that works or free-will receive any detriment, or come to be accounted for nothing.

Although it is above all things praiseworthy to greatly serve God our Lord out of pure love, yet we ought much to praise the fear of His Divine Majesty, because not only is filial fear a pious and most holy thing, but even servile fear, when a man does not rise to anything better and more useful, is of great help to him to escape from mortal sin; and, after he has escaped from it, he easily attains to filial fear, which is altogether acceptable and pleasing to God our Lord, because it is inseparable from Divine love.

C. The Council of Trent Decrees Reform and Condemns Protestant Doctrine

The universal Church has always understood that the penance complete confession of sins was instituted by the Lord, and is of divine right necessary for all who have fallen into sin after baptism; because our Lord Jesus Christ, when about to ascend from earth to heaven, left priests, his own vicars, as leaders and judges, before whom all the mortal offenses into which the faithful of Christ may have fallen should be carried, in order that, in accordance with the power of the keys, they may pronounce the sentence of forgiveness or of retention of sins. For it is manifest that priests could not have exercised this judgment without knowledge of the case. . . .

This holy Council enjoins on all bishops and others who are charged with teaching, that they instruct the faithful diligently concerning the intercession and invocation of saints, the honor paid to relics, and the legitimate use of images. Let them teach that the saints, who reign together with Christ, offer up their own prayers to God for men; that it is good and useful suppliantly to invoke them, and to have recourse to their prayers and aid in obtaining benefits from God, through his Son, Jesus Christ our Lord, who is our sole Redeemer and Saviour; and that those persons think impiously who deny that the saints, who enjoy eternal happiness in heaven, are to be invoked; or who assert that the saints do not pray for men, or that the invocation of them to pray for each of us individually is idolatry; or who declare that it is repugnant to the word of God, and opposed to the honor of the "one mediator of God and men, Christ Jesus," or that it is foolish to supplicate, orally or mentally, those who reign in heaven. . . .

If any one saith that the New Testament does not provide for a distinct, visible priesthood; or that this priesthood has not any power of consecrating and offering up the true body and blood of the Lord, and of forgiving and retaining sins, but is only an office and bare ministry of preaching the gospel; or that those who do not preach are not priests at all; let him be anathema. . . .

If any one saith that by sacred ordination the Holy Ghost is not given, and that vainly therefore do the bishops say, "Receive ye the Holy Ghost"; or that a character is not imprinted by that ordination; or that he who has once been a priest can again become a layman; let him be anathema. . . .

If any one saith that in the Catholic Church there is not a hierarchy instituted by divine ordination, consisting of bishops, priests, and ministers; let him be anathema.

If any one saith that the sacraments of the new law were not all instituted by Jesus Christ, our Lord; or that they are more or less than seven, to wit, baptism, confirmation, the eucharist, penance, extreme unction, orders, and matrimony; or even that any one of these seven is not truly and properly a sacrament; let him be anathema. . . .

In order that the faithful may approach and receive the sacraments with greater reverence and devotion of mind, this Holy Council enjoins on all bishops that, not only when they are themselves about to administer them to the people they shall first explain, in a manner suited to the capacity of those who receive them, the efficacy and use of those sacraments, but they shall endeavor that the same be done piously and prudently by every parish priest; and this even in the vernacular tongue, if need be, and if it can be conveniently done.

Such instruction shall be given in accordance with the form which will be prescribed for each of the sacraments by this holy Council in a catechism, which the bishops shall take care to have faithfully translated into the vulgar tongue, and to have expounded to the people by all parish priests. They shall also explain in the said vulgar tongue, during the solemnization of mass, or the celebration of the divine offices, on all festivals or solemnities, the sacred oracles and the maxims of salvation; and, setting aside all unprofitable questions, they shall endeavor to impress them on the hearts of all, and to instruct their hearers in the law of the Lord. . . .

It is to be desired that those who undertake the office of bishop should understand what their portion is, and comprehend that they are called, not to their own convenience, not to riches or luxury, but to labors and cares, for the glory of God. For it is not to be doubted that the rest of the faithful also will be more easily excited to religion and innocence if they shall see those who are set over them not fixing their thoughts on the things of this world, but on the salvation of souls and on their heavenly country. Wherefore this holy Council, being minded that these things are of the greatest importance towards restoring ecclesiastical discipline, admonishes all bishops that, often mediating thereon, they show themselves conformable to their office by their actual deeds and the actions of their lives; which is a kind of perpetual sermon; but, above all, that they so order their whole conversation that others may thence be able to derive examples of frugality, modesty, continency, and of that holy humility which so much commends us to God.

Wherefore, after the example of our fathers in the Council of Carthage, this Council not only orders that bishops be content with modest furniture, and a frugal table and diet, but that they also give heed that in the rest of their manner of living, and in their whole house, there be nothing seen which is alien to this holy institution, and which does not manifest simplicity, zeal toward God, and a contempt of vanities.

It strictly forbids them, moreover, to strive to

enrich their own kindred or domestics out of the revenues of the Church; seeing that even the canons of the apostles forbid them to give to their kindred the property of the Church, which belongs to God; but if their kindred be poor, let them distribute to them thereof as poor, but not misapply or waste the Church's goods for their sakes: yea, this holy Council, with the utmost earnestness, admonishes them completely to lay aside all this human and carnal affection towards brothers, nephews, and kindred, which is the seed plot of many evils in the Church. And what has been said of bishops, the same is to be observed by all who hold ecclesiastical benefices, whether secular or regular, each according to the nature of his rank. . . .

Document Set 15.8 References

A. Gasparo Contarini Attacks Superstition and Impiety, 1516
Contarini, *De Officio Episcopi,* in John C. Olin, ed., *The Catholic Reformation: Savoranola to Ignatius Loyola* (New York: Harper & Row, 1969), 105–106.

B. St. Ignatius Loyola Codifies the Rules for Thinking with the Catholic Church
Loyola, *Spiritual Exercises,* trans. Burns and Oates, 4th ed. (1908).

C. The Council of Trent Decrees Reform and Condemns Protestant Doctrine
Acts of the Council of Trent, in Robinson, 2:156–161.

DOCUMENT SET 15.9
The Triumph of the State

Document A, an extract from an early sixteenth-century description of the French monarchy by Claude de Seyssel, *The Grand Monarchy of France,* sets forth a very traditional view of how kings and subjects ought to relate to one another. Point out elements in his description that might have been written in the Middle Ages. How realistic does such a political order seem under sixteenth-century conditions? Specifically, how would Seyssel's views be received by his near contemporary, Niccolò Machiavelli (1469–1527)? An extract from Machiavelli's *The Prince* appears as Document B. Why did Machiavelli's ideas so shock his contemporaries, even though the practices he described were commonplace? How would you evaluate Emperor Charles V's instructions to his high official Matthias Held, bearing in mind Seyssel's remarks on how a ruler ought to behave and Machiavelli's observations on how princes actually acted?

The Peace of Augsburg in 1555 ended Catholic resistance to legalizing Lutheranism (not Calvinism or radical Protestantism) within the Holy Roman Empire. How would you evaluate the provisions, excerpted in Document D, from the standpoint of "reasons of state"? What decisions did the Peace leave to the princes?

A. Claude de Seyssel Describes the Traditional Values of the French Monarchy

The authority and power of the king in France is regulated and restrained by three checks . . . the first is Religion, the second, Justice and the third, Police. . . .

With regard to the first, it is an indisputable fact that the French have always been, and still are . . . pious and god-fearing . . . For that reason it is both proper and necessary that whoever is king should make it known to the people by example and by visible and outward signs that he is a zealot, an observer of the Faith and of the Christian religion, and that he is resolved to use his power to sustain and strengthen it . . . so long as the king respects . . . the Christian religion he cannot act as a tyrant. If he is guilty of such an act, it is permissible for a prelate or any other devout man of religion who respects the people, to remonstrate with and to upbraid him, and for a simple preacher to rebuke and accuse him publicly as well as in private. . . .

Justice, which is the second check . . . indubitably carries more weight in France than in any other country in the world, especially because of the institution of the *Parlements,* whose principal rose is to bridle the absolute power which kings might seek to use. . . . In the matter of distributive justice the king has always been subject to these courts, so that in civil cases an individual may gain satisfaction and justice indiscriminately against the king or against his subjects. As far as criminal cases are concerned, royal pardons and remissions are so contested, and those who obtain them are the subject of such violent argument that, lacking hope and confidence in such remissions, few people dare to act in an ill-advised, much less in a thoroughly odious manner. . . . Besides, justice is that much more powerful because those who are deputed to administer it have permanent possession of their offices and the king has no power to remove them, save in the event of forfeiture. . . .

The third check is that of Police, by which is intended those many ordinances that have been promulgated, and subsequently confirmed and approved from time to time, by the kings themselves, which help to preserve the kingdom as a whole and the rights of the individuals who compose it. . . .

Regarding the monarchical state, since everything depends upon the monarch it appears that no other remedy for abuse is required, no other means of maintaining order is necessary than that the king should be good. Because he commands the entire obedience of his subjects he can, without difficulty, enforce the observance and maintenance of good laws, ordinances and customs, he can correct and annul those which are not beneficial or completely faultless, and he can make new laws if necessary; by living in a law-abiding way himself he can induce his subjects to follow his example and . . . do what is right. . . .

B. Niccolò Machiavelli Asks "Whether It Is Prudent for a Prince to Keep His Promises," 1513

Every one understands how praiseworthy it is in a prince to keep faith, and to live uprightly and not craftily. Nevertheless we see, from what has taken place in our own days, that princes who have set little store by their word, but have known how to over-reach men by their cunning, have accomplished great things, and in the end got the better of those who trusted to honest dealing.

Be it known, then, that there are two ways of contending,—one in accordance with the laws, the other by force; the first of which is proper to men, the second to beasts. But since the first method is often ineffectual, it becomes necessary to resort to the second. A prince should, therefore, understand how to use well both the man and the beast.... But inasmuch as a prince should know how to use the beast's nature wisely, he ought of beasts to choose both the lion and the fox; for the lion cannot guard himself from the toils, nor the fox from wolves. He must therefore be a fox to discern toils, and a lion to drive off wolves.

To rely wholly on the lion is unwise; and for this reason a prudent prince neither can nor ought to keep his word when to keep it is hurtful to him and the causes which led him to pledge it are removed. If all men were good, this would not be good advice, but since they are dishonest and do not keep faith with you, you in return need not keep faith with them; and no prince was ever at a loss for plausible reasons to cloak a breach of faith. Of this numberless recent instances could be given, and it might be shown how many solemn treaties and engagements have been rendered inoperative and idle through want of faith among princes, and that he who has best known how to play the fox has had the best success.

It is necessary, indeed, to put a good color on this nature, and to be skilled in simulating and dissembling. But men are so simple, and governed so absolutely by their present needs, that he who wishes to deceive will never fail in finding willing dupes. One recent example I will not omit. Pope Alexander VI had no care or thought but how to deceive, and always found material to work on. No man ever had a more effective manner or asseverating, or made promises with more solemn protestations, or observed them less. And yet, because he understood this side of human nature, his frauds always succeeded....

In his efforts to aggrandize his son the duke [Caesar Borgia], Alexander VI had to face many difficulties, both immediate and remote. In the first place, he saw no way to make him ruler of any state which did not belong to the Church. Yet, if he sought to take for him a state of the Church, he knew that the duke of Milan and the Venetians would withhold their consent, Faenza and Rimini [towns in the province of Romagna] being already under the protection of the latter. Further, he saw that the forces of Italy, and those more especially of which he might

have availed himself, were in the hands of men who had reason to fear his aggrandizement,—that is, of the Orsini, the Colonnesi [Roman noble families] and their followers. These, therefore, he could not trust....

And since this part of his [Caesar Borgia's] conduct merits both attention and imitation, I shall not pass it over in silence. After the duke had taken Romagna, finding that it had been ruled by feeble lords, who thought more of plundering than of governing their subjects,—which gave them more cause for division than for union, so that the country was overrun with robbery, tumult, and every kind of outrage,—he judged it necessary, with a view to rendering it peaceful, and obedient to his authority, to provide it with a good government. Accordingly he set over it Messer Remiro d' Orco, a stern and prompt ruler, who, being intrusted with the fullest powers, in a very short time, and with much credit to himself, restored it to tranquillity and order. But afterwards the duke, apprehending that such unlimited authority might become odious, decided that it was no longer needed, and established the center of the province a civil tribunal, with an excellent president, in which every town was represented by its advocate. And knowing that past severities had generated ill feeling against himself, in order to purge the minds of the people and gain their good will, he sought to show them that any cruelty which had been done had not originated with him, but in the harsh disposition of this minister. Availing himself of the pretext which this afforded, he one morning caused Remiro to be beheaded, and exposed in the market place of Cesena with a block and bloody ax by his side. The barbarity of this spectacle at once astounded and satisfied the populace.

C. Monarchy in Practice: Charles V Secretly Instructs Vice-Chancellor Mathias Held, 1536

In addition to the instructions which you, Messire Mathias Held, our dear and faithful councillor and Vice-Chancellor of the Empire, have already received, drawn up in German, and relating to the business for which we have sent you to Germany, we think it essential to confide in you the following secret instructions, which you are to impart confidentially to the king, our good brother [Ferdinand I] and to the most reverend cardinal of Trent, without, however, allowing the matter to reach the ears of any one else.

First you shall inform my lord, our brother concerning what you saw and heard of public matters up to the time of your departure, and of the existing relation with the pope, the Venetians, an other powers of Italy, as well as with the kings of France and of England. Of these matters we shall say no more here since we do not wish to lengthen this instruction unduly, and are, morever, expecting more exact information of the status of affairs. You will also speak of the conditions in Flanders, and of various other matters which can be more advantageously communicated by you than written.

The information which you might otherwise convey to our brother, as to the policy which we desire and are in a position to adopt, cannot well be formulated without learning first what action the said king of France will take in regard to peace and the conditions which we have offered in the case of Milan. These you have seen, and of them you have a copy. We must, moreover, learn what further violence the said king will resort to. Inform our brother of the measures we have taken to learn as soon as possible if matters can be arranged. He must, moreover, be made aware of the measures which the pope, the Venetians and the other powers will take should the king of France obstinately continue the war. It is further very essential to learn the aim and intentions of the electors, princes and estates of the Empire in respect to the matters with which you are commissioned, not only as regards the question of the faith, but concerning the sympathy and assistance which we may expect and hope from them. You must exercise the greatest diligence and prudence in this matter, and inform us of the disposition which you find.

In view of the ill-will which the king of France has always shown, and the frequent negotiations for peace which have come to naught, we are inclined to doubt whether any results will be reached in the present case, hence it is especially important that you should make every effort to learn what can be done to gain the favor and assistance of Germany in case of the continuance of the war.

It must always be kept in mind that the division in Germany is at bottom entirely due to the controversy in regard to our holy religion. This prevents Germany from being united as it should be in obedience to us and the holy Empire. This encourages the king of France, moreover, to persist in the war, and furnishes him an obvious excuse for impeding, in a most unwarrantable fashion, the meeting of the council.[1] The confusion may even become worse in view of the said king's favorable attitude towards the

Turks, should no means be found to restore peace. This point must be emphasized in Germany, and some agreement ought to be reached as to the measures which should be adopted in case the pope, through the influence of the said king of France or through fear on the part of the Holy Father of losing his authority in the kingdom of France, should refuse to consent to the calling of the council, on the ground of the war between us and the king of France, or for other reasons. To say the truth it would seem, in spite of the evil deeds of the king of France, which are notorious and proven beyond the chance of doubt, that the Holy Father does not care to take any measure against the king, but that he will, in a word, remain neutral until he discovers which is in the wrong, as if the king of France had committed no offences up to the present and our actions belonged in the same category as his. He would seem to excuse himself and escape responsibility on the ground that he ought to arbitrate between us as a father and that, especially, he fears the loss of his authority in France. He may in this way be simply disguising the partiality which he constantly showed towards France before he became pope.

It is, however, none the less true that, in spite of the anxiety caused by the attitude of the Holy Father and the obstinacy of the king of France, we do not wish to use our power in any way against the apostolic authority and dignity [the papacy],or do anything prejudicial, directly or indirectly, to the essentials of our religion or the holy Catholic institutions. But we see clearly that should the pope continue to maintain his attitude of indifference or dissimulation, and not frankly consent to a council, it is all the more necessary that some means should be devised as soon as possible to prevent an increase of confusion in Germany, which will cause the destruction both of religion and the imperial authority. Owing to this disorder we are prevented from doing anything for Christianity itself or towards the defence against the Turks, whom the king of France is constantly encouraging. Our power is thus paralyzed to an extent which manifestly jeopardizes our realms and estates and those of our brother.

For these reasons, while maintaining the great secrecy which the affair demands, you should confer very particularly with my lord our brother, as to whether there be any way of celebrating the council, should Germany consent, even if the said pope and king of France should not agree to it, and as to how this may be done and with what certainty. This would seem to be a plan based upon perfect right and reason, and all the more, because the Holy Father has already promised a council and pledged himself expressly for

---

[1] That is, an ecumenical council to settle issues raised by the Reformation.

the king of France. The principal need of a council is, moreover, for the German nation. The king of Portugal will consent to and support the plan, as will probably the king of Poland, and the most of the powers of Italy. As for England, since it is utterly schismatic, the pope and the king of France cannot validly allege against the legitimacy of the council the fact that that country was not included.

Should the resort to a council in Germany, with the approbation of all or the greater part of that nation, prove impracticable, it should be determined whether there is not some other expedient, for example, to assure those who have fallen from the faith that no further coercion will be used if they will but sincerely conform with the other members of Germany in maintaining peace at home and in cooperating with our said brother and ourselves, or might not the treaty of Nuremberg by modified, or such a new one drawn up as the change of times and altered circumstances might dictate. Or may it not be advisable to call a national assembly in Germany and adjust, or neglect, such matters as may not be essential to our holy religion. Or let some other expedient be devised so that the imperial, Roman authority be not sacrificed, as well as our said brother and ourselves, even should it not supply a remedy in the matter of religion. For we can but wait until God grants such remedy as he shall judge fitting to his holy service, since he knows the regret with which our said brother and we behold the sad state of affairs, and that our aim and desire is to serve him and apply ourselves to cure the existing evils so soon as any means shall offer themselves.

We are thus placed in a difficult and critical position, for we cannot have peace if our enemy does not consent, for, as it is well known, he is as obstinate as he is powerful, and regards neither God nor good faith, placing his chief hope in the division of Germany and the difference in religious matters which exists there, as well as in the approach of the Turk, whom, as it is reported, he spares no efforts to encourage. In view of this it behooves our brother to turn his attention to this matter, since everything is at stake, and to find some way of settling his difficulties in Hungary, and any other complications in which he may be involved. For it would be quite impossible for us to lend him any assistance, being, as we are, far in arrears for the outlays we have been forced to make in the past. Our kingdoms and countries are so surcharged with burdens that we do not know where we are to look for the absolutely necessary means of continuing this war. This is one of the chief motives which induces us to return to our Spanish kingdoms in order to take council there as to what may be done.

D. The Triumph of State Interests: The German Princes Conclude the Peace of Augsburg, 1555

. . . In order that . . . peace, which is especially necessary in view of the divided religions, as is seen from the causes before mentioned, and is demanded by the sad necessity of the Holy Roman Empire of the German nation, may be the better established and made secure and enduring between his Roman Imperial Majesty and us, on the one hand, and the electors, princes, and estates of the Holy Empire of the German nation on the other, therefore his Imperial Majesty, and we, and the electors, princes, and estates of the Holy Empire will not make war upon any estate of the empire on account of the Augsburg Confession and the doctrine, religion, and faith of the same, nor injure nor do violence to those estates that hold it, nor force them, against their conscience, knowledge, and will, to abandon the religion, faith, church usages, ordinances, and ceremonies of the Augsburg Confession, where these have been established, or may hereafter be established, in their principalities, lands, and dominions. Nor shall we, through mandate or in any other way, trouble or disparage them, but shall let them quietly and peacefully enjoy their religion, faith, church usages, ordinances, and ceremonies, as well as their possessions, real and personal property, lands, people, dominions, governments, honors, and rights. . . .

On the other hand, the estates that have accepted the Augsburg Confession shall suffer his Imperial Majesty, us, and the electors, princes, and other estates of he Holy Empire, adhering to the old religion, to abide in like manner by their religion, faith, church usages, ordinances, and ceremonies. They shall also leave undisturbed their possessions, real and personal property, lands, people, dominions, government, honors, and rights, rents, interest, and tithes. . . .

But all others who are not adherents of either of the above-mentioned religions are not included in this peace, but shall be altogether excluded. . . .

No estate shall urge another estate, or the subjects of the same, to embrace its religion.

But when our subjects and those of the electors, princes, and estates, adhering to the old religion or to the Augsburg Confession, wish, for the sake of their religion, to go with wife and children to another place in the lands, principalities, and cities of the electors, princes, and estates of the Holy Empire, and settle there, such going and coming, and the sale of property and goods, in return for reasonable compensation for serfdom and arrears of taxes, . . . shall be everywhere unhindered, permitted, and granted. . . .

Document Set 15.9 References

A. Claude de Seyssel Describes the Traditional Values of the French Monarchy
De Seyssel, *La Monarchie de France,* in J. H. Shennan, *Government and Society in France, 1461–1661* (London: George Allen & Unwin, 1969), 77–78.

B. Niccolò Machiavelli Asks "Whether It Is Prudent for a Prince to Keep His Promises," 1513
Machiavelli, *The Prince,* trans. N. H. Thomson, in James Harvey Robinson, ed., *Readings in European History* (Boston: Ginn, 1904), 2:10–13.

C. Monarchy in Practice: Charles V Secretly Instructs Vice-Chancellor Mathias Held, 1536
Translations and Reprints from the Original Sources of European History (Philadelphia: University of Pennsylvania Press, 1898), 2/6:31–34.

D. The Triumph of State Interests: The German Princes Conclude the Peace of Augsburg, 1555
"The Religious Peace of Augsburg," in Robinson, 2:114–116.

DOCUMENT SET 15.10
Courtiers and Patrons

Amid the Reformation era's wars and doctrinal disputes, court life throughout Europe was becoming more refined, though not notably more moral. The great model for courtly behavior—it was translated into most European languages—was *The Courtier,* a series of dialogues written by the Italian diplomat Baldassare Castiglione (1478–1529). An extract appears as Document A. What conclusion do you draw from the *tone* of the dialogue—the rather light-hearted bantering, the advice that the "perfect courtier" adopt the pose of "nonchalance" even when he performs difficult feats, and the apparently equal participation of men and women in the conversation?

A very different view of court life came from the *Heptameron* of Marguerite de Navarre (1492–1549), the queen of Navarre and sister of Francis I, who spent most of her life at the French court. A gifted writer and woman of strong, rather unorthodox, religious convictions, Marguerite in the *Heptameron* tells a series of stories. In the one excerpted here, a nobleman has attempted to rape a princess, a woman of great beauty and virtue, but she fights off her assailant with the assistance of her lady-in-waiting. After hearing the story, the male and female characters in *Heptameron* comment: Hircain claims that male honor justifies even murder, to which the noblewoman Nomerfide responds with horror.

Still another classic literary account of court life comes from Thomas More's *Utopia* (1516). Scholars still debate the meaning of More's famous book, describing an imaginary land of "nowhere" (Utopia) and contrasting it with the injustices of sixteenth-century life. But the passage quoted here as Document C seems to have a clear meaning: in it More expresses his own ambivalence about serving King Henry VIII at court because he will not be able to give his king truly honest advice. (As it happened, More did become a royal servitor but was beheaded in 1535 because he refused to support Henry's break with Rome.)

Document D offers still another perspective on court life. As noted in Set 14.2, the treatment of Renaissance artists ranged from peremptory to highly deferential. In the sixteenth century the trend toward regarding *some* artists as inspired geniuses continued. Michelangelo (1475–1564) was unquestionably regarded with awe—often mixed with exasperation—by his contemporaries, including the cardinal who sent him this obsequious letter.

After examining these documents and using *The Challenge of the West* for background, prepare an analysis of the place of courts and artistic patronage in early sixteenth-century life. It would also be helpful to consider Set 15.9.

A. Baldassare Castiglione Describes the Perfect Courtier

Messer Federico replied: "Get Marquess Febus to tell you, who has often seen them in France; and perhaps they were done to him."

Marquess Febus replied: "I have seen nothing of the kind done in France that is not also done in Italy; but every thing that is good among the Italians in the way of dress, sports, banquets, handling arms, and everything else that befits a Courtier— they have gotten it all from the French."

"I do not say," replied messer Federico, "that very fine and modest cavaliers are not also to be found among the French, and I myself have known many that are truly worthy of every praise. Still, there are some who are careless; and, generally speaking, it strikes me that the customs of the Spaniards suit the Italians better than do those of the French, because the calm gravity that is peculiar to the Spaniards is, I think, far more suited to us than the ready vivacity we see in the French in almost all their movements: which is not unbecoming to them, nay, is charming, because it is so natural and proper to them as not to appear an affectation on their part. There are indeed many Italians who devote every effort to imitating that manner; and they do nothing but shake their heads as they speak, bowing clumsily to the side; and when they pass through town they walk so fast that their lackeys cannot keep up with them. By way of such manners they deem themselves to be good Frenchmen and to have the free manner of the French, which actually happens rarely save in those who have been reared in France and have acquired the manner from childhood.

"The same is true of knowing many languages, which is something I very much approve of in the Courtier, especially Spanish and French, because

From *The Book of the Courtier* by Baldesar Castiglione, Illus. edited by Edgar Mayhew. Copyright © 1959 by Charles S. Singleton and Edgar de N. Mayhew. Used by permission of Doubleday, a division of Bantam Doubleday Dell Publishing Group, Inc.

intercourse with both of these nations is very frequent in Italy, and they have more in common with us than any of the others; and their two princes, being very powerful in war and most magnificent in peace, always have their courts full of noble cavaliers, who are then spread abroad in the world; and we do indeed have occasion to hold converse with them.". . .

"Now I would not go on to speak in any more detail of things too well known, such as that our Courtier ought not to profess to be a great eater or drinker, or be dissolute in any bad habit, or be vile or disorderly in his way of life, or have certain peasant ways that bespeak the hoe and the plow a thousand miles away; because a man of this sort not only may not hope to become a good Courtier, but no suitable job can be given him other than tending sheep.

"And, to conclude, I declare that it would be well for the Courtier to know perfectly all we have said befits him, so that everything possible may be easy for him, and that everyone may marvel at him and he at no one. It is understood however, that in this there is to be no proud and inhuman rigidity, such as some have who refuse to show any wonder at all at what others do, because they think they are able to do much better, and by their silence they scorn those things as unworthy of any mention; and act as if they wished to show that no one is their equal, let alone able to undersand the profundity of their knowledge. The Courtier must avoid these odious ways, and praise the good achievements of others with kindness and good will; and, although he may feel that he is admirable and much superior to all others, yet he ought not to appear to think so.

"But because such complete perfection as this is very rarely, and perhaps never, found in human nature, a man who feels himself wanting in some particular ought not to lose confidence in himself or the hope of reaching a high mark, even though he cannot attain to that perfect and highest excellence to which he aspires. For in every art there are many ranks besides the highest that are praiseworthy, and he who aims at the summit will seldom fail to mount more than half the way. Therefore if our Courtier knows himself to be excellent in something besides arms, I would have him with propriety derive profit and honor from it; and let him have the discretion and good judgment to know how to bring people adroitly and opportunely to see and hear what he considers himself to excel in, always seeming to do this without ostentation, casually as it were, and rather when begged by others than because he wishes it. And in everything that he has to do or say, let him, if possible, always come prepared and ready, but give the appearance that all is done on the spur of the moment. But, as for those things in which he feels himself to be mediocre, let him touch on them in passing, without dwelling much upon them, though in such a way as to cause others to think that he knows much more about them than he lays claim to know: like certain poets who have sometimes suggested the most subtle things in philosophy or other sciences, when probably they understood very little about them. Then, in those things wherein he knows himself to be totally ignorant, I would never have him claim ability in any way or seek to gain fame by them; on the contrary, when need be, let him confess openly that he knows nothing."

"That," said Calmeta, "is not what Nicoletto would have done, who, being an excellent philosopher, but with no more knowledge of law than of flying, when a certain mayor of Padua decided to give him a lectureship in law, was never willing (although many students so urged him) to undeceive that mayor and confess his ignorance; saying always that he did not agree with the opinion of Socrates in this matter, and that it was not for a philosopher ever to declare himself ignorant in anything."

"I do not say," replied messer Federico, "that the Courtier, unrequired by others, should venture of himself to confess his own ignorance; for I too dislike this folly of accusing and depreciating oneself. And sometimes therefore I laugh to myself at certain men who are so ready, without any coercion, to tell of certain things, which, even though they may have happened through no fault of theirs, yet imply a certain disgrace; like a cavalier you all know, who, every time mention was made of the battle fought against King Charles in the Parmesan, would begin at once to tell how he had fled, making it clear that on that day he had seen and heard nothing else; or, whenever a certain famous joust was mentioned, would always tell how he had fallen; and in his conversation he often appeared to try to create the occasion for telling how one night, when he was on his way to speak with a certain lady, he had gotten a sound beating.

"I would not have our Courtier say such silly things; but rather, should the occasion arise when he might show his ignorance in something, then I think he ought to avoid it; and if compelled by necessity, then he ought openly to confess his ignorance rather than expose himself to that risk. And in this way he will escape the censure that many nowadays deserve who (out of I know not what perverse instinct or imprudent judgment) are always attempting things of which they are ignorant and avoiding things they know how to do. And, in proof of this, I know a very excellent musician who has abandoned music and given himself over entirely to composing verses, and, thinking himself very great at that, has made himself the laughingstock of everyone, and by now has lost even his music. Another, one of the first painters of the world, scorns that art wherein he is most rare, and has set about studying philosophy; in which he comes up with such strange notions and new chimeras that, for all his art as a painter, he would never be able to paint them. And countless instances like these are to be found.

"There are of course some who know their own excellence in one thing and yet make a profession of something else, though something in which they are not ignorant; and every time they have an occasion to show their worth in the thing wherein they feel they have talent, they give evidence of their considerable ability. And it sometimes happens that the company, seeing this ability of theirs in something that is not their profession, think they must be able to do far better in what is their profession. Such an art, when accompanied by good judgment, does not displease me in the least."

B. Marguerite de Navarre Observes Honor and Sexuality at Court

"And that, Ladies, is a story that should strike fear into the hearts of any man who thinks he can help himself to what doesn't belong to him. The Princess's virtue and the good sense of her lady-in-waiting should inspire courage in the hearts of all women. . . ."

"In my opinion," said Hircan, "the tall lord of your story lacked nerve, and didn't deserve to have his memory preserved. What an opportunity he had! He should never have been content to eat or sleep till he'd succeeded. And one really can't say that his love was very great, if there was still room in his heart for the fear of death and dishonor."

"And what," asked Nomerfide, "could the poor man have done with two women against him?"

"He should have killed the old one, and when the young one realized there was no one to help her, he'd have been half-way there!"

"Kill her!" Nomerfide cried. "You wouldn't mind him being a murderer as well, then? If that's what you think, we'd better watch out we don't fall into your clutches!"

"If I'd gone that far," he replied, "I'd consider my honor ruined if I didn't go through with it!"

C. Sir Thomas More and His Fictional Friend, Just Back from Utopia, Discuss the Advice that a Courtier Can Safely Give His King

"Do not you think that if I were about any king, proposing good laws to him, and endeavoring to root out all the cursed seeds of evil that I found in him, I should either be turned out of his court or at least be laughed at for my pains? For instance, what could it signify if I were about the King of France, and were called into his Cabinet Council, where several wise men, in his hearing, were proposing many expedients, as by what arts and practices Milan may be kept, and Naples, that had so oft slipped out of their hands, recovered; how the Venetians, and after them the rest of Italy, may be subdued; and then how Flanders, Brabant, and all Burgundy, and some other kingdoms which he has swallowed already in his designs, may be added to his empire. One proposes a league with the Venetians, to be kept as long as he finds his account in it, and that he ought to communicate councils with them, and give them some share of the spoil, till his success makes him need or fear them less, and then it will be easily taken out of their hands. Another proposes the hiring the Germans, and the securing the Switzers by pensions. Another proposes the gaining the Emperor by money, which is omnipotent with him. Another proposes a peace with the King of Aragon, and, in order to cement it, the yielding up the King of Navarre's pretensions. Another thinks the Prince of Castile is to be wrought on, by the hope of an alliance; and that some of his courtiers are to be gained to the French faction by pensions. The hardest point of all is what to do with England: a treaty of peace is to be set on foot, and if their alliance is not to be depended on, yet it is to be made as firm as possible; and they are to be called friends, but suspected as enemies: therefore the Scots are to be kept in readiness, to be let loose upon England on every occasion: and some banished nobleman is to be supported underhand (for by the league it cannot be done avowedly) who had a pretension to the crown, by which means that suspected prince may be kept in awe.

"Now when things are in so great a fermentation, and so many gallant men are joining councils, how to carry on the war, if so mean a man as I should stand up, and wish them to change all their councils, to let Italy alone, and stay at home, since the Kingdom of France was indeed greater than could be well governed by one man; that therefore he ought not to think of adding others to it: and if after this, I should propose to them the resolutions of the Achorians, a people that lie on the southeast of Utopia, who long ago engaged in war, in order to add to the dominions of their prince another kingdom, to which he had some pretensions by an ancient alliance. This they conquered, but found that the trouble of keeping it was equal to that by which it was gained; that the conquered people were always either in rebellion or exposed to foreign invasions, while they were obliged to be incessantly at war, either for or against them, and consequently could never disband their army; that in the meantime they were oppressed with taxes, their money went out of the kingdom, their blood was spilt for the glory of their King, without procuring the least advantage to the people, who received not the smallest benefit from it even in time of peace; and that their manners being corrupted by a long war, robbery and murders everywhere abounded, and their laws fell into contempt; while their King, distracted with the care of two kingdoms, was the less able to apply his mind to the interests of either.

"When they saw this, and that there would be no end to these evils, they by joint councils made an humble address to their King, desiring him to choose which of the two kingdoms he had the greatest mind to keep, since he could not hold both; for they were too great a people to be governed by a divided king, since no man would willingly have a groom that should be in common between him and another. Upon which the good prince was forced to quit his new kingdom to one of his friends (who was not long after dethroned), and to be contented with his old one. To this I would add that after all those warlike attempts, the vast confusions, and the consumption both of treasure and of people that must follow them; perhaps upon some misfortune, they might be forced to throw up all at last; therefore it seemed much more eligible that the King should improve his ancient kingdom all he could, and make it flourish as much as possible; that he should love his people, and be beloved of them; that should live among them, govern them gently, and let other kingdoms alone, since that which had fallen to his share was big enough, if not too big for him. Pray how do you think would such a speech as this be heard?"

"I confess," said I, "I think not very well."

D. A Cardinal Respectfully Addresses "My Dearest Michelangelo," 1518

We have received your letter dated the eighth, to which we reply that we are vastly pleased to hear of the diligence you have shown, and that one Hieronimo of Porto Venere has promised on good security to deliver the marble for the tomb of Pope Julius of happy memory, because as you know we want to see the said tomb finished. We are very sorry to hear that you have been ill, but thank God for restoring you to health as you write and as we have understood from Leonardo [Sellaio], the bearer of your letter. We beg you to take care to regain your strength and keep well, both for your own sake and so that we may see the completion of the said tomb. We wait with eagerness to see the two figures ready at the time you have promised. Be of good spirit and do not be carried away by any passion; we put more trust in your slightest word than whatever the rest may say to the contrary. We know your good faith, and believe in it as much as we possibly can, and as we have said at other times, want you to take every care for your safety, because we love you from the heart and want to do everything we can for you.

Farewell. Rome, 23 October 1518
Your Cardinal San Pietro ad Vincula

To the discreet Michelangelo, the excellent sculptor, our most dear friend

Document Set 15.10 References

A. Baldassare Castiglione Describes the Perfect Courtier
Castiglione, *The Courtier,* trans. Charles S. Singleton (Garden City, N.Y.: Anchor Books, 1962), 134–138.
B. Marguerite de Navarre Observes Honor and Sexuality at Court
Marguerite de Navarre, *Heptameron,* trans., P. A. Chilton (Harmondsworth: Penguin, 1984), 96–97.
C. Sir Thomas More and His Fictional Friend, Just Back from Utopia, Discuss the Advice that a Courtier Can Safely Give His King
Thomas More, "Dialogue of Counsel" in *Utopia* (New York: Colonial Press, 1901), 22–24.
D. A Cardinal Respectfully Addresses "My Dearest Michelangelo," 1518
Cardinal Leonardo Grosso della Rovere to Michelangelo, in D. S. Chambers, *Patrons and Artists in the Italian Renaissance* (Columbia, S.C.: University of South Carolina Press, 1971), 35.

16

Religious Warfare and Crises of Authority, 1560–1640

DOCUMENT SET 16.1
Rebellion and Civil War

Chapter 15 of *The Challenge of the West* analyzed the authoritarian bent of institutions in most European states during the era of struggles over religion known as the Reformation. Set 16.1 traces the backlash against this authoritarianism.

Reflecting the clarity and dispassion characteristic of the genre, the Venetian ambassador's report on France in 1559 (Document A) sets forth the social and political order of that kingdom on the eve of the great upheavals of the Wars of Religion, 1560–1598. What mutual relationships bound the various strata of French society together, and what differences separated them? Going by this report, would you expect the nobility to oppose royal authoritarianism? On whom would the monarchy tend to depend for support? Why, according to the ambassador, was it proving difficult to maintain religious unity?

Document B describes one of the most notorious events of the Wars of Religion, the St. Bartholomew's Day massacre of 1572. The author of this selection, Charlotte de Mornay (1550–1606), is an example of the many able and intellectually sophisticated Huguenot noblewomen who strongly influenced the religious choices of their families and friends. In 1572 she was a young widow (her first husband had died in the wars before he was twenty), and she was planning to spend the winter with her sister. Later she married Philippe de Mornay, a French Protestant political leader. Read this document bearing in mind the picture of the French state that you are evolving from your other source readings—especially Document C, an extract from the *Vindiciae contra*

Tyrannos (1579). The most likely author of this anonymously published work was the Huguenot leader François Hotman. The word *tyranny* is often used indiscriminately; what does it mean here, and how does Hotman's idea of tyranny compare with the traditional concept of French monarchy? What implications do you see in Hotman's call for resistance to tyranny? With Document D we are witnessing the other great European revolution of the 1550s to 1570s, the Dutch revolt. The author, a former official in Antwerp, fled to Germany in 1567 after witnessing the events of the previous year, described here. What concerns for the social order does he express? How do you reconcile his evident conservatism with his support for rebels against the Spanish crown? Can a conservative become a revolutionary?

Document E takes us to Eastern Europe, where Tsar Ivan IV (known as "The Terrible," *1533–1584) was throwing Russia into turmoil with his attack on the noble boyar class. One of his councillors, Prince Andrei Kurbsky, broke with Ivan in 1564 and fled to Poland-Lithuania (with which Russia was then at war), denouncing the tsar as a bloodthirsty tyrant. Kurbsky's defection drove Ivan to even more gory repression at home. The ensuing exchange of letters between Kurbsky and Ivan, which was published at the time, is regarded as authentic by most historians. How does the picture of tyranny and the resistance to it compare with similar conflicts in the sixteenth-century West? How do you regard Ivan's account (largely accurate) of how as a young boy he was dominated and mistreated by a boyar conspiracy?

A. A Venetian Ambassador Sketches the Hierarchy in France, 1558

The inhabitants of the kingdom are divided into four classes of persons, viz: nobles; men of the long robe; peasantry; and clergy. The nobles, under which designation are included lords and princes, do not dwell in the cities, but in the villages, in their castles, and for the most part give little attention to letters, but are either soldiers or follow the court, leaving the management of the house and the revenues to their wives.

The French are, generally speaking, suspicious, high spirited and impatient of restraint, wherefore it is noticeable that in war, after the first dash is over, they are almost useless. They are more liberal away from home than at home; nevertheless, whoever accommodates himself to their moods will find them for the most part courteous. They avoid labor in so far as they are able, and above all it is a peculiarity of the Frenchman that he reflects little, and therefore very many of their conclusions are hastily arrived at; whence it often happens that they have no sooner finished an undertaking than they perceive its error and repent of it; but the strength of the kingdom is great enough to overcome all these errors.

There is no special burden upon the nobility beyond that which arises from their feudal holdings, which is to go to war at their own expense with such a number of horsemen as may be determined by the conditions of their investiture, in default of which they are condemned to pay money, and now the burden has become so great by reason of continued warfare that the nobility of France is seen to be almost wholly impoverished.

This militia is called the *arrière-ban,* because those who compose it are the last who are obliged to go to war and are for the defence of the kingdom. They are able to bring out about 16,000 horse, and they do not all come out at one time, but only that part for which an immediate need is felt; and from the fact that it is a very inferior soldiery, since the lords do not themselves go to war, but send their retainers and these badly equipped, it is understood that the king intends to do away with the obligation to send men to war and substitute a proportionate money payment, with which he may increase the number of his men-at-arms.

The second class embraces those who are called men of the long robe, and is divided into two groups. The first, which is the better bred, is made up of those who occupy judicial positions and all the other officials of the palace and those as well who manage the finances and accounts of the king. All these offices his majesty sells for the lifetime of the purchaser, and their honor and advantage is so great that they are bought at high prices. They enjoy also many important privileges, as though they were nobles, and easily secure the same for their descendants.

The other group is that of the merchants, who have personally no way of gaining a share in any sort of distinction, but if they wish to give a certain position to their sons they have them made doctors, whereby a judicial career is open to them equally with the members of the former group; and it may be said moreover that in them principally the wealth of France is to be found. No special burden is laid upon this class beyond the maintenance of 50,000 infantry for four months, for the defence of the kingdom in time of war, which contribution has been for some time so modified that all the inhabitants of the cities and other walled places now contribute to it. But because the greater part of these who have offices from the king are exempt by special privilege, the burden has come to rest wholly upon those who are least able to bear it.

The third class is the peasantry, who are extremely poor, principally on account of the heavy taxes which they pay to the king, since they are obliged to pay an ordinary *taille* of four millions of francs; and also on account of the *aides,* which amount to six hundred thousand; in addition to this a million francs to augment the number of men-at-arms; and, outside of all this, in times of war, the *taille* has at times been increased in amount two millions of francs; to which burdens those peasants alone contribute who work the soil. The assessments are made first upon the provinces, are then distributed by villages, and the peasants arrange the further *per capita* assessment, each one being responsible for the others, in such a way that the king actually receives the whole amount that he has demanded.

The fourth class is the clergy, in which are comprised the 117 bishoprics, 15 archbishoprics and 1230 abbacies, besides an infinite number of priories and benefices, which altogether amount in value to six million francs of income, and in ordinary time the king levies upon these an annual tax of four-tenths; and sometimes, in case of war, even up to six-tenths. But from the fact that the assessment is made very loosely and upon an estimate of incomes as they existed many years ago, they do not render more than 300,000 francs for each tenth. The disposition of all these benefices belongs to the king, except in the case of those which become vacant through the death of those prelates who die at the Roman court, and these belong to the pope. The authority for this disposition was first granted by pope Leo; then enlarged by Clement and finally confirmed by pope Julius II; nor shall I omit to say that these benefices are for the most part awarded with little respect for sacred things and by simple favor, or to recompense benefits conferred, with little consideration for the personality of the applicant; in such a way that whoever has served the king in war or otherwise desires no better thing by way of being rewarded than with benefices; wherefore it is a common thing to see a man who yesterday was a soldier or merchant, today a bishop or abbot: and if he has a wife and cannot assume ecclesiastical garb he is allowed to put his benefice under the name of another and retain the revenues for himself. And it is on this account, as well as through the evil tendencies of the time, that heresy has increased to such an extent in this realm, that they say there are at present 400,000 Lutherans,[1] so united by intercourse and mutual understanding that it is with great difficulty that any method may be found of remedying this state of affairs.

B. Charlotte de Mornay Describes the St. Bartholomew's Day Massacre

While I was still in bed, one of my kitchen servants, who was of the religion [Huguenot] and was coming from the city, came very terrified to find me. She told me that people were being killed everywhere. . . . Looking from my windows into Saint Antoine Street where I lived, I saw that everyone was very agitated, and several guards were wearing white crosses in their hats [to identify themselves as Catholics]. . . . I sent my daughter, who was then three and a half years old, in the arms of a servant to Mister de Perreuze . . . one of my closest relatives and friends, who let her in the back gate, received her, and sent word to ask if I would come, saying I would be welcome. I accepted his offer and left myself. . . . There was sedition all over the city. It was then eight in the morning, and I had no sooner left my lodgings than the servants of the Duke of Guise came in, called my host to find me, and looked for me everywhere. Finally, they sent to my mother telling her that if I wanted to bring them 100 *écus,* they would spare my life and my goods. . . . After having thought a little, I decided it was not a good idea to let it be known where I was or to go to find them, but I begged my mother to let them know that she did not know where I was and to offer them the sum that they were

demanding. Having heard nothing from me, they pillaged by lodgings. . . .

[Mister de Perreuze] was obliged to hide us . . . me with one of my servants in a hollow of the roof vaulting; the rest of our people were disguised and hidden as well as possible. Inside the vaulting, at the top of the attic, I heard the strange cries of men, women, and children who were being massacred in the streets, and having left my daughter below, I was in such perplexity and almost despair that, without fearing that I offended God, I would sooner have thrown myself out the window than to fall alive into the hands of the populace and see my daughter massacred—something I feared more than my death. . . . [After fleeing from one house to another, she hid for five days in the home of a grain merchant, then took a boat out of Paris, where she was stopped because she did not have a passport. She narrowly escaped capture and certain death by posing as a servant and hiding in the house of a vineyard worker. Throughout the ordeal, she steadfastly refused to go to mass in order to save herself.]

C. A Huguenot Leader Justifies Resistance to Tyranny

A king, we have said, is someone who has obtained the kingdom in due form, either by descent or by election, and who rules and governs in accordance with the law. Since a tyrant is the opposite of a king, it follows either that he has seized authority by force or fraud, or that he is a king who rules a kingdom freely given him in a manner contrary to equity and justice and persists in that misrule in violation of the laws and compacts to which he took a solemn oath. A single person can, of course, be both of these at once. The former is commonly called a "tyrant without title," the latter, "a tyrant by conduct." But it sometimes happens that a kingdom occupied by force is governed justly; a kingdom legally conveyed, unjustly. And since justice is here more important than inheritance, and performance more important than title to possession, it appears that a ruler who performs his office badly is more properly a tyrant than one who did not receive his office in due form. Similarly, a Pope who enters office illegally is called an "intruder," one who governs badly, an "abuser." . . .

In sum, a king promotes the public interest, a tyrant seeks his own. But since men are only human, no king can have the public interest in view on every question, and no tyrant can exist for long who seeks his own advantage in all respects whatever. Therefore,

[1] "Lutherans" was the label that Roman Catholics in the sixteenth century often applied to all Protestants, irrespective of confession. Here, these "Lutherans" were in fact mostly Calvinists.

if the public interest is generally uppermost we may speak of a king and of a kingdom, and if the ruler's interest generally predominates, we speak of a tyrant and a tyranny. . . .

The next question is whether a tyrant may be lawfully resisted and, if so, by whom and by what means. And we shall begin by considering tyranny without title, as it is commonly called. Suppose, then, that a Ninus invades a people over which he has no legal claim and which has not done him any injury; or that a Caesar subjugates the Roman Republic, his fatherland; or that a Popelus uses murder and deceit in an attempt to make the kingdom of Poland hereditary rather than elective; or that a Bruenhilde takes over the entire government of France for herself and her Protadius; or that an Ebroinus, encouraged by Theodoric's negligence, seizes the governorships of the kingdom and enslaves the people. What is the law in all these cases?

In the first place, nature instructs us to defend our lives and also our liberty, without which life is hardly life at all. If this is the instinct of nature implanted in dogs against the wolf, in bulls against the lion, in pigeons against the falcon, and in chickens against the hawk, how much stronger must it be in man against another man who has become a wolf to man. To fight back is not only permitted, but enjoined, for it is nature herself that seems to fight here.

Next, there is the law of peoples (*jus gentium*), which distinguishes countries and establishes boundaries that everyone is obligated to defend against any person whatsoever. . . . An Alexander pillaging a country may be opposed no less than the vagabond who steals a cloak; an invader battering the ramparts of a city, no less than the burglar breaking into buildings.

Last and most important is the civil law, which is the legislation that societies establish for their particular needs, so that here is one and there another kind of government, some being ruled by one man, others by a few, and still others by all. Some peoples deny political authority to women, others admit them; with some, kings are chosen from a particular line, among others the choice is free; and so forth. If anyone tries to break this law through force or fraud, resistance is incumbent upon all of us, because the criminal does violence to that association to which we owe everything we have, because he subverts the foundations of the fatherland to which we are bound—by nature, by the laws, and by our oath. Therefore, if we do not resist, we are traitors to our country, deserters of human society, and contemners of the law.

Thus, the law of nature, the law of peoples, and civil law command us to take arms against tyrants without title, nor is there any legal scruple to detain us—no oath or compact whatsoever, entered into either publicly or privately. Therefore, when this kind of tyranny occurs, anyone may act to drive it out, including private individuals. . . .

D. Jacob van Wesenbeke Analyzes the Drift Toward Rebellion in the Netherlands, 1566

All people were made to hope that the States General of the country would be called to draft a definitive and good ordinance concerning religion. Such an ordinance, intended to be really binding, to restore calm, to bring no harm to the country and give satisfaction to the inhabitants had been awaited, longed for and yearned for by every one. Shortly afterwards the hope and the satisfaction of the population turned to sadness, hatred and suspicion, because it was discovered that at court men had secretly devised a moderation or new edict which was sent to His Majesty in Spain. And although it had been hoped that the States General would be convoked thereupon, as had been asked in the petition of the nobles and had moreover been promised them, some persons schemed so ingeniously and successfully that it was resolved to present this moderation, not to the States General convoked for that purpose but to the provincial States of every province one after the other and, in the same order, to the provincial councils. Learning this many people feared and concluded that no good would arise from such a procedure and that things would grow worse every day, for they were far from confident that the result would come up to the hope deeply cherished by the people. No one, it was feared, would like to be subjected to such private consultation and the population continued to favour the convocation of the States General as an alternative acceptable to everybody. This suspicion, this distrust and this embitterment greatly increased and took root in people's hearts when they saw clearly, that some provincial States were ordered to meet separately (according to the aforementioned plan) in the presence of their governors or other knights of the Order or lords of high rank who were sent there to persuade them to accept the proposed moderation.

Excerpt from "The Revolt of the Netherlands" from Kossman and Mellink, eds., *Texts Concerning the Revolt of the Netherlands,* Cambridge University Press, 1975, pp. 66–69. Reprinted with the permission of Cambridge University Press.

Moreover, people's perplexity and despair about the results were complete when it was found that the provincial States were left so little liberty in convoking the meeting that only a few selected members were summoned and many, who also belonged there, were omitted and in several places people were even excluded who usually attended the meetings. Moreover, discussion was almost impossible; members were not allowed the usual time or means to deliberate and consult others, and were made to swear that they would not notify anyone of the proceedings or inform any members of the councils in the town they came from except the magistrates. In short the approval of States meeting in such circumstances was generally considered to be an extorted rather than a free and frank opinion. People who attended the discussions in the States of Artois, Hainault, Namur and Tournay know that this was the way it went.

A further important reason for scandal and discontent was the fact that the States were first convoked in the provinces which were least accustomed to show that they have some freedom and were most subject to the inquisition and the persecutions, while in the provinces which were most influenced by the novel developments, possessed the greatest privileges and had through words and deeds most boldly defended the freedom of the country, the States were not convoked at all. This was the case . . . above all [in] Brabant, the principal and most important province. As to the province second in importance, Flanders, this was only convoked after the States mentioned previously had met and passed judgment. And though every attempt was made to keep secret the contents of the new edict as well as the opinion of the States assembled to discuss it (which made things look even more suspicious to the common people), there were nevertheless some people who succeeded in discovering part of the truth and got to know still more about it when the States and Members of Flanders, told of the limitations prescribed for their meeting, with the utmost difficulty obtained at first four days' and later eight days' delay. And it became known that these States had given their approval to the new edict (though with some restrictions and conditions added by the secular States) without having, in the old way, convoked and heard all their members and councillors. All this caused a violent commotion among the people. Many different booklets and pamphlets were immediately written and distributed in various places arguing that the new edict was illegal, that it was no better than all the previous edicts, that the inquisition was still in force, that all this was the work of the adherents of Cardinal

Granvelle, some of them mentioned by name, and of the inquisitors who wanted to cause bloody disturbances, that it was done contrary to the promise made to the nobles and to the freedom of the country, that this way of assembling the States was an innovation never before witnessed, that this could not therefore be called approval of the edict and that it was entirely null. People were earnestly exhorted to oppose it forcefully and not to allow the enemies of the country to deceive the king and the governess and to give them false information any longer but to arrest and punish them. All this was accompanied by yet more strong and violent arguments and exclamations. It proved impossible to stop the flood of publications by prohibiting them, for the more the court issued edicts against them, the more the number of such booklets and writings increased. One complained that the commonalty was deprived of its liberty to explain and to discover the truth openly, whether in the councils of the provinces and the towns or in clear remonstrances and writings, although on this depended the prosperity of the country. People wrote that these outrages would very soon have all sort of evil consequences and suggested that the men who thus wanted to keep the king and the country in servitude, were afraid that their treachery would be revealed if the States General were convoked in the proper fashion and allowed to give their opinion freely. Soon, because of the refusal and delay in convoking the States, the commotion, embitterment and grumbling that had existed among the people before the nobles presented their petition, began anew.

This, however, was much more serious than before because the inhabitants, made much more hard-hearted and embittered by the course of events, gave up all hope of improvement and redress since the distinguished assembly and well-founded petition of the nobles as well as the promises made to them had been of no avail, and because they saw clearly that it was not the intention of the court to convoke the States General, or, if it was its intention, that there would be people to prevent it from being brought about although the meeting of the States General was considered by all sensible people to be the only remedy against the troubles. What else could be concluded when neither the supplication of the nobles, nor the desire of various provinces and towns intimated long before, nor the consent of many of the most important lords, including those who sat in the council and agreed to it and thought it necessary, had succeeded in persuading the court to do it? There seemed nothing left to give them hope that the promises given to the nobles might be kept, or that the inhabitants might be released from the hated persecutions and odious inquisition, or might be given some relief or exemption from the slavery and servitude of their consciences which they had been enduring for such a long time. Despair made those who dissented in religion more obdurate and made them prefer to oppose the government openly and confess their belief frankly, rather than to remain for ever oppressed and subdued. This was the reason why they started to hold their meetings and services each day more openly, thus getting so many more adherents. The others too now became embittered and opposed to the way in which the matter was being dealt with, and began to turn against the doctrines of the authorities who, in their opinion, were the cause of all these troubles, commotions and outrages.

E. Prince Andrei Kurbsky and Ivan the Terrible Trade Accusations, 1564

Kurbsky to Ivan IV: To the tsar, exalted above all by God, who appeared (formerly) most illustrious, particularly in the Orthodox faith, but who has now, in consequence of our sins, been found to be the contrary of this. If you have understanding, may you understand this with your leprous conscience—such a conscience as cannot be found even amongst the godless peoples. And I have not let my tongue say more than this on all these matters in turn; but because of the bitterest persecution from your power, with much sorrow in my heart will I hasten to inform you of a little. . . .

What evil and persecution have I not suffered from you! What ills and misfortunes have you not brought upon me! And what iniquitous tissues of lies have you not woven against me! But I cannot now recount the various misfortunes at your hands which have beset me owing to their multitude and since I am still filled with the grief of my soul. But, to conclude, I can summarize them all [thus]: of everything have I been deprived; I have been driven from the land of God without guilt [*lit.* in vain], hounded by you. I did not ask [for aught] with humble words, nor did I beseech you with tearful plaint; nor yet did I win from you any mercy through the intercession of the hierarchy. You have recompensed me with evil for good and for my love with implacable hatred. My blood, spilled like water for you, cries out against you to my Lord. God sees into [men's] hearts—in my

mind have I ardently reflected and my conscience have I placed as a witness [against myself], and I have sought and pried within my thoughts, and, examining myself [*lit.* turning myself around], I know not now—nor have I ever found—my guilt in aught before you. In front of your army have I marched—and marched again; and no dishonor have I brought upon you; but only brilliant victories, with the help of the angel of the Lord, have I won for your glory, and never have I turned the back of your regiments to the foe. But far more, I have achieved most glorious conquests to increase your renown. And this, not in one year, nor yet in two—but throughout many years have I toiled with much sweat and patience; and always have I been separated from my fatherland, and little have I seen my parents, and my wife have I not known; but always in far distant towns have I stood in arms against your foes and I have suffered many wants and natural illnesses, of which my Lord Jesus Christ is witness. Still more, I was visited with wounds inflicted by barbarian hands in various battles and all my body is already afflicted with sores. But to you, O tsar, was all this as nought; rather do you show us your intolerable wrath and bitterest hatred, and, furthermore, burning stoves.[2]

Ivan IV to Kurbsky: Wherefore, O Prince, if you regard yourself to have piety, have you lost your soul? What will you give in its place on the day of the terrible judgment? Even if you should acquire the whole world, death will reach you in the end! Why have you sold your soul for your body's sake? Is it because you were afraid of death at the false instigation of your demons and influential friends and counselors? . . .

Are you not ashamed before your slave Vaska Shibanov,[3] who preserved his piety and, having attached himself to you with a kiss of the cross, did not reject you before the tsar and the whole people, though standing at the gate of death, but praised you and was all too ready to die for you? But you did not emulate his devotion: on account of a single angry word of mine, have you lost not only your own soul, but the souls of all your ancestors: for, by God's will, had they been given as servants to our grandfather, the great tsar, and they gave their souls to him and served him up to their death, and ordered you, their children, to serve the children and grandchildren of our grandfather. But you have forgotten everything and traitorously, like a dog, have you transgressed the oath and have gone over to the enemies of

---

Excerpt from Chapter 33 of *Medieval Russia's Epics, Chronicles, and Tales,* Serge A Zenovsky, ed., E. P. Dutton, 1963, pp. 289–291, 296–298. Reprinted by permission.

[2] An allusion to one of Ivan's favorite methods of torture.
[3] Kurbsky's servant, whom Ivan tortured to death without forcing him to betray Kurbsky.

Christianity, and, not considering your wrath, you utter stupid words, hurling, as it were, stones at the sky.
. . .

It had pleased God to take away our mother, the pious Tsarina Helen, from the earthly kingdom to the kingdom of heaven. My brother George, who now rests in heaven, and I were left orphans and, as we received no care from anyone, we laid our trust in the Holy Virgin, and in the prayers of all the saints, and in the blessing of our parents. When I was in my eighth year, our subjects acted according to their will, for they found the empire without a ruler, and did not deign to bestow their voluntary attention upon us, their master, but were bent on acquiring wealth and glory, and were quarreling with each other. And what have they not done! How many boyars, how many friends of our father and generals they have killed! And they seized the farms and villages and possessions of our uncles, and established themselves therein. The treasure of our mother they trod underfoot and pierced with sharp sticks, and transferred it to the great treasure, but some of it they grabbed themselves; and that was done by your grandfather Mikhaylo Tuchkov. The Princes Vasily and Ivan Shuysky took it upon themselves to have me in their keeping, and those who had been the chief traitors of our father and mother they let out of prison, and they made friends with them. Prince Vasily Shuysky with a Judas crowd fell in the court belonging to our uncle upon our father confessor Fedor Mishurin, and insulted him, and killed him; and they imprisoned

Prince Ivan Fedorovich Byelsky and many others in various places, and armed themselves against the realm; they ousted metropolitan Daniel from the metropolitan see and banished him: and thus they improved their opportunity, and began to rule themselves...

Document Set 16.1 References

A. A Venetian Ambassador Sketches the Hierarchy in France, 1558
Giovanni Sorano, in *Reports of the Venetian Ambassadors,* in *Translations and Reprints from the Original Sources of European History* (Philadelphia: University of Pennsylvania Press, 1902), 3/2:16–19.
B. Charlotte de Mornay Describes the St. Bartholomew's Day Massacre
Memoires de Madame de Mornay (Paris: J. Nenouard, 1868–1869), 1:59–62. Translated by Lynn Hunt.
C. A Huguenot Leader Justifies Resistance to Tyranny
Julian H. Franklin, *Constitutionalism and Resistance in the Sixteenth Century* (New York: Pegasus, 1969), 185–197 passim.
D. Jacob van Wesenbeke Analyzes the Drift Toward Rebellion in the Netherlands, 1566
Van Wesenbeke in E. H. Kossman and A. F. Mellink, eds., *Texts Concerning the Revolt in the Netherlands* (Cambridge: Cambridge University Press, 1974), 66–69.
E. Prince Andrei Kurbsky and Ivan the Terrible Trade Accusations, 1564
Serge A. Zenkovsky, ed. and trans., *Medieval Russia's Epics, Chronicles, and Tales* (New York: E. P. Dutton, 1963), 289–299.

DOCUMENT SET 16.2
Alternatives to Wars of Religion

Secular governments' insistence on unity of belief was the primary reason why differences in religion escalated into civil war or degenerated into persecutions. Overwhelmingly, sixteenth-century men and women felt their convictions strongly enough to believe that theirs was the only true path prescribed by God. Read the documents in this set with the question in mind of how faith in the correctness of one's "inner" religious vision was giving way as the sixteenth century wore on and as the consequences of religious wars became ever more appalling.

The French nobleman Michel de Montaigne (1533–1592) was the first great writer of the literary essay (a term he invented), devoted to the examination of one's own character and experiences. Particularly at the outset of his literary career, he was deeply influenced by the ancient philosophical tradition of skepticism, with its radical doubt of all received wisdom. During the civil wars, Montaigne conformed to Catholicism because it was the traditional religion of France, but he never expressed serious conviction. In Document A he characteristically exposes the frailty of human understanding, and its vulnerability to prejudice and subjective experience.

Jean Bodin (c. 1530–1596), one of the foremost political philosophers of the era, unequivocally rejected the right of revolution, which Hotman and other Huguenot writers (Set 16.1, Document 4) had advocated. In Document B, an extract from his *Six Books of the Republic* (1676), Bodin argued that every state should have a sovereign authority which could never be divided or ended and which no subject could legally or morally oppose. Yet in another work, the *Colloquium Heptaplomeres* (1587), the nominally Catholic Bodin presented seven men differing radically in religion (including a Jew, a Muslim, and an ancient Epicurean) and concluded that they must live together in peace. (Lest you give Bodin too much credit as an advanced-thinking liberal, however, compare his views on witchcraft: Set 16.7, Document A.) In what respects—and why—was Bodin making a case for substituting a religion of obedience to the sovereign, peace-keeping state for a religion of obedience to God?

Unlike most of the rest of sixteenth-century Europe, the Polish-Lithuanian commonwealth experienced neither serious religious persecution nor civil war, although all the religious currents of the age flowed through it. In 1572–1573, facing a potentially devastating crisis with the dying-out of the national dynasty and with rival religious interests vying to elect as their next king someone favorable to their viewpoint, the commonwealth's nobility instead pledged to maintain religious toleration among themselves. The Warsaw Confederation of 1573 (excerpted here as Document C) formalized this agreement; thereupon the Poles elected the candidate Henry of Valois, whose hands (unbeknownst in Warsaw) were drenched with the blood of St. Bartholomew's. At the same time, however, they placed severe limitations on royal power—restrictions so onerous that the new king fled Poland as soon as word arrived that he had succeeded to the French crown as Henry III. In what ways do you think that the Poles' determination to modify authoritarian government—a step that Jean Bodin greatly disapproved—reflected a response to the sixteenth-century experience with religious warfare? Comment also on the fact that the Warsaw Confederation's guarantee of religious liberty was limited to the nobility.

In the final reading of this set (Document D), the Venetian Republic in 1606 reacts to a papal interdict, a prohibition against holding any Catholic services (including giving last rites to the dying) in Venice until the republic brought its foreign policy into alignment with Rome's. As you will recall from Set 12.3, Document E, the papacy had used such a threat in 1309 to humble Venice. What was different in 1606? The Venetian Republic was strongly Catholic, but it would not allow the papacy to dictate its policies. How did its defiance of the papacy raise the issue of religious wars and reflect the growing power of the state?

A. Michel de Montaigne Ponders the Fallibility of Human Understanding

I do not know what to say about it, but it is evident from experience that so many interpretations disperse the truth and shatter it. Aristotle wrote to be understood; if he did not succeed, still less will another man, less able, and not treating his own ideas. By diluting the substance we allow it to escape and spill it all over the place; of one subject we make a thousand, and, multiplying and subdividing, fall back into Epicurus' infinity of atoms. Never did two men judge alike about the same thing, and it is impossible to find two opinions exactly alike, not only in different men, but in the same man at different times. Ordinarily I find subject for doubt in what the commentary has not deigned to touch on. I am more apt to trip on flat ground, like certain horses I know which stumble more often on a smooth road.

Who would not say that glosses increase doubts and ignorance, since there is no book to be found, whether human or divine, with which the world busies itself, whose difficulties are cleared up by interpretation? The hundredth commentator hands it on to his successor thornier and rougher than the first one had found it. When do we agree and say, "There has been enough about this book; henceforth there is nothing more to say about it"?

This is best seen in law practice. We give legal authority to numberless doctors, numberless decisions, and as many interpretations. Do we therefore find any end to the need of interpreting? Do we see any progress and advance toward tranquillity? Do we need fewer lawyers and judges than when this mass of law was still in its infancy? On the contrary, we obscure and bury the meaning; we no longer find it except hidden by so many enclosures and barriers.

Men do not know the natural infirmity of their mind: it does nothing but ferret and quest, and keeps incessantly whirling around, building up and becoming entangled in its own work, like our silkworms, and is suffocated in it. *A mouse in a pitch barrel* [Erasmus]. It thinks it notices from a distance some sort of glimmer of imaginary light and truth; but while running toward it, it is crossed by so many difficulties and obstacles, and diverted by so many new quests, that it strays from the road, bewildered. . . .

It is more of a job to interpret the interpretations than to interpret the things, and there are more books about books than about any other subject: we do nothing but write glosses about each other. The world is swarming with commentaries; of authors there is a great scarcity.

Is it not the chief and most reputed learning of our times to learn to understand the learned? Is that not the common and ultimate end of all studies?

Our opinions are grafted upon one another. The first serves as a stock for the second, the second for the third. Thus we scale the ladder, step by step. And thence it happens that he who has mounted highest has often more honor than merit; for he has only mounted one speck higher on the shoulders of the next last.

How often and perhaps how stupidly have I extended my book to make it speak for itself! Stupidly, if only for this reason, that I should have remembered what I say of others who do the same: that these frequent sheep's eyes at their own work

testify that their heart thrills with love for it, and that even the rough, disdainful blows with which they beat it are only the love taps and affectations of maternal fondness; in keeping with Aristotle, to whom self-appreciation and self-depreciation often spring from the same sort of arrogance. For as for my excuse, that I ought to have more liberty in this than others, precisely because I write of myself and my writings as of my other actions, because my theme turns in upon itself—I do not know whether everyone will accept it.

I have observed in Germany that Luther has left as many divisions and altercations over the uncertainty of his opinions, and more, as he raised about the Holy Scriptures.

Our disputes are purely verbal. I ask what is "nature," "pleasure," "circle," "substitution." The question is one of words, and is answered in the same way. "A stone is a body." But if you pressed on: "And what is a body?"—"Substance."—"And what is substance?" and so on, you would finally drive the respondent to the end of his lexicon. We exchange one word for another word, often more unknown. I know better what is man than I know what is animal, or mortal, or rational. To satisfy one doubt, they give me three; it is the Hydra's head.

Socrates asked Meno what virtue was. "There is," said Meno, "the virtue of a man and a woman, of a magistrate and of a private individual, of a child and of an old man." "That's fine," exclaimed Socrates; "we were in search of one virtue, and here is a whole swarm of them."

B. Jean Bodin Defines Sovereignty

Sovereignty is that absolute and perpetual power vested in a commonwealth which in Latin is termed *majestas* . . . The term needs careful definition, because although it is the distinguishing mark of a commonwealth, and an understanding of its nature fundamental to any treatment of politics, no jurist or political philosopher has in fact attempted to define it. . . .

I have described it as *perpetual* because one can give absolute power to a person or group of persons for a period of time, but that time expired they become subjects once more. Therefore even while they enjoy power, they cannot properly be regarded as sovereign rulers, but only as the lieutenants and agents of the sovereign ruler, till the moment comes when it pleases the prince or the people to revoke the gift. The true sovereign remains always seized of his power. Just as a feudal lord who grants lands to another retains his eminent domain over them, so the ruler who delegates authority to judge and command, whether it be for a short period, or during pleasure, remains seized of those rights of jurisdiction actually exercised by another in the form of a revocable grant, or precarious tenancy. For this reason the law requires the governor of a province, or the prince's lieutenant, to make a formal surrender of the authority committed to him, at the expiration of his term of office. In this respect there is no difference between the highest officer of state and his humblest subordinate. If it were otherwise, and the absolute authority delegated by the prince to a lieutenant was regarded as itself sovereign power, the latter could use it against his prince who would thereby forfeit his eminence, and the subject could command his lord, the servant his master. This is a manifest absurdity, considering that the sovereign is always excepted personally, as a matter of right, in all delegations of authority, however extensive. . . .

C. The Polish-Lithuanian Nobles Promise Mutual Religious Toleration, 1573

We, the Spiritual and Temporal Counselors, the Gentry and the other Estates of the one and indivisible Republic, from Old and New Poland, from the Grand Duchy of Lithuania, etc.—and from the Cities of the Crown (declare):

".... Whereas there is a great dissidence in affairs of the Christian Religion within our Country, and to prevent any sedition for this reason among the people—like what we see clearly in other Kingdoms—we promise each other, on behalf of ourselves and our descendants, for perpetuity, under oath and pledging our faith, honor and consciences, that we who are *dissidentes de religione*[1] will keep peace between ourselves, and neither shed blood on account of differences of faiths or kinds of churches, nor punish one another by confiscation of goods, deprivation of honor, imprisonment or exile. . . ."

D. Venice Rejects the Papal Interdict, 1606

It has come to our knowledge that on the 17th of April last past, by the order of the most holy father, Pope Paul V, there was published and posted up in Rome a so-called brief, which was fulminated against us, our senate, and the whole of our state; and that one was addressed to you, the tenor and contents whereof were similar to those of the other. We there-

[1] Dissidents in religion—Catholics, Orthodox, and Protestants.

fore find ourselves constrained to preserve in peace and tranquility the state which God has given us to rule; and, in order to maintain our authority as a prince, who in temporal matters recognizes no superior saving the Divine Majesty, we, by these our public letters, do protest before the Lord God and the whole world that we have not failed to use every possible means to make his Holiness understand our most valid and irrefragable case; first, by means of our ambassador residing at the court of his Holiness; then, by letters of ours in answer to briefs addressed to us by his Holiness; and, lastly, by a special ambassador sent to him to this effect. But having found the ears of his Holiness closed against us and seeing that the brief aforesaid is published contrary to all right reason and contrary to the teaching of the divine Scriptures, the doctrine of the holy fathers, and the sacred canons, to the prejudice of the secular authority given us by God, and of the liberty of our state, inasmuch as it would cause disturbance in the quiet possession which, by divine Grace, under our government our faithful subjects hold of their properties, their honor and their lives, and occasion a most grave and universal scandal throughout the state; We do not hesitate to consider the said brief not only as unsuitable and unjust, but as null and void and of no worth or value whatever, and being thus invalid, vain, and unlawfully fulminated, *de facto nullo juris ordine servato*, we have thought fit to use in resisting it the remedies adopted by our ancestors and by other sovereign princes against such pontiffs as, in using the power given them by God to the use of edifying, have overstepped their due limits. . . . And we pray the Lord God to inspire him [the pope] with a sense of the invalidity and nullity of his brief and of the other acts committed against us, and the He, knowing the justice of our cause, may give us strength to maintain our reverence for the holy apostolic see, whose most devoted servants we and our predecessors, together with this republic, have been and ever shall be.

Document Set 16.2 References

A. Michel de Montaigne Ponders the Fallibility of Human Understanding
Montaigne, *Essays*, trans. Donald Frame (Stanford, Cal.: Stanford University Press, 1957), 817, 818–819.
B. Jean Bodin Defines Sovereignty
Bodin, *Six Books of the Republic*, abridged and edited by M. J. Toole (Oxford, England: Basil Blackwell, 1956), 25.
C. The Polish-Lithuanian Nobles Promise Mutual Religious Toleration, 1573
Manfred Kridl, ed. and trans., *For Your Freedom and Ours* (New York: Unger, 1943), 32–33.
D. Venice Rejects the Papal Interdict, 1606
Translations and Reprints from the Original Sources of European History (Philadelphia: University of Pennsylvania Press, 1898), 4/4:32–33.

DOCUMENT SET 16.3
The Greatness and Tragedy of Spain

Spain was the greatest power in sixteenth-century Europe. Yet it became badly overstretched by wars and international commitments, and by the early seventeenth century stood on the brink of a long descent. This set offers some basis for reflecting on Spain's greatness and impending decline.

Document A is another of those Venetian ambassadorial reports that historians find so useful for grasping the character of sixteenth-century political figures and understanding the mentality of the age. What is your assessment of the young Philip II, judging by this report?

The Spanish Inquisition, for all its fervent Catholicism, was primarily an instrument of state policy, intended to unify Spain and crush all manifestations of religious dissent. From Document B you can get some idea of how the Inquisition worked and what befell someone accused of being a "Lutheran" (which could mean any kind of Christian religious heterodoxy). Note that the person accused in this extract is a *converso*—an individual of converted Jewish parentage. Such people were primary targets of inquisitorial suspicion.

The destruction of the Spanish Armada in its futile attempt to defeat English intervention in the Netherlands and to crush the Dutch Republic's revolt is described in Document C in words that were spread throughout Europe in the Fugger Newsletters—one of the first instances of what we would today call journalism. The great Spanish novel of Miguel de Cervantes (1547–1616), *Don Quixote,* is often interpreted as a satire on the decline of medieval chivalry; like all great comedies, it not only pokes fun but also expresses great sympathy with the essential human condition. Document D is an extract from very early in *Don Quixote.* What elements of satire do you detect?

The final document in this set comes from the early seventeenth century. The foremost statesman of this era, the count-duke of Olivares (1587–1645), who served Philip IV as prime minister, tried valiantly to stem the monarchy's decline by instituting administrative reforms and by squeezing money out of the provinces despite their protests about local liberties. Document E is an extract of Olivares' plan for "union of arms" that would bring all Iberia together. This plan instead provoked both Portugal and Catalonia to rebel in 1640 and led to the count-duke's downfall a year later.

Using *The Challenge of the West* and the documents of this set, write a brief analysis of the strengths and weaknesses of the Spanish monarchy from the mid-sixteenth century to the mid-seventeenth century.

A. The Venetian Ambassador Suriano Takes the Measure of Philip II, 1559

. . . Although his actions display that royal dignity and gravity which are natural and habitual to him, he is none the less agreeable for this; on the contrary, his courtesy toward all seems only the more striking. His pleasing figure, his manly air, and his suavity of speech and manner serve to enhance the pleasing effect. He is slight in stature, but so well built, so admirably proportioned, and dressed with such taste and discernment that one could hardly imagine anything more perfect. . . .

Although the king resembles his father in his face and speech, in his attention to his religious duties, and in his habitual kindness and good faith, he nevertheless differs from him in several of those respects in which the greatness of rulers, after all, lies. The emperor was addicted to war, which he well understood; the king knows but little of it and has no love for it. The emperor undertook great enterprises with enthusiasm; his son avoids them. The father was fond of planning great things and would in the end realize his wishes by his skill; his son, on the contrary, pays less attention to augmenting his own greatness than to hindering that of others. The emperor never allowed himself to be influenced by threats or fear, while the king has lost some of his dominions owing to unreasonable apprehensions. The father was guided in all matters by his own opinion; the son follows the opinions of others.

In the king's eyes no nation is superior to the Spaniards. It is among them that he lives, it is they that he consults, and it is they that direct his policy; in all this he is acting quite contrary to the habit of his father. He thinks little of the Italians and Flemish and still less of the Germans. Although he may employ the chief men of all the countries over which he rules, he admits none of them to his secret counsels, but utilizes their services only in military affairs, and then perhaps not so much because he really esteems them, as in the hope that he will in this way prevent his enemies from making use of them.

B. The Spanish Inquisition Interrogates a Converso "Lutheran" and Sends Him to an *Auto Da Fé*, 1559

Sentencing of Pedro de Cazalla for Lutheranism in 1559 by the Valladolid tribunal.

The accused " . . . having confessed to us that for four years he had communicated with a certain person who had been his friend for fourteen years and who had instructed him in [the Lutheran explanation] of justification . . . [this friend] had suggested to him that there was no need to stop at the denial of purgatory, and from this inferred the uselessness of indulgences and things conceded by the Pope . . . [It was pointed out that] Pedro de Cazalla was descended from converted Jews on both sides . . . [and had] instructed and indoctrinated many others about the passion and merits of our redeemer, Jesus Christ, who had justified all sinners without recourse to works, penance. . . .

"Item . . . Cazalla believed in faith alone without works . . . penance, fasts, prayers . . . [none of the latter being] meritorious nor profitable for sinner's salvation, saying they were only justified by Christ's passion and merits.

"Item . . . believed there was no purgatory in the next life . . . and held the same error about the sacrifices, offerings, prayers, and aids in the Catholic Church for the deceased . . . [considering] all such aids superfluous and without effect.

"Item . . . believed that Christians who had faith did not have to have recourse to the saints, saying that the saints' intercession . . . had no effect concerning the salvation of sinners.

"Item . . . believed that the Apostolic Roman Catholic Church had no power or authority to force any Christians to observe its precepts, fast, vigils, celebrations, nor prohibit or make [special] distinctions about foods.

"Item, [he asserted] that the Pope or other eminence . . . had no power to excommunicate or absolve any Christian by means of indulgences, jubilees, and pardons . . . which were worthless . . . concerning the pardoning of sins.

"Item, [he denounced monasticism].

"Item . . . believed that oral confession . . . is not necessary, nor is a sacrament, nor is useful for the pardon and absolution of sins . . . [instead Cazalla recommended a kind of mental confession to God, directly and alone].

"Item . . . believed that the Catholic Church should have no more than two sacraments (cf. the nun Guevara, from the same group), baptism and communion in memory of the passion and [last] supper of the savior while the others . . . were not sacraments [this seems to be a quasi-Zwinglian view of the Eucharist, which testified to the book-smugglers' diligence in getting other than Lutheran Protestant works into Spain. Ed.] . . . .

"Item . . . believed that the . . . Eucharist of the consecrated host and chalice is not . . . Christ . . . nor sacramental, but only spiritual through the faith of the recipient and [He is] not really or corporeally [present] as our Holy Catholic faith and mother church has taught us. [This probably can be interpreted in several Protestant ways. Ed.]

"Item . . . believed that all Christians, priests and laymen, could administer and receive the . . . Eucharist under both kinds, of bread and of wine . . . [Classic statement of priesthood of all believers. Ed.]

"Item . . . Cazalla had made communion . . . with many others . . . according to the Lutheran usage . . . many times in diverse places, while hearing and preaching before this supper a sermon about the sect and errors of Luther in which [Lutheranism] was praised as the truth.

" . . . Item, in Cazalla's house were such [heretical] meetings held and . . . [he owned and loaned out] the heretical books of Luther and Calvin, and many other heretics.

"Item . . . declaring our definitive sentence that he is an apostate heretical Lutheran [Cazalla is sentenced to relaxation, confiscation of all goods, etc.]. . . ."

Auto de fe at Valladolid, May 21, 1559, attended by Don Carlos and the Regent, Princess Juana, Philip II's son and sister respectively; the King had not yet returned from the Netherlands.

"This *auto* was held in the Plaza de San Francisco on a very large platform [there follows a very minute, detailed description of the local arrangements for the occasion and the social eminence of the onlookers, including high clergy as well as laymen] . . . before the *auto* began a letter from the Holy Office was read imploring the princes [Carlos and Juana] and others . . . to aid the Inquisition [and the true faith generally] to punish and extirpate all errors, heresy, and apostacy . . . and Don Carlos and Princess Juana swore [to do as much] on the Gospels and the Cross . . . which all received with great admiration, joy, and contentment. Friar Melchor de Cano [the noted Dominican supporter of the tribunal and the ongoing scholastic revival of Thomism in Spain. Ed.] began to read the sentences in a very impressive manner . . . [fifteen burnt, sixteen reconciled]. . . . "

"Continuation of this *auto*, pp. 449–452. "Agustin de

Cazalla, Francisco de Vivero, and Alonso de Pérez [to be burnt] passed by the Princes' platform to the heretics'. The Bishop of Palencia and the grandly apparelled ponifical representative . . . formally degraded [unfrocked] these three clerics.

". . . Cazalla, at this, gave great indications of contrition with tears before all; . . . Vivero was smiling while Pérez displayed no feelings at the moment of this humiliation. Cazalla went down on his knees before the Princes saying in tear [he pleaded for his several relations arrested and sentenced with him, especially for an aged sister; otherwise he seemed to collapse pathetically] . . . [the executions start] Cazalla [, hysterical], proclaiming his belief in the Holy Mother Church of Rome for which he is dying . . . Vivero, Pérez, and Antonio Herrezuelo silent . . . Cazalla in a great voice said he died for having been Lutheran . . . but was repenting . . . and all those dying with him were dying for his doctrine, and by his inducement and great sympathy persuaded Herrezuelo to convert to Christ's faith [i.e., Cazalla's repudiation of his "Lutheranism" drove the latter to also deny it and revert to Catholicism; Herrezuelo subsequently went back on this recantation]. . . . the others did not show any feelings or demonstrate repentance.

. . . and thus were burnt alive . . . .

"Tuesday, the next day, dawn came to the Plaza and the scaffold. . . ."

c. The Fugger Newsletters Comment on the Destruction of the Armada

Report from England about the Spanish Armada, received in Augsburg from Hamburg on the 19th day of November 1588.

The Armada of the King of Spain set sail from Portugal with one hundred and thirty-five ships, to wit: four galleasses from Naples, four galleons from Portugal, ten vessels with victuals, fourteen Venetian ships, among them several galleons. The remainder was made up of other large and small craft. The Armada arrived in Corunna on the 5th day of July, from whence it intended to sail for Flanders, there to join forces with the Duke of Parma and invade England. At that time the English Armada was in Plymouth Port.

After they had been under sail from Corunna eight days they arrived in Ostend and thereupon lay south of the shores of England, where for four or five days they had various skirmishes with the English Armada. On that occasion the English took two

ships. On one of these there was Don Pedro di Mendoza, whom they took prisoner and so to the loss of four Portuguese galleons which remained England. Storms south of England caused them stranded on the French coast. They then proceeded and cast anchor off Calais, since they could no longer get as far as Dunkirk. They wished to wait for the Duke of Parma in Calais, but he sent word that he could not be ready under eight days. Thereupon the admiral sent reply that he would again set sail for Spain. Meanwhile the English sent forth against the Spanish Armada several burning ships, so that they were forced to cut their moorings and to retire hastily. Each ship left two anchors behind and four of the largest galleasses were stranded and wrecked off Calais. The following day at eight o'clock, the two Armadas had a further encounter, heavily bombarding each other for eight hours. In this battle the Spanish lost four ships, namely two Portuguese galleasses, a vessel from Biscay and one other. All four went to the bottom of the sea. Three large Venetian craft remained behind off the coast of Flanders and were in great peril of going under. The inhabitants of Flushing took two of these ships, and the third was shipwrecked. One of them had on board the Colonel commanding the garrison of Seville. According to the prisoners' report the Spaniards lost four thousand men in the battle off Calais, amongst them the Commander-in-Chief of the cavalry at Naples and Seville. The Spaniards are said to have left one hundred and twenty ships, although others could count only one hundred and ten. The big galleon, which the Duke of Florence had sent, was not to be seen anywhere after the battle.

Hereafter the Armada made off and was pursued by the English for five days as far as Scotland. When they counted their men there they found that they had already lost eight thousand, most of whom had been killed or died of disease. From thence they set sail for Ireland without taking provisions on board. Off Ireland they lost two ships, the *San Sebastian* and the *San Mathias*, which had four hundred and fifty-six men on board. Lacking fresh water, the fleet threw many horses and mules overboard off Ireland. When they sailed away from Ireland, the Commander-in-Chief, the Duke of Medina Sidonia, ordered each one of his captains to set his course for Corunna or the first Spanish port. They thus sailed together throughout ten days. Then the storm separated the Duke of Medina Sidonia with twenty-seven of his ships from them and no one knew where they had gone. The last time the Armada was assembled it counted no more than seventy-eight ships. Of the big galleasses not one was left. Two of the Duke of Medina Sidonia's ships ran ashore. Only two or three of the men were saved. They say that the Chief Admiral had left on board only five-and-twenty more barrels of wine, but little bread and no water. His masts had been so weakened by firing that he could not carry full canvas. . . .

From Middleburg, the 14th day of November 1588.

It is said that news has arrived from Ireland that a further nine ships of the Spanish Armada have perished there. Sixteen hundred men are reported to be still alive, to whom the Irish are lending help. For that reason the Queen of England has dispatched thither six hundred men who are to take up hostilties against these people. From Sicily there comes information that the General Duke of Medina in Seville organized there a great procession to celebrate his return. Ninety ships of the Armada are missing, and every one has been forbidden to mourn his friends who were lost with the Armada. A forty days' fast has been ordered, hoping that thereby the return home of the missing ships will be obtained.

D. Don Quixote, Gone Mad, Turns Knight-Errant

In fine, he gave himself up so wholly to the reading of Romances, that a-Nights he would pore on 'till 'twas Day, and a-Days he would read on 'till 'twas Night; and thus by sleeping little, and reading much, the Moisture of his Brain was exhausted to that Degree, that at last he lost the Use of his Reason. A world of disorderly Notions, pick'd out of his Books, crouded into his Imagination; and now his Head was full of nothing but Inchantments, Quarrels, Battles, Challenges, Wounds, Complaints, Amours, Torments, and abundance of Stuff and Impossibilities; insomuch, that all the Fables and fantastical Tales which he read, seem'd to him now as true as the most authentick Histories. He would say, that the *Cid Ruy liaz* was a very brave Knight, but not worthy to stand in Competition with the *Knight of the Burning Sword,* who with a single Backstroke had cut in sunder two fierce and mighty Giants. He liked yet better *Bernardo del Carpio,* who at *Roncesvalles* depriv'd of Life the inchanted *Orlando,* having lifted him from the Ground, and choak'd him in the Air, as *Hercules* did *Antoeus* the Son of the Earth. . . .

Having thus lost his Understanding, he unluckily stumbled upon the oddest Fancy that ever enter'd into a Madman's Brain; for now he thought it convenient and necessary, as well for the Increase of his own Honour, as the Service of the Publick, to turn Knight-Errant, and roam through the whole World arm'd Cap-a-pee, and mounted on his Steed, in quest of Adventures; that thus imitating those Knight-Errants of whom he had read, and following their Course of Life, redressing all manner of Grievances, and exposing himself to Danger on all Occasions, at last, after a happy Conclusion of his Enterprizes, he might purchase everlasting Honour and Renown. Transported with these agreeable Delusions, the poor Gentleman already grasp'd in Imagination the Imperial Sceptre of *Trapizonde,* and, hurry'd away by his mighty Expectations, he prepares with all Expedition to take the Field.

The first Thing he did was to scour a Suit of Armour that had belong'd to his Great-Grandfather, and had lain Time out of Mind carelessly rusting in a Corner.

E. The Conde-Duque Olivares Attempts to Unify Iberia

Today, the common people look on the various nationals as if they were little better than enemies, and this happens in all the kingdoms. If Castile can be seen as feudatory of Aragon, and Aragon of Castile, Portugal of both and both of Portugal, and the same for all the kingdoms of Spain, those of Italy and Flanders being brought into a close relationship, then the blindness and separation of hearts which has existed hitherto must necessarily be ended by the close natural bond of a union of arms. For when the Portuguese see the Castilians and the Castilians the Portuguese, they will know that each sees the friend and feudatory of the other, who will help him with his blood and his men in time of need.

This closer union would bring immediate relief to Castile, while going a long way towards solving that problem of imperial defence which first brought home the need for more adequate co-operation among the provinces of the Monarchy.

Document Set 16.3 References

A. The Venetian Ambassador Suriano Takes the Measure of
   Philip II, 1559
   James Harvey Robinson, ed., *Readings in European History*
   (Boston: Ginn, 1904), 2:168–169.
B. The Spanish Inquisition Interrogates a Converso "Lutheran"
   and Sends Him to an *Auto Da Fé*, 1559
   Paul Hauban, ed. and trans., *The Spanish Inquisition* (New
   York: John Wiley, 1969), 70–76.
C. The Fugger Newsletters Comment on the Destruction of the
   Armada
   G. T. Matthews, ed., *The Fugger Newsletters* (New York:
   G. P. Putnam's Sons, 1959), 161–163.
D. Don Quixote, Gone Mad, Turns Knight-Errant
   Miguel de Cervantes, *Don Quixote,* Ozell's revision of the
   translation of Peter Motteux (New York: Modern Library,
   1930), 3–4.
E. The Conde-Duque Olivares Attempts to Unify Iberia
   J. H. Elliott, *The Revolt of the Catalans: A Study in the
   Decline of Spain (1598–1640)* (Cambridge: Cambridge
   University Press, 1903), 206.

DOCUMENT SET 16.4
England from Elizabeth to the Early Stuarts

William Shakespeare (1564–1616) expressed with incomparable eloquence the generally accepted ideas of his day. In the extracts from his play *Troilus and Cressida* (Document A), set in the time of the Trojan War, he puts into the mouth of Ulysses a magnificent defense of social hierarchy. In what ways does this reflect sixteenth-century ideas of authority and deference? Can you also find such ideas expressed in Elizabeth I's speech to Parliament quoted in Document B? Notice here how the queen recognizes the mutual dependence of crown and Parliament; do you think her remarks are sincere?

Social policy in Elizabethan and early Stuart England depended heavily on the willingness of local authorities to accept responsibility for maintaining order. Read Document C for insights into what their obligations were; do you see any echo of ideas expressed in Documents A and B?

Documents D and E show two sides of the battle for individual conscience in late sixteenth-century England. In Document D, Jesuit Robert Johnson faces the gallows in 1582; what line does he draw between loyalty to the crown and his understanding of his duty to God, and how do the authorities respond? In Document F, the important Puritan writer William Perkins, a Cambridge divine, urges his noble patron (and all readers of his book) to listen closely to the voice of conscience. In Puritan teaching, it was through conscience that God called sinners to repentance and into the body of the elect. Compare the two examples of appeal to conscience across the religious divide.

The Stuarts were to find it impossible to govern England arbitrarily after they inherited the crown with James I's accession in 1603. Elizabeth, who understood the craft of ruling better than most of her colleagues among Europe's crowned heads, offered her cousin James VI of Scotland (who would become James I of England after her death) some shrewd advice on how to behave as a monarch. Her advice was prompted by news of a palace conspiracy against James in 1592. How well does this counsel (in Document F) fit with the ideas of governance and deference expressed elsewhere in this set? James's own notion of his prerogatives appears in Document G, a report on a church conference at which the new king had to listen to an English Puritan clergyman recall his many clashes with the Scottish Presbyterians. James's son Charles I (*1625–1649) tried to rule by combining heavy-handed arbitrariness, after dispens-

ing with Parliament, and wooing ordinary English people's loyalty away from the strict Puritan regimen. His decree in favor of Sunday sports (Document H) was typical of the Stuarts' claim to have the interests of humble subjects at heart.

The final document (I) returns us to the voice of conscience. The lay Puritan John Winthrop had to search his soul deeply before deciding that emigration to America was the right course for him. Ultimately he decided to go, and he became one of the leaders of Massachusetts Bay Colony. What considerations passed through this prominent gentleman's mind, and what did he hope that emigration would accomplish? How did his decision reflect tensions within Tudor-Stuart England?

A. William Shakespeare Defends the Social Order

The heavens themselves, the planets and this center,
Observe degree, priority, and place,
Insisture, course, proportion, season, form,
Office, and custom, in all line of order.
And therefore is the glorious planet Sol [the sun]
In noble eminence enthroned and sphered
Amidst the other, whose medicinable eye
Corrects the ill aspécts of planets evil,
And posts like the commandment of a king,
Sans check to good and bad. But when the planets
In evil mixture to disorder wander,
What plagues and what portents, what mutiny,
What raging of the sea, shaking of earth,
Commotion in the winds, frights, changes, horrors,
Divert and crack, rend and deracinate,
The unity and married calm of states
Quite from their fixure! Oh, when degree is shaked,
Which is the ladder to all high designs,
The enterprise is sick! How could communities,
Degrees in schools and brotherhoods in cities,
Peaceful commerce from dividable shores,
The primogenitive and due of birth,
Prerogative of age, crowns, scepters, laurels,
But by degree, stand in authentic place?
Take but degree away, untune that string,
And hark, what discord follows! Each thing meets
In mere oppugnancy. The bounded waters
Should lift their bosoms higher than the shores,
And make a sop of all this solid globe.
Strength should be lord of imbecility,

And the rude son should strike his father dead.
Force should be right, or rather, right and wrong,
Between whose endless jar justice resides,
Should lose their names, and so should justice too.
Then everything includes itself in power,
Power into will, will into appetite,
And appetite, a universal wolf,
So doubly seconded with will and power,
Must make perforce a universal prey,
And last eat up himself. . . .

B. The Young Elizabeth I Beguiles Her Subjects

Now, if ever any person had either the gift or the
style to win the hearts of people, it was this
Queen. . . . Every motion seemed a well guided
action; her eye was set upon one, her ear listened to
another, her judgment ran upon a third, to a fourth
she addressed her speech; her spirit seemed to be
everywhere, and yet so entire in her self, as it seemed
to be nowhere else.

. . . She was a Lady, upon whom nature had
bestowed, and well placed, many of her fairest favors;
of stature average, slender, straight, and amiably composed; of such state in her carriage, as every motion
of her seemed to bear majesty.

. . . In life, she was most innocent; in desire, moderate; in purpose, just; of spirit, above credit and
almost capacity of her sex; of divine wit, as well for
depth of judgment, as for quick conceit and speedy
expedition; of eloquence, as sweet in the utterance, so
ready and easy to come to the utterance; of wonderful knowledge both in learning and affairs; skilfull
not only in Latin and Greek, but also in diverse other
foreign languages: none knew better the hardest art of
all others, that is, of commanding men.

C. Parliament Imposes Compulsory Poor Rates, 1572

And forasmuch as charity would that poor, aged and
impotent persons should as necessarily be provided
for, as the said rogues, vagabonds and sturdy beggars
repressed, and that the said aged, impotent and poor
people should have convenient habitations and abiding places throughout this realm to settle themselves
upon, to the end that they nor any of them should
hereafter beg or wander about; It is therefore enacted
. . . that the justices of peace of . . . the shires of
England and Wales . . . and all other justices of the
peace, mayors, sheriffs, bailiffs, and other officers of

all and every city, borough, riding and franchises
within this realm . . . shall at or before the . . . feast of
St. Bartholomew [August 24] next coming . . . make
diligent search and enquiry of all aged, poor, impotent and decayed persons born within their . . . divisions and limits, or which were there dwelling within
three years next before this present parliament, which
live or of necessity be compelled to live by alms . . .
and shall . . . make a register book containing [their]
names and surnames . . . And when the number of the
said poor people forced to live upon alms be by that
means truly known, then the said justices . . . and
other officers shall within like convenient time devise
and appoint, within every their said several divisions,
meet and convenient places by their discretions to
settle the same poor people for their habitations and
abidings, if the parish within the which they shall be
found shall not or will not provide for them; and shall
also within like convenient time number all the said
poor people within their said several limits, and
thereupon (having regard to the number) set down
what portion the weekly charge towards the relief
and sustentation of the said poor people will amount
unto within every their said several divisions and limits; and that done, they . . . shall be their good discretions tax and assess all and every the inhabitants,
dwelling in all and every city, borough, town, village,
hamlet and place known within the said limits and
divisions, to such weekly charge as they and every of
them shall weekly contribute towards the relief of the
said poor people, and the names of all such inhabitants taxed shall also enter into the said register book
together with their taxation, and also shall be their
discretion within every their said divisions and limits
appoint or see collectors for one whole year to be
appointed of the said weekly portion, which shall
collect and gather the said proportion, and make
delivery of so much thereof, according to the discretion of the said justices . . . and other officers, to the
said poor people, as the said justices . . . and other
officers shall apoint them: and also shall appoint the
overseers of the said poor people by their discretions,
to continue also for one whole year; and if they do
refuse to be overseers, then every of them so refusing
to forfeit ten shillings for every such default . . .

D. An English Jesuit Goes to the Gallows, 1582

Johnson. I am a Catholic, and am condemn'd for
conspiring the queen's death at Rheims, with the
other company who were condemn'd with me. I
protest, that as for some of them with whom I was

condemn'd to have conspired withal, I did never see them before we met at the barr, neither did I ever write unto them, or receive letters from them: and as for any treasons, I am not guilty in deed nor thought . . .

Sheriff. Dost thou acknowledge the queen for lawful queen? Repent thee, and notwithstanding thy traitorous practices, we have authority from the queen to carry thee back.

Johnson. I do acknowledge her as lawful as Queen Mary was. I can say no more; but pray to God to give her grace, and that she may now stay her hand from shedding of innocent blood.

Sheriff. Dost thou acknowledge her supreme head of the church in ecclesiastical matters?

Johnson. I acknowledge her to have as full and great authority as ever Queen Mary had; and more with safety and conscience I cannot give her.

Sheriff. Thou art a traitor most obstinate.

Johnson. If I be a traitor for maintaining this faith, then all the kings and queens of this realm heretofore, and all our ancestors, were traitors, for they maintain'd the same.

Sheriff. What! You will preach treason also, if we suffer you!

Johnson. I teach but the Catholic religion.

Hereupon the rope was put about his neck, and he was willed to pray, which he did in Latin. They willed him to pray in English, that they might witness with him; he said, "I pray that prayer which Christ taught, in a tongue I well understand." A minister cried out, "Pray as Christ taught": to whom Mr. Johnson replied, "What! do you think Christ taught in English?" He went on, saying in Latin his *Pater, Ave,* and Creed, and *In manus tuas,*[1] etc. And so the cart was drawn away, and he finish'd this life as the rest did . . .

E. A Puritan Searches His Conscience: William Perkins, 1586

Sir, I pray you consider with me an especial point of God's word, carefully to be weighed. It is this: (a) Many professors of Christ, in the day of grace, persuade themselves that they are in the estate of grace, and so the true church esteemeth of them too; yet when the day of grace is past, they contrariwise shall find themselves to be in the estate of damnation, remediless. A doleful case, yet a most resolute truth, and the reason is plain. Men that live in the church are greatly annoyed with a fearful security and deadness

of heart, by which it comes to pass that they think it enough to make a common protestation of the faith, not once in all their lifetimes examining themselves whether they be in the estate of grace before the eternal God or not. (b) And indeed it is a grace peculiar to the man elect, to try himself whether he be in the estate of grace or not.

F. Elizabeth I Advises James VI on Ruling

The dear care, my dear brother, that ever I carried, from your infancy, of your prosperous estate and quiet, could not permit [me to] hear of so many, yea so traitorous attempts, without unspeakable dolour and unexpressful woe. . . . To redouble crimes so oft, I say with your pardon, most to your charge, which never durst have been renewed if the first had received the condign reward; for slacking of due correction engenders the bold minds for new crimes. And if my counsels had as well been followed as they were truly meant, your subjects had now better known their king, and you no more need of further justice. You find by sour experience what this neglect hath bred you.

I hear of so uncouth a way taken by some of your conventions, yea, agreed to by yourself, that I must [wonder] how you will be clerk to such lessons. Must a king be prescribed what councillors he will take as if you were their ward? Shall you be obliged to tie or undo what they list make or revoke? O Lord, what strange dreams hear I, that would God they were so, for then at my waking I should find them fables. If you mean, therefore, to reign, I exhort you to show you worthy the place, which never can be surely settled without a steady course held to make you loved and feared. I assure myself many have escaped your hands more for dread of your remissness than for love of the escaped; so oft they see you cherishing some men for open crimes, and so they mistrust more their revenge than your assurance. My affection for you best lies on this, my plainness, whose patience is too much moved with these like everlasting faults.

And since it so likes you to demand my counsel, I find so many ways your state so unjointed, that it needs a skilfuller bonesetter than I to join each part in his right place. But to fulfil your will, take, in short, these few words: For all whose you know the assailers of your courts, the shameful attempters of your sacred decree, if ever you pardon I will never be the suitor. Who to peril a king were inventors or actors, they should crack a halter if I were king. Such is my charity. Who under pretence of better[ing] your

---

[1] *Pater,* etc.: Catholic prayers, in Latin.

estate, endangers the king, or needs will be his school-masters, if I might appoint their university they should be assigned to learn first to obey; so should they better teach you next. I am not so unskilful of a kingly rule that I would wink at no fault, yet would be open-eyed at public indignity. Neither should all have the whip though some were scourged. But if, like a toy, of a king's life so oft endangered nought shall follow but a scorn, what sequel I may doubt of such contempt I dread to think and dare not name. The rest I bequeath to the trust of your faithful servant, and pray the Almighty God to inspire you in time, afore too late, to cut their combs whose crest may danger you. I am void of malice. God is judge. I know them not. Forgive this too too long a writing.

G. James I Tells the Presbyterians: "No Bishop, No King"

At which speech his Majesty was somewhat stirred, yet, which is admirable in him, without passion or show thereof; thinking that they aimed at a Scottish presbytery which, saith he, as well agreeth with a monarchy as God and the devil. "Then Jack and Tom and Will and Dick shall meet and at their pleasure censure me and my council and all our proceedings. Then Will shall stand up and say it must be thus; then Dick shall reply and say, 'Nay, marry, but we will have it thus.'" . . .

"I will tell you a tale. After that the religion restored by King Edward the Sixth was soon overthrown by the succession of Queen Mary here in England, we in Scotland felt the effect of it. Whereupon Master Knox writes to the queen regent [2] (of whom, without flattery, I may say that she was a virtuous and moderate lady), telling her that she was supreme head of the Church, and charged her, as she would answer it before God's tribunal, to take care of Christ, his Evangel, and of suppressing the popish prelates, who withstood the same. But how long, trow ye, did this continue? Even so long, till by her authority, by the popish bishops were repressed. He [Knox] himself and his adherents were brought in and well settled, and by these means made strong enough to undertake the matters of reformation themselves. Then, lo, they began to make small account of her supremacy, nor would longer rest upon her authority, but took the cause into their own hand; according to that more light wherewith they

were illuminated, made a further reformation of religion. How they used that poor lady, my mother, is not unknown, and with grief I may remember it; who, because she had not been otherwise instructed, did desire only a private chapel wherein to serve God, after her manner, with some few selected persons; but her supremacy was not sufficient to obtain it at their hands. And how they dealt with me in my minority you all know; it was not done secretly, and though I would, I cannot conceal it. . . . But if once you [my lords the bishops] were out, and they in place, I know what would become of my supremacy. No bishop, no king, as before I said."

H. Charles I Allows Sunday Sports, 1633

Our dear father of blessed memory, [James I], in his return from Scotland, coming through Lancashire, found that his subjects were debarred from lawful recreations upon Sundays after evening prayers ended and, upon holydays; and he prudently considered that if these times were taken from them, the meaner sort, who labor hard all the week, should have to recreations at all to refresh their spirits; and after his return he further saw that his loyal subjects in all other parts of his kingdom did suffer in the same kind, though perhaps not in the same degree; and did therefore, in his princely wisdom, publish a declaration to all his loving subjects concerning lawful sports to be used at such times . . . in the year 1618. . . .

Our pleasure likewise is, that the bishop of that diocese take the like strait order with all the Puritans and precisians within the same, either constraining them to conform themselves or to leave the county, according to the laws of our kingdom and canons of our Church, and so to strike equally on both hands against the contemners of our authority and adversaries of our Church; and as for our good people's lawful recreation, our pleasure likewise is, that after the end of divine service our good people be not disturbed, letted, or discouraged from any lawful recreation, such as dancing, either men or women; archery for men, leaping, vaulting, or any other such harmless recreation, nor from having of May-games, Whitsun-ales, and Morris-dances, and the setting up of Maypoles and other sports therewith used, so as the same be had in due and convenient time, without impediment or neglect of divine service; and that women shall have leave to carry rushes to the church for the decorating of it, according to their old custom; but withal we do here account still as prohibited all

2 Mary Queen of Scots' mother

unlawful games to be used upon Sundays only, as bear and bull baitings, interludes, and at all times in the meaner sort of people by law prohibited, bowling.

I. John Winthrop Ponders a Puritan Migration to New England, 1629

1. It will be a service to the Church of great consequence to carry the gospel into those parts of the world, to help on the coming of the fullness of the Gentiles, and to raise a bulwark against the kingdom of Antichrist which the Jesuits labor to rear up in those parts.

2. All other churches of Europe are brought to desolation, and our sins, for which the Lord begins already to frown upon us and to cut us short, do threaten evil times to be coming upon us; and who knows but that God hath provided this place to be a refuge for many whom he means to save out of the general calamity, and seeing the Church hath no place left to fly into but the wilderness, what better work can there be than to go and provide tabernacles and food for her against she comes thither?

3. This land grows weary of her inhabitants, so as man, who is the most precious of all creatures, is here more vile and base than the earth we tread upon, and of less price among us than an horse or a sheep; masters are forced by authority to entertain servants, parents to maintain their own children; all towns complain of the burden of their poor, though we have taken up many unnecessary—yea, unlawful—trades to maintain them, and we use the authority of the law to hinder the increase of our people, as by urging the statute against cottages and inmates, and thus it is come to pass that children, servants, and neighbors, especially if they be poor, are counted the greatest burdens, which, if things were right, would be the chiefest earthly blessings.

4. The whole earth is the Lord's garden, and he hath given it to the sons of men with a general commission (Gen. i. 28) to increase and multiply, and replenish the earth and subdue it, which was again renewed to Noah; the end is double and natural, that man might enjoy the fruits of the earth and God might have his due glory from the creature. Why then should we stand here striving for places of habitation, etc. (many men spending as much labor and cost to recover or keep sometimes an acre or two of land as would procure them many, and as good or better, in another country), and in the meantime suffer a whole continent as fruitful and convenient for the use of man to lie waste without any improvement?

5. We are grown to that height of intemperance in all excess of riot as no man's estate almost will suffice to keep sail with his equals; and who fails herein must live in scorn and contempt. Hence it comes that all arts and trades are carried in that deceitful and unrighteous course as it is almost impossible for a good and upright man to maintain his charge and live comfortably in any of them.

6. The fountains of learning and religion are so corrupted as (besides the insupportable charge of their education) most children (even the best wits and of fairest hopes) are perverted, corrupted, and utterly overthrown by the multitude of evil examples and the licentious government of those seminaries where men strain at gnats and swallow camels, use all severity for maintenance of caps and other accompliments, but suffer all ruffianlike fashions and disorder in manners to pass uncontrolled.

7. What can be a better work and more honorable and worthy a Christian than to help raise and support a particular church while it is in its infancy, and join his forces with such a company of faithful people as by a timely assistance may grow strong and prosper, and for want of it may be put to great hazard, if not wholly ruined? . . .

Document Set 16.4 References

A. William Shakespeare Upholds the Social Order
Shakespeare, *Troilus and Cressida*, Act I, Scene 3, lines 85–124.
B. The Young Elizabeth I Beguiles Her Subjects
Sir John Hayward in Alan Glover, ed., *Gloriana's Glass* (London: Nonesuch Press, 1953), 57–58.
C. Parliament Imposes Compulsory Poor Rates, 1572
H. E. S. Fisher and A. R. J. Jurica, eds., *Documents in English Economic History* (London: G. Bell, 1977), 2:427–428.
D. An English Jesuit Goes to the Gallows, 1582
Richard Johnson, Scaffold Speech, in Lacey Baldwin Smith and Jean Reeder Smith, eds., *The Past Speaks*, 2d ed. (Lexington, Mass.: D. C. Heath, 1993), 1:305–306.
E. A Puritan Searches His Conscience: William Perkins, 1586
Perkins, Letter, in Smith and Smith, 1:311–312.
F. Elizabeth I Advises James VI on Ruling
John Bruce, *Letters of Queen Elizabeth and James VI of Scotland* (London: Camden Society, 1849), orig. series, 46:75–76.
G. James I Tells the Presbyterians: "No Bishop, No King"
James I, 1604, in James Harvey Robinson, ed., *Readings in European History* (Boston: Ginn, 1904), 2:218–219.
H. Charles I Allows Sunday Sports, 1633
Declaration of Sports, in Robinson, 2:228–230.
I. John Winthrop Ponders a Puritan Migration to New England, 1629
Winthrop, "Reasons to be Considered . . .," in Robinson, 2:225–226.

Henry VIII broke w/ Rome.
—for land
—divorce
catholicism w/ pope
Investiture — never solved
rest of Europe · build national churches
→ later, religious tension

DOCUMENT SET 16.5
Recovering from the Wars of Religion: France from Henry IV to Richelieu

monarch is sun of all positions but not all positions have same powers.

has ate pts by?

The Edict of Nantes (Document A) must be read against the background of Set 16.1 and Set 16.2. Henry IV, formerly the Huguenots' leader and now having succeeded to the French crown, made a political decision to switch religions in order to be accepted as France's legitimate king, yet he conceded important rights to his former Huguenot followers. How well did these rights guarantee the Huguenots' status as a protected minority? In what respects does the Edict accord with Bodin's ideas on undivided sovereignty as the only solution to a society suffering an authority crisis (compare Set 16.2, Document B)?

The remaining documents in the set all reflect various strategies attempted in the early seventeenth century for reestablishing order in the land. The law of 1604 known as the Paulette regularized the sale of offices by royal officials, a practice that had been going on de facto for a very long time. Considering the implications of this practice—bestowing life-time rights to important judicial and other state offices for a fee—how do you suppose that such a law, as enacted by men like Henry IV and his minister Sully, could be the means of ending political disorder? In Document D, the great royal minister Cardinal Richelieu (1585–1642) recalls in his *Memoirs* the disastrous state of French affairs at the time he was summoned to power by Louis XIII (1624). Notice in particular his remarks about the aristocracy and the Huguenots. Why was he so determined to break these adversaries? Why too, in Document E, should Richelieu's regime have been so concerned to put down false claims of nobility—continuing a policy that nobles in the Estates General had demanded in 1614? It may be easier to understand the motivation behind Document F, the edict that Richelieu had the king promulgate ordering the demolition of nobles' castles. Likewise it was at Richelieu's instigation that in 1635 Louis XIII established the French Academy (Document G); what political and social purpose do you see in this measure? Considering all these documents together and drawing upon *The Challenge of the West,* write a brief essay on the consolidation of royal authority in early seventeenth-century France, keeping in mind this country's social background.

borders are not fixed (fluid)
Charles V (1519–1556)
—largest landowner.
—descendant of Burgundians
—got Latin America

English + France were exceptions not rules.

Religion.
Augsburg (1558) — leader picks religion (cath or Luth)

A. Henry IV Promises the Huguenots Limited Toleration: the Edict of Nantes, 1598

King of Navarre; Protestant
→ converted when he got the throne, but allows toleration.

Among the infinite benefits which it has pleased God to heap upon us, the most signal and precious is his granting us the strength and ability to withstand the fearful disorders and troubles which prevailed on our advent in this kingdom. The realm was so torn by innumerable factions and sects that the most legitimate of all the parties was fewest in numbers. God has given us strength to stand out against this storm; we have finally surmounted the waves and made our port of safety,—peace for our state. For which his be the glory all in all, and ours a free recognition of his grace in making use of our instrumentality in the good work. . . . We implore and await from the Divine Goodness the same protection and favor which he has ever granted to this kingdom from the beginning. . . .

We have, by this perpetual and <u>irrevocable</u> edict, *later revoked?* established and proclaimed and do establish and proclaim:

I. First, that the recollection of everything done by one party or the other between March, 1585, and our accession to the crown, and during all the preceding period of troubles, remain obliterated and forgotten, as if no such things had ever happened.

III. We ordain that the Catholic Apostolic and Roman religion shall be restored and reestablished in all places and localities of this our kingdom and countries subject to our sway, where the exercise of the same has been interrupted, in order that it may be peaceably and freely exercised, without any trouble or hindrance; forbidding very expressly all persons, of whatsoever estate, quality, or condition, from troubling, molesting, or disturbing ecclesiastics in the celebration of divine service, in the enjoyment or collection of tithes, fruits, or revenues of their benefices, and all other rights and dues belonging to them; and that all those who during the troubles have taken possession of churches, houses, goods or revenues, belonging to the said ecclesiastics, shall surrender to them entire possession and peaceable enjoyment of such rights, liberties, and sureties as they had before they were deprived of them.

VI. And in order to leave no occasion for troubles or differences between our subjects, we have permitted, and herewith permit, those of the said religion

Counter Reformation (Council of Trent)
→ no compromise w/ Luth

called <u>Reformed</u> to live and abide in all the cities and places of this our kingdom and countries of our sway, without being annoyed, molested, or compelled to do anything in the matter of religion contrary to their consciences, . . . upon conditions that they comport themselves in other respects according to that which is contained in this our present edict.

VII. It is permitted to all lords, gentlemen, and other persons making profession of the said religion called Reformed, holding the right of high justice [or a certain feudal tenure], to exercise the said religion in their houses.

IX. We also permit those of the said religion to make and continue the exercise of the same in all villages and places of our dominion where it was established by them and publicly enjoyed several and divers times in the year 1597, up to the end of the month of August, notwithstanding all decrees and judgments to the contrary.

XIII. We very expressly forbid to all those of the said religion its exercise, either in respect to ministry, regulation, discipline, or the public instruction of children, or otherwise, in this our kingdom and lands of our dominion, otherwise than in the places permitted and granted by the present edict.

XIV. It is forbidden as well to perform any function of the said religion on our court or retinue, or in our lands and territories beyond the mountains, or in our city of Paris, or within five leagues of the said city.

XVIII. We also forbid all our subjects, of whatever quality and condition, from carrying off by force or persuasion, against the will of their parents, the children of the said religion, in order to cause them to be baptized or confirmed in the Catholic Apostolic and Roman Church; and the same is forbidden to those of the said religion called Reformed, upon penalty of being punished with special severity.

XXI. Books concerning the said religion called Reformed may not be printed and publicly sold, except in cities and places where the public exercise of the said religion is permitted.

XXII. We ordain that there shall be no difference or distinction made in respect to the said religion, in receiving pupils to be instructed in universities, colleges, and schools; or in receiving the sick and poor into hospitals, retreats and public charities.

XXIII. Those of the said religion called Reformed shall be obliged to respect the laws of the Catholic Apostolic and Roman Church, recognized in this our kingdom, for the consummation of marriages contracted, or to be contracted, as regards to the <u>degrees of consanguinity and kinship</u>.

B. The Sale of Offices Is Regulated: the Paulette, 1604

Henry, by the grace of God, king of France and Navarre, etc. Having never desired anything more than the opportunity to indicate to our subjects in general and to our officers in particular the effects of our favour we have recently listened with a good deal of satisfaction to the supplications and remonstrances which have been made to us by a number of the chief and most senior officers of this kingdom seeking to persuade us to introduce some regulation into the practice of resignation of office so that they should not be forced, when they are elderly and consequently more capable of exercising them worthily, to resign their offices in favour of younger and less experienced men in order to avoid the loss of such a large sum as the value of their offices entails: consequently, recognizing the considerable interest of our officers, the good which we will do in this kingdom by keeping offices in the hands of those most skilled in affairs and their readiness to pay the four *deniers per livre* tax on the estimated value of their offices which we will collect annually from those who are prepared to raise the said tax in order to redeem themselves from the severity of the forty day rule.

For all these reasons after having deliberated over this matter in our council, in which were a number of princes of the royal blood, officers of our crown and other *seigneurs* and notable personages who have judged this proposal just and advantageous to our officers and worthy of the affection that we have for our subjects; with their advice and in conformity with the decree already issued on this matter, and with our certain knowledge, full power and royal authority we have by this present declaration . . . decreed and declared . . . that hence-forward, the officers of our kingdom, whether judicial, financial or of any other kind, whatever their station . . . who are subject to the forty day rule . . . shall be dispensed from the rigour of the forty days which each of these officers must survive after his resignation, counting from the day and date of the receipt of money paid into the *Parties Casuelles,* by the annual payment of four *deniers per livre* of the estimated value of their offices by those who wish voluntarily to avail themselves of this favour and dispensation . . . in return for this money, if they should die during the year, their offices will not be declared vacant and obtainable for our profit, but will be kept in favour of their resignees as far as those offices which are subject to suppression are concerned; and as for those which are not subject to suppression, they will go to the widows and heirs who may dispose of them as they see fit and

*economy : sets own prices.
entrepreneurs*

world of antiquity moved fm. med. to Atlantic.
Spain + Italy became unimportant.

became modern.
became nations

What is modern?

to their own profit, as something belonging to them; . . . all officers who will have paid the said tax shall enjoy the said favour and dispensation during the year for which they have paid, their guarantee being simply the receipt for the money contributed for the said annual right of dispensation duly signed by *maître* Charles Paulet, a secretary of our chamber. . . .

antiquity barbarous ma. [illegible] ar religious tension. rather than fall.

C. Richelieu Assesses the State of France in 1624

At the time when your Majesty resolved to admit me both to your council and to an important place in your confidence for the direction of your affairs, I may say that the Huguenots shared the state with you; that the nobles conducted themselves as if they were not your subjects, and the most powerful governors of the provinces as if they were sovereign in their offices.

I may say that the bad example of all these was so injurious to this realm that even the best regulated *parlements* were affected by it, and endeavored, in certain cases, to diminish your royal authority as far as they were able in order to stretch their own powers beyond the limits of reason.

I may say that every one measured his own merit by his audacity; that in place of estimating the benefits which they received from your Majesty at their proper worth, all valued them only in so far as they satisfied the extravagant demands of their imagination; that the most arrogant were held to be the wisest, and found themselves the most prosperous.

I may also say that the foreign alliances were unfortunate, individual interests being preferred to those of the public; in a word, the dignity of the royal majesty was so disparaged, and so different from what it should be, owing to the malfeasance of those who conducted your affairs, that it was almost impossible to perceive its existence.

It was impossible, without losing all, to tolerate longer the conduct of those to whom your Majesty had instrusted the helm of state; and, on the other had, everything could not be changed at once without violating the laws of prudence, which do not permit the abrupt passing from one extreme to another.

The sad state of your affairs seemed to force you to hasty decisions, without permitting a choice of time or of means; and yet it was necessary to make a choice of both, in order to profit by the change which necessity demanded from your prudence.

Thoughtful observers did not think that it would be possible to escape all the rocks in so tempestuous a period; the court was full of people who censured the temerity of those who wished to undertake a reform; all well knew that princes are quick to impute

to those who are near them the bad outcome of the undertakings upon which they have been well advised; few people consequently expected good results from the change which it was announced that I wished to make, and many believed my fall assured even before you Majesty had elevated me.

Notwithstanding these difficulties which I represented to your Majesty, knowing how much kings may do when they make good use of their power, I ventured to promise you, with confidence, that you would soon get control of your state, and that in a short time your prudence, your courage, and the benediction of God would give a new aspect to the realm.

I promised your Majesty to employ all my industry and all the authority which it should please you to give me to ruin the Huguenot party, to abase the pride of the nobles, to bring back all your subjects to their duty, and to elevate your name among foreign nations to the point where it belongs.

D. Bogus Claims of Nobility Are Forbidden, 1614–1634

His Majesty is most humbly entreated to ensure . . . that those who have taken advantage of the times to give themselves unjustly the title of nobleman and to enjoy the privileges appertaining thereto should be deprived to their title and declared *roturiers;* and so that non-nobles should not infiltrate into the ranks of the nobility an exact register should be drawn up of all the noblemen in the kingdom, together with their coats of arms and an account of the honours and ancient lineage of their families. . . . In future letters of knighthood should be bestowed only upon persons of worth whose public service greatly merits such a reward . . . it should be lawful for the nobility to take part in wholesale trading without forfeiture of nobility, this without prejudice to the custom of Brittany. Also, only noblemen ought to hold the rank of port-captain.

Louis XIII forbids fraudulent claims of nobility, 1634

We forbid any of our subjects to usurp the status of nobility, to take the title of esquire and to bear coats of arms if they are not of a noble house and extraction, under pain of a fine of 2,000 *livres.*

E. The Demolition of Feudal Castles Is Ordered, 1626

Whereas formerly the assemblies of the estates of this realm and those of notable persons chosen to give advice to ourselves, and to the late king, our very honorable lord and father, on important affairs of this realm, and likewise the assembly of the estates of the province of Brittany held by us in the year 1614, have repeatedly requested and very humbly supplicated our said lord and father and ourselves to cause the demolition of many strongholds in divers places of this realm, which, being neither on hostile frontiers nor in important passes or places, only serve to augment our expenses by the maintenance of useless garrisons, and also serve as retreats for divers persons who on the least provocation disturb the provinces where they are located; . . .

For these reasons, we announce, declare, ordain, and will that all the strongholds, either towns or castles, which are in the interior of our realm or provinces of the same, not situated in places of importance either for frontier or defense or other considerations of weight, shall be razed and demolished; even ancient walls shall be destroyed so far as it shall be deemed necessary for the well-being and repose of our subjects and the security of this state, so that our said subjects henceforth need not fear that the said places will cause them any inconvenience, and so that we shall be freed from the expense of supporting garrisons in them.

F. Louis XIII Establishes the French Academy, 1635

When God called us to the headship of the state we cherished the purpose not only of putting an end to the disorders caused by the civil wars which had so long distracted the realm, but we also aimed to adorn the state with all the ornaments appropriate to the oldest and most illustrious of existing monarchies. Although we have labored without intermission to realize this purpose, it has been impossible hitherto fully to accomplish it. . . . [But now] the confusion has at last given way to good order, which we have reëstablished by the best of all means, namely, by reviving commerce, enforcing military discipline in our armies, adjusting the taxes, and checking luxury. Every one is aware of the part that our very dear and beloved cousin, the cardinal, duke of Richelieu, has had in the accomplishment of all these things.

Consequently when we communicated our intention to him, he represented to us that one of the most glorious proofs of the happiness of a realm is that the sciences and arts flourish within it, and that letters as well as arms are held in esteem, since these constitute one of the chief ornaments of a powerful state; that, after so many memorable exploits, we had now only to add the agreeable to the essential, and to adorn the useful. He believed that we could not do better than to commence with the most noble of all arts, namely, eloquence. The French language, which has suffered much hitherto from neglect on the part of those who might have rendered it the most perfect of modern tongues, is now more capable than ever of taking its high place, owing to the great number of persons who possess a special knowledge of the advantages which it enjoys and who can augment these advantages. The cardinal informed us that, with a view of establishing fixed rules for the language, he had arranged meetings of scholars whose decisions in these matters had met with his hearty approval, and that in order to put these decisions into execution and render the French language not only elegant but capable of treating all the arts and sciences, it would only be necessary to perpetuate these gatherings. This could be done with great advantage should it please us to sanction them, to permit rules and regulations to be drawn up for the order of procedure to be observed, and to reward those who compose the association by some honorable marks of our favor.

For these reasons, and in view of the advantages which our subjects may derive from the said meetings, acceding to the desires of our said cousin:

We do permit, by our special favor, power, and royal authority, and do authorize and approve by these presents, signed by our hand, the said assemblies and conferences. We will that they continue hereafter in our good city of Paris, under the name of the *French Academy;* that our said cousin shall be designated as its head and protector; that the number of members be limited to forty persons. . . .

Document Set 16.5 References

A. Henry IV Promises the Huguenots Limited Toleration: the Edict of Nantes, 1598
   Edict of Nantes, excerpted in James Harvey Robinson, ed., *Readings in European History* (Boston: Ginn, 1904), 2:183–185.
B. The Sale of Offices Is Regulated: the Paulette, 1604
   J. H. Shennan, ed. and trans., *Government and Society in France, 1461–1661* (London: G. Allen and Unwin, 1969), 137–138.
C. Richelieu Assesses the State of France in 1624
   Richelieu, "Political Testament," in Robinson, 2:268–269.
D. Bogus Claims of Nobility Are Forbidden, 1614–1624
   Edict of Louis XIII, January 1634, in Shennan, 107.
E. The Demolition of Feudal Castles Is Ordered, 1626
   Edict of Louis XIII, in Robinson, 2:270.
F. Louis XIII Establishes the French Academy, 1635
   Letters Patent Establishing the French Academy, in Robinson, 2:271.

Confusion of religious + national interests.

DOCUMENT SET 16.6   defenestration of Prague
The Ultimate War of Religion: The Thirty Years' War

The three documents in this set have been chosen to illustrate aspects of the climactic struggle of the religious confessions born of the Reformation, the Thirty Years' War of 1618–1648.

Document A is an extract from the novel *Simplicissimus* by H. J. C. von Grimmelshausen (c. 1622–1676), the introduction to which was discussed at the beginning of *The Challenge of the West,* Chapter 16. The present extract, from later in the novel, describes how soldiers spent much of their time scrounging for food. (Grimmelshausen wrote from personal experience, having served in the Imperial Army; his book was published in 1669.) Document B describes the horrors of the siege, capture, and destruction of Magdeburg, a Protestant city in north-central Germany, by the Imperial forces. (The Catholic General Tilly did not order the massacre and burning of the city; these acts were the results of undisciplined soldiers running amuck.) In Document C, the pope, having heard that an end to the war had finally been negotiated, condemned the peace as injurious to people's interests. Write an essay drawing upon these documents and *The Challenge of the West,* placing the Thirty Years' War in its social and political context as a watershed event.

A. Simplicissimus Endures

. . . Truth to tell, a musketeer is a miserable creature who has to live this way in a garrison and who has to get by on dry bread—and not half enough of that. He's no better than a prisoner who is prolonging his poor life with the bread and water of tribulation. In fact, a prisoner is better off, for he does not have to stand watch, go the rounds, or do sentry duty; he stays quietly in bed and has just as much hope as a sad garrison trooper of getting out of his prison in time. There were a few who, by various means, had it a little better; but none of these ways of getting a bite more to eat were to my liking. In their misery, a few troopers took on wives (some of these formerly were two-bit sluts) who could increase their income by such work as sewing, washing, spinning, or by selling second-hand clothing or other junk, or even by stealing. Among the women was a female ensign who drew her pay like a corporal! Another was a midwife, and she was given many a good meal for herself and her husband. Another took in laundry and ironing; she washed shirts, socks, nightshirts, and other apparel for the bachelors among the officers and men, and she had quite a reputation. Others sold tobacco and furnished pipes for those who needed them. Still others sold brandy; it was generally thought that they were adulterating it with water distilled by their own bodies—but that didn't change the color of the liquor in the least! Another was a seamstress who was able to earn money through hemstitching and embroidery. Still another could pick a living off the field; in the winter she dug up snails, in the spring she picked salad herbs, in summer she took the young out of birds' nests, and in fall she could gather hundreds of other tidbits. Some sold kindling wood, which they carried to market like donkeys; others peddled still other merchandise. To earn my keep that way was not for me, since I already had a wife. Some of the men made a living by gambling (which they could do better than professional sharps), and by means of false dice and cards they got what they wanted from their simple-minded fellow soldiers. I despised such a trade. Others worked at building fortifications or at other odd jobs; for this I was too lazy. Some carried on a trade, but I had learned none. If a musician had been needed I could have served, but this starvation district got along on pipes and drums. Some took over others' guard duty and stood watch day and night. I would rather have starved than wear out my body that way. Some made both ends meet by going on raids, but I wasn't even permitted to step outside of the gate. Some could "organize" things better than a general; I hated such actions like sin. To make it brief, no matter where I turned, I could pick up nothing with which to fill my stomach. And what made me maddest was having to take it when the gang said, "You're a doctor and yet don't know how to cure starvation?"

Finally, necessity made me juggle a couple of good-sized carp out of the moat into my hands as I stood on the rampart; but as soon as the colonel heard of it I was in dutch and he forbade further prestidigitation on pain of hanging. At last, others' misfortune turned out to be my luck. Having cured a few cases of jaundice and fever—these patients must have had special faith in me—I was allowed to wander out of the fortress to gather (so I said) medicinal roots and herbs. But instead I set snares for rabbits and was lucky to catch two the first night. These I took to the colonel and he gave me not only a thaler as a present but also permission to go out after rabbits when I was off duty. Since the country was rather deserted and nobody was catching these animals, which had multiplied over the years, I had grist in my mill again, especially as it seemed that rabbits turned up everywhere or that I could charm them into my snares. When the officers saw that they could trust me, I was allowed to go raiding with the others, and I resumed the life of Soest, except that I could not be in charge. For that, one had to know all the roads and byways and the course of the Rhine.

B. Magdeburg Is Destroyed, 1631

So the General Pappenheim collected a number of his people on the ramparts by the New Town, and brought them from there into the streets of the city. Von Falckenberg [an emissary of Gustavus Adolphus] was shot, and fires were kindled in different quarters; then indeed it was all over with the city, and further resistance was useless. Nevertheless some of the soldiers and citizens did try to make a stand here and there, but the imperial troops kept bringing on more and more forces—cavalry, too—to help them, and finally they got the Kröckenthor open and let in the whole imperial army and the forces of the Catholic League,—Hungarians, Croats, Poles, Walloons, Italians, Spaniards, French, North and South Germans.

Thus it came about that the city and all its inhabitants fell into the hands of the enemy, whose violence and cruelty were due in part to their common hatred of the adherents of the Augsburg Confession, and in part to their being imbittered by the chain shot which had been fired at them and by the derision and insults that the Magdeburgers had heaped upon them from the ramparts.

Then was there naught but beating and burning, plundering, torture, and murder. Most especially was every one of the enemy bent on securing much booty. When a marauding party entered a house, if its master had anything to give he might thereby purchase respite and protection for himself and his family till the next man, who also wanted something, should come along. It was only when everything had been brought forth and there was nothing left to give that the real trouble commenced. Then, what with blows and threats of shooting, stabbing, and hanging, the poor people were so terrified that if they had had anything left they would have brought it forth if it had been buried in the earth or hidden away in a thousand castles. In this frenzied rage, the great and splendid city that had stood like a fair princess in the land was now, in its hour of direst need and unutter-

able distress and woe, given over to the flames, and thousands of innocent men, women, and children, in the midst of a horrible din of heartrending shrieks and cries, were tortured and put to death in so cruel and shameful a manner that no words would suffice to describe, nor no tears to bewail it. . . .

Thus in a single day this noble and famous city, the pride of the whole country, went up in fire and smoke; and the remnant of its citizens, with their wives and children, were taken prisoners and driven away by the enemy with a noise of weeping and wailing that could be heard from afar, while the cinders and ashes from the town were carried by the wind to Wanzleben, Egeln, and still more distant places. . . .

In addition to all this, quantities of sumptuous and irreplaceable house furnishings and movable property of all kinds, such as books, manuscripts, paintings, memorials of all sorts, . . . which money could not buy, were either burned or carried away by the soldiers as booty. The most magnificent garments, hangings, silk stuffs, gold and silver lace, linen of all sorts, and other household goods were bought by the army sutlers for a mere song and peddled about by the cart load all through the archbishopric of Magdeburg and in Anhalt and Brunswick. Gold chains and rings, jewels, and every kind of gold and silver utensils were to be bought from the common soldiers for a tenth of their real value. . . .

C. Pope Innocent X Condemns the Peace of Westphalia, 1648

Consumed by zeal for the house of the Lord, we are especially concerned with the endeavor everywhere to maintain the integrity of the orthodox faith and the authority of the Catholic Church, so that the ecclesiastical rights of which we have been appointed guardian by our Saviour shall not in any way be impaired by those who seek their own interest rather than God's, and that we may not be accused of negligence when we shall render account to the Sovereign Judge. Accordingly it is not without deep pain that we have learned that by several articles in the peace concluded at Osnabrück, August 6, 1648, between our very dear son in Christ, Ferdinand, king of the Romans and emperor elect, his allies and adherents, on the one hand, and the Swedes, with their allies and adherents, on the other, as well as in that peace which was likewise concluded at Münster in Westphalia on the twenty-fourth day of October of this same year 1648, between the same Ferdinand, king of the Romans, etc., and our very dear son in Jesus Christ, Louis, the very Christian king of the French, his allies and adherents, great prejudice has been done to the Catholic religion, the divine service, the roman apostolic see, the ecclesiastical order, their jurisdictions, authority, immunities, liberties, exemptions, privileges, possessions, and rights; since by various articles in one of these treaties of peace the ecclesiastical possessions which the heretics formerly seized are abandoned to them and to their successors, and the heretics, called those of the Augsburg Confession, are permitted the free exercise of their heresy in various districts. They are promised places in which they may build temples for their worship and are admitted with the Catholics to public offices and positions. . . . Many other things have been done too shameful to enumerate and very prejudicial to the orthodox religion and the Roman see. . . .

[Accordingly] we assert and declare by these presents that all the said articles in one or both of the said treaties which in any way impair or prejudice in the slightest degree, or that can be said, alleged, understood, or imagined to be able in any way to injure or to have injured the Catholic religion, divine worship, the salvation of souls, the said Roman apostolic see, the inferior churches, the ecclesiastical order or estate, their persons, affairs, possessions, jurisdictions, authorities, immunities, liberties, privileges, prerogatives, and rights whatsoever,—all such provisions have been, and are of right, and shall perpetually be, null and void, invalid, iniquitous, unjust, condemned, rejected, frivolous, without force or effect, and no one is to observe them, even when they be ratified by oath . . .

Document Set 16.6 References

A. Simplicissimus Endures
  J. J. C. von Grimmelshausen, *Simplicius Simplicissimus,* trans. George Schutz Behrend (Indianapolis: Bobbs-Merrill, 1965), 220–222.
B. Magdeburg Is Destroyed, 1631
  Contemporary Account, in James Harvey Robinson, ed., *Readings in European History* (Boston: Ginn, 1904), 2:211–212.
C. Pope Innocent X Condemns the Peace of Westphalia, 1648
  Innocent X, in Robinson, 2:214.

This and Set 16.8 should be read together as you ask why and how the early seventeenth century saw the climax of Europe's bloody obsession with witchcraft and, simultaneously, several major breakthroughs in what has become known as the Scientific Revolution.

Ask, for example, how the rational political philosopher Jean Bodin could also have written Document A, a ferocious call upon magistrates to do their duty in prosecuting witchcraft. When you read Documents B through D, consider how accusations of witchcraft, once set in motion, could engulf whole communities in hysteria. Was there any validity to the accusations, or anything that victims might have done to attract suspicion? Do you see evidence here of systematic misogyny (hatred of women) at work? How did those in authority respond? You should also look back at Set 14.8, Document E—the infamous fifteenth-century witch-hunters' handbook, *Malleus Maleficarum.*

A. Jean Bodin Insists That Magistrates Have a Duty to Prosecute Witchcraft, 1580

There are two means by which states are maintained in their weal and greatness—reward and penalty: the one for the good, the other for the bad. And, if the distribution of these two be faulty, nothing else is to be expected than the inevitable ruin of the state....

But those greatly err who think that penalties are established only to punish crime. I hold that this is the least of the fruits which accrue therefrom to the state. For the greatest and the chief is the appeasing of the wrath of God, especially if the crime is directly against the majesty of God, as is this one.... Now, if there is any means to appease the wrath of God, to gain his blessing, to strike awe into some by the punishment of others, to preserve some from being infected by others, to diminish the number of evildoers, to make secure the life of the well-disposed, and to punish the most detestable crimes of which the human mind can conceive, it is to punish with the utmost rigor the witches.... [Bodin lists fifteen horrid crimes of which every witch is guilty; in default of proof, presumption is enough to merit death.]

Now, it is not within the power of princes to pardon a crime which the law of God punishes with the penalty of death—such as are the crimes of witches.

Moreover, princes do gravely insult God in pardoning such horrible crimes committed directly against his majesty, seeing that the pettiest prince avenges with death insults against himself. Those too who let the witches escape, or who do not punish them with the utmost rigor, any rest assured that they will be abandoned by God to the mercy of the witches. And the country which shall tolerate this will be scourged with pestilences, famines, and wars; and those which shall take vengeance on the witches will be blessed by him and will make his anger to cease. Therefore it is that one accused of being a witch ought never to be folly acquitted and set free unless the calumny of the accuser is clearer than the sun, inasmuch as the proof of such crimes is so obscure and so difficult that not one witch in a million would be accused or punished if the procedure were governed by the ordinary rules....

B. An Eyewitness Describes the Witch-Hysteria at Trier, 1589

Inasmuch as it was popularly believed that the continued sterility of many years was caused by witches through the malice of the Devil, the whole country rose to exterminate the witches. This movement was promoted by many in office, who hoped wealth from the persecution. And so, from court to court throughout the towns and villages of all the diocese, scurried special accusers, inquisitors, notaries, jurors, judges, constables, dragging to trial and torture human beings of both sexes and burning them in great numbers. Scarcely any of those who were accused escaped punishment. Nor were there spared even the leading men in the city of Trier. For the Judge, with two Burgomasters, several Councilors and Associate Judges, canons of sundry collegiate churches, parish-priests, rural deans, were swept away in this ruin. So far, at length, did the madness of the furious populace and of the courts go in this thirst for blood and booty that there was scarcely anybody who was not smirched by some suspicion of this crime.

Meanwhile notaries, copyists, and innkeepers grew rich. The executioner rode a blooded horse, like a noble of the court, and went clad in gold and silver; his wife vied with noble dames in the richness of her array. The children of those convicted and punished were sent into exile; their goods were confiscated;

plowman and vintner failed—hence came sterility. A direr pestilence or a more ruthless invader could hardly have ravaged the territory of Trier than this inquisition and persecution without bounds: many were the reasons for doubting that all were really guilty. This persecution lasted for several years; and some of those who presided over the administration of justice gloried in the multitude of the stakes, at each of which a human being had been given the flames.

At last, though the flames were still unsated, the people grew impoverished, rules were made and enforced restricting the fees and costs of examinations and examiners, and suddenly, as when in war funds fail, the zeal of the persecutors died out.

C. A French Witch Confesses, 1652

Asked how long she has been in subjugation to the devil.

—Says that it has been about twenty-five or twenty-six years, that her lover also then made her renounce God, Lent, baptism, that he has known her carnally three or four times, and that he has given her satisfaction. . . .

Asked if the devil did not advise her to steal from Elisabeth Dehan and to do harm to her.

—Said that he advised her to steal from her and promised that he would help her; but urged her not to do harm to her; and that is because she [Elisabeth Dehan] had cut the wood in her [Suzanne Gaudry's] fence and stirred up the seeds in her garden, saying that her lover told her that she would avenge herself by beating her.

D. The Toll of a Witch-Hunt at Bonn

Those burned are mostly male witches of the sort described. There must be half the city implicated: for already professors, law-students, pastors, canons, vicars, and monks have here been arrested and burned. His Princely Grace has seventy wards who are to become pastors, one of whom, eminent as a musician, was yesterday arrested; two others were sought for, but have fled. The Chancellor and his wife and the Private Secretary's wife are already executed. On the eve of Our Lady's Day there was executed here a maiden of nineteen who bore the name of being the fairest and most blameless of all the city, and who from her childhood had been brought up by the Bishop himself. A canon of the cathedral, named Rotenbahn, I saw beheaded and burned. Children of three or four years have devils for their paramours. Students and boys of noble birth, of nine, ten, eleven, twelve, thirteen, fourteen years, have here been burned. In fine, things are in such a pitiful state that one does not know with what people one may talk and associate.

Document Set 16.7 References

A. Jean Bodin Insists That Magistrates Have a Duty to Prosecute Witchcraft, 1580
   Jean Bodin, "De la Démonomanie des Sorciers," in *Translations and Reprints from the Original Sources of European History* (Philadelphia: University of Pennsylvania Press, 1902), 3/2:5–6.
B. An Eyewitness Describes the Witch-Hysteria at Trier, 1589
   Linden, *Gesta Tevirorum*, in *Translations and Reprints*, 3/2:13–14.
C. A French Witch Confesses, 1652
   J. Français, *L'Eglise et la Sorcellerie* (Paris: 1910), 236–251, quoted in Alan Kors and Edward Peters, eds., *Witchcraft in Europe* (Philadelphia: University of Pennsylvania Press, 1972), 266–275.
D. The Toll of a Witch-Hunt at Bonn
   Duren, Letter, in *Translations and Reprints*, 3/2:18–19.

Copernicus, as we saw in Set 15.3, set the agenda for what we now call the Scientific Revolution; the problems raised by his heliocentric theory had to be answered. Notice in Document A how Galileo's epoch-making observations of the moons of Jupiter in 1610 suggested confirmation of some Copernican ideas while also casting doubt on some of Aristotle's ancient ideas about the incorruptibility of the heavens. Even more explicitly, the German astronomer Johann Kepler (Document B) saw Galileo's discoveries as a vindication of the Copernican vision.

Sir Francis Bacon (1561–1629), the English politician and author of *Novum Organum* (1620), from which Document C is taken, was an ambitious, grasping, obsequious courtier, fully convinced of his own unparalleled genius. He was not a scientist and can hardly be called a philosopher. His greatness lay in his insistence that experiment, not authority, should guide scientific inquiry; no one ever attacked medieval philosophy and its Aristotelian foundations so relentlessly, nor called so vigorously for science to exploit nature for humanity's benefit. To what extent does Bacon's onslaught seem to you characteristic of the Scientific Revolution? And how do you react to Bacon's argument that there is no conflict between science and religion? Bear in mind that Protestants (and especially Puritans, of which company Bacon was not) tended to be less fearful than Catholics that scientific inquiry would undermine religious truths.

René Descartes (1596-1650), whose *Discourse on Method,* 1637, is excerpted in Document D, was one of the great philosophical minds of the seventeenth century. His "method" rested on radical doubt of all sensory evidence while he searched for and ultimately found a new principle of knowledge based on the realization that he could trust the fact of his own existence as a thinking being. The extract in Document D explains how Descartes arrived at his fundamental insight. He had to be especially wary of being identified as a Copernican, but his support of rationalism (particularly in France) was tremendously important in undermining Aristotelianism and scholasticism, which by the seventeenth century had become identified merely with citing ancient authority and predetermined propositions.

The dangers that anyone in Catholic Europe, including Descartes, faced in endorsing Copernicus's theories is apparent from Galileo's ordeal before the Papal Inquisition (Document D) after he had ridiculed

Aristotelianism in his *Dialogue of the Two-World Systems* (1632).

A. Galileo Turns His Telescope on Jupiter, January–March 1610

On the seventh day of January in this present year 1610, at the first hour of night, when I was viewing the heavenly bodies with a telescope, Jupiter presented itself to me; and because I had prepared a very excellent instrument for myself, I perceived (as I had not before, on account of the weakness of my previous instrument) that beside the planet there were three starlets, small indeed, but very bright. Though I believed them to be among the host of fixed stars, they aroused my curiosity somewhat by appearing to lie in an exact straight line parallel to the ecliptic, and by their being more splendid than others of their size. Their arrangement with respect to Jupiter and each other was the following:

East   *   *   O   *   *West*

that is, there were two stars on the eastern side and one to the west . . . on January eighth—led by what, I do not know—I found a very different arrangement. The three starlets were now all to the west of Jupiter, closer together, and at equal intervals from one another as shown in the following sketch:

East   O   *   *   *   *West*

At this time, though I did not yet turn my attention to the way the stars had come together, I began to concern myself with the question how Jupiter could be east of all these stars when on the previous day it had been west of two of them. . . .

On the tenth of January, however, the stars appeared in this position with respect to Jupiter:

East   *   *   O   *West*

that is, there were but two of them, both easterly, the third (as I supposed) being hidden behind Jupiter. As at first, they were in the same straight line with Jupiter and were arranged precisely in the line of the zodiac. Noticing this, and knowing that there was no way in which such alterations could be attributed to Jupiter's motion, yet being certain that these were still the same stars I had observed (in fact no other was to be found along the line of the zodiac for a long way on either side of Jupiter), my perplexity was now transformed into amazement. I was sure that the apparent changes belonged not to Jupiter but to the observed stars, and I resolved to pursue this investigation with greater care and attention.

And thus, on the eleventh of January, I saw the following disposition:

East   *   *   O   *West* . . .

I had now decided beyond all question that there existed in the heavens three stars wandering about Jupiter as do Venus and Mercury about the sun, and this became plainer that daylight from observations on similar occasions which followed. Nor were there just three such stars; four wanderers complete their revolutions about Jupiter, and of their alterations as observed more precisely later on we shall give a description here. Also I measured the distances between them by means of the telescope, using the method explained before. Moreover I recorded the times of the observations, especially when more than one was made during the same night—for the revolutions of these planets are so speedily completed that it is usually possible to take even their hourly variations. [Galileo continues to make similar observations until March 2, noting the changes in the "stars" adjacent to Jupiter.] . . .

Such are the observations concerning the four Medicean planets recently first discovered by me, and although from this data their periods have not yet been reconstructed in numerical form, it is legitimate at least to put in evidence some facts worthy of note. Above all, since they sometimes follow and sometimes precede Jupiter by the same intervals, and they remain within very limited distances either to east or west of Jupiter, accompanying that planet in both its retrograde and direct movements in a constant manner, no one can doubt that they complete their revolutions about Jupiter and at the same time effect all together a twelve-year period about the center of the universe. That they also revolve in unequal circles is manifestly deduced from the fact that at the greatest elongation from Jupiter it is never possible to see two of these planets in conjunction, whereas in the vicinity of Jupiter they are found united two, three, and sometimes all four together. It is also observed that the revolutions are swifter in those planets which describe smaller circles about Jupiter, since the stars closest to Jupiter are usually seen to the east when on the previous day they appeared to the west, and vice versa, while the planet which traces the largest orbit appears upon accurate observation of its returns to have a semimonthly period.

Here we have a fine and elegant argument for quieting the doubts of those who, while accepting with tranquil mind the revolutions of the planets about the sun in the Copernican system, are mightily disturbed to have the moon alone revolve about the earth and accompany it in an annual rotation about the sun. Some have believed that this structure of the universe should be rejected as impossible. But now we have not just one planet rotating about another while both run through a great orbit around the sun; our own eyes show us four stars which wander around Jupiter as does the moon around the earth, while all together trace out a grand revolution about the sun in the space of twelve years. . . .

B. Johann Kepler Speculates on the Implications of Galileo's Discoveries

. . . I rejoice that I am to some extent restored to life by your work. If you had discovered any planets revolving around one of the fixed stars, there would now be waiting for me chains and a prison amid Bruno's innumerabilities, I should rather say, exile to his infinite space. Therefore, by reporting that these four planets revolve, not around one of the fixed stars, but around the planet Jupiter, you have for the present freed me from the great fear which gripped me as soon as I had heard about your book from my opponent's triumphal shout.

Wackher of course had once more been seized by deep admiration for that dreadful philosophy. What Galileo recently saw with his own eyes, it had many years before not only proposed as a surmise, but thoroughly established by reasoning. It is doubtless with perfect justice that those men attain fame whose intellect anticipates the senses in closely related branches of philosophy. Theoretical astronomy, at a time when it had never set foot outside Greece, nevertheless disclosed the characteristics of the Arctic Zone. Who then would not rank it in nobility above Caesar's experience of learning from the water-clocks that the nights on the coasts of Britain are a little shorter than the nights in Rome, or above the Dutchmen's spending the winter in the north, an expedition which was indeed wonderful, but which would have been impossible without that theoretical knowledge? Who does not honor Plato's myth of Atlantis, Plutarch's legend of the gold-colored islands beyond Thule, and Seneca's prophetic verses about the forthcoming discovery of a New World, now that the evidence for such a place has finally been furnished by that Argonaut from Florence? Columbus himself keeps his readers uncertain whether to admire his intellect in divining the New World from the direction of the winds, more than his courage in facing unknown seas and the boundless ocean, and his good luck in gaining his objective.

In my own field too, the prodigies will naturally be Pythagoras, Plato, and Euclid. Borne aloft by the preeminence of their reason, they argued that God could not have done otherwise than to arrange the world on the model of the five regular solids. But they mistook the pattern. On the other hand, the plaudits of the average man will go to Copernicus who, equipped with a mind that was not average, yet drew a picture of the universe virtually as it is seen by the eye. But he brought to light only the bare facts. Trailing far behind the ancients will be Kepler. From the visual outlook of the Copernican system he rises, as it were, from the facts to the causes, and to the same explanation as Plato from on high had set forth deductively so many centuries before. He shows that the Copernican system of the world exhibits the reason for the five Platonic solids. It is not an act of folly or jealousy to set the ancients above the moderns; the very nature of the subject demands it. For the glory of the Creator of this world is greater than that of the student of the world, however ingenious. The former brought forth the structural design from within himself, whereas the latter, despite strenuous efforts, scarcely perceives the plan embodied in the structure. Surely those thinkers who intellectually grasp the causes of phenomena, before these are revealed to the senses, resemble the Creator more closely than the others, who speculate about the causes after the phenomena have been seen.

Therefore, Galileo, you will not envy our predecessors their due praise. What you report as having been quite recently observed by your own eyes, they predicted, long before you, as necessarily so. Nevertheless, you will have your own fame. Copernicus and I, as a Copernican, pointed out to the ancients the mistaken way in which they considered the five solids to be expressed in the world, and we substituted the authentic and true way. Similarly, you correct and, in part, unsettle Bruce's doctrine, borrowed from Bruno. These men thought that other celestial bodies have their own moons revolving around them, like our earth with its moon. But you prove that they were talking in generalities. Moreover, they supposed it was the fixed stars that are so accompanied. Bruno even expounded the reason why this must be so. The fixed stars, forsooth, have the quality of sun and fire, but the planets, of water. By an indefeasible law of nature these opposites combine. The sun cannot be deprived of the planets; the fire, of its water; nor in turn the water, of the fire. Now the weakness of his reasoning is exposed by your observations. In the first place, sup-

pose that each and every fixed star is a sun. No moons have yet been seen revolving around them. Hence this will remain an open question until this phenomenon too is detected by someone equipped for marvelously refined observations. At any rate, this is what your success threatens us with, in the judgment of certain persons. On the other hand, Jupiter is one of the planets, which Bruno describes as earths. And behold, there are four other planets around Jupiter. Yet Bruno's argument made this claim not for the earths, but for the suns.

Meanwhile I cannot refrain from contributing this additional feature to the unorthodox aspects of your findings. It is not improbable, I must point out, that there are inhabitants not only on the moon but on Jupiter too or (as was delightfully remarked at a recent gathering of certain philosophers) that those areas are now being unveiled for the first time. But as soon as somebody demonstrates the art of flying, settlers from our species of man will not be lacking. Who would once have thought that the crossing of the wide ocean was calmer and safer than that of the narrow Adriatic Sea, Baltic Sea, or English Channel? Given ships or sails adapted to the breezes of heaven, there will be those who will not shrink from even that vast expanse. Therefore, for the sake of those who, as it were, will presently be on hand to attempt this voyage, let us establish the astronomy, Galileo, you of Jupiter, and me of the moon. . . .

C. Francis Bacon Announces the March of Progress

The discoveries which have hitherto been made in the sciences are such as lie close to vulgar notions, scarcely beneath the surface. In order to penetrate into the inner and further recesses of nature, it is necessary that both notions and axioms derived from things by a more sure and guarded way, and that a method of intellectual operation be introduced altogether better and more certain. . . .

There is no soundness in our notions, whether logical or physical. Substance, quality, action, passion, essence itself are not sound notions; much less are heavy, light, dense, rare, moist, dry, generation, corruption, attraction, repulsion, element, matter, form, and the like; but all are fantastical and ill-defined. . . .

There are and can be only two ways of searching into and discovering truth. The one flies from the senses and particulars to the most general axioms, and from these principles, the truth of which it takes for settled and immovable, proceeds to judgment and the discovery of middle axioms. And this way is now in fashion. The other derives axioms from the senses and particulars, rising by a gradual and unbroken ascent, so that it arrives at the most general axioms last of all. This is the true way, but as yet untried. . . .

It is not to be forgotten that in every age natural philosophy has had a troublesome adversary and hard to deal with,—namely, superstition and the blind and immoderate zeal of religion. For we see among the Greeks that those who first proposed to man's uninitiated ears the natural causes for thunder and for storms were thereupon found guilty of impiety. Nor was much more forbearance shown by some of the ancient fathers of the Christian Church to those who, on most convincing grounds (such as no one in his senses would now think of contradicting), maintained that the earth was round and, of consequence, asserted the existence of the antipodes.

Moreover, as things now are, to discourse of nature is made harder and more perilous by the summaries and systems of the schoolmen; who, having reduced theology into regular order as well as they were able, and fashioned it into the shape of an art, ended in incorporating the contentious and thorny philosophy of Aristotle, more than was fit, with the body of religion. . . .

Lastly, some are weakly afraid lest a deeper search into nature should transgress the permitted limits of sobermindedness; wrongfully wresting and transferring what is said in Holy Writ against those who pry into sacred mysteries to the hidden things of nature, which are barred by no prohibition. Others, with more subtlety, surmise and reflect that if secondary causes are unknown everything can be more readily referred to the divine hand and rod,—a point in which they think religion greatly concerned; which is, in fact, nothing else but to seek to gratify God with a lie. Others fear from past example that movements and changes in philosophy will end in assaults on religion; and others again appear apprehensive that in the investigation of nature something may be found to subvert, or at least shake, the authority of religion, especially with the unlearned.

But these two last fears seem to me to savor utterly of carnal wisdom; as if men in the recesses and secret thoughts of their hearts doubted and distrusted the strength of religion, and the empire of faith over the senses, and therefore feared that the investigation of truth in nature might be dangerous to them. But if the matter by truly considered, natural philosophy is, after the word of God, at once the surest medicine against superstition and the most approved nourishment for faith; and therefore she is rightly given to religion as her most faithful handmaid, since

the one displays the will of God, the other his power. . . .

D. René Descartes Conceives a New Method of Reasoning

I was then in Germany, attracted thither by the wars in that country, which have not yet been brought to a termination; and as I was returning to the army from the coronation of the Emperor, the setting in of winter arrested me in a locality where, as I found no society to interest me, and was besides fortunately undisturbed by any cares or passions, I remained the whole day in [a stove-heated room,] with full opportunity to occupy my attention with my own thoughts. Of these one of the very first that occurred to me was, that there is seldom so much perfection in works composed of many separate parts, upon which different hands have been employed, as in those completed by a single master. Thus it is observable that the buildings which a single architect has planned and executed, are generally more elegant and commodious than those which several have attempted to improve, by making old walls serve for purposes for which they were not originally built. Thus also, those ancient cities which, from being at first only villages, have become, in course of time, large towns, are usually but ill laid out compared with the regularly constructed towns which a professional architect has freely planned on an open plain; so that although the several buildings of the former may often equal or surpass in beauty those of the latter, yet when one observes their indiscriminate juxtaposition, there a large one and here a small, and the consequent crookedness and irregularity of the streets, one is disposed to allege that chance rather than any human will guided by reason, must have led to such an arrangement. . . .

It is true . . . that it is not customary to pull down all the houses of a town with the single design of rebuilding them differently, and thereby rendering the streets more handsome; but it often happens that a private individual takes down his own with the view of erecting it anew, and that people are even sometimes constrained to this when their houses are in danger of falling from age, or when the foundations are insecure. With this before me by way of example, I was persuaded that it would indeed be preposterous for a private individual to think of reforming a state by fundamentally changing it throughout, and overturning it in order to set it up amended; and the same I thought was true of any similar project for reforming the body of the Sciences, or the order of teaching them established in the Schools [scholastic philosophy]: but as for the opinions which up to that time I had embraced, I thought that I could not do better than resolve at once to sweep them wholly away, that I might afterwards be in a position to admit either others more correct, or even perhaps the same when they had undergone the scrutiny of Reason. I firmly believed that in this way I should much better succeed in the conduct of my life, than if I built only upon old foundations, and leant upon principles which, in my youth, I had taken upon trust. . . .

Among the branches of Philosophy, I had, at an earlier period, given some attention to Logic, and among those of the Mathematics to Geometrical Analysis and Algebra,—three arts or Sciences which ought, as I conceived, to contribute something to my design. But, on examination, I found that, as for Logic, its syllogisms and the majority of its other precepts are of avail rather in the communication of what we already know . . . than in the investigation of the unknown; and although this Science contains indeed a number of correct and very excellent precepts, there are, nevertheless, so many others, and these either injurious or superfluous, mingled with the former, that it is almost quite as difficult to effect a severance of the true form the false as it is to extract a Diana or a Minerva form a rough block of marble. . . . By these considerations I was induced to seek some other Method which would comprise [their] advantages . . . and be exempt from their defects. And as a multitude of laws often only hampers justice, so that a state is best governed when, with few laws, these are rigidly administered; in like manner, instead of the great number of precepts of which Logic is composed, I believed that the four following would prove perfectly sufficient for me, provided I took the firm and unwavering resolution never in a single instance to fail in observing them.

The *first* was never to accept anything for true which I did not clearly know to be such; that is to say, carefully to avoid precipitancy and prejudice, and to comprise nothing more in my judgment than what was presented to my mind so clearly and distinctly as to exclude all ground of doubt.

The *second,* to divide each of the difficulties under examination into as many parts as possible, and as might be necessary for its adequate solution.

The *third,* to conduct my thoughts in such order that, by commencing with objects the simplest and easiest to know, I might ascend by little and little, and, as it were, step by step, to the knowledge of the more complex; assigning in thought a certain order even to those objects which in their own nature do not stand in a relation of antecedence and sequence.

And the *last,* in every case to make enumerations so complete, and reviews so general, that I might be assured that nothing was omitted.

The long chains of simple and easy reasonings by means of which geometers are accustomed to reach the conclusions of their most difficult demonstrations, had led me to imagine that all things, to the knowledge of which man is competent, are mutually connected in the same way, and that there is nothing so far removed from us as to be beyond our reach, or so hidden that we cannot discover it, provided only we abstain from accepting the false for the true, and always preserve in our thoughts the order necessary for the deduction of one truth from another. . . .

E. Galileo Faces the Inquisition

I, Galileo, son of the late Vincenzo Galilei, Florentine, aged seventy years . . . have been pronounced by the Holy Office [of the Inquisition] to be vehemently suspected of heresy, that is to say, of having held and believed that the Sun is the center of the world and immovable and that the Earth is not the center and moves: . . . with sincere heart and unfeigned faith I abjure, curse, and detest the aforesaid errors and heresies.

Document Set 16.8 References

A. Galileo Turns His Telescope on Jupiter, January–March 1610
Stilman Drake, ed., *Discoveries and Opinions of Galileo* (Garden City, N.Y.: Doubleday, 1957), 51–57.
B. Johann Kepler Speculates on the Implications of Galileo's Discoveries
Edward Rosen, ed., *Kepler's Conversation with Galileo's Sidereal Messenger* (New York: Johnson Reprint Co., 1965), 36–39.
C. Francis Bacon Announces the March of Progress
Bacon, *Novum Organum,* in James Harvey Robinson, ed., *Readings in European History* (Boston: Ginn, 1904), 2:601–603.
D. René Descartes Conceives a New Method of Reasoning
Descartes, *Discourse on Method,* trans. John Veitch (Edinburgh, 1873), 11–14, 17–20.
E. Galileo Faces the Inquisition
Giorgio de Santillana, *The Crime of Galileo* (Chicago: University of Chicago Press, 1955), 292–293, 312.

Rebellion and State Building, 1640–1690

DOCUMENT SET 17.1
The English Revolution

The two documents of this set starkly contrast the two sides, parliament and king, at the outset of the English Civil War. By an eleven-vote margin the House of Commons enacted the Grand Remonstrance (Document A) in November 1641, a time of rising tension between Parliament, in which radical Puritans were gaining the upper hand, and Charles I, who was ever more determined to resist. Open civil war was only nine months away. Read the document for an understanding of how positions had hardened on both sides: not everything in the Grand Remonstrance was strictly true.

Document B comes from the end of the Civil War. Charles had been defeated and eventually put on trial for his life—as "Charles Stuart, Esq.," not as King Charles I—before Parliament, which claimed to "have the supreme power in the nation." How do you react to Charles's insistence that he had become the persecuted defender of tradition and law?

A. Parliament Confronts the King: The Grand Remonstrance, 1641

The Commons in this present Parliament assembled, having with much earnestness and faithfulness of affection and zeal to the public good of this kingdom, and His Majesty's honour and service for the space of twelve months, wrestled with great dangers and fears, the pressing miseries and calamities, the various distempers and disorders which had not only assaulted, but even overwhelmed and extinguished the liberty, peace and prosperity of this kingdom, the comfort

and hopes of all His Majesty's good subjects, and exceedingly weakened and undermined the foundation and strength of his own royal throne, do yet find an abounding malignity and opposition in those parties and factions who have been the cause of those evils, and do still labour to cast aspersions upon that which hath been done, and to raise many difficulties for the hindrance of that which remains yet undone, and to foment jealousies between the king and Parliament, that so they may deprive him and his people of the fruit of his own gracious intentions, and their humble desires of procuring the public peace, safety and happiness of this realm.

For the preventing of those miserable effects which such malicious endeavours may produce, we have thought good to declare the root and the growth of these mischievous designs: the maturity and ripeness to which they have attained before the beginning of the Parliament: the effectual means which have been used for the extirpation of those dangerous evils, and the progress which hath therein been made by His Majesty's goodness and the wisdom of the Parliament: the ways of obstruction and opposition by which that progress hath been interrupted: the courses to be taken for the removing those obstacles, and for the accomplishing of our most dutiful and faithful intentions and endeavours of restoring and establishing the ancient honour, greatness and security of this Crown and nation.

The root of all this mischief we find to be a malignant and pernicious design of subverting the fundamental laws and principles of government, upon which the religion and justice of this kingdom are firmly established. The actors and promoters hereof have been:

1. The Jesuited papists, who hate the laws, as the obstacles of that change and subversion of religion which they so much long for.

2. The bishops, and the corrupt part of the clergy, who cherish formality and superstition as the natural effects and more probable supports of their own ecclesiastical tyranny and usurpation.

3. Such councillors and courtiers as for private ends have engaged themselves to further the interests of some foreign princes or states to the prejudice of His Majesty and the state at home. . . .

In the beginning of His Majesty's reign the [Catholic] party began to revive and flourish again. . . .

[There follows a long list of protests against arbitrary and excessive taxation.]

37. The Court of Star Chamber hath abounded in extravagant censures, not only for the maintenance and improvement of monopolies and other unlawful taxes, but for divers other causes where there hath been no offence, or very small; whereby His Majesty's subjects have been oppressed by grievous fines, imprisonments, stigmatising, mutilations, whippings, pillories, gags, confinements, banishments; after so rigid a manner as hath not only deprived men of the society of their friends, exercise of their professions, comfort of books, use of paper or ink, but even violated that near union which God hath established between men and their wives, by forced and constrained separation. . . .

48. Titles of honour, judicial places, sergeantships at law, and other offices have been sold for great sums of money, whereby the common justice of the kingdom hath been much endangered, not only by opening a way of employment in places of great trust, and advantage to men of weak parts, but also by giving occasion to bribery, extortion, partiality, it seldom happening that places ill-gotten are well used. . . .

51. The bishops and the rest of the clergy did triumph in the suspensions, excommunications, deprivations, and degradations of divers painful, learned and pious ministers, in the vexation and grievous oppression of great numbers of His Majesty's good subjects.

52. The [ecclesiastical court of] High Commission grew to such excess of sharpness and severity as was not much less than the Romish Inquisition, and yet in many cases by the archbishop's power was made much more heavy, being assisted and strengthened by authority of the Council Table.

53. The bishops and their courts were as eager in the country; although their jurisdiction could not reach so high in rigour and extremity of punishment, yet were they no less grievous in respect of the generality and multiplicity of vexations, which lighting upon the meaner sort of tradesmen and artificers did impoverish many thousands.

54. And so afflict and trouble others, that great numbers to avoid their miseries departed out of the kingdom, some into New England and other parts of America, others into Holland. . . .

B. Charles I Defies Parliament, 1649

Having already made my protestations, not only against the illegality of this pretended court, but also, that no earthly power can justly call me (who am your king) in question as a delinquent, I would not any more open my mouth upon this occasion, more than to refer myself to what I have spoken, were I in this case alone concerned: but the duty I owe to God in the preservation of the true liberty of my people will not suffer me at this time to be silent: for, how can any freeborn subject of England call life or anything he possesseth his own, if power without right daily make new, and abrogate the old fundamental laws of the land which I now take to be the present case? Wherefore when I came hither, I expected that you would have endeavored to have satisfied me concerning these grounds which hinder me to answer to your pretended impeachment. But since I see that nothing I can say will move you to it (though negatives are not so naturally proved as affirmatives) yet I will show you the reason why I am confident you cannot judge me, nor indeed the meanest man in England: for I will not (like you) without showing a reason, seek to impose a belief upon my subjects.

There is no proceeding just against any man, but what is warranted, either by God's laws or the municipal laws of the country where he lives. Now I am most confident this day's proceeding cannot be warranted by God's laws; for, on the contrary, the authority of obedience unto kings is clearly warranted, and strictly commanded in both the Old and New Testament, which, if denied, I am ready instantly to prove.

And for the question now in hand, there it is said, that "where the word of a king is, there is power; and who may say unto him, what dost thou?" Eccles. viii. 4. Then for the law of this land, I am no less confident, that no learned lawyer will affirm that an impeachment can lie against the king, they all going in his name: and one of their maxims is, that the king can do no wrong. Besides, the law upon which you ground your proceedings, must either be old or new: if old, show it; if new, tell what authority, warranted by the fundamental laws of the land, hath made it, and when. But how the House of Commons can erect a court of judicature, which was never one itself (as is well known to all lawyers) I leave to God and the world to judge. And it were full as strange, that they should pretend to make laws without king or Lords' House, to any that have heard speak of the laws of England.

And admitting, but not granting, that the people of England's commission could grant your pretended power, I see nothing you can show for that; for certainly you never asked the question of the tenth man in the kingdom, and in this way you manifestly wrong even the poorest ploughman, if you demand not his free consent; nor can you pretend any color for this your pretended commission, without the consent at least of the major part of every man in England of whatsoever quality or condition, which I am sure you never went about to seek, so far are you from having it. Thus you see that I speak not for my own right alone, as I am your king, but also for the true liberty of all my subjects, which consists not in the power of government, but in living under such laws, such a government, as may give themselves the best assurance of their lives, and property of their goods. . . . Then for anything I can see, the higher house is totally excluded; and for the House of Commons, it is too well known that the major part of them are detained or deterred from sitting; so as if I

had no other, this were sufficient for me to protest against the lawfulness of your pretended court. Besides all this, the peace of the kingdom is not the least in my thoughts; and what hope of settlement is there, so long as power reigns without rule or law, changing the whole frame of that government under which this kingdom hath flourished for many hundred years? (nor will I say what will fall out in case this lawless, unjust proceeding against me do go on) and believe it, the commons of England will not thank you for this change; . . . and by this time it will be too sensibly evident, that the arms I took up were only to defend the fundamental laws of this kingdom against those who have supposed my power hath totally changed the ancient government.

Thus, having showed you briefly the reasons why I cannot submit to your pretended authority, without violating the trust which I have from God for the welfare and liberty of my people, I expect from you either clear reasons to convince my judgment, showing me that I am in an error (and then truly I will answer) or that you will withdraw your proceedings. . . .

Document Set 17.1 References

A. Parliament Confronts the King: The Grand Remonstrance, 1641
   Lacey Baldwin Smith and Jean Reeder Smith, eds., *The Past Speaks: Sources and Problems in English History*, 2d ed. (Lexington, Mass.: D. C. Heath, 1993), 1:341–343.
B. Charles I Defies Parliament, 1649
   Charles I, in Smith and Smith, 1:349–350.

DOCUMENT SET 17.2
English Radicals and Republicans

Radical voices began to echo as soon as king and Parliament clashed in 1641. The anonymous *A Glimpse of Sion's Glory* shows that radical millennial ideas appealed even to respectable middle-class Puritans.

In 1649, the end of the Civil War raised the urgent question of what kind of government should succeed the monarchy. In May 1649 *An Agreement of the Free People of England* (Document B) was published containing a defense of four Levellers (army and lower-class radicals) accused of treason for publishing seditious pamphlets. The tone was moderate, but the demands extreme for the time. To assess how radical the Levellers were, see Document C, an account of a debate between two army officers, Colonel Thomas Rainsborough (a radical) and General Henry Ireton (a conservative). How do Ireton's sentiments reflect mainstream contemporary values?

As *The Challenge of the West* makes clear, the English Revolution brought women into considerable prominence in the radical sects. In Document D, feisty Susannah Parr recalls her difficulties with the (male) elders of her congregation. Among other insights, notice how she speaks of the procedure (normal in Puritan congregations) of having a prospective new member publicly reveal the private experiences in which she had received assurance of God's grace—that is, her "conversion experience." What is significant in her minister's criticism of her "censoriousness"? Notice that the minister who criticized her was himself of extremely radical (Quaker) leanings.

Oliver Cromwell (1599–1658), the leader of the parliamentary army, became England's military dictator. He has always been a controversial figure. Edward Hyde (later named the Earl of Clarendon), a member of parliament who early turned against the Revolution and lived to write its history, paid an eloquent tribute to his opponent Cromwell in the extract from his *History of the Rebellion* that forms Document E.

One of the noblest spirits among the English revolutionaries was the Puritan poet John Milton (1608–1674), who served the parliamentary cause and the Commonwealth as a pamphleteer and Latin secretary. But a proposal to censor controversial religious and political books brought forth in 1644 one of Milton's most eloquent efforts, the essay *Areopagitica*, defending freedom of expression. It is

difficult to extract a short passage from this moving plea; the excerpt in Document F, however, makes a powerful statement that it is precisely out of the clash of ideas that a new, freer, and more glorious England shall arise.

Using these documents and relying on *The Challenge of the West*, write a brief analysis of the mid-seventeenth century English Revolution as a battlefield of political and religious ideas.

A. A Puritan Visionary Catches "A Glimpse of Sion's Glory," 1641

Rev. 19.6: *And I heard as it were the voice of a great multitude, and as the voice of many waters, and as the voice of mighty thunderings, saying: Hallelujah, for the Lord God Omnipotent reigneth.*

At the pouring forth of the first vial, there was a voice saying: *Babylon is fallen, it is fallen.* At the pouring forth of the sixth, John hears a voice as the voice of many waters, and as the voice of thunderings, saying: *Hallelujah, the Lord God Omnipotent reigneth,* immediately following the other. Babylon's falling is Sion's raising. Babylon's destruction is Jerusalem's salvation. The fourth vial was poured upon the sun, which is yet doing, namely upon the emperor and that house of Austria, and will be till that house be destroyed. . . . This is the work that is in hand. As soon as ever this is done, that Antichrist is down, Babylon fallen, then comes in Jesus Christ reigning gloriously; then comes in this *Hallelujah, the Lord God Omnipotent reigneth.* . . . It is the work of the day to cry down Babylon, that it may fall more and more; and it is the work of the day to give God no rest till he sets up Jerusalem as the praise of the whole world. Blessed is he that dasheth the brats of Babylon against the stones. Blessed is he that hath any hand in pulling down Babylon. And beautiful likewise are the feet of them that bring glad tidings unto Jerusalem, unto Zion, saying, *The Lord God Omnipotent reigneth.* This is the work of this exercise: to show unto you how, upon the destruction of Babylon, Christ shall reign gloriously, and how we are to further it. . . .

From whence came this hallelujah? *I heard as it were the voice of a great multitude, and as the voice of many waters.* By waters we are to understand people: the voice of many waters, of many people. . . .

The voice, of Jesus Christ reigning in his Church, comes first from the multitude, the common people. The voice is heard from them first, before it is heard from any others. God uses the common people and the multitude to proclaim that the Lord God Omnipotent reigneth. As when Christ came at first the poor receive[d] the Gospel—not many wise, not many noble, not many rich, but the poor—so in the reformation of religion, after Antichrist began to be discovered, it was the common people that first came to look after Christ. . . . The business, brethren, concerning the Scots, it is a business in the issue whereof we hope there will be great things. Where began it? At the very feet, at the very soles of the feet. You that are of the meaner rank, common people, be not discouraged; for God intends to make use of the common people in the great work of proclaiming the kingdom of his Son. . . .

Though the voice of Christ's reign came first from the multitude; yet it comes but in a confused manner, as the noise of many waters. Though the multitude may begin a thing, and their intention may be good in it, yet it is not for them to bring it to perfection: that which they do commonly is mixed with much confusion and a great deal of disorder. . . . After the beginning of this confused noise among the multitude, God moves the hearts of great ones, of noble, of learned ones; and they come in to the work, and their voice is as the voice of mighty thundering, a voice that strikes terror, and hath a majesty in it to prevail. . . . This is the work of the day, for us to lift up our voice to heaven, that it might be mighty to bring forth more and more the voice of our Parliament as a voice of thunder, a terrible voice to the Antichristian party, that they may say, *The Lord God Omnipotent reigneth.* And let us not be discouraged, for our prayers, though they be poor and mean, and scattered, they may further the voice of thunderings. . . .

Though Christ's kingdom be for a while darkened, Christ shall reign gloriously. That is implied. It is revealed to John as a great wonder, as a glorious thing. Why, did not Christ reign before? Yes, but not in that manner that now he is to reign: the kingdom of Christ hath been exceedingly darkened in the world: though it now begins to appear a little more brightly, it hath been exceedingly darkened. . . .

You see that the Saints have little now in the world; now they are the poorest and the meanest of all; but then when the adoption of the sons of God shall come in the fulness of it, the world shall be theirs; for the world is purchased for them by Jesus Christ. *Not only heaven shall be your kingdom, but this world bodily.* . . .

B. The Levellers Demand a Thorough-Going Revolution: The Agreement of the People

We the free People of England . . . agree to ascertain our Government, to abolish all arbitrary Power, and to set bounds and limits both to our Supreme, and all Subordinate Authority. . . .

I. That the Supreme Authority of England and the Territories therewith incorporate, shall be and reside henceforward in a Representative of the People consisting of four hundred persons, but no more; in the choice of whom (according to naturall right) all men of the age of one and twenty yeers and upwards (not being servants, or receiving alms, or having served the late King in Arms or voluntary Contributions) shall have their voices; and be capable of being elected to that Supreme Trust. . . .

VIII. . . . That the next and al future Representatives, shall continue in full power for the space of one whole year: and that the people shall of course, chuse a Parliament once every year. . . .

X. That we do not impower or entrust our said representatives to continue in force, or to make any Lawes, Oaths, or Covenants, whereby to compell by penalties or otherwise any person to any thing in or about matters of faith, Religion or Gods worship or to restrain any person from the profession of his faith, or exercise of Religion according to his Conscience, nothing having caused more distractions, and heart burnings in all ages, then persecution and molestation for matters of Conscience in and about Religion.

C. Major Rainsborough and Major General Ireton Debate the Levellers' Demands at Putney

Rainsborough: For my part, I think we cannot engage one way or other in the army if we do not think of the people's liberties. If we can agree where the liberty and freedom of the people lies, that will do all.

Ireton: I cannot consent so far. As I said before: when I see the hand of God destroying king, and Lords, and Commons too, [or] any foundation of human constitution, when I see God hath done it, I shall, I hope, comfortably acquiesce in it. But . . . if the principle upon which you move this alteration, or the ground upon which you press that we should make this alteration, do destroy all kind of property or whatsoever a man hath by human constitution, [I cannot consent to it]. The law of God doth not give me property, nor the law of Nature, but property is of human constitution. I have a property and this I shall enjoy. Constitution founds property. If either the thing itself that you press or the consequence [of] that you press [do destroy property], though I shall acquiesce in having no property, yet I cannot give my heart or hand to it; because it is a thing evil in itself and scandalous to the world, and I desire this army may be free from both. . . .

D. Susanna Parr, Independent, Searches Her Soul and Is Disciplined by Her Congregation, 1650s

They who desired admission into the society were sometimes desired in a private meeting to speak what experience they had of the work of grace upon their souls. After which we were every one of us, both men and women, to declare our thoughts of what was spoken; it being laid down as a ground, that we must have an account of a change from a natural and legal estate, into an estate of grace and believing, of those whom we admitted into communion with us. I among the rest did according to my weak measure declare myself against that which I thought would not stand for grace. I was so far from delighting in this work as that it was a trouble to me, an employment from which I would willingly have been freed. I conceived it more needful for myself to study the Word, and compare my own heart with the rule, than to be so taken up about the condition of others. But this was our principle: we were to keep the house of God pure, we were set as porters at the door; it was our duty, we were not to be wanting at such times; yea, it was our liberty that we, who were to have communion with those who came to be admitted, should give in our assent or dissent in reference to their admission. I did therefore at such times declare my thoughts as well as the rest, but left the determination to themselves, as it appears in Ganicle, who was admitted though I was at the first against his admission. I mention him because he was brought by Mr. Eveleigh as an instance of my censoriousness. I was blamed for disliking him whom they said was one of the most eminent among them, and yet it was not long after before he discovered himself, by renouncing the principles of Christianity and turning Quaker. He, in speaking out his experiences, pretended unto much joy and ravishment of spirit, but (the Lord knows) when he spake of such enjoyments, he spake as a stranger that never intermeddled with this joy, never declaring any powerful effect thereof, but only that which was only but a Balaam's wish. I the

rather instance in him because he was the first that kindled the fire of contention, which then brake out in that manner as it is not quenched to this day; here began the quarrel on their part. When I was called by the Elder to give in my thoughts concerning a person proposed, he most disorderly intercepted me, for which there was not the least admonition given him: but not long after, his folly was made manifest by his casting off the very form of godliness. This is one and the chief one of those persons whom I disliked, though approved of by the church. If I be contentious for opposing such a one, let me be contentious still; though none among them will witness for me, yet he doth, he stands to this day as a sad witness between me and them, whether I were contentious in my oppositions, or they infallible in their determinations. Besides, as for some who continue among them, if you look for distinguishing characters they are scarcely visible, much less easy to be discerned.

E. A Great, Bad Man: The Earl of Clarendon Pays Tribute to His Opponent Cromwell

He was one of those men . . . [who] could never have done half that mischief without great parts of courage and industry and judgment. And he must have had a wonderful understanding in the natures and humours of men, and as great a dexterity in the applying them, who from a private and obscure birth (though of a good family), without interest of estate, alliance, or friendships, could raise himself to such a height, and compound and knead such opposite and contradictory tempers, humours, and interests into a consistence that contributed to his designs and to their own destruction, whilst himself grew insensibly powerful enough to cut off those by whom he had climbed in the instant that they projected to demolish their own building. . . . Without doubt, no man with more wickedness ever attempted anything, or brought to pass what he desired more wickedly, more in the face and contempt of religion and moral honesty; yet wickedness as great as his could never have accomplished those trophies without the assistance of a great spirit, an admirable circumspection and sagacity, and a most magnanimous resolution.

When he appeared first in the Parliament, he seemed to have a person in no degree gracious, no ornament of discourse, none of those talents which use to reconcile the affections of the standers-by; yet as he grew into place and authority, his parts seemed to be renew[ed], as if he had concealed faculties till he had occasion to use them; and when he was to act the part of a great man, he did it without any indecency through the want of custom.

After he was confirmed and invested Protector by the humble Petition and Advice, he consulted with very few upon any action of importance, nor communicated any enterprise he resolved upon with more than those who were to have principal parts in the execution of it; nor to them sooner than was absolutely necessary. What he once resolved, in which he was not rash, he would not be dissuaded from, nor endure any contradiction of his power and authority, but extorted obedience from them who were not willing to yield to it. . . .

In all other matters which did not concern the life of his jurisdiction, he seemed to have great reverence for the law, and rarely interposed between party and party. And as he proceeded with this kind of indignation and haughtiness with those who were refractory and dared to contend with his greatness, so towards those who complied with his good pleasure, and courted his protection, he used a wonderful civility, generosity, and bounty.

To reduce three nations, which perfectly hated him, to an entire obedience to all his dictates; to awe and govern those nations by an army that was indevoted to him and wished his ruin; was an instance of a very prodigious address. But his greatness at home was but a shadow of the glory he had abroad. It was hard to discover which feared him most, France, Spain, or the Low Countries, where his friendship was current at the value he put upon it. And as they did all sacrifice their honour and their interest to his pleasure, so there is nothing he could have demanded that either of them would have denied him. . . .

F. John Milton Sees a Free England Rising in Majesty

Methinks I see in my mind a noble and puissant Nation rousing herself like a strong man after sleep, and shaking her invincible locks. Methinks I see her as an Eagle muing her mighty youth, and kindling her undazl'd eyes at the full midday beam, purging and unscaling her long abused sight at the fountain itself of heav'nly radiance, while the whole noise of timorous and flocking birds, with those also that love the twilight, flutter about, amaz'd at what she means, and in their envious gabble would prognosticat a year of sects and schisms.

What should ye doe then, should ye suppresse all this flowry crop of knowledge and new light sprung up and yet springing daily in this City, should ye set an *Oligarchy* of twenty ingrossers over it, to bring a

famin upon our minds again, when we shall know nothing but what is measur'd to us by their bushel? Beleeve it, Lords and Commons, they who counsell ye to such a suppressing doe as good as bid ye suppresse yourselves; and I will soon shew how. If it be desir'd to know the immediat cause of all this free writing and free speaking, there cannot be assign'd a truer then your own mild and free and human government; it is the liberty, Lords and Commons, which your own valorous and happy counsels have purchast us, liberty which is the nurse of all great wits; this is that which hath rarify'd and enlightn'd our spirits like the influence of heav'n; this is that which hath enfranchis'd, enlarg'd and lifted up our apprehensions degrees above themselves. Ye cannot make us now lesse capable, lesse knowing, lesse eagerly pursuing of the truth, unlesse ye first make your selves, that made us so, lesse the lovers, lesse the founders of our true liberty. We can grow ignorant again, brutish, formall, and slavish, as ye found us; but you then must first become that which ye cannot be, oppressive, arbitrary, and tyrannous, as they were from whom ye have free'd us. That our hearts are now more capacious, our thoughts more erected to the search and expectation of greatest and exactest things, is the issue of your owne vertu propagated in us; ye cannot suppresse that unlesse ye reinforce an abrogated and mercilesse law, that fathers may dispatch at will their own children. . . .

Document Set 17.2 References

A. A Puritan Visionary Catches "A Glimpse of Sion's Glory," 1641 .
   Hanserd Knollys or Thomas Goodwin, "A Glimpse of Sion's Glory," in Lacey Baldwin Smith and Jean Reeder Smith, eds., *The Past Speaks,* 2d ed., (Lexington, Mass.: D. C. Heath, 1993), 1:351–353.
B. The Levellers Demand a Thorough-Going Revolution: The Agreement of the People
   William Haller and Godfrey Davies, eds. *The Leveller Tracts, 1647–1653* (New York: Columbia University Press, 1944), 318–328.
C. Major Rainsborough and Major General Ireton Debate the Levellers' Demands at Putney
   Thomas Rainsborough and Henry Ireton, in Smith and Smith, 1:385.
D. Susanna Parr, Independent, Searches Her Soul and Is Disciplined by Her Congregation, 1650s
   Elspeth Graham et al., eds., *Her Own Life: Autobio-graphical Writings by Seventeeth-Century English Women* (London: Routledge, 1989), 108–109.
E. A Great, Bad Man: The Earl of Clarendon Pays Tribute to His Opponent Cromwell
   Clarendon, *History of the Rebellion,* in James Harvey Robinson, ed., *Readings in European History* (Boston: Ginn, 1904), 2:249–250.
F. John Milton Sees a Free England Rising in Majesty
   Milton, *Areopagitica* (London: Oxford University Press, 1875), 49–50.

DOCUMENT SET 17.3
In Search of Stability: The Restoration and the Glorious Revolution

The anonymous pamphlet excerpted in Document A recites grievances that had grown steadily in English minds at all social levels under the dictatorship of Oliver Cromwell. Drawing on your understanding of the Commonwealth (as informed by Set 17.2 and *The Challenge of the West*), consider the nature and gravity of the complaints that this pamphleteer sets forth. What picture of a stable, peaceful England does the author seem to invoke? And does it persuade you?

Sir William Petty (1623–1687) is one of the first European thinkers who merits being called an economist in the modern sense. In 1672 he wrote *Political Arithmetic* as an inquiry into how an understanding of national statistics can help guide state policy. Petty enjoyed considerable favor (including being named to the Royal Society) under Charles II. Compared to the oceans of statistics in which governments now find themselves awash, the data at the Stuarts' disposal were obviously puny. In what ways could the kind of information catalogued in Document B (Petty's Table of Contents) be of use in designing policy? Notice the jumble of significant and (to us) fantastic topics; what does this reveal about the late seventeenth-century mind?

Documents C and D come from the Glorious Revolution, the overthrow of the Stuarts in 1688–1689 and the installation of a regime willing to recognize Parliament's ultimate control of England's political destiny. Sir John Evelyn (1620–1706), a diarist who seemed to be everywhere and in contact with everyone in late seventeenth-century England, in Document C records the fall of James II very much from the perspective of a member of the politically active Anglican elite. The Bill of Rights (Document D) enshrined the Glorious Revolution's outcome and takes its place next to Magna Carta and the U.S. Bill of Rights as a statement of fundamental liberties in the English-speaking world. Using *The Challenge of the West* to supplement your fund of information, analyze the outcome of the Glorious Revolution using these materials. Consider, in particular, the willingness of the elite to close ranks before Catholics or lower-class radicals found an opening to exploit.

Document E should be read—or better, sung—partly for fun and partly as a wry comment on the continuities of local authority despite revolutionary upheavals. (It has a very catchy tune, and recordings exist.) The verses were composed anonymously sometime in the early eighteenth century, and "the vicar of Bray" remains Britain's proverbial political opportunist.

A. A Call for the Stuarts' Restoration, 1659

If we take a view of the several pretensions, carried on in the nation apart, we shall find the most considerable to be the Roman Catholic, the Royalist, the Presbyterian, the Anabaptist, the Army, the Protectorian, and that of the Parliament.

1. 'Tis the Roman Catholic's aim not only to abrogate the penal laws, and become capable of all employments in the Commonwealth, but to introduce his religion, to restore the rights of the Church, and utterly eradicate all that he esteems heresy.

2. 'Tis the Royalist's desire to bring in the king as a conqueror, to recover their losses in the late war, be rendered capable of civil employments, and have the former government of the Church.

3. 'Tis the Presbyterian's desire to set up his discipline, to have the covenant reënforced, and only such as take it to be employed in church or state; to be indemnified in reference to what they have done, and secured of what they possess.

4. 'Tis the wish of the baptized churches that there might be no ecclesiastical government of any kind, nor ministerial function, or provision for it; and that only persons so minded should be capable of employment; likewise to be indemnified for what they have done.

5. 'Tis the aim of the Army to govern the nation, to keep themselves from being disbanded, or engaged in war, to secure their pay, and to be indemnified for all past action.

6. 'Tis the desire of the family of the late Protector to establish the heir of the house, that they may rule him, and he the nation, and so both preserve and advance themselves.

7. 'Tis the wish of the present Parliament (as far as they have one common design) to continue themselves in absolute power by the specious name of a popular government; to new-model and divide, and, at last, take down, the Army; and, finally, under the pretences of a committee of Parliament, or council of state, set up an oligarchy resembling that of the Thirty Tyrants in Athens.

Lastly, 't is the general interest of the nation to establish the ancient fundamental laws, upon which every one's propriety and liberty are built, to settle religion, to procure a general indemnity for all actions past, to revive their languishing and almost dead trade, gain an alliance with our neighbour states; to put the government in such hands as, besides present force, can plead a legal title to it; into the hands of such with whose private interest that of the public not only consists, but in which 't is necessarily involved, which likewise does least contradict the aims of particular parties; lastly, the hands of such whose counsel is fit to direct in matters of deliberation, and courage fit to vindicate the injuries of the nation.

From which premises we may conclude that the pretensions of no party now on foot in the nation are attainable; or, if attained, are consistent with the good of other parties, or of the nation; or, in fine, with their own; and from hence likewise one would be apt to conclude that the ruin of the public is inevitable; there being no door of hope left open to receive, no method visible to unite, such distant and incompatible ends.

But, notwithstanding all this, 't is not impossible —no, nor hard—to find an expedient that shall evacuate all these difficulties; not only establish the general concernment, but (exorbitant passion only retrenched) satisfy the real interest of every party— nay, single person—in the nation.

Now to the cheerful reception of such an overture, I suppose there is no need to persuade, nor even to admonish, that words and names, however rendered odious, ought not to frighten us from our certain benefit and dearest interest. All that is demanded here is that if , upon serious consideration, the proposal be found reasonable, men would be so kind to themselves as to receive it. The assertion I doubt not to make most plain and evident, and therefore shall as plainly pronounce it. 'T is this: the calling in the king is the certain and only means for the preservation of the kingdom, and also of the rights and interests of all single persons in it.

B. Sir William Petty Searches Statistics for the Key to Progress and Stability, 1672

The scope of this essay is concerning people and colonies, and to make way for another essay concerning the growth of the City of London. I desire in this first essay to give the world some light, concerning the number of people in England, with Wales, and in Ireland; as also, of the number of houses and families wherein they live and of acres they occupy.

2. How many live upon their lands, how many upon their personal estates and commerce, and how many upon art and labour; how many upon alms, how many upon offices and public employments, and how many as cheats and thieves; how many are impotents, children and decrepit old men.

3. How many upon the poll-taxes in England do pay extraordinary rates, and how many at the level.

4. How many men and women are prolific, and how many of each are married or unmarried.

5. What the value of people are in England, and what in Ireland, at a medium, both as members of the church or commonwealth, or as slaves and servants to one another; with a method how to estimate the same in any other country or colony.

6. How to compute the value of land in colonies, in comparison to England and Ireland.

7. How 10,000 people in a colony may be, and planted to the best advantage.

8. A conjecture in what number of years England and Ireland may be fully peopled, as also all America, and lastly the whole habitable earth.

9. What spot of the earth's globe were fittest for a general and universal emporium, whereby all the people thereof may best enjoy one another's labours and commodities.

10. Whether the speedy peopling of the earth would make first, for the good of mankind. Secondly, to fulfill the revealed will of God. Thirdly, to what prince or state the same would be most advantageous.

11. An exhortation of all thinking men to salve the Scriptures and other good histories, concerning the number of people in all ages of the world, in the great cities thereof, and elsewhere.

12. An appendix concerning the different number of sea-fish and wild-fowl at the end of every thousand years, since Noah's flood.

13. An hypothesis of the use of those spaces (of about 8,000 miles through) within the globe of our earth, supposing a shell of 150 miles thick.

14. What may be the meaning of glorified bodies, in case the place of the Blessed shall be without the convex of the orb of the fixed stars, if that the whole system of the world was made for the use of our earth's men.

C. Sir John Evelyn Records the Glorious Revolution in His Diary, January 1689

1689. 15th January. I visited the archbishop of Canterbury, where I found the bishops of St. Asaph, Ely, Bath and Wells, Peterborough, and Chichester, the earls of Aylesbury and Clarendon, Sir George Mackenize Lord-Advocate of Scotland, and then came in a Scotch archbishop, etc. After prayers and dinner, divers serious matters were discoursed, concerning the present state of the public, and sorry I was to find there was as yet no accord in the judgments of those of the Lords and Commons who were to convene; some would have the princess made queen without any more dispute, others were for a regency; there was a Tory party (then so called), who were for inviting his Majesty again upon conditions; and there were republicans who would make the Prince of Orange like a stadtholder [an elected chief prince, as in the Dutch Republic]. The Romanists were busy among these several parties to bring them into confusion: most for ambition or other interest, few for conscience and moderate resolutions. I found nothing of all this in this assembly of bishops, who were pleased to admit me into their discourses; they were all for a regency, thereby to salve their oaths, and so all public matters to proceed in his Majesty's name, by that to facilitate the calling of a Parliament, according to the laws in being. Such was the result of this meeting. . . .

The great convention being assembled the day before, falling upon the question about the government, resolved that King James having by the advice of the Jesuits and other wicked persons endeavoured to subvert the laws of church and state, and deserted the kingdom, carrying away the seals, etc., without any care for the management of the government, had by demise abdicated himself and wholly vacated his right; they did therefore desire the Lords' concurrence to their vote, to place the crown on the next heir, the Prince of Orange, for his life, then to the princess, his wife, and if she died without issue, to the Princess of Denmark (Anne), and she failing, to the heirs of the prince, excluding forever all possibility of admitting a Roman Catholic. . . .

29th. The votes of the House of Commons being carried up by Mr. Hampden, their chairman, to the Lords, I got a station by the prince's lodgings at the door of the lobby to the House, and heard much of the debate, which lasted very long. Lord Derby was in the chair (for the House was resolved into a grand committee of the whole House); after all had spoken, it came to the question, which was carried by three voices against a regency, which 51 were for, 54 against; the minority alleging the danger of dethroning kings, and scrupling many passages and expressions in the vote of the Commons, too long to set down particularly. Some were for sending to his Majesty with conditions; others that the king could do no wrong, and that the maladministration was chargeable on his ministers. There were not more than eight or nine bishops, and but two against the regency; the archbishop was absent, and the clergy now began to change their note, both in pulpit and discourse, on their old passive obedience, so as people began to talk of the bishops being cast out of the House. In short, things tended to dissatisfaction on both sides; add to this, the morose temper of the Prince of Orange, who showed little countenance to the noblemen and others, who expected a more gracious and cheerful reception when they made their court. The English army also was not so in order, and firm to his interest, nor so weakened but that it might give interruption. Ireland was in an ill posture as well as Scotland. Nothing was yet done towards a settlement. God of His infinite mercy compose these things, that we may be at last a nation and a church under some fixed and sober establishment. . . .

D. Parliament Enacts the English Bill of Rights, 1689

Whereas the said late King James II having abdicated the government, and the throne being thereby vacant, his Highness the prince of Orange (whom it hath pleased Almighty God to make the glorious instrument of delivering this kingdom from popery and arbitrary power) did (by the device of the lords spiritual and temporal, and diverse principal persons of the Commons) cause letters to be written to the lords spiritual and temporal, being Protestants, and other letters to the several counties, cities, universities, boroughs, and Cinque Ports [five port towns on the English Channel, having special privileges], for the choosing of such persons to represent them, as were of right to be sent to parliament, to meet and sit at Westminster upon the two and twentieth day of January, in this year 1689, in order to such an establishment as that their religion, laws, and liberties might not again be in danger of being subverted; upon which letters elections have been accordingly made.

And thereupon the said lords spiritual and temporal and Commons, pursuant to their respective letters and elections, being now assembled in a full and free representation of this nation, taking into their most serious consideration the best means for attaining the ends aforesaid, do in the first place (as their ancestors in like case have usually done), for the vindication and assertion of their ancient rights and liberties, declare:

1. That the pretended power of suspending laws, or the execution of laws, by regal authority, without consent of parliament is illegal.

2. That the pretended power of dispensing with the laws, or the execution of law by regal authority, as it hath been assumed and exercised of late, is illegal.

3. That the commission for erecting the late court of commissioners for ecclesiastical causes, and all other commissions and courts of like nature, are illegal and pernicious.

4. That levying money for or to the use of the crown by pretense of prerogative, without grant of parliament, for longer time or in other manner than the same is or shall be granted, is illegal.

5. That it is the right of the subjects to petition the king, and all commitments and prosecutions for such petitioning are illegal.

6. That the raising or keeping a standing army within the kingdom in time of peace, unless it be with consent of parliament, is against law.

7. That the subjects which are Protestants may have arms for their defense suitable to their conditions, and as allowed by law.

8. That election of members of parliament ought to be free.

9. That the freedom of speech, and debates or proceedings in parliament, ought not to be impeached or questioned in any court or place out of parliament.

10. That excessive bail ought not to be required, nor excessive fines imposed, nor cruel and unusual punishments inflicted.

11. That jurors ought to be duly impaneled and returned, and jurors which pass upon men in trials for high treason ought to be freeholders.

12. That all grants and promises of fines and forfeitures of particular persons before conviction are illegal and void.

13. And that for redress of all grievances, and for the amending, strengthening, and preserving of the laws, parliament ought to be held frequently.

E. The "Vicar of Bray" Achieves Stability, c. 1725

In good King *Charles's* golden days,
  When Loyalty no harm meant;
A Furious High-Church Man I was,
  And so I gain'd Preferment.[1]
Unto my Flock I daily Preach'd,
  Kings are by God appointed,

And Damn'd are those who dare resist,
  Or touch the Lord's Anointed.
    And this is Law, I will maintain
      Unto my Dying Day, Sir,
    That whatsoever King shall Reign,
      I will be Vicar of *Bray,* Sir!

When Royal *James* possest the Crown,
  And Popery grew in fashion,
The Penal Law I hooted down,
  And read the Declaration:
The Church of *Rome,* I found would fit,
  Full well my Constitution,
And I had been a Jesuit,
  But for the Revolution.
    And this is Law, etc.

When *William* our Deliverer came,
  To heal the Nation's Grievance,
I turned the Cat in Pan again,
  And swore to him Allegiance;
Old Principles I did revoke,
  Set Conscience at a distance,
Passive Obedience is a Joke,
  A Jest is Non-resistance.
    And this is Law, etc.

When glorious *Ann* became our
    Queen,
  The Church of *England's* Glory,
Another face of things was seen,
  And I became a Tory:
Occasional Conformists base,
  I Damn'd, and Moderation,
And thought the Church in
    danger was,
  From such Prevarication.
    And this is Law, etc.

When *George* in Pudding time[2]
    came o'er,
  And Moderate Men looked big, Sir,
My Principles I chang'd once more,
  And so became a Whig, Sir:
And thus Preferment I procur'd,
  From our Faith's Great Defender,
And almost every day abjur'd
  The Pope, and the Pretender.
    And this is Law, etc.

The Illustrious House of *Hannover,*
  And Protestant Succession,

---

[1] Appointment to office

[2] A lucky or favorable time

To these I lustily will swear,
　　Whilst they can keep possession:
For in my Faith, and Loyalty,
　　I never once will falter,
But *George,* my Lawful King shall be,
　　Except the Times shou'd alter,
　　　　And this is Law, etc.

Document Set 17.3 References

A. A Call for the Stuarts' Restoration, 1659
　　Contemporary Pamphlet, Quoted in James Harvey Robinson,
　　ed., *Readings in European History* (Boston: Ginn, 1904),
　　2:251–252.

B. Sir William Petty Searches Statistics for the Key to Progress
　　and Stability, 1672
　　Petty, "Concerning the Encrease of People and Colonies," in
　　Lacey Baldwin Smith and Jean Reeder Smith, eds., *The Past
　　Speaks,* 2d ed. (Lexington, Mass.: D. C. Heath, 1993), 1:413.

C. Sir John Evelyn Records the Glorious Revolution in His
　　Diary, January 1689
　　Evelyn, *Diary,* in Walter L. Arnstein, *The Past Speaks,* 2d ed.
　　(Lexington, Mass.: D. C. Heath, 1993), 2:3–10 passim.

D. Parliament Enacts the English Bill of Rights, 1689
　　The Statutes, rev. ed. (London: Eyre and Spotiswoode, 1871),
　　2:10–12.

E. The "Vicar of Bray" Achieves Stability, c. 1725
　　Anonymous Poem, in Arnstein, 2:22.

Summing Up the English Revolution: Baxter, Milton, Hobbes, and Locke

The authors of the four selections in this set are among the foremost names of mid to late seventeenth-century English thought. Their commentaries offer a valuable perspective on England's fate in these revolutionary decades.

Richard Baxter (1615–1691) was one of England's notable Puritan voices as a preacher during the Civil War. He was most influential, however, as a spokesman for defeated Puritanism after the Restoration, when he was hounded out of his position for being too vocal a nonconformist. His advice (Document A) on how a good Protestant ought to behave in the world, taken from his 1673 book *A Christian Directory,* is a classic summary of what we now call the Protestant Ethic: hard work reveals godliness. Countless English nonconformists took this path with particular vigor after the fall of the Puritan regime shut them out of the political realm.

Milton's *Paradise Lost,* the great blind poet's epic interpretation of God's purpose, was also composed after Puritanism had ceased to be England's established faith. The passage quoted as Document B is the famous opening invocation. Since God had apparently "spit in our faces"—as one Puritan, shocked by events after 1659, put it—Milton's courageous reassurance that God indeed had "ways" that could be justified was no small comfort.

Thomas Hobbes (1588–1679), one of the greatest philosophical minds of Western culture, wrote *Leviathan* (1651) as a reflection on the turmoil set in motion by the fall of traditional authority in England. He surpasses even Machiavelli as a realistic analyst of why human beings form and maintain civil societies. What echoes of the Civil War era do you see in the extract from *Leviathan* that appears as Document C?

John Locke (1632–1704), a more comfortable, less daring, and more influential thinker than Hobbes, wrote his *Second Treatise of Government* (Document D) early in the 1680s and published it in 1689. It is notable for refuting Robert Filmer's thoroughly traditional justification of government as patriarchy writ large. Instead, Locke saw government as a pragmatic contract for guaranteeing life, liberty, and property. His was the right book at the right time; he perfectly vindicated the Glorious Revolution. It became virtual holy writ for eighteenth-century Americans.

A. Richard Baxter Justifies the Puritan Ethic, 1673

Every man that is able, must be steadily and ordinarily employed in such work as is serviceable to God, and to the common good. . . . Everyone that is a member of a church or commonwealth must employ their parts to the utmost for the good of the church and commonwealth, public service is God's greatest service. To neglect this, and to say, I will pray and meditate, is as if your servant should refuse your greatest work, and to tie himself to some lesser easy part; and God has commanded you some way or another to labour for your daily bread, and not to live as drones on the sweat of others only. Innocent Adam was put into the Garden of Eden to dress it, and fallen man must eat his bread in the sweat of his brow (Genesis 3:19). And he that will not work must be forbidden to eat (2 Thes. 3:6, 10 and 12). And indeed, it is necessary for ourselves, for the health of our bodies, which will grow diseased with idleness. And for the health of our souls, which will fail if the body fail. And man in flesh must have work for his body as well as his soul. And he that will do nothing but pray and meditate, it's like will (by sickness or melancholy) be disabled ere long to pray or meditate, unless he have a body extraordinary strong . . .

It gloryeth God, by showing the excellency of faith, when we contemn the riches and honor of the world, and live above the worldling's life, accounting that a despicable thing, which he accounts his happiness, and loses his soul for . . . When seeming Christians are worldly and ambitious as others, and make as great matter of the gain, and wealth and honour, it shows that they do but cover the base and sordid spirit of worldlings, with the visor of the Christian name . . .

As labour is thus necessary so understand how needful a state a calling is, for the right performance of your labours. A calling is a stated course of labour. This is very needful for these reasons: (1) Out of a calling a man's labours are but occasional or inconstant, so more time is spent in idleness than labour; (2) A man is best skilled in that which he is used to; (3) And he will be best provided for it with instruments and necessaries; (4) Therefore he does it better than he could do any other work, and so wrongs not others, but attains more the end of his labour; (5) And he does it more easily, when a man unused and unskilled and unfurnished, toils himself much in doing little; (6) And he will do his work more orderly, when another is in continual confusion, and his business knows not its time and place, but one part contradicts another. Therefore some certain calling or trade of life is best for everyman . . .

The first and principal thing to be intended in the choice of a trade or calling for yourselves or children is the service of God, and the public good. And, therefore, *ceteris paribus* [other things being equal], that calling which most conduces to the public good is to be preferred. The callings most useful to the public good are the magistrate, the pastor, the teacher of the church, schoolmaster, physician, lawyer, etc., husbandmen (ploughmen, graziers and shepherds); and next to them are mariners, clothiers, booksellers, tailors and such others that are employed about things most necessary to mankind. And some callings are employed about matters of so little use, as tobacco-sellers, lace-sellers, feather-makers, periwig-makers, and many more such, that he that may choose better, should be loath to take up with one of these, though possibly in itself it may be lawful. It is a great satisfaction to an honest mind, to spend his life in doing the greatest good he can, and a prison and a constant calamity, to be tied to spend one's life in doing little good at all to others, though he should grow rich by it . . .

If thou be called to the poorest laborious calling, do not carnally murmur at it; because it is wearisome to the flesh, nor imagine that God accepts the less of thy work and thee. But cheerfully follow it, and make it the matter of thy pleasure and joy that thou art still in thy heavenly master's services, though it be the lowest thing. And that He who knows what is best for thee, has chosen this for thy good, and tries and values thy obedience to Him the more, by how much the meaner work thou stoopest to at His command. But see that thou do it all in obedience to God, and not merely for thy own necessity. Thus every servant must serve the Lord, in serving their master, and from God expect their chief reward . . .

In doing good to others we do good to ourselves: because we are living members of Christ's body, and by love and communion feel their joys, as well as pains.

Good works are comfortable evidence that faith is sincere, and that the heart dissembles not with God.

Good works are much to the honour of religion, and consequently of God, and much tend to men's conviction, conversion and salvation.

B. John Milton Justifies God's Ways to Man, 1663

Of man's first disobedience, and the fruit
Of that forbidden tree, whose mortal taste
Brought death into the world, and all our woe,
With loss of Eden, till one greater Man
Restore us, and regain the blissful seat,
Sing, Heavenly Muse, that on the secret top
Of Oreb, or of Sinai, didst inspire
That shepherd, who first taught the chosen seed,
In the beginning how the Heavens and Earth
Rose out of Chaos; or if Sion hill
Delight thee more, and Siloa's brook that flowed
Fast by the oracle of God, I thence
Invoke thy aid to my adventurous song,
That with no middle flight intends to soar
Above the Aonian mount, while it pursues
Things unattempted yet in prose or rhyme.
And chiefly thou, O Spirit, that dost prefer
Before all temples the upright heart and pure,
Instruct me, for thou know'st; thou from the first
Wast present, and with mighty wings outspread
Dove-like sat'st brooding on the vast abyss
And mad'st it pregnant: what in me is dark
Illumine, what is low raise and support;
That to the highth of this great argument
I may assert Eternal Providence,
and justify the ways of God to men. . . .

C. Thomas Hobbes Justifies the State as Leviathan, 1651

Hereby it is manifest, that during the time men live without a common power to keep them all in awe, they are in that condition which is called war; and such a war, as is of every man, against every man. For war, consisteth not in battle only, or the act of fighting; but in a tract of time, wherein the will to contend by battle is sufficiently known: and therefore the notion of *time*, is to be considered in the nature of war; as it is in the nature of weather. For as the nature of foul weather, lieth not in a shower or two of rain; but in an inclination thereto of many days together: so the nature of war, consisteth not in actual fighting; but in the known disposition thereto, during all the time there is no assurance to the contrary. All other time is peace.

Whatsoever therefore is consequent to a time of war, where every man is enemy to every man; the same is consequent to the time, wherein men live without other security, than what their own strength, and their own invention shall furnish them withal. In such condition, there is no place for industry; because the fruit thereof is uncertain: and consequently no culture of the earth; no navigation, nor use of the commodities that may be imported by sea; no commodious building; no instruments of moving, and removing, such things as require much force; no knowledge of the face of the earth; no account of time; no arts; no letters; no society; and which is worst of all, continual fear, and danger of violent death; and the life of man, solitary, poor, nasty, brutish, and short.

It may seem strange to some man, that has not well weighed these things; that nature should thus dissociate, and render men apt to invade, and destroy one another: and he may therefore, not trusting to this inference, made from the passions, desire perhaps to have the same confirmed by experience. Let him therefore consider with himself, when taking a journey, he arms himself, and seeks to go well accompanied; when going to sleep, he locks his doors; when even in his house he locks his chests; and this when he knows there be laws, and public officers, armed, to revenge all injuries shall be done him; what opinion he has of his fellow-subjects, when he rides armed; of his fellow citizens, when he locks his doors; and of his children, and servants, when he locks his chests. Does he not there as much accuse mankind by his actions, as I do by my words? But neither of us accuse man's nature in it. The desires, and other passions of man, are in themselves no sin. No more are the actions, that proceed from those passions, till they know a law that forbids them: which till laws be made they cannot know: nor can any law be made, till they have agreed upon the person that shall make it.

It may peradventure be thought, there was never such a time, nor condition of war as this; and I believe it was never generally so, over all the world: but there are many places, where they live so now. For the savage people in many places of America, except the government of small families, the concord whereof dependeth on natural lust, have no government at all; and live at this day in that brutish manner, as I said before. Howsoever, it may be perceived what manner of life there would be, where there were no common power to fear, by the manner of life, which men that have formerly lived under a peaceful government, use to degenerate into, in a civil war.

But though there had never been any time, wherein particular men were in a condition of war one against another; yet in all times, kings, and persons of sovereign authority, because of their independency, are in continual jealousies, and in the state and posture of gladiators; having their weapons pointing, and their eyes fixed on one another; that is, their forts, garrisons, and guns upon the frontiers of their kingdoms; and continual spies upon their neighbours; which is a posture of war. But because they uphold thereby, the industry of their subjects; there does not follow from it, that misery, which accompanies the liberty of particular men.

To this war of every man, against every man, this also is consequent; that nothing can be unjust. The notions of right and wrong, justice and injustice have there no place. Where there is no common power, there is no law: where no law, no injustice. Force, and fraud, are in war the two cardinal virtues. Justice, and injustice are none of the faculties neither of the body, nor mind. If they were, they might be in a man that were alone in the world, as well as his senses, and passions. They are qualities, that relate to men in society, not in solitude. It is consequent also to the same condition, that there be no propriety, no dominion, no *mine* and *thine* distinct; but only that to be every man's, that he can get; and for so long, as he can keep it. And thus much for the ill condition, which man by mere nature is actually placed in; though with a possibility to come out of it, consisting partly in the passions, partly in his reason.

The passions that incline men to peace, are fear of death; desire of such things as are necessary to commodious living; and a hope by their industry to obtain them. And reason suggesteth convenient articles of peace, upon which men may be drawn to agreement. These articles, are they, which otherwise are called the Laws of Nature. . .

D. John Locke Justifies the Glorious Revolution as the Essence of the Social Contract, 1690

87. Man being born, as has been proved, with a Title to perfect Freedom, and an uncontrouled enjoyment of all the Rights and Privileges of the Law of Nature, equally with any other Man, or Number of Men in the World, hath by Nature a Power, not only to preserve his Property, that is, his Life, Liberty and Estate, against the Injuries and Attempts of other Men; but to judge of, and punish the breaches of that Law in others, as he is perswaded the Offence deserves, even with Death it self, in Crimes where the heinousness of the Fact, in his Opinion, requires it. But because no *Political Society* can be, nor subsist without having in it self the Power to preserve the Property, and in order thereunto punish the Offences of all those of that Society; there, and there only is *Political Society,* where every one of the Members hath quitted this natural Power, resign'd it up into the

hands of the Community in all cases that exclude him not from appealing for Protection to the Law established by it. And thus all private judgement of every particular Member being excluded, the Community comes to be Umpire, by settled standing Rules, indifferent, and the same to all Parties; and by Men having Authority from the Community, for the execution of those Rules, decides all the differences that may happen between any Members of that Society, concerning any matter of right; and punishes those Offences, which any Member hath committed against the Society, with such Penalties as the Law has established: Whereby it is easie to discern who are, and who are not, in *Political Society* together. Those who are united into one Body, and have a common establish'd Law and Judicature to appeal to, with Authority to decide Controversies between them, and punish Offenders, *are in Civil Society* one with another: but those who have no such common Appeal, I mean on Earth, are still in the state of Nature, each being, where there is no other, Judge for himself, and Executioner; which is, as I have before shew'd it, the perfect *state of Nature*.

88. And thus the Commonwealth comes by a Power to set down, what punishment shall belong to the several transgressions which they think worthy of it, committed amongst the Members of that Society, (which is the *power of making Laws*) as well as it has the power to punish any Injury done unto any of its Members, by any one that is not of it, (which is the *power of War and Peace;*) and all this for the preservation of the property of all the Members of that Society, as far as is possible. But though every Man who has enter'd into civil Society, and is become a member of any Commonwealth, has thereby quitted his power to punish Offences against the Law of Nature, in prosecution of his own private Judgment; yet with the Judgment of Offences which he has given up to the Legislative in all Cases, where he can Appeal to the Magistrate, he has given a right to the Commonwealth to imploy his force, for the Execution of the Judgments of the Commonwealth, whenever he shall be called to it; which indeed are his own Judgments, they being made by himself, or his Representative. And herein we have the original of the *Legislative* and *Executive Power* of Civil Society, which is to judge by standing Laws how far Offences are to be punished, when committed within the Commonwealth; and also to determin, by occasional Judgments founded on the present Circumstances of the Fact, how far Injuries from without are to be vindicated, and in both these to imploy all the force of all the Members when there shall be need.

89. Where-ever therefore any number of Men are so united into one Society, as to quit every one his Executive Power of the Law of Nature, and to resign it to the publick, there and there only is a *Political, or Civil Society.* And this is done where-ever any number of Men, in the state of Nature, enter into Society to make one People, one Body Politick under one Supreme Government, or else when any one joyns himself to, and incorporates with any Government already made. For hereby he authorizes the Society, or which is all one, the Legislative thereof to make Laws for him as the publick good of the Society shall require; to the Execution whereof, his own assistance (as to his own Decrees) is due. And this *puts Men* out of a State of Nature *into* that of a *Commonwealth,* by setting up a Judge on Earth, with Authority to determine all the Controversies, and redress the Injuries, that may happen to any Member of the Commonwealth; which Judge is the Legislative, or Magistrates appointed by it. And where-ever there are any number of Men, however associated, that have no such decisive power to appeal to, there they are still *in the state of Nature.*

90. Hence it is evident, that *Absolute Monarchy,* which by some Men is counted the only Government in the World, is indeed *inconsistent with Civil Society,* and so can be no Form of Civil Government at all. For the *end of Civil Society,* being to avoid, and remedy those inconveniencies of the State of Nature, which necessarily follow from every Man's being Judge in his own Case, by setting up a known Authority, to which every one of that Society may Appeal upon any injury received, or Controversie that may arise, and which every one of the Society ought to obey; where-ever any persons are, who have not such an Authority to Appeal to, for the decision of any difference between them, there those persons are still *in the state of Nature.* And so is every *Absolute Prince* in respect of those who are under his *Dominion.*

91. For he being suppos'd to have all, both Legislative and Executive Power in himself alone, there is no Judge to be found, no Appeal lies open to any one, who may fairly, and indifferently, and with Authority decide, and from whose decision relief and redress may be expected of any Injury or Inconveniency, that may be suffered from the Prince or by his Order: So that such a Man, however intitled, *Czar,* or *Grand Signior,* or how you please, is as much *in the state of Nature,* with all under his Dominion, as he is with the rest of Mankind. For where-ever any two Men are, who have no standing

Rule, and common Judge to Appeal to on Earth for the determination of Controversies of Right betwixt them, there they are still *in the state of Nature,* and under all the inconveniencies of it, with only this woful difference to the Subject, or rather Slave of an Absolute Prince: That whereas, in the ordinary State of Nature, he has a liberty to judge of his Right, and according to the best of his Power, to maintain it; now whenever his Property is invaded by the Will and Order of his Monarch, he has not only no Appeal, as those in Society ought to have, but as if he were degraded from the common state of Rational Creatures, is denied a liberty to judge of, or to defend his Right, and so is exposed to all the Misery and Inconveniencies that a Man can fear from one, who being in the unrestrained state of Nature, is yet corrupted with Flattery, and armed with Power.

92. For that thinks *absolute Power purifies Mens Bloods,* and corrects the baseness of Humane Nature, need read but the History of this, or any other Age to be convinced of the contrary. He that would have been insolent and injurious in the Woods of *America,* would not probably be much better in a Throne; where perhaps Learning and Religion shall be found out to justifie all, that he shall do to his Subjects, and the Sword presently silence all those that dare question it. For what the *Protection of Absolute Monarchy* is, what kind of Fathers of their Countries it makes Princes to be, and to what a degree of Happiness and Security it carries Civil Society where this sort of Government is grown to perfection, he that will look into the late Relation of *Ceylon,* may easily see.

Document Set 17.4 References

A. Richard Baxter Justifies the Puritan Ethic, 1673
   Baxter, *A Christian Directory: Or a Summa of Practical Theologie and Cases of Conscience,* in H. E. S. Fisher and A. R. J. Jurica, eds., *Documents in English Economic History* (London: G. Bell, 1977), 1:519–521.
B. John Milton Justifies God's Ways to Man, 1663
   Milton, *Paradise Lost,* book I, lines 1–26.
C. Thomas Hobbes Justifies the State as Leviathan, 1651
   Hobbes, *The Leviathan,* 252–257.
D. John Locke Justifies the Glorious Revolution as the Essence of the Social Contract, 1690
   Locke, *Second Treatise on Government,* §§ 87–92.

DOCUMENT SET 17.5
Louis XIV's France: State, Court, and Subjects

Taxation and the threat—or outbreak—of popular revolt were the two fundamental realities of life in seventeenth century France. The letter quoted as Document A was a report by the royal governor of Guyenne province about 1645, conveying typical details in such cases. And although the nobility was exempt from paying the *taille* and other onerous exactions, it often felt keenly the need to hold down commoners' taxes as Document B—an appeal to the government in 1661—reveals. It is obvious why these nobles should want to see the price of offices reduced, but why were they concerned about the welfare of the lower classes?

Louis XIV was one of the handful of kings who took the trouble to write extensive, self-serving memoirs, a task he undertook for the benefit of his heir. Document C is an excerpt from the king's recollections of his early years. Judging by other evidence in the set and from what you have learned from *The Challenge of the West,* how do you evaluate the case he makes for authoritarian royal government?

Another famous set of memoirs of Louis XIV's reign was written by the Duc de Saint-Simon (1675–1755) (Document D). An acute though acerbic observer of the Sun King's court in its later years, after 1695, Saint-Simon was as eager as anyone to gain royal favor. In interpreting his remarks, we must remember that they describe the king in his pious old age. A somewhat younger Louis appears in Document E, a letter written by Elizabeth Charlotte, Duchess of Orleans, the German wife of Louis's brother. During her fifty years at the French court she wrote about forty long letters per week. Why, as this letter seems to indicate, should Louis's every act have influenced the behavior of court nobles?

Not everything that went on at the Versailles court turned on matters of etiquette and place. Louis XIV's chief minister, Jean-Baptiste Colbert (1619–1683), was busy supervising the revival of French finances and encouraging industry and colonization. The anonymous pamphlet excerpted in Document F was written at Colbert's behest in 1664 to argue the advantages of colonial trade and to urge the foundation of the French East India Company. Why does it make so much of the Dutch success, and why, when translated into English, did it cause alarm in England?

A. A Tax Revolt Brews, 1645

I learned at Grenade in a letter from the aldermen [*jurats*] of Bordeaux that a revolt was feared there as a result of the rumour of a new imposition of the *sou* per *livre* tax, and upon receiving this news I set out at once for Bordeaux. Yesterday in letters sent by the same aldermen and by the first president [of the *parlement* of Bordeaux] I learned that Monsieur de Lanson (the *intendant*) whom the people suspected of being at Bordeaux to supervise this imposition, had left the town on the advice of the *parlement* and had been accompanied by the aldermen, as he himself wished, as far as the boat that was to take him to Bourg . . . With God's help I shall reach Bordeaux in two days and do all that I can to maintain order and stifle a sedition which could flare up and spread very easily in this province because of the extraordinary expense of supporting soldiers which it has borne for five months and is still sustaining, the difficulty of paying *tailles* and other royal revenues, the discontent of the office-holders in the *parlement* and in the *présidial* courts because of the half-yearly arrangements [*semestres*], the separation of jurisdictions and the establishment of new tribunals with which they are threatened.

B. The Nobility of Troyes Plead for a Reduction Both in the Price of Offices and in Taxes, 1651

Now to come to the matter of the reformation of justice in your kingdom, Your Majesty is entreated to listen to the general complaints of the whole of France, concerning venality and the excessive price of judicial and financial offices, which is the cause of the widespread corruption discernible in those who exercise them. . . . The cause of this immensely high cost of offices may be traced to that enemy of the state, the *paulette,* palotte [sic] now called the annual due which in the manner of a canker is gradually undermining and consuming all the families of this kingdom, and therefore the nobility begs His Majesty most humbly to revoke the wretched annual due immediately and forever, with orders forbidding its re-establishment under any pretext whatsoever.

And may this be done on the last day of next December since the officers have not paid any loans nor made any advance payments since it has been continued and re-established this last time and all the nobility of the kingdom are entreated to unite in order to secure this present article, for it has an interest in seeing the prices of offices reduced and restored if possible to what they were in our fathers' time fifty or sixty years ago when a nobleman of the *robe* could call three or four of his children into public offices; now only tax-farmers can do that and it is even impossible for a nobleman who follows the profession of arms to place any of his children (although they are capable) into offices of the *robe* because of their excessive and enormous price, and truly it is monstrous to witness this great superfluity and cost of office, not previously heard of nor even contemplated and unlikely to be believed by posterity.

We are therefore now obliged most humbly to entreat Your Majesty to re-establish the ancient order, which obtained before the time of Louis XII; under that régime when a judicial office became vacant whether in the sovereign courts, on the royal benches or in subordinate jurisdictions, the officers in the place concerned elected three suitable persons capable of exercising the vacant office and the king conferred it upon one of the three, who did not have to spend a single *denier;* and because such offices had cost nothing their holders rendered justice freely and without fees (*épices*), content with the honour of being judges. Moreover, His Majesty's conscience was clear before God and his people.

C. Louis XIV Recalls the Problems He Faced at the Outset of His Reign

From my early infancy the very name of *rois fainéants* or *maires du palais*[1] displeased me when mentioned in my presence. But I must point out the state of affairs: grievous disturbances throughout the kingdom before and after my majority; a foreign war in which these troubles at home had lost to France thousands and thousands of advantages; a Prince of my blood and of great name at the head of my enemies; many Cabals in the State; the Parliaments still in the possession and enjoyment of a usurped authority; at my Court very little disinterested fidelity and, on this account, my subjects, though outwardly most submissive, as much a responsibility and cause of misgiving to me as the most rebellious; a minister re-established in power despite so many factions, very

[1] "Do-nothing kings" and mayors of the palace: terms dating from the time of the weak Merovingian kings of France and their Carolingian successors.

skilful and very adroit, but whose views and methods were naturally very different from mine, whom, nevertheless, I could not gainsay, nor abate the least portion of his credit, without running the risk of again raising against him by some misleading appearance of disgrace those very storms which had been allayed with so much difficulty. I myself was still very young, though I had reached the majority of kings, which the State laws anticipate in order to avoid still greater evils, but not the age at which mere private persons begin to regulate freely their own affairs. I only knew to its full extent the greatness of my burden, without having yet learned my own capabilities. . . .

I made a beginning by casting my eyes over all the different parties in the State, not indifferently, but with the glance of experience, sensibly touched at seeing nothing which did not invite and urge me to take it in hand, but carefully watching what the occasion and the state of affairs would permit. Everywhere was disorder. . . .

The finances, which give movement and action to the great organisation of the monarchy, were entirely exhausted, so much so that we could hardly find the ways and means. Much of the most necessary and most privileged expenses of my house and my own privy purse were in arrears beyond all that was fitting, or maintained only on credit, to be a further subsequent burden. At the same time a prodigality showed itself among public men, masking on the one hand their malversations by every king of artifice, and revealing them on the other in insolent and daring luxury, as though they feared I might take no notice of them.

The Church, apart from its usual troubles, after lengthy disputes on matters of the schools, a knowledge of which they allowed was unnecessary to salvation for any one, with points of disagreement augmenting day by day through the heat and obstinacy of their minds, and ceaselessly involving fresh human interests, was finally threatened with open schism by men who were all the more dangerous because they were capable of being very serviceable and greatly deserving, had they themselves been less opinionated. . . .

The least of the ills affecting the order of Nobility was the fact of its being shared by an infinite number of usurpers possessing no right to it, or one acquired by money without any claim from service rendered. The tyranny exercised by the nobles over their vassals and neighbours in some of my provinces could no longer be suffered or suppressed save by making severe and rigorous examples. The range for dueling—somewhat modified by the exact observance of the latest regulations, over which I was always inflexible—was only noticeable in a now well advanced recovery from so inveterate an ill, so that there was no reason to despair of the remedy.

The administration of Justice itself, whose duty it is to reform others, appeared to me the most difficult to reform. An infinity of things contributed to this state of affairs: the appointments filled haphazard or by money rather than by selection and merit; scant experience and less knowledge on the part of some of the judges; the regulations referring to age and service almost everywhere eluded; chicanery firmly established through many centuries, and fertile in inventing means of evading the most salutary laws. And what especially conduced to this was the fact that these insatiable gentry loved litigation and fostered it as their own peculiar property, applying themselves only to prolong and to add to it. Even my Council, instead of supervising the other jurisdictions, too often only introduced disorder by issuing a strange number of contrary regulations, all in my name and as though by my command, which rendered the confusion far more disgraceful.

All this collection of evils, their consequences and effects, fell principally upon the people, who in addition, were loaded with impositions, some crushed down by poverty, others suffering want from their own laziness since the peace, and needing above all to be alleviated and occupied. . . .

D. The Duke of Saint-Simon Characterizes Louis XIV

The king's great qualities shone more brilliantly by reason of an exterior so unique and incomparable as to lend infinite distinction to his slightest actions; the very figure of a hero, so impregnated with a natural but most imposing majesty that it appeared even in his most insignificant gestures and movements, without arrogance but with simple gravity; proportions such as a sculptor would choose to model; a perfect countenance and the grandest air and mien ever vouchsafed to man; all these advantages enhanced by a natural grace which enveloped all his actions with a singular charm which has never perhaps been equaled. He was as dignified and majestic in his dressing gown as when dressed in robes of state, or on horseback at the head of his troops.

He excelled in all sorts of exercise and liked to have every facility for it. No fatigue nor stress of weather made any impression on that heroic figure and bearing; drenched with rain or snow, pierced with cold, bathed in sweat or covered with dust, he was always the same. I have often observed with admiration that except in the most extreme and exceptional weather nothing prevented his spending considerable time out of doors every day.

A voice whose tones corresponded with the rest of his person; the ability to speak well and to listen with quick comprehension; much reserve of manner adjusted with exactness to the quality of different persons; a courtesy always grave, always dignified, always distinguished, and suited to the age, rank, and sex of each individual, and, for the ladies, always an air of natural gallantry. So much for his exterior, which has never been equaled nor even approached.

In whatever did not concern what he believed to be his rightful authority and prerogative, he showed a natural kindness of heart and a sense of justice which made one regret the education, the flatteries, the artifice which resulted in preventing him from being his real self except on the rare occasions when he gave way to some natural impulse and showed that,—prerogative aside, which choked and stifled everything,—he loved truth, justice, order, reason,— that he loved even to let himself be vanquished.

Nothing could be regulated with greater exactitude than were his days and hours. In spite of all his variety of places, affairs, and amusements, with an almanac and a watch one might tell, three hundred leagues away, exactly what he was doing. . . . Except at Marly, any man could have an opportunity to speak to him five or six times during the day; he listened, and almost always replied, "I will see," in order not to accord or decide anything lightly. Never a reply or a speech that would give pain; patient to the last degree in business and in matters of personal service; completely master of his face, manner, and bearing; never giving way to impatience or anger. If he administered reproof, it was rarely, in few words, and never hastily. He did not lose control of himself ten times in his whole life, and then only with inferior persons, and not more than four or five times seriously. . . .

Louis XIV's vanity was without limit or restraint; it colored everything and convinced him that no one even approached him in military talents, in plans and enterprises, in government. Hence those pictures and inscriptions in the gallery of Versailles which disgust every foreigner; those opera prologues that he himself tried to sing; that flood of prose and verse in his praise for which his appetite was insatiable; those dedications of statues copied from pagan sculpture, and the insipid and sickening compliments that were continually offered to him in person and which he swallowed with unfailing relish; hence his distaste for all merit, intelligence, education, and, most of all, for all independence of character and sentiment in others; his mistakes of judgment in matters of importance; his familiarity and favor reserved entirely for those to whom he felt himself superior in acquirements and ability; and, above everything else, a jealously of his own authority which determined and took precedence of every other sort of justice, reason, and consideration whatever.

E. The Duchess of Orleans Describes the Court of Louis XIV

Although I had not hurt myself or fallen on my head, he would not rest until he had personally examined my head on all sides . . . he also led me back to my room and even stayed with me for a while to see whether I might become dizzy. . . . I must say that even now the King still shows me his favor every day. . . . This is also the reason that I am now very much à la mode; whatever I say or do, whether it be good or awry, is greatly admired by the courtiers, to the point that when I decided to wear my old sable in this cold weather to keep my neck warm, everyone had one made from the same pattern, and sables have become quite the rage. This makes me laugh, for five years ago the very people who now admire and wear this fashion so laughed at me and made so much fun of me with my sable that I could no longer wear it. This is what happens at this court: if the courtiers imagine that someone is in favor it does not matter what the person does, one can be certain that the courtiers approve of it; but if they imagine the contrary, they will think that person ridiculous, even if he has come straight from heaven.

F. Colbert Sponsors a Pamphlet on "The Advantages of Overseas Trade"

Now of all commerces whatsoever throughout the whole world, that of the East Indies is one of the most rich and considerable. From thence it is (the sun being kinder to them, than to us) that we have our merchandise of greatest value and that which contributes the most not only to the pleasure of life but also to glory, and magnificence. From thence it is that we fetch our gold and precious stones and a thousand other commodities (both of a general esteem and a certain return) to which we are so accustomed that it is impossible for us to be without them, as silk, cinnamon, pepper, ginger, nutmegs, cotton cloth, oüate (vulgarly [cotton] wadding), porcelain, woods for dyeing, ivory, frankincense, bezoar [an antidote for poisons], etc. So that having an absolute necessity

upon us, to make use of all these things, why we should not rather furnish ourselves, than take them from others, and apply that profit hereafter to our own countrymen, which we have hitherto allowed to strangers, I cannot understand.

Why should the Portuguese, the Hollanders, the English, the Danes, trade daily to the East Indies possessing there, their magazines, and their forts, and the French neither the one nor the other? . . . To what end is it *in fine* that we pride ourselves to be subjects of the prime monarch of the universe, if being so, we dare not so much as show our heads in those places where our neighbors have established themselves with power? . . .

What has it been, but this very navigation and traffic that has enabled the Hollanders to bear up against the power of Spain, with forces so unequal, nay, and to become terrible to them and to bring them down at last to an advantageous peace? Since that time it is that this people, who had not only the Spaniards abroad, but the very sea and earth at home to struggle with, have in spite of all opposition made themselves so considerable, that they begin now to dispute power and plenty with the greatest part of their neighbors. This observation is no more than truth, their East India Company being known to be the principal support of their state and the most sensible cause of their greatness.

Document Set 17.5 References

A. A Tax Revolt Brews, 1645
Letter of the duc d'Epernan [governor of Guyenne] to Seguier, in J. H. Shennan, ed. and trans., *Government and Society in France, 1461–1661* (London: G. Allen and Unwin, 1969), 151.
B. The Nobility of Troyes Plead for a Reduction Both in the Price of Offices and in Taxes, 1651
Cahier of the Remonstrances of the Nobility in the Bailiwick of Troyes, in Shennan, 154–155.
C. Louis XIV Recalls the Problems He Faced at the Outset of His Reign
Louis XIV, *Memoirs,* trans. Herbert Wilson (Port Washington, N.Y.: Kennikat), 41–45.
D. The Duke of Saint-Simon Characterizes Louis XIV
James Harvey Robinson, ed., *Readings in European History* (Boston: Ginn, 1904), 2:285–286.
E. The Duchess of Orleans Describes the Court of Louis XIV
A Woman's Life in the Court of Sun King: Letters of Liselotte von der Pfalz, 1652–1722 (Elisabeth Charlotte, Duchesse d'Orleans), trans. Elborg Forster (Baltimore: Johns Hopkins University Press, 1984), 17–18.
F. Colbert Sponsors a Pamphlet on "The Advantages of Overseas Trade"
Colbert, "A Discourse . . .," trans. R. L'Estrange (London: 1664), in Geoffrey Symcox, ed., *War, Diplomacy, and Imperialism, 1618–1763* (New York: Walker, 1974), 257–260.

DOCUMENT SET 17.6
Louis XIV's France: Religion and Sensibility

Religion was taken seriously in Louis XIV's France. Not only did memories of the sixteenth-century wars of religion still fester; the monarchy was also acutely aware that religious heterodoxy could have serious political implications. Louis himself grew more pious as he aged, and the court followed suit. But religious controversies were exceedingly convoluted. Royal Catholicism did not mean accepting papal dictation to France's "Gallican" church. An intense controversy grew up within French Catholicism over Jansenism, pitting the strongly pro-papal Jesuit order against what the papacy had declared to be an almost Protestant heresy, of which the royal government also disapproved without bowing to the Jesuits and Rome.

The documents of this set explore various dimensions of the religious and social tensions coursing through the French elite. Document A is an extract from *The Provincial Letters* (1656–1657) of Blaise Pascal (1623–1662). One of the great mathematical minds of the ages, Pascal suffered from intense religious anxiety, which we will explore further in Set 17.8. He joined the Jansenists, a religious movement within Catholicism that stressed deep piety and came close to agreeing with the Calvinist doctrine of predestination. The Jansenists' great enemy was the Jesuit Order, which they had accused of making religion too "easy" by encouraging well-born sinners to interpret their transgressions in a favorable light. Pascal's *Provincial Letters,* purporting to be the correspondence of a country gentleman, ridiculed the Jesuit position mercilessly.

In 1685 Louis made one of the great mistakes of his reign, revoking the Edict of Nantes on the wildly misinformed grounds that practically no Huguenots remained in France. As a consequence, more than 50,000 Huguenot families who refused to convert to Catholicism were expelled from the Kingdom. The magnitude of this mistake became apparent at once, and the Duc de Saint-Simon commented bitterly on it in his *Memoirs* (Document B).

The novels of the Countess de Lafayette (1634–1693) are an excellent barometer of the sensibilities of Louis XIV's court. Her *Princess of Cleves*, excerpted in Document C, balances sensuality and propriety exquisitely, while also making one more contribution to that perennially belabored topic of court life, "What is true nobility?" Molière (1622–1673), the great playwright, wrote comedies

satirizing both religious hypocrisy and social climbing; his *Bourgeois gentilhomme* (1671), on the latter subject, is excerpted in Document D, a scene in which the soberly bourgeois Mme. Jourdain expresses her doubts about her rich husband's foolish aspirations to buy his way into the nobility.

What was the reality, meanwhile, of French Catholicism at the grassroots? In Document E a reform-minded Catholic clergyman suggests that a century of Counter-Reformation had done little to make ordinary rural parishioners behave in a seemly, pious manner.

Pulling together the material in this set, use these documents and *The Challenge of the West* to write a brief analysis of the anxieties and aspirations of France's middle class and elite. Considering also the materials in Set 17.5 will enhance your analysis.

A. Blaise Pascal Satirizes Jesuitical Reasoning

"Show me, with all your directing of the intention," returned I, "that it is allowable to fight a duel."

"Our great Hurtado de Mendoza," said the [Jesuit] father, "will satisfy you on that point in a twinkling. 'If a gentleman,' says he, in a passage cited by Diana, 'who is challenged to fight a duel, is well known to have no religion, and if the vices to which he is openly and unscrupulously addicted are such as would lead people to conclude, in the event of his refusing to fight, that he is actuated, not by the fear of God, but by cowardice, and induce them to say of him that he was a *hen,* and not a man—*gallina, et non vir;* in that case he may, to save his honor, appear at the appointed spot—not, indeed, with the express intention of fighting a duel, but merely with that of defending himself, should the person who challenged him come there unjustly to attack him. His action in this case, viewed by itself, will be perfectly indifferent; for what moral evil is there in one stepping into a field, taking a stroll in expectation of meeting a person, and defending one's self in the event of being attacked? And thus the gentleman is guilty of no sin whatever; for in fact it cannot be called accepting a challenge at all, his intention being directed to other circumstances, and the acceptance of a challenge consisting in an express intention to fight, which we are supposing the gentleman never had.'"

"You have not kept your word with me, sir," said

I. "This is not, properly speaking, to permit duelling; on the contrary, the casuist is so persuaded that this practice is forbidden, that, in licensing the action in question, he carefully avoids calling it a duel."

"Ah!" cried the monk, "you begin to get knowing on my hand, I am glad to see. I might reply, that the author I have quoted grants all that duellists are disposed to ask. But since you must have a categorical answer, I shall allow our Father Layman to give it for me. He permits duelling in so many words, provided that, in accepting the challenge, the person directs his intention solely to the preservation of his honor or his property: 'If a soldier or a courtier is in such a predicament that he must lose either his honor or his fortune unless he accepts a challenge, I see nothing to hinder him from doing so in self-defence.' The same thing is said by Peter Hurtado, as quoted by our famous Escobar; his words are: 'One may fight a duel even to defend one's property, should that be necessary; because every man has a right to defend his property, though at the expense of his enemy's life!'"

I was struck, on hearing these passages, with the reflection that while the piety of the king appears in his exerting all his power to prohibit and abolish the practice of duelling in the State, the piety of the Jesuits is shown in their employing all their ingenuity to tolerate and sanction it in the Church. But the good father was in such an excellent key for talking, that it would have been cruel to have interrupted him; so he went on with his discourse.

"In short," said he, "Sanchez (mark, now, what great names I am quoting you!) Sanchez, sir, goes a step further; for he shows how, simply by managing the intention rightly, a person may not only receive a challenge, but give one. And our Escobar follows him." ...

B. The Duke of Saint-Simon Deplores the Revocation of the Edict of Nantes

The revocation of the Edict of Nantes, without the slightest pretext or necessity, and the various proscriptions that followed it, were the fruits of a frightful plot, in which the new spouse was one of the chief conspirators, and which depopulated a quarter of the realm; ruined its commerce; weakened it in every direction; gave it up for a long time to the public and avowed pillage of he dragoons; authorized torments and punishments by which many innocent people of both sexes were killed by thousands; ruined a numerous class; tore in pieces a world of families; armed relatives against relatives, so as to seize their property and leave them to die of hunger; banished our manufactures to foreign lands; made those lands flourish and overflow at the expense of France, and enabled them to build new cities; gave to the world the spectacle of a prodigious population proscribed without crime, stripped, fugitive, wandering, and seeking shelter far from their country; sent to the galleys nobles, rich old men, people much esteemed for their piety, learning, and virtue, people carefully nurtured, weak, and delicate;—and all solely on account of religion; in fact, to heap up the measure of horror, filled the realm with perjury and sacrilege, in the midst of the echoed cries of these unfortunate victims of error, while so many others sacrificed their conscience to their wealth and their repose, and purchased both by simulated abjuration, from which without pause they were dragged to adore what they did not believe in, and to receive the divine body of the Most Holy whilst remaining persuaded that they were only eating bread which they ought to abhor!

Such was the general abomination born of flattery and cruelty. From torture to abjuration, and from that to communion, there was often only a space of twenty-four hours; and executioners were the guides of the converts and their witnesses. . . . The king received from all sides detailed news of these conversions. It was by thousands that those who had abjured and taken the communion were counted; ten thousand in one place, six thousand in another,—all at once and instantly. The king congratulated himself on his power and his piety. He believed himself to have brought back the days of the apostles, and attributed to himself all the honor. The bishops wrote panegyrics of him; the Jesuits made the pulpit resound with his praise. All France was filled with horror and confusion; and yet there was never such triumph and joy, such boundless laudation of the king.

C. Madame de Lafayette's *Princess of Cleves* Suggests the Proper Values for a Young Noblewoman

Now there appeared at the Court a beauty. All eyes were upon her and she must indeed have been a paragon to be so much admired in a place where lovely women were the rule. She belonged to the same family as the Vidame de Chartres, and was one of the greatest heiresses in France. Her father had died young, leaving her to be brought up by his widow, Madame de Chartres, a good, noble, and distinguished person. For some years after her husband's death she left the Court and devoted herself to her daughter's education, not only cultivating her mind and caring for her beauty, but also trying to make her good and give her a real love of virtue. Most mothers think that they can best protect their children by never speaking of love in their presence, but Madame de Chartres had different ideas; she often described it to her daughter, minimizing none of its charm so that the girl should more readily understand what she told her of its dangers. She told her that men were not very sincere, not very faithful and not above deceit; she spoke of the unhappiness that love affairs can bring to a family, and then, on the other hand, she showed her the life of a good woman—happy, serene, and enjoying the particular glamor that attaches to noble birth when there is also virtue. She impressed upon her that this virtue can only be kept by vigilance and by following the one line of conduct which can make a woman happy—that is to say, loving her husband and being loved by him.

D. Mme. Jourdain Has Her Doubts

M. Jourdain: Shut up, saucebox. You're always sticking your oar in the conversation. I have enough property for my daughter; all I need is honor; and I want to make her a marquise.

Mme Jourdain: Marquise?

M. Jourdain: Yes, marquise.

Mme Jourdain: Alas, God forbid!

M. Jourdain: It's something I've made up my mind to.

Mme Jourdain: As for me, it's something I'll never consent to. Alliances with people above our own rank are always likely to have very unpleasant results. I don't want to have my son-in-law able to reproach my daughter for her parents, and I don't want her children to be ashamed to call me their grandma. If she should happen to come and visit me in her grand lady's carriage, and if by mistake she should fail to salute some one of the neighbors, you can imagine how they'd talk. "Take a look at that fine Madame la Marquise showing off," they'd say. "She's the daughter of Monsieur Jourdain, and when she was little, she was only too glad to play at being a fine lady. She wasn't always so high and mighty as she is now, and both her grandfathers sold dry goods besides the

Porte Saint Innocent. They both piled up money for their children, and now perhaps they're paying dear for it in the next world; you don't get so rich by being honest." Well, I don't want that kind of talk to go on; and in short, I want a man who will feel under obligation to my daughter, and I want to be able to say to him: "Sit down there, my boy, and eat dinner with us."

M. Jourdain: Those views reveal a mean and petty mind, that wants to remain forever in its base condition. Don't answer back to me again. My daughter will be a marquise in spite of everyone; and if you get me angry, I'll make her a duchess.

E. Catholic Priest Noël Chomel Denounces Dancing on Holy Days

During these holy days, the air is filled with the worst sort of filth; impudence knows no bounds; and because of negligence great enough to make one cry, even the most moderate persons approve what on other occasions they would judge to be a scandal and an atrocious crime. . . . To see the lewd and violent gyrations of the girls mixed in dance with the young men, does it not seem that one is watching bacchantes and savages rather than Christians?

Document Set 17.6 References

A. Blaise Pascal Satirizes Jesuitical Reasoning
   Pascal, *Provincial Lettes,* Thomas M'Cree, trans. (New York: Modern Library, 1941), 406–408.
B. The Duke of Saint-Simon Deplores the Revocation of the Edict of Nantes
   James Harvey Robinson, ed., *Readings in European History* (Boston: Ginn, 1904), 2:291–293.
C. Madame de Lafayette's *Princess of Cleves* Suggests the Proper Values for a Young Noblewoman
   Mme. de Lafayette, *The Princess of Cleves,* trans. Nancy Mitford (Westport, Conn.: Greenwood, 1977), 11–12.
D. Mme. Jourdain Has Her Doubts
   Molière, *Le Bourgeois Gentilhomme,* in Morris Bishop, trans., *Eight Plays by Molière* (New York: Modern Library, 1957), 372.
E. Catholic Priest Noël Chomel Denounces Dancing on Holy Days
   Paul T. Hoffman, *Church and Community in the Diocese of Lyon 1500–1780* (New Haven, Conn.: Yale University Press, 1984), 88.

DOCUMENT SET 17.7
Varieties of Liberty on the Continent

Seventeenth-century Poland-Lithuania was one of the great exceptions to the era's trend toward more authoritarian—or at least better organized—states. The right of the commonwealth's nobility to elect a king and hold him in obedience to a contentious parliament typified Poland-Lithuania's "golden freedom." Jan Chrzyzostom Pasek, a Polish nobleman of middling fortune and great but untutored literary skill, left fascinating memoirs of his experiences that have only recently been translated into English. His uproarious account of the royal election of 1669 (Document A), out of which a weak national candidate named Michał Wiśniowiecki (*1669–1673) was elected king despite lavish bribery by a French-sponsored candidate, gives a vivid picture of "gentry democracy" at work.

The expulsion of the Huguenots from France (Set 17.6, Document B) provided a great opportunity for the Protestant powers of Europe not only to demonstrate their liberality but also to gain industrious new subjects. Energetic at crushing the liberties of his own burgher- and noble-dominated provincial legislatures, Brandenburg's great elector Frederick William (*1640–1688) eagerly welcomed the Huguenot refugees to his lands (Document B). Some of their descendants, still bearing French names, remained prominent in the Prussian aristocracy until the twentieth century. In view of his otherwise repressive policies, what do you make of the Great Elector's welcome to the Huguenots?

Another citadel of liberty (as contemporaries would have expressed it) in seventeenth-century Europe was the Dutch Republic, then at the peak of a prosperity that was the envy of the rest of the continent. One foreigner who understood the connection was Sir William Temple (1628–1699), an English essayist and diplomat. Do you agree with his assessment? It may help to recall that the republic had a stormy history, including several French invasions and a violent mob uprising in 1672.

The latter event profoundly shook the great Dutch-Jewish philosopher Baruch Spinoza (1632–1677), who was personally close to the de Witt brothers, important Dutch leaders lynched by the mob. Spinoza recognized that civil society poised precariously above a cauldron of violence; in Document D he pleads for moderation of the passions (a central theme of his philosophy) and for the tempering of free thought with responsibility for maintaining legitimate authority.

A. Golden Freedom: The Polish Nobility Elects a King, 1669

The election of the king took place then. Announcements went out to the districts from the archbishop, urging *ordines Reipublicae* [the estates of the Commonwealth] to accomplish a speedy election, tendering the wish that the election be carried off *per deputatos* [by the deputies]. But the provinces refused their assent and, indeed, ordered everyone to horse as if for war. . . .

But when the sessions of the Diet began, divers men were of divers minds: this one'll be king, that one will, yet no one mentioned the one whom God himself had forseen. All those who sent deputies were scheming and hoping that things would turn out as they'd planned. While he, our future king, expects nothing, knowing the likelihood to be nil. The French deputies, as if cowed, work in secret, but the Neuburg and Lorraine deputies work openly. Not a word about a Polish candidate. The others are handing out money, giving it away, wining, dining, making promises; while he bestows nothing on anybody, promises nothing, requests nothing: and yet he carries off the crown. . . .

[At first the French candidate, the Duke of Lorraine, appeared to have the upper hand, although his supporters had to fight some serious brawls with advocates of other candidates—all very colorfully described.]

As this is going on, [the nobles from the province of] Wielkopolska now gives a shout: *"Vivat rex!"* Several from our delegation dash over to see whom they are cheering; they returned with the news that it was Charles of Lorraine. In Łęczyce and Kujawy they were saying, "we don't need a rich man for, upon becoming the king of Poland, he'll be rich. We don't need anyone related to other royalty, for 'tis a *periculum libertatis,* [danger to liberty] but we need a *virum fortem,* a *virum bellicosum* [a strong, bellicose man]. Were Czarniecki[1] here, he'd surely have sat on the throne; but as God took him from us, let us elect his disciple, let us elect [Alexander] Polanowski."

This is going on here; meanwhile I, *per curiositatem* [out of curiosity] dashed over to the deputies from Sandomierz, they were standing the closest to us, and what should I find but that they prefer some-

[1]A notable magnate, recently deceased

one *de sanguine gentis* [of native blood], and they're saying: "We have not far to look for a king, he's in our midst. Recalling the virtue and decency, and the many services to this country of the deceased Prince [Jeremi] Wiśniowiecki, right and fitting would it be to pay our debt of gratitude to his *posteritas*. Here is Prince Michał Wiśniowiecki; why should we not elect him? Is he not from an ancient family of great princes? Is he not worthy of the crown?"

And he is sitting there among the gentry, humble as pie, wincing, saying nothing. I rush back to my own delegation and say: "Gentlemen, already several delegations are putting forth a Piast."[2] Our Kraków lordship inquires: "Who is it?" Say I: "Polanowski and Wiśniowiecki." And meanwhile there's a roar from Sandomierz: "*Vivat Piast!*" Debicki, the chamberlain, hurls his cap into the air, yelling at the top of his voice: "*Vivat Piast! Vivat Rex Michael!*" And now our Kraków deputies too: "*Vivat Piast!*" A few of us run off to the other provincial delegations with the news, shouting "*Vivat Piast!*" Those from Łęczyce and Kujawy, thinking it's for their Polanowski, at once started shouting too; other delegations too. Returning to my own, they're now taking his arm, they're leading him to the assembly.

Our Kraków officers *negant, contradicunt*, [do not wish it, oppose it] (having taken a great deal of money from others and made big promises), in particular, Pisarski and Lipski who were saying: "For God's sake, what are we doing? Have we gone mad? Wait! This cannot be." Our Kraków lordship has now withdrawn from us, the nominee being his kinsman; there he is, next to the candidate. Many other senators are coming toward us. Some protest, others remain silent. Pisarski says to me (he nonetheless held me in esteem); "My dear fellow, what think you of this situation?" I reply: "I think what God has put in my heart: *Vivat Rex Michael!*" Where upon, I ride out of the line and dash after Sandomierz; in all haste the squadrons with their standards follow after me, only Pisarski, slamming his cap on his head, rode off to the side.

We led Wiśniowiecki then to the assembly. Now come the *gratulationes* [congratulations], now was there rejoicing for men of good will, heartache for the evildoers.

[2] A native-born candidate

B. The Great Elector Welcomes French Huguenot Refugees to Brandenburg

In view of the sympathy which we ought to, and do, feel for our brethren of the reformed evangelical religion in France, who have been driven by persecution to leave their homes and settle in other countries, we, Frederick William, etc., desire by this edict to offer them a free and safe refuge in all our lands and possessions and to specify what rights, privileges, and prerogatives we are graciously minded to grant them. . . .

3. . . . We particularly specify the towns of Stendal, Werben, Rathenow, Brandenburg, and Frankfurt in the electorate of Brandenburg, Magdeburg, Halle, and Calbe in the duchy of Magdeburg, and Königsberg in Prussia, as places where living is cheap and opportunities for trade and other means of support abundant; and we command herewith that when any of the said French people of the reformed evangelical religion make their appearance, they shall be well received in the said towns, and that every opportunity and assistance shall be given them in establishing themselves there. They shall, moreover, be free to establish themselves in any other place in our lands and dominions outside the above-mentioned towns which shall seem to them more convenient for the purposes of their trade or calling.

4. They shall be permitted to bring with them any furniture, merchandise, or other moveable property free of all duties or imposts of any kind whatever. . . .

6. In towns or other places where there are unoccupied or waste lands or properties, we ordain that these shall be given over to our said French brethren of the reformed evangelical religion, free of all and every incumbrance, to hold and enjoy for themselves and their posterity. We further ordain that the necessary materials for the cultivation of these lands shall be furnished them gratis. . . .

7. So soon as any of our said French brethren of the reformed evangelical religion shall have settled themselves in any town or village, they shall be invested, without payment of any kind, with all the rights, benefits, and privileges of citizenship enjoyed or exercised by our subjects who live and were born in said town or village.

8. If any of them shall desire to establish manufactories of cloth, stuffs, hats, or other articles, we will not only bestow on them all the necessary permissions, rights, and privileges, but will further aid

them, so far as is in our power, with money and requisite materials.

9. Those who wish to settle in the country shall be given a certain amount of land to cultivate, shall be furnished with the requisite utensils and materials and encouraged in every way, as has been done in the case of certain families who have come from Switzerland to settle in our country. . . .

11. In every town where our said French brethren in the faith are established, we will support a special preacher and set apart a proper place where they may hold their services in the French language, and with such usages and ceremonies as are customary in the reformed evangelical churches in France.

12. As for the members of the French nobility who have placed themselves under our protection and entered our service, they enjoy the same honors, dignities, and prerogatives as our own subjects of noble birth, and several of them have been given some of the most important offices at our court as well as in our army; and we are graciously disposed to show like favor to all such of the French nobility as may in future present themselves to us.

Given at Potsdam, the 29th of October, 1685.

Frederick William, Elector.

C. Sir William Temple Observes Liberty and Prosperity in the Dutch Republic

In this city of Amsterdam is the famous bank, which is the greatest treasure, either real or imaginary, that is known any where in the world. The place of it is a great vault under the Stadthouse, made strong with all the circumstances of doors and locks, and other appearing cautions of safety, that can be: and it is certain, that whoever is carried to see the bank, shall never fail to find the appearance of a mighty real treasure, in bars of gold and silver, plate, and infinite bags of metals, which are supposed to be all gold and silver, and may be so for aught I know. But, the Burgomasters only having the inspection of this bank, and no man ever taking any particular account of what issues in and out, from age to age, it is impossible to make any calculation, or guess, what proportion the real treasure may hold to the credit of it. Therefore the security of the bank lies not only in the effects that are in it, but in the credit of the whole town or state of Amsterdam, whose stock and revenue is equal to that of some kingdoms; and who are bound to make good all monies that are brought into their bank: the tickets or bills hereof make all the usual great payments, that are made between man and

man in the town; and not only in most other places of the United Provinces, but in many other trading parts of the world. So as this bank is properly a general cash, where every man lodges money, because he esteems it safer, and easier paid in and out, than if it were in his coffers at home; and the bank is so far from paying any interest for what is there brought in, that money in the bank is worth something more in common payments, than what runs current in coin from hand to hand; no other money passing in the bank, but in the species of coin the best known, the most ascertained, and the most generally current in all parts of the Higher as well as the Lower Germany. . . .

It is certain, that, in no town, strength, beauty, and convenience are better provided for, nor with more unlimited expence, than in this, by the magnificence of their public buildings, as the Stadthouse and Arsenals; the number and spaciousness, as well as order and revenues, of their many hospitals; the commodiousness of their canals, running through the chief streets of passage; the mighty strength of their bastions and ramparts; and the neatness, as well as convenience, of their streets, so far as can be compassed in so great a confluence of industrious people; all which could never be achieved without a charge much exceeding what seems proportioned to the revenue of one single town. . . .

[At the beginning of the next chapter Temple notes that the Dutch must import all their raw materials:]. Nor has Holland grown rich by any native commodities, but by force of industry; by improvement and manufacture of all foreign growths; by being the general magazine of Europe, and furnishing all parts with whatever the market wants or invites; and by their seamen being, as they have properly been called, the common carriers of the world.

Since the ground of trade cannot be deduced from havens, or native commodities (as may well be concluded from the survey of Holland, which has the least and the worst; and of Ireland, which has the most and the best, of both) it were not amiss to consider, from what other source it may be more naturally and certainly derived: for, if we talk of industry, we are still as much to seek, what it is that makes people industrious in one country, and idle in another. I conceive the true original and ground of trade to be, great multitude of people crowded into small compass of land, whereby all things necessary to life become dear, and all men, who have possessions, are induced to parsimony; but those, who have none, are forced to industry and labour, or else to want. Bodies, that are vigorous, fall to labour; such, as are not, supply that defect by some sort of inventions or ingenuity. These customs arise first from necessity, but increase by imitation, and grow in time to be habitual in a country; and where-ever they are so, if it lies upon the sea, they naturally break out into trade, both because whatever they want of their own, that is necessary to so many men's lives, must be supplied from abroad; and because, by the multitude of people, and smallness of country, land grows so dear, that the improvement of money that way is inconsiderable, and so turns to sea, where the greatness of the profit makes amends for the venture.

This cannot be better illustrated, than by its contrary, which appears no where more than in Ireland; where, by the largeness and plenty of the food, and scarcity of people, all things necessary to life are so cheap, that an industrious man, by two days labour, may gain enough to feed him the rest of the week; which I take to be very plain ground of the laziness attributed to the people: for men naturally prefer ease before labour, and will not take pains, if they can live idle: though when, by necessity, they have been inured to it, they cannot leave it, being grown a custom necessary to their health, and to their very entertainment: nor perhaps is the change harder, from constant ease to labour, than from constant labour to ease.

This account of the original of trade agrees with the experience of all ages, and with the constitutions of all places, where it has most flourished in the world, as Tyre, Carthage, Athens, Syracuse, Agrigentum, Rhodes, Venice, Holland; and will be so obvious to every man, that knows and considers the situation, the extent, and the nature, of all those countries, that it will need no enlargement upon the comparisons.

By these examples, which are all of commonwealths, and by the decay and dissolution of trade in the six first, when they came to be conquered, or subjected to arbitrary dominions, it might be concluded, that there is something, in that form of government, proper and natural to trade, in a more peculiar manner. But the height it arrived to at Bruges and Antwerp, under their Princes, for four or five descents of the house of Burgundy, and two of Austria, shews, it may thrive under good Princes and legal monarchies, as well as under free States. Under arbitrary and tyrannical power it must of necessity decay and dissolve, because this empties a country of people, whereas the others fill it; this extinguishes industry, whilst men are in doubt of enjoying themselves what they get, or leaving it to their children; the others encourage it, by securing men of both: one fills a country with soldiers, and the other with merchants; who were never known yet to live well

together, because they cannot trust one another. And as trade cannot live with mutual trust among private men; so it cannot grow or thrive, to any great degree, without a confidence both of public and private safety, and consequently a trust in the government, from an opinion of its strength, wisdom, and justice; which must be grounded either upon the personal virtues and qualities of a Prince, or else upon the constitutions and orders of a State.

D. Baruch Spinoza Balances Freedom of Thought and Political Authority

Of the Functions of Supreme Authorities

The right of the supreme authorities is limited by their power; the most important part of that right is, that they are, as it were, the mind of the dominion, whereby all ought to be guided; and accordingly, such authorities alone have the right of deciding what is good, evil, equitable or iniquitous, that is, what must be done or left undone by the subjects severally or collectively. And, accordingly, they have the sole right of laying down laws, and of interpreting the same, whenever their meaning is disputed, and of deciding whether a given case is in conformity with or violation of the laws; and, lastly, of waging war, and of drawing up and offering propositions for peace, or of accepting such when offered.

As all these functions, and also the means required to execute them, are matters which regard the whole body of the dominion, that is, are affairs of state, it follows that affairs of state depend on the direction of him only who holds supreme dominion. And hence it follows that it is the right of the supreme authority alone to judge the deeds of every individual, and demand of him an account of the same; to punish criminals, and decide questions of law between citizens, or appoint jurists acquainted with the existing laws, to administer these matters on its behalf; and, further, to use and order all means to war and peace, as to found and fortify cities, levy soldiers, assign military posts, and order what it would have done, and, with a view to peace, to send and give audience to ambassadors; and, finally, to levy the costs of all this.

Since, then, it is the right of the supreme authority alone to handle public matters, or choose officials to do so, it follows that that subject is a pretender to the dominion, who, without the supreme council's knowledge, enters upon any public matter, although he believe that his design will be to the best interest of the commonwealth.

But it is often asked, whether the supreme authority is bound by laws, and, consequently, whether it can do wrong. Now as the words "law" and "wrong-doing" often refer not merely to the laws of a commonwealth, but also to the general rules which concern all natural things, and especially to the general rules of reason, we cannot, without qualification, say that the commonwealth is bound by no laws, or can do no wrong. For were the commonwealth bound by no laws or rules, which removed, the commonwealth were no commonwealth, we should have to regard it not as a natural thing, but as a chimera. A commonwealth then does wrong, when it does, or suffers to be done, things which may be the cause of its own ruin; and we can say that it then does wrong, in the sense in which philosophers or doctors say that Nature does wrong; and in this sense we can say, that a commonwealth does wrong, when it acts against the dictate of reason. For a commonwealth is most independent when it acts according to the dictate of reason; so far, then, as it acts against reason, it falls itself, or does wrong. And we shall be able more easily to understand this if we reflect that when we say, that a man can do what he will with his own, this authority must be limited not only by the power of the agent, but by the capacity of the object. If, for instance, I say that I can rightfully do what I will with this table, I do not certainly mean that I have the right to make it eat grass. So, too, though we say, that men depend not on themselves, but on the commonwealth, we do not mean, that men lose their human nature and put on another; nor yet that the commonwealth has the right to make men wish for this or that, or (what is just as impossible) regard with honor things which excite ridicule or disgust. But it is implied that there are certain intervening circumstances which supposed, one likewise supposes the reverence and fear of the subjects towards the commonwealth, and which abstracted, one makes abstraction likewise of that fear and reverence, and therewith of the commonwealth itself. The commonwealth, then, to maintain its independence, is bound to preserve the causes of fear and reverence, otherwise it ceases to be a commonwealth. For the person or persons that hold dominion can no more combine with the keeping up of majesty the running with harlots drunk or naked about the streets, or the performances of a stage-player, or the open violation or contempt of laws passed by themselves, than they can combine existence with non-existence. But to proceed to slay and rob subjects, ravish maidens, and the like, turns fear into indignation and the civil state into a state of enmity.

We see, then, in what sense we may say, that a commonwealth is bound by laws and can do wrong. But if by "law" we understand civil law, and by "wrong" that which, by civil law, is forbidden to be done, that is, if these words be taken in their proper sense, we cannot at all say that a commonwealth is bound by laws or can do wrong. For the maxims and motives of fear and reverence which a commonwealth is bound to observe in its own interest, pertain not to civil jurisprudence, but to the law of Nature, since they cannot be vindicated by the civil law, but by the law of war. And a commonwealth is bound by them in no other sense than that in which in the state of Nature a man is bound to take heed that he preserve his independence and be not his own enemy, lest he should destroy himself; and in this taking heed lies not the subjection, but the liberty of human nature. But civil jurisprudence depends on the mere decree of the commonwealth, which is not bound to please any but itself, nor to hold anything to be good or bad, but what it judges to be such for itself. And, accordingly, it has not merely the right to avenge itself, or to lay down and interpret laws, but also to abolish the same, and to pardon any guilty person out of the fullness of its power.

Contracts or laws, whereby the multitude transfers its rights to one council or man, should without doubt be broken, when it is expedient for the general welfare to do so. But to decide this point, whether, that is, it be expedient for the general welfare to break them or not, is within the right of no private person, but of him only who holds dominion; therefore of these laws he who holds dominion remains sole interpreter. Moreover, no private person can by right vindicate these laws, and so they do not really bind him who holds dominion. Notwithstanding, if they are of such a nature that they cannot be broken without at the same time weakening the commonwealth's strength, that is, without at the same time changing to indignation the common fear of most of the citizens, by this very fact the commonwealth is dissolved, and the contract comes to an end; and therefore such contract is vindicated not by the civil law, but by the law of war. And so he who holds dominion is not bound to observe the terms of the contract by any other cause than that, which bids a man in the state of Nature to beware of being his own enemy, lest he should destroy himself.

Of the Best State of a Dominion

We have shown that man is then most independent when he is most led by reason, and, in consequence, that that commonwealth is most powerful and most independent which is founded and guided by reason. But, as the best plan of living, so as to assure to the utmost self-preservation, is that which is framed according to the dictate of reason, therefore it follows that that in every kind is best done, which a man or commonwealth does, so far as he or it is in the highest degree independent. For it is one thing to till a field by right, and another to till it in the best way. One thing, I say, to defend or preserve oneself, and to pass judgment by right, and another in defend or preserve oneself in the best way, and to pass the best judgment; and, consequently, it is one thing to have dominion and care of affairs of state by right, and another to exercise dominion and direct affairs of state in the best way. And so, as we have treated of the right of every commonwealth in general, it is time to treat of the best state of every dominion.

Now the quality of the state of any dominion is easily perceived from the end of the civil state, which end in nothing else but peace and security of life. And therefore that dominion is the best, where men pass their lives in unity, and the laws are kept unbroken. For it is certain, that seditions, wars, and contempt or breach of the laws are not so much to be imputed to the wickedness of the subjects, as to the bad state of a dominion. For men are not born fit for citizenship, but must be made so. Besides, men's natural passions are everywhere the same; and if wickedness more prevails, and more offenses are committed in one commonwealth than in another, it is certain that the former has not enough pursued the end of unity, nor framed its laws with sufficient forethought; and that, therefore, it has failed in making quite good its right as a commonwealth. For a civil state, which has not done away with the causes of seditions, where war is a perpetual object of fear, and where, lastly, the laws are often broken, differs but little from the mere state of Nature, in which every one lives after his own mind at the great risk of his life.

But as the vices and inordinate license and contumacy of subjects must be imputed to the commonwealth, so, on the other hand, their virtue and constant obedience to the laws are to be ascribed in the main to the virtue and perfect right of the commonwealth. And so it is deservedly reckoned to Hannibal as an extraordinary virtue, that in his army there never arose a sedition.

Of a commonwealth, whose subjects are but hindered by terror from taking arms, it should rather be said, that it is free from war, than that it has peace. For peace is not mere absence of war, but is a virtue that springs from force of character: for obedience is the constant will to execute what, by the general decree of the commonwealth, ought to be done. Besides, that commonwealth whose peace depends on the sluggishness of its subjects, that are led about like sheep to learn but slavery, may more properly be called a desert than a commonwealth.

When, then, we call that dominion best, where men pass their lives in unity, I understand a human life, defined not by mere circulation of the blood, and other qualities common to all animals, but above all by reason, the true excellence and life of the mind.

But be it remarked that, by the dominion which I have said is established for this end, I intend that which has been established by a free multitude, not that which is acquired over a multitude by right of war. For a free multitude is guided more by hope than fear; a conquered one, more by fear than by hope: inasmuch as the former aims at making use of life, the latter but at escaping death. The former, I say, aims at living for its own ends, the latter is forced to belong to the conqueror; and so we way that this is enslaved, but that free. And, therefore, the end of a dominion, which one gets by right of war, is to be master, and have rather slaves than subjects. And although between the dominion created by a free multitude, and that gained by right of war, if we regard generally the right of each, we can make no essential distinction; yet their ends, as we have already shown, and further the means to the preservation of each are very different.

But what means a prince, whose sole motive is lust of mastery, should use to establish and maintain his dominion the most ingenious Machiavelli has set forth at large, but with what design one can hardly be sure. If, however, he had some good design, as one should believe of a learned man, it seems to have been to show, with how little foresight many attempt to remove a tyrant, though thereby the causes which make the prince a tyrant can in no wise be removed, but, on the contrary, are so much the more established, as the prince is given more cause to fear, which happens when the multitude has made an example of its prince, and glories in the parricide as in a thing well done. Moreover, he perhaps wished to show how cautious a free multitude should be of entrusting its welfare absolutely to one man, who, unless in his vanity he thinks he can please everybody, must be in daily fear of plots, and so is forced to look chiefly after his own interest, and, as for the multitude, rather to plot against it than consult its good. And I am the more led to this opinion concerning that most far-seeing man, because it is known that he was favorable to liberty, for the maintenance of which he has besides given the most wholesome advice.

Document Set 17.7 References

A. Golden Freedom: The Polish Nobility Elects a King, 1669
Jan Chrzysostom Pasek, *Memoirs of the Polish Baroque,* trans.
Catherine Leach (Berkeley and Los Angeles: University of
California Press, 1976), 210–211, 214–215.

B. The Great Elector Welcomes French Huguenot Refugees to
Brandenburg
Frederick William, Edict, in James Harvey Robinson, ed.,
Readings in European History (Boston: Ginn, 1904),
2:316–317.

C. Sir William Temple Observes Liberty and Prosperity in the
Dutch Republic
The Works of Sir William Temple (London: 1814), 1:119–121,
183–185.

D. Baruch Spinoza Balances Freedom of Thought and Political
Authority
Spinoza, "A Political Treatise," in *The Philosophy of Spinoza
Selected from His Chief Works,* ed. Joseph Ratner (New York:
Modern Library, 1927), 324–332.

Regaining Coherence: Faith and Rationalism at the End of the Seventeenth Century

". . . All coherence gone," lamented John Donne (1572–1631), the English metaphysical poet of the early seventeenth century, thinking of how Copernican astronomy had destroyed the world-picture of European tradition without having established any new basis for understanding God's universe. But by the late seventeenth century, a new sense of coherence began to gain ground.

One manifestation of the intense spiritual uneasiness wrought by the challenge of a new cosmology—with its assumption that the universe must be a terrifying place of almost infinite dimensions, with God's earth a mere speck of cosmic dust whirling through the void—was the tortured conscience of Blaise Pascal, whom we have already met (Set 17.6). His *Pensées* (Thoughts), a jumble of notes found after his death in 1662, are excerpted as Document A. Notice his famous wager on God's existence; how close do you think Pascal came to atheism?

Thomas Hobbes, probably England's greatest philosophical mind in the seventeenth century, took a decidedly pessimistic view of humanity (Document B). Convinced that careful education could temper the passions, John Locke viewed humanity more optimistically (Document C). Does this, too, bespeak a growing faith in reason?

Sir Isaac Newton (1642–1729) formulated the laws of classical physics that framed the modern world-view until supplemented by Einstein's theory of relativity in the early twentieth century. Newton's epochal work at last provided rigorous mathematical confirmation of the Copernican universe and by the early eighteenth century had helped convince educated Europeans that God had indeed created a reasonable, ordered, and comprehensible universe that, figuratively speaking, ran like clockwork. As we shall see in *The Challenge of the West*'s Chapters 18 and 19, Newton's world-view underlay the eighteenth-century Enlightenment. Document D, taken from Newton's masterpiece, *Principia mathematica* (1687), shows the extent to which, for Newton, modern scientific method had already come into focus, leaving behind the scholastic practice of deducing conclusions from theory or authority and substituting a *quantitative* for the traditionally *qualitative* approach to unraveling nature's secrets.

Newton remained a devout theist; indeed, he devoted enormous energy throughout his career to

trying to predict when the world would end by uncovering secret patterns in the numbers given in biblical texts. But did he see theological implications in his laws of physics? Document E, his response to an English theologian named Bentley who tried to draw such conclusions, suggested that Newton was cautiously neutral about the ultimate meaning of his discoveries—an attitude that most modern scientists would heartily endorse.

A. Blaise Pascal Wagers on God's Existence

199. Let us imagine a number of men in chains, and all condemned to death, where some are killed each day in the sight of the others, and those who remain see their own fate in that of their fellows, and wait their turn, looking at each other sorrowfully and without hope. It is an image of the condition of men. . . .

205. When I consider the short duration of my life, swallowed up in the eternity before and after, the little space which I fill, and even can see, engulfed in the infinite immensity of spaces of which I am ignorant, and which know me not, I am frightened, and am astonished at being here rather than there; for there is no reason why here rather than there, why now rather than then. Who has put me here? By whose order and direction have this place and time been allotted to me? *Memoria hospitis unius diei praetereuntis.*

206. The eternal silence of these infinite spaces frightens me. . . .

229. This is what I see and what troubles me. I look on all sides, and I see only darkness everywhere. Nature presents to me nothing which is not matter of doubt and concern. If I saw nothing there which revealed a Divinity, I would come to a negative conclusion; if I saw everywhere the signs of a Creator, I would remain peacefully in faith. But, seeing too much to deny and too little to be sure, I am in a state to be pitied; wherefore I have a hundred times wished that if a God maintains nature, she should testify to

Him unequivocally, and that, if the signs she gives are deceptive, she should suppress them altogether; that she should say everything or nothing, that I might see which cause I ought to follow. Whereas in my present state, ignorant of what I am or of what I ought to do, I know neither my condition nor my duty. My heart inclines wholly to know where is the true good, in order to follow it; nothing would be too dear to me for eternity.

I envy those whom I see living in the faith with such carelessness, and who make such a bad use of a gift of which it seems to me I would make such a different use.

230. It is incomprehensible that God should exist, and it is incomprehensible that He should not exist; that the soul should be joined to the body, and that we should have no soul; that the world should be created, and that it should not be created, etc.; that original sin should be, and that it should not be. . . .

346. Thought constitutes the greatness of man.

347. Man is but a reed, the most feeble thing in nature; but he is a thinking reed. The entire universe need not arm itself to crush him. A vapour, a drop of water suffices to kill him. But, if the universe were to crush him, man would still be more noble than that which killed him, because he knows that he dies and the advantage which the universe has over him; the universe knows nothing of this.

All our dignity consists, then, in thought. By it we must elevate ourselves, and not by space and time which we cannot fill. Let us endeavour, then, to think well; this is the principle of morality.

348. *A thinking reed.*—It is not from space that I must seek my dignity, but from the government of my thought. I shall have no more if I possess worlds. By space the universe encompasses and swallows me up like an atom; by thought I comprehend the world.

. . . If there is a God, He is infinitely incomprehensible, since, having neither parts nor limits, He has no affinity to us. We are then incapable of knowing either what He is or if He is. This being so, who will dare to undertake the decision of the question? Not we, who have no affinity to Him. . . .

. . . But you must wager. It is not optional. You are embarked. Which will you choose then? Let us see. Since you must choose, let us see which interests you least. You have two things to lose, the true and the good; and two things to stake, your reason and your will, your knowledge and your happiness; and your nature has two things to shun, error and misery. Your reason is no more shocked in choosing one rather than the other, since you must of necessity choose. This is one point settled. But your happiness? Let us weigh the gain and the loss in wagering that

God is. Let us estimate these two chances. If you gain, you gain all; if you lose, you lose nothing. Wager, then, without hesitation that He is.— "That is very fine. Yes, I must wager; but I may perhaps wager too much."—Let us see. Since there is equal risk of gain and loss, if you had only to gain two lives, instead of one, you might still wager. But if there were three lives to gain, you would have to play (since you are under the necessity of playing), and you would be imprudent, when you are forced to play, not to chance you life to gain three at a game where there is an equal risk of loss and gain. But there is an eternity of life and happiness. And this being so, if there were an infinity of chances, of which one only would be for you, you would still be right in wagering one to win two, and you would act stupidly, being obliged to play, by refusing to stake one life against three at a game in which out of an infinity of chances there is one for you, if there were an infinity of an infinitely happy life to gain. But there is here an infinity of an infinitely happy life to gain, a chance to gain against a finite number of chances of loss, and what you stake is finite. It is all divided; wherever the infinite is and there is not an infinity of chances of loss against that of gain, there is no time to hesitate, you must give all. And thus, when one is forced to play, he must renounce reason to preserve his life, rather than risk it for infinite gain, as likely to happen as the loss of nothingness.

For it is no use to say it is uncertain if we will gain, and it is certain that we risk, and that the infinite distance between the *certainty* of what is staked and the *uncertainty* of what will be gained, equals the finite good which is certainly staked against the uncertain infinite. It is not so, as every player stakes a certainty to gain an uncertainty, and yet he stakes a finite certainty to gain a finite uncertainty, without transgressing against reason. There is not an infinite distance between the certainty staked and the uncertainty of the gain; that is untrue. In truth, there is an infinity between the certainty of gain and the certainty of loss. But the uncertainty of the gain is proportioned to the certainty of the stake according to the proportion of the chances of gain and loss. Hence it comes that, if there are as many risks on one side as on the other, the course is to play even; and then the certainy of the stake is equal to the uncertainty of the gain, so far is it from fact that there is an infinite distance between them. And so our proposition is of infinite force, when there is the finite to stake in a game where there are equal risks of gain and loss, and the infinite to gain. This is demonstrable: and if men are capable of any truths, this is one.

B. Thomas Hobbes Takes a Bleak View of Humanity's Natural State

... In the nature of man, we find three principal causes of quarrel. First, competition; secondly, diffidence; thirdly, glory.

The first, maketh men invade for gain; the second, for safety; and the third, for reputation. The first use violence, to make themselves masters of other men's persons, wives, children, and cattle; the second, to defend them; the third, for trifles, as a word, a smile, a different opinion, and any other sign of undervalue, either direct in their persons, or by reflection in their kindred, their friends, their nation, their profession, or their name.

Hereby it is manifest, that during the time men live without a common power to keep them all in awe, they are in that condition which is called war; and such a war, as is of every man, against every man. For war, consisteth not in battle only, or the act of fighting; but in a tract of time, wherein the will to contend by battle is sufficiently known: ... so the nature of war, consisteth not in actual fighting; but in the known disposition thereto, during all the time there is no assurance to the contrary. All other time is peace.

Whatsoever therefore is consequent to a time of war, where every man is enemy to every man; the same is consequent to the time, wherein men live without other security, than what their own strength, and their own invention shall furnish them withal. In such condition, there is no place for industry; because the fruit thereof is uncertain; and consequently no culture of the earth; no navigation, nor use of the commodities that may be imported by sea; no commodious building; no instruments of moving, and removing, such things as require much force; no knowledge of the face of the earth; no account of time; no arts; no letters; no society; and which is worst of all, continual fear, and danger of violent death; and the life of man, solitary, poor, nasty, brutish, and short ...

The desires, and other passions of man, are in themselves no sin. No more are the actions, that proceed from those passions, till they know a law that forbids them: which till laws be made they cannot know: nor can any law be made, till they have agreed upon the person that shall make it ...

To this war of every man, against every man, this also is consequent; that nothing can be unjust. The notions of right and wrong, justice and injustice have there no place. Where there is no common power, there is no law; where no law, no injustice. Force, and fraud, are in war the two cardinal virtues. Justice, and injustice are none of the faculties neither of the body, nor mind ... They are qualities, that relate to men in society, not in solitude. It is consequent also to the same condition, that there be no propriety, no dominion, no *mine* and *thine* distinct; but only that to be every man's, that he can get; and for so long, as he can keep it. And thus much for the ill condition, which man by mere nature is actually placed in; though with a possibility to come out of it, consisting partly in the passions, partly in his reason.

The passions that incline men to peace, are fear of death; desire of such things as are necessary to commodious living; and a hope by their industry to obtain them. ...

C. John Locke Views More Hopefully the Natural Human Condition

... The first capacity of human intellect is that the mind is fitted to receive the impressions made on it, either through the senses by outward objects or by its own operations when it reflects on them. This is the first step a man makes towards the discovery of anything and the groundwork whereupon to build all those notions which ever he shall have naturally in this world. All those sublime thoughts which tower above the clouds and reach as high as heaven itself take their rise and footing here; in all that great extent wherein the mind wanders in those remote speculations it may seem to be elevated with, it stirs not one jot beyond those ideas which sense or reflection have offered for its contemplation. ...

D. Sir Isaac Newton Explains the Rules for Reasoning in Natural Science, 1687

Rule I

We are to admit no more causes of natural things than such as are both true and sufficient to explain their appearances.

To this purpose the philosophers say that Nature does nothing in vain, and more is in vain when less will serve; for Nature is pleased with simplicity, and affects not the pomp of superfluous causes.

Rule II

Therefore to the same natural effects we must, as far as possible, assign the same causes.

As to respiration in a man and in a beast; the descent of stones in *Europe* and in *America;* the light of our culinary fire and of the sun; the reflection of light in the earth, and in the planets.

Rule III

The qualities of bodies, which admit neither intensification nor remission of degrees, and which are found to belong to all bodies within the reach of our experiments, are to be esteemed the universal qualities of all bodies whatsoever.

For since the qualities of bodies are only known to us by experiments, we are to hold for universal all such as universally agree with experiments; and such as are not liable to diminution can never be quite taken away. We are certainly not to relinquish the evidence of experiments for the sake of dreams and vain fictions of our own devising; nor are we to recede from the analogy of Nature, which is wont to be simple, and always consonant to itself. We no other way know the extension of bodies than by our senses, nor do these reach it in all bodies; but because we perceive extension in all that are sensible, therefore we ascribe it universally to all others also. That abundance of bodies are hard, we learn by experience; and because the hardness of the whole arises from the hardness of the parts, we therefore justly infer the hardness of the undivided particles not only of the bodies we feel but of all others. That all bodies are impenetrable, we gather not from reason, but from sensation. The bodies which we handle we find impenetrable, and thence conclude impenetrability to be an universal property of all bodies whatsoever. That all bodies are movable, and endowed with certain powers (which we call the inertia) of persevering in their motion, or in their rest, we only infer from the like properties observed in the bodies which we have seen. The extension, hardness, impenetrability, mobility, and inertia of the whole, result form the extension, hardness, impenetrability, mobility, and inertia of the parts; and hence we conclude the least particles of all bodies to be also all extended, and hard and impenetrable, and movable, and endowed with their proper inertia. And this is the foundation of all philosophy. Moreover, that the divided but contiguous particles of bodies may be separated from one another, is matter of observation; and, in the particles that remain undivided, our minds are able to distinguish yet lesser parts, as is mathematically demonstrated. But whether the parts so distinguished, and not yet divided, may, by the powers of Nature, be actually divided and separated from one another, we cannot certainly determine. Yet, had we the proof of but one experiment that any undivided particle, in breaking a hard and solid body, suffered a division, we might by virtue of this rule conclude that the undivided as well as the divided particles may be divided and actually separated to infinity.

Lastly, if it universally appears, by experiments and astronomical observations, that all bodies about the earth gravitate towards the earth, and that in proportion to the quantity of matter which they severally contain; that the moon likewise, according to the quantity of its matter, gravitates towards the earth; that, on the other hand, our sea gravitates towards the moon; and all the planets one towards another; and the comets in like manner towards the sun; we must, in consequence of this rule, universally allow that all bodies whatsoever are endowed with a principle of mutual gravitation. For the argument from the appearances concludes with more force for the universal gravitation of all bodies than for their impenetrability; of which, among those in the celestial regions, we have no experiments, nor any manner of observation. Not that I affirm gravity to be essential to bodies: by their *vis insita* [force of inertia] I mean nothing but their inertia. This is immutable. Their gravity is diminished as they recede from the earth.

Rule IV

In experimental philosophy we are to look upon propositions inferred by general induction from phenomena as accurately or very nearly true, notwithstanding any contrary hypotheses that may be imagined, till such time as other phenomena occur, by which they may either be made more accurate, or liable to exceptions.

This rule we must follow, that the argument of induction may not be evaded by hypotheses.

E. Newton Declines to Derive Wider Implications from His Discoveries

The Hypothesis of deriving the Frame of the World by mechanical Principles from Matter evenly spread through the Heavens, being inconsistent with my System, I had considered it very little before your Letters put me upon it, and therefore trouble you with a Line or two more about it, if this comes not too late for your Use.

In my former I represented that the diurnal Rotations of the Planets could not be derived from Gravity, but required a divine Arm to impress them. And tho' Gravity might give the Planets a Motion of Descent towards the Sun, either directly or with some little Obliquity, yet the transverse Motions by which they revolve in their several Orbs, required the divine Arm to impress them according to the Tangents of their Orbs. I would now add, that the Hypothesis of Matter's being at first evenly spread through the Heavens, is, in my Opinion, inconsistent with the Hypothesis of innate Gravity, without a Supernatural Power to reconcile them, and therefore it infers a Deity. For if there be innate Gravity, it is impossible now for the Matter of the Earth and all the Planets and Stars to fly up from them, and become evenly spread throughout all the Heavens, without a Supernatural Power; and certainly that which can never be hereafter without a Supernatural Power, could never be heretofore without the same Power.

You queried, whether Matter evenly spread throughout a finite space, of some other Figure than spherical, would not in falling down towards a central Body, cause that Body to be of the same Figure with the whole Space, and I answered, yes. But in my Answer it is to be supposed that the Matter descends directly downwards to that Body, and that that Body has no diurnal Rotation.

This, Sir, is all I would add to my former Letters.

Document Set 17.8 References

A. Blaise Pascal Wagers on God's Existence
   Pascal, *Pensées*, trans. W. F. Trotter (New York: Modern Library, 1941), 73–82.

B. Thomas Hobbes Takes a Bleak View of Humanity's Natural State
   Hobbes, *Leviathan*, in Lacey Baldwin Smith and Jean Reeder Smith, eds., *The Past Speaks*, 2d ed. (Lexington, Mass.: D. C. Heath, 1993), 1:377–378.

C. John Locke Views More Hopefully the Natural Human Condition
   Locke, *Essay Concerning Human Understanding*, in Smith and Smith, 1:410–411.

D. Sir Isaac Newton Explains the Rules for Reasoning in Natural Science, 1687
   Newton, *Principia Mathematica*, trans. Andrew Motte (1729), rev. Florian Cajori (Berkeley and Los Angeles: University of California Press, 1947), 398–400.

E. Newton Declines to Derive Wider Implications from His Discoveries
   Isaac Newton's Papers and Letters on Natural Philosophy and Related Documents, I. Bernard Cohen, ed. (Cambridge, Mass.: Harvard University Press, 1978), 310–312.

18

New Societies and the Early Enlightenment, 1690–1740

DOCUMENT SET 18.1
The Rise of the European Colonial Empires

In 1700, according to Document A of this set, the English Parliament severely restricted the import of various kinds of Asian cloth. Besides attesting to the expansion of world-wide trading links by the early eighteenth century, in what ways does this legislation reflect mercantilist concerns? Why import *any* of the banned goods if they were simply to be warehoused under lock and key?

Slave trading and the creation of slave-labor plantation economies were central to the rise of eighteenth-century colonial empires. In Document B a Dutch sea captain explains the details of slaving in West Africa. In Document C a West African named Olaudah Equiano narrates a victim's experience. Converted to Christianity and literate in English, he had the rare good luck eventually to become emancipated and settle in London, where in the late eighteenth century he published his moving description of what it meant to be enslaved.

England's Virginia colony developed full-fledged black slavery by the beginning of the eighteenth century, distinguishing such hereditary bondage from the temporary loss of freedom endured by white indentured servants. A 1705 law (Document D) enacted by the Virginia legislature authorized local sheriffs to hunt down runaway black slaves. The harshest conditions of slavery, however, prevailed on the large plantations of Brazil, the West Indies, and South Carolina, on which sugar was raised and milled for export under conditions that effectively worked the slaves to death. A Swiss traveler in the mid eighteenth century left a description of the French colony of Saint-Domingue

(today Haiti) that makes clear why the colony's labor supply had to be constantly replenished with fresh bodies from Africa (Document E). Such accounts moved a French priest, the Abbé Raynal, in 1780 to call for liberation of the West Indian slaves by any means possible, including violent insurrection (Document F).

Of foreign lands, the French Baron de Montesquieu (1689–1755) in reality knew only England well. He published his *Persian Letters* (Document G) in 1721, knowing practically nothing about Persia, to debunk French customs of which he disapproved by having exotic foreigners express amazement at them. In writing the *Letters* he demonstrated that European ways of life were neither natural nor inevitable. What, in your opinion, is the value of considering Montesquieu's satire in the context of Europe's increasingly aggressive encounter with the wider world?

A. Parliament Imposes Import Controls and Forbids Smuggling, 1700

Whereas it is most evident, that the continuance of the trade to the East Indies, in the same manner and proportions as it hath been for two years last past, must inevitably be to the great detriment of this kingdom, by exhausting the treasure thereof, and melting down the coin, and taking away the labor of the people, whereby very many of the manufacturers of this nation are become excessively burdensome and chargeable to their respective parishes, and others are thereby compelled to seek for employment in foreign parts: for remedy whereof be it enacted . . . That from and after [September 29, 1701] all wrought silk, bengalls,[1] and stuffs mixed with silk or herba, of the manufacture of Persia, China, or East India, and all calicoes, painted, dyed, printed, or stained there, which are or shall be imported into this kingdom, shall not be worn, or otherwise used within this kingdom of England, dominion of Wales, or town of Berwick upon Tweed, but under such limitations as are herein after mentioned and expressed.

II. And for the better effecting the same, be it enacted . . . that all such . . . [goods] which are or shall be imported into this kingdom[2] shall, after entry thereof, be forthwith carried and put into such warehouse or warehouses, as shall be for that purpose approved of by the commissioners of his Majesty's customs for the time being. . . .

III. And for preventing all clandestine importing or bringing into this kingdom . . . any of the aforesaid goods hereby prohibited, or intended to be prohibited, from being worn or used in England; be it further enacted by the authority aforesaid, That if any person or persons, or bodies corporate, from and after [September 29, 1701], shall import or bring into any port of or in this kingdom . . . other than the port of London, any of the aforesaid prohibited goods, or into the port of London, and shall not make due entries of such goods so imported, or brought in, the same shall be, and is hereby adjudged, deemed, accounted, and taken to be clandestine running thereof, and such person or persons, or bodies corporate so offending therein, and their abettors, shall not only forfeit and lose the said goods so clandestinely run, as aforesaid, but also the sum of fine hundred pounds. . . .

IV. And be it further enacted, That if any question or doubt shall arise where the said goods were manufactured, the proof shall lie upon the owner or owners thereof, and not upon the prosecutor; any law, usage, or custom to the contrary notwithstanding.

V. And be it further enacted by the authority aforesaid, That if any action, bill, plaint, suit, or information, shall be commenced, or prosecuted against any person or persons, for any seizure, or other thing to be made or done, in pursuance or in execution of any thing before in this act contained,

such person or persons, so sued in any court whatsoever, may plead the general issue, and give this act and the special matter in evidence, for their excuse or justification. . . .

VI. And for preventing clandestinely carrying out of the said warehouses any of the said goods hereby prohibited, and by this act intended for exportation, as aforesaid; be it further enacted by the authority aforesaid, That the warehouse-keeper or warehouse-keepers shall keep one or more book or books, wherein he or they shall fairly enter or write down an exact, particular, and true account of all and every chest, bale, and number of pieces therein contained, of such of the aforesaid goods only, which shall be brought into, and carried out of, his or their said warehouse or warehouses, and the days and times when the same shall be so brought in and carried out; and shall every six months in the year transmit in writing an exact account thereof, upon oath, to the said commissioners, together with an exact account how much shall be remaining in his or their said warehouse or warehouses respectively; and the said commissioners are hereby impowered and injoined, within one month after the same shall be transmitted to them, as aforesaid, to appoint one or more person or persons to inspect the said book or books, warehouse or warehouses, and examine the said accounts, and to lay a true account of the same before the Parliament. . . .

VIII. Provided always, and be it further enacted, That it shall and may be lawful to and for the proprietor or proprietors of the said goods so lodged in any warehouse or warehouses, as aforesaid, to affix one lock to every such warehouse or warehouses, the key of which shall remain in the custody of the said proprietor or proprietors; and that he or they may view, sort, or deliver the said goods, in order for exportation, as aforesaid, in the presence of the said warehouse-keeper or warehouse-keepers, who is and are hereby obliged, at seasonable times, to give attendance for that purpose. . . .

B. The Dutch Captain Willem Bosman Describes Trading for Slaves in Guinea, c. 1700

Not a few in our country fondly imagine that parents here sell their children, men their wives, and one brother the other. But those who think so, do deceive themselves; for this never happens on any other account but that of necessity, or some great crime; but most of the slaves that are offered to us, are prisoners of war, which are sold by the victors as their booty.

---

[1] A type of cloth imported from Bengal, India
[2] Scotland and Ireland are excluded from the law.

When these slaves come to Fida, they are put in prison all together; and when we treat concerning buying them, they are all brought out together in a large plain; where, by our surgeons, whose province it is, they are thoroughly examined, even to the smallest member, and that naked both men and women, without the least distinction or modesty. . . .

The invalids and the maimed being thrown out, as I have told you, the remainder are numbered, and it is entered who delivered them. In the meanwhile, a burning iron, with the arms or name of the companies, lies in the fire, with which our are marked on the breast. This is done that we may distinguish them from the slaves of the English, French, or others (which are also marked with their mark), and to prevent the Negroes exchanging them for worse, at which they have a good hand. I doubt not but this trade seems very barbarous to you, but since it is followed by mere necessity, it must go on; but we yet take all possible care that they are not burned too hard, especially the women, who are more tender than the men.

We are seldom long detained in the buying of these slaves, because their price is established, the women being one fourth or fifth part cheaper than the men. The disputes which we generally have with the owners of these slaves are, that we will not give them such goods as they ask for them, especially the *boesies* [cowry shells] (as I have told you, the money of this country) of which they are very fond, though we generally make a division on this head, in order to make one part of the goods help off another; because those slaves which are paid for in *boesies,* cost the company one half more than those bought with other goods. . . .

When we have agreed with the owners of the slaves, they are returned to their prison; where, from that time forwards, they are kept at our charge, cost us two pence a day a slave; which serves to subsist them, like our criminals, on bread and water: so that to save charges, we send them on board our ships with the very first opportunity, before which their masters strip them of all they have on their backs; so that they come to us stark-naked, as well women as men: in which condition they are obliged to continue, if the master of the ship is not so charitable (which he commonly is) as to bestow something on them to cover their nakedness.

You would really wonder to see how these slaves live on board; for though their number sometimes amounts to six or seven hundred, yet by the careful management of our masters of ships, they are so [well] regulated, that it seems incredible. And in this particular our nation exceeds all other Europeans; for

as the French, Portuguese, and English slave-ships are always foul and stinking; on the contrary, our are for the most part clean and neat.

The slaves are fed three times a day with indifferent good victuals, and much better than they eat in their own country. Their lodging place is divided into two parts; one of which is appointed for the men, the other for the women, each sex being kept apart. Here they lie as close together as it is possible for them to be crowded. . . .

C. The West African Olaudah Equiano Is Brought Aboard a Slave Ship

The first object which saluted my eyes when I arrived on the coast was the sea, and a slave ship, which was then riding at anchor, and waiting for its cargo. These filled me with astonishment, which was soon converted into terror, which I am yet at a loss to describe nor the then feelings of my mind. When I was carried on board I was immediately handled, and tossed up, to see if I were sound by some of the crew; and I was now persuaded that I had got into a world of bad spirits, and that they were going to kill me. Their complexions too differing so much from ours, their long hair, and the language they spoke, which was very different from any I had ever heard, united to confirm me in this belief. Indeed, such were the horrors of my views and fears at the moment, that, if ten thousand worlds had been my own, I would have parted with them all to have exchanged my condition with that of the meanest slave in my own country. When I looked around the ship too, and saw a large furnace or copper boiling, and a multitude of black people of every description chained together, every one of their countenances expressing dejection and sorrow, I no longer doubted of my fate; and, quite overpowered with horror and anguish, I fell motionless on the deck and fainted. When I recovered a little, I found some black people about me, who, I believed were some of those who brought me on board, and had been receiving their pay; they talked to me in order to cheer me, but all in vain. I asked them if we were not to be eaten by those white men with horrible looks, red faces, and long hair? They told me I was not; and one of the crew brought me a small portion of spirituous liquor in a wine glass; but, being afraid of him, I would not take it out of his hand. One of the blacks therefore took it from him, and gave it to me, and I took a little down my palate, which, instead of reviving me, as they thought it would, threw me into the greatest consternation at the strange feeling it produced, having never tasted any such liquor before. Soon after this, the blacks who brought me on board went off, and left me abandoned to despair. I now saw myself deprived of any chance of returning to my native country, or even the least glimpse of hope of gaining the shore, which I now considered as friendly; and I even wished for my former slavery, in preference to my present situation, which was filled with horrors of every kind, still heightened by my ignorance of what I was to undergo. I was not long suffered to indulge my grief; I was soon put down under the decks, and there I received such a salutation in my nostrils as I had never experienced in my life; so that, with the loathsomeness of the stench, and crying together, I became so sick and low that I was not able to eat, nor had I the least desire to taste any thing. I now wished for the last friend, Death, to relieve me; but soon, to my grief, two of the white men offered me eatables; and, on my refusing to eat, one of them held me fast by the hands, and laid me across, I think, the windlass, and tied my feet, while the other flogged me severely. . . .

D. Virginia Prescribes the Laws of Slavery

It shall be lawful for any person or persons whatsoever, to kill and destroy such slaves by such ways and means as he, she, or they shall think fit, without accusation or impeachment of any crime for the same: And if any slave, that hath run away and lain out as aforesaid, shall be apprehended by the sheriff, or any other person, upon the application of the owner of the said slave, it shall and may be lawful for the county court, to order such punishment to the said slave, either *by dismembering*, or any other way, not touching his life, as they in their discretion shall think fit, for the reclaiming any such incorrigible slave, and terrifying others from the like practices.

E. A Swiss Traveler Observes Plantation Slave Labor in Saint-Domingue, 1785

They were about a hundred men and women of different ages, all occupied in digging ditches in a canefield, the majority of them naked or covered with rags. The sun shone down with full force on their heads. Sweat rolled from all parts of their bodies. Their limbs, weighed down by the heat, fatigued with the weight of their picks and by the resistance of the clayey soil baked hard enough to break their imple-

ments, strained themselves to overcome every obstacle. A mournful silence reigned. Exhaustion was stamped on every face, but the hour of rest had not yet come. The pitiless eye of the Manager patrolled the gang and several foremen armed with long whips moved periodically between them, giving stinging blows to all who, worn out by fatigue, were compelled to take a rest—men or women, young or old.

F. The Abbé Reynal Calls for a Black Liberator of America

If self-interest alone prevails with nations and their masters, there is another power. Nature speaks in louder tones than philosophy or self-interest. Already are there established two colonies of fugitive negroes, whom treaties and power protect from assault. Those lightnings announce the thunder. A courageous chief only is wanted. Where is he, that great man whom Nature owes to her vexed, oppressed and tormented children? Where is he? He will appear, doubt it not; he will come forth and raise the sacred standard of liberty. This venerable signal will gather around him the companions of his misfortune. More impetuous than the torrents, they will everywhere leave the indelible traces of their just resentment. Everywhere people will bless the name of the hero who shall have reestablished the rights of the human race; everywhere will they raise trophies in his honour.

G. Montesquieu's Imaginary Persian Observes European Ways

The King of France is the most powerful ruler in Europe. . . . He has been known to undertake or sustain major wars with no other funds but what he gets from selling honorific titles, and by miracle of human vanity, his troops are paid, his fortresses supplied, and his fleets equipped.

Moreover, this king is a great magician. He exerts authority even over the minds of his subjects; he makes them think what he wants. If there are only a million crowns in the exchequer, and he needs two million, all he has to do is persuade them that one crown is worth two, and they believe it [Montesquieu is referring here to currency debasement]. . . .

You must not be amazed at what I tell you about this prince: there is another magician, stronger than he, who controls his mind as completely as he controls other people's. This magician is called the Pope. He will make the king believe that three are only one [the doctrine of the trinity], or else that the bread one eats is not bread, or that the wine one drinks not wine [the sacrament of communion], and a thousand other things of the same kind.

Document Set 18.1 References

A. Parliament Imposes Import Controls and Forbids Smuggling, 1700
Walter Arnstein, ed., *The Past Speaks*, 2d ed. (Lexington, Mass.: D. C. Heath, 1993), 2:62–63.
B. The Dutch Captain Willem Bosman Describes Trading for Slaves in Guinea, c. 1700
Bosman, *"A New and Accurate Description . . ."* (London: 1721), in David Northrup, ed., *The Atlantic Slave Trade* (Lexington, Mass.: D. C. Heath, 1994) 72–73.
C. The West African Olaudah Equiano Is Brought Aboard a Slave Ship
The Interesting Narrative of the Life of Olaudah Equiano (London: 1793), in Northrup, 77–78.
D. Virginia Prescribes the Laws of Slavery
A. Leon Higginbotham, Jr., *In the Matter of Color: Race and the American Legal Process (The Colonial Period)* (New York: Oxford University Press, 1978), 56.
E. A Swiss Traveler Observes Plantation Slave Labor in Saint-Domingue, 1785
Girod-Chantrans, in C. L. R. James, *The Black Jacobins*, 2d ed. (New York: Vintage Books, 1963), 10.
F. The Abbé Reynal Calls for a Black Liberator of America
Abbé Reynal, *Philosophical and Political History . . .* , in James, 25.
G. Montesquieu's Imaginary Persian Observes European Ways
Montesquieu, *Persian Letters,* trans. C. J. Betts (Harmondsworth, England: Penguin, 1973), 72–73.

DOCUMENT SET 18.2
Modernizing Muscovite Russia

The emergence of Russia as a major political and military power, and as a society westernizing on orders from the tsar, was one of the most significant changes in eighteenth-century Europe. Yet the Russia that Peter the Great (*1685–1725) painfully pushed onto the European stage remained a highly distinctive country, still deeply influenced by its old Muscovite past. For example, serfdom had gained the force of law in the Muscovite Code of Law of 1649 (Document A), more than a generation before Peter's time. Serfdom depended on the power conceded to landlords to prevent their peasants from migrating to escape debts, and it permitted landlords to recover peasants at any time. Determined as well to force the nobility into life-long service, Peter tightened the bonds of serfdom to assure his bureaucrats and army officers a stable income from their estates.

Peter turned the Russian Orthodox church into an arm of the government—for example, by abolishing the office of patriarch and substituting a committee of laymen called the Holy Synod—so that the old church had lost its independence by the late seventeenth century. Popular sentiment was probably on the side of the sectarians called Old Believers, who resisted the liturgical and organizational changes accepted by the official state church. To gauge the Old Believers' state of mind, read Document B, an extract from the autobiography of the Archpriest Avvakum (1620–1682), a passionate opponent of the new order who eventually died at the stake. The struggle between schismatics and the state continued throughout Peter's reign—and for a very long time thereafter—but the supremacy of the state was never in doubt.

Peter's most visible internal reforms featured the creation of a European-looking capital city—St. Petersburg—and a Western-style ruling class. Documents C to F all comment on aspects of this transformation: building St. Petersburg, legislation ordering officials to wear German-style clothes and to shave (a practice repugnant to traditional Russian males, who regarded cutting the beard as an affront to the presumably bewhiskered God the Father), and the advancement of technically skilled foreign recruits like the Scottish general Alexander Gordon.

Using these documents and relying also on the *Challenge of the West,* prepare an analysis of Peter's aims and methods in modernizing Muscovite Russia.

A. The Muscovite Law Code of 1649 Prescribes the Rules of Serfdom

1. Any peasants of the Sovereign and labourers of the crown villages and black volosts [administrative areas] who have fled from the Sovereign's crown villages and from the black volosts . . . are to be brought to the crown villages of the Sovereign and to the black volosts to their old lots according to the registers of inquisition with wives and children and with all their peasant property without term of years.

2. Also should there be any lords holding an estate by inheritance of service who start to petition the Sovereign about their fugitive peasants and labourers and say that their peasants and labourers who have fled from them live in the crown villages of the Sovereign and in black volosts or among the artisans in the artisan quarters of towns or among the musketeers, cossacks or among the gunners, or among any other serving men in the towns . . . [there follows a long list of all the possible places to which fugitives might have fled] then those peasants and labourers in accordance with law and the [right of] search are to be handed over according to the inquisition registers which the officers handed in to the Service Tenure Department.

20. But if any people come to anyone in an estate held by inheritance or service and say that they are free and those people want to live under them as peasants or as labourers, then those people to whom they come are to question them: who are those free people, and where is their birthplace and under whom did they live and where have they come from, and are they not somebody's runaway people, peasants and labourers, and whether they have charters of manumission. And if any say they do not have charters of manumission on them, those holding estates by service and inheritance are to get to know genuinely about such people, are they really free people; and after genuinely getting to know, to take them the same year to be registered. . . .

22. And if any peasants' children deny their fathers and mothers they are to be tortured.

B. The Archpriest Avvakum Defends the Old Believers' Faith and Practices

Thus having remained ten weeks in Pafnutiev in chains, they took me again to Moscow, and in the room of the Cross the bishops held disputation with me. They led me to the Cathedral church, and after the Elevation of the Host they sheared me and the deacon Theodore, and then they cursed us and I cursed them back. And I was heavy at heart for the Mass. And after I had stayed for a time at the patriarchal court, they took us by night to Ugresha,[1] to the monastery of St. Nicholas—and the enemies of God shaved off my beard. . . .

And poor Prince Ivan Vorotynsky came there without the tsar to pray, and he asked to be admitted to my prison cell. But they would not let the hapless man in. I could only, looking through the window, weep over him. My sweet friend feared God, he was Christ's orphan. Christ will not cast him away. Thus always was Christ on our side, and all the boyars were good to us, only the devil was malicious and what could we have done if Christ had left us? They beat my dear Prince Ivan Khovansky with rods and they burnt Isaiah, and the lady Theodosia Morozova they brought to ruin, and they killed her son and tortured her and her sister Eudoxia, beating them with rods; and they parted her from her children and divorced her from her husband, and him they say, Prince Peter Urusov, they married to another wife. But what was there to do? Let them torture those dear ones, they will go to their heavenly bridegroom. In every wise God will cause to pass this troublesome time and will call to himself the bridegroom to his heavenly palace, he the true Sun, our Light and our Hope. . . .

I will tell you yet more of my wanderings when they brought me out of the Pafnutiev Monastery in Moscow and placed me in the guesthouse, and after many wanderings they set me down in the Miracle Monastery, before the patriarchs of all Christendom, and the Russian Nikonites sat there like so many foxes. I spoke of many things in Holy Writ with the patriarchs. God did open my sinful mouth and Christ put them to shame. The last word they spoke to me was this: "Why," said they, "art thou stubborn? The folk of Palestine, Serbia, Albania, the Wallachians, they of Rome and Poland, all these do cross themselves with three fingers, only thou standest out in thine obstinacy and dost cross thyself with two fingers; it is not seemly." And I answered them for Christ thus: "O you teachers of Christendom, Rome

---

[1] A village in the vicinity of Moscow.

fell away long ago and lies prostrate, and the Poles fell in the like ruin with her, being to the end the enemies of the Christian. And among you orthodoxy is of mongrel breed; and no wonder—if by the violence of the Turkish Mohmut you have become impotent, and henceforth it is you who should come to us to learn. By the gift of God among us there is autocracy; till the time of Nikon, the apostate, in our Russia under our pious princes and tsars the Orthodox faith was pure and undefiled, and in the church was no sedition. Nikon, the wolf, together with the devil, ordained that men should cross themselves with three fingers, but our first shepherds made the sign of the cross and blessed men as of old with two fingers, according to the tradition of our holy fathers, Meletina of Antioch, Theodoret, the blessed Bishop of Cyrene, Peter of Damascus and Maxim the Greek; and so too did our own synod of Moscow, at the time of the Tsar Ivan, bid them, putting their fingers together in that wise, make the sign of the cross and give the blessing, as of old the holy fathers Melety and others taught. Then in the time of Ivan [IV] the Tsar, there were the standard-bearers, Gury and Varsanophy, wonder-workers of Kazan, and Phillip the Abbot of Solovki among the Russian saints. And the patriarchs fell to thinking, and our people began to howl like wolf cubs and to belch out words against their fathers saying, "Our Russian holy men were ignorant, and they understood nothing, they are unlearned folk," said they. "How can one trust them? they have no letters." O Holy God! How hast thou suffered so great reviling of thy holy ones? I, miserable one, was bitter in my heart, but I could do nothing. I abused them as hard as I could . . . them, poor things! Woe to the hapless followers of Nikon! They have perished of their own wickedness and their stubbornness of soul!

Then they brought us from the Vorobiev hills to the guest-house of the Andreevsky Monastery to the Savin suburb, and as though we were robbers, followed after us and left us not, nay, even when we relieved nature. It was both pitable and laughable, as though the devil had blinded them.

Then again we were taken to the St. Nickolas Monastery at Ugresha. And there the tsar sent to me the officer Yury Lutokhin, that I might bless him, and we had much converse concerning this and that.

Then again they brought me to Moscow, to the guesthouse of the Nikolsky Monastery, and they demanded of us yet again a statement of the true faith. After that there were sent more than once to me gentlemen of the bedchamber, diverse persons, Artemon and Dementy. And they spake to me in the name of the tsar; "Archpriest!" they said, "I see thy life that it is pure and undefiled and pleasing unto God, I and the tsarina and our children, be entreated of us." The envoy wept as he spake, and for him I weep always. I was exceeding sorry for him. And again he spake: "I beg of thee, hearken to me. Be thou reconciled with the patriarchs." And I said, "Even if God will that I should die, I will not be joined together with apostates. Thou art my tsar, but they, what have they to do with thee? They have lost their tsar and they have come here to gobble you up. I—say I—will not cease to uplift my hands to heaven until God give thee over to me."

The last word I got from the tsar was, "Wherever," said he, "thou shalt be, do not forget us in thy prayers." And I, sinful one, now, as far as I may, pray to God for him.

XV. Banishment to Pustozersk

After scourging my friends, but not me, they banished me to Pustozersk. And I sent from Pustozersk to the tsar two letters, the first not long but the other longer, what I had said to him, that I wrote also in the letters, and also certain signs of God, which had appeared to me in my prison. Who reads will understand. Also a letter written by the deacon was sent to Moscow by me and the brotherhood as a gift to the True Believers.

C. Peter the Great Founds St. Petersburg

In the year 1703 the tsar took the field early, cantoned his troops in the month of March, and about the 20th of April brought the army together; then marched and invested another small but important place called Nyen-Chance, which surrendered on the 14th of May. The commodious situation of this place made the tsar resolve to erect on it a considerable town, with a strong citadel, consisting of six royal bastions, together with good outworks; this he soon put into execution and called it St. Petersburg, which is now esteemed so strong that it will be scarcely possible for the Swedes ever to take it by force.

As he was digesting the scheme of this, his favorite town, which he designed not only for the place of his residence but the principal harbor of his shipping, as having a communication with the sea by the river Nyen; having duly observed and sounded it all over, he found it would be a very natural project to erect a fort in the isle opposite to the island of Ratusary; which for a whole league over to the land is not above four feet deep. This is a most curious work scarcely to be matched. He went about it in winter, in

the month of November, when the ice was so strong that it could bear any weight, causing it to carry materials such as timber, stone, etc. The foundation was thus laid; trees of about thirty feet in length and about fifteen inches thick were taken and joined artfully together into chests ten feet high; these chests were filled with stones of great weight, which sunk down through the sea, and made a very solid foundation, upon which he raised his fort, called Cronstat. . . .

About two hundred fathoms distant from the island Ratusary there is also erected another strong fort, with a tolerable small town, called Cronburgh, where sea officers are commonly lodged. Betwixt Cronstat and Cronburgh is all sea, deep only in the middle, about thirty fathoms broad, so that ships of great burden can pass only one after another. These two forts secure St. Petersburg from any insult by sea, and make it perhaps one of the best and safest harbors in the known world. . . . The work gave no small umbrage to the Swedes. In carrying materials for it there were upwards of eight thousand horses destroyed and near as many men.

D. Peter the Great Orders Certain Subjects to Wear Western Dress and to Shave, 1701–1705

Peter's Decree on Wearing German Clothes, 1701

[All ranks of the service nobility, leading merchants, military personnel, and inhabitants of Moscow and the other towns, except the clergy] are to wear German clothes and hats and footwear and to ride in German saddles; and their wives and children without exception are also so to dress. Henceforth nobody is to wear [traditional] Russian or cossack clothes or to ride in Russian [i.e., Tatar-style] saddles; nor are craftsmen to make such things or to trade in them. And if contrary to this the Great Sovereign's decree some people wear such Russian or cossack clothes and ride in Russian Saddles, the town gatekeepers are to exact a fine from them, [so much] for those on foot and [much more] from those on horseback. Also, craftsmen who make such things and trade in them will be, for their disobedience, severely punished.

Peter's Decree on Shaving, 1705

All courtiers and officials in Moscow and all the other towns, as well as leading merchants and other townsmen, except priests and deacons, must henceforth by this the Great Sovereign's decree shave their beards and mustaches. And whosoever does not wish to do so, but to go about with [traditional Russian] beard and mustache, is to pay a [hefty] fine, according to his rank. . . . And the Department of Land Affairs [in Moscow] is to give [such persons] a badge in receipt, as will the government offices in the other towns, which badges they must wear. And from the peasants a [small] toll is to be exacted every day at the town gates, without which they cannot enter or leave the town. . . .

E. A Frenchman Describes the Enforcement of Peter's Decree on Dress

The tsar labored at the reform of fashions, or, more properly speaking, of dress. Until that time the Russians had always worn long beards, which they cherished and preserved with much care, allowing them to hang down on their bosoms, without even cutting the moustache. With these long beards they wore the hair very short, except the ecclesiastics, who, to distinguish themselves, wore it very long. The tsar, in order to reform that custom, ordered that gentlemen, merchants, and other subjects, except priests and peasants, should each pay a tax of one hundred rubles a year if they wished to keep their beards; the commoners had to pay one kopeck each. Officials were stationed at the gates of the towns to collect that tax, which the Russians regarded as an enormous sin on the part of the tsar and as a thing which tended to the abolition of their religion.

These insinuations, which came from the priests, occasioned the publication of many pamphlets in Moscow, where for that reason alone the tsar was regarded as a tyrant and a pagan; and there were many old Russians who, after having their beards shaved off, saved them preciously, in order to have them placed in their coffins, fearing that they would not be allowed to enter heaven without their beards. As for the young men, they followed the new custom with the more readiness as it made them appear more agreeable to the fair sex.

From the reform in beards we may pass to that of clothes. Their garments, like those of the Orientals, were very long, reaching to the heel. The tsar issued an ordinance abolishing that costume, commanding all the boyars (nobles) and all those who had positions at the court to dress after the French fashion, and likewise to adorn their clothes with gold or silver according to their means.

As for the rest of the people, the following method was employed. A suit of clothes cut accord-

ing to the new fashion was hung at the gate of the city, with a decree of enjoining upon all except peasants to have their clothes made on this model, under penalty of being forced to kneel and have all that part of their garments which fell below the knee cut off, or pay two grives every time they entered the town with clothes in the old style. Since the guards at the gates executed their duty in curtailing the garments in a sportive spirit, the people were amused and readily abandoned their old dress, especially in Moscow and its environs, and in the towns which the tsar oftenest visited.

The dress of the women was changed, too. English hairdressing was substituted for the caps and bonnets hitherto worn: bodices, stays, and skirts, for the former undergarment. . . .

The same ordinance also provided that in the future women, as well as men, should be invited to entertainments, such as weddings, banquets, and the like, where both sexes should mingle in the same hall, as in Holland and England. It was likewise added that these entertainments should conclude with concerts and dances, but that only those should be admitted who were dressed in English costumes. His Majesty set the example in all these changes.

F. The Scottish General Alexander Gordon Describes Peter the Great

This great emperor came in a few years to know to a farthing the amount of all his revenues, as also how they were laid out. He was at little or no expense about his person, and by living rather like a private gentleman than a prince he saved wholly that great expense which other monarchs are at in supporting the grandeur of their courts. It was uneasy for him to appear in majesty, which he seldom or never did, but when absolutely necessary, on such occasions as giving audience to ambassadors or the like; so that he had all the pleasure of a great emperor and at the same time that of a private gentleman.

He was a lover of company, and a man of much humor and pleasantry, exceedingly facetious and of vast natural parts. He had no letters; he could only read and write, but had a great regard for learning and was at much pains to introduce it into the country. He rose early; the morning he gave to business till ten or eleven o'clock at the farthest; all the rest of the day, and a great part of the night, to diversion and pleasure. He took his bottle heartily, so must all the company; for when he was merry himself he loved to see everybody so; though at the same time he could not endure habitual drinkers, for such he thought unfit for business.

When he paid a visit to a friend he would pass almost the whole night, not caring to part with good company till past two o'clock in the morning. He never kept guards about his person. . . . He never could abide ceremony, but loved to be spoke to frankly and without reserve.

Document Set 18.2 References

A. The Muscovite Law Code of 1649 Prescribes the Rules of Serfdom
Code of 1649, in Thomas G. Barnes and Gerald D. Feldman, eds., *Renaissance, Reformation, and Absolutism, 1400–1650* (Berkeley and Los Angeles: University of California Press, 1972), 148–151.

B. The Archpriest Avvakum Defends the Old Believers' Faith and Practices
Avvakum, in Serge A. Zinkovsky, ed. and trans., *Medieval Russia's Epics, Chronicles, and Tales* (New York: E. P. Dutton, 1963), 358–359, 362–364.

C. Peter the Great Founds St. Petersburg
Alexander Gordon, *History*, in James Harvey Robinson, ed., *Readings in European History* (Boston: Ginn, 1904), 2:309.

D. Peter the Great Orders Certain Subjects to Wear Western Dress and to Shave, 1701–1705
Laws of Peter I, in James Cracraft, ed., *Major Problems in the History of Imperial Russia* (Lexington, Mass.: D. C. Heath, 1994), 110–111.

E. A Frenchman Describes the Enforcement of Peter's Decree on Dress
Jean Rousset (Ivan Nestesuranoi), in Robinson, 2:310–311.

F. The Scottish General Alexander Gordon Describes Peter the Great
Gordon, in Robinson, 2:308–309.

DOCUMENT SET 18.3
Before the Industrial Revolution: Life and Death in Eighteenth-Century Europe

Spanning a larger chronology than Chapter 8, the documents of this set illustrate important aspects of life in Europe before industrialization (beginning in the mid-eighteenth century and extending well into the next century) transformed society forever.

Document A serves as a reminder of the way in which middle-class English families ate at the end of the seventeenth century. Such a diet was not only characteristic of well-off urbanites but also of the country gentry and prosperous yeomen and tenant farmers. The contrast with the presumably more fastidious French diet is apparent from the writer's comments. Left unsaid is how such fare differed from that consumed by poor tenants, farm laborers, and continental peasants; typically they made do with a monotonous diet of porridge, bread, beer or ale, and sometimes root vegetables like carrots—and a bit of meat on only the rarest of occasions.

Between 1709 and 1720, Mr. and Mrs. Edmund Williamson, gentry in the English county of Bedfordshire, took the trouble to record their family's births and deaths. The terse entries speak for themselves. But they should be weighed against statistics like those tabulated in Document C. These statistics come from eighteenth-century Norway, where sufficiently careful records were being kept (by church and state officials) to permit modern demographers to measure gross trends. What patterns do you notice? What differences do you see between patterns for farmers (rural people with substantial holdings) and cotters (the rural poor)? What do such statistics suggest to you about marriage, reproduction, and premarital sexuality?

Urban crime, to judge from Document D, was not an easily manageable problem even before our own disorderly times. Henry Fielding (1707–1754), the English novelist who wrote *Tom Jones,* was also a London magistrate who founded the forerunner of the modern police force. His *Inquiries into the Causes of Robbers* repays close reading for his analysis of the demoralization and class conflict that he saw as "root causes" of crime—certainly a modern explanation.

The final two documents of this set provide an interesting contrast. Both are reports by traveling, carefully inquiring Englishmen dating from the late eighteenth century. Arthur Young (1741–1820) was an English agricultural expert whose travels through France are an extremely valuable source for understanding the society of that country on the eve of revolution; his contrasting descriptions (Document E) of prosperous and backward regions are a reminder of the unevenness of change and of the dangers of generalizing too broadly. William Coxe (1747–1828), a clergyman and historian, published in 1783 an account of his extensive travels in Poland (Document F), in which he sympathetically pondered the plight of the desperately poor, enserfed peasantry, utterly dependent on a land-owning nobility that had only recently begun to experiment with freeing their villages from bondage.

A. A French Visitor Comments on the Middle-Class English Diet, About 1695

The English eat a great deal at dinner; they rest a while, and to it again, till they have quite stuffed their paunch. Their supper is moderate: gluttons at noon and abstinent at night. I always heard they were great flesh-eaters, and I found it true. I have known several people in England that never eat any bread, and universally they eat very little: they nibble a few crumbs, while they chew the meat by whole mouthfuls. Generally speaking, the English tables are not delicately served. There are some noblemen that have both French and English cooks, and these eat much after the French manner. But among the middling sort of people . . . they have ten or twelve sorts of common meats, which infallibly take their turns at their tables, and two dishes are their dinners; a pudding, for instance, and a piece of roast beef: another time they will have a piece of boiled beef, and then they salt it some days beforehand, and besiege it with five or six heaps of cabbage, carrots, turnips, or some other herbs or roots, well prepared and salted, and swimming in butter: a leg of roast or boiled mutton, dished up with the same dainties, fowls, pigs, ox-tripes, and tongues, rabbits, pigeons, all well moistened with butter, without larding. Two of these dishes, always served up one after the other, make the usual dinner of a substantial gentleman, or wealthy citizen. When they have boiled meat, there is sometimes one of the company that will have the broth; this is a kind of soup with a little oatmeal in it, and some leaves of thyme or sage, or other such small herbs. They bring up this in as many porringers as there are people that desire it; those that please crumble a little bread into it, and this makes a king of *potage*. The pudding is a dish very difficult to be described, because of the several sorts there are of it; flour, milk, eggs, butter, sugar, suet, marrow, raisins, &c., &c. are the most common ingredients of a pudding. They bake them in an oven, they boil them with meat; they make them fifty several ways. Blessed be he that invented pudding, for it is a manna that hits the palates of all sorts of people; a manna, better than that of the wilderness, because the people are never weary of it. Ah, what an excellent thing is an English pudding! To come in pudding-time, is as much as to say, to come in the most lucky moment in the world. Give an Englishman a pudding, and he shall think it a noble treat in any part of the world. The dessert they never dream of, unless it be a piece of cheese. Fruit is brought only to the tables of the great, and of a small number even among them. It would be unjust to take, in a rigorous sense, all that I have said of these common dishes; for the English eat everything that is produced naturally, as well as any other nation. I say naturally, in opposition to the infinite multitude of your made dishes; for they dress their meat much plainer than we do.

B. Edmund Williamson and His Second Wife Record Births and Deaths, 1709–1720

1709

March 29. My wife fell into labor and a little after 9 in the morning was delivered of a son. Present: aunt Taylor, cousin White, sister Smith, cousin Clarkson, widow Hern, Mrs. Howe, midwife, Mr[s]. Wallis, nurse, Mrs. Holms, Eleanor Hobbs, servants.
April 4. He was baptised by Doctor Battle by the name of John. . . .
[April] 16. The child died about 1 o'clock in the morning.

1711

Sept. 17. My said wife was delivered of a son just before 4 in the morning. Present: Mrs. Thomas Molyneux's lady and maid, Mrs. Mann, midwife, Margaret Williamson, nurse, Susan Nuthall, servant.
Oct. 4. He was baptised by Mr. Trabeck by the name of Talbot after my grandmother's name. Sir John Talbot and John Pulteny esquire were gossips,[1] with my sister Smith godmother. . . .

1713

June 9. About 8 at night my said wife began her labor.
[June] 10. Half an hour after 1 in the morning was brought to bed of a son. Present: Mrs. Molyneux, Mrs. Bisset, Mrs. Mann, midwife, Nurse Williamson, Susan Nuthall and Betty Ginger, servants.
[June] 30. Baptised by Mr. Mompesson of Mansfield by the name of Edmond. . . .

1715

March 7. My said wife was brought to bed of a daughter 10 minutes before 6 in the morning. Present: Mrs. Molyneux, Mrs. Mann, midwife, Nurse Williamson, Mary Evans, Mary Cole and Mary Wheeler, servants.
[March] 29. Was baptised by Dr. Mandivel, chancellor of Lincoln, by the name of Christian.

1716

March 9. My wife was delivered of a daughter at 7 at night. Present: aunt Taylor, Mrs. Molyneux, Mrs. Oliver, Mrs. Mann, midwife, Mary Smith, nurse, Jane Kensey, and Mary Wheeler, servants.
[March] 31. Was baptised by Mr. Widmore, the reader of St. Margaret's, by the name of Elizanna. . . . Registered in St. Margaret's, Westminster, as all the rest were.
April 27. Died, was buried in the new chapel yard in the Broadway.

1718

Jan. 21. [Mrs. Williamson:] I was brought to bed of a son about 2 in the morning, Mrs. Mann, midwife, nurse Chatty, dry-nurse, present; Mrs. Taylor, Mrs. White and Mrs. Molyneux, Jane Beadle; servants: Mary Wells, Jane Griffith, Edmond Kinward. He was baptised by Mr. Widmore, reader of St. Margaret's, Westminster, by the name of Francis. . . .

1719

Feb. 21. [Mrs. Williamson:] I was brought to bed of a son between 6 and 7 in the evening, Mrs. Mann, midwife, nurse Chatty, dry-nurse; present: aunt Taylor, Mrs. Molyneux and Jane Beadle; servants: Rebecca Shippy, Betty Hall and Mathew Dowect.
March 7. He was baptised by Mr. Widmore, reader of St. Margaret's, Westminster, by the name of William. . . .
[N.d.] Died and buried at Hadley.

1720

June. My wife brought to bed of a daughter, but the child did not live a minute.
July 21. My wife died and was buried at Isleworth.
Sept. 9. [Francis] died of the smallpox at Nurse Ward's in Hampstead, and was buried at Hadley.

[1] Godfathers

C. Vital Statistics from Eighteenth-Century Norway

Comparative Demographic Profile, Eastern Norwegian Towns, Eighteenth Century

Median Age at Marriage, First Marriages, Both Sexes.

Men		Farmers	Cottars[2]	Miners/Ironworkers
Ullensaker	1733–1789	29.1	28.6	—
Nesodden	Information lacking			
Bø	1727–1815	26.3	27.6	26.5
Sandsvær	1750–1801	29.2	29.2	27.1
Rendalen	1733–1780	28.2	33.3	—
Women				
Ullensaker	1733–1789	26.0	28.6	—
Nesodden	1710–1800	25.4	31.0	—
Bø	1727–1815	22.8	26.9	24.8
Sandsvær	1750–1780	24.7	27.8	26.3
Rendalen	1733–1780	24.5	30.5	—

Remarriage for Social Groups. Percentage. Both Sexes.

	Men Ullensaker 1733–1789	Bø 1727–1815	Sandsvær 1750–1801	Ullensaker 1790–1839	Women Ullensaker 1733–1789	Bø 1727–1815	Sandsvær 1750–1801	Ullensaker 1790–1839
Farmers	54	69	48	44	37	45	39	33
Cottars	67	70	50	55	39	36	26	25
Miners	—	67	67	—	—	14	31	—
Total	59	69	54	49	38	39	33	30

Permanent Celibacy. Percentage of Age Groups 45–49, 50–54 Not Married, Both sexes.

	Ullensaker	Nesodden	Bø	Sandsvær	Rendalen
Men	5.7	11.4	4.5	6.6	18.5
Women	4.3	10.3	9.8	9.9	10.7

Percentage of Brides That Had First Birth Before or 0–7 Months After the Wedding.

		Farmers	Cottars	Miners/Ironworkers
Ullensaker	1733–1789	26	58	—
Nesodden	1710–1800	29	49	—
Bø	1727–1815	33	47	67
Sandsvær	1750–1801	33	60	53
Rendalen	1733–1780	45	61	—

[2] A cottar is a tenant renting land from a farmer or landlord.

Survivors per 1,000 Liveborn Babies at Different Age. Different Social Groups.

		1 Year	5 Years	10 Years	15 Years
Ullensaker	Farmers	802	637	593	569
	Cottars	724	565	511	470
Bø	Farmers	811	704	676	652
	Cottars	804	705	655	626
	Ironworkers	800	700	663	625
Sandsvær	Farmers	835	737	704	690
	Cottars	833	755	722	710
	Miners	737	600	570	558
Rendalen	Farmers	879	811	755	730
	Cottars	841	732	620	588

Expected Numbers of Years Still to Live at the Age of 0. Both Sexes.

		1727–49	1750–69	1770–89	1790–1815
Bø	Women	38.3	39.2	41.8	41.7
	Men	36.6	37.3	39.7	39.6

Average Number of Children per Family. Different Social Groups and Total.

	Farmers	Cottars	Miners	Total
Ullensaker	4.31	3.51	—	3.91
Nesodden	No information			
Bø	4.90	3.60	—	4.20
Sandsvær	4.44	3.10	3.95	3.86
Rendalen	5.02	2.78	—	3.85

D. Henry Fielding Studies London's Crime Wave, 1751

The great increase of robberies within these few years is an evil which to me appears to deserve some attention; and the rather as it seems (though already become so flagrant) not yet to have arrived to that height of which it is capable, and which it is likely to attain; for diseases in the political, as in the natural body, seldom fail going on to their crisis, especially when nourished and encouraged by faults in the constitution. In fact, I make no doubt, but that the streets of this town, and the roads leading to it, will shortly be impassable without the utmost hazard; nor are we threatened with seeing less dangerous gangs of rogues among us, than those which the Italians call the banditti. . . .

I cannot help thinking it high time to put some stop to the farther progress of such impudent and audacious insults, not only on the properties of the subject, but on the national justice, and on the laws themselves. The means of accomplishing this (the best which suggest themselves to me I shall submit to the public consideration after having first inquired into the causes of the present growth of this evil, and whence we have great reason to apprehend its farther increase. . . .

First then, I think, that the vast torrent of luxury,

which of late years hath poured itself into this nation, hath greatly contributed to produce, among many others, the mischief I here complain of. I am not here to satirize the great, among whom luxury is probably rather a moral than a political evil. But vices no more than diseases will stop with them; for bad habits are as infectious by example, as the plague itself by contact. In free countries, at least, it is a branch of liberty claimed by the people to be as wicked and as profligate as their superiors. Thus while the nobleman will emulate the grandeur of a prince, and the gentleman will aspire to the proper state of the nobleman, the tradesman steps from behind his counter into the vacant place of the gentleman. Nor doth the confusion end here; it reaches the very dregs of the people, who aspiring still to a degree beyond that which belongs to them, and not being able by the fruits of honest labor to support the state which they affect, they disdain the wages to which their industry would entitle them; and abandoning themselves to idleness, the more simple and poor-spirited betake themselves to a state of starving and beggary, while those of more art and courage become thieves, sharpers [swindlers], and robbers. . . .

But the expense of money, and loss of time, with their certain consequences, are not the only evils which attend the luxury of the vulgar; drunkenness is almost inseparably annexed to the pleasures of such people. A vice by no means to be construed as a spiritual offense alone, since so many temporal mischiefs arise from it; amongst which are very frequently robbery, and murder itself. . . .

The drunkenness I here intend [refer to] is that acquired by the strongest intoxicating liquors, and particularly by that poison called *Gin*; which I have great reason to think is the principal sustenance (if it may be so called) of more than a hundred thousand people in this metropolis. Many of these wretches there are who swallow pints of this poison within the twenty-four hours; the dreadful effects of which I have the misfortune every day to see, and to smell too. But I have no need to insist on my own credit, or on that of my informers; the great revenue arising from the tax on this liquor (the consumption of which is almost wholly confined to the lowest order of people) will prove the quantity consumed better than any other evidence.

E. Arthur Young Tours France to Observe Agricultural Practices, 1787

9th. Enter a different country, with the new province of Quercy, which is part of Guienne; not near so

beautiful as Limosin, but, to make amends, it is far better cultivated. Thanks to maize [American corn], which does wonders! Pass Noailles, on the summit of a high hill, the chateau of the Marshal Duke of that name.—Enter a calcareous country, and lose chestnuts at the same time.

In going down to Souillac, there is a prospect that must universally please: it is a bird's-eye view of a delicious little valley sunk deep amongst some very bold hills that enclose it; a margin of wild mountain contrasts the extreme beauty of the level surface below, a scene of cultivation scattered with fine walnut trees; nothing can apparently exceed the exuberant fertility of this spot.

Souillac is a little town in a thriving state, having some rich merchants. They receive staves from the mountains of Auvergne by their river Dordonne, which is navigable eight months in the year; these they export to Bourdeaux and Libourn; also wine, corn, and cattle, and import salt in great quantities. It is not in the power of an English imagination to figure the animals that waited upon us here, at the Chapeau Rouge. Some things that called themselves by the courtesy of Souillac women, but in reality walking dung-hills.—But a neatly dressed clean waiting girl at an inn will be looked for in vain in France.—34 miles.

10th. Cross the Dordonne by a ferry; the boat well contrived for driving in at one end, and out at the other, without the abominable operation, common in England, of beating horses till they leap into them; the price is as great a contrast as the excellence; we paid for an English whisky, a French cabriolet, one saddle-horse, and six persons, no more than 50 sous (2s. Id.) I have paid half-a-crown a wheel in England for execrable ferries, passed over at the hazard of the horses' limbs.—This river runs in a very deep valley between two ridges of high hills: extensive views, all scattered with villages and single houses; an appearance of great population. Chestnuts on a calcareous soil, contrary to the Limosin maxim.

Pass Payrac, and meet many beggars, which we had not done before. All the country, girls and women, are without shoes or stockings; and the ploughmen at their work have neither sabots [wooden shoes] nor feet to their stockings. This is a poverty that strikes at the root of national prosperity; a large consumption among the poor being of more consequence than among the rich: the wealth of a nation lies in its circulation and consumption; and the case of poor people abstaining from the use of manufactures of leather and wool ought to be considered as an evil of the first magnitude. It reminded me of the misery of Ireland. Pass Pont-de-Rodez, and come to high land, whence we enjoyed an immense and singular prospect of ridges, hills, vales, and gentle slopes, rising one beyond another in every direction, with few masses of wood, but many scattered trees. At least forty miles are tolerably distinct to the eye, and without a level acre; the sun, on the point of being set, illumined part of it, and displayed a vast number of villages and scattered farms. The mountains of Auvergne, at the distance of 100 miles, added to the view. Pass by several cottages, exceedingly well built of stone and slate or tiles, yet without any glass to the windows; can a country be likely to thrive where the great object is to spare manufactures? Women picking weeds into their aprons for their cows, another sign of poverty I observed, during the whole way from Calais.—30 miles.

F. An English Traveler Comments on the Consequences of Serfdom in Eighteenth-Century Poland

Peasants belonging to individuals are at the absolute disposal of their master, and have scarcely any positive security, either for their properties or their lives. Until 1768 the Statutes of Poland only exacted a fine from a lord who killed his slave; but in that year a decree passed, that the murder of a peasant was a capital crime; yet, as the law in question requires such an accumulation of evidence as is seldom to be obtained, it has more appearance of protection than the reality.

How deplorable must be the state of that country, when a law of that nature was thought requisite to be enacted, yet is found incapable of being enforced. The generality, indeed, of the Polish nobles are not inclined either to establish or give efficacy to any regulations in favour of the peasants, whom they scarcely consider as entitled to the common rights of humanity. A few nobles, however, of benevolent hearts and enlightened understandings, have acted upon different principles, and have ventured upon the expedient of giving liberty to their vassals. The event has showed this project to be no less judicious than humane, no less friendly to their own interests than to the happiness of their peasants: for it appears that in the districts, in which the new arrangement has been introduced, the population of their villages is considerably increased, and the revenues of their estates augmented in a triple proportion.

The first noble who granted freedom to his peasants was [Andrzej] Zamoiski, formerly great chancellor, who in 1760 enfranchised six villages in the palatinate of Masovia. These villages were, in 1777, visited by the author of the Patriotic Letters [advocating

political reform], from whom I received the following information: on inspecting the parish-registers of births from 1750 to 1760, that is, during the ten years of slavery immediately preceding their enfranchisement, he found the number of births 434; in the first ten years of their freedom, from 1760 to 1770, 620; and from 1770 to the beginning of 1777, 585 births.

By these extracts it appeared that
During the first period there were only 43 births
second period   62 } each year.
third period   77 }

If we suppose an improvement of this sort to take place throughout the kingdom, how great would be the increase of national population!

The revenues of the six villages, since their enfranchisement, have been augmented in a much greater proportion than their population. In their state of vassalage Zamoiski was obliged, according to the custom of Poland, to build cottages and barns for his peasants, and to furnish them with feed, horses, ploughs, and every implement of agriculture; since their attainment of liberty they are become so easy in their circumstances, as to provide themselves with all these necessaries at their own expence; and they likewise cheerfully pay an annual rent, in lieu of the manual labour, which their master formerly exacted from them. By these means the receipts of this particular estate have been nearly tripled.

Document Set 18.3 References

A. A French Visitor Comments on the Middle-Class English Diet, About 1695
M. Missor's Memoirs and Observations in His Travels Over England, trans. J. Ozell (1719), in H. E. S. Fisher and A. R. J. Jurica, eds., Documents in English Economic History (London: G. Bell, 1977), 1:455–456.
B. Edmund Williamson and His Second Wife Record Births and Deaths, 1709–1720
Edmond Williamson, "An Account of the Birth of My Children by My Second Wife (1709–1720)," in Walter Arnstein, ed., The Past Speaks, 2d ed. (Lexington, Mass.: D. C. Heath, 1993), 2:33–34.
C. Vital Statistics from Eighteenth-Century Norway
Bonnie G. Smith, Changing Lives: Women in European History Since 1700 (Lexington, Mass.: D. C. Heath, 1989), 16–17.
D. Henry Fielding Studies London's Crime Wave, 1751
Henry Fielding, An Inquiry into the Causes of the Late Increase of Robbers (1751), in Arnstein, 2:43–44.
E. Arthur Young Tours France to Observe Agricultural Practices, 1787
Arthur Young, Travels in France, in James Harvey Robinson, ed., Readings in European History (Boston: Ginn, 1904),
F. An English Traveler Comments on the Consequences of Serfdom in Eighteenth-Century Poland
William Coxe, Travels into Poland . . . (London, 1785; reprinted New York: Arno Press, 1971), 115–117.

CHAPTER

19

The Promise of a New Order, 1740–1787

DOCUMENT SET 19.1
Fundamental Values of the Enlightenment

There is no better way to begin inquiring into the nature of the Enlightenment than with Document A, the essay "What is Enlightenment" by the German philosopher Immanual Kant (1724–1804). With one of the world's greatest minds, Kant formulated a philosophy of daunting complexity, aimed at refuting both skepticism and mechanistic materialism. His university lectures and essays, such as the one quoted here, are far more accessible to the general reader.

As Chapters 18 and 19 of the *Challenge of the West* explain, an essential quality of the Enlightenment movement was its *sociability,* and all the remaining selections of this set is one way or another comment on this quality. Salons in a few key cities, for example, were indispensable to the flow of ideas among the well-born or well-connected men and women committed to thinking "without prejudice." Document B offers extracts from a single letter (August 7, 1765) of Mme. Marie Therèse Geoffrin, a Parisian hostess who corresponded tirelessly with "enlightened" writers and political leaders all over Europe. One of her most faithful correspondents was the king of Poland, Stanislaw August Poniatawski (*1764–1794), to whom she wrote long letters at least once a month between 1765 and 1777. The letter quoted here suggests the range of her concerns.

The word *philosopher* normally suggests someone of lofty intellect, accustomed to commune with abstract ideas (a definition that would fit Kant perfectly). But in the eighteenth century the French word *philosophe*—which literally translates as "philosopher"—actually meant something quite different. The

essay by Denis Diderot (1713–1774) entitled "The Philosopher," written for that great compendium of Enlightenment ideas, the *Encyclopedia* (of which he was editor), applies this designation to any enlightened person devoted passionately to the life of reason (Document C). Evaluate his portrait of the Enlightenment *philosophe.* Does such an individual strike you as a professional or academic thinker? Notice particularly Diderot's stress on living usefully and sociably within the practical world. An excellent example of a man who lived by such a creed was the Marquis de Condorcet (1773–1794), a mathematician and *Encyclopedia* contributor who eventually took part in the French Revolution. Jailed by the extremist Jacobin party, he escaped the guillotine only by committing suicide. Hiding out before his arrest, Condorcet wrote one of the Enlightenment's great confessions of faith (Document D).

Two contrasting perspectives on Enlightenment sociability appear in the last two documents. The famous portrait painter Elizabeth Vigée-Lebrun (1755–1842), who worked for Marie Antoinette and numerous other wealthy patrons, supported herself by her work but evidently knew how to relax after hours with the most "amiable" and reasonable of Parisian company (Document E). On the other hand, that strange, contorted genius Jean-Jacques Rousseau (1712–1757) hated the sophisticated urban scene. As he relates in his *Confessions* (Document F), he left Paris "forever" in 1756 to live in the countryside, away from the corruptions, temptations, and deceitful habitués of the salon life. In fact, his rural

485

exile was not permanent, and Rousseau had largely himself to blame for his unhappiness. But his account is a useful corrective to other Enlightenment figures' seemingly irrepressible attraction to the world of witty repartée.

A. Immanuel Kant Asks, "What Is Enlightenment?"

Enlightenment is man's release from his self-incurred tutelage. Tutelage is man's inability to make use of his understanding without direction from another. Self-incurred is this tutelage when its cause lies not in lack of reason but in lack of resolution and courage to use it without direction from another. *Sapere aude!*[1] "Have courage to use your own reason!"—that is the motto of enlightenment.

Laziness and cowardice are the reasons why so great a portion of mankind, after nature has long since discharged them from external direction . . . , nevertheless remains under lifelong tutelage, and why it is so easy for others to set themselves up as their guardians. It is so easy not to be of age. If I have a book which understands for me, a pastor who has a conscience for me, a physician who decides my diet, and so forth, I need not trouble myself. I need not think, if I can only pay—others will readily undertake the irksome work for me.

That the step is competence is held to be very dangerous by the far greater portion of mankind (and by the entire fair sex)—quite apart from its being arduous—is seen to by those guardians who have so kindly assumed superintendence over them. After the guardians have first made their domestic cattle dumb and have made sure that these placid creatures will not dare take a single step without the harness of the cart to which they are tethered, the guardians then show them the danger which threatens if they try to go alone. Actually, however, this danger is not so great, for by falling a few times they would finally learn to walk alone. But an example of this failure makes them timid and ordinarily frightens them away from all further trials.

For any single individual to work himself out of the life under tutelage which has become almost his nature is very difficult. He has come to be fond of this state, and he is for the present really incapable of making use of his reason, for no one has ever let him try it out. Statutes and formulas, those mechanical tools of the rational employment or rather misem-

ployment of his natural gifts, are the fetters of an everlasting tutelage. Whoever throws them off makes only an uncertain leap over the narrowest ditch because he is not accustomed to that kind of free motion. Therefore, there are few who have succeeded by their own exercise of mind both in freeing themselves from incompetence and in achieving a steady pace. . . .

B. Mme. Geoffrin Writes to the King of Poland

I am sending to you a banker named Claudel who is returning to Warsaw. He will have with him a printed memoir on a new kind of mill. The more I have learned about it, the more I see that this machine is very well-known. Your Majesty is best advised to invite a miller to come from France; he will know how to set it up and show how to use it, and use of it can spread from there.

Prince Sulkowski [a Polish nobleman] met Mr. Hennin at my salon. Mr. Hennin had been for a long time in Warsaw, and they talked together about Poland. I see with pain that it has a very bad government [Stanislaw was elected king only in 1764]; it seems almost impossible to make it better. . . .

I sent you the catalogue of the diamonds of Madame de Pompadour [King Louis XV's mistress had died recently and her diamonds were auctioned off] . . .

Do not forget, my dear son, to send the memoir on commerce to Mr. Riancourt when he returns. . . .

I cannot report any news yet on your project for paintings; I am very sad about the death of poor Carle Vanloo [a leading French painter who died in July 1765]. It was a horrible loss for the arts.

C. Denis Diderot, in the *Encyclopedia,* Defines "the Philosopher"

There is nothing which costs less to acquire nowadays than the name of *Philosopher*; an obscure and retired life, some outward signs of wisdom, with a little reading, suffice to attach this name to persons who enjoy the honor without meriting it.

Others in whom freedom of thought takes the place of reasoning, regard themselves as the only true philosophers, because they have dared to overturn the consecrated limits placed by religion, and have broken the fetters which faith laid upon their reason. Proud of having gotten rid of the prejudices of edu-

[1] "Dare to know!" was the motto adopted in 1736 by the Society of the Friends of Truth, an important circle in the German Enlightenment.

cation, in the matter of religion, they look upon others with scorn as feeble souls, servile and pusillanimous spirits, who allow themselves to be frightened by the consequences to which irreligion leads, and who, not daring to emerge for an instant from the circle of established verities, nor to proceed along unaccustomed paths, sink to sleep under the yoke of superstition. But one ought to have a more adequate idea of the philosopher, and here is the character which we give him:

Other men make up their minds to act without thinking, nor are they conscious of the causes which move them, not even knowing that such exist. The philosopher, on the contrary, distinguishes the causes to what extent he may, and often anticipates them, and knowingly surrenders himself to them. In this manner he avoids objects that may cause him sensations that are not conducive to his well being or his rational existence, and seeks those which may excite in him affections agreeable with the state in which he finds himself. Reason is in the estimation of the philosopher what grace is to the Christian. Grace determines the Christian's action; reason the philosopher's.

Other men are carried away by their passions, so that the acts which they produce do not proceed from reflection. These are the men who move in darkness; while the philosopher, even in his passions, moves only after reflection. He marches at night, but a torch goes on ahead.

The philosopher forms his principles upon an infinity of individual observations. The people adopt the principle without a thought of the observations which have produced it, believing that the maxim exists, so to speak, of itself; but the philosopher takes the maxim at its source, he examines its origin, he knows its real value, and only makes use of it, if it seems to him satisfactory.

Truth is not for the philosopher a mistress who vitiates his imagination, and whom he believes to find everywhere. He contents himself with being able to discover it wherever he may chance to find it. He does not confound it with its semblance; but takes for true that which is true, for false that which is false, for doubtful that which is doubtful, and for probable that which is only probable. He does more—and this is the great perfection of philosophy; that when he has no real grounds for passing judgment, he knows how to remain undetermined.

The world is full of persons of understanding, even of much understanding, who always pass judgment. They are guessing always, because it is guessing to pass judgment without knowing when one has proper grounds for judgment. They misjudge of the capacity of the human mind; they believe it is possible to know everything, and so they are ashamed not to be prepared to pass judgment, and they imagine that understanding consists in passing judgment. The philosopher believes that it consists in judging well: he is better pleased with himself when he has suspended the faculty of determining, than if he had determined before having acquired proper grounds for his decision. . . .

The philosophic spirit is then a spirit of observation and of exactness, which refers everything to its true principles; but it is not the understanding alone which the philosopher cultivates; he carries further his attention and his labors.

Man is not a monster, made to live only at the bottom of the sea or in the depths of the forest; the very necessities of his life render intercourse with others necessary; and in whatsoever state we find him, his needs and his well-being lead him to live in society. To that reason demands of him that he should know, that he should study and that he should labor to acquire social qualities.

Our philosopher does not believe himself an exile in the world; he does not believe himself in the enemy's country; he wishes to enjoy, like a wise economist, the goods that nature offers him; he wishes to find his pleasure with others; and in order to find it, it is necessary to assist in producing it; so he seeks to harmonize with those with whom chance or his choice has determined he shall live; and he finds at the same time that which suits him: he is an honest man who wishes to please and render himself useful. . . .

D. The Marquis de Condorcet Predicts the March of Progress

The aim of the book that I have undertaken to write, and what it will prove, is that man by using reason and facts will attain perfection. Nature has set no limits to the perfection of the human faculties. The perfectibility of mankind is truly indefinite; and the progress of this perfectibility, henceforth to be free of all hindrances, will last as long as the globe on which nature has placed us. Doubtless his progress will be more or less rapid, but it will never retrograde, at least as long as the globe occupies its present place in the system of the universe; and unless the general laws that govern this system bring to pass a universal cataclysm, or such changes as will prevent man from maintaining his existence, from using his faculties, and from finding his needed resources. . . .

Since the period when alphabetical writing flourished in Greece the history of mankind has been linked to the condition of man of our time in the most enlightened countries of Europe by an unbroken chain of facts and observations. The picture of the march and progress of the human mind is now revealed as being truly historical. Philosophy no longer has to guess, no longer has to advance hypothetical theories. It now suffices to assemble and to arrange the facts, and to show the truths that arise from their connection and from their totality. . . .

If man can predict with almost complete certainty those phenomena whose laws he knows; and if, when he does not know these laws, he can, on the basis of his experience in the past, predict future events with assurance why then should it be regarded as chimerical to trace with a fair degree of accuracy the picture of man's future on the basis of his history? The sole foundations for belief in the natural sciences is the principle that universal laws, known or unknown, which regulate the universe are necessary and constant. Why then should this principle be less true for the development of the intellectual and moral faculties of man than it is for the other operations of nature? Finally, since beliefs, based on past experience under like conditions, constitute the only rule according to which the wisest men act, why then forbid the philosopher to support his beliefs on the same foundations, as long as he does not attribute to them a certainty not warranted by the number, the constancy, and the accuracy of his observations. . . .

E. The Painter Elisabeth Vigée-Lebrun Describes an Artist's Life and Pleasures

The business of the day over, twelve or fifteen amiable people would gather to finish their evening in their hostess's home. The relaxed and easy gaiety that reigned over these light evening meals gave them a charm that formal dinners could never have. A sort of confidence and intimacy spread among the guests; and because well-bred people can always eliminate stiffness, it was in these suppers that Parisian high society showed itself superior to the rest of Europe.

At my house, for instance, we gathered about nine o'clock. We never talked of politics, but of literature or recounted the story of the day. Sometimes we amused ourselves with charades and sometimes [authors] read us a few of their verses. At ten we seated ourselves; my suppers were the simplest, composed always of a fowl, a fish, vegetables, and salad; but it mattered little, we were gay, amiable, hours passed as if they were minutes, and at about midnight, everyone departed.

One evening my brother was reading me the *Travels of Anacharis.* When he got to the place where a description of a Greek dinner appears, it explained how to make several sauces. I called my cook and we decided to have such and such a sauce for the fowl and another for the eels. As I was expecting very pretty women [for dinner], I decided to dress all of us in Greek fashions. My studio, full of everything necessary to drape my models, would furnish enough clothes, and the Count de Parois also had a superb collection of Etruscan vases. The charming Madame de Bonneuil arrived, then Madame Vigée, my sister-in-law, and soon both had been transformed into veritable Athenians. Lebrun-Pindar entered; we removed his hair powder, and I put a crown of laurel on his head. I also found costumes for Monsieur de Riviere, Guinguene, and Chaudet, the famous sculptor.

Besides the two dishes that I have already mentioned, we ate a cake of honey and raisins, and two plates of vegetables. We also drank a bottle of old wine from Cyprus that someone had given me as a guest. We spent a long time at dinner where Lebrun recited us several odes of Anacreon that he translated himself. I don't believe I ever had a more amusing evening.

F. Jean-Jacques Rousseau Leaves Paris, "Never to Live in a City Again," 1756

It was on the 9th of April, 1756, that I left Paris, never to live in a city again, for I do not reckon the brief periods for which I afterwards stayed in Paris, London and other cities, only when passing through them, or against my will. Madame d'Epinay took us all three in her carriage; her farmer took charge of my small amount of luggage, and I was installed in my new home the same day. I found my little retreat arranged and furnished simply, but neatly and even tastefully. The hand which had attended to these arrangements conferred upon them in my eyes an inestimable value, and I found it delightful to be the guest of my friend, in a house of my own choice, which she had built on purpose for me. Although it was cold, and there was still some snow on the ground, the earth was beginning to show signs of vegetation: violets and primroses could be seen, the buds were beginning to open on the trees, and the night of my arrival was marked by the first song of the nightingale, which made itself heard nearly under my window, in a wood adjoining the house. When I awoke, after a light sleep, forgetting my change of abode, I thought that I was still in the Rue de Grenelle, when suddenly this warbling made me start, and in my delight I exclaimed, "At last all my wishes are fulfilled!" My first thought was to abandon myself to the impression caused by the rural objects by which I was surrounded. Instead of beginning to set things in order in my new abode, I began by making arrangements for my walks; there was not a path, not a copse, not a thicket, not a corner round my dwelling, which I had not explored by the following day. The more I examined this charming retreat, the more I felt that it was made for me. This spot, solitary rather than wild, transported me in spirit to the end of the world. It possessed those impressive beauties which are rarely seen in the neighbourhood of cities; no one, who had suddenly been transported there, would have believed that he was only four leagues from Paris. . . .

. . . Although for some years I had visited the country pretty frequently, I had rarely enjoyed it; and those excursions, always taken in the company of pretentious persons, and always spoiled by a feeling of restraint, only whetted my appetite for country pleasures, and, the nearer the glimpse I had of them, the more I felt the want of them. I was so weary of salons, waterfalls, groves, flower-gardens, and their still more wearisome exhibitors; I was so tired of stitching, pianos, sorting wool, making bows, foolish witticisms, insipid affectations, trifling story-tellers, and big suppers that, when I caught a glimpse of a simple thorn-bush, a hedge, a barn, or a meadow; when I inhaled, while passing through a hamlet, the fragrance of a savoury chervil omelette; when I heard from a distance the rustic refrain of the *bisquières* [female goatherds], I wished all rouge, furbelows, and ambergris [perfume] at the devil; and, regretting the good-wife's homely dinner and the native wine, I should have been delighted to slap the face of M. le chef and M. le maître, who forced me to dine at my usual supper-hour, and to sup at a time when I am usually asleep; above all, I should have liked to slap MM. les laquais [the servants], who devoured with their eyes the morsels I ate, and, if I was not prepared to die of thirst, sold me their master's adulterated wine at ten times the price I should have paid for wine of a better quality at an inn.

Behold me, then, at last, in my own house, in a pleasant and solitary retreat, able to spend my days in the independent, even, and peaceful life, for which I felt that I was born. Before describing the effect of this situation, so new to me, upon my heart, it behoves me to recapitulate its secret inclinations, that the progress of these new modifications may be better followed up in its origin. . . .

Document Set 19.1 References

A. Immanuel Kant Asks, "What Is Enlightenment?"
   L. W. Beck, ed. and trans., *Immanuel Kant on History* (Indianapolis: Bobbs-Merrill, 1963), 3–4.

B. Mme. Geoffrin Writes to the King of Poland
   Charles de Mouy, ed., *Correspondance inédite due roi Stanislaw-Auguste Poniatowski et de Madam Geoffrin (1764–1777)* (Geneva: Satine, 1970, reprint of 1875 edition, 164–168. Translated by Lynn Hunt.

C. Denis Diderot, in the *Encyclopedia*, Defines "the Philosopher"
   Diderot, *Encyclopedia*, in *Translations and Reprints from the Original Sources of European History* (Philadelphia: University of Pennsylvania Press, 1898), 6/3:20–22.

D. The Marquis de Condorcet Predicts the March of Progress
   Condorcet, *Esquisse d'un Tableau historique des progrès de l'esprit humain,* in J. Salwyn Schapiro, ed., *Liberalism: Its Meaning and History* (Princeton, N.J.: D. Van Nonstrand, 1958), 103–104.

E. The Painter Elisabeth Vigée-Lebrun Describes an Artist's Life and Pleasures
   Elisabeth Vigée-Lebrun, *Souvenirs* (Paris: Des Femmes, 1984), 1:85–88, in Bonnie Smith, *Changing Lives: Women in European History Since 1700* (Lexington Mass.: D. C. Heath, 1989), 31.

F. Jean-Jacques Rousseau Leaves Paris, "Never to Live in a City Again," 1756
   Rousseau, *Confessions* (London: Dent, 1904), 2:54, 62–63.

DOCUMENT SET 19.2
Breaking with Traditional Religion

"Crush the infamous thing" was the battle cry of Voltaire (1694–1778), the archetypal man of the Enlightenment. The target of his wrath was institutional religion, which backed its ancient dogmas with the power to destroy dissenters' lives. He professed a religion devoid—so he claimed—of "superstition" and revelation, but instead envisioned a benevolent "divine clockmaker" who had set the universe in motion according to Newton's reasonable laws. Such a faith was called deism, and from its lofty heights Voltaire pleaded that reasonable people of all religious backgrounds could agree on simple truths and practice universal toleration (Document A). A similar hope and faith, together with a passionate cry against "blind religious zeal," breathes from every pore of Diderot's *Encyclopedia* article "Fanaticism," (Document B).

The minority touched by the Enlightenment faced two major untraditional choices. The German-born Baron d'Holbach (1723–1789) broke entirely with Christianity, insisting that science had proved that human beings were simply living machines (Document C). Rousseau followed the more mainstream Enlightenment impulse to dissolve Christianity into deism, combined with his own brand of nature worship (Document D).

The vast majority of Europeans continued to adhere to traditional religion, though, as we shall see, eighteenth-century cultural currents had their effects here, too. In Great Britain and North America the rapid emergence of Methodism at mid-century testified to the hunger ordinary people felt for an emotionally satisfying form of Christianity. John Wesley, the father of Methodism, was not an Enlightenment figure, but in examining Document E, look for evidence of concerns that he shared with the *philosophes*. Among the Jews of Poland-Lithuania, the eighteenth century saw the rapid rise of a movement called Hasidism, which interpreted Judaic law in a less formal, more joyful sense. Document F, written by the twentieth-century Jewish philosopher Martin Buber, recreates oral-tradition tales relating to the Baal Shem Tov, the rabbi and faith-healer most influential in revitalizing eastern European Judaism at the grass roots. Remember, however, that Judaism itself was the target of sophisticated scorn by Enlightenment intellectuals like Voltaire (Document G), for whom the Jews' religion was simply one more archaic "superstition."

A. Voltaire Pleads for Toleration

One does not need great art and skilful eloquence to prove that Christians ought to tolerate each other—nay, even to regard all men as brothers. Why, you say, is the Turk, the Chinese, or the Jew my brother? Assuredly; are we not all children of the same father, creatures of the same God?

But these people despise us and treat us as idolaters. Very well; I will tell them that they are quite wrong. It seems to me that I might astonish, at least, the stubborn pride of a Mohammedan or a Buddhist priest if I spoke to them somewhat as follows:

This little globe, which is but a point, travels in space like many other globes; we are lost in the immensity. Man, about five feet high, is certainly a small thing in the universe. One of these imperceptible beings says to some of his neighbours, in Arabia or South Africa: "Listen to me, for the God of all these worlds has enlightened me. There are nine hundred million little ants like us on the earth, but my ant-hole alone is dear to God. All the others are eternally reprobated by him. Mine alone will be happy."

They would then interrupt me, and ask who was the fool that talked all this nonsense. I should be obliged to tell them that it was themselves. I would then try to appease them, which would be difficult....

B. Diderot Excoriates "Fanaticism"

FANATICISM, noun (philosophy) is blind and passionate zeal born of superstitious opinions, causing people to commit ridiculous, unjust, and cruel actions, not only without any shame or remorse, but even with a kind of joy and comfort. *Fanaticism*, therefore, is only superstition put into practice.... The particular causes of *fanaticism* are to be found:

1) In the nature of dogmas. If they are contrary to reason, they overthrow sound judgment and subject everything to imagination whose abuses are the greatest of all evils.... Obscure dogmas produce a multitude of interpretations thereby creating the dissension of the sects. Truth does not make any *fanatics*. It is so clear that it hardly allows any contradiction; it so penetrates the mind that the most demented people cannot diminish its enjoyment....

5) In the intolerance of one religion is regard to others, or of one sect among several of the same reli-

gion, because all hands join forces against the common enemy. . . .

6) In persecution, which arises essentially from intolerance. . . .

Fanaticism has done much more harm to the world than impiety. What do impious people claim? To free themselves of a yoke, while *fanatics* want to extend their chains over all the earth. Infernal zealomania! Have we ever seen sects of unbelievers gather into mobs and march with weapons against the Divinity? Their souls are too weak to spill human blood.

C. Baron d'Holbach Denounces Intellectual Conservatism and Questions the Idea of the Soul

Man's ignorance has endured so long, he has taken such slow, irresolute steps to ameliorate his condition, only because he has neglected to study nature, to scrutinize her laws, to search out her resources, to discover her properties. His sluggishness finds its account in permitting himself to be guided by precedent, rather than to follow experience which demands activity; to be led by routine, rather than by his reason which exacts reflection. Hence may be traced the aversion man betrays for everything that swerves from these rules to which he has been accustomed; hence his stupid, his scrupulous respect for antiquity, for the most silly, the most absurd institutions of his fathers; hence those fears that seize him, when the most advantageous changes are proposed to him, or the most probable attempts are made to better his condition. He dreads to examine, because he has been taught to hold it a profanation of something immediately connected with his welfare; he credulously believes the interested advice, and spurns at those who wish to show him the danger of the road he is traveling.

This is the reason why nations linger on in the most scandalous lethargy, groaning under abuses transmitted from century to century, trembling at the very idea of that which alone can remedy their misfortunes. . . .

The more man reflects, the more he will be convinced that the soul, very far from being distinguished from the body, is only the body itself considered relatively to some of its functions, or to some of the modes of existing or acting of which it is susceptible, whilst it enjoys life. Thus, the soul in man is considered relatively to the faculty he has of feeling, of thinking, and of acting in a mode resulting from his peculiar nature; that is to say, from his properties,

from his particular organization, from the modifications, whether durable or transitory, which the beings who act upon him cause his machine to undergo. . . .

An organized being may be compared to a clock, which, once broken, is no longer suitable to the use for which it was designed. To say that the soul shall feel, shall think, shall enjoy, shall suffer after the death of the body, is to pretend that a clock, shivered into a thousand pieces, will continue to strike the hour and have the faculty of marking the progress of time. Those who say that the soul of man is able to subsist notwithstanding the destruction of the body, evidently support the position that the modification of a body will be enabled to conserve itself after the subject is destroyed; but this is completely absurd.

D. Rousseau Advocates a Deistic Religion of Feeling

Christianity is a purely spiritual religion, occupied solely with heavenly things; the country of a Christian is not of this world. He does his duty, it is true, but he does it with a profound indifference as to the good or ill success of his efforts. Provided he has nothing to reproach himself with, it matters little to him whether things go well or ill here below. If the state is flourishing, he scarcely dares enjoy the public felicity; he fears to become proud of the glory of his country. If the state degenerates, he blesses the hand of God which lies heavy upon his people. . . .

Should the depository of this [political] power abuse it, he regards this abuse as the rod with which God punishes his children. People would have scruples about driving out the usurper: it would be necessary to disturb the public repose, to use violence, to shed blood; all this accords ill with the gentleness of the Christian, and, after all, what matters it whether one is a slave or free in this vale of misery? The essential thing is to go to paradise, and resignation is but one more means to accomplish it.

Should some foreign war supervene, the citizens march to combat without difficulty. None among them think of flying; they do their duty, but without passion for victory; they know better how to die than to win. Whether they are victors or vanquished, what matters it? Does not Providence know better than they what they need? . . .

But I am in error in speaking of a Christian republic; each of these words excludes the other. Christianity preaches only servitude and dependence. Its spirit is too favorable to tyranny not to be taken advantage of by it. Christians are made to be slaves: they know it and do not care; this short life has too little value in their eyes. . . .

There is, however, a profession of faith purely civil, of which it is the sovereign's [i.e. the people's] duty to decide upon the articles, not precisely as dogmas of religion, but as sentiments of sociality without which it is impossible to be a good citizen or a faithful subject. Without being able to oblige any one to believe them, the sovereign can banish from the state whoever does not believe them; the sovereign should banish him, not as impious, but as unsocial, as incapable of loving law and justice sincerely, and of sacrificing at need his life to his duty. If any one, having publicly acknowledged these dogmas, conducts himself as if he did not acknowledge them, he should be punished with death; he has committed the greatest of crimes,—he has lied before the law.

The dogmas of civil religion should be simple, few in number, announced with precision, without explanation or commentary. The existence of a powerful, intelligent, benevolent, prescient, and provident Divinity, the life to come, the happiness of the just, the punishment of the wicked, the sacredness of the social contract and the law,—these are the positive dogmas.

As to the negative dogmas, I limit them to one,—intolerance: it enters into the religions which we have excluded. Those who make a distinction between civil intolerance and theological intolerance deceive themselves, to my mind. These two intolerances are inseparable. It is impossible to live in peace with people whom one believes to be damned, to love them is to hate God, who punishes them; they must be redeemed or else tortured. Wherever theological intolerance is admitted, it must have some civil effects; and as soon as it has them the sovereign is no more a sovereign even in temporal matters. From that time priests are the true masters; kings are but their officers.

E. John Wesley Explains Methodism

1. About ten years ago my brother [Charles Wesley] and I were desired to preach in many parts of London. We had no view therein but, so far as we were able (and we knew God could work by whomsoever it pleased Him) to convince those who would hear, what true Christianity was, and to persuade them to embrace it.

2. The points we chiefly insisted upon were four: First, that orthodoxy or right opinions is, at best, but a very slender part of religion, if it can be allowed to be any part of it at all; that neither does religion consist in negatives, in bare harmlessness of any kind, nor merely in externals in doing good or using the means of grace, in works of piety (so called) or of charity: that it is nothing short of or different from the mind that was in Christ, the image of God stamped upon the heart, inward righteousness attended with the peace of God and joy in the Holy Ghost.

Secondly, that the only way under heaven to this religion is to repent and believe the gospel, of (as the apostle words it) repentance toward God and faith in our Lord Jesus Christ.

Thirdly, that by this faith, he that worketh not, but believeth in Him that justifieth the ungodly, is justified freely by His grace, through the redemption which is in Jesus Christ.

And lastly, that being justified by faith we taste of the heaven to which were are going; we are holy and happy; we tread down sin and fear, and sit in heavenly places with Christ Jesus. . . .

4. Immediately . . . [those who accepted this new way] were surrounded with difficulties. All the world rose up against them; neighbors, strangers, acquaintances, relations, friends began to cry out amain, "Be not righteous overmuch: why shouldst thou destroy thyself? Let not much religion make thee mad.". . .

You are supposed to have the faith that "overcometh the world." To you, therefore, it is not grievous:

I. Carefully to abstain from doing evil; in particular:
1. Neither to buy nor sell anything at all on the Lord's day.
2. To taste no spiritous liquor, no dram of any kind, unless prescribed by a physician.
3. To be at a word [to be honest] both in buying and selling.
4. To pawn nothing, no, not to save life.
5. Not to mention the fault of any behind his back, and to stop those short that do.
6. To wear no needless ornaments, such as rings, earrings, necklaces, lace, ruffles.
7. To use no needless self-indulgence, such as taking snuff or tobacco, unless prescribed by a physician.

II. Zealously to maintain good works; in particular:

1. To give alms of such things as you possess, and that to the uttermost of your power.
2. To reprove all that sin in your sight, and that in love and meekness of wisdom.
3. To be patterns of diligence and frugality, of self-denial, and taking up the cross daily.

III. Constantly to attend on all the ordinances of God; in particular:

1. To be at church and at the Lord's table every week, and at every public meeting of the bands.

2. To attend the ministry of the word every morning unless distance, business or sickness prevent.

3. To use private prayer every day; and family prayer, if you are at the head of a family.

4. To read the scriptures, and meditate therein, at every vacant hour. And

5. To observe, as days of fasting or abstinence, all Fridays in the year. . . .

F. Hasidism Spreads Through East European Jewry: Tales of the Baal Shem

The disciples of the Baal Shem heard that a certain man had a great reputation for learning. Some of them wanted to go to him and find out what he had to teach. The master gave them permission to go, but first they asked him: "And how shall we be able to tell whether he is a true zaddik?"

The Baal Shem replied. "Ask him to advise you what to do to keep unholy thoughts from disturbing you in your prayers and studies. If he gives you advice, then you will know that he belongs to those who are of no account. For this is the service of men in the world to the very hour of their death; to struggle time after time with the extraneous, and time after time to uplift and fit it into the nature of the Divine Name." . . .

The Sermon

Once they asked the Baal Shem to preach after the prayer of the congregation. He began his sermon, but in the middle of it he was shaken with a fit of trembling, such as sometimes seized him while he was praying. He broke off and said: "O, Lord of the world, you know that I am not speaking to increase my own reputation . . . " Here he stopped again, and then the words rushed from his lips. "Much have I learned, and much have I been able to do, and there is no one to whom I could reveal it." And he said nothing further.

Like Locusts

Rabbi Mikhal of Zlotchov told:

"Once when we were on a journey with our teacher, Rabbi Israel Baal Shem Tov, the Light of the Seven Days, he went into the woods to say the Afternoon Prayer. Suddenly we saw him strike his head against a tree and cry aloud. Later we asked him about it. He said: "While I plunged into the holy spirit I saw that in the generations which precede the coming of the Messiah, the rabbis of the hasidim will multiply like locusts, and it will be they who delay

redemption, for they will bring about the separation of hearts and groundless hatred."

Before the Coming of the Messiah

The Baal Shem said:

"Before the coming of the Messiah there will be great abundance in the world. The Jews will get rich. They will become accustomed to running their houses in the grand style and moderation will be cast to the winds. Then the lean years will come; want and a meagre livelihood, and the world will be full of poverty. The Jews will not be able to satisfy their needs, grown beyond rhyme or reason. And then the labor which will bring forth the Messiah, will begin.". . . After prayer, the Baal Shem asked him: "Did you go to the bath yesterday?" He answered "No." Then the Baal Shem said: "It has already come to pass, and after this there is nothing more."

G. Voltaire Sneers at Judaism

. . . the Hebrews have ever been vagrants, or robbers, or slaves, or seditious. They are still vagabonds upon the earth, and abhorred by men, yet affirming that heaven and earth and all mankind were created for them alone. . . .

You ask, what was the philosophy of the Hebrews? The answer will be a very short one—they had none. Their legislator himself does not anywhere speak expressly of the immortality of the soul, nor of the rewards of another life. Josephus and Philo believe the soul to be material; their doctors admitted corporeal angels. . . . The Jews, in the latter times of their sojourn at Jerusalem, were scrupulously attached to nothing but the ceremonials of their law. The man who had eaten pudding or rabbit would have been stoned; while he who denied the immortality of the soul might be high-priest. . . .

Their law must appear, to every polished people, as singular as their conduct; if it were not divine, it would seem to be the law of savages beginning to assemble themselves into a nation; and being divine, one cannot understand how it is that it has not existed from all ages, for them, and for all men. . . .

In this law it is forbidden to eat eels, because they have no scales; and hares, because they chew the cud, and have cloven feet. Apparently, the Jews had hares different from ours. The griffin is unclean, and four-footed birds are unclean, which animals are somewhat rare. Whoever touches a mouse or a mole is unclean. The women are forbidden to lie with horses or asses. The Jewish women must have been subject to this sort of gallantry. The men are forbidden to offer up their seed to Moloch; and here the term seed is not metaphorical. It seems that it was customary, in the deserts of Arabia, to offer up this singular present to the gods; as it is said to be used in Cochin and some other countries of India, for the girls to yield their virginity to an iron Priapus in a temple. These two ceremonies prove that mankind is capable of everything. The Kaffirs, who deprive themselves of one testicle, are a still more ridiculous example of the extravagance of superstition.

Another law of the Jews, equally strange, is their proof of adultery. A woman accused by her husband must be presented to the priests, and she is made to drink of the waters of jealousy, mixed with wormwood and dust. If she is innocent, the water makes her more beautiful; if she is guilty, her eyes start from her head, her belly swells, and she bursts before the Lord. . . .

It is true that, considering the carnage that was made of them under some of the Roman emperors, and the slaughter of them so often repeated in every Christian state, one is astonished that this people not only still exists, but is at this day no less numerous than it was formerly. Their numbers must be attributed to their exemption from bearing arms, their ardor for marriage, their custom of contracting it in their families early, their law of divorce, their sober and regular way of life, their abstinence, their toil, and their exercise.

Their firm attachment to the Mosaic law is no less remarkable, especially when we consider their frequent apostasies when they lived under the government of their kings and their judges; and Judaism is now, of all the religions in the world, the one most rarely abjured—which is partly the fruit of the persecutions it has suffered. Its followers, perpetual martyrs to their creed, have regarded themselves with progressively increasing confidence, as the fountain of all sanctity; looking upon us as no other than rebellious Jews, who have abjured the law of God, and put to death or torture those who received it from His hand. . . .

Document Set 19.2 References

A. Voltaire Pleads for Toleration
Voltaire, *Essay on Toleration,* J. McCabe, trans. (New York: Putnam's, 1912).

B. Diderot Excoriates "Fanaticism"
Stephen J. Gendzier, ed. and trans., *Denis Diderot's The Encyclopedia: Selections* (New York: Harper and Row, 1967), 104–106.

C. Baron d'Holbach Denounces Intellectual Conservatism and Questions the Idea of the Soul
d'Holbach, *The System of Nature,* in *Translations and Reprints frm the Original Sources of European History* (Philadelphia: University of Pennsylvania Press, 1898), 3/1:26–27.

D. Rousseau Advocates a Deistic Religion of Feeling
James Harvey Robinson, ed., *Readings in European History* (Boston: Ginn, 1904), 2:384–386.

E. John Wesley Explains Methodism
John Wesley, *A Plain Account of the People Called Methodists (1749),* in Walter Arnstein, ed., *The Past Speaks,* 2d ed. (Lexington, Mass.: D. C. Heath, 1993), 2:87–89.

F. Hasidism Spreads Through East European Jewry: Tales of the Baal Shem
Martin Buber, *Tales of the Hasidim: The Early Masters,* Olga Marx, trans. (New York: Schocken, 1947), 66–67, 82–83.

G. Voltaire Sneers at Judaism
Richard Levy, ed., *Antisemitism in the Modern World* (Lexington, Mass.: D. C. Heath, 1992), 40–43.

In Search of an Enlightened Society

"Reasonableness" and "usefulness" were the Enlightenment's watchwords in weighing the political institutions of the age, and by these standards the status quo (except in Britain) was usually found wanting. In his masterpiece *The Spirit of the Laws*, Montesquieu looked for rules by which a polity could be designed to best fit its geography and population (Document A). From his knowledge of England, he developed exceedingly influential advice—heeded by the framers of the United States Constitution—that liberty is best safeguarded by dividing authority within the state (Document B). Without ever visiting Pennsylvania, Voltaire decided that the moderate and tolerant regime established there by William Penn was the ideal society for Europeans to emulate (Document C). Rousseau redefined the social-contract theory of government (see Chapter 17 for Hobbes's and Locke's versions of it) to incorporate the universal moral law, which he called the General Will, under which human beings acknowledged their interdependence (Document D).

Even the institution of marriage was examined according to Enlightenment criteria. The first English feminist, Mary Astell, was sufficiently ahead of her time to argue in her anonymously published *Reflections upon Marriage* (1700) that celibacy as an alternative to marriage could give upper-class women some measure of independence. (Astell was quite conventional in her conservative and Tory-Anglican politics.)

A. Montesquieu Speculates on the Optimal Sizes of Various Kinds of States

It is natural for a republic to have only a small territory; otherwise it cannot long subsist. In an extensive republic there are men of large fortunes, and consequently of less moderation; there are trusts too considerable to be placed in any single subject; he has interests of his own; he soon begins to think that he may be happy and glorious by oppressing his fellow-citizens; and that he may raise himself to grandeur on the ruins of his country.

In an extensive republic the public good is sacrificed to a thousand private views; it is subordinate to exceptions, and depends on accidents. In a small one the interest of the public is more obvious, better understood, and more within the reach of every citizen; abuses have less extent, and, of course, are less protected.

A monarchical state ought to be of moderate extent. Were it small, it would form itself into a republic; were it very large, the nobility, possessed of great estates, far from the eye of the prince, with a private court of their own, and secure, moreover, from sudden executions by the laws and manners or the country—such a nobility, I say, might throw off their allegiance, having nothing to fear from too slow and too distant a government.

A large empire supposes a despotic authority in the person who governs. It is necessary that the quickness of the prince's resolutions should supply the distance of the places they are sent to; that fear should prevent the remissness of the distant governor or magistrate; that the law should be derived from a single person, and should shift continually, according to the accidents which necessarily multiply in a state in proportion to its extent.

B. Montesquieu Advocates the Separation of Powers

In every government there are three sorts of power: the legislative; the executive in respect to things dependent on the law of nations; and the executive in regard to matters that depend on the civil law.

By virtue of the first, the prince or magistrate enacts temporary or perpetual laws, and amends or abrogates those that have been already enacted. By the second, he makes peace or war, sends or receives embassies, establishes the public security, and provides against invasions. By the third, he punishes criminals, or determines the disputes that arise between individuals. The latter we shall call the judiciary power, and the other simply the executive power of the state.

The political liberty of the subject is a tranquillity of mind arising from the opinion each person has of his safety. In order to have this liberty, it is requisite the government be so constituted as one man need not be afraid of another.

When the legislative and executive powers are united in the same person, or in the same body of magistrates, there can be no liberty; because apprehensions may arise, lest the same monarch or senate should enact tyrannical laws, to execute them in a tyrannical manner.

Again, there is no liberty, if the judiciary power be not separated from the legislative and executive. Were it joined with the legislative, the life and liberty of the subject would be exposed to arbitrary control; for the judge would be then the legislator. Were it joined to the executive power, the judge might behave with violence and oppression.

There would be an end of everything, were the same man or the same body, whether of the nobles or of the people, to exercise those three powers, that of enacting laws, that of executing the public resolutions, and of trying the causes of individuals.

Most kingdoms in Europe enjoy a moderate government because the prince who is invested with the two first powers leaves the third to his subjects. In Turkey, where these three powers are united in the Sultan's person, the subjects groan under the most dreadful oppression.

In the republics of Italy, where these three powers are united, there is less liberty than in our monarchies. Hence their government is obliged to have recourse to as violent methods for its support as even that of the Turks; witness the state inquisitors, and the lion's mouth into which every informer may at all hours throw his written accusations.

C. Voltaire Sees Utopia Among the Pennsylvania Quakers

About this time there appeared on the scene the illustrious William Penn, who established the power of the Quakers in America, and who would have secured them respectability in Europe if men were able to respect virtue when it lies beneath a ridiculous exterior. . . .

. . . He founded [in Pennsylvania] the city of Philadelphia, today [ca. 1755] a very flourishing one. He began by making an alliance with the Americans, his neighbors. This is the only treaty between these peoples and the Christians that was never sworn to and has never been broken. The new sovereign was also the legislator of Pennsylvania; he enacted wise laws, none of which has since been altered. The first is to mistreat no one for his religion, and to regard all those who believe in a God as brothers.

Hardly had he established his government, when a number of American merchants arrived to people this colony. The natives of the country, instead of fleeing into the forests, gradually got used to the peaceable Quakers; to the degree that they hated the other Christians, conquerors and destroyers of America, they loved these newcomers. Before long, delighted with the gentleness of their neighbors, a great crowd of these supported savages came to ask William Penn if he would receive them as his vassals. It was quite a new sort of spectacle: a sovereign whom everyone familiarly *thee'd* and *thou'd,* and spoke to with one's hat on; a government without priests, a people without weapons, citizens all of them equals—magistrates excepted—and neighbors free from jealousy.

William Penn could boast of having brought forth on this earth the Golden Age that everyone talks so much about, and that probably never was, except in Pennsylvania . . .

D. Rousseau Proclaims the Sovereignty of the People, United by the General Will

Since no man has any natural authority over his fellowmen, and since force is not the source of right, conventions remain as the basis of all lawful authority among men. [Book I, Chapter 4].

Now, as men cannot create any new forces, but only combine and direct those that exist, they have no other means of self-preservation than to form by aggregation a sum of forces which may overcome the resistance, to put them in action by a single motive power, and to make them work in concert.

This sum of forces can be produced only by the combination of many; but the strength and freedom of each man being the chief instruments of his preservation, how can he pledge them without injuring himself, and without neglecting the cares which he owes to himself? This difficulty, applied to my subject, may be expressed in these terms.

"To find a form of association which may defend and protect with the whole force of the community the person and property of every associate, and by means of which each, coalescing with all, may nevertheless obey only himself, and remain as free as before." Such is the fundamental problem of which the social contract furnishes the solution. . . .

If then we set aside what is not of the essence of the social contract, we shall find that it is reducible to the following terms: "Each of us puts in common his person and his whole power under the supreme direction of the general will, and in return we receive every member as an indivisible part of the whole." [Book I, Chapter 6].

But the body politic or sovereign, deriving its existence only from the contract, can never bind itself, even to others, in anything that derogates from the original act, such as alienation of some portion of itself, or submission to another sovereign. To violate the act by which it exists would be to annihilate itself, and what is nothing produces nothing. [Book I, Chapter 7].

It follows from what precedes, that the general will is always right and always tends to the public advantage; but it does not follow that the resolutions of the people have always the same rectitude. Men always desire their own good, but do not always discern it; the people are never corrupted, though often deceived, and it is only then that they seem to will what is evil. [Book II, Chapter 3.]

The public force, then, requires a suitable agent to concentrate it and put it in action according to the directions of the general will, to serve as a means of communication between the state and the sovereign, to effect in some manner in the public person what the union of soul and body effects in a man. This is, in the State, the function of government, improperly confounded with the sovereign of which it is only the minister.

What, then, is the government? An intermediate body established between the subjects and the sovereign for their mutual correspondence, charged with the execution of the laws and with the maintenance of liberty both civil and political. [Book III, Chapter 1.]

It is not sufficient that the assembled people should have once fixed the constitution of the state by giving their sanction to a body of laws; it is not sufficient that they should have established a perpetual government, or that they should have once for all provided for the election of magistrates. Besides the extraordinary assemblies which unforeseen events may require, it is necessary that there should be fixed and periodical ones which nothing can abolish or prorogue; so that, on the appointed day, the people are rightfully convoked by the law, without needing for that purpose any formal summons. [Book III, Chapter 13.]

So soon as the people are lawfully assembled as a sovereign body, the whole jurisdiction of the government ceases, the executive power is suspended, and the person of the meanest citizen is as sacred and inviolable as that of the first magistrate, because where the represented are, there is no longer any representative. [Book III, Chapter 14.]

These assemblies, which have as their object the maintenance of the social treaty, ought always to be opened with two propositions, which no one should be able to suppress, and which should pass separately by vote. The first: "Whether it pleases the sovereign to maintain the present form of government." The second: "Whether it pleases the people to leave the administration to those at present entrusted with it."

I presuppose here what I believe I have proved, viz., that there is in the State no fundamental law which cannot be revoked, not even this social compact; for if all the citizens assembled in order to break the compact by a solemn agreement, no one can doubt that it could be quite legitimately broken. [Book III, Chapter 18.]

E. Mary Astell Considers the Institution of Marriage

Tis true, thro' Want of Learning, and of that Superior Genius which Men as Men lay claim to, she was ignorant of the *Natural Inferiority* of our Sex, which our Masters lay down as a Self-Evident and Fundamental Truth. She saw nothing in the Reason of Things, to make this either a Principle or a Conclusion, but much to the contrary. . . .

That the Custom of the World has put Women, generally speaking, into a State of Subjection, in not deny'd; but the Right can no more be prov'd from the Fact, than the Predominancy of Vice can justifie it. . . .

The Domestic Sovereign [husband] is without Dispute Elected, and the Stipulations and Contract are mutual, is it not then partial in Men to the last degree, to contend for, and practise that Arbitrary Dominion in their Families, which they abhor and exclaim against in the State? For if Arbitrary Power is evil in itself, and an improper Method of Governing Rational and Free Agents, it ought not to be Practis'd any where; Nor is it less, but rather more mischievous in Families than in Kingdoms, by how much 100000 Tyrants are worse than one.

Document Set 19.3 References

A. Montesquieu Speculates on the Optimal Sizes of Various Kinds of States
   Montesquieu, *The Spirit of Laws*, book VIII, chap. 16–20 passim, in *Translations and Reprints from the Original Sources of European History* (Philadelphia: University of Pennsylvania Press, 1902), 3/1:4–5.
B. Montesquieu Advocates the Separation of Powers
   Montesquieu, *The Spirit of Laws*, trans. T. Nugent (New York: Hafner, 1949), 151–152.
C. Voltaire Sees Utopia Among the Pennsylvania Quakers
   Voltaire, *Philosophical Letters*, trans. Ernest Dilworth (Indianapolis: Bobbs-Merrill, 1961), 16, 18–19.
D. Rousseau Proclaims the Sovereignty of the People, United by the General Will
   Jean-Jacques Rousseau, *The Social Contract*, in *Translations and Reprints*, 1/6:14–16.
E. Mary Astell Considers the Institution of Marriage
   Mary Astell, *Reflections Upon Marriage*, in Bridget Hill, ed., *The First English Feminist: Reflections Upon Marriage and Other Writings by Mary Astell* (New York: St. Martin's, 1986), 71, 72, 76.

DOCUMENT SET 19.4
Inculcating Enlightenment

Education and the proper upbringing of children were obviously the keys to securing a truly enlightened society; otherwise the superstitious violence and ignorance of the masses would always threaten the well-bred from below and give the state a perfect excuse to maintain despotism. Rousseau pondered the problem of educating children in the spirit of generous humanitarianism and wrote a much-discussed didactic novel on the subject, *Emile,* excerpted in Document A. Unfortunately, his own record on raising children leaves much to be desired. He placed all of his illegitimate offspring in foundling homes, where they vanished without a trace, the sad fate of most abandoned children in this era. His lachrymose, self-justifying account of this episode forms a memorable passage in his *Confessions* (Document B). In a more practical vein, the Polish writer Stanislaw Konarski (1700–1773) advanced in 1773 a moderate pedagogical program for the Noble's College founded in Warsaw to train young boys from the gentry in the enlightened spirit that, it was hoped, would enable the Commonwealth from its century-long decline (Document C).

A. Rousseau Recommends Learning a Virtuous Trade

If you cultivate the arts whose success depends upon the reputation of the artist, if you turn your attention to those employments which are obtained only by favor, of what use will it all be to you, when, rightly disgusted with the world, you disdain the means without which you cannot hope to succeed? You have studied diplomacy and the interests of princes? Good; but what will you do with this knowledge, unless you know how to conciliate the ministers, the ladies of the court, the heads of the bureaus; unless you possess the secret of pleasing them; unless all find in you the rascal that suits their purposes? You are architect or painter? Good; but it is necessary that you should make your talent known. Do you expect to go straightway and exhibit your work at the salon? Alas! that doesn't happen so easily! It is necessary to be in the Academy; it is necessary to be a favorite in order to obtain even a dark corner of the wall. Give up your model and your brush, take a cab and go from door to door; it is in this way that you will acquire celebrity. But you ought to know that all these illustrious doors have Swiss or porters who understand only by motions, and whose ears are in their hands. Do you wish to impart what you have learned, and become a teacher of geography, or mathematics, or languages, or music, or drawing? For that it is necessary to find pupils, and consequently somebody to recommend you. Remember, it contributes more toward success to be plausible than to be able, and that, if you know no trade but your own, you will never by anything but a dunce.

See then how little solidity all these brilliant resources possess, and how many other resources are necessary in order to derive any advantage from them. And then, what will become of you in this cowardly abasement? Reverses, instead of instructing you, debase you. More than ever the creature of public opinion, how will you elevate yourself above those prejudices, arbiters of your lot? How will you despise baseness and the vices of which you have need for your subsistence? You were dependent only on wealth, and now you are dependent on wealth; you have only deepened your slavery and surcharged it with your poverty. You are poor without becoming free; it is the worst state into which a man can fall.

But instead of resorting for a livelihood to those high knowledges which are made for nourishing the soul and not the body, if you resort, in time of need, to your hands and the use which you know how to make of them, all difficulties vanish, all artifices become useless. Your resources are always ready at the moment their use is required; probity and honor are no longer an obstacle to living; you have no need to be a coward and a liar before the great, to bend and cringe before rascals, a vile pander to all the world, a borrower or a thief, which are almost the same thing when one has nothing. The opinion of others concerns you not; you have your court to make to no one, no fool to flatter, no Swiss to knuckle to, no courtier to fee, or what is worse, to worship. That rogues manage the affairs of the great is of no consequence to you. That does not prevent you in your obscure life from being an honest man and having bread. You enter the first shop whose trade you have learned: "Master, I need work." "Journeyman, go there and get to work." Before the dinner hour arrives you have earned your dinner. If you are diligent and sober, before eight hours have passed you will have wherewith to live eight hours more. You will have lived free, sound, true, industrious and just. To gain it thus is not to lose one's time.

B. Rousseau Places His Own Children in a Foundling Home

While philosophising upon the duties of man, an event occurred which made me reflect more seriously upon my own. Thérèse [Rousseau's mistress] became pregnant for the third time. Too honest towards myself, too proud in my heart to desire to belie my principles by my actions, I began to consider the destination of my children and my connection with their mother, in the light of the laws of nature, justice, and reason, and of that religion—pure, holy and eternal, like its author—which men have polluted, while pretending to be anxious to purify it, and which they have converted, by their formulas, into a mere religion of words, seeing that it costs men little to prescribe what is impossible, when they dispense with carrying it out in practice.

If I was wrong in my conclusions, nothing can be more remarkable than the calmness with which I abandoned myself to them. If I had been one of those low-born men, who are deaf to the gentle voice of Nature, in whose heart no real sentiment of justice or humanity ever springs up, this hardening of my heart would have been quite easy to understand. But is it possible that my warm-heartedness, lively sensibility, readiness to form attachments, the powerful hold which they exercise over me, the cruel heartbreakings I experience when forced to break them off, my natural goodwill towards all my fellow-creatures, my ardent love of the great, the true, the beautiful and the just; my horror of evil of every kind, my utter inability to hate or injure, or even to think of it; the sweet and lively emotion which I feel at the sight of all that is virtuous, generous, and amiable; is it possible, I ask, that all these can ever agree in the same heart with the depravity which, without the least scruple, tramples underfoot the sweetest of obligations? No! I feel and loudly assert—it is impossible. Never, for a single moment in his life, could Jean Jacques have been a man without feeling, without compassion, or an unnatural father. I may have been mistaken, never hardened. If I were to state my reasons, I should say too much. Since they were strong enough to mislead me, they might mislead many others, and I do not desire to expose young people, who may read my works, to the danger of allowing themselves to be misled by the same error. I will content myself with observing, that my error was such that, in handing over my children to the State to educate, for want of means to bring them up myself, in deciding to fit them for becoming workmen and peasants rather than adventurers and fortune-hunters, I thought that I was behaving like a citizen and a father, and considered myself a member of Plato's Republic. More than once since then, the regrets of my heart have told me that I was wrong; but, far from my reason having given me the same information, I have often blessed Heaven for having preserved them from their father's lot, and from the lot which threatened them as soon as I should have been obliged to abandon them. If I had left them with Madame d'Epinay or Madame de Luxembourg, who, from friendship, generosity, or some other motive, expressed themselves willing to take charge of them, would they have been happier, would they have been brought up at least as honest men? I do not know; but I do know that they would have been brought up to hate, perhaps to betray, their parents; it is a hundred times better that they have never known them.

My third child was accordingly taken to the Foundling Hospital, like the other two. The two next were disposed of in the same manner, for I had five altogether. This arrangement appeared to me so admirable, so rational, and so legitimate, that, if I did not openly boast of it, this was solely out of regard for the mother; but I told all who were acquainted with our relations. I told Grimm and Diderot. I afterwards informed [several other friends]. . . . In a word, I made no mystery of what I did, not only because I have never known how to keep a secret from my friends, but because I really saw no harm in it. All things considered, I chose for my children what was best, or, at least, what I believed to be best for them. I could have wished, and still wish, that I had been reared and brought up as they have been. . . .

C. Stanislaw Konarski Establishes a Program of Enlightened Education in Poland, 1753

If it were possible to eliminate from our schools corporal punishment this should be very desirable. Let us then at least behave in such a way as to take care lest the schools earn the name of "torture chambers" and "children's shambles", and the teachers the name of floggers, whippers, executioners and butchers. Therefore, one should follow that important counsel urging moderation which is given to educators by wise persons, and always observe the principles recommended by mere prudence: *viz.*, the boys should not be flogged for negligence in their school duties or assignments, etc., or even for more frequently occurring excesses, outbursts of anger or even slight disrespect of religion in church, for arrogant answers, improper fulfillments of some duty, or some other offense, but solely and exclusively for obstinacy, stubbornness and headstrongness. When one says for obstinacy and headstrongness in evil, the concept of the cause is very wide and contains much in itself. But where this cause is actually absent, one should refrain from flogging, and instead appeal rather to reason, double one's watchfulness, admonish, chastise, and in general try all other means tending to the improvement of youth, namely, to the extirpation of laziness, lying or any other wickedness. . . .

Well born lads should refrain from the practices of deceitfulness into which youth so easily falls; as from the worst disgrace, the deepest shame, and the gravest evil. For lying is the proof of a false, perverted and unworthy nature, and whosoever falls into this loathsome habit loses his reputation for the whole of life. He will never get free from it. . . . A youth of good character and honest spirit will always tell the truth even though he be afraid of what it entails; for lying is worse than losing a good name. He will prefer to suffer rather than compromise his own credit and the Divine patience. . . .

One of the greatest benefits of the school should be the habit engendered in the student of reading good books: books treating of life, history, public questions, books about literature and the sciences. Reading alone can make men learned and great in their nation, and those who take good books for their tutors need no others. . . . It is also clear that when one leaves school the only way to make up for time ill-used there is by reading. And what hope is there that he who does not form a love for books while at school will find time for them, when out in the world and facing so many distractions? Whoever while young learns to love books will certainly not forsake them the rest of his days. . . .

The youth should have often in mind their country for which they were born; learning from earliest days to love her, and not disappointing the hopes she entertains of them. They should school themselves in good habits and a life worthy of great sons of their nations. They should keep ever before their eyes the name and honor of their own families, whose ornament and strength they must become. Above all they should ground themselves in the love of our Holy Faith, for which their fathers shed their blood: as also, in godly fear, in Christian duties and excellence, without which no one can be of use either to himself or to the commonwealth.

We do not wish that students should find the studies in the college a burden, or too severe a business. If the truth be told there is nothing so hard that it does not become easy, if only one gets under it!

Document Set 19.4 References

A. Rousseau Recommends Learning a Virtuous Trade
Jean-Jacques Rousseau, *Emile*, book 3, in *Translations and Reprints from the Original Sources of European History* (Philadelphia: University of Pennsylvania Press, 1898), 1/6:18–20.

B. Rousseau Places His Own Children in a Foundling Home
Jean-Jacques Rousseau, *Confessions* (London: Dent, 1904), 1:8–9.

C. Stanislaw Konarski Establishes a Program of Enlightened Education in Poland, 1753
Konarski, *Ordinationes* (*School Regulations*), in Manfred Kridl, ed. and trans., *For Your Freedom and Ours* (New York: Unger, 1943), 51–55.

DOCUMENT SET 19.5
Enlightened Despotism in Central and Eastern Europe

Enlightened despotism, a term sanctioned by long usage among historians, may be a contradiction in terms. But it does refer usefully to a specific phenomenon: the efforts of the bureaucratic monarchies of continental Europe to enact Enlightenment-inspired reforms while maintaining or enhancing their own totalitarian power. In different ways, Austria, Prussia, and Russia all pursued such aims.

Thus Document A shows Holy Roman Emperor Joseph II (*1780–1790) removing by decrees-from-above in 1781 and 1782 the worst disabilities traditionally borne by Jews in the Habsburg lands. The extracts here show influence of the Enlightenment—and also the deep-rooted antisemitism of Austria's gentile population. Prussia's Frederick II (*1740–1786), the archetypal enlightened despot and friend of Voltaire, in 1752 instructed one of his officials in the proper implementation of a mercantilist policy for Prussia, drawing on the Enlightenment idea of promoting socially useful innovations (Document B). And Russia's Catherine the Great (*1762–1796), a German-born ruler of great intelligence, energy, and ruthlessness, in 1767 filled her instructions to her Legislative Commission with Enlightenment precepts. All this, however, was lost on the enserfed peasantry, the vast majority of Russia's population. For their view of justice, see Document D, a pathetic 1774 petition from the Upper Volga region to "Peter III," the name that the Cossack rebel Pugachev adopted. See also Document E, an extract from a book that a genuine Russian admirer of the Enlightenment, the nobleman Alexander Radishchev, tried to publish in 1790—only to find himself exiled to Siberia as a subversive by Catherine.

A. Joseph II Emancipates the Austrian Jews

In order to make the Jews more useful, the discrimination hitherto observed in relation to their clothing is abolished in its entirety. Consequently the obligation for the men to wear yellow armbands and the women to wear yellow ribbons is abolished. If they behave quietly and decently, then no one has the right to dictate to them on matters of dress.

Within two years the Jews must abandon their own language. . . . Consequently the Jews may use their own language only during religious services.

Those Jews who do not have the opportunity to send their children to Jewish schools are to be compelled to send them to Christian schools, to learn reading, writing, arithmetic and other subjects.

Jewish youth will also be allowed to attend the imperial universities.

To prevent the Jewish children and the Jews in general suffering as a result of the concessions granted to them, the authorities and the leaders of the local communities must instruct the subjects in a rational manner that the Jews are to be regarded like any other fellow human-beings and that there must be an end to the prejudice and contempt which some subjects, particularly the unintelligent, have shown towards the Jewish nation and which several times in the past have led to deplorable behaviour and even criminal excesses. On the other hand the Jews must be warned to behave like decent citizens and it must be emphasised in particular that they must not allow the beneficence of His Majesty to go to their heads and indulge in wanton and licentious excesses and swindling.

B. Frederick the Great Demands an Industrial Policy for Prussia

To Privy Finance Councillor Faesch

Since I have seen from your report of the ninth that you are of the opinion that except for the few factories listed by you, which in themselves are very good and necessary, we need no more factories in this country, but have more than enough, I cannot refrain from informing you that I must conclude that you can have made only a very superficial survey and examination of the extracts and balance sheets of imports and exports sent in by the Cameral; certainly, if you had looked attentively at the rubrics in them of imports from foreign countries, you would easily have seen from the details specified in them how very many objects there are which at present we have to get from abroad, and that we could spare ourselves that necessity by setting up our own factories here or sometimes by extending beginnings already made. The example of silk alone will make my ideas clearer to you. We have made a small beginning in setting up silk factories here, but they are still very far from sufficient to meet all our domestic demand for silken goods of all kinds, much less to meet the demands of neighboring countries; so that we are forced to use a very considerable quantity of foreign silks, importing them, and sending the money for them abroad. I cannot accept it if you object that you could not see this out of the Cameral extracts; if you had only taken the total or sum cost of the imported foreign silks and had reckoned out, taking approximate prices, how much this worked out to per piece and ell and then how many pieces can be made in a year on one frame and how many frames we are still short of, you would have seen that we are still lacking in a considerable number of such frames, which could be established here with assurance of success. The same attention would have shown you that we still have in our provinces no vellum factories, or not nearly enough, yet the consumption of vellum is so large that big sums of money have to go out of the country for it.

Besides these examples, you would have found a hundred more similar things for which we have at present no factories and will gradually have to establish them. I therefore require you to go through the extracts (which are being returned to you) again, with closest attention, and report accordingly. You must pay special attention to the question of which factories are particularly advantageous to each province and whether there are too many of any kind in some province, in which case they must be established in another, in which they are lacking. You appeal, indeed, to the order issued by the Cameral President that shortage of factories is the Camera's business; but when you consider with how many different questions the President is charged, whereas the Fifth Department has no other business, you will see yourself that it is its duty to work on the question with all attention.

FRIEDRICH

Potsdam, August 11, 1752

C. Catherine the Great Gives Directions to the Legislative Commission, 1767

. . . 6. Russia is a European state.

7. This is clearly demonstrated by the following observations: the alterations which Peter the Great undertook in Russia succeeded with greater ease because the manners which prevailed at that time, and had been introduced amongst us by a mixture of different nations and the conquest of foreign territories, were quite unsuitable to the climate. Peter the First, by introducing the manners and customs of Europe among the *European* people in his domains, found at that time such means [success] as even he himself did not expect. . . .

9. The Sovereign is absolute; for there is no other authority but that which centers in his single person that can act with a vigor proportionate to the extent of such a vast Dominion. . . .

13. What is the true end of Monarchy? Not to deprive people of their natural liberty but to correct their actions, in order to attain the Supreme Good. . . .

15. The intention and end of Monarchy is the glory of the Citizens, of the State, and of the Sovereign. . . .

66. All laws which aim at the extremity of rigor, may be evaded. It is moderation which rules a people, and not excess of severity.

67. Civil liberty flourishes when the laws deduce every punishment from the peculiar nature of every crime. The application of punishment ought not to proceed from the arbitrary will or mere caprice of the Legislator, but from the nature of the crime. . . .

68. Crimes are divisible into four classes: against religion, against manners [morality], against the peace, against the security of the citizens. . . .

74. I include under the first class of crimes [only] a direct and immediate attack upon religion, such as sacrilege, distinctly and clearly defined by law. . . . In order that the punishment for the crime of sacrilege might flow from the nature of the thing, it ought to consist in depriving the offender of those benefits to which we are entitled by religion; for instance, by expulsion from the churches, exclusion from the society of the faithful for a limited time, or for ever. . . .

76. In the second class of crimes are included those which are contrary to good manners.

77. Such [include] the corruption of the purity of morals in general, either publick or private; that is, every procedure contrary to the rules which show in what manner we ought to enjoy the external conveniences given to man by Nature for his necessities, interest, and satisfaction. The punishments of these crimes ought to flow also from the nature of the thing [offense]: deprivation of those advantages which Society has attached to purity of morals, [for example,] monetary penalties, shame, or dishonor . . . expulsion from the city and the community; in a word, all the punishments which at judicial discretion are sufficient to repress the presumption and disorderly behavior of both sexes. In fact, these offenses do not spring so much from badness of heart as from a certain forgetfulness or mean opinion of one's self. To this class belong only the crimes which are prejudicial to manners, and not those which at the same time violate publick security, such as carrying off by force and rape; for these are crimes of the fourth class.

78. The crimes of the third class are those which violate the peace and tranquillity of the citizens. The

punishments for them ought also to flow from the very nature of the crime, as for instance, imprisonment, banishment, corrections, and the like which reclaim these turbulent people and bring them back to the established order. Crimes against the peace I confine to those things only which consist in a simple breach of the civil polity.

79. The penalties due to crimes of the fourth class are peculiarly and emphatically termed Capital Punishments. They are a kind of retaliation by which Society deprives that citizen of his security who has deprived, or would deprive, another of it. The punishment is taken from the nature of the thing, deduced from Reason, and the sources of Good and Evil. A citizen deserves death when he has violated the public security so far as to have taken away, or attempted to take away, the life of another. Capital punishment is the remedy for a distempered society. If publick security is violated with respect to property, reasons may be produced to prove that the offender ought not in such a case suffer capital punishment; but that it seems better and more conformable to Nature that crimes against the publick security with respect to property should be punished by deprivation of property. And this ought inevitably to have been done, if the wealth of everyone had been common, or equal. But as those who have no property are always most ready to invade the property of others, to remedy this defect corporal punishment was obliged to be substituted for pecuniary. What I have here mentioned is drawn from the nature of things, and conduces to the protection of the liberty of the citizens. . . .

348. The rules of Education are the fundamental institutes which train us up to be citizens. . . .

350. It is impossible to give a general education to a very numerous people and to bring up all the children in schools; for that reason, it will be proper to establish some general rules which may serve by way of advice to all parents.

351. Every parent is obliged to teach his children the fear of God as the beginning of all Wisdom, and to inculcate in them all those duties which God demands from us in the Ten Commandants and in the rules and traditions of our Orthodox Eastern Greek religion.

352. Also to inculcate in them the love of their Country, and to ensure they pay due respect to the established civil laws, and reverence the courts of judicature in their Country as those who, by the appointment of God, watch over their happiness in this world.

353. Every parent ought to refrain in the presence of his children not only from actions but even from words that tend to injustice and violence, as for instance, quarreling, swearing, fighting, every sort of cruelty, and such like behavior; and not to allow those who are around his children to set them such bad examples. . . .

511. A Monarchy is destroyed when a Sovereign imagines that he displays his power more by changing the order of things than by adhering to it, and when he is more fond of his own imaginations than of his will, from which the laws proceed and have proceeded.

512. It is true there are cases where Power ought and can exert its full influence without any danger to the State. But there are cases also where it ought to act according to the limits prescribed by itself.

513. The supreme art of governing a State consists in the precise knowledge of that degree of power, whether great or small, which ought to be exerted according to the different exigencies of affairs. For in a Monarchy the prosperity of the State depends, in part, on a mild and condescending government. . . .

522. Nothing more remains now for the Commission to do but to compare every part of the laws with the rules of this Instruction.

D. Serfs Petition "Peter III," 1774

Most brilliant and autocratic Great Sovereign Peter Fedorovich, Autocrat of Little and White Russia, etc., etc.!

This declaration comes from the Guselinkova part of the village of Spasskoe in Kungurskii district, in the name of an entire community through its authorized representatives, Kornilo Prokopov'ev Shiriaev and Ustin Ananienich Medvidev. It addresses the following points:

1. By the grace of God, we have heard that Your Imperial Majesty—from the southern part of the country, in Orenburg province—has great strength. We praised God that our beautiful sun of old, after having been concealed beneath the soil, now rises from the east and wishes to radiate mercy on us, Your most humble and loyal slaves. We peasants bow to the ground [before You] in total unanimity.

2. We slaves, all the peasants in this community, most humbly petition for tsarist mercy from the military officers and do not wish to oppose [them]. Your Majesty did not declare his anger and punishment toward us, and we request that the commanding officers spare us of the destructive sword and that they obey Your Majesty's orders.

3. We also nourish the great hope that his tsarist majesty will mercifully spare us of vicious, wild, poi-

sonous animals and break off the sharp claws of the miscreants, the aristorcrats and officers—like those in the Iugov state factories, Mikhail Ivanovich Bashmakov, also (in the city of Kungurov) Ivan Sidorovich Nikonov, Aleksei Semenovich Elchanov, and Dmitrii Popov. . . . These magnates make us indignant through their order that whoever invokes the name of the great Peter Fedorovich ["Peter III"] is a great evildoer and [to be punished] with death.

4. Therefore we slaves, all peasants, have sent reliable people to discover the truth about Your Majesty and to bow down before Your military commanders, not to resist them. Therefore, if you please, give them encouragement so that we slaves know of Your Tsarist Majesty's health, for which we slaves would have great jubilation.

5. Show Your merciful judgment upon our most humble petition, so that we suffer no damages from Your armies.

E. Alexander Radishchev Learns About Serfdom from a Serf, 1790

[Village of Liubani.] . . . A few steps from the road I saw a peasant ploughing a field. The weather was hot. I looked at my watch. It was twenty minutes before one. I had set out on Saturday. It was now Sunday. The ploughing peasant, of course, belonged to a landed proprietor, who would not let him pay [dues in money or kind (obrok)]. The peasant was ploughing very carefully. The field, of course, was not part of his master's land. He turned the plough with astonishing ease.

"God help you," I said, walking up to the ploughman, who, without stopping, was finishing the furrow he had started. "God help you," I repeated.

"Thank you, sir," the ploughman said to me, shaking the earth off the ploughshare and transferring it to a new furrow.

"You must be a Dissenter [Old Believer], since you plough on a Sunday."

"No, sir, I make the true sign of the cross," he said, showing me the three fingers together. "And God is merciful and does not bid us starve to death, so long as we have strength and a family."

"Have you no time to work during the week, then, and can you not have any rest on Sundays, in the hottest part of the day, at that?"

"In a week, sir, there are six days, and we go six times a week to work on the master's fields; in the evening, if the weather is good, we haul to the master's house the hay that is left in the woods; and on holidays the women and girls go walking in the woods, looking for mushrooms and berries. God grant," he continued, making the sign of the cross, "that it rains this evening. If you have peasants of your own, sir, they are praying to God for the same thing."

"My friend, I have no peasants, and so nobody curses me. Do you have a large family?"

"Three sons and three daughters. The eldest is nine years old."

"But how do you manage to get food enough, if you have only the holidays free?"

"Not only the holidays: the nights are ours, too. If a fellow isn't lazy, he won't starve to death. You see, one horse is resting; and when this one gets tired, I'll take the other; so the work gets done."

"Do you work the same way for your master?"

"No, sir, it would be a sin to work the same way. On his fields there are a hundred hands for one mouth, while I have two for seven mouths: you can figure it out for yourself. No matter how hard you work for the master, no one will thank you for it. The master will not pay our head [soul] tax; but, though he doesn't pay it, he doesn't demand one sheep, one hen, or any linen or butter the less. The peasants are much better off where the landlord lets them pay a commutation tax [obrok] without the interference of the steward. It is true that sometimes even good masters take more than three rubles a man; but even that's better than having to work on the master's fields. Nowadays it's getting to be the custom to let [lease] villages to [noble] tenants, as they call it. But we call it putting our heads in a noose. A landless tenant skins us peasants alive; even the best ones don't leave us any time for ourselves. In the winter he won't let us do any carting of goods and won't let us go into town to work; all our work has to be for him, because he pays our head tax. It is an invention of the Devil to turn your peasants over to work for a stranger. You can make a complaint against a bad steward, but to whom can you complain against a bad tenant?"

"My friend, you are mistaken; the laws forbid them to torture people."

"Torture? That's true; but all the same, sir, you would not want to be in my hide." Meanwhile the ploughman hitched up the other horse to the plough and bade me good-bye as he began a new furrow.

The words of this peasant awakened in me a multitude of thoughts. I thought especially of the inequality of treatment within the peasant class. I compared the [state] peasants with the [proprietary] peasants. They both live in villages; but the former pay a fixed sum, while the latter must be prepared to pay whatever their master demands. The former are judged by their equals; the latter are dead to the law, except, perhaps, in criminal cases. A member of society becomes known to the government protecting him, only when he breaks the social bonds, when he becomes a criminal! This thought made my blood boil.

Document Set 19.5 References

A. Joseph II Emancipates the Austrian Jews
   T. C. W. Blanning, *Joseph II and Enlightened Despotism* (London: Longman, 1970), 142–144.
B. Frederick the Great Demands an Industrial Policy for Prussia
   Frederick the Great in C. A. Macartney, ed., *The Hadsburg and Hohenzollern Dynasties in the Seventeenth and Eighteenth Centuries* (New York: Harper and Row, 1970), 346–347.
C. Catherine the Great Gives Directions to the Legislative Commission, 1767
   Catherine II, *The Grand Instruction to the Commissioners Appointed to Frame a New Code of Laws for the Russian Empire,* in James Cracraft, ed., *Major Problems in the History of Imperial Russia* (Lexington, Mass.: D. C. Heath, 1994), 200–205.
D. Serfs Petition "Peter III," 1774
   Petition From Serfs in Kungurskii District to Peter III, in Gregory Freeze, ed. and trans., *From Supplication to Revolution* (New York: Oxford University Press, 1988), 84–85.
E. Alexander Radishchev Learns About Serfdom from a Serf, 1790
   Radishchev, *A Journey from St. Petersburg to Moscow,* in Cracraft, 212–213.

DOCUMENT SET 19.6
France Tries Enlightened Despotism

Financial and administrative troubles dominated Louis XVI's reign from his accession in 1774 to the onset of the Revolution in 1789. Authoritarian reform figured prominently among the strategies by which the monarchy tried to escape the consequences of hundreds of years of traditional muddling along. Jacques Turgot (1727–1781), a man with connections to the philosophes who served as Louis's principal reforming minister from 1774 to 1776, tried to overhaul finances and abolish guilds (Documents A and B), before political intrigues and the unpopularity of belt-tightening forced him out. The Genevan banker Jacques Necker (1732–1804), who followed Turgot from 1777 to 1781, managed to achieve piecemeal reforms (Document C).

Arbitrary state power remained a reality in French life, though it was under strong challenge from public opinion. The right of the royal government to jail an individual indefinitely under a secret order—*Lettre de Cachet*—was, for example, protested by the lower courts (Document D). And, as we shall see in Chapter 20, absolute monarchy itself was increasingly rejected by the French public.

A. Turgot Outlines His Reform Program to Louis XVI, 1774

Compiègne, August 24, 1774.

Sire:

Having just come from the private interview with which your Majesty has honored me, still full of the anxiety produced by the immensity of the duties now imposed upon me, agitated by all the feelings excited by the touching kindness with which you have encouraged me, I hasten to convey to you my respectful gratitude and the devotion of my whole life.

Your Majesty has been good enough to permit me to place on record the engagement you have taken upon you to sustain me in the execution of those plans of economy which are at all times, and to-day more than ever, an indispensable necessity.... At this moment, sire, I confine myself to recalling to you these three items:

No bankruptcy.

No increase of taxes.

No loans.

No *bankruptcy*, either avowed or disguised by illegal reductions.

No *increase of taxes;* the reason for this lying in the condition of your people, and, still more, in that of your Majesty's own generous heart.

No *loans;* because every loan always diminishes the free revenue and necessitates, at the end of a certain time, either bankruptcy or the increase of taxes. In times of peace it is permissible to borrow only in order to liquidate old debts, or in order to redeem other loans contracted on less advantageous terms.

To meet these three points there is but one means. It is to reduce expenditure below the revenue, and sufficiently below it to insure each year a saving of twenty millions, to be applied to redemption of the old debts. Without that, the first gunshot will force the state into bankruptcy.

The question will be asked incredulously, "On what can we retrench?" and each one, speaking for his own department, will maintain that nearly every particular item of expense is indispensable. They will be able to allege very good reasons, but these must all yield to the absolute necessity of economy....

These are the matters which I have been permitted to recall to your Majesty. You will not forget that in accepting the place of comptroller general I have felt the full value of the confidence with which you honor me; I have felt that you intrust to me the happiness of your people, and, if it be permitted to me to say so, the care of promoting among your people the love of your person and of your authority.

At the same time I feel all the danger to which I expose myself. I foresee that I shall be alone in fighting against abuses of every kind, against the power of those who profit by these abuses, against the crowd of prejudiced people who oppose themselves to all reform, and who are such powerful instruments in the hands of interested parties for perpetuating the disorder. I shall have to struggle even against the natural goodness and generosity of your Majesty, and of the persons who are most dear to you. I shall be feared, hated even, by nearly all the court, by all who solicit favors. They will impute to me all the refusals; they will describe me as a hard man because I shall have advised your Majesty that you ought not to enrich even those that you love at the expense of your people's subsistence.

And this people, for whom I shall sacrifice myself, are so easily deceived that perhaps I shall encounter their hatred by the very measures I take to defend them against exactions. I shall be calumniated (having, perhaps, appearances against me) in order to deprive me of your Majesty's confidence. I shall not regret losing a place which I never solicited. I am ready to resign it to your Majesty as soon as I can no longer hope to be useful in it. . . .

Your Majesty will remember that it is upon the faith of your promises made to me that I charge myself with a burden perhaps beyond my strength, and it is to yourself personally, to the upright man, the just and good man, rather than to the king, that I give myself.

I venture to repeat here what you have already been kind enough to hear and approve of. The affecting kindness with which you condescended to press my hands within your own, as if sealing my devotion, will never be effaced from my memory. It will sustain my courage. It has forever united my personal happiness with the interest, the glory, and the happiness of your Majesty. It is with these sentiments that I am, sire, etc.

B. Turgot Decrees the Abolition of Guilds

In almost all the towns the exercise of the different arts and trades is concentrated in the hands of a small number of masters, united in corporations, who alone can, to the exclusion of all other citizens, make or sell the articles belonging to their particular industry. Any person who, by inclination or necessity, intends following an art or trade can only do so by acquiring the mastership [i.e. freedom of the corporation] after a probation as long and vexatious as it is superfluous. By having to satisfy repeated exactions, the money he had so much need of in order to start his trade or open his workshop has been consumed in mere waste. . . .

Citizens of all classes are deprived both of the right to choose the workmen they would employ, and of the advantages they would enjoy from competition operating toward improvements in manufacture and reduction in price. Often one cannot get the samplest work done without its having to go through the hands of several workmen of different corporations, and without enduring the delays, tricks, and exaction which the pretensions of the different corporations, and the caprices of their arbitrary and mercenary directors, demand and encourage. . . .

Among the infinite number of unreasonable regulations, we find in some corporations that all are excluded from them except the sons of masters, or those who marry the widows of masters. Others reject all those whom they call "strangers,"—that is, those born in another town. In many of them for a

young man to be married is enough to exclude him from the apprenticeship, and consequently from the mastership. The spirit of monopoly which has dictated the making of these statutes has been carried out to the excluding of women even from the trades the most suitable to their sex, such as embroidery, which they are forbidden to exercise on their own account. . . .

God, by giving to man wants, and making his recourse to work necessary to supply them, has made the right to work the property of every man, and this property is the first, the most sacred, the most imprescriptible of all. . . .

It shall be free to all persons, of whatever quality or condition they may be, even to all foreigners, to undertake and to exercise in all our kingdom, and particularly in our good city of Paris, whatever kind of trade and whatever profession of art or industry may seem good to them; for which purpose we now extinguish and suppress all corporations and communities of merchants and artisans, as well as all masterships and guild directories. We abrogate all privileges, statutes, and regulations of the said corporations, so that none of our subjects shall be troubled in the exercise of his trade or profession by any cause or under any pretext whatever.

C. Necker Reviews His Administration, 1781

The review I take of my past administration occasions, it is true, neither remorse nor repentance: possibly I may even find in it some actions the remembrance of which will shed a happy influence over the remainder of my days; possibly I may think that, if it had not been for the revival and support of public confidence, the enemies of the king, who relied on the effects of the former disorder and low state of public credit in France, might have gained advantages that have escaped them; possibly I may think that if, in the first years of the war, I had been obliged to furnish the resources of a prudent government to taxes or rigorous operations, the poor would have been very unhappy, and the other classes of citizens would have taken alarm.

Yet, to balance these pleasing recollections, I shall always behold the empty shadow of the more lively and pure satisfactions that my administration was deprived of; I shall have always present to my mind those benefits of every kind which it would have been so easy to have effected if the fruits of so many solicitudes, instead of being appropriated solely to the extraordinary expenses of the state, could have been applied daily to augment the happiness and prosperity of the people.

Alas! what might not have been done under other circumstances! It wounds my heart to think of it! I labored during the storm; I put the ship, as it were, afloat again, and others enjoy the command of her in the days of peace! But such is the fate of men; that Providence which searches the human heart and finds even in the virtues on which we pride ourselves some motives which are not perhaps pure enough in its sight, takes a delight in disappointing the most pardonable of all passions, namely, that of the love of glory and of the good opinion of the public. . . .

I regret, and I have made no secret of it, that I was interrupted in the middle of my career, and that I was not able to finish what I had conceived for the good of the state and for the honor of the kingdom. I have not the hypocritical vanity to affect a deceitful serenity, which would be too nearly allied to indifference to deserve a place among the virtues. That moment will be long present to my mind when, some days after my resignation, being occupied in assorting and classifying my papers, I came across those that contained my various ideas for future reforms, and more especially the plans I had formed for ameliorating the salt tax, for the suppression of every customhouse in the interior parts of the kingdom, and for the extension of the provincial administrations:—I could proceed no farther, and pushing away all these notes by a kind of involuntary motion, I covered my face with my hands, and a flood of tears overpowered me.

D. A French Court Protests a *Lettre de Cachet*, 1770

Sire:

Your Court of Excises, having been impeded in the administration of justice by illegal acts which cannot have emanated from your Majesty personally, have determined that a very humble and very respectful protest should be made to you concerning the matter. . . .

Certain agents of the "farm" arrested an individual named Monnerat without observing any of the restrictions imposed by law. Shortly afterwards an order from your Majesty was produced in virtue of which the man was taken to the prison of Bicêtre and held there for twenty months. Yet it is not the excessive length of the imprisonment that should most deeply touch your Majesty. There exist in the fortress of Bicêtre subterranean dungeons which were dug long ago to receive certain famous criminals who, after having been condemned to death, saved themselves by exposing their accomplices. It would seem that they were condemned to a life which would have made death the preferable alternative. While it was desired that their cells should be absolutely dark, it was necessary to admit enough air to sustain life. Accordingly hollow pillars were constructed which established some connection with the outer air without letting in any light. The victims that are cast into these damp cells, which necessarily become foul after a few days, are fastened to the wall by a heavy chain and are supplied with nothing but a little straw, and bread and water. Your Majesty will find it difficult to believe that a man simply *suspected* of smuggling should be kept in such a place of horror for more than a month.

According to the testimony of Monnerat himself, and the deposition of a witness, it appears that after emerging from his subterranean cell, which he calls "the black dungeon," he was kept for a long time in another less dark. This precaution was taken for the welfare of the prisoner, since experience has shown— perhaps at the cost of a number of lives—that it is dangerous to pass too suddenly from the black dungeon to the open air and the light of day.

Monnerat, upon being released from prison, brought suit for damages against the farmers general. Up to that point the question was one of an individual. But the arrest was illegal in form and the imprisonment a real injustice. If this man was a smuggler, he should have been punished according to the laws, which are very severe in this matter. But when your Majesty grants an order for the imprisonment of one suspected of smuggling, it is not your intention to have the suspected person kept in confinement for nearly two years waiting for proofs of his guilt. Now Monnerat has always maintained, both during and since his imprisonment, that he was not even the person for whom the order was obtained. . . .

According to the prevailing system, whenever the farmer of the revenue has no proof of smuggling except such as the courts would regard as suspicious and insufficient, he resorts to your Majesty's orders, called *lettres de cachet,* in order to punish the offense. . . .

The result is, sire, that no citizen in your kingdom can be assured that his liberty will not be sacrificed to a private grudge; for no one is so exalted that he is safe from the ill will of a minister, or so insignificant that he may not incur that of a clerk in the employ of the farm. The day will come, sire, when the multiplicity of the abuses of the *lettres de cachet* will lead your Majesty to abolish a custom so opposed to the constitution of your kingdom and the liberty which your subjects should enjoy.

Document Set 19.6 References

A. Turgot Outlines His Reform Program to Louis XVI, 1774
   Turgot, Letter, in James Harvey Robinson, ed., *Readings in European History* (Boston: Ginn, 1904), 2:386–388.
B. Turgot Decrees the Abolition of Guilds
   Preamble to Turgot's Edict Abolishing Guilds, in Robinson, 2:389.
C. Necker Reviews His Administration, 1781
   Necker, *A Treatise on the Administration of the Finances of France,* in Robinson, 2:390–391.
D. A French Court Protests a *Lettre de Cachet,* 1770
   Robinson, 2:362–364.

DOCUMENT SET 19.7
Britain and America in the Age of the Atlantic Revolutions

Foreigners admired the unwritten British Constitution, under which the king reigned but did not rule and Parliament, in which the crown had an important part, made the laws. But the reality was not as pretty as the theory. Politics was by our standards blatantly corrupt; where voting took place (which was not everywhere in the country), electoral procedures could be almost ludicrously unfair, as one member of Parliament complacently related in the letter quoted as Document A. The court—a term that also embraced the nation's banking system and political patronage network—seemed a cesspool of shady dealing and backstabbing to the opposition politician Lord Chesterfield (1694–1773) in his famous letters of advice to his son (Document B). George III, immortalized in the American Declaration of Independence as a tyrant, considered himself a faithful participant in the British constitutional system and sincerely tried to do well by his country (Document C).

The American colonists, however, regarded Parliament's plan of extending effective British sovereignty over the hitherto rather autonomous outposts as not only destructive of their liberties but also as a threat to involve a virtuous New World in the corrupt politics of the old. Britain's great empire builder William Pitt (1708–1788), who disapproved of coercing the Americans for fear of driving them to rebellion, clearly understood that the colonists were fighting the same battle against a corrupt political system that British reformers at home were waging—a struggle that would not succeed until at least the 1830s (Document D).

Declaring independence in 1776, the American revolutionaries raised their original rather local quarrel with the British Parliament into a universal cause: the right of a people to create a new government for themselves if their old one becomes oppressive (Document E). The author of the Declaration, Thomas Jefferson (1723–1826), was a man of the Enlightenment, equally at home among the intellectuals of Europe and the farmers of Virginia. His *Notes on the State of Virginia* (1781–1782), intended for foreign readers, was written while he was American minister to France. It is part of the extensive contemporary literature explaining America to Europeans (Document F). Notice his thoughts on slavery, an institution that deeply embarrassed him but on which he was economically dependent.

The most profound work of political philosophy ever written by Americans, *The Federalist,* originated as a series of political pieces in support of ratifying the new United State Constitution in 1776 to 1787. James Madison, the chief draftsman of that document and author of *The Federalist No. 51* (Document G), makes a compelling argument for dispersing power among rival branches of government and for exploiting the natural failings of human nature to ensure the survival of free institutions. This was a stunning break from the traditions of Western political thought going back to Plato and Aristotle, which held that only human virtue could ensure good government.

The readings in Sets 19.1 to 19.7 should be considered as a group in evaluating the meaning of the Enlightenment. Supplement your analysis by consulting *The Challenge of the West,* Chapters 18 and 19. Who were the men and women of the Enlightenment? How did they stand in relation to ordinary people? What were their ideals? What were their religious and philosophical principles, and in what ways did these ideals represent something new in history? How did they approach the age-old problems of governing human society? Do you consider them idealistic benefactors of humanity, élitist dreamers, or subverters of tradition—or are any such generalizations valid?

A. Sir George Selwyn's Supporters Get "Shopped," 1761

Two of my voters were murdered yesterday by an experiment which we call shopping, that is, locking them up and keeping them dead drunk to the day of election. Mr. Snell's agents forced two single Selwyns into a post chaise, where, being suffocated with the brandy that was given them and a very fat man that had the custody of them, they were taken out stone dead. Here follows a hanging; in short, it is one roundeau of delights.

B. Lord Chesterfield Warns His Son About Courts, 1749

You will soon be at Courts, where though you will not be concerned, yet reflection and observation upon what you see and hear there may be of use to you when hereafter you may come to be concerned in courts yourself. Nothing in courts is exactly as it appears to be,—often very different, sometimes directly contrary. Interest, which is the real spring of everything there, equally creates and dissolves friendship, produces and reconciles enmities; or rather, allows of neither real friendships nor enmities; for as Dryden very justly observes, "Politicians neither love nor hate." This is so true that you may think you connect yourself with two friends to-day and be obliged to-morrow to make your option between them as enemies. Observe therefore such a degree of reserve with your friends as not to put yourself in their power if they should become your enemies, and such a degree of moderation with your enemies as not to make it impossible for them to become your friends.

Courts are unquestionably the seats of politeness and good breeding; were they not so, they would be the seats of slaughter and desolation. Those who now smile upon and embrace, would affront and stab each other, if manners did not interpose; but ambition and avarice, the two prevailing passions at courts, found dissimulation more effectual than violence; and dissimulation introduced that habit of politeness which distinguishes the courtier from the country gentleman. In the former case the strongest body would prevail; in the latter, the strongest mind.

A man of parts and efficiency need not flatter everybody at court, but he must take great care to offend nobody personally, it being in the power of very many to hurt him who cannot serve him. Homer supposes a chain let down from Jupiter to the earth to connect him with mortals. There is at all courts a chain which connects the prince of the minister with the page of the backstairs or the chambermaid. The king's wife, or mistress, has an influence over him; a lover has an influence over her; the chambermaid or the valet de chambre has an influence over both; and so *ad infinitum.* You must therefore not break a link of that chain by which you hope to climb up to the prince.

C. George III Upholds the British Constitution, 1760

. . . Born and educated in this country, I glory in the name of Briton; and the peculiar happiness of my life will ever consist in promoting the welfare of a people, whose loyalty and warm affection to me, I consider as the greatest and most permanent security of my throne; and I doubt not but their steadiness in these principles will equal the firmness of my invariable resolution, to adhere to and strengthen this excellent constitution in church and state, and to maintain the toleration inviolable. The civil and religious rights of my loving subjects are equally dear to me with the most valuable prerogatives of my crown: and, as the surest foundation of the whole, and the best means to draw down the divine favor on my reign; it is my fixed purpose to countenance and encourage the practice of true religion and virtue. . . .

[The king describes recent successes of British arms in the Seven Years' War.]

Gentleman of the House of Commons, The greatest uneasiness which I feel at this time is, in considering the uncommon burthens necessarily brought upon my faithful subjects: I desire only such supplies as shall be requisite to prosecute the war with advantage, be adequate to the necessary services, and that they may be provided for in the most sure and effectual manner: you may depend upon the faithful and punctual application of what shall be granted.

I have ordered the proper estimates for the ensuing year to be laid before you; and also an account of the extraordinary expenses, which, from the nature of the different and remote operations, have been unavoidably incurred.

It is with peculiar reluctance that I am obliged, at such a time, to mention any thing which personally regards myself; but, as the grant of the greatest part of the civil list revenues is now determined, I trust in your duty and affection to me, to make the proper provision for supporting my civil government with honor and dignity: on my part, you may be assured of a regular and becoming economy.

My Lords, and gentlemen, The eyes of all Europe are upon you. From your resolutions the Protestant interest hopes for protection; as well as all our friends, for the preservation of their independency; and our enemies fear the final disappointment of their ambitious and destructive views. Let these hopes and fears be confirmed and augmented, by the vigor, unanimity, and dispatch, of your proceedings.

In this expectation I am the more encouraged, by a pleasing circumstance, which I look upon as one of the most auspicious omens of my reign. That happy extinction of divisions, and that union and good harmony which continue to prevail amongst my subjects, afford me the most agreeable prospect: the natural disposition and wish of my heart are to cement and promote them: and I promise myself, that nothing will arise on your part, to interrupt or disturb a situation so essential to the true and lasting felicity of this great people.

D. William Pitt Links American Resistance and British Reform, 1775

This resistance to your arbitrary system of taxation might have been foreseen; it was obvious from the nature of things and of mankind, and, above all, from the Whiggish spirit flourishing in that country. The spirit which now resists your taxation in America is the same which formerly opposed loans, benevolences, and ship money in England; the same spirit which called all England on its legs, and by the Bill of Rights vindicated the English constitution; the same spirit which established the great, fundamental, essential maxim of your liberties, that no subject of England shall be taxed but by his own consent.

This glorious spirit of Whiggism animates three millions in America, who prefer poverty with liberty to gilded chains and sordid affluence, and who will die in the defense of their rights as men, as free men. What shall oppose this spirit, aided by the congenial flame glowing in the breast of every Whig in England, to the amount, I hope, of double the American numbers? Ireland they have to a man. In that country, joined it is with the cause of the colonies, and placed at their head, the distinction I contend for is and must be observed. This country superintends and controls their trade and navigation, but they tax themselves. And this distinction between external and internal control is sacred and insurmountable; it is involved in the abstract nature of things. Property is private, individual, absolute. Trade is an extended and complicated consideration; it reaches as far as ships can sail or winds can blow; it is a great and various machine. To regulate the numberless movements of the several parts and combine them into effect for the good of the whole, requires the superintending wisdom and energy of the supreme power in the empire. But this supreme power has no effect towards internal taxation, for it does not exist in that relation; there is no such thing, no such idea in this constitution, as a supreme power operating upon property. Let this distinction then remain forever ascertained: taxation is theirs, commercial regulation is ours. As an American, I would recognize to England her supreme right of regulating commerce and navigation; as an Englishman by birth and principle, I recognize to the Americans their supreme unalienable right in their property,—a right which they are justified in the defense of to the last extremity. To maintain this principle is the common cause of the Whigs on the other side of the Atlantic and on this. "'Tis liberty to liberty engaged," that they will defend themselves, their families, and their country. In this great cause they are immovably allied: it is the alliance of God and nature,—immovable, eternal, fixed as the firmament of heaven.

E. The United States Declares Independence, 1776

When, in the course of human events, it becomes necessary for one people to dissolve the political bands which have connected them with another, and to assume, among the powers of the earth, the separate and equal station to which the laws of nature and of nature's God entitle them, a decent respect to the opinions of mankind requires that they should declare the causes which impel them to the separation.

We hold these truths to be self-evident: That all men are created equal; that they are endowed by their Creator with certain unalienable rights; that among these are life, liberty, and the pursuit of happiness; that, to secure these rights, governments are instituted among men, deriving their just powers from the consent of the governed; that whenever any form of government becomes destructive of these ends, it is the right of the people to alter or to abolish it, and to institute new government, laying its foundation on such principles, and organizing its powers in such form, as to them shall seem most likely to effect their safety and happiness. Prudence, indeed, will dictate that governments long established should not be changed for light and transient causes; and accordingly all experience hath shown that mankind are more disposed to suffer, while evils are sufferable, than to right themselves by abolishing the forms to which they are accustomed. But when a long train of abuses and usurpations, pursuing invariably the same object, evinces a design to reduce them under absolute despotism, it is their right, it is their duty, to throw off such government, and to provide new guards for their future security. Such has been the patient sufferance of these colonies; and such is now the necessity which constrains them to alter their former systems of government. The history of the present King of Great Britain is a history of repeated injuries and usurpations, all having in direct object the establishment of an absolute tyranny over these states. To prove this, let facts be submitted to a candid world. . . .

F. Thomas Jefferson Describes Virginia to European Readers

Query XIII: Constitution

This constitution [of the state of Virginia] was formed when we were new and unexperienced in the science of government. It was the first too which was formed in the whole United States. No wonder then that time and trial have discovered very capital defects in it.

1. The majority of the men in the state, who pay and fight for its support, are unrepresented in the legislature, the roll of freeholders intitled to vote, not including generally the half of those on the roll of the militia, or of the tax-gatherers.

2. Among those who share the representation, the shares are very unequal. . . .

3. The senate, is by its constitution, too homogeneous with the house of delegates. . . .

Query XIV: Laws

[In this section Jefferson advocates emancipating the slaves, educating girls of former slave families to age eighteen and boys to twenty-one, and then sending them away to unspecified colonies.]

It will probably be asked, Why not retain and incorporate the blacks into the state, and thus save the expence of supplying, by importation of white settlers, the vacancies they will leave? Deep rooted prejudices entertained by the whites; ten thousand recollections, by the blacks of the injuries they have sustained; new provocations; the real distinctions which nature has made; and many other circumstances, will divide us into parties, and produce convulsions which will probably never end.

G. James Madison Meditates on Why Limited Government Is Necessary

To what expedient than shall we finally resort for maintaining in practice the necessary partition of power among the several departments, as laid down in the constitution? The only answer that can be given is, that as all these exterior provisions are found to be inadequate, the defect must be supplied, by so contriving the interior structure of the government, as that its several constituent parts may, by their mutual relations, be the means of keeping each other in their proper places. . . .

. . . [T]he great security against a gradual concentration of the several powers in the same department, consists in giving to those who administer each department, the necessary constitutional means, and personal motives, to resist encroachments of the oth-

ers. The provision for defense must in this, as in all other cases, be made commensurate to the danger of attack. Ambition must be made to counteract ambition. The interest of the man must be connected with the constitutional right of the place. It may be a reflection on human nature, that such devices should be necessary to control the abuses of government. But what is government itself but the greatest of all reflections on human nature? If men were angels, no government would be necessary. If angels were to govern men, neither external nor internal controls on government would be necessary. In framing a government which is to be administered by men over men, the great difficulty lies in this: You must first enable the government to control the governed; and in the next place, oblige it to control itself. A dependence on the people is no doubt the primary control on the government; but experience has taught mankind the necessity of auxiliary precautions.

This policy of supplying by opposite and rival interests, the defect of better motives, might be traced through the whole system of human affairs, private as well as public. We see it particularly displayed in all the subordinate distributions of power; where the constant aim is to divide and arrange the several offices in such a manner as that each may be a check on the other; that the private interest of every individual, may be a sentinel over the public rights. These inventions of prudence cannot be less requisite in the distribution of the supreme powers of the state.

Document Set 19.7 References

A. Sir George Selwyn's Supporters Get "Shopped," 1761
   Selwyn, in Lewis B. Namier, *The Structure of Politics at the Accession of George III* (New York: St. Martin's, 1968), 78.
B. Lord Chesterfield Warns His Son About Courts, 1749
   Edward Gilpin Johnson, ed., *The Best Letters of Lord Chesterfield* (Chicago: McClure, 1890), 131–133.
C. George III Upholds the British Constitution, 1760
   George III, in Walter Arnstein, ed., *The Past Speaks*, 2d ed. (Lexington, Mass.: D. C. Heath, 1993), 2:94, 95.
D. William Pitt Links American Resistance and British Reform, 1775
   William Pitt, in James Harvey Robinson, ed., *Readings in European History* (Boston: Ginn, 1904), 2:354–355.
E. The United States Declares Independence, 1776
   The Declaration of Independence.
F. Thomas Jefferson Describes Virginia to European Readers
   Thomas Jefferson, *Notes on the State of Virginia*, in Harvey C. Mansfield, Jr., ed., *Thomas Jefferson: Selected Writings* (Arlington Heights, Ill.: AHM, 1979), 28–29, 37.
G. James Madison Meditates on Why Limited Government Is Necessary
   James Madison, *The Federalist*, No. 51, February 6, 1778.

DOCUMENT SET 19.8
The Agricultural Revolution and Early Industrialization in Britain

The intellectual revolution of the Enlightenment coincided with another fundamental change of direction in the Western world: the beginnings of industrialization.

In cause-effect relationships that scholars still debate, rising population in the eighteenth century created demand for both more food and more manufactured goods. Eastern England was a particularly important center of improvements in agriculture that helped boost productivity, but the "improving" landlords who enclosed traditional village lands and evicted tenants exacted a high price for the progress they wrought. Document A juxtaposes Arthur Young's approving judgment and the victims' protests.

Besides marking the American Declaration of Independence, the year 1776 was epoch-making also for the publication of Adam Smith's *The Wealth of Nations,* the first fully modern treatise on capitalism and the market economy. Document B offers two key passages from this massive book: Smith's famous demonstration of the efficiency of mass production in the case of pins, and his argument for absolute advantage and specialization in international trade. It was in letting the efficiencies of the marketplace work their effects through such mechanisms as these, Smith argued, that the "invisible hand" of competition would function to humanity's natural advantage. Documents C and D suggest how the freeing of the "invisible hand" worked in practice, as the city of Manchester arose from an obscure village to a thriving industrial town in just a generation, while "Luddites"—displaced and despairing artisans—tried to halt mechanization by destroying machinery.

The eighteenth century saw the birth of an idea that most Westerners now take for granted: progress. From the days of ancient Israel and Greece, the key to understanding history had been the notion that humanity had degenerated from an Age of Gold (or Garden of Eden) to its present state of corruption. The Enlightenment and the promise of more abundant production held out the hope that humanity's path might lead upward, not downward. But as the eighteenth century was about to close, the English clergyman and economist Robert Malthus (1766–1834) published a somber correction to his century's optimism, the *Essay on Population* (Document E), which argued that the natural increase of population outstrips the increase in the means of subsistence. Whether Malthus was right in the long run is a question still to be answered.

A. Two Views of Enclosure, Late Eighteenth Century

1. Arthur Young, 1771

As I shall presently leave Norfolk it will not be improper to give a slight review of the husbandry which has rendered the name of this county so famous in the farming world. Pointing out the practices which have succeeded so nobly here, may perhaps be of some use to other countries possessed of the same advantages, but unknowing in the art to use them.

From forty to fifty years ago, all the northern and western, and a part of the eastern tracts of the county, were sheep walks, let [leased] so low as from 6d. to 1s. and 2s. an acre. Much of it was in this condition only thirty years ago. The great improvements have been made by means of the following circumstances.

First. By inclosing without the assistance of parliament.

Second. By a spirited use of marl and clay.

Third. By the introduction of an excellent course of crops.

Fourth. By the culture of turnips well hand-hoed.

Fifth. By the culture of clover and ray-grass.

Sixth. By landlords granting long leases.

Seventh. By the country being divided chiefly into large farms.

The Course of Crops

After the best managed inclosure, and the most spirited conduct in marling, still the whole success of the undertaking depends on this point: No fortune will be made in Norfolk by farming, unless a judicious course of crops be pursued. That which has been chiefly adopted by the Norfolk farmers is,

1. Turnips.
2. Barley.
3. Clover: or clover and ray-grass.
4. Wheat.

Large Farms

If the preceding articles are properly reviewed, it will at once be apparent that no small farmers could effect such great things as have been done in Norfolk. Inclosing, marling, and keeping a flock of sheep large enough for folding, belong absolutely and exclusively to great farmers. . . . Nor should it be forgotten that the best husbandry in Norfolk is that of the largest farmers. . . . Great farms have been the soul of the Norfolk culture: split them into tenures of an hundred pounds a year, you will find nothing but beggars and weeds in the whole county.

2. A PETITION AGAINST ENCLOSURE

A Petition of the hereunder-signed small Proprietors of Land and Persons entitled to Rights of Common [at Raunds, Northamptonshire].

That the petitioners beg leave to represent to the House that, under the pretence of improving lands in the same parish, the cottages and other persons entitled to right of common on the lands intended to be enclosed, will be deprived of an inestimable privilege, which they now enjoy, of turning a certain number of their cows, calves, and sheep, on and over the said lands; a privilege that enables them not only to maintain themselves and their families in the depth of winter, when they cannot, even for their money, obtain from the occupiers of other lands the smallest portion of milk or whey for such necessary purpose, but in addition to this, they can now supply the grazier with young or lean stock at a reasonable price, to fatten and bring to market at a more moderate rate for general consumption, which they conceive to be the most rational and effectual way of establishing public plenty and cheapness of provision; and they further conceive, that a more ruinous effect of this enclosure will be the almost total depopulation of their town, now filled with bold and hardy husbandmen, from among whom, and the inhabitants of other open parishes, the nation has hitherto derived its greatest strength and glory, in the supply of its fleets and armies, and driving them, from necessity and want of employ, in vast crowds, into manufacturing towns, where the very nature of their employment, over the loom or the forge, soon may waste their strength, and consequently debilitate their posterity, and by imperceptible degrees obliterate that great principle of obedience to the Laws of God and their country, which forms the character of the simple and artless villagers, more equally distributed through the open counties, and on which so much depends the good order and government of the state. These are some of the injuries to themselves as individuals, and of the ill consequences to the public, which the petitioners conceive will follow from this, as they have already done from many enclosures, but which they did not think they were entitled to lay before the House (the constitutional patron and protector of the poor) until it unhappily came to their own lot to be exposed to them through the Bill now pending.

B. Adam Smith Presents the Case for Economic Efficiency

To take an example, therefore, from a very trifling manufacture; but one in which the division of labour has been very often taken notice of, the trade of the pin-maker; a workman not educated to this business (which the division of labour has rendered a distinct trade), nor acquainted with the use of the machinery employed in it (to the invention of which the same division of labour has probably given occasion), could scarce, perhaps, with his utmost industry, make one pin in a day, and certainly could not make twenty. But in the way in which this business is now carried on, not only the whole work is a peculiar trade, but it is divided into a number of branches, of which the greater part are likewise peculiar trades. One man draws out the wire, another straights it, a third cuts it, a fourth points it, a fifth grinds it at the top for receiving the head; to make the head requires two or three distinct operations; to put it on, is a peculiar business, to whiten the pins is another; it is even a trade by itself to put them into the paper; and the important business of making a pin is, in this manner, divided into about eighteen distinct operations, which, in some manufactories, are all performed by distinct hands, though in others the same man will sometimes perform two or three of them. I have seen a small manufactory of this kind where ten men only were employed, and where some of them consequently performed two or three distinct operations. But though they were very poor, and therefore but indifferently accommodated with the necessary machinery, they could, when they exerted themselves, make among them about twelve pounds of pins in a day. There are in a pound upwards of four thousand pins of a middling size. Those ten persons, therefore, could make among them upwards of forty-eight thousand pins in a day. Each person, therefore, making a tenth part of forty-eight thousand pins, might be considered as making four thousand eight hundred pins in a day. But if they had all wrought separately and independently, and without any of them having been educated to this peculiar business, they certainly could not each of them have made twenty, perhaps not one pin in a day; that is, certainly, not the two hundred and fortieth, perhaps not the four thousand eight hundredth part of what they are at present capable of performing, in consequence of a proper division and combination of their different operations.

In every other art and manufacture, the effects of the division of labour are similar to what they are in this very trifling one: though, in many of them, the labour can neither be so much subdivided, nor reduced to so great a simplicity of operation. The division of labour, however, so far as it can be introduced, occasions, in every art, a proportionable increase of the productive powers of labour. The separation of different trades and employments from one another, seems to have taken place, in consequence of this advantage. This separation too is generally carried furthest in those countries which enjoy the highest degree of industry and improvement; what is the work of one man in a rude state of society, being generally that of several in an improved one....

... As every individual, therefore, endeavours as much as he can both to employ his capital in the support of domestic industry, and so to direct that industry that its produce may be of the greatest value; every individual necessarily labours to render the annual revenue of the society as great as he can. He generally, indeed, neither intends to promote the public interest, nor knows how much he is promoting it. By preferring the support of domestic to that of foreign industry, he intends only his own security; and by directing that industry in such a manner as its produce may be of the greatest value, he intends only his own gain, and he is in this, as in many other cases, led by an invisible hand to promote an end which was no part of his intention. Nor is it always the worse for the society that it was no part of it. By pursuing his own interest he frequently promotes that of the society more effectually than when he really intends to promote it. I have never known much good done by those who affected to trade for the public good. It is an affectation, indeed, not very common among merchants, and very few words need be employed in dissuading them from it....

The natural advantages which one country has over another in producing particular commodities are sometimes so great, that it is acknowledged by all the world to be in vain to struggle with them. By means of glasses, hotbeds, and hotwalls, very good grapes can be raised in Scotland, and very good wine too can be made of them at about thirty times the expence for which at least equally good can be brought from foreign countries. Would it be a reasonable law to prohibit the importation of all foreign wines, merely to encourage the making of claret and burgundy in Scotland? But if there would be a manifest absurdity in turning towards any employment, thirty times more of the capital and industry of the country, than would be necessary to purchase from foreign countries an equal quantity of the commodities wanted, there must be an absurdity, though not altogether so glaring, yet exactly of the same kind, in turning towards any such employment a thirtieth, or even a three hundredth part more of either. Whether the

advantages which one country has over another, be natural or acquired, is in this respect of no consequence. As long as the one country has those advantages, and the other wants them, it will always be more advantageous for the latter, rather to buy of the former than to make. It is an acquired advantage only, which one artificer has over his neighbour, who exercises another trade; and yet they both find it more advantageous to buy of one another, than to make what does not belong to their particular trades. ...

C. Manchester Becomes a Thriving Industrial City, 1795

... No exertions of the masters or workmen could have answered the demands of trade without the introduction of *spinning machines*.

These were first used by the country people on a confined scale, twelve spindles being thought a great matter; while the awkward posture required to spin on them was discouraging to grown up people, who saw with surprise children from nine to twelve years of age manage them with dexterity, whereby plenty was brought into families formerly overburthened with children, and the poor weavers were delivered from the bondage in which they had lain from the insolence of spinners. ...

The improvements kept increasing, till the capital engines for twist were perfected, by which thousands of spindles are put in motion by a water wheel, and managed mostly by children, without confusion and with less waste of cotton than by the former methods. But the carding and slubbing preparatory to twisting required a greater range of invention. The first attempts were in carding engines, which are very curious, and now brought to a great degree of perfection; and an engine has been contrived for converting the carded wool to slubbing, by drawing it to about the thickness of candlewick preparatory to throwing it into twist. ...

These machines exhibit in their construction an aggregate of clock-maker's work and machinery most wonderful to behold. The cotton to be spun is introduced through three sets of rollers, so governed by the clock-work, that the set which first receives the cotton makes so many revolutions than the next in order, and these more than the last which feed the spindles, that it is drawn out considerably in passing through the rollers; being lastly received by spindles, which have every one on the bobbin a fly like that of a flax wheel; ...

Upon these machines twist is made of any fineness proper for warps; but as it is drawn length way of the staple, it was not so proper for weft; wherefore on the introduction of fine callicoes and muslins, mules were invented, having a name expressive of their species, being a mixed machinery between jennies and the machines for twisting, and adapted to spin weft as fine as could be desired. . . .

These mules carry often to a hundred and fifty spindles, and can be set to draw weft to an exact fineness up to 150 hanks in the pound, of which muslin has been made, which for a while had a prompt sale; but the flimsiness of its fabric has brought the finer sorts into discredit, and a stagnation of trade damped the sale of the rest. . . .

The prodigious extension of the several branches of the Manchester manufactures has likewise greatly increased the business of several trades and manufactures connected with or dependent upon them. The making of paper at mills in the vicinity has been brought to great perfection, and now includes all kinds, from the strongest parcelling paper to the finest writing sorts, and that on which banker's bills are printed. To the ironmongers shops, which are greatly increased of late, are generally annexed smithies, where many articles are made, even to nails. A considerable iron foundry is established in Salford, in which are cast most of the articles wanted in Manchester and its neighborhood, consisting chiefly of large cast wheels for the cotton machines; cylinders, boilers, and pipes for steam engines; cast ovens, and grates of all sizes. This work belongs to Batemen and Sharrard, gen[tle]men every way qualified for so great an undertaking. Mr. Sharrard is a very ingenious and able engineer, who has improved upon and brought the steam engine to great perfection. . . .

The tin-plate workers have found additional employment in furnishing many articles for spinning machines; as have also the braziers in casting wheels for the motion-work of the rollers used in them; and the clock-makers in cutting them. Harness-makers have been much employed in making bands for carding engines, and large wheels for the first operation of drawing out the cardings, whereby the consumption of strong curried leather has been much increased. . . .

Within the last twenty or thirty years the vast increase of foreign trade has caused many of the Manchester manufacturers to travel abroad, and agents or partners to be fixed for a considerable time on the continent, as well as foreigners to reside at Manchester. And the town has now in every respect assumed the style and manners of one of the commercial capitals of Europe. . . .

D. Yorkshire Luddites Resist Machinery

Sir,
Information has just been given in, that you are a holder of those detestable Shearing Frames, and I was desired by my men to write to you, and give you fair warning to pull them down, and for that purpose I desire that you will understand I am now writing to you, you will take notice that if they are not taken down by the end of next week, I shall detach one of my lieutenants with at least 300 men to destroy them, and further more take notice that if you give us the trouble of coming thus far, we will increase your misfortunes by burning your buildings down to ashes. . . . We hope for assistance from the French Emperor in shaking off the Yoke of the Rottenest, wickedest and most Tyrannical Government that ever existed. . . . We will never lay down our arms till the House of Commons passes an act to put down all the machinery hurtfull [sic] to the Commonality and repeal that to the Frame Breakers. . . .

Signed by the General of the Army of Redressers,
Ned Ludd, Clerk

E. Robert Malthus Doubts Human Perfectibility, 1798

I have read some of the speculations on the perfectibility of man and of society with great pleasure. I have been warmed and delighted with the enchanting picture which they hold forth. I ardently wish for such happy improvements. But I see great, and, to my understanding, unconquerable difficulties in the way to them. These difficulties it is my present purpose to state; declaring, at the same time, that so far from exulting in them, as a cause of triumphing over the friends of innovation, nothing would give me greater pleasure than to see them completely removed. . . .

I think I may fairly make two postulata.
First, That food is necessary to the existence of man.
Secondly, That the passion between the sexes is necessary, and will remain nearly in its present state. . . .

Assuming, then, my postulata as granted, I say, that the power of population is indefinitely greater than the power in the earth to produce subsistence for man.

Population, when unchecked, increases in a geometrical ratio. Subsistence only increases in an arithmetical ratio. A slight acquaintance with numbers will show the immensity of the first power in comparison of the second.

By that law of our nature which makes food necessary to the life of man, the effects of these two unequal powers must be kept equal.

This implies a strong and constantly operating check on population from the difficulty of subsistence. This difficulty must fall some where; and must necessarily be severely felt by a large portion of mankind. . . .

The ultimate check to population appears then to be a want of food arising necessarily from the different ratios according to which population and food increase. But this ultimate check is never the immediate check, except in cases of actual famine.

The immediate check may be stated to consist in all those customs, and all those diseases which seem to be generated by a scarcity of the means of subsistence; and all those causes, independent of this scarcity, whether of a moral or physical nature, which tend prematurely to weaken and destroy the human frame.

In every country some of these checks are, with more or less force, in constant operation; yet, notwithstanding their general prevalence, there are few states in which there is not a constant effort in the population to increase beyond the means of subsistence. This constant effort as constantly tends to subject the lower classes of society to distress, and to prevent any great permanent melioration of their condition.

These effects, in the present state of society, seem to be produced in the following manner. We will suppose the means of subsistence in any country just equal to the easy support of its inhabitants. The constant effort toward population, which is found to act even in the most vicious societies, increases the number of people before the means of subsistence are increased. The food, therefore, which before supported eleven millions, must now be divided among eleven millions and a half. The poor consequently must live much worse, and many of them be reduced to severe distress. The number of laborers also being above the proportion of work in the market, the price of labor must tend to fall, while the price of provisions would at the same time tend to rise. The laborer therefore must do more work to earn the same as he did before. During this season of distress, the discouragements to marriage and the difficulty of rearing a family are so great, that the progress of population is retarded. In the meantime, the cheapness of labor, the plenty of laborers, and the necessity of an increased industry among them, encourage cultivators to employ more labor upon their land, to turn up fresh soil, and to manure and improve more completely what is already in tillage, till ultimately the means of subsistence may become in the same proportion to the population as at the period from which we set out. The situation of the laborer being then again tolerably comfortable, the restraints to population are in some degree loosened; and, after a short period, the same retrograde and progressive movements, with respect to happiness, are repeated. . . .

Document Set 19.8 References

A. Two Views of Enclosure, Late Eighteenth Century
   A. Young, *The Farmer's Tour,* 1771, in A. E. Bland, P. E. Brown, and R. H. Tawney, eds., *English Economic History: Selected Documents* (London: G. Bell, 1915), 530–532.
B. Adam Smith Presents the Case for Economic Efficiency
   Adam Smith, *The Wealth of Nations,* Edwin Cannan, ed. (New York: Modern Library, 1937), 4–5, 423, 425–426.
C. Manchester Becomes a Thriving Industrial City, 1795
   John Aikin, *A Description of the Country from Thirty to Forty Miles Round Manchester,* in Walter Arnstein, ed., *The Past Speaks,* 2d ed. (Lexington, Mass.: D. C. Heath, 1993), 2:148–149.
D. Yorkshire Luddites Resist Machinery
   G. D. H. Cole and A. W. Filson, eds., *British Working Class Documents: Selected Documents 1789–1875* (London: Macmillan, 1951), 113–115.
E. Robert Malthus Doubts Human Perfectibility, 1798
   Malthus, *An Essay on the Principle of Population,* in Arnstein, 2:144–146.